Dictionary of Literary Biography

1 *The American Renaissance in New England,* edited by Joel Myerson (1978)

2 *American Novelists Since World War II,* edited by Jeffrey Helterman and Richard Layman (1978)

3 *Antebellum Writers in New York and the South,* edited by Joel Myerson (1979)

4 *American Writers in Paris, 1920–1939,* edited by Karen Lane Rood (1980)

5 *American Poets Since World War II,* 2 parts, edited by Donald J. Greiner (1980)

6 *American Novelists Since World War II, Second Series,* edited by James E. Kibler Jr. (1980)

7 *Twentieth-Century American Dramatists,* 2 parts, edited by John MacNicholas (1981)

8 *Twentieth-Century American Science-Fiction Writers,* 2 parts, edited by David Cowart and Thomas L. Wymer (1981)

9 *American Novelists, 1910–1945,* 3 parts, edited by James J. Martine (1981)

10 *Modern British Dramatists, 1900–1945,* 2 parts, edited by Stanley Weintraub (1982)

11 *American Humorists, 1800–1950,* 2 parts, edited by Stanley Trachtenberg (1982)

12 *American Realists and Naturalists,* edited by Donald Pizer and Earl N. Harbert (1982)

13 *British Dramatists Since World War II,* 2 parts, edited by Stanley Weintraub (1982)

14 *British Novelists Since 1960,* 2 parts, edited by Jay L. Halio (1983)

15 *British Novelists, 1930–1959,* 2 parts, edited by Bernard Oldsey (1983)

16 *The Beats: Literary Bohemians in Postwar America,* 2 parts, edited by Ann Charters (1983)

17 *Twentieth-Century American Historians,* edited by Clyde N. Wilson (1983)

18 *Victorian Novelists After 1885,* edited by Ira B. Nadel and William E. Fredeman (1983)

19 *British Poets, 1880–1914,* edited by Donald E. Stanford (1983)

20 *British Poets, 1914–1945,* edited by Donald E. Stanford (1983)

21 *Victorian Novelists Before 1885,* edited by Ira B. Nadel and William E. Fredeman (1983)

22 *American Writers for Children, 1900–1960,* edited by John Cech (1983)

23 *American Newspaper Journalists, 1873–1900,* edited by Perry J. Ashley (1983)

24 *American Colonial Writers, 1606–1734,* edited by Emory Elliott (1984)

25 *American Newspaper Journalists, 1901–1925,* edited by Perry J. Ashley (1984)

26 *American Screenwriters,* edited by Robert E. Morsberger, Stephen O. Lesser, and Randall Clark (1984)

27 *Poets of Great Britain and Ireland, 1945–1960,* edited by Vincent B. Sherry Jr. (1984)

28 *Twentieth-Century American-Jewish Fiction Writers,* edited by Daniel Walden (1984)

29 *American Newspaper Journalists, 1926–1950,* edited by Perry J. Ashley (1984)

30 *American Historians, 1607–1865,* edited by Clyde N. Wilson (1984)

31 *American Colonial Writers, 1735–1781,* edited by Emory Elliott (1984)

32 *Victorian Poets Before 1850,* edited by William E. Fredeman and Ira B. Nadel (1984)

33 *Afro-American Fiction Writers After 1955,* edited by Thadious M. Davis and Trudier Harris (1984)

34 *British Novelists, 1890–1929: Traditionalists,* edited by Thomas F. Staley (1985)

35 *Victorian Poets After 1850,* edited by William E. Fredeman and Ira B. Nadel (1985)

36 *British Novelists, 1890–1929: Modernists,* edited by Thomas F. Staley (1985)

37 *American Writers of the Early Republic,* edited by Emory Elliott (1985)

38 *Afro-American Writers After 1955: Dramatists and Prose Writers,* edited by Thadious M. Davis and Trudier Harris (1985)

39 *British Novelists, 1660–1800,* 2 parts, edited by Martin C. Battestin (1985)

40 *Poets of Great Britain and Ireland Since 1960,* 2 parts, edited by Vincent B. Sherry Jr. (1985)

41 *Afro-American Poets Since 1955,* edited by Trudier Harris and Thadious M. Davis (1985)

42 *American Writers for Children Before 1900,* edited by Glenn E. Estes (1985)

43 *American Newspaper Journalists, 1690–1872,* edited by Perry J. Ashley (1986)

44 *American Screenwriters, Second Series,* edited by Randall Clark, Robert E. Morsberger, and Stephen O. Lesser (1986)

45 *American Poets, 1880–1945, First Series,* edited by Peter Quartermain (1986)

46 *American Literary Publishing Houses, 1900–1980: Trade and Paperback,* edited by Peter Dzwonkoski (1986)

47 *American Historians, 1866–1912,* edited by Clyde N. Wilson (1986)

48 *American Poets, 1880–1945, Second Series,* edited by Peter Quartermain (1986)

49 *American Literary Publishing Houses, 1638–1899,* 2 parts, edited by Peter Dzwonkoski (1986)

50 *Afro-American Writers Before the Harlem Renaissance,* edited by Trudier Harris (1986)

51 *Afro-American Writers from the Harlem Renaissance to 1940,* edited by Trudier Harris (1987)

52 *American Writers for Children Since 1960: Fiction,* edited by Glenn E. Estes (1986)

53 *Canadian Writers Since 1960, First Series,* edited by W. H. New (1986)

54 *American Poets, 1880–1945, Third Series,* 2 parts, edited by Peter Quartermain (1987)

55 *Victorian Prose Writers Before 1867,* edited by William B. Thesing (1987)

56 *German Fiction Writers, 1914–1945,* edited by James Hardin (1987)

57 *Victorian Prose Writers After 1867,* edited by William B. Thesing (1987)

58 *Jacobean and Caroline Dramatists,* edited by Fredson Bowers (1987)

59 *American Literary Critics and Scholars, 1800–1850,* edited by John W. Rathbun and Monica M. Grecu (1987)

60 *Canadian Writers Since 1960, Second Series,* edited by W. H. New (1987)

61 *American Writers for Children Since 1960: Poets, Illustrators, and Nonfiction Authors,* edited by Glenn E. Estes (1987)

62 *Elizabethan Dramatists,* edited by Fredson Bowers (1987)

63 *Modern American Critics, 1920–1955,* edited by Gregory S. Jay (1988)

64 *American Literary Critics and Scholars, 1850–1880,* edited by John W. Rathbun and Monica M. Grecu (1988)

65 *French Novelists, 1900–1930,* edited by Catharine Savage Brosman (1988)

66 *German Fiction Writers, 1885–1913,* 2 parts, edited by James Hardin (1988)

67 *Modern American Critics Since 1955,* edited by Gregory S. Jay (1988)

68 *Canadian Writers, 1920–1959, First Series,* edited by W. H. New (1988)

69 *Contemporary German Fiction Writers, First Series,* edited by Wolfgang D. Elfe and James Hardin (1988)

70 *British Mystery Writers, 1860–1919,* edited by Bernard Benstock and Thomas F. Staley (1988)

71 *American Literary Critics and Scholars, 1880–1900,* edited by John W. Rathbun and Monica M. Grecu (1988)

72 *French Novelists, 1930–1960,* edited by Catharine Savage Brosman (1988)

73 *American Magazine Journalists, 1741–1850,* edited by Sam G. Riley (1988)

74 *American Short-Story Writers Before 1880,* edited by Bobby Ellen Kimbel, with the assistance of William E. Grant (1988)

75 *Contemporary German Fiction Writers, Second Series*, edited by Wolfgang D. Elfe and James Hardin (1988)

76 *Afro-American Writers, 1940–1955*, edited by Trudier Harris (1988)

77 *British Mystery Writers, 1920–1939*, edited by Bernard Benstock and Thomas F. Staley (1988)

78 *American Short-Story Writers, 1880–1910*, edited by Bobby Ellen Kimbel, with the assistance of William E. Grant (1988)

79 *American Magazine Journalists, 1850–1900*, edited by Sam G. Riley (1988)

80 *Restoration and Eighteenth-Century Dramatists, First Series*, edited by Paula R. Backscheider (1989)

81 *Austrian Fiction Writers, 1875–1913*, edited by James Hardin and Donald G. Daviau (1989)

82 *Chicano Writers, First Series*, edited by Francisco A. Lomelí and Carl R. Shirley (1989)

83 *French Novelists Since 1960*, edited by Catharine Savage Brosman (1989)

84 *Restoration and Eighteenth-Century Dramatists, Second Series*, edited by Paula R. Backscheider (1989)

85 *Austrian Fiction Writers After 1914*, edited by James Hardin and Donald G. Daviau (1989)

86 *American Short-Story Writers, 1910–1945, First Series*, edited by Bobby Ellen Kimbel (1989)

87 *British Mystery and Thriller Writers Since 1940, First Series*, edited by Bernard Benstock and Thomas F. Staley (1989)

88 *Canadian Writers, 1920–1959, Second Series*, edited by W. H. New (1989)

89 *Restoration and Eighteenth-Century Dramatists, Third Series*, edited by Paula R. Backscheider (1989)

90 *German Writers in the Age of Goethe, 1789–1832*, edited by James Hardin and Christoph E. Schweitzer (1989)

91 *American Magazine Journalists, 1900–1960, First Series*, edited by Sam G. Riley (1990)

92 *Canadian Writers, 1890–1920*, edited by W. H. New (1990)

93 *British Romantic Poets, 1789–1832, First Series*, edited by John R. Greenfield (1990)

94 *German Writers in the Age of Goethe: Sturm und Drang to Classicism*, edited by James Hardin and Christoph E. Schweitzer (1990)

95 *Eighteenth-Century British Poets, First Series*, edited by John Sitter (1990)

96 *British Romantic Poets, 1789–1832, Second Series*, edited by John R. Greenfield (1990)

97 *German Writers from the Enlightenment to Sturm und Drang, 1720–1764*, edited by James Hardin and Christoph E. Schweitzer (1990)

98 *Modern British Essayists, First Series*, edited by Robert Beum (1990)

99 *Canadian Writers Before 1890*, edited by W. H. New (1990)

100 *Modern British Essayists, Second Series*, edited by Robert Beum (1990)

101 *British Prose Writers, 1660–1800, First Series*, edited by Donald T. Siebert (1991)

102 *American Short-Story Writers, 1910–1945, Second Series*, edited by Bobby Ellen Kimbel (1991)

103 *American Literary Biographers, First Series*, edited by Steven Serafin (1991)

104 *British Prose Writers, 1660–1800, Second Series*, edited by Donald T. Siebert (1991)

105 *American Poets Since World War II, Second Series*, edited by R. S. Gwynn (1991)

106 *British Literary Publishing Houses, 1820–1880*, edited by Patricia J. Anderson and Jonathan Rose (1991)

107 *British Romantic Prose Writers, 1789–1832, First Series*, edited by John R. Greenfield (1991)

108 *Twentieth-Century Spanish Poets, First Series*, edited by Michael L. Perna (1991)

109 *Eighteenth-Century British Poets, Second Series*, edited by John Sitter (1991)

110 *British Romantic Prose Writers, 1789–1832, Second Series*, edited by John R. Greenfield (1991)

111 *American Literary Biographers, Second Series*, edited by Steven Serafin (1991)

112 *British Literary Publishing Houses, 1881–1965*, edited by Jonathan Rose and Patricia J. Anderson (1991)

113 *Modern Latin-American Fiction Writers, First Series*, edited by William Luis (1992)

114 *Twentieth-Century Italian Poets, First Series*, edited by Giovanna Wedel De Stasio, Glauco Cambon, and Antonio Illiano (1992)

115 *Medieval Philosophers*, edited by Jeremiah Hackett (1992)

116 *British Romantic Novelists, 1789–1832*, edited by Bradford K. Mudge (1992)

117 *Twentieth-Century Caribbean and Black African Writers, First Series*, edited by Bernth Lindfors and Reinhard Sander (1992)

118 *Twentieth-Century German Dramatists, 1889–1918*, edited by Wolfgang D. Elfe and James Hardin (1992)

119 *Nineteenth-Century French Fiction Writers: Romanticism and Realism, 1800–1860*, edited by Catharine Savage Brosman (1992)

120 *American Poets Since World War II, Third Series*, edited by R. S. Gwynn (1992)

121 *Seventeenth-Century British Nondramatic Poets, First Series*, edited by M. Thomas Hester (1992)

122 *Chicano Writers, Second Series*, edited by Francisco A. Lomelí and Carl R. Shirley (1992)

123 *Nineteenth-Century French Fiction Writers: Naturalism and Beyond, 1860–1900*, edited by Catharine Savage Brosman (1992)

124 *Twentieth-Century German Dramatists, 1919–1992*, edited by Wolfgang D. Elfe and James Hardin (1992)

125 *Twentieth-Century Caribbean and Black African Writers, Second Series*, edited by Bernth Lindfors and Reinhard Sander (1993)

126 *Seventeenth-Century British Nondramatic Poets, Second Series*, edited by M. Thomas Hester (1993)

127 *American Newspaper Publishers, 1950–1990*, edited by Perry J. Ashley (1993)

128 *Twentieth-Century Italian Poets, Second Series*, edited by Giovanna Wedel De Stasio, Glauco Cambon, and Antonio Illiano (1993)

129 *Nineteenth-Century German Writers, 1841–1900*, edited by James Hardin and Siegfried Mews (1993)

130 *American Short-Story Writers Since World War II*, edited by Patrick Meanor (1993)

131 *Seventeenth-Century British Nondramatic Poets, Third Series*, edited by M. Thomas Hester (1993)

132 *Sixteenth-Century British Nondramatic Writers, First Series*, edited by David A. Richardson (1993)

133 *Nineteenth-Century German Writers to 1840*, edited by James Hardin and Siegfried Mews (1993)

134 *Twentieth-Century Spanish Poets, Second Series*, edited by Jerry Phillips Winfield (1994)

135 *British Short-Fiction Writers, 1880–1914: The Realist Tradition*, edited by William B. Thesing (1994)

136 *Sixteenth-Century British Nondramatic Writers, Second Series*, edited by David A. Richardson (1994)

137 *American Magazine Journalists, 1900–1960, Second Series*, edited by Sam G. Riley (1994)

138 *German Writers and Works of the High Middle Ages: 1170–1280*, edited by James Hardin and Will Hasty (1994)

139 *British Short-Fiction Writers, 1945–1980*, edited by Dean Baldwin (1994)

140 *American Book-Collectors and Bibliographers, First Series*, edited by Joseph Rosenblum (1994)

141 *British Children's Writers, 1880–1914*, edited by Laura M. Zaidman (1994)

142 *Eighteenth-Century British Literary Biographers*, edited by Steven Serafin (1994)

143 *American Novelists Since World War II, Third Series*, edited by James R. Giles and Wanda H. Giles (1994)

144 *Nineteenth-Century British Literary Biographers*, edited by Steven Serafin (1994)

145 *Modern Latin-American Fiction Writers, Second Series*, edited by William Luis and Ann González (1994)

146 *Old and Middle English Literature*, edited by Jeffrey Helterman and Jerome Mitchell (1994)

147 *South Slavic Writers Before World War II*, edited by Vasa D. Mihailovich (1994)

148 *German Writers and Works of the Early Middle Ages: 800–1170*, edited by Will Hasty and James Hardin (1994)

149 *Late Nineteenth- and Early Twentieth-Century British Literary Biographers*, edited by Steven Serafin (1995)

150 *Early Modern Russian Writers, Late Seventeenth and Eighteenth Centuries*, edited by Marcus C. Levitt (1995)

151 *British Prose Writers of the Early Seventeenth Century,* edited by Clayton D. Lein (1995)

152 *American Novelists Since World War II, Fourth Series,* edited by James R. Giles and Wanda H. Giles (1995)

153 *Late-Victorian and Edwardian British Novelists, First Series,* edited by George M. Johnson (1995)

154 *The British Literary Book Trade, 1700–1820,* edited by James K. Bracken and Joel Silver (1995)

155 *Twentieth-Century British Literary Biographers,* edited by Steven Serafin (1995)

156 *British Short-Fiction Writers, 1880–1914: The Romantic Tradition,* edited by William F. Naufftus (1995)

157 *Twentieth-Century Caribbean and Black African Writers, Third Series,* edited by Bernth Lindfors and Reinhard Sander (1995)

158 *British Reform Writers, 1789–1832,* edited by Gary Kelly and Edd Applegate (1995)

159 *British Short-Fiction Writers, 1800–1880,* edited by John R. Greenfield (1996)

160 *British Children's Writers, 1914–1960,* edited by Donald R. Hettinga and Gary D. Schmidt (1996)

161 *British Children's Writers Since 1960, First Series,* edited by Caroline Hunt (1996)

162 *British Short-Fiction Writers, 1915–1945,* edited by John H. Rogers (1996)

163 *British Children's Writers, 1800–1880,* edited by Meena Khorana (1996)

164 *German Baroque Writers, 1580–1660,* edited by James Hardin (1996)

165 *American Poets Since World War II, Fourth Series,* edited by Joseph Conte (1996)

166 *British Travel Writers, 1837–1875,* edited by Barbara Brothers and Julia Gergits (1996)

167 *Sixteenth-Century British Nondramatic Writers, Third Series,* edited by David A. Richardson (1996)

168 *German Baroque Writers, 1661–1730,* edited by James Hardin (1996)

169 *American Poets Since World War II, Fifth Series,* edited by Joseph Conte (1996)

170 *The British Literary Book Trade, 1475–1700,* edited by James K. Bracken and Joel Silver (1996)

171 *Twentieth-Century American Sportswriters,* edited by Richard Orodenker (1996)

172 *Sixteenth-Century British Nondramatic Writers, Fourth Series,* edited by David A. Richardson (1996)

173 *American Novelists Since World War II, Fifth Series,* edited by James R. Giles and Wanda H. Giles (1996)

174 *British Travel Writers, 1876–1909,* edited by Barbara Brothers and Julia Gergits (1997)

175 *Native American Writers of the United States,* edited by Kenneth M. Roemer (1997)

176 *Ancient Greek Authors,* edited by Ward W. Briggs (1997)

177 *Italian Novelists Since World War II, 1945–1965,* edited by Augustus Pallotta (1997)

178 *British Fantasy and Science-Fiction Writers Before World War I,* edited by Darren Harris-Fain (1997)

179 *German Writers of the Renaissance and Reformation, 1280–1580,* edited by James Hardin and Max Reinhart (1997)

180 *Japanese Fiction Writers, 1868–1945,* edited by Van C. Gessel (1997)

181 *South Slavic Writers Since World War II,* edited by Vasa D. Mihailovich (1997)

182 *Japanese Fiction Writers Since World War II,* edited by Van C. Gessel (1997)

183 *American Travel Writers, 1776–1864,* edited by James J. Schramer and Donald Ross (1997)

184 *Nineteenth-Century British Book-Collectors and Bibliographers,* edited by William Baker and Kenneth Womack (1997)

185 *American Literary Journalists, 1945–1995, First Series,* edited by Arthur J. Kaul (1998)

186 *Nineteenth-Century American Western Writers,* edited by Robert L. Gale (1998)

187 *American Book Collectors and Bibliographers, Second Series,* edited by Joseph Rosenblum (1998)

188 *American Book and Magazine Illustrators to 1920,* edited by Steven E. Smith, Catherine A. Hastedt, and Donald H. Dyal (1998)

189 *American Travel Writers, 1850–1915,* edited by Donald Ross and James J. Schramer (1998)

190 *British Reform Writers, 1832–1914,* edited by Gary Kelly and Edd Applegate (1998)

191 *British Novelists Between the Wars,* edited by George M. Johnson (1998)

192 *French Dramatists, 1789–1914,* edited by Barbara T. Cooper (1998)

193 *American Poets Since World War II, Sixth Series,* edited by Joseph Conte (1998)

194 *British Novelists Since 1960, Second Series,* edited by Merritt Moseley (1998)

195 *British Travel Writers, 1910–1939,* edited by Barbara Brothers and Julia Gergits (1998)

196 *Italian Novelists Since World War II, 1965–1995,* edited by Augustus Pallotta (1999)

197 *Late-Victorian and Edwardian British Novelists, Second Series,* edited by George M. Johnson (1999)

198 *Russian Literature in the Age of Pushkin and Gogol: Prose,* edited by Christine A. Rydel (1999)

199 *Victorian Women Poets,* edited by William B. Thesing (1999)

200 *American Women Prose Writers to 1820,* edited by Carla J. Mulford, with Angela Vietto and Amy E. Winans (1999)

201 *Twentieth-Century British Book Collectors and Bibliographers,* edited by William Baker and Kenneth Womack (1999)

202 *Nineteenth-Century American Fiction Writers,* edited by Kent P. Ljungquist (1999)

203 *Medieval Japanese Writers,* edited by Steven D. Carter (1999)

204 *British Travel Writers, 1940–1997,* edited by Barbara Brothers and Julia M. Gergits (1999)

205 *Russian Literature in the Age of Pushkin and Gogol: Poetry and Drama,* edited by Christine A. Rydel (1999)

206 *Twentieth-Century American Western Writers, First Series,* edited by Richard H. Cracroft (1999)

207 *British Novelists Since 1960, Third Series,* edited by Merritt Moseley (1999)

208 *Literature of the French and Occitan Middle Ages: Eleventh to Fifteenth Centuries,* edited by Deborah Sinnreich-Levi and Ian S. Laurie (1999)

209 *Chicano Writers, Third Series,* edited by Francisco A. Lomelí and Carl R. Shirley (1999)

210 *Ernest Hemingway: A Documentary Volume,* edited by Robert W. Trogdon (1999)

211 *Ancient Roman Writers,* edited by Ward W. Briggs (1999)

212 *Twentieth-Century American Western Writers, Second Series,* edited by Richard H. Cracroft (1999)

213 *Pre-Nineteenth-Century British Book Collectors and Bibliographers,* edited by William Baker and Kenneth Womack (1999)

214 *Twentieth-Century Danish Writers,* edited by Marianne Stecher-Hansen (1999)

215 *Twentieth-Century Eastern European Writers, First Series,* edited by Steven Serafin (1999)

216 *British Poets of the Great War: Brooke, Rosenberg, Thomas. A Documentary Volume,* edited by Patrick Quinn (2000)

217 *Nineteenth-Century French Poets,* edited by Robert Beum (2000)

218 *American Short-Story Writers Since World War II, Second Series,* edited by Patrick Meanor and Gwen Crane (2000)

219 *F. Scott Fitzgerald's* The Great Gatsby: *A Documentary Volume,* edited by Matthew J. Bruccoli (2000)

220 *Twentieth-Century Eastern European Writers, Second Series,* edited by Steven Serafin (2000)

221 *American Women Prose Writers, 1870–1920,* edited by Sharon M. Harris, with the assistance of Heidi L. M. Jacobs and Jennifer Putzi (2000)

222 *H. L. Mencken: A Documentary Volume,* edited by Richard J. Schrader (2000)

223 *The American Renaissance in New England, Second Series,* edited by Wesley T. Mott (2000)

224 *Walt Whitman: A Documentary Volume,* edited by Joel Myerson (2000)

225 *South African Writers,* edited by Paul A. Scanlon (2000)

226 *American Hard-Boiled Crime Writers,* edited by George Parker Anderson and Julie B. Anderson (2000)

227 *American Novelists Since World War II, Sixth Series,* edited by James R. Giles and Wanda H. Giles (2000)

228 *Twentieth-Century American Dramatists, Second Series,* edited by Christopher J. Wheatley (2000)

229 *Thomas Wolfe: A Documentary Volume,* edited by Ted Mitchell (2001)

230 *Australian Literature, 1788–1914*, edited by Selina Samuels (2001)

231 *British Novelists Since 1960, Fourth Series*, edited by Merritt Moseley (2001)

232 *Twentieth-Century Eastern European Writers, Third Series*, edited by Steven Serafin (2001)

233 *British and Irish Dramatists Since World War II, Second Series*, edited by John Bull (2001)

234 *American Short-Story Writers Since World War II, Third Series*, edited by Patrick Meanor and Richard E. Lee (2001)

235 *The American Renaissance in New England, Third Series*, edited by Wesley T. Mott (2001)

236 *British Rhetoricians and Logicians, 1500–1660*, edited by Edward A. Malone (2001)

237 *The Beats: A Documentary Volume*, edited by Matt Theado (2001)

238 *Russian Novelists in the Age of Tolstoy and Dostoevsky*, edited by J. Alexander Ogden and Judith E. Kalb (2001)

239 *American Women Prose Writers: 1820–1870*, edited by Amy E. Hudock and Katharine Rodier (2001)

240 *Late Nineteenth- and Early Twentieth-Century British Women Poets*, edited by William B. Thesing (2001)

241 *American Sportswriters and Writers on Sport*, edited by Richard Orodenker (2001)

242 *Twentieth-Century European Cultural Theorists, First Series*, edited by Paul Hansom (2001)

243 *The American Renaissance in New England, Fourth Series*, edited by Wesley T. Mott (2001)

244 *American Short-Story Writers Since World War II, Fourth Series*, edited by Patrick Meanor and Joseph McNicholas (2001)

245 *British and Irish Dramatists Since World War II, Third Series*, edited by John Bull (2001)

246 *Twentieth-Century American Cultural Theorists*, edited by Paul Hansom (2001)

247 *James Joyce: A Documentary Volume*, edited by A. Nicholas Fargnoli (2001)

248 *Antebellum Writers in the South, Second Series*, edited by Kent Ljungquist (2001)

249 *Twentieth-Century American Dramatists, Third Series*, edited by Christopher Wheatley (2002)

250 *Antebellum Writers in New York, Second Series*, edited by Kent Ljungquist (2002)

251 *Canadian Fantasy and Science-Fiction Writers*, edited by Douglas Ivison (2002)

252 *British Philosophers, 1500–1799*, edited by Philip B. Dematteis and Peter S. Fosl (2002)

253 *Raymond Chandler: A Documentary Volume*, edited by Robert Moss (2002)

254 *The House of Putnam, 1837–1872: A Documentary Volume*, edited by Ezra Greenspan (2002)

255 *British Fantasy and Science-Fiction Writers, 1918–1960*, edited by Darren Harris-Fain (2002)

256 *Twentieth-Century American Western Writers, Third Series*, edited by Richard H. Cracroft (2002)

257 *Twentieth-Century Swedish Writers After World War II*, edited by Ann-Charlotte Gavel Adams (2002)

258 *Modern French Poets*, edited by Jean-François Leroux (2002)

259 *Twentieth-Century Swedish Writers Before World War II*, edited by Ann-Charlotte Gavel Adams (2002)

260 *Australian Writers, 1915–1950*, edited by Selina Samuels (2002)

261 *British Fantasy and Science-Fiction Writers Since 1960*, edited by Darren Harris-Fain (2002)

262 *British Philosophers, 1800–2000*, edited by Peter S. Fosl and Leemon B. McHenry (2002)

263 *William Shakespeare: A Documentary Volume*, edited by Catherine Loomis (2002)

264 *Italian Prose Writers, 1900–1945*, edited by Luca Somigli and Rocco Capozzi (2002)

265 *American Song Lyricists, 1920–1960*, edited by Philip Furia (2002)

266 *Twentieth-Century American Dramatists, Fourth Series*, edited by Christopher J. Wheatley (2002)

267 *Twenty-First-Century British and Irish Novelists*, edited by Michael R. Molino (2002)

Dictionary of Literary Biography Documentary Series

1 *Sherwood Anderson, Willa Cather, John Dos Passos, Theodore Dreiser, F. Scott Fitzgerald, Ernest Hemingway, Sinclair Lewis*, edited by Margaret A. Van Antwerp (1982)

2 *James Gould Cozzens, James T. Farrell, William Faulkner, John O'Hara, John Steinbeck, Thomas Wolfe, Richard Wright*, edited by Margaret A. Van Antwerp (1982)

3 *Saul Bellow, Jack Kerouac, Norman Mailer, Vladimir Nabokov, John Updike, Kurt Vonnegut*, edited by Mary Bruccoli (1983)

4 *Tennessee Williams*, edited by Margaret A. Van Antwerp and Sally Johns (1984)

5 *American Transcendentalists*, edited by Joel Myerson (1988)

6 *Hardboiled Mystery Writers: Raymond Chandler, Dashiell Hammett, Ross Macdonald*, edited by Matthew J. Bruccoli and Richard Layman (1989)

7 *Modern American Poets: James Dickey, Robert Frost, Marianne Moore*, edited by Karen L. Rood (1989)

8 *The Black Aesthetic Movement*, edited by Jeffrey Louis Decker (1991)

9 *American Writers of the Vietnam War: W. D. Ehrhart, Larry Heinemann, Tim O'Brien, Walter McDonald, John M. Del Vecchio*, edited by Ronald Baughman (1991)

10 *The Bloomsbury Group*, edited by Edward L. Bishop (1992)

11 *American Proletarian Culture: The Twenties and The Thirties*, edited by Jon Christian Suggs (1993)

12 *Southern Women Writers: Flannery O'Connor, Katherine Anne Porter, Eudora Welty*, edited by Mary Ann Wimsatt and Karen L. Rood (1994)

13 *The House of Scribner, 1846–1904*, edited by John Delaney (1996)

14 *Four Women Writers for Children, 1868–1918*, edited by Caroline C. Hunt (1996)

15 *American Expatriate Writers: Paris in the Twenties*, edited by Matthew J. Bruccoli and Robert W. Trogdon (1997)

16 *The House of Scribner, 1905–1930*, edited by John Delaney (1997)

17 *The House of Scribner, 1931–1984*, edited by John Delaney (1998)

18 *British Poets of The Great War: Sassoon, Graves, Owen*, edited by Patrick Quinn (1999)

19 *James Dickey*, edited by Judith S. Baughman (1999)

See also DLB 210, 216, 219, 222, 224, 229, 237, 247, 253, 254, 263

Dictionary of Literary Biography Yearbooks

1980 edited by Karen L. Rood, Jean W. Ross, and Richard Ziegfeld (1981)

1981 edited by Karen L. Rood, Jean W. Ross, and Richard Ziegfeld (1982)

1982 edited by Richard Ziegfeld; associate editors: Jean W. Ross and Lynne C. Zeigler (1983)

1983 edited by Mary Bruccoli and Jean W. Ross; associate editor Richard Ziegfeld (1984)

1984 edited by Jean W. Ross (1985)

1985 edited by Jean W. Ross (1986)

1986 edited by J. M. Brook (1987)

1987 edited by J. M. Brook (1988)

1988 edited by J. M. Brook (1989)

1989 edited by J. M. Brook (1990)

1990 edited by James W. Hipp (1991)

1991 edited by James W. Hipp (1992)

1992 edited by James W. Hipp (1993)

1993 edited by James W. Hipp, contributing editor George Garrett (1994)

1994 edited by James W. Hipp, contributing editor George Garrett (1995)

1995 edited by James W. Hipp, contributing editor George Garrett (1996)

1996 edited by Samuel W. Bruce and L. Kay Webster, contributing editor George Garrett (1997)

1997 edited by Matthew J. Bruccoli and George Garrett, with the assistance of L. Kay Webster (1998)

1998 edited by Matthew J. Bruccoli, contributing editor George Garrett, with the assistance of D. W. Thomas (1999)

1999 edited by Matthew J. Bruccoli, contributing editor George Garrett, with the assistance of D. W. Thomas (2000)

2000 edited by Matthew J. Bruccoli, contributing editor George Garrett, with the assistance of George Parker Anderson (2001)

2001 edited by Matthew J. Bruccoli, contributing editor George Garrett, with the assistance of George Parker Anderson (2002)

Concise Series

Concise Dictionary of American Literary Biography, 7 volumes (1988–1999): *The New Consciousness, 1941–1968; Colonization to the American Renaissance, 1640–1865; Realism, Naturalism, and Local Color, 1865–1917; The Twenties, 1917–1929; The Age of Maturity, 1929–1941; Broadening Views, 1968–1988; Supplement: Modern Writers, 1900–1998.*

Concise Dictionary of British Literary Biography, 8 volumes (1991–1992): *Writers of the Middle Ages and Renaissance Before 1660; Writers of the Restoration and Eighteenth Century, 1660–1789; Writers of the Romantic Period, 1789–1832; Victorian Writers, 1832–1890; Late-Victorian and Edwardian Writers, 1890–1914; Modern Writers, 1914–1945; Writers After World War II, 1945–1960; Contemporary Writers, 1960 to Present.*

Concise Dictionary of World Literary Biography, 10 volumes projected (1999–   ): *Ancient Greek and Roman Writers; German Writers; African, Caribbean, and Latin American Writers; South Slavic and Eastern European Writers.*

Dictionary of Literary Biography® • Volume Two Hundred Sixty-Seven

Twenty-First-Century British and Irish Novelists

Dictionary of Literary Biography® • Volume Two Hundred Sixty-Seven

Twenty-First-Century British and Irish Novelists

Edited by
Michael R. Molino
University of Southern Illinois, Carbondale

A Bruccoli Clark Layman Book

GALE®

Detroit • New York • San Diego • San Francisco • Cleveland • New Haven, Conn. • Waterville, Maine • London • Munich

THOMSON
GALE

Dictionary of Literary Biography
Volume 267: Twenty-First-Century
British and Irish Novelists
Michael R. Molino

Advisory Board
John Baker
William Cagle
Patrick O'Connor
George Garrett
Trudier Harris
Alvin Kernan
Kenny J. Williams

Editorial Directors
Matthew J. Bruccoli and Richard Layman

Senior Editor
Karen L. Rood

LIBRARY OF CONGRESS CATALOGING-IN-PUBLICATION DATA

Twenty-first-century British and Irish novelists / edited by Michael R. Molino.
    p. cm. — (Dictionary of literary biography ; v. 267)
"A Bruccoli Clark Layman book."
Includes bibliographical references and index.
    ISBN 0-7876-6011-6
    1. English fiction—21st century—Bio-bibliography—Dictionaries.
    2. English fiction—Irish authors—Bio-bibliography—Dictionaries.
    3.Novelists, English—21st century—Biography—Dictionaries.
    4. Novelists, Irish—21st century—Biography—Dictionaries.
    5. English fiction—Irish authors—Dictionaries.
    6. English fiction—21st century—Dictionaries.
    7. Ireland—In literature—Dictionaries.
    I. Title: 21st century British and Irish novelists. II. Molino, Michael R., 1956– III. Series.
PR889 .T86 2002
823'.9209'03—dc21   2002010923

Printed in the United States of America
10 9 8 7 6 5 4 3 2 1

To Mary

Contents

Plan of the Series xv
Introduction xvii

G. E. Armitage (Robert Edric)
(1956–) 3
  Anne-Marie Obilade

Kate Atkinson (1951–) 13
  Roger Clark

Stephen Blanchard (1950–) 22
  Dominic Head

Clare Boylan (1948–) 26
  Mary L. Bogumil

Amit Chaudhuri (1962–) 39
  Mary Robertson Ellen

Michael Collins (1964–) 50
  Aiping Zhang

Peter Cunningham (Peter Lauder,
Peter Benjamin) (1947–) 57
  Annette Gilson

Emma Donoghue (1969–) 68
  Stacia L. Bensyl

Helen Dunmore (1952–) 75
  Ann Hancock

Anne Enright (1962–) 88
  Caitriona Moloney

Giles Foden (1967–) 94
  Annette Rubery

Christopher Fowler (1953–) 101
  Philip Lockwood Simpson

Romesh Gunesekera (1954–) 111
  Rocío G. Davis

Hugo Hamilton (1953–) 121
  Steven Belletto

James Hamilton-Paterson (1941–) 130
  Michael R. Molino

Philip Hensher (1965–) 141
  Dirk Van Hulle

Michael Ignatieff (1947–) 148
  R. Victoria Arana

John Lanchester (1962–) 157
  Robert A. Morace

Toby Litt (1968–) .164
  Claire Squires

Bernard MacLaverty (1942–) 172
  Michael R. Molino

Colum McCann (1965–) 181
  Joseph Lennon

Duncan McLean (1964–) 192
  Desmond Fitzgibbon

Candia McWilliam (1955–) 203
  Benjamin G. Lanier-Nabors

Livi Michael (1960–) 211
  Roxanne Harde

Andrew Miller (1960–) 222
  Eva Roa White

Magnus Mills (1954–) 228
  Mary L. Bogumil

Mary Morrissy (1957–) 234
  Ann Owens Weekes

Julie Myerson (1960–) 241
  Ann Hancock

Jeff Noon (1957–) 250
  David Ian Paddy

Lawrence Norfolk (1963–) 261
  Barry Lewis

Joseph O'Connor (1963–) 271
  Tim Middleton

Kate O'Riordan (1960–) 279
  Kersti Tarien

Deirdre Purcell (1945–) 285
  Ellen Crowell

Ian Rankin (Jack Harvey)
(1960–) 294
  Mariadele Boccardi

Contents

James Ryan (1952–) 304
   Moira E. Casey

Madeleine St John (1942–) 310
   Shannon Forbes

Ahdaf Soueif (1950–) 314
   Geoffrey P. Nash

Rupert Thomson (1955–) 322
   Ben Saunders

Jonathan Treitel (1959–) 330
   Peter Brigg

Robert McLiam Wilson (1964–) 336
   Gregory Dobbins

Books for Further Reading 349
Contributors 353
Cumulative Index 357

Plan of the Series

The advisory board, the editors, and the publisher of the *Dictionary of Literary Biography* are joined in endorsing Mark Twain's declaration. The literature of a nation provides an inexhaustible resource of permanent worth. Our purpose is to make literature and its creators better understood and more accessible to students and the reading public, while satisfying the needs of teachers and researchers.

To meet these requirements, *literary biography* has been construed in terms of the author's achievement. The most important thing about a writer is his writing. Accordingly, the entries in *DLB* are career biographies, tracing the development of the author's canon and the evolution of his reputation.

The purpose of *DLB* is not only to provide reliable information in a usable format but also to place the figures in the larger perspective of literary history and to offer appraisals of their accomplishments by qualified scholars.

The publication plan for *DLB* resulted from two years of preparation. The project was proposed to Bruccoli Clark by Frederick G. Ruffner, president of the Gale Research Company, in November 1975. After specimen entries were prepared and typeset, an advisory board was formed to refine the entry format and develop the series rationale. In meetings held during 1976, the publisher, series editors, and advisory board approved the scheme for a comprehensive biographical dictionary of persons who contributed to literature. Editorial work on the first volume began in January 1977, and it was published in 1978. In order to make *DLB* more than a dictionary and to compile volumes that individually have claim to status as literary history, it was decided to organize volumes by topic, period, or

genre. Each of these freestanding volumes provides a biographical-bibliographical guide and overview for a particular area of literature. We are convinced that this organization—as opposed to a single alphabet method—constitutes a valuable innovation in the presentation of reference material. The volume plan necessarily requires many decisions for the placement and treatment of authors. Certain figures will be included in separate volumes, but with different entries emphasizing the aspect of his career appropriate to each volume. Ernest Hemingway, for example, is represented in *American Writers in Paris, 1920–1939* by an entry focusing on his expatriate apprenticeship; he is also in *American Novelists, 1910–1945* with an entry surveying his entire career, as well as in *American Short-Story Writers, 1910–1945, Second Series* with an entry concentrating on his short fiction. Each volume includes a cumulative index of the subject authors and articles.

Since 1981 the series has been further augmented by the *DLB Yearbooks,* which update published entries, add new entries to keep the *DLB* current with contemporary activity, and provide articles on literary history. There have also been nineteen *DLB Documentary Series* volumes which provide illustrations, facsimiles, and biographical and critical source materials for figures, works, or groups judged to have particular interest for students. In 1999 the *Documentary Series* was incorporated into the *DLB* volume numbering system beginning with *DLB 210: Ernest Hemingway.*

We define literature as the *intellectual commerce of a nation:* not merely as belles lettres but as that ample and complex process by which ideas are generated, shaped, and transmitted. *DLB* entries are not limited to "creative writers" but extend to other figures who in their time and in their way influenced the mind of a people. Thus the series encompasses historians, journalists, publishers, book collectors, and screenwriters. By this means readers of *DLB* may be aided to perceive literature not as cult scripture in the keeping of intellectual high priests but firmly positioned at the center of a nation's life.

DLB includes the major writers appropriate to each volume and those standing in the ranks behind them. Scholarly and critical counsel has been sought in deciding which minor figures to include and how full their entries should be. Wherever possible, useful references are made to figures who do not warrant separate entries.

Each *DLB* volume has an expert volume editor responsible for planning the volume, selecting the figures for inclusion, and assigning the entries. Volume editors are also responsible for preparing, where appropriate, appendices surveying the major periodicals and literary and intellectual movements for their volumes, as well as lists of further readings. Work on the series as a whole is coordinated at the Bruccoli Clark Layman editorial center in Columbia, South Carolina, where the editorial staff is responsible for accuracy and utility of the published volumes.

One feature that distinguishes *DLB* is the illustration policy—its concern with the iconography of literature. Just as an author is influenced by his surroundings, so is the reader's understanding of the author enhanced by a knowledge of his environment. Therefore *DLB* volumes include not only drawings, paintings, and photographs of authors, often depicting them at various stages in their careers, but also illustrations of their families and places where they lived. Title pages are regularly reproduced in facsimile along with dust jackets for modern authors. The dust jackets are a special feature of *DLB* because they often document better than anything else the way in which an author's work was perceived in its own time. Specimens of the writers' manuscripts and letters are included when feasible.

Samuel Johnson rightly decreed that "The chief glory of every people arises from its authors." The purpose of the *Dictionary of Literary Biography* is to compile literary history in the surest way available to us—by accurate and comprehensive treatment of the lives and work of those who contributed to it.

The *DLB* Advisory Board

Introduction

At ten minutes past two o'clock on the afternoon of 3 June 1997, a handful of spectators gathered in the Round Reading Room of the British Library at Great Russell Street, awaiting the appearance of Enoch Soames, who had mysteriously vanished from that same room—then known as the British Museum reading room—precisely one hundred years before. These few dutiful, if not gullible, souls shyly awaited Soames's scheduled return because they had read Max Beerbohm's story "Enoch Soames: A Memory of the Eighteen-nineties," from his *Seven Men and Two Others* (1919). In Beerbohm's account, Soames, an arrogant young poet eager to learn the extent of his influence on British literature, agrees to an eternity of damnation in exchange for a quick visit to the future. The devil, with whom Soames makes this Faustian pact, grants Soames a short visit to the reading room at the end of the next century to search the card catalogue and the *Dictionary of National Biography* for signs of his place in the British canon. Soames returns to the nineteenth century long enough to convey a mixed utopian/dystopian vision of the future in which, among other changes, "some sort of phonetic spelling" had replaced traditional spelling. Soames also reports the sad news that he will be remembered only as an "immajnari Karrakter kauld 'Enoch Soames'—a thurd-rait poit hoo beleevz imself a grate jeneuz." Once the doomed Soames is spirited away, Beerbohm opines confidently:

> You realize, therefore, that on that afternoon, when it comes round, there the selfsame crowd will be, and there Soames will be, punctually, he and they doing precisely what they did before. Recall now Soames's account of the sensation he made. You may say that the mere difference of his costume was enough to make him sensational in that uniformed crowd. You wouldn't say so if you had ever seen him, and I assure you that in no period would Soames be anything but dim. The fact that people are going to stare at him and follow him around and seem afraid of him, can be explained only on the hypothesis that they will somehow have been prepared for his ghostly visitation. They will have been awfully waiting to see whether he really would come. And when he does come the effect will of course be—awful.

Beerbohm's confidence is, of course, tempered by the fact that he is writing a satiric ghost story of sorts. Nonetheless, Beerbohm reveals confidence in the continuity of the past and present to extend into the future and an even greater assurance, despite his shock to the contrary, that his judgment as a critic forecasts the aesthetic and cultural values of succeeding generations. Beerbohm does not demonstrate, however, an ability to anticipate the fact that the reading room itself in the venerable British Museum—haven for and archive of civilization—would cease to exist in the form he knew it. The room was renamed as a result of the British Library Act of 1972, which merged the library departments of the British Museum with other government libraries to create the British Library in 1973. In fact, if it were not for various delays the reading room would have been moved to the new British Library building at Euston years before Soames's scheduled arrival. If that building had opened in the early 1980s as originally projected and not in June 1998, those curious and awe-inspired figures Soames encounters would not have been able to congregate in anticipation of Soames's return in the manner Beerbohm so confidently asserted. Beerbohm has great fun at Soames's expense, placing himself in the annals of British letters as the sole source of Soames's literary heritage. It never dawns on Beerbohm to question whether the place Soames left in 1897 would be the same place a century later. In Beerbohm's mind, England and its monuments of culture would no doubt remain in place over the next one hundred years. Beerbohm was accurate when he assumed that Great Britain would still exist one hundred years later, but Beerbohm, despite an imagination for the fantastic, could never have anticipated the Britain waiting for Soames in 1997.

Beerbohm looks forward in time, certain that some things will improve, while others, such as spelling, will sadly diminish. In contrast, writers of the period Soames briefly visits look backward in time to re-envision a past they no longer feel confident they understand. The social and cultural reality of contemporary Britain demands that earlier articulations based on narrow, homogeneous, or unitary concepts of Englishness be expanded, even discarded, in favor of a variety of new perspectives that stress regional influences within the geographical boundaries of the United Kingdom—such as Welsh, Scottish, Northern Irish—or even local influences. Moreover, these new perspectives of Englishness often also express the mixture of British influences with those of former colonies and other non-Western countries, many of whose citizens have come to call Great Britain home. Because of, not in spite of, the influx of such varying voices and perspectives, the last years of the twentieth century and first years of the twenty-first century have been extraordinarily bright for British literature. *Dictionary of Literary Biography 267: Twenty-First-Century British and Irish Novelists* includes entries on some of those writers who exemplify the state of British literature at the millennium, mostly either up-and-coming novelists or those previously ignored by critics. Books of various genres and those that blend or redefine genres have appeared in great numbers, as have books and writers from Australia, the Indian subcontinent, and Africa. Included in this volume, for example, are entries on Amit Chaudhuri, who divides his time between Calcutta and Cambridge; Romesh Gunesekera, from Sri Lanka; and Ahdaf Soueif, who is based in London but returns frequently to her native Egypt. Old boundaries designating nationality, genre, or gender have been broached or blurred in bursts of creative output and experimentation in fiction.

The major British and Commonwealth literary prizes have been quick to acknowledge and reward such efforts. The celebrity lavished upon award-winning writers and the attendant boost in sales have resulted in an intriguing intermingling of the private experience of literary writing and reading with public questions of national character, identity, and history. A quick examination of several prize winners at the turn of the twenty-first century reveals some of the trends in current fiction. Zadie Smith won the 2000 Guardian First Book Prize and the 2001 Commonwealth Writers First Novel Prize for *White Teeth,* a seriocomic novel of hybrid voices in a narrative that hopscotches its way over 150 years. The 2000 Whitbread Book of the Year Award went to *English Passengers,* Matthew Kneale's novel in which conversations during a voyage to Tasmania reveal imperial policies that lead beyond colonization to include persecution and even genocide. Trinidad-born novelist V. S. Naipaul, long a writer of the postcolonial experience, won the 2001 Nobel Prize in literature. Australian Peter Carey won the 2001 Booker Prize for his novel *True History of the Kelly Gang.* Carey's novel went on to win the Victoria Premier's Literary Award, the Commonwealth Writers Prize, and the Townville Foundation of Australian Literary Studies Award. Included in *DLB 267* is an entry on Andrew Miller, whose debut novel, *Ingenious Pain* (1997), won the James Tait Black Memorial Fiction Prize and whose third novel, *Oxygen*

(2001), was short-listed for the Booker Prize that Carey's novel won.

Eighteenth-century novelists told fictional stories that they purported to be true in order to convince or cajole a reading public unused to nakedly fictional accounts of ordinary life, particularly in an age when art focused primarily on the actions and ideas of great men. Contemporary novelists, though, reverse that tendency. Aware that their audience has a clearer sense of constructed identities and the problematic nature of objective historical fact, contemporary novelists can, as Carey does, tell fictional stories of factual people and events knowing that narratives of all types are contingent upon the narrator's subjectivity, cultural context, and chronological perspective. They use fiction to reimagine factual characters and events. Carey's novel exemplifies this intriguing mixture. Carey took as the starting point for the novel a letter in which Ned Kelly justifies one of his many bank robberies: "If my lips taught the public that men are made mad by bad treatment, then my life will not have been thrown away." In the novel, Carey presents imaginary letters by Kelly that some reviewers praised as the literary articulation of an unforgettable voice expressed in a kind of vernacular poetry, while other reviewers dismissed Carey's narrative as mere literary ventriloquism.

The versions of Englishness portrayed in contemporary British fiction are understandably characterized by heterogeneity, open-endedness, and multiethnicity. In their introduction to *New Writing 8* (1999), novelists and editors Tibor Fischer and Lawrence Norfolk make the case for the vitality of contemporary British literature by exchanging the older notions of Englishness as the defining trait that literature exemplifies for those in which Britain appears as a conceptual space in which varied voices, techniques, outlooks, and sources coexist:

> If Britain has largely become more launch-pad than terrain in its own right it is because its writers have actively chosen to seek out new challenges: a sign of writerly confidence. In turn, the diversity of what they have surveyed and logged speaks well of this country as a cultural entrepôt, a place of flux and reflux, differently but intricately connected to both Europe and the United States, historically and more problematically to the Indian subcontinent and Africa. Plenty of grist still passes through this mill called Britain.

Fischer and Norfolk's intriguing definition replaces older, pejorative versions of imperialistic Britain with one that celebrates diversity, a space in which various factors interact and thereby revitalize all in the process. Beyond this portrait of Britain as a "place of flux and reflux," Fischer and Norfolk conflate seemingly incompatible metaphors of their country. On the one hand, Britain is a "launch-pad," suggesting a contemporary and technologically advanced society looking to the future. On the other hand, Britain is also a "mill," an anachronism of Victorian industrialization and old-world politics and economics. These two editors correctly envision contemporary Britain as a new country filled with many new literary voices but also a country with a long history that needs to be re-envisioned and many stories as yet untold. Thus, for many contemporary novelists the launchpad to which Fischer and Norfolk refer is a starting point for an exploration of the past.

In her novel *The Giant, O'Brien* (1998) Hilary Mantel—subject of an entry in *DLB 271*—portrays the dangers of cultural and moral amnesia when a society blindly subjects itself to scientific pragmatism and blithely seeks entertaining distractions in human misery. The voice Mantel chooses to express the consequences of such behavior is an eighteenth-century Irish giant who represents a fading tradition of storytelling that connects humans both to their place in the present and to their past: "When human memory runs out, there is memory of animals; behind that, the memory of plants, and behind that the memory of rocks. But the wind and the sea wear the rocks away; and the cell-line runs to its limit, where meaning falls away from it, and it loses knowledge of its own nature. Unless we plead on our knees with history, we are done for, we are lost." The giant's words suggest an ineluctable link between history and memory and that the denial of one leads to the devastation of all else. Many contemporary novelists seem to agree with Mantel's giant, for they explore the past and the stories it tells. In other words, history proves surprisingly uncertain and open to interpretation, and one vehicle for exploring and rearticulating the past is narration.

Rather than being the study of the past as it "really was," history for many contemporary novelists entails a study of the textuality through which conflicting accounts of the past are mediated. History is thus always incomplete, always provisional, because it cannot do without the perspective of an observer or interpreter who creates a narrative in which, or through which, the past is re-created or interrogated. This practice does not deny historical fact or waive historical references, nor does it ignore the influence of memory and representation upon them. Considering historical events and figures from multiple perspectives opens possibilities of understanding; it does not necessarily foreshadow a decline in certainty or reliability. Historical novels represent the process of history itself and reveal how all attempts to narrate, negotiate, and re-envision history are inside the narrative rather than outside it. In the preface to his book *Ornamentalism: How*

the British Saw Their Empire (2001), which attempts to present the worldview held by those running, and working within, the British empire, David Cannadine acknowledges the impact of literary explorations of the past on the study of history itself: "And instead of concentrating on the official records of government, or the unofficial documents of business and trade, literary scholars have insisted on the need to address and analyse a wider range of imperial texts, which disclose much more about systems of power and domination, and about how what they like to call the 'hegemonic imperial project' was primarily concerned with the production of derogatory stereotypes of other, alien, subordinated societies."

Pat Barker, who appears in *DLB 271,* offers a particularly powerful example of this practice with her war trilogy—*Regeneration* (1991), *The Eye in the Door* (1993), and *Ghost Road* (1995). The trilogy focuses broadly on an historical event, World War I, and a biographical fact, Siegfried Sassoon's protest against the war and his subsequent treatment for shell shock as an alternative to the charge of desertion and court-martial. The novels present a linear and developing story in real, rational, or historical time that, like the therapy sessions Sassoon receives, offers every expectation of completion and resolution. The story of Dr. W. H. R. Rivers's treatment of Sassoon's alleged shell shock by means of the recently developed science of psychoanalysis leads quickly away from linear time to a form of unreal, irrational, nonsuccessive time that comprises the unconscious mind and dreams of Sassoon and other patients. The exchanges between patients and physician often fluctuate between these two realms of time, and Rivers's journal and thoughts represent some of the most pointed conflicts between the two. Through the intrusion of memories and thoughts unearthed during Rivers's sessions with his patients, the supposed linearity and certainty of rational or historical time is ruptured, revealing gaps, alternatives, and unexpected connections that undermine the reader's expectation that linear time will ultimately regain command and bring a sense of closure or ordered resolution to the events portrayed in the narrative.

For writers living in the late twentieth and early twenty-first centuries, events in the first half of a remarkable and horrifying century act as a backdrop to the world they know. As a girl, Barker saw the bayonet scar on her grandfather that acted as a physical reminder of the war; however, her grandfather never spoke of his war experiences until late in life. In an interview with Lynn Karpan in *The New York Times Book Review* (29 March 1992) Barker acknowledged that "World War I was the first subject I ever wanted to write about." Included in this volume is an entry on

Giles Foden, who found both personal and historical factors motivating him to write *Ladysmith* (1999), his novel set during the Boer War (1899–1902). The historical events of the war seem dusty and forgotten; however, Foden believes that in some ways the twentieth century began with concentration camps, in a war fought by powerful nations over colonized territory. In an essay for *The Guardian* (9 October 1999) titled "The First Camps," Foden makes the link between the Boer War and events occurring later in the twentieth century: "A century ago on Monday, the Boer war broke out. The conflict between Afrikaner settlers and an expanding British empire, is best remembered for the concentration camps in which the British interned some 200,000 refugees. Approximately 20,000 Afrikaners died in the camps, together with an estimated 12,000 black Africans."

Beyond an interest in an historical event whose impetus and practices echo throughout the century, in "A Family Story," another essay published in *The Guardian* (18 June 1999), Foden recalls his great-grandfather, whose experiences in the war Foden discovered through letters written by a young man, eager for adventure, who left his home to help run the empire:

> A century ago when my great-grandfather went out to fight in the Boer war as a British trooper, Africa was a place not just of strangeness, but also of opportunity. In his letters home he writes of how different things were from England: the capering crowds of Zulu hustlers who greet him at the quayside in Durban are "oddly garbed in horn and feather," and the rabbits he sees running before the army column when it begins its march on the besieged town of Ladysmith are "like a cross between a rabbit and a hare." All the same, "I have seen something of a beautiful, if terrible continent." That last observation of Trooper Foden's has the characteristic Victorian drifts towards the twin exoticisation and demonisation of Africa as classically registered in Joseph Conrad's *Heart of Darkness* [1899].

Several critics have offered paradigms that reveal the recurring interest in history among contemporary novelists. In her book *Traces of Another Time: History and Politics in Postwar British Fiction* (1990), Margaret Scanlan explores what she calls the "spectral historical novel," in which the past is not valorized nor its triumphs and achievements glorified. Instead, such novels focus on defeat rather than victory, drawing attention to shortcomings or arrogance that facilitated the loss; begin with a troubling event whose veracity can never be proved; dismantle once-potent myths, such as the benign nature of "civilizing" practices by those advocating a natural superiority over those deemed uncivilized; and undercut traditional narrative techniques that might convey a sense of a singular or insular past. Rep-

resented in this volume is Philip Hensher, whose novel *The Mulberry Empire* (2002) is a retelling of the events of the first Afghan War (1839–1842), in which British overconfidence and arrogance resulted in a massacre and a resounding defeat for the invading British forces.

Conrad's *Heart of Darkness* represents the modern root of this type of historical novel from which other offshoots branch out. Colonials on their heels, vainly trying to hold their ground as imperial status wanes, appear in the works of authors who have appeared in earlier *DLBs*, such as Graham Greene's *The Heart of the Matter* (1948) and William Boyd's *A Good Man in Africa* (1981). Foden's *The Last King of Scotland* (1998) is a fictionalized account of Idi Amin's dictatorship, narrated by a Scottish doctor who is a representative of the former colonial power. Also included in this volume is an entry on G. E. Armitage (who writes under the name Robert Edric), whose novel about nineteenth-century British mapmakers in the Congo, *The Book of the Heathen* (2000), is a rewriting of Conrad's novella from a postcolonial perspective. Salman Rushdie has aptly referred to the efforts of writers to articulate the story of those subjugated by imperialistic imposition as "the empire writes back." Novels of such postcolonial critique include Chinua Achebe's *Things Fall Apart* (1958), Naipaul's *A Bend in the River* (1979), Rushdie's *Midnight's Children* (1981), and even Armitage's retelling of the story of the last full-blooded Tasmanian aborigine, *Elysium* (1995). Between the narratives of deteriorating imperialism and swelling postcolonialism lie novels such as Norfolk's *Lemprière's Dictionary* (1991), Barry Unsworth's *Sacred Hunger* (1992), and Kneale's *English Passengers,* which blend elements of the voyage or quest with expressions of imperialistic greed and economic expansion—recurring themes in Conrad's novel as well.

Novelist and critic A. S. Byatt has written the first piece of detailed criticism analyzing contemporary British fiction published in the new millennium. In her collection of essays *On History and Stories* (2000), Byatt attempts to "map" the new terrain of British fiction. In order to make her argument, Byatt juxtaposes older and more established authors with those of a younger generation. She classifies the approaches to history taken by many contemporary novelists under three headings: "Fathers," "Forefathers," and "Ancestors." In her discussion of "Fathers," Byatt first asks, "why has history become imaginable and important again?" She then compares novelists of an older generation whose experience leads back to World War II. This older generation of novelists is subdivided into three categories: recorders of the immediate, Henry Green and Elizabeth Bowen; comic chroniclers, Evelyn Waugh and Anthony Powell; and moral investigators, Penelope Fitzgerald, Muriel Spark, Anthony Burgess, and William Golding. Juxtaposed with these authors who lived through the war are those writers who live in its aftermath and must cope "with clichés, with popular images of wartime derived from films they saw as boys about the bravery of Spitfire pilots and secret agents, or spies under interrogation." This postwar generation of novelists includes such already well-established writers as Julian Barnes, Graham Swift, Barker, and Martin Amis. Byatt argues that this generation of writers is turning to history, despite the fact that they were raised on popular images of war, because they have lived to see the modernist preoccupation with the construction of the self played out, thus the historical figure who is not totally knowable and only partially imaginable offers an intriguing option to modernist narratives that dwell upon impressionistic experiences and infinitely regressing memories. Byatt identifies a common trait among contemporary novelists, "Something that surprised me in the war novels of the post-war generation was the fact that the interest common to all of them, in linear time and the finiteness of the single biological life, is always accompanied by some teasing or puzzling image of infinity and indestructibility."

Byatt's second category, "Forefathers," involves the question of how novelists approach the facts of the past. As she did with "Fathers," Byatt reveals the intention of contemporary novelists to move away from the techniques of modernist fiction and its immediate successors: "This new interest in narration can, I think, be related to the novelists' need for, and essential interest of, storytelling, after a long period of stream-of-consciousness, followed by the fragmented, non-linear form of the *nouveau roman,* and the experimental novel." Two types of techniques employed by novelists in this category are "maggot" and "ventriloquism." In the case of the former, which directly echoes the title of John Fowles's novel *A Maggot* (1985), novelists connect with the past through metaphor rather than specific events. Byatt includes in this group Jeanette Winterson, specifically her novel *The Passion* (1987), Richard Sennatt in *The Fall of Public Man* (1977), and John Fuller in *Flying to Nowhere* (1983). Byatt uses the word *ventriloquism* in a specific way to identify the latter group. While the word suggests pastiche or parody, both of which recur in contemporary British fiction, Byatt champions these novelists because they breathe new life into the past and raise "the spirits of the dead." This group includes Peter Ackroyd, Golding, Byatt herself, Burgess, Barnes, and Swift. Byatt takes particular pleasure, though, in identifying three novels for special attention: Mantel's *A Place of Greater Safety* (1992), Norfolk's *Lemprière's Dictionary,* and Fitzgerald's *The Blue Flower* (1995).

Byatt's last category, "Ancestors," is more broadly defined and involves the connection between stories and the "large paradigmatic narratives we inhabit," which in the past took the form of biblical or national narratives. Byatt offers an extended reading of Mantel's *A Change of Climate* (1996) to support her overall point that a new sense of the past is needed that differs from the grand narratives available in the past: "History is neither the working-out of the divine plan, nor simply the history of political progress and destruction. A new kind of historical novel might be possible. The process of adaptation, as Darwin said, is slow and gradual, and much current fiction springs out of a resistance to the implications of his ideas—a resistance sometimes nostalgic, sometimes combative." Byatt's new "map," of course, is incomplete. The psychological novel delving into family conflicts and marital infidelities may be less fashionable today, but such novels nonetheless recur among the works of excellent novelists. Included in *DLB 267* are entries on Helen Dunmore, who writes thrillers that are also psychological studies of complex family relationships, such as her *With Your Crooked Heart* (1999); and Candia McWilliam, whose novels examine the choices that middle-class women are forced to make both within and without marriage. Kate Atkinson, Anne Enright, and Magnus Mills are among the authors represented in this volume who are writing novels that have a distinctive comic edge. Intriguing mysteries, thrillers, and science-fiction novels appear from novelists who receive both vigorous sales and positive critical reviews. Included in *DLB 267,* for example, are entries on Ian Rankin, whose best-selling Inspector John Rebus crime novels have met with critical success; Peter Cunningham, who has successfully bridged the divide between author of thrillers and writer of serious fiction; Christopher Fowler, whose horror fiction also manages to transcend genre labels; and Jeff Noon, whose dystopic novels set in a near-future Manchester have been hailed by critics for their linguistic innovation. However, as one of the first critical studies of the new millennium that focuses specifically on contemporary fiction, Byatt's study points readers and scholars in a fruitful direction. Byatt is less open to charges of insularity and elitism than one might suspect, considering her preference for literature that explores the past. As Elaine Showalter states in "Showing Off," an essay in *The Guardian* (11 May 1999) on the state of contemporary fiction written by women, the changes in British fiction are not isolated to a select few writers determined to interpret the past:

But it may also be that as we reach the millennium, British women's writing may be coming to the end of its history as a separate and distinct "literature of its own." The self-consciousness that is the legacy of two decades of feminist literary criticism has made British women's writing self-reflexive in a new way. Now, every book is written in the shadow of feminist theory as well as Jane Austen, and in the consciousness of such female themes, metaphors, and iconographies as the mother tongue, embroidery, cookery, eating disorders, sisterhood, madwomen in the attic, lesbian eroticism and mother-daughter attachment. In addition, the insularity and locality of setting that characterized British women's writing a century ago has now largely disappeared. The new generation of novelists is responding and assimilating influences that are global.

In this volume a variety of women writers are included, ranging from Deirdre Purcell, a best-selling author of romance novels, to Livi Michael, the writer of feminist-influenced novels frequently set in the grim reality of Manchester housing estates, to Australian-born Madeleine St John, whose third novel, *The Essence of the Thing* (1997), was short-listed for the Booker Prize. Emma Donoghue, an Irishwoman who now lives in Canada, has written lesbian revisions of fairy tales that have attracted critical attention. In addition to Purcell and Donoghue, other Irishwomen included in *DLB 267* are Clare Boylan, who writes about the situation of women in Ireland; Mary Morrissy, whose novel *The Pretender* (2000) is a fictionalized account of the Romanov pretender Anna Anderson; and Kate O'Riordan, whose works encompass a range of moods and styles.

Many of the trends at work in contemporary British fiction are simultaneously occurring in contemporary Irish fiction—though for completely different reasons. As with their British counterparts, Irish novelists now challenge older notions of national identity and portray newer versions that would have been unknown even to their immediate literary ancestors. Gerry Smyth argues in his *The Novel and the Nation: Studies in the New Irish Fiction* (1999) that "the new Irish novelists combine a willingness to confront the formal and conceptual legacies of a received literary (and wider social) tradition alongside a self-awareness of the role played by cultural narratives in mediating modern (or perhaps it would be better now to say *postmodern*) Ireland's changing circumstances." Smyth cites *Cowboys & Indians* (1991) by Joseph O'Connor, subject of an entry in this volume, as an example of the older notions of Ireland and their expression in fiction being challenged by a newer generation of writers. In a tone dripping with anger and satire, the speaker in O'Connor's novel identifies themes once resonant and powerful in Irish literature that now seem little more than cliché and are certainly lacking any immediacy and relevance for contemporary writers. Nonetheless, contemporary writers feel compelled to participate in and perpetuate the tradition offered them. Smyth concludes that the "tension generated as a

result of this contradictory structure, in which the subject is forced to operate constantly on the interface between discourses of change and discourses of continuity, is the defining characteristic of both the modern Irish experience and the new Irish fiction which seeks to represent that experience."

There has been a long-held tradition in Ireland that links cultural and political conflicts with the struggle for autonomy and self-definition. For many Irish citizens the history of struggle against the influences and power of outsiders stretches back to 1 May 1169 when the Normans, having subdued and organized England, looked westward and landed on Irish shores. Since that time, the people who have defined themselves as Irish alternately employed tactics of armed rebellion and strategic diplomacy in their attempts to bring—or retrieve—political and cultural independence to their island.

In the oft-cited passage from James Joyce's novel *A Portrait of the Artist as a Young Man* (1916), a seething Stephen Dedalus contemplates his conversation with the British dean of studies and concludes that the British influence upon his identity reaches back to the point at which thought and word meet: "The language in which we are speaking is his before it is mine. How different are the words *home, Christ, ale, master,* on his lips and on mine! I cannot speak or write these words without unrest or spirit. His language, so familiar and so foreign, will always be for me an acquired speech. I have not made or accepted its words. My voice holds them at bay. My soul frets in the shadows of his language." Language, history, and cultural influences conspire against young Stephen to hold his soul back from artistic freedom. Stephen is well on his way to reaching the same conclusion many other Irish citizens and writers have made—namely, that he has two options, fight or flight. Despite his exalted proclamation that he plans "to forge in the smithy of my soul the uncreated conscience of my race," Stephen chooses flight in the final pages of the novel. The twin options of physical exile and strident nationalism still exist for contemporary novelists, though neither seems particularly appealing. The question then becomes what, if any, other options afford themselves to contemporary novelists.

The nationalist mythos, so potently articulated in both artistic expression and political rhetoric, carried over into the modern Irish Free State, which gained the freedom to run its own affairs in 1922. Despite their newfound independence, the Irish had a long-established conviction that the British adversely influenced, or even determined, Irish identity. This conviction was sustained when the small island was partitioned into two parts, the six counties in the north that retained ties to England and the twenty-six counties in the south that eventually became the Republic of Ireland. The political struggle of an entire country was then even further delimited by a small group of nationalists whose identity was shaped by religious, cultural, and economic factors in the north.

In the closing years of the century in which Ireland ended one violent struggle only to experience another, in which independence led to separation, it became increasingly clear to novelists that older versions of Irish identity act more as an encumbrance to their literary efforts than a foundation for them. Since the conflicts and borders have not faded with time, they have to be re-envisioned, challenged, or transgressed. In the introduction to *Contemporary Irish Fiction: Themes, Tropes, Theories* (2000), Liam Harte and Michael Parker explain the choices made by many contemporary Irish novelists who find the past rife with an untenable version of Irishness: "Such literary partitionism, moreover, is rendered increasingly anachronistic by the proliferation of recent fictional narratives that engage in the determined subversion of actual and metaphorical borders. The transgression of boundaries, both literal and figurative, appears as a familiar trope in contemporary Irish fiction, as novelists attempt to reimagine 'Ireland' as a syncretic space, thereby interrogating established narratives of identity and difference."

Harte and Parker's description of Ireland as a "syncretic space" bears remarkable similarity to Fischer and Lawrence's description of England as a "cultural entrepôt." Both pairs of editors, moreover, identify their respective countries as spaces of flux and change where old definitions are replaced by newer hybrid definitions. Here lies one of the intriguing similarities between novelists from two countries that have long defined themselves in contradistinction to one other. Both England and Ireland must accept the changes they have experienced in recent decades and acknowledge the new voices and perspectives that such changes facilitate. Likewise, both must explore and interrogate the past in order to exorcise lingering ghosts and discover previously disavowed versions of themselves.

Perhaps no Irish novelist represents these changes in Irish fiction more than Roddy Doyle, the subject of an entry in *DLB 194*. After five novels that explore the lives of working-class Dublin families, Doyle changes his focus in *A Star Called Henry* (1999)—the first in a series of novels, perhaps a trilogy, that will follow the Irish experience throughout the twentieth century, including the mass migration of the Irish to America. The first in the series is a memoir-style novel about the violent birth of the Irish Free State. *A Star Called Henry* follows Henry Smart, a bright and precocious young man full of charm and courage, from his early years in the grinding poverty of Joyce's Dublin, through the

1916 Easter Uprising, and up to independence, partition, and the Civil War. Henry, an Irish Republican Army (IRA) assassin during the struggle for independence, escapes the retaliation of British troops, which become increasingly sophisticated in their tactics toward terrorism, only to discover he cannot escape the factional splintering and betrayals that followed victory over Britain.

Doyle's novel, thus, tells the story of a fictional character surrounded by historical figures and events. In the course of the novel, rather than simply portraying figures and events, Doyle opens up possible interpretations of them. Was, for example, the Easter Uprising ill conceived and executed, a doomed but mythically potent romantic quest, or a prelude or precipitating cause of latter events leading eventually to independence? The picture of politicians positioning themselves for power, jostling allegiances, and expelling the unwanted leads to questions about the myths the Free State government would eventually embrace: middle-class, conservative, romantic, and Catholic values. These are the very values, diluted if not impotent over time, that inform the Irish society of Doyle's earlier novels.

Doyle, of course, is not the only novelist exploring the lingering incongruities of the old Ireland and the problems facing the new Ireland. While Doyle's novels tend to blend comic dialogue with serious cultural analysis, Patrick McCabe—also the subject of an entry in *DLB 194*—has made a career of exposing the dark underbelly of Irish cultural values. McCabe's best-known novel, *The Butcher Boy* (1992), portrays the debilitating effects of indifferent parenting, alcoholism, economic hopelessness, and institutional care on the developing psyche of its young protagonist, Francie Brady. While Irish society seems to offer little more to Francie than nostalgic images and expressions of its own past, many of which turn out to be lies, contemporary Irish culture, as it is in Doyle's comic novels, revolves around images and expressions derived from American television shows, movies, and comic books.

Even the concept of Irish identity has been distorted by American media images, as the Belfast-born novelist Robert McLiam Wilson, subject of an entry in this volume, observes in his essay "Sticks and Stones: Irish Identity," published in *Grand Street* (1997). Wilson describes the phenomenon of the Irish adopting green kilts and bagpipes after learning that "New Yorkers are marching in green-kilted bagpipe bands," and he remarks, "Over the years I've watched the fundamental concepts of what it is to be Irish being altered by common-currency American errors. . . . Yet I've always believed that such Americans have it just about right. Their ideas of Irishness are as fake as a hooker's tit, but then so are ours." The results of the cross-generation of Irish and American culture can be seen in a more positive light in the works of two other writers included in this volume, Michael Collins and Colum McCann. Collins, who now lives in Seattle, and McCann, who lives in New York City, have both written novels that reflect the Irish, American, and Irish American experiences. Collins's *Emerald Underground* (1998), for example, is about the lives of illegal Irish immigrants in the United States, and McCann's *This Side of Brightness* (1998) incorporates the story of the African American and Irish workers who built the New York City subway system.

Identifying which contemporary novelists will influence British and Irish literature well into the twenty-first century demands foresight and imagination that would have humbled even Beerbohm. If the past several years are any indication, though, then the cultural space in which British and Irish fiction is written will undoubtedly allow, if not encourage, novelists to redefine the very space they occupy. If the modernist period in British literature is any indication of success, then one can assert that the incubator of great literature begins with the conviction of writers to explore important ideas that they are uniquely suited to address. Little can be imagined that is more important than one's relationship to the past and one's identity in the present.

–Michael R. Molino

Acknowledgments

This book was produced by Bruccoli Clark Layman, Inc. Karen L. Rood is senior editor. Jan Peter F. van Rosevelt was the in-house editor.

Production manager is Philip B. Dematteis.

Administrative support was provided by Ann M. Cheschi and Carol A. Cheschi.

Accountant is Ann-Marie Holland.

Copyediting supervisor is Sally R. Evans. The copyediting staff includes Phyllis A. Avant, Brenda Carol Blanton, Caryl Brown, Melissa D. Hinton, Philip I. Jones, Rebecca Mayo, Nancy E. Smith, and Elizabeth Jo Ann Sumner. Freelance copyeditors are Brenda Cabra, Thom Harman, and Alice Payne.

Editorial associates are Michael S. Allen, Michael S. Martin, Catherine M. Polit, and Amelia B. Lacey.

Permissions editor and database manager is Amber L. Coker.

Layout and graphics supervisor is Janet E. Hill. The graphics staff includes Zoe R. Cook and Sydney E. Hammock.

Office manager is Kathy Lawler Merlette.

Photography supervisor is Paul Talbot. Photography editor is Scott Nemzek.

Digital photographic copy work was performed by Joseph M. Bruccoli.

Systems manager is Marie L. Parker.

Typesetting supervisor is Kathleen M. Flanagan. The typesetting staff includes Patricia Marie Flanagan, Mark J. McEwan, and Pamela D. Norton. Freelance typesetters are Wanda Adams and Rebecca Mayo.

Walter W. Ross did library research. He was assisted by Jo Cottingham and the following other librarians at the Thomas Cooper Library of the University of South Carolina: circulation department head Tucker Taylor; reference department head Virginia W. Weathers; reference department staff Brette Barron, Marilee Birchfield, Paul Cammarata, Gary Geer, Michael Macan, Tom Marcil, Rose Marshall, and Sharon Verba; interlibrary loan department head John Brunswick; and interlibrary loan staff Robert Arndt, Hayden Battle, Alex Byrne, Bill Fetty, Marna Hostetler, and Nelson Rivera.

Dictionary of Literary Biography® • Volume Two Hundred Sixty-Seven

Twenty-First-Century British and Irish Novelists

Dictionary of Literary Biography

G. E. Armitage
(Robert Edric)
(14 April 1956 –   )

Anne-Marie Obilade
Southern Illinois University

BOOKS: *A Season of Peace: A Novel* (London: Secker & Warburg, 1985; New York: St. Martin's Press, 1985);
Winter Garden, as Robert Edric (London: Deutsch, 1985);
Across the Autumn Grass: A Novel (London: Secker & Warburg, 1986);
A New Ice Age, as Edric (London: Deutsch, 1986);
A Lunar Eclipse, as Edric (London: Heinemann, 1989);
In the Days of the American Museum, as Edric (London: Cape, 1990);
The Broken Lands, as Edric (London: Cape, 1992); republished as *The Broken Lands: A Novel of Arctic Disaster* (New York: Thomas Dunne Books, 2002);
The Earth Made of Glass, as Edric (London: Picador, 1993);
Hallowed Ground, as Edric (Lincoln: Sunk Island, 1993);
Elysium, as Edric (London: Duckworth, 1995);
In Desolate Heaven: A Novel, as Edric (London: Duckworth, 1997);
The Sword Cabinet, as Edric (London: Anchor, 1999);
The Book of the Heathen, as Edric (London: Anchor, 2000; New York: Thomas Dunne Books, 2002);
Peacetime, as Edric (London: Doubleday, 2002).

G. E. Armitage has written a few works under his own name and several under his pseudonym, Robert Edric. His status in contemporary British fiction is rising, and critics have placed his work under categories ranging from murder mystery, horror, and crime to historical fiction. Although many of Armitage's fictional works are related to broad historical events, his themes focus on the everyday reality of individuals.

Gary Edric Armitage was born on 14 April 1956 in Sheffield, England, the son of E. H. Armitage (a store

G. E. Armitage (Hulton-Deutsch/Corbis; from the dust jacket for the U.S. edition of The Broken Lands, *2002)*

manager) and A. Armitage, née Gregory. He attended the University of Hull, where he graduated in 1977, with honors, with a B.A. degree in geography. On 12 August 1978 he married Sara Jones, a teacher, and in 1980 he graduated with a Ph.D. in geography, writing his Ph.D. thesis on the spatial imagination in Victorian literature. He lives in East Yorkshire in England.

Armitage's literary career began suddenly when two novels written within a few years of each other were accepted for publication; one under his own name, *A Season of Peace* (1985), and the other under his pseudonym, Robert Edric, *Winter Garden* (1985). Although written at about the same time, the two novels have different styles that represent Armitage's shift in technique when writing under his own name and pseudonym, respectively.

A Season of Peace was well received by critics. Writing for *Publishers Weekly* (11 April 1986), Sybil Steinberg called it a work examining "the nature of loss and grief, marriage and parenthood, and the disappointments and compromises of which most lives are composed." In the novel Armitage tells the story of a former military engineer mourning the death of his son in an Irish Republican Army (IRA) bombing. The unnamed first-person narrator tells the reader that he cannot relate to his wife, who seems to have secluded herself in her own form of grieving. Instead, the narrator engages in memories of the past involving a period of time spent at Cable Point, an old coastal anti-aircraft battery, thirty-two years earlier. The novel, therefore, comprises two separate accounts, one concerning the narrator's contemporary relationship with his wife, and the other involving his past relationship with Mary, a young girl with whom he occasionally converses at Cable Point. The reader can easily find parallels within the two accounts. As the narrator awaits the body of his son, killed while serving in Northern Ireland, so also Mary awaits the return of her father, who was injured in World War II. While in the present the narrator tries to reconstruct the truth about his relationship with his son, in the past he tries to decipher the truth about Mary's family and her father in particular. In both accounts the narrator criticizes the government for its treatment of soldiers, questioning the amount of fear and uncertainty soldiers and their families are forced to live with. In the end, innocent lives are lost; Michael, the narrator's son, is killed, and Mary perishes, perhaps at her father's hands—her body is found and it seems that her father is responsible for her death.

Character types and situations that Armitage further develops in his later works are already present in his first novel. For instance, the inability of couples to communicate is a recurrent motif in Armitage's works. The narrator states early in the novel, "Because my own means of dealing with Michael's death do not correspond with hers we have grown even further apart, and now his absence rather than his presence is the wall between us." Within this statement rests another of Armitage's major themes: his concern with the roots of difficulty in communication, especially in a marriage. For the narrator and his wife in *A Season of Peace* the

roots most likely lie in their many differences; for example, in the different ways in which they communicate with their son and cope with his military service. In Armitage's novels, problems related to marriage are often located within a couple's lack of desire to accept, appreciate or understand one another. *A Season of Peace* received special notice as a runner-up to the Betty Trask Award in 1985.

In his second novel, *Winter Garden,* marriages break down completely, and reconciliation is not always possible. *Winter Garden* is of much greater complexity than Armitage's preceding novel, and in it Armitage continues to explore themes of miscommunication and isolation but with more depth and gravity than in his previous work. He also involves a larger number of characters whose lives reflect a desperation and hopelessness not seen in his first work. The result is a tale that foreshadows the focus on crime and disillusionment that marks many of the Edric works. *Winter Garden* is about a missing fourteen-year-old schoolgirl, Tracey Morton, who is later found murdered. Through the course of the novel, the reader learns about the lives of several characters residing at the lodging of the Protheroes; Alice Protheroe is an old housewife, and her husband, Norman, is the police inspector who has been assigned to the investigation. Using the omniscient narrative voice, Armitage brings several situations to the reader's attention. There is the story of the Priestleys, a disgruntled married couple performing magic tricks for children; Mighty Morgan, a midget who delights in the discomforts of others; Rita, a lonely former stripper; Roland Tripper, the rich but dissatisfied theater owner; Vincent, a married man separated from his wife; and Malcolm Devlin, a stagehand at Tripper's theater, who turns out to be the murderer of Tracey Morton. Although the novel won the James Tait Black Memorial Prize in 1985, Steinberg—who had earlier reviewed *A Season of Peace*—writing for *Publishers Weekly* (26 June 1987), found it to be "a grim, slow-moving novel" that left the reader with a "totally bleak view of life."

Indeed, the theme of the work does not reflect an encouraging view of the community, for each individual exists in a relationship that is broken down. Veronica Priestley, for instance, resents her husband for their plight. Their professional career has been deteriorating, and Veronica cannot determine whether Derek is to blame or if they are both responsible in their decline. Again, Armitage explores possible roots of the broken relationship, paralleling it with the accounts of other broken lives. Unlike *A Season of Peace,* in which the narrator's retrospective point of view is used to show characters' development from their past, *Winter Garden* is written primarily in the present from an omniscient point of view. There is no narrator to interpret the events in a person's life. Speaking in a 2000 interview for the on-line literary magazine *ArtsReaders* (published on the Arts Council of England website, www.artsonline.com), Armitage explained his desire to trust his readers as opposed to telling them all the details:

> I don't much care for writing that says, the following week they met again and the week after that they—I don't like that kind of writing. I don't want to be told everything. I'd much rather be shown individual little flashes of actions and interaction and for the spaces in between literally to be left blank.

This method of reading through different scenes in quick succession produces a cinematic effect in *Winter Garden* and Armitage's successive works. Characters' dialogues provide the reader with ideas about their past, but the reader is not given a straightforward chronicle of events as in the two Armitage novels.

Winter Garden and *A Season of Peace,* however, follow a similar cyclical pattern. The former work begins with the recovery of Tracey Morton's body on Christmas Day and ends with a similar scene. Armitage reveals the identity of the girl's murderer to the reader relatively early in the book. As a result, readers know more than do the characters in the book and can thus analyze the characters' situations more than can the characters themselves. Knowing early on that Devlin is the murderer of Tracey gives readers the ability to study his actions and to determine the psychological reasons for his attitude toward women in general. His flirtation with Tripper's teenage daughter and his sexual advances toward women can no longer be seen as comic gestures. Devlin is a troubling character because he assumes a normal life and position in society, even though by the end of the story he has committed two murders, having killed both Tracey and his own mother.

As critics have noted, Armitage is unafraid to delve into the distasteful aspects of life, and he explicitly describes the rape and murder of Tracey Morton. Armitage's attention to harrowing crimes that might make the reader cringe has won him wide acclaim. Mark Sanderson declared, in a 30 July 2000 review of *The Book of the Heathen* (2000) for *The Sunday Telegraph* (London), "The worst in men has brought out the best in Edric." Armitage's focus on depraved deeds of individuals, however, may have affected his literary success, as D. J. Taylor remarked in a 2 September 2000 review of the same novel in *The Spectator* (London), "Every year or so Mr. Edric produces a work which half-a-dozen metropolitan critics garland with the most luxuriant adjectives ('thoroughly arresting . . . utterly believable . . . gloriously discomforting') to the complete indifference of the book-buying public." Taylor claimed that publishers were still hesitant to work with a writer

Dust jacket for the U.S. edition of Armitage's 1985 novel, in which a retired military engineer reflects on his experiences in World War II (Richland County Public Library)

who focused explicitly on the troubling and unglamorous side of life.

Murder and crime scenes are written in great detail and specificity in many of Armitage's novels, yet what is still fascinating to critics is Armitage's ability to describe horror in surprisingly calm narration. In *Winter Garden,* for instance, Tracey's murder is related with chilling calm, as if a news report is being given. The calm depiction of horror is a trademark of Armitage's finesse and control as a writer. By writing the narrative in a steady, calm style, Armitage brings the immediacy of the horror closer to readers in a way that allows them to view scenes of murder with an eerie calm that would probably not be present if they were viewing such a description on film.

Themes regarding the difficulty of communicating in marriage, however, are still pervasive in *Winter Garden* despite the recurring focus on Tracey's death. The first characters introduced are the Protheroes, Alice and Norman. Theirs is a marriage of commitment and respect, but the reader can see signs of isolation early on. For instance, Alice assumes that her husband's fascination with geography and nature magazines is a childish thing. Norman, however, reads these magazines in order to relax. Later on in the book, Alice begins to wonder whether or not she has missed something in her life; when she attempts to communicate with Norman, he ignores her advances, silently brooding over the discovery of the girl's body. The narrative reads, "She wanted to talk about the holiday, but he remained with the girl's body, outlining the months ahead and already guessing at the outcome."

Veronica and Derek drift apart because of the frustration of their failing careers. While Derek keeps trying to believe things will improve, Veronica resents him for his optimism. She admits to herself that she does not know whether she hates her work because of her husband or if her hatred of her husband is caused by their circumstances. Other characters, such as Rita and Morgan, though single, are every bit as lonely as their married counterparts. Rita has given up on holding onto any self-respect, allowing men to buy her drinks and acknowledging "her own unspoken part of the bargain." By the end of the novel, as Steinberg noted, all seems hopeless for the characters. *Winter Garden* is a much more ambitious novel than *A Season of Peace* and its complexities of character, style, and situation are features of all the Edric novels.

Across the Autumn Grass (1986), the second work published under the name Armitage, contains the same straightforward narration of events found in *A Season of Peace*. Here the unnamed narrator, a writer, recounts the stories told to him by a war veteran, George. As he listens to George's harrowing tales, the narrator begins to recall the details of his own separation from his wife, remembering the nuances of their marriage and his scarred relationship with his two daughters. In the meantime he also begins to learn of the townspeople's artificiality. A couple invites the narrator to dinner, and he sees through all their outward gestures of courtesy, being fully aware of the role he has to play in order to amuse them. He comes to find that much of what occurs on the surface is in actuality different from underlying truths. By the end of the novel, George has finished retelling his tale but is not immediately released from the past. He undergoes a violent outburst of emotion that truly sets him free, the same kind of outburst symbolized in the rain that begins to fall on the village following a long drought.

In both *Across the Autumn Grass* and *Winter Garden,* Armitage introduces secretive characters who have either a hidden past or a private identity. In *Across the Autumn Grass* the narrator's literary agent, Alex, is a homosexual, a fact that is discovered only after his death. In his novels Armitage often engages indirectly in social commentary. In *Across the Autumn Grass,* for instance, George utters grievances against a society that expects men to return home from war unchanged and unscathed: "You can't take away from somebody everything they ever had or were likely to have, to know or were likely to know and expect them to feel the same afterwards." He later shares with the narrator the confusion he felt after killing his first enemy soldier, as he asks, "How can a man come back and expect to carry on as a husband or a son or brother as though none of it has happened?" Social commentary is also implied in *Winter Garden* when comments are made about how representatives of various charities near the scene of Tracey Morton's murder are too busy collecting funds to hear the young girl's screams.

Themes found in past works are again explored in Armitage's later works. He explores another failed marriage in *Across the Autumn Grass,* this time between the narrator and his estranged wife. Again differences in expectations and ambitions play an important part in the demise of the marriage. Ruth prefers a conventional husband, like the professors that she encounters. The narrator recalls, "The hairline cracks of our separation were with us from the start. My writing alienated her. She never understood. Most of our friends taught in schools, and at the beginning she had used the word 'college' as I imagine the wives of university lecturers would have said the word 'university' to her. As the cracks widened, my work became to her just another wedge."

Realism is an integral part of Armitage's works, which feature a range of social commentary on all aspects of human life, from the political to the domestic. In *Across the Autumn Grass* the narrator describes the manner in which his relationship with his daughters has changed since the divorce, saying, "They still wrote to me regularly, but their letters were filled with the stilted adolescent listing of facts, people and events—as though they were already dividing their lives into two halves, one secret, one public, and I was being shown only the latter."

In his novels Armitage prompts the reader to reflect on socially accepted gestures. For instance, in *A Season of Peace* one finds commentary on the procedures involved in a military burial:

> The military presence at a funeral is not for the benefit of those who suffer genuine grief—for they would hardly notice—but for those peripheral witnesses who want to believe in something more heroic rather than to understand the circumstances of the death itself. There can be few things more final than a volley of gunfire over an open grave, few things more loaded with contradictory meaning than a line of rifles pointed Heavenwards.

A New Ice Age (1986), Armitage's fourth novel, follows closely upon the style and themes of *Winter Garden.* The novel was a runner-up for the Guardian Fiction Prize in 1986 and received generally good reviews. The story is about a group of tenants in a boardinghouse that is about to be torn down. Each of the tenants is slow to look for a new place to live, and each possesses various idiosyncrasies. Mrs. Devine, known as Mrs. D, is always speaking about her two dead husbands; Atlas, the bodybuilder, despises the rest for not being as health conscious as himself; and Mrs. Patel dominates her husband without saying a word. While commenting on actions of his neighbors, the narrator also tells the reader about the demise of his own life, remembering the details of his marriage from its start to its finish. As he did with *Winter Garden,* Armitage has constructed this novel in a circular fashion—the book begins and ends with almost identical scenes—so that the reader progressively learns about the narrator's life in the interim. Again, the primary setting is a boardinghouse with several characters, but instead of giving each full attention, their conveyance to the reader comes through the narrator's own interest in them. Through his narration, the narrator indirectly reveals information about his character.

While marriage is of importance in all of Armitage's works, it takes center stage in *A New Ice Age.* The unnamed first-person narrator gives the reader a chronology of events leading up to the divorce, and Armitage leaves the lives of the narrator and his wife open for the reader's interpretations. From the start of the relationship, there is tension. The narrator sees that differences in their natures will affect the relationship. He finds Lynette to be a focused woman who has her own definition of success and merely acknowledges his dreams of becoming a writer. When her dog-breeding business escalates, he resents her and her dogs. He recalls, "I remained home each weekend during Lynette's absence, feeding and cleaning out the dogs and guarding the house. . . . I resented the dogs their easy successes, but I kept that to myself. Hearing the excitement in her voice I knew precisely how far apart we had grown." Lynette represents the frustrated female figure, a recurring motif in Armitage's early works. Like Veronica Priestley of *Winter Garden,* Ruth of *Across the Autumn Grass* has great plans for the future but finds herself thwarted by her circumstances. In these novels, neither the woman nor the man is unified with the other prior to the marriage or afterward. A similar dilemma occurs both in *A New Ice Age,* in which neither partner can accept the other's occupation or goals, and in *Across the Autumn Grass,* in which neither the narrator nor Ruth accepts the other. In Armitage's works people remain individuals in marriage, as isolation becomes an aspect of social relationships. In *A New Ice Age* the narrator is frustrated over his failure at becoming a writer; his wife, on the other hand, has little regard for his feelings and pursues her own career successfully.

The narrator is also openly hostile toward his wife. He says words that he knows will be taken badly and even becomes sick all over the floor, expressing little remorse the next day when he learns that her mother has had to clean it up. He engages in lying to the degree of ludicrousness and does little to advance his own career. Armitage makes neither character completely likable, but both are responsible to the extent that they are aware of the failing relationship but continue to engage in hostile activities that worsen the situation. In many ways the narrator and Lynette are ordinary people and can be laughed at as well as pitied, an aspect of Chekhovian humor critics have noted. For instance, Lynette's obsession with her dogs causes the narrator to appear less important and, thus, pitiable. The reader can laugh at Lynette's kissing and cuddling of the dogs as well as pity her for the manner in which the narrator provokes her to rage. The little actions eventually lead to a divorce.

Although the marriage account of the narrator and Lynette traverses much of the book, the narrator also talks about the desperate lives of those around him. All seem shrouded in uncertainty and immobility. The Patels have another child on the way, without adequate resources to support their present family. *A New Ice Age* presents another Armitage character with a double or secret identity—Farouk, a male prostitute who is also a pedophile. Aspects of Farouk's life remain a mystery to the reader. Atlas and the Irishman survive precariously, one continually obsessed with bodybuilding, the other involved with excessive drinking and women. The black couple shows signs of breaking up. Mrs. Devine, the landlady, is portrayed in a comedic light. She progressively breaks down as time comes closer the date of to her eviction, and in the end she remains alone with the narrator, both in a house devoid of electricity and heat. The title *A New Ice Age* implies that they are about to embark on a cold and hostile future. Like the boarders in *Winter Garden,* the characters of *A New Ice Age* possess a sense of togetherness in their shared plight of broken dreams and desperate scenarios.

The style found in Armitage's earlier novels, whereby the narrator listens to successive complaints of other characters, is again present in *A New Ice Age,* but in a more subdued manner than in the previous books. In the early novels the narrator listens to the other characters, who usually confide in him, in a sense offering himself as a therapeutic medium for those who are in need of a confidant. George and Mary find avenues of release in *Across the Autumn Grass* and *A Season of Peace,* respectively. In *A New Ice Age,* however, the narrator's response to the complaints of other characters varies from his genuine concern for Mr. Patel to his sense of obligation and duty when he lis-

*Dust jacket for Armitage's 1986 novel, about tenants
in a boardinghouse slated for demolition
(Richland County Public Library)*

tens to Mrs. Devine. Indeed, he feels that he humors her when he pretends to be interested in her dilemma.

Armitage's next novel, *A Lunar Eclipse* (1989), follows along the same line as *A New Ice Age,* with its ending predicting little sense of hope. The novel is about Rachel and Colin and their apparently perfect but problematic relationship. It begins with a prologue, in which the couple's wedding party is described, but in the next chapter, time has passed and the reader learns that Colin is dead. The rest of the novel involves a series of recollections made by Rachel as she revisits her relationship with Colin; the unnamed female narrator, a friend of the couple, also recollects her talks with Colin. Throughout, the narrator listens to Rachel and confronts her with the truth about her marriage. In the end Rachel, who has been moving in and out of clinics, attempts suicide and, though she survives, is left in despair.

As in his previous novels, Armitage again examines the roots of misunderstandings in relationships.

From the onset of Rachel's and Colin's marriage, the cracks exist; all appears to be well on the outside, but within their small circle the narrator is aware that neither Colin nor Rachel is happy, recollecting that Colin's face was as "distant and as far removed from what was happening as the telegrams of congratulations." Following Colin's death, Rachel is revealed to have been highly upset with the relationship, perhaps resenting the fact that while Colin continued to succeed in his job as a reporter, she became increasingly stagnant in her own work. Rachel's attitude is a reversal of what is usually found in the Edric novels, where the man is left pondering his lack of success. In *A Lunar Eclipse* Rachel cannot understand her predicament and, as does the narrator of *A New Ice Age,* tries to recall the past so as to understand her present situation. The narrator explains that Rachel "returned to the events of five, three, and two years ago to make sense of the immediate future, which, for her, remained uncertain." Such is the plight of many of Armitage's characters. In his early works there is an attempt by the characters to return to the past in search of answers to their present. In *A Lunar Eclipse* the word *detail* is examined. The narrator states that in every situation, whether it is dating or marriage, events are the same and only details differ. In essence, only details make a situation personal to the individual; otherwise, that situation is common to all. For instance, the narrator states, "The details of Scotland, the honeymoon, are perfect. Except that like the memories of the wedding they are the memories of any honeymoon." By saying that only the details of lives differ while events remain the same, the narrator seems to put little significance on the lives of individuals; in a sense, however, something greater is being said about humanity as a whole. Through his novels, Armitage seems to be showing that details of people's lives are the same even though the individual circumstances surrounding those details may differ. In life there are characters with failed marriages and people with secret passions. Some are like Derek and Veronica, others like Lynette, but they still belong to the same broken society, undergoing experiences that are common to all. Only the details of situations may differ, but the situations, whether they are occurrences like heartbreak or divorce, remain the same.

Following *A Lunar Eclipse,* Armitage wrote three works of historical fiction. *In the Days of the American Museum* (1990), *The Broken Lands* (1992), and *The Earth Made of Glass* (1993) are either based on actual events or structured around actual occurrences. *In the Days of the American Museum* is based on the display of human freak exhibitions at P. T. Barnum's nineteenth-century museum in New York City. Humans involved in the freak show express themselves, and the reader is thereby able to see behind the artificial glamour of the exhibition to the personal lives affected. Roy Kaveney stated in *TLS: The Times Literary Supplement* (6 April 1990) that "at its most painful and tragic, the novel becomes a set-piece, in which pain and misery are delivered as sensational entertainment; and the grand finale completes a set of metaphors about misery." Indeed, Armitage's historical novels of the 1990s are generally considered grim.

The Broken Lands is a fictionalized account of Sir John Franklin's disastrous nineteenth-century expedition to find the Northwest Passage, while *The Earth Made of Glass* recounts the vicious religious persecution prevalent in seventeenth-century England. In the latter novel, a church inquisitor travels to a village to investigate a past witch-hunt and finds a place given over to religious fanaticism and superstition with a priest at its head. The novel includes depictions of the religious beliefs of seventeenth-century Christianity, and Tom Shone, in *TLS* (11 February 1994), credited Armitage for its realistic depictions. Commenting on the prevalent theme of Hell in these historical novels in a 20 August 2000 review for *The Sunday Times* (London), Peter Kemp remarked, "*The Broken Lands* (1992), which opens with a talk of the strangeness of thinking of 'Hell as a burning, fiery place' while suffering the unbearably cold torments of the Arctic, glacially surveyed the miseries of Franklin's doomed expedition to find the North-West Passage." In *In the Days of the American Museum, The Earth Made of Glass,* and successive novels, Armitage focuses on the evil that men do to one another.

Hallowed Ground (1993) takes place just after World War II and is about American and British officers stationed in 1945 in the small German town of Waldsdorf, a town that has largely escaped the physical ravages of the war. Much to the displeasure of the townspeople, space is being progressively given up for refugees, and the townspeople are required to work in the refugee camps and hospitals. The unnamed narrator, a translator for the British army, records the interactions between the mayor of the town and an American officer, an unlikable controlling figure named Nash. Tensions rise when Nash requisitions an isolated building called the Waldsdorf Estate as a base for his troops. There is a likelihood that the townspeople have executed several prisoners of war or forced them to work on the estate, and have also provided temporary refuge for war criminals. They guard the estate with hostility and in the end would rather destroy any incriminating evidence at the site than betray their secrets or give away the Waldsdorf Estate, which has become a symbol of their pride.

In the novel, Armitage does not focus on the details of World War II but focuses more on aspects such as the suffering of refugees and the atrocities of battle, as well as human nature. For instance, the novel begins with the description of a young man who has been burned over his entire body. The doctor at the refugee camp is overwhelmed with casualties, loses sleep, and yet works diligently. Angry villagers rise up in spontaneous violence on the streets, and the narrator's companion, an American officer named Monroe, drinks and has recurring nightmares. Again critics praised Armitage for his realistic yet controlled depiction of scenes of carnage. Jason Cowley, writing for *TLS* (12 November 1993), remarked, "Although he may be describing the cruelest of scenes, he remains detached and fastidiously calm." Several noteworthy characters representing different aspects of the war are portrayed in the novel. For instance, there is Monroe, who incessantly drinks as a means of escape, but there is also Nash, who wields his power for his own gain. Although people warn Nash not to acquire the Waldsdorf Estate, he persists and thus represents the greed and selfishness of individuals even in precarious situations such as war.

The narrator of *Hallowed Ground* is a significant character in the tale. He goes through a process of discovery, learning about the complexities of issues and of human nature. He is glad for the opportunity to work in Waldsdorf because he is able to escape his stationary life back home in England. Now, as a translator, he sees at firsthand complex issues and can no longer imagine life and people to be innocent and simple to understand. Armitage sets the narrator in the midst of a chaotic situation; there is a gradual breakdown of order in Waldsdorf, and much of the novel thrives on the tension of the reader knowing that something is wrong, without knowing exactly what it is.

In Armitage's next novel, *Elysium* (1995), there are more accounts of man's evil toward his fellowman, as the reader learns of the true story of William Charles Edward Albert Lanne, the last surviving pure-blooded aborigine of Tasmania. Set in 1869, the novel is based on Lanne's ordeal, following the eradication of his people by colonialists. An English scientist, James Fairfax, is then sent to study him, and through the course of the novel Lanne undergoes humiliation after humiliation from the colonialists, who are not as educated as Lanne himself. Critics have noted the two forces at work in the novel, namely, those trying to adapt to the new presences in the land and those who remain outcast because of their drive to retain the old ways. Elements typical to Armitage's past novels are again found in this work. For instance, there is the clear but calm depiction of violence. Opinions vary as to the success of the work. While some find that the novel fully examines cultural history and the horrors of colonialism, Robert Brain argued in *TLS* (15 December 1995) that perhaps it collapses under its weighty records of atrocities: "*Elysium* is a wayward novel. The relationship between

Lanne and Fairfax is clouded by subplots hinting at the dark world of extermination and tragic loss, a world which is only fitfully described. In many ways, the book appears to be the remnant of a wider vision, and, as the horrors begin to overwhelm the slight story, the reader begins to wonder if the unsettled author abandoned what was originally a much grander scheme." According to Brain, Armitage might have written a more accessible novel had he chosen to narrow his subject matter.

In his next two works, *In Desolate Heaven* (1997) and *The Sword Cabinet* (1999), Armitage continues to explore disillusionment and broken lives in different mediums. In *In Desolate Heaven* he examines the lives of individuals affected by World War I. *In Desolate Heaven* is the story of Elizabeth, a woman whose brother has died in the war. The story unfolds around both her and her sister-in-law, Mary's, attempts to find meaning and purpose. They develop a relationship with two men, Jameson and Hunter, who have suffered from the war. Critics praise Armitage's ability unflinchingly to portray the psychological and physical effects of war with a sense of truthfulness. George Moore, in a 24 January 1999 review for *The Sunday Star-Times* (Auckland), identified the strong sense of the visual in the novel, comparing the experience of reading it to "Watching an art-house film," while Linda Grant in *The Guardian* (27 November 1997) credited Armitage for his boldness in looking pain in the eye without flinching. Suffering is a concept Armitage often writes about. Whether such suffering is a result of world catastrophe or personal failure, Armitage narrates painful reality and the ways in which people try to cope: what James Harkin, in an 11 July 1999 review of Armitage's next novel, *The Sword Cabinet* (1999), in *The Independent* (London), called a "passion for laying bare aspects of human suffering."

In *The Sword Cabinet* Armitage deals with the underside of show business, as he examines the lives of those who have fallen from their high status in the entertainment industry. In a 3 June 1999 review in *The Times* (London), Ruth Scurr compared it to Johann Wolfgang von Goethe's *Wilhelm Meisters Lehrjahre* (Wilhelm Meister's Apprenticeship, 1795–1796; translated as *Wilhelm Meister,* 1824) and Graham Greene's *Brighton Rock* (1938), two works that also involve the world of "showbusiness, seasides and crime." *The Sword Cabinet* is the story of Mitchell King, an illusionist, who tries to find out about his mother's relationship to the family line of the once-famous Kings. His mother is the former assistant of Morgan King, the famed escapologist who has been accused of being a serial murderer; Morgan King eventually dies while attempting to perform Harry Houdini's freezing act. Mitchell King is himself an illusionist, and his own career, plagued by financial

trouble and other problems, is already over by the end of the novel. As is *Winter Garden,* which assumes a circular kind of narration, *The Sword Cabinet* is written in a circular pattern. The reader learns of Morgan King's career and decline and of Mitchell's failing relationship with his partner, Laura, as the novel moves structurally between the past and the present, with Mitchell King the main narrator and the flashback sequences told to him by Quinn, a former assistant to Morgan King.

In *Winter Garden,* a couple is about to break up, and in *The Sword Cabinet* Laura similarly knows that her relationship is failing. She remarks, concerning herself and Mitchell, "The cruelties, maneuverings and deceptions had grown like beautiful crystals, intricate and ever-extending, and ready to shatter at the first sharp tap of unguarded truth." Mitchell, however, is mesmerized by the story of Morgan King. He does not appear to learn from the infamous showman's mistake, and by the time he has finished examining the showman's life, Mitchell's own career has ended. There is little he can learn for the future. As does Devlin in *Winter Garden,* characters such as Morgan have secret lives that make them suspect. There is a sinister darkness in the lives of the entertainers, and each seems doomed to failure regardless of preliminary success.

Critics did not believe *The Sword Cabinet* to be Armitage's best work. Harkin, in his review in *The Independent* (London), complained about the shifts in its structure, saying, "Written in short epigrammatic chapters, *The Sword Cabinet* moves between past and present rather too quickly, often dizzying the reader." Similarly, in a 6 June 1999 review for *The Sunday Herald* (London) Teddy Jamieson complained about the difficulty of finding one's bearings amid the narrative shifts. In Armitage's next novel the shifts in narrative structure are kept to a minimum, and the work has received largely favorable reviews.

Published in 2000, *The Book of the Heathen* was shortlisted for the Booker Prize and has been compared to such works as Dino Buzzati's *Il deserto dei Tartari* (1940; translated as *The Tartar Steppe,* 1952), J. M. Coetzee's *Waiting for the Barbarians* (1980), and Greene's *A Burnt-Out Case* (1961), all of which depict colonialism and the exploration of the unknown. Armitage has also been likened to such authors as William Boyd, George Orwell (Eric Arthur Blair), and Ronan Bennett. The novel has many echoes of Joseph Conrad's *Heart of Darkness* (1899), and it includes features seen in Armitage's earlier works. James Charles Russell Frasier, the narrator, has come to the Congo in 1897, seeking a life of adventure and promise, but ends up in a stagnant position. When the novel begins, he is trying to find out more about the accusations being made against his friend and fellow Englishman, Nicholas Frere, who has been accused of killing a girl and of cannibalism. With Frere, Armitage presents another character with a secret—this time a character who becomes fascinated with, and is suspected of engaging in, cannibalism while in the Congo. The young and inexperienced narrator, Frasier, is unaware of the events that have occurred in the Congo and only slowly comes to understand what the reader often already knows.

Like other Armitage narrators, Frasier reverts to the past in order to understand his present, hence the flashbacks intermittently spread throughout the novel. The narrator, however, tells his tale in a way that gives it continuity as opposed to confusion. He recounts the love story of Cornelius van Klees, a senior quartermaster who married a native woman, describing the manner in which Father Klein, a domineering priest, derides Cornelius regarding the disappearance of his wife and the death of his daughters. When Father Klein enters the story line, the reader learns to dislike him even more as the narrator describes a scene in which Klein flogs his so-called nuns (actually former prostitutes who work with him) in church. Flashback is used to enhance the plot, and the technique does not disrupt the narrative structure, as has been the case in some of Armitage's previous works.

Another significant difference in the work is Armitage's creation of a narrator and characters whom the reader accepts even though disliking them. Both Frere and Frasier come from England expecting more than what they receive in the Congo. They find themselves having to work as mapmakers and surveyors, and it is out of desperation that Frere engages in his adventures outside the station. The past lives of the two characters do not necessarily make them likable, but it does give them fuller identities, in which both their strengths and weaknesses can be appreciated.

Critics have commented on aspects of the book ranging from its sensational motif to its prosaic style. In a 26 August 2000 review in *The Independent* (London), Aamer Hussein praised Armitage for holding the reader's interest throughout the novel. He also noted the symbolism of minor characters such as Hammad, "the vaguely Arab slave trader, whom the Belgian authorities humor and encourage, and other stock caricatures from Imperial fictions." Hussein called the book not just a revision of Conrad's work, but "a fable about versions of truth and moral responsibility." Sukhdev Sandhu, writing for *The Guardian* (19 August 2000), praised Armitage's "linguistic minimalism" but said that occasionally "the fastidiousness of his writing denies us that woozily hallucinogenic sense of colonial place that we find in European authors such as Ryszard Kapuscinski or Sven Lindqvist. One finishes the novel thinking not 'The horror! The horror!,' but 'The unseemliness! The unseemliness!'" For the most part, however, the work has received favorable reviews from

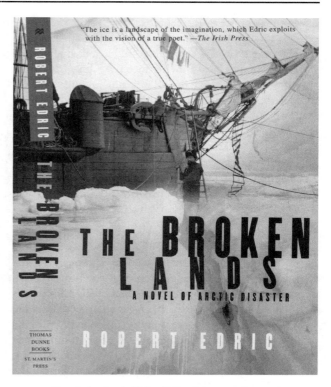

Dust jacket for the U.S. edition of the 1992 historical novel Armitage based on Sir John Franklin's ill-fated 1845–1847 search for the Northwest Passage (Richland County Public Library)

critics, ranging from those who praised its thriller motif to those who appreciated the authentic representations of gruesome aspects of the historical period.

All critics agree that the book evokes a strong sense of horror because of Armitage's description of the young girl's torture and murder. They believe it to be a physical representation of the "horror" hinted at in Conrad's *Heart of Darkness*. In a 20 August 2000 review in *The Sunday Times* (London), Kemp remarked, "Where Conrad leaves 'The horror' at the center of history unspecific, Edric gives his a hideously charred and screaming actuality that sears into the memory." In his *ArtsReaders* interview Armitage responded to the comparisons made about his book, stating that he disliked Conrad's ending, and indeed, his work is a kind of rewriting of Conrad's novel: "I always felt the ending of 'Heart of Darkness' was wrong. I always felt that there needed to be a little more." In Armitage's rewriting, the setting for *The Book of the Heathen* is the Middle Station of Conrad's tale, a place of disarray and chaos into which the young and inexperienced narrator, similar to the narrator of Conrad's novel, enters.

Armitage's *The Book of the Heathen* has received as much acclaim for its description of African culture as for its exploration of the human psyche. This desire to keep human experience at the center of his work is one of the reasons for Armitage's success, and it is a motivating factor in his next novel, *Peacetime* (2002). He talked about the then-forthcoming novel in his interview for *ArtsReaders,* saying, "I'm trying to write a book now about a concentration camp survivor without any reference whatsoever to those old ideas of barracks, starvation, tattoos, skeletons, barbed wire, gas chambers, crematoria." Once again history is the backdrop of his work, but man and his dealings with suffering take center focus. In the interview Armitage insisted that he trusts the reader to fill in the gaps of history that are omitted from the tale, for in so doing, the reader receives more from the story.

Peacetime is set in 1946 in a remote community in the fens of the east coast of Britain, to which has come James Mercer, a recently demobilized captain of the Royal Engineers, whose peacetime assignment is to demolish obsolete gun emplacements. While Mercer is thus engaged, an assortment of unrepatriated German POWs and displaced persons are occupied in dismantling a no-longer-needed airfield nearby. Mercer, an outsider in the village, befriends two of these workers: Mathias Weisz, a German soldier taken prisoner at Normandy, and Jacob Haas, a Dutch Jew and concentration-camp survivor. Mercer in turn is befriended by Mary Lynch, a local girl whose father is shortly to be released from the military prison where he has been held for the duration, allegedly for desertion. After Lynch returns, he begins to foment conflict between the insular locals and the foreigners in their midst, leading to what reviewer Ian Thomson called, in *The Guardian* (15 June 2002), a "startling denouement" and "an enduring image of prejudice."

Thomson described *Peacetime* as "a marvel of psychological insight and subtly observed relations," praising the "poetic resonance" of Armitage's "spare, unadorned prose." He concluded his review with the remark "Why Edric has not yet been shortlisted for the Booker Prize is a mystery." This sentiment was echoed by John de Falbe, in a 29 June 2002 review in *The Spectator* (London), who declared, "If other novels deserve this year's Booker Prize more than *Peacetime,* then they must be very remarkable indeed." The novelist Patrick Gale, in an 8 June 2002 review in *The Independent* (London), described Armitage as "one of those immensely skilled novelists who, because little noise is made on his behalf, seems fated to be discovered insultingly late in a productive career when caught in the arbitrary spotlight of Booker nomination or television adaptation." He called *Peacetime* "less a war novel than an effects-of-war novel," praising Armitage's "masterly" descriptions of the countryside and "the desolation peculiar to the redundant architecture of warfare," as well as his "refusal to let the mounting tension slacken,"

declaring that the "gathering menace is heightened by the mournful emptiness of the landscape described."

In a sense, many of Armitage's works can be said to be historical in nature. Both *A Season of Peace* and *Across the Autumn Grass* are about the world wars or their effects, as are the later works *Hallowed Ground, In Desolate Heaven,* and *Peacetime.* Armitage likes to use true events as settings in his works. He has admitted, however, that even in such a case as *The Book of the Heathen,* which is loosely based on the colonial past of the Belgian Congo, his main concern remains people and not the specific event. In the interview for *ArtsReaders,* Armitage stated, "I look upon the research as the scaffolding around the novel. Just as you take away scaffolding around a building when it's finished, you take the research out. . . . It's interesting to be able to look at some point in history and treat it almost as if it was happening today."

G. E. Armitage's focus on the dark and sordid part of humanity may have curtailed his popularity with publishers, as Taylor asserted in his review of *The Book of the Heathen* in *The Spectator* (London); however, he has not been overlooked for praise by reviewers. In her review of *In Desolate Heaven* for *The Guardian,* for instance, Grant stated that he is "one of the very small group of contemporary novelists whose work is able to look at pain and suffering without tricks or trendiness." Armitage's attention to aspects of life that others prefer to leave untouched has set him apart and given him a position as a writer of what Kemp called in his review of *The Book of the Heathen* "concentrated horror." Yet, his ability to take historical events and give them a sudden immediacy through characters with whom the reader can identify allows his work to have the depth that might otherwise be missing in a purely sensational text. Hence, Armitage can often reach a wider audience because of his narrative and stylistic techniques. Armitage continues to write reviews of contemporary novels for such periodicals as *The Spectator* (London) and served as a mentor to younger writers in the Asham Literary Endowment Trust writing competition and mentoring project, First Edition, the results of which were published as *Don't Think of Tigers* (2001), edited by Peter Guttridge. His works range from topics such as colonialism in *The Book of the Heathen* to the displacement of one culture by another in *Elysium;* however, Armitage's focus remains on the darkness and complexity of the human soul and the consequences of individual choices. Admired by many reviewers, yet still critically and commercially overlooked, he continues to build up a steady following of readers.

Interview:
"Interview with Robert Edric," *ArtsReaders,* 2000 <www.artsonline.com/space/reader/edric_intro.html>.

Kate Atkinson

(20 December 1951 –   )

Roger Clark
York St John College

BOOKS: *Behind the Scenes at the Museum* (London & New York: Doubleday, 1995; New York: St. Martin's Press, 1996);

Human Croquet (London & New York: Doubleday, 1997; New York: Picador USA, 1998);

Emotionally Weird: A Comic Novel (London & New York: Doubleday, 2000); republished as *Emotionally Weird: A Novel* (New York: Picador USA, 2000);

Abandonment (London: Nick Hern, 2000);

Not the End of the World (London: Doubleday, 2002).

PLAY PRODUCTIONS: *Nice,* adapted by Atkinson from her short story "Inner Balance," Edinburgh, Traverse Theatre, 31 May 1996;

Abandonment, Edinburgh, Traverse Theatre, 11 July 2000.

PRODUCED SCRIPT: "Karmic Mothers–Fact or Fiction?" television, adapted by Atkinson from her short story of that title, *Tartan Shorts,* BBC 2, 7 December 1997.

OTHER: "Karmic Mothers–Fact or Fiction?" in *Snapshots: 10 Years of the Ian St James Awards* (Tunbridge Wells: Angela Royal, 1999), pp. 156–164.

SELECTED PERIODICAL PUBLICATIONS–
UNCOLLECTED:
FICTION
"In China," *Woman's Own* (London), 1988;
"Leaves of Light," *Scotsman* (Edinburgh), 1996;
"This Dog's Life," *Daily Mail* (London), 1997;
"A Partner for Life," *Sunday Express Magazine* (London), 12 March 2000, p. 41;
"The Bodies Vest," *Daily Telegraph* (London), 17 March 2001, pp. 1–8.
NONFICTION
"Behind the Scenes . . . ," *Observer* (London), 13 August 2000.

Kate Atkinson (photograph by John Foley/Opale; from the dust jacket for Emotionally Weird, *2000)*

Kate Atkinson gained sudden prominence as an important contemporary British novelist when her first novel, *Behind the Scenes at the Museum,* won the prestigious Whitbread Book of the Year Award in 1995, overcoming formidable competition that included well-established figures such as Salman Rushdie. Atkinson's arrival caused something of a stir with sensationalist headlines appearing in the press, such as that in *The Guardian* (24 January 1996) remarking that an unknown writer described as "a 44-year-old chambermaid" had won one of the leading British literary awards.

In fact, Atkinson was neither a chambermaid nor entirely unknown, since she had won her first major literary prize in 1993, when her characteristically quirkily titled short story, "Karmic Mothers–Fact or Fiction?" won the prestigious Ian St James Award for short fiction. Five years before that she had won a short-story competition in *Woman's Own,* a national British women's magazine, with "In China." The critical reception of *Behind the Scenes at the Museum* says more, perhaps, about the London literary establishment than about the novel itself. A challenging yet accessible postmodern text, bridging high and popular culture and written by a middle-aged woman, was clearly perceived by critics as an oddity or aberration. Oddly enough, as Hilary Mantel suggested in a spirited defense of Atkinson and her novel that appeared in the *London Review of Books* (4 April 1996) a few months after the Whitbread brouhaha, Atkinson's novel has much in common with Rushdie's work, given its dizzying imaginative energy, merging of dream- and real worlds, and melding of past, present, and future. Atkinson mixes magic realism, postmodern disjuncture, and a corrosive satire of "provincial" English life into a heady fictional and metafictional cocktail, and initial reviews of the novel identified the unusual mix of Yorkshire realism with North American experimentalism. *Behind the Scenes at the Museum* went on to win the 1996 Exclusive Books–Ama Boeke Prize in South Africa.

Atkinson was born 20 December in 1951 in the "provincial" and ancient northern city of York, which provides the essential historical and cultural backdrop for her first novel. Her parents ran a medical-supplies shop in the center of the city, and for the first two years of Atkinson's life the family lived in the flat above the store, a location she re-created in her first novel. As an only child Atkinson read eagerly as a way of further populating her world. In an interview with E. Jane Dickson, published in the 24 February 2001 issue of *The Times* (London), Atkinson described "devouring" a grandparent's encyclopedia as well as the classic texts of childhood, ranging from *Just William* (1922), Richmal Compton's comic account of a boy causing untold chaos in the adult world, to Lewis Carroll's *Alice* books. Atkinson's favorite was *Alice in Wonderland* (1865), which she claimed to have read once a week between the ages of five and ten and that clearly operates as a vital intertext in all her fiction. Atkinson attended Queen Anne's Grammar School for Girls in York (1963–1970) and then studied English literature at Dundee University (1970–1974), the setting for her third novel, *Emotionally Weird: A Comic Novel* (2000). After graduating with an M.A. she began a doctoral

study of the American postmodern story in its historical context and developed a particular interest in the narrative innovations of such American writers as Donald Barthelme, John Coover, and Kurt Vonnegut, who have clearly influenced her narrative style.

One of the most remarkable facets of Atkinson's fiction is her interweaving of American prose experimentalism with an English concern for the particularities and oddities of the everyday–what might perhaps be described as "Kurt Vonnegut meets Jane Austen." Hence, a key text in Atkinson's literary pantheon is Vonnegut's extraordinary 1969 novel, *Slaughterhouse Five,* which, along with *Alice in Wonderland,* was influential in forming her view of fiction. Vonnegut's philosophical probings of time and human identity suffused with wild comedy have been acknowledged by Atkinson as important influences on her own work. Interestingly, Vonnegut himself has had his work consistently neglected by academics–perhaps because, as does Atkinson, he traverses the high wire between popular and high culture with provoking ease.

Atkinson began writing short stories in the early 1980s after the birth of her second child. She had married a fellow student at Dundee in 1973 when she was twenty-one. She had her first daughter there a year later, having begun work on her doctorate. The politics of academia are treated mercilessly in *Emotionally Weird,* a result, perhaps, of Atkinson's residual discomfort at having her Ph.D. refused at its viva voce, an event she now sees as crucial, as it eventually impelled her to take her first steps as a writer. Atkinson's first marriage lasted only two years and ended in divorce, but in 1982 she married a Scots teacher, had a second daughter, and moved to Edinburgh. Atkinson began to write for herself while doing a variety of part-time jobs and raising her two daughters after the end of her second marriage. In an interview with Alex Clark for *The Guardian* (10 March 2001) Atkinson has described writing as a process of self-validation, her early efforts as combining biography and therapy, putting something of the self down in words.

The need to narrate as a fundamental act of self-creation is embedded in the opening lines of her first and most acclaimed novel, *Behind the Scenes at the Museum.* The narrator of the novel, Ruby Lennox, proclaims her existence at the moment of conception in 1951, declaring "I exist! I am conceived to the chimes of midnight on the clock on the mantelpiece in the room across the hall," immediately interweaving images of time and being that proliferate and grow along with the narrative as it traces Ruby through her childhood and adolescence into mature adulthood in the last decade of the twentieth century. The novel is superficially a kind of family saga, as Ruby portrays her dysfunctional parents and siblings as well as the gaps and absences that deny her a full sense of self. The simple pleasures of this conventional narrative genre are soon disrupted by interchapters dealing with the lives and losses of Ruby's family predecessors back into the nineteenth century. Atkinson employs a variety of inventive narrative strategies including footnotes that reveal invisible lives, particularly women's lives, which have been lost in history. Reviewers of the novel agreed that among the most successful of these interchapters are the sections that deal with World War I, in which Atkinson gives an intensely powerful yet understated account of the impact of war on ordinary life. As it progresses the novel develops into a complex meditation on the nature of time and death, the power of inheritance, and the workings of chance. Ruby's uncertain history, which provides the backbone for the novel, requires her repeatedly to reiterate her selfhood in the face of a world that seems bent on denying it, as in the affirmation with which the novel ends, "I am alive . . . I am Ruby Lennox."

Atkinson told Megan Tresidder in a 27 January 1996 interview for *The Guardian* of the way in which the idea for the novel came to her from a dream, in which museum displays came to life while she was visiting the Festival of Britain rooms in the famous Castle Museum of Yorkshire Life in York. These rooms in reality present a series of frozen tableaux depicting domestic life through the ages—rooms full of objects and artifacts that carry the fingerprints of invisible and nameless owners lost in time. The novel itself becomes a museum of lost lives and objects. The image of existence as akin to a lost property cupboard is perhaps the most resonant in Atkinson's evocation of the randomness and chaos of experience that human beings attempt to order through storytelling and narration. The novel also evokes a powerful sense of place in both cultural and topographical terms with its plethora of actual street names and buildings and its overt references to, among others, that earlier York writer Lawrence Sterne, whose *Tristram Shandy* (1759–1767) Atkinson playfully echoes in her digressive layering of story upon story and her acknowledgment of the sheer difficulty of "telling" a life. Atkinson belongs in a long line of English fiction, not just in relation to Sterne but the great tradition of the English novel and its exploration of the relationship between the self and a sense of place and environment. Reviewers of the novel remarked that Atkinson's writing shares some of the density and profusion of detail that characterize the great nineteenth-century novelists, such as Charles Dickens, George Eliot, and Thomas Hardy, in their creation of seemingly actual worlds. In her 2001 interview with Clark, Atkinson cited Eliot's *Middlemarch* (1871–1872) as an influence, with its picture of society as an organic, synthesized whole, and she shares Eliot's concern with the interaction of place, the spatial worlds that

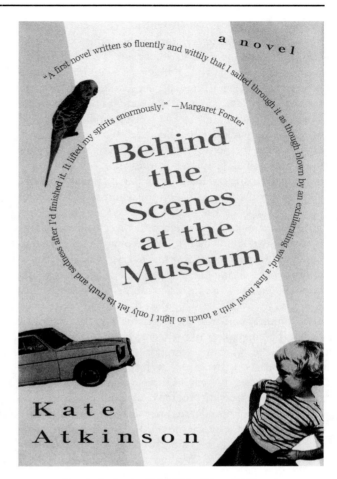

Dust jacket for the 1996 U.S. edition of Atkinson's 1995 novel, about a family in York (Richland County Public Library)

characters inhabit, and their impact on character and identity. By and large these nineteenth-century precursors held a relatively organicist view of the family and social life—a sense of society evolving and developing. For a later novelist such as Atkinson such a view is considerably more problematic. She has been criticized for apparently holding negative opinions on the family—the family as tyranny over the individual, over women—but her doubts about the family are perhaps only part of a wider perspective in her writing that suggests a continual fracturing of familial, social, and cultural ties.

This perspective takes on a particularly ironic note in *Behind the Scenes at the Museum,* given its self-conscious use of the York landscape as its setting—a landscape that contains almost the whole of English history within its architecture and archaeological remains: "These streets seethe with history," proclaims the narrator in recognition of the burden of history, personal and cultural, that weighs down the individual. The repeated images of literal and metaphorical flight that pervade the fabric of the novel suggest a need for escape from the burden of the past. In all her novels Atkinson's characters attempt to shed the weight of self and history while in the process of discovering their various pasts. The very soil on which the city of York is built exists as a kind of multilayered text that narrates, perhaps in an arbitrary and random way, the story of England and Englishness. York is, of course, a major center for archaeology and offers a useful analogy for the novel, which itself is multilayered, in the sense that it piles individual histories upon individual histories, accrues and collects nearly innumerable objects, lost property that appears and disappears—crockery, photos, buttons, and so on. As in an archaeological dig the past is retrieved and dusted off, but in an inevitably random and piecemeal way. History in this novel is akin to archaeology—so much rubble with bits to retrieve from it—every piece tells part of a story but piecing these together is a difficult if not impossible task. False histories can be constructed, false narratives woven that will affect the way lives are lived and families constructed, crucially for the narrator, Ruby. The metaphor of archaeology—of carefully clearing back the layers of accretion and debris—illustrates Ruby's progress toward some form of identity or selfhood that comes by way of the psychoanalytic "archaeology" of regression therapy as she confronts the missing piece of her identity, her dead twin sister, Pearl. In a pivotal scene in the novel, Ruby's therapist holds her like a baby and rocks her to and fro as she reaches the base level of memory and narrates the fate of her sister, finally finding some sort of truth about her story.

Atkinson has an intimate knowledge of York and provides detailed descriptions of the settings of the novel, which takes place in and around the city. Ruby's family begins in the pet shop at the heart of the Roman city and gradually moves out to the suburbs, tracing the shift toward suburbanization characteristic of post–World War II England. The web of streets that the novel traces matches the web of family relations upon which the narrative is based. Atkinson's novel is based on the topography of her own life—though Ruby is not Atkinson and she has strongly resisted the idea that this book or any of her other novels are autobiographical. Nonetheless Atkinson has been identified as one of several contemporary British writers who have, particularly in their early fiction, intermingled fictional and autobiographical elements, another example being Jeanette Winterson in *Oranges Are Not the Only Fruit* (1987). This kind of narrative mode is favored by women writers concerned with writing those lives that are often absent from history—those of lost women such as Alice or Nell in *Behind the Scenes at the Museum*. In the closing pages of her novel Atkinson uses her portrayal of place, the topography of York, to address another characteristic postmodern dilemma—that associated with the apparent replacement of any substantial authenticity of experience in the so-called postmodern condition by the provisional, by the pervasive simulacra of theme-park culture. The rejection of contemporary York and the flight to the furthest reaches of Scotland seem to be part of a search for authenticity of experience that has eluded all of the characters in the novel. Escape is also a search for agency, the capacity to shape and influence events in any meaningful way—even in any way at all. The feeling of subjection—of being dominated by events beyond the individual's control—is another characteristic element in the portrayal of experience in the novel. For the reader this point of view could lead to a fairly profound feeling of pessimism and determinism, particularly given the Vonnegut-like awareness of death as ever present and random, but like her American mentor Atkinson finds redemption through a sustained comic sensibility and a belief in the power of words to make some sense of the world.

Adaptations of Atkinson's work followed on the popular and critical success of *Behind the Scenes at the Museum:* in 1996 she adapted her prize-winning story "Karmic Mothers" for BBC 2 television, and she adapted her story "Inner Balance" for the stage; it was performed under the title *Nice* at the Traverse Theatre, Edinburgh. Two short stories, "Leaves of Light" (1996) and "This Dog's Life" (1997), were written for nationally circulated U.K. newspapers. In 1996 she received an E. M. Forster Award from the American Academy of Arts and Letters.

Human Croquet (1997) is the second of the three published novels that Atkinson described to Kim Bunce in a 12 March 2000 interview for *The Observer* (London) as a trilogy based in one way or another on *Alice in Wonderland*. Carroll's unerring sense of the child's rationality in a world populated by volatile, unpredictable, childish, and sometimes downright murderous adults finds echoes in Atkinson's work, with its young central protagonists adrift in a chaotic, illogical, and arbitrary world. It is the metamorphic view of reality emerging from Carroll's story of the dream-child Atkinson has acknowledged as a key influence. Indeed her second novel takes metamorphosis as its central image—as in the *Alice* books, there are countless references to physical transformation. Atkinson draws on a range of literary antecedents for this project—from fairy tales, Ovid's narrative poetry, through William Shakespeare's *Midsummer Night's Dream* (1595–1596) to Franz Kafka's *Metamorphosis* (1916). As the central heroine, Isobel Fairfax, says in response to the constantly shifting patterns of nature, "Everything in the whole world seems capable of turning into something else."

Human Croquet opens with the pubescent Isobel celebrating her sixteenth birthday on April Fool's Day 1960. She then sets out on a quest for understanding

*Dust jacket for the 1998 U.S. edition of Atkinson's 1997 novel, a magic-realism story of a teenage girl
growing up in a British suburb (Richland County Public Library)*

about her own self and history, the relationship between her immediate family and the first Elizabethans. Sections of the novel are headed "Past," "Present," and "Future"—with the final section presenting an apocalyptic vision of the natural cycles of death and renewal, in which the primeval forests evoked earlier in the novel return to the English landscape. The enthusiastic critical reception of the novel again focused on Atkinson's ability to combine the serious and the comic and to draw on a vast literary heritage, particularly Shakespeare, in an inventive and liberating fashion.

As in *Behind the Scenes at the Museum,* Atkinson conjures up multiple images of Englishness. In the earlier novel, characters' lives are punctuated by a series of cultural and historical "moments"—the coronation of Elizabeth II and the English victory in the World Cup in 1964 sit alongside the cataclysmic events of the two world wars and provide a context for the changing nature of English life in the twentieth century. In *Human Croquet* the time span is much greater. The novel begins with another moment of "conception," only this time it is the beginning of time itself and the birth of the universe, suggesting a world where time slips about arbi-

trarily, Wonderland fashion, and where characters, in their uncertainty about the real world of the here and now, speculate on the existence of parallel universes, time travel, and alien beings. Once again there are echoes of Vonnegut's narrative strategies in the intermingling of fantasy and reality. Atkinson's main point of cultural reference in this novel is the forested England of the sixteenth century and before. Called Lythe Forest in the novel, it is a version of Shakespeare's Forest of Arden, a lost mythic/idyllic pastoral evoked in *As You Like It* (1599–1600) and *A Midsummer Night's Dream.* Atkinson portrays a primeval, wolf-inhabited, fairy-tale landscape of trees that existed prior to the processes of deforestation, "civilization," and urbanization that are described in the early parts of the novel. In her interview with Bunce, Atkinson said, with some seriousness, that the novel is about "trees."

The present of the novel is set in a house ironically called "Arden," built on the foundations of the Elizabethan Fairfax mansion that was once visited, according to the novel, by the Bard himself. Arden was constructed by the unnamed twentieth-century "master builder" who has created the quintessential English suburban setting—a dreary, soulless, mock-pastoral land-scape where trees really survive only in the ironic names of the streets, Chestnut Avenue and Sycamore Terrace. Nature is tamed and regulated in this apparently ordered environment, where fathers grow vegetables and roses while mothers take afternoon tea. It is a triumph of nature over culture. *Human Croquet* offers both sharply observed social satire and dark-hued meditation on time and change. At one point in the novel Isobel is writing a school essay on Shakespeare's *Twelfth Night* (1599–1600) and perceptively remarks that it is about "darkness and death," much to the consternation of her English teacher, who conventionally retorts that "it's one of his lyrical comedies." Darkness and death are arguably at the heart of Atkinson's novel, despite its undoubted comic verve.

Atkinson is recognized as a notable addition to the line of significant English novelists—such as Muriel Spark and Beryl Bainbridge—whose fiction has explored the darker side of English middle-class life. *Human Croquet* traces the heroine's feelings of alienation from the deadening world of The Widow and Aunt Vinny, her temporary surrogate parents after the disappearance of her mother and father. Through Isobel's vivid imagination and her elaborate fictional narratives that give her a sense of her own being, Atkinson writes a sharply comic account of the surrealism of suburban life. Among the memorable characters is the hapless Debbie, Isobel's stepmother, who appears with her long-lost father partway through the novel. Debbie is the polar opposite of Isobel's natural mother, the flamboyant and exotic Eliza, who embodies the anarchic, sensual spirit of the ancient woods. The mundane Debbie plays out the role of the ultimate suburban wife, locked into an inherited blueprint for family life, barbecues and all, but suffers increasingly from a kind of rampant paranoia and literal fear of losing control, believing as she does that all the objects in the house move whenever she turns her back. Similarly, the next-door neighbors, the Baxters, turn out to hide dark, incestuous, and ultimately murderous secrets behind the lace curtains and cake baking. Suburban life clearly does not offer the kind of fixity and predictability that it appears to promise; rather, it is more of a Mad Hatter's tea party in which social rituals barely disguise an advancing chaos. Such settings and characters could be seen as easy targets for the novelist's acidic wit, and Atkinson has been criticized for this aspect of her work. Other critics, though, have remarked on the way in which Atkinson infuses the satire with a rich narrative concoction of fantasy, magic realism, postmodern playfulness, slippage, and disjuncture. These narrative elements appear as well in another key English novelist of the late twentieth century, Angela Carter.

The process of uncovering, of disinterring the past, takes on this dark tone in the novel as questions of gender and power inform the characters' relationships. The game after which the novel is named has obvious echoes of Alice's surreal game of croquet with hedge-hogs and flamingoes—a characteristic Carrollian defamiliarizing of a politely competitive upper-middle-class pastime. In this novel the croquet game acts as a multiple metaphor. At one level it offers a nostalgic image of childhood innocence, as the kindly but victimized and abused Mrs. Baxter, emblematic of the facade and reality of suburban respectability, remembers the party games of her idyllic youth. Its darker meanings connote the sexual politics and the power structures implicit in the patriarchal order that constructs male as active and female as passive as well as a more general sense of human subjection to arbitrary and ultimately chaotic forces of fate and chance. At one of the more feverish and climactic moments in Isobel's imaginings, a Christmas party at a neighbor's house, she is pursued by a pack of loutishly Dionysian youths across what turns out to be a croquet lawn. She escapes by apparently metamorphosing into a tree—"Call me Daphne," she tells the reader. This encounter is part of a sustained motif throughout the novel that explores the conflict between nature and culture in terms of gender. At points this exploration seems to follow a familiar pattern, the identification of woman with nature, an identification for which Atkinson gives a stream of examples—from the Elizabethan Lady Fairfax, a timid heart at home only in the green of the forest, to the mysterious Eliza (described as "as slender as a willow, as straight as a Douglas fir"), to Isobel herself. The novel seems to follow another familiar pattern, as male patriarchal order tames and controls female otherness, and rationality extinguishes instinct. Both of these women disappear mysteriously into the wilderness, apparently victims of male power and envy.

Atkinson resists conventional narrative strategies and, as does Carter in her rewriting of fairy tales, *The Bloody Chamber* (1979), she uses that most gendered of narrative modes to subvert the reader's expectations. Isobel reenacts various fairy tales, notably Goldilocks, Cinderella, and Sleeping Beauty, but each time the conventionally passive construction of the female is subverted in unexpected ways. At one point Isobel pricks her finger in characteristic fairy-tale fashion, and near the end of the novel she encounters a red apple. This encounter occurs at a moment when she has a fleeting, visionary encounter with her vanished mother, Eliza, in the suitably suburban and mundane setting of a supermarket. The scene metamorphoses the usual Snow White story of female antagonism into a moment of intimacy and unity, with the red apples connoting the transference of knowledge and mature sexuality rather than the poison of envy and temptation. Similarly, in a multiple parody of Sleeping Beauty, Isobel is awakened from her sleep not by the kiss of her imagined prince but by her stepmother, the traditionally evil figure and persecutor of the heroine in the fairy tale. The apparently mundane Debbie, the opposite, mirror image of her mother, has saved her by giving her the kiss of life. Eventually, like Alice, Isobel awakes from her dream, and the reader is presented with a completion of the narrative in the final sections. Atkinson's heroine awakes from her long sleep as well as the multiple narratives of female identity that her unconscious has played out. In the final section, "Street of Trees," Atkinson presents a résumé of her characters' future lives, which some critics felt to be an unnecessarily concrete conclusion to a narrative that powerfully celebrates the process of unfixing.

In her third novel, *Emotionally Weird,* subtitled "A Comic Novel," Atkinson completes her "trilogy" of *Alice*-inspired fictions with a narrative that updates Wonderland to a 1970s English department at a Scottish university, Dundee, where Atkinson studied English during the same period in which the novel is set. Published in 2000, the novel consists of several interwoven narratives, delineated for the reader by differing fonts often appropriate to their subject matter, but is dominated by two narratives in particular. The first, printed in a flintily sharp sans serif, takes place on a remote and wind-swept Scottish island where two women, Effie and Nora, are telling stories as a way of killing time. Effie's full name, Euphemia Stuart-Murray, links her in genealogical terms with a regal line of Scottish ancestry and comically echoes the past-in-present motif found throughout Atkinson's work. Effie's story, which is interrupted and critiqued by Nora as it unfolds, is the major narrative strand and concerns her experience as a hapless student in the English department and her relationships with other students and academic staff. Effie's narrative has a relentlessly Shandyesque quality to it—literally a "shaggy dog" story whose digressions and circumlocutions echo those of Sterne.

Atkinson's central themes of family loss and abandonment emerge in Nora's story, which is concerned with Effie's apparently unknown parentage. Effie's narrative begins with the enigmatic statement "MY MOTHER IS A VIRGIN" and ends with revelations about her origins that confirm Atkinson's repeated sense of the family as a site of anger, jealousy, violence, introversion, and only occasionally love. The other narratives and fictions that cut into these two main strands are the products of aspiring novelists among the students and staff of the university, including Effie herself, who is writing a crime novel, *The Hand of Fate,* for a creative- writing assignment. This novel is the first text that is presented to the reader and is printed throughout in a font that resembles that produced by a typewriter.

Atkinson's well-recognized talent for pastiche and parody is paramount here; among the most memorable of these fragments is an impenetrably dire, sub-Kafka piece ostensibly written by an English professor who is a better theorist than novelist. The fabric of the novel is a patchwork of these fragments of writing but there is no "figure in the carpet" here, in Henry James's sense of an underlying and unifying pattern, as they appear to lead nowhere, testaments only to the human need to narrate, to tell stories, to invent lives and selves. References to James and Eliot appear often throughout the novel—Effie is desperately trying to write an essay on *Middlemarch,* and her dissertation title is "Henry James—Man or Maze"—but this particular example from the "House of Fiction" (in James's phrase) is more like a drawing by M. C. Escher. Like her mentor Vonnegut, Atkinson is concerned to explore the ways in which humans use words and stories to invent and reinvent themselves in the face of chaos and silence. By the end of the novel Effie has effectively narrated and written herself into being, as her revealed parentage gives her some anchorage for identity. As in her first two novels, Atkinson gives readers a coda of sorts in the final section, "Last Words." Here the reader learns that Effie's creative writing was not in vain and she has become a mildly successful crime writer. With her penchant for a good joke, Atkinson cannot resist adding that one of the other characters has gone on to win the 2001 Booker Prize for fiction—the most prestigious literary award in the United Kingdom.

Among its preliminaries *Emotionally Weird* has a disclaimer denying any connection with real places or people; as with her other novels, Atkinson has taken autobiographical material and transmuted it through her copiously inventive imagination. The novel also has at its opening the most explicit reference to Carroll in a direct quotation from *Through the Looking Glass* (1872): Humpty Dumpty's dictum about words and meaning from chapter 6 of Carroll's fantasy that anticipates Saussurean structuralist linguistics. The quotation is particularly appropriate given that the novel includes among its fragments of narrative a parody seminar on post-structuralism during which, much to his students' bewilderment, Archie McCue, one of the Literature faculty, deconstructs the word *post-structuralism,* employing the theories of Walter Benjamin, Jacques Derrida, Susan Sontag, and John Barth. The opening also introduces Atkinson's Alice-like puzzling over words and meaning that gives the novel its philosophical underpinning. Effie, the heroine, is in many ways a further version of Alice, adrift in a world of competing narratives, including her own, and colliding with a plethora of characters who

Dust jacket for the U.S. edition of the novel Atkinson set in the English department of a Scottish university during the 1970s (Richland County Public Library)

Bach's popular allegorical novel, *Jonathan Livingston Seagull* (1970). The slightly stoned inarticulacy of the title fits the fabric of the novel well as the narrative takes on an increasingly hallucinatory quality. *Emotionally Weird* has received the least critical acclaim of Atkinson's novels. Some reviewers, such as Stephanie Zacharek in *The New York Times* (25 June 2000), contended that Atkinson was covering ground familiar from her first two novels, and others complained of the inconsequentiality of the central narrative, which was deemed to be less interesting than the unfinished fragments. In contrast, the many positive responses, such as Clark's review in *The Guardian* remarked on her continuing narrative inventiveness and willingness to take risks in her storytelling.

In July 2000 a stage version of *Behind the Scenes at the Museum* adapted by the leading British playwright Bryony Lavery was given its first performance, appropriately at the Theatre Royal, York, setting of one of the central scenes in the novel. This critically acclaimed version imaginatively recasts the narrative as a "memory play," focusing on the relationship between Ruby and her therapist as they unravel the web of the past in order to allow Ruby her full existence. Atkinson has also been commissioned to adapt the novel for television serialization, confirming its place as a major text of the 1990s.

The politics of the personal are central to the play *Abandonment,* which was first performed during the 2000 Edinburgh Festival. This work is Atkinson's first full-length play for the stage and marks a significant development in her work. *Abandonment* focuses with a Chekhovian intensity on a group of contemporary women: two sisters—Elizabeth, who is an historian, and Kitty, a journalist—their meddling and deeply conventional adoptive mother, and a scientist friend. Their lives and loves are closely juxtaposed and interwoven with the nineteenth-century "ghosts" who "inhabit" Elizabeth's Victorian Gothic apartment and whose story is one of seduction and abandonment. Elizabeth was abandoned as a baby and barely survived the ordeal; the audience learns in the course of the play that she has separated from her husband after discovering that he has slept with her sister.

The play displays Atkinson's delight in elaborate contouring of plot and narrative, with the past intersecting with the present as a scene between a caddish photographer and Elizabeth merges at the flash of his camera into a moment in 1865 when a governess is being photographed by her employer and lover, an upright middle-class Victorian gentleman who dabbles in amateur photography. The date and photographic context offer some obvious connections to the ever-present Carroll: *Alice in Wonderland* was published in 1865, and Carroll was one of the first great Victorian amateur photographers. But the implications here have less to do with Car-

populate the novel like so many Duchesses, Red Queens, and White Knights. Atkinson's characters, like Carroll's, seem trapped within their own egos, unable to understand or communicate with one another despite their professional facility with words and ideas.

Despite its setting, *Emotionally Weird* is not a campus novel in the tradition of David Lodge and Malcolm Bradbury. Atkinson's third novel is another meditation upon "words, language and writing" as Atkinson intimated in her 2000 interview with Bunce. The open-endedness implied by this description of the novel is perhaps reinforced by the absence of a centrally informing metaphor. At a simple but important level the titles of her previous two novels gave a central focus to the dominant themes of time, order, chaos, convention, and ritual. As a title *Emotionally Weird* is strongly resonant of the period in which the action largely takes place, 1972, a date that is pictorially depicted at the beginning of the novel in psychedelic script. The narrative is infused with evocative period detail, such as references to the rock group Deep Purple, the television show *Doctor Who,* and Richard

rollian absurdity and more to do with questions of representing the past, the validity of scientific truth, and the possibility of female agency within a patriarchal social order. Photographs are always powerful signifiers in Atkinson's work, beginning with the picture of Alice in *Behind the Scenes at the Museum,* carrying as they do the promise of representation and fixity, of a scientific process that will somehow cheat all-powerful time, an illusion of identity or essence.

In *Abandonment* the two male characters associated with photography, one modern and the other Victorian, are both ultimately shallow beings merely interested in the exercise of male power and sexual gratification. Atkinson is more concerned with the interaction of flesh-and-blood relationships on human subjectivity than on chemical reactions with light on paper. The play juxtaposes the sexual identities open to contemporary women with their nineteenth-century counterparts, but there is no easy acknowledgment of contemporary woman's liberation and freedom of choice. Even if the main Victorian strand of the play ends in Gothic melodrama with the murder of the transgressive woman—her history literally intrudes into the contemporary action as her skeletal remains are found under the floorboards—the contemporary figures themselves face still an albeit less murderous burden of familial and social pressure.

The play ends with what is perhaps the most complete and resolved statement by any of Atkinson's characters in prose or drama. Elizabeth ends the play having given birth to her own child, fathered by the now absent and forgotten photographer, and suggests "I've got everything I need now," as she poses for a final photograph with the other female characters. It is a rare moment of affirmation in Atkinson's often provisional and problematic portrayal of the self, although the final ghostly appearance of the murdered and pregnant governess that immediately follows saves the moment from an uncharacteristic excess of reassuring closure. As with her third novel, critical reaction to the play was mixed. Some critics felt that *Abandonment* was insufficiently dramatic in conception and attempted to cover too many subjects at once, thereby lacking tension and concentration. Atkinson herself has remarked on the problems that she has writing dialogue for the stage and wrote a witty and honest account of the genesis of the play, "Behind the Scenes . . ." (2000), for *The Observer* (London) newspaper. The play also received considerable acclaim; the leading commentator on British drama, Michael Billington, remarked in *The Guardian* (7 August 2000) that *Abandonment* represents a significant addition to contemporary drama by women and expressed the belief that Atkinson clearly was capable of making further contributions to the theater.

Kate Atkinson is a generous and inclusive writer whose eclecticism of style and content has drawn considerable praise and occasional criticism. Her major achievement has been to take some key elements of the late-twentieth-century English novel—the concern with history as filtered through a postmodern consciousness, the first-person narrative as a vehicle for the exploration of particularly female selfhood and subjectivity, and the representation of what might be meant by Englishness at the turn of the millennium—and fuse them into writing that is highly personal and idiosyncratic. Her debt to writers as diverse as Carroll and Vonnegut may indicate something of the breadth of her narrative. If some criticism of her work has suggested that this breadth is in fact too great and ultimately overambitious, such observations have been counterbalanced by the popularity of her work among a wide range of readers and by the extensive recognition given to her inventiveness and originality of voice. Her appeal extends far beyond her native shores, with her first two novels having been translated into many languages. Atkinson has also returned to the short story, the genre with which she began her writing career. Her stories contain in compressed form many of the central concerns of her novels and are characterized by the sharpness of observation and dark humor that give her narratives their highly distinctive savor. Published in *The Daily Telegraph* (London), "The Bodies Vest" (2001) follows the trajectory of a life from the earliest years to death and transcendence as Vincent, the central character, negotiates family, identity, the death of his lover, and finally his own death and transfiguration. In it Atkinson explores further the relationship between the physical and metaphysical, the body and soul, humanity and mortality, that she began in her earliest fiction. The title of a collection of her stories scheduled to be published by Doubleday in November 2002, *Not the End of the World,* suggests that her fictional meditations on life and death in the twenty-first century will continue to display her hallmarks of experimental verve and playful seriousness.

Interviews:

Megan Tresidder, "Big sister of the anti-family," *Guardian,* 27 January 1996, p. 25;

Kim Bunce, "Emotionally Weird? Moi?" *Observer* (London), 12 March 2000;

E. Jane Dickson, "Word of Mouth," *Times* (London), 24 February 2001;

Alex Clark, "The Fragility of Goodness," *Guardian* (London), 10 March 2001.

Stephen Blanchard

(8 December 1950 –   )

Dominic Head
Brunel University

BOOKS: *Gagarin and I* (London: Chatto & Windus, 1995); *Wilson's Island* (London: Chatto & Windus, 1997); *The Paraffin Child* (London: Chatto & Windus, 1999).

SELECTED PERIODICAL PUBLICATIONS–UNCOLLECTED: "Clive's Dog," *London Magazine,* 31 (December 1991–January 1992): 25–30; "The Fat People," *Interzone,* 61 (July 1992): 45–49; "The Gravity Brothers," *Interzone,* 67 (January 1993): 55–61.

In the 1990s there was a "second wave" of the renaissance of the novel in Britain. If the first wave of the 1980s is generally characterized by the emergence of a British school of magic realism–in Salman Rushdie, Jeanette Winterson, and the consolidation of Angela Carter's reputation–a key strand of the second wave is the resurgence of a revitalized form of realism. Stephen Blanchard is a principal exponent of this method, a writer whose laconic style is deceptive, and who can extract great poignancy from simple, prosaic description. Like that of Andrew Cowan, winner of a Betty Trask Award for traditional fiction, awarded for his novel *Pig* (1994), Blanchard's prose is finely wrought, creating an intensity that can take his readers by surprise.

Stephen Thomas Blanchard was born in Hull, England, on 8 December 1950, the son of George Blanchard, a brewery worker, and Evelyn (née Staniforth) Blanchard. He told Dominic Head in an unpublished 2001 interview that "there weren't any books at home except for odd copies of *Reader's Digest* and my mother's *My Life and Loves* by Frank Harris which I couldn't make much sense of. . . . The adults around me didn't read and weren't especially talkative. So my starting to write was an anomaly really."

If Blanchard's home life did not supply the "bookish" background that some writers enjoy, it did provide a rich seam of human drama upon which he was able to draw. According to Blanchard, what he did have "was lots of people (odd, quarrelsome) and drama, jealousy, scandal etc. It was like Dostoevsky but a bit more cold-blooded.

My mother and her friend Vera ran a lodging house not far from the town and Vera's mother (Mrs. Black) had the house next door so that there was a floating population of mainly single working-men but sometimes runaway couples and melancholy middle-aged women."

As a child in Hull just after World War II, Blanchard experienced a city that conveyed conflicting impressions. Hull had been bombed heavily, and the bomb sites and derelict buildings remained until the 1960s, making "wonderful, dangerous playgrounds." As a boy he discerned a related ambivalence in the city itself. Because of its geographical location "the city was very much a world on its own–isolated by the Humber on one side and Holderness and the North Sea on the other–and there was always a sense of space and possibility. The light's different there–damper and clearer."

In a search for some respite from the comings and goings of the lodging house Blanchard would find himself a private space and read, becoming a self-described "heavy user of the local library," borrowing and reading many books, particularly works of historical fiction such as Rosemary Sutcliff's *Sword at Sunset* (1963), her retelling of the Arthurian legend. Blanchard developed an interest in narrative slightly at odds with the realistic focus his writing took, telling himself "bedtime stories in which I was the boy leader of a tribe of red Indians. I think I kept it up for a few years, three or four–running with the same characters and introducing new ones as needed. As puberty approached the stories took on an erotic coloring which broke the spell. . . ."

Blanchard attended Liverpool University between 1968 and 1970 where he began a degree in geology. The experience did not suit him, so he gave up his studies and moved to London where he led what he described as "a grim, rackety life south of the river for about twenty years before having kids and starting seriously to write at the same time." He and his partner, Sarah Rookledge, still live in South London. The couple has three children: Thomas (born 9 March 1992), Catherine (born 2 November 1994), and Lily (born 24 September 1997). He worked as a carpenter from 1975 to 1985, a dealer in secondhand

Stephen Blanchard (courtesy of the author)

goods from 1985 to 1990, and a postman from 1990 to 1997. He also wrote short stories, some of which were published in the British science-fiction magazine *Interzone*.

Blanchard's first novel, *Gagarin and I* (1995), establishes his distinctively terse style, characterized by judicious understatement and reticence. Nicholas Lezard's praise in his 24 May 1996 review in *The Guardian* is representative: Lezard considered the novel to be a "masterpiece" on account of its "poised, stately prose" that enables it to fulfill "the highest responsibilities to art, without letting on that it is doing so." The book, set in the 1960s, is narrated from the point of view of Leonard, a fourteen-year-old boy afflicted with an unusual wasting disease and obsessed with Yuri Gagarin. Leonard lives with his mother and aunt in the boardinghouse they run in a city based on Hull. Blanchard makes full use of his childhood memories in lending solidity to the setting of the book and to its range of quirky characters. The boardinghouse is based on the one in which the author grew up, and the descriptions of the bomb sites and derelict buildings are drawn from memory. Yet, the ambivalence of Hull, registered in the author's own account of an "isolated" place that still suggests "a sense of space and possibility," is conveyed effectively in the mood of the novel. The setting registers both the drabness of domestic detail and the sense of opportunity associated with the rites-of-passage narrative.

This latter quality is assisted by the motif of space flight, but in a way that is less obvious. In the 2001 interview Blanchard remarked that "Gagarin came in at quite a late stage" and that "the book seemed to use him and the idea of space flight as a sort of armature." The lateness of the concept in the process of composition is surprising. Indeed, the analogy with an armature—the framework on which a clay sculpture is molded—implies something more integrated about the design of the book. Most critics have detected something organic in the use of space travel as a motif. Albert Read, for example, in *TLS: The Times Literary Supplement* (18 January 1995) observed that "the novel is loaded with numerous portentous references to the moon and gravity . . . as if Gagarin's weightlessness is somehow desirable for a boy suffering from a wasting disease." The boyish fascination with Gagarin, in Leonard's case, thus denotes something more personal and poignant than the usual boyish enthusiasm for adventure. For Leonard, Gagarin represents his subliminal yearning for a cure. And the achievement of space travel has a wider significance, too. Read noted how the differences between Leonard and his mother and aunt locate a key moment of social change: "Blanchard identifies the chasm that cuts through the twentieth century: here are two generations on a cusp—one battling with superstition and morality, the other with technology and disease."

Leonard's father is absent for most of *Gagarin and I*—presumed dead by Leonard—until the boy is taken by his aunt to visit his father at an asbestos factory. The ground is covered in white dust, evocative of a lunar landscape, as befits this "other worldly" scene. The discovery of the father and the apparent intimacy between the father and the aunt suggest an indeterminacy about Leonard's origins which, by implication, might turn his own world upside down. In 1996 *Gagarin and I* won both the *Yorkshire Post*

Best First Work Award and the McKitterick Prize from the Society of Authors.

In Blanchard's second novel, *Wilson's Island* (1997), the father figure becomes more of a focus. Again Blanchard drew on his personal experience, this time ranging across the different phases of his life. He told Head that "Dad—or a dad—makes an appearance in *Wilson's Island*. By which time I had a boy of my own so that I was crossing between father and son. The book seemed strangely to be set in the future and the past at the same time. The seedy business of the junk-shop and local small-scale gangsterism is an import from my time in the second-hand trade in South London."

The novel centers on the return of Ralph, a drifter in his thirties, to his hometown after a period away "along the coast." The setting is vague, and Ralph's motivation is unclear. An atmosphere of aimlessness, decrepitude, and seediness hangs over the book. Ralph's father, Cliff, a dealer in secondhand domestic appliances, persuades Ralph to lend a hand in the business and also to apply his talent at playing darts for cash. Ralph's brooding resentment against his father dominates the narrative. He has called his father "Cliff" ever since he abandoned his family for a time when Ralph was little. Another key figure in the book is the grandmother, Ma, or Marion, a fading matriarch who now spends most of her time in bed. As in the first novel Blanchard's descriptive skills are finely tuned here, producing a rich and deceptively economical style. As Hal Jensen observed in his *TLS* review (7 February 1997), "Blanchard seems to know instinctively what sort of thing will most clearly and unobtrusively express a person's character. His apprehensive powers are of the highest order; he not only selects his objects with precision and ingenuity, but judges well which senses will most bring them alive for the reader."

The true locus of power of the novel, however, lies in the recurring motif of Wilson's Island and the memory of something witnessed there long ago. In some versions of this piece of local mythology a naked man was seen on a shed roof. But there is also a suggestion that something more mystical and less prosaic may have been witnessed, possibly something with a religious significance. Certainly, memories of the island for some of the characters become imbued with a distant spiritual potential. However, this spirituality has been overlaid, subverted into something smutty, as befits the presentation of the characters of the novel, who are all in need of redemption. In one recollected scene, Cliff alludes to the "vision" in seeking to persuade the young Ralph that there is nothing in it. The scene conveys both Cliff's failure as father and the community's broader imaginative failure, which is a kind of spiritual bankruptcy.

In his third novel, *The Paraffin Child* (1999), Blanchard uses his characteristically understated style to tell-

ing effect, especially in building effects that can take the reader by surprise. This understated style is particularly evident in his treatment of character. In a 20 June 1999 review for the *Independent on Sunday* (London), Matthew Sweet observed that Blanchard "doesn't feel obliged to blab on his characters, spoon out their potted histories, stage conversations that enumerate their pasts or presents. The result is that after a hundred or so pages of puzzling over quite who these people are and what they're up to, there comes a point when you suddenly have enough information to bring them sharply into focus." The power of understatement also contributes to the effectiveness of the principal themes of the book. The setting is a familiar one to readers of Blanchard's fiction: a seedy seaside town in the north of England with snooker halls and caravan parks. Protagonist John Drean is a pill-popping taxi driver struggling to rebuild his life after the disappearance of his four-year-old daughter, Pearl, who went missing in the woods, in the manner of a luckless Little Red Riding Hood. The allusions are various, from the fairy tales of Jacob and Wilhelm Grimm to Daphne du Maurier's *Don't Look Now* (1971). In *TLS* (25 June 1999) David Utterson suggested that "the presiding haunting image of the dead child, Pearl, recalls the steady presence in [Nathaniel] Hawthorne's *The Scarlet Letter* [1850] of a child of that name who also determines the plot in a persistent, infernal way."

The narrative switches between Drean's own first-person narrative and a series of letters addressed to him, written by his former partner, Anna. She becomes involved with the former policeman who investigated Pearl's disappearance and who now collects information about missing people, though he has never found anyone. As the novel unfolds, it becomes clear that both parents have been traumatized by the loss of their daughter and that their lives have been arrested. It is an intense and difficult subject and one that has clearly engaged the author's own emotions.

The novel opens with Drean dousing every photograph of Pearl he can find with paraffin and setting them alight, thus establishing the pervasive motif of fire. Drean's self-destructiveness is epitomized in his relationship with Enid, a woman drawn to arson, who at one point stubs a cigarette out on Drean, in the attempt to share with him the language of fire. Eventually she sets her own caravan alight. Fire—and, specifically, paraffin flame—is the central symbolic element of the book. Paraffin burns rapidly and nearly invisibly in daylight. As Phil Baker pointed out in *The Guardian* (5 June 1999), paraffin is employed as "a vivid image of evanescence" but also to evoke that which is painful and destructive. As with the use of gravity in *Gagarin and I*, Blanchard's imagery evokes the emotional lives of his characters powerfully and economically.

Cover for Blanchard's 1999 novel, about a taxi driver whose four-year-old daughter
has disappeared (Bruccoli Clark Layman Archives)

The writers Blanchard cites as important or influential for him are Joseph Conrad, H. G. Wells, Saul Bellow, Vladimir Nabokov, Fyodor Dostoevsky, Hermann Hesse, and Flann O'Brien. But he is also interested in popular forms of writing, such as fantasy and children's fiction, remarking in the 2001 interview that "The idea of 'literary' fiction becomes a bit stultifying—or the idea of 'quality' fiction." He cited other forms of inspiration as well, including movies, galleries, and walking in London. Since writing *The Paraffin Child* Blanchard has finished three books—"Little Egypt," "Kark" (a novel for children), and "Dog Hill." All three are yet to be published.

Blanchard takes a pragmatic view of postwar Britain and its international standing. He remarked that "there's a decline of power, influence etcetera, punctuated by brief spells of overblown self-confidence. We're a bit small, a bit mediocre in lots of ways." This sober assessment of national status has an important bearing on Blanchard's regionalism: "British, Britain, Britishness etcetera seems not a very useful idea nowadays whereas Hull, South London, Birmingham, are actual places." Blanchard is also a little skeptical about the much-vaunted renaissance of fiction in Britain since 1979, pointing out that "some of the best writing in English seems to come from outside this country—not only the US and Ireland which are always strong but also Canada, India, Sri Lanka, Scotland. . . . Our own output seems a bit dullish."

Asked if there was anything else he would like future readers and critics of his work to know, Stephen Blanchard referred to "the generative effect of the friction of being a transplanted northerner." He explained the ambivalent feelings of someone from Hull who has chosen to settle in South London: "I'm a little surprised as I seem to be more 'in place' than the Africans, Croats, Mauritians, Vietnamese I live among but there's a feeling of loss and discomfort which I write to escape or come to terms with. Also a little guilt as I've no wish to go back." That feeling of personal dislocation is reflected in the haunting ambiguity of his novels.

Clare Boylan

(21 April 1948 –)

Mary L. Bogumil
Southern Illinois University, Carbondale

BOOKS: *Holy Pictures: A Novel* (London: Hamilton, 1983; New York: Summit, 1983);

A Nail on the Head (London: Hamilton, 1983; Harmondsworth, U.K. & New York: Penguin, 1985);

Last Resorts (London: Hamilton, 1984; New York: Summit, 1986);

Black Baby: A Novel (London: Hamilton, 1988; New York: Doubleday, 1989);

Concerning Virgins: A Collection of Short Stories (London: Hamilton, 1989; New York: Viking Penguin, 1989);

Home Rule (London: Hamilton, 1992); republished as *11 Edward Street* (New York: Doubleday, 1992);

That Bad Woman: Short Stories (London: Little, Brown, 1995);

The Stolen Child (London: Phoenix, 1996);

Room for a Single Lady (London: Little, Brown, 1997);

Another Family Christmas: A Collection of Short Stories (Dublin: Poolbeg, 1997);

Ladies' Night at Finbar's Hotel, by Boylan, Kate O'Riordan, Maeve Binchy, Emma Donoghue, Anne Haverty, Éilis Ní Dhuibhne, and Deirdre Purcell, edited by Dermot Bolger (London: Picador, 1999; Dublin: New Island, 1999; San Diego: Harcourt Brace, 2000);

Beloved Stranger (London: Little, Brown, 1999; Washington, D.C.: Counterpoint, 2001).

Collection: *The Collected Stories* (London: Abacus, 2000; Washington, D.C.: Counterpoint, 2002)—comprises *A Nail on the Head, Concerning Virgins,* and *That Bad Woman.*

OTHER: *The Agony and the Ego: The Art and Strategy of Fiction Writing Explored,* edited, with an introduction, by Boylan (London & New York: Penguin, 1993);

The Literary Companion to Cats: An Anthology of Prose and Poetry, compiled by Boylan (London: Sinclair-Stevenson, 1994).

Clare Boylan (photograph © Mike Bunn)

SELECTED PERIODICAL PUBLICATIONS—UNCOLLECTED: "Growing Pains," *Guardian,* 15 September 1997, II: 4;

"Lady in Red," *Guardian,* 7 September 1998, II: 6;

"Always Larger than Life," *Daily Telegraph* (London), 28 August 1999, p. 7;

"Ring Cycle," *Guardian,* 30 August 1999, II: 6;

"My Mother, Myself," *Guardian,* 3 April 2000, II: 6.

Often compared to her contemporaries Edna O'Brien and Julia O'Faolain, Clare Boylan writes fiction that focuses on the lives of family members, particularly the women of the house whose lives have been shaped less by personal will and choice than by societal and religious strictures. In her novels Boylan blends moments of humor, in which she reveals an unusual imagination, with moments of poignant seriousness. Her exploration of such subjects as virginity, motherhood, and domesticity suggests a feminist reading of relationships and life for women in a patriarchal society—though her views are never stated dogmatically and her characters are always developed thoroughly and carefully.

Novelist, short-story writer, newspaper and magazine journalist, and editor, Clare Catherine Boylan was born on 21 April 1948 in Dublin, Ireland—a fifth generation Dubliner. The youngest of three daughters born to Patrick Boylan and Evelyn (neé Selby) Boylan, Clare Boylan experienced a creatively stimulating environment as a child. Her grandfather was a singer and is identified in Peter Costello's biography *James Joyce* (1980) as the model for the character Blazes Boylan in Joyce's novel *Ulysses* (1922). In a 1999 article for *The Daily Telegraph* (London) newspaper titled "Always Larger than Life," Boylan describes the kind of creativity and emotional expression that surrounded her as a child. Her father was always inventing gadgets and seeking financial support for his work. When Patrick Boylan's plans failed, as they often did, the Boylan household was plunged into a state of dark depression. Clare Boylan describes her mother as a "thwarted writer":

Creativity was her religion. Kitchen walls were painted black to facilitate full-scale expression. From my father, we got the gift of yearning, of never tailoring our ambitions, of believing that beneath the dust of any pavement we pounded there was yellow brick—possibly even gold.

Boylan comments on the profound influence her mother had on her as a writer in a 3 April 2000 article for *The Guardian,* "My Mother, Myself," writing

Now that she is gone, I can clearly see the real and enormous influence she effected. She made me feel that I was capable of anything and worthy of love. But the kind of writer I became is all her own work. In the end, the relationship, which dominated most of my life, became the substance and motivation of my fiction. All of my books, in one way or another, concern mothers and daughters.

Educated in Dublin as a journalist, Boylan began her career as a reporter for the *Evening Press* in 1966. Boylan then became the Dublin editor for *Young Woman* magazine in 1968, a position she held for two years. In September of 1970 she married Alan Wilkes, a journalist. Boylan worked as a features writer for the *Evening Press* from 1972 to 1978, winning the Benson & Hedges Journalist of the Year Award in 1974. From 1981 to 1984 she was the Dublin editor for *Image* magazine, at which time she began to explore fiction as a way to express the complex emotional and social issues that intrigued her. However, Boylan's fascination with fiction extends back to her childhood. In the introduction to *The Agony and the Ego: The Art and Strategy of Fiction Writing Explored* (1993), a collection of essays on writing she edited, Boylan explains what has always fascinated her about the art of fiction:

My earliest feelings, upon reading fiction were not, 'I want to be a writer', but 'How was that made?' As a child, I was not very interested in toys. I wanted to dismantle stories to find out: what held them together, what was underneath, what made them work, where was trick and where was truth, why some stories made you feel better, why some put out leafy branches in one's own imagination. . . . When I grew up this curiosity did not go away, but got stronger, so that when I began my career as a journalist I spent most of my time interviewing writers, trying to find out how particular effects of style or structure were achieved.

Boylan's first novel, *Holy Pictures* (1983), centers on the fourteen-year-old Nan Cantwell, who struggles to understand the world of adults from the uncertain vantage point of early adolescence. Unlike her younger sister, Mary, who is still thoroughly immersed in the world of childhood, Nan is beginning to mature physically and senses the imposition of the outside world upon her. When the novel opens it is four days prior to Christmas, and Nan and Mary travel from their impoverished 1920s Catholic Dublin neighborhood for a picnic in the snowy woods. The picnic is a respite from the hardscrabble home life of the Cantwells; even the church bell summons thoughts in Nan's mind of floating corpses in the Liffey—corpses of desperate victims of crime, poverty, and broken dreams. This grim scene also acts as a foreshadowing of the eventual suicide of Nan's father. Despite the fairy-tale innocence of her life, Nan has begun to encounter the less-than-innocent adult world. Prepubescent innocence, like that revealed on the face of unblemished virginal saints depicted on Holy Cards, proves impossible to sustain. In response to physical changes she cannot control, Nan straps down

*Dust jacket for the 1986 U.S. edition of Boylan's 1984 novel, about a middle-aged divorcée who decides to make
a new life for herself on a Greek resort island (Richland County Public Library)*

her breasts; similarly, she mentally corsets herself from those feelings she cannot understand.

The corset is a central motif in many of Boylan's novels, representing the constraining roles inflicted upon women in a patriarchal culture. Nan binds her transforming figure as an act of resistance against those who impose traditional roles upon her, yet Nan still revels in escapist childhood thoughts of being a fairy in the school pageant. In one scene Nan goes to a Jewish enclave, "Little Israel," and there proudly celebrates a female rite of passage, menstruation, with Mrs. Schweitzer and her daughters. Through these acts of evasion, regression, and exploration, Nan questions the traditional assumptions about her identity as a female. As Linda Taylor suggested in *TLS: The Times Literary Supplement* (11 March 1983), "Nan bandages her breasts, only to be accused of unnaturalness by her father. Mr. Cantwell's view of female sexuality is concerned with another kind of bondage—the corset, which he manufactures and which is becoming increasingly unfashionable. Nan's gesture appears to

him like an act of treason, both against her body and his life's work."

As the eldest daughter, hence a surrogate maternal figure in her family, Nan is responsible for her younger sister, Mary; Doll Carter, her Protestant neighbor; and Doll's cousin, Anastasia. Like her mother, Marguerite, who accepts but does not always approve of Cecil Cantwell's foolish business schemes, his love letters and photograph of a dark and exotic woman from his cavalry days in India, and his penchant for bringing strange boarders into their home, Nan must cultivate forbearance and exhibit compassion. Nan must also adhere to the nuns' parochial constraints at school, viewing her developing body as a vehicle for the eventual consummation of the sacrament of marriage and blissful motherhood. Nan must, in other words, perceive herself as subordinate to the patriarchal order of her society.

Nan's bewilderment over patriarchal order becomes clear when her father, Cecil, plans to escape the burden of the failing Cantwell Corset business by changing his name to Cecil Webster in order to disassociate himself from a product no longer in demand. Cecil explains that "Names do not matter to women. They are only of interest to people in the world. Women do not have a name until they marry." In reaction to her father's declaration Nan contemplates running away with her friend Dandy Tallon, whose father beat her when she came home late from a date. Like Nan, Dandy questions male authority. Unlike her mother, Nan attempts to glimpse and comprehend the world outside her immediate family and to pursue her own course in life, which includes a university education. Nan's dream is never realized, however, because Cecil Cantwell's suicide leaves his family in debt, and her mother, through financial necessity, decides that Nan must help operate a boardinghouse for fine gentlemen.

Late in the novel, the girls return to the forest in December to search for a tree to decorate. They locate one and Nan tries to put an angel atop the tree while the other girls place candles upon it, but the winter wind disrupts their activities: the angel is crooked, and they must hastily make their wishes upon the lit candles, following the Irish tradition that prayers said over candles at Christmastime all come true. *Holy Pictures* concludes almost as it began, though Nan is no longer caught between the worlds of childhood and adulthood, for fate has dictated the direction of her life for now—one of obligation, responsibility, and limitation.

In contrast to Nan, the adolescent central character of *Holy Pictures,* Harriet Bell, the main character of *Last Resorts* (1984), is a middle-aged divorcée dominated by her three egocentric, rude children: Tim, Lulu, and Kitty. Harriet is unfulfilled in life. She has an unsatisfactory, intermittent relationship with her married lover, Joe Fisher, secretly aspires to become a watercolor artist, and dreams of finding contentment amid the demands of others. For Harriet the solution to these problems is to vacation on Keptos, an exotic island off the coast of Greece, a place near where her former husband, Martin, and his new family holiday. With her modest income as an office worker Harriet had begun to take the children to Keptos after Martin left her. Although she initially dwells on Martin's infidelity during their marriage, Harriet envelops herself in the dreams of passion Joe Fisher evokes and the solace these vacations provide. But now that her children are older, these excursions to Greece are costly and have become a chore as Harriet tries unsuccessfully to please her teenage children.

In "Figuring the Mother in Contemporary Irish Fiction" (2000) Anne Owen Weekes addresses the problematic portraits of Irish mothers in the works of

Dust jacket for the 1989 U.S. edition of Boylan's 1988 novel, about an elderly Irishwoman who assumes a black British woman is the African child that she sponsored with her First Communion money (Richland County Public Library)

Boylan and other Irish writers, such as O'Brien, Mary Lavin, and Jennifer Johnston. Weekes suggests that Harriet, while residing in a postfeminist age, nonetheless is not truly liberated from the earlier Irish religious and social concept of maternal perfection, which is evident in her confrontations with her daughters. Wingate Packard in *The Seattle Times* (23 March 1986) noted that "Harriet finds with 'regret and relief' that not only will the children leave her, but she must also leave them—in the past—as they outgrow childhood. She is shocked to find herself thinking that 'the treachery of children was far worse than that of men, after years of nurturing and training,' and this presents a powerful image of family intimacy." This realization regarding the separation of a mother from her children, which is essential for the formation of the children's individual identities, is an epiphany to which Harriet must reconcile herself.

Returning to Edward Street Daisy
found that all her other feelings were
swept aside by a surge of melancholy melancholy
and regret. So much was poe freine
so much might never again returns.
The little house was folded in on itself
like an owl. Now that she was back
-r did not feel like home at all and
she knew it was something other than the

Returning to Edward Street Daisy suffered
a surge of melancholy and regret. The
little house was folded in on itself
like an owl. Pa and all the boys
gone. Maisie, Lena, Fanny. She stood
in the street with her valise.

Returning to Edward Street, Daisy
suffered a surge of melancholy &
regret. The house was no longer her
home. She stood in the street with
her valise, occasionally banging her
lids down uneasily on tears, trying to
keep the narrow limits humbly back in
focus with the picture she had carried
in her mind. The little house seemed
folded in on itself like an owl.
You and all to home were gone —
Missie, Cora, Janey. But it wasn't
The exodus that had let her down.
It was the view from the window

Dust jacket for the retitled U.S. edition of Home Rule
(Richland County Public Library)

Boylan employs the motif of a telescope, which becomes a vital image of transformation in Harriet's life. The telescope is a present given to Tim by his father and acts for Harriet as a window into a world of choices and freedom from domestic responsibility. When Harriet peers through its lens at the modernization of a formerly bucolic neighboring island, Psiros, with its newly constructed Paradise Hotel and bustling tourists, she begins to construct a narrative about the inhabitants of the island. At the same time she reconstructs the narrative of her own life, thus embarking on a journey into her past: her parents' ennui during family vacations, the seduction of Joe Fisher, and the changes in her children that seem to have distanced them from her. Harriet realizes that she married at the age of nineteen to escape a cloistered life under her parents' domination and connects that desire to her children's rebellion.

These telescopic adventures are not without consequences, though, for just as reality interfered

with her life in the past—an unsuccessful marriage and love affair—her encounters with Lulu's boyfriend, Roger; the meddlesome Melina, mother of the owner of the cottage, Stefan; and Apollo, a Greek fisherman with whom Harriet plans a sexual tryst, all prove unsettling. The relationship that seems to matter the most to Harriet is the one with Kitty, for Kitty's emotional outbursts—such as running away into the arms of a young man named Christos and clandestinely communicating with her father for parental guidance—mirror Harriet's inward struggles with others, specifically her mother, from whom she sought both love and independence.

As she did in *Holy Pictures,* Boylan uses a corset in *Last Resorts* to connect the past with the present and explore the need for women to liberate themselves. Harriet considers corseting Kitty's zaftig figure and recalls the time her own mother purchased a corset but pulled out all the bones. In this way Harriet's mother symbolically tried to lessen the confinement of her own domesticity, just as Harriet wishes to do. As a result of this realization Harriet writes a letter to her mother, whom she has neglected for many years. When a letter from her mother arrives later in the novel, Harriet learns that her father has left her mother. With this news an astounded Harriet realizes that she must make changes in her own life and travel to Psiros, the island she has only viewed through the telescope. Harriet realizes that unexpected events that affect one's life are also what give one's life meaning. Boylan concludes *Last Resorts* with Harriet clutching a suitcase, seeking employment, and gazing through the bars of a gate at a sand castle where little children play in their imaginary world, a world that nonetheless anticipates their future adult lives: "She sat down on a rocking chair which was painted to look like a kangaroo and watched the children living out lives that were prescribed for them, falling helpless into the trap of generation building, destroying, swinging, tumbling, laughing."

Boylan's most critically acclaimed novel, *Black Baby* (1988), begins with an epigraph from the Epistle of St. Paul to the Hebrews: "Be not forgetful to entertain strangers: for thereby some have entertained angels unawares." Chapter 1 presents an African adaptation of Genesis. The epigraph from St. Paul and the Africanized version of the Christian doctrine act as a preface for the main narrative of *Black Baby,* in which the main character, a sixty-seven-year-old cantankerous pensioner named Alice Boyle, briefly interacts with Dinah, a thirty-five-year-old black woman supposedly from Africa, whom Alice assumes to be the now grown "pagan" child she adopted with the money she received on the day of her First Communion.

Alice is a lonely and self-isolated spinster, repeatedly portrayed as looking through her window as though she were just a spectator in life. During the course of the novel the reader learns that Alice was a compliant child of domineering parents, that she had no children of her own, and that she is pitied by her two nephews and their avaricious wives. Her nephews visit Alice only at Christmas and on her birthday; during one birthday visit the nephews give Alice an old gramophone on which to play her late father's records. Alice describes the gramophone as a small coffin–a detail, like Alice's tendency to stare out the window, that Boylan uses to foreshadow facts revealed at the end of the novel.

After the nephews and their wives leave, Dinah appears at Alice's door. Thinking that Dinah might be a burglar, Alice is startled by the visitor who quietly utters the word "home" and kisses her upon the cheek. In fear, Alice claims that she has a husband resting in the other room. Dinah knows this claim is a ruse and quips that marriage causes more trouble than elation, referring to her own problems with marriage, which opens the door for Alice's ruminations later in the novel on her only marriage prospects. Dinah announces that she is a "daughter of Christ" on mission work and begins to win Alice's trust when she says that she had seen Alice crying, tears Alice claims were caused by the coffin-like present her nephews gave her. Alice asks Dinah, "Do you believe spirits of the dead live on?" to which Dinah replies, "yes." It is in this interchange that Boylan reveals Alice's need for Dinah, the stranger in her life.

While Dinah attempts to console Alice, Boylan describes the record spinning on the gramophone. The record becomes a eucharistic wafer, a segue into Dinah's supposed "communion" connection to Alice; Dinah's life with the Sisters of the Good Shepard in Africa; her worn King James Bible, the origin of her adoptive name, and a Christian song sung in child-like fashion by the visitor. Here Boylan blurs the line between dreams and reality in Alice's mind, for Dinah's stories are a confluence of the two. In his 1996 essay "Joyce and Boylan's *Black Baby:* 'Swiftly and Silently,'" Jean-Louis Giovannangelli argues that this blurring of the line between dreams and reality is a stylistic device and compares Boylan's use of the "comatic hallucination" to Joyce's *Finnegans Wake* (1939): "In both works this lost or repressed something is linked with memory and desire, with indeterminacy and wit. In Joyce's work Ireland's father tongue is personified as a traumatized Everyman; in Boylan's work it is personified as a woman (Alice) in a coma, a virgin in search of a black baby called Dinah." Giovannangelli also notes thematic similarities between Boylan's novel and Joyce's *Ulysses:* "At a structural level, just as *Ulysses* is built on the narrative pattern of the father/son motif, largely used as pretext, *Black Baby* bearing on theme of the lost parental link plays on the mother/daughter relationship, similarly impossible and unaccomplished."

Chapter 6 begins with Dinah, having left Alice's home in frustration, securing a room at a bed-and-breakfast; yet, remnants of the elder woman's psyche intrude upon Dinah's narrative: "Alice's house had been full of stories. Each object had its memory. And Alice? Alice was a box, full of stuff, which had thrown away its own key." Dinah becomes a somewhat ambivalent accomplice in Alice's narrative, and through Dinah's emerging narrative of self as she encounters other Dubliners, Boylan depicts a woman who, like Alice, is unable to respond to genuine human contact. Although more assertive than Alice, Dinah also feels an overwhelming sense of isolation. Unlike Alice, however, Dinah is a black woman negotiating a white world, prompting a need for commitment or "communion" on her own terms.

After Dinah's visit Alice dreams of her past, of a cradle she thought would hold a baby, which then awakens more memories: two ill-fated youthful romances, one with the older Burton Gosling and another, more passionate, with the "coloured" African, Dr. Henry Makwaia, that was cut off by her mother's intervention. After the twenty-five-year-old Alice was forced to renounce Makwaia, her "whole body went into rebellion" and she experienced early menopause. As Christine St. Peter argues in "*Black Baby* Takes Us Back: Dreaming the Postcolonial Mother" (1997), "Thus disappeared her possibility of biological motherhood. The black baby that might have issued from the match serves as a symbol of lost hope and reconciliation. . . . the novel writes the dream of a glorious vision of life's possibilities beyond the sundry practices of colonization." Simply put, Dinah represents that dream baby to Alice. For Dinah, Alice becomes for a moment a maternal figure to replace her natural, African-born mother, who raised her in a Brixton slum dwelling in London. Further, St. Peter suggests that *Black Baby* could be perceived as "a complex satire of the way Irish Catholics, themselves victims of historical abuse, could become in turn righteous colonizers and wily spiritual bankers, storing up credit in heaven."

History for Alice is clouded by the past as she rummages through the attic and discovers old issues of *National Geographic,* including one containing pictorials of black aborigines. Those pictures remind her of her uncle's racial prejudices, stereotypes she never espoused but latently expresses toward Dinah. She

*Dust jacket for the 2001 U.S. edition of Boylan's
1999 novel, about a daughter who is forced to
care for her parents when her father begins
showing signs of senile dementia (Richland
County Public Library)*

also thinks of the time her mother tried to destroy all of her father's beloved clocks. It is as if Boylan signals to the reader that the temporal world has been suspended in Alice's mind from the moment that Dinah left her home. Life changes for Alice after Dinah's fateful visit, and she seemingly becomes more compassionate and less reclusive. While living by herself, Alice becomes the victim of a burglary whose aftermath is a stroke and hospitalization. It is not until the conclusion of the novel that Boylan reveals to the reader that most of the narrative is a product of the mind of the comatose Alice Boyle. In the concluding chapter, the reader finds Dinah phoning Alice's home only to hear that "Miss Boyle had died peacefully in the hospital earlier that day."

Boylan's next novel, *Home Rule* (1992), was published in the United States as *11 Edward Street*. Set in 1890s Dublin and centering on the travails of the Devlin family, the novel is a companion piece to *Holy Pic-*

tures. As reviewer Deborah Singmaster in *TLS* (11 June 1992) reported, "The larger historical events—war, the sinking of the Titanic, the Easter Rising—merely serve as chronological pointers: *Home Rule* is neither a historical nor a political novel, its title is one of many jokes. . . . Buried deep underneath the surface fun runs a wry lament for the unhappy lot of Irish wives, shackled to rotten men and dogged by the threat of perpetual pregnancy." In the opening chapter Boylan provides the reader with a brief panoramic view of the city landscape, including the River Liffey, the Guinness Brewery, and The Magdalen Institute for wayward girls. The last landmark ironically foreshadows the plight of young girls, victims of verbal and physical abuse, incest, rape, attempted suicide, and domestic isolation, who, not unlike the Devlin sisters, naively attempt to find a place for themselves in this provincial society. The mother is an aristocratic English Protestant woman, Elinore DuBois, who against her family's wishes married a young Catholic Irishman, Danny Devlin, a dreamer and concocter of medicinal cures. Elinore's family claimed Devlin would desert her and leave her penniless with ten children. In a way Devlin does desert the family, dying and leaving his overbearing and apathetic wife impoverished and his nine children—Daisy, Will, Tom, Janey, Essie, Beth, Weenie, Lena, Bertie—fatherless.

The protagonist in the story is the empathetic Daisy Devlin, the eldest daughter, whom the reader discovers was sexually molested by her father. The spirited Daisy acts as surrogate mother to the other children and secretly fights for her own sense of self-worth, while her domineering mother schemes of ways to improve the family's monetary situation, such as her plan to open a secondhand shoe shop. Boylan renders Daisy's Dublin neighborhood as a spectacle of the grotesque: poor, dirty, and inhabited by the unfortunate. At one point the girls visit Granny Devlin, who offers the girls advice on how to repel sexual advances from their future husbands and claims that their mother is too "dainty," meaning that a romantic nature might be fine for luring a husband but impractical in "normal married life."

Driven away by her mother's draconian control and influenced by some kindly nuns, Daisy decides to enter a convent in Manchester, believing a spiritual life will offer her solace and a sense of worth apart from being a factory girl or her mother's problem. One day, when Daisy is off on an errand for the convent, she encounters the charming Cecil Cantwell, a young military man home on leave, who is a younger version of the character who appeared in *Holy Pictures*. Even though Daisy is in a nun's habit, the attraction between the two is strong. Boylan comically suffuses their meeting with the conventions of a romance novel: a gallant soldier and the virginal young woman on the verge of reconsidering a cloistered asexual life who exchange sentimental missives. At this point in the novel Daisy, who Cecil calls Marguerite, returns home to her mother and the drudgery of her life on 11 Edward Street, and she and Cecil embark on a five-year courtship via the mail. Actually Daisy stops writing Cecil, and it is Daisy's sister Janey, a cosmopolitan free spirit, who assumes the nom de plume of Daisy and composes sensually explicit letters to him. Just like her mother, Daisy marries the man of her dreams only to suffer through pregnancy, infidelity, and Cecil's outlandish business ventures: including hair restoration and the infamous Cantwell Corset.

Boylan's next novel, *Room for a Single Lady* (1997), is set in the 1950s at the Dublin home of the Raffertys, a Catholic family of five: Eugene, the father, who experiences constant bouts of unemployment; Edith, the mother, who is frustrated by their lack of money; and three girls, Bridie, Kitty, and Rose. Eugene resolves to pay the bills by taking in lodgers. Into this plot Boylan cleverly situates colorful vignettes of the tenants who reside with the Raffertys, these scenes providing insight into the girls' characters, their mother's protectiveness, and their father's indifference.

Boylan explains in "Growing Pains," an article published in *The Guardian* (15 September 1997), that the female tenants of the boardinghouse illustrate the limited options available to women during the 1950s:

> When I set out to write my novel, *Room for a Single Lady,* it was as a tribute to a lost era of imaginative richness. I wanted to press in its pages the magical episodes of my own growing up. Play was safe in the 1950s. With no television or telephones, we grew up in a fantasy world, childhood a series of hilarious dress rehearsals for the great drama of growing up. But behind the comedy and the charm, I found something less heartwarming. As my sisters and I grew older, our role play developed an edge of anxiety, verging on panic. When we reached adolescence, we realised we were about to be pushed out on stage with no script and without proper costume. There was the awful discovery that there was no such thing as a woman. That is to say, there was no definition for a woman. There were only different kinds of women; married women or spinsters, beautiful women or plain ones, saints or sinners, fat women, brainy women, unstable women, man eaters, ball breakers, bitches, bags.

From the tenants' lives the girls learn about loss, love, superstition, and sex. From their infirm maternal grandmother they witness the ravages of old age—dependency on relatives and incontinence. From gen-

tle, countrified Selena Taylor, a victim of incest who marries wealthy widower and invalid Boris Carson, they learn compassion for those less fortunate. From the educated, pro-communist and erratic Ruth Kandinsky and her scholarly husband Daniel Fine they learn of love, loss, rage, and the Holocaust. From the flamboyant, sensuous Sissy Sullivan they learn about the customary rites of passage for girls: cosmetics, sex, and a desperate hope for marriage. From the commercially enterprising, older, Jewish tenant, Minnie Mankievitz, they learn about self-reliance, devotion, and adaptability in the midst of change. From Gladys Partridge, a tenant recommended by the Rafferty's well-to-do neighbors, the Bates, they learn about relationships outside the sanctity of marriage. From the reclusive, supposed schoolteacher, Mrs. Heaslip, "the Werewolf," a lodger who urinates in bottles stored beneath her bed, they learn about eccentricity. In a review in *The New Statesman* (9 December 1997) Katy Emck commented on the relationship between the Rafferty girls and their boarders: "The lodgers focus the girls' confused desires for adventure and, most importantly of all, for that mystical state of womanhood . . . *Room for a Single Lady* paints a vivid sketch of life's losers and victims and then shows them coming out on top—while remaining as weird as ever." In other words, through this procession of tenants, some more significant then others, Boylan invites the reader to inhabit the minds of Bridie, Kitty, and Rose as they awkwardly and honestly experience the joys and hardships of the adult world.

Boylan was awarded a Ford/Sunday Independent Spirit of Life Arts Award in 1997. Founded in that year, the award is meant to honor the achievements of Irish artists in a variety of disciplines who have made an impact both at home and abroad. That same year she received a Hawthornden Foundation fellowship. In 1996 Boylan was made a member of Aosdána, an organization established by the Arts Council to honor those artists whose work has made an outstanding contribution to the arts in Ireland. Boylan was also invited by Dermot Bolger to join six other well-known Irish women authors—Kate O'Riordan, Maeve Binchy, Emma Donoghue, Anne Haverty, Éilis Ní Dhuibhne, and Diedre Purcell—in contributing to the group novel *Ladies' Night at Finbar's Hotel* (1999). This book was a sequel to *A Night at Finbar's Hotel* (1997), also edited by Bolger, which had featured unsigned contributions by several Irish writers, including Roddy Doyle, Anne Enright, Hugo Hamilton, and Joseph O'Connor, depicting the clientele of a rundown Dublin hotel scheduled to be closed. *Ladies' Night at Finbar's Hotel* is set in the reopened and

As to the strange alliance of opposites
known as marriage, I became,
in due course, as most women do, an
expert on the subject. Habit and
kindness form its strong weave. Passion
and intellect are but adornments to the
garment. Fabric. As it requires a
strong degree of commonsense, a wealth of
organisational skill and sufficient mettle
to sustain it under seige, a strong fortress
may endure better than a good passion.
Indeed, if a wife ever loves a husband
so much that a harsh word or a
cold look cuts her to the heart, — she
is a fool - foolish. If she ever loves so
much that her husband's will be her law —
and that she has got into the habit of
watching his looks in order that she may
anticipate his wishes she will soon
be a neglected fool.

Looking at Albert and I as
years progressed and we took happiness
from such children as had been planted.
To one came, anyone would have said

Page from the manuscript for Boylan's novel "Emma Brown," scheduled for publication in 2003 (courtesy of the author)

trendily refurbished hotel, and the anonymous chapters follow the often funny activities of a different set of characters. Bolger adapted the novel into a radio play for the British Broadcasting Corporation (BBC), broadcast on BBC Radio 4 on 10 May 2000.

Boylan's sixth novel, *Beloved Stranger* (1999), shares some common themes with her earlier novels— female children attempting to separate themselves from their parents in a quest for their own identity and discovering what it means physically and emotionally to be female. Rather than writing about youthful characters, however, Boylan shifts her focus to an already independent-minded, middle-aged daughter and her elderly mother who must face the father's descent into madness. This madness is manic depression, which wreaks havoc on the staid married life of Dick and Lily Butler, both in their seventies, and warrants the intervention of Ruth, the couple's distant daughter who believes herself quite happy in her own life as an architect.

Boylan commented upon her interest in the subject of marriage as a topic for her novel in "Ring Cycle," an article published in *The Guardian* (30 August 1999):

> Increasingly as I get older, I find myself fascinated by the idea of marriage. My new novel is largely an analysis of this changeless institution in a vastly altered world. The idea of tying two strangers together for life because of sexual attraction, sympathy or even deep and lasting love seems odd and I don't believe that marriage is necessarily a natural state. At the same time, the yearning for a happy marriage seems an absolutely natural thing. Happy marriages do exist. . . .

Despite the septuagenarian Butlers' fifty years of seemingly blissful marriage, the reader learns that Lily Butler was a closet feminist before the term existed, and that the now retired Dick, whose life was defined by his work and ability to keep his family financially comfortable, is reduced to merely carrying his old business cards. Ruth recalls once reading Simone de Beauvoir's *The Second Sex* (1949), specifically the phrase "marriage incites a man to capricious imperialism," and thinks this statement perfectly encapsulates the tenor of her father's role in the marriage. Therefore, when Ruth leaves home, she decides never to marry nor to enhance herself to please a man the way her mother did, but to enjoy sex without the contract of marriage and to select a profession her father thought suitable only for a man. The departure of Ruth changes Lily, too, when Lily discovers and begins to read her daughter's feminist texts. Through the books on her daughter's bedroom bookshelves Lily begins to comprehend that she has shelved her

own identity, the woman she might have been and still is in some ways, prior to her marriage to Dick.

The signs of Dick's manic depression become manifest to Lily in his mood swings and actions. Dick's paranoia causes him one night to crouch on all fours with a shotgun in hand, ready to fend off an imaginary intruder. He opens all the doors and the windows despite the cold weather outside and the lack of central heating inside. Dick hides his check stubs from secret transactions. He also demonstrates a heightened sexual appetite: purchasing a new mattress and desiring an expensive trip to a tropical island for a second honeymoon. Lily at first tries to dismiss all these signs but then contacts Ruth with the excuse that her father is a bit depressed. Convinced that her father is becoming dangerous to himself and her mother, Ruth quickly seeks professional help, and Dick is sent to a local psychiatric hospital to be observed by a doctor named Tim Walcott. When Walcott enters the lives of the three characters, the family is forced to make adjustments: Dick resists the diagnosis that he is mentally ill and must be hospitalized; Lily accepts the fact that Dick is ill; Dick dreams that she conspired to have him institutionalized and that she is having an illicit affair with Walcott; Lily attempts to drink away her anguish; and Ruth acknowledges that her parents are now dependent upon her.

The plot is not entirely grim in *Beloved Stranger*. Boylan sporadically shows a medicated Dick in good humor and sanity, as when he sells their new mattress for more than it is worth. Lily finds that for a brief time she can thrive in a world outside the confines of marriage, though the reader detects the extent of Lily's loneliness without Dick when she befriends a pet mouse in the flat where she lives temporarily. Ruth realizes that many of her mother's traits are not entirely unlike many of her own, and the two even take a mother-daughter vacation together, during which Ruth dons more-attractive clothes and lipstick and decides she, too, wants a child. Ruth eschews the traditional gender roles set forth in the institution of marriage when she forgoes the obligation of the marriage contract and asks the kindly, but gay, Doctor Walcott to be the father of her child. The novel concludes on a joyous, celebratory note. At Dick's grave Ruth announces to Lily that she is pregnant by Walcott, and a bemused, naively optimistic Lily claims, "'I knew he wasn't really gay. It's just a matter of meeting the right girl. I wouldn't mind you marrying him. . . . Next time we come we'll bring a flask . . . Of course, you realise who this child will be? . . . It'll be your father, coming back.'" Lily's longing for her late husband and her wish for him to be reincarnated in Ruth's unborn child is explicable. As E. Jane Dickson pointed out in an 11 September 1999 review in *The Independent* (London), from the start of Dick's dementia Lily finds it difficult to perceive her life without him at the helm: "For the first time, Lily finds herself unable to follow where her husband leads and is utterly disorientated by this freedom."

In her 1999 article "Always Larger than Life" Boylan relates events from her own life that parallel events in *Beloved Stranger:* "When I came back home to Dublin from a summer holiday in 1987, my father, Patrick, had undergone a terrible change. The mild old gentleman, in his late seventies, with his pipe and his highly polished shoes, his love of music and corny jokes, was now a frightened and frightening alien." Symptoms of her own father's dementia are ascribed to the character of Dick in the novel: the shotgun episode, opening the windows in freezing weather, and unfounded jealousies and suspicions of conspiracies. Like his fictional counterpart, Dick Butler, Patrick Boylan was committed to a locked psychiatric ward and eventually placed in a nursing home.

In reviewing *Beloved Stranger* for *The New York Times* (11 April 2001), Richard Elder noted Clare Boylan's skill as a novelist and suggested why the reader empathizes with the characters in what on the surface appears to be a bleak novel: "They do not prevail over what happens to them but neither they, nor we, are swamped. We read from the vantage of little boats, not that of the dismal waves they sail against." Elder's comment about this novel may suggest why many readers enjoy Boylan's novels. What Arminta Wallace, a reviewer for *The Irish Times* (25 October 1997), wrote about *Home Rule* seems applicable to all of Boylan's novels: Wallace noted that Boylan

"smashes the mould" of the usual Irish novel "to joyful smithereens," presenting characters with "a pulsating vividness, never stooping to stereotype or stage Oirish effects; her characters are persuasively human, their adventures poignant and hair-raising, their spirit absolutely indomitable." Boylan's female characters are typically persevering to various degrees despite their ordeals, whether they experience a loss of innocence or find themselves confounded by their Catholicism, their traditional gender-bound roles, male morality, or sexual relationships. Boylan is a member of a generation of Irish women novelists who see the need for such topics to be explored through fiction with wit, sensitivity, and insight.

Interview:

Penny Wark, "Interview: Clare Boylan," *Sunday Times* (London), 28 July 1996, p. 1.

References:

Jean-Louis Giovannangelli, "Joyce and Boylan's *Black Baby:* 'Swiftly and Silently,'" in *The Comic Tradition in Irish Women Writers,* edited by Theresa O'Connor (Gainesville: University Press of Florida, 1996), pp. 171–182;

Christine St. Peter, "*Black Baby* Takes Us Back: Dreaming the Postcolonial Mother," *Canadian Woman Studies,* 17, no. 3 (1997): 36–38;

Anne Owen Weekes, "Figuring the Mother in Contemporary Irish Fiction," in *Contemporary Irish Fiction: Themes, Tropes, Theories,* edited by Liam Harte and Michael Parker (New York: St. Martin's Press, 2000), pp. 100–124.

Amit Chaudhuri
(15 May 1962 –)

Mary Robertson Ellen
University of East Anglia

BOOKS: *A Strange and Sublime Address* (London: Heinemann, 1991);

Afternoon Raag (London: Heinemann, 1993);

Freedom Song (London: Picador, 1998);

A New World (London: Picador, 2000; New York: Knopf, 2000);

Real Time: Stories and a Reminiscence (London: Picador, 2002; New York: Farrar, Straus & Giroux, 2002).

Collection: *Freedom Song: Three Novels* (New York: Knopf, 1999); republished as *Three Novels* (London: Picador, 2001)—comprises *A Strange and Sublime Address, Afternoon Raag,* and *Freedom Song.*

OTHER: *The Picador Book of Modern Indian Literature,* edited by Chaudhuri (London: Picador, 2001); republished as *The Vintage Book of Modern Indian Literature* (New York: Vintage, 2002).

SELECTED PERIODICAL PUBLICATIONS—
UNCOLLECTED: "A Small Bengal, NW3," *Granta,* 65 (February 1999): 308–310;

"Lure of Hybridity: What the Post-colonial Indian Novel Means to the West," *TLS: The Times Literary Supplement* (3 September 1999): 5–6.

Amit Chaudhuri (photograph by Jerry Bauer; from the dust jacket for Freedom Song: Three Novels, *1999)*

The novelist Mulk Raj Anand often spoke of the double burden carried by Indian writers who choose English as their literary language. On the one shoulder, Anand contended, sat the Alps of European tradition, and on the other shoulder, the Himalayas of an Indian past. Some Indian writers of the first half of the twentieth century—such as Anand, R. K. Narayan, and Raja Rao, considered the founding fathers of the Indian novel in English—chose that dual burden, while other writers, such as Rabindranath Tagore, who wrote in his native Bengali, and Premacanda, who wrote in both Urdu and Hindi, eschewed the language of European modernism and its narrative techniques. In the foreword to his novel *Kanthapura* (1938) Raja Rao explains the problematic relationship facing Indian writers writing in English: "One has to convey in a language that is not one's own the spirit that is one's own."

Among contemporary Indian novelists writing in English, this problematic relationship and dual burden has been mediated by a postmodern narrative style that allows bilingual or multilingual playfulness, panhistorical time compression, and magic-realist description. This postmodern narrative is most closely associated with Salman Rushdie, whose novel *Midnight's Children* (1981) evades the either or opposition earlier novelists faced in favor of an approach blending both traditions. Novelists such as Amitav Ghosh, I. Allan Sealy, Upamanyu Chatterjee, and Kiran Desai—writers often referred to as "Midnight's Grandchildren"—have followed Rushdie's lead. Several Indian writers, however, have chosen to write in English without embracing Rushdie's postmodern style. Vikram Seth, Rohinton Mistry, and Amit Chaudhuri instead choose close descriptive detail that explores and reveals the lives of characters rooted in their particular Indian experience. Chaudhuri is one such novelist, whose novels and stories focus on the lives of Indian characters told in a style that has more in common with Virginia Woolf than Rushdie. It is a style, though, particularly suited for a writer trained in England who sets his early fiction in the India he remembers.

Amit Prakash Chaudhuri was born 15 May 1962 in Calcutta, West Bengal, to Hindu parents of East Bengali origin. His father, Nages Chandra Chaudhuri, and mother, Bijoya Chaudhuri (née Nandi Majumdar), were both from Sylhet in East Bengal but left soon after Indian independence in 1947, when the Indian subcontinent was partitioned into India and Pakistan, and East Bengal became East Pakistan (now Bangladesh). Amit Chaudhuri's parents both settled in Shillong, in the Indian state of Assam, where they became engaged in 1948. In 1949, at the age of twenty-seven, Nages Chandra Chaudhuri left India for England to study to be a chartered accountant (equivalent to a certified public accountant in the United States). His fiancée, Amit Chaudhuri's mother, had to wait until 1955 before she could join him in London. There the two were married in a Hindu ceremony. In "A Small Bengal, NW3" (1999) Chaudhuri recalls his parents' experiences living in Belsize Park in the borough of Camden during the 1950s. The transitory nature of Chaudhuri's parents' lives—they were part of a shifting student population that Chaudhuri terms "itinerant" rather than "emigrant"—was matched by their attempts to install or translate certain aspects of Bengali culture into their new "homeland." His mother, for instance, insisted on practicing the Tagore songs that she had learned as a child in Sylhet, only to receive complaints from the landlady for singing too loudly, and took pride in her reputation as a Bengali cook so far from home. The early experiences of the marriage of Chaudhuri's mother, a new wife to an Indian living in England, form an episode or scene of cross-cultural exchange.

As Chaudhuri notes, in Belsize Park the new bride was received not by her in-laws (as would be traditional) but by a surrogate family of male students (including her husband), and she arrived not at her husband's Indian house but at a one-room apartment "with wallpaper and cooking hobs which was now to be her own, and which cost three pounds and ten shillings a

week." Any cultural dissonance felt by Chaudhuri's parents was balanced by a strong desire to assimilate English metropolitan culture: their working days were punctuated by shared lunches or teas at Lyons restaurant and weekly Chinese dinners at the Cathay restaurant in Piccadilly. Chaudhuri's narrative of his parents' process of settlement in a foreign land centers on these issues of cross-cultural "translation."

The decade of the 1950s was a period of increased emigration from newly independent, or soon-to-be independent, British colonial territories to Britain, especially to London. These immigrant experiences form an important episode in the Anglo-Indian tradition of cross-cultural writings, of what since the late 1980s has increasingly been called postcolonial literature. In his *Imaginary Homelands* (1991) Rushdie outlines many of the features of "the phenomenon of cultural transplantation" associated with migrant writing: "To be an Indian writer in this society is to face, every day, problems of definition. What does it mean to be 'Indian' outside India? . . . How are we to live in the world?" Rushdie's answers center on the need to embrace the positive aspects of writing in English: "To conquer English may be to complete the process of making ourselves free . . . Having been borne across the world, we are translated men. It is normally supposed that something always gets lost in translation; I cling, obstinately to the notion that something can also be gained." Chaudhuri's parents' experiences form an important "generational" aspect to such issues; as a second-generation short-term migrant, Chaudhuri took a course that had been already outlined by their experiences during the 1950s, as well as Rushdie's own negotiations with Englishness. Chaudhuri's novels can be viewed as a supplement to both Anglo-Indian writing and writing of the contemporary condition of migrancy in the Indian diaspora. However, like the Bengali poet and writer Tagore, who in 1913 became the first non-European to win the Nobel Prize in literature, Chaudhuri is primarily interested in celebrating his native Bengal, with an added focus on its capital, Calcutta. A concern for the local, with an emphasis on its sense of "*un*translatable strangeness," continuously interacts with the larger transnational framework most associated with postcolonial migrant literature.

In 1961 Chaudhuri's parents left England for Bombay, where his father had a new job that paid for their fares back to India by ship, a journey that took two weeks. Amit, their only child, was born in Calcutta the following year. He grew up in Bombay, where as a schoolboy he was taught what he has termed "the creation-myth of the nation," or the "official historical narrative of India." Chaudhuri's perspective on the official narrative of the partition and independence is viewed through a highly personal and individualized family lens where exile, displacement, and resettlement become the scenes of family memory not allowed for in official versions of history. As his parents' experiences had already testified, movement from one house to another, from one country to another, had always been central to their lives—and thus to Chaudhuri's own life, as narrator of family memory—both before and after 1947. Chaudhuri has argued that the partition must also be seen as an ever-present moment of transition where the "old" country is never fully left behind and where the "new" country of India remains slightly "foreign."

Chaudhuri's personalized rewritings of the events of 1947 are also a reworking of certain literary histories written during the fiftieth anniversary of Indian independence. He has argued that too many English-language novels produced by Indian writers since the 1980s have focused mainly on those events highlighted in the official "creation-myth of the nation." This argument holds serious implications for those Indians writing in English during the period that is now referred to as the post-Rushdie boom. The critical and commercial success in 1981 of *Midnight's Children*—a novel that takes the moment of Independence as its own "creation-myth"—transformed the Anglo-Indian novel. It succeeded in redrawing the literary map of India by drawing attention to a new crop of Indian authors writing in English, particularly during the late 1980s, many of whom modeled themselves on Rushdie. Chaudhuri's comments act as an important reminder that "India" remains a political and historical construct and that regional differences and earlier Indian writings must be remembered. In 1986 Chaudhuri graduated with honors from University College, London.

Chaudhuri's first book, *A Strange and Sublime Address,* was published in Britain in 1991 by William Heinemann, Ltd. It is divided into two parts: the opening novella, which gives the book its title, followed by nine short stories. Chapter 7 of the novella had already appeared in the *London Review of Books,* and the short story "Lakshmi Poornima Night" had been published in the *London Magazine.* His work had also appeared in *TLS: The Times Literary Supplement, Oxford Poetry,* and the *Oxford Companion to Twentieth Century Poetry.* The book won first prize in the Betty Trask Awards of 1991, the Commonwealth Writers Prize for Best First Book (Eurasia) in 1992, and was short-listed for the 1991 Guardian Fiction Prize. The title of the novella—*A Strange and Sublime Address*—is identified by Sandeep, the ten-year-old boy into whose world the author invites the reader, as the address written by his cousin Abhi on the first page of his schoolbooks:

Abhijit Das,
17 Vivekananda Road,
Calcutta (South),
West Bengal,
India,
Asia,
Earth,
The Solar System,
The Universe.

This written address resembles the inscription that Stephen Dedalus, the protagonist of James Joyce's *Portrait of the Artist as a Young Man* (1916), makes on the flyleaf of his geography book. The physical address represented forms the central focus of the book. The house on Vivekananda Road is the home of Sandeep's maternal uncle, his wife, and their two young sons, Abhi and Babla, where Sandeep and his mother spend their holidays. In his preface Chaudhuri explains that in Bengali his uncle's name, Chotomama, means "Junior Uncle," and his wife is called Mamima, translated as "motherly maternal aunt": "All in all, the Bengali family is a tangled web, an echoing cave, of names and appellations, too complicated to explain individually."

This Bengali household is set against Sandeep's life in Bombay, where he attends an English-language school and lives with his parents in a twenty-five-story apartment building. Home for Sandeep, however, is where the heart is—in Calcutta—amid the noise, dust, smoke, and day-to-day family life on the outskirts of the city, where he can forget the loneliness and artificiality of his other life. Whenever Bombay is recalled by Sandeep, it is as a site of absence: "Alone in the big apartment on the twenty-third floor, he was like Adam in charge of paradise, given dominion over the birds and fishes; he was too much in the foreground. . . . But here, in Chotomama's house, he pulsed into life and passed into extinction according to his choice; he had liberty." Freedom, for Sandeep, lies with being able to forget oneself and exist in the moment as a passive recipient of all that is most routine and unremarkable in daily life. The absences experienced by Sandeep later in the tale as he gazes out across Bombay—"No sounds, no smells, only a pure, perpetually moving picture"—serve to recall the reader, and Sandeep, back to the greater physicality of Calcutta. And yet, the minutiae of everyday life are presented in a multiplicity of impressions that serve to soften this physicality.

Sandeep's ten-year-old visitor's gaze is particularly suited to this vision of city life. He watches and listens to all the city has to offer him, its characters in the lanes outside the house, his extended family inside, including their daily rituals of cooking, washing, sweeping, singing, sleeping, reading, praying, watching, thinking—all the "untidy but regular activity" that continually threatens to turn to chaos but that always emerges as the material of a particularly poetic and meditative vision. On one occasion, when meeting a distant relative, Sandeep announces that when he grows up he will be a writer of horror stories. As he walks out one evening with his uncle and two cousins, the reader is reminded of Sandeep's future as a writer. "Why," the narrator asks, "did all these houses seem to suggest that an infinitely interesting story might be woven around them?" The answer suggests that Calcutta works against constructing any unified narrative of the city, that its irrelevancies and digressions are the "point," that the "'real' story, with its beginning, middle and conclusion, would never be told, because it did not exist." Chaudhuri's characterization of Calcutta is central to this novella; the city enacts a modernist drama from which it cannot or does not wish to fully emerge. Its representations as a "city of dust" or as part of "that primitive, terracotta landscape of Bengal . . . the Bengal of the bullock-cart and the earthen lamp" encourage a new, as-yet-unknown, or unknowable, aesthetic: "At such times, Calcutta is like a work of modern art that neither makes sense or has utility, but exists for some esoteric aesthetic reason." The "sublime address" of the title becomes a reworked version of a suburbanized, Bengali aesthetic tradition.

The search for meaning within Calcutta as text has been the subject of a wide range of writings by a variety of authors: the records of the colonial officials of the East India Company; the short stories of Rudyard Kipling; the various works of Tagore; the Indian travelogues of Allen Ginsberg, W. Somerset Maugham, Eric Newby, Vikram Seth, and David Foster; and the novels of Amitav Ghosh. Chaudhuri's fictionalized Calcutta belongs to a genre in which questions of how to "map" or imagine the city—in particular the city as a site of postcolonial difference—have been colored by postmodern theories. The two-dimensional aspects of "mapmaking," where epistemological knowledge has been linked to Western ideas of the Oriental, have given way to more unstable cartographies in which, as Edward Said in *Culture and Imperialism* (1993) has suggested, the experience of exile encourages the "charting of new territories in defiance of the classic, canonic enclosures." Chaudhuri's personal tribute to Calcutta adds an extra dimension to these ideas; the character Sandeep, like himself, is a visitor, an outsider who attempts to incorporate his extended family's sense of "exile" from East Bengal as they live out their new Indian life in Calcutta.

Sandeep has grown up as an English-speaking, English-writing Indian with little knowledge of his own provincial Bengalese: "He was one of the innumerable language-orphans of modern India." His childish attempts to learn the Bengali "characters," or script, and

to understand his uncle's singing are portrayed as examples of premodern moments when the text itself "remembers" an older family-based history. Chotomama is able to grant a new perspective, for example, on pre-Independence Indian history by informing the young boys—Sandeep, Abhi, and Babla—that it was Subhas Chandra Bose, the Bengali freedom fighter, who was the true "Father of the Nation" and not Mohandas Gandhi, as Sandeep supposed: "'Gandhi! Gandhi was no freedom-fighter! He was a sham yogi who knew no economics!' He began to deify Subhas Bose, the brilliant side-tracked Bengali . . . pride shone in his eyes, the pride a son feels when he remembers a calumniated father." An alternative Bengali tradition is asserted throughout this short novella, including a localized pre-Independence version of Indian history, the novels and prayer-songs of Tagore, the movies of Satyajit Ray, the stylized Bengali script, the fish-based cuisine, and the unfinished nature of Calcutta's industrial status.

Of the nine short stories that make up the second half of *A Strange and Sublime Address,* eight are set in India—Calcutta and Bombay—and one in London. The main characters belong to the Hindu middle classes, with particular emphases on their relations with the servant class: shopkeepers, cleaners, cooks, plumbers, electricians. As in the title novella, the routine details of daily life are foregrounded. In "Lakshmi Poornima Night" two servants, Savitri, the maidservant, and Panna, the toilet cleaner, ask for extra money after finishing their work for the narrator's family, as part of a tradition associated with the goddess Lakshmi. Both the precarious nature of their work and the need for careful supervision are represented; the narrator and his mother must ensure the servants do not step out of line, yet their characters and abilities to negotiate are sympathetically represented. Indeed, the intradependence of their relationship is strongly noted: religious observance by the servants acts as a cultural reminder to the more laissez-faire attitudes of their middle-class employers. In "The Happiest Man in the World" the narrator's uncle and his meager existence in Chalk Farm, London, are explored during a short visit by the young narrator from Oxford. His uncle had previously lived in Belsize Park at the same time as had the narrator's parents, a fact that suggests the story has autobiographical elements. The uncle is represented as "an impossible man" whose idiosyncrasies are acknowledged as part of his lonely immigrant existence. When asked, "What exactly do you have against going back [to India]?" he replies, "I can't go back. Everyone has his own life. I want to return to everyone living in the same place . . . as we used to do in Shillong . . . Let's not talk about it." Waiting at the bus stop he tells his nephew a story from his childhood, where his dream of touching the inside of a clock was inspired when he saw "the happiest man in the world," a watch-repairer, "touching the black hands of the clock with his fingers . . . My uncle was overwhelmed by this vision of perfect peace and joy."

On 12 December 1991 Chaudhuri married Rinka Khastgir. Between 1992 and 1995 he held a creative-arts fellowship at Wolfson College, Oxford. In 1993 he received a D.Phil. from Balliol College, Oxford, submitting as his thesis "Text and Intertextuality in the Poetry of D. H. Lawrence." That same year *Afternoon Raag* was published and won the 1993 Southern Arts Literature Prize and the Encore Award for Best Second Novel. Chapter 4 was first published in *New Writing 2* (1993), edited by Malcolm Bradbury and Andrew Motion. The apparently autobiographical nature of its subject matter—a first-person account of student life at Oxford University—could be read as a direct adolescent successor to the childhood experiences explored in *A Strange and Sublime Address*. When asked, in an on-line Internet chat hosted by www.rediff.com (14 February 2000), how his "Bengaliness" has influenced his writing, however, Chaudhuri explained that "Lots of novels are based on actual experiences or real characters, but once the character is transmuted for some reason into fiction, it assumes a mythic separateness which doesn't have all that much to do with the person it was based on. So, however related to reality it might be, autobiographical fiction is never simply a confession or a revealing snapshot of reality."

Afternoon Raag is prefaced by a poem written "in memory of Pandit Govind Prasad Jaipurwale (1941–1988)," the family's music teacher, or "guru," and centers on one particular lesson:

> My mother plays the harmonium; she begins to sing.
> Her fingers on the black and white keys make, of her hand, a temple with many doors.
> When the music-teacher joins in intermittently, he shows what a strange thing the human voice is,
> . . . .
> The music-teacher is dying.
> He does not know it, but he will be dead in less than a
>   year's time.

The song, or *raag,* provides Chaudhuri with material, both metaphoric and real, with which to explore the nuances of Indian and English lives while studying at Oxford. Song and *raag* are also an integral part of Chaudhuri's own life; he is an accomplished Hindustani musician who has given concerts throughout India. The famous dream-like quality of Oxford consists of many specifically English ingredients: "then, after the exams, the town is nearly empty, and the days, because of that peculiar English enchantment called Summer Time, last one hour longer; and,

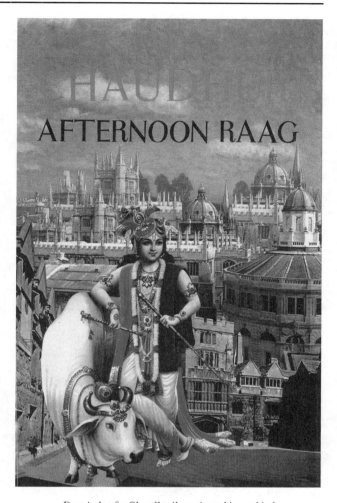

Dust jacket for Chaudhuri's semi-autobiographical 1993 novel, about a young Indian who leaves Bombay to study at Oxford University (Bruccoli Clark Layman Archives)

Oxford, in the evening, resembles what an English town must have looked like in wartime. . . . It is because of its smallness, repetition, and the evanescence of its populace, that Oxford is dream-like."

As a member of a postwar Indian elite, Chaudhuri's "outsider" status is marked, not by an absence of recognizable "Indian" faces—he describes three Indians as close friends, Shehnaz, Mandira, and Sharma, as well as the multicultural nature of the Oxford suburbs—but by his own personal "evanescent" or temporary status as a "short-stay" visitor or "passenger." Images of "dream-like" impermanence prevail. Chaudhuri's parents' postwar experiences in Belsize Park are recalled as a shared migrant rite of passage within the family, while his father's student days in Calcutta prior to Independence are interwoven with memories of the narrator's childhood visits to unknown relatives and the sense of artistic inheritance he now inhabits: "For the first time I could see where my own private joys came from—the love of songs, of music, of pride and delight in creation. That delight is my family's gift."

His parents' move from Bombay to Calcutta, during the narrator's time at Oxford, also invites a sense of Proustian reminiscence, while the remembered presence of his music teacher acts as an important central "melody" throughout. This *raag*-like quality works as a palimpsest-like layering, weaving its musical echoes between different locations and the narratives that both unite and separate them. The "architecture" of the *raag* links the spires and lanes of Oxford to the urban geography of Bombay and Calcutta, Chaudhuri's birthplace, with the regional folk-melodies of different *raags* likened to an "airy, skeletal frame, with holes and gaps in it . . . woven together [they] are a history, a map, a calendar, of Northern India, they are territorial and temporal, they live and die with men, even though they seem to be timeless and exist outside them." On his return to India the narrator understands the ritualistic and impermanent nature of student life: "We were children sent here who, for a period of time till the exams began, behaved and felt like adults. Once the exams were finished the childhood was over, the childhood of which even Shehnaz, Mandira, and I . . . were part."

The closing chapters thwart the reader's expectations by returning the narrative to Oxford. Chapter 26 is a third-person account of the narrator's relationship with an unnamed "she," whose identity can be surmised as Shehnaz, his student girlfriend. The narrator's earlier account of their relationship is overturned in favor of the girl's version, written from her point of view; her feelings of leaving Oxford and returning home echo the sense of loss and excitement felt by the narrator himself, but they also invite a gendered comparison between foreign students' future expectations: "If she could choose, what would she choose? She is going back home to her parents and her wonderful, wisecracking sister, she will never mention it to them, and then she will get married. . . . She will begin another life." The final chapter returns to a first-person narrative voice and recalls the narrator's friendship with his fellow student Sharma, who is from a poor, rural location in northern India. Their common love of the English language (especially poetry) and of Indian food and culture serve to overcome their class-based differences, which persist within the commonality of migrant life. And yet, their different ways of managing "Englishness" are also maintained: Sharma "did not exchange his persona for a new one, as many city-educated Indians do in England; he remained still and deep. The choices that

existed in my world—between clinging to my Indianness, or letting it go, between being nostalgic or looking toward the future—did not exist in his." Their shared conversations enhance Chaudhuri's first-person account by bringing together many of his earlier themes: the function of memory, an Indian's love of the English language, the beauty of singing, the poignancy of past friendships, the passing away of childhood, the death of his music teacher, and his all-important decision to retain and enhance his "Indianness" through writing.

Chaudhuri's third novel, *Freedom Song,* was first published by Picador, released in Calcutta in February 1998 and in London in August 1998. In the United States it was published the following year by Alfred A. Knopf along with his first two books in an omnibus volume, *Freedom Song: Three Novels*. The U.S. edition was awarded the Los Angeles Times Book Prize for Fiction in April 2000. It also achieved recognition as a New York Times Notable Book of the Year, Independent Bestseller and was chosen by the New York Public Library as one of its "25 Books to Remember" of 1999. When asked by Nitish S. Rele, in an on-line interview (22 May 2000), what these awards meant to him, Chaudhuri replied, "Not a great deal in the long term, but to be honoured means to feel, at least briefly, somewhat assured of the legitimacy of what you are doing." Responding to Rele's question as to whether Indian novelists had "finally made it on the world stage," Chaudhuri replied that "There have been Indian novelists of world stature—in English and, most importantly, in other languages—for more than a hundred years now." He went on to remark that "Whether they have a worldwide audience or not is really not a measure of the kind of significance they have in our national life, culture, and mental landscape."

Western and Indian reviewers praised Chaudhuri's achievement. The citation for the *Los Angeles Times* prize proclaimed, "The three short novels introduce us to a voice as intimate, homely and elaboratively imaginative as young Marcel's in Proust's *Remembrance of Things Past* [1913–1927]." Reviewing the British edition for *The New Statesman* (11 September 1998), Pankaj Mishra declared that Chaudhuri was "one of the two or three Indian writers in English who seem aware of the peculiar poignancies of a sheltered upper-middle-class existence in India, and is able to describe them in measured prose of an unvaryingly high quality," and praised his "rather lonely attempt to generate artistic capital out of the neglected small change of everyday middle-class life in India." In *World Literature Today* (Spring 1999), reviewer Bruce King called the novel

A STRANGE AND SUBLIME
ADDRESS
'Funny, delicate, sensuous, evocative
... made me laugh out loud. The
best portrait of India today I've read'
Margaret Drabble

'This evocation of the routine,
quotidian magic of normality strikes
me as an extraordinary thing to have
brought off ... mesmerizing'
John Lanchester, *Vogue*

AFTERNOON RAAG
'Enchanting, studded with moments of beauty more arresting than
anything to be found in a hundred busier and more excitable narratives
... Chaudhuri has proved that he can write better than just about
anyone of his generation'
Jonathan Coe, *London Review of Books*

'This immensely subtle novel both estranges and gently strokes the
surface of English and Indian life. I know of nothing in English fiction
that begins to resemble it'
Tom Paulin

'A fine reminder that writing about India need not rush towards magic
realism for its effect, here we have real magic instead'
James Wood, *Guardian*

'Amit Chaudhuri's languorous, elliptic, beautiful prose is impressively
impossible to place in any category at all'
Salman Rushdie

ISBN 0-330-34423-4

AMIT CHAUDHURI   FREEDOM SONG

freedom song
**AMIT
CHAUDHURI**

PICADOR

9 780330 344234

*Dust jacket for Chaudhuri's 1998 novel, about two middle-class families in Calcutta
(Bruccoli Clark Layman Archives)*

"finely wrought" and remarked that Chaudhuri "has a justifiable reputation for a remarkable prose style." Alice Truax, reviewing the Knopf edition for *The New York Times* (28 March 1999), described Chaudhuri as "an immensely gifted writer" and remarked that his novels "are crammed with breathtaking sentences, sharp characterizations, comic set pieces and melancholy grace notes." In an undated review for the on-line *IndiaStar Review of Books* (www.indiastar.com), however, C. J. S. Wallia was slightly more critical of Chaudhuri's "surface observations" of upper-middle-class life in Calcutta, remarking that "the details of daily Indian life Chaudhury [*sic*] so masterfully depicts will appeal more to the Western reader's exotic quest, and will probably seem all too ordinary to the Indian reader."

An Indian author who chooses to write in English continues to attract criticism, especially from his or her compatriots. If such an author acquires an international audience, he or she is frequently accused of belonging to a third-world elite, particu-larly if he or she has been educated at Oxford or Cambridge. There is also the risk that the author may become wholly dependent on the patronage of publishers in the West and on a cosmopolitan readership in Europe and the United States and thus consciously or unconsciously begin writing for that readership, to present a picture of India tailored for Western consumption. Western expectations concerning the authentic nature of "India" and how it should be written are matched, however, by similar demands voiced by Indian critics: writers in regional languages are often viewed as superior to those writing in English, while the "India" or "Indias" demanded by Indian critics of their writers can be as formulaic as those demanded by Western critics. In his review, for example, Wallia criticized Chaudhuri's representation of Calcutta for "confining itself to the thin segment of the upper-middle class," and he complained that "Nowhere is there a mention of the squalor and abysmal poverty of the Calcutta slums, even though the point of view chosen is third-person omniscient."

Freedom Song is set in the early 1990s and describes the life history of two interrelated middle-class families and their friends, living in North and South Calcutta. The first consists of an elderly couple, Khukhu and her husband, Shib, who works part-time in the "public sector" at Little's Confectionary, a government-owned factory. Their only child, a son, is living in California "doing research in economics." A rendition of the political and economic history of Calcutta provides the background, reminding the reader that the city has one of the last socialist governments in the world. Shib's job as adviser to a failing company within the "public sector" reflects the historical changes affecting the city: "ever since the Communist Party came to power, the atmosphere had changed to a benign, co-operative inactivity, with a cheerful trade unionism replacing the tensions of the past . . . and the whole thing becoming a relaxed, ungrudging family affair." Economic deregulation, or "liberalisation" as it was called in India during the early 1990s, threatens the future of such companies. Shib's response is to preempt such changes by investing "some money in the Mutual Fund and uncharacteristically to buy a few shares in a company that made biscuits, and in another one that made shoes. Now, in the last quarter of his life, a business and speculative curiosity, long suppressed in the interests of his managerial skills, began to come into play, and also a silent, watchful interest in political issues. . . . his gaze and concentration as he absorbed the curve and energizing shape of the time were intent."

The second family is that of Khukhu's brother Bhola, whose son, Bhaskar, much to the consternation of all his relatives, is a committed member of the CPI (Communist Party of India): he delivers their newspaper, the *Ganashakti* (People's Power), to local houses; attends local party meetings where debates over the economic future of India take place, including the effects of the "imperialist" International Monetary Fund; and partakes in a street play, "an allegorical tale about life in capitalist Russia, called *The Fall of Ashoke,* written by the talented young man whose mind engendered almost all their plays, Arjun Dastidar." Chaudhuri's interests lie in its tangential or background aspects, particularly of family life: how, with the set dismantled, "the larger family scattered and became, temporarily, little islands, each with its own memories and pastimes." Bhaskar's arranged marriage to Sandhya and the initial moments of getting to know one another—"In marrying each other they had in effect embraced the unknown and the inconsequential"—represents one of these "islands," set against the shared background of communal violence that occurred during this period:

They read the headlines each day, in newspapers that were already old when they'd finished reading them, of a country that had turned upon itself, without really being able to take them in: "Where hate comes in a communal garb"; then the smaller headings: "Seven killed in violence"; or the same sentence, with eight substituting for seven. Was it really as bad as that? . . . They did not know what the appropriate reaction should be: shock; a certain sense of being vindicated; or a lingering sense of unpleasantness.

The Hindu middle-class Bengali families, whom Chaudhuri describes as "tangential" to the communal violence of India, do voice their alignment against the Muslims, albeit in domestic, almost nonreligious, terms. The *azaan* (Muslim call to prayer) that opens the novel, for example, is viewed as a nuisance from Khukhu's point of view: its sound wakes her too early. Mini, her childhood friend and guest, commiserates, proclaiming, "'Really . . . They are going too far! And,' she said, 'it isn't really Indian, it sounds like Bedouins.'" Daily discussions follow, in which are invoked the anti-Muslim propaganda of the Hindu nationalist BJP (Bharatiya Janata Party):

They talked of how, by the next century, there would be more Muslims than Hindus in the country. Mini, being the teacher, had the facts and figures. She told Khukhu that "population control" was meant for Hindus alone, and Khukhu, listening to Mini, began to see Muslims everywhere . . . "BJP," said Khukhu, her eyes larger than usual. "I might even vote for the BJP. Why not?" They spoke defiantly and conspiratorially, as if they were playing a prohibited game. They would stop once Shib arrived at the house.

Religious conviction is not represented as a serious, all-consuming subject; Chaudhuri's families may be Hindu, but they seem unlikely to embrace the more militant tendencies of Hinduism. Khukhu's childhood memories—when, for example, her brother Pulu explained that "Musholmaans . . . were ghosts who haunted the dark and hilly regions of Sylhet"—are presented as equally important narrative material, providing a series of overlapping connections between the various characters and India, both the India of the past in which they once lived and present-day India.

Bhaskar remains the only member of this extended family to commit himself wholeheartedly to any political cause; after his marriage he continues to insist that the *Ganashakti* contains "all the real and important news," even though Sandhya knows it was used to make "cartons and containers in the market; and its pages were swept away in lanes and alleys." Even here, the narrator's attitude toward such "devo-

Dust jacket for the U.S. edition of Chaudhuri's 2000 novel, about an economics professor from
Ohio visiting his family home in Calcutta (Richland County Public Library)

tional" acts appears indulgent and ironically knowing, as if Bhaskar is merely rehearsing for a future that is already here or may never happen. Chaudhuri details these family miniatures with a cinematic eye, while the open-ended nature of the "off-stage" scenes of *Freedom Song* creates the open-ended, stanza-like sectioning of the various narratives that the reader is invited to resolve. Time is measured out according to what does not happen–reminiscent of Woolf's "moments of non-being"–the gaps, or hiatuses, within the narrative reflecting the older characters' modes of remembering and forgetting, their sense of waiting for the next development that life and death might bring: "Much would change in the next few months in subtle ways, but much would seem to remain unchanged. And the change was probably only a phase, a development as short-lived as anything else. . . . It was as if life, or history, were a spirit that kept transforming its features, discontented to be one thing at one time." The patterning of words–"spun pink-white winter smoke," for instance–reflects Chaudhuri's poetic sensibilities and, in similar fashion to the language of

Afternoon Raag, alerts the reader to the internal architecture of language itself.

Chaudhuri's fourth novel, *A New World,* was launched at the 14th World Book Fair in New Delhi, held 5–13 February 2000, and released at The Seagull Bookstore in Calcutta on 25 February 2000. *A New World* was Chaudhuri's first novel to be released in his home country before it was available in the United Kingdom, where it was officially published 9 June 2000. The novel traces the arrival of Jayojit Chatterjee, an economics professor, and his seven-year-old son, Vikram, or "Bonny," at his parents' apartment in Calcutta, where they spend their summer vacation before returning "home" to Cleveland, Ohio. A recent divorce from his wife, Amala, makes this a highly awkward reunion for Jayojit: this trip is Jayojit's first visit without her, and the divorce contrasts strongly with the routine nature of his parents' married life. His father, an admiral retired from the Indian navy, "could not reconcile himself to the fact that the boy had to tag along part of the year with Jayojit, and then go back to his mother, who was living elsewhere on the vast American map, with some-one else," while Jayojit's mother, Ruby, fulfills her domestic duties toward all three males with an anxious air, attempting to bridge the gap left by Amala's absence—overfeeding her son, persuading her grandson to try the local cuisine, forever submissive to her overbearing husband.

A sense of failure pervades all attempts to incorporate this new stage in their family drama. During his visit Jayojit tries to begin writing his second book on economics—"I hope it will deal with the ethics of developmental policy," he tells Dr. Sen, a family friend—but the project is put aside in favor of his domestic concerns. This economic subtext provides an important addition to Chaudhuri's earlier depictions of the Indian approach to economic liberalization. A central question is whether India should fully embrace Western ideas of a deregulated market economy or be wary of the loss of culture and native traditions that might ensue. As an economics student inspired by Amartya Sen (a fellow Bengali), Jayojit has an understanding of Indian policies based on its position within a global economy and "whether, in a poor country, healthcare and literacy needed to be a prerequisite to deregulation, or whether deregulation would provide the economic wherewithal for literacy and healthcare."

A New World sets these ideas against the everyday economies of Indian life, those "off-duty" moments with which Chaudhuri is so fascinated. Jayojit's visits to Grindlays Bank, where he discovers that interest rates are much higher than in the United States, reveal his ignorance concerning the basics of localized market forces. Intent on establishing an account that would take care of his new arrangements as part-time father, Jayojit's "fragile pride of the dollar-earner" is further undermined by his lack of knowledge concerning which account to use: "'Sir, do you wish to deposit fifteen hundred dollars into which account, savings or fixed?' . . . 'Fixed,' he said after a moment. He was probably not as conversant with these terms as he should be." Jayojit's earning capacity as a "westernised" Indian is juxtaposed against his parents' current difficulties in "making ends meet." The exigencies of retirement and ill health are a constant source of worry for his father—"If you were unemployed or had retired, the Admiral said, it was better not to be in India but somewhere else." For her part, Jayojit's mother continues to find "the different rhythms of expenditure" difficult after a life where the value of money was never thought about and where "everything had been done for them."

The difficulties of adapting to a "new world" make an important narrative link between all aspects of the Chatterjee household and the wider world, from the absorption of new items into a traditional Bengali framework—such as a washing machine, Dove soap, Colgate toothpaste, a laptop computer, and Bonny's "western" toys—to a new generational negotiation of East/West differences. According to Chaudhuri, the novel symbolizes the "transition in Bengali middle class life where the Nehruvian India that shaped Jayojit and the Admiral has come to an end but their means of self-definition belong to the old India." The difficulties faced by Jayojit in adapting to divorced parenthood are evidence of this. During a discussion on feminism with a colleague "back home" in the United States, Jayojit had "argued vociferously that America had taken away the constraints of the institution of marriage, but replaced them with nothing else." A direct link is made between the constraining influence of "old" India—arranged marriage within a strictly delineated caste system—and a deregulated "new world" economy: "'We can't live without constraints,' he'd said. 'Even the—no, *especially* the free-market economy is held together by tiny rules more subtly graded than the caste system!'" Efforts to arrange a second marriage for Jayojit had, however, failed; the girl's family finally decided that he required a governess, not a wife.

Caught between two worlds, Jayojit approaches daily life with some irritation—he is critical of the local traffic, the unhealthy effects of the weather and food of Calcutta, and the general lack of efficiency—but his new "tourist" point of view renews his appreciation of Indian tradition. While buying presents from a local branch of "Cottage Industries," Jayojit finds himself staring at a *pichwa,* a Hindu "devotional" of Krishna, aware that "his mind had been caught in the rippling dance in the picture." But the moment is short-lived; the picture reminds him of his marriage and the anxieties it produces.

In contrast to Chaudhuri's earlier novels, *A New World* appears to resist the spiritual aesthetics belonging to Bengali traditions, and yet a similar focus on the mysterious impermanence of "ironic, qualified continuity" between the past and present is sustained throughout. A corresponding attentiveness to the emotional dramas of middle-class Bengalis as they attempt to negotiate social change is granted extra "territorial" force in this novel by Chaudhuri's focusing on the diasporic realities of living between two worlds: North America and India. North America is now the most favored location for professional Indians attempting to find employment outside their own country. Chaudhuri's novel can be read within a new genre of Indian writing that extends the more traditional Anglo-Indian framework to include America as a new "imaginary homeland." Writers such as Bharati Mukherjee, Anita Desai, and Rohinton Mistry trace the results of such immigrant experiences from India to the United States and Canada.

Chaudhuri's particular emphasis on the impact of such cross-cultural encounters from a Bengali point of view not only highlights the current position of India within a global framework but also continues his localized narrativizations of "the physical immediacy of the spaces we inhabit." His work as editor of *The Picador Book of Modern Indian Literature* (2001), an anthology of Indian literature since the nineteenth century, reveals his interest in demonstrating the full range of Indian writing, including as it does both selections written in English and translations of works by twenty authors who wrote in seven indigenous languages. Chaudhuri, who divides his time between Cambridge and Calcutta, was a judge for the prestigious International IMPAC Dublin Literary Award in 2001. In his collection *Real Time: Stories and a Reminiscence* (2002) Chaudhuri continues his narrative practice of minute and sensuous detail, which recalls Woolf's "moments of being" in stories that explore a wide range of Indian characters in various Indian cities. Reviewing the collection for *The Los Angeles Times* (21 April 2002), the novelist Shashi Tharoor remarked that Chaudhuri had made "virtually his own" the sub-genre of the "meticulously observed depiction of daily life in contemporary India" with his "rare delicacy of description" and "keen sense of the unwritten, unspoken rules that govern human relationships." Amit Chaudhuri continues to be a fiction writer whose explorations of the relationships between the Indian past and the Indian present, between colonial India and its postcolonial state, impress and delight readers and critics alike.

Interviews:

Fernando Galvan, "On Belonging and Not Belonging: A Conversation with Amit Chaudhuri," *Wasafiri,* 30 (1999): 42–50;

"Rushdie, in the West, Has Been Confused with Indian Writing Itself, If Not with India Itself at Times," *Rediff on the Net,* 14 February 2000 <http://www.rediff.com/chat/amicchat.htm>;

Nitish S. Rele, "'To be honoured means to feel somewhat assured of the legitimacy of what you are doing,'"*Rediff on the Net,* U.S. edition, 22 May 2000 <http://www.rediff.com/us/2000/may22us1.htm>.

References:
Anita Desai, "Indian Fiction Today," *Daedalus,* 118 (1989): 207–231;

Geetha Ganapathy-Doré, "A Dawnlight Raag: Amit Chaudhuri's *Freedom Song,*" *Commonwealth Essays and Studies,* 22, no. 1 (1999): 73–79;

R. K. Gupta, "Trends in Modern Indian Fiction," *World Literature Today,* 68 (1994): 299–307;

Salman Rushdie, *Imaginary Homelands* (London: Granta, 1991);

Edward Said, *Culture and Imperialism* (New York: Knopf, 1993);

Rumina Sethi, "The Writer's Truth: Representation of Identities in Indian Fiction," *Modern Asian Studies,* 31 (1997): 951–965.

Michael Collins

(4 June 1964 –   )

Aiping Zhang
California State University, Chico

BOOKS: *The Meat Eaters* (London: Cape, 1992); republished as *The Man Who Dreamt of Lobsters* (New York: Random House, 1993);
The Life and Times of a Teaboy (London: Phoenix House, 1994);
The Feminists Go Swimming (London: Phoenix House, 1996);
Emerald Underground (London: Phoenix House, 1998);
The Keepers of Truth (London: Phoenix House, 2000; New York: Scribner, 2001);
The Resurrectionists (London: Weidenfeld & Nicolson, 2002; New York: Scribner, 2002).

Michael Collins's literary debut, *The Meat Eaters,* a collection of short stories published in 1992, did not cause a great stir in literary circles, but most reviewers of the book regarded Collins as a perceptive and imaginative writer able to explore Irish and Irish American sensibilities. Since then, Collins, who lives in Seattle, has won several awards, including being short-listed for the Booker Prize and the 2002 International IMPAC Dublin Literary Award. His writing has consistently revolved around the dramatization of the underside of life and the marginalized people who either struggle merely to survive at home or feel compelled to leave their country for a better life. Collins's style—which relies on candid and lean narrative, familiar but often sublime settings, and passionate and sharp prose—combines Irish and American influences in a manner likely to enrich the tradition of both James Joyce and William Kennedy.

Michael D. Collins was born on 4 June 1964 in Limerick, Ireland. Although his childhood in the ancient town had its share of rough times, it gave Collins many fond memories and planted an attachment to his hometown that is still strong. When his parents, Joe Collins, a manager of media and public relations with Dublin Bus, and Patricia Collins, moved to Dublin in the early 1970s Collins begged to return to school in Limerick. In an interview with Susan Katz Keating, Collins credited his mother with "sparking an interest

Michael Collins (photograph by Kevin L. Delahunty; from the cover for the U.S. edition of The Keepers of Truth, *2001)*

in literature. She always had books around the house: [Albert] Camus, Thomas Mann and others. So, there was a canon of literature. And she told stories." During his youthful years Collins wanted to be a computer scientist rather than a professional writer. It was his mother's storytelling that helped nurture his passion for reading and writing.

At the age of eighteen Collins was arrested for his involvement with local troublemakers who committed some assaults and robberies. Although not convicted of any crime, Collins lost his track scholarship and missed a year of school. This incident led to his immigration to the United States. At the age of nineteen Collins was a student on a scholarship as a cross-country runner at the University of Notre Dame, where he met his wife, Heidi. They married in 1987, and she became a doctor who specializes in rehabilitative medicine at the University of Washington. Unable to work legally during the summer, Collins traveled in an old station wagon to see the United States. Over the course of three summers in the early 1980s Collins visited most of the continental United States. More important, his daily runs took him far away from the manicured campus and into various bleak neighborhoods of run-down industrial towns in America. Through these encounters, as he noted in a 4 November 2000 interview with Kevin L. Delahunty in *The Times* (London), Collins "felt the intangible ethos of loss and deprivation in these dying cities" and "began to understand Americans' fears and hopes, [and] feel the cadence of how they said what they had to say."

Although Irish by birth, Collins writes short stories and novels in and often about the United States, his adopted home. His experience in America has been essential to his personal growth and his writing. "My conscious life," he told Delahunty, "begins not in Ireland, but as an immigrant in America. It is through America that I have understood my own Irish background and come to terms with what America is." Collins calls himself "an exile" in America of his own choosing. Collins did not make any serious attempt at writing until he faced a problem with his graduation from college. Because of his rigorous training and frequent participation in running races, he found himself behind in credits. To improve his academic standing in his final year at college (1987), Collins decided to take a writing course, assuming that he could write stories about what he had seen on his travels all over America. The course work was more difficult than he anticipated because he did not have enough of a grasp of American vernacular to describe, let alone capture, "the tone and cadence" of what he had seen. What Collins wrote in that writing course, instead, was a series of stories he had heard from people while growing up in his native country.

Collins's rewarding experience in this writing course kindled his passion for writing. After his graduation from college, Collins took a job at Merrill Lynch as a computer analyst, but left there in 1989 to travel around Europe for a year and half, often writing stories on trains. He returned to Notre Dame and entered the Creative Writing Program, submitting his thesis, "The Meat Eaters: A Collection of Short Stories," in 1991, and became one of the first recipients of an M.A. in Creative Writing from Notre Dame. Unable to find an agent or a publisher, Collins used the newly available Pagemaker desktop publishing software and a scanner to produce a collection of stories, *The Meat Eaters,* an enlarged version of his master's thesis. Then, as he told Keating in their 2000 interview, Collins purchased "an off-the-shelf company in the Isle of Man" named Matavia, which came complete with a prestigious London mailing address and "an answering service with a British-voiced girl answering the phone and taking messages." He had his sister distribute review copies to British newspapers, and the collection garnered a few reviews. A representative from the publisher Jonathan Cape, Ltd., thinking that Matavia was a legitimate small press, contacted Collins, asking if he would be interested in switching publishers for his next book. Collins "wrote a fake contract, and phonied up an argument with Matavia," convincing Jonathan Cape to "republish" his first collection of stories in 1992.

The nine stories in this collection cover various aspects of life in modern Ireland, from family relationships to coming-of-age experiences, games, drinking, violence, and love. All characters are caught up in social upheavals and driven by cultural myths, illusions, and sentimentalism in their struggle for survival. The title story, "The Meat Eaters," is about a young man's escape to America from his involvement with the Irish Republican Army (IRA) and his failure to find solace and good fortune despite his flight from Irish sectarian violence. "First Love," which is widely regarded as the best story in the collection, is primarily set in a dirty old car, in which three children watch their wounded dog dying slowly and contemplate their sad life, while their father drinks at the pub. The children have many questions about the misfortunes in their family and in life, but no one is there to give them answers. The other stories in the collection deal with more serious issues and absurd situations: among these stories, "The Butcher's Daughter" describes a young and pregnant Irish girl's bombing of a Protestant pub in retaliation for her lover's sectarian murder; "The Dead" is a horrific story of the butchering of a man; and "The Enemy" is a hilarious but often chilling tale of a handicapped young man who is on holiday with his cartoon-like parents.

"In truth," Collins admitted to Delahunty, "the collection of stories entitled *The Meat Eaters* had a trenchant Forties bleakness, and seemed like they had been written by a man in his seventies. But that was the intention, since the Ireland of my youth had the feeling of an island adrift from Europe, a place that had more in common with the nineteenth century." The world depicted in these stories seems to have the kind of raw-

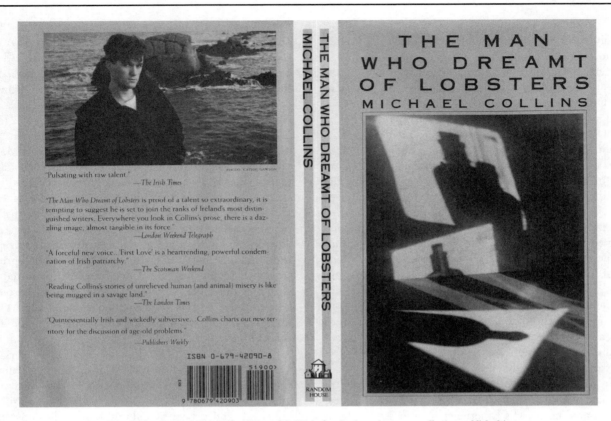

Dust jacket for the 1993 U.S. edition of Collins's first book, a short-story collection published in London the preceding year as The Meat Eaters *(Richland County Public Library)*

ness, menacing sounds, and repulsive smells that are prevalent in Dickens's novels. All the stories have horrendous images of evil, treachery, tyranny, violence, deformity, abnormality, or death, and their endings are frequently shocking or terrifying.

Although *The Meat Eaters* received only a few desultory reviews when first published in Britain, its republication as *The Man Who Dreamt of Lobsters* by Random House in New York in 1993 attracted more favorable attention from reviewers. It was cited as a *New York Times* Notable Book of the Year. Many reviewers saw it as an exceptionally strong and imaginative first book. In his review for *The Washington Post* (16 May 1993) George O'Brien observed that "The nine stories cover all aspects of modern Irish life," and they are "outlandish, reactionary yet provocative expressions of the revisionist mood of contemporary cultural debate in Ireland, unnerving and dismal reminders that it's still not easy being Green." Michael Harris, in his review in *The Los Angeles Times* (13 June 1993), asserted that these stories give readers a great sense of "the endurance that has sustained the Irish for centuries."

That same year Collins returned to the United States to pursue his interest in writing and literature, beginning his doctoral studies in English at the University of Illinois in Chicago. He was again lured away into computer programming after teaching an introductory course in literature. Collins found a job with the Computer Science Department of the University of Illinois, working with programming languages and creating web pages and network applications for interface learning. Although he was at the forefront of the Internet revolution, Collins realized that he was unable to give up his passion for writing. While working for a living and completing his doctorate, Collins managed to finish writing three books.

The Life and Times of a Teaboy (1994), Collins's first novel, is set in an Irish border town during the years after World War II. Under the December twilight the father and daughter of the Feeney family are waiting anxiously for the birth of a calf, a calf that "would pay for Christmas." Unfortunately, the calf is stillborn, creating a bloody and ominous scene. From this distressful and terrifying episode, the novel soon shifts its focus to the erratic life of the eldest son Ambrose Feeney, "a brooding schoolboy in black trousers." "Introspective, mother-fixated, wary of his intense, preoccupied father, Ambrose is," as D. J. Taylor suggested in his 30 June 1994 review of the book for *The Independent* (London), "clearly set on an incorrigible, downward path."

Ambrose's nickname, Tea Boy, comes from a task he has performed since childhood of boiling water in the kettle for his mother. Every day Ambrose is forced to cope with his father's angry disappointments and his mother's stultifying religious beliefs. After he grows up and gets a job as a lighthouse keeper on the coast, Ambrose finally has a chance to enjoy his independence and to pay for his mother's charities. Yet, he is still unable to escape from his parents' control. Ambrose is stunned to discover that his mother has betrayed him by using his money to pay for his brother's college education. He wants to be an architect, but every time he reveals his aspirations to his parents they become outraged. Perplexed and depressed, Ambrose soon slips into schizophrenia and suffers confinement in an asylum under constant medication and shock therapy. At the end of the novel Ambrose attempts to write his story, which is "to be sociological and not psychological," and tries to figure out how he can free himself from the endless constraints of his family and the society.

If the reader interprets the whole novel "at a heightened level," as Collins suggested in a conversation with Philip Marchand published in *The Toronto Star* (5 December 1998), the reader will certainly realize that this novel delivers more than just the story of a "tea boy." In many ways Ambrose represents thousands of others who descend into disillusionment and insanity, just as he does. Symbolically, Ambrose's wretched life epitomizes the ordeal of his nation, Ireland, which has been searching desperately for its identity through numerous political and religious conflicts. One thing that has done more in honing such an implication is Collins's use of his dreary and confining hometown, Limerick, as the backdrop for the novel and as a microcosm of his society under deprivation. Collins's personal experience there enabled him to portray his characters with distinct traits and give his novel an authentic Irish voice.

Collins's third book, *The Feminists Go Swimming* (1996), is a collection of eleven darkly funny stories that read like morality tales and religious satires. The stories offer a survey of the preoccupations in modern Ireland—women's demand for a greater role in society, political corruption, drinking, emigration, and the conservative Catholic status quo. One theme underlying all the stories is Collins's consistent fascination with the absurdities of human folly and the intricacies of human cruelty. The stories present a gallery of victims and victimizers in Ireland, from wife beaters to zealots, alcoholics, and fornicators. However, Collins seems to have little sympathy toward his characters, as they often appear to have neither will nor resources to confront the adversity in their life.

The title story is based on a true incident and tells how a quaint morning swimming ritual for a group of old men, including a priest and a policeman, ends in tragedy. "The daily swim," a ritual that has been handed down through generations, "gave a certain order to their lives." A group of feminists suddenly appears naked on the beach, with the "wavering word LIBERTY" written on their stomachs, demanding their right to swim in the same place, thus preventing the men from coming out of the water. As a result, an old man drowns, and two young swimmers also drown while trying to save him. The narrative voice in the story might sound somewhat nonchalant and often amusing, but the real message becomes evident when Collins ends the story by revealing that the other swimmers are more concerned with the public's reaction to the tragedy than the loss of lives. Collins clearly presents an example of human indifference and hypocrisy in the people's ensuing cover-up of what actually led to the drowning of the men in the name of giving the dead "a decent, quiet burial without scandal."

The second story in the collection, "The End of the World," won the Pushcart Prize in 1996. Based on a story that his mother had told Collins, it details the tragic consequence of a boy's fanatic obsession with the end of the world. At first, Patsy gets a blow on the nose from his teacher and rugby coach for writing the word "Armageddon" in his notebook. Soon, everyone in town is predicting how the world is going to end, but no one, including Father Mackey, has a definite answer. During the supposed last mass, everyone confesses his or her sins and impure thoughts and reveals what they know about some of the unsolved mysteries in the past. That night Patsy, like everyone else in town, closes his eyes for one last time, and whispers his last words on earth, "I am sorry for what I done, Jesus." But the world does not end as predicted, and the next day things seem as usual. Feeling afraid, shaking in loneliness, and waving his fists at the ceiling, Patsy shouts with a trembling voice, "Yes, you up there! You ol' fuckin' bastard, God!" People grab him and clasp his mouth "to keep him quiet, to stop the devil in him." Beneath the pile of bodies, Patsy is "crushed and twisted" and becomes the only casualty "associated with the end of the world." In contrast to the first story, this one presents a darker and more disturbing picture of a young boy's mind that has been misguided by false convictions. The narrative offers no relief through humor or hilarity, and it becomes increasingly forlorn and disheartening as the story progresses.

The reception of this collection was mixed. Some critics liked Collins's unflinchingly blunt representation of a nihilistic vision. Gavin Drummond, for example, pointed out in a 15 February 1997 review in *The Gazette*

SHORTLISTED FOR THE BOOKER PRIZE

The Keepers
of Truth

"Unflaggingly brilliant . . .
cool and ironically self-aware."
—Jonathan Raban

A NOVEL

Michael Collins

*Paperback cover for the U.S. edition of Collins's 2000 novel,
about a newspaperman in an economically depressed
Midwestern town (Richland County
Public Library)*

(Montreal) that all the stories "exhibit Collins' remarkable feel for content and pacing, and all reveal the power of an elegantly savage style." They display the riveting effect of using humor and horror in equal measure, and mingling love and betrayal with defiance and laughter. Other critics, such as the novelist Hugo Hamilton, in his review in *The Irish Times* (17 February 1996), found Collins's portrayal of contemporary Ireland full of old stereotypes and inaccuracies.

After receiving his Ph.D. in English in 1997, Collins started working for Microsoft. Between his job as an encryption software engineer and running eighty or more miles a week, Collins still found time and energy for his fiction writing.

In *Emerald Underground* (1998), his fourth book and second novel, Collins writes for the first time at length about his travels and observations in America. The novel was well received in England and Canada and was soon translated into several languages. Critics

have given Collins rave reviews for his convincing descriptions of America and his knack for capturing the American voice. In *The Irish Times* (3 October 1998) John Kenny called the novel "the best attempt yet in Irish fiction to deal with the sub-species of Irish illegals in the Eighties." The novel, Collins told Delahunty, is written in "two distinct parts": one part is a story that captures "the interminable purgatory of the illegal world"; the other part is a road novel that experiments with an outsider's interpretation of the American experience. Collins wants his readers to read the novel as "the indictment of Ireland's practice of forcing young men into emigration" and to learn about their predicament in their adopted country.

The novel centers on Liam, an illegal Irish immigrant in New York in the early 1980s. Liam has come to the United States determined to prove to his father and others that he can make something of himself. After his arrival Liam discovers that he must endure humiliating abuse, backbreaking labor, horrible living conditions, and an irritable skin disease, all in the company of overseers, bullies, drug addicts, drunkards, and prostitutes. It is a life of isolation brought on by poverty, fear, and exploitation. Liam laments, "There wasn't much for me in America, not that I expected much of anything. But this was shite beyond my wildest dreams." For Liam and others like him, New York is a godless, grim, and grotesque place, where even the city skyline takes on a demonic grandeur, and "Nobody coming to America saw the Statue of Liberty any more. There was nothing to signify a new beginning." Immigrants discover that their personalities, hopes, and dignity are taken from them and that their sense of identity disintegrates into disillusionment, depression, and paranoia. Liam leaves his seedy New York motel with a drug addict, Sandy, and Sandy's sixteen-year-old pregnant girlfriend, Angel, heading for "the heart of America." The three end up living in a trailer park, making ends meet by doing odd jobs. They bet all their hopes for a better life on Liam's winning of a road race. At the end Liam wins the race, but the reward is no more than a chance to restart his immigrant life in America; whether or not he will achieve the success of which he has been dreaming is still uncertain.

The portrait of Liam is based on Collins's own experience. Fittingly, Collins adopts the first-person narrative mode and mixes the narrative with many flashbacks of the past. Liam was born and raised in Limerick, as Collins was, and he takes a similar route of emigrant adventure. Similar to the experiences of his three main characters in the novel, Collins used to live at a campground while doing menial jobs and running races for money because he did not have a work visa. He had been exposed to the tawdry and sordid aspects of American society, and he had at least partially experienced the kind of life that he depicted in the novel. As a whole, the novel presents a steely, realistic story that shows what living on the edge means in America. For Liam and other illegal immigrants in the 1980s, the world around them is a dreamy but dangerous place, where human cruelty prevails, and only the aggressive and heartless can overcome the adversity and win the battle of survival. Some critics, however, argue that the novel relies a little too much on imprecations and ridicule in its dealings with the unpleasant and undesirable in life. In his review for *The Irish Times* (3 October 1998) John Kenny noted that the novel "is considerably damaged by the aggressive hipness of the sordidness, by the imprecations being heightened to such a degree that they become histrionic, unreal, and quickly incense the reader."

Collins's third novel, *The Keepers of Truth* (2000), garnered a few prominent awards. It won the Kerry Food Ingredients Book-of-the-Year Award, which was presented by Irish president Mary McAleese at the thirtieth annual Writers Week in Listowel in 2000; it was short-listed for the Booker Prize in 2000 and for the 2002 International IMPAC Dublin Literary Award; and the movie rights were sold for a hefty sum, according to a review in *Canadian Business and Current Affairs* (18 April 2000). *The Keepers of Truth* struck critics as a distinctive and emotionally enthralling work that is apocalyptic in perspective and magnificent in style. In a brief review in *The Guardian* (19 February 2000) Isobel Armstrong declared that "Collins creates a gripping picture of slow-moving, small-town life, and packs it into a treat of a murder mystery." An unsigned 9 June 2001 review in *The Independent* (London) called the novel "a complex and literary book, but also a fast-paced and cinematic one." Although the novel did not win the Booker Prize, being short-listed was a major achievement for Collins and has resulted in his being considered one of the most promising writers in Ireland and the United States.

Collins claimed in his interview with Delahunty that he got the idea for *The Keepers of Truth* one day while running in the hills around his workplace, Microsoft. He stopped and scribbled down the first words of the story. Late at night over the next three months, Collins turned away from the computer and wrote the story about an American town with pen and paper. The novel starts with a description of the town that sounds like a eulogy, and later it shows how the inhabitants of the town have turned into "a lost people," and the town has become "a Pompeii of the twentieth century." Bill, the narrator and a reporter for the moribund local newspaper, *Daily Truth,* has been trying to "slide" the requiem, a piece he wrote in his journalism class years ago, into the paper, but the hardworking

and old-school newspaper editor, Sam Perkins, blocks it because he believes that both in a town and newspaper that are "going under," "Language changes. It ain't worth a damn." Bill does not give in so easily because he never sees himself as a hack in a down-and-out small town; his prose is "ambitious beyond the scope of journalism as we know it." What dismays him is that the life of the town is so static that he has nothing but a baking contest to report. Unexpectedly, however, everything changes when an old man in town goes missing. Rumors fly, and all suspicions fix on Ronny Lawton, the old man's son, and the local police are determined to fix the murder of the old man on Ronny, a notorious ne'er-do-well. With the tremendous attention from national news media and the public, both the paper and the town come to life instantly. At first reluctantly following his editor's orders, Bill starts his pursuit of the case. But because of his sympathetic character and his yearning for passion, Bill soon gets personally involved with the suspects. By the end of the novel, the case is still unsolved.

The core of the story, therefore, is Bill, rather than the murder case. Through his deft use of Bill's dual role as an investigative reporter and a new friend of the suspects in the case, Collins manages to move the narrative along effortlessly, alternating between presenting Bill's discoveries of the dark secrets of the case and revealing his often painful inner thoughts on the complex entanglement, distrust, and hatred among the townspeople. The novel offers a perceptive sketch of the discontented families and disillusioned youth who are trying desperately to survive the disintegration of their community and to hold on to their faith in the American Dream in the postindustrial era. That the town is not named and its location never specified accentuates Collins's intention to portray the town in the novel as the epitome of thousands of run-down towns in America. The novel is more than a tense mystery of murder and obsession. Collins brings style and substance together by integrating raucous hilarity with chilling reality.

After the publication of *The Keepers of Truth* Collins took a leave of absence from his lucrative job at Microsoft in order to have more time to work on another novel. Published in 2002, *The Resurrectionists* is another take on postindustrial small-town America, portraying a character, Frank Cassidy, haunted by his childhood memories of the deaths of his parents in a house fire, who leaves his dead-end job in a New Jersey fast-food restaurant and returns to the desolate northern Michigan town in which he was raised by his uncle, Ward, after learning that Ward has been murdered. Robert MacFarlane, in a 14 April 2002 review in *The Observer* (London), noted that *The Resurrectionists* "occupies approximately the same time frame as *The Keepers of Truth* and treads the same metaphysical territory"; however, while the earlier novel "read, in the words of its narrator, like 'a roar of despair,' the moral of *The Resurrectionists* turns out to be a mutedly positive one." MacFarlane called *The Resurrectionists* "a powerful, subtle and uplifting account of happiness being found against the odds" but tempered his praise somewhat, complaining that this account was "muffled by melodrama" and remarking that "one senses a gifted writer trying to punch just above his weight." A *New Statesman* review (22 April 2002) by Jason Cowley and Matt Thorne suggested, "The plot is deceptively complex, including comatose characters, secret identities, murder, bankruptcy and fear of madness. While this drives the action, Collins concentrates on individual dramas. . . . There is something unusually comforting about the world Collins creates, and the resilience of his unfortunate characters. His is a tarnished American dream, but a dream none the less."

Writing is not the only passion that demands considerable time and energy from Collins. When he is not writing novels, he is running in the forests near Seattle. A world-class runner and extreme-sports enthusiast, he runs 120 to 150 miles a week and frequently participates in various endurance competitions. In 1999 he won the Himalayan Ultra Marathon, a three-day event with a course that runs 100 miles at more than 14,000 feet above sea level, finishing with a record time of fifteen hours and twenty minutes. Despite his rising fame in Europe, Collins has had a hard time attracting attention from American publishers. After *The Keepers of Truth* was short-listed for the Booker Prize in 2000, however, Collins has gradually gained recognition in American literary circles.

Although he has lived in the United States since 1983 and much of his fiction has focused on small-town life in America, Collins still considers himself an Irish writer. Laurence Phelan pointed out in his 5 May 2002 review for *The Independent on Sunday* (London), "Three of Collins's four novels all describe these insignificant-seeming but hard-fought for existences that are usually hidden amid the vastness of America, and it's something he does compassionately but precisely." Collins himself was quoted in an article by Helen Meany, published in *The Irish Times* (17 April 2002): "I want to show the level of desperation that exists among people in rural areas especially, where the American dream is sold." His dark and sometimes fiercely cynical representation of American consumer culture has won him both plaudits and criticisms from reviewers. His new novel, as Phelan

observed, does not have the same kind of "politically informed anger" that dominates *The Keepers of Truth*. David Robson argued in his 14 April 2002 review for *The Sunday Telegraph* (London) that "all American life is here" in *The Resurrectionists* and Collins "has captured its quirks, its daily rhythms, its underlying despair and, most impressively of all, its quiet optimism." Collins is hopeful that, with Scribner's release of *The Keepers of Truth* and *The Resurrectionists* in the United States, his new Irish American voice and style will reach a larger American audience.

All of Michael Collins's work either looks back on life in Ireland with remorse and outrage or satirizes the human miseries that he has witnessed in the United States. Collins never attempts to hide the social implications in his books. In fact, he writes like a sociologist who is keen to offer his version of a society. Some readers find it difficult to read Collins and not think of Joyce. As Brian McCombie pointed out in a review of *The Man Who Dreamt of Lobsters* in *Studies in Short Fiction* (Fall 1994), "the emotional and intellectual paralysis that Joyce detailed is so apparent in these stories, too. Yet Collins is his own writer, his voice strong, as capable of the lyric as of the harsher tones of a difficult world. He's writing of an Ireland that's not so much new as contemporary, its paralysis more fixed, the cycle of victims and victimizers more vicious. Joyce would have recognized the terrain, though maybe not the intensity."

Interviews:

Philip Marchand, "When You're Young, Irish—and Illegal," *Toronto Star,* 5 December 1998, Arts section, p. K6;

Kevin L. Delahunty, "Once Upon a Time in America," *Times* (London), 4 November 2000, p. 92;

Susan Katz Keating, "One on One with Michael Collins," *Pif Magazine* (2000) <http://www.pifmagazine.com/2000/11/i_m_collins1.php3>.

References:

Alan Hubbard, "Inside Lines: Too Bookish for Football?" *Independent* (London), 5 November 2000, Sport section, p. 2;

Susan Katz Keating, "Booked for the Limelight," *Seattle Times,* 30 October 2000, Scene section, p. E1;

Helen Meany, "Sleepless in Seattle," *Irish Times,* 17 April 2002;

Anthony Wilson-Smith, "His Irish Eyes Are Smiling," *Maclean's* (1 May 2000): 52.

Peter Cunningham
(Peter Lauder, Peter Benjamin)
(10 May 1947 –)

Annette Gilson
Oakland University

BOOKS: *Noble Lord,* as Peter Lauder (London: Collins, 1986; New York: Stein & Day, 1986);

All Risks Mortality (London: Joseph, 1987; Boston: Little, Brown, 1988);

The Snow Bees (London: Joseph, 1988);

The Bear's Requiem (London: Joseph, 1989);

Hostile Bid (London: Joseph, 1991);

Who Trespass Against Us: A Novel (London: Century, 1993);

Tapes of the River Delta (London: Century, 1995; New York: St. Martin's Press, 1996);

Consequences of the Heart (London: Harvill, 1998);

Love in One Edition (London: Harvill, 2001);

Terms and Conditions, as Peter Benjamin (London: Simon & Schuster/Townhouse, 2001).

Until 1993 Peter Cunningham was best known as a writer of popular international thrillers. In September of 1990, however, his eldest son was killed in an automobile accident. The loss of a child at the threshold of adulthood became the subject of Cunningham's next novel, *Who Trespass Against Us* (1993), which Cunningham describes as a generic transition between the earlier thrillers and the literary fiction of his acclaimed Monument saga that followed. Although the loss of his son compelled him to write *Who Trespass Against Us,* Cunningham reported, in an unpublished August 2001 e-mail interview with Annette Gilson, that he had also "grown impatient" with the thriller genre (which he termed "entertainment," as distinct from his later literary novels). *Who Trespass Against Us* draws on the knowledge base Cunningham accumulated while researching political thrillers; in the Monument novels Cunningham fuses the political material with psychological realism and a nascent, lyrical sensitivity to place, in this way winning an international reputation as a writer of highly crafted plots and enigmatic dreaminess. In addition to his novels, he also writes a column for the *Irish Independent* (Dublin) magazine.

Peter Cunningham (from the dust jacket for the U.S. edition of Tapes of the River Delta, *1996)*

Born 10 May 1947 in Dublin to Redmond Cunningham and Mory "Nicky" McIntyre Cunningham, Peter Cunningham was heir to the complex intertwining of politics and religion that is so common in Ireland. His father was a Catholic of Waterford, whose family was intensely political. His paternal grandfather, Bryan Cunningham, who ran a business from 1900 to 1932 exporting live pigs to the United Kingdom from the Waterford port, was a friend of John Redmond, Charles Stewart Parnell's successor as leader of the

Irish parliamentary party at Westminster. When Redmond, who had first been elected to the House of Commons from New Ross, Wexford, in 1881, stood as a candidate for Waterford in 1891, Cunningham's grandfather was his election agent. Cunningham's father was born in 1916 and was named after Redmond, who was also his godfather. As Redmondites, Cunningham's family deplored the Easter 1916 Uprising and Sinn Féin, the extremist Irish nationalist party, and supported the continuing political connection between Ireland and Britain. Redmond was an advocate of Home Rule and encouraged Irishmen to enlist in the British army in World War I. It comes as no surprise, then, that his godson enlisted in the British Royal Engineers in 1943 to fight in World War II. Redmond Cunningham was part of the D-Day offensive and the only Irishman to win a Military Cross that day. He won another in the Rhineland and was awarded the croix de guerre by the French.

Nicky McIntyre, born in 1920, was a Protestant from Sutton, County Dublin. Her family, though Protestant, was not part of the "Anglo-Irish Ascendancy," Cunningham explained in the e-mail interview, calling this term a "quaint Irish pigeon-hole." Nicky's father, Fred McIntyre, was an Australian gambler who disappeared in 1933 and was presumed dead. Cunningham discovered in 1999, while researching his family line, that Fred McIntyre's real name was Arthur Albert Lester, a name that Cunningham supposes his grandfather left behind that he might leave his past behind as well. When her husband disappeared, Rhoda McIntyre, Cunningham's maternal grandmother, came south to Waterford with her daughter, Nicky. She chose Waterford because her father, Edmund Lauder, an Edwardian court photographer, used to holiday in Tramore, a seaside village about eight miles south of Waterford. Edmund Stanley Lauder's career as a photographer was nurtured by his father, Edmund Stanley Lauder Sr., and brother James Stack Lauder, both of whom had their own businesses in the field. James Stack Lauder rose to prominence by taking portraits of British royalty and aristocracy. His fame persisted through his lifetime and his prints helped define photography in the early days of its syndication. At Waterford, Rhoda McIntyre married Redmond Cunningham's maternal uncle, Danny Bowe.

Redmond Cunningham and Nicky McIntyre met in the late 1930s, presumably through their family connections, and were married in 1946 when he returned from the war. Redmond Cunningham was by this time a major in the British army and for the rest of his life was referred to by everyone as "the Major." He had been an architect's draftsman before the war and now, through a correspondence course, became an architect.

His brother Willie was an engineer, and together in 1947 they set up a practice in Waterford. The Cunningham siblings numbered thirteen, and so the extended family was enormous, but in Peter Cunningham's words in the 2001 interview with Gilson, Redmond Cunningham "was always going to be the one who 'made it' in terms of business. He became a very successful businessman, started a number of enterprises, built up a chain of hotels and accumulated property." As Redmond Cunningham was getting started, the family lived with Danny Bowe in nearby Tramore. In 1955, when Peter Cunningham was eight, they moved to one of the finest residences in Waterford, where he became "conscious growing up that we were better off than my first cousins." However, Cunningham remarked in the Gilson interview, his family maintained "strong associations with my father's family in Ballybricken where my widowed grandmother Pigeon (Bowe) Cunningham lived with various members of her by then grown up family. This was a family of pig-dealers and livestock traders. They were famous for their storytelling. I learned a lot of what I know about storytelling from these people."

Despite the family's continued connection with the extended Cunningham clan, Redmond Cunningham wanted badly to move up in the world, into the Irish middle class. Peter Cunningham attended the local Christian Brothers school until the age of twelve, yet his father discouraged him from making friends because, Cunningham said, he was "suspicious of his original peer group," speculating that his father was afraid of being drawn back into that social class. This ban left Cunningham a solitary child, but he remembers his childhood as "intensely happy." Beginning at the age of nine, he wrote essays for the Christmas editions of the local newspaper, for each of which he was paid one guinea (£1 1s.). Although bad at sports he "had ponies and hunted, both with the Waterfords and with Mrs Crosbie's pack, the Gaultier Harriers (Woodstown, Callaghan, and environs)." One reason for his intense experience of happiness may have been the contiguity to his mother, who was also a solitary person with few friends.

Unusually for the time, neither of Cunningham's parents converted to the other's faith. Nicky Cunningham remained Protestant, while Redmond Cunningham was a devout Catholic who attended weekly Mass. Although the five children were raised Catholic, Nicky Cunningham went to services in the Protestant cathedral once a year and the children accompanied her. The preservation of his dual religious heritage may have been part of the reason that Cunningham could say of himself in the 2001 e-mail interview: "I knew both the Catholic middle-class Waterford and the

Anglo-Irish Protestant Waterford in growing up." He added, "My father, a larger than life character (all his life he drank nothing but champagne), made a number of friends among the local Anglo Irish and brought them into his business ventures. In this way, I came to know that side of Waterford society."

In 1959, when Peter Cunningham was twelve, his father decided to send him to the Benedictines in Glenstal Abbey, Limerick, for his schooling. The choice of this Catholic boarding school was, in Cunningham's words, "a significant statement from my father," less in terms of religion than of class. Cunningham explained to Gilson, "Catholic boarding schools—and Glenstal was one of the top such—were the expensive preserve of the children of the established professional classes and of wealthy farmers. None of my very many cousins would be educated like this." He added,

My school friends were all from the comfortable Irish middle class, the place my father wished so hard to be. This position reflected a number of givens: that your parents had money, that you lived in a certain type and standard of house. This meant you could invite friends to stay and be invited back, all gliding along on safe assumptions. None of the friends who came to our lovely home in Waterford would ever be brought to meet my grandmother in the very modest terraced house she lived in. Sixty years before it might have been respectable but by the 1960s it was just another street in a working-class part of Waterford.

This attempt on Redmond Cunningham's part to claim middle-class status for his immediate family was not one that sat easily with his son. Peter Cunningham noted that "a part of me wanted to fill the gap that my father had leapt, so to speak. I admired my father's family, valued their stories. They were very real people. It was their home patch I would return to write about."

Cunningham was ambivalent about the Glenstal Abbey school. In the beginning Cunningham missed home desperately, and his mother missed him with equal intensity, writing him a letter a day until the headmaster instructed her to cease. Cunningham described himself to Gilson as hopeless at almost all subjects, though he loved English. He had two inspiring teachers and was greatly encouraged to write. He became co-editor of the school magazine, at which point he "began to learn the business of writing." Both of his parents encouraged him to write, his mother in particular. She told him: "'You might be the next Tennessee Williams.' When I pointed out the drawbacks in such an achievement, she replied, 'I don't care what he was. He was very successful.'" In addition he read prodigiously, about fifty books a term, including such authors as Ian Fleming, Eric Ambler, Michael Innes,

Dust jacket for the U.S. edition of Cunningham's pseudonymous 1986 thriller about a terrorist plot to assassinate Elizabeth II (Richland County Public Library)

Evelyn Waugh, Joseph Conrad, and Kingsley Amis. He matriculated in 1964.

From 1964 to 1967 Cunningham attended University College Dublin (UCD), receiving a B.A. in English, economics, and French. He told Gilson, "I had absolutely no interest in university—although in my first year I did win a short story competition in the college magazine, *Awake*." During the summer term of 1965 the nineteen-year-old Cunningham went to London, where he worked as a barman and a barge painter. He shared a flat with "(tellingly, I suppose) two aspirant professional gamblers and a cat-burglar from New Zealand." His flatmates' professions were telling because they point to a nascent fascination with marginal groups and criminal behavior, subjects that later appear in Cunningham's fiction.

After graduating from the university in 1967, Cunningham worked in the office of an accountant, became apprenticed to him, and sat and passed accountancy exams. He stayed in this position for three years, after which he went to New York. He went "without many contacts, or a job, or a visa." Cunningham stayed less than one year, sharing an apartment "with two Wall Street types, one Irish, one US, in Claremont Avenue on the Upper West Side. We drank a lot. I eventually got a job on Wall Street and hated every moment of it." He worked for six months on the floor of the New York Stock Exchange, "basically as a messenger boy. . . . It was the only job I could get." In addition, he went to Ivy League football games, dated girls, and felt homesick, noting that "My first adult published story would reflect the homesickness of this period."

Despite Cunningham's feeling that he went to the United States without many contacts, his existence, like that of most Irish expatriates in New York, depended upon his ability to place himself in the social network of Irish abroad. He acknowledged this connectedness to Gilson: "I had a cousin who ran a bar near Wall Street; her name was Peggy Doyle and she lived in New Jersey. She had friends 'down town' who came to the rescue when my visa problems arose." In the end Cunningham left the United States because he "hated the claustrophobia of New York," but he acknowledged experiencing the enervation common to expatriates, saying that it was a "major undertaking . . . to leave the city."

Although he escaped the Wall Street job, Cunningham returned to accountancy when he arrived back in Ireland. These forays into the world of business may reflect another pull in his life: that of his father's desires for him. When he returned to Ireland in 1971, he told Gilson, "I think I was acting out my father's wishes in this period: that I become a successful businessman like him. (Although he was getting into the sauce big-time himself around then and would eventually lose almost everything.) I went into business as an accountant, got married. Although I did not know it then, I was intensely frustrated—I wasn't writing, not even thinking of writing, but unconsciously I was burning up. I drank a lot." In 1973 he married Carol Powell, who came from a well-to-do Tipperary farming family. Members of her father's family had represented Limerick in Parliament. Although her father was Protestant, her mother was Catholic, and so, Cunningham remarked to Gilson, "she and her siblings were raised as Catholics, as these things were arranged back then." Cunningham is four years older than his wife; he told Patricia Deevy, in a 9 December 2001 interview for *The Sunday Independent* (Dublin), that "We'd been in love for many years. We had to wait till she was 21 to get married." A musician with a master's degree in music, Carol Cunningham later became a practicing Jungian psychotherapist. The couple lives on a farm in County Kildare, Ireland.

Cunningham worked in business from 1971 until 1989. On the book jackets of his thrillers he is described as having had "a career on Wall Street" and subsequently as having "worked in Paris and London in the commodities market." In 1984 on his way to Antigua he read a thriller by Peter James called *Billionaire* (1983), and, as he told Gilson, thought, "I could do that. And did." He found himself surprised at how easy it was to get published. He wrote the first book, *Noble Lord* (1986), under the pseudonym Peter Lauder, because he "thought people in business would think I'd lost the run of myself." He "wryly" admitted to Deevy that he adopted the pseudonym because "I think I felt that by simply the act of having a book published I was going to become an international celebrity overnight." However, by using his maternal grandmother's maiden name, it is possible that Cunningham was also affiliating himself with his family's artistic heritage.

Cunningham continued to write international thrillers for the next five years, his last one coming out in 1990. At this time he wrote between six and nine each morning, then went off to his office. Cunningham views the thrillers as entertainments, not serious literature; however, he did acknowledge to Gilson that "The thrillers made me learn pace and tension," and added that it is because of them that he knows "how to keep the pages turning." The thrillers include *Noble Lord*, *All Risks Mortality* (1987), *The Snow Bees* (1988), *The Bear's Requiem* (1989), and *Hostile Bid* (1991). Each engages some aspect of international intrigue, usually connected with high finance and international politics.

Noble Lord brings together international terrorism, the criminal underworld, and the hidden connections of these to international law enforcement, when an Antiguan sergeant, in the process of investigating the murder of his brother-in-law, a jewel thief in New York, learns that terrorists are plotting to murder Queen Elizabeth II. The novel also explores the international world of horse racing and adds to this the underworld actions of Arab and Irish terrorists. The dust jacket blurb, attempting to promote the unknown author by turning him into a character out of a thriller novel, states: "Unlike thriller writers who write about Irish terrorists from afar, Peter Lauder, as he calls himself, lives in the thick of it. An Irishman whose name will now be known around the world, he is descended from great athletes and daring gamblers and men of courage and drive. All those qualities flow through the veins of his heroes, while he sits at his secret typewriter, and his friends and neighbors know him only as a successful accountant, commodities dealer, and farmer."

After the success of *Noble Lord*, Cunningham's next novel was published under his own name. *All Risks Mortality* focuses on a former Nazi who is living in the

United States under the assumed name of Galatti; he has fraudulently collected millions of dollars in insurance on a racehorse that he had killed. The hero of the book is Matt Blaney, an insurance adjuster sent to investigate the insurance fraud, who, in the course of his investigation, discovers Mossad Nazi hunters who also seek Galatti. The book also incorporates financial double-dealing on Wall Street, nuclear terrorism, and the arms industry, as well as the oil industry.

The third thriller Cunningham published, titled *The Snow Bees,* concerns a half-English, half-Spanish assessor who is sent out from London to finalize the sale of a French vineyard, but discovers a trail of international hostile takeovers and money laundering instead, leading back to the bombing of Guernica during the Spanish Civil War. The novel connects drug trafficking and the black-market diamond trade with the agitations of Basque separatists, who use illegal means to attempt to liberate their land.

The next novel, *The Bear's Requiem,* also treats Wall Street and the Arab oil industry, focusing on the fortune made and lost by a young commodities broker who is mysteriously set up on the eve of his marriage to respectability in the form of a society heiress, with the result that he is left bankrupt and alone. The novel traces his determination to regain his fortune, which takes him to Japan, where crooked officials try to control the price of oil by faking the discovery of a vast reserve.

The last of Cunningham's early thrillers, *Hostile Bid,* returns to Japan, this time to probe the workings of the *yakuza* (the Japanese mafia), as well as illegal drug running and corrupt politics, finally circling back to the treacherous maneuverings of Wall Street. All of these early works received praise from critics of the thriller genre: the novels were described as readable, well written, gripping, and original.

Hostile Bid was in press when, on 22 September 1990, the Cunninghams' eldest son, Peter Cunningham Jr., was killed in a car accident. Cunningham wrote Gilson:

> Peter was 16. I don't need to describe the effect, but our lives were changed forever. In my case, I decided to write a book that would not depend on plot and special effects, but would say something special about its characters. *Who Trespass Against Us* was my first attempt to find a voice. It is, looking back, a raw novel written in the shadow of intense grief. It is too close to the suffering to succeed as an art form. It combines thriller and literary format. Importantly for me, however, part of the novel is written in the first person.

Who Trespass Against Us is set in the 1980s in Ireland and England and centers around an Irish Republi-

can Army (IRA) bombing in London that kills a young woman. The woman's father, Adam Coleraine, is devastated by his daughter's death. He is a member of the antiterrorist division of the British Home Office and gets hold of a top-secret file on Irish revolutionaries put together by Dublin-based detective superintendent Brian Kilkenny, who for fifteen years has been in contact with an operative from within the IRA organization named Vincent Ashe. Kilkenny does not know Ashe's status in the IRA but has maintained a relationship of mutual respect with the man, and he has received from him names of particularly aggressive operatives in the IRA who, Ashe says, are damaging North-South relations in Ireland. The information has led to arrests that have allowed Kilkenny to advance up the ranks in the Special Detective Unit of the Garda Síochána (Guardians of the Peace; the Irish national police force). Yet, beyond the political usefulness of his relationship to Ashe, Kilkenny feels a complex sense of admiration and envy for the man. He is attracted to Ashe's passionate love for Ireland and moved by his eloquent speeches on the plight of the Irish people whose cultural identity is in his view forever blighted by their continued affiliation with the British. In contrast, Kilkenny feels the weight of years of ambivalence and compromise that are part of his career in the Garda Síochána. He protects Ashe's identity from political figures who want to use the man to eradicate the IRA, and in this way feels he has remained at least partially true to his sense of moral duty. When Coleraine takes the report and disappears, presumably on a mission of revenge, Kilkenny pursues him to Northern Ireland and into the thick of IRA activity. He discovers that Ashe is the head of the IRA and has been using Kilkenny all along to control the information being passed to the Republic of Ireland regarding IRA activities.

The novel is clearly written in thriller format, but Cunningham is also interested in the emotional evolution of his characters. Coleraine is caught between his feelings of outrage and grief over the murder of his daughter and his awareness that, by seizing the report in an effort to exact revenge, he is only perpetuating the cycle of violence that has embroiled Britain and Ireland for so many years. In contrast, Kilkenny finds himself trapped in the gray area of Irish revolutionary politics, where questions of nationality, religious and social culture, and political stance become complexly interwoven. In the end readers discover that Kilkenny has recorded his narrative in prison, from which place he also corresponds with Coleraine, now a monk. Both men, after careers as political operatives, have ended up living as recluses, reflecting on life but no longer a part of it.

The removal from life depicted at the end of *Who Trespass Against Us* is the final position adopted by all

'This dramatic tale physically brings to life the continuing horror of
the Northern Ireland conflict.'
TIM PAT COOGAN

ISBN 0-7126-5678-2

9 780712 656788

C
CENTURY

PETER CUNNINGHAM

Who Trespass Against Us

*Dust jacket for Cunningham's 1993 novel, about a father whose daughter
is killed in an IRA bombing (Bruccoli Clark Layman Archives)*

Cunningham's male protagonists in the novels that follow. In the interview with Gilson, Cunningham said of
his own position in Ireland, "I was only political in so far
as I voted along Redmondite lines—but this would not be
unusual in Ireland." This statement is at once a repudiation of politics and an acknowledgment of the politicized
nature of Irish identity. As Cunningham remarked to
Deevy, his family "would argue incessantly how Ireland
would have been better off had there been no Rising. A
futile exercise, I suppose." But beyond representing characters who are, like himself, opposed to the political and
terrorist activities of radical republicans, Cunningham
does not use his novels to preach his views. Instead he
explores the texture of contemporary Irish life, composed as it is of people with widely varying social and
religious backgrounds and political views. To place this
broad mix of characters, Cunningham turned to his own
hometown, Waterford, renaming it Monument.

Cunningham had several reasons for turning
Waterford into Monument. He is a man for whom matters of family and personal history exert a tremendous
pull. As an adult he has spent considerable time

researching his family history and has used the
unearthed material in his novels. He feels the same
draw to the town inhabited by his family; Waterford,
he explained to Gilson, was and is extremely important
to his imaginative life: "Never a day goes by that my
mind does not flit, however briefly, to a street in Waterford. When I am writing of Monument, I am writing of
a place and of people I intimately know and understand." However, he added: "At the beginning I didn't
want to get into a discussion in which I might have
been asked, 'If it's Waterford, why not call it such?'
That is why I invented Monument. Monument is a fictional celebration of Waterford. Monument has its own
map and its own identity. Although when I think of a
street in Monument, I probably think of one in Waterford, the fact that what I am writing about is invented
gives me complete freedom."

Cunningham also felt liberated by his use of
first-person narrative in the Monument series. Although
he experimented with it in *Who Trespass Against Us,* he
feels that it was not until *Tapes of the River Delta* (1995),
the first of his novels depicting Waterford, that he really

perfected his use of this narrative device, and, as he told Gilson, "I have stuck to it ever since." Indeed, in Cunningham's own opinion, *Tapes of the River Delta* is seminal in his development as a writer. He remarked to Deevy that the book "was an entirely new departure for me because it was writing really from the heart." A densely layered novel narrated by Theo Love Shortcourse, *Tapes of the River Delta* chronicles the narrator's ambivalent relationships with his various family members and exposes his own lack of self-knowledge in emotional matters. As are all of Cunningham's Monument novels, the story is concerned with the ways in which the often unknown past creates the present as well as the particular nature of that present in the atmosphere of enforced intimacy that prevails in a small town in Ireland.

Theo's childhood is marked by family mysteries he cannot understand and secret relationships he cannot discuss. When he grows up, he leaves Monument and eventually becomes the head of the Department of Customs and Excises. Only then does he discover that his mother, Sparrow, is the daughter of her own sister, Baby Love, and their father, Sammy, who sent the fourteen-year-old Baby Love to the United States after she gave birth in secret to Sparrow, the child that was a product of rape and incest. Furthermore, Theo discovers that he himself is not the son of Sparrow but of Baby and her American husband, stolen in infancy by Sparrow from her sister (and mother). Baby pursued her sister/daughter and her infant son, Theo, but was killed by a bomb in London during World War II; thus, Sparrow's claim that Theo was her own child was never disproved. Nevertheless, Theo feels that Sparrow prefers his cousin, Bain, to him, and he cannot reconcile himself to her preference. He continues to compete with his cousin even after Bain has grown up to become *taoiseach* (prime minister) of Ireland. Bain becomes involved in gunrunning for the IRA and blackmails Theo into taking part in it, and the novel ends with a sequence of spectacular action scenes, culminating in the murder of Bain by Theo.

The complexity of the background plots as well as the dramatic action scenes remind the reader that Cunningham began his career as a writer of thrillers. Indeed, in stylistic terms, all the novels published after 1993 are marked in this way. Each is dramatically and intricately plotted, and each uses information that is unknown by the characters in the present to create suspense and build toward an end that is climactic, revelatory, and violent. This intricacy in the plot of *Tapes of the River Delta* drew fire from some critics such as Mike Milotte and Mary Leland. On 24 March 2001 Leland notes in *The Irish Times* (Dublin) that "There is the hindrance of dates, the structural mystery of sequence, place-names which are difficult to accommodate in the imagination, contradic-

tions in the flow of fervent prose." Other critics, such as Vincent Banville in the 24 June 1995 issue of *The Irish Times* (Dublin) admitted that the complexity of relationships and the shifts in time and story demand that the reader remain attentive and active, but they claimed that the novel is worth the effort, delivering a narrative whose registration of complexity and ambiguity approximates that of life itself.

Other legacies of the thriller genre, in particular the high-paced action and larger-than-life drama, have also drawn criticism. Several reviewers of *Tapes of the River Delta* accused Cunningham of melodrama and found the plot far-fetched. For example, Milotte of *The Sunday Tribune Magazine* (Dublin) wrote on 25 June 2001: "It is hard to know just what Peter Cunningham hoped to achieve with this book. Are we supposed to laugh or cry? Is any of it, or all of it, to be taken seriously? Is it deliberately over the top or is the in-built hyperbole a terrible mistake? Does it matter that we lose our way in a series of confusing time sequences and multi-generational conundrums?" Critics such as Milotte seemed unsure as to how to place the novel generically, but this very defiance of category was hailed by other critics, such as an unnamed reviewer for *The Times* (London), writing in the "Novels in Brief" section on 23 March 1996, who found the mixing of family saga and thriller to transcend the limits of both genres.

Even those critics who disliked the thriller components of *Tapes of the River Delta* praised Cunningham's lyrical writing, finding the prose full of powerful images that show great descriptive power. Milotte, for example, acknowledged that Cunningham writes "sparkling prose with great inventiveness," as well as "powerful images that reveal a rare talent for descriptive writing." But again he tempered this praise by claiming that "the writing at times seems too good for the throwaway plot, creating an unresolved tension between form and content."

Overall, however, the response to the publication of *Tapes of the River Delta* was enthusiastically favorable. Many Irish and English newspapers and periodicals short-listed the book as one of the best of the week or season; it also received notice in the United States. In large part this notice is a result of the thematic content of the novel; Kevin Myers, in his 10 August 1995 "An Irishman's Diary" column in the *Irish Times* (Dublin), noted that unlike many Irish novelists whose themes are thoroughly predictable, *Tapes of the River Delta* "is a truly original work; original in its themes, its style, its content. Since it is in part set today, there are obviously references to the IRA and the North. But these do not come in the normal kit-form of caricatures, and they are simply the inevitable ingredients of the lives which Peter has written about . . . a class, a society, which has been largely ignored in most Irish literature in recent decades—the non-Dublin, com-

*Dust jacket for the 1996 U.S. edition of Cunningham's
1995 novel, about an incestuous family and political
intrigue in the Republic of Ireland
(Richland County Public Library)*

fortable, Catholic commercial classes." In a press release distributed by the publisher, Century Press, the British novelist Barry Unsworth, winner of the Booker Prize, is quoted as describing *Tapes of the River Delta* as "an eloquent meditation on recent Irish history" and adding, "It is difficult to know what to admire most in this gifted novel," thereby pointing to the fact that its importance is not limited to its ability to record Irish life. In Unsworth's view the novel is also "a subtle and perceptive study of the pains of adolescence" and "a powerful story of betrayal and corrupted political practice and lost dreams."

The complex and sensitive rendering of Irish politics connects *Tapes of the River Delta* to the earlier *Who Trespass Against Us*. Both novels demonstrate a sophisticated grasp of the intricacies of contemporary Irish life, moving with ease from the IRA, drug and gun running, party politics, the role of British Intelligence in Dublin and Northern Ireland governmental affairs, to the social alliances and breakdowns that link Catholics and Protestants, lower- and middle-class Irish, the Church and the

government. But in his next novel Cunningham seems to have decided to forego for the most part the representation of that complex and dangerous world in favor of a more interior exploration of character. *Consequences of the Heart* (1998) moves the highly politicized public world into the background—so much so that the larger context of his characters at times disappears.

The novel is narrated by Chud Conduit, a child of barely legitimate birth whose "simple" mother, Hilda, was forced by his grandmother to marry a sailor with whom she had spent a single night. After the marriage the sailor vanished for good, leaving Chud effectively a bastard child. Chud was born into the Church family, a powerful Monument clan who support both Empire and Union. Theirs is a large and eccentric tribe; for example, his grandmother, a doctor's wife and the family matriarch, is a former prostitute. The colorful characters that help to define Chud's childhood give the novel a generational epic sweep. But the novel is less concerned with the family than with the evolution of Chud's lifelong friendships with Jack Santry and Rosa Bensey.

Jack Santry is the scion of Main, the Anglo-Irish big house that stands just outside of Monument. His family received the land from Oliver Cromwell as a reward for their role in the taking of Monument by the British. This detail is a good example of the way in which Cunningham refers to Irish history in his work. After executing Charles I and establishing a Protectorate in England, Cromwell turned his attention to the conquest of Ireland in 1649, and his forces soon overran the country. Waterford managed to hold out for several months before it fell to the British. After the struggle had ended, one quarter of the Catholic population of Ireland was dead and many of the survivors found themselves transported to the West Indies as slaves. In 1652 the Act of Settlement was drawn up, confiscating land from Catholics on a massive scale. By alluding thus to Cromwell, Cunningham implies that the descendants of the native Irish population of Monument would not have forgotten how the Anglo-Irish Santrys acquired their land, despite their ability to accept the family's presence as a part of their daily lives.

Jack and Chud are good friends, and they are both in love with Rosa, the daughter of the wealthiest bookkeeper in Monument. Although Jack and Rosa are not supposed to keep company with Chud because of his questionable heritage, the three teenagers spend summers together in the mountains, skinny-dipping and experimenting sexually. One day they discover that they are being spied on by Bruno, the son of Italian immigrants, and a childhood friend of Chud. They decide to punish Bruno, but their actions inadvertently result in his death. Chud takes the blame for the killing and is sent away to reformatory school. Rosa goes to a convent, and Jack, to England.

In 1941, in the midst of World War II, Chud is released from the school. His grandmother secures him a job working in Omagh, a town in Northern Ireland, as a civilian laborer for the British army. In order to gain a commission—not the easiest feat for a Catholic Irishman—Chud spies on the republican activities of the locals and reports back to the British army commander. In this way Chud is responsible for the deaths of several IRA operatives. He gets his commission and goes to England.

Chud and Jack meet again on the advent of the D-Day offensive. In this section of the novel Cunningham returns to the international political concerns of his earlier works. He told Gilson, "If there was a contest to select one defining day which stands out over all others in the 20th century, D-Day, 6th June 1944, would be on the short list. Although the outcome of W.W. II was never in doubt by 1944, the sheer size of the D-Day operation and the spirit of freedom which it symbolised, galvanised the hopes of a generation." But Cunningham's interest in this day is not simply prompted by its place in history, as he explained: "My father's career in the BA [British Army], and the fact that he left me original D-Day papers, are central to the plot of *Consequences*." Thus, for Cunningham this section of the novel is both a return to the public world and an intensely intimate, interior glimpse into the life of the man whose interests and charismatic character importantly shaped Cunningham's own. Like Chud, Redmond Cunningham distinguished himself in France on D-Day. But in *Consequences of the Heart* it is not Chud who receives the Military Cross, as did Redmond Cunningham, but Jack, despite the fact that Jack had caused the death of several of his men when he lost his nerve. Because no one knows about his moment of paralyzing fear, Jack is hailed as a hero in Monument upon his return. He marries Rosa and settles down to life in Main, while Chud goes into the Church family business of warehousing trade goods. The rest of the novel traces the evolution of the relationship between Chud and Rosa and Jack, which is marked by such sensational elements as a ménage à trois, compulsive gambling, blackmail, and murder.

The sensational qualities of *Consequences of the Heart* were defended by several critics. Jim Clarke, writing in the Living Section of *The Sunday Independent* (Dublin) on 25 October 1998 said of the plot: "It's often unrealistic, but that's because it deals with the extremes of human bonding, blind loyalty and true love. The intense passion of this book, like the nature of love it attempts to portray, is seductive, courageous and spellbinding. Peter Cunningham provides proof, if any were needed, that the boundaries of the romantic novel exist a million miles away from the cosy world of Mills and Boon." John

Kenny, writing in *The Irish Times* (Dublin) on 31 October 1998 stated "Unlike Cunningham's last book, *Tapes of the River Delta,* this novel stays nicely on the right side of melodrama." He added, "Peter Cunningham has performed the feat of investing a clichéd, Mills-and-Boon title with a new credibility."

Critics agree that the key to Cunningham's successful negotiation of the melodramatic lies in his skillful deployment of the first-person narrative. David Horspool pointed out in the 9 October 1998 issue of *TLS: The Times Literary Supplement* that, though there is at times a "romanticized tone of reminiscence" that can obscure the clarity of Cunningham's writing, for the most part Chud's narrative is compelling and engrossing. He noted that "One of the achievements of Peter Cunningham's ambitious novel is that his narrator—who confesses in the course of the book to murder, betrayal, adultery and a clutch of other crimes and deceptions—is, none the less, a sympathetic, even an admirable person. Chud's story, however, is not one of simple self-justification, or of defiance of convention; with great care, Cunningham constructs instead a narrative in which the characters' actions and reactions, no matter how shocking they are, appear logical, even inevitable." Cunningham's characters are, he concluded, "people in a realm governed by its own rules, so completely self-absorbed that the real world can barely touch them." The contrast between Chud's private realm and the external one has, in Horspool's opinion, been brought into effective relief.

The fact that the public world of large-scale political and social upheavals is still visible, though in a less dominant capacity than in earlier novels, seemed particularly impressive to some critics. Many noted with enthusiasm the perspective from which Irish and European history is presented, both its interiorized aspect in the form of Chud's narrative, and its presentation as one facet of a larger European history. Arminta Wallace, writing in *The Historical Novels Review* in August 1999 was particularly impressed by Cunningham's sensitivity of a "deep underlying sadness . . . at the modern male psyche broken by this century's wars." The elegiac and lyrical power of the novel caused Daire Dolan writing in *The Irish Post* (Dublin) on 8 June 2001 to say that *Consequences of the Heart* should earn the same massive critical success that *Tapes of the River Delta* received, while Dermot Bolger writing in *The Sunday Tribune* (Dublin) on 11 October 1998 described Cunningham as being "at the height of his powers as a novelist." Some reviewers did offer some negative criticism as well: James Zug, writing in *The New York Times* (21 January 2001) found the narrative structure that has Chud organizing his life into a series of ring-binders "an annoying conceit that only gets worse when he also fills us in on many generations of the town's

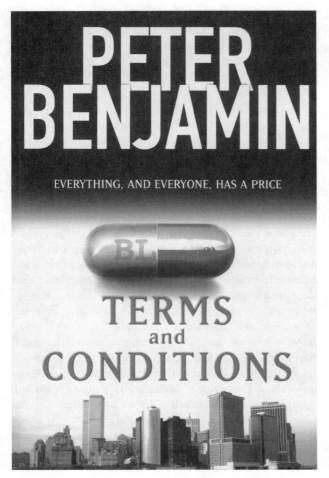

Paperback cover for Cunningham's pseudonymous 2001 novel, about the search for a missing scientist who may have discovered a cure for AIDS (Bruccoli Clark Layman Archives)

limited narratives, and these stories, in combination with her own narrative and Kaiser's, create an effect of layers of voices moving backward and forward in time.

The plot of the novel centers around the Monument newspaper where Kaiser works as a janitor. Founded in the late nineteenth century by Boss Pender's father, it was expanded by his son into a lucrative and powerful industry. Boss becomes a larger-than-life figure in Monument. He has three sons, his favorite being "Black," the dark-haired boy whose twin brother, "White," is more or less ignored by their father. Boss rapes Black's fiancée, a Protestant girl named Cushy, and her brother curses the family when Cushy gets pregnant, threatening to expose Black, whom he thinks is the father. Boss goes to see the brother and ends up murdering him but persuades Black to take the rap. Black escapes to the north and lives the rest of his days under a false name, while Boss has White marry Cushy. Many years later, Jasmine discovers that Kaiser is in fact Black's son, who was smuggled back into Monument by Boss when Black died, so that Boss's favorite son's issue would inherit the newspaper. Boss himself dies soon after this act, and Kaiser's true identity is covered up by Ollie, the daughter of Cushy and Boss, who wants to keep the newspaper for herself and her own son, Tim. Tim kills Jasmine when she uncovers the truth of Kaiser's parentage, and Kaiser is left to contemplate the tangle of events and the legacy of passion and deceit that is his family inheritance, from his place in the Monument mental hospital.

The critical response to *Love in One Edition* echoed much of the earlier criticism of Cunningham's work. Several reviewers praised Cunningham enthusiastically. On 17 April 2001 Myers, writing again in "An Irishman's Diary," called Cunningham "the most critically underrated author we have," while Jerome Boyd Maunsell, writing in *The Times* (London) on 10 March 2001, described Cunningham's novel as beginning "with a lyrical evocation of provincial life before descending swiftly into darker territory," and added that the book is "beautifully written and pierced with moments of calm insight." Bolger extended this praise, writing in *The Sunday Independent* (Dublin) on 11 March 2001, when he asserted that Cunningham's work "is skilled and solid storytelling," adding that Cunningham's unique world is "quite unlike anything I have read in contemporary Irish fiction."

Monument itself is the focus of many critics' praise. Bolger, again in *The Sunday Independent* (Dublin), spoke for many critics when he stated that "the overriding character" bringing the Monument books to life "is the closeknit town of Monument itself." Myers concurred and pointed out in *The Irish Times* (Dublin) in his "An Irishman's Diary" (17 April 2001), that the melodramatic elements, fast-paced action, and surprise revela-

eccentric residents. Yet the story of the three lovers and their alternating bouts of infatuation and disenchantment is told with delicacy and skill."

The third novel in the Monument series is *Love in One Edition* (2001). The fusion of thriller and literary first-person novel is here given a twist by the use of two different narrators. Kaiser, a deaf janitor and graduate of reform schools, whose inheritance has, unbeknownst to him, been stolen from him, is the frame narrator. But over the course of his narrative Kaiser also reads from a journal kept by his lover, Jasmine, an educated research librarian who is both alarmed by and drawn to Kaiser's moody eccentricities and latent violent behavior. As he reads, Kaiser discovers that Jasmine had been attempting to solve the mystery of his past, but in piecing together his history, she also inadvertently reconstructed the hidden histories of many of the most important people of Monument, revealing hidden injustices and cruelty. She tells the different characters' histories in the form of third-person-

tions that have been the subject of some criticism emerge directly out of the social world Cunningham is depicting. He stated "All such worlds have dark and terrible secrets . . . This is a narrative truth which the ancients understood." Graeme Woolaston, writing in *The Herald* (Glasgow) on 17 March, 2001, expanded on this point, observing that Cunningham's novel

> belongs to a genre which now enjoys little literary respectability on this side of the Irish Sea. In England (which in this context means London) it would be dismissed as a 'provincial' novel. In other words, it's set in a specific, tightly-knit community where secrets are kept for decades and are arguably best left unexplored. In less competent hands than Cunningham's this kind of story can become little more than upmarket soap. But his careful delineation of the impact on his characters of their developing discoveries lifts *Love in One Edition* into another class altogether.

But there are critics who disagree with this enthusiastic praise of Cunningham's creation. Gregory Dart, writing in *TLS* (16 March 2001), called *Love in One Edition* "pure Gothic melodrama." He argued, however, "The problems with the novel have less to do with the story, than with the manner in which it is told. Ostensibly, it is mediated in a number of different ways—multiple narrators, a mixture of written and oral testimonies, competing versions of the same event—as if an analysis of the way in which knowledge is produced and circulated in communities were a real concern. When it comes to the actual writing, however, there is something homogenous about the final result." Indeed, Dart pointed out, "In Kaiser, we are told, we have an eccentric loner, a man scarcely articulate, often misunderstood; in Jasmine, a restless spirit, sexy, outgoing. So why do they sound identical on the page? And why do they both seem at one remove from the emotional drama they are taking part in?" Dart added that the forced quality of the lyricism creates an effect that is pedantic yet inexact, and concludes that *Love in One Edition* would have been better "if it had been told straight, as an old-fashioned thriller; Cunningham is skilled as a storyteller but is not interested in the way characters and their stories express themselves in small-town life."

Dart is not the only critic who finds the language of the novel overwrought. Gerry Dukes, writing in the Review Books Section of *The Irish Independent* (Dublin) on 24 February 2001, faulted the novel for its forced and clichéd plot, what he described as "Narrative ham-fistedness." He noted that in itself this "would not count for much if the writing itself was in any way sustaining" and concluded that "*Love in One Edition* is one unlovely edi-

tion." Leland, writing again in *The Irish Times* (Dublin) on 24 March 2001, agreed, calling the habit of "contrived lyricism . . . wearying and often inaccurate until a startling image singes a paragraph into resonance." Leland acknowledges that the confusion of dates, sequences, and contradictions is slow and difficult going, but notes that once she pieced together the narrative it became completely engrossing. She holds that the complexities of the narrative method are justified because they are a metaphor for the world Cunningham portrays, reflecting the complexities of history, politics, and social behavior in a small town that is affected indirectly and often obliquely by the events of the larger world beyond its bounds.

Despite the negative critiques, Cunningham's literary novels have been generally well received. His success led Simon & Schuster/Townhouse to publish for the first time a book he completed many years earlier, *Terms and Conditions* (2001). A thriller involving Wall Street speculators, villainous multinational pharmaceutical companies, and corruption at the highest levels, the novel centers on the Dublin financial analyst Joe Grace, who is hired to search for Carlos Penn, a missing scientist who may have a cure for AIDS. *Terms and Conditions* was published under the pseudonym Peter Benjamin (Benjamin is the name of his youngest son); Cunningham does not want readers to confuse his literary novels with his thrillers. Although he was happy to see the earlier work republished, and he told Deevy that another Joe Grace novel is forthcoming, he has no intention of returning exclusively to the thriller genre.

Peter Cunningham's Monument novels are both interesting and compelling contributions to British and Irish literature of the late twentieth and early twenty-first centuries. Their provocative fusion of popular genres such as the thriller and the detective novel with literary forms such as the historical novel, the family saga, and the novel of provincial life make them at once readable and lyrically moving. As several critics have noted, at times Cunningham's experiments seem forced, both stylistically and in emotional terms, while his attempts to construct "believable" narrative conceits can become intrusive and annoying. However, in many critics' estimation he also succeeds at capturing the lives and perceptions of characters whose stories are not often found in contemporary Irish literature. His explorations of genre, class, and locale are welcome and timely additions to the experiments within the novel form that are currently ongoing in Ireland and Britain.

Interview:
Patricia Deevy, "Writing of the Heart," *Sunday Independent* (Dublin), 9 December 2001.

Emma Donoghue

(24 October 1969 –   )

Stacia L. Bensyl
Missouri Western State College

BOOKS: *Passions Between Women: British Lesbian Culture 1668–1801* (London: Scarlet, 1993; New York: HarperCollins, 1995);

Stir-fry (London: Hamilton, 1994; New York: Harper-Collins, 1994);

Hood (London: Hamilton, 1995; New York: Harper-Collins, 1996);

Kissing the Witch (London: Hamilton, 1997); republished as *Kissing the Witch: Old Tales in New Skins* (New York: HarperCollins, 1997);

Ladies and Gentlemen (Dublin: New Island, 1998);

We Are Michael Field (Bath: Absolute, 1998);

Ladies' Night at Finbar's Hotel, by Donoghue, Maeve Binchy, Clare Boylan, Anne Haverty, Éilis Ní Dhuibhne, Deirdre Purcell, and Kate O'Riordan, edited by Dermot Bolger (London: Picador, 1999; Dublin: New Island, 1999; San Diego: Harcourt Brace, 2000);

Slammerkin (London: Virago, 2000; New York: Harcourt Brace, 2001);

The Woman Who Gave Birth to Rabbits (New York: Harcourt Brace, 2002; London: Virago, 2002).

PLAY PRODUCTIONS: *I Know My Own Heart,* Dublin, Glasshouse Productions, March 1993;

Ladies and Gentlemen, Dublin, Glasshouse Productions, 18 April 1996; Minneapolis, Outward Spiral Theatre, 14 April 2000;

Kissing the Witch, adapted by Donoghue from her short-story collection of that title, San Francisco, Magic Theatre, 9 June 2000.

PRODUCED SCRIPTS: *Trespasses,* radio, RTÉ, 1996;

Expecting, radio, BBC Radio 4, 1996;

Error Messages, radio, RTÉ, 1999;

A Short Story, radio, BBC Radio 4, May 2000;

The Lost Seed, radio, BBC Radio 4, May 2000;

Figures of Speech, radio, BBC Radio 4, May 2000;

Night Vision, radio, BBC Radio 4, May 2000;

Daddy's Girl, radio, BBC Radio 4, May 2000;

Exes, radio, BBC Radio 4, 2001;

Emma Donoghue (photograph © Tadhy Hayes; from the dust jacket for Stir-fry, *1994)*

Pluck, motion picture, Language / Irish Film Board / RTÉ / Zanzibar Productions, 2001.

OTHER: "Noises from Woodsheds: Tales of Irish Lesbians, 1886–1989," in *Lesbian and Gay Visions of Ireland: Towards the Twenty-first Century,* edited by Ide O'Carroll and Eoin Collins (London: Cassell, 1995), pp. 158–170; revised as "Noises from Woodsheds: The Muffled Voices of Irish Lesbian

Fiction," in *Volcanoes and Pearl-Divers: Essays in Lesbian Feminist Studies,* edited by Suzanne Riatt (London: Onlywomen Press, 1995), pp. 169–200;

What Sappho Would Have Said: Four Centuries of Love Poems Between Women, edited by Donoghue (London: Hamilton, 1997); republished as *Poems Between Women: Four Centuries of Love, Romantic Friendship, and Desire* (New York: Columbia University Press, 1997);

The Mammoth Book of Lesbian Short Stories, edited by Donoghue (London: Robinson, 1999; New York: Carroll & Graf, 1999);

I Know My Own Heart, in *Seen and Heard: Six New Plays by Irish Women,* edited, with an introduction, by Cathy Leeney (Dublin: Carysfort Press, 2001).

SELECTED PERIODICAL PUBLICATION–
UNCOLLECTED: "Coming Out a Bit Strong," *Index on Censorship,* 24, no. 1 (1995): 87–88.

Emma Donoghue is one of the most prolific young Irish writers to emerge since the 1970s. While Donoghue may be best known for her treatment of lesbian themes in her writing, her work is also intrinsically Irish and deeply rooted in her sense of both sexuality and nationality. Her name is often associated with Irish writer Mary Dorcey, who also explores in her writings the place where sexuality and nationalism merge. Donoghue has written in diverse genres and has proven herself equally adept at fiction, drama, and criticism.

Emma Donoghue was born in Dublin, Ireland, on 24 October 1969, the youngest of eight children. Both Donoghue's father and mother were teachers. Her father, the literary critic Denis Donoghue, taught in the English department at University College Dublin (UCD) from 1966 to 1979. Her mother, Frances (Rutledge) Donoghue, taught English at the secondary-school level. Donoghue traveled to the United States as a child, spending a year there when her father became the Henry James Professor of Letters at New York University. After graduating from UCD in 1990, with a B.A. degree in English and French, Donoghue went on to attend Cambridge University, receiving her Ph.D. in 1997.

In an interview with Stacia Bensyl for *Irish Studies Review* (2000) Donoghue remarked that growing up in an academic household

provided a number of advantages. It was a house literally lined with books, so I spent most of my childhood mooching around, reading whatever I wanted and quite a few of these books had my father's name on the spine because he's a critic, and this gave me the sense that this was something one could do; one could grow up and publish books with one's name on the spine. So

I had this rather illusory feeling that publishing books was an easy business, which gave me great confidence.

Although Donoghue had always written and had entered many competitions, the confidence she received from her family's support inspired her to begin writing a book-length fiction project while she was still an undergraduate: "I started my first novel, *Stir-Fry,* when I was in third year UCD, so to be honest I didn't know anything else. I'd been to school and I'd been to college and that was about it; that's probably why I've written all those details."

Stir-fry (1994) is indeed full of details of life in the late 1980s and early 1990s. In her review in *The Guardian* (8 February 1994) Miranda Carter commented on Donoghue's "feel for the authentic." Indeed, Donoghue has captured both the looks and the feel of the UCD campus and the "flatlands" of college housing in south Dublin. She told Bensyl that she

liked the eccentricity of the campus. I'd grown up there; it was my sort of childhood space, playing around the lake and in the trees and so on. I liked the combination of lovely green areas, hideously ugly buildings, and a lot of students just doing their thing. I liked the fact that nobody cared what they had to wear, . . . it was also big and grubby and anonymous. I found that quite a thrill.

The young protagonist of the novel, Maria, answers an advertisement for a roommate. Her discovery that her new roommates, Jael and Ruth, both "mature" college students, are lovers, initially shocks, then intrigues her. At the same time, Maria is making discoveries about other aspects of her life. Although she is a student, she finds she must find employment to supplement her university stipend, and her job as a cleaner at an office building in the city center allows her time to think about Jael and Ruth. Her trips home to visit her traditional Irish family become stifling and repugnant.

While some critics might well classify *Stir-fry* as a coming-of-age novel, the sexual discoveries Maria makes surpass those of most college freshmen. Her roommates are lovers, her heterosexual love interest turns out to be bisexual, and she becomes attracted to Ruth. Ultimately, the value of Maria's university experience pales in comparison to the practical education she receives about interpersonal relationships and personal fulfillment.

Donoghue's second novel, *Hood* (1995), earned her the Gay, Lesbian and Bisexual Book Award for Literature from the American Library Association in 1997. In *Hood* she chronicles the relationship between Pen and Cara, a lesbian couple who live with Cara's separated father. Pen and Cara come from different eco-

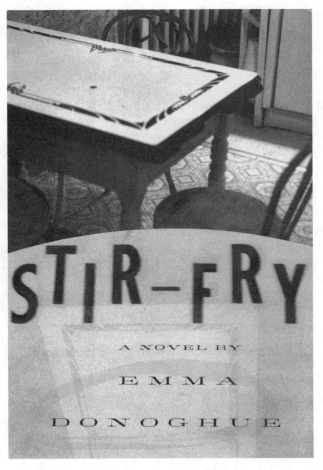

Dust jacket for the U.S. edition of Donoghue's first novel, about a first-year student at University College Dublin who becomes fascinated by her older, lesbian roommates (Richland County Public Library)

the Greek-born U.S. writer's 1977 collection, *Beginning with O.* The speaker of Broumas's poem is a Little Red Riding Hood character whose hood hides a secret she shares only with other women like her. Donoghue takes the story and gives it a particularly lesbian association in the epigraph. Donoghue has Pen, at the end of the novel, going to visit her mother, basket of homemade cookies in hand, to finally come out about her own sexuality. Pen thus becomes a Little Red Riding Hood character herself, extending the myth in the epigraph to the reality of the contemporary Irish lesbian experience.

One area in which *Hood* breaks new ground in the Irish lesbian novel is in its sexual frankness and, at times, explicitness. In ways much different from Irish lesbian narratives that came before, such as Dorcey's *A Noise from the Woodshed* (1989), Linda Cullen's *The Kiss* (1990), or Donoghue's own *Stir-fry,* or after—such as Dorcey's *Biography of Desire* (1997)—Donoghue creates in Pen a character who, while matter-of-fact about her lesbian identity, is also highly graphic and emphatic when she recounts her memories of her sexual relationship with Cara.

Just as Donoghue uses language to establish the existence and primacy of lesbian sexuality, she establishes the Irishness of her characters through language, as well as other means. One of Pen's duties as a primary-school teacher is to teach the Irish language. Pen's sexual identity is important to her, but her national identity is clearly important as well. She listens intently to the girls' choir at her day school singing Thomas Moore's "The Meeting of the Waters," from his *Irish Melodies,* part 1 (1808):

> Where the storms that we feel
> in this cold world should cease
> And our hearts like thy waters
> be mingled in peace.

Although Pen is quick to point out that a field trip to the actual Meeting of the Waters, the region in the Vale of Avoca, County Wicklow, where the River Avonmore and the River Avonbeg converge, was a great disappointment to her as a schoolgirl, she finds the lyrics of the song give her a comfort that she could well use after Cara's death. Pen's comfort comes from her sense of place and nationality, as well as her sexuality. She is clearly Irish, and she clearly belongs in Ireland. Kate, Cara's sister, tells Pen that "Ireland has nothing but a past tense. Did you know there are more Irish living in America than in Ireland?" to which Pen replies, "Not real ones." Pen is really, truly Irish—a Dubliner born and bred, a Roman Catholic, and a lesbian. Kate lives in the United States, but emigration seems unnatural to Pen, who cannot imagine not living in Ireland. Pen's aversion to America and to emigration weaves a subtle subtext in the novel. Donoghue fills *Hood* with Irish

nomic backgrounds, but their cultural backgrounds are the same, the result of being raised Catholic in Ireland, attending the same school, and being the same age. While Cara is an active, "out" lesbian, Pen's attitude toward her own sexuality is much more pragmatic. The novel begins as Pen learns of Cara's death in a car accident and alternates between Pen's present-time account of the funeral arrangements, her own grieving and attempt to maintain a sense of normalcy in her day-to-day activities, and Pen's memories of their thirteen-year-long relationship.

While *Hood* focuses on the relationship between Pen and Cara, it is also clearly a coming-out novel of sorts. Pen, after Cara's death, comes out to one of her male coworkers, to Cara's sister, and at the end of the novel, to her own mother. The form of the novel reflects Irish as well as lesbian identity, as it is framed by folktale. The epigraph is taken from the lesbian feminist poet Olga Broumas's "Little Red Riding Hood," a poem in

markers, including references to the popular television series *Glenroe,* Bourbon Creams, the largest cemetery in Ireland (and burial place of the patriot Daniel O'Connell, among others), Glasnevin Cemetery, and *The Irish Times.* She creates a character in *Hood* who relies heavily on her cultural identity to define who she is.

Pen and Cara meet and become sexually intimate while they are still in secondary school, but they both resist the label "lesbian" at that time. "Just . . . get on with it," is Pen's attitude toward her sexuality. Eventually, she becomes comfortable with the word "lesbian" and refers to herself as a lesbian or as gay; however, for Pen her sexuality is only one part of her personality. Cara is much more the stereotypical, politically active lesbian. Pen sometimes goes with Cara to workshops or rallies, but Pen is much more likely to define herself by her relationship with Cara than by the generic term "lesbian."

While Cara has sexual relationships with both men and women during this thirteen-year period, Pen remains monogamous: "'I've been faithful to Cara for thirteen years. I've never been to bed with anyone else.'" Pen, however, knows of Cara's infidelities and tolerates them. Although lesbian relationships often emphasize autonomy more than do heterosexual relationships, Pen's personal autonomy does not take the form of sexual infidelities. Pen is the constant figure in the novel; her life revolves around her work, her home, and her relationship with Cara. While Cara and Pen have definite agreed-upon roles, they do not conform to prescribed "butch" or "femme" stereotypes; rather, they define themselves and their roles within their relationship.

In *Hood* Donoghue answers the question of how contemporary Irish lesbian writers are to merge ideas of lesbianism and Irishness. "How was I to conceive of myself as a practicing Catholic and a furious lesbian feminist, a sweet colleen and a salty sinner?" Donoghue asks in her essay "Noises from Woodsheds" in *Lesbian and Gay Visions of Ireland: Towards the Twenty-first Century* (1995). In *Hood* Pen grapples with some of the same questions. Ultimately, however, Pen's image of herself as both Irish and lesbian supercedes any questions or doubts she may have. Pen loses her partner in *Hood,* but she retains her sense of self–her cultural and sexual identity. As Ellen Orleans commented in *Lambda Book Report* (August 1996), "With droll humor and heartbreaking insight, *Hood* examines this relationship, as well as questions of identity, family, sex, Catholicism and loss." Ultimately, however, Donoghue focuses on what Pen gains through that loss.

Because of the themes of *Stir-fry* and *Hood,* readers might not be surprised to find that *Kissing the Witch* (1997) features "lesbian revisionist" fairy tales. But Donoghue's rewriting transcends what could be a narrow definition. The characters in this collection of short stories, or linked fiction, often find a sense of self in their relationships to other women, and, as Patricia A. Dolisch observed in her June 1997 *School Library Journal* review, they are "complex enough to be neither entirely good nor entirely evil." As a result of their complexity, and of the "magic" of creative women working with and supporting one another, Donoghue's characters overcome poverty, fear, and loneliness by establishing nurturing relationships with women. Based on European fairy tales, the stories in *Kissing the Witch* are more akin to the works of the Brothers Jacob and Wilhelm Grimm than those of Walt Disney. These are not children's fairy stories, though the U.S. publisher of the book, HarperCollins, marketed it as a "young adult" title because of the fairy-tale plots.

As she told Bensyl in a portion of their 2000 *Irish Studies Review* that was not published, Donoghue is not the first to rewrite fairy tales, and others, such as Angela Carter, have examined the themes of several of the European fairy tales of the nineteenth-century Brothers Grimm through the eyes of a modern woman. Donoghue's approach is distinctive, however, for its emphasis on relations between women.

Donoghue's take on Thumbelina, for example, presents the protagonist as a woman who is made to feel small and unworthy by those around her. While Donoghue has not included traditional Irish folktales in *Kissing the Witch*–in fact she told Bensyl that there is little or no conscious effort on her part to meld Irish and European fairy tales–she has included the theme of the wise old woman who is not as she might appear, which permeates much of Irish folklore. The common theme calls on women to trust themselves, to rewrite their myths, to find the handsome princess in the mirror. The collection was short-listed for the 1997 James Tiptree, Jr. Award; Donoghue's stage adaptation, which dramatizes five stories from the collection, premiered at the Magic Theatre in San Francisco in 2000.

In her *Irish Studies Review* interview Donoghue remarked that as a college student, "I was very drawn to research, so I loved the fact that I could just bury myself in the library and work away on my own." This love of research found an outlet in her *We Are Michael Field* (1998), a biographical account of Katherine Harris Bradley and Edith Emma Cooper, Victorian poets and playwrights who wrote under the pseudonym Michael Field. *We Are Michael Field* is the first critical work dealing with Bradley and Cooper's voluminous unpublished journals and letters.

While these women shared a working relationship, they were also a committed lesbian couple who created for themselves a literary and aesthetic world that sometimes strained their personal relationships with others.

*Dust jacket for the U.S. edition of Donoghue's 1995
novel, about a woman coming to terms with the
death of her lesbian partner (Richland
County Public Library)*

such impassioned research, Donoghue's prose reflects the brightness and wonder of the discoveries she made while researching *We Are Michael Field*. Through her dedication to careful scholarship and research, Donoghue illuminates the work of these women who have been mostly forgotten and, when remembered, are recalled mainly for their poetry. "A reading of the Michaels' complete works," suggests Donoghue, "offers many surprises, especially among their plays, a handful of which are riveting."

Donoghue continues the theme of giving voice to lesbian couples in the arts who support each other in committed relationships in *Ladies and Gentlemen* (produced 1996; published 1998). This play is based on the historical Annie Hindle, an English-born American vaudevillian whose "act" was male impersonation. Hindle's most striking claim to fame, however, came not from her cross-dressing but from her marriage to theater dresser Annie Ryan. Hindle and Ryan's wedding, although unconventional, was presided over by a Unitarian minister, and their married life in New Jersey equaled the domesticity of their heterosexual neighbors.

The success of the role-playing and cross-gendering that the characters in the play experience is, of course, not without its hardship and difficulty. Ella Wesner, an American male-impersonator who follows Annie Hindle's act with her own, never does find the enduring love that Hindle and Ryan share. Gilbert Saroney, a female impersonator in the vaudeville troupe, experiences dissatisfaction and estrangement in his heterosexual marriage. And the owner of the troupe, Tony Pastor, appears to be blatantly heterosexual, as his overtures to Annie Ryan might indicate. But at one point in the play Saroney hints that Pastor made a pass at him, thus implying that Pastor's sexual preference is not so definite.

In 1998, after years of commuting between England, Ireland, and Canada, Donoghue moved to London, Ontario, and became a permanent resident of Canada. Her partner (since 1994) is Chris Roulston, a professor of French at the University of Western Ontario, where Donoghue has been a writer-in-residence. Although she spends most of her time in Canada, she continues to travel to England and Ireland, and, as she told Linda Richards in an interview for the on-line *January Magazine* (November 2000), "I clearly am an Irish writer and that's my, kind of, language and the particular flavor of English that I write," though she went on to say that "I think these geographical labels aren't as relevant nowadays. Especially as people move around so much. So I'm happy to be Irish Canadian or whatever mixture."

The couple, however, "were careful not to shock friends or family by claiming to be married; they saved that audacious metaphor of union for their private writings." Complicating the matter further, Bradley and Cooper were also aunt and niece. Their twenty-five-year relationship, nurtured by an unfailing commitment to each other and to writing, resulted in thirty plays and eleven volumes of poetry.

Most of the subject matter for their plays came from male figures in European history, such as Henry VI of Germany, Otto the Great, and King Canute. Their poetry, however, often focuses on their love for each other, as in their volume *Underneath the Bough* (1893), or women's love for women, as in *Long Ago* (1889), which takes as its inspiration the poems of Sappho. The bibliography in the text gives evidence both to Donoghue's exhaustive research and the Michael Fields' voluminous creative work. However, the most successful aspect of *We Are Michael Field* is the way in which Donoghue's passion for research and scholarship shines through the narrative about these two often overlooked writers: "In the British Library's Manuscript Room, the reader turns a brittle page and a pressed flower falls out, a souvenir of some walk the lovers took and wanted to remember, still bright yellow after more than a century." As a result of

Donoghue participated in one of her most creative projects, the collaborative novel *Ladies' Night at*

Finbar's Hotel (1999), a women-authored sequel to *Finbar's Hotel* (1997). The earlier book, which had featured unsigned chapters by several Irish writers, including Roddy Doyle, Anne Enright, Hugo Hamilton, and Joseph O'Connor, was a group novel set in a decrepit Dublin hotel about to be shut down. *Ladies' Night at Finbar's Hotel,* "devised" and edited by Dermot Bolger (who had also directed the first novel), brings together seven of the most successful, well-known contemporary Irish women writers: in addition to Donoghue, Maeve Binchy, Clare Boylan, Anne Haverty, Éilis Ní Dhuibhne, Dierdre Purcell, and Kate O'Riordan all contributed chapters. In the reopened, now-chic Finbar's Hotel, each character moves through his or her own subplot; each subplot links to the next, creating a novel with intertwining themes and characters written by seven different women. But, as the editor points out, "Each chapter in the book has been written by a different author. . . . We leave it to discerning readers to identify them." Bolger dramatized the novel for the British Broadcasting Corporation (BBC), and the play adaptation was broadcast on BBC Radio 4 on 10 May 2000.

In a move away from dealing with contemporary Irish lesbian themes in fiction and toward her predilection for history and research, Donoghue based her third novel, *Slammerkin* (2000), on the life of Mary Saunders, a London prostitute turned seamstress who brutally murdered her mistress in 1763 because she desired "fine clothes." Donoghue uses *Slammerkin* to challenge the privilege of class and the worth of the individual.

Mary, the child of a piecework seamstress and a cobbler killed as a result of his involvement in the "calendar riots" of 1752, lives with her mother and brutal stepfather in a London cellar. Mary goes to the charity school, the result of a promise her mother made to her deceased father, and wishes for a life other than the one she sees destroying her mother. Lured by the finery of the prostitutes she sees working around the Seven Dials, and contrasting that with the gray smock that is her only garment and a life that promises nothing but drudgery, Mary bargains with a peddler for a bright red ribbon but ends up being raped and is impregnated. Upon her parents' discovery of her pregnancy, Mary is driven from their home and ends up walking the streets, where she is eventually gang-raped and left for dead. Doll Higgins, a Seven Dials prostitute, finds Mary and nurses her back to health, arranges for her to have an abortion, and introduces her to the life of a "miss." Throughout the novel Donoghue juxtaposes Mary's "illegal" or "immoral" activity with verses she learned at the charity school, "Grateful we must always be / For the gifts of charity," and sage advice from Doll, "Be sure and always carry half a crown to prove you're not a whore." Doll's wis-

Dust jacket for the U.S. edition of Donoghue's 1997 collection of "lesbian revisionist" fairy tales (Richland County Public Library)

dom proves much more useful than the empty verses Mary learned by heart as a child.

Slammerkin contrasts with Donoghue's earlier novels in its treatment of grinding poverty, despair, and commercialized sex. While Mary's only loving relationship is with Doll, just a few years her senior, who becomes her protector, adviser, and surrogate mother, it is not a sexual relationship. Mary uses men solely for survival and is incapable of envisioning a mutually satisfying sexual relationship between a man and a woman.

After Doll's death, Mary leaves London and takes a position with Mr. and Mrs. Jones, dressmakers in the small Welsh town of Monmouth, and she appears to begin her life again as an "honest woman." The Joneses have come up in the world, from the back lanes of Monmouth. However, the penury of the lower middle classes holds no appeal for Mary. Her desire for finery and a life of more than servitude drives her back to prostitution. She has anonymous sex in the dark behind the local pub, dividing her profits with the publican and putting aside her earnings, planning to escape her position and return to London with a nest egg. On one occasion, however, she meets Mr. Jones, her master, while she is waiting for a customer and seduces him to keep him quiet; although the encounter is not repeated, it changes the dynamics of the relationships of the entire household.

Mrs. Jones discovers Mary's cache of coins and puts them in the church poor box, hoping in some way to expiate Mary from whatever wrongdoing gained her the money. Out for revenge, Mary steals Mrs. Jones's own savings and piles of the finery she had helped sew and embroider. When Mrs. Jones catches her in the act, Mary murders Mrs. Jones with a meat cleaver. Mary is caught and tried, then hanged and burned.

The note at the end of the novel cautions that it "is a fiction, inspired by the surviving facts of the real Mary Saunders' life, which are disputed and few." Donoghue's talent for research becomes apparent. Although she acknowledges "little contemporary commentary," she cites both *The Gentleman's Magazine* and a broadside, *The Confession and last Dying-Words of Mary Saunders* (1764), as historical sources for the novel. Other characters who appear in the novel are based on or inspired by real people, according to Donoghue. She told Richards in the *January Magazine* interview that the book involved "years and years and years of research" into eighteenth-century life, though "maybe only two percent" of her research made it into the finished novel.

The Woman Who Gave Birth to Rabbits (2002) is a collection of short fictions that are based on odd incidents in British and Irish history. Previously broadcast in 2000 on BBC 4, "A Short Story" is about the smallest surviving baby then-known to exist, a girl who was exhibited as a freak until her death in 1823. "The Last Rabbit" is the account of the woman after whom the volume is titled, Mary Toft, who hoaxed much of England in 1726 into believing her story of her miraculous birthing abilities, while "The Fox on the Line"—which previously appeared in *Circa 2000: Lesbian Fiction at the Millennium* (2000), edited by Terry Wolverton and Robert Drake—focuses on the relationship between the Irish journalist Frances Power Cobbe and the Welsh sculptor Mary Charlotte Lloyd, nineteenth-century animal rights activists. Donoghue told Richards in the *January Magazine* interview, "To me history is a kind of warehouse of stories for me to burgle," and in *The Woman Who Gave Birth to Rabbits* Donoghue has liberated many quirky and fantastic stories from the warehouse of history.

In January 2002 Donoghue announced on her website that she was working on "Life Mask," a novel set in eighteenth-century London and based on the historical triangle of the sculptor Anne Damer, the actress Elizabeth Farren, and Edward Stanley, twelfth Earl of Derby. The novel is scheduled to be published in the United Kingdom and Ireland by Virago Press and in the United States by Harcourt Brace and Company in 2003 or 2004. In her interview with Richards and in a 7 October 2000 interview with Alexandra Gill of *The Globe & Mail* (Toronto), Donoghue indicated that she was also working on a contemporary novel about long-distance relationships. She told Gill that the novel would be about an Irish woman and a Canadian woman who fall in love; although the book will be based on some of her own experiences, Donoghue told Gill that "the main character is far more glamorous. She's half-Indian, half-Irish. She's a flight attendant. And she drinks chocolate martinis."

Donoghue's dedication to research and history, as well as her ability to express her literary skill in several genres, marks her as an important contemporary Irish writer. Her contributor's note in *Circa 2000* declares, "Emma Donoghue's vision of lesbian writing in the 21st century is that lesbians will write about anything, and anyone will write about lesbians, thus making the business of defining and anthologizing more delightfully impossible than ever." Her dedication to giving a voice to lesbian characters and lesbian history places her squarely in the midst of lesbian and gay writers of the twenty-first century who find it imperative to convey to their audience the importance of establishing and maintaining those often unheard voices.

Interviews:

Stacia Bensyl, "Swings and Roundabouts: An Interview with Emma Donoghue," *Irish Studies Review,* 8, no. 1 (2000): 73–81;

Alexandra Gill, "Emma's Exploits," *Globe & Mail* (Toronto), 7 October 2000;

Linda Richards, "Emma Donoghue," *January Magazine* (November 2000) <http://www.januarymagazine.com/profiles/donoghue.html>.

References:

Emma: Emma Donoghue <http://www.emmadonoghue.com> [29 May 2002];

Marti Hohmann, "Women's Passions of the Millennium: Emma Donoghue," *Harvard Gay and Lesbian Review,* 6, no. 4 (1999): 14–16;

Antoinette Quinn, "New Noises from the Woodshed: The Novels of Emma Donoghue," in *Contemporary Irish Fiction: Themes, Tropes, Theories,* edited by Liam Harte and Michael Parker (New York: St. Martin's Press, 2000), pp. 145–167.

Helen Dunmore

(12 December 1952 –   )

Ann Hancock
University of the West of England, Bristol

BOOKS: *The Apple Fall* (Newcastle upon Tyne, U.K.: Bloodaxe, 1983);

The Sea Skater (Newcastle upon Tyne, U.K.: Bloodaxe, 1986);

The Raw Garden (Newcastle upon Tyne, U.K.: Bloodaxe, 1988);

Short Days, Long Nights: New & Selected Poems (Newcastle upon Tyne, U.K.: Bloodaxe, 1991);

Going to Egypt (London: Julia MacRae, 1992);

In the Mon£y (London: Julia MacRae, 1993); republished as *In the Money* (London: Red Fox, 2001);

Zennor in Darkness (London: Viking, 1993);

Burning Bright (London: Viking, 1994);

Recovering a Body (Newcastle upon Tyne, U.K.: Bloodaxe, 1994);

Secrets (London: Bodley Head, 1994);

A Spell of Winter (London & New York: Viking, 1995; New York: Atlantic Monthly Press, 2001);

Go Fox! illustrated by Colin Mier (London: Young Corgi, 1996);

Amina's Blanket, illustrated by Judith Lawton (London: Heinemann, 1996);

Talking to the Dead (London & New York: Viking, 1996; Boston: Little, Brown, 1997);

Fatal Error (London: Corgi Yearling, 1996);

Bestiary (Newcastle upon Tyne, U.K.: Bloodaxe, 1997);

Allie's Apples, illustrated by Simone Lia (London: Mammoth, 1997);

Love of Fat Men (London: Viking, 1997);

Clyde's Leopard, illustrated by Gerry Ball (Cambridge: Cambridge University Press, 1998);

Your Blue-Eyed Boy (London: Viking, 1998; Boston: Little, Brown, 1998);

Great-Grandma's Dancing Dress, illustrated by Sam Thompson (Cambridge: Cambridge University Press, 1998);

Brother, Brother, Sister, Sister (London: Scholastic, 1999; New York: Scholastic, 2000);

Allie's Rabbit, illustrated by Lia (London: Mammoth, 1999);

Helen Dunmore (photograph by Jerry Bauer; from the dust jacket for The Siege, *2001)*

With Your Crooked Heart (London: Viking, 1999; New York: Atlantic Monthly Press, 2000);

Bouncing Boy: And Other Poems, engravings by Ros Cuthbert (Winscombe, U.K.: Yellow Fox Press, 1999);

Zillah & Me (London: Scholastic, 2000; New York: Scholastic, 2001);

Ice Cream (London & New York: Viking, 2000);

Allie Away, illustrated by Lia (London: Mammoth, 2000);

Aliens Don't Eat Bacon Sandwiches: Short Stories (London: Mammoth, 2000);

The Ugly Duckling, illustrated by Robin Bell Corfield (London: Scholastic, 2001);

The Siege (London: Viking, 2001; New York: Grove, 2002);

Snollygoster (London: Scholastic, 2001);

The Zillah Rebellion (London: Scholastic, 2001);

Out of the Blue: Poems 1975–2001 (Tarset, U.K.: Bloodaxe, 2001).

OTHER: "An Unlikely Ambition," in *How Poets Work*, edited by Tony Curtis (Bridgend, U.K.: Seren, 1996), pp. 82–87;

"The Red Dress," in *A Second Skin: Women Write about Clothes,* edited by Kirsty Dunseath (London: Women's Press, 1998), pp. 61–64.

Helen Dunmore already had a distinguished reputation as a poet before she began writing novels in the 1990s. Since then she has reached a much larger, and diverse, audience with a series of children's fictions and adult novels, several of which have won major awards. Her distinctive style and thrilling narratives have earned her a secure place as one of the most accomplished contemporary British writers.

Dunmore was born 12 December 1952 in Beverley, Yorkshire, the second of four children. Her father, a manager for an industrial firm, was frequently transferred, and the family often relocated. As a child, Dunmore was fascinated by poetry, and by the time she was seven or eight years old she was already on her way to becoming a poet, learning poems by heart at school and practicing writing sonnets at home on scraps of card. From an early age she aspired to be a writer, at no time considering another career, and was experimenting with poetic form before the age of ten, when her first published poem appeared in a local newspaper. Moreover, her family background may have stimulated her interest in literature. Both parents had benefited from higher education, her mother taking degrees at the universities of Manchester and Oxford, and they fostered intellectual values at home. While Dunmore was the first member of her family to become a professional writer, others were interested in the arts, and a sister became a painter.

Dunmore attended York University to study English and Related Literature. She found it a dynamic place that offered her a broad range of study—from Anglo-Saxon and medieval literature to French literature—and the opportunity to develop her own poetry through presenting a creative-writing paper for formal assessment and credit toward her degree. Works by women writers were largely absent from her course of study, texts by Jane Austen and Virginia Woolf being the exceptions, but Dunmore discovered the writing of Katherine Mansfield and read Russian poetry, in which women writers had a more assured position.

Dunmore's undergraduate studies were followed by a period (from 1973 to 1975) teaching English as a Foreign Language in Finland, an experience that is reflected in many of her short stories. At that time she began seriously to write poetry, and shortly after her return from Finland she began to publish her poems in literary magazines. She faced the excitement and challenge of defining herself as a woman poet in the mid 1970s and combining the writing of her first collections, in the early 1980s, with motherhood. Dunmore married at the age of twenty-seven to Francis, gaining a stepson, Oliver; her son, Patrick, was born in 1981. In her contribution to *How Poets Work* (1996) she states that writing while having "the sense of every faculty being stretched beyond what I'd thought possible" was difficult, but Dunmore has carefully honed her creative process to incorporate the demands of family life. She became adept at using such time as she had available: "When I was writing the poems for my first collections my main working time was in the mornings when my baby usually slept. If he did not I had the playpen beside me and would drop in a different toy as I shot back the carriage return."

During the 1980s Dunmore published three volumes of poetry: *The Apple Fall* (1983), *The Sea Skater* (1986)—which won the Alice Hunt Bartlett Award—and *The Raw Garden* (1988), a Poetry Book Society Choice. Her poems have also appeared in many magazines and anthologies, and she has won several prizes for her work, including second prize in the *Times Literary Supplement*/Cheltenham Literature Festival Poetry competition (1989) and first prize in the Cardiff International Poetry Competition (1990). In addition to writing, Dunmore has engaged in a wide range of literary activities: conducting writing workshops for adults and children; giving readings at literary festivals; accepting writing residencies, for example at the Polytechnic of Wales in 1990; and teaching, both university teaching at various institutions, among them the University of Glamorgan and Bristol University, and school teaching.

Dunmore discovered her versatility in the 1990s. Although she had experimented with prose-writing earlier in her career, she was not satisfied with the results. In the early 1990s, however, Dunmore began to write fiction, not only for adults but also for children and teenagers, while maintaining her production of poetry, publishing three more collections and a book of poetry for children, *Secrets* (1994). Dunmore does not see any of the genres in which she works as dominant but perceives herself as a writer who is able to move readily from one to the other, following where her curiosity leads. Her comments at the presentation of the Orange Prize, quoted in the 16 May 1996 issue of *The Times* (London), typify her view: "I wouldn't define myself as a children's writer, a poet or a novelist because I want to feel that we can push the boundaries of what we are." Children's fiction allowed her to develop her interest in strong, bold narratives and to explore fictional modes, for example science fiction, which would be inappropriate for her realist adult novels. She thinks that writing for children has taught her a great deal, as she explained in a 2 May 1998 interview with Lottie Moggach for *The Times* (London): "Poetry makes you very economical. You realise what every word does. And with children's books too, you have to make sure every sentence works, because your audience can leave you just like that. You learn a lot."

Her first book of children's fiction, *Going to Egypt* (1992), was quickly followed by an adult novel, *Zennor in Darkness* (1993). *Going to Egypt* is a coming-of-age novel for young adults about a young girl, Colette, who dreams of traveling to distant, exotic lands but instead discovers her first love in a British seaside town. An inspiration for *Zennor in Darkness* was Dunmore's curiosity about D. H. Lawrence, a writer whom she has researched and lectured on, and with whom she has occasionally been compared with in regard to her frank writing about sex. In the novel she takes the period in Lawrence's life when he went to the village of Zennor, in Cornwall, initially with Mansfield and John Middleton Murray, with the dream of establishing an artistic community. Mansfield and Murray did not stay, but Lawrence and his wife, Frieda, did, and the novel relates some of their experiences in the summer of 1917, setting them amid the lives of fictional villagers. Dunmore was anxious that the period details be as accurate as possible and worked carefully on establishing the right clothes, food, furnishings, and songs to generate authenticity. The passion for lived detail is a trait she has shown in all her subsequent fictions.

The Treveal family, with its matriarchal grandmother and young men vulnerable to conscription, constitute the core of the story, especially Clare, a girl whose strivings for personal identity and artistic aspirations are nourished by her meeting with Lawrence. The deprivations and pressures of wartime are vividly evoked. Food is scarce and unpalatable, consisting of gray bread, metallic rhubarb jam, and margarine that "tastes like axle-grease." Patriotism is the order of the day, but even Clare's conformist father privately loses faith in the war: "We are like children whose game has gone terribly wrong." Like children, the villagers of Zennor vent their anxieties through hostility aimed at the pacifist strangers, the Lawrences. As war intensifies and more men die, they "need more enemies. Even the Germans are not enough any more." Yet, the girls, Hannah, Clare, and Peggy, still have their fun in the unexpected sunshine, held together by childhood mem-

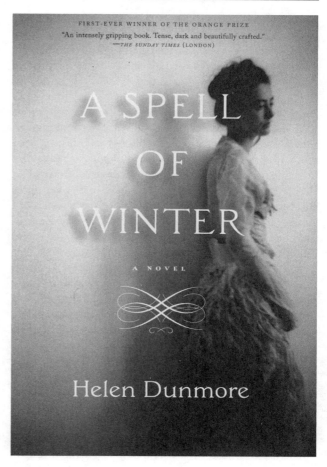

Dust jacket for the 2001 U.S. edition of the 1995 novel that Dunmore has described as a "story about painful losses" (Richland County Public Library)

ories, rare pleasures—a small piece of chocolate and Clare's "body starts to tingle"—and by a strength fostered by adversity. Despite the horrors of fear and loss, Dunmore asserts the resilience of youth and the triumph of life over death.

Along with keeping house for her widowed father, Clare paints, but her achievements are limited by the demands of her father, Francis Coyne, whom she feels obliged to assist by producing botanical illustrations for his book. Lawrence sees the drawings she has done and kept to herself and appreciates her talent. Francis Coyne, from a rather grander background than his Treveal wife, is a repressive influence on his daughter and is starkly juxtaposed with Lawrence, whom Dunmore portrays with sympathy. Francis wants Clare's drawing to be "meticulous," but Lawrence encourages her in what she wants, work that is "flowing and alive." When Clare visits the Lawrences in their isolated cottage, the marital relationship is characterized by warmth, spontaneity, openness, and energy; in contrast, Francis Coyne finds sexual release through furtive visits twice a month to May Foage, whom he pays for her services. Both men are outsiders in the community, Francis separated by class, Lawrence suspect because of his German wife and because, as Clare says, he is "different from anyone else." It is Francis who finally rids the village of the Lawrences by writing an anonymous letter to the authorities that results in their being given official notice to leave. The hypocrisy of wartime society, where patriotism is professed but sons are saved by any means possible from the draft boards, is overt in the treatment of the Lawrences and in the cover-up of the suicide of John William, Clare's shell-shocked cousin. Francis believes that Lawrence has seduced his daughter, but in fact it is John William who has sexually initiated Clare. When John William, who has already been in combat, came home on leave from an officers' training camp for further wartime preparations, their childhood friendship was intensified into passion, but his odd behavior hid memories Clare could not share; shortly after their sexual encounter he returns to the training camp and blows off his head.

By the end of the novel Clare is pregnant with her cousin's child, but she insists on finding her own way rather than being defeated by circumstances. As Judy Cox remarked in *Socialist Review* (July/August 1997), Dunmore's novels "expose how social hierarchies and restrictions invade the most intimate parts of our lives, and how, on a personal level, women resist." Dunmore herself said of the novel in a 9 March 1995 *Guardian* interview with Marianne Brace: "I wanted to look at what happens to a society that's under pressure. It's when people are tested that you see real quality." *Zennor in Darkness* won the £5,000 McKitterick Prize, awarded for a first novel by a writer over forty, and was generally well received. The unsigned reviewer for *The Times* (5 March 1994) found it a "fine first novel," showing a "sure hand" with character. Dunmore's writing was compared with Woolf's in its "poetic incandescence" and use of multiple viewpoints.

In the same year Dunmore published a novel for teenagers, *In the Money* (1993), in which two children, whose father has mysteriously come into money, move to a large country house away from the friends and the life that they know. The loneliness and anxiety of the narrator, Paul, whose suspicions about the source of the money are realized when the police arrive at the end of the novel, is both echoed and relieved by the discovery in the house of Sarah-Louise, a ghostly servant girl whose fear of mistreatment has kept her in the house for a hundred years. Parallels are drawn between the dubious activities of Sarah-Louise's employer and Paul's present-day problems in a well-plotted narrative about the "trap of fear."

With her children moving through their teenage years, Dunmore was surprised at the age of forty-one by a late pregnancy. In February 1994 her daughter, Tess, was born, an event that had an enormous impact on Dunmore's life, though her writing continued unabated. In the afterword to her fifth poetry collection, *Recovering a Body* (1994), Dunmore discusses how her pregnancy concentrated her thoughts on the physical and psychological effects of female aging: "Forty is a good age for thinking about the body." The tangible presence of the body and sensory experience are perhaps the most constant features of Dunmore's writing. Her characters do not exist in the abstract but are constructed through their physical engagement with the world. Precise rendering of tastes, sights, sounds, and, in particular, smells, gives her writing a visceral quality that has made its mark on her readers.

Almost simultaneously with the arrival of her new baby, Dunmore's second novel, *Burning Bright* (1994), was published. As with many of Dunmore's novels, *Burning Bright* takes its title from literary sources, and the allusion here is to William Blake's "The Tyger" (1806). Like Clare in *Zennor in Darkness,* the central characters of both *Burning Bright* and Dunmore's next novel, *A Spell of Winter* (1995), are young motherless girls facing difficult challenges and entering unconventional, potentially shocking, sexual relationships. In *Burning Bright,* Nadine, just sixteen years old and virtually ignored by her parents, who are absorbed in the problems of a younger disabled child, sets up with Kai, a Finnish pimp passing himself off as a property dealer, in a dilapidated London house, and is quickly duped into an encounter with a psychologically scarred cabinet minister, Paul Parrett, whose unusual sexual requirements, such as wanting to be tied up to watch women masturbate, have been difficult to satisfy with Kai's regular girls. Paul is a sympathetic character, offering no threat to Nadine, who faces dangers elsewhere when Kai nearly kills Enid, an old woman who, because of her squatter's rights, lives precariously at the top of the house, knowing that Kai is desperate to be rid of her for financial profit. Enid is well aware of the vicious world Nadine has entered and hopes to protect her from it, succeeding where she failed many years ago to save her lover, Sukey, from being murdered by Caro, the third member of an uneasy lesbian triangle. The novel opens with Enid's sharp memories of the bloody death of Sukey, which establishes an expectation of violence culminating in Kai's attack on Enid:

She's never seen a bull charge, but it must be like this. He runs at her and she's lifted with him, the butt of it thwacking out her breath. The air is tearing around her; everything's so fast, so much stronger than her.

Suddenly he's close, his breath in her face, his eyes glaring at something she wants to say isn't in her, isn't here at all. But she has no breath. He's got her, she's in the air, lifted high by the arms so her feet dabble against the floor. . . . She sees her doorknobs whip past, her heavy door, and then he hurls and she flies but doesn't know where she's going as the air hisses in the white downpour of her falling.

Dunmore makes no judgments on her characters. She said in an interview with Tom Morris for *The Guardian* (19 April 1994), "I'm not taking a moralistic stand in any way." Evil is a presence, and passion can lead to murder, but the darker areas of the human psyche are explored in a way that is intimate without being prurient and that leaves the readers to decide for themselves.

Burning Bright was praised for its seductive narrative and the management of suspense. Penny Perrick, in a 20 February 1994 review in *The Sunday Times* (London), found Nadine "one of the most convincing 16-year-olds in fiction, with that strutting assertiveness that masks insecurity." Dunmore's economical visual prose and rich sense of physicality were also applauded. In a 13 February 1994 review for *The Observer* (London), David Buckley dubbed it a "surprisingly uplifting novel which touches sordidness with grace." The impact of the novel is enhanced by Dunmore's bold use of the present tense for Enid's memories of long ago and the events of present time, unusual in fiction but used to great effect in all her novels, not only giving immediacy to incidents in the here and now but also suggesting the inescapable pull of the past.

Interviewers are often puzzled by the apparent disparity between Dunmore's startling subject matter and her life as a polite, reserved mother of three. In her 1998 conversation with Moggach she recalled the comments of a Finnish interviewer: "Oh, you look so nice and friendly, how can you write about such dark things?" Dunmore's public persona reveals little of her, as her answer testifies: "there are lots of layers to a human being and you're not going to see them all in the shop window, are you?" Dunmore strenuously avoids self-disclosure in discussions of her life and work, preferring to allow the writing, where "readers get the full picture," to speak for itself.

Gritty subject matter and the legacy of the past again dominate in *A Spell of Winter,* published in 1995. Although she is a young woman, Cathy dwells morbidly on her childhood and adolescence, alone in her disintegrating house in a chilly winter: "A spell of winter hangs over it and everyone is gone." Place and time are not specified, but as events unfold it becomes clear that the setting is the same as that of *Zennor in Darkness,* England during World War I. This novel, however, is much more insular than the earlier one, as Dunmore

Dust jacket for the 1997 U.S. edition of Dunmore's 1996 novel, about the troubled relationship of two sisters, one of whom may have murdered their infant brother (Richland County Public Library)

has exchanged the multiple viewpoints of her first two novels for a single, first-person voice. She described it to Brace in their 1995 interview as a "story about painful losses," in which grief and isolation cause Cathy to withdraw further and further into herself.

Cathy recalls her life with her brother, Rob, and her grandfather in a house increasingly given up to decay as the family fortunes decline. Their mother leaves with no explanation, and their father, overtaken by grief, has a breakdown, ending his life in an asylum. Cathy looks to their servant, Kate, for love but is hounded by their old governess, Miss Gallagher, whose possessive love inspires in her only fear and disdain. As the siblings grow up, they become closer, united against the world, until an intense, consuming, incestuous relationship develops, resulting in a secret and messy abortion. The relationship is reminiscent of that of Cathy and Heathcliff in Emily Brontë's *Wuthering Heights* (1847): "we're turning into one another." Finally, everyone Cathy loves has left her, her grandfather and brother through death, and the claustrophobic narrative is dominated by Cathy's inner world and the richly drawn landscape that echoes her feelings. There is, however, a potentially happy ending when Cathy, in the company of a rich, older lover, seeks out her mother in France, seemingly released from the spell of the past.

The novel is not always totally convincing. When Cathy takes up a spade and leads Miss Gallagher deep into the woods, where fear precipitates a fatal heart attack, her cold malice seems excessive, even if the governess does know her secret. It is one thing to feel anger at a woman "breathing her threats like sugar," quite another thing to deliberately engineer her death, as it seems Cathy may have done. As Louisa Kamps, reviewing the U.S. edition for *The New York Times* (25 February 2001), noted, "Cathy displays a weird lack of empathy toward human beings that makes her not very credible, or likable. The hatred she feels for her needy, overly solicitous tutor, Miss Gallagher, seems gratuitous, to say the least." The passionate relationship with Mr. Bullivant, a father figure, is also a surprise when the final chapter brings the story up to date, though it attests to Dunmore's underlying optimism about the capacity of people to recover from profound psychological damage and go on with their lives. Reviewers had mixed feelings about *A Spell of Winter*. Dunmore's considerable literary talents were not in doubt; the craftsmanship and the sheer beauty of the erotic, lyrical writing gave much readerly pleasure. Many found the novel powerful, unsettling, and magical. Some reservations were articulated by critics such as Gill Hornby in a 23 March 1995 review in *The Times* (London) about the possible monotony of a first-person narrative in which everything is pervaded by Cathy's feelings and sensations, and the dangers of writing that is too insistently poetic.

In these first three novels Dunmore marked out her distinctive territory: forbidden or repressed passion, the secrets and deceptions within family life, and the addictive quality of love. Talking to Giles Coren for a 23 February 1995 interview in *The Times* (London), she said: "I am interested in addictive relationships, people who are drawn towards something that will harm them and in the ways they try to break free from it." She investigates dark subjects—betrayal, incest, abortion, murder—in an intensely physical and almost matter-of-fact way. The girls in the early novels find a way out of the darkness, given direction by a substitute parent—Lawrence for Clare, Enid for Nadine, Mr. Bullivant for Cathy—but escaping an oppressive past through their own strength of will. The conclusions of these novels are positive; in Dunmore's later works endings are harsher, with limited possibilities for rescue.

Given that Dunmore was already well known as a poet before she began publishing novels, it is unsur-

prising that her fiction has been viewed as "poetic," with a few commentators suggesting that the poet's voice was paramount in her prose. Dunmore is dismissive of this view, telling Moggach that "I think the word 'poetic' is really horrible. People who write 'poetic' novels aren't poets, they're just throwing their adjectives around." In a 31 May 1997 review of *Bestiary* (1997) and *Love of Fat Men* (1997) in *The Independent* (London) the poet Carol Rumens pointed out that there is a "holistic quality" to Dunmore's imagination and that she does not write "what is disparagingly known as 'poet's prose.'"

In 1996 Dunmore published several works, including a novel for teenagers and a novel for adults. The teenage science-fiction thriller *Fatal Error,* about a virtual-reality theme park ride and villains plotting to sabotage it, was welcomed by the reviewer Maureen Owen of *The Times* (London), who noted in a 3 August 1996 review that in her portrayal of Nicky, the heroine, Dunmore had "done an impressive switch into the mind and dialogue of an adolescent girl." However, the major event of the year for Dunmore was her winning of the first Orange Prize for fiction, for *A Spell of Winter*. An award offered only to women novelists writing in English, the Orange Prize came with a purse of £30,000, which at that time made it the most valuable award in Britain for a single book. The establishment of a women-only literary prize attracted a degree of controversy and publicity that was heightened by disputes between the five female judges over the quality of the 146 entries. When she won against strong competition from Amy Tan and Anne Tyler, Dunmore professed herself unconcerned by the arguments the prize had spawned, quoted in the 16 May 1996 issue of *The Times* (London) as declaring "We have a unique tradition of women writing fiction in England. . . . We are foolish if we don't celebrate something we are so strong in." The prize continued to court debate the following year when A. S. Byatt was quoted in an 18 March 1997 article in *The Independent* (London) as having protested that women should not be "ghettoised" in this way.

In *How Poets Work,* Dunmore expresses regret at the way that literary prizes "pit writer against writer," having throughout her career maintained a strong sense of comradeship with other writers, in particular women, suggesting that they "have a common work which belongs to none of us." However, she felt that the Orange Prize did draw attention to the way in which such awards are given and foregrounded women's writing. Dunmore is supportive of women's writing and critical of its debasement. In her February 1995 interview for *The Times* (London) she stated: "Women are doing all sorts of things with fiction, but there is still this attitude that the big boys Martin Amis, Julian Barnes,

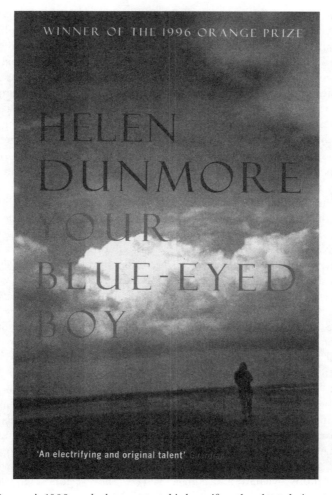

*Dust jacket for Dunmore's 1998 novel, about a respected judge, wife, and mother, who is sent nude photographs
of herself, taken many years earlier by a former lover (Bruccoli Clark Layman Archives)*

Kazuo Ishiguro are the ones doing all the experimenting." In her own writing Dunmore likes to explore different narrative possibilities but, though she is a lifelong feminist, she does not see herself as bound to a particular feminist agenda or as a writer who addresses her work only to women. A consequence of winning the Orange Prize was that Dunmore became much more widely known as a novelist. Sales of *A Spell of Winter* quadrupled after the award was given, and the tag "Orange Prize winner" was often attached to her name in the press.

Despite the celebrity attendant on winning a major literary prize Dunmore continued to maintain a private life in Bristol, where she has lived since 1977. She has always worked at home, though in 1999 she bought a nearby studio apartment to use for writing. Although she has been involved in reviewing for national newspapers for some years and has participated in radio programs, she avoids television appearances and defends her privacy fiercely. On the whole she maintains her distance. In a 26 May 2001 interview for *The Daily Telegraph* (London) she revealed her distaste for publicity: "Celebrity is very frightening, it's not something I've ever found appealing."

Talking to the Dead (1996) is the first in a set of novels that she referred to in an unpublished interview with Ann Hancock on 3 November 2000 as a "triplet," the other two being *Your Blue-Eyed Boy* (1998) and *With Your Crooked Heart* (1999). *Talking to the Dead* continues Dunmore's exploration of intense sibling relationships and dangerous secrets shared by siblings. Told in the first person and almost entirely in the present tense by Nina, the novel begins with the funeral of Nina's older sister, Isabel, who has committed suicide by drowning. The remainder of the novel is retrospective, focusing upon Isabel's last, hot summer, when Nina comes to stay in her house in the country after the difficult birth of Isabel's baby, Antony. The sisters are close but not at all alike. Isabel is beautiful and loves her house and garden but is rather distant from those around her, including Richard, her husband. Nina, a photographer and unmarried, enjoys sex and food, both of which feature prominently in the novel. The birth of Antony brings to the fore the jealousies experienced by the two sisters, both of each other and of their younger brother, Colin, born when Isabel was seven and Nina four, who died when only three months old, supposedly of crib death.

Through conversations between the sisters and through snatches of memory and dream by Nina, key moments of their childhood are re-created. Like Cathy and Rob in *A Spell of Winter,* they receive little attention from their artistic parents, and Isabel becomes an erratic surrogate mother for Nina. Isabel is the "sensible one," Nina the difficult toddler. Both sisters are clearly annoyed by the birth of a brother who will use up what little maternal affection exists in the house. Nina remembers: "I didn't want it. She was my mother, mine and Isabel's." But Nina also has a memory of Isabel smothering the baby and of Isabel's illness after the death of Colin. The truth of her recollection is put in doubt when Isabel, all love and concern, tells Nina that it was she who killed Colin: "You were only four. . . . You were jealous, of course you were." The complexities of the sisters' relationship and the mystery surrounding Colin's death are played out within a claustrophobic household that consists of Richard, Isabel's husband; Edward, her gay friend; and Susan, a local girl acting as nanny to Antony. Richard and Nina begin a torrid affair, everyone worries about Isabel's physical and mental health, and no one speaks of the things that matter: "This house is stiff with things which can't be said." Nina seems to see food as the road to freedom. When Isabel suggests a celebration feast, for which each of them will present a course, Nina responds with enthusiasm and prepares for gourmet cooking; lingering descriptions of food preparation and consumption are prominent in the novel. However, the feast does not take place and the food and the flowers are thrown away, because on the day of the feast Isabel walks into the sea.

As a whodunit thriller the novel is intriguing. Nina is not a reliable narrator, and the reader is never sure which competing view of events is the right one. Sometimes Isabel is the victim, scarred by the past and drifting into madness as motherhood recalls her lost brother. Yet, she is also manipulative, unlikable, and lacking in feeling. Similarly, Nina, while seeming at a disadvantage in comparison to her lovely sister with the beautiful house, the husband, and the baby, is also callous, having sex with Richard as the police search for Isabel's body, seeming almost to claim Antony as her

own at the end. The plot is managed with great control, reaching a chilling yet ambiguous conclusion when, on the final page, Nina remembers a moment when it seems that she asked Isabel to get rid of Colin for her.

Talking to the Dead was favorably reviewed; there was agreement that Dunmore had now mastered the novel form, producing a compelling, riveting narrative that retained her sparkling, visual prose without sacrificing narrative development, what Caroline Gascoigne called in a 7 July 1996 review for *The Sunday Times* (London) "a memorable and assured work." The novel was seen as erotic and disturbing, the writing concentrated and sharp. Joan Smith, in a 10 August 1996 review in *The Financial Times* (London), called the novel "outstanding for its near-perfect control and deceptively limpid prose." In 2001 it was featured on the BBC Radio 4 program *Book Club,* a show in which a group of readers discusses a novel with its author.

In 1997 *Talking to the Dead* became the first of Dunmore's novels to be published in the United States. Publication in the United States enhanced her standing, with reviewers echoing their British counterparts. Reviewing the novel for *The Washington Post Book World* (10 August 1997), Carolyn Banks remarked that "Helen Dunmore . . . takes a tale that could drive a thriller and weaves her linguistic spell around it. The result is brilliant and terrifying, an unbeatable combination. . . . Without sacrificing any literary merit, *Talking to the Dead* provides a textbook example of structuring for suspense." Carol Kino, reviewing the book for *The New York Times* (1 June 1997), noted that "In the hands of another writer, these elements—murder, adultery, repressed memory, familial love—might well have become a fevered, one-note drama," but that what makes Dunmore's novel "so gripping and complex is her ability to convey many different layers of experience at once," with "language dense with imagery and metaphor, as compacted as poetry."

Published in 1997, *Love of Fat Men,* her first collection of short stories, includes nineteen stories, none longer than a dozen pages, many set in a cold Scandinavia. They represent the work of many years: some of them were written before Dunmore began to write novels and were previously published in magazines. About half of the stories concern fragments from the life of a Finnish girl, Ulli, depicted in "Family Meeting" as a child seeking attention from her family and elsewhere as a young woman, self-contained, elusive. Dunmore reveals Ulli's life through hints and silences, and the last Ulli story, "Girls on Ice," written in a postmodern mode, ends bleakly and without resolution. The remaining stories are generally snapshots of relationships. Reviewers such as Susanna Rustin in a 9 August 1997 review in *The Financial Times* (London), found quite different qualities in these stories. Those who valued a strong plot found the spareness of story and characterization somewhat disappointing and felt that the poet in Dunmore was more to the fore than the novelist. Others saw great merit in the collection, finding the stories polished, profound, and perceptive in their examination of the mundane. While some emphasized the darkness of these "icy" tales, others were struck by the warmth and humor.

Also published in 1997 was a volume of poems, *Bestiary*. Influenced no doubt by Dunmore's success as a novelist, reviewers found narrative qualities in her poetry, as previously they had seen the poet at work in her fiction. In the 20 July 1997 issue of *The Independent on Sunday* (London) the reviewer, Sarah Maguire, described the best poems as having "the deft punch of a powerful short story," while Ruth Padel, in *The Independent on Sunday* (London) on 10 October 1999, discussed "The Surgeon Husband," from this collection, as turning "story fragments into little lyrical epiphanies."

Published in 1998, *Your Blue-Eyed Boy* follows *Talking to the Dead* in some respects. The novel begins, "There are things you should know about blackmail," and an element of the plot concerns embarrassing youthful nude photographs sent by a former lover to the protagonist, a respectable judge with a husband and two children. It is, however, by no means confined by the thriller genre, but is rather an examination, as in the earlier novel, of past hurts and buried sadness, and the need to carry on. The first-person narrator, Simone, shares with Nina a kind of hardness that enables survival, though perhaps at a cost: "My face is soft, but you have to be hard to get where I am." Again the use of the present tense gives a tactile immediacy to the narrative, but the landscape of *Your Blue-Eyed Boy* is bleaker and harsher than in Dunmore's previous work. Passion is absent, and gorgeous descriptions of food do not appear in this novel of a family that is dogged by poverty: greasy margarine rather than butter, "a cake of soapy cheddar" and cheap bread rather than the "shiny purple aubergines" fresh from the market that Simone once bought. The crisis in this novel has been precipitated by the near bankruptcy of Simone's architect husband, Donald. The family has escaped absolute ruin by Simone's taking on a job, district judge, for which she feels not fully prepared, and which has taken them out of London to a damp, cold, and remote house by the sea. This cheerless existence does not bring them financial security as Simone's improved earnings disappear in debt repayment. Already the situation is tense; Donald is depressed and angry, the children unsettled and confused. Most of the difficulties between husband and wife remain unspoken, but

Dust jacket for the 2000 U.S. edition of Dunmore's 1999 novel, the third in a series of thrillers Dunmore has described as a "triplet" (Richland County Public Library)

Dunmore conveys with skill the anxieties and hidden resentments between them.

Into an already fragile situation come the photographs, sent by Michael, the Vietnam veteran who was Simone's lover in the (fictional) New England resort town of Annassett when she was eighteen. Uncertain of what Michael may want from her, Simone dreads the post and the telephone but starts to recapture that time, and the present-day narrative is interspersed by graphic scenes of Simone, Michael, and Calvin, the friend who took the photographs. When Michael appears in the flesh, older, fatter, and damaged by years of hospitalization—the legacy of his Vietnam experience—the past presses more forcibly on Simone: "Memory spreads over my senses like a film of oil, brilliant and treacherous." She recalls the stories Michael told of the horrors of war, alongside memories of her childhood and the misery of her parents' deaths. Of her father's early death she thinks, "I let the blow sink into me silently, and I'm still reeling from it."

While her personal dilemmas accumulate, her work as a judge continues: child custody disputes, domestic violence, other people's tragedies.

Walking with Michael on the marshland that borders her home, Simone finds out that Michael has come to take her back with him, plane tickets already in his pocket. They have sex out on the beach, and she feels at ease with him, physically if in no other way. On the walk back along the sea wall, high above the beach, however, Michael falls and is killed instantly. Simone, perhaps used to coping, is strangely detached from the scene but realizes there is no one but she to take responsibility for the situation. A grueling chapter describes in great detail how Simone drags Michael's body into a small boat and takes it out to sea, because she does not want any evidence of her whereabouts exposed, particularly to her husband. As he has always worked in the boating industry, boats have been Michael's life, and it seems an appropriate end.

Afterward, life returns to normal, but Simone's guilt and anxiety affect her confidence, and she feels haunted by Michael's ghost. It is uncertain how her life will go on. *Your Blue-Eyed Boy* was mentioned frequently as a contender for the 1998 Booker Prize, and there was little critical dissent from the assessment in the 3 May 1998 review in *The Sunday Times* (London): a "powerful read, but one that is not at all comfortable." Neil Spencer, writing for *The Observer* (London), found room for criticism, remarking in a 3 May 1998 review on the "improbability of its basic scenario" and the "sketchbook" characterization of Donald. In *The New York Times Book Review* (6 September 1998) Mark Lindquist tempered a generally favorable review with the remark that Dunmore "writes gracefully and has an excellent sense of place, but overloads her story with peripheral detail. By the end, the reader may be skimming pages, but not necessarily to find out what happens next."

The last novel in the "triplet" of thrillers, *With Your Crooked Heart,* appeared in 1999. In this novel Dunmore continues her complex psychological study of family relationships, particularly between siblings. Johnnie, the beautiful but hopeless younger brother, is a source of perpetual anxiety to Paul, who has become a successful businessman, specializing in the redevelopment of contaminated land. Paul loves Johnnie like a son and has indeed taken over the rearing of him from their grief-stricken mother, depressed after the death of her husband. However, Johnnie persists in exploring the seamier side of business, becoming involved with drugs and in schemes for moneymaking that never quite come off. As he tells his former sister-in-law, Louise, toward the end of the novel, Paul has suffocated him with attention: "I can't move without

him knowing. I can't even breathe. Everything I've done, he knows." Included in what Paul knows is the fact that Johnnie fathered Louise's child, Anna, though this is never discussed and only acknowledged by Louise right at the end. Johnnie himself never quite lives up to what the reader is told of him—his beauty, his charm—and the reader has to take on trust the love he inspires in Paul, Louise, Anna, and in most of those who meet him.

Many chapters of the novel tell of the significant events in the past: Louise's decline into an overweight, irresponsible alcoholic. Just as Paul took Johnnie away from their mother, so he takes Anna from Louise, installing her in a house in Yorkshire with a young and beautiful, but vacuous, stepmother, Sonia. What motivates the characters is a key question, but one that is also hard to answer. As with Dunmore's previous two novels, the characters are all curiously unlovable and enigmatic. Paul clearly wants to escape his working-class past through worldly success, but his obsession with Johnnie is less comprehensible. Louise professes to love both brothers and her daughter but spends most of her time in a drunken lethargy. Johnnie appears to be on a course of self-destruction, careless of his own safety or of the feelings of others. For Johnnie "not to be able to trust yourself is the biggest thrill of all." The three of them are bound irrevocably together, Louise saying on several occasions that she is married to Paul until death despite the fact that they are legally divorced.

The most positive character is Anna, ten years old and bravely supporting herself when no one else seems able to. After being ostracized as an outsider in Yorkshire, she is saved from loneliness by finding both a kitten, which she nurtures as determinedly as Paul does his waif-and-stray brother, and David, a local boy she befriends. Unlike her family, Anna has a sane hold on the world as is demonstrated when Dunmore juxtaposes two journeys in the closing chapters. Louise and Johnnie, having run away to Brighton to escape the hoods who are pursuing Johnnie because he owes them money, are on a ferry to Denmark, red-eyed with drink and fearful of discovery. Anna and David are on a train from Leeds to London to see Anna's mother, a journey carefully planned and successfully accomplished. When they find Louise is not at home, they set up camp in the garden to wait for her return, still tending the growing kitten. Meanwhile, on the ship Johnnie is having his face slashed and his legs broken, a punishment for his own misdeeds but also a payback to Paul from a crook he had crossed in the past. When Louise intervenes, the maiming turns into a double murder and she is thrown overboard, and it seems that the obsessive love of Paul and Louise for Johnnie—the two continually having indulged and bailed out Johnnie and thus contributed

PRAISE FOR *THE SIEGE*:

"Deeply moving . . . A world-class novel."
—ANTONY BEEVOR, *THE TIMES* (LONDON)

"Dunmore writes beautifully of privation and desire.
She writes about food as though it were art, and about
art as though it were hunger. She writes with piercing
tenderness about the way in which nurturing can be
both a burden and a joy."
—JANE SHILLING,
THE SUNDAY TELEGRAPH (LONDON)

"Deeply moving, unsentimental, restrained and powerful, [*The Siege*] is a stunningly well-conceived portrayal of a city under siege, and a stark, honest
account of the ravages of war and its effect on the
lives of ordinary people."
—GREG EDEN,
SCOTLAND ON SUNDAY

"This remarkable, affecting and extremely accomplished novel represents a pinnacle in Dunmore's fiction, and in the year's fiction too. There are few more
interesting stories than this; and few writers who
could have told it better."
—RACHEL CUSK, *THE TELEGRAPH* (LONDON)

"[*The Siege*] is a moving and powerful novel in which
Dunmore employs all her celebrated descriptive and
narrative skills while bravely extending her range."
—MICHAEL ARDITTI, *THE DAILY MAIL* (LONDON)

ISBN 0-8021-1700-7

Dust jacket for the 2002 U.S. edition of Dunmore's 2001 novel, set during the siege of Leningrad in
World War II (Richland County Public Library)

to his inadequacies as an adult–has merely brought about Johnnie's and Louise's deaths.

The novel ends as it began, in Louise's London garden. The opening is a characteristic Dunmore scene, a sensual and visual description of a heavily pregnant Louise sunbathing naked on the warm stone of the terrace. At the end of the book Paul comes in search of Anna and finds her asleep in her sleeping bag beside David, already moving on from Paul to "somewhere he cannot go."

As a narrative, *With Your Crooked Heart* builds up tension and a sense of inescapable fate: that the adult characters are all in some way doomed is early established. The presence of the past, which Dunmore emphasized in both *Talking to the Dead* and *Your Blue-Eyed Boy,* is here preeminent, and the fragmentary quality of the storytelling is more marked. No constant voice holds the narrative together as it moves from first person to third and, uncommon in fiction, to second, a device that can be confusing for the reader.

Carole Morin, in a 4 September 1999 review in *The Daily Telegraph* (London), was disappointed by the novel, saying that Dunmore's "life-affirming sensibili-ties appear to be struggling with the chic aesthetic of self-destructiveness that is imposed on the narrative. In the process, what might have been a satisfying midlife-crisis novel becomes a failed attempt at passion-ate prose." Reviewing the paperback edition of the novel for the 1 March 2000 issue of the same newspa-per, Marc Davidson demurred slightly, calling the book a "powerful but frustrating novel" but one with "pas-sages of eloquence and poignancy." In her review for *The Guardian* (4 September 1999), however, Katy Emck called *With Your Crooked Heart* "a peculiarly direct and gripping read . . . a novel that stays close to the visceral experiences of life."

Dunmore's second collection of stories, *Ice Cream,* was published in 2000. The stories are adventurous and varied in both form and subject matter. In some, Dunmore foregrounds narrative, moving beyond her usual realist mode, as in her experimental writing for children. "Leonardo, Michelangelo and SuperStork" is a science-fiction story about cloning, in which the idea of keeping up with the neighbors takes a sinister turn.

Next-door neighbors Susie and Pat are both pregnant; in their gardens they compare conditions in the summer heat and bemoan the price of a child these days. Natural conception is illegal, and all babies are produced to order, selected from catalogues, and Pat is curious to know whether Susie can top her superior Michelangelo product. Susie claims to have used Leonardo, the most expensive service at more than £100,000, but is reluctant to show Pat her brochure. It transpires that Susie has committed a crime, conceiving a child naturally with the help of a medical student who has secretly removed her birth-control device (called a "Rubicon") to allow conception to take place. When Pat's husband is about to inform on Susie and her husband, Reuben, the couple flee, with Susie giving birth Madonna-like in a pigsty.

An element of social comment is also present in the title story, "Ice Cream," in which a beautiful, famous young woman, Clara, celebrates her twenty-fourth birthday in a restaurant with her sleek, well-dressed friends. Clara "never eats ice cream," and as the craving takes hold of her, her personal trainer, Elise, tries to divert her, reminding her of the days when the teenage Clara was "wide and sleek as a whale." The friends suggest avoidance strategies—spitting it out, vomiting it up, taking pills to kill the appetite—while the waiter looks on stiff and frowning. After Clara gives a slight nod to the waiter, he brings Clara a platter of the finest ice cream. Clara takes a mouthful and swallows. The sensuous pleasures of physical existence win over the enforcement of repressive dictates.

Several of the stories deal with painful material. In "Lisette" a Jewish doctor who devotes his life in Paris to treating tuberculosis in the poor is taken to Auschwitz with his wife and delicate young daughter. This story ends the collection, and the final sentence is perhaps a reflection on many of the stories included: "I felt I had to tell it, even if you're tired of it, even if you've heard it all before." In "The Clear and Rolling Water" Dunmore deals with the despair of a failing sheep farmer in a remote area who puts all his hopes into an unsuccessful scheme building holiday cottages on his property.

Three of the stories offer further snapshots from the life of Ulli, the Finnish girl featured in *Love of Fat Men*. "The Kiwi-Fruit Arbour" follows up her adolescent relationship with Jorma from "Spring Wedding," a story in *Love of Fat Men*. Here she is pregnant, away from home as is often the case in her tales, staying with a French family and wondering if they are aware of her condition. She ponders on what Jorma is doing and whether he will understand what is happening to her. "The Icon Room" and "Living Out" both show Ulli living alone and having slightly bizarre encounters with men she meets by chance.

In her 30 March 2000 review for *The Times* (London) Amanda Craig observed that the title of *Ice Cream* encapsulates the nature of Dunmore's work. On the one hand, there is the soothing sensuality of the writing that has been consistently admired, designating her the "celebrant of the senses." On the other hand, chilliness is pervasive too, a dispassionate seriousness that renders the world disturbing. Readers and reviewers have been entranced by the brilliance of her thriller plots, but underlying the stories, as Craig noted, is "a deep disquiet about the way our society works." Dunmore's protagonists usually survive, but they never quite know when the ground will give way beneath them.

Dunmore's seventh novel, *The Siege* (2001), marked another change of direction, away from the thriller to historical fiction. Having had for many years a strong interest in Russia and its literature—she cited Leo Tolstoy as her favorite novelist in a 19 September 1999 interview with *The Sunday Times* (London)—she developed the idea of giving an inner view, through the intimate experiences of a family struggling for survival, of the siege of Leningrad in World War II. Like her first novel, *Zennor in Darkness*, it was carefully researched and became for the author a major preoccupation during, and for some time after, the writing. The novel centers around Anna Levin, who has become responsible for both her four-year-old brother, Kolya, and her ineffectual father, Mikhail, a writer whose work is considered unpublishable under Joseph Stalin's regime. Although the setting and subject matter are much different from her previous work, she continues in *The Siege* to demonstrate her skills in storytelling, in rendering the sensuousness of everyday life, and in observing human behavior in extreme circumstances. She told interviewer Robert McCrum of *The Guardian* (10 June 2001) that she found the "rapid and catastrophic decline" that Leningrad experienced during the siege "chilling and fascinating." In an interview with Sybil Steinberg for *Publishers Weekly* (21 January 2002) Dunmore indicated that her theme in the novel was more than the survival of a single individual or family; referring to the 11 September 2001 terrorist attack on the World Trade Center, she said, "I think we have an expectation that civil society is quite fragile, but often it turns out that society is capable of a huge effort in order to preserve the whole. What history shows is that people often do survive, and their resilience was quite miraculous."

Rachel Cusk, in a 2 June 2001 review for *The Daily Telegraph* (London), called the novel "remarkable, affecting and extremely accomplished" and said that it "represents a pinnacle in Dunmore's fiction, and in the year's fiction too. There are few more interesting stories than this; and few writers who could have told it better." Reviewing the novel for *The New York Times* (31 March 2002), Janice P. Nimura observed that the "best historical fiction delivers emotional truth through the lives of imaginary but ordinary people, making it possible to feel the texture of events that have been smoothed out by the generalizations of conventional histories" and declared that in *The Siege* "the specific becomes epic as five people huddle in one freezing room and Dunmore describes what is happening to them in language that is elegantly, starkly beautiful." The novel was short-listed for both the Whitbread Novel Award and the Orange Prize in 2002.

In October 2001 Bloodaxe Books published *Out of the Blue: Poems 1975–2001,* a collection that comprises twenty-nine new poems, selections from her 1994 collection for children, *Secrets,* and those poems from Dunmore's earlier Bloodaxe collections that she thought worthy to stay in print. In addition to her still-growing reputation as a novelist and short-story writer, Helen Dunmore's reputation as a poet remains high, and she continues to attend poetry festivals as well as give readings from her novels. In November 1996 she was a member of a panel of three, including Andrew Motion (who later became the Poet Laureate), judging entries for the T. S. Eliot Prize for poetry, and she was chairwoman of the panel that awarded the T. S. Eliot Prize to the Canadian poet Anne Carson in January 2002, making Carson the first woman recipient of that award. Evidence of her literary distinction can also be drawn from her election in 1998 as a Fellow of the Royal Society of Literature. She has become internationally known, with her work translated into many languages, including Japanese. Her novels have sold particularly well in France and Scandinavia, while her children's writing is popular in Germany.

Interviews:

Tom Morris, "Life's a Pimp," *Guardian,* 19 April 1994, pp. G2, G9;

Giles Coren, "Behind the Last Taboos," *Times* (London), 23 February 1995, p. 5;

Marianne Brace, "Gruelling Passions," *Guardian,* 9 March 1995, pp. G2, G14;

Anne Taylor, "The Difference a Day Made," *Guardian,* 12 September 1996, pp. G2, G25;

Lottie Moggach, "Well Versed," *Times* (London), 2 May 1998, Metro section, p. 14;

"Bibliophile," *Sunday Times* (London), 19 September 1999, Books section, p. 15;

Serena Allott, "Moments of Truth," *Daily Telegraph* (London), 26 May 2001, p. A7;

Robert McCrum, "The Siege is a Novel for Now," *Observer* (London), 10 June 2001, Review section, p. 16;

Sybil Steinberg, "History and Human Frailty: Helen Dunmore," *Publishers Weekly,* 249 (21 January 2002): 59.

Reference:

Pamela Norris, *The Story of Eve* (London: Picador, 1998), pp. 328–329.

Anne Enright

(11 October 1962 –   )

Caitriona Moloney
Bradley University

BOOKS: *The Portable Virgin* (London: Secker & Warburg, 1991);

The Wig My Father Wore (London: Cape, 1995; New York: Grove, 2001);

Finbar's Hotel, by Enright, Dermot Bolger, Roddy Doyle, Hugo Hamilton, Jennifer Johnston, Joseph O'Connor, and Colm Tóibín, edited by Bolger (London: Picador / Dublin: New Island, 1997; San Diego: Harcourt Brace, 1999);

What Are You Like? (London: Cape, 2000; New York: Atlantic Monthly Press, 2000);

The Pleasure of Eliza Lynch (London: Cape, 2002).

PLAY PRODUCTION: *Thank God, Fasting,* Dublin Youth Theatre, 1994.

PRODUCED SCRIPT: "Revenge," television, *Two Lives,* RTÉ, 1994.

OTHER: "Seascape," in *Irish Love Stories,* edited by David Marcus (London: Sceptre, 1994), pp. 125–130;

"Felix," in *Class Work: The Best of Contemporary Short Fiction,* edited by Malcolm Bradbury (London: Sceptre, 1995), pp. 141–151;

"My Generation," in *My Generation: Rock 'N' Roll Remembered, An Imperfect History,* edited by Anthony Farrell, Vivienne Guinness, and Julian Lloyd (Dublin: Lilliput, 1996), pp. 80–81.

SELECTED PERIODICAL PUBLICATIONS–
UNCOLLECTED: "Diary," *London Review of Books,* 22 (5 October 2000), pp. 34–35; republished as "My Milk," *Harper's* (14 May 2001): 26;

"Pale Hands I Loved, Beside the Shalimar," *Paris Review,* 42 (Winter 2000–2001): 269–279;

"In the Bed Department," *New Yorker,* 77 (May 2001): 92–95.

Anne Enright, one of the most promising fiction writers to appear in Ireland in the 1990s, has received considerable critical attention and literary accolades for her short stories and novels. She also writes essays and columns for such periodicals as the *London Review of Books, The Irish Times, Harper's,* and *The New Yorker.* Most critics agree that her work is postmodern and deconstructionist while utilizing a cinematic style suggestive of both the celluloid quality and pace of contemporary life. The term "magic realism" is often employed to describe her work. In a 9 March 2000 interview with Caitriona Moloney, Enright explained her focus: "I am also fascinated by the problem of Goodness. The characters in my novels are damaged, but though they are interested in badness (or evil), they are more interested in/bewildered by goodness." Reviewers consider Enright's forte to be comedy, often invoking the Irish comedic tradition of Jonathan Swift, Oscar Wilde, James Joyce, and Samuel Beckett in descriptions of her work. Enright's comedy challenges traditional belief systems and epistemologies; she conflates the genres of journalism, history, and fiction to make problematic the official records and shared memories of the past.

Enright was born in Dublin, Ireland, on 11 October 1962 to Donal and Cora Enright, who were both civil servants. She grew up in the suburbs of Dublin, went to St. Louis High School in Rathmines, and attended Pearson College in Canada on a scholarship from 1979 to 1981. From 1981 to 1985 she completed her degree in modern English and philosophy at Trinity College, Dublin. At that time she was acting with Dublin theater groups Rough Magic Theatre and The Abbey and writing for Irish television and theater. Both her play *Thank God, Fasting,* written for Dublin Youth Theatre, and her script "Revenge," written for the Radio Telefis Éireann (RTÉ; Irish Radio Television) series *Two Lives,* were produced in 1994. After graduating from Trinity College in Dublin, Enright received a scholarship to the University of East Anglia and completed an M.A. in creative writing with Malcolm Bradbury and Angela Carter. Her first short story was published in 1989 in the Faber & Faber, Ltd. anthology series *First Fictions,* and

Anne Enright (courtesy of the author)

netted Enright an agent and an advance on a short-story collection. When she returned to Dublin, she got a job as a television producer and director for RTÉ on a show called *Nighthawks,* which she described in the interview with Moloney as "a fairly subversive programme . . . a very busy mixture of chat and sketches . . . where anything could happen, sketches and pieces of art or literature."

While she worked on *Nighthawks* at RTÉ, Enright wrote the short stories that were later published as *The Portable Virgin* in 1991. When *The Portable Virgin* was published, Enright left television to make a living as a full-time writer. She married actor and director Martin Murphy in 1993.

The title story of *The Portable Virgin* juxtaposes virginity and portability, two concepts whose conjunction suggests radical theoretical constructs but also refers on a literal level to the little plastic statuettes of the Virgin Mary that people place on the dashboards of their cars, whose little blue crown is a screw-off top and whose body is filled with holy water. Enright's style makes the literal self-parodic and irreverent, while remaining naively factual—a technique that recalls how Joyce uses Leopold Bloom's naive perspectives to satirize Dublin society in his novel *Ulysses*

(1922). Enright's style in *The Portable Virgin* fragments and reassembles elements of history and journalism to question the past. The story "Historical Letters" addresses an absent lover who was present in Dublin in 1914, New Orleans in 1926, Moscow in 1937, the Spanish Civil War, and Berlin in 1989. Enright deliberately invokes Joyce's Stephen Dedalus—protagonist of *A Portrait of the Artist as a Young Man* (1916) and a central character in *Ulysses*—when writing of a character in Dublin who was "walking, pretentiously enough, on the beach"; she also recalls Joyce's "nightmare" of history: "History is just a scum on reality as far as you are concerned. You scrape it away."

Enright's story "The Brat" is stylistically Joycean; in it her portrait of the grandiosity of the alcoholic rivals Joyce's Farrington, a character in the short story "Counterparts," included in his *Dubliners* (1914). Her portrait of a self-described "bon vivant" captures both the illusions of the drinker and the clinical observation of the narrator:

> He is a man much given to speaking aloud when company is absent, and to silence when the nicer of social obligations might urge him into speech. Those contributions he does make are as counterpoint to the

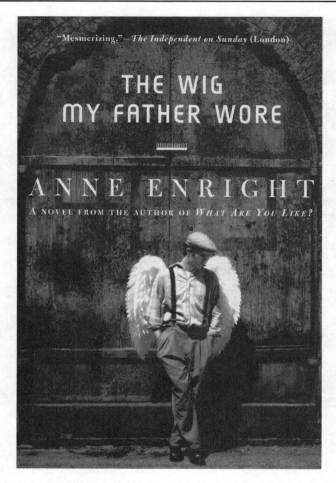

Cover for the 2001 U.S. edition of Enright's 1995 novel, in which a woman is impregnated by an angel (Richland County Public Library)

sounds of liquid consumption only, the sweetest of which is the sound of a pint drawing creamily at the bar, a music only those born with the gift, or those who spend a minimum of three thousand hours acquiring the gift, can hear.

Readers of *The Portable Virgin* note Enright's gift for comedy and the postmodern quality of her imagery. Ann Owens Weekes calls Enright's style in *The Portable Virgin* "unconventional," describing her narrative technique as "precisely focused shots into a character's consciousness" and the characters as "intelligent, keen and ironic observers." In her review of Enright's novel *What Are You Like?* (2000) in the *London Review of Books* (5 March 2000) Penelope Fitzgerald characterized the earlier stories as being "concerned with the crucial moment when human nature cannot stand any more." Fitzgerald described Enright's writing as "eloquent" and "dazzlingly funny," noting that "for Enright, the recognisable dimensions of time, speech

and thought (though not of place) are fluid and interchangeable, while metaphors often become the things they stand for." *The Portable Virgin* won the Rooney Prize for Irish Literature in 1991.

Published in 1995, Enright's first novel, *The Wig My Father Wore,* was written between 1993 and 1995, after Enright stopped working in television. The novel uses cinematic techniques of fast cutting and rewinding to create and interweave multiple plots and perspectives into the narrative. All of Enright's plots have a suggestive duality. In one plot the protagonist Grace/Grainne works on an hour-long television game show called *Love Quiz* that is slated either to be expanded to two hours or to be cancelled. In another an angel moves in with Grace, redecorates her house, turns up on *The Love Quiz,* and impregnates Grace; in the third, Grace's father has a stroke and is intermittently demented and remarkably astute. The wig itself, like Enright's other realistic symbols, represents the fragility of individual constructions of reality. During her father's illness

Grace's mother manages to launder his wig without ever speaking directly about it, demonstrating the care her family takes to preserve her father's fragile beliefs about his life.

Grace's relationship with her angelic lover caught the attention of many reviewers, who categorized the novel as magic realism. The angel plot, a deliberate reproduction of the Annunciation, results in Stephen stripping Grace's wallpaper and uncovering bits of old newspapers, which are then woven into the novel. Their lovemaking is quite bizarre, resulting in a metamorphosis of Grace's body parts and then pregnancy. In her 19 March 1995 review for *The Independent* (London) Christina Patterson wrote that "the celestial and physical worlds come together even more dramatically in the love scenes between Stephen and Grace, beautifully and erotically described." Grace's erotic and fulfilling affair with the angel Stephen contrasts with her more jarring relationships with "real" people, her family and work colleagues. For example, Grace is not sure if her boss, a woman she calls the Love Wagon, is her best friend and mentor or "a bitch who is out to get her."

The strength of the novel lies in its stream-of-consciousness humor and psychological portrayals of the unconscious. The novel satirizes just about every aspect of Irish life: newspaper headlines proclaim "The Archbishop says no to AIDS test," and there is a recurring "Ceasefire in Belfast." Enright's humor is terse, dark, and complex. Grace's coproducers of *The Love Quiz* are portrayed as neurotic, driven, and occasionally vicious, characters whose personal lives are all wrecks. When the show is threatened, the crew goes out to lunch, queuing up for food "like our own lives cooked up, cooled down, and reheated": lunch includes "paranoid peas . . . chicanery chips . . . Sole on the Dole." At one point Grace decides to take a day off and call her friends, realizes that she has none, and comes into work. In a commentary on the possible consequence of a television-addicted society Enright's television crew's lives have been structured by television.

In *The Wig My Father Wore* identity is perilously permeable, and boundaries are maintained only temporarily against a constant metamorphosis that resembles how one story can blend into another for a channel surfer or a postmodern novelist. Reviewers of *The Wig My Father Wore* remarked on the cinematic or televisual nature of the novel. In *The Guardian* (4 April 1995) Elizabeth You wrote that "the reader adjusts the horizontal, adjusts the vertical, normal service is restored and the pattern emerges"; in *The Irish Times* (18 March 1995) Katie Donovan noted, "the every day is seen with the revelation afforded by an off kilter angle, with a probing and unpredictable Flannery O'Connoresque zoom

Enright in Venice, 1999 (photograph by Martin Murphy; courtesy of Anne Enright)

lens"; and Tom Gilling, in *The New York Times* (18 November 2001), remarked on Enright's playing "wry games with the idioms of pop culture," noting that the "effect of these pastiches is like the crackle of an unprogrammed television signal, background noise that lends an elemental urgency to the voice of Grace herself." *The Wig My Father Wore* has been translated into French, German, Dutch, and Russian.

Enright contributed to the group novel *Finbar's Hotel* (1997), a project organized by Dermot Bolger, who invited six fellow Irish writers each to devise a chapter about one night in a decrepit Dublin hotel scheduled for demolition. In addition to Enright and Bolger, the novelists Roddy Doyle, Hugo Hamilton, Jennifer Johnston, Joseph O'Connor, and Colm Tóibín all contributed unsigned chapters, which form a loosely linked narrative. In her review in *The New York Times* (2 May 1999) Katharine Weber called the book "quite funny," remarking that "the very occasional jolts that come when one chapter ends and the next begins are more than offset by the sustained excellence of the writing."

Enright's second solo novel, *What Are You Like?* (published in 2000), examines themes of exile, loss, and the multiple identities attached to "Irishness" in

Dust jacket for the U.S. edition of the 2000 novel that prompted reviewer James Wood to call Enright "a spry surrealist who challenges the world with extraordinary, lancing sentences" (Richland County Public Library)

the Irish diaspora in the United States and England. Issues of motherhood and Catholicism play a role in this novel also: the protagonists, twins, are separated at birth because their mother dies in childbirth, victim to the Catholic policy of saving the child's life over the mother's. One twin is sent to England by the clandestine adoption apparatus of the Catholic Church. Maria, the twin raised by her father and stepmother in Dublin, immigrates to New York as an adult, and experiences Irish American culture, while Rose, the adopted twin, grows up in England as an Irish transplant. The experiences of both twins demonstrate the problems of immigrant identity within a global culture. Through her discovery of the life stories of her mother and sister, Maria (the narrator) enacts a theme of recovering women's stories to fill in the silences, slippages, and gaps to which women's history is so often subjected.

Although some complained that Enright's style can be artificial and alienating, most reviewers praised *What Are You Like?* for thematic complexity and stylistic achievement. In *The Irish Times* (4 March 2000) John Kenny criticized a "surrealism that appears too consciously designed to shock," and in his review in *The Guardian* (11 March 2000) James Wood noted that at times Enright's ambitious prose style risks overreaching, sounding "unnaturally sealed off from the ordinary" or making the characters seem like "neurasthenic clowns." Wood, however, went on to write, "Anne Enright is a very original writer—a spry surrealist who challenges the world with extraordinary, lancing sentences. . . . overwhelmingly, redeemingly common—are moments and whole passages when Enright captures something subterranean with a strange flick of her marvelous insight." In a 16 April 2000 review in *The Observer* (London) Justine Ettler commented, "With stylistic echoes of early Joyce, in particular *Dubliners,* Enright's writing dazzles the reader with its control." Reviewers have generally concluded that Enright's prose, while challenging, more than compensates readers for their efforts.

Enright herself considers *What Are You Like?* to be an investigation of the "dead mother" icon in Irish culture. The novel begins with Anna literally dying as she gives birth and ends with her blaming her survivors: "I am not dead. I am in hell. And I blame the feet that walk over me." The novel investigates the process through which women are erased from public life in Ireland while simultaneously being "iconized" as sacrificing mothers, virgins, and so on. In the Moloney interview Enright reflected:

> Men can't write the iconized mother figure in Irish literature; they are either dead or left out. In *What Are You Like?* I split that big iconic mother presence, which for the small child is so large and unfeasible. The difficulty with the mother daughter relationship is establishing difference, the daughter is trying to separate, to become someone else. Anna is the omnipresent dead mother in Irish fiction—never explained, never made manifest—and the stepmother, Evelyn, a perfectly likeable person rears Maria, the child that is left, but Maria never forgives her for something.

The uncovering of the dead mother's and the lost sister's stories represents a process of giving voice to the women historically silenced in and by Irish literature. *What Are You Like?* received the Encore Prize of the Society of Authors, was short-listed for the Whitbread Award and the Kerry Ingredients Listowel Writer's Week Prize.

Enright and Murphy's first child, Rachel Charis Murphy, was born on 29 June 2000. Enright moved the following spring from central Dublin to CoWicklow, where, as she told Moloney, she is "really happy, writing non-stop and thinking mostly about the future."

Judging from Enright's publication of the essay "Diary" in the *London Review of Books* (5 October 2000)—republished as "My Milk" in *Harper's* (14 May 2001)—and the short story "In the Bed Department" in *The New Yorker* (May 2001), Enright is following up on her interest in the mother-daughter theme, possibly because she is now a mother herself. She also published the short story "Pale Hands I Loved, Beside the Shalimar" in *The Paris Review* (Winter 2000–2001). Enright's return to the short story will please some of her critics who judge *The Portable Virgin* to be her best work. However, Anne Enright's novels contribute more significantly to the tradition of Irish fiction, extending and developing the modernist techniques and themes of Joyce, while bringing refreshingly new constructions of Irishness to literature.

Interviews:

Ruth Padel, "Anne Enright: Twin Tracks and Double Visions," *Independent* (London), 26 February 2000, p. 9;

Caitriona Moloney, "Anne Enright," in *Conversations with Contemporary Irish Women Writers,* edited by Moloney and Helen Thompson (Syracuse, N.Y.: Syracuse University Press, 2003).

References:

Maryanne Felter, "Anne Enright," in *Dictionary of Irish Literature,* revised and enlarged edition, edited by Robert Hogan, volume 1 (Westport, Conn. & London: Greenwood Press, 1996), pp. 410–411;

Ann Owens Weekes, "Anne Enright," in *Unveiling Treasures: The Attic Guide to the Published Works of Irish Women Literary Writers: Drama, Fiction, Poetry* (Dublin: Attic Press, 1993), pp. 120–121.

Giles Foden

(11 January 1967 –   )

Annette Rubery
University of Warwick

BOOKS: *The Last King of Scotland* (London: Faber & Faber, 1998; New York: Knopf, 1998);
Ladysmith (London: Faber & Faber, 1999; New York: Knopf, 2000);
Zanzibar (London: Faber & Faber, 2002).

OTHER: *The Guardian Century,* edited by Foden, foreword by Alan Rusbridger (London: Fourth Estate, 1999);
"Weekenders," in *The Weekenders: Travels in the Heart of Africa* (London: Ebury, 2001), pp. 269–297.

SELECTED PERIODICAL PUBLICATIONS–
UNCOLLECTED: "Aftermath of Genocide," *Evening Standard* (London), 22 March 1999, p. 47;
"Bringing It All Back Home," *Guardian,* 4 September 1999, Saturday Review section, pp. 1–2;
"The First Camps," *Guardian,* 9 October 1999, p. 24;
"Blood and Ink," *Guardian,* 6 November 1999, Saturday Review section, p. 9;
"Tony Blair is reported to have swotted up on Afghanistan from a bestselling book. So what does it say?" *Guardian,* 10 October 2001, G2 section, p.9;
"When Authors Take Sides," *Guardian,* 27 April 2002, Saturday Review section, p. 8.

Giles Foden's novels are characterized by his meticulous craftsmanship and careful research. Foden is an editor and writer for the nationally circulated British newspaper *The Guardian,* and his approach to fiction shares the toughness, pragmatism, and unsentimentality of newspaper journalism. Much of Foden's writing has been about Africa, a subject that continues to inspire him. His first novel achieved widespread acclaim, earning praise for its intelligence and verisimilitude. An outsider's view of Africa, the relationship between beauty and terror, warfare, and the plight of black Africans are major themes in both his fiction and nonfiction works.

Giles William Thomas Foden was born in Warwickshire on 11 January 1967. After the death of his grandfather, which resulted in the sale of the family farm, he moved, aged five, with his family to Malawi. His father, Jonathan Foden, became an agricultural adviser in the Malawian Ministry of Agriculture, and his mother, Mary Foden, eventually became a teacher. At thirteen Giles Foden returned to England, where he was educated at Malvern College (1980–1985) and Fitzwilliam College, Cambridge (1986–1989), where he studied English. Meanwhile, his parents remained in Africa, moving to Tanzania, Nigeria, Ethiopia, and Uganda. Foden spent his school holidays in Africa and still visits regularly. After graduating from Cambridge, he was awarded a £7,000 scholarship to travel and write for one year; he chose to visit East Africa, planning to write a novel about a fictitious African dictator. In practice, though, the image of the real-life Idi Amin increasingly occupied Foden's mind, convincing him to steer the book toward a representation of Amin's rule in 1970s Uganda. On his return to England he postponed work on the novel while he started his first job as a reporter for *Media Week* magazine. In 1991 he became an assistant editor at *TLS: The Times Literary Supplement,* before moving to his current position as deputy literary editor for *The Guardian.* He has worked as a novelist while living in Uganda, Islington (North London), and Bantry Bay, Ireland.

Foden's debut novel, *The Last King of Scotland* (1998), was applauded as a triumph. In addition to the 1998 Whitbread First Novel Award, *The Last King of Scotland* won a Somerset Maugham Award, a Betty Trask Award, and the Winifred Holtby Memorial Prize. Drawing closely on historical events, the book paints a portrait of the charismatic Amin, whose regime of casual violence began in 1971 with a coup that overthrew President Milton Obote and ended in 1979 with Amin fleeing Uganda to take refuge in Saudi Arabia. The title is a reference to one of the dictator's many bizarre obsessions. Having completed his military training in Stirling, Amin developed a fixation on the Scots, whom he saw as fellow victims of English imperialism. In the novel Amin writes a letter to the queen in which he observes: "Unless the Scots achieve their independence peacefully . . . they will take up arms and fight the English . . . Many of the Scottish people already con-

Giles Foden (© Poppypix; courtesy of the author)

sider me the Last King of the Scots." Significantly, Amin's rule and the events leading to his deposition are described through the fictional journals of a Scottish doctor, Nicholas Garrigan, who has taken up an assignment at a remote Ugandan hospital. A freak traffic accident involving Amin's sports car and a cow eventually brings him into the dictator's orbit, and, a few months later, Garrigan finds himself recalled from his rural hospital and named personal physician to the president.

The opening chapters, which document Garrigan's arrival in Uganda and the collapse of Obote's rule, create an almost palpable sense of foreboding. Foden hints at the corruption to come by the use of disturbing imagery. On his first trip around the medical compound at Mbarara, for example, Garrigan narrowly avoids stepping into the hospital cesspit, which is concealed under a crust of brown earth. The pit, he is told, is almost unnoticeable during the dry season, but with the rains it turns into a "Tidal wave of shit." Similarly, on his first night in the compound Garrigan has a nightmare about a Godzilla-like encounter between a cricket and a bullfrog, which seems to forecast the predatory nature of his relationship with Amin. Even the map of Africa, he notices, resembles a gun in a holster. These and other examples of threatening imagery are

enhanced by Foden's unfailing eye for the absurd. Early on in the novel Garrigan's encounter with a white South African, Freddy Swanepoel, is made both strange and humorous by Foden's description of the man's physical characteristics: "His body, his manner, everything about him was chunky and muscular, even his face: it was as if, above the sprouting black hair, he had biceps for cheeks." The unease that Garrigan feels at being a stranger in a strange land is constantly heightened by this inventive use of metaphor. Watching the townspeople smash melons on which are painted Obote's face, Garrigan reflects that the comic and the sinister can sometimes be one and the same thing: an observation that could also apply to Foden's method in writing the novel.

Although *The Last King of Scotland* largely concerns itself with historical events, the portrait of Amin is filtered through Garrigan's fictional journals, which are themselves supported by tape-recorded interviews with Amin—known as "the dictatorphone tapes"—that the doctor has supposedly sent back to Scotland for safekeeping. The first-person narrative operates on several levels, with Garrigan's account of the dictator interrupted by tantalizing glimpses into the doctor's own past. Garrigan clearly wants to be considered as a detached observer and trusted guide, something that is evidenced by his love of order, the methodical nature of his job, and his solid upbringing. The only son of a Scots Presbyterian minister, Garrigan was raised to observe a rigid moral code: "I had learned that feelings . . . must be strictly controlled," he remarks. The reader discovers that after qualifying in Edinburgh, Garrigan went to Africa to improve his prospects and to escape the oppressive influence of his family. Now Garrigan has resolved to set down a genuine eyewitness account and a fair judgment on the blood, misery, and foolishness that characterized Amin's rule. This sentiment seems closely related to Foden's epigraph, a quotation from Alexander Trocchi's *Cain's Book* (1960): "Loose ends, things unrelated, shifts, nightmare journeys, cities arrived at and left, meetings, desertions, betrayals, all manner of unions, adulteries, triumphs, defeats . . . these are the facts."

Yet, as the story unfolds, the reader sees Garrigan steadily losing his grip on the facts. Far from being a dispassionate scientist gathering impartial data, Garrigan is sensitive and artistic. His observations on life are filled with fanciful and descriptive detail (even his medical colleague notices that he is "not clinical enough about things"). Garrigan has a tendency to obfuscate and, when recalling particularly shocking and barbaric acts, even leaves gaps in his narrative, claiming that he cannot remember or that his journal is indecipherable. This blindness and lack of inner strength is a key part of Garrigan's character and helps to explain why, even when Amin's crimes are made known to him, he fails to take positive action. Throughout the novel Garrigan's responses vacillate between guilt and passive disengagement. Foden resists making him a highly fictionalized, epic figure, implying that Garrigan is in fact just an ordinary man, trapped in an extraordinary and, indeed, nightmarish situation. It is in some ways a reverse of the traditional concern of fiction, namely the heroism of the ordinary individual. Garrigan's weakness and his lack of insight are made plain through his brief affair with an Israeli doctor, Sarah Zach, who leaves suddenly with a group of engineers and later (to his great surprise) reveals herself to be an intelligence operative. Undoubtedly, Garrigan suffers from a detachment common to expatriate whites living in Africa. In a 28 August 1999 interview with Jayne Dowle of *The Times* (London), Foden (who had visited Rwanda the year before the Hutus massacred more than eighty thousand Tutsis) observed: "As a white expatriate in Africa you are always a little disengaged though. I went to Rwanda the year before everything blew up there. It seemed placid and pleasant and even sophisticated compared to Uganda where we lived at the time."

Despite his attempts to marshal the facts and to present a truthful chronicle of the times, Garrigan is forced to admit that it is a struggle to deal with himself squarely.

Indeed, the violence that Garrigan witnesses proves powerfully seductive, leaving a question mark over his real role in Amin's program of terror. The initial link between Garrigan's nationality and Amin's kinship with the Scots is emphasized by the doctor's growing panic that he is not only the dictator's accomplice but also his double. These fears culminate when Garrigan is called to attend Amin, whom he finds lying on a massage table at the Imperial Hotel. Noticing that he could easily reach Amin's gun, Garrigan thinks how satisfying it would be to pull the trigger, sending "his hoggish brains over the wall." At this moment he realizes, with horror, that he has "crossed the line" because he has become enough like Amin to want to kill for pleasure. From here onward the novel changes pace as Garrigan partly overcomes his fascination with the dictator and plans to flee Uganda. Garrigan attempts to escape under cover of the advancing Tanzanian army, who are launching an aggressive attack on Uganda. At this point in the narrative Foden demonstrates his talent for evoking scenes of warfare, combining military detail with medically accurate descriptions of the wounded. Finally, Julius Nyerere's troops seize Kampala, and Amin slips away to retirement in Saudi Arabia, leaving Garrigan to face the press in London.

While *The Last King of Scotland* is undoubtedly an examination of Garrigan's internal struggle between good and evil, the novel is also a realistic portrait of an historical figure. Amin's charisma, his cunning, his childishness, and occasional flashes of insight are all drawn with great attention to detail. The surreal aspects of Amin's regime are demonstrated through various theatrical set pieces, such as the monstrous banquet of bee larvae, bush crickets, and flying ants that he presents to his staff, or his unexpected appearance, rising out of the center of a swimming pool in a custom-built hydraulic cubicle. In a 1998 interview with the Internet magazine *Bold Type* Foden said that he used a combination of fact, memory, and imagination in re-creating the character of Amin; his main problem was keeping "the research at bay," as "I kept discovering these amazing things about Amin which I wanted to put in the book." The "strangest things in the book are all factually true," he told the interviewer—yet, Amin's world, and the image that he presented to the people, was so bizarre that Amin was, in a sense, like a living work of fiction, and "long before I got to him [Amin] was 'already a novel,' so to speak." Foden's main difficulties in writing the book were that events were not properly documented and many of the participants were no longer alive. The Saudi government also refused his request to interview Amin, though Foden had come to know him, he felt, through his extensive research. Interestingly, when asked about Amin's motives, Foden observed that Amin was not driven by politics but rather by "appetite"; it was, he remarked, simply a case of wanting an excess of everything: "more guns, more money, more women." He also felt that Amin's "lack of a father figure led him to worship his original colonial officers, and when Britain effectively abandoned him, he struck out like a sulky child."

Foden did not limit his careful and exact groundwork to the character of Amin. The inspiration for Nicholas Garrigan came partly from Bob Astles, a former sergeant in the British Royal Engineers known as "Amin's White Rat," seen by many as the dictator's right-hand man. Astles spent ten years in a Kampala jail after Amin was overthrown; when Foden met and interviewed "Major Bob," then living in the London suburb of Wimbledon, he was struck by the way in which he had "come to believe his own version of events." Foden told the *Bold Type* interviewer that even though Astles had publicly disassociated himself from Amin, he still "seems to live in the same fantasy world as Amin." Despite Astles's obvious influence on the character of Nicholas Garrigan, Foden does make the distinction that, unlike Major Bob, Garrigan is an unresisting, passive figure. His weak temperament is no greater than that of the average person when faced with things too disturbing to acknowledge. Indeed, while gathering material for the novel, Foden interviewed four doctors who were working in Uganda, all of whom remained in the country, trying to live normal lives.

At the time of Amin's fall those who had been closely involved with the dictator were attacked in the British press (indeed, at the close of the novel Garrigan faces such an assault). Although Foden acknowledged that this vilification of Amin and his cronies was in some cases deserved, he commented to the *Bold Type* interviewer that "a lot of the time it seemed like a way of drumming up racist sentiment or (and these things to some degree went hand in hand) assuaging colonial guilt by using Amin as a way of pointing out how wonderful things had been under the auspices of Empire." Foden's handling of Garrigan's humiliating return to Britain is also intended to provoke questions about the relationship between "sensationalism" and the "writing of fiction"; as he remarked in the *Bold Type* interview, "Where does the chain of responsibility and voyeurism that wraps itself around Garrigan end?" How much has Foden or, for that matter, "you, the reader" been part of the "glamourisation of Amin's deeds?" In this way Foden powerfully demonstrates the difficulty, in postimperial Africa, of knowing which is the "right side." Garrigan's brief foray into London at the close of the novel stands in stark contrast to the breathtaking scenery of Uganda. Both places are threatening: Garrigan learns that a bomb had gone off in a dustbin by the Baker Street tube station just before his arrival, shutting off part of the underground. Despite the fact that this is, technically, his home soil, Garrigan feels dislocated and confused. London is both menacing and drab, whereas Africa seems compelling, exciting, and mercurial.

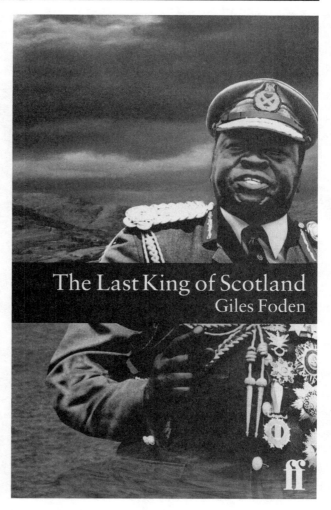

Dust jacket for Foden's 1998 novel, about Ugandan dictator Idi Amin, who considered the Scots fellow victims of English imperialism (Bruccoli Clark Layman Archives)

As a fiction based closely on actual events, *The Last King of Scotland* has been compared to Truman Capote's *In Cold Blood* (1966), Norman Mailer's *The Armies of the Night* (1968), and Beryl Bainbridge's *Every Man for Himself* (1996). Foden's portrayal of Amin has been likened in particular to Polish writer Ryszard Kapuścinski's evocation of Haile Selassie in his *Cesarz* (1978; translated as *The Emperor: Downfall of an Autocrat,* 1983). At the time of publication critical responses to the novel were on the whole enthusiastic and encouraging, with only a few exceptions. In an 8 March 1998 review in *The Sunday Times* (London), critic Hugo Barnacle compared Foden's "remarkable" battle scenes with those of Leo Tolstoy and paid tribute to Foden's beautifully realized African background. However, Russell Celyn Jones wrote in *The Times* (London) on 12 March 1998 that Foden's topographical descriptions, beautiful though they are, occasionally go on for too long, distracting attention from the heart of the story. In a 9 March 1988 review Anthony Daniels of *The Evening Standard* (London) considered Foden's portrait of Amin "superlatively well done" and added that the weaknesses of the book could have been avoided by stronger editing: "It seems to cleave too closely and obviously to the author's personal experience to count quite as fiction." In an 8 March 1998 review in *The Sunday Telegraph* (London) Edward Smith commented on Foden's failure to evoke psychological sympathy for the doctor but, again, felt that this was countered by his believable rendering of the charismatic Amin. On the publication of the paperback edition by Faber and Faber in 1999, Trevor Lewis wrote in a 14 March 1999 notice in *The Sunday Times* (London) that Foden had re-created a "fragment of modern history" where "fact and imagination are artfully intertwined."

This adroit merging of fact and fiction is also a key characteristic of Foden's next novel, *Ladysmith* (1999). Turning his attention to the dying days of the nineteenth century, Foden imaginatively re-creates events in the small South African town of Ladysmith, which, along with Mafeking and Kimberley, was surrounded and besieged by Boer troops in the autumn of 1899. The inhabitants spent a total of 118 days under fire, waiting for General Sir Redvers Buller's relief forces. With the arrival of the British troops came two years of guerrilla fighting, during which thousands of Boer civilians were interned in concentration camps. Peace was signed at Vereeniging in May 1902. The British were victorious and, having annexed the Transvaal and the Orange Free State as colonies, promised the Boers eventual self-government. Black Africans were excluded from this political transaction, an act that led to conflict in that area throughout much of the twentieth century.

In contrast to *The Last King of Scotland,* in which the action is seen exclusively from the perspective of Nicholas Garrigan, in *Ladysmith* Foden introduces a host of characters whose limited observations cross and complement one another, gradually building up a coherent picture of historical events. These core characters pin the narrative together, while a cast of minor individuals lends the book its sweeping perspective. To add to the sense of realism, Foden gives walk-on parts to recognizable historical figures: Winston Churchill appears as a cub reporter, and Mohandas Gandhi is pictured offering medical aid to the British. At the center of the novel is Bella Kiernan, the daughter of an Irish hotelier whose romantic adventures stand in sharp contrast to the harrowing conditions in the beleaguered town. Bella's father, Leo Kiernan, and sister, Jane, also have major parts to play, as do Muhle Maseku, the head of a poor Zulu family; the British troopers Tom and Perry Barnes; real-life British war correspondents

George W. Steevens and Henry W. Nevinson; and Antonio Torres, a barber from Portuguese East Africa.

The novel was inspired by letters written by Arthur Foden, the author's great-grandfather, a British trooper at Ladysmith, letters the sixteen-year-old Giles Foden had stumbled across while looking for fishing tackle in his aunt's attic. Reading the letters, Foden realized how ordinary people became caught up in the tide of historical events. These letters, which his great-grandfather, a farmer's son who enlisted as a trooper in the Imperial Yeomanry, sent home throughout the war, became the inspiration for *Ladysmith* and, in particular, the character of Tom Barnes. "In many ways Ladysmith was a crucible for the century which came afterwards," Foden remarked to Dowle in their 1999 interview, "All these things seemed to start there–like modern warfare and telecommunications in battle. By 1899 all the great lights of what we understand as Victorianism had gone out. The Victorians knew they were on the verge of a great change and the Boer War to some degree signalled that." One of the means by which Foden emphasizes technical innovation is to introduce a nameless character, known simply as the Biographer, who crops up from time to time, recording incidents through his camera lens. He is aboard the *Dunottar Castle* with Churchill and Buller when it first docks in South Africa; the latter he captures on still plates: "the heavy moustache, the Crombie with a buttonhole of violets, the felt hat, the stolid figure and big, kindly face." Like Garrigan, the Biographer is an observer, working in close proximity to important historical figures. However, Foden also highlights the vital importance of the Biographer's role in the great historical scheme; he is something of an unsung hero, risking his life to record the horrific events of "modern" warfare. As the story progresses the reader also picks up subtle hints about his character. The Biographer's shyness clearly is bound up with his trade; the huge elm-wood box of his motion-picture camera is like armor plating, behind which he is protected and completely anonymous. A glance at the author's acknowledgments reveals that Foden used, among other things, William Kennedy Laurie Dickson's *The Biograph in Battle: Its Story in the South African War* (1901) as source material for *Ladysmith*.

Other important sources include the works of three war correspondents. Foden consulted the memoirs of Nevinson–one of the greatest journalists of the age–along with his *Ladysmith: The Diary of a Siege* (1900) and *Essays in Freedom* (1909). He also referred to Donald MacDonald's *How We Kept The Flag Flying: The Story of the Siege of Ladysmith* (1900) and Steevens's posthumously published *From Capetown to Ladysmith: An Unfinished Record of the South African War* (1900). Nevinson, MacDonald, and Steevens (who died of fever before Buller's arrival) appear as characters in Foden's story. The action opens with them surveying the town of Ladysmith through spyglasses from a vantage point on the hillside. Like the Biographer, they are observers who make use of new technology to record their impressions of war. Their dispatches are sent with the help of heliograph and flag men, who relay them in Morse code and semaphore to troops at other stations. With the siege of Ladysmith, however, the Boer troops block the channels of communication, forcing Nevinson to resort to using the Zulu boy Wellington as a runner. Partly because of the lack of information about the relief troops, and partly as a means of distraction from the perils of Ladysmith, the correspondents pass the time by writing a satirical news sheet called *The Ladysmith Lyre,* the masthead of which proclaims as its content "news which you can absolutely rely on as false." In this way Foden points up the burgeoning issue of propaganda in warfare, as well as suggesting interesting links between journalism and the writing of fiction. In an article for *The Guardian,* "Bringing It All Back Home" (4 September 1999), Foden explores in greater detail the idea that the Boer War was the first mass-media war. He also shows how such men as Nevinson and Steevens paved the way for a new breed of journalist: the war correspondent.

Perhaps the most original angle that Foden takes in writing about the Boer War is that of the involvement of Irish nationalists. The novel opens with a first-person narrative by Leo Kiernan, who recalls his days in Dublin and his violent involvement with the Republican Brotherhood led by John MacBride. The story shifts to Ladysmith, where, years later, Kiernan is running a hotel with the help of his grown-up daughters, Bella and Jane. Although Bella provides much of the romantic focus of Foden's novel, this issue of Irish Nationalism resurfaces at various points in the story. The reader learns, for example, that the Boers, like the British, have their own Irish regiment whose second-in-command is the aggrieved MacBride. Bella, though largely ignorant of her father's involvement in the Nationalist cause, is nevertheless swept up with events surrounding it. However, Bella's main role is to point up the changing attitudes of women at the end of the nineteenth century. This change is demonstrated through her relationships with two men: the British trooper, Barnes, and the Portuguese barber, Torres. Foden explores Bella's confusion over the dual issues of sex and marriage and shows how her eventual rebellion against her father reflects the emergence of the New Woman and, eventually, the feminist movement.

With so much material to handle, Foden makes repeated use of narrative techniques that provide structure and focus. Much of the impact of the story is created by the use of dramatic set pieces, such as the ludicrous Home versus Colonial Born cricket match (conducted under shellfire) or the powerful description of the Battle of Spion Kop. Another device used by Foden is the linking of chapters either by word association or matching imagery. Just as one chapter ends with the Biographer sipping coffee with Churchill on the *Dunottar Castle,* for example, so the next opens with the Zulu Maseku noticing the blossoms on the coffee bushes. As in *The Last King of Scotland,* Foden chooses to describe the more ghastly moments in a dispassionate style, thus creating a greater impact on the reader. For instance, the gruesome death of Perry Barnes causes the Biographer to become hysterical, yet the narrative voice matter-of-factly informs the reader that he was riding his horse "when a shell struck off his head." This technique is employed to great effect in the battle scenes themselves, which recall the fast-paced style of John Buchan (as a child Foden avidly read Buchan's works, along with those of Buchan's fellow adventure writer H. Rider Haggard). Foden reflects on the difficulties of depicting military conflict in a review of two anthologies, *The Penguin Book of War: Great Military Writings* (1999), edited by John Keegan, and *The Vintage Book of War Stories* (1999), edited by Sebastian Faulks and Jörg Hensgen. In this review, published as "Blood and Ink" in *The Guardian* (6 November 1999), Foden observes that "Writing about war is notoriously difficult, which is perhaps why only a few novelists have written great battle scenes. . . . Writing conflict is also technically tricky because battle often involves multiple points of view—wide panoramas as well as individual escapades. The direction of the writing is always being pulled here and there as the hapless author tries to convey the full picture."

For all Foden's skill in depicting the battlefields, however, the theme of *Ladysmith* is not solely human conflict but how history is written. This theme is underlined at the close of the novel when Foden draws his characters together and anticipates the events that followed the Boer War. Thus, Churchill is represented by two documents: the script of a speech he gave in 1931 and a telegraph dated 1944 and addressed to the viceroy of India. Similarly, the Biographer is represented by a newsreel script beginning with the words: "British Movie-tone News: It Speaks For Itself!" along with a narrative fragment from 1945 in which he muses on the defeat of the Nazis. Meanwhile, the end of Bella's story is told years later by her sister, Jane, and Nevinson leaves the reader with an eyewitness account of the landing of the troops at Gallipoli in 1915. In this way Foden offers the reader a clear sense of the ways in which the Boer War shaped modern life. However, Foden's account of the war itself is, necessarily, a biased one. His characters tend to support the theory expounded in Thomas Pakenham's seminal history, *The Boer War* (1979)—namely, that the British governor in Cape Town wanted ownership of the Boers' gold and diamond mines. Interestingly, Foden outlines

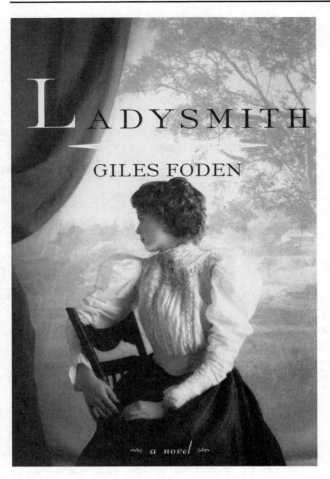

Dust jacket for the 2000 U.S. edition of Foden's 1999 novel, set during the 1899 Boer siege of a strategically important South African town (Richland County Public Library)

his personal responses to the British part in the Boer War in his *Guardian* article "The first camps" (9 October 1999). Referring to it as "Britain's Vietnam," Foden outlines the appalling conditions in the concentration camps where, under the orders of General Horatio Herbert Kitchener, the British interned approximately two hundred thousand refugees. An estimated twenty thousand Afrikaners and twelve thousand black Africans died in these camps. "What Britain did in South Africa," writes Foden, "was not some common-or-garden omission, but institutional barbarism, setting the tone for events in that country for years to come."

Despite its historical breadth and impressive battle scenes, *Ladysmith* had a much less enthusiastic critical reception than *The Last King of Scotland* did. Much of the criticism of the novel was directed toward what reviewers saw as Foden's problematic handling of the eyewitness accounts and historical documentation of the period. In a 29 August 1999 review in *The Sunday Times* (London) Bar-

nacle complained that Foden's material had "got the better of him," with the opening chapters reading like research notes passed off as dialogue. Barnacle also objected to the "half-digested portions" of Pakenham's *The Boer War,* which he claims are clearly recognizable, as are excerpts from the memoirs of Dickson, Nevinson, and Churchill. Jones, too, found little to recommend in this siege story, remarking in his 9 September 1999 review for *The Times* (London) that the book seems "shackled to historiography," which, Jones concludes, makes the characters seem "wooden" and the prose "curiously inert." However, the novelist Penelope Fitzgerald remarked in the *Evening Standard* (23 August 1999) that *Ladysmith* was "The best siege novel" she had encountered since reading J. G. Farrell's *The Siege of Krishnapur* (1973), adding that Foden's writing "excels in quietly unexpected terms." Fitzgerald praised Foden's bold move from the central narrative perspective of *The Last King of Scotland* into the more demanding territory of historical overview, adding that the close of the novel—with its references to the impact of the Boer War on the subsequent decades of the twentieth century—enables Foden to bring the narrative up to date and "to remind us that history has no stopping places." Similarly, in a 4 September 1999 review for *The Daily Telegraph* (London) W. F. Deedes complimented Foden on his handling of dialogue and observed that "The strength of this very good novel lies in its credibility."

Giles Foden continues to divide his time between working as a novelist and writing for *The Guardian*. He edited *The Guardian Century* (1999), an anthology of journalism, feature stories, illustrations, and photographs drawn from the pages of that newspaper published during the twentieth century. According to Dable, *The Last King of Scotland* and *Ladysmith* have been optioned as motion pictures by Channel Four and Working Title Films respectively. Foden's work combines the excitement of the old-fashioned adventure story and the complexity of the historical epic. Foden's third novel, *Zanzibar* (2002), is set on the African island of the title and centers on a marine biologist, Nick Karolides, who gets swept up in the 1998 terrorist plot to bomb the U.S. embassies in East Africa. Despite his passion for travel Foden has no interest in becoming a foreign correspondent. Neither is he worried about being typecast as an author who can write only about Africa. As he told Dowle, "I'm glad people think I can write anything really! You can only write what you write."

Interviews:

"An Interview with Giles Foden," *Bold Type,* 2, no. 9 (1998) <http://www.randomhouse.com/boldtype/1298/foden/interview.html>;

Jayne Dowle, "Not that Boer-ing," *Times* (London), 28 August 1999, p. 16.

Christopher Fowler
(26 March 1953 -   )

Philip Lockwood Simpson
Brevard Community College, Palm Bay Campus

BOOKS: *How to Impersonate Famous People,* illustrated by Stuart Buckley (London: Quartet, 1984; New York: Crown, 1985);

The Ultimate Party Book: The Illustrated Guide to Social Intercourse, illustrated by Buckley (London: Unwin, 1985);

City Jitters (London: Sphere, 1986; New York: Dell, 1988; revised edition, with a new introduction by Fowler, London: Warner, 1992);

More City Jitters (New York: Dell, 1988);

Roofworld (London: Legend, 1988; abridged edition, New York: Ballantine, 1988);

The Bureau of Lost Souls (London: Century, 1989; New York: Ballantine, 1991);

Rune (London: Century, 1990; New York: Ballantine, 1991);

Red Bride (London: Little, Brown, 1992; New York: Roc, 1993);

Sharper Knives (London: Warner, 1992);

Darkest Day (London: Little, Brown, 1993);

Spanky (London: Warner, 1994);

Psychoville (London: Warner, 1995);

Flesh Wounds, illustrated by Richard Parker (London: Warner, 1995);

Disturbia (London: Warner, 1997);

Menz Insana, illustrated by John Bolton (New York: DC Comics, 1997);

Personal Demons (London: Serpent's Tail, 1998);

Soho Black (London: Warner, 1998);

Uncut: Twenty-one Short Stories (London: Warner, 1999);

Calabash (London: Warner, 2000);

The Devil in Me (London: Serpent's Tail, 2001).

Christopher Fowler is one of the most versatile and prolific of twenty-first-century British novelists. He also writes advertising campaigns for motion pictures, television and movie scripts, graphic novels, music, stage shows, reviews, and magazine articles and columns. In addition to his creative work, Fowler is the director of a motion-picture production company, The Creative Partnership. Although Fowler has yet to achieve a wide audience in the United States, he is well known, commercially successful, and critically respected not only in his native country but around the world. His fiction has been translated into Dutch, Japanese, Romanian, Russian, and Spanish.

Fowler's work has changed over the years into fiction that defies easy genre categorization, though publishers tend most often to classify it as "horror." However, Fowler himself prefers the term "urban unease." In terms of writing style and thematic content, various critics have favorably compared Fowler to the distinguished likes of Ray Bradbury, H. Rider Haggard, H. P. Lovecraft, George Orwell, Edgar Allan Poe, and Bram Stoker. As literary influences or inspirations, Fowler has cited J. G. Ballard, Peter Barnes, Alan Bennett, Bradbury, John Collier, Charles Dickens, E. M. Forster, Joe Haldeman, James Hawes, Charlie Higson, Henry James, B. S. Johnson, Magnus Mills, Joyce Carol Oates, Christopher Priest, Bruce Robinson, Alan Sillitoe, Keith Waterhouse, Evelyn Waugh (Fowler's personal favorite), Tennessee Williams, and Virginia Woolf.

Fowler was born in London on 26 March 1953 to William Edward Fowler, a glassblower, and Lilian Kathleen Upton Fowler, a legal secretary. He has a younger brother, Steven. Fowler's mature interest in darker themes—horror—can be traced in part back to his youth, when Fowler was an unabashed devotee of written science fiction, fantasy, and horror. At age fifteen he read the fantasy fiction of J. R. R. Tolkien and then "graduated" to the equally fantastic but more psychological works of Ballard. In a 2000 interview with David Mathew for the website *SF Site,* Fowler called Ballard "a genius" who "doesn't explore science fiction as much as he does the psyche." Fowler's work suggests something of those early influences—his cityscapes are richly imagined borderlands of Tolkienesque wonder and darkness, while his characters often manifest a pathological urban angst amid grimly fantastic settings reminiscent of Ballard's most disturbing creations in works such as *Crash* (1973), *Concrete Island* (1974), and *High Rise* (1975).

Christopher Fowler (from the dust jacket for the U.S. edition of Rune, *1991)*

Fowler began his professional education by attending the London guild school of Colfes, where he studied languages such as Russian. He left in 1972 to enroll in Goldsmith's College of Art. However, he soon decided to leave the university setting to be trained as an advertising copywriter. He worked for six advertising agencies, such as J. Walter Thompson, before at the age of twenty-four forming a partnership with a producer, Jim Strugeon, and striking out on their own into the then-undeveloped field of cinema marketing. Fowler founded a Soho-based company called The Creative Partnership in 1979 to create advertising campaigns for movies. A self-confessed movie obsessive, Fowler desired to revitalize the then-sorry state of cinema attendance in the United Kingdom. As Fowler and his creative team achieved marketing success and a higher profile, their organization expanded to the point where Fowler opened an office in Beverly Hills, California. After four years, however, Fowler decided to return home to London to focus his efforts there. Shortly thereafter, The Creative Partnership boasted a full art studio and editing suites.

The agency is now one of the largest of its kind in Europe, with approximately fifteen staff members. Primarily, the organization produces and markets advertising campaigns for both major and independent motion-picture companies in the United Kingdom. Over the years, the company has distinguished itself by opening small "problem films," such as *The Cook, the Thief, His Wife and Her Lover* (1989), to wider audiences in the United Kingdom. According to Fowler, in an unpublished 19 December 2000 e-mail correspondence with Philip Lockwood Simpson, he and The Creative Partnership team "have been writing TV and radio scripts, documentaries, trailers and promos for everyone from John Cleese and Leslie Nielsen to Ewan McGregor and Harry Enfield." They have worked with such directors as Quentin Tarantino, Bernardo Bertolucci, Franco Zeffirelli, David Cronenberg, Peter Greenaway, Mike Leigh, and Ridley Scott, creating the campaigns for such movies as *Reservoir Dogs* (1992), *Pulp Fiction* (1994), *Romeo and Juliet* (1996), *Trainspotting* (1996), *The Talented Mr. Ripley* (1999), *eXistenZ* (1999), *The Beach* (2000), and *Hannibal* (2001). Fowler noted that "Our productions include James Bond specials, title sequences, and Channel 4's advertising." In particular, Fowler enjoyed "working on the Bond films because we traveled the world, and the 700-strong unit was like an Army on the march, only with more memorable meals."

While developing and expanding his business, Fowler also began writing humor, working for a BBC comedy program titled *Say Hello to Your Radio* and publishing such books as *How to Impersonate Famous People* (1984) and *The Ultimate Party Book: The Illustrated Guide to Social Intercourse* (1985). In this same period, Fowler was inspired by the publication of the first volumes of friend and fellow horror-writer Clive Barker's fiction collections, *Clive Barker's Books of Blood* (six volumes; 1984–1985), to submit his own short-story collection to a publisher. No one was more surprised than Fowler when his work was accepted for publication on the first try. The collection is titled *City Jitters* (1986). Each story is introduced by segments of a master narrative centering on English business traveler Paul Norris attempting to reach Florida. The stories end with the gruesomely ironic deaths of the main characters. Fowler repeated this formula, including another Paul Norris narrative as structuring device, with the publication of *More City Jitters* (1988). These and later short-story collections typically manifest a darkly comic mix of the macabre and the whimsical.

Fowler has published stories in such periodicals as *The Big Issue, The Independent on Sunday* (London), *The Mail on Sunday* (London), and *Time Out*. Additionally, his stories have appeared in diverse anthologies. "Mother of the City" appeared in *The Time Out Book of London Short Stories* (1993), edited by Maria Lexton, and was republished in *The Best New Horror: Volume Five* (1994), edited by Stephen Jones and Ramsey Campbell, before being collected in Fowler's *Flesh Wounds* (1995). "Permanent Fixture" and "The Grande Finale Hotel" were anthologized, respectively, in *A Book of Two Halves* (1996), edited by Nicholas Royle, and *Dark of the Night* (1997), edited by Jones, before appearing in Fowler's *Personal Demons* (1998). Other short stories subsequently included in Fowler's own collections have appeared in such anthologies as volumes one, three, four, and five of *Dark Terrors: The Gollancz Book of Horror* (1995–2000), edited by Jones and David Sutton; *London Noir* (1994), edited by Maxim Jakubowski; *Love in Vein II* (1997), edited by Poppy Z. Brite and Martin H. Greenberg; volumes seven, nine, and ten of *The Mammoth Book of Best New Horror* (1995–1997), and *The Mammoth Book of Dracula* (1997), all edited by Jones; and *The Time Out Book of New York Short Stories* (1997), edited by Royle.

One of Fowler's stories, "Left Hand Drive," which first appeared in *City Jitters,* was made into a movie that won the Best British Short Film award in 1993, ran in cinemas, and aired on Channel Four in the United Kingdom. The story was included in *100 Fiendish Little Frightmares* (1997), edited by Stefan Dziemianowicz, Robert Weinberg, and Greenberg. "The Master Builder," a story collected in Fowler's *The*

Bureau of Lost Souls (1989), was anthologized in *I Shudder at Your Touch* (1991), edited by Michele Slung, and was adapted by Solomon Isaacs as the CBS television movie *Through the Eyes of a Killer,* which starred Richard Dean Anderson and aired on 15 December 1992.

Following the publication of his first short-story collection, Fowler began writing novels set in a London in which he says, in the standard biography he sends critics, that "characters cross in each other's tales to build a portrait of an alternative London, a city that might have been, and may well be." Fowler's first three novels establish the foundational themes of "urban unease" throughout his work. Fowler's first novel, *Roofworld* (1988), an otherworldly tale about gangs who live and fight on London rooftops above a mostly unsuspecting populace, is what Pauline Morgan, in the *St. James Guide to Horror, Ghost & Gothic Writers* (1998), calls "a fast-paced detective novel with elements of farce, a tiny hint of the supernatural, and a feeling that a lot of the basics of the situation have really been glossed over." This first novel, while rough, still sets up Fowler's later and more polished works of urban and suburban unease. Fowler's interest in cinema also influences his literary style and thematic content. Significantly, Fowler relates the genesis of his idea for his first novel, *Roofworld,* in part to the cinematic flourish of Alfred Hitchcock. Fowler explained to Mathew: "With *Roofworld,* the idea I came up with was because, in the place where I used to work, all the buildings were joined, and the burglars used to come in through the top floor. We were burgled, and they let in thousands of pigeons. I went in to the office on Monday morning, and it was like a scene from [Hitchcock's 1963 movie] *The Birds*! Thousands of these things flying around. Terrified me. . . ."

The conjoined image of human and avian attack is a consistent motif throughout *Roofworld*. The villain of the novel ties a savagely clawing raven to a traitor's face and throws him from a building, poisons another man while dressed as (or perhaps literally transformed into) a giant, Zeus-like swan, and leaves a peacock feather in another victim's throat. Like the threatening swarm of birds that infested Fowler's office building, the cloaked and hooded villain and his renegade gang swoop through the night skies, raining corpses down upon the London streets. Replete with such spectacularly gory highlights, Fowler's first novel, indeed, betrays the cinematic and comic-art background of its creator. The grotesque but cinematic deaths are just one such indicator. Another is the profession of the protagonist, who is a screenwriter for a London-based movie-production company. Indeed, most of Fowler's heroes have connections, in one way or another, to the

Cover for the U.S. edition of Fowler's 1988 novel, about rooftop gangs whose clashes are undetected by most Londoners (Bruccoli Clark Layman Archives)

British motion-picture industry, and thus may have some autobiographical elements.

Roofworld establishes many of the key themes and plot devices that remain consistent throughout Fowler's body of work. For example, Fowler typically structures his plots around fantastic yet oddly feasible premises. In *Roofworld* the narrative conceit centers on the existence of a secret rooftop society originating in a utopian experiment of the 1920s. The original inhabitants of this rooftop world are the disillusioned, the disadvantaged, the disenfranchised, and the disenchanted. Opting to drop out of the economic exploitation of the ground-level modern world, the alienated and the dispossessed take to the rooftops of London to create their own world, with its own codes and laws and means of survival. The founders of Roofworld built aerial "runs," consisting of nearly invisible cables anchored to a series of platforms on the tops of various architectural structures. The Roofworlders have ever since clipped themselves with belts and lines to these cables to soar above the unsuspecting populace under cover of night.

As originally conceived, the Roofworld was an idealistic alternative to the dehumanization of modern economic and industrial practice. Those tired of life on the ground could literally transcend it, returning to the streets only when scavenging raids or other practical concerns demanded. Some even lived dual lives—the street by day and the rooftops by night. In successive decades the utopian vision has at once been augmented by pilfered technology—laser sights, air guns to cast cables to create new runs, computers to hack multinational corporate accounts, and the like—but plagued by defections and rebellions. As the novel opens, a renegade faction of Roofworlders called the New Age has begun a savage internecine war against the remaining guardians of the utopian ideals of Roofworld. The idealists, led by a man named Steven Zalian, are in danger of extermination by the skinhead armies of Chymes, who styles himself after a melodramatic stage villain, right down to the grandiose rhetoric and theatrical costumes. The Roofworld scenario sounds implausible, yet Fowler grounds his incredible plot in enough mundane detail and explanation to convince the reader to accept the notion that a secret society's civil war rages mostly unseen above the complacent heads of Londoners.

Another of Fowler's creative signatures is to structure two parallel investigations—one amateur, one professional—that eventually converge at the narrative climax. Fowler himself wrote in his e-mail to Simpson, "If you look for recurrent themes in my fiction you'll find pairs and opposites." In *Roofworld,* for instance, the murder by the New Age faction of a woman writer who threatens to expose their existence brings the young scriptwriter, looking to option the woman's novel, into confluence with a police detective investigating the executions of traitors and informants by Chymes's skinheads. Throughout most of the novel, the scriptwriter, named Robert Linden, follows clues left behind by the dead woman. Accompanied by the dead woman's building superintendent, a black female photographer named Rose who has captured the Roofworlders on film, Robert is able not only to find the secret society but also to cast his lot with the idealists of Zalian's inner circle. Meanwhile, the detective, named Ian Hargreave, a recurring character in Fowler's novels, conducts his own investigation with his own ally and lover—a fellow officer named Janice Longbright. Hargreave remains on the outside of the secret society, unlike Robert, but he too manages to uncover the mystical code behind the series of ritual murders. Following the clues, Hargreave's police forces collide with Chymes in an apocalyptic but ultimately inconclusive showdown atop the Telecom Tower.

Thus, while the larger society represented by Hargreave achieves temporary respite from evil but no definitive resolution of the social issues that contributed to the problem in the first place, the smaller society of alienated, cinema-raised youth represented by Robert and Rose finds itself embroiled in the ultimate B-movie spectacular. Fowler's amateur sleuths/movie fanatics typify the postmodern fascination with genre formula, providing at the narrative level an apotheosis of such "geeks." Yet, Fowler, wryly subverts this kind of movie fetishism.

Throughout *Roofworld* Fowler exhibits a fascination with ancient mythology and its intrusion upon the agnostic present. In Fowler's urban landscape the myths of pre-Christian and Christian tradition find unexpected resurrection. The Roofworld society, as a secret organization in the style of the famous, or infamous, Hermetic Order of the Golden Dawn, structures its rituals according to mythic qualities represented by the Greco-Roman deities: Hermes, Apollo, Diana, Mercury, Venus, Mars, Jupiter, and Saturn. The renegade New Age, in opposition to the ethereal ideals of its parent organization, appropriates the alchemical, or metal-based, associations of the Greco-Roman names as a structuring framework. For example, Mercury becomes quicksilver, Venus becomes copper, and so forth. The New Age faction's link to earth metals places it firmly in the chthonic tradition of subterranean gods, which arguably leads into the Christian conception of Satan as an underground rival (resembling in most medieval depictions a horned satyr from the pagan tradition) of God in heaven. Chymes, named after the first alchemist, is a Satanic figure who rebels against the heavenly order represented by Zalian's beleaguered but sympathetic true believers. Fowler continued to develop this interest in the Satanic in his next few novels, which clearly belong to the genre of supernatural horror.

Rune is Fowler's second novel, published in 1990. In a review of the novel in *The Library Journal* (January 1991) A. M. B. Amantia praised it as bringing "black magic into the video age with excitement and suspense." The novel owes a great conceptual debt to Jacques Tourneur's motion picture *Night of the Demon* (1957). Morgan also notes that the novel pays "homage" to the M. R. James story "Casting the Runes" (1911). In this novel the reader can see Fowler's theme of urban paranoia extended from the street, or rooftops, into the corporate world of postmodern media. Fowler exploits the apprehension of the many people who mistrust media agencies by depicting a world on the verge of being taken over by a ruthless media conglomerate literally in thrall to the devil. The protagonist is an advertising executive named Harry Buckingham, who is drawn into a conspiratorial netherworld following the death of his father in an apparent street accident. The conspiracy Harry uncovers is a Luddite's worst fears confirmed. Video signals do indeed contain hidden messages capable of brainwashing otherwise ordinary people into committing murder and suicide, and product bar codes are literally the Mark of the Beast. Harry, as an executive in a London advertising agency called Instant Image, is in the right place and possesses the appropriate technical knowledge to untangle the series of mysterious clues and "random" deaths, beginning with his father's, that all seem to center around Harry.

Suspected of involvement in the deaths by Fowler's continuing detective characters Arthur Bryant and John May, Harry must not only untangle the mystery of the deaths but clear his own name in the process. Harry is aided in his investigation by his romantic interest, Grace Crispian, a typically Fowlerian movie buff whose apartment is decorated with posters of movies such as Ruggero Deodato's cult classic, *Cannibal Holocaust* (1979); Dorothy Huxley, a librarian who can provide the knowledge of ancient lore that Harry needs to complete the puzzle; and Frank Drake, a young assistant librarian who spends his spare time seeking to discover the back-masked messages in heavy metal music and compiling a file of seemingly accidental deaths to prove that there is an occult purpose and design behind the deaths. Reviewing the novel in *The Library Journal,* Amantia noted that Harry as a hero does not possess much "substance" but that these secondary characters are "delightful."

Of course, as genre fiction demands, these fringe characters with their esoteric interests and quixotic agendas are instrumental in saving the world from the evil machinations of a media corporation known as ODEL. Harry and his small team find that ODEL is nothing less than the Antichrist of biblical prophecy. Contrary to millennial expectation, the Beast turns out not to be one individual but rather a multinational, Fortune 100 company that eliminates business enemies by incorporating ancient runic symbols into modern media formats and then cursing those who view the runes. Harry learns that the runes are pre-Christian, Germanic characters that lack curves and symbolically represent various aspects of nature. Known as the Devil's Prayers in earlier centuries, the runes constitute an underground pagan language that has manifested itself in various consistent ways throughout human history, even in urban graffiti spray-painted on crumbling walls. The runes are magical in that their lines evoke universal or Jungian responses from those who view them. Some runes create terminal or murderous hallucinations, invariably resulting in the death of the sufferer, while other runes protect against the malign effect of such curses.

Dust jacket for the 1991 U.S. edition of Fowler's 1990 novel, in which a media conglomerate in thrall to the devil is about to take over the world (Richland County Public Library)

Thus, Fowler's persistent theme of urban paranoia finds its most sinister and farthest-ranging expression. ODEL, as headed by the villain of the book, Daniel Carmody, has married these runes to modern technology to create an invincible corporate entity. Grafting the runes projected in the right sequence into diverse media formats such as videotape and television signals, ODEL uses the runes not only to protect itself but also to kill those (including Harry's father) who threaten to expose its ultimate plot. To complete its monopoly on media technology, ODEL has digitized the runes and plans to transmit via satellite a worldwide program designed to drive all of its business rivals into terminal psychosis. As events unfold, Carmody wants Harry, as a key executive at Instant Image, to create a global publicity campaign for ODEL—a campaign that, of course, will brainwash millions through the subliminal use of the runes. Harry refuses and is saved only when Carmody's embittered wife uses her own set of runes against Carmody to fuse him, literally, with his

own computer system. The ending of the novel is decidedly ambiguous. Carmody is now disincorporated, so to speak, but now is perhaps more powerful than ever as a free-floating consciousness existing within the limitless freedom of cyberspace.

The troubling conclusion of the novel fits well with one of Fowler's key themes. The reader is right, Fowler suggests, to be paranoid in an urban existence so heavily dependent on capitalism, profit motive, and survival-of-the-fittest notions of competition. Business success trumps all other considerations, including such sentimental abstractions as morality, preservation of the environment, and the sanctity of the individual human life. Or, as the villainous Carmody says so eloquently: "What's right in business anymore? Is industrial espionage right? What about the tobacco cartels who print death warnings on their products, the alcohol companies who advertize glamorous life-styles to their addicts, the insurance companies who only pay up when every get-out clause has failed them? What about the manufacturers of sugar drinks and junk food, the corporations that condone immigrant labor and support apartheid, the industries that destroy the rain forests so they can print leaflets telling you how caring they are?" Within this context, ODEL and its Satanic CEO seem only slightly more extreme than the megalithic corporations and capitalist chieftains many people fear, envy, worship, and emulate every day.

Red Bride (1992), Fowler's third novel, moves away from the social apocalypse of his earlier works and narrows in on a much more personal apocalypse—the power of urban evil to seduce and destroy an individual. The book marks a transition between the melodramatic, larger-than-life sweep of Fowler's first two novels to the much more intimate and psychologically realistic focus of his later work. Like *Rune*, *Red Bride* presents a straightforwardly supernatural menace, but this time the horrific menace threatens only unfortunate lovers, not the entire world. The book chronicles the travails of a London businessman named John Chapel who, while switching careers from accountancy to motion-picture public relations, finds himself bewitched by a beautiful young woman named Ixora De Corizo. Chapel first sees Ixora running through Waterloo Station—unbeknownst to him, she has just committed the first of her series of London murders—and is so mesmerized by her feral beauty that time seems to slow and he dreams of her that night. Shortly thereafter, Chapel is astounded to discover that the beautiful stranger he saw running for the train in Waterloo Station is a client in his new business venture, whom he is to be responsible for personally escorting to business functions. In the course of his duty he becomes so smitten by her beauty and mystery (she refuses to reveal details of her past) that he begins an affair with Ixora and eventually leaves his wife, Helen, and son, Joshua, for her.

The unraveling of the Chapel family is juxtaposed with a series of sensational murders taking place in London. The first victim is discovered in his apartment stabbed to death with his feet bound; a cross on a chain has been removed from his throat and placed in a glass of water in the kitchen. The subsequent murders are all connected by the removal of a religious symbol from the victim's body and the placement of that symbol in water. For example, after a photographer named Feldman is murdered by having a film roll containing compromising photographs of Ixora hammered down his throat with a tripod leg, the assailant takes a gold "hai," the Jewish symbol for life, and drops it into a toilet. Another victim is slashed to death with a razor, his crucifix thrown into a nearby fountain. Chapel's boss is killed with a sword and his gold crucifix immersed in a bottle of spring water. Detective Sergeant Michael Sullivan, Detective Constable Deborah Mace, Detective Chief Inspector Ian Hargreave, and Sergeant Janice Longbright—the latter two first introduced in *Roofworld*—investigate the murders, with Sullivan himself becoming one of the victims along the way. Eventually, Hargreave, as lead investigator, realizes that all of the victims are in one fashion or another threats to Ixora. She is systematically murdering all those who would jeopardize her relationship with John Chapel.

Of course, in the supernatural world of *Red Bride,* Ixora is a lethal incubus, a demon who must remove the holy icons from her victims so as to ensure their damnation. As her name symbolizes, and reminiscent of the cyclones that eternally hurl the lustful around the Second Circle of Dante's Inferno, Ixora is like a wind that demolishes John Chapel as she has others before him. Squalls and gales herald several of her key appearances in the novel. Originally from St. Lucia in the West Indies and supposedly born in the middle of a fierce hurricane, Ixora and her parents drowned after their boat sank in another hurricane in 1979. Spared from death and ensured fame by a bargain with Satan, she is literally the Devil's Mistress. In return for cinematic success and the subsequent worship of millions, her special mission is to single out men like Chapel for destruction at the exact instant they believe completely in her innocence and loyalty. Her affair with Chapel destroys his home life, gets him fired from his new job, throws him into despair-induced drinking binges that end in debt and memory lapse, finds him arrested as a suspect in the murder of his former boss following a highly public argument over Ixora, and culminates in the death of his wife and unborn child. In her pivotal role as temptress of the solid family man Chapel, Ixora

is the demonic personification of masculine fears of unleashed female sexual appetite.

The demonization of female sexuality in the text is made evident in an early chapter of the book, when Chapel and his wife uncomfortably discuss Ixora while a nature-documentary program on the television behind them announces that "The male . . . Common Garden Spider . . . must mate its partner very carefully to avoid being eaten by her immediately following intercourse." The subliminal reference to the voracious female's literal engulfing of the hapless male foreshadows the unease Chapel feels about Ixora, even as he becomes more attracted to her: "For the first time in his life, he felt that all that he held dear had been placed in danger. And that the almost mystical intensity of that first innocent, grateful kiss [with Ixora] was the vanguard of all future misery and destruction." Chapel's unease increases as both he and Ixora are followed and attacked by mysterious men with romantic claims to Ixora's past, including a man named Anthony Saunders who was married to her briefly. One of the attackers, a photographer named Matteo, says of Ixora: "She's a special kind of jinx. A bad omen. Like, if you saw her at sea, your ship would straightaway hit a . . . rock, you know what I mean? Bitches like that shouldn't be allowed to walk around." Ixora's former husband, Anthony Saunders, tells Chapel: "She—causes bad things to happen."

In spite of these warnings and his own intuitive misgivings about Ixora, Chapel cannot help but risk his marriage and surrender his principles for his adulterous affair. Even as he abandons himself to Ixora, he continues to mistrust her, periodically interrogating her about a plethora of concerns both trivial and profound: her disappearances, her suspicious withdrawal of money from their joint account, her past relationships, and her mysterious past. Ixora herself acknowledges that she uses her sexuality as a means of male domination: "This is woman's territory. The bedroom. . . . This is the easiest way to control your sex. There is nothing more pliable than a man in a state of constant expectation." Ixora, in turn, strikes out at men because of her own fear, which she claims to result from a childhood incidence of sexual abuse by her father but in reality stems from her bargain with Satan. She speaks euphemistically of her fear of Satan to Chapel: "sometimes I still believe that out there, somewhere, concealed in the dark, there is a man like my father, someone who wants to cause me the worst harm in the world." Ixora seeks to avoid this harm by victimizing the men chosen by Satan. By the end of the novel, however, Ixora reneges on her diabolical compact by falling in love with Chapel and then ultimately saving him from death. All she ever really wanted, she says in a farewell note to Chapel, is to live and love, and so who would not have agreed to the devil's terms when facing a premature death? Having ironically found divinely sanctioned love with Chapel, the damned Ixora is free to renounce her contract with Satan and die in peace. In Fowler's hands, then, the horror-genre cliché of the lethal temptress finds a poignant recasting in the story of Chapel and Ixora's tragic, but finally redemptive, love. Fowler runs a high risk by working in such heavily traveled genre territory; however, his critics generally acknowledge his stylistic skill. A. J. Wright, reviewing the novel for *The Library Journal* (January 1993), noted that the "unbelievable" narrative "in the hands of a lesser writer would seem excessive, if not ridiculous," but that Fowler "manages to pull it off with good writing and swift plotting."

Red Bride is a transitional text in Fowler's move away from supernatural horror into what can be most accurately described as "psychological thrillers" that incorporate both horror elements and more overtly autobiographical references. Four novels followed *Red Bride* in quick succession: *Darkest Day* (1993), *Spanky* (1994), *Psychoville* (1995), and *Disturbia* (1997). *Darkest Day* features the return of Detectives Arthur Bryant and John May as they investigate a series of occult-linked deaths in the rarefied world of high finance and upper-crust families of proud but corrupt lineage. As is to be expected in a Fowler novel, Bryant and May are aided by some decidedly eccentric allies—a troubled young woman named Jerry Gates and a white witch. The theme of familial dysfunction at the highest levels of society furthers the indictment of modern business practice established in Fowler's earlier work. Fowler revisits the *Red Bride* territory of the personal demonic in *Spanky,* wherein a young urban loser named Martyn finds short-term professional, financial, and romantic success but eventual disaster by striking a Faustian bargain with a devil named Spancialosaphus ("Spanky") Lacrimosae. When Martyn refuses to let Spanky possess his body as repayment for the debt, Spanky retaliates by taking away Martyn's successes and killing people. An interesting aspect of this particular novel is how Fowler's style has markedly improved since the previous book. Morgan, for one, says of this novel that it "has a quality not found in Fowler's earlier work." The "urban unease" of Fowler's increasingly polished style is extended into "suburban unease" in *Psychoville.* The March family moves from inner London into a suburb, where the snobbish residents quickly decide to mount an ultimately lethal campaign to force the Marches out of town and back to the city. Ten years later, the son, Billy March, marries a woman who also was victimized as a child by the townspeople. Billy and his wife return to the town to destroy it in an apocalyptic finale.

Disturbia continues Fowler's signature theme of the brutality of wealth and privilege—the novel opens with the murder of a black man by aristocrats outside a concert. The League of Prometheus, a secret society of powerful men who really run London, is the covertly institutionalized form of such brutality. Its leader, Sebastian Wells, challenges a working-class journalist named Vince Reynolds to solve ten puzzles in the space of one night or face death. Fowler's dramatization of class warfare, so much a part of *Roofworld* in particular, is stronger than ever in this novel.

During the late 1990s Fowler's versatility and output expanded. Fowler wrote *Menz Insana,* a 1997 graphic novel for DC Comics drawn by John Bolton of *Batman* fame. As a sign of his increasing critical acclaim, Fowler's short story "Wage slaves," collected in *Personal Demons,* won the BFS Best Short Story of the Year in 1998. He also published his eighth novel, *Soho Black,* in 1998. This novel, a good example of Fowler's matured "urban unease" body of work, is one of his favorites, which, he revealed in his correspondence with Simpson, "was written as a catharsis just after I survived a near-death experience." The book reveals the author's insider knowledge of the movie industry through the character of a motion-picture executive, Richard Tyler, who is on the brink of personal, financial, and professional ruin as a seemingly unrelated wave of violence sweeps through the bohemian London district of Soho. The violence is the result of a powerful new drug—distilled from a naturally occurring narcotic found on the backs of Australian trough caterpillars—being given away in the streets of Soho by a lower-level studio errand boy named Lucas Fox. The potent drug, called Imago, causes profound hallucinatory and psychotic episodes in its users and thus creates an outbreak of violence investigated by Fowler's ubiquitous detective duo, Bryant and May. As they close in on the source of the drug, the hallucinogen finds its way from the street to the executive inner sanctum of Tyler's studio, Film Creation Incorporated. Tyler, a sensitive soul reminiscent of John Chapel, who is too timid to survive within the vicious corporate world of the motion-picture industry, has been cuckolded by his boss, Berry, is separated from his wife, owes money he cannot possibly pay back to a Soho loan shark, and is about to be fired, when he snorts a line of Imago-poisoned cocaine in a restaurant washroom. Under the psychoactive influence of the drug, Tyler believes he has died of a heart attack but has returned as a reanimated zombie—a hallucination derived directly from his expansive knowledge of the horror-movie genre. Thinking he only has a few days left before his "dead" body decomposes in the Soho heat wave past the point of functionality, Tyler ferociously asserts himself in his work to set up enough lucrative movie projects to provide for his wife and autistic son after he is gone. He also hallucinates that he kills his boss Berry in a particularly brutal fashion. In actuality, Berry is not even in town but scuba diving in the Maldive Islands.

The other disparate plot threads of the novel, involving a club owner named Midas Blake, a woman named Judy seemingly under a spell of enchantment cast by Midas, which imprisons her in her apartment, a dangerously seductive stripper named Glory, and a pair of hit men named One-Eighty and Waldorf, all come together in the last third of the novel as the drug causes a minor apocalypse in Soho. The plot device that ties all the characters together is the Imago drug—that, and the fact that all of the characters inhabit the underworld of Soho. In Fowler's mythscape, Soho is dangerous but potentially redemptive as well, precisely because of the bizarre characters who inhabit it. Barbara, a friend of Tyler's, is present as he begins to shake off the effects of Imago and realize he is still alive and not a zombie. She expresses the celebration of urban existence of the novel when she tells him, "You're here in Soho because there's something very wrong with you, something that prevents you from fitting in. . . . Just keep away from normal people. Brick up the wall. Stay in the ghetto where you belong. Ghettos are the last bastions of individuality." The "something" that prevents Tyler from fitting in with "normal" suburbia is his encyclopedic knowledge of cinema, which has given his drug-overdosed system a horrific waking nightmare. However, the Imago-induced nightmare has also ensured his future success as a moviemaker, as he crafts his experience into a cult movie titled *Soho Black,* starring Brad Pitt, Cameron Diaz, Drew Barrymore, and Ethan Hawke. In this eighth novel, then, the reader can see Fowler's craft in its mature form, where he skillfully blends horror-genre convention and psychological realism to create a self-referential critique of contemporary London life.

In his ninth novel, *Calabash* (2000), Fowler expands his range beyond not only London but also the more sensational trappings of the horror genre. However, the novel is still concerned with the realm of the fantastic and the imagination. *Calabash* is set half in ancient Persia and half in a small rundown resort town named Cole Bay on the British coast during the 1970s. The protagonist of the novel is an adolescent boy, Kay Goodwin, who spends most of his waking hours lost in fantasy because his family and school existence is so dreary. "Calabash" refers to the name of the Persian fantasy land into which Kay imagines himself, a place where he can escape his mother and school bullies and find beautiful people in an exotic setting who actually want him around. Kay's escape into a delusional state resembles that of Tyler in *Soho Black* and represents a new phase in Fowler's work, where the realm of the fantastic exists intrinsically and not extrinsically. Fowler's novelistic work reveals an extraordinary ability to take chances and to develop. He does so in many ways. He transcends and blurs easy genre classifications, explodes

Paperback cover for Fowler's 2001 collection of short stories (Richland County Public Library)

mainstream horror conventions, and expresses an intellectual and artistic complexity more often associated with "non-genre" fiction.

Fowler's success, both artistically and personally, continues to grow. Many Fowler novels, including *Roofworld, Rune, Spanky, Psychoville,* and *Disturbia,* are in various stages of cinematic development by studios such as Granada (*Roofworld*) and Columbia-Tristar (*Spanky*). As he told Mathew, "What I try to do is turn each manuscript into a screenplay as soon as I've finished it—to clean the palatte [*sic*], as it were. . . . I've sold options on all the books so far. Nothing ever happens, but hey, it pays for the hallway carpet, so I'm not complaining." Notable motion-picture industry names reportedly associated with Fowler projects include Jonathan Hales (screenwriter of *Roofworld*), Guillermo Del Toro and Martin Scorsese (director and producer, respectively, of *Spanky*), and Stefan Elliot and Jude Law, director and star, respectively, of *Psychoville*. In addition to his advertising campaigns, Fowler writes scripts (including the adaptation of *Pychoville*) for Ewan MacGregor's production company, Natural Nylon. He advised the director of (and had a walk-on part in) a short movie titled *On Edge,* directed by Frazier Lee and starring Charley Boorman, that had a theatrical release in 1999. A successful businessman and writer, Fowler divides his time between London and the South of France, where he has a house just outside Monte Carlo. He keeps busy. As he told Mathew in their interview, Fowler publishes a book a year and a short-story collection every other year, with most of his mornings devoted to his movie-advertising business and his afternoons spent in writing. Besides novels and short stories, he writes reviews and essays for *The Edge, The Independent on Sunday* (London), *Pure Magazine, Time Out,* and *The Third Alternative.*

Reflecting on his approach to "horror" fiction, Fowler told Mathew that his biggest challenge is "choice of subject matter: how to balance real life with grand guignol, which I am strongly drawn towards." Indeed, Fowler's work is noted, or notorious, for its spectacularly violent, almost operatic, set pieces of mayhem. Yet, the over-the-top quality of the violence is, in some absurd way, humorous. Fowler does revel in black comedy, which he told Mathew is "the correct response to the times in which we live. . . . it's impossible for me to keep a sense of fun out of what I write. That's just part of living in England, a country very absurd in many ways." In a 1998 interview with Carlos Ruiz Zafon for the Internet magazine *The Barcelona Review,* Fowler termed his work "social satire with an edge of black comedy," saying, "I was never very happy with the straitjacket of horror fiction." In his 2000 e-mail to Simpson he remarked "I abhor horror's late misanthropic streak, and love stories that create fatally flawed humans. I don't like the ghettoization of the genre, and many of the stories I consider to be horrific do not fit into easy horror categories. I . . . don't enjoy much 'comfortable' mainstream horror fiction. This creates a problem for me, because I drift across the genre into other areas, and it confuses readers looking for a consistent backlist. I have trouble with the supernatural, and tend to avoid it now because reality holds more useful keys to unsettling psychological situations." Indeed, the supernatural, which some readers consider synonymous with "horror," plays a prominent role in only a few of Fowler's novels. The most obvious unifying element throughout most of Fowler's work is the London setting. When explaining his persistent focus on London to Mathew, Fowler confessed that rural life does not appeal to him: "I hate the countryside. The outdoors is the place you empty the ashtray. It's the bit between your vehicle's door and your house's door."

He told Zafon that "Working in the centre of a city of over eight million people encourages a healthy sense of paranoia. But I only get paranoid when I go to the country—because I don't enjoy pastoral peace, and can't get the mindset to enjoy it."

Since Fowler defines himself as a Londoner and has primarily lived and worked in London, his familiarity with that city lends his fabulations of the paranoia of contemporary city life a verisimilitude that establishes Fowler as a sort of postmodern Dickens. Referring to Fowler's love of the London setting, Suzi Feay wrote in her review of *Disturbia* in *The New Statesman* (3 October 1997) that Fowler as a horror writer should not be grouped with Stephen King and James Herbert but rather "with the mythographers and psychic geographers, the scribes, mystics and poetasters of London: Ian Sinclair, Jah Wobble, Aidan Dun, Peter Ackroyd."

Christopher Fowler is an ever evolving novelist of the twenty-first century who has transcended the genre classifications foisted upon him by publishers but still remains influenced by the fantastic and the horrific. With each novel and short story, his skill at creating complex characters and plot oppositions increases. But at every stage of his career, throughout his extensive body of writing, Fowler has made the nightmare city of London a metaphor for the cares and concerns that face human beings in the postindustrial world. Paranoia about multinational corporations, the media, the effect of violent images and lyrics upon impressionable minds, secret cabals and conspiracies, the occult, skinheads, and punk rockers all find expression in Fowler's fiction. He is a dark fabulist of contemporary existence who nevertheless grounds his Grand Guignol tales in a sharp brand of psychological realism.

Interviews:

Stan Nicholls, "Christopher Fowler: Won't Breathe Anything He Can't See," in his *Wordsmiths of Wonder* (London: Orbit, 1993);

Carlos Ruiz Zafon, "Christopher Fowler: A Very Personal Demon," *The Barcelona Review,* 1998 <http://www.barcelonareview.com/eng/cf_in08.htm>;

David Mathew, "London in the Blood: An Interview with Christopher Fowler," *SF Site,* 2000 <http://www.sfsite.com/07b/cf85.htm>.

Reference:

Pauline Morgan, "Fowler, Christopher," in *St. James Guide to Horror, Ghost & Gothic Writers,* edited by David Pringle (Detroit: St. James Press, 1998), pp. 218–220.

Romesh Gunesekera

(26 February 1954 –)

Rocío G. Davis
University of Navarre

BOOKS: *Monkfish Moon* (London: Granta, 1992; New York: New Press, 1993);
Reef (London: Granta, 1994; New York: New Press, 1995);
The Sandglass (London: Granta, 1998; New York: New Press, 1998);
Heaven's Edge (London: Bloomsbury, 2002).

OTHER: "Wild Duck," in *New Writing 3,* edited by Andrew Motion and Candice Rodd (London: Minerva/British Council, 1994), pp. 271–275;
"The Lover," in *New Writing 5,* edited by Christopher Hope and Peter Porter (London: Vintage, 1996), pp. 329–333.

SELECTED PERIODICAL PUBLICATIONS–
UNCOLLECTED: "The Green Line," *London Magazine,* 29, nos. 3–4 (1989): 3–11;
"Stringhoppers," *Granta,* 52 (1995): 189–193;
"Ealing," *London Magazine,* 26, nos. 9–10 (1996–1997): 109–113.

Romesh Gunesekera (photograph by Barbara Piemonte; from the dust jacket for the U.S. edition of The Sandglass, *1998)*

In his fiction Romesh Gunesekera engages the reality of Sri Lankan immigrants to England, who must deal with separation from their country in the midst of ethnic violence, the consequences of postcolonial history, and their role in the complex cultural situation of the Asian diaspora. With the short-listing of his first novel, *Reef* (1994), for the Booker Prize in 1994, Gunesekera established himself as an important figure in the field of British Asian writing. The versatility of his narrative techniques and choices, his exploration of the immigrant experience, and his engagement with fundamental issues of meaning in the context of the Asian diaspora, have made Gunesekera's works an essential part of the discourse of immigration and ethnicity in Britain.

Romesh Gunesekera was born in Colombo, the capital of Sri Lanka (then Ceylon), on 26 February 1954, the second son of Douglas and Miriam Gunesekera. For the first years of his life, Gunesekera's family lived in Colombo, then, because of his father's various jobs in international development programs, moved briefly to the United States in the late 1950s and to the Philippines in the mid 1960s. Gunesekera moved to England in 1972 to prepare for university entrance and attended the University of Liverpool from 1973 to 1976, where he enrolled in the Combined Honours Program, majoring in English and philosophy, and where he was awarded the Rathbone Prize in Philosophy in 1976. Gunesekera's early employment included a variety of jobs, ranging from manual work to bookselling. Subsequent professional employment was in education, internal development, and cultural relations. His last post prior to becoming a full-time writer in 1996 was Assistant Regional Director, East Asia, for the British Council. Gunesekera lives in London with his wife, Helen, and daughters, Shanti and Tanisa.

Gunesekera's prose publications include stories that have appeared in journals such as *London Magazine, Granta,* and *Wasafiri,* and anthologies such as *Telling Stories: The Best of BBC Radio's Recent Short Fiction* (1992), edited by Duncan Minshull; and volumes three and five of *New Writing* (1994; 1996). Some previously published stories, notably "A House in the Country," first published in *Granta,* and "A Storm Petrel," first published in *Stand,* were later collected in *Monkfish Moon* (1992). The diasporic experience is the central framing theme of Gunesekera's work, though many of his narratives are set in Sri Lanka.

The island nation of Sri Lanka, located in the Indian Ocean and independent from Britain since 1948, has long been racked by sectarian conflicts. Relations between the majority Sinhalese, who are mostly Buddhist and speak Sinhala, and the minority Tamil, who are mostly Hindu and speak Tamil, began deteriorating rapidly in the 1960s, when Sinhalese nationalist leaders put into effect laws that made Sinhala the sole official language and gave state support to Buddhism and Sinhalese culture. In the 1970s such organizations as the Tamil United Liberation Front began calling for the establishment of an independent Tamil state in Tamil-dominated areas in the northern and eastern provinces. Tamil groups—the most prominent being the Liberation Tigers of Tamil Eelam—began insurgent activities aimed at establishing such a state; their activities provoked systematic mob violence against Tamils living in Sinhalese-dominated areas in July 1983, which in turn provoked further paramilitary actions, most notably a series of terrorist suicide bombings against Sinhalese politicians and other targets that continued throughout the 1990s. This sectarian violence has led to the displacement of both the Sinhalese and Tamil populations, both within the island and abroad, especially to Britain, the former colonial power. Gunesekera repeatedly highlights, through the use of continually evolving and highly original metaphors, the destruction of the island by violence, and the people's resort to flight as the only reasonable alternative. Significant elements in his writing include Sri Lanka, diaspora, violence, fiction, and memory. Gunesekera's engagement with public events also foregrounds private experience, and, ultimately, his writing focuses on the approaches people have to reality and the manner in which they deal with what it means to be human, to be alive amid diverse forms of conflict. These epistemological concerns encompass fundamental issues of meaning, such as language, art, memory, imagination, beauty, truth, and life. Set against the background of Sri Lankan and immigrant reality, these themes expand the contexts of Gunesekera's writing, as his engagement with private

lives illuminates and complicates his examination of public manifestations.

Gunesekera's works have received several literary awards and recognitions. His first collection of stories, *Monkfish Moon,* was a finalist for the David Hingam Prize and won for the author an Art Council Writers' Bursary. In 1993 the collection was a *New York Times* Notable Book of the Year and a finalist for the Commonwealth Writers' Regional Prize. An epigraph set on the page before the table of contents states: "There are no monkfish in the ocean around Sri Lanka." This cryptic introduction suggests a link between fiction and other realities, of the word as a path toward renewed perception, and of a possible shift between what is real and what may be imagined; it also insinuates a representational, rather than a literal, reading of the stories. The collection is composed of nine stories set in either Sri Lanka or England, each engaging with the vacilating political and ethnic climate of the country, as well as the situation of immigrants. Certain motifs recur in the stories, creating a web of images and meanings that extend to Gunesekera's later fiction. The image of the house, for instance, appears in several stories: dilapidated houses figure in "Ullswater" and "Ranvali"; characters in "A House in the Country" and "Captives" refurbish old houses; CK in "Storm Petrel" dreams of building a little guest house on the beach, as the country is being destroyed. The narrator in "Carapace" uses the image of an aging building to tell Vijay that he must move on: "The Beach Hut isn't going to be here forever. The bamboo and coconut will split. The wood on the window-frame is already rising, turning itself inside out." These varied houses suggest, more than simply the position and fortunes of the people who own them, the situation of the country itself and the imperative to leave, to which many of the characters succumb.

The first story, "A House in the Country," sets the tone for the others: "These were troubled times in Sri Lanka." The questions *"What has happened? Why? Who's responsible?"* are repeated in several of the stories, as characters cannot comprehend the escalating ethnic tension in Sri Lanka. Gunesekera's descriptions of the paradisiacal beauty of the country are overshadowed by the awareness that a subtle but steady destruction is being worked behind it. Sometimes the danger is manifested only in the jungle sounds; at other times, as in "A House in the Country," a shopkeeper burns inside his store after it is set on fire, and Siri's brother is hanged from a lamppost. In "Captives," the narrator of the story, a hotel manager, provides a description of the jungle at night in the middle of a brownout that is emblematic: "Outside I could hear the jungle flex and move. The jungle grass growing. Leaves unfurling. Things slithering around, searching, circling, fornicating. In between there was the terrible sound of metal on metal." Moreover, the author's emphasis on darkness and night as the setting for many scenes in the stories contributes to a sinister atmosphere, the suggestion of a world of shadows replete with unknown dangers. In contrast, the narrator in "Ullswater," looking around the English pub in which he is sitting, concludes that "it feels wholesome and safe, blessed, as if the air had been licked clean." This description differs sharply with the images of Sri Lanka as a place where even nature can be menacing.

A sense of vulnerability permeates many of the stories. Characters cannot stand firm in the midst of growing tension and actual violence. Roads are not safe from young militarists, and curfews are routine. Things are not what they seem: the hotel manager in "Captives" is shocked to realize that the "honeymooning" couple he was showing around were not actually married; Tissa in "Straw Hurts" is betrayed by his friends; the successful businessman in the title story, "Monkfish Moon," a victim of his own overindulgence, still dreams of becoming a monk. Tellingly, as Ray in "A House in the Country" sits on his veranda quietly at night, he realizes that "he never expected that such peace would come so close to war." The instinct toward self-preservation is thus heightened, and characters must either escape the threat or delude themselves into believing that it will never come close. Yet, as Gunesekera shows in several stories, and, as Ray replies to his servant Siri's question about where a "good place" might be, the answer–"It has happened all over the world"–confirms that violence cannot be escaped. Allusions to violence at home are tempered by the reminder that this history is shared by people around the world. Nonetheless, fear becomes one of the most prevalent sentiments in the stories. Peter, the overweight businessman in the title story, declares: "In this country now everybody is frightened. . . . They are frightened because they feel guilty. They feel guilty for all the things they have done and all the things they haven't done."

Reconnection is another recurring theme in the stories. Gunesekera suggests that the land one has left behind always haunts the expatriate and that the myth of return, as well as the current condition of the homeland, are pivotal to the construction of immigrant identity and self-definition. Each story offers a nuanced account of the exile's longing for home and a struggle to redefine the very notion of "home." Ray returns from London to rebuild his house, because he "hoped he would find out what he wanted once he had freed himself from the constraints of his London life, and once he had retrieved his past." Yet, he finally understands that it is really impossible to go back, though the old world "never quite passes away." This theme is tellingly analyzed in "Batik," as Nalini, who is Sinhalese and lives in London with her Tamil husband, sees him become increasingly caught up in the struggle for the independent Tamil homeland of Eelam. Nalini has her own belief that life "was first to do with where she was rather than where she had come from" challenged by her husband's growing coldness toward her.

The dichotomy between the expatriate's need to preserve an unchanged image of the island and the brutal reality of what the island has become permeates many of the stories. The destruction of the myth of the island invalidates the possibility of a return, condemning the immigrant to perpetual nostalgia for what once was. In "Storm Petrel," CK, though he dreams of returning, finds he cannot leave London: "You see you can't rush these things. You know how it is, going home." In "Batik," the narrator muses that "The barbarity made the common memories Tiru and Nalini had found earlier of sesame oil and pink rose sherbet seem like so many sad and pathetic illusions. . . . The bright green tropical island they thought of as their own turned into grotesque images of smoke and devastation strewn across the news-stands, litter bins, subway walls and train stations of the whole city." As Neloufer de Mel argued in a review in *Wasafiri* (September 1993), this frustrated longing leads to the homeland being represented as a place where resolution is impossible or endlessly deferred. All the stories set in Sri Lanka end in displacement and fracture, while two of the three set in England conclude with a sense of reconnection–the couple in "Batik" beginning to move back toward each other–or on the path to closure, as when the uncle attempts to help his nephew come to terms with his father's life in "Ullswater." The setting in which Ranjit asks his uncle to tell him his father's story–a pub on a summer's day as they sit drinking English beer–ironically stresses the distance between father and son, the land of the past and that of the present.

Gunesekera's use of violence is primarily metaphoric, and he writes to uncover the effects of violence on the wider society, on the people's conceptions of themselves, and their strategies for survival. Moral questions as to positions and stances taken become imperative for the characters, who must make decisions as to whether they will stay or leave. On the one hand, if they leave, they must deal with the guilt that ensues; remaining in Sri Lanka, on the other hand, becomes, on occasion, a death sentence. Yet, the real issues are wider existential ones. Gunesekera consistently pits his individual stories and characters against the larger frame of history, foregrounding his epistemological concerns. Art and truth, language and memory, beauty and imagination have their place in this scheme, Gunesekera sug-

Dust jacket for the 1995 U.S. edition of Gunesekera's 1994 novel, which was short-listed for the Booker Prize (Richland County Public Library)

gests, and an essential element in the characters' development and presentation is the manner in which they engage these fundamental questions.

Reef, Gunesekera's first and most critically acclaimed novel, is a postcolonial bildungsroman presented as a novel of memory and has garnered several awards, including the Premio Mondello Five Continents Asia Prize 1997 and the Yorkshire Post First Work Prize in 1995. *Reef* was also short-listed for the Booker Prize in 1994, named a finalist for the Guardian Fiction Prize the same year, and nominated for the 1995 New Voice Award. The novel opens with Triton in England meeting a fellow Sri Lankan working at a petrol station but finding that they are unable to communicate because the Tamil attendant cannot speak Sinhala. The encounter with this new immigrant who is also "painting a dream" reminds Triton of the home he had left behind, "a sea of pearls. Once a diver's paradise. Now a landmark for gunrunners in a battle zone of army camps and Tigers . . . I remembered a

bay-fronted house six thousand miles away." From that point the narrative moves back to the moment the boy arrives from his village home to Mister Salgado's house, where he is to work. Gunesekera employs the voice of the child as the central controlling consciousness. The story is focalized through Triton, who introduces the reader to the country and the events that will lead to his immigration. The tale and the teller thus create an ambience, a world distant in time and space from the narrative present, that has been lost to everything except memory and imagination, a fitting analogy to the diasporic condition. In his 1995 essay "Images of Sri Lanka through Expatriate Eyes," Walter Perera criticizes the novel, arguing that Triton's "'voice' articulates attitudes that are chauvinistic and problematic" in their representation of Sri Lanka, specifically referring to women and the exoticism of the landscape and culture. Perera's concern for political correctness is at odds with Gunesekera's apolitical intention: to present the development of a child's perception and imagination, filtered through the nostalgia of recall.

The setting for the boy's education is Ranjan Salgado's house. Little information is given about Triton's past, not even his real name. "Triton" is the name Salgado gives the boy, connecting him to the sea that surrounds the island. In an interesting subversion of the traditional bildungsroman, Triton is given the opportunity to begin again; his arrival at the house is an opportunity for completely reinventing himself. Triton's erasure of the past is a conscious choice, and he remembers how he "liked to sit unfettered in a room of my own, emptied of all the past, nothing inside, nothing around, nothing but a voice bundled in paper, a pattern of marks entering my own stillness." Triton sees the possibility he has of constructing himself into the form he chooses. And he elects to make himself like Mister Salgado. Triton's childhood admiration for his master is wholehearted and endearing: "'All I have to do is watch you, Sir. Watch what you do. That way I can really learn.' . . . So I watched him, I watched him unendingly, all the time, and learned to become what I am." As such, the house becomes, for a time, the center of Triton's universe, "and everything in the world took place within its enclosure. Even the sun seemed to rise out of the garage and sleep behind the del tree at night." The boy's celebration of the place arises from the unlimited possibilities that life in the house seems to offer: "I felt I could spend my life growing in the house, making something of myself. . . . I felt safer than I had ever felt before in my life." His admiration for Mister Salgado makes him want to care for his master, as he begins to know and understand the man who employs him.

Yet, as time goes by, Triton begins to regard his life in Mister Salgado's household with a certain ambivalence. He places himself and his position in the house against larger events of the outside world and realizes that his life in the house with Salgado is limited and limiting: "I had no real opening to the outside world; only walls everywhere . . . I was trapped inside what I could see, what I could hear, what I could walk to without straying from my undefined boundaries." When Miss Nili visits for the first time, Triton hopes she will visit more and "lift the monkishness from our monastic house." Triton craves to move beyond reading, cooking, and his other domestic duties, to see the ocean. Eventually, Salgado does take him to see the ocean and, later, to England. Salgado's house has profound representational value in the text. As Charles Sarvan notes, in his "*Reef*: A Chekhovian Awareness and Mood"(1998), the house reflects past importance, status, and lifestyle, yet there is a contradiction between the proportions and the valuable and solid contents of Salgado's home and the emptiness and air of neglect of "that extraordinary house, headed for nothing but oblivion." Much in the house is unused, stored away, and quietly decaying, much like Salgado himself. The slow decay and eventual abandonment of the house is a metaphor for the disintegration of the nation, suggesting the process that leads to the diaspora.

In his review of *Reef* in *The New York Review of Books* (22 June 1995) Pico Iyer described Triton and Salgado as representatives of science and superstition who blend to make their home a model of the island around them; through specific details, Gunesekera acknowledges the mixed influences of an island in a state of flux. The web of relationships that Triton sees and recalls illustrates a world marked by differences and diverse points of view. Salgado and Triton have disparate manners of perceiving reality and contrasting reactions to many fundamental issues. Salgado, a scientist for whom there were no boundaries to knowledge, believed that science would transform people's lives by lifting them from the "swamp of our psychotic superstitions." Triton had learned as a child that language was what made humans different from animals, and wanted to listen to Salgado because he "had never heard language spoken so gently." Salgado's ordered view of the world opens up another dimension to the poetic, religious, even superstitious, child, who lives in a world of spirits. Triton's attitude toward nature is primal, and he is captivated by the colors and smells of his world, as well as by the mysteries he believes lurk behind the commonplace.

The diverse attitudes these characters have toward the reef is emblematic of their distinct worldviews. For Salgado, it is an object of study; water mea-

surements and temperature changes define the life of the reef for him. Triton, on the contrary, was "frightened by its exuberance" the day he swam out to it. In this manner Gunesekera contrasts adult and child perception, not only through Salgado and Triton but also between the representation of Triton as a child and Triton as an adult narrating his childhood experiences. In this context Nili becomes a catalyst for specific types of development of both characters: a representative of the middle class, she is the only woman living in the house and offers Salgado a chance to escape from his solitary existence. Her presence also signals an awakening for Triton, as he becomes aware of her as a woman.

The central metaphor of the novel, the eponymous reef, comes alive with meaning as its inevitable disintegration implies the destruction of the island itself. Set in the 1960s, the novel reflects the development of political tensions in Sri Lanka. The reef is regarded by politicians as a marketable resource, and the coral is being torn up by developers and turned into cement for tourist hotels. Triton's initial obliviousness to the chaos of the outside world ends when stirrings of dissent explode into full-scale violence. The boy can no longer find comfort in his religion, as sectarian battles erupt. Illustrative of the change in the times is a folktale Triton recalls about a gentle young prince who is told by his corrupt teacher to make a necklace out of a thousand human fingers and, as a result, becomes a blood-crazed mass murderer. The boy eventually understands that this tale is not merely a fantasy, and he considers how "the whole country had been turned from jungle to paradise to jungle again, as it has been even more barbarically in my own life." An important part of Triton's education thus involves his growing awareness of political violence and the choices one is obliged to make.

Reef is also a *künstlerroman,* a novel about the development of an artist. Triton's artistry is culinary. The first section of the novel narrates Triton's apprenticeship and discovers his talent in the kitchen, developing his own ideas on the concept and the preparation of food, turning the task of cooking into a craft and an art of love. For Triton food becomes more than mere nourishment; it becomes a way to signify caring and to express love. He plays culinary Cupid and helps Salgado court Miss Nili by plying her with love cakes. "I wanted her to taste the world through my fingers," he proclaims, "so I cooked like a magician—tiger prawns to rum soufflés." As he does in several stories in *Monkfish Moon,* Gunesekera utilizes images of food and the preparation of food to symbolize mood and intent, art and human emotions, turning it into a strategy for multilayered meanings. Triton's process of creative development is manifested primarily as he learns how to cook and to make his mark on the world through culinary art. In this context Gunesekera has discussed the fundamental concerns of this novel, which extend to the rest of his fiction. As Gunesekera explained in a 1997 interview with Rocío G. Davis, the novel is

> about identity, gaining a voice, finding a voice, which to me again is linked with the whole idea of an artist. It is an artistic enterprise, which is about finding a voice. And what you get in the book is the idea that actually we are all artists, we are all artists of our own lives. We make our own lives. And, in a sense, we do two things: we make our own lives by living the way we do, and then we recreate it in our memory, trying to deal with the things we didn't do right, for example. There is a creation and a recreation process, which is the artistic process as well.

At the end of *Reef,* Triton takes another step toward reinventing himself. Some years after settling in London, Salgado decides to return to Sri Lanka and to Nili, leaving Triton in England. Triton understands that the only way he can succeed is by repeating the strategy he successfully enacted years before: by beginning again "without a past, without a name," only this time "without Ranjan Salgado standing by my side." Gunesekera suggests that Triton's attitude toward the past, his ability to overcome or ignore it, makes him a survivor. Triton can move away from his home and build a new life anywhere because he is free of any restrictions the past may impose. Triton's ability to adapt stems precisely from his openness, the absence of a history to weigh down his flight or force him to conform. In contrast, Salgado, who begins the novel as a privileged man with a history, "a line of people who believed in making their own future," ends up trapped in a closed space that he cannot leave. Neither his sense of the past nor his past privileges have helped him make his mark upon the world and choose his destiny. If Triton's liberation from the fetters of the past allows him to survive anywhere, it is clear that Salgado's clinging to the past will hinder his ever moving away from the life he has physically left behind. Triton comprehends the future of the country he left behind: "The older houses would all be eclipsed by the premium on land, the reformed regulations. Even ours, I could see, would one day have to give way and disappear behind a façade of somebody else's concrete. Our walls would crumble. The whole geography of our past would be reconstructed. It seemed nothing could remain the same." And the question Triton asks at the end echoes the diasporic subject's nostalgic concern: "I wondered who would come to live in the house after us: what sort of a world would they build on our remains?" On the one hand, Salgado, who believes that "we are only

what we remember, nothing more . . . all we have is the memory of what we have done or not done; whom we might have touched, even for a moment," remains chained to the past. Triton, on the other hand, understands that human history is the story of repeated diasporas, of the struggle between those who expel and those who remember, and that the individual must deal with his or her links with the past.

In his review of Gunesekera's second novel, *The Sandglass* (1998), Paul Binding, writing in the 23 February 1998 *The Independent on Sunday* (London), highlighted the concerns that link Gunesekera's fiction: "For all the delicacy of his art, for all his preference for ambiguous inference over overt judgement, throughout his work one emotional truth plainly reverberates: Sri Lanka compels the leaving of it." The colonial past of the tear-shaped island, the uncertainties of the civil war, and its unpredictable future make it seem unable to provide a home for its inhabitants. Gunesekera engages once again with the question of home and belonging, as well as the exile's plight. Memory occupies center stage in the narrative, and the complex relationship with the land becomes the driving force that influences characters' lives and decisions.

The novel centers on two neighboring families, the Ducals and the Vatunases, and the decades-long relationship between them. The chapters are titled and arranged to suggest both an Aristotelian unity of time—chapter titles include "Daybreak," "Morning," "Ten O'Clock," "Late Morning," "Midnight," "Dawn," and "Later"—as well as the inexorable passing of time, also implicit in the title of the novel. The action takes place over two days, during which Prins Ducal arrives in London for his mother's funeral and his niece Naomi gives birth to Dawn. This structure implies an attempt to order history, the task that the narrator, Chip, finds himself engaged in as he weaves the account of those days with his memories of Prins's mother, Pearl, and her stories.

A friend of the Ducals, Chip finds himself the custodian of the family secrets. Once more the narrative is structured as a flashback: Chip begins his story in a hotel room in an unspecified country, a metaphor for his state of perpetual travel. Because of Pearl's recent death and Prins's disappearance after his mother's funeral, Chip cannot untangle himself from the memories of his past: "In every place I have been to since then, I seem to end up in a low-lit hotel room going over the story of Prins and Pearl—the whole Ducal family and the scheming Vatunases, who seemed forever coiled around them—trying to untangle the truth." The narrative becomes Chip's recounting of this family history—a history that spans colonial and postcolonial Sri Lanka and England, from the 1950s to the 1990s—using

Dust jacket for the U.S. edition of Gunesekera's 1998 novel, about two feuding
Sri Lankan families (Richland County Public Library)

the fragments of stories he has been given or has recovered through letters or diaries. Interestingly, he does not tell his own story but rather Pearl's, which he has appropriated and tries to understand. As with Triton in *The Reef,* Chip appears not to have a real past previous to his arrival at Pearl's apartment in London in 1975. Facts about Chip's life are unveiled in reference to the Ducals: his mother, as did Naomi's, died in childbirth; the reader learns that Chip's father's death came shortly after Pearl's, but Chip only reveals this information during the course of a meditation on the matriarch's death. Chip's apparent lack of a history makes him the ideal receiver of the Ducal story, and its most faithful preserver. But beyond merely romance and family saga, as Shirley Chew noted in her 13 February 1998 review in *TLS: The Times Literary Supplement,* Chip's account leads to an indictment of the landowning and professional classes of Sri Lanka.

As the first day moves on, Chip unravels the story of the complex personal and business connec-

tions between the feuding Ducals and Vatunases, beginning from when they shared land that had been developed by an Englishman who named his house Arcadia, and ending with both families depleted and dispersed. The family names are cleverly chosen: in Sinhala, "Ducal" derives from *dhukka,* meaning "sadness," and *Vatunas* means "the fallen." Jason Ducal is at the center of the narrative: first, because Pearl's life and memories revolve around him and, later, because of Prins's obsession with his possible murder. The difficulty of finding out the truth about the past is a central theme; Prins describes trying to find out about their lives in Sri Lanka as "swimming in treacle." "How to find out anything?" he asks. "The entire bloody country seems to have always been one big barrel of rumour and conspiracy."

Land figures as the central metaphor in the novel, with profound consequences on people's lives. For the Vatunases, it "was the result of a deep and intense relationship between the sleeping earth and the ambitions of a line of modern dynasts . . . from the first to the last, land defined everything: the shape of their lives, the shape of their bodies and their heads and the shape of their dreams." Jason's buying the land adjacent to the Vatunases's property leads to unforeseen consequences, specifically the enmity of Esra Vatunas, who was probably involved in the former's death. His obsession with the land reflects his preoccupation with place and status, both geographical and social. Occupying this land, described as a "magnified tear," and the house, Arcadia, leads to the family's destruction and eventual exile. The conflict with the land reflects the larger political situation and violent ethnic confrontations that serve as the background to the lives being recounted. Gunesekera sets the story of the feud between the Ducals and Vatunases against specific moments in Sri Lankan history. In this manner the author engages the Sri Lankan political and economic situation of the 1950s, and the idiosyncratic behavior of the players in the dangerous games of business and politics.

Exile becomes an imperative for most of the characters. Chip appears completely disconnected from Sri Lanka. Searching for a way to shape his life, Chip converts Pearl, then Prins, into "the cardinal points for my uncertain identity." His abandonment of Sri Lanka allows him to adopt a new mother, and appropriate that family's stories. It is he who tells Jason's story and who will keep the biscuit tin with Jason and Pearl's diaries and letters, "for me to dig my hands in and feel her life slip through my fingers, again and again." He will also continue to discover aspects of the story he did not hear from Pearl, such as her relationship with Tivoli Vatunas. Pearl, who immigrates to England after Jason's death, survives exile by turning to the past and making it continually present through her storytelling. As a young married couple, Pearl and Jason had traveled to England, where Pearl had spent the happiest time of her marriage, and she describes this "exotic past of hers" to Chip "as though it were the ordinary precursor to any immigrant life."

Pearl's children deal with exile differently. Anoja, her oldest daughter, marries an Englishman but dies in childbirth. Anoja's daughter, Naomi, will also come to live with Pearl and share her stories. This character, the child of a Sri Lankan mother and English father, is "the only one who knew no boundaries, or seemed to cross wherever she wished, and whenever she wished." Naomi's daughter, Dawn, born at the end of the novel, is the promise of the continuation of the family line, though not of the name. Prins, the second son, returns to Sri Lanka, his "dreamland," partly because of his growing obsession with his father's death, which—conveniently for the Vatunases—had been labeled an acci-

dent and because of his relationship with Lola, youngest of the Vatunas children. He returned promising never to come back: "an emigrating immigrant" escaping from the "confusion of being nowhere." Prins was obsessed about the future, as though it were a place he had to reach, where everything would be ordered. This attitude toward the world contrasts sharply with Pearl's view. She believed that all the important places were those of the past or of the present and that the future was a fantasy. These two attitudes are integral to the tone and the manner in which the novel unravels, as well as the constant references to time, fate, and death. Prins does become a success in Sri Lanka, running the Shangri-La hotel, "selling the paradise experience between death camps and suicide bombers to tourists who didn't care," until he begins to work with Dino Vatunas. The rivalries and political maneuvers that characterized the end of Jason's life appear to be replayed in his son's. The suspicious events surrounding Prins's disappearance suggest that the cycle of greed and lust for power continues in the second generation, as his vanishing may be connected to his search for the truth about his father's death.

Ravi, Pearl's younger son, chooses a life of isolation. Immigration from Sri Lanka alienated him from the world. Chip describes Ravi's process in the following terms: "He not only tried not to make any impression in his daily life, but he tried to undo all past impressions. Sand down every surface he touched so that there was no imprint left; wear away the shape of his image, and dull the daily perception of him until nothing remained to distinguish the figure from the background." When he eventually commits suicide, his manner of death is the culmination of his "particular ambition," which was "to absent himself for longer and longer periods, until it became so long that one could not remember when he had left one's company and when he was due to come back." When they look at his possessions, they find nothing but a few volumes of American poetry and used tickets, "proof of any journey." Again, the obsession with travel haunts the displaced immigrant. Ravi is perhaps the most memorable character in the novel, precisely because of the systematic manner in which he tries to efface himself. His suicide becomes the final, logical step in his gradual withdrawal from life. But, as Chip notes, Ravi had not counted on Naomi and himself, who were hungry for history, "even one of disappearance," and would keep him alive in their memories.

As Chip describes the family history, he exalts the written word as a source: he transcribes pages of the journal Jason had kept the week before his death, he looks at Pearl's letters, he attaches significance to the poetry Ravi read, and he receives Prins's journal at the end. As such, he stresses the power of the written word as a preserver of stories and, conversely, as a way of hiding the truth between the lines. At the end of the novel, the last member of the Ducal family is gone. Prins's disappearance is unexplained and unresolved. Only Chip, who has taken on the task of reclaiming the family, will remember their story, as he continues his own life as an exile: "I would be perpetually on the road, retracing the footsteps of the past . . . I know how to live with only a modem and a slip of plastic, but with each jolt I find I yearn for a story without an end." This character, like many other of Gunesekera's exiles, seems condemned to travel and to keep struggling to understand the complex lines of history and family that compose the fabric of Sri Lankan life and its inevitable diaspora. Yet, this ending obliges the reader to reconsider the primary focus of the novel: imagination and memory rather than the story of the Ducals and Vatunases. Ultimately, the narrative is Chip's, as his mind engages his memories and the stories he has been given, and the story is about what he needs to stay alive.

In *Heaven's Edge* (2002) Gunesekera revisits many of the themes and issues previously dealt with in his earlier fiction, through the central character, Marc, who travels to a place known only as "the Island," where his grandfather was born and where his father had died. The Island is never identified, and the cities in it have fictional names, though readers will recognize Sri Lanka because Gunesekera describes it in terms he has used previously: the Island is in the Indian Ocean and is characterized as a paradise that has been destroyed by escalating violence. But the omission of specific geographical and even temporal references moves the novel beyond the particular to signify on a wider sphere. Once again, the juxtaposition of beauty and destruction become constitutive elements in the definition and search for home.

Marc travels from Britain to the Island he has never been to, led by his sense of isolation and his father's posthumous invitation, to find a place for himself that appears to be marked for him by his forebears. Eldon, his grandfather, who raised the boy, left the Island at seventeen and settled in England, where he married a Caribbean immigrant. Their only son, Lee, went to the Island to fly planes and died there, leaving for his wife and son a videotape in which he describes the beauty of the place and promises to bring them over. His untimely, and largely unexplained, death curtails that dream. After his mother and his grandparents die, Marc finds the videotape and responds to his father's invitation. Once on the Island, he witnesses firsthand the nature and extent of the destruction and the underground culture that evolves to survive, and he meets Uva, a woman with whom he falls in love, who

introduces him to terrible truths about the paradisiacal place. Themes of reconnecting, of the need to leave the place of the beginning as well as the need to recover it, color the narrative.

In this novel, more than in any of his others, Gunesekera explores the nature of violence, both physical and psychological. He describes a war that pits siblings against each other and makes killing a strategy for survival. As Marc engages the increasingly frightening reality of the Island, he continually recalls his grandfather, Eldon, and the old man's advice, as well as ideas on memory, belonging, and survival. His grandfather's stories of the Island had made it an imaginary home for him long before his arrival there, and meeting Uva, herself a rebel, made him realize that, in spite—or perhaps because—of its history of loss and destruction, it would become his true home. Here, the home must be literally fought for and the loss of human lives the required price to pay for possession of that home. Yet, the sensational bellicose confrontations in the novel serve as background to the even more dramatic struggle within the protagonist to find his place in the midst of a changing world. The twofold movement of the novel constitutes a harrowing contrast: as the Island is being systematically destroyed, Marc engages in the process of creating himself from the ruins of a lost home and family, a misunderstood history, and the experience of his own insecurity.

This notion challenges the idea of the stabilization of identity to demonstrate once again how postcolonial and immigrant identity is never finished or completed but keeps transforming itself in stories and in the context of the place within which this identity is enacted. Storytelling thus also becomes essential to Marc's evolving sense of self, intricately woven with his search for his father. As Marc travels through much of the Island and escapes from those who pursue him, in search of a more peaceful location, the reader may be reminded of Odysseus, himself a reluctant warrior. The diverse locations that Marc inhabits become points in his itinerary of belonging. The portrayal of the violence-laden Island as a "promised land" for the protagonist, led there as he was by his grandfather's stories, his father's death, and his dream of a future with Uva, thus radically subverts the traditional notion of a homecoming while offering a suggestion of hope in the face of destruction, the possibility of a future change and renewal of life. The multilayered ending of the novel obliges readers to revisit the entire story, as well as the enduring concerns of Gunesekera's writing: the nature of beauty and the reality of violence, morality, the meaning of the journey, the role of imagination and of stories, evolving identity, and hope.

As one of the most important contemporary British writers, Romesh Gunesekera's position is a significant one. An insightful and poetic craftsman of the word, he builds narratives that engage the Sri Lankan diaspora and the issues with which immigrants must deal: guilt, adaptation, violence, and the question of home and family, simultaneously engaging profound epistemological questions of art, memory, and truth. Gunesekera juxtaposes the paradise image of the island with stories of violence, creating a nuanced portrait of a land and a people in search of their own history and who struggle for self-definition. In recognition of his work, in 1998 he was awarded the BBC Asia Award for Achievement in Writing and Literature. Gunesekera's narratives widen the scope of British fiction, as they examine the immigrant's relationship with the homeland and the place of exile, art and memory as strategies for survival, and the boundaries between the public and private spheres, formulating a complex vision of societies in the process of transformation.

Interview:

Rocío G. Davis, "'We Are All Artists of Our Own Lives': A Conversation with Romesh Gunesekera," *Miscelanea: A Journal of English and American Studies,* 18 (1997): 43–54.

References:

Paula Burnett, "The Captives and the Lion's Claw: Reading Romesh Gunesekera's *Monkfish Moon,*" *Journal of Commonwealth Literature,* 30, no. 2 (1997): 3–15;

Rocío G. Davis, "'I am an Explorer on a Voyage of Discovery': Myths of Childhood in Romesh Gunesekera's *Reef,*" *Commonwealth Essays and Studies,* 20, no. 2 (1998): 14–25;

Jose Santiago Fernandez Vazques, "Subverting the Bildungsroman in Postcolonial Fiction: Romesh Gunesekera's *Reef,*" *World Literature Written in English,* 36, no. 1 (1997): 30–38;

Senath W. Perera, "The Perils of Expatriation and a 'Heartless Paradise': Romesh Gunesekara's *The Sandglass,*" *Commonwealth Essays and Studies,* 22, no. 2 (2000): 93–106;

Walter Perera, "Images of Sri Lanka through Expatriate Eyes: Romesh Gunesekera's *Reef,*" *Journal of Commonwealth Literature,* 30, no. 1 (1995): 63–78;

Charles Sarvan, "*Reef:* A Chekhovian Awareness and Mood," *Toronto Review of Contemporary Writing Abroad,* 16, no. 2 (1998): 44–53.

Hugo Hamilton

(28 January 1953 –)

Steven Belletto
University of Wisconsin–Madison

BOOKS: *Surrogate City* (London: Faber & Faber, 1990);

The Last Shot (London: Faber & Faber, 1991; New York: Farrar, Straus & Giroux, 1992);

The Love Test (London & Boston: Faber & Faber, 1995);

Dublin Where the Palm Trees Grow (London: Faber & Faber, 1996);

Headbanger (London: Secker & Warburg, 1997; New York: Four Walls Eight Windows, 2001);

Finbar's Hotel, by Hamilton, Dermot Bolger, Roddy Doyle, Anne Enright, Jennifer Johnston, Joseph O'Connor, and Colm Tóibín, edited by Bolger (London: Picador / Dublin: New Island Books, 1997; San Diego: Harcourt Brace, 1999);

Sad Bastard (London: Secker & Warburg, 1998; New York: Four Walls Eight Windows, 2001);

Yeats Is Dead! A Novel By Fifteen Irish Authors, by Hamilton and others, edited by O'Connor (London: Cape, 2001); republished as *Yeats is Dead! A Mystery By Fifteen Irish Writers* (New York: Knopf, 2001).

OTHER: Francis Stuart, *The Pillar of Cloud,* introduction by Hamilton (Dublin: New Island Books, 1994).

SELECTED PERIODICAL PUBLICATIONS–
UNCOLLECTED: "A Touch of the Blarney," *Irish Times,* 17 February 1996, Supplement, p. 9;

"Ireland–the Snug of Europe Joining Europe," *Irish Times,* 29 June 1996, p. 12;

"Morals in Our Pockets," *Irish Times,* 6 May 1997, p. 12;

"That Summer," *Irish Times,* 17 August 1998, p. 21;

"Thanks for Nothing, Michael Flatly," *Observer* (London), 6 September 1998, p. 5.

Born of Irish-German parentage, author Hugo Hamilton is committed to exploring the intricacies of his bipartite heritage and has noted, in an interview with Liam Fay published 30 August 1998 in *The Sunday Times* (London), that, coincidentally, he was born in 1953, the same year the last of the Blasket Islanders–recognized in Ireland for their adherence to traditional culture–abandoned their homes to live on the mainland. Hamilton likens himself to a "modern-day Peig Sayers," a Blasket Island diarist who left a record of her life on the island and thus helped to preserve her culture. Accordingly, Hamilton is known for saturating his characters in a complex cultural and political milieu and documenting precisely their relationships with one another given the strictures of their environment.

Often praised for his taut, economical prose style, Hamilton tries to strip away his authorial presence while still insisting on the political dimension of his work; as he told Victoria White in an interview for *The Irish Times* (4 January 1996): "I don't think I'll ever get away from the sense of my characters being haunted by the political landscape they live in." Hamilton explores this haunting through the intersections between personal experience, contemporary political situations, and the lingering effects of the past, which are major thematic concerns in Hamilton's first three novels, all set in Germany. In his characteristically spare prose Hamilton writes of subtly damaged relationships, the inescapability of history, and the often conflicted nature of European experience.

Hugo O'Urmoltaigh was born to Sean O'Urmoltaigh and Irmgard (Kaiser) O'Urmoltaigh on 28 January 1953, in Dun Laoghaire, a suburb of Dublin. Hugo O'Urmoltaigh grew up with three siblings: an older brother, Franz, and two younger sisters, Maire and Ita. His father, Sean O'Urmoltaigh, an engineer from West Cork, built the children toys and wagons throughout their youth. German by birth, Hugo's mother, Irmgard, went to Ireland to work as a governess for a Killiney family, and, as Hamilton recalled in an interview with *Books Ireland* (March 1995), she met her future husband through a German language group. Growing up, Hamilton spoke Irish to his father and German to his mother, while learning English in school and on the streets of South Dublin. Hamilton's awareness that the very language one speaks contains a political history was heightened as a boy when his family took summer trips to Connemara, in the west of Ireland, where Irish was more

Hugo Hamilton (photograph by John Carlos; from the dust jacket for the 1992 U.S. edition of The Last Shot, *1991)*

frequently spoken than it was in Dublin. In Connemara his father was "elated at the contact with the Irish language," Hamilton recalls in "That Summer," a piece published in *The Irish Times* (17 August 1998). Hamilton often felt out of place as a young boy, a phenomenon he traces back to his exposure to the languages of three distinct cultures. Of living in Dublin, Hamilton told *Books Ireland:* "Being half German, I felt like an outsider from an early age." Speaking German to his mother on the streetcars of Dublin meant that Hamilton and his siblings were ostracized as children; he records a version of the discrimination he encountered in 1950s Dublin in the short story "Nazi Christmas," collected in *Dublin Where the Palm Trees Grow* (1996), about three German-Irish children vilified as Nazis by angry Irish youth.

Hamilton's literary interest in Germany and Ireland in relation to Europe as a whole is reflected in a life spent divided largely between the two countries. After school he landed a job as a copy boy at *The Irish Press,* but he told *Books Ireland* that he found journalism

to be "a very narrow way of looking at the world, because it's very much in the moment." Restless in Dublin, Hamilton moved to Berlin, where he worked in a publishing company until the mid 1980s. When he returned to Dublin, Hamilton got a job with Gael-Linn, a nonprofit organization devoted to preserving Irish culture, and wrote his first novel, *Surrogate City* (1990), while on a six-month sabbatical. Besides writing, Hamilton's other passion is music, and as he remarked in his interview with *Books Ireland,* he has "always been a musician," and he "probably should have pursued a career in music." There is thus a keen musical awareness in all of Hamilton's work, and lines from pop songs often float through the minds of his characters as they think through their problems.

In his introduction to the 1994 republication of prominent Irish author Francis Stuart's *The Pillar of Cloud* (1948), Hamilton writes that Stuart's honesty made him an "inspiring" writer to read in the 1970s, when Hamilton himself had begun "to think seriously about writing."

He did not publish, however, until 1985, when he sent some stories to *The Irish Press* editor David Marcus, who recognized the emergence of a talented writer. Following publication of Hamilton's stories in *The Irish Press,* other works quickly appeared in *The Irish Times.* Three stories—"Above and Beyond," "The Compound Assembly of E. Richter," and "The Supremacy of Grief," all subsequently collected in *Dublin Where the Palm Trees Grow*—were published in *First Fictions: Introductions 10* (1989), an anthology series published by Faber and Faber, Ltd.; that publishing house soon agreed to publish *Surrogate City.* All this success occurred, Hamilton told *Books Ireland,* without his receiving a single rejection slip. Although he burst onto the Irish literary scene with a few stories and his first novel, Hamilton maintains that he had been gestating as a writer since the early 1970s, writing in his introduction to *The Pillar of Cloud:* "I first started to write short stories when I was twenty, and although nothing ever came of those stories, the very act of writing them made me alert to certain things in a literary way."

In 1995 Hamilton moved from Dublin to eastern Europe and from 1995 to 1996 was a visiting lecturer in Irish Studies at the University of Bucharest in Romania. As he writes in an article for *The Irish Times* (29 June 1996): "Teaching Irish literature abroad gave me a chance to assess the real impact of Irish culture on Europe. It allowed me to see Europe from both ends." He has since written several newspaper articles about his experiences in Romania and told Fay in their 1998 interview in *The Sunday Times* (London) that, on the whole, they have "left him feeling empathy for our [Ireland's] immigrant population." When his term in Bucharest finished, Hamilton returned to Dublin, where he lives with his wife, author Mary Rose Doorly, with whom he has three children.

Hamilton's interest in examining European culture from multiple angles is evident in his first novel, *Surrogate City,* set in Berlin in the late 1970s, as Helmut Schmidt is being elected to the chancellorship. Irishwoman Helen Quinn is one of the principal characters of the novel; the story is driven by her search for Dieter, the German father of her unborn child. The narrator, Alan, helps Helen search for Dieter and falls in love with her in the process. One of the hallmarks of Hamilton's early fiction is that he builds a novel from two interwoven stories. In the case of *Surrogate City,* the story of Alan and Helen moves around that of Hadja and Wolf. Hadja is a forceful woman, half-Turkish, half-German. Alan's narrative devotes long passages to Hadja, allowing Hamilton to explore the experience of the Turkish minority in Berlin, which seems to serve Germany as an undocumented reserve for manual labor. Hamilton's musical interests turn up in Wolf, a rock musician of some repute in Germany who employs Alan as his chief lighting technician.

As Helen and Alan search Berlin for Dieter, the relationship between Hadja and Wolf grows increasingly troubled when she discovers he has had an affair. Hamilton sets these personal events against the backdrop of Berlin in the 1970s, and the political landscape through which the characters move is ever present. In fact, in a February 1991 review John Dunne wrote that in *Surrogate City,* "Berlin, even Germany itself, is the principal character, and thus we have what seems like endless observation and analysis." Through this observation and analysis Hamilton develops a multilayered picture of modern Berlin, seen through the eyes of expatriates who are forced to negotiate German bureaucratic and cultural systems in their search for Dieter. With Hadja, Hamilton offers his reader Berlin from yet another perspective—the Turkish-German—which adds a dimension to Germany that moves beyond Europe itself. Thus, Hamilton explores not only the general elections and the music subculture of the city but also working-class Turkish neighborhoods, Iranians living in Berlin, and quiet cultural truisms such as "In Germany, the sign that you're moving in with somebody is to bring your coffee grinder." Through the outsider Alan, who can speak German but often chooses not to, Hamilton meditates on the various things that need to be "declared" in modern Germany: the popularity of Ireland in Germany, the divide between East and West Berlin, and even the future of the city.

The title of the novel suggests that for Hamilton's characters Berlin is a substitute for other cultures and other countries. In fact, the characters themselves become surrogates. As Alan falls in love with Helen, he clearly becomes the surrogate father to her baby, a role that he ultimately cannot fill. Perhaps Helen's child, born of Irish-German parentage, represents for Hamilton the confluence of cultures that he senses modern Europe to be, and he signals that no single cultural experience is adequate to nurture that child. In any case, the characters in *Surrogate City* express the wish to be free of their current cultural constraints. As Wolf confides to Alan: "I would love to belong to a minority. . . . I would love to belong to a small race of people with nothing to lose. Palestinians. Kurds. Dispossessed." Despite Wolf's longing to be dispossessed, each person in the novel is a creature of his or her political climate; indeed, when Hadja retaliates for Wolf's infidelity, not only does she sleep with a Turk, she also spends her days putting up posters for the rivals of the political party Wolf supports. As Hadja's actions confirm, the political and personal in *Surrogate City* affect one another so absolutely that they seem permanently bound together.

When asked in the 1995 *Books Ireland* interview why he set so much of his work in Germany, Hamilton responded: "when I began to write my first novel, Berlin

Dust jacket for the 1992 U.S. edition of Hamilton's 1991 novel,
set in Germany during the final days of World War II
(Richland County Public Library)

seemed like the right place to start. . . . The fact that, politically and socially, Germany is such an interesting place, particularly in recent years, is another factor. There has been so much to write about, and the political element of my work is something which is very important to me. I believe that people are very much steeped in, and shaped by, their political environment, and that's especially evident in Germany, though Germans strongly deny this." *Surrogate City* demonstrates not only how people are "shaped by" their political environment but also how this environment is shaped by the accretions of small acts by ordinary people, which description finally yields a more complex picture of both Berlin and its residents. The German composer Heiner Goebbels borrowed some of Hamilton's images of the city—and his very title—for his musical *Surrogate Cities*. This work, which premiered in Frankfurt in 1994, seeks to explore various facets of the modern city through music by Goebbels and words by Hamilton and author Paul Auster, among others.

In 1991, scarcely six months after *Surrogate City* appeared, Faber and Faber published Hamilton's second novel, *The Last Shot*. Like *Surrogate City, The Last Shot* concerns the intersections between individuals and their political environment, but takes this exploration through time with dual story lines—a technique Hamilton reprises in *The Love Test* (1995). *The Last Shot* is narrated with the air of cool detachment that pervades all of Hamilton's novels set in Germany. One story in *The Last Shot* takes place during the final days of World War II and records the flight of German officer Franz Kern from a small Wehrmacht fort in Laun, Czechoslovakia. Franz is technically deserting his post, and there is an urgency in his plan because he wants to escape before the Russians liberate the area. Franz offers Bertha Sommers, a young secretarial assistant posted in Laun, the opportunity to escape back to Nuremberg with him. Franz is in an unhappy marriage to a wife he has not seen in a long time, and he and Bertha fall in love as they flee by bicycle from Laun to Nuremberg. The "last shot" of the title refers to the last gunshot of World War II, which Franz must eventually fire to protect Bertha from an attack by starving, half-crazed Czech refugees. With Franz's act, Hamilton suggests not only that his characters are subject to their political environment but also that even the smallest of love affairs or individual acts can affect the sweep of history.

Folded into the tale of Franz and Bertha is a story that takes place in 1990 just after Communism has fallen in Czechoslovakia and involves an unnamed American searching through Prague and Laun for clues to the flight of Franz and Bertha, who—as the reader ultimately learns in the surprise ending of the novel—are his parents, and to the last shots of Worlds War II. As is typical in Hamilton's "German" novels, the narrator is embroiled in a complicated love affair—with Anke, his former lover, who married a mutual friend, Jürgen. When the narrator breaks from his work in Prague and Laun, he drives to Germany, where he stays with Anke and Jürgen, soon renewing his affair with Anke. Thus, like Franz and Bertha, the narrator finds himself tangled in an illicit relationship as the tide of history flows around him. However, modern Berlin is too stifling to allow Anke and the narrator the sort of joyful freedom Franz and Bertha enjoy as they pedal from Laun. In his review of *The Last Shot* for *The Los Angeles Times* (18 June 1992), Richard Eder wrote: "Quietly, as if opening a gas-cock, Hamilton steeps us in claustrophobia: 'Another feeble wintry evening. Kitchen windows begin to steam up. . . . TVs came on. Cartoons. News. Football results. People from all over Germany sealed into their own luck.'" Modern Germany's atmosphere of "claustrophobia" is set against the collapsing Third Reich in 1945, the Germany "on the move" in which the seeds of the narrator's existence were sown: "All over Germany, the retreat went on, relentless. Everybody in Europe was on the move. Some going home, some going to find new homes. New places where they could find peace. Everywhere, people now discovered the destruction of the war." With this juxtaposition of a free-form and mobile 1945 Germany and a developed though nearly stagnant 1990 Germany, Hamilton suggests not only that contemporary Europe is informed by its history but also that one must explore and understand this past in order to reconcile oneself with the modern world.

Hovering around the center of *The Last Shot* is the question of Alexander, Anke and Jürgen's son, a boy afflicted with Down's Syndrome. When Alexander develops leukemia, Jürgen's medical background tells him that his son has a painful existence ahead of him with no chance of recovery; he and Anke struggle with their decision to euthanize the boy. The narrator becomes involved in the ethical questions surrounding euthanasia, and as he continues to uncover more facts about Franz and Bertha's flight from Laun, he discovers the existence in Laun of a boy with Down's Syndrome who in the mid 1940s was the same age as Alexander. Although this boy is mentioned only in passing, there is a sense of doom pervading the descriptions of him, as Down's Syndrome would have been grounds for extermination under the Nazi eugenic plan. When Jürgen finally determines to euthanize Alexander, then, the act carries an historical valance that transcends even the personal, familial decision. Hamilton's parallels between Jürgen's choice and the Nazi goals of race purity are clear: the narrator senses that Jürgen hates the "efficiency of his plan," the final component of which requires a quiet scene in which Alexander's body is cremated. Several reviewers have commented on the power of Hamilton's association of Alexander's death with the Holocaust. Dunne, writing for *Books Ireland* (October 1991), found that much of the strength of the novel comes after "we learn just how closely and absolutely convincingly the stories are related." More so than *Surrogate City,* Hamilton's second novel was a uniformly critical success, and in 1992, *The Last Shot* was awarded the prestigious Irish £3,500 Rooney Prize for Irish Literature.

Hamilton's third novel, *The Love Test,* published in 1995, exploits many of the same themes and techniques used in *Surrogate City* and *The Last Shot.* Set in newly reunified Berlin, *The Love Test* plots relationships that are twisted and shattered first by the East-West divide, then by new Cold War realities. Mathias Hauser is a reporter for a Berlin newspaper, *Tagezeitung,* who has a rocky relationship with his wife, Claudia. They have a son, Werner, who, like Alexander in *The Last Shot,* represents the innocent person who has little control over his environment, and who is subject to the whims of the adults.

Early in the novel Mathias meets Christa Süsskind, an East German who had been imprisoned in the infamous Hohenschönhausen prison with her lover, Ralf Krone. At Hohenschönhausen Christa and Ralf were exposed to unimaginable psychological torture at the hands of Erwin Pückler, an official of the Stasi (secret police). While incarcerated, Christa gave birth to a child, who was immediately taken from her. She comes to Mathias fourteen years later, after the fall of the Berlin Wall and the dissolution of the German Democratic Republic (GDR), with the hope of finding her lost child. Partly because of his crumbling home life, Mathias throws himself into the case, printing a feature article and searching relentlessly for the whereabouts of Pückler, who has yet to be prosecuted.

As Christa slowly reveals her story to Mathias, and as he conducts further investigations into the matter, the narrative switches from the present time to the early 1980s, when the Stasi began to monitor Ralf and Christa. Ralf, a married professor of chemical engineering at the Karl Marx University in Leipzig, meets Christa, a woman almost half his age, and they begin a passionate affair. When the Stasi agents discover this affair, they use their leverage to force Ralf from Leipzig and into work for them in the "foreign department" in Berlin. When Christa eventually joins him there, the Stasi force her to report information about him, and it soon seems that even their closest friends are on the payroll of the secret police. When Ralf and Christa finally decide to defect to the West, they are double-crossed by their best friends and imprisoned in Hohenschönhausen. There Pückler exacts special pleasure in separating the lovers, then thrusting them together for an hour, separating them, forcing them nude into frigid rooms, separating them, and inflicting assorted other psychological tortures. After Christa has her baby, the prison nurses tell her it is stillborn, and she thinks Ralf has been shot.

Like *The Last Shot, The Love Test* does not comprise a single tale but intertwines the story of Ralf and Christa's imprisonment in the GDR with the collapse of Mathias's marriage in contemporary, unified Berlin. The transitions and connections between these two tales were impressive enough to prompt David Buckley, in *The Guardian* (15 January 1995), to call Hamilton's work "as complex and smooth as an onyx egg." In his explorations of Mathias's marriage Hamilton works at some of the themes that preoccupy him in his later novels; namely, the commercialization of Europe and the reduction of Irish culture to clichéd trends. In addition to the subtle rendering of romantic relationships that he developed in his first two novels, Hamilton becomes in *The Love Test* a more pointed cultural critic, a facet of his writing that dominates *Headbanger* (1997) and *Sad Bastard* (1998). While Mathias and Claudia drift apart,

Hamilton describes in detail the commercialized world in which they live: they drink from "chipped *Jurassic Park* mugs," at parties their friends dance "a cross between Tai Chi and Michael Jackson," and Claudia finds expression for her deepest emotions in Neil Young lyrics. Late in the novel, when Claudia attempts desperately to reconcile with Mathias, her lone outlet of expression is a credit card binge, a "consumer rampage," as Mathias calls it. He returns home to discover that "The whole apartment was full of stuff . . . too many things for Werner to grasp."

This saturation of mass culture is funneled into an exploration of "Irishness," as Claudia begins to pursue an affair with Kevin, an Irishman living in Berlin. Kevin is to some extent representative of Ireland itself, and in having Claudia turn to him for her affair, Hamilton demonstrates how Irish culture is being reduced to an imaginary land for the benefit of the rest of Europe and the world. For Claudia, the affair is permissible because it is almost unreal; she even conducts her trysts with Kevin in English, to ensure they do not "overlap" with her German existence:

> On the first night she even became practical, calmly putting down all kinds of rules which would belong to their affair. She called them the 'Oscar Wilde' rules, after the Irish bar where they would have to practise maximum discretion in case Mathias should go there. . . . There would be no display of affection in public and they would speak English at all times, ensuring that the relationship was always conducted in a semi-imaginary, foreign land; a territory which would never overlap that of her family. They would behave as though they were on holiday in Ireland.

In developing these "Oscar Wilde rules," Claudia not only relegates Kevin to a "semi-imaginary" person but also similarly trivializes Ireland, a phenomenon that Hamilton sees happening all over Europe. Hamilton is worried that, for the rest of Europe, the scope of Irish history and culture is being reduced to a cliché as time-worn as the "traditional" Irish pub. His concern is echoed in his careful description of Claudia and Kevin's meeting place:

> The pub was a piece of Ireland, imported straight from Derry. The wood, the barmen, the pictures of Irish authors and singers on the walls; sepia-coloured Irish street scenes from long ago and posters advertising Irish breakfast. Over the speakers there was Irish music; some song about a woman's heart. . . . Claudia was struck by Ireland-fever. Berlin soon became a small enclave of Ireland.

This interest in the presentation of Irish culture informs Hamilton's next two novels and much of the nonfiction he has published since *The Love Test*.

In 1996 Hamilton collected thirteen short stories written over the span of his career into a volume titled *Dublin Where the Palm Trees Grow*. This short-story collection, which exhibits many of the same themes as Hamilton's novels, was praised by Buckley in a 7 January 1996 review in *The Observer* (London) as "humming with silence." This silence arises from the understatement of stories such as the title piece, in which a couple can barely speak to one another, or "Mad Dog," one of Hamilton's earliest stories, in which a couple resolves to skip out on their lunch without paying for it. *Dublin Where the Palm Trees Grow* also includes some thinly veiled autobiographical tales, such as "Nazi Christmas," in which young Irish-German siblings living in Dublin are accosted by their peers, accused of being Nazis, and pelted with snowballs. In all, Hamilton's stories confirm the preoccupations found in his novels, offering as they do brief glimpses into lives of characters stuck in cultures as varied as they are.

The compartmentalization of Irish culture is a frequent topic of Hamilton's nonfiction articles, which can be used as a point of entry into his political thinking following the publication of *The Love Test*. In his 1998 *Sunday Times* (London) interview, Hamilton told Fay that "every contemporary Irish writer is forecasting the end of Ireland. . . . We're going to be drinking in Irish bars, which is the most European thing you can do." In his many nonfiction articles of the mid to late 1990s, Hamilton returns again and again to this idea of "the end of Ireland," as Irish culture is being subsumed in a global trend of commercialization. In an article titled "Thanks for Nothing, Michael Flatly" (6 September 1998), for example, Hamilton remarks, "We are very happy to have become tourists in our own country. Thirty years ago, everybody would have laughed at the Hollywood image of 'faith and begorrah.' Now we seem chuffed to be reminded." Even in his own reviews of other books, a special target for Hamilton is the "cliched paddywhackery" he uncovers in his *Irish Times* review (17 February 1996) of Michael Collins's short-story collection *The Feminists Go Swimming* (1996). Despite this defense of traditional Irish culture, Hamilton finally told Fay: "I'm not interested in retaining Ireland as a museum culture. . . . I realise it has to move on and I'd prefer it to move on with U2 and Sinead O'Conner. That strikes me as more honest than all this watered-down diddley-aye [such as Riverdance, a popular stage show purporting to be traditional Irish dance]."

Continuing to write articles and publish novels throughout the 1990s, Hamilton has become one of the most respected authors in Ireland, as evidenced by his

Paperback covers for the U.S. editions of Hamilton's novels about the adventures
of a Dublin police officer (Richland County Public Library)

inclusion in the 1997 collaborative novel *Finbar's Hotel.* Conceived and edited by another prominent Irish author, Dermot Bolger, *Finbar's Hotel* has seven authors, each of whom composed a different chapter about the guests of the once-glorious Finbar's Hotel, now rundown and scheduled to be closed. Fellow contributors included Roddy Doyle, whose novel *Paddy Clarke, Ha Ha Ha* won the 1993 Booker Prize, the most prestigious literary award in Britain. One of the most intriguing aspects of *Finbar's Hotel* is that nobody knows which author wrote which chapter, since they were arranged in anonymous order by Bolger, who claimed that even the contributors themselves did not know which of their fellow writers wrote which chapter. *Finbar's Hotel* garnered a good deal of attention from the media in Britain and Ireland and earned generally favorable reviews.

In 1997 Hamilton also published his fourth novel, *Headbanger,* in which he takes his exploration of contemporary Irish culture to the extreme. Both *Headbanger* and its 1998 sequel, *Sad Bastard,* chronicle the adventures of Pat Coyne, a *garda* (police officer) in the Dublin police

force. Beyond the fact that these novels are set in Dublin, they are radical departures from Hamilton's previous work because they are hard-boiled, cop-and-robbers thrillers narrated in a cheeky tone that critics, such as Tim Haigh of *The Independent* (London) (20 September 1998), have labeled "black comedy." In the Coyne novels Hamilton portrays his hero not through quiet emotional interplay as in his previous work but during shoot-outs and car chases and in his reactions to the world of contemporary Dublin. In his review for *The Guardian* (29 May 1997) D. J. Taylor called *Headbanger* a "psychological study masquerading as a thriller," and Hamilton indeed succeeds in creating a sympathetic picture of Coyne amid a Dublin that seems to be falling down around him.

A middle-aged *garda,* Coyne is in a shaky marriage to Carmel, an amateur painter, and he struggles to raise his young son, Jimmy. Coyne has intimate knowledge of the lees and dregs of contemporary Dublin and asserts early in the novel that "The world is fucked, basically." This conviction informs Coyne's loathing for humanity, which he sets against the animal world, a realm he idealizes because it has not yet developed civilization, an absolutely corrupting force. He feeds his interest in the animal kingdom with nature magazines and animal programs on television. In Coyne's world, reality (typified by violence and crime) is directly opposed to art—including the movies, television, and his wife's paintings—which he sees as promoting whitewashed, false versions of Ireland and the world. In order to begin to clean up the mess of reality, Coyne administers "Coyne's Justice," a personal brand of vigilantism that does not necessarily fix the problem and could well end up perpetuating the cycle of violence.

The novel is driven by Coyne's determination to bring down a local Dublin "druglord" called Drummer Cunningham. When official channels have been exhausted, and it looks as though Drummer will emerge scot-free from a murder everybody knows he committed, Coyne decides to take matters into his own hands, to become the "Dublin Dirty Harry." To get Drummer, Coyne crosses the "thin membrane between good and evil" and embraces vigilantism, setting fire to Drummer's Range Rover in the street outside his nightclub. This act touches off a personal war between the two men, which affords Hamilton several cinematic scenes that critics have remarked seem written for the big screen. As Coyne carries on this guerilla warfare, however, his marriage is crumbling—as marriages are in much of Hamilton's work—and his wife's new interest in painting leads to a sexual encounter with her sophisticated teacher. So Coyne's task is clear: to save Dublin from the menace of Drummer Cunningham while rescuing his own failing marriage. This task becomes further complicated when he meets Drummer's girlfriend, Naomi, who is also in need of rescuing, and Coyne himself stumbles into adultery. With this component of the plot, then, the familiar aspects of Hamilton's work emerge. What is much different in Headbanger is the comic tone, the fast-paced action, and the sheer cultural saturation that Coyne senses and the novel performs.

In his quest to "connect the shite back to the arsehole it came from," Coyne launches into another sort of warfare, a battle against a contemporary existence saturated—and indeed defined—by mass-market commercial products. While Coyne goes around criticizing incorrect grammar on street signs and offering anthropological explanations for the behavior of his friends, he bemoans those who "remove reality by watching MTV" and thinks that "The streets of Dublin were like one big movie anyway." Hamilton returns again to the idea that cultural saturation has reached a critical mass in a 6 May 1997 article for The Irish Times:

"We're all suffocating in culture," the misunderstood hero of my novel, Headbanger, bawls at his artist wife across the dinner table. The fact is that we have reached a point, once quaintly termed the "end of history," when there is no experience or political impulse left to engage us that has not already found its way into the TV commercial. There is no mystery. No place left unexplored. No original rainforest without dozens of anthropologists and natural scientists crossing each other's paths and discovering each other's discarded Coke cans.

Coyne's experience in Headbanger, then, is not simply that of a vigilante cop out to bring down a local drug kingpin; it is that of a man as metaphysically and culturally lost as the characters in Hamilton's earlier novels. The difference is that Coyne deals with his feelings of alienation through humor and violence, which allows Hamilton to place him in a script-like action thriller.

For Coyne, the commercialization of Irish culture is also often committed under the guise of "art," about which he seems ambivalent: Carmel comes to represent art, and though Coyne can secretly appreciate the beauty of her paintings, he can never bring himself to tell her so. What seems more familiar to Coyne are the paintings for sale in Merrion Square, a well-known Dublin site near Trinity College: "For amateurs and enthusiasts who drew nice pictures of Irish life with no rubbish in the streets, no puke and no poverty. Trinity College without the kids holding out empty Coke cups. People who drew the faces of Joyce and Beckett five hundred times a week. Liffey paintings with the severed heads of Swift and Wilde floating along the water." Thus, in Headbanger art itself can be guilty of whitewashing Irish culture and promoting the sort of suffocating admonished by both Coyne and Hamilton.

Hamilton followed Headbanger with Sad Bastard, the title of which again refers to Coyne, who has been divorced from Carmel and is no longer a member of the Garda. In the first line of Sad Bastard, Coyne sits "drinking his pint" in a Dublin pub, the very act Hamilton has cited as the ultimate Irish cliché. So, perhaps, more alone than ever, estranged from his wife and his career, nursing injuries sustained in a fire, Coyne has become as contradictory as Ireland itself: unconsciously enacting old clichés while openly trying to deny them. The plot of Sad Bastard is driven by the fruits of Coyne's lackluster parenting in Headbanger: his son, Jimmy, now grown to a teenager, is a headbanger like his father and has a comparable talent for creating trouble for himself. When Jimmy inadvertently makes off with a bagful of cash belonging to Mongi O'Docherty, the villain of the novel, he becomes a marked man, and Coyne has a new mission: to foil Mongi's plans and save his son. Like the Turks in Surrogate City, Romanians figure prominently in

Sad Bastard as a sort of lens through which Hamilton can display Irish culture more clearly (Hamilton composed the Coyne novels following his year of teaching in Bucharest). In his attempt to protect Jimmy, Coyne discovers that Mongi runs a ring that smuggles Romanians into Ireland to serve as little more than slaves. During his investigation he meets Corina Stanescu, a beautiful Romanian immigrant who is the archetypal damsel in distress, much like Naomi in *Headbanger*. Although Coyne is stuck in "The endless loop of heroic failure," he sets out to save his son and Corina, and foil Mongi, all while moving through a changing Ireland that he can barely negotiate.

Many of Hamilton's themes and concerns in *Headbanger* are present again in *Sad Bastard*. If anything, he has amplified them and identified Coyne more closely with Ireland itself. While emphasizing that all humans are fundamentally connected by their biological urges (with techniques such as describing in detail the eating habits of the principal characters of the book—a technique that recalls James Joyce's *Ulysses* [1922]), Hamilton again delivers a Dublin driven by the mandates of popular culture. It is a world that Coyne finds increasingly difficult to navigate, and his son, Jimmy, represents the new Ireland that is slipping from his grasp. Struggling to understand contemporary Irish culture, Coyne meditates: "It was really all about being cool. . . . Cool probably meant the same as being 'holy' used to mean. Being right and sacred with God and all that stuff. Nowadays it was all to do with listening to the right music and being with the right woman. 'Cool' was just the new word for 'holy.'" Coolness is then another culprit in the loss of Irish culture, and as the novel progresses, it is clear that Coyne is far from cool. Coyne's personal life crumbles side by side with Irish culture, as Carmel cultivates a romance with Councillor Hogan, a man whose "weekend love-shacks have nothing to do with Irish culture." Coyne also discovers that the Irish language, a beloved holdover from his youth, has been reduced to a language merely for insults and is spoken only when people threaten one another. Forsaken by this new culture, Coyne is left at the end of *Sad Bastard* with a single, impotent act of defiance: he steals decorative lawn rocks from people's front yards and moves them to a hill where he erects a small monument, his personal "assault on the idea of suburbia."

While many critics agree with Antonia Logue's assessment in her 3 April 1997 review in *The Times* (London) that Coyne is a "majestic creation," some are unsure about Hamilton's overarching project in the Coyne books, especially compared to his three previous novels. John Kenny, for example, writing for *The Irish Times* (3 October 1998), maintained that with *Sad Bastard* "Hamilton has basically written the same flawed novel twice." Kenny's reasoning is that both *Headbanger* and *Sad Bastard* are too

"self-conscious" in their criticism of "Irish social ills," and that if Hamilton "wants to return to form while maintaining his current state-of-the-nation project he should calm down a little and aim to make his view of Ireland more panoramic and his irreverence more stylistically cohesive." Other critics have expressed reservations about the narrative technique of the Coyne novels, suggesting that it is more conducive to a screenplay than a "literary" novel. In a particularly critical review for *Books Ireland* (May 1997) Desmond Traynor speculated that the fact that the Coyne novels are thrillers could itself be an ironic performance of the consumer culture Coyne bemoans: "Perhaps Coyne's anti-art stance is an ironic tongue-in-cheek by Hamilton on how he knows his new work will be received by the more literary of literary critics. . . . *Headbanger* is an average to good thriller, but it represents Hamilton indulging in the opportunism of latching on to a hot topic, this time Dublin's rising crime rate." Despite such initial reluctance from some critics, *Headbanger* and *Sad Bastard* have managed to weather Hamilton's abrupt stylistic change to garner generally warm reviews. Logue in fact acknowledges that "Hamilton took a tremendous risk in moving so dramatically from the territory staked out in his previous three novels, but his gamble has added an extra dimension to his writing." This "extra dimension" of Hamilton's abilities generated enough sales to have prompted an American imprint, Four Walls Eight Windows, to publish *Headbanger* and *Sad Bastard* in the United States in 2001. Hamilton also appeared as a contributor to the collaborative detective novel *Yeats Is Dead! A Novel By Fifteen Irish Authors* (2001), a lighthearted mystery conceived to raise funds for Amnesty International.

Hugo Hamilton is recognized as one of the most important writers in contemporary Ireland. First exploiting his dual cultural identity to gain special entry into German culture, then flipping this perspective to view Ireland against its European backdrop, Hamilton has proven himself an apt cultural critic with an eye for the humane. Throughout his career he has displayed equal dexterity in composing spare and detached narratives of loss and comic thrillers in which irony abounds. As Hamilton continues to write, he seems a new version of the Blasket Island writer: documenting the changes in his natural and adopted homelands while offering persistent critiques undergirded by a quiet awareness of the presence of the past.

Interviews:

"Breaking the Bounds of Nationality," *Books Ireland* (March 1995): 45–46;

Victoria White, "Words Between Languages," *Irish Times,* 4 January 1996, pp. 10–11;

Liam Fay, "Novel Green Gauge," *Sunday Times* (London), 30 August 1998, p. 20.

James Hamilton-Paterson

(6 November 1941 –   )

Michael R. Molino
Southern Illinois University, Carbondale

BOOKS: *Flight Underground* (London: Faber & Faber, 1969);

The House in the Waves (London: Faber & Faber, 1970; New York: S. G. Phillips, 1970);

A Very Personal War: The Story of Cornelius Hawkridge (London: Hodder & Stoughton, 1971); republished as *The Greedy War (A Very Personal War)* (New York: McKay, 1972);

Option Three (London: Gollancz, 1974);

Mummies: Death and Life in Ancient Egypt, by Hamilton-Paterson and Carol Andrews (London: Collins/British Museum Publications, 1978; New York: Viking, 1979);

Hostage! (London: Gollancz, 1978; London: Collins, 1980);

Dutch Alps (Bristol, U.K.: Redcliffe Poetry, 1984);

The View from Mount Dog (London: Macmillan, 1986);

Playing with Water: Passion and Solitude on a Philippine Island (London: Macmillan, 1987; New York: New Amsterdam Books, 1987); republished as *Playing with Water: Alone on a Philippine Island* (Sevenoaks, U.K.: Sceptre, 1988);

Gerontius (London: Macmillan, 1989; New York: Soho Press, 1990);

The Bell-Boy (London: Hutchinson, 1990); republished as *That Time in Malomba* (New York: Soho Press, 1990);

Seven-Tenths: Meditations on the Sea and Its Thresholds (London: Hutchinson, 1992); republished as *The Great Deep: The Sea and Its Thresholds* (New York: Random House, 1992);

Griefwork (London: Cape, 1993; New York: Farrar, Straus & Giroux, 1994);

Ghosts of Manila (London: Cape, 1994; New York: Farrar, Straus & Giroux, 1994);

The Music: Stories (London: Cape, 1995);

Three Miles Down: A Hunt for Sunken Treasure (London: Cape, 1998; New York: Lyons, 1999); republished as *Three Miles Down: A Firsthand Account of Deep Sea Exploration and a Hunt for Sunken World*

James Hamilton-Paterson (photograph by Jerry Bauer; from the dust jacket for Loving Monsters, *2001)*

War II Treasure (San Diego & New York: Harcourt Brace, 2000);

America's Boy: The Rise and Fall of Marcos and Other Misadventures of U.S. Colonialism in the Philippines (London: Granta, 1998); republished as *America's Boy: A Century of Colonialism in the Philippines* (New York: Holt, 1999); republished as *America's Boy: The Marcoses and the Philippines* (London: Granta, 1999);

130

Loving Monsters (London: Granta, 2001; New York: Granta, 2002).

PRODUCED SCRIPT: *Gerontius,* radio, adapted by Hamilton-Paterson from his novel of that title, BBC, 1990.

OTHER: "The Cultural Impact of Oceans," in *Sea Change: The Seascape in Contemporary Photography,* edited by Trudy Wilner Stack (Tucson: Center for Creative Photography, University of Arizona, 1998), pp. 9–12.

SELECTED PERIODICAL PUBLICATIONS–UNCOLLECTED: "Waiting for Che," *New Statesman* 77 (4 April 1969): 473–474;
"Sea Burial," *Granta,* 61 (January 1998): 7–49;
"Asking for It," *Granta,* 68 (December 1999): 228–232;
"When I Was Lost," *Granta,* 72 (December 2000): 235–246;
"The Separate World of Seaports," *Granta,* 75 (October 2001): 129–168;
"What We Think of America," *Granta,* 77 (March 2002): 44–47.

James Hamilton-Paterson is one of those writers who, like James Joyce, chose to forsake his native country for a life of self-imposed exile. Unlike Joyce, however, Hamilton-Paterson has not spent his artistic life writing about the country of his birth, much the opposite in fact. Although he was forty-eight years old when he published his first literary novel, *Gerontius* (1989), by that time Hamilton-Paterson had been writing for more than twenty years. His nonfiction work reflects his expatriate status, in part because Hamilton-Paterson does not want to remain in England writing for an audience of literary critics but also because it reveals his preference for travel, the sea, and the purity of life in what many would call unrefined surroundings. Today Hamilton-Paterson shuttles between two worlds: a house in the mountains of southern Tuscany, where he lives for about nine months out of the year, and the even more rustic setting of a hut on a Philippine island, where he lives the other three months. In such surroundings, free of the trappings of modern life, Hamilton-Paterson has written novels that are notable for their divergent topics, subtle social satire, unblinking critical judgment, and lush and meditative prose. Among his contemporaries Hamilton-Paterson is most commonly compared to Bruce Chatwin, another peripatetic writer of travel and fiction. Among his predecessors Hamilton-Paterson recalls the probing wit and irony of Evelyn Waugh.

In a 1990 interview with David Finkle, Hamilton-Paterson explained his relationship with his homeland:

"I actually don't think of myself as being particularly English. Everybody tells me I'm absolutely, characteristically English, but it's not something I either think about or, indeed, react to very happily when I hear it. It's not to say that I think of myself as wonderfully cosmopolitan. I just don't think of myself as having a particular cultural center." The adult Hamilton-Paterson may not have a "cultural center," but as a child he benefited from the best that British culture had to offer.

The offspring of physicians, Hamilton-Paterson was born in war-torn London on 6 November 1941. His father, John Hamilton-Paterson, was a neurologist, and his mother, Ursula Im Thurn Hamilton-Paterson, an anesthetist. Because his father was serving in the Royal Army Medical Corps (RAMC), Hamilton-Paterson did not know him well, and their relationship was strained after the elder Hamilton-Paterson was discharged in 1945. Solidly middle-class, Hamilton-Paterson's parents did what was common for people of their status: they sent their children away to boarding school. At the age of eight Hamilton-Paterson was sent to the first of three schools: Windlesham House, a country house among the South Downs of Sussex; then to a school in Kent, whose lush landscape Hamilton-Paterson describes in *Playing with Water: Passion and Solitude on a Philippine Island* (1987) as an "island amid suburbia"; and finally to King's School in Canterbury.

The reference to an island is no idle metaphor for Hamilton-Paterson. In June 1953, at the age of twelve, his imagination wandering during class, Hamilton-Paterson drew a map of an island in his exercise book. When his mother returned that exercise book to him thirty-three years later, Hamilton-Paterson was stunned to discover that the map he had drawn so idly as a child represented the contours of the Philippine island on which he had then been living for many years. In *Playing with Water* Hamilton-Paterson claims "to disdain the slow chronology of childhood and adolescence" but nonetheless admits that the map in the exercise book is one of those events that "echo down a life and go on appearing weirdly relevant and even influential in what one is and does." Thus, the trajectory of Hamilton-Paterson's life represents a course away from the "cultural center" of his youth inexorably toward a place far from home.

In 1961 Hamilton-Paterson continued his education at Exeter College, Oxford. Two events stand out in Hamilton-Paterson's years at Oxford. The first occurred in his first year, when his father died at the age of forty-seven. Hamilton-Paterson admits to having had an unhappy relationship with his father, and portions of his nonfiction book *Playing with Water* involve critical self-examination of the antagonism he held toward his father while growing up. The other event

*Dust jacket for the 1991 U.S. edition of Hamilton-Paterson's
1989 novel, a fictionalized account of composer Edward
Elgar's 1923 cruise up the Amazon River
(Richland County Public Library)*

occurred in his final year at Oxford. In 1964, at the age of twenty-two, Hamilton-Paterson won the prestigious Newdigate Prize for poetry, the same award Oscar Wilde won while attending Oxford. Upon graduation, though, rather than parlay his award into a career as a poet, Hamilton-Paterson left England and taught in a government-run school in Tripoli, Libya, for about a year. During that time Hamilton-Paterson wrote his first novel. Although never published, this first effort revealed one of the directions Hamilton-Paterson's life would take: he had decided that he wanted to make his living as a writer.

When he returned to England a year later, Hamilton-Paterson took a job as an orderly and operating-room technician at St. Stephen's Hospital, where he worked for the next three years. His writing career began in 1968 when he took a trip—much like the one portrayed in his first novel, *Gerontius*—up the Amazon. After spending several months traveling in South America, particu-

larly Bolivia, Hamilton-Paterson submitted a piece to *The New Statesman,* "Waiting for Che," which published it on 4 April 1969 and offered him a job filling in for vacationing writers. This first job was Hamilton-Paterson's introduction to journalism, a field he pursued during the early 1970s–traveling in Latin America and Indochina, writing as a freelance journalist for *TLS: The Times Literary Supplement, The New Statesman,* and *The Sunday Times* (London). While writing books based on his journalistic travels—such as *A Very Personal War: The Story of Cornelius Hawkridge* (1971), about U.S. involvement in the Vietnam War—Hamilton-Paterson also began writing children's novels. The first novel for children, *Flight Underground,* was published in 1969, followed by *The House in the Waves* in 1970, and then *Hostage!* in 1978.

Although he wrote extensively during the 1970s and 1980s, including volumes of short stories and poems, Hamilton-Paterson's nonfiction memoir of his life in the Philippines, *Playing with Water,* marks a point of transition at which his writing gained greater recognition. When *Playing with Water* was first published in the United States in 1987, it sold a mere 150 copies and garnered a single review in a Midwestern newsletter. Three years later, however, reviewing the paperback publication of *Playing with Water,* William H. Gass brought Hamilton-Paterson to the attention of the American reading public with a glowing review in *The New York Times Book Review* (29 April 1990). Praising the descriptive passages of the book, Gass particularly acknowledged Hamilton-Paterson's ability to draw a reader into a world that links author with reader: "I was reminded . . . while reading *Playing with Water* of those intense and aimlessly happy hours spent in pages of books before I became a professional skimmer and scanner and interpreter of texts, and how immersed my soul was in the superior spirit of another." Gass also identified what most reviewers agree is Hamilton-Paterson's strength as a writer, his style: "What makes this book so remarkable is not its ostensible subjects, interesting though they are, but its style: a style of mind, the poise of one who knows that everything is matter-of-fact and nothing is, a sensibility that allows a graceful dialogue between meaning and emotion, a talent that achieves that unity of word and reality that is the poet's special gift."

Known to be prickly in interviews and other publishing activities but lyrical and reflective in his writing, Hamilton-Paterson explains his relationship with his home country best in *Playing with Water:*

Sooner or later I shall have to visit England, see people. Such trips fill me with mixed pleasure and dread. . . . The last time I was in London I was bemused and stunned by it. . . . Now the sea felt immeasurably far away and it was in any case the wrong sea. . . . In rhetorical moments I say: 'I don't know how on earth people can live in England.' What I actually mean, of course, is that I no longer know of any way in which I could. I have lost the knowledge of how to get by in a predominantly urban society. I am no longer intrigued enough by arcana, blandished enough by its pleasures, consoled enough by its facilities. Provided the climate is warm I don't mind a leaky roof, washing dishes in the sea, fetching water on my shoulder. They are neither pressures nor hardships, simply the minimal terms on which one lives in a way one chooses in a landscape of one's choice.

In *Playing with Water* Hamilton-Paterson lends some insight into his views of national identity as well as his preoccupation with travel and the sea. If landscape is the source of longing for the past, then its opposite may hold the key to contemplation of the eternal:

Nostalgia is very much the home province of the English and when they tap into its rich vein they become adult-children perpetually grieving over some indefinable passing, a whole nation in mourning for the pre-lapsarian. How easy it becomes to view a landscape in these terms and how full our school poetry-books were of its afforded vision. . . . Now the thought comes: in my private war with my own past the English landscape really serves as the battlefield. I love foreignness in landscapes to the exact degree with which they violently contrast with my inherited notions of how a landscape ought to look. Whatever my sense of loss it now needs other metaphors to express itself.

By the time he published *Gerontius* in 1989, Hamilton-Paterson was dividing his time between Italy and the Philippines. He chose a trip up the Amazon as the framework for *Gerontius,* a novel based on a real event. In 1923, at the age of sixty-six, the British composer Edward Elgar took a trip up the Amazon on the cruise ship *Hildebrand.* Biographers acknowledge the trip but know little regarding Elgar's motivation for taking it or what happened during it. Hamilton-Paterson makes these unknown factors in Elgar's trip the topic of his novel, which follows the composer from the time he boards the train in England in anticipation of his trip to his return. In between, the elderly composer, now well past his prime, looks back on a career and sees failure rather than success. Well-known and respected though he may be, Elgar views his career as one in which financial considerations rather than artistic inspiration motivated his work. Elgar also believes that when his artistic inspiration was expressed, it reached only ignorant or indifferent ears. Thus, *Gerontius* is a novel both about an external journey filled with the wonders of an untamed and exotic landscape

and also an internal journey filled with old-age doubts about the supposed timelessness of art.

Hamilton-Paterson makes the journey worthwhile for both character and reader by populating the ship with a variety of interesting characters, some of whom spur serious contemplation in Elgar, others comic moments. Elgar shares a dining table with two elderly women, Mrs. Dora Bellamy and Mrs. Kate Hammond, who seem benign enough on the surface but prove a wily pair of card sharks who earn a living luring unsuspecting passengers into games of chance. Two of the other passengers Elgar encounters are planning, each in his or her own way, to represent the Amazon. The first is a World War I aviator who has begun a scheme to map the Amazon region from the air. A new breed of explorer and entrepreneur, Fortescue represents an exciting and affirmative side of the modern technology that proved so devastating during the war. The most interesting relationship during the voyage is the one between Elgar and a young aspiring artist named Molly Air. Molly is traveling to the Amazon because she wants to paint the vivid plant life of the Amazon in a way never seen before. The exchanges between Elgar, prone to pessimism bordering on self-indulgent excess, and the naive but earnest young painter probe contrasting views of the relationship between artist and art as well as the demands and potential pitfalls of the artistic life.

The title of the novel is derived from Elgar's masterpiece, his oratorio *The Dream of Gerontius* (1900), which is in turn based on the nineteenth-century poem by Cardinal John Henry Newman, in which Gerontius travels from his deathbed to the edge of Purgatory, with Judgment Day and God referred to as a distant promise by his escorting angel. Thus, Elgar's physical trip up the Amazon and his concurrent emotional journey expressed in his journal are complemented by Elgar's musical creation and the metaphysical journey it represents. Elgar's physical and emotional journey, however, does not end with eternal rest or even a renewed spirit. At the far side of the world, at the halfway point in his journey, Elgar encounters a former love, Lena von Pussels, who years earlier married a fabulously wealthy rubber baron and moved to the small Amazonian town of Manaos. Lena has not forgotten Elgar over the years but instead kept close record of his accomplishments and compositions. A fervent patron of the arts, Lena has built the Schiller Institute in the town, which stands as a kind of cultural beacon amid the encroaching jungle: "Here in the middle of however many million square kilometers of jungle dotted with naked savages still occupied with blowpipes and shrinking each others' heads, a cultivated young man had just tuned a very beautiful instrument on which later that

Dust jacket for the U.S. edition of Hamilton-Paterson's 1990
novel, published in London as The Bell-Boy
(Richland County Public Library)

after all these years, yet she also reveals the inherent dependency between the arts and commerce. The glorious Opera House and her own Schiller Institute stand in Manaos precisely because wealthy patrons built them. These buildings and the artistry they contain are as much victims of the transience of commerce as any local business.

Reviewers, as well as admirers of Elgar's music, responded favorably to *Gerontius*. In a review in *The New York Times Book Review* (30 June 1991), John Rockwell praised both the tale and its telling: "But if this tale is inhabited by Elgar, it embodies even more Mr. Hamilton-Paterson's own quietly ecstatic response to nature and the uneasy balance he has struck between protean forces and civilized veneer. The writing throughout this novel is a joy, the kind of prose that instantly seizes attention. But it is the description of nature, the rapturous effusions in the face of alien wonder, that transforms this book." Walter Nash also praised *Gerontius,* not for Hamilton-Paterson's response to the world around him, but because the novel focuses so relentlessly on the decline of creativity and the potential failure of art and civilization to survive the simple passage of time. Writing for *The London Review of Books* (4 May 1989), Nash asserted that "There is no romantic consequence, there is no comfortable restoration of the old artist's fading powers. Instead there is confrontation, never quite over, realized mostly in Lena's affronted musings, a moral confrontation in which, if the truth be told, Elgar is found wanting. . . . This is a fine book, but painful reading for those who grimly abide the lapse of craft, the loss of energy, the decline of perception and feeling." *Gerontius* went on to win the 1989 Whitbread Prize for First Novel.

Published in 1990 as *The Bell-Boy* in Great Britain and *That Time in Malomba* in the United States, Hamilton-Paterson's second novel could not have been more different from his first. *The Bell-Boy* tells the story of Tessa Hemony, a 1960s holdover and devotee of Eastern mysticism, and her children as they travel to the fictional city of Malomba, in Southeast Asia, in search of psychic surgery. Malomba, known as one of the most spiritual cities in the world, is the crossroads of thirty-nine different religions, their churches, mosques, temples, synagogues, and so on. Upon their arrival in Malomba, Tessa and her daughter, Zoe, and her son, Jason, meet a young bellboy, Laki, who has moved to the city from his small village in search of wealth and success. When the four meet, East meets West to comic effect as Hamilton-Paterson reveals the fantasies of wealth those from the East have about those from the West, as well as the assumptions of innocence and spirituality those from the West have regarding those from the East.

evening an Italian girl was to play Scarlatti, Mendelssohn, Schumann and Busoni. It was going on. It was proceeding. The darkness would have to take a further step backwards."

The echoes of Joseph Conrad's *Heart of Darkness* (1899) are inescapable throughout the novel. However, Hamilton-Paterson takes a different approach to the topics of civilization, commerce, and culture. Unlike Elgar, whose pessimism has waxed as his creative powers have waned, Lena has remained faithful in her commitment to art, even in the face of the physical and spiritual devastation of the war. Although the character of Lena is an invention of Hamilton-Paterson, she serves the theme of the novel well. While Elgar continually grouses about making money and his penurious state, which diminishes him as an artist in some people's eyes, Lena represents the opposite perspective. Lena's dedication to the value of the magic mountain of artistic achievement remains unshaken

The city of Malomba is as much a character in the novel as any of the people who find themselves navigating its streets. With streets named for states of grace or pillars of virtue, every physical journey carries a spiritual subtext, often one that contrasts with the actual purpose of the journey. For example, when Laki follows Zoe to a local nightclub with hopes of a romantic interlude, "He knew where she was heading even before she left Justice and turned into Sobriety. . . . Her walk was purposeful and she didn't hesitate when she reached the junction with Awareness." Later in the novel Laki's dream comes true when the two spend several unusual and awkward hours in a pagoda on the grounds of the Redemptorist Fathers' monastery. Zoe turns out to be something other than the beautiful, virginal goddess Laki imagines her to be, and Zoe turns the tables on Laki, rendering him confused and vulnerable.

Laki, whose name the Hemonys mistake as "Lucky," is not so much a con-man as a boy who dares to dream of bettering himself financially in a city where commerce and religion indistinguishably meld. Malomba, after all, is the place where billboards read, "'The Bank of the Divine Lotus. Where Purity Meets Security.'" Eventually, Laki's sexual fantasies are realized, not with Zoe, however, but with Tessa. As a result of spending several nights with Laki, the chronic back pain from which Tessa has suffered for ten years disappears. The probing fingers of the psychic surgeon have been preempted, making Tessa's impending surgery and indeed her trip to Malomba unnecessary. In the end everyone seems to get what he or she wants. Tessa is cured but visits the renowned psychic surgeon anyway, and Laki makes out financially when Tessa gives him a gift of money whose amount exceeds even Laki's powers of imagination. As valued Western tourists, the Hemonys enter and leave Malomba unmolested by the authorities. Laki, on the other hand, is simply another undesirable from the provinces. The novel ends with the safe return of the Hemonys to their world while the physical forces that keep the spiritual city running smoothly, namely Malomba's police thugs, enlighten Laki to third-world justice. The money the Hemonys give to Laki in a fit of guilty conscience or misguided beneficence leads to Laki's plight at the end of the novel. While he dreams of his recent financial windfall, what amounts in Malomba to a small fortune, Laki is visited by a group of off-duty police thugs who beat the boy and steal his money. Thus, the novel ends on a note of sadness and irony. The Hemonys came to Malomba seeking both physical relief and spiritual enlightenment. Despite the fact that they do not wish to harm Laki, they do not appreciate their own privileged status well enough to anticipate the consequences of their actions for Laki.

Reviewers of the novel agreed that the story of innocence abroad represents a well-worn path in literature, but most reviewers also agreed that Hamilton-Paterson's description of Malomba and his ironic portrait of those innocents (and those not so innocent) steers the novel away from that path. In his review for *The Boston Globe* (17 December 1990) Robert Taylor argued that "Although the plot of *That Time in Malomba* is a shade too schematic and derivative of Waugh, Angus Wilson, P. H. Newby and others . . . the novel's prismatic descriptions and scintillations of wit promise a bright future." In *The New York Times Book Review* (14 October 1990) the novelist Michael Malone saw the same literary antecedents as Taylor but believed Hamilton-Paterson had found his place among their membership: "But what makes this book more like the dark comedy of Evelyn Waugh than the spoofery of [E. F.] Benson is that its irony cuts all ways—faith healers are shysters *and* healers, cynics are disabused as well as confirmed, and belief—that is, the capacity for belief—is left, like life, undestroyed by all the Armageddons to which religions have for millenniums subjected it. . . . Few books since E. M. Forsters's *Passage to India* [1924] (whose formal perfection this novel shares) have conveyed more intensely the allure (and revulsion) the East holds for Westerners." David Williams, however, writing for the *Los Angeles Times* (16 September 1990), dismissed the novel as just another "form of literary Orientalism, a beautifully written fantasy about the East for people who will never go there. It is in the tradition of European chinoiserie."

In some ways Hamilton-Paterson's third novel, *Griefwork* (1993), recalls his first, *Gerontius*. Both novels focus on a lonely figure who has dedicated his life to creating beauty, for Elgar musical compositions and for Leon an exotic botanical garden. Both men see their creations through times of great cultural upheaval, World War I and World War II respectively. Both men believe that others, with a few exceptions, fail to appreciate their creations and that most treat their works merely as convenient forms of entertainment and escape. In contrast, though, Leon commands none of the awe Elgar does, nor does he move within respectable society as freely as does Elgar. Any respect directed at Leon comes from his clear genius for creating and maintaining Palm House, a beautiful greenhouse that endures and even thrives during the years the Nazis occupy the unnamed country in which the novel is set. However, Leon's unkempt appearance and unusual behavior make him an outsider at a time when such traits could be life threatening. Leon's dedication to his plants continues and even strength-

*Dust jacket for the U.S. edition of Hamilton-Paterson's 1994
novel, whose setting reviewer Edward T. Wheeler
compared favorably to "the borderland territory
so well traveled by Graham Greene"
(Richland County Public Library)*

ens despite the condition of the outside world, whereas Elgar's attitude toward his music diminishes as his reputation wanes. This unwavering dedication to his creation and his antagonism to the commercial forces at work in the city after the war drive Leon to the brink of madness. In contrast, by deciding to conduct and record his compositions when he returns to England, Elgar envisions a new form of commercial gain for himself that also ensures him a respected place in the pantheon of composers. Bach and Beethoven, after all, never had the opportunity to record their own compositions. The nature and importance of art, or a created world, recur as central concerns in both *Gerontius* and *Griefwork*. Art may not prevent human calamities such as world wars, but it perseveres despite them. Art may be subject to commercial concerns, but its worth cannot be underval-

ued. In an uncharacteristically impassioned outburst, Leon explains to Dr. Anselmus, the director of the Botanical Gardens, why the Palm House must be saved despite the cost: "Within my Palm House I'm authentic, and so is it. Far, far away there's a vast natural simulacrum of what I already live in. Part of our job as I see it is to train the public to understand that museum, memorial, research centre—whatever it is, the place is priceless. It's *because* it's so unnatural it can make people think and change their minds. We must preserve it at all costs. At any cost at all, really, since it'll never be rebuilt."

In *Gerontius*, Hamilton-Paterson chose a traditional method of plumbing the depths of his character's conscience by having Elgar write in a journal during his travels. In *Griefwork*, however, Hamilton-Paterson chose a more innovative but, for some reviewers, too peculiar technique. From his youth in a small coastal North Sea town, Leon was an unusual child who could sense, perhaps even hear and interpret, the natural world around him. As a child, Leon learns the language of the birds, wind, and sea—fashioning a vocabulary that articulates the voices of nature around him. When he moves to the capitol of the unnamed country where he lives, Leon's ability has matured to the point that he seems capable of conversing with the plants that populate his beloved Palm House. Each chapter in the novel thus ends with a soliloquy or dialogue by various plants in the Palm House, whose comments act as a kind of chorus on the action that has just taken place.

In *The Boston Review* (December 1995/January 1996) James Hynes claimed that this narrative technique "takes some getting used to, because the plants turn out to be chattier and funnier than anybody else in the book—certainly more so than Leon, who has the grimness of obsession." Novelist Philip Hensher in his review for *The Guardian* (18 May 1993) challenged the technique more forcefully: "The fantasy is a good idea, but it is difficult to suppress doubts about the way Hamilton-Paterson has put it into the novel. . . . It's such a bold device, which at every moment suggests whimsy; and it doesn't quite justify itself by telling us enough about Leon through his fantasy." Both reviewers noted the device Hamilton-Paterson employs at the end of each chapter when the plants speak up to assess the thoughts, actions, and intentions of the humans around them. The device functions much in the way Elgar's journal does in *Gerontius*, as a bridge between the main character's external world of words and deeds and his internal world of thoughts and dreams. Hamilton-Paterson thus creates a device that easily can be described as a variation on interior monologue or stream of consciousness, in which Leon's overt and unambiguous affection for his plants articulates the loss and longing for which Leon finds no other outlet. The internal urges of the self find clearest expression through the others closest to him, his plants: "Sometimes these dialogues told him things he hadn't known he knew. Not the least strange aspect of this odd man was that he was thus able to be unself-aware while providing a half-amused, knowing commentary as though he were standing a long way off from himself or as if it were all happening in a distant country."

In a 10 June 2001 interview with Bella Bathurst of *The Sunday Herald* (London), Hamilton-Paterson remarked, "Perhaps I'm a dinosaur, but I do quite like a chronological thread or narrative thread." The shift in narrative at the end of each chapter acts as that thread in *Griefwork,* because long-held grief and long-desired love find expression by plants that cannot be expressed by their human counterpart. Leon's mother was killed by a falling piece of glass when Leon was just a child. His relatives and neighbors withheld the news of his mother's death from the boy to save him the pain of knowing his mother would never return. For all their good intentions, these relatives and friends only ensured that Leon's grief would never cease. Years later, Leon finds contentment of a sort, caring for his trees and plants under the glass of the Palm House. The novel ends when Felix, an apparently mute human whom Leon has imprisoned inside the garden, breaks the panes of glass protecting the inside of the Palm House from the hostile elements, ensuring the death of the physical plants Leon loves as well as the expressions of Leon's love those plants articulate. As the bits of glass fall and the winter winds blow into the wrecked Palm House, the plants realize their imminent fate, and the tamarind confesses his love for the misplaced hemlock plant that grew by its side for years. In the midst of its expression of grief and love, the tamarind refers to the hemlock by its scientific name, *Conium,* and then as Cou Min, the name of a Chinese servant girl the youthful Leon knew for just a short while but adored for a lifetime. The two words are anagrams of each other, a kind of transference, through which the world and the words of plants express the love and loss of the human, and Leon can say good-bye to one he has always loved.

Ghosts of Manila (1994), Hamilton-Paterson's fourth novel, reflects a change from his earlier novels in both storytelling technique and topic. Although the novel is framed by the arrival and departure of one of its main characters, John Prideaux, *Ghosts of Manila* is a story of many perspectives told by many characters, each of whom gain access to different parts of the Philippine capital and offer different interpretations and knowledge of life therein. To a greater extent than do his earlier novels, *Ghosts of Manila* links Hamilton-Paterson's journalistic interests in and writings on Southeast Asia with his fiction. The novel *Ghosts of Manila* provides a fictional account of the Philippines few Westerners have seen or wish to see.

Unlike his earlier novels, which focus on the lives of one or two characters, *Ghosts of Manila* weaves together the story of many characters: John Prideaux, a British anthropology student who, paradoxically, questions the possibility that someone from one culture can study another; Rio Dingcas, a reasonably honest Filipino police inspector who works within an unreasonably corrupt system; Sharon Polick, a displaced American archaeologist whose discovery changes the lives of countless Filipinos; Ysabella Bastiaan, a British archaeologist who uncovers a personal past while digging for a cultural one; Vic Agusan, a zealous but realistic Filipino reporter whose tabloid stories of corruption and violence seem eerily accurate in the backstreets and slums of Manila; and Epifania Tugos, a Filipino squatter who organizes a sewing co-op in an attempt to eke out a living. These main characters encounter a chauffeur- turned-Filipino-senator; several Catholic priests, both real and fake; various colleagues, lovers, and family members; many unseen nefarious figures who haunt the daily life of almost all Filipinos; and a host of named and unnamed ghosts, victims of a corrupt system, who inhabit the buildings and streets of Manila with nowhere else to go.

Ghosts of Manila aggressively explores topics of political and social relevance in contemporary Filipino society as well as lingering vestiges of colonial power and domination. Hamilton-Paterson's cast of characters exposes in various ways aspects of a country tourists choose not to see, governments prefer to ignore, and academics refuse to accept. For example, John Prideaux comes to the Philippines to study the phenomenon of *amok*–a point at which an individual, usually a male, snaps and goes on a killing spree that is later occluded by amnesia. With a background in documentary moviemaking, Prideaux wants to understand, explain, and then relate the reason the psyche of an otherwise ordinary person just snaps: "Underneath, though, anyone could recognize that injustice piled on hardship and topped with ever more injustice bedded down into something not unlike a permanent state of pain: that pain which so many carried and which now and then could break out in frenzy with a gun spraying bullets or a machete flailing in a last, desperate attempt to clear a

Dust jacket for the 2001 novel in which a fictional
character sets out to write a biography of an author
who shares Hamilton-Paterson's interest in the
Philippines (Richland County Public Library)

ties while others will wind up in the homes of wealthy Filipino senators.

The Filipino characters Rio Dingcas, Vic Agusan, and Epifania Tugos function within a corrupt system without being thoroughly corrupted by it. These three characters not only take the reader to virtually every part of Manila but also reveal forms of human dignity and conscience at odds with their surroundings. Hamilton-Paterson is thus able to plunge deep into the heart of a society and its political machinery and dig into its archaeological and colonial past in a novel that also reveals a place as home to millions. Michael Harris, in his review for the *Los Angeles Times* (20 February 1995), praised Hamilton-Paterson's mixture of Filipino personal and political life: "For a novel that is so much of an intellectual construct, *Ghosts of Manila* is remarkably alive. Hamilton-Paterson crams it with gaudy prose, lurid and hyper-exact detail, outrageous stories (many undoubtedly true) and humor. . . . The Op-Ed musings are provocative, but not so loud that we can't hear the cries of the victims." In a review for *Commonweal* (21 April 1995) Edward T. Wheeler favorably compared Hamilton-Paterson to one of his well-known contemporaries: "The novel inhabits the borderland territory so well traveled by Graham Greene. . . . But there is also a bluntness of language in the characterization and description of violence alien to Greene."

After *Ghosts of Manila*, Hamilton-Paterson published *The Music: Stories* (1995), a short-story collection that reflects his interest in music, and *Three Miles Down: A Hunt for Sunken Treasure* (1998), a nonfiction account of his experiences accompanying an unsuccessful 1995 attempt to salvage gold from two vessels, a Japanese submarine and a British troopship, that were sunk during World War II. In September 1998, about seven months after *Three Miles Down* appeared, Hamilton-Paterson published a nonfiction account of Ferdinand Marcos's years ruling the Philippines, titled *America's Boy: The Rise and Fall of Marcos and Other Misadventures of U.S. Colonialism in the Philippines*. As the subtitle indicates, the book is a reexamination of the dictator's rule in a way that neither demonizes Marcos in the manner common to Western journalism nor excuses the abuses of power and rampant corruption endemic to his government. In *Ghosts of Manila*, Hamilton-Paterson skillfully combines his knowledge of the Filipino people, based largely on his experience of living in the Philippines for many years, with his journalistic research into the Filipino government. In that sense, fact informs fiction in *Ghosts of Manila*, though the two remain distinguishable.

path for the soul through a tangling darkness." While interviewing people as background for his thesis on amok, Prideaux realizes that he does not and probably never will fully understand the society he has come to study, that the myriad factors leading to such a snap are as deeply ingrained in the culture as they are in the individual's psyche. Sharon Polick and Ysabella Bastiaan discover a seven-hundred-year-old Chinese burial ground that may be the most important archaeological discovery in years. Unfortunately, the dig site is in the middle of a squatters' enclave where thousands of displaced people reside in horrifying poverty. A convenient, unexplained, and uninvestigated fire then clears the area of squatters. From past events, the reader is then able to see the future: a government institute will present itself to oversee the site and the precious artifacts uncovered therein, many of which will unaccountably find their way onto the black market in antiqui-

In his fifth novel, *Loving Monsters* (2001), Hamilton-Paterson blurs the distinction between fact and fiction in order to write a novel about a fictional character, Raymond Jerningham Jebb, who solicits a kind of gentlemen's agreement from a writer named James to write his biography. The prospective biographer, author of several books on the sea, lives on a hill in Tuscany and worries about impending interviews and deadlines for a book he is writing on Marcos, the former dictator of the Philippines.

To confuse matters further, Jerningham Jebb, known as Jayjay, describes himself as a professional impostor who has made his way through life apparently freely donning identities as need or whim demanded: "'To maintain a consistent character from one end of your life to the other takes just as much energy and subterfuge and self-deception as it does to slip into interesting roles as they're offered. More, probably. One easily gets carried along by the sheer thrill of transgressing.'" Even more confounding is the fact that the novel is punctuated by photographs, some ostensibly derived from Jayjay's extensive collection of pre–World War II pornography, several that could be Jayjay's relatives, and one of Jayjay's gravestone, which James is planning to purchase as the novel begins. Scattered among these photographs that in part document the life of a fictional character—no photos of the adult Jayjay appear in the book—are photographs of the Tuscan landscape, including one of James's beehive, which commands the view from both Jayjay's and James's windows. The end result is a novel that draws the reader into a world in which a fictional author has to pull the true story out of a fictional impostor, while the real author occasionally breaks from the conversation to interview real members of the brutal Marcos regime who willingly tell their stories in the hope they will recuperate their damaged reputations.

Jayjay approaches James one day in the local co-op in Castiglion Fiorentino near the place both men live. Jayjay's charm and graciousness intrigue James, who finds himself slowly drawn into Jayjay's world, where a personally signed photograph of Henry Kissinger hangs in the guest bathroom, a thank-you letter from Margaret Thatcher sits on the desk, and a silver replica of Benjamin Disraeli's genitals lies flattened, though intact, on the bookshelf. From that moment James is hooked, and he agrees to write Jayjay's biography. The two men work together and eventually become as close friends as an old impostor and an unrepentant loner can be. In fact, the two become close because Jayjay eventually reveals more than he intended, after James astutely peels away the patina of fraud in Jayjay's stories and

demands that Jayjay fill in the ellipses with details. Jayjay's biography, then, changes from being a lively story about a young man who leaves a pedestrian life in England for a ribald and thrilling life in the Middle East before and during World War II to being a poignant story of love imagined in youth and longed-for over a lifetime.

If Hamilton-Paterson has one recurring feature in his fiction, it is the use of a frame narrative around his story. The train ride before and after Elgar's voyage up the Amazon frames *Gerontius*. Laki leaving his hutch on top of the hotel one morning and Laki driven from his hutch one evening frame *The Bell-Boy*. In *Griefwork*, the Palm House in its prime and in its demise frames the novel. *Ghosts of Manila* is framed by John Prideaux's arrival in and departure from the Philippines. The last flickers of Jayjay's life frame *Loving Monsters,* with his final conversation with James beginning the novel and it ending with James opening a package that holds the pornography Jayjay has left James in his will.

Between the frame in *Loving Monsters,* though, Hamilton-Paterson does more than simply play with the boundaries distinguishing fact from fiction, for the story of Jayjay and James working together on Jayjay's biography carries into James's work on Marcos and his henchmen. As a result, the question of identity and personality as constructs that can be created and reinvented recurs in various forms throughout the novel. On the one hand, Jayjay, the admitted impostor, is not seeking redemption through his biography. If it were not for James's careful attention to detail, Jayjay's prevarications might have stood as his lasting legacy, resulting in a biography that was little more than a ribald jaunt through the years between World War I and World War II. The story of Jayjay's compassion and love would have been obscured by his selective revelations, and the subsequent biography would be just another impersonation donned by Jayjay. On the other hand, Marcos's former generals display all the good manners of proper society while they hide in well-protected homes that overlook beautiful beaches or breathtaking skylines. Their civility and wealth were purchased at the high cost of human lives. James's reputation as an unbiased journalist motivates these former henchmen to tell their stories as well. Unlike Jayjay, however, these men do not define themselves as impostors, certainly not as butchers, but as patriots. These men nonetheless are impostors of a sort. They, like Jayjay, have something they wish to hide, something they have never said out loud before, but something they paradoxically wish to reveal as well.

Hamilton-Paterson admitted in his 2001 interview with Bathurst that his disparate interests satisfy him but frustrate his publisher: "My problem is that I refuse to write the same kind of book over and over again and therefore it's very difficult to market me." Despite any marketing difficulties he presents to publishers, James Hamilton-Paterson has developed a reputation for writing carefully crafted prose in a wide variety of genres, publishing, in addition to novels, volumes of poetry, short-story collections, children's fiction, and nonfiction works. He also writes a fortnightly column on marine and scientific matters for *Das Magazin,* a Swiss weekly. If becoming well-known demands that he spend more time in England placating the marketing desires of publishers, then Hamilton-Paterson is more than willing to remain unknown. If being known by select readers as a fine stylist who entertains with lively wit and challenges with blunt details, then Hamilton- Paterson, as he told Bathurst, will be content to write his books from either his hilltop home in Tuscany or his small hut in the Philippines, just as long as he does not have to repeat himself. Readers tend to feel the same way, responding favorably to Hamilton-Paterson's wide-ranging topics and styles. As John de Falbe admitted in his 12 May 2001 review for *The Spectator* (London), "It is a tribute to the power of *Loving Monsters* that, on finishing it, I ignored the plaintive pile of unread books on the bedside table and instead hunted down and read some of the author's earlier work."

Interviews:

David Finkle, "James Hamilton-Paterson: The Peripatetic Author Weaves the Theme of Cultural Disorientation into His Work," *Publishers Weekly* (21 September 1990): 56–57;

Jean W. Ross, "James Hamilton-Paterson," *Contemporary Authors,* volume 137, edited by Susan M. Trosky and Donna Olendorf (Detroit: Gale Research, 1992), pp. 181–185;

Charles Nicholl, "Gone Fishing for the Truth," *Independent* (London), 26 September 1998, p. 26;

Bella Bathurst, "Books: Swimming against the Tide in a Sea of Diversity," *Sunday Herald* (London), 10 June 2001.

References:

Robert Anderson, *Elgar* (New York: Schirmer/Maxwell Macmillan International, 1993);

William Conger and others, "Autobiography, Biography, Fiction: A Symposium," in *Psychoanalytic Studies of Biography,* edited by George Moraitis and George H. Pollock (Madison, Conn.: International Universities Press, 1987), pp. 349–404;

Carolyn G. Heilbrun, "Is Biography Fiction?" *Soundings,* 76, nos. 2 and 3 (1993): 295–304;

Luke Jenning, "Expatriate Games," *Vanity Fair,* 55, no. 8 (August 1992): 80–89;

Ira Nadel, *Biography: Fiction, Fact, and Form* (New York: St. Martin's Press, 1984).

Philip Hensher

(20 February 1965 –   )

Dirk Van Hulle
University of Antwerp

BOOKS: *Other Lulus* (London: Hamilton, 1994);
Powder Her Face: An Opera in Two Acts and Eight Scenes, libretto by Hensher for the opera by Thomas Adès (London: Faber & Faber, 1995);
Kitchen Venom (London: Hamilton, 1996);
Pleasured (London: Chatto & Windus, 1998);
The Bedroom of the Mister's Wife (London: Chatto & Windus, 1999);
The Mulberry Empire (London: Flamingo, 2002; New York: Knopf, 2002).

PLAY PRODUCTION: *Powder Her Face,* libretto by Hensher, music by Thomas Adès, Cheltenham Festival, 1 July 1995; Aspen, Col., Aspen Music Festival, 25 July 1997.

RECORDING: *Powder Her Face,* libretto by Hensher, music by Thomas Adès, London, EMI Classics CDC 5 56649 2, 1998.

OTHER: "A Geographer," in *New Writing 4,* edited by A. S. Byatt and Alan Hollinghurst (London: Vintage, 1995), pp. 246–259;
Geoffrey Willans and Ronald Searle, *Molesworth,* introduction by Hensher (London: Penguin, 1999);
Nancy Mitford, *Love in a Cold Climate and Other Novels,* introduction by Hensher (London: Penguin, 2000).

SELECTED PERIODICAL PUBLICATIONS–
UNCOLLECTED: "Summer Houses," *Critical Quarterly,* 35 (Summer 1993): 32–37;
"Trying to Understand," *Granta,* 56 (December 1996): 152–171;
"The Dying of the Light: Two Elegies for Iris Murdoch," *New Statesman,* 11 (21 August 1998): 48–49;
"Why Do They All Love Marcel?" *Independent* (London), 12 February 1999, Friday review section, p. 4;
"To Feed the Night," *Granta,* 65 (February 1999): 241–254;

Philip Hensher (from the dust jacket for Pleasured, *1998)*

"The Country and the City," review of the Library of America edition of the novels of Dawn Powell, *Atlantic Monthly* (September 2001);
"This plan sounds like a right royal recipe for disaster," *Independent* (London), 5 October 2001;
"Brandy," *Granta,* 76 (December 2001): 53–72.

One of the youngest writers to be elected to the Royal Society of Literature, Philip Hensher was more or less "canonized" with an entry in the eighth edition of *The Oxford Companion to English Literature* (1995), edited by Margaret Drabble. A respected novelist and the only author of his generation to be included in *The Oxford Book of English Short Stories* (1998), edited by A. S. Byatt, Hensher is also a sharp critic, reviewing books for *The Spectator* (London) on a regular basis and writing a column for *The Independent* (London). His critical reflections, both in his columns and in his fiction, are an important contribution to the shape of the British literary scene at the beginning of the twenty-first century.

Hensher was born in London on 20 February 1965. His father, R. J. Hensher, was a bank manager, his mother, M. Foster Hensher, a university librarian. He grew up in Kingston on Thames and Sheffield, where he attended comprehensive school. For most of his teenage years Hensher wanted to become a musician or a composer, playing the piano and writing music until he was about twenty years old. Hensher went to Oxford, reading English between 1983 and 1986, and he finished his doctorate on eighteenth-century satire and English painting at Cambridge in 1992. In the meantime he had started working at the House of Commons in 1990, first as a clerk to the Energy Select Committee, then as a clerk in the Journal Office, and finally as a clerk to the Treasury Committee. While he was working at the House of Commons, he started publishing journalism from time to time, writing reviews of fiction and musical performances in newspapers and magazines such as *The Spectator, The Telegraph, The Mail on Sunday, The Atlantic Monthly,* and columns for *The Independent*. Some of his stories have appeared in *Granta* and the *New Writing* anthology series.

Hensher's first novel, *Other Lulus* (1994), is written from a female perspective. When Friederike, the narrator, goes to Vienna to take singing lessons, a British teacher, Archy, finds out that her grandfather was a student of the composer Alban Berg. Archy, who marries Friederike, claims he possesses a version of the third act of Berg's unfinished opera, *Lulu* (1935). It appears to be a kind of journal in which Berg expresses his passion for a woman whom he cannot name "except by negative. She is not Hanna, she is not Helene." When Friederike's grandmother Helga, who was once physically attracted to Berg and now realizes that the unnamed woman is herself, reads this manuscript after the death of her husband, the fake journal gives her the idea that Berg only taught her husband composition lessons to be near her, and she thus considers Berg's influence on her husband's music as a poison and destroys almost all the manuscripts of her husband's music. Eventually, however, it turns out that Archy forged the *Lulu* manuscript, hoping to become famous as its discoverer. Ironically, Archy's forgery shatters his prospects of setting himself up as the great discoverer of

Friederike's grandfather, the unknown but brilliant student of Berg, since scarcely any of his music exists anymore. Friederike, now a great singer, gives a performance of Berg's *Lulu* during which she adds several lines from the forged third act for reasons not stated in the novel. After this performance Archy gives her a farewell letter, in which he compares their situation to the plot of *Lulu,* with a villain dispatched to live out a life of exile, a wicked witch in a hell of her own, and a heroine who, against all odds, will live happily everafter. But Archy is quick to add that "even *Lulu* has a third act."

Hensher thematizes the completion of stories at various points in his novel, for example, after the *Lulu* performance, when Berg's composition is compared to Richard Strauss's *Der Rosenkavalier* (The Cavalier of the Rose, 1911), which may be more "finished" than *Lulu* but is paradoxically less complete. Earlier in the novel Friederike tells a story about her grandmother leaving a mark with her shooting stick on the floor in front of her favorite paintings in the Berlin art gallery. But there is no point or punch line to the story, and Friederike leaves her audience "waiting for the surprising rabbit." When she remarks that it seemed like a story in itself, Hensher's poetics come to the surface. His works are unfinished but more complete than if they lacked this feeling of unfinishedness. Hensher constantly plays with the reader's desire for completeness. In a review in *The Atlantic Monthly* (September 2001) he praised the American writer Dawn Powell's novels for "their distrust of the naive wish to be explicit," which he said "propels them into a rewarding vein of aesthetically rich implication and suggestion and emotional ambiguity."

In 1995 Hensher wrote the libretto for an opera by the British composer Thomas Adès. *Powder Her Face* is what Andrew Porter calls in the EMI CD pamphlet included with the recording of *Powder Her Face* (1998) a "cabaret opera," for four singers and an unconventional orchestra of only fifteen players, because of its cabaret-like scenes, reminiscent of Kurt Weill's *Seven Deadly Sins* (1962) and Berg's *Lulu*. *Powder Her Face,* which was commissioned by the Almeida Opera and had its first performance at the Cheltenham Festival on 1 July 1995, has been performed many times since, recorded, and filmed for Channel 4. Originally, Adès thought of Nabokov's *Lolita* (1955) as a subject for his first opera, but he and Hensher decided instead to dramatize the life of the socialite Margaret Whigham Campbell. Her first marriage, to the American stockbroker Charles Sweeney (called Freeling in the opera), ended in an amicable divorce in 1947, but her second marriage, to Ian Campbell, Eleventh Duke of Argyll, ended in 1963 after a prolonged and bitter divorce trial. The divorce case was extremely sensational—Campbell produced graphic evidence of his wife's multiple infidelities, and the British public was scandalized by reports of her proclivity for performing fellatio on servants. In his verdict the judge described the duchess as "a highly-sexed woman who had ceased to be satisfied with normal sexual relations and had started to indulge in disgusting sexual activities to gratify a debased sexual appetite." After the divorce she gradually lost her social status, until she was evicted from her Dorchester Hotel suite in 1990, dying in poverty in 1993. The opera begins and ends in the Dorchester Hotel suite, with the six intervening scenes evoking different stages in the Duchess's life. In his stage directions Hensher emphasizes the melodramatic aspect of the Duchess, dressed in a "grotesquely enormous" fur coat. Apart from this "dramatic soprano," three other singers play various roles. A high soprano acts as several women who envy the Duchess; a tenor plays the roles of young men who are seduced by the Duchess; and a bass plays the stern roles of the hotel manager, the brutish duke, and the judge. In Hensher's condensed version of the verdict, the judge characterizes the Duchess as "a woman who can be described as modern." What "modern" means is explained in the subsequent lines: "She is a woman who has no scruples, and the morals of a bed-post. . . . She is a Don Juan among women. She is insatiable." The theme of insatiability crystallizes in the only two lines of the epilogue: "Enough. / Or too much!"

The combination of the desire for completeness in *Other Lulus* and the insatiability in *Powder Her Face* assumes Faustian proportions in the Nietzsche-esque notion of *omnivolence* (willing and wanting everything) that forms the theme of Hensher's second novel. *Kitchen Venom* (1996), which won the Somerset Maugham Award in 1997, starts with a dream of the female prime minister implicitly modeled after Margaret Thatcher. In a white room she finds a shelf with twenty-six books and takes down the volume comprising all the words beginning with the letter *O*. When she comes to the words beginning with *omni-*, "the words of power," they are erased before she is able to read them. As she wakes up, *omnipotence* and *omniscience* are still in her own dictionary, but not *omnivolence*. Two hundred and fifty pages later, after having been forced out of office by her fellow Conservatives, she also loses her role as the omniscient narrator. The short last chapter, "The City Overhead," is a first-person narrative devoid of any omniscience.

Hensher drew on his six-year experience as a House of Commons clerk to write this novel. It opens with the funeral of an unnamed mother. Her daughters, Jane and Frances (who calls herself Francesca), are the

Dust jacket for Hensher's 1998 novel, set in East Germany before the fall of the Berlin Wall (Bruccoli Clark Layman Archives)

two female protagonists. Their father, John, is Clerk of the Journals in the House of Commons. Together with his younger colleagues, Henry and Louis, he keeps the minutes of the House in an eighteenth-century code that only a few people can decipher. Hensher ridicules the sophistic belief that truth is secret and the more secret it remains, the truer it is. John likes secrecy more than anything else, although he is not aware of it. "It was something only I knew," the narrator wittily adds. Hensher provides the reader with what the clerks of the Journal are not interested in: the ephemera surrounding their lives. The loves of the fat homosexual Louis are indeed ephemeral, whereas the immaculate and natty Henry is a virgin who has had a long relationship with John's eldest daughter. Jane's love-hate relationship with Henry is compared to poison in a place where nourishment should be produced, the "kitchen venom" of the title. When Henry eventually decides to marry her younger sister, Francesca, Jane grabs a kitchen knife. She does not use it, however, until she is alone. What happens next is merely implied, as Jane's apparent suicide is not depicted. Hensher continually refrains from explicit descriptions of crucial scenes. His suggestive style is the antithesis of the explicitness of such authors as Bret Easton Ellis. John's secret—his relationship with an Italian boy, whom he kills—is revealed in the most unspectacular way. Hensher whets his readers' curiosity, but not in order to appease it, which may explain why Jane Charteris in the *Literary Review* (June 1996) described *Kitchen Venom* as an "enjoyable but somehow vaguely dissatisfying novel."

In 1996 Hensher took up writing full-time after the publication of *Kitchen Venom,* when he was fired from the House of Commons for, as interviewer Jason Steger noted in the 17 June 2002 issue of *The Age* (Melbourne), "allegedly bringing the institution into disrepute" with his novel. His dismissal was neither a disappointment nor a surprise to Hensher, who commented to Steger of the scandal, "That was great fun. I orchestrated it to get sacked." Hensher's detached description in the novel of John's job is revealing with regard to his own poetics: "Everything needs its minutes to be kept. Everything needs to be reduced from what occurs to what it means." But in order to do so, a novelist has to evoke "Everything" first, creating an effect of reality by means of hundreds of details. The urge to reduce events to their significance is an essential human trait; however, this reduction is so extreme in the minutes that it implies a lesson in vanity: "In the perspective of the Journal, men and women vanished." This awareness of human vanity is always present in Hensher's polished and fluent prose. He never fails to take a bird's-eye view once in a while and look at everyday life from a distance. But one thing that distinguishes his fiction from the minutes of the House is what Amanda Craig, reviewing *The Bedroom of the Mister's Wife* (1999) in the *Literary Review* (August 1999), called "his fastidious eye for detail."

Hensher's plots are often provided by history, events such as the prime minister's retirement or the fall of the Iron Curtain. He is not so much interested in these important historical events in themselves, however, but in the contingencies, that is, the small histories of common people that are not mentioned in history books, that accompany them. A trip from Cologne to Berlin is Hensher's starting point in his story of the Berlin Wall in his third novel, *Pleasured* (1998), which was short-listed for the Guardian Fiction Prize in 1998 and nominated for the 1999 W. H. Smith Literary Award. In the opening scene of the novel Friedrich Kaiser and a girl called Daphne celebrate New Year's Eve 1988 on a transit road in the Deutsche Demokratische Republik (DDR; East Germany) some thirty kilometers from

Berlin, where the driver, Peter Picker, has left them to go and find someone to fix his blown-out tire. Not fate, but the Mitfahrzentrale, an organization that arranges lifts in private cars, has brought these three people together, and this coincidence will have a major impact on their lives. Daphne is a literature student in Berlin. She joins a group of left-wing activists, encouraged by her friend Mario who, as she later finds out in files belonging to the Stasi (the East German secret police), actually works for the Stasi. Peter Picker devises a plan to precipitate the fall of the Wall by smuggling the drug ecstasy into the DDR and distributing "pleasure" for free to give the East Germans an idea of what they are missing by being separated from the West. Friedrich encourages him in this scheme but then swindles Picker by providing him with tablets of the nonprescription analgesic paracetamol (known in the United States as acetaminophen), passing them off as ecstacy pills.

On the whole, Hensher's book was well received in Britain, but for divergent reasons. In an 8 August 1998 review in *The Telegraph* (London) the novelist Barry Unsworth praised *Pleasured* as a "highly original and accomplished novel." The desire for consolation is emphasized by Jane Shilling in her positive review of *Pleasured* in *The Telegraph* (22 August 1998). She called it "a novel whose ambitious scale is matched only by the steely elegance of its author's control over what he is up to." According to Francis King, however, the novel is loose-textured and episodic, and "makes no demands," as he describes the book in his review "Ecstasy in Germany," from *Literary Review* (August 1998).

In *Pleasured* Hensher misleads his readers by first creating the impression that the book will be a love story between Daphne and Friedrich, whereas in fact he focuses on the totally different and unexpected relationship between Friedrich and Peter Picker, shortly after the latter's son has died of meningitis. The last scene, in the gardens of Sans Souci, Frederick the Great's palace in Potsdam, where Friedrich Kaiser and Peter Picker find comfort in each other's presence, is a masterly example of what Thomas Mann called *Zeitentiefe* (temporal depth). Friedrich Kaiser is literally the opposite of Kaiser Friedrich. By leading his protagonist to the place where his famous namesake lived a few centuries earlier, Hensher confronts the "careworn" present with the "sans souci"(carefree) past, fully aware that history tends to gild the past.

The awareness that memory distorts the remembered events gives this text a Proustian aspect, echoing the narrator's recognition of this effect in Marcel Proust's *A La Recherche du Temps Perdu* (1913–1927). Moreover, both the opening and closing chapters of *Pleasured* are marked by a vivid "involuntary memory," both times in a car. Proust is explicitly referred to by one of the supporting characters in the novel. In a 12 February 1999 review of Edmund White's *Marcel Proust* (1999) in *The Independent* (London) Hensher called Proust "the funniest and most entertaining novelist ever to have laid his hands on the French language." Another link with Proust is the subtle way in which Hensher treats the subject of homosexuality. He does not write so-called coming-out fiction. His central characters are often gay, but this fact is never the main issue. Instead, he focuses on time, human transitoriness, and the ways in which the past can be misused, for instance, as a way of making excuses for oneself.

The question of whether history repeats itself comes up as well, when Hensher reminds the reader of the 9–10 November 1938 Nazi pogrom, the *Reichskristallnacht* (Imperial Crystal Night), to show how "winners" need "losers" and "how much life rests on *Schadenfreude*." Hensher's analysis of the fall of the Berlin Wall on 9 November 1989–which he calls "the second Imperial Crystal Night"–shows the same tendency toward abstraction that characterized the accounts of the Journal in *Kitchen Venom*. By leaving out of consideration the obvious differences between *Kristallnacht* and the fall of the Wall, Hensher comes to the conclusion that the emotions during both events–"the fierce exhilaration" of destruction supported by the "unarguable right of the State"–teach the same lesson: that suffering is inevitable. While pointing out the similarity of the emotion involved in both events, Hensher simultaneously remarks in *Pleasured* that "it is in poor taste to point it out." Understandably, the reactions of former citizens of the DDR focus on this painful analogy. In a review of the German translation in *Berliner LeseZeichen* (October 2000) Dorothea Körner emphasized that the Berlin Wall eventually fell because of the pressure exerted by the people on the government of the DDR, though she readily admits that in the long run, indeed, nothing much has changed for the East Germans. In *Pleasured,* Friedrich laconically points out to Picker that in Germany "Happy End" is a brand of toilet paper.

Hensher focuses not on the immediate causes of these historical moments but on the long-term forces underlying the European condition and human history in general. The inexplicable urge for "more" recurs in all of Hensher's works. Part 2, "Genug," in *Pleasured* starts with the chapter "Enough," which ends with a series of unanswerable questions: "What was enough? Was money enough? Was *enough* enough?" The sexual insatiability in *Powder Her Face* is translated into an intellectual thirst for knowledge in his story "Dead Languages," included in *The Oxford Book of English Short Stories* and in Hensher's 1999 short-story collection, *The Bedroom of the Mister's Wife:* "Once I wanted to learn and learn, until I knew enough. But now I know that I will never

know enough." "Enough" is an "unmastered subject," which makes it such an inexhaustible theme. Even the characters who make a serious attempt to resign themselves to their fate and be content with their situation cannot enjoy this static state of satisfaction, because of, for example, disturbing e-mails in the story "In the Net" or noisy neighbors in "Quiet Enjoyment," both included in *The Bedroom of the Mister's Wife*. In the latter story Hensher builds up the tension between a quiet man and his new young neighbors who–possibly deliberately–play loud music during the night. The man devises all kinds of destructive plans to retaliate, but Hensher ends the narrative just in time–resisting the "naive wish to be explicit"–applying the idea that anticipation is better than fulfillment, brought up in *Pleasure* with a venomous twist: "Planting the seed is a better feeling than plucking the fruit. Whatever. There are a million proverbs, aren't there, to get you to accept that things aren't going to work out for you?"

Hensher further explores the difference between the potential courses history might have taken versus the course it actually took in his opulent historical novel, *The Mulberry Empire* (2002), focusing on a moment in history when "things did not work out" for the British. Their adventure in Afghanistan in the 1830s resulted in a catastrophic slaughter. When the Persian shah invades the Afghan city of Herat with the support of the Russians, Dost Mohammed, Amir of Afghanistan, asks the British–in the person of Alexander Burnes–for help, which Burnes cannot promise, because such a commitment would interfere with British diplomatic relations elsewhere. Despite Burnes's diplomatic efforts, Dost Mohammed considers calling in the help of the Russian tsar. Meanwhile, the British discover the double game the Russians are playing and decide that Dost Mohammed must go. In the interest of the stability of the region, they will reinstall the deposed Shah Shujah-ul-mulk as the new amir. Eventually, Dost Mohammed's son Akbar takes revenge on Burnes and slaughters all sixteen thousand men of the Army of the Indus, sparing the life of only one messenger to report on the massacre to the rest of the British army, under the command of General Sale. As the only survivor, the messenger bears the heavy burden of both his story and history.

In the first essay of her *On Histories and Stories: Selected Essays* (2000), "Fathers," Byatt emphasizes that self-consciousness about the writing of history coincided with the so-called renaissance of the historical novel. This self-consciousness also characterizes *The Mulberry Empire,* most explicitly in chapter 18, focusing on the similarity between the omniscient narrator and the historian, who "knows everything." The chapter closes with a blatant example of foreshadowing, pre-

*Flamingo publishing director Philip Gwyn Jones, Hensher, and Georgia Garrett of the Wylie Agency at a party celebrating
the publication of* The Mulberry Empire, *March 2002 (from* The Bookseller, *5 April 2002)*

dicting the lamentable fate of Dost Mohammed. But
Hensher also examines the opposite mechanism: the
tendency to project retrospectively the shadow of
important historical events backward onto the preceding period, what Michael André Bernstein calls "back-
shadowing," in his *Foregone Conclusions: Against
Apocalyptic History* (1994). The alternative "sideshadow-
ing," which Bernstein illustrates by means of Proust's
A La Recherche du Temps Perdu, applies to *The Mulberry
Empire* as well. With his seemingly traditional historical novel Hensher undermines the belief that it is possible to make sense of one's past by reconstructing a
single, comprehensive narrative. Hensher deliberately
draws attention to this rectilinear narrative structure
by disturbing his own story with a single, anachronistic white line, drawn by a jet plane in the blue Afghan
sky. On the narrative level the story line is interrupted
at the end of part 2 by an "anthropological interlude"
and again continued at the beginning of part 3 with a
description of the rectilinear movement of one of the
first trains traversing the English landscape at the
beginning of part 3.

Hensher's book explores the tension between
chance and choice, between the several routes not taken
and the one taken, which only seems inevitable in retrospect. The "sideshadowed" possibilities usually crystal-
lize in small details, but Hensher formally enlarges
some of these by presenting them as the side-panels of a
triptych: part 2, "Burnes," is flanked by parts 1 and 3,
respectively called "Bella" and "Akbar." Bella Garr-
away is the woman whom Burnes has left behind in
gloomy Gloucestershire. Their son, Henry, is the incarnation of sideshadowed potential: Burnes dies without
even knowing of his existence. Akbar, who is responsible for his death, makes an end to the short, vainglori-
ous British adventure in Kabul, the "Mulberry Empire"
for which thousands of men died. In the epilogue General Sale's failure is remodeled in the "latest triumph" of
Astley's circus in London, where the same catastrophic
history is dramatized, ending with the reunion of the
general and his "brave wife." That is the way little
Henry is confronted with a dramatized and fictionalized
version of the Afghan War in which his father was
killed and prepared for his own future of glorified impe-

rialism and Faustian pursuits. Hensher confronts the boy's innocence with his unwitting employment of one of the "words of power," as called in the novel, by making him wish to take the omnibus before going home. The urge for omniscience and the desire to get a grip on everything, thematized more hesitantly in earlier novels, is fully elaborated upon in *The Mulberry Empire* and presented as being as equally pernicious as the imperialist longing for omnipotence. Hensher suggests that the real reason underlying British imperialism was the British desire to lose their empire and give up what they had taken possession of. The greater the empire, the nobler the gesture of surrender, according to the example set by Prospero in William Shakespeare's *The Tempest* (1611). As one of Burnes's Afghan friends says: "You are not adventurers; you are all Prosperos, waiting for the day you can give it up, drown your book, and return nobly." By analogy, the same goes for *The Mulberry Empire:* Hensher had to expand a monumental story first in order to be able to surrender and nobly admit that it is impossible to "conquer" the complexity of life in a linear narrative.

Zeitentiefe and the question of whether history repeats itself is a major theme in the novel, which Hensher wrote before the terrorist attacks on the Pentagon and the World Trade Center in New York City on 11 September 2001, but took on a new significance after those tragic events. In his column in *The Independent* (London) of 5 October 2001 Hensher explicitly compared the deposed Afghan king, Zahir Shah, whom the Western antiterrorist coalition considered reinstalling, to Shah Shujah-ul-mulk: "The US delegation is obviously under the impression that Afghanistan thinks of Zahir as the heir of Dost Mohammed, the great 19th-century amir. The real analogy is with Shah Shujah-ul-mulk, the discredited old king the British fondly believed Kabulis longed for, and who, without his western bodyguards, came to a swift and unregrettedly bloody end." *The Mulberry Empire* is more than just another self-conscious historical novel concerned with the linguistic representation of the past. The observation that the mechanics of historiography distort the past has almost become a commonplace since it was theorized by scholars such as Linda Hutcheon, in her *A Poetics of Postmodernism: History, Theory, Fiction* (1988). In this novel and his post–11 September columns Hensher, however, moves on beyond Hutcheon's formulation by showing how historiography not only distorts the past but, more importantly, influences the politics of the present as it provides the molds in which the future is often cast.

In 2001 Philip Hensher was one of the judges of the Booker Prize, which may be regarded as a recognition of the special blend of fictional and critical writings that characterizes Hensher's work and defines his position within the British literary scene. The adjectives— "ambiguous," "unsettling," "puzzling," and "unpredictable"—that Hensher employs in his assessment of the 2001 Booker Prize winner, Peter Carey's *True History of the Kelly Gang* (2000), are not only revealing with reference to Hensher's own poetics but also suggest that he is unconcerned with best-seller lists. The ambiguity and complexity of Hensher's work may not attract the largest of readerships, but these qualities do guarantee its lasting literary merit.

Interview:

Jason Steger, "Literary Mischief," *The Age* (Melbourne), 17 June 2002.

References:

Michael André Bernstein, *Foregone Conclusions: Against Apocalyptic History* (Berkeley: University of California Press, 1994);

A. S. Byatt, *On Histories and Stories: Selected Essays* (Cambridge, Mass.: Harvard University Press, 2000);

Linda Hutcheon, *A Poetics of Postmodernism: History, Theory, Fiction* (New York & London: Routledge, 1988);

Karin Littau, "Reading Thieving Theorizing: Philip Hensher's *Other Lulus* and Kathy Acker's *The Selling of Lulu*," *Dedalus: Revista Portuguesa de Literatura Comparada*, 6 (1996): 37–50;

Andrew Porter, "Powder Her Face," *Powder Her Face* (EMI Classics, 1998): 10–17.

Michael Ignatieff

(12 May 1947 –   )

R. Victoria Arana
Howard University

BOOKS: *A Just Measure of Pain: The Penitentiary in the Industrial Revolution, 1750–1850* (London: Macmillan, 1978; New York: Pantheon, 1978);

The Needs of Strangers (London: Chatto & Windus, 1984; New York: Viking, 1985);

Nineteen Nineteen, by Ignatieff and Hugh Brody, afterword by John Berger (London & Boston: Faber & Faber, 1985);

The Russian Album (London: Chatto & Windus, 1987; New York: Viking, 1987;);

Asya: A Novel (New York: Knopf, 1991; London: Chatto & Windus, 1991);

Blood and Belonging: Journeys into the New Nationalism (London: BBC Books, 1993; New York: Farrar, Straus & Giroux, 1994);

Scar Tissue (London: Chatto & Windus, 1993; New York: Farrar, Straus & Giroux, 1994);

Isaiah Berlin: A Life (London: Chatto & Windus, 1998; New York: Metropolitan Books, 1998);

The Warrior's Honor: Ethnic War and the Modern Conscience (New York: Metropolitan Books, 1998); republished as *The Warrior's Honour: Ethnic War and the Modern Conscience* (London: Chatto & Windus, 1998);

The Rights Revolution (Toronto: House of Anansi Press, 2000);

Virtual War: Kosovo and Beyond (London: Chatto & Windus, 2000; New York: Metropolitan Books, 2000);

Human Rights as Politics and Idolatry, edited, with an introduction, by Amy Gutmann (Princeton: Princeton University Press, 2001).

PRODUCED SCRIPTS: *1919,* motion picture, by Ignatieff and Hugh Brody, British Film Institute / Channel Four Films, 1985;

Guardian's of Chaos, television, BBC, 1995;

Getting Away with Murder, television, BBC, 1997;

Onegin, motion picture, by Ignatieff and Peter Ettedgui, 7 Arts International / Baby Productions / Canwest, 1999;

Michael Ignatieff (photograph by Miriam Berkeley; from the dust jacket for Asya, *1991)*

One World? television, Channel Four, 1999;

Future War, television, BBC, March 2000.

OTHER: *Religion and International Affairs: International Teach-In,* edited by Ignatieff and Jeffrey Rose (Toronto: House of Anansi Press, 1968);

Wealth and Virtue: The Shaping of Political Economy in the Scottish Enlightenment, edited, with an introduction, by Ignatieff and Istvan Hont (Cambridge & New York: Cambridge University Press, 1983);

Psychoanalysis, edited by Bill Bourne, Udi Eichler, and David Herman (Nottingham, U.K.: Spokesman /

Atlantic Highlands, N.J.: Hobo Press, 1987)–includes contributions by Ignatieff.

SELECTED PERIODICAL PUBLICATIONS–
UNCOLLECTED: "Second thoughts of an interventionist," *Observer* (London), 16 May 1993, World News section, p. 21;
"The Danger of a World without Enemies: Lemkin's Word," *New Republic* (26 February 2001): 26.

Michael Ignatieff has made his mark as a public intellectual primarily in the fields of history, public and foreign policy analysis, cultural journalism, and media broadcasting. He has held important academic administrative and teaching positions, written critically acclaimed books on social ethics and modern warfare, contributed to several motion-picture projects, served on international commissions dedicated to the resolution of ethnic conflicts, and written two novels. A key feature of many of Ignatieff's intellectual and artistic achievements is his personal involvement as an eyewitness in the developments he recounts and upon which he reflects.

Ignatieff is interested in human dignity and in human pain and, accordingly, in an array of liberal humanitarian endeavors–including those to develop ethical designs for social welfare, to defuse the volatile dynamics of multigenerational ethnic conflicts, and to comprehend the psychologies of national and tribal loyalty, of human abandonment and betrayal. His nonfictional books on these topics resemble, in spirit, the fiction of Graham Greene, Malcolm Lowery, and others adept at seeing postcolonial debacles with an ethnographic eye and describing them in a nuanced style, but succinctly, as a trenchant travel writer might do.

Ignatieff was born on 12 May 1947 in Toronto to George Ignatieff, a Canadian diplomat of Russian aristocratic extraction, and Alison Grant Ignatieff, a Canadian painter of English and Scottish ancestry. Michael–the elder of two sons; his brother Andrew is three years younger–spent his earliest days in New York City, where his father represented Canada at the United Nations. Following that assignment, George Ignatieff was posted to different countries every two years, and the family moved with him. When Michael was twelve, he was sent for seven years to Upper Canada College, an elite boarding school that he described to Sandra Martin in a 1992 interview as a "little monastery for the making of Tory patricians," and at which, despite "the snobberies" and "absurd authoritarianism of the place," he distinguished himself, in Martin's words, as "brilliant, the most able student in his class." From there, Ignatieff went to Trinity College at the University of Toronto, where he majored in his-

tory, pursued his love of reading, wrote for the student newspaper, immersed himself in liberal causes, worked in Pierre Trudeau's national campaign of 1968, and determined that he "lacked the necessary ruthlessness" to succeed in politics.

After graduation in 1969 Ignatieff pursued the study of history at Harvard, where he earned a doctoral degree but was denied a position as assistant professor, owing to what Martin Peretz–one of his professors there, subsequently editor in chief of *The New Republic*–called "irrelevant prejudices against a talented young scholar." Following that rejection, Ignatieff taught history at the University of British Columbia for two years, from 1976 to 1978, wrote for *The Globe and Mail* (Toronto), broadcast radio and television commentaries for the Canadian Broadcasting Corporation (CBC), and launched his writing and lecturing career–all of which led to a six-year research fellowship at King's College, Cambridge, from 1978 to 1984.

Ignatieff's earliest publications scrutinize the development of civic humanism against that ideology's backdrop of human suffering and privation. An outgrowth of his doctoral dissertation, his first book, *A Just Measure of Pain: The Penitentiary in the Industrial Revolution, 1750–1850* (1978), traces the history of prison reforms over the past two centuries. Besides laying out the contradictions and evolving cultural assumptions concerning ways to define, incarcerate, and reform convicted criminals, Ignatieff looks at the physical and spiritual pain that reformists "carefully legitimated and scientifically inflicted" on prisoners and argues that, ironically, as democratic empowerments increased, so did "intolerance toward 'deviant' minorities."

Ignatieff pursues the connections between unjust privation and depravity to another level of inquiry in *Wealth and Virtue: The Shaping of Political Economy in the Scottish Enlightenment* (1983). He claims, in the introduction to that collection of academic papers co-edited with Istvan Hont, that Adam Smith wrote *An Inquiry into the nature and causes of the Wealth of Nations* (1776) to find "a market mechanism capable of reconciling inequality of property with adequate provision for the excluded," or the poorest classes. In his *TLS: The Times Literary Supplement* review (15 June 1984) D. D. Raphael severely criticized the editors' premises, scholarship, and logic, emphatically pointing out, among other alleged errors, that Smith "did not regard the needs of the poor as an issue of justice, but one of humanity" and charity.

That review, so negative and in so prominent a place, may have prompted Ignatieff to address the topic of human needs and civic responsibility with even greater passion and scholarly latitude in his next book, *The Needs of Strangers* (1984). Here, Ignatieff avoids the historical method and tries "to leave the rutted road of

*Ignatieff's paternal grandparents, Paul and Natasha
Ignatieff, in Quebec, 1944 (from Ignatieff,
The Russian Album, 1987)*

contemporary political philosophy altogether" in order to meditate publicly on the inability of the welfare state's money "to buy the human gestures which confer respect" on its purported beneficiaries. Ignatieff raises questions about "what humans need in order to be human" or "free" or "happy," and he claims that "to raise these questions is to raise the possibility that there are human needs which escape the domain and competence of political action altogether." Ignatieff warns politicians, therefore, to "be careful not to conjure up the fierce and bitter emotions of disillusion." He vividly describes strangers he has seen suffering from injustice, confinement, and isolation, and he examines how human needs for justice, liberty, and solidarity are registered in drama, especially *King Lear* (1605) and the various and richly descriptive works of such writers as Saint Augustine, Hieronymus Bosch, Erasmus, Blaise Pascal, David Hume, James Boswell, Adam Smith, and Jean-Jacques Rousseau. His book, he hopes, will help

readers decide "which needs can be satisfied through politics and which cannot."

Reviewers, however, reacted negatively to *The Needs of Strangers.* Janet Daley, in a 27 January 1990 review in *The Times* (London), described Ignatieff's style as "pompous" and hyperbolic; Jeremy Waldron, in *TLS* (21 December 1984), called his claims exaggerated; and Alan Tonelson, in *The New York Times Book Review* (5 May 1985), dismissed his arguments as "half-hearted." In *The New Republic* (13 May 1985), Michael Walzer wrote, apologetically, that he understood Ignatieff's straining after "a poetic revelation" and explained that "it is a common temptation among political theorists dissatisfied with their trade, who sense deep meanings they cannot quite express." Richard Eder in *The Los Angeles Times* (10 April 1985) called the book "a highly non-systematic ramble" marred by "a good deal of wandering and murky purposes." The book was a commercial success, however, and inspired a certain degree of begrudging respect, drawing critical attention to the most basic needs of a world full of strangers in the midst of the "greedy 1980s." Dennis Duffy, in a 31 August 1985 review in *The Globe and Mail* (Toronto), noted what even Ignatieff's detractors, for the most part, had acknowledged as well: "The book has texture, richness and depth of intellect and feeling. It is not, finally, fully integrated and coherent; it offers no solution to the difficulties beyond moral ones." Duffy wrote that the value of the book "lies in challenging and heartening the rest of us, to move us to deeper understanding and broader compassion."

Ignatieff spent 1985 as visiting professor at the Ecole des Hautes Etudes, Paris. By 1985 Ignatieff had abandoned the "thought of becoming a distinguished professor" and jumped into freelance work. He dropped academia, as he told Martin, because he "wanted to be a writer." Ignatieff's next few projects probed the relationship of family and love to personal identity. The first of these was *Nineteen Nineteen* (1985), a screenplay written with Hugh Brody that was made into a distinguished motion picture starring Paul Scofield and Maria Schell. It recalls the romantic story of Alexander and Sophie, lovers who had been psychoanalyzed by Sigmund Freud and later endured the Nazi occupation of Europe. Ignatieff's continuing interest in the relationship between psychology and identity led to his contribution to *Psychoanalysis* (1987), a collection of essays on that subject.

In 1987 Ignatieff published his highly acclaimed family memoir, *The Russian Album,* the story of his grandparents Count Paul Ignatieff and Princess Natasha Mestchersky, their aristocratic childhoods in their respective family estates, their romance and marriage, their escape from Russia when the Russian Revolution began in earnest in 1917, their ten years as émigrés in France and England, and their eventual immigration to and settlement in Canada. In a conversation with Caroline Moorehead about its composition, Ignatieff confessed that he had spent "ten years pondering *The Russian Album*: one year writing it." "The break came," Moorehead reported in a story in the 12 June 1987 issue of *The Times* (London), "with the realization that it [this book] did not, as he had always thought, have to be about his own roots: it was their story, not his." In his introductory chapter, titled "The Broken Path," Ignatieff recounts the process by means of which he determined how to tell their story: "I had to respect the distance between us. I had to pay close attention to what they left unsaid. . . . I could not elide these silences by the artifice of fiction."

Paradoxically, the decision to try to render their lives faithfully and truthfully meant that Ignatieff needed to abandon the archival historian's methods and instead, by retracing their trajectories, enter vicariously the space-time continuum of their emotional lives, more or less the way a novelist might do. Ignatieff traveled to their landscapes, their resorts, their city streets and—from such primary experiential data—reconstructed a sense of their psychological and material existences. After determining to cleave to whatever facts he could recover, Ignatieff discovered that the art of epic storytelling involves piecing together the grand sagas—of empires and their dissolution, of conflicts and migrations, of impressions and possessions—out of myriad tiny, well-observed details. He found that he could recapture something of his grandparents' reality by combining the information in old family snapshots with the family's various memoirs, his own firsthand impressions of the places they had lived in and traveled through, and his judicious use of facts from the material history of everyday life. The book is full of evocative sentences, such as that describing the visits of Vladimir Nabokov to the young Paul Ignatieff: "When Nabokov visited Kroupodernitsa [the family estate in the Ukraine] in the summer holidays, he would sit under an umbrella in the cabriolet in a broad-brimmed hat and a cream linen suit and read while his earnest friend in the heavy corduroys [Paul Ignatieff] discussed seed-drilling techniques with his peasant foremen in the dusty beet fields."

Ignatieff concludes *The Russian Album* by observing that "you can inherit loyalties, indignation, a temperament, the line of your cheekbones, but you cannot inherit yourself. You make yourself with your own hands, here and now, alone or with others." *The Russian Album*, Ignatieff's tribute as a writer to his father's heritage, is not, he insists, "a voyage of self-discovery":

I have just been keeping a promise to two people I never knew. These strangers are dear to me not because their lives contain the secret of my own, but because they saved their memory for my sake. They beamed out a signal to a generation they would never live to see. They kept faith with me and that is why I must keep faith with them and with those who are coming after me. There is no way of knowing what my children will make of ancestors from the age of dusty roads and long afternoons on the shaded veranda deep in the Russian countryside. But I want to leave the road marked and lighted, so that they can travel into the darkness ahead, as I do, sure of the road behind.

The Russian Album won Canada's Governor General's Award in 1988 and the W. H. Heinemann Prize of the Royal Society of Literature, prizes awarded for literary merit. Critical reception by Duffy in *The Globe and Mail* (Toronto; 22 August 1987), Suzanne Massie in *The New York Times* (23 August 1987), and Elena Brunet in the *Los Angeles Times* (15 January 1989) concurred in pointing to the highly detailed, novelistic texture of the writing. Duffy pronounced it "a family memoir written with acute intelligence and sensitivity," and Massie concluded that "Mr. Ignatieff is Russian to his fingertips—in his sensibility, his nostalgia, his philosophic musings and in the Chekhovian poignancy of the details he chooses to record a vanishing time." Walter Goodman of *The New York Times* (1 August 1987) remarked that what is "fascinating" is having "the account of the revolution through aristocratic eyes." In his *TLS* review (17 July 1987) Roger Scruton asserted, quite contrary to the author's protestations, that "the book is a conscious search for roots, and the reader never loses sight of the anxious, nomadic author standing in the wings, identifying with his characters and attending to their words and gestures with a vivid personal concern." In a 1998 scholarly analysis, "Identity, the State, and Masculinity: The Representation of the Male Subject in Michael Ignatieff's *The Russian Album*," Paul Hjartarson argues that the book is a son's novel-like exploration of an inherited but "fatally flawed" Ignatieff male narrative and should be read as "a second-generation immigrant male's struggle to rewrite the narrative of masculinity he inherits." It cannot be denied that Ignatieff is, though not the key figure of the book, certainly its pivotal consciousness.

From the mid 1980s through the 1990s Ignatieff assiduously cultivated his talents as a public intellectual from his London base: he hosted the television show *Thinking Aloud* (1986) for the British Broadcasting Corporation (BBC); the program *Voices* (1986) for Channel Four; *The Late Show* (1989–1992) for BBC2; and various television documentaries: *Blood and Belonging* (1993), on ethnic nationalism, *Guardians of Chaos* (1995),

Dust jacket for the U.S. edition of Ignatieff's 1991 novel, a fictionalized biography of a Russian princess (Richland County Public Library)

on the United Nations, *One World?* (1999), on the fall of the Berlin Wall, and *Future War* (2000). He also wrote for several periodicals, including *The Observer* (London), from 1990 to 1993.

In 1991 Ignatieff published *Asya: A Novel*. It is the omnisciently narrated, full-length, fictional biography in five parts of Anastasia Vladimirovna Galitzine, "born with the century." Asya, as she is called familiarly, is a Russian princess, "exuberant, godless, and unworldly," whose childhood conviction is that she is "immortal." Part 1 of the novel takes place in Russia and involves a large cast of characters that revolve around the central figures. When Asya's mother dies of cancer, imploring the fourteen-year-old Asya to live life and not let anything stop her, Asya's childhood comes to an abrupt end. World War I soon alters the tenor of life: Asya trains as a nurse; her brother Lapin is sent away to a safe school in England; the beautiful country estate is abandoned; the elegant Moscow house is ransacked by Red revolutionaries; and her

father dies of a heart attack. Asya sings the "Viechnaya Pamyat" herself because the town Soviet does not allow Christian burials. Orphaned, suddenly impoverished, and trapped by a standoff between the Soviet and royalist armies, Asya offers her medical services to a hospital filled with starving children dying of scurvy. From there she is kidnapped by royalist officers to serve in their medical corps, where she meets and falls in love with the wounded Sergei Apollonovich Gourevich, a cynical young royalist lieutenant. Her real life, her "fate," she feels, begins at this point, with their brief and secret sexual liaison. Sergei rejoins his troops without saying goodbye. Desperate, not wanting to admit her abandonment, Asya finally escapes Russia: by rail to the Black Sea port of Novorossisk, by steamship to Constantinople, and from there (now four months pregnant) by sea to Provence. In part 1 Ignatieff fuses the emotional and the historical stories of his cast of characters to portray the transformation of Imperial Russia into the Revolutionary Soviet Republics on an epic scale.

Part 2 is set some years later in France, between St. Rémy and Paris, where Asya draws around her a makeshift family of Russian émigrés. The cast of characters of the novel expands to include her young son Niki; an "entirely unsuitable" suitor, Vladimir Botynsky, the myopic editor of the émigré journal *The Russian Voice*, "penniless, vague, frantically energetic, a typical Russian madcap"; Ilya Ilyonovich Razumkin, a physician leading a double life as an émigré society doctor and an underworld abortionist and stool pigeon; and a stream of other suitors attracted by Asya's spirit and astonishing beauty. After six years of living precariously off of her wits and the generosity of men caught in the web of her charms, Asya is stunned by the dramatic reappearance of Sergei, and her life takes another sensational turn. After confessing that he has been broken by torture and a prison term in Siberia, Sergei dedicates himself coldly to making a fabulous fortune, deliberately misinforms Asya about his real business, involves himself in Soviet and other intelligence operations that benefit his moneymaking schemes, antagonizes his idealistic but Nazi- and royalist-leaning son, sets up his family in a luxurious lifestyle in Paris, disappears from home for long terms and, finally, vanishes for good. Ignatieff limns this story with a running account of Asya's veering emotions and of Asya's willfully blind, fatalistic, and fierce loyalty to Sergei, her "fate." The subtext of part 2 bears on how the Communists established their hegemony over the U.S.S.R.

Part 3 recounts Asya's life during World War II, caught in the vortices of war, espionage, and mind-boggling personal betrayals. Part 4 finds her in England, recuperating from tuberculosis, then training to read the news on the BBC, her son meanwhile fighting with the German forces in the Nazi invasion of Soviet Russia. Asya meets all sorts of people. She becomes intimately involved with Gaby, a bisexual high-fashion model, and with Nick Isvolsky, a Canadian soldier whom Asya knew as a child in Russia. The plot twists and turns through multiple discoveries and betrayals. Asya learns from Gaby, for instance, that Gaby has had affairs with both Sergei and Sergei's son, Niki. She learns from Nick, her Canadian lover, that her son Niki–Prince Nikita Galitzine, a translation officer with a German Panzer division–was killed in January 1942 by sniper fire, ironically, on the grounds of Marino, the Galitzine country estate. Asya finds out what has become of many people she once knew but lost track of. She seeks information about Sergei but can find nothing concrete, nothing official. Asya does not believe those who tell her that Sergei is dead. Part 4 ends with Nick's leaving for Canada to see his little boy there and to obtain a divorce so that he will be free to marry Asya. He never sees her again.

Part 5 celebrates Asya's tenacity and love of life. Nick's grown son Peter, armed with his father's wartime diaries, visits the ninety-year-old Asya in London, sure that he will learn from Asya something he needs to know in order to pick up the pieces of his own calamitous life. Abruptly, Asya and Peter determine to travel to Russia to seek Sergei's final resting place. At the cemetery Peter meets a Soviet official who knows all about Sergei's multiple identities and patriotic career as a Russian spy and who, claiming to be Sergei's son, subtly leads Peter to conclude that Sergei may well not yet be dead. But Peter, caught up in the mystique of the impetuous Princess Anastasia Galitzine, does not have the heart to share this potentially devastating information with the gallant old aristocrat whose "unchecked tears" are running down what she believes is her husband's unmarked, basalt gravestone.

Reviewers of *Asya* appreciated the historical sweep of the novel, but many did not credit Ignatieff with much artistic skill as a novelist. The reviews were mixed. Writing for *The Globe and Mail* (Toronto) on 26 October 1991, Antanas Sileika noted that much of the material in *Asya* appeared earlier in *The Russian Album,* and he called it a "terrible novel": "Why he chose to write a romance based on the same material is best known to himself. The reader only wishes he had written it well. . . . the characters . . . are pushed across 20th-century history, and like many forced characters, they become stiff and dull. . . . this novel is poorly written even by romance standards. Narrative point of view changes confusingly in mid-paragraph and the gush of purple prose is deeply cloying." Sabine Durrant, in a 28 February 1991 review for *The Times* (London), quipped

that *Asya* "must have been written on the bus between libraries" but acknowledged that it "is above all a gripping yarn." In a *TLS* review (22 February 1991) Zinovy Zinik observed that "the logic of the narrative is not unlike that of a typical socialist realist novel where every step the hero makes is dictated not by conflict of personalities but by historic upheavals carefully set up in advance by the author." While critics variously panned Ignatieff's plot, character development, or what Muriel Spanier, in *The New York Times Book Review* (1 December 1991), termed his "fervid pen," they nevertheless were reminded of Mikhail Bulgakov, Boris Pasternak, Nabokov, F. Scott Fitzgerald, Henry Miller, and the classic motion picture *Casablanca* (1943). "It is hard to decide whether all this signifies merely that Mr. Ignatieff is easily influenced, or that he has written a dashing work emblematic of our hectic century. It hardly matters. It is charming," concluded John Banville in his piece in *The New York Review of Books* (21 November 1991). In her profile of Ignatieff, Martin recounts in detail how English reviewers "savagely flogged" and "hugely panned" *Asya,* and she adds, "The problem with *Asya* is that it is not a novel; it is a monument . . . a form of bereavement therapy." So dense is it with allusions to the whirl of world history that it serves a pedagogical purpose. Epic in scope, it honors the Russian aristocrat's heroic grace under pressure and psychological tenacity in the face of cataclysmic change and holds up to ethical scrutiny the emotional lives of survivors of all stripes–foremost among them the passionate Asyas, the Machiavellian Sergeis, the fraudulent Razumkins, and the innocent later generations represented by Peter Isvolsky.

Whereas *Asya* proffers Ignatieff's tribute to his Russian parentage, *Scar Tissue* (1993) ostensibly pays homage to his mother's memory while functioning as a philosophical meditation on the meaning of life. The central figure is the narrator, whose thoughts and feelings about his mother's decline and death from Alzheimer's disease mirror Ignatieff's own. The novel takes the shape of a memoir, written by a middle-aged professor of philosophy. It begins with a harrowing physical description of the mother's death throes, but segues into family lore, his mother's life as a painter, her marital relationship with his Russian émigré father, her gradual mental deterioration, his father's death from exhaustion and a heart attack, the narrator's foundering marriage, his guilt, an extramarital affair with one of his mother's nurses, his quarrels with his neuropathologist brother, and his collapse into brooding about disease, dying, and neurological degeneration and its relationship to religious belief and to artistic creativity. The family drama is punctuated time and again by the narrator's acute awareness of his personal ten-

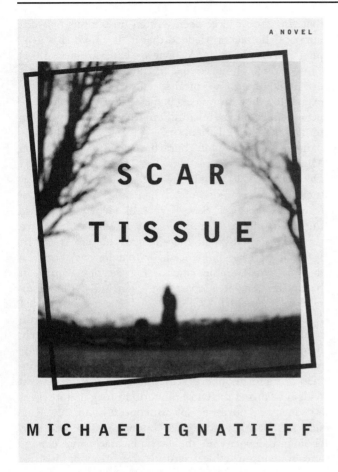

A NOVEL

S C A R
T I S S U E

M I C H A E L   I G N A T I E F F

*Dust jacket for the 1994 U.S. edition of Ignatieff's
1993 novel, a fictional memoir by a philosophy
professor whose mother is suffering from
Alzheimer's disease (Richland
County Public Library)*

dency to turn whatever he "at first found fearful into something interesting." When his mother's condition reaches the point where her shattered mind no longer seems to inhabit her body, the narrator advocates stoicism, "refusing to succumb to the contagion of fear." When he meets one of his brother's patients who suffers from Stephen Hawking's disease (amyotrophic lateral sclerosis), the narrator is forced to contemplate how it might feel to inherit an opposite fate: a body disintegrating while the mind is still sharp; and he is forced to ask, "Does understanding *anything* make a difference, if there is nothing you can do to stop it happening?" It is a question he is unable, finally, to answer.

Scar Tissue received strong, positive reviews. In a 16 May 1993 review in *The Observer* (London) Boyd Tonkin wrote: "A limpid prose gazes unafraid at everyday terror and finds meaning, if not comfort, there. It redeems the hideous indignities of dying not by hope or uplift, but by reclaiming them for thought." In his *TLS*

review (16 April 1993) Mark Wormald concluded that, whereas "Ignatieff's rhetoric stimulates us by the precision of its detachment from the predicament described," its "metaphors and the moments they illuminate make *Scar Tissue* much more than the personal tribute for lost parents it clearly is for its author as well as its narrator. It will speak to anyone who has endured, or only contemplated, equivalent suffering." *Scar Tissue* was nominated in 1993 for the Booker Prize and for a Whitbread Award, two of the most prestigious British awards for fiction.

The two nonfiction works that followed *Scar Tissue*—*Blood and Belonging: Journeys into the New Nationalism* (1993) and *The Warrior's Honor: Ethnic War and the Modern Conscience* (1998)—combine attributes of travel writing with those of political journalism. They depict locations, people, and conversations—once again—with first-person immediacy. The companion volume to the BBC documentary series of that title, *Blood and Belonging* is based on Ignatieff's trips to Serbia, Croatia, Germany, the Ukraine, Quebec, Kurdistan, and Northern Ireland. Ignatieff concludes: "Until I had spent some time at the checkpoints of the new world order, until I had encountered my quotient of young males intoxicated by the power of the guns on their hips, I had not understood how deeply pleasurable it is to have the power of life and death in your hands. It is a characteristic liberal error to suppose that everyone hates and fears violence." In 1996 Ignatieff inaugurated a show featuring interviews with intellectuals for the CBC program *Newsworld*. In July 1998 he was named to head the Cultural Journalism Program at the Banff Center for the Arts in Canada.

In *The Warrior's Honor* Ignatieff reports on his voyages to speak with International Red Cross workers in the war zones of Serbia, Croatia, Bosnia, Rwanda, Burundi, Angola, and Afghanistan. In this book he decides that ethnic conflicts, ethnic cleansing campaigns, and genocidal massacres conducted by irregulars and armed gangs have obliterated the distinctions between justifiable war and barbarism. The only hope for preventing the latter is not to appeal, as the International Red Cross does, to the warrior's honor or to some liberal notion of victim's rights, at which the new ethnic warlord laughs, but to work to establish strong civil states that can put an end to lawless rampage. In his 10 April 1994 review of *Blood and Belonging* in *The New York Times Book Review*, Francis Fukuyama asserted that Ignatieff "is much better at observing small details, where he can bring to bear the talents of a journalist and novelist, than in making broad generalizations" and rebuked Ignatieff's "nostalgia for the old imperial systems." An unsigned review in *The Economist* (14 March 1998) agreed: "Mr. Ignatieff's writing, though taut in reportage, sags . . . when he turns analytical." Time and again, while they sometimes find fault with his specific policy counsels, Ignatieff's critics and reviewers invariably praise his talent for making one see and feel what he has seen and felt.

On many occasions Ignatieff has drawn public attention to his belief that journalistic writing about such subjects must of necessity move "right up to the frontier with fiction"–a point he made to Andrea Marantz in 1998, describing his vision for the Cultural Journalism program he was then directing at the Banff Center in Canada. "Cultural journalism," Ignatieff explained to Marantz, springs from "that borderline where you use fictional technique in non-fiction writing." Ignatieff's two novels also straddle "that border-line." Both novels–according to Ignatieff himself–incorporate significant measures of family history and of his own spiritual autobiography.

For Ignatieff, as his remark about the "border-line" suggests, fiction is not so much a departure from fact as it is a communicative strategy: the best way of distilling and conveying the emotions that attend any act of eyewitnessing. Even, for example, in his most straightforward study of war and genocide, *The War-rior's Honor,* Ignatieff considers it his moral responsibility to take his readers narratively where he has gone. *The Warrior's Honor* begins:

> The British nurse was picking her way through the mass of women and children squatting in the dust at the entrance to the field hospital of the refugee camp at Korem in Ethiopia. She was selecting which children could still be helped. . . . A television reporter approached with a mike and asked her how she felt about what she was doing. It was not a question she felt capable of answering. The look she gave the camera came from very far away.

Ignatieff's larger purpose–to examine how the new moral interventionists such as relief workers, reporters, and diplomats mediate "moral relations between strangers . . . in the modern world"–requires that he transmit how he feels about what he has seen and heard. He distinguishes his own genre of conscientious reportage, however, from the "promiscuous voyeurism a visual culture makes possible." To produce striking vignettes about his authentic personal encounters with, for instance, "the new warriors: the barefoot boys with Kalashnikovs, the paramilitaries in wraparound sun-glasses, the turbaned zealots of the Taliban who checked their prayer mats next to their guns," Ignatieff applies the techniques of storytellers: metonymic and synecdochic details, striking dialogue, and fast-paced chronicle. These narrative strategies give his nonfiction books their compelling character and distinctive appeal.

Isaiah Berlin: A Life (1998) is Ignatieff's intimate record of friendship with an intellectual father figure, the influential liberal philosopher Berlin. In a C-Span interview with Brian Lamb (24 January 1998) Ignatieff explained how he came to write this biography: Berlin saw him on BBC TV, invited him to lunch, and they began a series of conversations that lasted for ten years, much of which Ignatieff captured on tape, his primary source material. In his review in *The New Republic* (16 November 1998), Ian Buruma praises Ignatieff's biography as "fine" and "light in the best sense: entertaining without ever lacking in seriousness." Christopher Clausen in the *New Leader* (14 December 1998) deemed Berlin "fortunate in his biographer."

The Rights Revolution (2000) is the published version of Ignatieff's fall 2000 CBC Massey Lecture Series. In a review in *Macleans* (4 December 2000) John Bemrose noted that in this volume Ignatieff holds up Canada as "in the forefront of attempts to create an equitable and inclusive politics for a multicultural age," arguing that the experience of reconciling the demands of anglophone and francophone Canadians "has made the country adept at accommodating a variety of viewpoints" and according "special rights for women, homo-sexuals, Aboriginal Peoples and children, not to mention language and constitutional rights" in order "to protect minorities from the democratic tyranny of the majority." In basic accord with Berlin's view that a society valuing curbs on authority is better than one touting a positive liberty of a specified kind, in *The Rights Revolution* Ignatieff applauds the open civil society of Canada.

In February 2001 Ignatieff assumed the director-ship of the Carr Center for Human Rights Policy at the Kennedy School of Government at Harvard University. Ignatieff has lectured at the Center for the Study of Professional Military Ethics at the U.S. Naval Academy, Princeton University, the University of Notre Dame, Brandeis University, the London School of Economics, the University of California at Santa Barbara and at Berkeley, and elsewhere. His Tanner Lectures, delivered at the Center for Human Values at Princeton University in 2000, were published as *Human Rights as Politics and Idolatry* (2001), with an introduction by the editor, Amy Gutmann, comments by K. Anthony Appiah, David A. Hollinger, Thomas W. Laqueur, and Diane F. Orentlicher, and Ignatieff's response. He served on the International Commission on Kosovo and on the Independent International Commission on Sovereignty and Intervention. He was awarded the Lionel Gelber Prize for Writing on Foreign Affairs, the Cornelius Ryan Award of the Overseas Press Club in New York, the Alastair Home Fellowship at St.

Anthony's College (Oxford University), and a Mac-Arthur Foundation Grant.

In his nonfiction writings as well as his novels, Ignatieff cannot help characterizing himself (the observer-commentator) by drawing constant attention to his own way of seeing and his evolving attitudes. Such self-reflexiveness does not detract from the fundamental impulse of his writing: to engage his topics with passion and respect and to try to get his readers to feel as well as to envision the phenomena he has experienced. In this respect Ignatieff demonstrates how, in the twenty-first century, sense and sensibility may be transmitted together. Referring to Ignatieff's career in *Peace Magazine* (April–June 2001), Andres Kahar noted both the epic sweep and the verbal flair of his achievement: "He's describing global politics: open-ended and rough going. Like any great storyteller, Michael Ignatieff is trying to explain where we're coming from [emotionally and historically] and where we are today." He told R. Victoria Arana in an unpublished 19 June 2002 correspondence that he thinks about the world as a novelist does, "I try to structure material as a fiction writer would do, and to visualize events and recreate them as a fiction writer would. What is true, and has always been true, about my conceptual work is that I'm as interested in the writing of my work as I am in the thinking of it–and think of myself primarily as a writer."

Interview:

Sandra Martin, "Favorite Son," in *Saturday Night* (July/August 1992): 42–47, 55–61.

References:

Paul Hjartarson, "Identity, the State, and Masculinity: The Representation of the Male Subject in Michael Ignatieff's *The Russian Album*," in *Cultural Identities in Canadian Literature/Identités culturelles dans la littérature canadienne,* edited by Bénédicte Mauguière (New York: Peter Lang, 1998), pp. 73–87;

Andres Kahar, "Michael Ignatieff's Surprising Habits," *Peace Magazine* (April–June 2001);

Caroline Moorehead, "Making Peace with the Past," *Times* (London), 12 June 1987, Arts section, p. 16;

Elaine Kalman Naves, "The Shape of a Life: Michael Ignatieff on Isaiah Berlin," *Queen's Quarterly,* 106 (Summer 1999): 169–180.

John Lanchester

(25 February 1962 –   )

Robert A. Morace
Daemen College

BOOKS: *The Debt to Pleasure: A Novel* (London: Picador, 1996; New York: Holt, 1996);

Mr Phillips (London: Faber & Faber, 2000; New York: Putnam, 2000);

Fragrant Harbour (London: Faber & Faber, 2002); also published as *Fragrant Harbor* (New York: Putnam, 2002).

OTHER: Vladimir Nabokov, *The Real Life of Sebastian Knight,* afterword by Lanchester (Harmondsworth, U.K.: Penguin, 1995).

SELECTED PERIODICAL PUBLICATIONS–
UNCOLLECTED: "Sour Plums," review of *The Letters of John Cheever,* edited by Benjamin Cheever; *Mary McCarthy,* by Carol Gelderman; and *The Company She Keeps,* by Mary McCarthy, *London Review of Books* (26 October 1989): 29–30;

"The Gourmet," *Granta,* 52 (Winter 1995): 221–246;

"To Croak For," review of *The Frog,* by John Hawkes, *New York Times Book Review* (22 December 1996): 11;

"Diary," *London Review of Books* (20 March 1997): 29–30;

"A Vision of England," interview with Julian Barnes, *Daily Telegraph* (29 August 1998): 5;

"Cash Is King," *Granta,* 65 (Spring 1999): 155–175;

"Mad Coke Disease," *New York Times Magazine* (4 July 1999): 6–7;

"Slapping the Clammy Flab," review of *Hannibal,* by Thomas Harris, *London Review of Books* (29 July 1999): 10–11;

"See You in Court, Pal," review of *The Nudist on the Late Shift,* by Po Bronson; *Infinite Loop,* by Michael Malone; and *Bum Rate,* by Michael Woolf, *London Review of Books* (30 September 1999);

"More of What's Bad for You May Be Good for You," *Washington Post,* 2 January 2000, p. B2;

"Secrets and Lies: The Impossible World of DI John Rebus," review of *Set in Darkness,* by Ian Rankin, *London Review of Books* (19 April 2000): 18–20;

"Be Interesting!" review of *Experience,* by Martin Amis, *London Review of Books* (6 July 2000): 3, 5–6;

"You Go, Girls," review of *Ten Women Who Shook the World,* by Sylvia Brownrigg, *New York Times Book Review* (9 July 2000): 8;

"The Counter Life," review of *Shopgirl,* by Steve Martin, *New York Times Book Review* (29 October 2000): 21;

"Edible Complex," *New Yorker* (27 November 2000): 170–173;

"The Land of Accidents," review of *White Teeth,* by Zadie Smith, *New York Review of Books* (8 February 2001): 29–31;

"Sherlock Holmes's Smarter Brother," review of *The Confessions of Mycroft Holmes,* by Marcel Theroux, *New York Times Book Review* (25 March 2001): 7;

"Love on a Laptop," review of *Thinks,* by David Lodge, *New York Review of Books* (9 August 2001): 27–28;

"The Dangers of Innocence," review of *Atonement,* by Ian McEwan, *New York Review of Books* (11 April 2002);

"Knowing and Not Knowing," review of *Spies,* by Michael Frayn, *New York Review of Books* (27 June 2002).

"A colonial childhood does strange things to your sense of where you're from," John Lanchester said in a 1996 interview with Candida Crewe. Because he was raised in former colonial settings, his early years were especially marked by that "element of dislocation or displacement" he believes characterizes the lives of many writers.

Born in Hamburg, Germany, 25 February 1962, Lanchester was raised in the Far East, wherever his father, who worked for the Hong Kong and Singapore Bank, was posted: Hong Kong, Rangoon, Calcutta, and Lubaun, off the coast of Borneo. In 1972, having decided to send their only child to Gresham's School in Norfolk, England, his parents purchased a home in the nearby village of Surlingham (comically renamed Fakingham in the author's first novel), where the young

John Lanchester (photograph © Ari Mintz/Newsday, Inc; from the dust jacket for the U.S. edition of Mr Phillips, *2000)*

Lanchester, whose family had no previous ties to the area, found the townspeople reserved. The family moved to Norfolk proper in 1983, the same year the elder Lanchester died.

After completing his undergraduate degree at Oxford (1981–1984) and two additional years of study toward an M.Litt., Lanchester began his writing career. He wrote football reports for the now-defunct *The Sunday Correspondent* (London) and *The Guardian,* as well as literary journalism for these papers and *The Literary Review, Poetry Review,* and *Vogue.* Meanwhile, Lanchester worked at the *London Review of Books,* starting out in 1987 as a low-paid editorial assistant and working his way up to assistant editor before leaving in June 1991 to become Classics editor at Penguin Books. The restaurant critic for *The Observer* (London) from 1992 to 1994, Lanchester returned to the *London Review of Books* in January 1993, serving as its deputy editor until August 1996, when the success of his first novel made it possible for him to devote himself to his writing.

A resident of London since the late 1980s, Lanchester lives just south of the Thames, with his wife, the writer Miranda Carter, whom he married in

Reno, Nevada, in 1994, and their son. He works in a loft, writing his essays directly on the computer but composing his fiction more deliberately, in longhand on note cards at the painstaking rate of five hundred words per day.

That deliberateness, along with his itinerant upbringing, is evident in Lanchester's startlingly accomplished and enthusiastically received first novel, *The Debt to Pleasure* (1996). Being long-listed for the Booker Prize was arguably the least of its many achievements: Whitbread First Novel Award, Hawthornden Prize, as well as, less prestigiously and more surprisingly, the Betty Trask Prize, intended for a literary work of a "romantic or traditional nature" (*The Debt to Pleasure* is neither), and the 1997 Julia Child Award for literary food writing. By then, prepublication reports about the size of Lanchester's advance—rumored to be £65,000 in the United Kingdom and $300,000 in the United States—had already fueled interest in the book and debate about its merits.

Even as the novel was on the fast track to becoming an international best-seller translated into more than twenty languages, several (mainly English) commentators questioned whether what Tim Warren called in the *Houston Chronicle* (5 May 1996) the "most ingenious novel of the year" was indeed a work of great literary merit or merely an entertainment, which Suzi Feay described in the 29 December 1996 issue of *The Independent* (London, 1996) as "too arch for some, and at times too clever, by half." Was it really the best novel of the year, or only "the most hyped"? Were the rave reviews, seen against the backdrop of the modest commercial success of the book in Britain, evidence of literary excellence or of the London literary establishment's willingness to take care of one of its own? Was its international success the measure of actual literary worth or only the global marketing reach of its British publisher's parent company, the German multinational, Holtzbrinck? Lanchester was apparently still smarting from the backlash in 1998 when he complained, in an interview with fellow novelist Julian Barnes, of the unwillingness on the part of many influential English critics and media academics to acknowledge what the international literary community did, namely the healthy state of contemporary English fiction.

The questions that were raised concerning the part that economic considerations and literary clubbiness play in shaping the critical and commercial reception of a book are not without merit, but then neither is this remarkably self-assured first novel. Indeed, it is the author's faultless poise that makes *The Debt to Pleasure* seem less a first novel than what it is, the work of an already seasoned writer. Lanchester's narrative skills—his handling of tone and structure in particular—are surpassed only by his command of the literary tradition and his adroit and playful mimicry of a broad range of literary predecessors. His "playgiarisms" (to use Raymond Federman's apt term) include what Kate Muir described in the 4 October issue of *The Times* (London) as the "over-garnished prose" of Anthelme Brillat- Savarin, and what John Walsh called in a 16 March 1996 review in *The Independent* (London) the "Obsessive-Digressive" style of Laurence Sterne's *Tristram Shandy* (1760–1767), the hyper-precision of Nicholson Baker, the peripatetic meditativeness of Barnes's *Flaubert's Parrot* (1984), the tongue-in-cheek neo-Gothicism of Patrick McGrath, along with heavy doses of Vladimir Nabokov, Marcel Proust, M. F. K. Fisher, Fyodor Dostoevsky, and Thomas De Quincey (author of the satirical essay "On Murder Considered as One of the Fine Arts," 1827). Lanchester seems also to have drawn on cinematic sources: there are echoes of Peter Greenaway's movie *The Cook, the Thief, His Wife, and Her Lover* (1989); Inspector Jacques Clouseau, the bumbling character originated by Peter Sellers in Blake Edwards's *The Pink Panther* (1963); and postmodern thrillers such as Joseph

L. Mankiewicz's *Sleuth* (1972) and Sidney Lumet's *Deathtrap* (1982). Lanchester's more immediate sources of inspiration for the novel were less numerous but similarly diverse: a schoolmate at Gresham's who later in life murdered his parents, sister, and her children, and Lanchester's learning to cook while a graduate student writing, or "not writing," as he put it in an interview with Alix Madrigal (1996), his thesis, "Rhetoric and Diction in Three English Poets of the 1590s." Learning to cook required reading cookbooks, which in turn quickly led to his realizing how much autobiographical narrative cookbooks include. From there it was a small step to his imagining a cookbook mutating into a novel.

Thus, a reader's advisory is issued early in the novel by Lanchester's narrator: "This is not a conventional cookbook." The full extent of the unconventionality of the novel is at first muted. The narrative is organized according to four seasonal menus, winter through autumn. Within this overt structure lies another: an account of the narrator's trip from England to the south of France, written (or rather tape-recorded) on the go (and in the present tense, though subsequently edited) and including notes and thoughts on the subject of food. But within this second structuring device lies still another, for what at first appears nothing more than a pleasure trip mutates into something quite different, as the narrator, no less variously disguised than his narrative, pulls out narrative lines the way he pulls wigs, fake beards, bugging devices, Mossad manuals, and range direction finders out of his bag of dirty tricks while stalking a newly married couple, with what sinister intent the narrative only later, and laughingly, makes clear. Something as banal (as the narrator would say) as story line or motivation is at first so deeply impacted and dispersed in the densely clotted, disarmingly digressive prose (six pages on blinis alone) as to be all but invisible even to "the attentive reader" whom the narrator several times addresses. As he closes in on his prey, however, the digressions become less frequent, the forward thrust of the now all-too-obvious story line more relentless, the narrator more impatient, and the narrative more hilarious (nowhere more so than in the scene in which the narrator discovers, just as he is about to prepare an omelet loaded with lethal mushrooms, that one of his two intended victims is allergic to eggs).

Long before he reveals his name, a little more than three-quarters of the way through the novel—the bathetically prosaic Rodney Winot, who has flamboyantly renamed himself Tarquin after "Shakespeare's charismatic villain"—the narrator has already and abundantly revealed himself as a snobbish, name-dropping Europhile. Fastidiously precise, venomously opinion-

*Paperback cover for the U.S. edition of Lanchester's
1996 book, a cookbook that evolves into a novel
in which the narrator reveals himself to be a
murderer (Bruccoli Clark Layman Archives)*

ated, wholly self-absorbed, pathologically insecure in his need "to demonstrate connoisseurship," Winot nurses an equally outsized sense of grievance and betrayal. Born in the caul, that is, with the amniotic sac intact, he believes that he is the one destined for greatness, not his elder brother, a successful artist. "There is an erotics of dislike," he contends, one that he has perfected in the absence of any actual erotic life, or personal relationship of any kind for that matter. Believing that "Genius is close to imposture," he devotes himself to a life of disguises of one kind or another—at times consciously, at others not. He is a *gastroposeur* and *poète maudit* whose art is murder and whose collected works are his ten ingeniously dispatched victims, starting with a hamster and moving on to two family servants, a young houseguest, a neighbor, both parents, his brother Bartholomew, and now Bartholomew's American biographer and her Welsh husband Hugh (whom Winot—pedantically? pretentiously? mockingly?—insists on call-

ing Hywl) while on their combined honeymoon-research trip. In these "memoirs of an esthete of dubious reliability and sinister intent," to use the apt description of Lanchester's editor, who prepared the book for publication, it is Winot's pursuit of Laura and Hywl that moves the narrative forward, but it is Winot's sense of sibling rivalry that motivates the larger action, the serial murders, and his side trips down memory lane. The relationship between Rodney/Tarquin and Bartholomew is not so much a study in contrast, however, as its caricature, at once fussily correct and over-the-top: the super-refined Tarquin, self-made gourmand, artiste, and pedant on the one hand, Bartholomew with his (to Tarquin) crude paintings and sculptures, his love of ketchup and fry-ups, and his "plain-man-speaks realism" on the other.

Tarquin's narrative is as far from his brother's "forthright expression" as one can get, in that it exists not in the realm of fantasy per se but of pretentiousness, self-delusion, and misdirection. In the early stages of both his narration and his cross-Channel, cross-country pursuit of his prey, Winot refers to Laura as "my biographer" and "my collaborator," albeit with a few slighting references to her unrefined American English. In his "Preface, Acknowledgment, and Note on Structure," the perhaps deluded and certainly deluding Winot claims that the reason he writes is that "Over the years, people have pleaded with me to commit to paper my thoughts on the subject of food"—a pleading he resisted until now because "I did not want to distract attention from my artistic work in other media," that is, his murders. Thus, Winot's actual reason for writing his unconventional cookbook is to create some record—an encyclopedic as well as confessional catalogue raisonné, as it were—of his art of Derrida-like absences and farewells. Arguably the most shocking, as well as shockingly funny, of his many unconventional opinions is this argument: rather than think of murderers such as Adolf Hitler as failed artists, one should think of the artist as "a timid megalomaniac, venting himself in the easy sphere of fantasy rather than the unforgiving arena of real life—Kandinsky a failed Stalin, Klee a Barbie manque." Winot's narrative has the glistening surface of a highly refined irony that manifests itself in the nesting of narrative Chinese boxes and a high-class game of Trivial Pursuit, but the deeper pleasure of Lanchester's intricately constructed and densely intertextual novel derives from another source insofar as the gamesmanship is itself a form of masquerade disguising a finely wrought self-portrait of Nietzschean resentment in a postmodern, neo-Gothic mode. Winot is thus right to ask whether the character who speaks for the author in Shakespeare's *Tempest* may be not Prospero after all, but instead "the bitter, maimed, deformed, unstoppable poet Caliban."

The enormous critical success of Lanchester's debut novel had several consequences in addition to positioning this former restaurant critic and deputy editor of the *London Review of Books* more conspicuously on the literary map and putting his career as a fiction writer on a firm financial and critical foundation. Suddenly a hot property, he was invited by *The New Yorker, The New York Times, The Washington Post,* and the online *Slate Magazine* to write book reviews and feature articles on topics as varied as food scares, Hillary Clinton, and London telephone codes. His reviews are especially notable for the intelligence and scope Lanchester brings to the topic at hand, whether the rarefied fiction of John Hawkes or the mass-appeal novels of Thomas Harris and Ian Rankin. One consequence of his debut success was the opportunity in 1999 to switch publishers, from Picador to Faber and Faber, Ltd., in a three-book deal reportedly worth £350,000—an offer that Lanchester accepted and that again generated some gratuitously negative attention in the London papers. Another consequence was less positive: the extent of its success made *The Debt to Pleasure* a difficult act to follow, especially with a second novel, *Mr Phillips* (2000), so unlike the first: the one all tour de force, the other a leisurely, low-key walking tour, the one Euro, the other metro, the one about a comical, even clownish megalomaniac, the other about a day in the life of its "downsized hero," as described by Thomas Lynch in the *Los Angeles Times Book Review* (9 April 2002), a "reluctant redundant" barely able to muster the courage to "murder a pint of lager," as Lanchester depicts him in the novel, let alone a brother.

In a 6 July 2000 review of Martin Amis's *Experience* published just a few months after *Mr Phillips,* Lanchester, writing of the "current memoir boom," including that "distinct and recent genre," the novelistic memoir, identifies what he calls the "defining problem" of the form: "how to give the memoir an artistically gratifying shape while remaining true to the messiness and quotidianness of lived life." One solution, he contends, is to structure the memoir as a fiction; the other is "to make no attempt to impose a shape on experience: to let life have its messiness, and let the book pay its necessary price in terms of formal imperfection." In a sense, *Mr Phillips,* though not technically a memoir, except at one remove, follows both roads and does so with much less flair and to less acclaim than *The Debt to Pleasure* but arguably to greater effect.

Told in the third person but rigorously limited to what its focal character sees, thinks, and experiences, and (like *The Debt to Pleasure*) in the present tense, *Mr Phillips* relates the story of a day in the life of an accountant. It is Monday, 31 July 1995, the first workday after Mr. Phillips unexpectedly lost his job the previous week after being employed for twenty-six years at the same catering-supply firm. He awakes, washes, dresses, eats breakfast, walks to the station at Clapham Junction as usual. All dressed up but with no place to go, and surrounded by people who do, Mr. Phillips impulsively (and therefore uncharacteristically) disembarks at Battersea, strolls around the park, crosses the Thames, visits the Tate, has lunch with his elder son (a budding entrepreneur who reads such books as *Hitler Wins! Management Skills of Germany's Greatest Leader*), watches a pornographic movie in Soho, lingers at the margins of a church meeting, walks around Piccadilly Circus, rides the bus to Knightsbridge, follows a television celebrity into a bank, as well as into a bank robbery, returns home a little late but otherwise as usual, his wife, a music teacher, still in the dark about his having lost his job.

The plot is as prosaic, plodding, and (in a sense) purposeless as its passive protagonist, its pace necessarily, riskily slow. Mr. Phillips is not "officially awake" until page 30 and not out of the house until page 38; the next 70 pages take the story to just 10:30, leaving nearly 200 pages and eight hours still to go before Mr. Phillips can return home and the novel end. With so much time to kill, Mr. Phillips drifts about, recalling the past, trying hard not to think too much about the future. He first appears cartoonishly two-dimensional, a figure of fun rendered in Buster Keaton deadpan who repeatedly finds himself in comical, Chaplinesque situations. His first impulsive act leaves the unemployed Mr. Phillips beside the Battersea Dog Hospital, where unwanted pets are put to sleep. In the park, a former redundant-turned-pornographer attempts to strike up a conversation. Sighting a neighbor's wife, Mr. Phillips guiltily flees the Tate. Exiting the porn theater, his eyes not yet adjusted to the light, the Mr. Magoo–like Mr. Phillips steps off a curb and is nearly run down by a truck. Much of his time is spent thinking, recalling, fantasizing (especially if unspectacularly) about sex, and mentally doing sums (the accountant's worry beads) of one kind or another that provide him with some relief from the larger and more vexing problem of what to do with himself.

Much as in *The Debt to Pleasure,* only in a much more pedestrian way perfectly suited to the decidedly prosaic protagonist, Lanchester's narrative resonates intertextually: the day-in-the-life plot is borrowed from James Joyce's *Ulysses* (1922); Mr. Phillips's fantasies echo those of James Thurber's eponymous daydreamer in "The Secret Life of Walter Mitty" (1939); and Mr. Phillips himself is only the most recent in a long line of English nondescripts that includes Charles Pooter from George and Weedon Gros-

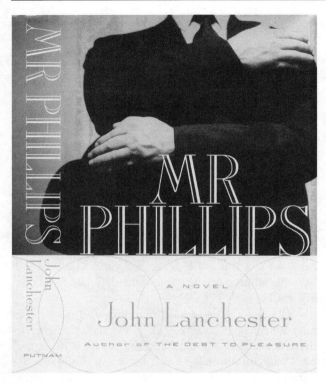

Dust jacket for the U.S. edition of Lanchester's 2000 novel, the story of one day in the life of an accountant who has unexpectedly lost his job (Richland County Public Library)

smith's *The Diary of a Nobody* (1872); Alfred Polly, the hapless shopkeeper and inadvertent hero whose exploits are recounted in H. G. Wells's *The History of Mr. Polly* (1910); the isolated, fretful, middle-aged speaker of T. S. Eliot's "The Love Song of J. Alfred Prufrock" (1917); and Mr. Bleaney, the focus of Phillip Larkin's poem of that title, in which the speaker speculates about the life of the previous tenant of the grim and shabby room into which he has just moved. There are also touches of Rowan Atkinson's blundering character Mr. Bean, from the 1989–1995 Thames Television series of that name; the daydreaming prevaricator Billy Fisher, played by Tom Courtenay in the movie *Billy Liar* (1963); as well as Gerald, Tom Wilkinson's character in the 1997 movie *The Full Monty,* who conceals his unemployment from his wife. Other sources and analogues include Zbigniew Herbert's Mr. Cogito, the central figure of the poem cycle published as *Pan Cogito* (1974; translated as *Mr. Cogito,* 1994); Italo Calvino's onlooker-philosopher Mr. Palomar, from his meditative fiction *Palomar* (1983; translated as *Mr. Palomar,* 1985); Paul Valery's M. Teste, the absent-minded and overly cerebral character introduced in *La Soirée avec M. Teste* (1896; translated as *An Evening with Mr. Teste,* 1925); John Cheever's Neddy Merrill (the obsessively swimming protagonist of the 1964 story "The Swimmer"); and perhaps most importantly,

Howie, the narrator-on-his-lunch-break in Baker's 1988 novel, *The Mezzanine*.

At fifty, Mr. Phillips is a child not of the war but of its aftermath. The rationing, which ended in 1954, with its "atmosphere of straitenedness and not quite privation," has profoundly affected this self-effacing, all but invisible man who "when he was training as an accountant . . . had fallen in love with the double-entry bookkeeping system." Although it focuses on a single day, the novel in fact recounts an entire life. As Mr. Phillips balances assets and liabilities, past and future, his uneventful life flashes fitfully before the eponymous hero's eyes, following much the same Proustian associative logic of *The Debt to Pleasure.* The loss of the job that has defined him for more than a quarter century causes Mr. Phillips to feel guilty and ashamed about not measuring up as a man and, worse, suddenly aware of having, like Prufrock, measured out his life in coffee spoons, having lived tentatively, more voyeur than participant. Not surprisingly, he fears exposure (thus Lanchester's deft use of third-person narration in recounting what one reviewer, Tom Shone, writing for the online magazine *Salon,* aptly terms "a catalog of pleasures deferred"). Mr. Phillips's carefully rationed life seems even drabber when contrasted with one of the chief objects of his sexual imagination, the television celebrity Clarissa Colingford, whose sole claim to fame is the fact that she is famous.

Stopping at a pub crowded with young professionals so unlike himself in age, temperament, and opportunity, Mr. Phillips, feeling even more alone and alien than ever, thinks, "If you started talking to strangers, where would it stop?" A little later, however, he does talk to a stranger, an elderly woman struggling with several bags of groceries, whom he first passes on his way home. Helping her with the bags, he learns that she is the widow of the man who had taught his Religious Education class decades earlier and about whom he had been thinking that very morning. Returning home, he sees his younger son engaged in an equally uncharacteristic act, washing the family car. Although the novel ends with Mr. Phillips walking through the door, having "no idea what would happen next," the effect on the reader is one, as Gabriele Annan described it in *The New York Review of Books* (29 June 2000), of "oddly Victorian uplift" well suited to the author's larger purpose, which is not to satirize—or not merely to satirize—Mr. Phillips, but to humanize him. This "uplift" is not necessarily as unambiguous, however, as some reviewers have claimed. The quiet affirmation of this downsized Odysseus's homecoming may be read more ironically, even sardonically, especially when read against the backdrop of the triumphant return of the wrongly accused father after a long absence to his jubilant family at the end of E. Nesbit's children's book *The Railway Children* (1906), the 1970 motion-picture adaptation of which, "in Mr. Phillips' opinion," is "the sexiest film ever made . . . though he knows you aren't supposed to say that."

Concerning Lanchester's first novel, Shone of *The Times* (London) wrote in a 17 March 1996 review that while "one can admire the will and the wit with which Lanchester has bodied forth his book . . . the book itself seems more hesitant, as if dragged into being only by the vacuum that would otherwise exist were 'John Lanchester's first novel' not to get itself written." The same cannot be said of Lanchester's second novel. *Mr Phillips* is less flamboyant but more purposeful and, as Barbara Trapido, in a 23 January 2000 review for *The Independent* (London), pointed out, only "as easy to read as it must have been difficult to write." Arguably, it may well have been more difficult to write than the pyrotechnic *The Debt to Pleasure,* not just for its remarkable control and understatement but for the way it combines postmodern playfulness and sincere interest in its retiring and redundant protagonist, "homage to the extraordinariness of the ordinary," as Alex Clark called it in his review for *The Guardian* (8 January 2000), and "the weird goulash of desire, shame, embarrassment, fear and desperation that characterises most people's lives," at least the lives of Londoners not found in the fiction of what Jason Cowley, in his 20 January 2000 review of *Mr Phillips* for *The Times* (London), disparagingly called "the drug and rave crowd." As this reviewer's remark suggests, part of the appeal of *Mr Phillips,* though not necessarily its intent, derives from its elegiac yet comic evocation of a vanishing England.

The monochromatic hues and taut structure of *Mr Phillips,* whose protagonist seems to have walked out of that quintessentially English film, *Brief Encounter* (1944), into the differently quintessential Ealing studio comedies of the postwar years, stand in stark contrast not only to the tour de force *Debt to Pleasure* but to Lanchester's third novel, scheduled to be published 8 July 2002. Set largely in Hong Kong, *Fragrant Harbour* follows its protagonist, Tom Stewart, from 1935 to the late 1990s, through the war to the rise of Hong Kong as a center for international business and criminal activities. Although it is clearly Lanchester's most historically expansive, most emotionally intense, and most adventurous work to date, *Fragrant Harbour* also evidences the same fine style and attention to closely observed detail that have made him one of the most interesting, acclaimed, and surprisingly versatile of contemporary English novelists.

Interviews:

Alix Madrigal, "The Novel Disguised as a Cookbook," *San Francisco Chronicle,* 5 May 1996, Books section, p. 4;

Candida Crewe, "Hometown," *Times* (London), 1 June 1996, Magazine, p. 54;

James Boyd Maunsell, "How I Write," *Times* (London), 5 February 2000, Metro section, p. 23.

References:

Jean Crichton, "How Holt Heated Up a First Novel," *Publishers Weekly,* 243 (1 April 1996); 26–27;

Boyd Tonkin, "Foodie Novel Finds the Gravy Train a Bumpy Ride," *Independent* (19 November 1996): News section, p. 3.

Toby Litt
(20 August 1968 –)

Claire Squires
Oxford Brookes University

BOOKS: *Adventures in Capitalism* (London: Secker & Warburg, 1996);
Beatniks: An English Road Movie (London: Secker & Warburg, 1997; New York: Marion Boyars, 2002);
Corpsing (London: Hamilton, 2000; New York: Marion Boyars, 2002);
deadkidsongs (London: Hamilton, 2001);
Exhibitionism (London: Hamilton, 2002).

OTHER: "Dada-Euro-Porn-Tale," in *The Erotic Review Bedside Companion,* edited by Rowan Pelling (London: Headline, 2000), pp. 188–193;
"A Small Matter for your Attention," in *New Writing 9,* edited by John Fowles and A. L. Kennedy (London: Vintage/British Council, 2000), pp. 344–350;
Henry James, *The Outcry,* edited, with an introduction, by Litt (London: Penguin, 2001);
James, *Notes of a Son and Brother,* introduction by Litt (London: Gibson Square, 2002).

SELECTED PERIODICAL PUBLICATION–UNCOLLECTED: "On Perversity," *Pretext,* 3 (Spring 2001): 56–66.

Toby Litt (courtesy of the author)

Toby Litt has been widely billed both as one of the best new writers of his generation and as one of its most accomplished chroniclers. The media has variously dubbed him "one of the foremost young lions of British hip-lit," as Maxim Jakubowski termed him in *The Guardian* (5 February 2000); "one of the leading voices of the young Brit-lit pack," according to Dominic Bradbury in the 17 February 2001 issue of *The Times* (London); and, in a 26 May 1996 roundup of "Young British Talent" in *The Independent on Sunday* (London), Emma Cook called him "the most exciting young talent on the literary scene."

Litt first became known for his witty, postmodern deconstructions of modern life, replete with references to the materiality of contemporary British society. In a literary marketplace often criticized for being awash with sprawling historical novels, this contemporaneity is perhaps one of the reasons Litt has acquired such prominence and is thought of as at the vanguard of–if not a new literary movement—at least a new generation of young writers. Litt is spoken of as a new Will Self or as the British equivalent to the Canadian writer Douglas Coupland. Yet, his writing has developed beyond such early hyperbolic promise, with work that transgresses and occasionally defies genre conventions.

Litt was born 20 August 1968 and grew up in Ampthill, Bedfordshire; his father was an antiques dealer, and his mother, a research assistant. Litt attended local Ampthill and Bedford schools before reading English Language and Literature at Worcester College, Oxford. While attending Oxford, Litt wrote a substantial amount of poetry, experimenting with different verse forms. After graduating in 1989, he traveled around the United States and lived for a short while in Glasgow before moving to Prague in 1990 to teach English. During his time in Prague, Litt worked on three unpublished novels, through which he acquired the interest of a publisher as well as an agent but not a publication contract.

On his return from Prague in 1992, Litt worked in an independent bookshop in Wimbledon, London. In 1994 he gained a place in the prestigious creative writing masters degree program at the University of East Anglia (UEA). He was attracted to the program by his reading of Angus Wilson's *Anglo-Saxon Attitudes* (1956) and Malcolm Bradbury's *The History Man* (1975), books written by past and present teachers at the program, as well as the work of their first student, Ian McEwan. While at UEA, Bradbury's influence gave Litt faith in what became a central concern in his work, as he stated in a 19 February 2000 interview with James Eve: "I learnt that one of the most exciting things you can do is to write about now. You take a gamble, and the gamble is whether the things that are happening now are going to be of interest in two years' time, and that they're not going to become incomprehensible."

In order to attempt as many different narrative voices as possible, Litt also decided to concentrate during the course on writing short stories rather than a novel, an experiment that bore fruit in *Adventures in Capitalism* (1996). Bradbury chose Litt to represent the most recent graduates of the program alongside more-established authors such as McEwan and Kazuo Ishiguro in his valedictory collection, *Class Work: The Best of Contemporary Short Fiction* (1995). Litt won the 1995 Curtis Brown Scholarship while at UEA, and shortly thereafter a publishing deal with Secker and Warburg for his first collection of short stories, after an editor had read his contributions to *Class Work*. After leaving UEA, Litt worked as a television subtitler for ITFC (Independent Television Facilities Centre).

Adventures in Capitalism, Litt's first major published work, is a bravura collection of eighteen stories. Litt divides the stories into two sections, "Early Capitalism" and "Late Capitalism," and as these titles indicate, he takes as his major theme contemporary consumer culture at the end of the twentieth century. Litt's style is frequently surreal, pushing fanciful ideas to their logical extreme in the pursuit of an astringent commentary upon capitalism's effects. An example is

to be found in the opening story, "It Could Have Been Me and It Was," the title of which echoes the slogan of the National Lottery. The conceit is of a lottery winner who decides to take advertisements literally and act on what they tell him to consume or buy, an enterprise that leads him through a litany of products, on holiday to Beijing, where he encounters a troubling lack of advertisements, and eventually back to a clinic in the United Kingdom, where he is protected from the reach of advertising and settles to reading the works of Charles Dickens, an allusion both to the fate of the protagonist of Evelyn Waugh's *A Handful of Dust* (1934) and also to a lost world of nineteenth-century fiction, where branding and marketing were far from their latter-day ascendancy. "Please Use a Basket" provides another instance of this technique as Litt's satire turns upon the cardboard cutout figure sited at the entrance to Boots, the chemists. He imagines a life for the woman photographed for the display, a Boots shop assistant who rebels against her employer, joining the Socialist Workers Party and decrying the "capitalist hegemony" of her former paymasters.

Other stories are also acts of character impersonation that cross gender and age barriers. In this collection Litt's characters are frequently beset by paranoia, neurosis, or self-delusion, such as the narrators of "Mr. Kipling" and "Flies II." Surveillance and voyeurism are encountered in several stories, including the chilling contemporary ghost story "Launderama." A writer, whose study overlooks an Ealing launderette, sees, quite literally, a ghost in the machine that disrupts his relationship with his girlfriend and his own new top-of-the-line Zanussi washer.

Contemporary celebrity culture is mocked in "IYouHeSheItWeYouThey," and the landscapes of trendy 1990s London provide the focus of the pièce de resistance of *Adventures in Capitalism,* "After Wagamama but Mostly Before." In this tale, one of the longest stories in the collection, Litt creates a cast of characters who flit through restaurants, bars, and cinemas, their lives entangling in an increasingly confused and kaleidoscopic way until the borderlines between fantasy and reality are completely occluded. Wagamama, the London-based chain of Japanese noodle bars, repaid Litt's homage by displaying sections of the story in their restaurants and selling copies of *Adventures in Capitalism.*

Two stories foreground their literary allegiances. "The Sunflower" is a self-consciously Kafkaesque tale of an aesthete who finds a flower growing out of his cheek, despite the best intentions of the protagonist, who is "more than well aware of the current dilapidated banality of the *Metamorphosis*-genre." This protagonist is a highly literary hero, who identifies his

Cover for the 1998 British paperback edition of Litt's 1997 novel, in which British characters re-enact Jack Kerouac's On the Road *(1957) in the mid 1990s (Bruccoli Clark Layman Archives)*

problem as "not one of physiology, but of genre. I was in the wrong kind of story—the wrong kind of story was happening to me." The hero is in a postmodern predicament, like many of his fellow adventurers in capitalism. The final story, "When I Met Michel Foucault," is a dream narrative whose two main characters are the French philosopher and a seemingly autobiographical narrator called Toby. As the dreamer/narrator follows Foucault through San Francisco bars, his Parisian apartment, and the sadomasochistic Heaven/Hell Club, the story reflects on the biography industry and the connections between a subject's life and the subject's writings.

More quietly reflective pieces complete the collection. The brief "Trains" is a deft vignette of a relationship refracted through the partners' feelings toward the trains passing close by the garden of their newly bought house. The subtle hallucinatory quality of "Moriarty" depicts two teenage girls, Holmes and Watson, in a provincial English village traversing

their summer holidays in an anxiety of nascent sexuality, fantasy, and intertextuality, that is, a worry about the effect of other stories and writers on the textual fabric of one's life. The story appeared earlier in the anthology *Harlequinned: New Writing* (1995), edited by Katherine Brown. The provincial setting and season foreshadow the atmosphere of the novel *deadkidsongs* (2001), and it is in "Moriarty" that Litt demonstrates a depth to his writing that extends beyond the pyrotechnic satire of some of the other stories.

Throughout *Adventures in Capitalism,* references to brand names, music, television, movies, and the Internet are liberally scattered, situating the stories at an extremely precise historical moment, fulfilling the imperative "to write about now" that Litt learned at UEA. Whether Litt succeeded in using the contemporary both as a weapon for his satire and as a means to literary acclaim is another matter. The reception to *Adventures in Capitalism* suggests a lack of consensus on this question. Lucy O'Brien, in a 29 June 1996 review in *The Independent* (London), expressed the dangerous line she felt Litt treads between satirizing consumer culture and lapsing into it himself, noting that "When he moves away from two-dimensional characters that merely echo the vacuity of our take-out culture, Litt forges a truly satirical comment on consumerism and capitalist gods." Reviewing the collection in the 16 June 1996 issue of *The Observer* (London), Tobias Jones had an equivocal reaction to the book, seeing "threads of beautifully short, intense narrative . . . a very lively, if not always coherent, collection . . . They are not all good, but they are all surprising." Reviewers generally noted a sense of uneven quality in the collection. There was also an occasional distaste or fear expressed by reviewers for a work that situated itself so unapologetically within the zeitgeist. Matt Seaton's 23 June 1996 review in *The Independent on Sunday* (London) provides a good summary of the reception to the book. He wrote: "At his best, Toby Litt seems to revive the spirit of Monty Python, mate it with a strain of magic realism, and let it roam about 1990s London. At his second-best he looks like an author in search of a subject. There's no doubt that *Adventures in Capitalism* marks the arrival of a fresh satirical voice, full of brio. One just hopes that he'll settle down to something more serious." Despite such variable praise, however, *Adventures in Capitalism* marked Litt's entry into the world of letters as a talent to be reckoned with, and an author whose future career would be monitored with serious interest.

Beatniks: An English Road Movie (1997), like *Adventures in Capitalism,* is also set in the 1990s, but it reaches back to earlier decades for its cultural references. It is a recasting of Jack Kerouac's Beat classic

On the Road (1957) in the unlikely setting of 1990s Bedfordshire. The year is 1995, but for the characters Jack and Neal time stopped on 29 July 1966, the day that Bob Dylan had a near-fatal road accident. Litt opens the novel with an imagined domestic scene at the Dylans' just before the accident that introduces some of his major themes in *Beatniks*: the difficulties and demands of growing up and facing adult responsibilities; conflict between the sexes; and a world in which what actually happened and what might have happened is blurred.

Twenty-nine years later, Mary, an unemployed graduate who has returned to live with her parents in Litt's hometown of Ampthill, goes to a party in nearby Bedford. She wanders through the house, passing groups representing various British subcultures: ravers, footballing "lads" (fans), Goths, and Crusties (members of a traveller and protest group with roots in the punk scene and the English folk tradition). Eventually, she enters an upstairs room and encounters Jack, Neal, and Maggie, in the throes of a Beat happening. Jack and Neal are self-named (Neal is in reality called Matthew; Jack's real name is not disclosed) for their heroes Kerouac and Neal Cassady, and the two try to live their lives as latter-day Beats, though they are three decades too late and a continent away. They dress in black turtlenecks, wear dark glasses to block out the incursions of the modern world, and fill their conversation with Beat parlance: "chick," "hip," "square," "cool," "cats," and "dig." Litt's plundering of this vernacular is simultaneously satirical and affectionate, wrapping his characters and their activities in layers of teasing linguistic play, as, for example, when they prepare for "Bedford's own renaissance"—a poetry reading at the local library:

> It was half past seven. Neal stood up again. I moved to follow him. Jack and Maggie were already out on the landing.
>
> "Are you okay?" asked Neal, quietly. "I'm glad you could—"
>
> "Neal, come on! We gotta go, go, go!" shouted Jack, from the stairs.
>
> "Go! Go! Go!" echoed Maggie.
>
> We put on our shoes and went, went, went.

Mary becomes entangled in the lives of these suburban "angelheaded hipsters," despite her reservations about Jack and Neal's obsession with the Beat lifestyle being "a little adolescent." When Jack and Neal realize that Mary has a car, her father's silver Vauxhall Chevette, they persuade her to join them on a road trip to Brighton, using only "a hip road atlas"—one without the post 1960s motorways—for directions. It is during this journey that the limitations of England as a location for a road trip, and for the Beat lifestyle, become all too apparent. Neal's "burst of jive" expresses his frustration: "'England is such a small island. You drive to the edge, then all you can do is stop. There's nowhere else to go. Unless you keep driving. Unless you go over the edge—off the road—into the sea. I want to keep going. I never want to stop. North, south, east, west—I don't care. Just get me off this island! Take me away! Take me to America!'"

The expedition to Brighton develops by way of bouts of torrid group sex, an exhilarating out-of-period visit to a 1970s disco night, and a nostalgic hymn to the contemporary world voiced by Mary, a world full of language-school students exiting McDonald's, AIDS sufferers in their emaciated last months, and mountain bikers in Day-Glo apparel. It climaxes in Neal's disappearance. Mary's car, in which he flees, is found teetering on the edge of Beachy Head—one of the most dramatic and literal edges of the country that he spoke of in his "burst of jive," and a notorious suicide spot.

The final stage of the novel takes Jack and Mary on a real American road trip from New York to San Francisco, in which they symbolically scatter the ashes of Neal's cat, Koko, on the east and west coasts of the United States. Their eventual reunion with Neal and the ambiguous ending rekindle the spirit of sexual jealousy, possession, and mental instability that hovers insistently around the narrative of Beatniks. Behind the satire upon Jack and Neal's pretensions also lies a recurrent question: what is the youth of England today to make of itself? Jack's ironic, cartoon-like emulation of the Beats is his "way of avoiding the pain." Neal's temporary answer is to turn from "this American myth stuff," or from suicide, to become a road protestor; that is, an activist who attempts to stop new highway construction. Litt's investigation of the opportunities, or their absence, for the new generation thus lends his first novel a deeper, darker strain than the comic plot would initially suggest.

This investigation received a mixed critical reception. For Alex O'Connell, writing in the 29 November 1997 issue of *The Times* (London), *Beatniks* was set to become a "suburban classic." In *The Guardian* (15 August 1998) Isobel Montgomery thought the work "masterful" as a "nineties youth novel." Others, however, such as Christina Patterson in *The Guardian* (21 September 1997), felt it to be "at best, mildly amusing and, at worst, irritating in the extreme." Litt's talent seems to inspire both high admiration and bitter disapproval.

Corpsing (2000), Litt's third book, is a stylish, metropolitan thriller, deriving its title from the two meanings of the verb "to corpse" glossed in an epigraph. They are, firstly, "To kill," and secondly, a piece of actors' slang, meaning "to confuse or put out (an actor), or spoil (a piece of acting), by some blunder." These definitions set the scene for the novel, a violently murderous tale played against the backdrop of the London media and acting worlds. In some senses, *Corpsing* marks a departure for Litt into more conventional genre territory than he had previously addressed, leading some reviewers to make comments that could be interpreted as meaning that this book was Litt's first publication. Jakubowski, for example, in *The Guardian* (5 February 2000), called it "a remarkable crime debut," an epithet that came to be used on the front cover of the U.K. mass-market edition, while *The Times* (London), in an unsigned review of the "Best of this year's crime novels" (30 September 2000), dubbed Litt "a strident new voice in British hard-boiled fiction." Litt's entry into the crime genre marks a temporary repositioning of his career from a literary niche to a literary/crime crossover. This genre shift is indicative both of the market awareness of a young writer such as Litt and of the conditions of the contemporary literary marketplace in the United Kingdom, where writing and marketing converge to shape the representation and interpretation of texts. It is worth noting that for *Corpsing* Litt changed publishers, moving from Secker and Warburg to Hamish Hamilton—both a moment for the author to reassess his career and for the new publisher to consider how to package and market their new acquisition. A motion-picture adaptation of the book is in development by Industry Entertainments, with a screenplay being written by Paul Mayersberg.

In *Corpsing,* Conrad Redman, a producer of trailers for satellite television, is summoned to supper in a trendily expensive Soho restaurant by his former girlfriend Lily, a beautiful actress with a lucrative advertising contract and prospective lead role in a controversial Royal Court play. Hoping but scarcely believing that the invitation will preface a reconciliation, Conrad instead finds that he and Lily are the target of a contract killer, who dispenses six bullets—three for Lily; three for Conrad. The trajectories of the six bullets are described in separate chapters, printed in italics. Their descriptive mode is that of the formal postmortem juxtaposed with an erotics of the body similar to the forensic violence of J. G. Ballard's *Crash* (1973), a novel Litt acknowledges in the appendix of his novel as invaluable in the writing of *Corpsing*. The first bullet to penetrate Lily exemplifies this forensic erotics, as autopsy-like precision is adduced by a pornography of violence. It

enters Lily's body approximately two inches beneath her left breast . . . that first bullet has traversed ten feet of air-conditioned air, has clipped through the floating grey viscose of Lily's ghost frock, has slit the slick black silk of her camisole. Now, however, that almost-perfect skin of hers begins slowly to stretch—resisting the onwardness of the bullet's metal apex, denting inwards above her delicate ribcage, tightening momentarily from shoulder to hip: but then—after this false, hopeless opposition—punctures easily enough.

Lily is killed in the attack, but after six weeks in a coma Conrad recovers and turns detective as he hunts both Lily's murderer and the paternity of the fetus that died with her. Conrad's search takes him from hospital morgue to a nightly front-row seat at a Royal Shakespeare Company production of William Shakespeare's *Macbeth* (1605–1606) at the Barbican—"All in all, as is usual with the Royal Shakespeare Company, there was far far too much acting going on"—to an insalubrious southeast London pub, where he acquires a sexily described gun, and eventually back to the Soho restaurant for a dramatic reenactment.

Corpsing is a tightly plotted story, one garnished with the lurid details of ballistic violence and shaped by the awareness of the contemporary environment notable in Litt's earlier work. Lily, for example, wears a dress by the designer Ghost to die in, from a line of clothing that later features the actual dress Lily wore when killed in a fashion shoot for *Face* magazine. Investigating the bedside-table reading of one of his suspects, Conrad notes "self-help books going back a couple of years, each generation of further knowledge piled on top of the half-read list—a sedimentary accumulation of shysterism: *Mars and Venus in the Bedroom* over-topped *Further along the Road Less Travelled* which rested upon *Toxic Parents* which surmounted *People of the Lie*."

Reviewers generally acknowledged the effectiveness of the plotting. Gerald Kaufmann approved, summoning up the spirit of the queen of crime writers to endorse Litt's writing in his 29 January 2000 *Daily Telegraph* (London) review. Kaufmann classified *Corpsing* as "a crime story constructed with punctilious skill and carefully laid clues worthy of Agatha Christie." Adam Piette, in the 31 January 2000 issue of *The Evening Standard* (London), however, thought it "heavy-handed" and accused Litt of once more falling into the trap that his own satire sets for him, though with the result this time of "displaying hysterical sarcasm rather than satirical energy." What is perhaps more interesting than this question, though, is the degree to which Litt creates a victim-protagonist in *Corpsing* for whom, as the story progresses, the reader's sympathy is tested and provoked, as the first-person narration enforces a sickening complicity of the reader with Conrad's fascination with Lily's death and his own revenge. As the narrative progresses, Conrad joins the ranks of Litt's narrators on the edges of sanity, and Litt's audience is placed in an increasingly uneasy reading position.

Published in 2001, *deadkidsongs,* like the earlier *Beatniks,* turns away from the allure of the postmodern bright lights of contemporary London, this time for the setting of the fictional Middle England county of Midfordshire in the 1970s and a distinctly unnostalgic exploration of provincial childhood. Yet, complicity—this time that of the author with his sadistic tale of childhood power games—is a theme that links Litt's third novel to *Corpsing.* It is one that certainly affected the reviewer Phil Baker, who, in the 8 February 2001 issue of *The Sunday Times* (London), saw the novel as "the writerly equivalent of pulling off insects' legs."

At the center of *deadkidsongs* are Andrew, Matthew, Peter, and Paul, the quartet of boys who make up Gang—"Not The Gang. Just Gang"—a quasi-military outfit based in the village of Amplewick during the Cold War but which often slips into the heroic mode of World War II. These children are not the sweet innocents of Friedrich Rückert's *Kindertotenlieder* (Songs on the Death of Children, 1872), whose freely translated verses introduce sections of the novel, but darker creations, who both abuse and suffer abuse. William Golding's *The Lord of the Flies* (1954) is a more obvious reference point for Litt's novel in its analysis of the moral depravity of an isolated community of boys. Throughout *deadkidsongs,* however, there is an emphasis on the tension between the generations and genders that is absent from the desert-island experiment of *The Lord of the Flies.* Mothers are described as "always with a worksurface in front of them, at approximately navel height: a pan-crowded hob, a sink full of dirty dishes, a sink full of dirty clothes, an ironing board." Fathers are less despised, but if, as does Paul's, they have "hippyish" leanings, they are viewed with suspicion. Only Andrew's father, "Best Father," is exonerated, and he acts as the honorary Major-General of Gang. Sometimes this role is simply one of organizing and arbitrating their war games, but at others his contributions are much more disturbing, such as his explanation of Matthew's death from meningitis as a necessary fact: "There are always going to be casualties in War."

The everyday brutality of Gang—animal torture, bullying, and the battle for supremacy—explodes one summer holiday, following Matthew's death. The remaining members of Gang blame "The Dinosaurs"—the orphaned Matthew's grandparents—

'*Corpsing* is a first-rate thriller' Muriel Spark
'tension, pace and a sharp wit...Litt will go far' *Daily Mail*

corpsing
toby litt

Paperback cover for the 2002 U.S. edition of the 2000 novel that inspired the reviewer for The Times *(London) to call Litt "a strident new voice in British hard-boiled fiction" (Bruccoli Clark Layman Archives)*

who failed to contact the doctor early enough. They set about a plan of persecution and "extinction," but the fissures in Gang start to show as narrative cohesiveness degenerates. The plot to deal with The Dinosaurs culminates in a bloodily comic mass murder in which Airfix plane models are used as weapons. Yet, it is uncertain whether this scene represents something that actually takes place or whether sick fantasy has taken over from warped reality. Narrative unreliability is introduced early into the novel, as Gang's Archives, though supposedly set down as "an accurate and truthful record of our achievements," are shown to be at variance to how these same events are related in other parts of the novel. The narrative is seemingly split into the four boys' separate voices, but the grammatical lacuna of the collective narratorial "we" induces further uncertainty. Page numbering stops at 419, then the next page is 375, followed by 376, and ascending chronologically, so providing two chapter thirteens and alternative endings. Textual integrity is also brought into question with the device of Matthew narrating his own death. The whole novel functions as a found manuscript read by the son of one of Gang the day after the funeral of his suicidal father.

deadkidsongs is also notable for its varying linguistic registers. Among these are elegiac, tourist-brochure descriptions of the English countryside in which Litt treats the pastoral with both sensitivity and irony. The sections narrated by the boys appear as if transcribed verbatim, and so include the grammatical tics of early adolescent speech. The Archives, written by Peter, are in militaristic shorthand:

> Went round to Andrew's then up to the Tree-Fort on bicycles. A discuss. Schedule for Operation Badger. Unanimous. Paul suggested small amendments. Worse revenge. Rejected as too risky. Hot day. Few clouds. Cleaned equipment. Did nothing. Morale low. Voiding fast. Andrew ordered rendezvous: Base Camp #1 this evening 1800 hours. Wise move.

In the novel Litt also experiments with typography and layout and includes a map drawn in a childish hand.

Reviewers of *deadkidsongs* were impressed and shocked, often expressing both reactions within the space of the same review. Christopher Tayler, writing in *TLS: The Times Literary Supplement* (23 February 2001), called it both "extremely compelling" and "vividly horrifying," claiming that "its view of boyhood, fatherhood and the battle between youth and age leaves an authentically bad taste in the mouth." In a 24 February 2001 review in *The Daily Telegraph* (London), John Preston called it "an extraordinary book, one of the most disturbing I have ever read." Peter Bradshaw, in *The Guardian* (24 February 2001), compared two visions of childhood in the 1970s by reviewing *deadkidsongs* alongside Jonathan Coe's *The Rotters' Club* (2001), introducing his comments by saying that "Coe's novel feels autobiographical. I very much hope Toby Litt's isn't." Bradshaw saw Litt's book as marking a genuine development in the author's career:

> *deadkidsongs* is about as far as it could be from the hip cosmopolitan sophistication of Litt's previous book, *Corpsing*. With its solidity and substance and its feel for the English countryside, it reads almost like a classroom classic itself. Litt has always been a smart writer, but *deadkidsongs* shows signs of something more than that. There is an effortless felicity in his prose, and a discreetly happy invention in almost every sentence. But the inflections of comedy and fun have been bleached out of his writing in favour of something much darker, tauter and more unsparing.

In Litt's second short-story collection, *Exhibitionism* (2002), he both revisits familiar themes and extends his repertoire of genres. "Dreamgirls," which opens the volume, is a comically psychoanalytic tale that investigates the results of the fulfilment of male desire, as the narrator is confronted first with a series of fantasy sexual companions, and then a wet nurse, his mother, and the Virgin Mary. Previously published in the first volume of *Neonlit: Time Out Book of New Writing* (1998), edited by Nicholas Royle, "A Higher Agency" plays on the contemporary vogue for London-based mobster movies, sending a would-be scriptwriter to wash dishes in a sinister restaurant kitchen, only to be rescued by an avenging angel of a literary agent. "Mapmaking Among the Middle-Classes" anatomizes a London dinner party with all its tensions, rivalries, and difficult alliances. Added to its menu of sushi, roast venison with apple purée and rosemary sauce, peas, and celeriac mash are the appetizers of depression, darkness, and cruelty. Its rehearsal of urban habitudes is complemented by "Unhaunted," a story of a lesbian relationship that begins in an Internet chatroom and ends with a ghostly visitation halfway between paranoia and, perhaps, a genuine haunting. The story appeared earlier in *The Time Out Book of London Short Stories,* volume two (2000), edited by Royle. A kinky gothic is evinced in "Mimi (Both of Her) and Me (Hardly There at All)," in which the narrator is lured from his research on Dante Gabriel Rossetti in the British Library to visit Elizabeth Siddall's grave in Highgate Cemetery West, and from thence to a illicit nighttime expedition with the strange Mimi. An atmosphere of uncertainty and unexplained circumstances, reminiscent of Roald Dahl's stories produced for the television show *Tales of the Unexpected* (1979–1984), pervade many of the stories, including the romantic "The Waters," set in a near-future world where the waters of the title start to intrude—first as drips and mist and later as raging torrents—into the controlled and hermetic environment of an apartment block. The scenario of "My Cold War [February 1998]" is similarly perturbing; this story, first collected in *Fortune Hotel: Twisted Travel Writing* (1999), edited by Sarah Champion, is a combination of spy thriller and existential boredom set in reunited Berlin.

The Internet appears in several of the stories in *Exhibitionism:* in "Unhaunted" it features as part of the social fabric of contemporary life; in a story earlier published in *The New English Library Book of Internet Stories* (2000), edited by Jakubowski, "On the Etiquette of Eye-Contact During Oral Sex," it is a satirical object; in "Alphabed," it is a structuring device. This last story had its origins as an actual Internet text. In 1999 Litt collaborated with James Flint, Penny Cotton, and Darren Francis on a hypertext project for the independent press Pulp Faction. Developed with the assistance of the London Arts Board as part of its Digital Initiatives project and launched in March 1999 as part of the London Festival of the Word, the collaborative novel *Babylondon* is online at www.pulpfact.demon.co.uk/babylondon/. Litt's contribution, "Alphabed," consists of twenty-six lettered sections, detailing the physical states of a man, a woman, and their bed. Pornography is also added to the themes and forms, with the occasionally explicit "Alphabed"; the spoof documentary of a porn star, "'Legends of Porn' (Polly Morphous) Final Shooting Script," a story that appeared earlier in *Piece of Flesh* (2001), edited by Zadie Smith; and the material copied from one tape to another by protagonists on rural retreat in "The New Puritans," a story previously published as "The Puritans," in *All Hail the New Puritans* (2000), edited by Nicholas Blincoe and Matt Thorne.

The prolific variety of the stories in *Exhibitionism,* Litt's fifth book, confirms his status as a writer of ingenuity and imagination. It is also one that suggests that Litt's aim of publishing twenty-six books, each title of which begins with a different letter of the alphabet, is an achievable goal, as he told Claire

Squires in an unpublished interview on 11 July 2001. Throughout his writing career, Litt has continued to publish short stories in magazines and anthologies. He also writes reviews and opinion pieces, thus building up a literary career that is not solely focused on major publications, which is confirmed by his text-based, self-constructed website, www.toby-litt.com, which he inaugurated 29 August 2000. As his list of publications grows, so his reputation continues to build: a reputation as an idiosyncratic and innovative writer, but also as a trenchant commentator on the mores and conventions of contemporary culture and society.

Interviews:

James Eve, "Screen Test," *Times* (London), 19 February 2000, Metro Section, p. 16;

Kevin Patrick Mahoney, "Toby Litt Interview," *Genre,* Summer 2000 <www.geocities.com/SoHo/Nook/1082/toby_litt_interview.html>;

Robert McCrum, "I Wrote it to be Honest about a Certain Kind of Violence. It's a Boy Book," *Observer* (London), 11 February 2001, p. 17.

Reference:

Toby Litt Website, 29 August 2000 <http: www.toby-litt.com>.

Bernard MacLaverty

(14 September 1942 –)

Michael R. Molino
Southern Illinois University, Carbondale

BOOKS: *Secrets: And Other Stories* (Belfast: Blackstaff, 1977; New York: Viking, 1984; London: Allison & Busby, 1984);

A Man in Search of a Pet (Belfast: Blackstaff, 1978);

Lamb (London: Cape, 1980; New York: Braziller, 1980);

Cal (London: Cape, 1983; New York: Braziller, 1983);

Andrew McAndrew (London: Walker, 1988; Cambridge, Mass.: Candlewick Press, 1992);

Columba (Edinburgh: Scottish Children's Press, 1997);

Grace Notes (London: Cape, 1997; New York: Norton, 1997);

The Anatomy School (London: Cape, 2001; New York: Norton, 2002).

Collections: *A Time to Dance: And Other Stories* (London: Cape, 1982; New York: Braziller, 1982)—includes "My Dear Palestrina," "Phonefun Limited," "No Joke," and "The Daily Woman";

The Great Profundo and Other Stories (London: Cape/Blackstaff, 1987; New York: Grove, 1988)—includes "The Break" and "Some Surrender";

The Best of Bernard MacLaverty: Short Stories, New Windmills series (Oxford: Heinemann, 1990);

The MacLaverty Collection, edited by Hamish Robertson (Harlow, U.K.: Longman, 1991);

Walking the Dog: And Other Stories (London: Cape, 1994; New York: Norton, 1995).

Bernard MacLaverty (photograph by Jude at One Degree North; from the dust jacket for the U.S. edition of The Anatomy School, *2002)*

PRODUCED SCRIPTS: *My Dear Palestrina,* radio, adapted by MacLaverty from his short story of that title, BBC, November 1980; television, BBC, December 1980;

Secrets, radio, adapted by MacLaverty from his short story of that title, BBC, 1981;

Phonefun Limited, television, adapted by MacLaverty from his short story of that title, BBC, 1982;

No Joke, radio, adapted by MacLaverty from his short story of that title, BBC, 1983;

Cal, motion picture, adapted by MacLaverty from his novel of that title, Warner Bros., 1984;

Lamb, motion picture, adapted by MacLaverty from his novel of that title, Channel Four Films / Flickers Limehouse, 1985;

The Daily Woman, television, adapted by MacLaverty from his short story of that title, BBC, 1986;

The Break, radio, adapted by MacLaverty from his short story of that title, BBC, 1988;

Some Surrender, radio, adapted by MacLaverty from his short story of that title, BBC, 1988;

Sometime.5 in August, television, BBC, 1989;

Hostages, television, Granada, 1992;

Grace Notes, radio, Radio Scotland, 1999– .

Equally as well known as a writer of short stories as he is a novelist, Bernard MacLaverty, as have many other Irish writers, has gone the way of exile—in his case, choosing life in Scotland over life in his native Northern Ireland. That choice does not make MacLaverty an anomaly among his peers, but the peace of mind that has come to him with exile does make MacLaverty something of a rare breed among Irish writers. In the forward to his anthology *Ireland in Exile: Irish Writers Abroad* (1993), editor Dermot Bolger identifies "a new breed of Irish writer abroad—writers who have turned their backs on a country which has long since turned its back on them." MacLaverty, however, is not one of Bolger's new breed. The authors Bolger identifies rage at their exile in London, Paris, or New York but feel out of place and uncomfortable visiting Dublin, eagerly awaiting the time they can leave Ireland again.

Unlike those who constitute this new breed of Irish writer, MacLaverty has found a peaceful life in Glasgow, which he claims is just like Belfast but without the violence. Moreover, MacLaverty has not turned his back on Ireland; much of his writing focuses on Ireland and its troubles, though not in a directly political or nationalistic manner. The distinction may be subtle to some, but in his interview with Rosa Gonzalez, published in *Ireland in Writing: Interviews with Writers and Academics* (1998), MacLaverty defined himself in relation to his native land: "I consider myself a writer who comes from Ireland. . . . I would be slightly less comfortable with being an Irish writer . . . But to be a writer from Ireland means that you could be examining certain concerns that any writer anywhere in the world could be examining." Although life in Scotland has afforded him the artistic freedom to examine whatever concerns he wishes, in his novels MacLaverty has chosen to stay at home in Ireland and examine the painful moments when personal belief, choice, and desire intersect with the intractable cultural conflicts of Northern Ireland.

MacLaverty was born 14 September 1942 in Belfast, Northern Ireland, to John MacLaverty, a commercial artist, and Molly (Boyd) MacLaverty. He has described his childhood as a happy time, growing up at 73 Atlantic Avenue in Belfast surrounded by a large extended family. The death of his father from lung cancer when MacLaverty was only twelve years old seems to be the only traumatic event from those early years that has stayed with MacLaverty into adulthood. As MacLaverty explained to Jeremy Hodges in a 12 October 1999 interview for *The Daily Mail* (London), his father's death occurred at a time when so many aspects of the father-son relationship had still to be resolved: "Because his death coincided with the onset of adolescence, I'd never had a row with him. He was a kind of

saint figure to me. I still sometimes dream about him, dreaming he's back and he's okay."

MacLaverty's writing career began in an unusual way. When he graduated from school, his grades were not good enough to gain him entrance into the university, so MacLaverty took a job in 1960 as lab technician in the Anatomy Department at Queen's University in Belfast. While working as a lab technician, MacLaverty published a short story in a medical-student magazine. Philip Hobsbawn, then a lecturer at Queen's, read the story and asked MacLaverty if he would like to join "The Group," a collection of young writers whom Hobsbawn mentored. Through his interaction with Hobsbawn and the others MacLaverty began to read and study writing more seriously. His peers in The Group included such future literary notables as Seamus Heaney, Paul Muldoon, Michael Longley, Stewart Parker, James Simmons, and Frank Ormsby. He married Madeline McGuckin 30 March 1967; the couple has four children: Ciara, Claire, John, and Judith.

Although he learned a great deal about writing during his time with The Group, MacLaverty was still years away from becoming a self-sufficient writer. In 1970, wishing to pursue the education unavailable to him earlier in his life, MacLaverty entered the university, took a degree in English, and earned his teaching certification. In 1975, his degree in hand, MacLaverty moved to Edinburgh, Scotland, where he taught until 1981. The move to Scotland occurred because the Troubles that had plagued Northern Ireland for years had taken a particularly violent turn. MacLaverty told Suzie MacKenzie in an interview for *The Guardian* (12 July 1997) that "All the bigotry, the Orange and the Green, the hatred between some Protestants and some Catholics had surfaced and had become death." In the midst of this death MacLaverty discovered that he did not have to live with the violence: "And suddenly it struck me that I could leave." So he did, though all the problems of Ireland did not disappear at the border.

From Edinburgh, MacLaverty moved to Islay, an island of four thousand inhabitants among the western isles of Scotland, where he lived until moving to Glasgow in 1988. His stay in Islay marked the beginning of MacLaverty's career as a professional writer. His first collection of short stories, *Secrets: And Other Stories* (1977), won the Scottish Arts Council Book Award. MacLaverty's first novel, *Lamb* (1980), likewise won the Scottish Arts Council Book Award, was selected runner-up for The Guardian Fiction Award, and subsequently was made into a motion picture, for which MacLaverty wrote the screenplay.

Lamb begins when Brother Sebastian returns to the reformatory at which he works after attending his father's funeral. He is immediately called into the office

*Dust jacket for the U.S. edition of MacLaverty's
1980 novel, which examines the wide-ranging
influence of the Roman Catholic Church in
Ireland (Richland County Public Library)*

of the Superior, Brother Benedict, who is more concerned with any inherited money Brother Sebastian will have to relinquish to the community than he is with Sebastian's grief. Brother Sebastian, whose lay name was Michael Lamb, hesitantly informs Brother Benedict that he plans to leave the community, with whom he feels no connection. Hesitant and even fearful toward the head of his community, Brother Sebastian does not tell Brother Benedict that he is leaving the church whose faith he no longer embraces and whose God he suspects is absent. Brother Sebastian specifically does not tell the elder Brother his plan to take twelve-year-old Owen Kane with him when he leaves. As Brother Sebastian leaves his office, Brother Benedict warns him of the web from which Sebastian is unlikely to escape: "And remember, if you do leave in hurried circumstances we can make it difficult for you to get a job. The Church in Ireland, Brother, has as many fingers as there are pies. Remember that." Despite Brother

Benedict's threat, secretly though guilelessly, Brother Sebastian becomes Michael Lamb once again and leaves with his young charge in hopes of saving Owen from the fate he knows awaits the boy–the unenviable future of life in a trade school.

Michael's plan is to obtain an advance on his inheritance and escape with Owen to London. As the two make their way through the busy streets of London, the reader is torn between feelings of compassion for these characters, who, perhaps for the first time, find some joy in their lives, and a sense of dread over the inevitable brevity of those joyous moments. Michael's plan, though simple enough, is so obviously filled with pitfalls that the reader can only wonder why Michael conceives and then executes such an improvident plan. Why, for instance, does Michael not realize that people will assume he kidnapped the boy, or worse? Why does Michael not recognize that his meager inheritance will not last long in a city such as London? What are Michael's long-range plans for himself and the boy? Such questions immediately spring to the reader's mind but not, apparently, to Michael's conscious mind. He is as innocent of such secular, and even practical, matters as he is of the guilt others will undoubtedly project upon him, assuming he has in some way harmed or exploited Owen.

Michael and Owen's escape from Ireland sparks contradictory feelings in the two. While they thrill to the sense of adventure new experiences bring, Michael and Owen also live in a recurring state of fear and confusion. The two travel around London, planning to visit important sites such as museums, but playing in amusement centers instead. The two live the good life, eating in restaurants and sleeping in nice hotels, but they also foolishly lose money in a curbside game of three-card monte. Almost every event has a double edge, both exhilarating and disquieting. When the two find a hotel with rates they can better afford, Michael can begin to relax and get some sleep; almost immediately, though, he meets an Irish maid who works in the hotel and dutifully listens to Irish radio. Michael, then, has to worry that this woman will hear news reports that claim Michael has kidnapped Owen. Thus, the two have to move on, this time ending up in a vacant building used by an odd assortment of squatters and homeless people whose attitudes and behavior seem far worse than anything the two experienced at the school in Ireland. Eventually, Michael concludes that the only option for the two is to return to Ireland and hide in plain sight. He tells Owen his plan, and the boy agrees to accompany Michael back to Northern Ireland. Once the two arrive back in Ireland, Michael takes the boy to see the beach where, after Owen has had every chance to play along the beach, Michael drowns Owen to protect the boy from the life that inevitably awaits him.

Since the 1980s several former inhabitants of Irish industrial schools have written memoirs depicting the harsh and sometimes brutal life boys endured at the hands of the Christian Brothers who ran the schools. Paddy Doyle in *The God Squad* (1988) and Patrick Touher in *Fear of the Collar* (1991), for example, have written about their experiences in the industrial schools, while in *Freedom of Angels* (1999) Bernadette Fahy presents her experiences in the schools for girls and young children run by the Sisters of Mercy. Mannix Flynn in *Nothing to Say* (1983) and Patrick McCabe in *The Butcher Boy* (1992) have written novels about the deleterious effects of the industrial schools on the psyches of young Irish children. Many of these novels and memoirs have sparked heated debate in Ireland over the fate of children handed over to the Church by the State. MacLaverty's *Lamb* predates these novels and memoirs—compassionately, yet unflinchingly, depicting the life that traps both Michael Lamb and Owen Kane.

Rather than attack the Church or the religious who ran the industrial schools, MacLaverty portrays Michael as having entered the congregation of brothers as an innocent and uneducated young man, and who has remained that way within its strict confines. Owen is portrayed as a young boy unwanted by his mother, whom Brother Benedict despises for her alcoholism and wantonness. Owen may not be the kind of innocent Michael was as a young man, but he too is a product of his environment. Ignored and discarded by his mother, Owen's future will be shaped by the strict, hierarchical, and occasionally violent world inside the industrial school. Neither Michael nor Owen expects much out of life, which makes their escape together so poignant and its consequences tragic.

MacLaverty never uses the words *Christian Brothers* or *industrial school* in the novel, choosing instead to emphasize the lives of his characters and their pursuit of freedom and happiness, even if those are only experienced for the briefest of time. Rather than rail against the institution of religion in Ireland, MacLaverty presents the way Michael's sense of self-awareness emerges as his religious beliefs recede, the way religious innocence paves the way for secular ignorance: "All his life he had been doing negative things, obedient things under pressure of religion and human respect. This was one decision he had arrived at by himself. . . . Ten years ago, on such a night as this, he would have assumed it was God talking to him. . . . Now that he ceased to believe in God he wondered who or what was pounding at him. . . . He allowed it finally to be his own decision." The decision to return to Ireland is Michael's as well, as is the decision to drown Owen rather than condemn the boy to a life in an industrial school. These particular choices may have been Michael's; however, MacLaverty's portrait of Michael suggests that, just as Brother Benedict warned, the Church's influence extends to both secular and religious matters in Ireland, and so too does its influence extend to psychological and emotional matters of the Irish people.

Reviewers of *Lamb* were taken by MacLaverty's ability to tell a tale that is simple but not simplistic, painfully predictable but not sentimentally suspenseful. In her review for *The New York Times Book Review* (2 November 1980) Julia O'Faolain compared *Lamb* to one of Aesop's fables: "Plain, suspenseful, streamlined, whittled down, it has the nerve to ignore verisimilitude in the interest of reminding us that reality is often more innocent and desperate than we think." In his review for *The Listener* (3 July 1980) John Naughton praised *Lamb* because "It's a story which could have easily degenerated into schmaltz, but Mr. MacLaverty keeps his nerve all the way, and brings off an ending which, though predictably tragic and moving, is in no way sentimental."

If *Lamb* represents one man's attempt to escape the strictures of Irish religion, then MacLaverty's second novel, *Cal* (1983), represents one man's attempts to escape the political violence of Northern Ireland. Michael Lamb seeks little out of life, just the chance for the kind of peaceful existence that will afford Owen an ordinary childhood; Cal McCluskey simply wants a job that does not sicken him and a home where he can live without fear of attack. *Cal* has its roots in the short story "Father and Son," which MacLaverty published in his collection *A Time to Dance: And Other Stories* (1982). The story portrays a love/hate relationship between a son and his father. The son loves his father and mourns his mother's death but also hates his father's timidity in the face of the sectarian conflicts of Northern Ireland. The boy locks himself in his room as a tactic for coping with his problems. In the end the boy is killed on his doorstep, apparently in retaliation for earlier sectarian violence. *Cal* presents many of the same predicaments and sentiments as "Father and Son" but provides a broader context for the events and attitudes presented in the story.

In one sense the McCluskeys, Shamie and Cal, are doing fairly well. Mr. McCluskey has a job in a slaughterhouse, and he and Cal live in a neighborhood where at one time they lived in relative peace. Such thin strands of normalcy, though, represent the extent to which Cal has achieved the life for which he longs. The sights and smells of the abattoir sicken him, so Cal quits the job his father has arranged for him—forcing Cal to live on the dole, or public assistance. As the only remaining Catholics in their neighborhood, Cal and his father receive threatening letters from militant members

*Dust jacket for the U.S. edition of MacLaverty's 1997 novel,
in which the protagonist composes a piece of music that
symbolically reconciles the conflict between Catholics
and Protestants in Nothern Ireland
(Richland County Public Library)*

of the Protestant Ulster Volunteer Force (UVF) who
want the two out of the now-Protestant neighborhood:
"GET OUT YOU FENYAN SCUM OR WE'LL BURN YOU
OUT. THIS IS YOUR 2NDWARNING. THERE WILL BE NO
OTHER. UVF." With such factors imposing themselves
into his life, the normal existence Cal desires seems an
unachievable dream.

Cal, however, is not an innocent like Michael
Lamb. Pressured to take up the cause of Irish nationalism, Cal reluctantly participates in an Irish Republican
Army (IRA) attack on a unionist reserve police officer,
Robert Morton. Although Cal was just the getaway
driver, he is nonetheless involved and thus culpable
when his friend, Crilly, a brutal young IRA member,
kills the Protestant policeman on the steps of the man's
home. Cal is haunted by the event and seeks to elude
Crilly and Skeffington, the IRA organizer. Cal discov-

ers that evading the reach of the IRA proves as difficult
as avoiding the hatred of the UVF. Cal also discovers
that he cannot escape the reproaches of his own conscience. As a result, Cal lives in a state of apprehension,
fear, loneliness, and guilt that marks his days and
haunts his nights. Cal's only escape occurs in church,
not because religion brings a message of hope or
redemption, but because the homily acts as a kind of
white noise to block the endless flow of thoughts running through Cal's mind: "He settled back for the ser-
mon. He liked this time. It was a time of comfort, of
hearing and not listening. The noise of the words kept
him from thinking his own black thoughts and yet the
words themselves were not interesting enough to make
him think of them."

Cal may not be moved by his parish priest, but he
is nonetheless moved by his sense of guilt over the
policeman's violent death. Seeking expiation, Cal
slowly approaches the policeman's widow, Marcella,
whose life he helped irreparably to alter. Marcella Morton, Cal discovers, is not Protestant but Catholic, not
Irish but Italian, and her beauty and seemingly normal
existence proves a powerful force over Cal. In an
attempt to avoid further involvement with Crilly and
Skeffington and to permit greater involvement with
Marcella, Cal takes a job at the Morton house, which
Marcella shares with Robert's family. The two eventually grow closer, which enables Cal to assume Robert's
place in Marcella's life. Just as the reader can foretell the
flaws in Michael Lamb's plan to escape Ireland with
Owen, the reader can sense that Cal and Marcella's
relationship is doomed from the beginning. Cal never
reveals his role in Robert's murder to Marcella, which
precludes any chance for Marcella to forgive–or to
reject–Cal. Moreover, in such a small town, Cal cannot
evade Crilly and Skeffington indefinitely, which means
Cal must risk IRA reprisals in order to escape recurring
calls to action. When the IRA does catch up with him,
Cal is forced to participate in a plot to plant a bomb in
the library where Marcella works. When the police raid
Crilly's house, Cal narrowly escapes, but he knows that
if either is captured, Crilly or Skeffington will betray
him to the police. Cal anonymously phones the police
about the bomb in the library and returns to the Morton house to be with Marcella. Cal knows the police will
arrive soon, and when they arrive the next day he does
not flee but rather embraces his fate and stands pas-
sively, "listening to the charge, grateful that at last someone was going to beat him to within an inch of his life."

Of all MacLaverty's books, *Cal* has received the
greatest critical attention–most, though not all, positive.
On the one hand, Valentine Cunningham in her review
for *The Observer* (16 January 1983) claimed that "no
novel that I've read about the Ulster of our times seems

so inward with the terrible plight of Northern Ireland as *Cal.*" Likewise, Michael Gorra in *The New York Times Book Review* (21 August 1983) concluded that "*Cal* is finally a most moving novel whose emotional impact is grounded in a complete avoidance of sentimentality." Gorra went on to predict that "*Cal* will become the *Passage to India* of the Troubles." On the other hand, writing in *The Washington Post* (21 August 1982), Jack Beatty argued that *Cal* fails because it provides neither an answer nor an alternative to the unremitting violence of Northern Ireland, but only more guilt and chastisement: "Ulster has had enough of that. It needs forgiveness, not more punishment."

Literary critics likewise disagree over *Cal.* Some, such as Gary Brienzo, believe that MacLaverty's novel explores sectarian violence in Northern Ireland without falling prey to stereotypical portraits of nationalists or unionists. Such critics tend to focus on Cal's attempt to flee or evade the violence plaguing Northern Ireland. Other critics, such as Margaret Scanlan, acknowledge the conflict between private and public spheres that the novel portrays but believe the novel fails because it offers no solution to or affirmative action in response to sectarian hatred and violence. Scanlan, for example, contends that "public life intersects with private lives only to destroy them. The novel itself is threatened when the contest between private and social life . . . is so manifestly unequal. The present is indeed unbearable, and the realistic novel does not imagine solutions." In an unpublished letter of 11 July 2002 MacLaverty responded to such criticism, remarking that there are those who "seem to imply that I have written a bad book because I have not found a way to solve the problems of Northern Ireland—which is daft." After examining the sexual dynamic informing the relationship between Marcella and Cal, Joe Cleary concludes that the novel ultimately moves away from realism: "The novel's sexual fantasy of two Catholics finding love in a Protestant bed must be paid for in the coin of a morality tale—with repentance and atonement . . . a secret desire, shamefully indulged, which must inevitably be exposed, punished, and disowned."

If, as some critics believe, *Cal* moves from realism to fantasy because the novel cannot offer solutions to the social and political conflicts it depicts, then MacLaverty's third novel, *Grace Notes* (1997), offers at least the hope of resolution, if only in symbolic form. During the fourteen years separating *Cal* from *Grace Notes,* MacLaverty seems to have envisioned fiction as a means of presenting affirmative responses to the Troubles of Northern Ireland. Although MacLaverty does not use his fiction as the medium for advocating specific political or social policy, he nonetheless creates characters and situations in his novels and short stories

that extend beyond the inevitable passivity and resignation of Cal's fate.

Several of the short stories in MacLaverty's collection *Walking the Dog: And Other Stories* (1994), for instance, present moments of kindness or forgiveness when Protestant and Catholics look beyond the long-standing hatred that divides them in order to recognize the things they have in common. In "The Wake House" a Catholic widow and her son cross the street to visit a house that is the mirror image of theirs to pay respects to a Protestant family whose deceased loved one routinely cursed his Catholic neighbors. In "A Silent Retreat," another story from *Walking the Dog,* a Catholic boy finds common ground with a Protestant B-Special (police reservist) who is guarding IRA prisoners. The two share a love of football and cigarettes, which brings them together, but the topic of politics brings fear and antagonism into the relationship. The title piece of the volume, "Walking the Dog," depicts a man abducted and interrogated concerning his allegiances by armed loyalist thugs posing as IRA members. The man, familiar with the usual markers that designate Catholics from Protestants, frustrates his interrogators by employing only ethnically neutral names, disavowing all religion, refusing to reveal what school he attended, and pronouncing the letter *h* as both *aitch* and *haitch*. In the end, determining that he is not a Catholic, his captors release the man. Like the loyalist interrogators, the reader never learns the man's identity, but the reader does experience his terror.

In *Grace Notes,* MacLaverty continues to explore affirmative responses to hatred and violence. *Grace Notes* begins with the social realism and psychological despair that has dominated the life of its central character, Catherine McKenna, but ends with the performance of Catherine's musical composition that symbolically expresses the need and means of reconciling Irish sectarian hatred. The novel is divided into two parts. The first part begins when Catherine returns to her mid-Ulster home to attend her father's funeral. Crying as she sits on the bus that takes her to the airport, Catherine is torn by conflicting emotions over her own life and her estranged relationship with her parents, which will never be resolved now that her father has died. Catherine's return to her childhood home evokes memories of growing up: her initial interest in music; her obvious musical talent, which offered her opportunities beyond the streets of her hometown; her eventual education and departure from Ireland; and her strained relationship with her family. The return home is fraught with painful moments. Catherine's mother is hurt that her daughter has stayed away for so long and excluded her parents from her life. Catherine has kept her life secret from her family for so long that mother and daughter hardly

*Dust jacket for the U.S. edition of MacLaverty's 2001
novel, which reviewers have compared to James Joyce's*
A Portrait of the Artist as a Young Man
(Richland County Public Library)

must make a living from her music. She moves to an island off the west coast of Scotland–close enough to see the coast of Northern Ireland, but far enough away to live in peace and safety. Part 2 of the novel reveals Catherine's life in Scotland, the deterioration of her love relationship, her move to Glasgow, and the composition and performance of her symphony, *Vernicle,* which occurs in the final pages of the novel.

Despite the trials of her personal life and bouts of self-doubt and despair, Catherine creates a musical composition that symbolically reconciles the sectarian conflicts of Northern Ireland. Incorporating the Lambeg drums, played by Protestants during their marches, into her musical score, Catherine creates a kind of musical violence in which competing sounds initially jar, rival, and overwhelm each other. Catherine chooses the unconventional instruments because they physically symbolize the ongoing conflicts that plague Northern Irish society. During the weeks surrounding 12 July, Orangemen stage parades celebrating the 1690 victory of the Protestant William III, known as William of Orange, over Catholic James II at the Battle of the Boyne. The battle was waged between contenders for the English throne, but the victory is recalled in contemporary Northern Ireland as a sign of British presence and Protestant rule in Northern Ireland. In the first part of the symphony the Lambeg drums forcefully mute the other instruments, but as the symphony reaches its conclusion the sound of the Lambeg drums is integrated into the score so that the drums' sound coexists rather than competes with the sound of other instruments. The audience, stunned and disturbed by the opening passages of the score, find the ending resounding and hopeful: "At the moment when the music comes to its climax, a carillon of bells and brass, the Lambegs make another entry at maximum volume. The effect this time is not one of terror or depression but the opposite. Like scalloped curtains being raised, like a cascade of suffocation being drawn back to the point it came from and lights appearing. The great drone bell sets the beat and the treble bells yell the melody. The whole church reverberates. The Lambegs have been stripped of their bigotry and have become pure sound." In a 2000 essay Liam Harte and Michael Parker make a connection among MacLaverty's two-part novel, Catherine's personal experiences as a woman and an Irish citizen, and Catherine's musical composition:

> Like the text that contains it, *Vernicle* endeavors to extend Northern Ireland's cultural consciousness by evoking a non-sectarian, politically inclusive space in which expressions of Catholic and Protestant identity might achieve mutual understanding and accommodation. In it, Catherine gestures towards an alternative narrative of identity in which states of plurality, mar-

know one another anymore. Eventually, Catherine reveals that she has a baby daughter, Anna, but not a husband. When her mother discovers the pills on her night stand, Catherine has to admit that she is taking medication for depression. The only positive experience for Catherine is her visit to her former music teacher, Miss Bingham. Aged now, Miss Bingham has followed Catherine's career and appreciates her music. Part 1 ends with Catherine's return to Scotland after the funeral and her joyful reunion with Anna.

Like Michael Lamb, Catherine flees Ireland, but unlike Michael, who lacks a clear plan or goal, Catherine seeks musical knowledge and inspiration. Her education and talent open doors for Catherine, allowing her to meet Chinese and Ukranian composers who expand her knowledge of music and convey its spirituality. Thus, Catherine recalls the beginning of her adult life with her hopes of artistic expression and creative success. Once her education is complete, Catherine

ginality and perceived Otherness might become sources of energy and potential change. The work is also an exercise in self-composition, an attempt to reconfigure the elements of her own troubled identity into a more satisfying "pattern."

In her review for *The Guardian* (24 July 1997) Natasha Walter located *Grace Notes* within MacLaverty's body of work: "Even if he never writes another word, MacLaverty won't be forgotten. He has written three books in which the trauma and poverty of Northern Ireland are squarely faced, but whose emotional emphasis is on joy, on snatched moments of happiness." Walter correctly identified the "moments of happiness" MacLaverty's characters eke out of the loneliness, poverty, and despair that typifies their lives. Unlike Michael Lamb and Cal McCluskey, however, Catherine McKenna experiences moments of joy at the end of the novel. In contrast to the experience of the earlier two protagonists who face their doomed existence with silent dignity, Catherine overcomes the forces in her life that may have held her back to create something that has never existed before. Catherine's tears that mark the end of *Grace Notes* are not the tears of suffering, guilt, or failure but the tears of hope, success, and possibility.

MacLaverty's novel *The Anatomy School* (2001) shares traits with James Joyce's *A Portrait of the Artist as a Young Man* (1916). So influential is Joyce's bildungsroman about his fictional protagonist Stephen Dedalus that the few Irish novelists to take up the genre have felt compelled to acknowledge Joyce's novel. In *Paddy Clarke Ha Ha Ha* (1993), for example, Roddy Doyle opens his novel with a line that recalls the Baby Tuckoo scene that opens Joyce's novel: "We were coming down our road." Likewise, in the opening chapter of *The Anatomy School*, MacLaverty sends his protagonist, Martin Brennan, off on a religious retreat–just as Stephen takes a retreat in the third chapter of Joyce's work–where he encounters the absolute demands of obedience by members of the Church. Martin, of course, is not a latter-day Stephen Dedalus, and MacLaverty is not writing a twenty-first-century counterpart to his predecessor's famous novel. Nonetheless, in his fourth novel MacLaverty ventures into territory many Irish novelists have been loath to travel for fear of being unfavorably compared to the master. MacLaverty's protagonist may not wish to forge the uncreated conscience of his race, the way Joyce's Stephen does, but Martin does, like his literary ancestor, seek what Stephen calls "the reality of experience." Once eighteen-year-old Martin discovers the reality of experience, he discovers a kind of freedom and joy that is often lacking in Joyce's somber and aloof protagonist.

The Anatomy School is divided into two parts. Part 1 occurs during a year's time when Martin and his friends–

the bright, arrogant Blaise Foley and the talkative, confident Kavanagh–plan an elaborate scheme to cheat on their exams. While making and implementing their plan, the boys encounter the authority of the Church and its attempt to control their lives. In contrast to his earlier novels, which portray characters in dire physical and psychological conditions, MacLaverty peppers *The Anatomy School* with moments of wit and humor. For example, in the name of sexual purity, teachers at Martin's school refuse to distinguish between pornography and art or science. Thus, photographs of Michelangelo's *David* are censored with a pair of ink-drawn shorts, and scientific explanations of human reproduction appearing in biology textbooks are literally torn out of existence.

Part 2 of the novel relates the events of a single day when Martin, having passed his exams, now works in a university science department, where he meets a visiting Australian student named Cindy. Assuming some of Kavanagh's confidence with girls, Martin seduces Cindy. The shift from the first to the second part of the novel allows the reader to see Martin moving away from childish schemes to avoid work and becoming a more motivated and analytical young man. The encounter with Cindy brings so much confidence to Martin that he spontaneously asks for a date with a girl whom he meets at a bus stop. The Martin Brennan who gleefully weaves his bicycle through traffic at the end of the novel is fundamentally different from the boy whose mother sent him on a retreat three years earlier. As the novel concludes, Martin reaches a point of maturity where he knows the joy that comes with the expectations of life.

Responses to *The Anatomy School* have been divided between those who find the two halves of the novel disconnected and those who do not. Writing for *Scotland on Sunday* (12 August 2001), Greg Eden argued that "Some powerfully evoked descriptions of the Troubles aside though, the second part of the novel is where it really falls down." Likewise, John Kenny in a 25 August 2001 review in *The Irish Times* (Dublin), after negatively comparing the novel to Joyce's *A Portrait of the Artist as a Young Man,* concluded that "Part Two proves deflationary . . . Comprised of a single chapter that has all the appearances of a stretched short story." Other reviewers, though, who did not have such problems with the structure of the book, focused instead on the positive conclusion of the novel. In his 26 August 2001 review for *The Sunday Times* (London) Peter Kemp recognized that "In marked contrast to the death and desolation with which so many of MacLaverty's previous works have concluded, *The Anatomy School* ends with an image of figures 'buoyed up on thermals of hope.'" Similarly, Hal Jenson in *TLS: The Times Literary Supplement* (7 September 2001) recognized the way "MacLaverty suggests that the big questions, such as how to find one's place in the world, are answered not through serious or conventional means but in unexpected, quietly subversive moments."

Exile seems to suit Bernard MacLaverty. Unlike many of his contemporaries, MacLaverty does not rant in his fiction over an Ireland that does not exist or an Ireland that failed him. In his early novels MacLaverty focused on the lives of ordinary people and explored the way religion and politics, woven as deeply as they are into the fabric of Irish society, bear upon the lives of people who desire only simple and ordinary lives. In his more-recent fiction MacLaverty has continued this line of inquiry into Irish life but has begun to create characters who finds ways out of the traps that hindered his earlier characters. Like his contemporary Brian Moore, MacLaverty has discovered that he can be a writer born in Ireland but living outside of Ireland. Like his predecessor Joyce, whether he considers himself an "Irish writer" or not, MacLaverty nonetheless spends his artistic energies writing about the country of his birth.

Interviews:

Christian Ganter, "Bernard MacLaverty, Glasgow, in Interview," *Anglistik: Mitteilungen des Verbandes Deutscher Anglisten,* 7 (1996): 5–22;

Suzie MacKenzie, "Day of Grace: Bernard MacLaverty Is an Irish Writer Who Lives in Scotland," *Guardian,* 12 July 1997, Weekend section, pp. 25–28;

Rosa Gonzalez, "Bernard MacLaverty," in *Ireland in Writing: Interviews with Writers and Academics,* edited by Jacqueline Hurtley and others (Amsterdam & Atlanta: Rodopi, 1998), pp. 21–38;

Jeremy Hodges, "A Graceful Note on Why Too Much Freedom Is Not Always the Answer," *Daily Mail* (London), 12 October 1999, p. 13.

References:

Gary Brienzo, "The Voice of Despair in Ireland's Bernard MacLaverty," *North Dakota Quarterly,* 57 (1989): 67–77;

James M. Cahalan, *Double Vision: Women and Men in Modern and Contemporary Irish Fiction* (Syracuse, N.Y.: Syracuse University Press, 1999);

Joe Cleary, "'Forked Tongued on the Border Bit': Partition and the Politics of Form in Contemporary Narratives of the Northern Irish Conflict," *South Atlantic Quarterly,* 95 (1996): 227–276;

C. J. Ganter, "Bleakness and Comedy: Stoic Humor in Bernard MacLaverty's Short Stories," *International Fiction Review,* 26 (1999): 1–7;

Benjamin Griffith, "Ireland's Ironies, Grim and Droll: The Fiction of Bernard MacLaverty," *Sewanee Review,* 106 (1998): 334–338;

Liam Harte and Michael Parker, "Reconfiguring Identities: Recent Northern Irish Fiction," in *Contemporary Irish Fiction: Themes, Tropes, Theories,* edited by Harte and Parker (New York: Macmillan, 2000), pp. 232–254;

Richard Haslam, "The Pose Arranged and Lingered Over: Visualizing the 'Troubles,'" in *Contemporary Irish Fiction: Themes, Tropes, Theories,* edited by Harte and Parker (New York: St. Martin's Press, 2000), pp. 192–212;

Michael R. Molino, "The 'House of a Hundred Windows': Industrial Schools in Irish Writing," *New Hibernia Review,* 5, no. 1 (2001): 33–52;

Lauren Onkey, "Celtic Soul Brothers," *Éire-Ireland,* 28 (1993): 147–58;

Arnold Saxton, "An Introduction to the Stories of Bernard MacLaverty," *Journal of the Short Story in English,* 8 (1987): 113–123;

Margaret Scanlan, "The Unbearable Present: Northern Ireland in Four Contemporary Novels," *Etudes Irlandaises,* 10 (1985): 145–161;

Paul Simpson and Martin Montgomery, "Language, Literature, and Film: The Stylistics of Bernard MacLaverty's *Cal,*" in *Twentieth Century Fiction: From Text to Context,* edited by Peter Verdonk and Jean-Jacques Weber (London & New York: Routledge, 1995), pp. 138–164;

Stephen Watt, "The Politics of Bernard MacLaverty's *Cal,*" *Éire-Ireland,* 28 (1993): 130–146.

Colum McCann

(28 February 1965 –   )

Joseph Lennon
Manhattan College

BOOKS: *Fishing the Sloe-Black River: Stories* (London: Phoenix House, 1994; New York: Metropolitan Books, 1996);

Songdogs: A Novel (London: Phoenix House, 1995; New York: Metropolitan Books, 1995);

This Side of Brightness: A Novel (London: Phoenix House, 1998; New York: Metropolitan Books, 1998);

Everything in This Country Must: A Novella and Two Stories (New York: Metropolitan Books, 2000; London: Phoenix House, 2000).

PLAY PRODUCTION: *Flaherty's Window,* adapted by McCann from his short story "Step We Gaily, on We Go," New York, Daedalus Theatre Company, April 1996.

PRODUCED SCRIPTS: *Fishing the Sloe-Black River,* motion picture, adapted by McCann and Brendan Bourke from McCann's short story of that title, Sloe Motion Pictures / Buena Vista International, 1996;

When the Sky Falls, motion picture, by McCann, Michael Sheridan, and Ronan Gallagher, Icon Entertainment International / Irish Screen Productions / Redeemable Features, 2000.

OTHER: "Tresses," in *The Hennessy Book of Irish Fiction,* edited by Ciaran Carty and Dermot Bolger (Dublin: New Island, 1995), pp. 60–69;

"Introduction: Ben Kiely: Let Us Hear Him," in *The Collected Stories of Benedict Kiely* (London: Methuen, 2001), pp. i–xvii.

SELECTED PERIODICAL PUBLICATIONS–UNCOLLECTED:

DRAMA

"Jalapeno Mon Amor: The Dried Apple Gambit," by McCann and Rick Ehrstin, *Analecta: The Student Literary Journal of the University of Texas at Austin,* 18 (1992): 73–85.

FICTION

"As Kingfishers Catch Fire," *Story,* 45, no. 2 (1997): 30–37;

"Sumac," *Story,* 47, no. 2 (1999): 104–106;

"As If There Were Trees," *Story,* 47, no. 4 (1999): 125–128;

"Whirligig," *Portal* (3 August 2000): 3–5, 14.

NON-FICTION

"Ten Days to Killarney," *Irish Times* (Dublin), 14 July 1994, p. 13;

"About Men, About Women," *Observer* (London), 30 October 1994, p. 25;

"Feeling Like the First Man to Whistle," *Irish Times* (Dublin), 25 August 1997, p. 9;

"The Mole People," *Irish Times* (Dublin), 27 September 1997, p. 60;

"International Bastards," *IE: A Supplement to the Irish Echo* (March 1998): 38;

"So Many Books, So Little Time," *Sunday Times* (London), 11 March 2001, p. 8;

"Are All the Bad Planes Gone, Dad?" *Irish Voice* (19 September 2001): 29–30;

"The Real Life of Anna V.," *New York Times,* 24 February 2002, p. 70.

Colum McCann, an Irish fiction writer who lives in New York City, has garnered literary prizes and critical attention in Europe, particularly Ireland, and North America. His writing compels such interest because of his inventive images and symbols, his rich poetic language, and his explorations of international characters who often live on the margins of society in Ireland and America.

McCann was born 28 February 1965 and raised in Deansgrange, south County Dublin, to Sean McCann and Sally (née McGonigle) McCann. His father, also a writer, had been born and raised in Dublin, while his homemaker mother had come from Garvagh, County Derry, in Northern Ireland; her family and community have greatly influenced McCann, who returns there annually. Sean McCann is known in Dublin journalistic and literary circles as an editor

*Colum McCann (photograph © Sigrid Estrada; from the dust jacket for
the U.S. edition of* This Side of Brightness, *1998)*

who encourages new writers; he has written
twenty-eight nonfiction and children's books and long
worked as the Features editor of the *Evening Press*
(Dublin) newspaper. In addition to his well-known
books on roses, gardening, and children's soccer, some
of Sean McCann's work includes volumes on Oscar
Wilde, Brendan Behan, and the Abbey Theatre. Sean
McCann's career familiarized his son at an early age
with the world of writing.

In a 1995 *Long Island Newsday* interview with Dan
Cryer, Colum McCann commented on his father's
career and family devotion, "I didn't appreciate it until
quite recently that he gave us this sort of comfortable,
middle-class Dublin existence when it was within his
ability to have run off with all these interesting journalist writers [like Brendan Behan] and gone drinking with
them. And to have done his own fiction, as well, something he always wanted to do." Like his father, Colum
McCann began his writing career by producing nonfiction, eventually moving to fiction.

Emigration has had an impact on McCann's
family for generations. Before Colum McCann was
born, the McCann family lived in England, where

Sean McCann's father had partly grown up. Colum
McCann's grandfather, Sean "Jack" McCann, who
had taken part in the Easter 1916 Uprising in Dublin,
had moved with his family to England in the late
1940s, and his family had grown up with a sense of
alienation from Ireland. Sean McCann as a younger
man had been a football (soccer) player for Charlton
Athletic, but after retiring from semiprofessional
sports, he and his wife, Sally McCann, returned to Ireland. By this time the McCanns had three children,
Siobhan, Sean, and Oona. Colum McCann became
their first child to be born in Ireland, followed by his
brother Ronan. McCann never met any of his grandparents, except for two visits to Jack McCann as he lay
dying from gangrene. These visits stood out as powerful moments for the young McCann, who attributes
the decrepit father figure in *Songdogs* (1995) to his
memory of these meetings.

McCann was educated at St. Brigid's Primary
School in Foxrock. Afterward, he attended St. Joseph's
Clonkeen College, a small Christian Brothers school,
until the age of seventeen. As a student McCann was
successful both in the classroom and in extracurricular

activities; in 1982 he was named "Student of the Year" at Clonkeen, and he excelled at sports. At an early age he was drawn to the world of his father, and by age eleven he was reporting the scores of soccer games to local newspapers. In a 3 January 1998 article by Vicki Reid in *The Daily Telegraph* (London), McCann is quoted as describing his childhood as happy, "non-traumatic and all that stuff." Apparently, his parents allowed him considerable freedom both at school and home. McCann spent many summers in the 1970s and early 1980s in rural County Derry at his uncle's farm, where his mother had grown up before moving to England. This time with his cousins, aunts, and uncles in rural Northern Ireland made a considerable impact on the author, who has used the setting and depicts strong familial ties, particularly those between mother and son, in his later fiction, which concerns the impact of sectarian conflict in Northern Ireland on three families.

McCann's father discouraged his son from going into journalism. Luke Clancy elaborates in his 21 June 1994 interview with McCann for *The Irish Times* (Dublin): "Sean McCann did not encourage his son to take up writing, and was distinctly lacking in enthusiasm for him making a career in journalism. 'He had seen what journalism does to people, the hardness, the cynicism it causes,' says McCann." Nevertheless, after school McCann stayed in the Dublin area, and, despite his father's reluctance, from 1982 to 1984 he attended the School of Journalism at Rathmine's College, where he earned the "Young Journalist of the Year" award in 1983. During this time he also worked at *The Connaught Telegraph* newspaper in Castlebar, County Mayo, which became a primary setting for much of his early fiction. McCann also first went to New York City in 1983, where he worked for six months at the Universal Press Syndicate, beginning as an office assistant and eventually receiving writing assignments. Returning to Ireland late in 1984, he worked as a freelance journalist with the Irish Independent Newspapers and the Irish Press Newspapers, serving as a "youth correspondent" for *The Evening Press* (Dublin) from 1984 to 1985. He decided that journalism would not be his field, however, and with the encouragement of his father he returned in 1986 to the United States to attempt a fiction-writing career.

In the 1995 *Long Island Newsday* interview Cryer noted, "When Sean McCann returned from lecture trips in the United States, he passed on to his son a fascination with the wonders of America: 'It's a silly idea now, but we always thought of the United States as Tir nan Og [*sic*], which means "the land of eternal youth" in Gaelic'." Upon arriving in Cape Cod, McCann worked and attempted to write, influenced by the legends of the American Beats. As he explained in an interview with Marjorie Kaufman in *The Sunday New York Times* (10 November 1996), "There was a whole enchantment of traveling to America, a wanderlust, with no real intention to stay, but to become a writer. I landed in Boston and got my first job driving a taxi in Cape Cod, bought a typewriter and had the same empty page in it for six months. I had nothing to write about." He soon set out on a solo two-year bicycle trip across the United States and Mexico seeking new experiences. During this time McCann worked for food and lodgings, variously taking positions as a journalist, fence builder, ranch hand, bicycle mechanic, house painter, ditch digger, and dishwasher. In *The Irish Times* (Dublin) Clancy records what McCann was reading: "At the time, he says, he was living on a diet of the Beats, [Jack] Kerouac, [William S.] Burroughs, [Allen] Ginsberg and [Lawrence] Ferlinghetti. (The only book he managed to carry from coast to coast, however, was a volume of Dylan Thomas poetry)." Much as it had done for earlier writers whom McCann admired, from John Dos Passos to Kerouac, these varied travel experiences gave McCann some of the most significant subjects, settings, characters, and themes for his fiction. McCann views these experiences within the context of being an Irish traveler or exile—of being both an outsider in another culture and walking in the footsteps of other Irish immigrants. Indeed, the exploration of his self-imposed exile and his musings on identity, along with the multitude of voices that McCann masters in his fiction, have been repeatedly remarked upon in reviews and essays on his work.

Ending his bicycle trip in San Francisco, McCann returned to Brenham, Texas, which he had visited during his journey; there he began again to attempt to write fiction seriously. For almost two years, from 1988 to 1990, he wrote and worked outside Brenham at Miracle Farm, a Christian-oriented institution for troubled teenage boys. McCann discussed his experience there in the Clancy interview:

> "I was a teacher," then corrects himself: "A wilderness educator. We took young boys who had come out of prison environments and broken homes into a wilderness setting, where we taught them forest and desert survival: how to go into a wilderness with nothing and survive for seven days and seven nights, and leave no mark on the environment . . . there are curative moments that become especially important when we are in the wilderness, when we are exposed, when we are out there. The wilderness puts you in very real mental and physical danger."

The wilderness found its way into much of McCann's early work. The mentoring he experienced at Miracle Farm also found representation in many of his works, most directly in several short stories—

*Dust jacket for the 1996 U.S. edition of McCann's 1994
collection of short stories, which includes fiction inspired by
his experiences as a "wilderness educator" of troubled
boys in Texas (Richland County Public Library)*

"Through the Field," "Stolen Child," "Around the
Bend and Back Again"—collected in *Fishing the Sloe-Black
River* (1994). But McCann did not begin these works at
this time; rather, he began a full-length novel, "Uncle
Saccharin," as Clancy notes: "At 24, juiced up on *The
Subterraneans* and *On the Road* he attempted a novel about
wandering through the United States and Mexico. It
remains unpublished, for very good reasons. According
to its author it was 'immature in every possible way.'"
McCann also wrote a nonfiction book, "Wilderness
Llamas," about his time with the young men that he
taught, which also remains unpublished. McCann
sought for several years in the early 1990s to find publishers for these books, but while some presses seriously
considered them, none accepted them. McCann says
that he needed to write these books "in order to write
myself out of my work." Indeed, his later work is
almost entirely fictional, although based on his personal
observations and travels.

McCann returned to college to study English in
1990, enrolling at the University of Texas in Austin. In
two busy years he completed his B.A. requirements
with a 4.0 average and was inducted into Phi Beta
Kappa. He also published his first short story while a
student—"Sister" in the student literary journal, *Analecta*. The story, which opens *Fishing the Sloe-Black River*
(retitled "Sisters"), opened many doors for McCann.
On its strength he was invited to enroll in graduate
writing courses in a non-credit capacity, despite the fact
that he was an undergraduate, albeit slightly older than
most undergraduates. McCann also had a poem, titled
"Songdogs," published in *Analecta* in 1992, as well as a
one-act drama, "Jalapeno Mon Amor: The Dried
Apple Gambit," co-authored with fellow student Rick
Ehrstin. This play reveals a strong sense of dialogue
and language and signified the beginning of his longtime work with scripts, plays, and screenplays. Then
surviving on bartender wages in Austin, McCann
wrote several of the stories for *Fishing the Sloe-Black
River;* in addition to "Sisters," these stories include
"Cathal's Lake," "Through the Field," and "Fishing
the Sloe-Black River."

In 1991 McCann's father had given a copy of
"Sisters" to David Marcus, who had asked the father
for a story by the younger McCann. Marcus organized
the highly regarded New Irish Writers Page for *The Irish
Press* (Dublin) and, later, for *The Sunday Tribune* (Dublin);
he liked "Sisters" so much that he sent it to Giles Gordon, who, with David Hughes, co-edited the *Best Short
Stories* series for William Heinemann, Ltd. Gordon
included it in the 1992 anthology *Best Short Stories 1992*
and in *The Best of Best Short Stories 1986–1995* in 1995.
This achievement led to two book contracts from Phoenix House for what became *Fishing the Sloe-Black River*
and *Songdogs. The Sunday Tribune* had also published his
second short story, "Tresses," which won two of the
annual *Sunday Tribune* Hennessy Literary Awards—for
Best First Story and Overall Winner. Included in *The
Hennessy Book of Irish Fiction* (1995), edited by Ciaran
Carty and Dermot Bolger, the story depicts a young
Irish couple working on Cape Cod and struggling with
their future; the protagonist, Grainne, aptly named
from Irish myth, is homesick and wonders about the
child growing in her womb.

Only a few stories in *Fishing the Sloe-Black River*
reflect the Texas milieu where McCann was living in
the early 1990s. His other experiences in Dublin, New
York, San Francisco, New Orleans, and the rural towns
and landscapes of western Ireland and the United States
inform the majority of the stories. Of the twelve stories
in the collection, only two are set in Texas, "Through
the Field" and "From Many, One." The other ten have
varied settings across the United States and Ireland. All

ten, however, have Irish characters in them, and the action of seven of the stories takes place partly or entirely in Ireland. Although not solely concerned with Ireland, it is the geographic and imaginative center in this volume. Other immigrants, however, are depicted; "A Basket Full of Wallpaper," for instance, depicts a Japanese American immigrant to a small town in Ireland and the townspeople's struggle to accept him. "Breakfast for Enrique" takes place in San Francisco and concerns a gay relationship between two emigrant men, one Irish and one Argentine. (Another gay-themed short story is "About Men, About Women," in which McCann writes about the time he first saw two men kiss.) Told through the voice of the Irish character, O'Meara, "Breakfast for Enrique" portrays the couple struggling with Enrique's impending death from AIDS as well as the fact that he will not see Argentina again.

> He pushed it [the mirror] away and turned his face to the wall, looked up at a photograph of himself rafting the Parana River. The photo is fading now, yellowing around the edges. The way he leans forward in the boat, going down through a rapid, with his paddle about to strike the water, looks ineffably sad to me these days. He hasn't been near a river in years and hasn't gone outside in almost a month.

The many voices and characters in this first collection reveal that McCann does not aim to limit his writing to Irish concerns; these stories evoke global themes and voices.

McCann's international characters and misfits range from Osobe, the Japanese wallpaper hanger in rural Ireland, to Flaherty, a retired Irish boxer in New Orleans, to Dana, a blind young African American woman in Brooklyn. These stories are realistic and psychologically revealing and yet symbolic; the language is often sensuous and freighted with rich metaphor. Both the title story, "Fishing the Sloe-Black River," and the closing story, "Cathal's Lake," present the Irish tragedies of emigration and violence in a magic-realist fashion. This closing story is based on an obscure Jewish myth that posits there are thirty-six hidden saints in the world who bury the sorrows of the world so that it may continue to exist. During these years McCann was also absorbing the fiction of the Americas, particularly that of Toni Morrison, Louise Erdrich, Cormac McCarthy, Michael Ondaatje, Jim Harrison, and Gabriel García Márquez. Magic realism employs supernatural symbolism, magical images, and surreal stories of animal and human interaction; and antecedents to McCann's employment of magic realism also can be found in the early-twentieth-century Irish novels of James Stephens and Flann O'Brien, particularly Stephens's *The Crock of Gold* (1912) and O'Brien's *At Swim-Two-Birds* (1939). As

do these novelists, McCann also intersperses images of the everyday, often the less savory physical details of life, with lyrical and magical moments.

During these years McCann also met his future wife, Allison Hawke, while on a trip to New York to find a literary agent. They married in 1992 in her home town of Lloyd Harbor, on Long Island, New York. Since that time Hawke has been the first reader of McCann's fiction, and it was she who first suggested that he focus on writing fiction, not autobiography or nonfiction. Soon after their marriage the couple moved to Japan to teach English as a second language (ESL), an occupation shared by many other Irish writers abroad, most notably, perhaps, James Joyce in Trieste. From January 1993 until the summer of 1994 they lived and taught in Kyoto and Kitakyushu and traveled around Asia. During these years in Japan and Asia, McCann noted how the Irish were all over the globe and how emigration and exile have shaped Irish culture. In the introduction to *Ireland in Exile: Irish Writers Abroad* (1993) Bolger cites a letter that McCann had written to him:

> Of course the nature of emigration has changed for all of us—when London is a one-hour flight away from Knock it's hard to say that we've actually emigrated. Not in the same way as people did before—flocks of wild geese, coffin ships, American wakes. In my travels it's been strange to find an Irishman in virtually every small town I've visited. Just two days ago I was out in the arse-end of Kyushu Island when out popped a young man from Limerick. In a town called Goodnight, Texas I met a Cavan man working as a ranch hand. When I bartended in Austin, Texas, there was seldom a week went by when I didn't see a new Irish face.

McCann's representation of these issues struck a positive chord with readers, scholars, and critics alike. Moreover, McCann recognized that he did not want to write about a single locale or place, as he told Clancy in their 1994 interview: "Travel is really central to what I do. Travel pushes within me and pushes within these characters. I don't know when, but I suppose I'm going to have to stop and take stock some time soon. But I can't see myself as a writer coming to terms with a single place." McCann wrote the remaining short stories in *Fishing the Sloe-Black River* while he and his wife were living in Japan. As the collection was being prepared for publication, McCann began his second novel, *Songdogs*.

On 16 June 1994 McCann received the Rooney Prize for Irish Literature, with its Irish £5,000 in prize money, given to an Irish writer under the age of forty. It was awarded for McCann's first collection, *Fishing the Sloe-Black River*, which had been published in Ireland

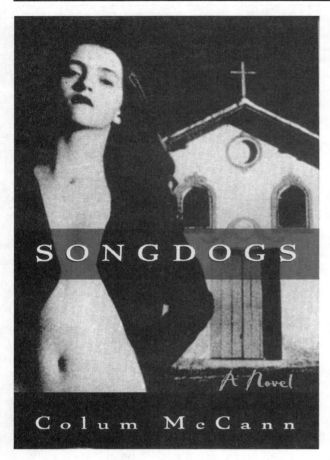

Dust jacket for the U.S. edition of McCann's 1995 novel, for which he drew on his experiences traveling across North America (Richland County Public Library)

strands of this aesthetic mode can be seen developing in this early nonfiction piece:

> At various times I find myself huddled in under trees talking to swans. I discover myself counting my footsteps. In Wexford I sing for seven serpentine miles, strung out on poteen. In Tipperary I find myself in the rain, swathed in black plastic bags. I wake up one morning in Cork and find that I've camped on top of a rather large piece of cow dung.
>
> When I walk over the Paps [of Dana] in Kerry I swear there is a quality of light that I'll never see again. . . . And the nasty stuff appears too. . . . There's filth in the lakes. The raw sewage being pumped into Killarney's River Flesk. There's the car that swerves towards me on a stretch of Tipperary road, six young fellas, one of them vomiting on the dashboard. There's the people gripped by an ineffable fear, afraid to open house doors or catch your eye, assaulted mentally by the recent spate of murders in the countryside. There's the men in youth hostel dormitories who snore and fart all night.
>
> But that's all right, I suppose, that's some of what it's about. . . . There's filth that exists in beauty. And vice versa.

McCann both dispels fanciful illusions about the Irish countryside and reveals the aesthetics that inform his major and more mature works.

Beginning in May 1994, *Fishing the Sloe-Black River* was reviewed in the British and Irish press, as well as in the Netherlands and Germany, where it was also released. The book was published in April, and its complete print run of three thousand copies sold out in less than two months, "a remarkable achievement for an unknown writer," as Graham Lord noted in *The Daily Telegraph* (28 July 1994). The collection was not published in the United States until 1996, but it received dozens of reviews in Europe. The reviews were mixed but generally favorable. A certain note was repeatedly struck; another young Irish writer, Philip MacCann, writing for *The Guardian* (17 May 1994), described McCann's achievement: "Colum McCann's debut—a collection of stories—promises a change. It gives refreshing imaginative narrative voices to the traditional Irish poetic idiom, producing a modern magical realism— rural, urban, Irish and American, with an impressive range of international characters authentic in dialogue and mannerisms." Both the international aspects of his work and McCann's evocative language and strong sense of story marked the collection for many reviewers. Some referred, however, to the manner in which some of McCann's language seemed overwritten, and his style comprised of an "uneasy mix of magic and

and England earlier that year. While on a trip back home to collect his prize, McCann took a ten-day walk from Dublin to Killarney in County Kerry and wrote about it in a piece for *The Irish Times,* "Ten Days to Killarney," published 14 July 1994. His description of the walk parallels descriptive sections of *Songdogs.* This essay reveals some of McCann's concerns, both ethical and stylistic, as a young writer:

> Sleeping along the banks of the Ow River in Wicklow, I have the first of many strange thoughts. I shall, I think, reincarnate myself as a trout. A rainbow perhaps, with a longitudinal red stripe. . . . Skip high from the copper coloured water and feed on these bloody midges that are crowding around me. It's dusk at the edge of the forest, near the Iron Bridge, and the midges are everywhere.

As reviewers and critics of McCann's work have noted, his writing blends both the lushness of magic realism and the spare details of a harsh realism. The two

social realism," as Victoria White and fellow Irish writer Mary Morrissy described it in their 28 May 1994 *Irish Times* review. But other reviewers lauded the book for this same quality.

McCann also began writing motion-picture scripts and working as a "script doctor" in 1994 and eventually became able to support himself as a full-time writer. He has worked on several screenplays over the years, including a short motion picture of his story "Fishing the Sloe-Black River," co-authored and directed by Brendan Bourke and released by Buena Vista with *Phenomenon,* starring John Travolta, in 1996. The fifteen-minute picture was shot with thirty-five millimeter cinemascope and captures the magic realism of the story, with its twenty-six mothers, representing the counties of Ireland, longing for their sons as they fish.

Songdogs was published in 1995 on both sides of the Atlantic and was reviewed in most major newspapers; it was also nominated for the then-new, prestigious International IMPAC Dublin Literary Award. Again the reviews were mixed but generally favorable. Morrissy, for example, in *The Irish Times* (20 June 1995) found the novel lacking in focus but praised the distinctive voice of the narrator and the "magical realism" running through the book. Others focused on the use of photographs in the plot, comparing McCann's work to that of Ondaatje and John Berger, as Tim Adams did in a 9 July 1995 review in *The Observer* (London). Much of the criticism of the novel concerned its language and pacing. As with *Fishing the Sloe-Black River,* some reviewers, such as Anthony Quinn in *The Financial Times* (5 August 1995), criticized McCann's prose for occasionally being "overwritten," using "crowded phrases" and "words that cloud the sense." Many criticized its pace; Ian Parker, for example, wrote in his 16 July 1995 review in *The Independent* (London): "It's a novel with the breathless, madcap pace of an overladen bicycle on an Irish country lane, going uphill." Nevertheless, Parker also emphasized that while "there is little sense of urgency, the book seems to know its destination." Other reviewers did not see the pace as problematic at all: in a 23 July 1995 review in *The Sunday Times* (London) Edward Platt declared, "*Songdogs* is a vivid, beautifully measured book"; writing in *The Ottawa Citizen* (24 September 1995), Iris Winston said, "the pace of *Songdogs* is as leisurely as that of a sleepy river. The result is a relaxing mood piece rather than a compelling read"; and Robert Cremins wrote in *The Houston Chronicle* (4 February 1996) that "McCann is far more interested in being a prose poet than in producing a page turner." Another reviewer, Joy Press of *The Baltimore Sun* (8 October 1995), described McCann's form of realism as an "emotional realism with poetic epiphanies . . . a strange, mongrelized version of magic realism–James

Joyce meets Gabriel Garcia-Marquez." McCann described himself to Cryer as a prose writer but acknowledged that his writing has poetic qualities: "I write poetry but I never publish any. I don't think I'm a poet. I don't think I have the strength to be a poet. I don't know anything about form or rhythm. Actually, 'Songdogs' was a poem long before it was a novel." The extended images and startling descriptions he uses are, in part, responsible for his widespread success, which continued to grow with *Songdogs*.

The novel recalls the settings of McCann's bicycle journey across the United States and Mexico as the central characters drift to and from Ireland through Spain, Mexico, and the American West. The wilderness McCann experienced while traveling across America appears as a backdrop to several short stories, but it is much more evident in his first published novel, *Songdogs,* the title of which, taken from a Navajo creation myth, is the name for a wanderer of wildernesses from the Mexican Pacific to the Canadian Atlantic: the coyote. As he explained to Cryer in his 1995 *Newsday* interview:

> I spent a lot of time in Wyoming on those long, empty roads where you go for days and days. And those huge dramatic landscapes down in Texas and New Mexico, and Mexico itself. I feel very free in places like that. There's a huge bursting out of land and space. And coming from Ireland, a small island, it was like discovering a whole new sense of yourself. By just even walking through the landscape, the landscape becomes a character in the work.

Landscape and place do fill significant roles in McCann's works, which often use geography as metaphors. While many settings and much autobiography made its way into his early writings, most of his published stories and novels are not autobiographical. As Eamonn Wall notes in his 2000 essay "Winds Blowing from a Million Directions: Colum McCann's *Songdogs*," the author overturned a common presentation of Ireland:

> Ireland is presented as being modern and polluted, whereas Mexico and Wyoming have retained more of the sense of traditional community. Such reversals are illuminating, problematic perhaps in their simplicity, but prophetic. In recent times, as Ireland has become more prosperous, the country has attracted immigrants from less-well-off parts of Europe and Africa who have experienced degrees of estrangement and hostility more often associated with the Irish Diaspora.

Songdogs is narrated by a young Irishman, Conor Lyons, who lives in America but has returned to County Mayo, Ireland, for a week, ostensibly in order to claim his green card in Dublin, but also to come to terms with his father, mother, and his family history. Using images from his father's old photographs, scant secondhand details, and a vivid imagination, Conor reconstructs his parents' lives. He narrates the story of his father's early life in Ireland and his work as a photographer in Spain during the Spanish Civil War. The narrative then retraces his father's footsteps in North America, relaying how Conor had done the same in his search for his Mexican-born mother—his parents moved from Mexico where they had met to California and the Rocky Mountains and eventually to New York City where Conor was born. After a few years, however, they returned to Ireland, where his father remained. Questions surrounding the family's eventual separation and the disappearance of his Mexican-born mother, an immigrant in Ireland, mount as Conor's investigation progresses. This story of diasporic origins is broken by alternating chapters in the present as Conor attempts to care for his aging father, who spends his days fishing in a polluted river, seeking to land a great salmon that he believes continues to inhabit the waters. But, as in the Irish myth of Fionn mac Cumhaill, instead of the old man acquiring the mythical wisdom of the salmon, it seems to pass on to the young man.

In a review of *This Side of Brightness* (1998) Hayden Murphy of *The Herald* (Glasgow; 29 January 1998) commented on the growth of McCann's popularity in the mid 1990s, recalling that McCann "was the surprise success of the 1995 Edinburgh Book Festival. Judging by the attendance at his one Scottish reading earlier this month the admirers are growing ardent and the praising has still to stop." McCann's work was also beginning to be put to the stage and screen. In December 1995 Dramsoc, a theater company at the University College, Dublin, adapted two of his short stories, "Sisters" and "Breakfast for Enrique," into monologues for the stage as a part of its "New Voices" season. Similarly, in 1996 McCann's play *Flaherty's Window,* an adaptation of the short story "Step We Gaily, on We Go" from *Fishing the Sloe-Black River,* was performed Off-Broadway in New York City and ran for six weeks. McCann also set to work on a screenplay for *Songdogs,* which was reportedly still in development by Redeemable Features in 2000.

Late in 1996 *Fishing the Sloe-Black River* was published in North America, where the reviews echoed earlier reviews but were even more positive. By this time McCann had been working full-time on his new novel for more than a year. Since 1995 McCann had been living with his wife in New York as a professional, established writer. A television version of his short story "A Basket Full of Wallpaper" was commissioned by the Irish Film Board and the Irish national broadcasting

organization, Radio Telefís Éireann (RTÉ). Produced by Samson Films and directed by Joe Lee, with a script written by Robert J. Quinn, the television movie was first broadcast by RTÉ on 3 June 1998 as part of its *Short Cuts* series. McCann contributed to the script for the motion picture *When the Sky Falls* (2000), directed by John MacKenzie and based on the life of Veronica Guerin, a crime correspondent for *The Sunday Independent* (Dublin) who was gunned down by a drug dealer in 1996. When McCann was brought into the project a screenplay written by Michael Sheridan was already extant and McCann is listed last in the writing credits; however, he essentially wrote an entirely new script for the motion picture. The director, MacKenzie, told Geoffrey Macnab in a 9 June 2000 interview in *The Independent* (London) that McCann was "the 'real' writer" of the movie, and his lack of full credit was an example of "the vagaries of how unjust a world we live in." McCann has been repeatedly drawn to motion pictures, perhaps because of their ability to present the visual images and tableaux that so often fill his fiction, which he has called "cinemagraphic detail." He was writing what became his most critically and financially successful novel to date, *This Side of Brightness.* Published in 1998, the novel is set in New York City and has two plot lines that eventually weave together: one concerns the construction of the subway tunnels in the early twentieth century, principally by African Americans and working-class immigrants, mostly Irish and Italian. The other follows several homeless inhabitants living in the labyrinthine network of passages toward the end of the century, focusing on one character, Treefrog. The idea for this novel reputedly came to McCann when someone at a party mentioned the thousands of homeless people living in the subway tunnels under New York. Intrigued, McCann began to research the construction of the subways and its denizens. In an essay, "The Mole People," published in the 27 September 1997 issue of *The Irish Times* (Dublin), McCann provides more details:

> There are 800 miles of tunnels in New York. They were built by Irishmen, Italians, and African-Americans, many of whom lost their lives in their construction. Steam tunnels, underground cellars, subway tunnels, railway tunnels, bunkers, lost passageways, abandoned tubes. Nowadays, the people who live underground are derisively called "The Mole People." There are between 2,000 to 5,000 living underground in Manhattan. A good 75 percent of them are African-American males.

McCann characterized these tunnel dwellers in a 1999 interview with Mark Fisher: "The most common denominator is that they are wounded. Something happened emotionally, physically, psychologically, and they're all carrying round these various wounds. To use an animal analogy, when a deer gets shot, it goes to the darkest place it can find to curl up into and die." Soon after hearing about these "wounded" people, he began to hang around some of the tunnel entrances to meet the subway dwellers. After weeks of talking to homeless people "topside," he ventured underground with a man named Marco, whom he had come to trust, if not fully understand. Over the course of the next year, McCann repeatedly returned to the tunnels and his new friends as he wrote the novel.

The opening chapters of the book alternate between 1991 and 1916 and develop in two disconnected plot lines that gradually reveal their connections, a structure that, in the words of Erica Wagner in a 1 January 1998 review in *The Times* (London), expresses "both the unifying and destructive power of the city of New York." The main character, a middle-aged African American man named Treefrog, once worked high above the city, but because of a lingering family trauma, he has moved into the tunnels. Much of the novel reveals his story and his family's history, presenting several other "wounded," mostly male, characters, in working-class neighborhoods, at subway and skyscraper construction sites, and within the tunnels.

The tone is suffused with wonder, boundary-breaking, and historical reference as the narrative traces a family's history. A series of spectacular images, sprinkled throughout the novel, bind the story with lyrical moments. In her review in *The Irish Times* (31 January 1998) Morrissy praised McCann's novel for this imagery: "In his poetic and atmospheric rendering of New York, he uses a number of tableaux vivants which reminded this reviewer of classic photographic images of the city—a group of street kids showering gleefully in the spray of a fire hydrant, a line of construction workers perched like swallow on a steel girder stretching out into nothingness." The first historical reference in the novel also provides the first spectacular image and event: the collapse of a subway tunnel between Manhattan and Brooklyn. Because of the rushing air spurting to the surface of the East River, the breach sucks four tunnel construction workers, "sandhogs," upward through the river bed, out of the tunnel, twenty feet into the air on a momentary muddy geyser. Although the accident actually occurred in 1915, McCann has it occur in 1916 as an homage to the 1916 Easter Uprising in Dublin. Indeed, McCann found his status as an Irishman to be helpful in researching the novel, as he told Philip Marchland in an interview for *The Toronto Star* (15 October 2000): "I would never have gone down into the tunnels if I hadn't been Irish. . . . Rightly or wrongly, these people

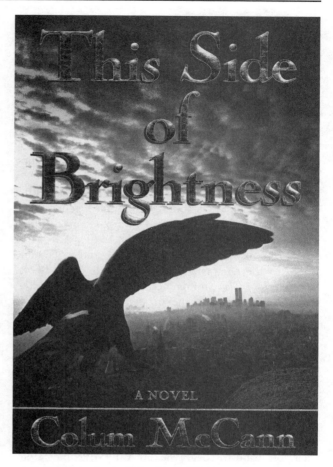

Dust jacket for the U.S. edition of McCann's 1998 novel, partly set in the early twentieth century during the construction of the New York subway system (Richland County Public Library)

saw a similarity between their history and the history of the Irish. 'You know what it means to be down, therefore I'll talk to you.' It gave me access."

The novel brought McCann even more critical attention. Critics generally reacted favorably—Michael Pakenham, in *The Baltimore Sun* (22 February 1998), called the book a "breath-takingly mature novel," and Eileen Battersby, in *The Irish Times* (15 January 1998), described the novel as a "major development" from *Songdogs*—but some reviewers, such as Sylvia Brownrigg, in a 21 January 1998 review in *The Independent* (London), described the novel as being "not so much plotted as built" and at times "overly symbolic." Some critics even saw it as somewhat sentimental, but the majority praised the book for its lyric imagery: "McCann is a bricoleur, making dream-catchers out of trash," Lorna Sage declared in a 25 January 1998 review in *The Observer* (London), adding, "it is the labour of love he puts in that distinguishes him." Other critics praised McCann's exploration of marginal characters who are disconnected from their histories, from an obsessive-compulsive, African American man living in the tunnels to the Irish, Italian, and African American construction workers. According to Richard Eder in *The Los Angeles Times* (22 March 1998), McCann tells stories of the dispossessed: "Those who have built New York are ground up and cast aside: This is McCann's theme."

Overall, the critical reception for *This Side of Brightness* was extensive and praiseful. Ambrose Clancy in *The Washington Post* (19 April 1998) called the novel "a rarity in this preciously cool era—the urban saga with a social conscience, spanning multiple generations, employing the large canvass." Translated into fifteen languages, the novel was listed in 1999 as a "Most Notable Book" by *The New York Times* and a "Notable Book" by the *Los Angeles Times;* named the "Best Book" by *The Boston Globe;* nominated for *The Irish Times* Literature Prize; and won the prestigious Butler Literary Award. Perhaps most significant, however, was the fact that the novel was one of seven books included on the shortlist for the 2000 International IMPAC Dublin Literary Award, at that time the most remunerative literary prize awarded for a single work of fiction.

During the time he was writing *This Side of Brightness,* McCann was busy with other projects and important events in his personal life. He and his wife had a daughter, Isabella Cara McCann, in January of 1997; their son, John Michael, was born in November 1998. McCann was also in demand for readings at Irish festivals from North America to Europe and Australia, and he continued to write short stories, notably "As Kingfishers Catch Fire," published in *Story* (1997), which won him a Pushcart Prize in 1999. In the 1990s McCann's stories were frequently anthologized in Ireland, Britain, the United States, and Germany.

Late in 1998 McCann began writing the novella and two short stories that comprise *Everything in This Country Must* (2000). These pieces concern the strains and effects of the sectarian tensions in Northern Ireland on families and individuals. The focus is on effects upon the characters rather than on more sensational and public events. The first story, "Everything in This Country Must," provides the missing verb for the title of the volume—"die." The story reveals a young woman's perspective on the way her father wrestles with the legacy of his dead son and the presence of British soldiers. The second story, "Wood," concerns a Protestant family who have tried not to be drawn into the conflict but find themselves inexorably drawn into it to an ending that satisfies none of them. Joyce Carol Oates described it in *The New York Review of Books* (29 June 2000): "As in the Joycean model of poetically rendered, elliptical fiction, the conclusion is only a poi-

gnant trailing off from overt confrontation." The novella, "Hunger Strike," which has received the most critical praise, most clearly illustrates the effects of sectarianism on individuals living at a slight remove. The novella follows the summer of a young teenager and his mother who have escaped from Belfast into rural Ireland. The young man's uncle has been arrested for IRA activity and goes on a hunger strike in order to be recognized as a political prisoner. Even though the boy has never met his uncle, his dead father's brother, he strongly identifies with him and is troubled that he is away from Belfast where the street violence continues.

McCann discussed his family's reaction, particularly that of his mother's family, to the sectarian clashes, or the "Troubles," in Northern Ireland in an interview with Thomas E. Mackin in *The World of Hibernia* (2000):

> All I could hear and feel from my immediate and extended family was all we want is peace. There was a real sad refrain. What the hell is going on? Why is this happening? There's an unspeakable sadness that people carry with them that really just says why, why, why? And there's a small minority who've decided what others should think and try to tell them why. . . . Most people are caught in the middle, in this sort of trough.

The book received praise for breaking new ground; an 18 June 2000 review in *The Independent* (London) was headlined "No Balaclavas or Colleens; A Novel Look at the Troubles Enthralls Maggie O'Farrell." In her review O'Farrell remarked, "Perhaps most crucially, his oldest protagonist is 15: he has chosen to write about a generation for whom all this mess is mired in distance and incomprehension. The surety of his grasp on the adolescent mind is by turns astonishing and painful." Most reviewers, including Oates in her review-essay in *The New York Review of Books,* saw the collection as a bold and "beautifully cadenced" look at how sectarian violence touches ordinary lives.

Since the late 1990s McCann's work has begun receiving attention from literary scholars, most notably in John Somer and John J. Daly's introduction to their 2000 anthology, *The Anchor Book of Irish Fiction: The New Gaelach Ficsean,* and Wall's essay in *New Perspectives on the Irish Diaspora* (2000). Somer and Daly situate McCann's work in a tradition of "deep realism," which incorporates both sensuous and symbolic language with stark realism. Somer and Daly trace this tradition back to the later episodes of Joyce's *Ulysses* (1922) and describe it as "a proper reaction to the cynicism of postmodernism. The thrust of this movement is to examine how we use, or misuse, myths and subliminal images and signs in order to infuse meaning and significance into our lives." Another significant critical perspective is put forward by Wall, who situates McCann in a tradition of recent Irish emigrant writers who are often seen wryly as "commuters" rather than "exiles": "These writers are different from other generations of Irish writers–Thomas Kinsella and Seamus Heaney most prominently–because they have come to America as young immigrants and not as fully fledged, mature writers. They have been formed, to a large extent at least, in, and by, America."

Although he participates in both Irish and American literary traditions, Colum McCann is not bound by a specific tradition or group; rather, he continually pushes the expectations of critics and reviewers. Presently, McCann lives in New York City with his wife and two children. He served as a judge for the International IMPAC Dublin Literary Award in 2001 and has paid tribute to one of his literary heroes, Benedict Kiely, writing the introduction to *The Collected Stories of Benedict Kiely* (2001). In 2001 McCann spent part of the summer on a short stint teaching creative writing in Russia, where he did research for a new novel, "Dancer," based on the life of the Russian dancer Rudolf Nureyev. McCann mentions this trip in "The Real Life of Anna V.," an article published in *The New York Times* (24 February 2002). At the end of 2001 he began co-directing (with Michael Garty) "The Last Run," an independent movie based in Irish neighborhoods in the Bronx, while finishing his novel and writing occasional essays. Scheduled for release in 2003, the movie co-stars the Pulitzer Prize–winning author Frank McCourt and his brother Malachy McCourt. He has completed the motion-picture adaptation of *This Side of Brightness* and has several other movie projects "in development," including an original screenplay about an Irish fisherman, co-authored with Bourke, with the working title of "Manlove." In 2002 McCann became the first recipient of the Princess Grace Memorial Literary Prize, for which he was nominated by poet Seamus Heaney and historian Roy Foster. Whether in his short stories, novels, or screenplays, McCann is a writer interested in telling those untold and marginal stories that reveal the common humanity of individuals in the unexamined creases of society in Ireland, in the Irish Diaspora, and across the globe.

Interviews:

Luke Clancy, "Writer and Wanderer,"*Irish Times* (Dublin), 21 June 1994, p. 9;

Dan Cryer, "Talking with Colum McCann," *Long Island Newsday,* 19 November 1995, p. 32;

Marjorie Kaufman, "An Author Fishing for Souls of Irish Emigres," *Sunday New York Times* (10 November 1996), Long Island edition, XIII: 21;

Mark Fisher, "People Who Live Down Below," *Herald* (Glasgow), 29 July 1999, p. 21;

Thomas E. Mackin, "Universal Truths," *World of Hibernia,* 6, no. 1 (2000): 156–157;

Philip Marchland, "Writers Without Borders," *Toronto Star,* 15 October 2000, Entertainment section, p. 1.

References:

Dermot Bolger, "Foreword," in *Ireland in Exile: Irish Writers Abroad,* edited by Bolger (Dublin: New Island Books, 1993), pp. 7–10;

John F. Healy, "Dancing Cranes and Frozen Birds: The Fleeting Resurrections of Colum McCann," *New Hibernia Review,* 4, no. 3 (2000): 107–118;

Joyce Carol Oates, "An Endangered Species," *New York Review of Books* (29 June 2000): 38–41;

John Somer and John J. Daly, "Introduction: Cathal's 'Peculiar Curse': Politics and the Contemporary Writer," in *The Anchor Book of New Irish Writing: The New Gaelach Ficsean,* edited by Somer and Daly (New York: Anchor, 2000), pp. xiii–xvii;

Eamonn Wall, "Winds Blowing from a Million Directions: Colum McCann's *Songdogs,*" in *New Perspectives on the Irish Diaspora,* edited by Charles Fanning (Carbondale: Southern Illinois University Press, 2000), pp. 281–288.

Duncan McLean

(3 October 1964 –)

Desmond Fitzgibbon
National University of Ireland, Maynooth

BOOKS: *The Druids Shite It, Fail To Show* (South Queens-ferry, Edinburgh: Clocktower Press, 1991);

Bucket of Tongues (London: Secker & Warburg, 1992; New York: Norton, 1999);

Blackden (London: Secker & Warburg, 1994; New York: Norton, 1997);

Bunker Man (London: Cape, 1995; New York: Norton, 1997);

Lone Star Swing: On the Trail of Bob Wills and His Texas Playboys (London: Cape, 1997; New York: Norton, 1998);

Duncan McLean: Plays 1 (London: Methuen, 1999)—comprises *Julie Allardyce, One Sure Thing, Rug Comes to Shuv, Blackden,* and *I'd Rather Go Blind.*

PLAY PRODUCTIONS: *The Ran-Dan,* touring Edinburgh and Glasgow, 1985;

Sharny Dubs, touring throughout Scotland, 1986;

The Country Doctor, touring throughout Scotland, 1987;

4 Goblins Hamburgers in Gravy, Edinburgh, Pilton Triangle Arts Centre, 1990;

Two Young Fuckers, Edinburgh, Pilton Triangle Arts Centre, 1990;

One Sure Thing, Glasgow, Castlemilk People's Theatre, 1992;

Julie Allardyce, Aberdeen, Boilerhouse Theatre Company/The Lemon Tree, 1993;

The Horseman's Word, Orkney, St. Magnus Festival, 1995;

Rug Comes to Shuv, Edinburgh, Traverse Theatre, 1996;

Blackden, Glasgow, Castlemilk People's Theatre, 1997;

I'd Rather Go Blind, Edinburgh, Traverse Theatre, 1999.

PRODUCED SCRIPTS: *The Doubles,* television, adapted by McLean from his short story of that title, BBC2, 1992;

Sittin' on Top of the World, television, BBC2, 1995;

Thought in Cold Storage, television, STV, 1999.

OTHER: *Safe/Lurch,* edited by McLean (South Queens-ferry, Edinburgh: Clocktower Press, 1990)—com-

Duncan McLean in Texas doing research for his 1997 book,
Lone Star Swing *(courtesy of the author)*

prises "Safe" by McLean and "Lurch" by James Meeks;

Zoomers: short sharp fiction, edited by McLean (South Queensferry, Edinburgh: Clocktower Press, 1991);

Alison Kermack, *Restricted Vocabulary,* edited by McLean (South Queensferry, Edinburgh: Clocktower Press, 1991);

Irvine Welsh, *Past Tense: four stories from a novel,* edited by McLean (South Queensferry, Edinburgh: Clocktower Press, 1992);

Parcel Of Rogues, edited by McLean (Stromness, Orkney: Clocktower Press, 1992);

Brent Hodgson, *Collected Works: three novels, two lessons, nine haikus and more,* edited by McLean (Stromness, Orkney: Clocktower Press, 1992);

Folk–More Zoomers, edited by McLean (Orkney: Clocktower Press, 1993);

David Crystal, *The Beetle House,* edited by McLean (Orkney: Clocktower Press, 1994);

"James Kelman Interviewed," in *Nothing Is Altogether Trivial: An Anthology of Writing from Edinburgh Review,* edited by Murdo MacDonald (Edinburgh: Edinburgh University Press, 1995), pp. 100–123;

John Aberdein, *The Can-Can, Ken? A Dose O Dorics,* edited by McLean, Clocktower Booklet, no. 10 (Stromness, Orkney: Clocktower Press, 1996);

Knut Hamsun, *Hunger,* translated by Sverre Lyngstad, introduction by McLean (Edinburgh: Rebel Inc., 1996);

Ahead of Its Time: A Clocktower Press Anthology, edited, with an introduction, by McLean (London: Cape, 1997);

James Kelman, *Tantalising Twinkles: Some Thoughts on a First Order Radical Thinker of European Standing,* edited by McLean (Stenness, Orkney: Emergency Eyewash Press, 1997);

Ghosts, edited by McLean (Stenness, Orkney: Swingtime/Clocktower Press, 1997);

"Singing Mrs. Murphy," in *Acid Plaid: New Scottish Writing,* edited, with an introduction, by Harry Ritchie (London: Bloomsbury, 1997; New York: Arcade, 1997);

Simon Crump, *My Elvis Blackout,* edited by McLean (Stenness, Orkney: Clocktower Press, 1998);

Richard Brautigan, *A Confederate General from Big Sur,* introduction by McLean (Edinburgh: Rebel Inc., 1999).

No treatment of Scottish literature since the 1990s can ignore the significant roles played by Duncan McLean. As a writer, McLean has produced a large and distinctive body of work, including the novels *Blackden* (1994) and *Bunker Man* (1995), an award-winning collection of short stories, and a travel book charting his quest for the heart of Western Swing music in Texas. As one of the cofounders of Clocktower Press, he has published, in photocopied booklets, many of the leading writers of his generation, including Irvine Welsh, James Kelman, and Alan Warner. McLean, and the writers he has promoted, may be seen as part of the resurgence in Scottish literature that started in the 1970s but came to wider notice only with the publication of Alasdair Gray's *Lanark: A Life in Four Books* (1981) and Kelman's *Not Not While the Giro* (1983).

Critics and commentators have labeled these authors variously as the "Scottish Renaissance," the "Scottish Beat Generation," and in the case of younger writers such as McLean and Welsh, as the "Repetitive Beat Generation," an ironic term coined to sum up their apparent affiliation with the dance music and fanzine culture of the 1990s. Although these writers reject any notion of a "school" or "movement," their work is generally influenced by debates surrounding language and representation, cultural production, and political identity. This influence is shown most notably in their shared commitment to the primacy of the spoken word in literature and in their related insistence that the people and places they know best are legitimate subjects for artistic consideration. In this commitment they see themselves as countering the cultural agenda set by a largely southern and metropolitan elite based around the large publishing houses and establishment press.

McLean's work is not overtly polemical, but it is politically informed, especially with regard to the disruptive potential that inheres to all language that is labeled as "non-standard." In this sense, he and his Scottish contemporaries belong to an established international tradition of writing. International literary figures cited as influences by McLean include Lu Xun, the father of modern vernacular Chinese literature; the Czech writer Bohumil Hrabal, author of *Hovory lidí* (People Talking, 1956); and the Nigerian writer Ken Saro-Wiwa, author of *Sozaboy: A Novel in Rotten English* (1985). McLean has also been called "Scotland's answer to Roddy Doyle" in a 26 February 1994 article in *The Irish Times* (Dublin), referring to Doyle, the Irish author of such works depicting working-class Dublin life as *The Barrytown Trilogy* (1992).

McLean was born 3 October 1964 in Fraserburgh, a fishing town with farming hinterland, thirty-five miles north of Aberdeen. His parents are Roddy McLean (an English teacher, retired 1996) and Alice Stevenson (a pharmacist, retired 2001). He has one sibling, a brother, Steve, who is three years younger and works in the oil industry. McLean started his primary education in Fraserburgh and completed it in Torphins, a village twenty miles west of Aberdeen, where his father had taken up a teaching post. Something of the self-help ethic that has informed McLean's career to date is evident even at this early stage of his life: he produced a comic called *Condor,* which he photocopied and sold to classmates. A subversive interest in the qualities of language is also hinted at in his inviting friends to

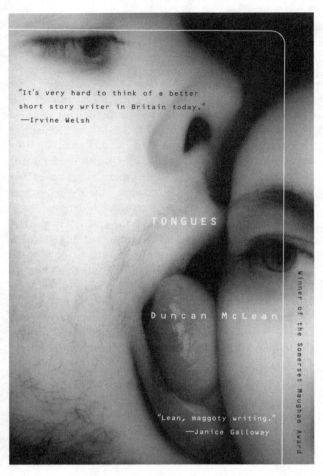

*Dust jacket for the 1999 U.S. edition of McLean's
1992 book, a collection of short stories for which he
drew on his experiences in Edinburgh during the
late 1980s and early 1990s (Richland
County Public Library)*

join the "Condor Club," which was, among other things, committed to "drppng th vwls frm wrds."

From 1976 to 1982 he attended Aboyne Academy and formed a punk band called "The Distorts." The title of a still-to-be-completed short story that deals with this period in his life, "Three Chords That Shook The World," reflects the seriocomic aspect of the musical endeavors he has carried on to the present day. Entering Edinburgh University on his eighteenth birthday, he studied philosophy and psychology for a year before switching to English language and literature. In an interview with Steve Redhead published in *Repetitive Beat Generation* (2000), McLean described encountering the work of Lewis Grassic Gibbon, the 1930s regionalist best known for *A Scots Quair* (1932–1934), and Kelman at this time: Gibbon's detailed treatment of the people, landscape, and language of northeast Scotland "came like a thunderbolt. He was writing about the area I grew up in—right down to individual roads and

villages and hills!" Gibbon's example showed McLean the artistic potential of the familiar and local. Kelman's *The Busconductor Hines* (1984), McLean told Redhead, "alerted me to the fact that there were folk writing now about the place I lived in right now. In the same way that Gibbon was writing about a place I knew, Kelman was writing about a time I knew: I recognized the people, the language, the predicaments, the politics, the culture, the world." McLean has also cited the influence of the Norwegian writer Knut Hamsun. In "Man-of-War," a paper presented at an Edinburgh symposium on Scandinavian writing (available on-line at www.galloway.1to1.org/Hamsun.html), McLean describes how Hamsun's "improvisatory approach" allows the writer greater freedom when dealing with his material. This approach is based on "not so much a *lack* of control, as a conscious decision not to attempt to control every moment of his creation."

While still at college, McLean edited several books, including R. A. Jamieson's *Thin Wealth* (1986) and Alex Cathcart's *The Comeback* (1986), for Polygon Books, Edinburgh. He also served on the editorial panel for Kelman's second novel, *A Chancer* (1985), and over the course of several months conducted a series of taped interviews with him, which were published in the *Edinburgh Review* (Spring 1986) and later republished in *Nothing Is Altogether Trivial: An Anthology of Writing from Edinburgh Review* (1995), edited by Murdo MacDonald. In 1986 he left college with an M.A. in English. He then experienced a period of unemployment before embarking on a career in performance as part of a comedy trio called The Merry Mac Fun Show. Much of the group's stand-up comedy and street theater took the form of political satire aimed at the Conservative government of the day. McLean has described the sociopolitical turmoil of the 1980s as having had a profound impact on his life and work. Long-standing grievances, such as the enquity generated by a class-riven society and the lack of Scottish political independence, were compounded by such events as the race-related riots in British cities in 1981, the Falklands War of 1982, and the miner's strike of 1984.

Apart from serving as a means of political expression, playing with the Merry Mac Fun Show also proved to be a useful literary apprenticeship for McLean. He began by writing plays, which the company performed around Scotland. It is clear that the vibrancy of the dialogue in his fiction owes as much to the patter and raillery of dramatic comedy as it does to his keen ear for the vernacular. The scabrous wit of the Glaswegian comedian Jerry Sadowitz is a noted influence.

Merry Mac enjoyed popular success throughout Britain, winning "Street Theatre Act of the Year" in

Covent Garden in 1986 and 1987 and making several appearances on national television. The group disbanded in the spring of 1988, after which McLean started a four-and-a-half-year stint as a janitor for Edinburgh District Council. This job allowed him time to start writing seriously, and, after a few false starts, he managed to place short stories with American "litzines," including *Hippo* and *Onionhead,* and established British publications such as the *Edinburgh Review* and *London Magazine*. Dissatisfied with the time it took for the "overworked underpowered magazines" to publish his work and inspired by the example of "litzines," McLean founded the underground Clocktower Press in 1990 with the writer James Meek and the artist Eddie Farrell. In his introduction to *Ahead of Its Time: A Clocktower Press Anthology* (1997), McLean writes

> Vanity publishing? No doubt we were caught up in the excitement of seeing our work in print. . . . Certainly it was a great feeling to write a story one week, and, with only a small amount of time, expertise and money, be able to send it out into the world the next in a neatly stapled card cover. . . . I'd come to the realisation that this was what publishing was really about: not a commercial, money-making venture, but a cultural intervention.

> The booklets were intended to be literary time-bombs. At first glance they looked slight and inoffensive, even lightweight, but once they were out in the world, once the stories and poems they contained lodged in the readers' minds, they'd start a chain reaction that would have disproportionately large effects.

Although Meek and Farrell's involvement in Clocktower lessened with time, McLean carried on, and from 1990 to 1998 thirteen booklets were produced, generally in print runs of a few hundred copies. Highlights include McLean's own work, early drafts of Welsh's *Trainspotting* (1993)—published as *Past Tense: four stories from a novel* (1992)—subsequently an international best-seller and movie, and *Parcel of Rogues* (1992), which included early drafts of Kelman's Booker Prize–winning novel, *How Late It Was, How Late* (1994). In the early 1990s McLean was involved in writers' groups in Edinburgh. He also started giving readings, and it was at one of these that a London editor noted the distinctive qualities of his work. This encounter led to McLean's first mainstream publication, *Bucket of Tongues* (1992), a collection of short stories largely inspired by his years living in Edinburgh. The work shows a writer willing to challenge the linguistic and formal conventions of an age-old form. His peers such as Janice Galloway praised the book for its "lean, maggoty writing"; Welsh referred to it as "inspirational." Claire Messud in *The Guardian* (15 March 1994) praised the book for capturing "the powerful rhythms of the down and out" while not neglecting "the grim humour which makes bleak lives bearable." *Kirkus Reviews* (15 March 1994) summarized the collection as "Short stories of broke, drink-sodden Scottish youths in various states of distress," adding that "McLean pumps underclass rage and considerable sensitivity through his fairly interchangeable Edinburgh characters, all in their 20s and 30s. His sensibility is dark, very male, and filled with an anger that borders on the irrational—but it's an anger that seems to be born from a head-on understanding of social injustice."

Most of the reviews by those McLean refers to in the introduction to *Ahead of Its Time* as the "Tartan Tories and middle-brow newspaper pundits" categorized him as one of the more potent and worrying forces to emerge from the already highly suspect "Scottish Renaissance." Some indication of the disquiet expressed at the time can be seen in such comments as those made in a 12 March 1993 review in *The Herald* (Glasgow), "His words are picked out of some lingual swill bin. . . . as foul and disgusting a diatribe as I have seen in print," and the description in the March 1993 issue of *The Face* (London): "Crisp snapshots of Scotland's seamier side . . . this could be the Scottish Tourist Board's worst nightmare." Regardless of the content of the stories, the titles themselves prove to be both evocative and provocative: "A/deen Soccer Thugs Kill All Visiting Fans," "The Druids Shite It, Fail To Show" (an earlier version of which was separately published in 1991), and "Jesus Fuckeroo." But to concentrate on the stories that portray dissolute characters often engaged in antisocial behavior would be a disservice to the collection as a whole.

McLean's depiction of alienated individuals struggling to communicate is encapsulated in a short piece, "Thistle Story," which, in its neat if rather obvious symbolism, says as much about the writer's condition in Scotland as it does about the lives of the characters that populate *Bucket of Tongues:*

> On my way to the pub one evening, I passed a public call-box. It was full of thistles.

> I stopped and looked more closely. It was a perfectly normal phone-box on the outside, but the inside was stacked full of thistles, right to the roof. Some of the thistles near the ground looked crushed, but the ones at eye level were crisp and green, prickles glistening in the light of a nearby streetlamp. Some of them had wee tartan ribbons twisted round their stalks in bows.

> I looked up and down the street: there was no one about. Who had put them there? I had no idea.

> Just then, the phone started to ring. I couldn't get in to answer it, because the box was full of thistles.

*Paperback cover for the 1997 U.S. edition of McLean's
1994 novel, written in the Orkney Islands, where
McLean settled in 1992 (Richland
County Public Library)*

McLean's interest in the notion of a character's troubled perception of reality is first seen in another story in *Bucket of Tongues*, "The Doubles," a story that was made into a short 1992 television movie. In an interview conducted with Ruth Thomas for *Scottish Book Collector* (1993) just after the release of this collection, he describes the genesis of the story and reveals details that have bearing on *Bunker Man*, the novel he wrote a few years later:

> It's an inversion of the well-worn tradition of the double in fiction: the fetch, the Doppelganger. This goes back to fairy and folk tales, with the best-known novel version being Hogg's Justified Sinner. . . . Hogg used it as a way of examining the Scottish psyche at a time before modern theories of the brain and the mind—psychoanalysis etc.—had developed.
>
> That's fine. But I think it's worn out now, no longer an honest way of describing the world. So I thought I'd do a wee semi-humorous parody of that tradition; in the story, instead of the central character having a dou-

ble, everything else in the world has: eventually he looks out of the window and thinks even the trees are imposters. Interestingly, I later found out that there is actually a mental illness which affects its sufferers in exactly the same way, so I suppose the story could also be read from that point of view.

Despite being lauded and lambasted in equal measure, *Bucket of Tongues* went on to win the Somerset Maugham Award in 1993. The prize money (intended for foreign travel) allowed him to visit Texas, where he carried out research on Western Swing music. His experiences are recorded in the often hilarious *Lone Star Swing: On the Trail of Bob Wills and His Texas Playboys* (1997). Following the success of *Bucket of Tongues*, McLean received an advance for a novel from his publisher, which enabled him to give up his job as a janitor and move to the island of Orkney in May 1992. Located off the northeast coast of Scotland, Orkney appealed to him because its mixed fishing and farming community was similar to the one he had known growing up in Fraserburgh. He had also spent several childhood holidays there with his family. McLean continued to publish Clocktower pamphlets and immersed himself in Orkney's social and cultural life. He assisted in the production of the *Orkney Arts Review (OAR)* and started performing with local musicians. In 1994 he married a native Orcadian, Ingrid Tait, who is a textile designer with her own business. Their daughter, Cara, was born in 1999. McLean assisted in the running of the Tait family's renowned jewelry-manufacturing business until late 2001.

Within two years of arriving in Orkney, McLean had produced a novel. Published in 1994, *Blackden* skillfully combines the regional lyricism of Gibbon and the narrative interiority found in such works as Hamsun's *Sult* (1890; translated as *Hunger*, 1899), James Joyce's *Ulysses* (1922), and Kelman's *The Busconductor Hines*. In his novels, however, McLean demonstrates he is not shackled to an artistic credo established by Kelman and other advocates of an uncompromising and urban realism. His literary editor, the poet Robin Robertson, remarked on the National Public Radio program *Morning Report* (15 April 1998) that he is a writer who instinctively eludes categorization: he is "one of those writers who is never going to write the same book twice. This, of course, dismays my sales department." In *Blackden* he shows that he may be—as he once half-jokingly contended—the missing link between Kelman and Gibbon.

Set in northeast Scotland, *Blackden* depicts a weekend in the life of eighteen-year-old Paddy Hunter, an auctioneer's apprentice. As he stands on the cusp of adulthood, he is faced with a challenge: either to remain in the eponymous Blackden or leave it to seek an alternative life that is as yet unknown. His movements around the village, and his interactions with family, friends, and community, may be seen as a test, which in fact becomes a last look at his old self and the world that has nurtured him.

Paddy's father is dead, and the strained but loving relationship he has with his mother is mainly enacted quite literally through emotional shorthand: they leave scrawled messages to one another on the kitchen table. He also feels overshadowed by the achievements of his sister, Helen, who is studying at Edinburgh University. When his mother goes to visit Helen for the weekend, he is left to fend for himself at home and must also cater to the needs of his infirm grandparents who live nearby.

Most reviews of *Blackden* depicted Paddy as a familiar literary character, an angry adolescent who feels alienated from his family and community. The most commonly cited fictional antecedents of Paddy include Holden Caulfield, the hero of J. D. Salinger's *Catcher in the Rye* (1951), and Stephen Dedalus of Joyce's *Portrait of the Artist as a Young Man* (1916). Other reviewers, however, such as Andrew Greig in the *Edinburgh Review* (Spring 1995), noted the distinctions between these adolescents, namely that Paddy "lacks the ego, narcissism and sense of personal superiority" found in Holden and Stephen, and that his relations with his family and community are essentially amicable. Greig also mentioned McLean's suggestion that the key to the book may be found in a quote from Jean-Paul Sartre: "We only become what we are by the deep-seated and radical refusal of that which others have made us." The existentialist aspect of *Blackden* is most obviously communicated through Paddy's examination of the factors that have created his identity: family, community, place, politics, history, and myth.

The structure of the book facilitates this investigation, being based around the social events of the village: the Friday night dance, the *roup* (auction) on Saturday, and a midnight game of the traditional Scottish sport of curling. These events are portrayed through Paddy's intimate narration, which is a detailed amalgam of the poignant and the hilarious. Although a non-Scottish reader is confronted with unfamiliar words, there is never a sense that they are used gratuitously, merely to provide local color; instead, the diction and rhythmic nuances of the spoken voice appropriately inform and enhance the narrative. The opening scene (describing Paddy's journey home from work on Friday evening) is a good illustration of McLean's use of Scotticisms:

> The track down from Goodman's Croft was rutted with mud, kirned up into a furrow of dried dubs and sharn in the middle, with more muck flung onto the long grass and tangled whins that lined it all the way to its junction with the denside road. For twenty years the only thing to come up to the half-mile hill had been Dod of Goodman's old grey Fordson, a bogey of neeps for the beasts bouncing along behind, Dod himself perched on top, bony arse padded from the iron seat by a thickfolded tattie-sack. But this morning the Murray Marts van had won through the dirt and shite and parked at the top of the brae. It'd stayed there all day till a few minutes before, when it rattled off downhill.

As *Blackden* is a novel concerned mainly with identity, it is fitting that Paddy should be offered various causes and ideas to identify with throughout the course of the weekend. For example, his aunt suggests he get involved in the Scottish National Party, but he says he would like it more if it did not have the words "Scottish" and "National" in its name. Paddy sees all labels and names as being exclusive and divisive. When his aunt asks if he likes his home area, he replies:

> Aye I like it, I said. This part of the world? I love it! I'd like to marry it! This part of the world with the Braes of Corse on one side and Ben MacDeamhain and the Aberdeen road on the other . . . aye. But once you start putting a name till it—Blackden—no! Cause that means we have to like this lump of land better than the next lump of land, cause that's called something else.

It becomes clear later on in the novel, however, that Paddy's identification with Blackden and Scotland in general is marked by a healthy skepticism rather than a destructive cynicism. Despite the menial aspect of his work as an auctioneer's apprentice, he refuses a job offer to write maudlin copy for a picture-postcard series called "The Sun Sets on the Great Scottish Industries." Paddy is told he may even progress to telephone sales if he loses his accent. Although he knows that two years will pass before he will get the opportunity to stand on the *kist* (auctioneer's box), he decides he would rather be the "orra loon" (odd-job boy) than a copywriter for "Bonnyview Cards." Paddy's family and friends realize to some extent that he is not quite himself: "I don't ken who else I'd be except myself, I said. I'm the loon . . . the orra loon . . . what else am I?" They refer to him variously as "the thinker," "the disappearing man," "Mr. Sensitive," and "the late Mr. Patrick Hunter." Although he is known to be unhappy with life in Blackden, nobody suspects he will ever leave. But he realizes that "Things come to an end, things change. . . . You're fed up of the sunlight on the faces you've memorised, and you want to cross over and be in the darkness, be with the folk who are new and unknown. . . . Darkness was coming to get me and I was glad."

Still, Paddy seeks reasons for staying. Finding no comfort in the social life of the village, he immerses himself in the beauty and history of the natural landscape that surrounds him. Shona, a young woman to whom he is attracted, tells him of her having witnessed a witches'

*Dust jacket for the 1997 U.S. edition of McLean's 1995 novel,
which he has called "a reworking of* Justified Sinner" *by the
nineteenth-century Scottish writer James Hogg
(Richland County Public Library)*

Sabbath in the local forest. He visits the pool he used to swim in as a child, and also the Sabbath Stane (stone). The thought of witches and possibly Shona dancing ecstatically around a fire leads him to masturbate. In a bizarre attempt at divination, he tries to read the pattern he has left on the grass: "It looked like nothing. Fuck that for a fortune telling."

He finally clambers up the side of the valley and surveys the village, recalling a local legend about a giant devil who had supposedly left the region after killing his wife. But Paddy thinks differently, speculating that the devil had "sneaked back some other dark night and laid himself down" and died, with his skeleton now underlaying the valley: "And now I was strolling through the devil's innards, approaching his thrapple's knot. And though the road was dry and solid beneath my feet, it was hard not to see it guttering black and wet with the devil's blood."

The end of the novel is ambiguous. There is a strong indication, however, that Paddy will manage to

escape the centrifugal force of the place that has kept him in a stable spin for so long:

> That was the problem with this part of the world, this hollow in the hills: if you didn't watch out you'd spend your whole life whizzing round and round the walls of the den like a motor-biker on a wall of death. Going a hell of a speed, maybe, but never actually getting anywhere. Round and round to the same places, round and round with the same people, round and round with the same thoughts going round and round in your head. I'd only been there eighteen years and three-quarters, and already I was feeling dizzy.

> My muscles had eased, my breath was even. I jumped up.

Although he has been criticized for the male-centeredness of his fiction, McLean also has been praised for his formal awareness and lyrical skill. For example, the topographical, folkloric, and social detail of *Blackden* is ideally suited to a novel intent on describing a young man's troubled relationship with the place that has both nurtured and hindered him. *Blackden* starts as a portrayal of the tedium of village life but evolves into a tentative deliberation on the sinister aspects of time and place. The power of history and geography is proven to be far from latent. Its effects on a sensitive spirit such as Paddy Hunter are considerable. It takes him an enormous effort to escape the weight of his heritage. In *Blackden,* McLean shows how a determined spirit can counter the forces that stifle the formation of a satisfactory sense of self.

Topographic and folkloric details are deliberately and appropriately eschewed in McLean's second novel, *Bunker Man* (readers are not even told the name of the town), which is primarily concerned with the internal world of a psychotic whose identity is devastated by unassailable forces. McLean relates the mental dissolution of Rob Catto, who, with his wife, Karen, has recently moved to her hometown, where he works as a janitor in the local school and she is employed as a credit controller for Scottish Petroleum. The equanimity of their life is disturbed when Rob develops an obsessive interest in the activities of a vagrant who lives in a disused military bunker close to the school. "Bunker Man" is clearly mentally unstable–he admits this himself–but he is no danger to society. Rob, however, invests him with despicable qualities, all of which are projections of his own sadistic fantasies.

Most of the effect of the novel is a result of McLean's skillful handling of "the double," a trope he had already treated, albeit unconventionally, in the short story "The Doubles." The depiction of "the double" in *Bunker Man,* however, is more in line with the tradition exemplified by James Hogg's *Private Memoirs and Confessions of a Justified Sinner* (1824), Nikolai Vasil'evich Gogol's "Zapiski sumasshedshego" (Diary of a Madman, 1835), Fyodor Dostoevsky's *Dvoinik* (1845, revised 1866; translated as *The Double,* 1956), Robert Louis Stevenson's *The Strange Case of Dr. Jekyll and Mr. Hyde* (1886), and Lu Xun's "K'uangjen jih-chi" (A Madman's Diary, 1918). McLean's Rob Catto is a contemporary amalgam of the classic figure of a man tortured by his alter ego. As with Gogol's Poproshin and Dostoevsky's Golyadkin, the mental collapse experienced by Rob finds its counterpart in the exalted sense of self-importance he constructs. In a similar fashion, it may be said that the final imperative of Xun's madman–"Save the children!"–is heeded by Rob, who assumes the role of "guardian angel" to the children who attend the school. He believes his mission is "to root out evil," to prevent a "vast blooming of filth and wrong-doing and perversity throughout the town–throughout the country!" Despite his heightened sense of pastoral duty, he still conducts an affair with an affection-starved fourteen-year-old schoolgirl.

Fiction that employs the figure of the "double" thrills and horrifies the reader at a superficial level but often presents a subtextual critique of society. McLean loads *Bunker Man* with allegorical possibility. In his interview with Redhead, he referred to the novel as "a reworking of *Justified Sinner* . . . though nobody seems to have noticed except me!" Such a reading is possible: the historico-religious tensions of late-seventeenth- and early-eighteenth-century Scotland, the setting of Hogg's novel, are replaced in McLean's work by the secular ennui of the late twentieth century, and the sources of "evil" are found in the psychological rather than the supernatural, with the figure of the "double" being best understood in terms of Freudian "projection" and perhaps Jungian "Shadow" rather than diabolical incarnation.

Recognizing the allegorical import of *Bunker Man,* however, is difficult because McLean exploits the conventions of the modern psychological thriller: suspense-filled scenes with graphic and, at times, gratuitous sex and violence. The effect of these in masking the subtext is considerable, and probably deliberate, for his use of them at times is parodic. The opening scene features a hushed bedroom exchange between Rob and his wife; she awakens him and tells him to listen: "He lay still, his ears straining into the dark. I can't hear anything, he said after a moment. There's somebody in the house, she whispered, and there was panic in her voice."

The situational and tonal clichés are carried forward into the rest of the novel to some extent, but McLean manages to reinvigorate them through a variety of narrative ploys, such as subversion and inversion. Kasia Boddy, in *TLS: The Times Literary Supplement* (9 June 1995), commented that the "novel's impact depends largely on reversals of expectation. Who is the 'weirdo'? Is it the Bunker Man, a gentle victim of the failure of care in the commu-

nity whose only crime is to live in the woods and keep the hood of his coat up on sunny days, or is it the 'Jannie Man' [Rob] himself, who tries to save Sandra, a fourteen-year-old schoolgirl, from pornography but ends up having an affair with her?"

Lori Dunn in *Library Journal* (1 June 1997) criticized *Bunker Man* on several levels. In particular, she thought McLean is remiss in not satisfactorily accounting for the genesis of Rob's psychosis: "For no apparent reason, Rob quickly degenerates into the school's resident lunatic and pervert. . . . Given Rob's complete lack of cunning, the only mystery is why the others fail to notice his painfully obvious dementia from the start. Sluggish, pointless, and predictable, the plot leads to an inconclusive and unsatisfying ending. Not recommended."

That human behavior is not easily explained is, to some extent, the theme of *Bunker Man.* It is thus similar to Bret Easton Ellis's *American Psycho* (1991) and Patrick McCabe's *The Butcher Boy* (1992). But the apparently motiveless malignity embodied in Rob Catto may be explained on several levels. For example, though McLean deliberately eschews overt didacticism in his literary work, he does imbue it with the political sensibility that informed his earlier creative output with the Merry Mac Fun Show. In *Bunker Man* he captures the zeitgeist of mid-1990s Britain, which was a period of social and economic disillusionment after the boom years of the 1980s. The plight of Bunker Man–sick and uncared for in the community–can be seen as but one example of how weaker members of the community suffer as a direct result of government cutbacks in public expenditure, and how they are marginalized still further by a society that needs to find palpable objects for its discontent. In effect, Bunker Man is a contemporary example of the age-old scapegoat. The uncaring attitude and largely unwarranted suspicions of a significant section of the British population at this time are given general expression in minor characters in *Bunker Man,* such as Rob's father-in-law and Karen's work colleagues, but an extreme form of this malaise is fatally realized in Rob's sadism and paranoia. The point is clear: Bunker Man's tragic fate is determined by far more than the psychotic machinations of Rob Catto.

At a more obvious and perhaps mundane level, Rob's disturbing behavior is also partly born of the low self-esteem he feels at being a janitor. Whereas Karen has a career, he has a job. When he socializes with her office friends, they can barely conceal their sniggers. In order to escape what he sees as his humiliatingly low station in life, he aggrandizes his work duties to the extent that he believes he is fulfilling a life-or-death mission:

> What they [Karen's workmates] don't appreciate is the responsibility I have. Six hundred kids, and I'm looking after the lot of them. It's down to me, just me, to

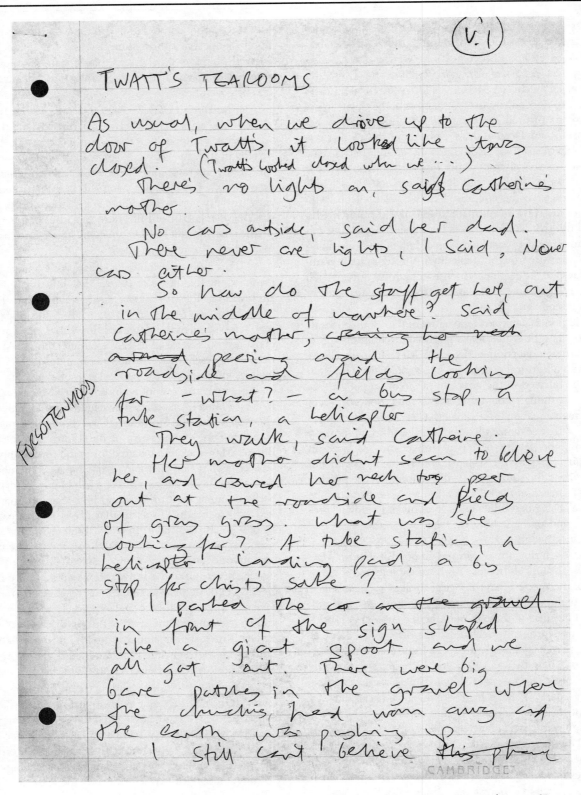

TWATT'S TEAROOMS

As usual, when we drove up to the door of Twatt's, it looked like it was closed. (Twatt's looked closed when we ...)

There's no lights on, said Catherine's mother.

No cars outside, said her dad.

There never are lights, I said, Nor cars either.

So how do the staff get here, out in the middle of nowhere? said Catherine's mother, ~~coming her neck around~~ peering around the roadside and fields looking for - what? - a bus stop, a tube station, a helicopter

They walk, said Catherine.

Her mother didn't seem to believe her, and craned her neck ~~too~~ peer out at the roadside and fields of grey grass. What was she looking for? A tube station, a helicopter landing pad, a bus stop for christ's sake?

I parked the ~~car on the gravel~~ in front of the sign shaped like a giant spoot, and we all got out. There were big bare patches in the gravel where the churchs had worn away and the earth was pushing up.

I still can't believe ~~this place~~

Pages from the manuscript for a work in progress (courtesy of Duncan McLean)

It's open, said Catherine's mum. Look,
there, grass ~~grow~~ in the gutters
and tiles off the roof.

~~It's~~ It's not what's on the
outside that matters, I said. It's
what they look up inside. Appearances
can be deceptive. (Come on)

I lead the way through the
big outer door with its peeling
blue paint, then ~~so~~ ~~through the~~
across the tiny lobby with its
pot of dried nozweed, and
on through the even bigger inner
door with its green baize
cover, like a billiard table upended
and set on hinges.

The ~~door~~ ~~edges~~ of the door
whooshed ~~behind~~ ~~is~~ ~~as~~ ~~we~~ its
~~their~~ rubber edges ~~against~~ the
~~door frame~~ as it shut ~~swung~~
slowly shut behind us, and
we stood looking down the
vast dark interior of the
tearoom. A row of ~~square~~ tables
down each edge, another
down the centre, each with
its half dozen seats, linen napkins,
silver cutlery — three or four
rows of it on the side of each
plate I and the centre of the
table with ~~an array of~~ glass & silver pots of
~~mustard~~, chutney, salt, pepper,
and as well as three glasses

guard them from perverts and drug pushers and god knows what lunatics. That's what I call responsibility, that's what I call a job: not just sitting around in an office playing computer games all day. But no, no, all they see is me in my dustcoat, me with a brush and shovel, me with a choked lavvie. They don't realise that's just a cover, they don't realise I'm really the kids' fucking guardian angel.

McLean is aware that job dissatisfaction cannot fully account for Rob's depraved behavior. It is not surprising, therefore, that a novel informed by twentieth-century psychology should look to the protagonist's childhood as another possible source of his adult difficulties. In a single but telling moment of flashback, the reader learns of Rob's friendless childhood and brutalization at the hands of an authoritarian father. Told by his father, "Don't play with your food!" the ten-year-old Rob responds, "Why not? I've no one else to play with!" Reacting to Rob's "cheek," the father "grabbed the back of Rob's head and pushed his face down into the plate of mince and doughballs. . . . When he straightened up there was gravy all over his face, and particles of mince up his nostrils."

Rob has no friends because his father is a skilled tradesman (a pipefitter) and does not like his son mixing with the children of unskilled workers who constitute most of the neighborhood. As an adult, Rob feels excluded from his wife's social circle because he is not good enough for them. Like Golyadkin in Dostoevsky's *The Double,* he is an "unimportant man" who craves recognition. But whereas Golyadkin is finally tricked by his doctor into entering a carriage that will take him to an asylum, Rob tricks his wife into the seaside bunker. Her rendezvous with Bunker Man and Jannie Man (Rob) is one of the most disturbing scenes in modern Scottish fiction.

McLean told Chris Wright in a 1997 interview that he was "aware that some people would be made uncomfortable reading it [*Bunker Man*] because I was uncomfortable writing it." Its graphic depiction of sex and violence, and, in particular, Rob's misogyny has led some readers to dismiss it as gratuitous and sensational. Such an assessment would be valid were it not for the parodic and allegorical dimensions that McLean builds into the text; these allow for varied interpretations. Its indebtedness to the tradition of the "double" is complemented by an awareness of the lives of the "hard men" and "weak silent types" that abound in twentieth-century Scottish literature. *Bunker Man* is an attempt to understand the causes and effects of an all-too-common mentality.

On a linguistic level *Bunker Man* is less idiosyncratic than *Blackden,* but its dialogue and narration still manage to capture the nuances of contemporary Scottish vernacu-

lar. As is all of McLean's work, these novels are shot through with varieties of comedy, including bawdry, slapstick, and the macabre.

Although McLean has not published any full-length fiction since 1995, he remains an important voice in Scottish literature. In Spring 1997 he participated in the "Great Scots" reading tour of several U.S. cities with Kelman and Welsh. In general, McLean has received more favorable notices in the United States than in Great Britain. When published in the United States, *Blackden* and *Lone Star Swing* were named "Notable Books of the Year" in the *Los Angeles Times.*

An anthology of selected work from McLean's Clocktower imprint was published by Jonathan Cape, Ltd. in 1997. Aptly titled *Ahead of Its Time,* it includes a history of the press written by McLean. Five of his plays were published in 1999. In 2002 he was reportedly working on a novel, a play, and a collection of short stories based on island life.

Judged on his innovative and challenging novels alone, Duncan McLean's contribution to Scottish and, indeed, British fiction at the turn of the millennium would be deemed significant; however, when his publishing endeavors are taken into account, his contribution should be regarded as exceptional. In his roles as writer and publisher, McLean has managed to focus attention on thematic and linguistic territory that remains largely unexplored by British writers and neglected by mainstream publishers.

Interviews:

Ruth Thomas, "Interview–Duncan McLean," *Scottish Book Collector* (Edinburgh), third series no. 6 (1992): 2–3;

Chris Wright, "Scotched–Interview with James Kelman, Irvine Welsh and Duncan McLean," *Boston Phoenix* (15–22 May 1997);

Steve Redhead, ed., "Bunkerman–Duncan McLean," in *Repetitive Beat Generation* (Edinburgh: Rebel Inc., 2000), pp. 101–111;

Alexander Laurence, "Duncan McLean: Scottish Writer," *Free Williamsburg,* 13 (May 2001) <http://www.freewilliamsburg.com/still_fresh/mclean.html>.

Reference:

Alastair Renfrew, "Them and Us?: Representation of Speech in Contemporary Scottish Fiction," in *Exploiting Bakhtin,* edited by Renfrew (Glasgow: Department of Modern Languages, University of Strathclyde, 1997), pp. 15–28.

Candia McWilliam

(1 July 1955 –)

Benjamin G. Lanier-Nabors
Louisiana State University

BOOKS: *A Case of Knives* (London: Bloomsbury, 1988; New York: Beech Tree, 1988);
A Little Stranger (London: Bloomsbury, 1989; New York: Doubleday, 1989);
Debatable Land (London: Bloomsbury, 1994; New York: Doubleday, 1994);
Change of Use (London: Bloomsbury, 1996);
Wait Till I Tell You (London: Bloomsbury, 1997).

OTHER: Elizabeth Taylor, *A Wreath of Roses,* introduction by McWilliam, Virago Modern Classics, no. 392 (London: Virago, 1994);
Shorts 2: The Macallan/Scotland on Sunday Short Story Collection, edited, with a foreword, by McWilliam (Edinburgh: Polygon, 1999);
Emma Tennant, *The Bad Sister: An Emma Tennant Omnibus,* introduction by McWilliam, Canongate Classics, no. 94 (Edinburgh: Canongate, 2000).

SELECTED PERIODICAL PUBLICATION–
UNCOLLECTED: "There was an atmosphere nicely poised between a séance and a chess game," *Guardian,* 13 March 1999, p. 3.

Candia McWilliam (photograph © Jerry Bauer; from the dust jacket for the U.S. edition of Debatable Land, *1994)*

Little more than a century after the publication of Robert Louis Stevenson's *The Strange Case of Dr Jekyll and Mr Hyde* (1886), another Edinburgh Scot made her novel-writing debut with a book that also deals with the mysteries of human psychology and the cultural implications of modern science. Candia McWilliam "loves ambiguity," she said in an unpublished 5 September 2001 interview with Benjamin G. Lanier-Nabors, and her treatment of mental and social concerns correspondingly evinces her preoccupation with linguistic nuance, moral complexity, the miraculous in the mundane, class relations, and identity—whether sexual, social, or national. Her connections to her Scottish background and her intimate knowledge of the English are also never far removed from her creative work.

Critics have compared McWilliam to such writers as Charlotte Brontë, Jane Austen, Henry James, Virginia Woolf, Angela Carter, and Iris Murdoch, and her writing has been both praised and criticized for perceived similarities to these authors: a serious interest in literary language, a tendency toward high concepts, an eye for minutiae, an affinity for classical mythology, and an empathic comprehension of people. She told Lanier-Nabors that her literary enthusiasms include James, Leo Tolstoy, Marcel Proust, Elizabeth Taylor, Philip Roth, John Updike, Patrick White, Eudora Welty, Alan Warner, Elizabeth Bowen, Muriel Spark, the metaphysical poets, and melodrama; she declared that James is "the best in the world—is preeminent. I never stop reading him." Her name is also frequently mentioned along with the names of other Scottish writers as part of the so-called renaissance of Scottish literature that began in the 1970s and 1980s; she has been listed with, for example, Janice Galloway, Alasdair Gray, James Kelman, A. L. Kennedy, Gordon Legge, Shena Mackay, Sheena McDonald, Duncan McLean, Allan Massie, Dilys Rose, Ali Smith, Alan Spence, Alice Thompson, and Irvine Welsh. With a growing list of prizes, awards, and other writing honors, McWilliam is undeniably a significant figure in contemporary British—and more specifically Scottish—letters.

Candia Francis Juliet McWilliam was born on 1 July 1955 in Edinburgh, Scotland. Her mother, Margaret Henderson McWilliam, had trained to be a fabric designer, and her father, Colin Edgar McWilliam, was an architectural historian. According to Helena de Bertodano, in a 5 June 1994 interview in *The Sunday Telegraph* (London), Candia McWilliam was "born to eccentric parents" and had "an unconventional upbringing." McWilliam's mother committed suicide when the writer was nine years of age.

McWilliam lived in and was educated in Edinburgh until she was thirteen, when she began to attend the Sherborne School for Girls in Dorset, England; there, she befriended Katie Howard, one of the four daughters of Donald Euan Palmer Howard, fourth Baron Strathcona and Mount Royal, and she was effectively adopted by Howard's family, reflecting the growing separation between McWilliam and her own father. While at Sherborne, McWilliam won the *Vogue* talent contest, but she was too young at fifteen to accept either the prize or a position at the magazine. Between 1973 and 1976 she pursued her postsecondary education at Girton College, Cambridge University, which culminated in her being awarded a B.A. with honors. After graduating college, McWilliam took a position at *Vogue* for three years, 1976 to 1979. From 1979 to 1981, she worked as a copywriter at the advertising firm Slade, Bluffix, and Bigg.

In 1981 the twenty-six-year-old McWilliam married for the first time. Given away by Lord Strathcona, she wed Quentin Gerard Carew Wallop, with whom she had her first two children, son Oliver Henry Rufus (born 1981) and daughter Clementine Violet Rohais (born 1983). Upon his grandfather's death in 1984 Wallop became tenth earl of Portsmouth; the following year he and McWilliam divorced. In 1986 McWilliam and Fram Eduljee Dinshaw, a Bombay-born English teacher and administrator at St. Catharine's College of Oxford University, were married. In 1989 the couple had a son, McWilliam's third child, Minocher Framroze Eduljee (Minoo). She and Dinshaw are currently separated. Although happy with her roles as writer and mother, McWilliam senses a competitive relationship between literature and motherhood, as she remarked to Joanna Coles in a *Guardian* (5 May 1993) interview: "With the birth of each child, you lose two novels."

In 1988 McWilliam published her first novel, *A Case of Knives,* its title and ethos reflecting lines from George Herbert's poem "Affliction (IV)"(1633): "My thoughts are all a case of knives, / Wounding my heart / With scattered smart." Filled with food imagery, literary allusions, and topical political undercurrents, *A Case of Knives* is the story of four people whose lives are interwoven but each one remains a virtual mystery to the other three. The son of Polish Jewish immigrants, Lucas Salik is a British hero because of his success as a pediatric cardiologist. Lucas is the character of focus, the center around which the other three personae revolve. He is a closeted homosexual, keeping his sexual identity secret except to his most intimate friends, and, as the novel discretely suggests, he has a taste for sadomasochistic trysts. His medical acumen and his masterfully concealed private life, however, enunciate his desire for a sterile, machine-like existence. Lucas's self-description is indicative: "I like the mechanical nature of medicine. It is why I have chosen not the magical zones of lymph and gland, but the engine, the pump, the heart." When, however, a bloody cow's tongue is discovered in the passenger's seat of Lucas's car and when his lover attempts to kill Lucas by stabbing him, McWilliam demonstrates how people cannot avoid what they might consider to be the unsanitary dimension of life: one cannot separate the machine of the heart from blood, the messy fluid of life.

With his closest friend, Anne Cowdenbeath, a Scottish aristocrat, Salik attempts to find a wife for his lover, Hal Darbo. To fit into mainstream British society, Hal desires to become married, and Lucas plans to orchestrate a marriage in order to remain close to his young lover and to have influence over the future Darbo family. Lucas and Anne find a suitable fiancée, Cora Godfrey, an apparently naive and common middle-class Englishwoman. Cora, though, proves to be a shrewd young woman who is searching for an affluent father for her unborn child. She is instantly captivated by Lucas but goes along with the plan of marrying Hal, following much the same logic as Lucas: she wants to be close to the famed doctor. Hal's physical characteristics, moreover, match those of the biological father of her unborn child. As the story progresses, Lucas is nearly mortally wounded by Hal. Before becoming involved with Lucas, Hal submits himself to the will of an animal-rights activist named Angelica, who is bent on making the cardiologist a high-profile example. The miracles that Lucas performs on children's cardiopulmonary systems are based on research that employs animal hearts. An object of attraction for Hal, Angelica is an anti-Semite, explaining in part her selection of Lucas as a victim. Angelica also seems to have harmful information about Hal, which he wants kept secret. Anne ulti-

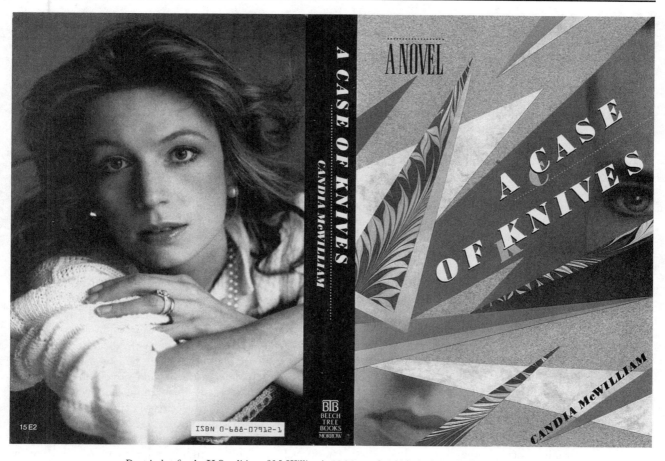

*Dust jacket for the U.S. edition of McWilliam's 1988 novel, which she has called an examination
of "people gaining power over other people" (Richland County Public Library)*

mately takes Lucas, Cora, and the newborn child into her border country Scottish estate, where they set up their new, pieced-together family.

The novel is structurally reminiscent of William Faulkner's *As I Lay Dying* (1930) or Geoffrey Chaucer's *The Canterbury Tales* (1387–1400): in distinct voices, each of the major characters narrates his or her own section—Lucas first, Cora second, Anne third, and Hal last. This format contributes to the mysterious and suspenseful nature of the novel. Conceptually, McWilliam establishes some of her dominant themes in her first book: the prevalence of human misperception, the futility of contrived moral judgments, and, as she remarked in the Lanier-Nabors interview, the horror of "people gaining power over other people." Perception and moral judgments are often based on presumptions dictated by class, ethnicity, sexuality, and politics, which therefore preclude any universally applied knowledge or moral standard. As with many other modern or postmodern writers, her sensitivity to diverse points of view and her ambivalence about

offering any bold proclamations or providing verdicts against her characters procure for McWilliam both praise and condemnation.

A Case of Knives earned the young novelist—she was thirty-three at the time the novel was published—the 1988 Betty Trask Award and one of the five Scottish Art Council 1988 Autumn Book Awards. These awards and other praise arose because of the writer's imaginative and conscientious writing style and because of her handling of difficult subject matter. Because of the AIDS epidemic, an upsurge in public awareness about the homosexual community occurred; nevertheless, McWilliam was one of a few novelists dealing sensitively and complexly with the relationships between and the social pressures on gay men. Her literary debut was not met with unmixed praise, however. An unexpected controversy arose when Bloomsbury used McWilliam's photograph on the cover. Some critics, such as Richard Lloyd Parry (*Sunday Times,* 17 January 1993), have argued that the publisher and the writer were trying to use her attractive features to sell her first book, an argument rebuffed by others, such as Liz Calder of Bloomsbury Publishing (*Sunday Times,* 24 January 1993), for being a sexually biased attack. McWilliam told Lanier-Nabors that "it is shocking to be marketed that way," but that she felt "she was lucky to be published at all," so having her photograph on the dust jacket or elsewhere in a book was a concession she was willing to make. As it is fairly common for writers (male or female) to have their photographs on dust jackets, McWilliam also observed that the furor over her photograph "would not have been a controversy in France, Italy, or America for that matter." A few critics have also accused McWilliam of purposefully employing arcane vocabulary, impenetrable syntax, and obscure subject matter. For example, in a *Times Literary Supplement* review (27 January 1989), Jonathan Keates asserts that McWilliam's sentences "parade like models on a catwalk, ruched and panniered with coy little inversions, sequined with similes, studded with hit-or-miss *jeux de mots* (a boiled shirtfront is compared to 'an unshriven sole'); McWilliam is the Ozbek and Lacroix of style, unwilling to let well alone if it can be adorned." In response to such criticisms, she told Lanier-Nabors: "I have always thought of language as an inclusive and democratic thing. I am not at all attempting to hold off people. I am not using a word like a jeweler. I do not believe in using a thesaurus; therefore, I am dealing with specificity, not synonyms." And as with the controversy surrounding her photograph on her books, she was "not sure" that the criticism surrounding her use of language "wasn't sexist." Along with awards earned after her first book and positive references to this novel in many reviews of later novels, both the superficial and substantive critical condemnations continue to haunt her.

Published in 1989, *A Little Stranger,* which won the writer another Scottish Arts Council Award in its year of publication, followed closely on the heels of McWilliam's first novel. This second novel takes the reader to the virtually isolated—and isolating—world of affluent British country estates. Daisy, daughter of a Dutch father and English mother, tells the story of loneliness, self-hatred, and domestic intrigue. She has become the wife of a wealthy landowning businessman, Solomon, and the mother of a kindergarten-aged son, John. Upon discovering that she is pregnant, she advertises for a nanny to help with raising John and maintaining the household. Margaret Pride, a lower-class Englishwoman, answers the advertisement and virtually replaces Daisy as wife and mother. By issuing subtle threats and by establishing the idea that she is having an affair with Solomon, who is frequently absent on business trips, Margaret pushes an already physically and psychologically fragile Daisy toward a mental breakdown. After Daisy's collapse the police remove Margaret from the house.

On its surface the prose form and plot follow a rather traditional and popular romantic line, akin to that of many domestic novels of the nineteenth century; however, the book unravels the themes and forms of the tradition from which it borrows. Up to the point of her collapse the narrator unwittingly shows how marginalized she is from the people and reality around her. She surrounds herself with food, and she uncritically abides by the conventions and institutions of her class, not realizing that both activities are driving her further away from her family and from herself: "My glowing feasts were celebrations of being a child. I lifted from myself the weight of thought as I donned that precious fat." Not until the last few chapters does Daisy consciously realize that she has effectively anesthetized herself to the world, and not until the conclusion of the narrative does she realize that Margaret was "carrying out her inverted worship of the same god," which manifests itself in another eating disorder, bulimia.

McWilliam's concern with the conflicting and often constricting societal views of women enunciates itself most boldly in the second novel, but it is a concern that is evident throughout her work. *A Little Stranger* hones in on the crisis of eating disorders, which are a result of cultural messages concerning women's beauty. The matter of beauty surfaces also in the first novel, particularly in reference to Cora Godfrey, as well as reappearing in the writer's subsequent stories and novels. The dysfunctional relationship between Daisy and Margaret, for example, has its precursor in the relationship between Anne Cowdenbeath and Cora Godfrey and is echoed by that of another pair of female characters in McWilliam's *Debatable Land* (1994).

McWilliam returns again and again to the multiple roles women play, frequently without being given notice or credit by a male-dominated society. Domestic, professional, economic, and emotional needs and responsibilities force women to make choices and alliances that either merely defer self-destruction or bring about self-destruction. Success or happiness is often measured in a manner similar to the final words of Thomas Hardy's novel *The Mayor of Casterbridge* (1886), as spoken by Elizabeth-Jane Henchard: happiness is "but the occasional episode in a general drama of pain." McWilliam—as a writer, self-proclaimed housewife, and divorcée—is intimately aware of the pressures experienced by women, particularly those pressures experienced by women of the middle classes. The earlier controversy about her photograph on the cover of her first novel serves as a testament to the significance of beauty and the potentially detrimental impact a cultural obsession with beauty can have on women. As is the case throughout her writing, McWilliam makes it difficult for readers to avoid the topics of wifehood, maternity, and child care. The unequal distribution of social and domestic obligations serves as a recurring theme in McWilliam's writing, a theme derived in part from the author's own experience. She elucidated this point in her 1993 interview with Coles: "When I say each child costs two novels, I mean in the energy and attention to detail needed. Of course it's a pleasure to pay one's children attention but it's difficult to write in a room in which you're always watching that they aren't trying to strangle one another. . . . I am over-concessive. Women, if they choose to link their lives with a man, have to be more consultative. I was brought up . . . to put others first." According to Coles, McWilliam's elite education, relative affluence, and literary success nevertheless have caused some critics to question how closely the writer is connected to the plight of most women and how sincerely she employs her feminist themes. Such criticisms, McWilliam suggested to Coles, could well be symptoms of the same sexual inequalities that McWilliam confronts in her work. Such skeptical views also did not keep the editors of *Granta* from including her on their list of the twenty best young British novelists in 1993.

In her third novel, *Debatable Land,* winner of the 1994 *Guardian* Prize for Fiction, McWilliam turns her attention directly to national and colonial concerns. Published in 1994, this book, on the one hand, discloses the claustrophobic world of soul-searching marine adventurers and, on the other, confronts the British colonial past and present. Logan Urquhart, an affluent Scottish American businessman, enlists for the last leg of a Pacific sailboat journey a crew that comprises his Scottish second wife, Elspeth; a Scottish artist, Alec Dundas; a young, attractive Englishwoman, Gabriel; and two experienced, nomadic seamen, Nick and Sandro. Aboard the *Ardent Spirit* the characters embark on external and internal odysseys. Logan, a perpetually angry man, attempts to escape the responsibilities of the "civilized" world by mastering the sea and by having an affair with Gabriel. Elspeth attempts to make her husband happy by assuaging and avoiding his wrath, which makes her as "happy as a person can be in rich emptiness." Alec searches the South Seas for something that will help him find his identity and give him a reason to exist, but he finds in those distant waters the Scot, the artistic vision, and the capacity for love that he could not as an adult find in the North Atlantic. Gabriel desires to experience excitement and adventure before she succumbs to the obligations of the adult world. Nick and Sandro are at home on the ocean, and they sometimes serve as oracles for their companions.

In a manner similar to her approach in *A Case of Knives,* McWilliam attempts to provide each character

with his or her own section of the novel. Alec nevertheless dominates the majority of the narrative, recollecting his childhood love of old architecture in Edinburgh and remembering his failed relationship with his wife, Lorna. His earliest memories, for instance, are filled with images of his mother, who—believing she was being merciful—drowned dock kittens whose fur had been burned off by packing salt and whose eyes had been pecked out by seagulls. The other persona who seems to dominate the book is Elspeth, reliving her trips to historic sites in the Scottish Highlands with her eccentric but loving parents. Both individuals, borrowing words from Nick, find Scotland "at the back end of the Pacific." Elspeth's memories bring the novel to bear, however, directly on the English colonization of Scotland. Her mother and father, who was a map publisher, take her as a child to visit Culloden, a battlefield where Highlanders were slaughtered by English soldiers. Alec's and Elspeth's recollections indicate the depth and breadth of the book.

As the novel shows, any voyage on the South Pacific will bring one face to face with the continuing effects of Western colonization. Pacific island natives are Mormons. Local economies are controlled by the whims of Western tourists and by businesses and banks headquartered in the United States, Britain, and France. The state of modern-day colonial activities links the characters and the book as a whole to historical imperialism, whether it has occurred north of the River Tweed, across the Irish Sea, on the banks of the Congo, in the Caribbean, on the Mississippi Delta, or between New Zealand and Tahiti. The macrocosmic concerns of history and culture find, furthermore, their parallel in the microcosmic concerns of the shipmates on the *Ardent Spirit.* Domination, exploitation, dispossession, legitimacy, and survival preoccupy both levels of the novel and the history to which it relates.

McWilliam is personally close to the global and mundane dimensions of her third book. By birth a Scot of the border region, the writer understands the complexity of being a descendent of former, if not current, colonial subjects—the imperial power being only a few dozen miles away. She is also aware of how colonialism makes the colonized both a victim and a complicit agent of imperial power. McWilliam observes, moreover, that being a Scot provides a distinctive position from which to observe and analyze the world. Catharine Bennet quotes McWilliam in a 13 January 1989 interview in *The Times* (London) as saying that she believes "'that the Scottish people have a very hardy inner life and they are unafraid of learning.'" Although she lives in Oxford, she is, Julia Llewellyn Smith reports in a 10 June 1994 interview in *The Times* (London), "fiercely Scots and badly home-

Dust jacket for the U.S. edition of McWilliam's 1989 novel, in which a nanny drives her employer to a mental breakdown (Richland County Public Library)

1999 article published in *The Guardian,* McWilliam describes her experience with Kubrick as

among the closest intellectual contact I've known. The construction of Stanley's brain was, to me who am solitary and fed by words and my eyes, like that of no other I have met. He was not distractible, nor was he narrow. He was a master of extraction; he could pull from one what he needed to make his own ideas complete. He was, if the word has meaning in this debased time, a genius. He took from one what he needed, but I didn't feel depleted, because his undivertable energy and strange openness refreshed my mind.

Her comments concerning Kubrick provide a glimpse of what she as an artist values in artists and thus what she strives for in her own work.

Even closer to McWilliam's home and personal life is her fourth book, *Wait Till I Tell You* (1997), a collection of twenty-four short stories that serve to document the writer's reflections on Britain. The title itself is an apparent homage to storytelling. Divided into two parts, "North" and "South," the collection explores the dynamic of being a Scot in Great Britain, which is always being Scottish in relation to England and, furthermore, in relation to the rest of the world. McWilliam explores this dynamic by carefully observing the nuances of diverse characters' lives. The stories are linked in many ways, with themes becoming the threads that tie together the narratives. None of the themes McWilliam explored in her earlier works is lost, and newer ones join the ranks: themes of personal identity, national and regional identity, domestic life, gender, class, age, provincialism, cosmopolitanism, and sexuality predominate.

This body of short stories in many regards echoes James Joyce's *Dubliners* (1914). Along with carefully controlling her writing in order to allow sociocultural undercurrents to emerge, McWilliam's language and overall authorial voice are more aligned with the speech patterns and worldviews of the characters about whom she writes: she conscientiously avoids overstatement, evincing instead a dedication to honoring and analyzing the people her characters represent. As Amanda Craig noted in a *New Statesman* (17 October 1997) review, McWilliam "explores her characters and situations through irony and indirection: you have to read each story twice, and concentrate hard." Although the various stories are all to some degree related, some seem more closely related according to certain general themes. There are, for example, those tales that concentrate on the theme of identity and on how identity is often dictated by national, regional, and gender norms. In "Carla's Face" the reader encounters how markedly American notions of female beauty are unhealthy and

sick." Her constant negotiations with her own cultural identity apparently make her sensitive to the precariousness of defining oneself; nevertheless, she maintains unwavering pride in being Scottish, which is in large part a result of the influence of her father, who took her as a child to visit historic Scottish buildings and ruins: these and other childhood experiences in Edinburgh during the 1950s and 1960s are reflected in those of Alec and Elspeth in *Debatable Land.* McWilliam remarked in her interview with Lanier-Nabors that she is often confronted with the fact that many "are surprised that I am a Scot because of my Oxford dialect," but "any Scottish blood I don't have is Irish. I am not racist against the English—I'm just not one."

From 1994 through 1996 McWilliam was invited to such programs as the Scottish Book Fortnight (1994), was named on the Booker Prize shortlist (1994), was asked by Stanley Kubrick to assist him as he was developing his last motion picture, *Eyes Wide Shut* (1994), and was invited to be a judge for the Whitbread Book of the Year (1996). In a 13 March

how such notions are detrimental to people throughout the world. As well as in "Ring if You Want Something," this motif resounds in "For After the Trains Have Stopped, a Woman Owes It to the Outside World to Take Proper Pride in Herself." Here McWilliam contrasts bourgeois American beauty obsession with the timeless practices of women in a small, working-class Scottish town—who go to the salon to fulfill certain communitarian needs, such as sharing information and planning community events. What one owes to the outside world and what one takes pride in are not necessarily superficial or self-centered, despite many commercial messages to the contrary. McWilliam's concern with the topic of body image furthermore engages, according to stories such as "Homesickness," a deeper cultural anorexia: people are ill because they are experiencing a spiritual and cultural homelessness.

"Sweetie Rationing" explores eating rituals and how these rituals reflect women's social condition. As elderly women eat candy they remember their marriages and contemplate the effects that matrimony had and will have on women. The theme of identity thus leads naturally to the relations between women and men and the cultural standards dictating those relations. In "Those American Thoughts" McWilliam depicts how a throwaway culture influences human relationships. Although a story of female empowerment, it is also a sobering testament to how even more remote from one another men and women are becoming. This division between women and men, as "The Buttercoat" demonstrates, does not merely injure women. Men such as young Lorne, a building plasterer, often lose those they love to the impersonal and often demoralizing effects of predominantly bourgeois male ideas of success. The promise of the upwardly mobile metropolis takes many, such as Lorne's beloved Nora, away from men of the islands, or of the peripheries, who might actually be capable of respect and love. Such phenomena are based deeply in economic, sexual, and societal stratification. Gender divisions accordingly extrapolate into sexual domination, as "A Jeely Place" shows, and into domestic and professional misogyny, as "Seven Magpies," "White Goods," and "Being a People Person" attest. "With Every Tick of the Heart" suggests, however, that some men learn from the mistakes of their fathers to become caring, egalitarian, lifelong lovers to their partners. The result is one that challenges the larger culture in subtle ways.

The global and particular problems presented by identity and human relationships can prove to be isolating and maddening; nevertheless, McWilliam sometimes sees—however remote or minute it might be— hope or the potential for hope in otherwise bleak circumstances. In "Shredding the Icebergs," the sketch of

an almost destitute wife and husband who run a seaside fish-and-chips shop in northern Scotland can still provide a glimpse of a subtle, unromantic vitality even when time is running out. A similar vitality is located in "The Only Only," "Writing on Buildings," and "Advent Windows." Despite the terrifying vision of death that it proffers—the decapitation of seven children in a dockside accident—"The Only Only" implies the importance of redefining the concept of family, which should be inclusive instead of isolating. In "Writing on Buildings," Bill is responsible for the upkeep of several historic Scottish buildings. His companion is his dog, Shona; nevertheless, he lives vicariously through others by reading the graffiti that young lovers make on the surfaces of the buildings he monitors. This story is not so much about voyeurism as it is about empathically loving humanity. In keeping with this familial or communitarian motif is "Advent Windows," which conveys how closely connected people actually are even if they attempt to live an anonymous existence in a city filled with a diverse and cramped population.

Careless and uncaring human beings can nevertheless create a horrifying environment, a reality that "Pass the Parcel" and "You Can't Be Too Clean" explore. In "Pass the Parcel," English middle-class morality produces a woman in a nursing home with self-perpetuating hatred and, as a consequence, loneliness. In "You Can't Be Too Clean," which is narrated by a schizophrenic homeless woman who eats soap and sleeps in the entranceway to a city bank, McWilliam again confronts a throwaway culture, in which some of the discards are human beings who exist on the fringes of society. She indirectly indicts a rich culture that not only permits but also seemingly encourages dispossession and isolation.

Isolation, though, can sometimes give way to humble but remarkable humane acts, as "A Revolution in China" and "Strawberries" illustrate. In "A Revolution in China," a seemingly impenetrable and eternally traditional department store saleswoman, Miss Montanari, begins unreservedly to buy items from other departments and from mail-order catalogues. Her colleagues conjecture that she is going through a midlife crisis. When she dies, however, and her fellow employees find gifts from her, they realize that she wanted to offer them friendship after her death. Generosity comes from another unpredictable source in "Strawberries," in which a devout, conservative Presbyterian nurse is the only adult who provides a sanctuary for children during a funeral gathering.

Multiple stories confront old age, a time of life that for many promises loneliness, homelessness, and lifelessness, but there are a few tales in particular that do not present old age as a death sentence but as a time of awakening. "On the Shingle," "Wally Dugs," "On the Seventh Day of Christmas," and "Change of Use" observe playfulness, sexuality, and vitality as elements of the later years of life. "A Change of Use," also published separately, is a representative narrative and is also the final story in the volume. The title echoes a passage from *Debatable Land:* "Do you know what demolition is called now? . . . Change of use, advice and salvage. . . ." This story is set in a nursing home. As with many of McWilliam's other writings, this concluding narrative engages a topical cultural issue—in this case, the desires and fates of the elderly in a youth-obsessed society. McWilliam also does not shy away from the sexual desires of older people. She implicitly questions, furthermore, the rationale underpinning society's use of nursing homes as a method for taking care of the aged. The concerns broached here connect to the writer's pursuit of complicated questions and her desire to uncover people's sensual existence, an existence not reserved for teenagers and young adults.

The more intimate, less determinate, and markedly less adorned approach that McWilliam takes in *Wait Till I Tell You* does not signal an abandonment of the bold moves she has made in her earlier books. Her foreword to a collection of Scottish short stories, *Shorts 2: The Macallan/Scotland on Sunday Short Story Collection* (1999), might explain her move toward shorter fiction: "We live in an inattentive time, whose preferred reading is not essays but captions. However, there is a thirst for something more, without the time—for most of us—to read those demanding baggy monsters, novels. I do not suggest that the short story is a tool for social engineering, but it is surely desired, and intensely appreciated." As with her three novels, though, she is no less concerned with aesthetics and the well-turned phrase; she is also no less occupied with serious social, historical, and psychological issues. McWilliam explained in the unpublished 2001 interview that she wants to communicate in different ways that human beings need "community as well as specificness." She consequently employs different dialects—in linguistic and sociocultural senses of the term—to explore further the intricate world to which McWilliam's Britons offer glimpses.

McWilliam has maintained her commitment to locating and creating new ways of telling stories. All of her books evince the sensitivity that she possesses when it comes to language, aesthetics, narrative, culture, and the intricacies of human beings' internal and external lives. As a Scot, McWilliam contributes to an exponen-

tially growing body of contemporary Scottish literature, and her Scottish background also greatly influences her subject matter and her writing methods. Through her own experience as a wife and mother, she is intimately familiar with the issues that surround domesticity and maternity, and she is aware of society's prejudices against women writers in general and women writers who are wives and mothers in particular. As a stylist, McWilliam has been both lauded and decried; these varying responses nonetheless affirm her unwavering desire to explore and to innovate. She is not afraid to contest zealotry, homophobia, sexism, ageism, and imperialism. As with her aesthetics, her ethical and political expressions have garnered her both praise and detraction. McWilliam is a writer who painstakingly interweaves language and life without neglecting the realities or possibilities of either.

Interviews:

Anne Bilson, "Love Affair with Language," *Times* (London), 22 January 1988;

Catharine Bennett, "Dis-syzygy blonde," *Times* (London), 13 January 1989, p. 1;

Joanna Coles, "An Unsuitable Job for a Woman," *Guardian,* 5 May 1993, p. 28;

Helen de Bertodano, "A vacuum wrapped in an enigma?" *Sunday Telegraph* (London), 5 June 1994, p. 3;

Jennifer Cunningham, "A Figure Too Often to the Fore," *Herald* (Glasgow), 14 June 1994, p. 13;

Dalya Alberge, "'Give me the boring life,' says literary world's newest star," *Times* (London), 25 January 1996, p. 1;

Catherine Lockerbie, "Strength of a Soft Touch," *Scotsman,* 1 November 1997, p. 4;

Lockerbie, "A Strong Faith in Readership," *Scotsman,* 21 August 1999, p. 4.

References:

Tom Adair, "Scotspotting: Reinvention or Renaissance?" *Irish Times* (Dublin), 5 August 1997, p. 66;

Liz Calder, "Shot Down," *Sunday Times* (London), 24 January 1993, p. 6;

Julian Critchley, "Why Roy Jenkins Was Robbed," *Daily Telegraph* (London), 25 January 1996, p. 12;

Rhoda Koenig, "Judging a Book by Its Cover," *Independent* (London), 25 May 1992;

Richard Lloyd Parry, "The Ploy of Sex," *Sunday Times* (London), 17 January 1993, p. 6.

Livi Michael

(15 March 1960 –   )

Roxanne Harde
Queen's University

BOOKS: *Under a Thin Moon* (London: Secker & Warburg, 1992);
Their Angel Reach (London: Secker & Warburg, 1994);
All the Dark Air (London: Secker & Warburg, 1997);
Inheritance (London & New York: Viking, 2000);
Frank and the Black Hamster of Narkiz (London: Puffin, 2002).

OTHER: "Daddy's Toy," in *Holding Out: Short Stories by Women* (Manchester: Crocus, 1988), pp. 21–26;
"Blue Sky Like Water," in *Shorts: New Writing from Granta Books* (London: Granta, 1998), pp. 212–225;
"Robinson Street," in *The City Life Book of Manchester Short Stories,* edited by Ra Page (London: Penguin, 1999), pp. 23–30;
"Feminism and the Class Ceiling," in *On the Move: Feminism for the New Generation,* edited by Natasha Walter (London: Virago, 1999), pp. 152–166;
"Sister, Sister," *Proof,* 1 (2000) <http://www.shu.ac.uk/proof/proof/livi.htm>.

From the publication of her first novel, Livi Michael has garnered both critical and popular attention for her work. While Michael's working-class fiction has won several literary awards and received largely favorable reviews from the popular press, some critics have dismissed her works as more political than literary. In a review of *Under a Thin Moon* (1992) for *The Guardian* (5 March 1992) Philip MacCann suggested that because Michael sacrifices literariness to politics, she ought to consider the House of Commons instead of authorship, and Jenny Turner in her 27 December 1994 *Guardian* review, of *Their Angel Reach* (1994) reprehended an "aesthetically unchallenging realism." Michael responded to such charges in an interview with Pat Wheeler and Sharon Monteith, published in *Critical Survey* (2000), by pointing out that her characters reflect the psychological impact of political economic policies. She also drew from her academic background to point out that for its entire history, working-class fiction has faced the accusation that "politics is not art," because it is a literary tradition that draws from the realities of poverty and unemployment.

Olivia Wood was born on 15 March 1960 in Stalybridge, Greater Manchester, in the north of England, where she grew up and where she still lives. Her story is one of a steady rise to the middle class. As Michael points out in her essay "Feminism and the Class Ceiling" (1999), there is no suitable term for the class of disadvantaged and impoverished people from which she rose: "we now have a large class of people for which there is no name. 'Working class' doesn't cover it, 'underclass' is both vague and derogatory." Like many of her characters, Michael was raised by a single parent, Ann Wood, who worked in various clerical and secretarial positions and then as a civil servant to support her daughter, and to whom her novel *Inheritance* (2000) is dedicated. In 1966, after several relocations, Michael's mother settled them into council housing at Ashton-under-Lyne in Greater Manchester. As Michael describes it, even though their new, award-winning high-rise was built to empty the slums, her mother had to prove that she was employed, and an inspector checked their standard of living. Their first neighbors were retirees and civil servants. However, this early atmosphere of low-rent gentility gradually degraded into the misery Michael depicts in her fictional tower blocks.

While Michael stands outside party politics, as she told Wheeler and Monteith, because of her years on the council estate, her "understanding of life and people is deeply economic." This stance is clear when she points out the culpability of changing government housing policies in the early 1970s in making the tower blocks the grim realities they are today. In "Feminism and the Class Ceiling" Michael describes the new generations of tenants as "people who couldn't be housed elsewhere, ex-cons, drug addicts. . . . we had neighbors who rode motorbikes *inside* their flats, played music so loud that five floors below you could feel your chest bone vibrate through the night, smeared shit in the

Livi Michael (courtesy of the author)

lifts." Living amid poverty, crime, and turmoil led to a deterioration in her mother's mental health, and Michael began to do poorly at school, though she had shown early promise. She left school, married, and had a son, Paul, born 24 February 1980, before her twentieth birthday, all while living in council housing.

If, however, the changes in government housing policy led to the deterioration of living conditions in the tower blocks and of the general well-being of their residents, then other government programs gave Michael her means to escape the estates. With her first husband she bought a house on a 100 percent mortgage (a government-guaranteed mortgage requiring no down payment). After they separated, she took an access course designed to prepare mature students for entrance to a university, at Tameside College of Technology, Ashton-under-Lyne, near Manchester. Her work in English and history in the access course led to her acceptance in 1986 at the University of Leeds, where Michael earned a first-class-honors bachelor of arts degree in English in 1989.

In "Feminism and the Class Ceiling," even as Michael describes her movement from the underpriv-

ileged class into a solid middle-class life, she takes little credit for her ability or hard work. She suggests that for herself, as for her mother, society has opened and closed many doors. Her education and feminist ideology are clear in her analysis of how she got out and why that path is no longer open: "Well, that was my route out. Not for everyone, obviously. But then, it isn't there any more. Grants have gone, cheap property has gone. . . . Other routes have also disappeared. Earlier this century the trade union movement, the co-operative movement, both offered women a measure of economic control and independence." Michael describes being almost paralyzed by a lack of confidence–a socially ingrained trait that holds back many of her characters–when she filled out the forms for entrance into the access course. She suggests that had she come along even ten years later, she likely would have ended up like the defeated and underprivileged women she met while researching "Feminism and the Class Ceiling," women who mirror the protagonists in her novels.

Besides living for a time as an unemployed single mother, Michael has seen how poverty affects the lives of women through her work with women's organizations and community centers. Her awareness of the many perspectives individual women bring to similar situations has influenced how she draws her characters. Michael tends to use a limited-third-person narrative that allows the reader to see the world through the eyes of poor and working-class women, to hear their usually silenced voices. Most of Michael's novels feature more than one female protagonist; in the *Critical Survey* interview she attributed her preference for "dealing with a cast of characters, rather than one central character in a novel" to her worldview, "I suppose this has something to do with the way I see society: people living isolated, alienated lives but are subject to the same forces and experiences."

Published in 1992, *Under a Thin Moon* focuses on the lives of Wanda and her daughter, Coral, and Laurie and her daughter, Valerie. They live in the ironically named Blenheim and Dunkirk towers on a sprawling council estate in Greater Manchester; these women are unemployed and alone. Michael draws from her own past as she explores the routes these women take: Wanda and Laurie fall from the working and middle classes; Coral and Valerie are born into hopeless poverty, all finding their own strategy for survival. When Wanda concludes that "being poor is like being ill all your life," she describes her personal experience as an unemployed single parent, but she also speaks for the rest of the women living in poverty in the tower block. For Wanda and Laurie, their survival strategies wind toward suicide; for their grown daughters, survival means escaping their mothers and their pasts, even as they reconstruct those pasts through the course of the novel. Mother-daughter relationships are at the forefront through the course of the novel. Wanda keeps her illegitimate child, the product of a joyless and happenstance coupling, in order to ensure she will not return to her mother's home. Laurie lets her mother down as she slides into alcoholism and escapes a world into which she cannot make herself fit. In its examination of the psychological effects of poverty and of the socioeconomic imbalances of power in Margaret Thatcher's Britain, the narrative makes clear these generations of women are the victims of their society.

Men in the novel are shadowy figures, kept to the periphery as symbols of power that the women might touch but never hold. For Wanda, men have the money she needs, and several are willing to exploit her need and her fair prettiness, but her foray into prostitution sends her mental health into a downward spiral. Coral mourns a relationship that failed when the man found a job and a way off the estate but would not take her along. Throughout her story Laurie is haunted by the image of the tutor who was the object of her great crush when she was at the university; as she repeatedly returns to memories of him, she focuses on language and how her early education and background made her deficient in her ability to articulate her thoughts. She remembers working "hours trying to adapt her language into a suitable mould" and credits her inability to adapt as the reason "she always felt so stupid when she was always the brightest girl in her class." Laurie eventually ties her powerlessness to language and realizes that her Cambridge-educated tutor represented for her power, not romance. Near the end of the novel "she remembers her mother's awe of the university, how she felt it would 'make something' out of Laurie. Laurie can see the irony in this now. All her life she was brought up to worship power, that was what it was in the end with her tutor, power, not sex."

If men are a symbol of power, money forms another major symbolic unit in the novel. Laurie gives herself a lecture in a schoolteacher's voice on how to make ends meet when one has £32 and needs £43 worth of goods. Valerie is more pragmatic as she realizes "all her options, every choice she has ever made came down to money in the end." Money takes on mythical proportions for these women, even as they equate its lack with their powerlessness. The socioeconomic critique of the novel is implicit as Wanda realizes that without money she cannot be a fit mother to Coral: "They will take Coral off her, she thinks, because she can't cope. But they have made it so she can't cope." Coral knows that "everything comes back to money," even her agoraphobia.

The four narratives are woven and knotted together in an episodic fashion, told in brief and detailed vignettes that are neither simultaneous nor chronological. Each of the four women self-consciously turns to memories as she sifts through her past in an attempt to make sense of her present. In his review for *TLS: The Times Literary Supplement* (6 March 1992) Nicholas Clee remarked that in her characterization Michael "achieves the difficult feat of getting inside the heads of people so overlooked by society that their own sense of their identities is dwindling." Clee found this narrative structure both distracting and apt, and he noted that Michael's "rawly musical present tense is somewhat confusing; but the disorientation is an appropriate effect for a work that unsparingly shows the alienation of those without money, jobs or support."

The third-person narrative point of view shifts from woman to woman, relating their interior monologues and external dialogues with others in an inner sort of fashion, so that all dialogue is filtered through each protagonist and becomes part of her personal and solitary experience. The narrative pattern develops the sense of isolation of each woman, even as they

[Olivia Michael]

Where does she live, Dan says.

Eveline looks up helplessly at the nurse.

She comes here ~~every~~ *usually once a* Sunday, the younger woman says without looking at us.

Now Mrs Crowther, I'm going to go and get your medication.

She turns towards us.

Perhaps you shouldn't stay too long, she says. She's getting tired.

Of course, we say, but Eveline is fiddling with her purse.

Here, here you are, she is saying, and a number of papers fall out.

She wrote it down for me, she says. In case I ever needed to – you know.

I take the scrap from her, not ~~liking to look at~~ *looking* at the expression in her eyes. ~~I scribble~~ *There, I have blandly at the name*

~~the address in my diary;~~ Mrs Mary Brennan, 202 Barthwaite Road, Greenbridge 46

~~3471.~~ *Why am I so surprised* *Well why not* *I think. Round here everyone*

Seems to be I put the paper back in her purse and close it for her, make myself look into her *related to everyone else*

eyes and smile. Unexpectedly she puts her hand on mine.

It'll all come right in the end, she says, and I have the oddest feeling she's not

talking to me at all, but I smile and pat her hand and leave.

On the way out we pass another nurse leading an old woman to the toilet. As

we pass the old lady breaks free and runs towards us.

My face, she cries in the greatest excitement. What's happened to my face?

Her fingers clutch the loose skin of her ~~face~~ *cheeks*.

Agnes, Agnes, the nurse says leading her away. Sorry about that, she says

over her shoulder.

I walk a little ahead of Dan and have nothing to say. Some bird seems to have

its talons around my skull. I'm sorry I ever started this; sorry that I've stirred up

4

176

Pages from the revised typescript for Michael's 2000 novel, Inheritance *(Collection of Livi Michael)*

Eveline's memories and left her to the mercy of them, because memories have no

mercy.

Would I have put my mother in a place like this?

Probably.

And where will I be at Eveline's age, ~~however old she is~~? (in my old age) Already my mind is

as full of holes as a cheese, where the unremembered, unrememberable bits of my life

have fallen through. And the bits I can remember slip in and out of the holes, *like fish*

appearing and disappearing ~~changing all the time~~. Maybe the holes will get bigger and bigger and swallow

everything else up. ~~Then my mind will be a broad windy place, like the sky.~~

Here I am, Louise Kenworthy, taking the huge step from being haunted by my

past to being haunted by my future.

Dan opens the car door. As he starts the engine he says,

Do you think you'll phone Eveline's *journal* daughter?

No, I say.

Livi Michael 2002

are in the midst of a crowded housing project. Michael deftly weaves the conclusions of the four stories together by using water as the symbol that unites the mothers and daughters. As the feminine element, water forms a major trope throughout the book: in the weather, in Wanda's attempt at inducing a miscarriage, then as the mothers wash their babies, and as each woman bathes herself and contemplates her body, in its strength and beauty, decay and ugliness. Throughout the book Laurie contemplates the river, while Valerie remembers summers when she was young and Laurie worked at holiday camps to give them a vacation at the beach. As she recalls her mother teaching her to swim and holding her up when the waves frightened her, Valerie comes to some understanding about the expectations and disappointments that have ruined their relationship. Water figures in Laurie's accident and in the dream that allows Valerie to accept and forgive her mother.

In a similar fashion the novel ends with water as the central symbol: Wanda's suicide in the bathtub becomes a quest toward the beauty life has denied her, and then Coral realizes as she is about to have a bath, that no matter what she does, "she is always running toward her mother." The novel concludes with a gesture toward the positive as Coral contemplates the stories she tells herself and decides that there is power in her ability to write the stories of those who cannot tell their own. This gesture may seem somewhat contrived; for example, Clee finds the ending of the novel its only false note. However, he appreciates the point that "all may not be completely hopeless if there are people to chronicle these desperate, marginalized lives." Michael finishes *Under a Thin Moon* at her most self-reflexive as Coral, a young woman from a background similar to that of the author, begins to write down the stories she tells herself: "Coral does not know what she will write. When you have no money it is like looking at the world through the chink of a door. She does not know if there is any other way of looking. Or maybe it is like looking by the light of a very thin moon; not just limited, but different."

Michael explained to Wheeler and Monteith that she shaped her first novel according to her research into working-class fiction, that she told the story of four women, then "divided it up, cut it up and interfaced." As she makes clear in "Feminism and the Class Ceiling," Michael's concerns are both feminist and economic. She takes a cultural-materialist view as she makes clear how society shapes women's views of themselves. For example, in *Under a Thin Moon,* Laurie, haunted by her past and aware that society deems most of her actions "foolish and terrible," wonders why she can remember only the bad: "she has come to

accept this shameful version of her history as truth, as a condition of her life. . . . She knows it is also a condition of powerlessness, this absorption of shame and guilt, for without a past she cannot possibly have a future." While discussing her technique with Wheeler and Monteith, Michael noted that "one of the results of extreme isolation is a form of extreme self-consciousness," and she uses a variety of narrative techniques, including stream of consciousness, to depict her characters as self-aware and often empowered from that cognition.

Under a Thin Moon proceeded to win the Society of Authors Award and the Arthur Welton Award. Continuing her education while writing her first novel, Michael completed her doctorate at the University of Leeds in 1993 with a dissertation titled "Towards a Theory of Working Class Writing: Lewis Grassic Gibbon's *A Scots Quair* in the Context of Earlier Working Class Fiction." During her time at Leeds, Michael married the poet Ian Pople, with whom she had a second son, Ben, born 22 February 1993.

Published in 1994, Michael's second novel, *Their Angel Reach,* was awarded the Geoffrey Faber Memorial Prize and a Society of Authors Award and was short-listed for the John Steinbeck and John Llewellyn Rhys/Daily Mail prizes. In this novel salvation and damnation are recurrent themes, and children are again seen having the capacity to redeem or condemn their mothers. Instead of a nameless council estate, the setting of the novel is the fictional Marley in Greater Manchester, which is based on Mosley, where Michael lived for a time. *Their Angel Reach* also focuses on the lives of underprivileged and working-class women, but Michael tells their stories in five separate narratives that function as discrete stories on their own but are connected in small, but important, ways. The daughter of the protagonist from one chapter goes to school with the protagonist from another; women from different stories ride the bus together and see each other in the market. The continuous presence of women provides a comforting counterpart to the darker elements also threaded through the novel: the ominous and repeated presence of bikers, Satanists, child pornographers, and a serial killer whose victims are girls. Where Michael used female symbols, the moon and water, to balance the patriarchal symbols of power in *Under a Thin Moon,* in her second book her chief tropes are angels and vampires, perpetuated in imagery, title, and section titles.

Michael links social reality to her method of characterization and uses cultural and political concerns to tie together characterization and narrative structure. In her *TLS* review (9 December 1994) Lavinia Greenlaw described these structural connections between the characters' interiority and plots that carry implicit cultural critique: "her narrative voice shares its characters' sense of estrangement, a quality that Michael uses most effectively in the gradual, relentless unfolding of her most harrowing scenes." Similarly, in her review for the *New Statesman & Society* (25 November 1994) Carol Birch found a veracity in the novel as Michael avoids the usual trap of depicting her working-class women as martyrs or victims, instead presenting them as neither idealized nor patronized. Birch suggested, however, that the continuous thread provided by the reporting of the crimes and capture of the Sandman "is too easy a metaphor." At the same time, serial killers have become a contemporary reality, and Michael pointed out to Wheeler and Monteith that this novel is about "violence generally and violence through the media" and was partly inspired by hearing that the Yorkshire Ripper was receiving thousands of fan letters from women.

Besides violence, *Their Angel Reach* is an exploration of sexual expression and deviation. Michael deals more explicitly with contemporary social issues. For example, eating disorders are portrayed in the fourth story with the narrative of the obese librarian who walks off her fear and loneliness on the moors at night, and the second story examines the power that entertainers hold in modern culture, with its tale of a teenage girl who worships a rock star as a means to escape from the reality of the rape and suicide of one classmate and the parental abuse of another. In her *TLS* review Greenlaw noted that while the cultural critique that drove *Under a Thin Moon* is present as well in Michael's second book, she "escapes repeating herself by concentrating here on her characters' subconscious fears and fantasies, in particular the darker areas of sexuality where desire is bound up with power and submission, violence and helplessness." The Sandman represents male violence against women, but he is not the only violent male in the book; each section touches on sexual assault, in passing fashion or as part of the plot.

Karen is the protagonist of the first story, and from its opening paragraph Michael builds a subtle interplay between the topics of homosexuality and homophobia. The story opens with Karen's husband, Steve, a former biker who once beat "an old queen . . . until blood streamed from every hole in his body." Karen's short narrative, told from her perspective but in the third person, focuses on her home and her dislike of housework. Michael describes the minutiae of Karen's day, in particular how she puts off her work until the last possible minute, then cleans in a flurry of fear that Steve will come home before she has made their home presentable. Her fears become tied up in

episodes from her past, in particular a rape she witnessed and did nothing to prevent. At the climax of the story Michael brings the homosexual undertones full circle when Karen seduces a woman friend, the first lesbian encounter for them both. During both the rape and the seduction Karen thinks, "she felt the lure of what you were not supposed to see." Both the seduction and Karen's subsequent confession to her husband are cathartic, and her perspective shifts as she refuses both the compulsive housework and her fear, things that were fundamental to her life.

Greenlaw argued that because of changing perspectives, each story ends "on a strangely hopeful note." The shift in perspective comes about for Rachel in the third section, when she leaves her unhappy marriage to run off with a New Age practitioner of the Old Religion (Wicca). Throughout the story Rachel is consumed with worry and frustration over her infant son, who dislikes food and touch and is not responsive to stimuli. She sees him through a battery of tests that tell her nothing, and she must cope with her baby's problems with little support from her husband. Dealing with the mystery of her child, Rachel finds Col, the cousin of a friend, a more welcome mystery. Attracted by his mystery and sensuality, she goes with him, though she suspects him of being linked to Satanists. In one of her darkly humourous twists Michael ends Rachel's adventure with Col ignoring her and the baby just as her husband had. Rachel's foray into the world of the New Age travelers exposes her to darkness and mystery and to real terror as the narrative view of her psyche allows the reader some powerful and disturbing imagery. As she escapes Col and carries her extremely ill child out of the dark forest, Rachel looks "down the long road in the mysterious autumn light," with a perspective that is bleakly hopeful.

Perspective as a theme becomes richer and more visual in the final piece of the book, the story of an artist, Lizzie, who hunts for but does not often find the right light needed to turn her emotions into imagery. Her story links her last major exhibition to key events in her life, meeting the boyfriend who would try to dictate the course of her art, selling a large painting to a woman who seemed to understand it better than Lizzie herself, and meeting the parents of a young woman who had vanished. They hire her to paint a portrait of their daughter as she would look had she reached maturity, and Lizzie's quest to fulfill their wish becomes tied to her ceaseless hunt for the right light. As in the other sections, Lizzie's story includes images of angels and vampires, and it focuses most clearly on blood imagery. When she is brutally raped, she pictures her attacker as a vampire, then imagines that he has infected her blood with AIDS, "like the kiss of a vampire." In the end Lizzie finds a perspective that combines images of salvation and damnation: swans on an early spring lake and the face of her attacker as Nosferatu. Her change in perspective is the most cleansing and hope filled of the novel.

Although Michael has received critical praise for her ability to depict women's lives, she has also been criticized for her neglect of male characters and men's lives. In her *TLS* review of *Their Angel Reach,* Greenlaw described Michael's male characters as "monolithically opaque," and in her *New Statesman & Society* review Birch found the lack of even one detailed and understandable male character to be a real weakness, suggesting that if Michael "could have brought her powers of tough, sympathetic observation to bear on even one male character, the book would have been even better."

After Michael completed her doctorate, she taught English literature and creative writing part-time at Manchester Metropolitan University until 1998. During that time Michael wrote her third novel, *All the Dark Air* (1997), which also received an award from the Society of Authors and was short-listed for the Mind Book of the Year Award. Where *Their Angel Reach* ends with Lizzie full of hope and considering the possibility of having a child, *All the Dark Air* charts the course of Julie's pregnancy. While children were seen more as worrisome burdens than as joys in Michael's earlier books, *All the Dark Air* sets forth Julie's love and hope for her child along with her fears about her capacity as she tries to cope in an untenable situation. Again using Marley for her setting, Michael revisits her concerns with social ills and injustices. The structure of this novel differs greatly from the earlier novels in that Michael focuses on one female protagonist and keeps her perspective at the center of the narrative. All other characters are seen in relation to Julie, and her increasingly unsettling world seems more disturbing than did those of characters whose lives played out in vignettes and short stories. As if to underscore the continuity of this narrative, Michael forgoes chapter divisions and separates the lengthy scenes with asterisks.

Michael sets this novel firmly below the working class, with the unskilled, unemployed, and impoverished. The book deals, in an implicit manner, with the points that Michael makes in "Feminism and the Class Ceiling," that "fifteen years ago there were not all these people in shop doorways," that mass homelessness is "the result of the economic policies of the last twenty years," and that there is no easy solution. Julie wanders in an aimless way toward homelessness, while Mick and his heroin-addicted friend Darren take a more direct route. The three of them end up living with Mick's Uncle Si in his derelict terraced house.

The relationships become increasingly complex and, because the narrative perspective is Julie's and since she does not understand all the details and nuances, they remain somewhat opaque to the reader. Mick and Darren carry on a mysterious relationship, laden with homoerotic undertones. The passion seems to be mostly Mick's, since Darren is constantly high, either on heroin or methadone, and has ceased to care about anything. Julie's passion for Mick reaches fruition when he crawls into her bed after a night of drinking and they have a sexual encounter. While Mick becomes a radical socialist and fills the rundown house with militants and drug addicts, Julie signs up for a New Age course meant to help people deal with their problems. Michael's humor is dark and cynical as Julie explores what the Mind-Power group has to offer, but only what they offer for free. She realizes that only those who do not need it can afford the help that she needs. Michael explained to Wheeler and Monteith that the novel was inspired in part by her youthful involvement with both New Age and socialist organizations, with her wish "to explore the experience of suffering to see how it strengthens some people and destroys others." *All the Dark Air* holds hope amid the darkness as Julie quietly draws on inner resources and grows stronger, finally realizing that Mick's radical socialism and her New Age remedies "don't work" at fixing problems any better than does Darren's drug addiction.

Poverty and the ensuing lack of power are again central questions in this novel. In her review of *All the Dark Air* in *TLS* (27 December 1996) Birch found in Michael's honest and direct portrayals "a brave writer tackling big themes by way of the lost, the unlovely, the tongue-tied and overlooked." Birch noted that for Julie, "money, or rather its lack, assumes an almost mythical presence, like the wolf in a fairy tale laying siege at the door." She went on to criticize the novel as having "a too clear sense of an agenda underlying an apparent slice of life." While the book does examine and critique contemporary society, Michael is not overtly didactic in her social critique. Rather, through the course of her pregnancy, Julie comes into contact with a variety of people dealing with issues and problems from a wide spectrum. Her radio at home provides a background chorus of crimes involving children, a series of murders, and pedophilia as she hears and tries to understand her friends' situations. One of her friends from the Mind-Power group, Annie, has to deal with difficult twin toddlers while her truck-driver husband is gone for long periods. Another friend, Alison, finds herself living with a man whose drug addiction, heroin trafficking, and voyeuristic sexual leanings seem to be major problems for

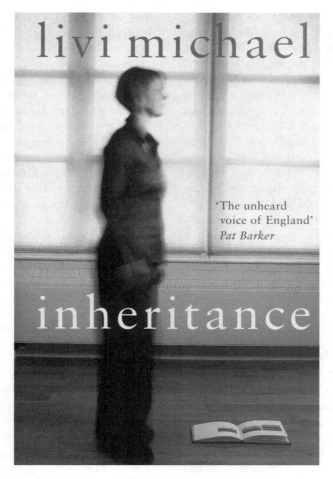

livi michael

'The unheard
voice of England'
Pat Barker

inheritance

*Paperback cover for Michael's novel in which a woman researches the history of an aunt who lost
contact with the rest of the family (Bruccoli Clark Layman Archives)*

her but that become trifling when he rapes her infant daughter. As Julie becomes part of each story, she gathers unknown resources of strength as she determines to stand up for herself and her child. Although Birch suggested that Michael's female characters "run the risk of fading into passivity," Alison prepares to fight to get her child back from the social services, and Julie decides how much Mick means to her now that she has a baby to take care of: "She tried to think, would she do anything for Mick, anything at all? She used to think so but not any more."

Even in the midst of such darkness Michael sets quiet, almost mundane flashes of insight. Darren relates lying on a dark street in the rain looking at the blank sky: "I felt—empty. . . . It was the best feeling I ever had, he said with his mouth full. And I remember thinking, this is what God is." Julie experiences a similarly quiet epiphany, again shaded by the themes of vision and seeing. After the novel details the minutiae of Julie's days, her cooking and cleaning, the ways in which she works to organize the house and the lives of

its inhabitants to prepare for her baby, she visits her mother's grave and realizes that her ordinary work carries great meaning, that the work one does not notice is the work that shapes lives: "Julie had thought that it was the ordinary, humdrum affairs of life that wiped you out, taking up your energy and time, never leaving you alone until there was no time or energy for anything else. But it was the routine work that lasted, she could see it now."

In *Inheritance,* her fourth novel, Michael continues to explore the idea of strength in the commonplace, in both the historical past and in the present. Published in 2000, *Inheritance* draws on the landscape and history of Saddleworth, the lovely Greater Manchester valley where Michael now lives; in fact, she lives a mere mile from the farm mentioned in the novel, where the workhouse children were taken and worked to death. The novel also draws from her working-class past and middle-class present but is a departure in genre. Michael explained in a 4 August 2001 e-mail interview with Roxanne Harde that after her third novel she no longer felt that she could write in the sociopolitical vein, "because I was no longer living the life of unemployment and single parenthood. . . . From my point of view it had to do with integrity." However, she went on in the interview to point out that she had not "abandoned the subject area—just gave it a broader and more historical canvas." Michael writes as a regionalist; her work is set in and dependent upon the area she knows best: Greater Manchester, Lancashire, and Yorkshire in the industrial north of England. In her *TLS* (12 May 2000) review of *Inheritance* Ali Smith called Michael's depictions of the north of England "spare, haloed and detached." As have other novelists who lived and wrote in the area, such as Elizabeth Gaskell and George Gissing in the nineteenth century and Alan Sillitoe in the twentieth, Michael's writing reflects the economic and social climate of her time and place. However, whereas her first three novels reflect the urban north of England in the later twentieth century, *Inheritance* focuses on rural and urban, past and present.

Part detective fiction, part historical novel, part melodrama—the genres that Michael argues are more closely associated with working-class fiction than any others—the thematic center of the book concerns endings and how women understand and deal with them. Structured in two interwoven narratives, *Inheritance* tells the stories of Louise, a London career woman who returns to Manchester to deal with two deaths as she sorts out her mother's effects; and Martha, Louise's aunt, a woman from the agrarian and working classes, whose memory has been erased from the family history. When Louise sees Martha's picture in the photograph album left by her mother, she begins to track down her mysterious relative, even as she comes to terms with her own memories, which include a fraught relationship with her mother and a love affair that ended in tragedy.

Throughout the novel Michael operates under the premise that the past is always part of the present. As Louise discovers Martha's history, she becomes involved in the history and present of her home village. Class divisions and economic and sexual politics are at play in both times as Martha regrets her arranged marriage and mourns leaving her beloved moors for the grim and grimy Manchester of the early 1900s, and as Louise becomes involved in the movement against the planned development of the village workhouse into luxury flats. Martha's marriage to a man deeply damaged by his childhood in that workhouse and Louise's determination not to think about the horrors of her own love affair that ended in a car wreck and death haunt their narratives. As Smith pointed out, the prose of this novel, "unlike the fast-moving fusion of the pedestrian

and the beautiful in the other novels, is soaked and sobered by grief." As both mysteries are brought to light and shown as past and present woven together, "invisible and powerful, like the mystery of the world," the language retains its somber tone.

Unlike in her other novels, Michael alternates in *Inheritance* between Louise's first-person narrative and a third-person relation of Martha's story. Smith found that in Louise's first-person sections, "the difference between said and unsaid becomes more complex, and this makes Louise a little uncomfortably self-conscious-seeming." At the same time, this novel is the first that Michael set in the middle class, in the place where she now lives, and in the relatively distant past as well as in the present, and is the first novel that has involved scholarly research. These factors may contribute to the self-reflexive aspects of Louise's role as narrator and author of Martha's history. Part of that history is linguistic as Martha and her family speak in their own Yorkshire dialect, for which Michael includes a glossary. The roles of writer and researcher as users of language are key to the narrative structure of the book as Louise sifts through the writings of her own time and of Martha's for clues to an understanding that she condenses and articulates on paper.

Time is the thematic guide in this novel. *Inheritance* juxtaposes a present-day working-class village with its wealthy outsiders and an historical, newly industrialized Manchester with its poor outsiders in the workhouse. The switching back and forth between times shifts perspectives about the past until Louise is able to put both her life and Martha's into some sort of order. Louise's constant attention to time allows a blurring of past and present that gives her an empathy with Martha, whom she resembles:

> her lips and cheeks have been tinted by the photographer, her hat is dark. She is printed there, forever, at the beginning of this century, me at the end of it, two world wars between. Nothing bridges that gap, I tell myself. Then I think about the stray gene that has printed the ghost of her into my features, my body. I think of it appearing and disappearing in the family line past and future, winking its way through eternity.

Martha reaches a similar conclusion about the past in her final section, the only one in which she speaks for herself, "Cold days, eccles hanging, I light fire in Matron's room while sculler maid looks on. Matron has a mirror with three sides, and a lamp with a candle. When I move it about in front of the mirror I can see light curving on all sides, bending back on itself, over and over. That's like time, I think." The connections between these women become more apparent as Louise uncovers enough of Martha's history to realize that, like herself, Martha was culpable in the death of the man who made her life unbearable.

This novel marks the first time Michael's heroines have fought back in a physical manner, and *Inheritance* also features her first detailed and fully sympathetic male characters. The hopefulness in this novel is made clear as Louise refuses to give up on men and live alone and bitter. While Martha has no choice but to descend into madness, Louise flirts with a handsome young librarian and has a brief affair with the cousin who helps her find Martha's history. In "Feminism and the Class Ceiling" Michael concludes that now is not the time for women to theorize about lives they have not lived, nor for individual heroines, such as the suffragettes, but rather now is the time for "structures and networks which will allow women from all classes of society the possibility of meeting and communicating."

In her review of *All the Dark Air,* Birch commented on Michael's lack of attention to her male characters but concluded that "Michael is a writer who is motivated by rage and compassion as well as by a true desire to fathom why so many people's lives are so awful." It seems clear that in her first three novels, at least, Michael's intention was to explore, specifically, why so many women's lives are so awful. Given that over the course of four novels she has drawn seven female protagonists, women's lives seem to be her overriding concern. While her third and fourth novels draw male characters and people from other cultures in more detail and sketch in enough background to make them somewhat understandable and empathetic, it seems clear that Michael's artistic and political focus will remain on women who continue to be largely silenced and oppressed. Her success

in this project is noted by Monteith, who argues in a 1996 essay published in *Critical Survey* that Michael creates "women whose fantasies and creativity and efforts at re-presenting themselves may garner them strength in the face of the debilitating standards against which their 'real' lives are measured."

Michael has been teaching English literature and creative writing at the undergraduate and postgraduate levels for the Department of Cultural Studies at Sheffield Hallam University since September 1998, prior to which she taught part-time at Manchester Metropolitan University. Separated from her second husband, Michael divides her time between teaching and writing. She also gives guest lectures and participates in writing workshops. With one son in university and a young son at home, Michael has written her first children's book, *Frank and the Black Hamster of Narkiz* (2002), with the animal-loving Ben in mind; "Frank's Quest," a sequel, is scheduled for publication in July 2003. While academic discourse about her work has just begun, Livi Michael's feminism, her awareness of her work as part of a literary tradition, and her readings of contemporary culture suggest promising routes of inquiry for twenty-first-century scholars.

Interview:

Pat Wheeler and Sharon Monteith, *Critical Survey,* 12, no. 1 (2000): 94–107.

Reference:

Sharon Monteith, "On the Streets and in the Tower Blocks: Ravinder Randhawa's 'A Wicked Old Woman' (1987) and Livi Michael's 'Under a Thin Moon' (1994)," *Critical Survey,* 8, no. 1 (1996): 26–36.

Andrew Miller

(29 April 1960 –   )

Eva Roa White
Southern Illinois University, Carbondale

BOOKS: *Ingenious Pain* (London: Sceptre, 1997; San Diego, New York & London: Harcourt Brace, 1997);

Casanova (London: Sceptre, 1998); republished as *Casanova in Love* (San Diego, New York & London: Harcourt Brace, 1998);

Oxygen (London: Sceptre, 2001; New York: Harcourt Brace, 2002).

SELECTED PERIODICAL PUBLICATIONS–UNCOLLECTED: "Zero Visibility," review of *Blindness* by Jose Saramango, *New York Times Book Review,* 4 October 1998, p. 8;

"The Power of the Past," *Waterstone Magazine,* 17 (Spring 1999): 48–56.

Andrew Miller made his debut on the British literary scene in 1997 with *Ingenious Pain,* a powerful and original first novel that won the prestigious James Tait Black Memorial Fiction Award that same year. Reviewers in Europe and the United States have raved about this new novelist who so decisively established himself from the first on the British literary scene.

Andrew Brooke Miller was born in Bristol on 29 April 1960, and he grew up in Bath and Wiltshire. He has one older brother who lives in Paris and a younger half sister in London. He also has eleven stepbrothers and stepsisters. His parents separated when he was four, and he and his older brother went to live in Bath with his mother, who used to work as a relationship counselor. His father, a doctor, is now retired and lives in Cyprus. Interestingly, it is not Miller but his brother who was a writer first and won a prize for poetry when he was twelve. He did not pursue a writing career, however, but went on to become a photographer. Andrew Miller's own scholastic prizes were for history, perhaps indicative of how he later brings history into his novels. Miller has said that he read whatever he could find, both the good and the bad. In an unpublished November 2000 interview with Eva Roa White, Miller comments that during his childhood, one of his favorite

Andrew Miller (photograph © Jerry Bauer; from the dust jacket for the U.S. edition of Ingenious Pain, *1997)*

books was Rosemary Sutcliff's *The Eagle of the Ninth* (1954). He also read many books by Alistair McLean and Hammond Innes. He particularly loved J. R. R. Tolkien. Historical romances such as E. L. Voynich's *The Gadfly* (1897) and John Meade Falkner's *Moonfleet* (1898) were also among his favorites.

As he got older, Miller was particularly influenced by Thomas Hardy's *Tess of the D'Urbervilles* (1891) and D. H. Lawrence's novel *The Rainbow* (1915). When he left school, Miller began to read European authors such as Fyodor Dostoevsky, Emile Zola, and

Samuel Beckett. He also enjoyed Japanese poetry and American Beat author Jack Kerouac.

Miller's extensive interest in international authors makes it difficult for him to choose a favorite book. However, during an unpublished November 2000 interview with White, Miller reported that "certain texts are constant": William Shakespeare's *A Midsummer Night's Dream* (1595), Giuseppe Tomasi di Lampedusa's *Il Gattopardo* (1958; translated as *The Leopard*, 1960), Italo Calvino's *I nostri antenati* (1960; translated as *Our Ancestors*, 1980), Henry James's "The Aspern Papers" (1888), James Joyce's *The Dead* (1914) and *A Portrait of the Artist as a Young Man* (1916), and Dostoevsky's *Igrok* (1866; translated as *The Gambler*, 1887). Some of Miller's favorite poets are Philip Larkin, T. S. Eliot, Seamus Heaney, and Matsuo Basho. He also reads a good deal of American fiction, particularly the works of Jim Harrison, Saul Bellow, and John Updike. Among British authors, he admires Beryl Bainbridge, Hilary Mantel, and Penelope Fitzgerald. Japanese writing continues to interest him, particularly that of Kenzaburo Oe. His affinity with Japan goes beyond literature: he is a martial arts practitioner. Miller also has said that he is influenced by cinema almost as much as by books. Among his favorite movies are Stanley Kubrick's *Paths of Glory* (1957), Federico Fellini's *Satyricon* (1969), and Ingmar Bergman's *Fanny and Alexander* (1982).

Miller was eighteen when he consciously decided to become a writer. He attended Middlesex Polytechnic in North London, receiving a degree in humanities in 1985, and later joined the M.A. creative writing program at the University of East Anglia, perhaps the most prestigious program of its kind in Britain, where Rose Tremain and Malcolm Bradbury were his tutors. He graduated in 1991. In December 2000 Miller told White about his time there: "It's hard to say how helpful it was. I think I gained a certain amount of confidence simply by being selected for the course. And I had time to experiment and make a lot of false moves. I was glad when it was over, that level of scrutiny is not always useful, but I think that it probably accelerated my progress. It was another five years however before I published my first book."

Miller spent those years living in different countries and working at various jobs, some of them distinctly unglamorous: he has worked in a poultry abattoir "pulling chicken legs out of hangers," driven an ice-cream van, and tended a bar. Before entering the Ph.D. program at Lancaster University, Miller lived in Spain, where he worked as a tour guide, and then moved to Japan in 1993. As he explained to White in December 2000, he went there for two reasons:

I wasn't making any progress with *Ingenious Pain* (or felt I wasn't) and I wanted to study a martial art called Aikido that I had practiced for some years in England. I worked (hard!) as an English teacher and lived in a traditional building in Tokyo. It was an exhausting but important year. I started working on the book again and began to see that it was not all bad and that it was "finishable." I stayed in Japan for a year and saved up some Yen, enough to mean I wouldn't have to get a job in England for a few months.

Miller also told White that his return from Japan "was a decisive moment for me. I think I'd been infused with a Samurai do or die spirit!" Miller decided that it was time to give himself the opportunity to finish this novel that he had been working on for so long and to see if indeed he was a writer:

I was 34 and felt (rightly or wrongly) that I either had to make it now or not at all. . . . I fretted a lot. To feel that you may, in some fundamental way, have fucked up, can lose you a lot of sleep. When *Ingenious Pain* was bought I had a strong (and contradictory?) sense both of being rescued and of having saved my own life.

It took Miller six years to write *Ingenious Pain*, and there were many occasions when he had to wrestle with self-doubt. His perseverance did indeed pay off; his first novel was accepted for publication in February 1996, appeared in print the following year, and was subsequently translated into eighteen languages, receiving international critical acclaim. Miller was visiting Cyprus at Christmas 1997 when he learned that his novel had won the James Tait Black Memorial Award; two years later *Ingenious Pain* received the coveted International IMPAC Dublin Literary Award. The idea for *Ingenious Pain* had come to him after reading about the Viennese doctor Franz Anton Mesmer, whose system of magnetic therapeutics, mesmerism, though discredited as spurious, influenced the development of hypnotism. Miller thought him both a tragic and comic figure. The fact that Miller's father was a doctor also influenced the book. As Miller told Enda Wyley in a 22 January 1998 interview for *The Irish Times* (Dublin), the opening autopsy scene in *Ingenious Pain* "was based on a promotional video for a drugs company which my father had been sent."

Ingenious Pain tells of a boy, James Dyer, who is born impervious to pain. He does not speak until the age of eleven, when after the death of his family he is taken into the care of Gummer, a traveling charlatan. Every night Gummer runs a needle through James's hand to demonstrate the supposed efficacy of the drug he is selling. James is later kidnapped by Canning, a wealthy collector of freaks, and James learns about books in Canning's library and about sex from two of Canning's other freaks, Siamese-twin girls. Conscripted

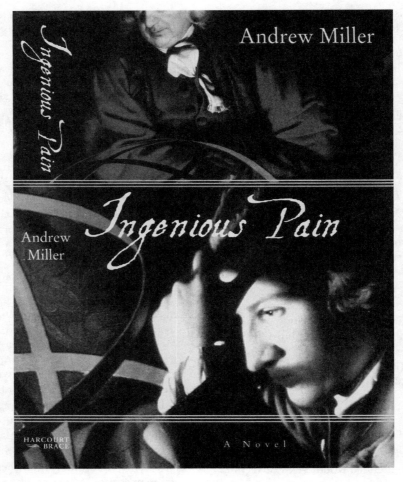

Dust jacket for the U.S. edition of Miller's 1997 novel, about a boy who does not feel pain
(Richland County Public Library)

into the navy, James becomes the apprentice to the ship surgeon, Munro. After Munro invites Dyer to join him in his medical practice in Bath, Dyer soon becomes the better-known of the two surgeons and seduces Munro's wife. James eventually journeys to the palace of Empress Catherine of Russia. There he meets a witch-like, mute woman named Mary, who, using supernatural, pagan powers, introduces him to the world of pain and humanity. Overwhelmed by these newfound feelings, James is driven mad and is consigned to an insane asylum in London. Once liberated, James is taken by Mary to the country to see the Reverend Lestrade, whom James and Mary had met in Russia. The reverend, a kindly man who admires Mary's pagan practices while trying to remain true to his Christian faith, takes in James, who comes to him a broken man. It is Lestrade who poses the crucial question of the novel as he contemplates Dyer's profound change: "Odd how a man can change. Finished as a doctor, of course. All that talent! True, he was a hard and unlovable man

before. But useful; by God he was. What does the world need most—a good, ordinary man, or one who is outstanding, albeit with a heart of ice, of stone?"

Christina Patterson discussed this central theme of the novel in a 23 February 1997 review in *The Observer* (London). Noting that "Miller's juxtaposition of the weirdly wonderful with the harsh reality and brutality of eighteenth-century life is a powerful vehicle for the themes he has chosen to explore," Patterson remarked, "Miller takes on no less a question than what makes an individual's life worthwhile. Is it better to be good or to be a genius? Is it better to experience pain than nothing at all?" In a 15 February 1997 review in *The Times* (London) Mary Loudon said of Miller's first novel: "*Ingenious Pain* shines like a beacon among the grey dross of much contemporary fiction." This admiration was also felt by Richard Dyer, who wrote in *The Boston Globe* (25 June 1997): "Miller is a virtuoso of description. . . . It is apparent that he is a born writer." Wyley praised *Ingenious Pain* in her interview with Miller for *The Irish Times* (Dublin), remarking that "Although the competition was stiff, it does not come as any great surprise that Miller's debut novel should receive this prestigious honour [The James Tait Black Memorial Award] . . . its . . . narrative burns with inventive, fresh prose and a strange imagination." Lucy Atkins, in *The Guardian* (10 April 1997), called *Ingenious Pain* "A true rarity: a debut novel which is original, memorable, engrossing and subtle." In *The New York Times Book Review* (13 April 1997) Patrick McGrath acknowledged the substantive nature of Miller's writing, calling the book "a mature novel of ideas soaked in the sensory detail of its turbulent times."

This combination of spirituality and worldliness can be found in all of Miller's novels. He addresses the theme of what makes life worthwhile by zeroing in on the turning point of a man's life and then focusing on the moment of reckoning. It is this moment in time that acts as a pivot to the story in his novels. Miller is able to identify the telling moment, the moment of truth, that will forever change the lives of his protagonists. Miller treats this vulnerability as the core of what makes us human. That is what attracted him to the historical figure of Giovanni Giacomo Casanova, the subject of his second novel, *Casanova* (1998). As Miller told White in December 2000:

> I chose Casanova after reading about his adventures in England and feeling that this was a very sympathetic character at a very interesting point in his life. I wanted to write about the moment when a life suddenly (or not so suddenly) stalls and you have to ask yourself some tough questions about what you're doing, about what the future might hold, about what's still possible. A moment that involves a lot of uncomfortable growing up. I wanted to treat the subject lightly and found Casanova an essentially comic figure in the best sense i.e. also a melancholy and perhaps even tragic figure.

Published in Great Britain in September 1998 as *Casanova* and published in the United States the following month as *Casanova in Love,* Miller's second novel is also set in the eighteenth century. When White asked him why he chose this century as an historical setting for his first two novels, Miller answered, "Both books are set in the eighteenth century because those particular stories could not exist in any other 'period.' I knew very little about the eighteenth century when I started. My interest came, so to speak, after the fact. It's a wonderful period, one I may return to at some point."

Casanova is the story of Casanova's later years and of his stay in England. Miller portrays an unknown side of the famous Venetian, whose name has become synonymous with *lover*. In fact, Casanova is the antithesis

of what the reader expects, being a broken-down old man, tormented by unrequited love. The reader first encounters Casanova ready to burn some old letters, when a mysterious woman comes unannounced. It is through their conversation that the story moves back to earlier years, to the time of Casanova's midlife crisis, when he goes to England to try to reinvent himself as a laborer, country squire, and writer. There he meets Marie Charpillon, the woman who will be his downfall. She constantly foils his plans to seduce her, though she always encourages him just enough to keep him in pursuit of her and thus manages to extract money from him with the aid of her family. Despairing of ever possessing her, Casanova tries to live as a laborer to see if he can find meaning in this new life but soon fails. The harshness of the London world quickly erodes his determination, as he finds no easy cure for his malaise. As Stephanie Merritt noted in a 5 September 1998 review in *The Daily Telegraph* (London), Casanova believes his failure to seduce Charpillon "to be the root of his disintegration, but Miller shrewdly reveals that the sexual frustration is merely a symptom, and that what truly ails him is nothing else than the ennui of his own existence." There is a moment of self-awareness and questioning when Casanova looks at his hands as the map of his life:

> He looked down at his hands, turned up the palms and gazed at the lines. He had come here, to this little island, to be healed, saved, confirmed. But what was he trying to save? Some heirloom of the self, a fragment, a romance, a dream. Must he hold on to a name, a certain style? Somehow he would have to think his way out of this mess, bludgeon it with his intelligence. He was a citizen of the Age of Light, not a Sicilian peasant, cowering in a world crammed with omens. He closed his hands, shut them like books, then quickly, with a little flush of shame, crossed his fingers and touched the table for luck.

Both *Ingenious Pain* and *Casanova* have similar moments of questioning, which mark turning points of men's lives. The question of what makes a good life, the courage to face one's past and move in a new direction, and the dilemmas of reason versus superstition in *Casanova* and faith versus paganism in *Ingenious Pain* are at the core of the human condition and of Miller's work. His innate sensibility allows Miller to link the eighteenth century to the contemporary world by exploring what it means to be human through a mixture of worldliness and spirituality. He presents the reader with the ephemeral transitional moment when one is still free to flit back and forth between magic and faith, superstition and reason, before taking the final step toward choice.

Dust jacket for the U.S. edition of Miller's 1998 novel, a fictional account of the famous lover's later years
(Richland County Public Library)

Critics praised *Casanova* as heartily as they had *Ingenious Pain*. Lorna Sage wrote in *The New York Times* (25 October 1998): "Miller is . . . . good at conjuring the phrases that get sensation onto the page, keeping you in obsessive, close-up focus." Robert McCrum, in a 20 September 1998 review in *The Observer* (London), named Miller's *Casanova* as one of the new novels worthy of "Britain's premier fiction award," the Booker Prize. In her review in *The Daily Telegraph* (London), Merritt wrote, "Miller has drawn an exquisite and convincing picture of 18th-century London," and she called *Casanova* "essentially an elegiac novel, beautifully and sensitively written, and painful in its observation of what it means to live past one's prime." The U.S. edition, *Casanova in Love,* was named *Publishers Weekly* Best Book of the Year for 1999. Both *Casanova* and *Ingenious Pain* are under option with Portobello Pictures in London.

Although Miller's third novel, *Oxygen* (2001), is set in the present rather than in the eighteenth century, it too deals with the human condition at the moment of reckoning. As he told White in December 2000: "It's about what we can do for each other when the moment of crisis comes. About holding out a hand, or not!" Short-listed for the 2001 Booker Prize, *Oxygen* explores the themes of identity and courage. Oxygen is the element lacking in all of the characters' lives. It is a metaphor for the freedom to live life fully. Short of air, albeit at different levels, all the characters in this novel are longing for the courage to act.

The plot of *Oxygen,* much like those of *Ingenious Pain* and *Casanova in Love,* is built around the emotional lives of its characters. Here, two much different brothers are brought back together by their mother's terminal illness. This time is one of reckoning and soul-searching, as they each strive to repair their own damaged life. Alice, the mother, is trying to come to terms with her illness. Alec, who returned home to care for his mother, is resentful of his older brother, Larry, and wrestles with old sibling rivalries. Larry, who left for the United States to become a movie star, is facing a deep personal crisis as his career and marriage are deteriorating. Alec is intermittently engaged in translating *Oxygène,* a play by the exiled Hungarian playwright László Lázár about miners trapped underground. A parallel narrative focuses on László, who, despite his artistic success and comfortable life in Paris, is also at a moment of reckoning in his life. He is haunted by a memory of the Hungarian uprising of 1956, when he failed to pull the trigger and perhaps save a man he loved.

All four protagonists are suffering from their own failures and inadequacies, which are slowly asphyxiating them, both physically and emotionally. Alice, slowly dying of lung cancer, is the physical manifestation of this lack of air. As the scholar who translates the work of others, Alec is too timid to take a deep breath and stand up for himself; Larry, once full of promise, has run out of wind as his career and personal life have disintegrated in the face of his alcoholism. Even László has trouble breathing freely as he is haunted by his own weakness. In the end, however, they all find the courage to act. Alice's heroism is a private one, as she strives to face her death gracefully in spite of her terrible suffering. For her sons and for László, their search for courage is a more conventional one as it focuses on ideas of heroism in the face of conflict. In an unpublished January 2002 interview, while talking about *Oxygen,* Miller told White that:

> The book is certainly about courage. All the main characters are constrained by a sense of failure and of their own weakness and inability to do the necessary thing. In the course of the book each—in some degree—does finally discover the strength to act. I think it's an optimistic book though not everyone agrees!

Oxygen, as had its predecessors, *Ingenious Pain* and *Casanova,* received much praise from the critics. In *The Birmingham Post* (13 October 2001) Marianne Nault wrote, "Oxygen is exactly what a modern inventive novel should do: to tell a complex tale about intersecting lives of characters trying to make sense of it all in disparate yet complementary ways." Alice Greenway, in her review in *The Scotsman* (10 September 2001), said that: "Miller's writing pulls this contemporary novel far

above the mundane. He writes beautifully of Alice's cancer, of how the disease eats away at her body and her sense of self." In a 2 September 2001 review in *The Independent* (London) Christopher Fowler noted that "Miller's great trick is the setting out of events in a deceptively relaxed fashion, the narrative gathering a steady accretion of detail that moves and involves." Caroline Gascoigne, in a 23 September 2001 review in *The Sunday Times* (London), declared *Oxygen* an unmitigated success, saying that with it Miller "confirms his reputation as one of our most skilful chroniclers of the human heart and mind" and describing the novel as "a thoughtful, complex and satisfying work."

Miller plans to return to the writing of historical novels. As he writes in "The Power of the Past," an essay published in *Waterstone Magazine* (Spring 1999), he believes that history is "one of the ways in which our experience of the contemporary is revived." As he explains:

> Even as a boy I understood that history is not out there, something apart from us, sealed off. It is in our blood, our music, our language, our food, the buildings we pass every day on the way to work. There is no break between us, no missing links in history, and we ourselves, of course, are part of the chain that will stretch on to the horizon of the future and beyond.

Andrew Miller exhibits this intrinsic human connection to history in all his novels. Whether he conducts his excavation of the human psyche in the eighteenth century, the twentieth, or the twenty-first, the result is the same. Thus, whether Miller chooses to set the private history of his protagonists in the present or in the past makes no difference. His talent and sensibility in exploring the human condition would seem to guarantee Miller continued success.

Interview:

Enda Wyley, "The Frozen Heart," *Irish Times* (Dublin), 22 January 1998, p. 12.

References:

Andrew Miller Website, 15 June 2002 <http://www.andrew miller-author.co.uk/>;

G. S. Rousseau, "*Ingenious Pain:* Fiction, History, Biography, and the Miraculous Eighteenth Century," *Eighteenth-Century Life,* new series 25, no. 2 (2001): 47–62.

Magnus Mills

(1954 –)

Mary L. Bogumil
Southern Illinois University, Carbondale

BOOKS: *The Restraint of Beasts: A Novel* (London: Flamingo, 1998; New York: Arcade, 1998);

Only When the Sun Shines Brightly (Tadworth, U.K.: Acorn, 1999);

All Quiet on the Orient Express (New York: Arcade, 1999; London: Flamingo, 1999);

Three to See the King (London: Flamingo, 2001; New York: Picador, 2001);

The Scheme for Full Employment (New York: Picador USA, 2002; London: Flamingo, forthcoming 2003).

Although many critics have compared his novels to those of Franz Kafka, Magnus Mills is perhaps still best known as the bus driver whose first novel, *The Restraint of Beasts* (1998), was short-listed for the prestigious Booker Prize in 1998, placing Mills among such literary notables as Beryl Bainbridge, Julian Barnes, Patrick McCabe, and Ian McEwan. While McEwan won the award that year for his novel *Amsterdam,* the publicity associated with a bus driver writing novels in his spare time catapulted Mills into the literary world. Mills's celebrity was enhanced when British newspapers published the rumor that he had received a £1 million advance for *The Restraint of Beasts.* Mills later revealed that he and his agent initiated the rumor to spark publicity about the novel, for which he had in fact received a £10,000 advance. Despite such sudden, unexpected, and slightly dubious notoriety, Mills is a serious novelist who has been influenced by such diverse writers as Joseph Conrad, Flann O'Brien, and Primo Levi, specifically Levi's account of his experiences in Auschwitz, *Se questo é un uomo* (1947; translated as *If This Is a Man,* 1959).

Mills was born in Birmingham, England, in 1954 but moved to Bristol when he was eleven. His father was an engineer and his mother worked in childcare. Mills attended the Riding School in Winterbourne until he was sixteen. Since Riding did not offer A levels, Mills had to move to Fulton. He then studied economics at Wolverhampton Polytechnic but decided at the age of twenty-one to take a job on a farm in the Lake District,

Magnus Mills (photograph by Steve Hogben; from the dust jacket for Three to See the King, *2001)*

where he worked at Pooley Bride for three years. Mills left the Lake District to join a fence-building crew in Scotland, a job he held from 1979 to 1986. During that time Mills also traveled in Australia for six months in 1981, working in a mill and in a factory, often in jobs where "he worked with dangerous machinery," as the dust-jacket blurb for his first novel reads.

On his return to England, Mills married Sue, and, after spending years traveling between Penrith and Gloucester, moved at his wife's request to London, where he drove a bus for the next twelve years. In an interview with Marcia Morgado for the on-line magazine *The Barcelona Review* (1999), Mills admitted that it was his wife, Sue, who urged him to write: "I never thought of being a writer when I was younger."

Mills wrote short pieces and a series of articles, *Life on the Buses,* for *The Independent* (London), the newspaper where his wife worked. He had not thought of becoming a novelist, but his wife suggested that the stories he told about his work experiences, particularly his jobs as a fence builder, should be written down. While still driving a bus in London, Mills borrowed an old Apple laptop computer and wrote his first novel. As novelist Julian Gough told Kelley Kawano in a 2001 interview for the on-line magazine *Bold Type,* that computer was later used by, among several others, Toby Litt to write a short story and Gough to write *Juno & Juliet* (2001).

Mills told Mark Campbell in a 1999 interview about why he kept working as a bus driver after he had made up his mind to become a professional writer: "The reason I stayed on was because for the last six years I had started writing and was waiting for a break, and they always take longer to come than you think. I didn't look for anything else, I just stuck with the job. Two years ago I got an agent, and then I knew everything else would follow soon." Then, in 1998, Mills's first novel was published.

The Restraint of Beasts is a dark comedy based on Mills's experiences as a fence builder in Scotland. The unnamed narrator is an English foreman hired to supervise two young, errant, and inseparable Scottish laborers named Tam Findlayson and Ritchie Campbell as they erect high-tensile fences in rural England. The fact that these two accident-prone men are not fond of work soon becomes apparent to the foreman. Tam and Ritchie's disappearing acts and frequent cigarette breaks take a toll on the narrator's patience, as he is under constant pressure by his menacing employer, Donald, and his boss's cohorts Robert and Ralph.

Tam, the son of a golf-course greens keeper, used to be foreman (though supervising only Ritchie) before the Englishman took his place, and Ritchie, a farmer's son, aspires to be a rock star one day and only works to pay the installments on an electric guitar. When not building fences or living amid self-perpetuated squalor in a dilapidated caravan they share with their fastidious English foreman, Tam and Ritchie frequent pubs, where they imbibe many pints of beer and ridicule the quality of said beer, other male patrons of the pub, and anything English. Simply put, they invest most of their time at these provincial English pubs championing their notion of Scottish nationalism.

"A demented, deadpan-comic wonder..." — THOMAS PYNCHON

THE RESTRAINT OF BEASTS

MAGNUS MILLS

Dust jacket for the U.S. edition of Mills's 1998 novel, about an inept crew of fence builders in Scotland (Richland County Public Library)

Their first job-related accident occurs when the crew is on the property of Mr. McCrindle, a dairy farmer, come to fix a newly installed high-tensile fence whose wires have gone slack. As Tam is tightening the topmost, and tautest, wire on the fence, he loses his footing, releasing the wire gripper, which then flies off and kills McCrindle. Tam and Ritchie finish the fence, prop McCrindle next to their truck, consult the narrator, and bury McCrindle feet first with a post on top of the grave. The narrator's comments about the cover-up of McCrindle's fate illustrate Mills's comic edge: "There were a lot of posts in the countryside which seemed to be there for no apparent purpose. Some had been waiting many years for a long-forgotten gate to be hung on them. Others started life as the straining posts of fences which, for some reason or other, were never completed. This spare post could join them. . . ."

Dust jacket for the 1999 novel in which, Mills says,
"A man accidentally spills a tin of paint and
thereby condemns himself to death"
(Richland County Public Library)

The plot is filled with Kafkaesque incidents, such as the trail of dead bodies the fencing gang leaves in its wake, most dismissed as accidents, most of them employers, except for a dog; Donald's attempt to electrocute Tam while demonstrating the power of an electric fence; and the fateful meeting of the fencing gang with the infamous, fear-inspiring Hall brothers—John, David, and Bryan—who are master fence builders as well as butchers. In his interview with Morgado, Mills was asked if "homicidal inclinations" were endemic to fencing gangs. Mills replied, "No . . . I just wanted to spice up the book so I put the deaths in and then I built on top of that." He went on to explain how his plot and characterization are analogous to the construction of a fence: "I tried to structure the book like I was building a fence: tension; major turning points; then it keeps going in a straight direction and in the end it comes back to where it started." Once the three fencers meet the Hall brothers, who contract them to erect a seven-foot fence to contain livestock, or "beasts," their lives change. The fencers are uneasy, trapped, and forced to conform to the brothers' regimentation, which includes company uniforms and control over their lodging, wages, comings and goings, meals, and work schedule. The atmosphere is similar to that of a concentration camp, which perhaps reveals the influence upon Mills of Levi's *If This Is a Man*. As Mills told Campbell, "One of my influences is Primo Levi, who wrote about the concentration camps, and there are hints of that in the novel." This atmosphere is enhanced when Mills describes in detail the sausages the crew must eat at the Hall Brothers' factory. Like the sausage meat that the factory machines force into casings, the lives of the crew are molded by the stern will of John Hall.

Mills's novel ends almost as it began. In the beginning of the novel, the narrator, seated uncomfortably in a chair, is hired by his demented boss, Donald, to supervise the child-like crew and instill in them a work ethic. At the end of the novel, Tam, Ritchie, and the narrator are summoned to John Hall's office, where he reprimands them for their idleness and puts them through a surreal mock trial. When Hall, acting as the voice of moral authority, remarks: "You've left a trail of very disappointed people behind you," meaning deceased people, the narrator reflects that "My chair had begun to feel very uncomfortable." *The Restraint of Beasts* concludes as Hall says, "Let's start with Mr. Crindle," their first unfortunate client.

The Restraint of Beasts received critical and popular acclaim. The reticent U.S. novelist Thomas Pynchon read an advance copy of the book and praised it highly, calling it—in words prominently displayed on the cover of the published novel—"A demented, deadpan comic wonder, this rude salute to the dark side of contract employment has the exuberant power of a magic word it might possibly be dangerous (like the title of a certain other Scottish tale) to speak out loud." In addition to making the Booker short-list, the novel was short-listed for the Whitbread and James Tait Black prizes. In 1999 Mills was awarded the McKitterick Prize for best first novel for a writer over forty. The novel sold more than fifty thousand copies and was translated into sixteen languages.

Mills published his first short-story collection, a slim volume comprising four short stories, *Only When the Sun Shines Brightly* (1999), with a firm specializing in poetry, the Acorn Book Company. In Mills's next novel, *All Quiet on the Orient Express* (1999), the narrator is a quiet, self-reliant young man who intends to spend a brief time in Cumbria in the Lake District at Hillhouse campsite, owned and operated by a Mr. Tommy Parker. It is the end of the holiday season; the tourists have left; and the narrator wants to leave as well. The narrator's only immediate plans are to fold up his tent, leave at the end of the week with his few possessions, including a vintage motorcycle, and embark on a journey to the East–Turkey, Persia, and India. The narrator has left his former job at an oil-drum recycling plant so that he could set off on this adventure, but the Eastern journey is postponed when he encounters the seemingly amicable Mr. Parker, who has other plans for the agreeable young man.

Parker, who has been watching the narrator, noting his humble financial state, initially hires him to do odd jobs around the campground. At first the narrator politely obliges Mr. Parker by painting a campsite gate for him in exchange for the rent. Then fate intervenes. The narrator's motorcycle fails him as he embarks on his journey to the East. Parker offers the narrator a ride and never fails to find some work for him to do thereafter. The narrator becomes Parker's on-call handyman and the tutor of his adolescent nymphet daughter, Gail. The narrator even begins doing Gail's homework—winning a contest for her with an essay he writes—and much more as the novel progresses. Naturally, the narrator becomes frustrated as one job always leads to another, whether it is painting the camp rowboats, sawing wood, or anchoring a new mooring. Once an outsider, a tourist, the narrator slowly becomes a member of the small community, most of whom patronize the Packhorse, the local pub. The narrator joins the pub darts team and takes over the route of Deakin, the milkman, when the latter meets with an unfortunate accident involving a galvanized chain.

Prior to the publication of *All's Quiet on the Orient Express,* Mills was asked by interviewer Morgado if in it he followed the same pattern of using an unnamed narrator as he had in his first novel. Mills replied, "Yep, the same sort of person is narrating it. In one line: 'A man accidentally spills a tin of paint and thereby condemns himself to death.'" He went on to elaborate upon the difference in setting between the two novels: "But there are a lot of other things going on. *The Restraint of Beasts* is linear; this takes place all in one area, by a lake, and everything ties—everybody is tied together, although they don't know it yet."

The moment the narrator becomes a part of the community and its politics, his identity is subverted by the needs of the community, and the dream trip to the East remains just that, a dream. Although he never experiences at firsthand Parker's rumored volatile temper, even after his first mishap with green paint while painting his employer's gate, eventually the narrator discovers that his position has been cavalierly offered to the former handyman, Mark, who calls himself Marco. Ironically, the derelict Marco, a romantic interest of Gail, has just come back from a trip to India. In *TLS: The Times Literary Supplement* (1 October 1999) reviewer Sam Gilpin discussed the problematic world of Mills's working-class hero. The narrator's trip to the East

"which never takes place, because of the narrator's susceptibility to manipulation, stands for all goals and aspirations which are delayed and lost in the compromises of the workaday world," Gilpin observed, reflecting that Marco, the narrator's competitor, "never pays his bills, does jobs so badly that he is not asked to do them again, eats other people's biscuits and generally gets everything he wants. The pessimistic implications of this are not difficult to divine: the unpleasant tend to benefit at the expense of the innocent." As Gilpin notes, however, at the conclusion of *The Restraint of Beasts* "not all is bleak in the narrator's life." He has not lost "his notion of karmic justice," and "As he contemplates preparing a length of galvanized chain, the narrator looks down at his new roommate, this prodigal handyman Marco, whom Parker claims is ' . . . just the right person for the job.'"

Martyn Bedford, in a review for *The New Statesman* (1 November 1999), remarked, "As in Kafka, a Mills hero is propelled by a series of circumstances that, taken individually, are logical and innocuous but which have the cumulative effect of entangling him in a life where he is no longer in control. Control is the key word here." Thus, the protagonist's lack of control over his destiny cannot be solely attributed to his relentless taskmaster, Parker, but is also a consequence of his own boundless ability to be cajoled by his employer and willingness to postpone his dream trip temporarily. In *The New York Times Book Review* (12 September 1999), James Polk commented on the passivity of Mills's protagonists: "the seductive nature of the familiar and the way in which a longing for comfort can diminish life's challenges emerge as central themes. . . . Once security becomes the only end, Mills suggests, growth, imagination and adventure fall by the wayside. Perhaps this is the real curse of the working class."

Mills's third novel, *Three to See the King* (2001), is set on a sandy and windy plain. The unnamed narrator employs the language of fairy tales: "I live in a house built entirely from tin, with four tin walls, a chimney and a door. Entirely from tin." He has three friends—Steve Treacle, Simon Painter, and Philip Sibling—but he lives far away from them because he relishes his solitude. Unlike the characters in Mills's two earlier novels, this narrator is unencumbered by employment or labor of any kind until the latter part of the novel. In the on-line "People in Tin Houses" interview, Mills explained why this novel is a departure from his earlier books with respect to work.

There's no paid employment in it. I just wanted to get away from any boundaries. I didn't want there to be any historical, geographical or economic references at all. I just wanted it to be pure literature. So I thought if I had a completely blank backdrop I could do whatever I wanted. I decided that they weren't going to be people with jobs.

Dust jacket for the U.S. edition of Mills's 2001 novel, in which he sought to avoid all
"historical, geographical or economic references" (Richland County Public Library)

Asked if the unnamed narrator was "a more highly evolved incarnation" of his earlier narrators, Mills replied:

> He's the same sort of guy. He's a bit more assertive in this one, in fact he's got a high opinion of himself and obviously as it progresses you realize that's self delusion. Not only him but all of them, all of them are deluding themselves in one way or another.

Shortly after the novel begins, the narrator's comfortable isolation is disrupted by the sudden appearance of a woman he hardly knows, Mary Petrie. Mary arrives with clothes, a washstand, a mirror—symbols of illusion, purgation or rebirth, and self-reflection—and moves in with him. As *TLS* (25 July 2001) reviewer Carol Birch pointed out, their coexistence is "a dry and elegant set piece of typical male-female relations—gently humourous and full of wry insight. Mary Petrie mothers and nags. Our tin-dwelling hero falls readily into the role of husband/child."

This comfortable existence is disturbed, however, when news comes of the enigmatic Michael Hawkins, who lives "even further out" along the plain and is "building a canyon" to contain a city. The narrator's three friends begin to visit him, much to the perturbation of the narrator. It seems the narrator once harbored dreams of living in a canyon, just not with a host of others. His three friends obsess over Hawkins's new community and eventually decide to dismantle their houses and move there. Other, more distant, neighbors, also join in digging the canyon. The narrator becomes obsessed with Hawkins's world, so he ventures through the wilderness to see for himself this canyon community—this experimental social construct—and its creator.

While Mary Petrie becomes Michael Hawkins's soul mate and Steve, Simon, and Philip his followers, the narrator is appointed by Hawkins to be his confidant and problem solver. When Hawkins's dutiful followers, who have a penchant for tin houses, discover that the new houses to be erected on the excavation site will be made not of tin but of clay instead, they revolt, tearing down Hawkins's tin house in retaliation for what they see as his betrayal. Mills's narrator exclaims that they should throw all the remaining tin over the precipice of the canyon and return from whence they came. They do so, and Hawkins becomes a king without a kingdom. Hawkins and his kingdom thus vanish like the sand the narrator sweeps away from his door.

As Birch pointed out in her review of the novel, though the five main characters are "clearly differentiated" and "memorable and endearing," Hawkins and his followers are less distinctly rendered. Birch argued that because of this lack of definition "the denouement is less successful than it might have been."

Mills's claim in the on-line interview that "the whole thing's allegorical in a sense" explains his ambiguous characterization of the Hawkins followers. In allegory, the characters are typically personifications of abstract qualities, and both setting and action represent the relationships among these abstractions. Thus, in allegory certain elements must be mitigated in order to represent meanings independent of, or greater than, those elements individually. Justine Jordan, a reviewer for *The Guardian* (7 October 2001), drew an analogy between the fanatical group consciousness portrayed in the Monty Python movie *Life of Brian* (1979) and Mills's characterization of Hawkins's followers. In doing so, Jordan indirectly addressed Birch's complaint regarding the scant characterization of Hawkins's followers. Jordan called the novel "philosophy for fiction-lovers," noting that "In his shifting, suggestive parable, Mills throws into relief the stark essences of leadership and individuality, community and solitude, progress and retreat."

The last chapter of *Three to See the King* is reminiscent of the first, with the narrator back in his tin house. If others look to him for guidance about living on a desolate plain in a tin house, he replies pragmatically: "I tell them they can find comfort here as long as they don't expect too much. . . . This house of mine has served me well. Though only built from tin, it held together while kingdoms were being swept away. It is my refuge and my fortress. Let it be your temple." These parting words represent the narrator's epiphany—an intuitive grasp of his own situation in a new light. There is an allusion here to Psalm 91:1–2, which reads in the King James Version "He that dwelleth in the secret place of the most High shall abide under the shadow of the Almighty. / I will say of the LORD, He is my refuge and my fortress: my God; in him will I trust." However, God is now the individual and his domain is a tin house.

Aside from referring to the unnamed protagonist's pilgrimage to the famed canyon city and his even-

tual meeting with its mysterious creator, Michael Hawkins, the title of *Three to See the King* refers to the narrator's three friends: Steve Treacle, Simon Painter, and Philip Sibling. Just as the title alludes to the Magi, who traveled a great distance to see the newborn Christ child, all the characters' names suggest biblical characters: the first-century Christian martyr Stephen; two of Jesus' apostles, Simon and Philip; Christ's mother, Mary; and an archangel, Michael. Although Mills proclaimed himself an atheist in the "People in Tin Houses" interview, he admitted that there are underlying religious references: "It's Old Testament in a sense. I don't know if you've ever seen these children's books where you see the construction of the pyramids, but I had the idea that there were all these people labouring for some sort of greater good. I was aware of the Old Testament sort of idea, that sort of religion—fire and brimstone, not spiritual." Mills also described *Three to See the King* as a fable: "I think there is a moral from the story, that's the bit about self-delusion. It's not like an Aesop fable with a definite ending. Aesop's fables tell us particular things, they tell us a particular message, mine doesn't do that but it's more of a fable than a novel."

In that same interview, Mills alluded to his forthcoming novel, *The Scheme for Full Employment,* scheduled for publication in December 2002, and mentioned his growing confidence as a writer. Mills remarked, "My plots are a bit pathetic, but because I write in a certain way I get away with it! My plots are like Victorian plots, full of coincidences, like *Jane Eyre* and all those." On the surface, Magnus Mills's writing in his darkly comic novels may appear deceptively simple, but beneath that surface lie empathetic though commonplace characters groping to find answers to the unanswerable in a mundane life that is nonetheless fraught with peril.

Interviews:

Mark Campbell, "On the Buses: Magnus Mills' Route to Success," *etcetera* (May/June 1999);

Marcia Morgado, "Interview with Magnus Mills," *Barcelona Review,* 13 (Mid-June–Mid-August 1999), <http://www.barcelonareview.com/13/e_mm_int.htm>;

Michelle Griffin, "Transports of Delight," *Age* (Melbourne), 23 September 2001;

"People in Tin Houses: An Interview with Magnus Mills" <http://www.fireandwater.com/Authors/interview.asp?interviewid=436> [7 June 2002].

Mary Morrissy

(25 January 1957 –)

Ann Owens Weekes
University of Arizona

BOOKS: *A Lazy Eye: Stories* (London: Cape, 1993; New York: Scribners, 1996);
Mother of Pearl (New York: Scribners, 1995; London: Cape, 1996);
The Pretender (London: Cape, 2000).

OTHER: "The Butterfly," in *Irish Sporting Short Stories,* edited by David Marcus (Belfast: Appletree Press, 1995);
"Clods," in *If Only* (Dublin: Poolbeg Press, 1997);
"Ceiling," in *The Whoseday Book* (Dublin: Irish Hospice Foundation, 1999).

SELECTED PERIODICAL PUBLICATIONS—UNCOLLECTED: "A Present for Julia Fortune," *Irish Times,* Christmas 1996;
"The Gender of Cars," *You Magazine, The Mail on Sunday,* April 2000.

Mary Morrissy (photograph by Matt Kavanagh, The Irish Times; *courtesy of the author)*

Subjects and style in Mary Morrissy's short stories and novels leave reviewers struggling for words to explain the appeal of her always compelling, yet bittersweet, stories; meticulous, exact, sensuous, exotic, they note, many remarking on her black humor and the almost too intelligent nature of plot and prose. Since her first story appeared on David Marcus's Young Writers Page in *The Irish Press* in 1976, Morrissy has had an eager, if small, Irish and British following, a following that swelled considerably with the publication of her first volume of short stories in 1993 and her first novel in 1995. Morrissy resists traditional identifications of Irish writers with place and time, setting much of her work in unnamed, unidentifiable places, creating characters arguably affected by an Irish Catholic upbringing but driven by strange, often disturbing, perspectives, as universal as they are Irish. Morrissy's voice is a significant one in Irish writing, one that, along with some few of her contemporaries, stretches the world of Irish fiction beyond the rich but well-worked canvas of the past into the often disaffected and sometimes violent world of modern psychology.

Born 25 January 1957, the third of four children, to a father from County Clare and a mother from County Kerry, both civil servants, Mary Morrissy grew up and attended school in Dublin. In a 1996 interview with Eileen Battersby, Morrissy recalled that her mother always read classics to the children, such as Charles Dickens's *The Personal History of David Copperfield* (1849–1850), Charlotte Brontë's *Jane Eyre* (1847), and Robert Louis Stevenson's *Treasure Island* (1883). Her father was also a great reader, and books were everywhere in the house. His death when she was thirteen marked a dividing line in her childhood: first there was the nuclear family, with parents, two older brothers, herself, and a sister eight years younger; after her father's death and her brothers' departures, Morrissy's family was all female, the influence of which, she suggested in a 1996 interview with Annie Callan, is more powerful in her work than that of the earlier, traditional nuclear family. Morrissy missed her father greatly, and this loss is reflected in the fatherless characters in her own work; she told Battersby, however, that had her father lived, she might never have written. A voracious reader, Morrissy never thought of writing during her years at the convent school of Notre Dame Des Missions in suburban Dublin. She received her school-leaving certificate in 1974, with honors in English, Irish, French, music, and Latin. Morrissy, whose parents and grandparents were civil servants and primary-school teachers, followed family tradition by applying for a position in the Irish Civil Service and for admission to a teaching school in Dublin; she diverged from tradition by applying for admission to a journalism course at the Dublin Institute of Technology. As was often the case at this time in Ireland, university was not a consideration, partly because of her family situation and partly because of her own lack of direction.

Although there were a few turns in the road, Morrissy soon took control of her own career. First she called the teaching college, which informed her that if she had not heard from them, she was not accepted. With this in mind, she accepted the place in the journalism course. Too late the teaching school called to explain that they had made a mistake. But the intensity of the journalism course initially overwhelmed her, so, dropping out, she took a job in the civil service. There, she encountered the same tedium as did her Irish predecessor Flann O'Brien, who spent eighteen years in the civil service and featured its inanities in his comic works. This tedium finally drove Morrissy to take a correspondence course, resulting in the writing of her first short story. This unpublished story, "The Bond," was so highly praised by an anonymous reviewer that Morrissy determined to become a writer, ending her short career in the civil service and returning to the journalism course. Upon completion of the course in 1977, Morrissy secured her first job for a provincial Irish newspaper in Tralee, County Kerry. The loneliness of her situation, reporting on everything from small-town "Bachelor of the Year" competitions to meetings of the "Kerry Sheep Dipping Committee," caused her to realize that she was a city person. She gave up the job after two years, exchanging the loneliness of an Irish village for the isolation of Sydney in the Australian desert. During 1979 she continued her journalism career in Australia working for a women's magazine, a press agency, and as a proofreader and a radio subedi-

tor. Returning to Ireland, she joined the staff of a Dublin newspaper, *The Irish Press,* in 1980, transferring to *The Irish Times* in 1985, where she remained until 2001.

As many Irish writers have been, Morrissy was first published by Marcus, an editor who has done a remarkable job of selecting the finest of new writers and introducing their work in the pages of a Dublin daily paper, grouping the works later as collections of new Irish writing. Between 1976 and 1993 Morrissy's short stories appeared in Irish newspapers, British and Irish magazines, and anthologies. Although no volume of her short stories appeared until 1993, her work was recognized and rewarded. As early as 1977, her short story "A Traveler's Paradise" took second place in the prestigious Listowel Writers Week Short Story Competition; in 1984 she won the Hennessy Award for Short Fiction with her story "Bookworm," and in 1992 she was awarded an Irish Arts Council Bursary in Literature.

Morrissy may have developed her precise, distinguished prose during her years as subeditor of a quality newspaper. In 1980 she realized that despite contemporary prejudice, editing, the least glamorous side of journalism, interested her more than reporting. The skills of a fine editor, tuning every word, playing every sentence for precision and nuance, underlie her use of language: "I have always felt that *style* is all," she acknowledged in a 1996 interview with Battersby. "What you are saying is determined by *how* you say it." All the stories that appeared in *A Lazy Eye* (1993) had already been published over the course of the previous ten years, so that Morrissy laughs at the idea of being discovered in 1993. The story of the publication is revealing: Morrissy sent the collection to an Irish publisher during the 1980s. Two years went by without any communication, then she received a letter noting that the editor had found the manuscript in his desk, was leaving his position, and would pass it on to his successor. She never heard from these publishers again. Finally, she hired an agent, who sold all the stories individually. In 1992 David Goodwin, an editor for the firm of Jonathan Cape, Ltd., saw one in *The London Magazine* and wrote to Morrissy asking to see more. As she told Callan in a 1996 interview for *Glimmer Train Stories:* "So after years of trying to flog them, a publisher actually came to me, which was kind of miraculous!"

Many critics remark on the arresting opening sentences of Morrissy's short stories, the attribute of an excellent journalist. "When I was at school you could buy a black baby," the narrator of "Bookworm"–the first story in *A Lazy Eye*–announces. This sentence transports Irish readers to the parochial and national schools of the 1950s, where children were encouraged to contribute stamps and money to the missionary sisters who regularly visited the schools with stories of the

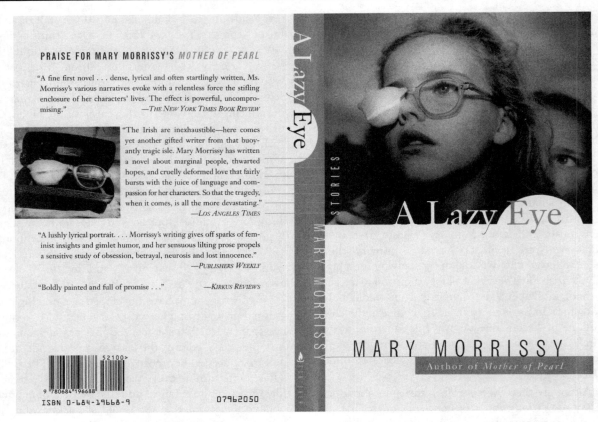

Dust jacket for the 1996 U.S. edition of Morrissy's 1993 book, a collection of stories about characters she calls "pretty ordinary people" who are "emotionally in extremis" and "have a skewed vision of the world" (Richland County Public Library)

poor, pagan, black babies. While Morrissy's stories are not specifically Irish or Catholic—they are usually set in unnamed locales—she sees her characters' obsessions with guilt as Irish and Catholic. She goes to great lengths to avoid naming a place, thinking that the connection of Irish writers and place has been overworked and her own urban background to be more universal. Most stories open with a journalistic hook: "At forty-one, Grave Davey's biggest fear was that she would dry up"; "Bella Carmichael woke in a pool of blood"; "By pity and contempt I have learned"; "Her teeth must have been rotting quietly for months but she only discovered this the morning after Jimmy left." Some implications of the opening sentences are apparent immediately, but further ironies are uncovered throughout the story. The disgruntled kleptomaniac of "Bookworm" is attracted to a black child because the child, like the narrator, is contemptuous of books, running her fingers over the shelves, toppling them onto the floor. Upset by the reverence of book lovers, the narrator steals books, ritually destroys them with her food blender, and leaves them for the garbage collectors, "pristine, clean, as pure as a child in a christening robe." The brief foray into memory and sentiment that

the black child's image evokes proves the narrator's downfall, as the child cries out, not in the expected exotic speech, but in a coarse Irish accent, "Mammy, mammy, look at her, look, she's taking them books."

Considering her characters and the detached voice of her work, critics and scholars often compare Morrissy to John Banville and Anne Enright, Irish contemporaries. The tone of the stories also resembles that of Julia O'Faolain's early stories; Morrissy's narrators often reflect the same jaundiced perspectives as O'Faolain's. In "Rosa" the older sister, comforter and protector of the pregnant and abandoned Rosa, cannot be with her sister for the birth of the baby. Slicing cold cuts in the store, she imagines the scene: "Rosa lay somewhere else on a cold slab, the midwife in a butcher's apron, the nurses gathered around like spectators at a bullfight, their urgent cries mixing with hers of pain." The narrator of "Moment of Downfall" recalls her mother's coming in from work: "she would tear off her tights as if she were being let out of harness, or extricate her bra down the sleeves of her dress muttering 'God, this thing is killing me!' My mother had very few private moments." The older-sister narrator in "Rosa" neither questions nor hesitates when she determines that Rosa does not want her baby, but takes the child when the store closes on Christmas Eve, removes the black baby Jesus from the store creche, and replaces it with Rosa's baby. Rosa, she realizes, was right: no one will know the difference. "The pale faces of Joseph and Mary looked down lovingly at the dark creature," but ironically she finds the "glassy eyes and puckered, rosebud smile" of the plastic baby Jesus she has put in her bag to be unsettling and covers it up. That night at midnight mass, it seems as if the women "wore scarves of children's arms, while other small hands clawed excitedly at the crooks of their elbows"; the odor of candle grease is everywhere, which, as a child, she remembers thinking "was the smell of hair singeing in hell."

Her position as a full-time subeditor naturally cut down on Morrissy's literary output; she believes that she would find full-time writing unnatural and balances her need to write with her need to be in the world. The characters and situations of the stories in *A Lazy Eye,* she told Helen Meany of *The Irish Times* (4 March 1993), "had come almost randomly, one at a time, at intervals." This gradual accumulation adds a richness and independence rarely seen in short-story collections: the tone, voice, mood, and characters all differ, reflecting the interests of particular moments, with the autonomy and originality of the characters and situations connected to those shifting interests. Tone changes with each distinctive narrator, and characters and situations reveal no connections: the kleptomaniac of the first story is followed by the story of a single, respectable woman whose chief worry is that she will "dry up" and be unable to delight in her sexual excursions; the young woman who abandons her baby; a woman whose menstrual blood stains the sheets on a train, for which offense she is forced to leave the train; a woman so starved for affection she pretends to be a thief; a ten-year-old girl who pushes her pregnant mother down the stairs; an abandoned lover who pours out her soul to an obscene phone-caller; and a baby-sitter so humiliated she stabs her employers' baby.

Almost all of Morrissy's narrators are women; indeed, the one story with a male narrator is the only story in which characters and situation seem stereotypical. She agrees with Callan that the males in the short stories are not necessarily developed. The women, however, are extreme instances of common female experiences, or more rarely, fulfillments of fantasies. When Callan remarked in her 1996 interview with Morrissy that she "turned each page with a mix of anticipation and dread," because the characters "have a disturbing undertone," Morrissy noted that "what most of the characters have in common is that they're pretty ordinary people but they're emotionally *in extremis,* and they have a skewed vision of the world." She sees them

as "verging on normal," except for Rosa, the mother who abandons her baby.

Morrissy's characters find themselves in, or create, situations that both shock and horrify themselves and readers, but Morrissy allows her readers not only to understand the actions but also to see them as predictable, perhaps even inevitable. She shows, for example, just why the sad fifteen-year-old baby-sitter in "A Curse" would wish to hurt a baby. Having witnessed the sad confines of Clara's widowed mother's house and personality, the reader can see why she welcomes working in the tatty but (for her) exciting atmosphere of the Skerritt home. With the baby in bed, she explores "every inch of the Skerritts' house. Their bedroom had all the abandon of a shared intimate life. A tousled double bed with clothes dripping off the end and trailing on the floor"; the bathroom, "sensual with its potent mix of male and female"; "the splashy silks and beaded boucles" of Joy Skerritt's clothes. In their home, Clara can see herself as an "extension" of the American television world she loves, so that, as Denis Skerritt drives her home, she imagines "them as parties to a secret, she and Mr. Skerritt, as if driving in the dark together was some kind of forbidden pleasure." When Joy Skerritt goes to hospital for the delivery of her second baby, Clara is called on to stay several nights to care for the older child, Marcus. She loves the role of housewife: cleans the kitchen, irons Denis Skerritt's shirts, and sits waiting "in front of the television hoping she looked as if she had been sitting there all evening." She prefers "the idea of his proximity and the imminence of his arrival to his actual presence," for the presence can clash with her fantasy. On the evening before Joy's return home, Clara realizes with a jolt that all the work she had so willingly and thoroughly undertaken with her fantasy husband was not part of a mutual fantasy, but simply his preparations for his wife's return. Dissolving into tears, Clara buries her head in her employer's chest; only the welcome sound of the ringing phone allows him to escape her sad clutch. Clara agonizes in embarrassment on the following days, an agony made unbearable when at last the Skerritts ask her to help with the baby's christening party, and she overhears her employers laugh with their guests over her "infatuation." Close to tears again, she resolves to escape but first picks up the baby, who "has never felt the slightest edge of a breeze," and in hatred of Joy's scorn, of Denis's pity, and of their pampered children, she undresses the baby and stabs it in the hip with the diaper pin. As she runs away, the Irish Catholic sense of guilt erupts, a sense that will haunt, mar, and distort her whole future, the knowledge that there "was a curse on her now."

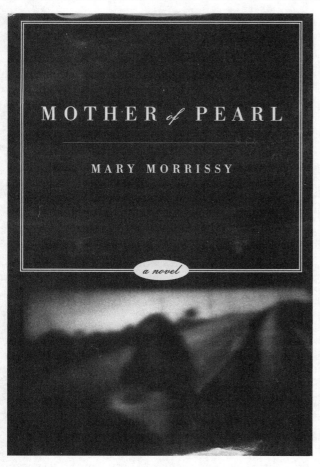

*Dust jacket for the 1995 novel that prompted Fay
Weldon to call Morrissy the "pride of a new
generation of fine young Irish writers"
(Richland County Public Library)*

Following the success of *A Lazy Eye* in Europe, Charles Scribner & Sons bought the U.S. publication rights, but the firm indicated that it would prefer to bring out a novel first. Morrissy was now offered an advance for a novel and faced new pressures. The stories had been written over the course of ten years, their subject matter and tone varying greatly, whereas the novel needed to be completed in a limited time frame and demanded consistent tone and sustained character development. Twice before, she had attempted and failed to write a novel; now she took three months of sabbatical leave from *The Irish Times* and went to Italy to write full-time. She extended her leave to six months and came home with the first and last sections of the novel written. *Mother of Pearl* was first published by Charles Scribner & Sons in the United States in 1995; the following year the firm published her short-story collection *A Lazy Eye* in the United States, and Jonathan Cape, Ltd. published the novel in Britain.

The Lannan Literary Award for Fiction was awarded to Morrissy in 1995 for *Mother of Pearl* and *A Lazy Eye* and was followed by enthusiastic reviews from Irish, British, and U.S. critics. The novel continues to focus unabashedly on women, with Morrissy examining their biological and emotional experiences as deeply and as matter-of-factly as any other major human experience. Her natural interest in women's issues was probably deepened by her female upbringing; also, she was married for less than two years, a relationship that ended amicably, though she told Battersby that "the failure of love always hurts." She uses the space of the novel, however, to develop more fully her secondary male characters.

Mother of Pearl is the story of three women. Irene Rivers, whom the reader meets in an Irish sanatorium in the 1950s, marries a middle-aged, impotent man. Distraught not so much by her childlessness as by the constant assessment of her interfering neighbors, Irene first conjures up a fantasy pregnancy and later actually steals a baby. Rita Golden, the second woman, marries Mel Spain when she's pregnant, and her unwanted baby, Mary, is stolen by Irene. Mary, called Pearl by Irene, is returned to Rita as a four-year-old. Rita lies to Mary about a dead older sister and tells her nothing of her own history. Mary, haunted by half-forgotten memories, struggles for a sense of self, but, as Battersby noted in her interview with Morrissy, her "personality collapses under the burden of her missing history." Besides questioning the traditional assumption of mothering as "natural," the novel also tenderly and unsentimentally examines the tragedy of involuntary childlessness. As do many characters in the short stories, all the women in the novel feel an undetermined but pressing weight of guilt, the residue of their unrecorded, Catholic Irish upbringing. This novel has an extraordinary tensile quality: the reader sees and feels the grim sanatorium, Granitefield; the tatty streets of Rita's and Irene's homes in a war-torn, fictional city, suggestive of contemporary Northern Ireland; the narrow, bitter, calculating perspectives of the inhabitants; the viciousness of the tuberculosis patients; and the rage of the impotent husband. While the story probes a topical, emotionally searing situation, Morrissy, as always, eschews sentimentality: her characters' desires are almost boringly "ordinary"; it is the steps they take, deliberately, pragmatically, to achieve these ordinary desires that move them from the mundane into the world of Jacob and Wilhelm Grimm's fairytales.

Economically and exactly, Morrissy uncovers the complicated, but logical, workings of her characters and situations. She is one of the first Irish novelists to take her readers into the world of Irish sanatoriums. During the 1950s, hospitals were built and existing institutions converted all over Ireland in an attempt to deal with rampant tuberculosis, a disease regarded as shameful, so secrecy surrounded both the patients and the hospitals. Women whispered of a neighbor's having contracted "it," or someone's being taken "there"–the words tuberculosis and sanatorium were rarely spoken. Despite the success of Thomas Mann's novel set largely in a tuberculosis sanatorium, *Der Zauberberg* (1924; translated as *The Magic Mountain,* 1927), Irish novelists shied away from the subject of disease. The opening section of Morrissy's novel takes the reader into a grim, insulated world of disease and deceit, where Irene's mother, "horrified by the notion that she might have contaminated the family . . . would have nothing more to do with her." Irene's illness, which her mother believes implies poverty and a lack of hygiene, shames the family, who "scour her room and burn her bedding." Irene's family only appear in the first four pages, but all, even the absent father, are fully realized characters. Similarly, the matron, doctor, staff, and patients, however peripheral their roles, are memorably drawn. The pain, discomfort, and unpleasantness of the disease is always evident, yet the foreshadowing prose, which layers the text, is also beautiful: Irene Rivers "didn't have to see the clouded blue picture of her lungs, the flowery clumps of infection. From the moment she surrendered to the embrace of a device that rendered her transparent, there was a shadow not only on Irene's lung, but on her life too."

Irene's marriage, to the dull, obtuse Stanley Godwin, initially offers some measure of contentment, hardly pleasure, as Stanley is impotent. Despite the poverty and meanness of the characters, the "neat, tight-lipped, righteous" neighbors and streets of this northern town, Morrissy injects whimsical humor. Brought up by his mother, who "had seemed to him large and mysterious enough, like a capacious cathedral, to have produced him on her own," Stanley, at her death, feels the "solitude of one who would not go forth and multiply. Like the last outpost of an empire, his memory would not outlast him." This distancing humor makes the excursion into the sad life of Irene and Stanley, and then of Rita and Mel Spain, bearable, but at the same time the distance is balanced and tempered by human sympathy and understanding of the situations that have shaped the characters.

In the last section, devoted to Pearl/Mary, the prose reaches beyond the material world, recording in first person Pearl/Mary's shadowy, nebulous sense of being, in a style that suggests the merging of subconscious with conscious. The story of a lost first child, which Rita had created, haunts Pearl/Mary. Obsessed with this lost, unnamed child, whom she christens Jewel, Pearl/Mary creates for her a life borrowed from the forgotten fragments of her own with her "first parents." Jewel has a father, who like Stanley is "suffused with a bewildered

but grateful reverence for the sight of a late and much-longed-for child. He would come into her room in the mornings to rouse her, carefully putting on her dressing gown and slippers, his breath a warm cloud on the icy air. . . . His big hands were clumsy with buttons; he often mismatched them. He carried her downstairs, his burly clasp around her waist, her arms tightly clutching his broad expanse of shoulder." Pearl/Mary longs for Rita to be as solicitous as the fictional mother she has given Jewel, but Jewel's life is tantalizingly elusive: "I would wake from the dream of her life and find little seams in the air as if the skin of a new world had for a moment been peeled back and then hurriedly sewn up again leaving behind only the transparent incision." The loss of Eden, from which Pearl was banished when her identity became known, haunts her life, determining its contours as surely as the shadow on Irene's lung determined her future. Reflecting on her loss of a presence that she believes she created, Pearl/Mary concludes: "Perhaps this is what all human beings feel in the world, an exquisite loneliness, an absence unaccounted for." There are no secrets, she now believes, no clues she has failed to see, but she is herself the "skeleton" in the family cupboard, "A vessel of guilt, carrier of original sin, a child of Eve."

Critics responded favorably to *Mother of Pearl.* In her 14 July 1996 review for *The Tribune Magazine,* Maxine Jones admired the "dream-like sequences," in which "Morrissy cleverly shows a personality in disintegration." Novelist Carol Birch noted in *The New Statesman & Society* (12 January 1996), "It's extremely unusual for a book to bring tears to my eyes these days, but *Mother of Pearl* managed it on the very last page, quite taking me by surprise. It is a very fine novel indeed and deserves wide recognition." Besides receiving the Lannan Literary Award, the novel was short-listed for the prestigious Whitbread Prize in 1996.

She remained with *The Irish Times,* publishing several stories between the publication of her novels *Mother of Pearl* in 1995 and *The Pretender* in 2000. Several previously published stories were also anthologized, in Irish, English, Swiss, Norwegian, and American collections. *Mother of Pearl* was translated and published in The Netherlands, Sweden, France, and Germany between 1996 and 1998, and *A Lazy Eye* was also published in The Netherlands in 1997. During these years Morrissy was involved in many aspects of literature, acting as judge for *The Irish Times* International Fiction Prize, adjudicating the Cork Campus Radio Short Story competition, directing and facilitating writing workshops in Ireland and the United States, teaching creative-writing seminars for both Trinity College, Dublin, and the University of Michigan, reviewing fiction for *The Irish Times,* as well as carrying on her duties as subeditor. In 1999 Morrissy won the Suspended Sentence residency in Australia. Given her busy schedule, it is surprising that she was able to research, write, and publish *The Pretender* by 2000.

Loss, identity, and guilt—all the familiar Morrissy preoccupations—dominate this novel, which is the fictional biography of the real woman known as Anna Anderson, who claimed to be the Grand Duchess Anastasia, youngest daughter of Czar Nicholas II, and the sole survivor of the massacre of the Romanov family in 1918, an identity refuted by DNA testing performed in 1994–1995, some ten years after her death in 1984. Morrissy told Callan that she agreed with Patrick White that "everything important that happens to you happens before you were born," and while she wrote less of childhood after *Mother of Pearl,* she added "there's always at the center the nugget of something that has happened a long time ago." The structure of *The Pretender* illustrates this idea: one layer conceals another, like the Matryoska doll that the young woman who becomes Anastasia takes from her childhood home. From the opening cameo of the elderly, senile, personally unattractive Anastasia, married to John Manahan, a retired academic twenty years her junior and living in squalor in Virginia, Morrissy journeys back to the 1920s, to a German asylum where a young unknown woman, an attempted suicide, refuses to speak for two years but finally, on hearing the story of the Romanovs, declares herself to be Anastasia, securing her release from the asylum and delivery to the media. Back the text goes to 1914, to a young Polish girl, Franziska Schanzkowska, working in a munitions factory in Berlin, and to the terrible industrial accident that left the scars later identified as Anastasia's bayonet wounds. Finally, the novel reaches Franziska's childhood in rural Poland, where she was the beloved—for a short time—youngest child of her father, who nicknamed her "Sissy" and "Princess," the child who rebelled against being ordinary. In the heartbreaking story of her childhood, the seeds are laid for both the desire for anonymity and the search for identity that define so many "celebrity" lives in the twentieth century.

While the facts of Franziska's life could lend themselves to a sensationalized treatment, Morrissy refuses to treat them thusly; rather, she shows how the brutal neglect of the father is more destructive of life and personality than even the awful moments and deprivations of history. Characters and situations are well realized. The living room in Virginia reeks of the squalor Anastasia creates: "Dreg-tided cups, plates with pools of congealed food, the sour tang of cat piss." Individually, the attendants in the mental hospital show kindness but seem particularly blind to a young woman's fears. Two orderlies strap Franziska to a table for a vaginal examination: "One grabbed the patient's arms and forced them over her head, the other clamped his hands around her ankles. Dr

Hanisch forced her legs open. She felt him enter her. Cold, metallic, he was using his rifle barrel. She screamed. One of the orderlies clapped a hand over her mouth." The war years in Berlin are depicted from the unusual perspective of the young Polish girl lodging with a German family, all of them impoverished and struggling against brutal odds to survive, the girls still young and optimistic enough to welcome eagerly every new dress, every hope of romance. The rural poverty of Franziska's Polish family contrasts with the urban poverty of the German family, the Wingenders; in Poland, there is little excitement, as the father rules over sons and daughters with a brutality not compensated by his moments of tenderness toward Franziska. All her life, Franziska regrets the loss of the golden years when she delighted in the rays of her father's love, a place lost to the five-year-old child by the birth of a more treasured sibling, a brother. Family life—its fragile potential for transcendence and its common brutality—is evoked here with a richness unmatched elsewhere in the text.

Unanswered questions and clues that appear in the early part of the narrative lead back to and are explained by the Polish childhood; similarly, foreshadowings in that childhood are brought to fulfillment in the beginning of the narrative, the end of Franziska's life. Whether it is the elderly wife of Jack Manahan demanding eggs imperiously, or the "Princess" pet name applied to the young Franziska, the clues and foreshadowings are so dense that it is difficult to know whether the assumption of the Grand Duchess's identity is a deliberate deception. The mystery and fragility of identity itself is the core of the novel, a core that refuses to surrender all its secrets in several journeys back and forth through the text and the life. In its ability to surprise to the last page, and in the mysteries it exposes but cannot explain, *The Pretender,* as does all of Morrissy's work, invites several readings.

The Pretender, as were Mary Morrissy's earlier works, was well received in Ireland and Britain. It was nominated, though not short-listed, for the 2002 International IMPAC Dublin Literary Award. It has been translated and published in The Netherlands, Sweden, Germany, and Poland but has not been published in the United States. This omission is a disappointment and surprise to Morrissy, who expected the subject to be of more interest in the United States. She left *The Irish Times* in 2001 to engage fully in conducting writing workshops as well as her own writing.

Interviews:

Eileen Battersby, "Still Waters," *Image Magazine* (February 1996): 28–30;

Annie Callan, "Interview," *Glimmer Train Stories,* 18 (Spring 1996): 89–103.

Julie Myerson

(2 June 1960 –)

Ann Hancock
University of the West of England, Bristol

BOOKS: *Sleepwalking* (London: Picador, 1994; New York: Doubleday, 1995);
The Touch (London: Picador, 1996; New York: Doubleday, 1996);
Me and the Fat Man (London: Fourth Estate, 1998; Hopewell, N.J.: Ecco Press, 1999);
Laura Blundy (London: Fourth Estate, 2000; New York: Riverhead, 2000).

PRODUCED SCRIPT: "Weekend Break," radio, *Fictuality,* BBC Radio 3, January 1997.

OTHER: "Maureen," in *City of Crime,* edited by David Belbin (Nottingham: Five Leaves, 1997), pp. 157–166.

SELECTED PERIODICAL PUBLICATIONS– UNCOLLECTED: "The Daddy of all Vengeance," *Observer* (London), 18 December 1994, p. 17;
"Dual Role Destiny," by Myerson and Jonathan Myerson, *Guardian,* 26 July 1995, pp. G2, G6;
"My Stepfather," *Observer* (London), 27 July 1997, p. 6;
"The Name of the Game is our Perfect Partnership," by Myerson and Myerson, *Independent* (London), 22 June 1998, pp. 10, 65;
"His Death Barely Touched Me," *Guardian,* 27 December 2000, p. 6.

Julie Myerson (photograph © Nigel Spalding; from the dust jacket for the U.S. edition of Laura Blundy, *2000)*

Julie Myerson's literary career began in the early 1990s amid considerable publicity, when she gained her first publishing contract after winning a writing competition in a popular women's magazine. She has subsequently acquired a reputation as a promising novelist with a particular talent for conveying physical experience in a frank and forthright manner not generally characteristic of contemporary British writers. The ease with which she represents sexual interactions led Ruth Padel to suggest in a 12 April 1998 review of her novel *Me and the Fat Man* (1998) in *The Independent on Sunday* (London) that she "writes about sex like an angel brought up in a brothel."

Born Julie Susan Pike on 2 June 1960 and brought up in Nottingham with two younger sisters, Amanda and Deborah, Myerson has attested in print on many occasions to traumatic experiences during her childhood. She portrays her parents as entirely mismatched. Her mother, Maritza Simpson Pike, daughter of a Hungarian Catholic mother and an English father, was only nineteen when she married the thirty-two-year-old Geoffrey Pike, a difficult and probably depressive man who owned a small plastics factory. In an 18 December 1994 article in *The Observer* (London) Myerson writes, "My parents should never have married each other and my father probably should not have married at all." Maritza Pike herself described the marriage in 1998 in her half of a pair of mother-daughter interviews with Ann McFerran as a "huge mistake" and seems to have entered into it largely because her father approved of the match. Although Myerson described her early years in a 19 April 1998 interview for *The Independent on Sunday* (London) as "very secure and normal," she was as a child well aware of the unhappiness of her parents' marriage, which manifested itself in fights, leading to broken plates and bruises on her mother's legs. Having a buoyant and optimistic personality, Myerson writes joyous reminiscences of summer holidays in Southwold and happy times with her sisters, but they are always juxtaposed with accounts of a home dominated by anger.

Myerson's initial interest in books came from her mother, as did her confidence. She told McFerran, "My mother is probably why I'm writing today. . . . What she gave us—which is probably the best gift you can give a child—was to make us think that anything was possible." At the age of nine she had decided that she wanted to be a writer and regularly wrote stories and poems. She entered competitions and sent work to publishers and established writers, among them Daphne du Maurier, whose *My Cousin Rachel* (1951) Myerson cited in a 19 April 1998 article by Kim Bunce in *The Observer* (London) as the novel that has most influenced her. At thirteen Myerson wrote to du Maurier about her desire to be an author and received half a dozen letters of encouragement from the reclusive writer.

In the summer of 1972 Myerson's parents abruptly separated when Maritza Pike left one night with the pets and half of everything commonly owned, later returning to collect the children. The escape had been carefully planned and was brought about in part by her mother's falling in love with another man, with whom they all went to live. As a consequence, Myerson's father became consumed by bitterness and hatred for his former wife, emotions that were played out before Julie and her sisters on their fortnightly visits. The visits were dominated by deprivation—no heat in the bedrooms or replacement of furniture his wife had taken with her—and bizarre injunctions not to mention their mother, her new partner, or his sons. She recalls in *The Guardian* (27 December 2000) that "There were so many rules, I was sometimes almost sick trying to remember them."

Myerson's fragile relationship with her father, in which she was constantly anxious for approval and affection she did not receive, halted when she was sixteen. She had been attending Nottingham High School for Girls and hoped to enter the sixth form, but her father wanted her to leave, though he was required to pay school fees until his daughters were eighteen. After her mother took her father to court for the money, the link with Myerson was broken, when her father wrote to say that he had been advised he should no longer see his daughters. Myerson's need for paternal love seems to have been answered by her stepfather, a genial and warm man—"I felt so fathered by Uncle Ray," she writes in a 27 July 1997 article in *The Observer* (London)—but his desertion of her mother some years later left a residue of pain about fathers. Her relationship with her mother, however, was always a close one. In her teens Myerson thought her a heroine whom she worshiped but perhaps found it difficult to live up to.

Myerson was a fervent reader throughout her teens and did well at school. Bunty Cardwell, her English teacher at Nottingham High School, described her in *The Guardian* (14 April 1998) as a "good, quiet, clever girl." After successfully completing her A levels, she stayed on at school for a term to apply for entry to Oxford or Cambridge university and then spent the remainder of 1979 as a nanny in Florence, looking after a three-year-old boy in an affluent Italian home. Afterward she attended Bristol University, the first person in her family to enter higher education, studying for a B.A. degree in English. There she was much influenced by her tutor, Roy Littlewood, to whom she had sent some of her poems. She graduated in 1982.

From 1983 until 1987 Myerson worked at the National Theatre, first in the press office, then as a publicist, but throughout that period she continued to foster a long-held ambition to write. In 1983 she was runner-up in a writing competition in *Vogue*. In 1987 she met the writer and director Jonathan Myerson, who was working as an assistant director at the National Theatre, and, having set up housekeeping with him in South London, she left the theater to work as press officer for Walker Books. Their first child, Jacob, was born in 1989; their second, Chloë, was born on New Year's Day 1991; and their third child, Raphael, was born in 1992. Myerson attempted reconciliation with her father when she first became a mother, on her partner's advice, but his polite indifference merely confirmed Myerson's sense of rejection; she remarks in the December 2000 article in *The Guardian* that "He was like a teacher tolerating a former pupil he'd never much liked or admired."

By a strange coincidence, on the very day of Chloë's birth, Geoffrey Pike killed himself. Although shocked, Myerson claims not to have been profoundly affected by the death of a man she did not love and who had renounced his role as father. However, his death did lead to major changes in her life. First, she changed her name by deed poll from Pike to Myerson, so that she no longer had the name of her father but shared a name with her children. She and Jonathan did not formally marry, but the change of name seemed to mark her now settled life. She remarks, in an article co-written with her partner that was published in the 22 June 1998 issue of *The Independent* (London), "I never felt happy when I was Julie Pike, but everything started to fit into place when I became Julie Myerson." More significantly, it was at this point that Myerson began work on the novel she had been contemplating for many years, which includes many autobiographical elements and focuses on the suicide of an estranged father. An extract from the novel, *Sleepwalking* (1994), won a competition in the magazine *Elle* in 1992, an event that launched her literary career. Her work attracted interest from several agents and publishers, finally being published by Picador in 1994, though the rights were also sold in the United States and Germany, and it was published in those countries the following year.

Sleepwalking was promoted with reference to the parallels between the novel and events in Myerson's life, guaranteeing press attention. Its main narrator, Susan, is a heavily pregnant woman dealing, in a rather somnambulistic way, with emotionally challenging circumstances: the death of her father and his frightening appearances to her in the form of a ghostly child, the decline of her marriage, and her absorption in a passionate affair. Myerson bravely confounds taboo by writing in intimate detail about the practicalities of sex when pregnant, to such a degree that, she reported in an on-line discussion sponsored by *The Guardian* in June 2000, a male publisher who wished to publish the novel asked if Susan could be made "a little less pregnant" in the scenes with her lover.

Although there is a great deal going on in Susan's life—she has ambitions as a painter, as well as managing her relationships, working in an office, and preparing for childbirth—paradoxically, it is the past that has the greatest resonance in the novel. Queenie and Douglas, Susan's grandmother and father, are far more vivid on the page than Susan, her husband, Alistair, or her lover, Lenny. The sheer hatred, selfishness, and vindictiveness of the "dead" characters are minutely represented in the many sections of narrative that chart their lives. Through juxtaposed passages Myerson contrasts the mean-spirited heartlessness of Queenie with the erotic fulfillment of Susan. A scene in which Lenny and Susan openly express their desire for each other is followed by an account of Queenie's disastrous wedding night, which solidifies her sexual disgust and hatred for her husband. A little later in the novel, when she discovers her husband, George's, adultery, Queenie's loathing is forcefully expressed: "Her eyes had the hot lithe look of a person who'd truly like to slice another's skull wide open and spill the gristly,

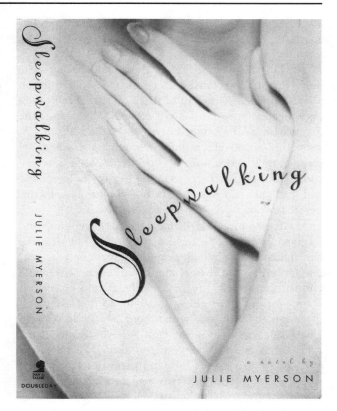

Dust jacket for the 1995 U.S. edition of Myerson's 1994 novel, a semi-autobiographical work about a woman in the late stages of pregnancy (Richland County Public Library)

sticky contents over their knees." When the young Susan and her even younger sisters visit their grandmother and are given homemade flapjacks containing pins, it does not seem merely a symptom of Queenie's senility that she should respond with calm, "almost smiling," to the children's pain and bewilderment. While the present-day sections of the narrative have Susan as first-person narrator, those dealing with Queenie's early life and Douglas's upbringing are related in a detached third-person narrative that intensifies the coldness of two generations of parents.

The death of her hated father—a "cruel and pathetic sort of man"—precipitates Susan into a painful reevaluation of her life, as she finds herself drawn into a new sexual relationship in the last weeks of pregnancy; for "when you make your own death as he did, you deliberately stir the black silt on the bottom." Memories of Susan's father are recalled that tally closely with Myerson's accounts of her relationship with her own father. Susan has always been living someone else's life—her father's as a child, her husband's, even Lenny's—and toward the end of the novel, during a weekend away with Alistair and their young baby, she is briefly tempted to commit suicide because she has lost all sense of who she is: "I don't feel like a mother anymore, nor anyone's wife or lover. I don't feel like anyone. I've been waiting to do this since I don't know when. I'm still waiting." The ghost child has become more threatening, causing her terror; her attempts to love her husband are half-hearted, and she has broken up with Lenny for the sake of the baby. She resists the urge to jump off a bridge but vows to leave Alistair. At the end of the novel it is unclear whether she will follow through on that decision, but in a dream Susan is reconciled with her father. By merging her father as a child with Jack, her son, she empathizes with her father's distress: "my poor, poor father, who had no love."

Myerson has stated that such understanding and forgiveness did not occur in her own life. The death of her father had an enduring, negative effect on his rejected family. In a final attempt to exert power and punish his former wife and his daughters, he left his entire fortune, around £400,000, to his youngest daughter, the only one with whom he was in contact. The result was a rift in the family; Myerson no longer communicates with her youngest sister. These consequences are dramatized fully in the novel when Penny, the younger of Susan's two sisters, excludes herself from the family after inheriting all of Douglas's money and making it clear that she does not intend to share it. Although her father withheld an inheritance from her, the novel in which Myerson attempted to come to terms with her father's behavior earned her the means to concentrate full-time on writing.

Many reviewers were impressed by Myerson's literary debut and thought she showed promise. An unsigned 20 August 1995 review in *The Observer* (London) called it "an impressive, affecting debut." The novel was short-listed for the Llewelyn Rhys Memorial Prize. Praise was given for the controlled writing, the fluency and seriousness of the narrative, and its affecting emotional intensity. Some critics, such as Valerie Grove, in her 22 October 1994 review in *The Times* (London), believed, however, that Myerson had been indiscreet in revealing so much autobiographical material to newspapers. At best such information could distract attention from the novel itself, at worst appear to be a cynical marketing ploy. The question arose over whether Myerson was genuinely a new literary talent or merely a woman making cathartic use of tragic personal experiences.

Having produced a successful first novel, Myerson turned also to journalism, writing a column for *The Independent* (London) from 1994 to 1996 and working for most of the major British newspapers and women's magazines, including *Vogue* and *Elle*. Her column in *The Independent* (London) provoked Mary Loudon, reviewing her second novel, *The Touch* (1996), in the 20 April

1996 issue of *The Times* (London), to skepticism, finding the newspaper writing "so smug and imaginatively thin that I found it hard to believe the same woman could produce a novel worth reading." In publishing a second novel Myerson had a reputation to live up to, with respect to those readers who had been impressed with her skills as a novelist, and perhaps one to live down, with respect to readers who were unimpressed by her prolific, generally lightweight journalism.

A rather longer novel than *Sleepwalking*, *The Touch* comprises several intertwined narratives written in the third person. The central character is Frank Chapman, a widower in his seventies who is dominated by religious fervor and spends much of his time offering evangelical rants to any he can persuade to listen. It is not clear how the reader is intended to interpret his unconventional behavior, which borders at times on menace. While he is often represented as pathetic rather than sinister, perhaps deranged by the death of his son of leukemia when the boy was only fourteen, and rendered eccentric by living alone, there are hints of his potential for violence, which are only fully realized at the end of the novel. A great deal of the narrative concerns Frank's past: his long but unfulfilling marriage to Lola, his fraught dealings with the regular church, his encounters with possible disciples, and his memories of his son, Tommy. These sections are too many and too prolonged; the narrator dwells unnecessarily on details that are established early in the text, such as Frank's physical strength, though he is seventy years old; his big face and large features; and the nature and content of his religious ramblings.

The other central characters are Gayle; her young daughter, Kitty; Gayle's sister, Donna; and Donna's boyfriend, Will. Donna's spine twists because of muscle spasms, causing her frequent pain and immobility, though doctors can find nothing physically wrong with her. She longs for a baby but has miscarried once and has been warned by the doctor that she would be unable to carry a pregnancy to full term. Her relationship with Will is dominated by her inexplicable disability. Gayle is a nurse who is bringing up a daughter on her own and offering help where she can to her troubled sister, though Will is unaccountably hostile toward her.

The novel opens with a scene in which Frank is lying on the ground in a local park, apparently having been mugged, but actually lying in wait for Donna and her family. Having seen her on a bus, he has discovered her problem and wants to offer to heal her by a laying on of hands, the "touch" of the title. Later, a reluctant Donna is persuaded by Gayle and Will, who have been visiting Frank after his stay in the hospital and hearing his claims as a healer, to try Frank's laying

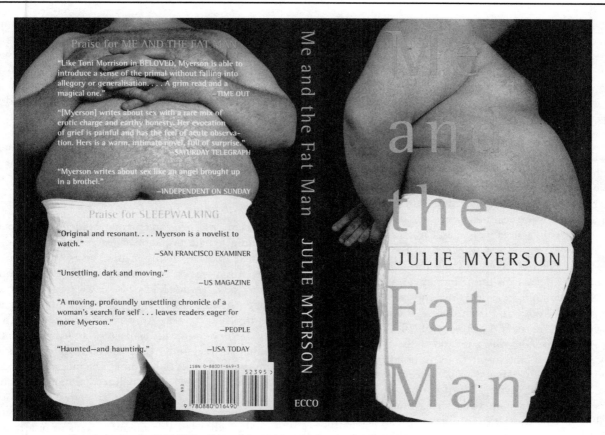

*Dust jacket for the 1999 U.S. edition of the 1998 novel that prompted one reviewer to comment that Myerson
"writes about sex like an angel brought up in a brothel" (Richland County Public Library)*

on of hands, and miraculously she is cured. Through gratitude and pity, the family incorporate Frank, albeit in a limited way, into their lives.

The slow and subtle changes Donna's new freedom of movement makes to her relationship with Will are carefully conveyed by Myerson. The relationship gradually loses its way, and Will finds himself in love with Gayle, at the point when Donna reveals that she is pregnant. The narrative seems to be drawing to a satisfactory conclusion when it becomes clear that Donna now has the prospect of what she most wants, a baby, and is unconcerned about Will's relationship with Gayle. In the closing pages, however, as Will paces the streets late at night, anxious about his future, he meets Frank, who attacks him viciously with Donna's walking stick, donated to him after her cure, and leaves him for dead. Frank's sudden extreme violence brings about a dramatic finale, but one insufficiently motivated. Frank's initial interest in Donna is explained by his belief that she looks like his lost son, and his desire to be accepted by her family is plausible. Their gradual withdrawal from him, however, does not seem marked enough to provoke such a devastating end. On the whole it is a bleak and macabre novel.

There are many minor characters in *The Touch*—Simon (Gayle and Donna's brother), Annie, Sarka, and Betty—who tend to distract from the core plot, as well as some gratuitous sex and violence. Annie is killed on her moped; Simon harbors incestuous desires toward Gayle; Frank may have murdered his brother when they were small children; and Gayle's child is conceived in a bondage session with her boyfriend, Harry, that is tantamount to rape.

Reviews were mixed, with criticism and praise equally served. Myerson was credited with powers of observation and an understanding of the workings of contemporary relationships. The intense physicality of her writing was generally appreciated. In an 11 May 1997 review for *The Observer* (London) Bunce found "perversity and brilliance" in this "captivating" novel that "has to be read in one sitting." There were, however, some disparaging comments. A few reviewers identified a lack of direction and conviction in the novel. In a 12 May 1996 review for *The Sunday Times* (London) Tom Deveson suggested that episodes were "merely aggregated together" rather than making a "coherent fiction." Accusations of self-indulgence were leveled at Myerson, reflected perhaps in what was perceived as the excessive self-absorption of her lonely characters. Responses might be summarized by an assertion by James Walton in *The Daily Telegraph* (London)–quoted by Harvey Porlock in a "review of reviews" in *The Sunday Times* (London) of 5 May 1996–that Myerson is "a skillful writer who has yet to find a way of being a skillful novelist."

In the late 1990s Myerson experimented briefly with the short-story form, taking part in two innovative writing events. She contributed "Weekend Break" to a Radio 3 series, *Fictuality,* in late January 1997, in which writers were asked to produce short stories based on an interaction between real news events and fictional characters. Myerson's story was about a couple's relationship deteriorating over a weekend in Jerusalem when an Israeli soldier is taken hostage by Palestinians and his mother appears on the television to appeal for his life. The monologue, read by the actress Harriet Walters, received praise from the radio critic Sue Gaisford in the 2 February 1997 issue of *The Independent on Sunday* (London) for the subtlety of the writing. The story was no doubt inspired by a holiday Myerson mentions in a 20 August 2000 interview with Ann McFerran in *The Sunday Times* (London), in which she refers to a visit she made with her partner to Jerusalem in 1996 as "the most extraordinary experience of my life." Myerson was one of four writers who were commissioned to write stories on the theme of "cold" for an evening of "Cold Short Stories." For the event, held at the Purcell Room on the South Bank in London, December 1998, she wrote a story titled "Mrs Pike," which remains unpublished. She has a short story in print, "Maureen," which was published in *City of Crime,* a collection of crime stories by writers from Nottingham in 1997.

Myerson's inclusion of explicit sexual content in her fiction has received much attention. Although she does not foreground sex in interviews quite to the extent that commentators have, she acknowledges that it forms an important part of her writing, especially the development of characters. In a 1998 interview with Ann Treneman for *The Independent on Sunday* (London) Myerson said, "To me, sex is a very obvious way into a character. I think sex is all about personality. . . . I want to write the way I think it is. I try to write about it without clichés. I try to be truthful." Later, during the June 2000 on-line discussion hosted by *The Guardian Unlimited,* she again emphasized her intention to represent sexual behavior without euphemism or fantasy: "I just try to write about sex as I truly perceive (or sometimes, let's face it, imagine) it to be–i.e. wonderful, terrifying, and with all the bodily fluids, the mess, the uncertainty, the no going backness, etc."

Published in 1998, *Me and the Fat Man* begins with a scene in which the protagonist performs oral sex for money, which confirms Myerson's preoccupation with unadorned description: "The rubbery odour hid the fish stink of his cock, a smell which'd lodge in the rough, screwy hairs at the base. I'd learned to hold my breath and turn my imagination off while doing it." In *Me and the Fat Man* the protagonist, Amy, devoid of love and emotionally numbed in a dead marriage, makes extra money by picking up men in the Garden for the Blind and taking them to a nearby room for brief sexual acts that are graphically and unpleasantly described on many occasions in the novel.

As in *The Touch,* an enigmatic older man seeks out the young female protagonist for reasons not entirely explained. Harris, in his sixties, visits the restaurant where Amy works as a waitress. He knew Amy's mother, Jody, a wild child who ran away to Greece as a teenager, giving birth to an illegitimate daughter and later drowning at sea. Amy has been brought up by unsatisfactory, mean foster parents and remembers little of her six years in Greece, so is drawn to Harris and to the stories he tells of her past. The fat man of the title is Gary, the manager of a small second-hand bookshop. He is supposedly Harris's lodger and surrogate son, whom Harris wants Amy to meet. Harris is a controlling figure whose benign manner seems to hide sinister intent. He obviously has plans for Gary and Amy, which are thwarted when the couple fall in love and have a child, Jimmy, threatening his dominance over them. As Gary becomes increasingly uneasy about Harris and reveals information at odds with what Amy has been told, the narrative changes gear.

The happiness of Gary and Amy and their joy in their son is shattered when Jimmy dies mysteriously in his pram while Harris is minding him. Amy and Gary are distraught, and in desperation Amy steals her baby's body from the hospital to take him in a carryall on a difficult journey to Eknos, where she was born. When she eventually arrives, having narrowly escaped being raped by her taxi driver, she finds Gary is already there and learns some more of the truth about her mother and Harris. Harris was the father of Jody's son, Amy's baby brother, a child Amy dimly remembers. Jody murdered the child and then killed herself, which locates Harris's search for Amy in revenge rather than love. Curiously, Harris fades from the story at the end. Although Gary and Amy fear that he will follow them to Greece, he does not appear, and his relationships with both Gary and Amy remain undeveloped. Amy and Gary are left finding a burial place for their son, after Gary has confessed, rather implausibly, that he is Greek, an identity that has hardly been hinted at earlier.

Everything is told from Amy's extremely limited point of view, allowing secrets to be withheld and mystery to develop. Yet, the thriller element of the novel lacks real suspense, and the unraveled complications in the end are redundant. Where the novel excels is in the delicate unfolding of the love affair between Amy and the sympathetically portrayed Gary, whose warmth and bulk allow Amy to come to life. As is the case in the previous two novels, *Me and the Fat Man* includes well-written passages and continues to explore what have become Myerson's major themes: emotional isolation and loss, the nature of motherhood, the presence of the past, and dark fears. In unpublished 26 June 2001 correspondence with Ann Hancock, she acknowledged that fear is a prime motivation for her writing: "I write about what frightens me. It's like peeking over into the abyss—but from a safe place."

The novel was more favorably received than *The Touch* had been, with Alex O'Connel, a reviewer for *The Guardian* (1 January 1998), announcing it in a list of 1998 "books to watch" as her return "to top form." Many reviewers applauded the sensitive portrayal of the love story and the vibrant immediacy of characters and situation. Reviewing the U.S. edition for *The New York Times* (6 June 1999), Deborah Weisgall remarked that Myerson "writes with consummate control, and her spare, lyrical language gives the novel its immediacy." Flaws were found in what the reviewer for *The Times* (London) in a 26 March 1998 review called the "sluggish and predictable" ending and in the lack of perspective given to the self-pitying, "whiny" Amy that threatens to distance the reader and prevent any genuine insight into her predicament. Padel, however, expressed considerable enthusiasm in her 12 April 1998 review in *The Independent on Sunday* (London) for this "sharp, original and vivid" novel.

Alongside her work as a novelist, Myerson has continued to write for newspapers and magazines and has appeared on the BBC Radio 4 arts program *Front Row*. She has been a book reviewer, a restaurant critic, and a regular columnist for the "Parents' Page" in *The Guardian*. Much of her journalism concerns her family. She has, for example, written several pieces with Jonathan Myerson about the problems of parenting three young children. They describe how their attempts at equal parenting have resulted in a traditional division of labor. In her half of a 26 July 1995 article co-authored with her partner for *The Guardian* she writes, "On an hour for hour, job for job basis we're equal, but still we've managed to end up providing exactly what we got from our respective 'old style' parents." Such writing is chatty, intimate, confessional

Dust jacket for the U.S. edition of Myerson's 2000 novel, in which the title character undergoes a long series of misfortunes in Victorian London (Richland County Public Library)

in style, revealing detailed information about the lifestyle and experiences of the family.

With *Laura Blundy* (2000) Myerson embarked on an ambitious project. The novel, set in Victorian London, is a first-person narrative told in nonsequential fragments by a protagonist whose life experiences would seem to cast her in melodrama. Orphaned at fifteen and left alone on the streets, Laura is soon raped, becomes pregnant, and is forced by her poverty to give up her newborn son to the foundling hospital; she is later unjustly jailed for killing a child in her care, then knocked down by a carriage, an accident necessitating the amputation of a leg. The surgeon, Ewan, who performs the gruesome operation, wants to marry Laura, and she agrees, though without enthusiasm. Her misery leads her to attempt suicide by jumping in the river, but Laura is saved from drowning by Billy, fifteen years younger than she is and married with five children. Passionately in love with Billy, Laura tries to leave Ewan but when he threatens Billy, she murders him, and Laura and Billy have to dispose of the body, a task that proves hazardous and problematic. Laura is not, however, a stereotypical, passive heroine, and Myerson claimed in *The Guardian* on-line chat that she wanted to avoid the "easy-on-the-eye history" of bland Victorian re-creation. She was inspired by photographs of London before the sewers and the underground were built, and she tries to reproduce life on the streets by the river without sanitizing it—everything "awkward, smelly, inept and skewed"—and with conversation that sounds natural without being anachronistic.

The novel is not for the squeamish reader, as it contains many lengthy episodes of violence, suffering, and squalor. Its opening pages shock and compel, as Laura carries out a horrifying murder with the same strange, child-like detachment characteristic of Amy in *Me and the Fat Man*. The death of Ewan occurs chronologically near the end of Laura's life story but is placed to good effect as the reader's introduction to the character. The process of killing is depicted by Myerson with uncompromising vigor: "At the first blow I felt a soft smashing, a caving-in of bone and brain. A slosh of blood came straight out, hit the wall beneath the dado which had just been done in a creamy color. Jam and cream. . . . I got his face—felt the bone that held his nose in place crunch like sugar. . . . Ewan was on the floor and he was crying like a baby animal. It was a snouty, fumbling noise. I hit him hard with my crutch."

Just before Laura attacks him with a bronze and marble ornament shaped like a spaniel, Ewan tells her that she is not a "level person" but a "strange woman." Throughout the novel the reader has to puzzle over Laura, as with Frank in *The Touch*, trying to determine whether she is psychotic or just desperate with maternal grief; the loss of her baby pervades the narrative. Certainly, she is a far more endearing character than Frank Chapman, despite her actions. Her amoral behavior has an innocence that almost gives her immunity from blame, and her status as traumatized victim in a male-dominated world is assured by the catalogue of mistreatment she has endured.

The raw physical details are riveting and unsettling: Laura's difficult survival on the street, the barbaric amputation, and Laura's enthusiastic amateur dismemberment of Ewan's body with his own surgical implements prior to packing the parts into bags for disposal in the river. Myerson follows through in full the practical consequences of murder. Ewan's head refuses to sink and has to be burned on the bank, but even then destruction proves difficult:

"The flesh does not burn to ashes as you might think. It stays like charred meat, like pork that is a little overdone. The sockets of his eyes are almost empty but seem to stare all the more for being so. His teeth are coated in shiny brown from the smoke and the fat." Some of the sexual scenes are similarly disturbing. When Laura tells Ewan that she was raped at the age of fifteen, he is aroused rather than horrified by details of her story and virtually reproduces the actions of the rapist: "Ewan gasped as he heard this, but I deduced it was a gasp of pleasure more than sympathy." In the on-line chat Myerson expressed her disappointment with those writers who are "coy about sex," among them many contemporary British women writers. In *Laura Blundy,* Myerson offers further provocative insights into the complexities of sexual response and behavior.

The dominant mood of the novel is despair, though there is something positive to be found in the strong attachment between Billy and Laura. Gradually, the two lovers become inseparable, as Billy fills the role of both sexual partner and lost child, making their relationship almost incestuous. Hints are offered that Billy could actually have been her son. He was at the foundling hospital at the right time, and the officials who told Laura of the death of her son, Jack, might have confused their records. Billy seems to embody what Laura has searched for all her adult life. Myerson avoids reinforcement of such a conclusion, however, by opting for a rather different and risky ending to the novel. In the final chapter Laura and Billy take the train to Folkestone, intending to run away together to France. Laura, however, seems to be losing substance: "Billy holds my hand. Holds it, but. But I am fading fast. Can barely feel his touch." At this point the reader might recall an earlier incident in the novel, when Billy tells Laura that his daughter Pinny had seen the grave of someone named Laura Blundy in a cemetery near London Bridge. Laura's panicky reaction to the news suggests that there is a mystery to be solved. When she begins to take on ghostly form, the reader's suspicions are confirmed. Laura soon tells the reader that she did in fact drown, that she was not rescued by Billy, did not murder Ewan. With this ending Myerson probably achieves what she had hoped for in terms of reader response: she remarked in the on-line chat that "I wanted the reader to be unsettled, confused, to have the rug pulled from under their feet a little." The effect is, however, also to undermine what is remarkable about the novel. Laura loses the identity that has been so carefully built up, and the reader is left bewildered.

Laura Blundy is Myerson's most critically successful novel. A minority thought the novel more melodrama than horror and questioned the authenticity of the dialogue, but the overwhelming response was that Myerson had produced an unusual and powerful fiction. Laura was regarded as convincing and intriguing, what E. Jane Dickson described in a 30 December 2000 review in *The Times* (London) as a "burningly original heroine." The strangeness of plot and character and Myerson's imaginative focus on the sensory, with what Alex Clark in his review in *The Guardian* (8 April 2000) termed her "exceptionally subtle understanding of the macabre and the desperate," made the novel haunting reading for many. She may still have a problem with endings that seem to be an easy way out, but *Laura Blundy* was pronounced "an accomplished novel" by Elizabeth Buchan in a 15 April 2000 review for *The Times* (London), with what Isobel Montgomery called in her 17 February 2001 review for *The Guardian* an "historical fiction with the comfort blanket of nostalgia pulled off."

Myerson specializes in confronting ideas often regarded as distasteful in British literature, particularly in respect to sexual mores: sex with amputees, obese or pregnant partners, rape, incest. She also explores common fears and anxieties, many of them her own. In *Laura Blundy,* for example, the heroine drowns, though Myerson herself is terrified of deep water. She remarks in a 24 May 1998 article in *The Observer* (London) that she is "still haunted by the idea of all that cold, heavy darkness, the tight, black panic of not seeing, of fighting for breath." Emotional and physical violence are prevalent in her writing, but Myerson denies the reader a comfortable identification of oppressor and victim. Openness to difficult subjects and exposure of vulnerabilities is perhaps a mark of Myerson's assurance as a writer. She has never doubted her vocation and asserted to Hancock that she has an "amazing confidence about writing," a belief that she has the ability to do it well. With her novels Myerson has established a territory of her own; what Stephanie Merritt noted in her 9 April 2000 review of *Laura Blundy* for *The Observer* (London) of the protagonists of her novels could be applied equally well to Myerson herself: "she has the same frankness, the same unsettling ability to describe the baser side of life, unselfconsciously and without squeamishness, oblivious to the unspoken rule that femininity means pretending not to notice the brutal and the disgusting."

Interviews:

Marianne Brace, "Sex and the Pregnant Wife," *Guardian,* 12 September 1994, pp. G2, G11;

Ann Treneman, "Julie Myerson–She's Not Quite Normal," *Independent on Sunday* (London), 19 April 1998;

Ann McFerran, "Maritza Simpson and Julie Myerson," *Motherland: Interviews with Mothers and Daughters* (London: Virago, 1998), pp. 162–180;

"Transcript: Julie Myerson live online," *Guardian Unlimited,* 29 June 2000 <http://www.guardian.co.uk/liveonline/story/0,6999,338339,00.html>.

Jeff Noon

(24 November 1957 –   )

David Ian Paddy
Whittier College

BOOKS: *Woundings* (Birmingham, U.K.: Oberon, 1986);

Vurt (Poynton, Manchester: Ringpull, 1993; New York: Crown, 1995);

Pollen (Poynton, Manchester: Ringpull, 1995; New York: Crown, 1996);

Automated Alice, illustrated by Harry Trumbore (New York: Crown, 1996; London: Doubleday, 1996);

Nymphomation (London & New York: Doubleday, 1997);

Pixel Juice: Stories from the Avant Pulp (London & New York: Doubleday, 1998);

Needle in the Groove (London: Anchor, 2000);

Cobralingus: Metamorphiction, illustrated by Daniel Allington; introduction by Michael Bracewell (Hove, U.K.: Codex, 2001);

Falling Out of Cars (London: Doubleday, 2002).

PLAY PRODUCTIONS: *Woundings,* Manchester, Royal Exchange Theatre, 1986;

Vurt, adapted by Noon from his novel of that title, Manchester, Contact Theatre, May 2000.

OTHER: "DJNA," in *Disco Biscuits,* edited by Sarah Champion (London: Hodder & Stoughton, 1997), pp. 171–187;

"Latitude 52," in *Intoxication: An Anthology of Stimulant-Based Writing,* edited by Toni Davidson (London: Serpent's Tail, 1998), pp. 1–23.

SELECTED PERIODICAL PUBLICATIONS–
UNCOLLECTED: "How I Write," *Times* (London), 2 October 1999, Metro section, p. 23;

"Film makers use jump cuts, freeze frames, slow motion. musicians remix, scratch, sample. Can't we writers have some fun as well?" *Guardian,* 10 January 2001, p. 15.

Jeff Noon has been described, according to Sean Coughlan in a 6 May 2000 interview in *The Times* (London), as a "cyberpunk, an acid-house novelist, a cult science fiction writer, rave author, and, at different stages,

*Jeff Noon (from the dust jacket for the
U.S. edition of* Pollen, *1996)*

he's been bracketed alongside writers as diverse as Irvine Welsh, J. G. Ballard, and Lewis Carroll." Noon has referred to his own writing as "Avant Pulp" and "Meta-morphiction." Resisting easy categorization, Noon's writing is exploratory–constructing strange, alternative realities in a language that emulates the mood and sound of contemporary underground music. Over the course of several novels and short-story collections, Noon has tried to reinvent himself with each new project. Initially labeled a science-fiction writer, Noon fears being pigeonholed and has stated that he does not want to feel constrained by any particular genre or style of writing, telling Bethan Roberts in a 1996 interview with the on-line journal *Spike Magazine,* "writers don't choose the labels, we just live them."

Writing at the "edges of science fiction," as Noon expressed it in an interview with Polly Marshall for *Interzone* (April 1999), Noon explores hallucinatory worlds of the near future where inner visions become external realities that are sometimes beautiful, sometimes nightmarish. He is also a postmodernist whose characters' identities are fluid and multiple and whose works explore the complex relationship of language and reality. His "Avant Pulp" fiction aims to be avant-garde and populist at the same time. It is plot driven, moving at a quick pace, but it is also linguistically and stylistically innovative. Merging science fiction and postmodernism, Noon is interested in the worlds that language can create. When Caroline Griffin asked, during a 1996 interview for the *Pure Fiction* website, where he saw himself in relation to such writers as Welsh, Noon responded that he saw his generation "trying to capture the rhythms of speech. And also a lot of us are trying to experiment more with language. One of the things I'm trying to do is bridge the gaps." By bridging the gaps, Noon means the modernist divide of high and low cultures, of difficult, experimental writing and accessible, plot-focused works: "I always wondered why isn't somebody writing American crime novels using the same techniques as James Joyce—try to imagine Raymond Chandler's version of *Ulysses* [1922]. That's maybe what I'm trying to hedge towards one day. Basically there are a lot of experimental things, sentences and words, but it's got to be a great story that you can't put down." Noon told Roberts in their 1996 interview, "I do want to be a popular writer whilst still satisfying my love for James Joyce and [Laurence Sterne's] *Tristram Shandy* [1759–1767]." Such a merger has manifested itself in Noon's dub or remix fiction, which adapts the techniques of electronic dance music to produce experimental writing.

Place is also deeply significant in Noon's fiction. Although he moved to Brighton in 1999, he is usually regarded as the writer who put Manchester on the contemporary literary map. Noon's Manchester is an archetype of the postindustrial British north, where postwar dreams of progress faltered in abandoned warehouses and bleak housing estates. As a former painter and punk musician, Noon has also drawn attention to the artists and musicians who have emerged from the city, praising bands such as Joy Division who expressed their desperate environment in sound. To him, punk and rave music provide hope. In the majority of his work Noon gives prominence to a dark urban landscape, but he sees his work as optimistic about the future, with imagination and the music of language offering a means of rescue from this grim world of postindustrial despair. As Alasdair Gray does for Glasgow, Noon transforms Manchester into an imaginary realm where despairing souls must find paths to transcendence.

Noon was born 24 November 1957 to James Noon, a presser, and Lilian (née Pearson) Noon, a clothing machinist, in Droylsden, just east of Manchester. About Droylsden he has said in "Biography," a piece posted on the www.jeffnoon.com website, "Definitely not the sort of place to grow up artistic in those days, unless (a) you don't mind getting beaten up and (b) you've got serious plans to escape." Noon was later raised in Ashton-under-Lyne. He describes his youth as a "classic writer's childhood, in the sense that I retreated into myself, built my own inner world, threw away the key." At a young age he developed a talent for painting and was exposed early on to modernist and Surrealist painters such as Pablo Picasso and Salvador Dali. This artistic perspective shaped Noon's narrative style, since his understanding of Cubism and Surrealism opened his imagination to writing that need not be linear or realistic. While he was studying for his A-level exams in art, he joined together with other students to form a group called "Stand and Deliver." In "Biography," Noon says this group "would go round pubs in the area, putting on little shows—music, comedy, poetry, etc. This is when I got hold of the mad idea of actually being serious about writing." He also played with a punk group called Manicured Noise. Noon continues to be aware of current musical forms and has said that music is essential to his writing process. In an article published in the 2 October 1999 issue of *The Times* (London), "How I Write," he states, "If I couldn't listen to music, I wouldn't be able to write. It feeds into my work." It is significant that throughout his career Noon has been received more openly by the British underground music press than by the British literary press.

After years of doing various jobs, Noon went on to Manchester University. From 1981 to 1984 he studied Combined Arts (Painting and Drama). In 1984, in an art show called Northern Young Contemporaries, Noon exhibited a painting that fused images with storytelling. That same year he gave up painting and music to focus on the art of playwriting, getting involved with the fringe theater scene in Manchester. After he graduated from university, Noon wrote a play titled *Woundings,* a draft of which he submitted to the Mobil Playwriting Competition. To his surprise, he won third prize. As part of the prize, *Woundings* was produced at the Royal Exchange Theatre in Manchester in 1986. Noon also became a writer-in-residence. The play was later produced at the Royal Academy of Dramatic Art in 1987 and Leicester Polytechnic in 1988, and in 1998 was made into a movie, adapted by Roberta Handley, who directed.

Set on a South Atlantic island where British soldiers are stationed, the play is clearly about the Falklands War. The conflict on this island, however, becomes a battle of sex and gender, as the male soldiers await the British government's shipment of volunteer women—"Roses of England"—whose duty to the nation is one of alleviating the pressures of war for the bored soldiers. Noon uses the backdrop of the war as a means to show how gender, sex, violence, war, and nationalism interrelate. Although the play bears few of the surrealist traits of Noon's later work, it does feature a few interludes that satirize advertising, which anticipate similar parodies found in his novels.

After the writing and production of *Woundings,* Noon spent years trying to write more plays but without much success. He took a job at Waterstone's bookstore in Manchester, where he worked for the next five years. A coworker, Richard Dodgson, who was a fringe theater director, asked Noon to write a play for his company. The play he set out to write became the source for his first novel, *Vurt* (1993). The play began as an adaptation of Octave Mirbeau's novel *Le Jardin des supplices* (1899; translated as *Torture Garden,* 1931), a decadent, anarchist work that explores the intersections of pain and pleasure. At the time, Noon was also inspired by emerging virtual-reality technology. Bringing these influences together, Noon imagined the idea of a garden of desire and torture existing in a virtual world. As the idea progressed, it eventually became the story of a man who enters this virtual world to rescue his lost sister, who is also his lover. Dodgson, the director who inspired Noon to write the play, left for a position in Hong Kong. Soon after this, though, another colleague at the bookstore, Steve Powell, who was starting his own publishing house, Ringpull Press, encouraged Noon to try writing a novel. Piecing together the scraps of the abandoned play, Noon crafted the novel that became his most popular work, seven years after his first success with *Woundings.* As Noon puts it in his on-line biographical statement, "I guess all those years of living inside my own head finally paid off."

After its initial publication with Ringpull Press in 1993, *Vurt* was published by Crown Publishers in the United States in 1995. An American literary agent found a copy in an English-language bookshop in Bern, Switzerland, contacted Ringpull, and sold the U.S. rights to Crown Publishers. The novel has since been translated into several languages. It won the Arthur C. Clarke Award and a Eurocon award in 1994, while Noon received the John W. Campbell Best New Writer Award for best new science-fiction writer in 1995. The Contact Theatre in London staged a theatrical production of Noon's "re-mix" of the novel in May 2000.

Rumors of a motion-picture adaptation of *Vurt* circulated for years, but nothing concrete emerged until 2002, when it was announced that Noon had begun writing the script for the movie, to be directed by Iain Softley, who directed *K-PAX* (2001).

Vurt is a fast-paced novel that depicts near-future Manchester as a dangerous urban world. Characters escape this setting by putting feathers in their mouths to enter the Vurt, a virtual fantasy world. The Vurt is like a hallucinatory movie that people navigate as they would a living video game. Unlike a drug trip, the "vurtual" world is a designed experience with a cast of characters that the user encounters after viewing trailers and credits. However, the experience is decidedly real for the user. As the novel progresses, the lines between the real and the "vurtual" become increasingly difficult to distinguish for the characters and the reader. Many reviewers regarded the novel as a British example of cyberpunk, the science-fiction movement of the 1980s and 1990s that explored near-future urban societies dominated by computer technology and contrasted high-tech computer simulations with gritty, hopeless realities. While Noon's novel does depend on a similar juxtaposition, *Vurt* is, as several critics noted, wholly organic in its imagery. It lacks the technological focus that characterizes much of the cyberpunk genre, from William Gibson's novel *Neuromancer* (1984) to the movie *The Matrix* (1999).

Vurt does share with cyberpunk a characteristic fluid reality that carries over into the construction of character and identity. The novel is populated with hybrid creatures, such as Dog People, Shadows, Robo People, and humans who have too much Vurt in them. Throughout the city, graffiti reads "Pure is poor," signaling a change in how identity is perceived in this near future world. Despite the fantastic nature of these characters, critics tended to praise *Vurt* for creating empathetic figures. Richard Gehr said in *The Village Voice Literary Supplement* (February 1995), "the novel diverges most radically from the cyberpunk template in its abundance of heart."

In addition to effective characterization, critics also noted how the novel draws attention to itself as fiction. Several reviewers, for instance, noted the mythological underpinning of the novel. This underpinning is most pronounced in the way the narrator, Scrib, and his friends try to find Scrib's sister, Desdemona, in the Vurt, echoing Orpheus's descent into the underworld to retrieve Eurydice. Noon himself notes, in an essay posted on the www.jeffnoon.com website, "Where the Stories Come From," that Joseph Campbell's *Hero with a Thousand Faces* (1949) influenced the structure of the novel. The novel also has a metafictional quality that can be seen in the many passages in which "Scribble," the narrator, interrupts the narrative to reflect on the writing of the narrative itself. Another feature of the novel that also draws attention to itself as text is the frequent appearance of the Game Cat. The Game Cat is a character who is an expert on the wide variety of legal and illegal Vurt feathers, and his words appear as intermittent chapters in the form of advice columns. Readers get their clearest understanding of the Vurt from these sections.

Many readers noted that it is not always clear what the Vurt is. For this reason, critics were divided over whether the novel succeeds as science fiction and whether it is even science fiction at all. Tom De Haven, in *The New York Times Book Review* (5 February 1995), argued that *Vurt* lacks a believable social context and as a result "it fails to convince." In his review for the British science-fiction magazine *Locus* (April 1994) Russell Letson also argued that the novel does not cohere within the genre of science fiction, primarily because it lacks rational explanations for the strange world it presents. Letson, however, did grant that *Vurt* functions well when considered as a blend of genres that relies on fantasy. Other reviewers, such as Gehr in *The Village Voice Literary Supplement,* contended that the novel should be regarded as an ironic revision of science fiction rather than a straight attempt at the genre.

Noon's first novel was reviewed widely, with frequent comparisons to Gibson's *Neuromancer,* Anthony Burgess's *A Clockwork Orange* (1962), and Carroll's *Alice's Adventures in Wonderland* (1865). The reviews raised issues and concerns that would reappear in the criticism of Noon's subsequent work. In general, critics were divided over the plot and language. For instance, David V. Barrett in *New Statesman & Society* (21 January 1994) called *Vurt* "an astonishing novel in story, style and emotion," while Hal Espen in *The New Yorker* (13 February 1995) dismissed Noon as "a woefully clumsy writer." While some readers may have desired a more crafted book, Noon has stated that he writes to explore where the writing will take him rather than fulfill a carefully designed plan, and that he is not interested in the kinds of well-written books that dominate contemporary British literature. He told Nile Southern and Mark Amerika in a 1995 interview for the website *Alt-X* that "I personally have trouble reading a well-written novel these days—I can appreciate the language, and appreciate that these are great sentences and interesting characters and so on, but by about page fifty I'm startin' to get bogged down in it, you know—because it's actually too well-written."

As Noon began working on his next book, *Pollen* (1995), he reflected critically on his first novel. In his on-line essay "Where the Stories Come From" he writes: "I look back on *Vurt* as an apprentice work, con-

Dust jacket for the U.S. edition of Noon's 1995 novel, about a future Britain stricken by a life-threatening hay-fever epidemic (Richland County Public Library)

structed out of other people's inspiration. Basically I was trying to import William Gibson into Manchester. You can see the joins. It was a book that had to be written, and I was lucky enough to be there at the time. Any number of other writers could have come up with the same basic book. But only one person could have written *Pollen*."

Pollen was published in the United Kingdom by the Ringpull Press in 1995 and published in the United States by Crown the following year. Noon's second novel is the sequel to *Vurt,* and at the time he had planned to continue the sequence as a four-volume series. As did *Vurt, Pollen* began life as an abandoned play, written before the first novel. Noon salvaged from this earlier work the idea of a hay-fever epidemic that could serve as a commentary on the new diseases and viruses that threaten humanity. Although a few minor characters from *Vurt* reappear, *Pollen,* as a sequel, is more concerned with developing the ideas and themes of the first novel, particularly the unstable conditions of reality, the complex relationship between nature and humanity, and the uses of mythology.

The novel begins as a crime story, as policewoman Sibyl Jones investigates the mysterious death of renegade cabdriver Coyote. The investigation exposes a plot involving Columbus, the head of the cab system, and characters from the Vurt. The novel explores several battles for control and freedom. Columbus seeks control of Manchester's maps, both real and "vurtual," while, in the Vurt, fertility figures John Barleycorn and Persephone try to break into the real world, thereby unleashing a lethal Pollen count. Extending the idea that the Vurt is a wonderland of all stories ever told, Noon shows his readers the plight of the mythological and folkloric characters who are condemned to being narrated when they would rather be narrators. In addition to furthering the mythological motifs of *Vurt, Pollen* also expands the cast of hybrid characters. The Dog People and Robo People of the earlier novel reappear, and *Pollen* also features Dodos, who are unaffected by Vurt feathers, zombies, and a new flower/human combination. Distancing himself further from the technological emphasis of cyberpunk, Noon uses *Pollen* to foreground humanity's relationship to nature and to explore classical themes of generation and decay, growth and harvest, and life and death.

As with *Vurt,* reviewers were torn between admiration for the wildness of Noon's imagery and language and dismay at what they regarded as the poor handling of plot and characters. Writing in *TLS: The Times Literary Supplement* (19 May 1995), Jason Cowley remarked that "the main weakness of the novel is that Noon never convinces us that the future will be like this . . . it is in the end unbelievable." Other reviewers noted, in contrast, that *Pollen* is a work of the imagination and that one either accepts or rejects it as a strange vision, not as an attempt to predict the future. Barrett, for example, in *New Statesman & Society* (18 August 1995), noted that the novel, like *Vurt,* is primarily a work of fantasy that happens to use the tropes of science fiction. Adam Mazmanian, reviewing the book for *Library Journal* (January 1996), regarded *Pollen* as a work that stemmed from a satirical rather than dystopian tradition of British literature, remarking "Who else but an ironist could imagine an England that is enslaved by its literature, poisoned by its flowers, and hated by its dogs." Noon himself commented in an interview with Eya Kuismanen and Ruud van de Kruisweg for *Albedo* (1997) that while Americans tended to view these books as science fiction, some British readers could see the books as visions of present-day Manchester, with an imaginary map superimposed:

for people who live in Manchester it's not really science fiction at all. It's a contemporary novel about what young people are up to. When I go to places like the U.S., they don't pick up on a single cultural clue at all. So to them it's pure SF. They think I made it all up.

When Noon set out to begin his third novel, he fully intended to continue the *Vurt* cycle. However, he found that it was not working. As he says in "Where the Stories Come From": "I wasn't getting into it, it felt like I was repeating myself." *Pollen* proved to be a difficult novel to write because the wild, free-flowing book was hard to control. He was looking for something more fun to write. Noon also became increasingly concerned that he was being pigeonholed as a science-fiction writer, whose style might become too predictable. In the interview for *Albedo,* Noon stated that he did not want to become a writer like Terry Pratchett, from whom readers would expect the twenty-fifth novel in the *Vurt* series. Noon wanted to extend his audience and range.

The novel that Noon began to write instead, *Automated Alice* (1996), began life as did his previous two novels, as an abandoned play. The original idea was to write an extension of Carroll's two Alice books, but as a piece of theater it proved unwieldy. When the time came for a new novel, the notion seemed ideal. Writing a book in the style of Carroll made perfect sense to Noon. Reviewers of Noon's first two novels had already noted the similarity to Carroll's works, especially in the playful use of language, the fluid relationship between imagination and reality, and the consistent use of wise, young girl figures (Twinkle in *Vurt* and Persephone in *Pollen*). Critics also noted that *Automated Alice* is a more comic novel than its predecessors that, as do Carroll's own books, suits a child's sense of joy, while probing deeper, darker themes.

Automated Alice was first published in October 1996 in the United States by Crown Publishing and the following month in the United Kingdom by Transworld Publishers, Ltd., under the Doubleday imprint. The independent Ringpull Press that gave Noon his start had gone out of business. The mainstream publisher Doubleday, however, gave Noon the opportunity to reach a wider readership and a design budget that allowed the inclusion of illustrations by Harry Trumbore. The novel sends Alice, struggling with a grammar lesson in her aunt's Victorian home, on a journey through a grandfather clock into the Manchester of the future, 1998. It is the future, though, as a Victorian fantasist might imagine it. As Noon stated in his 1996 interview with Griffin, "I wanted to take Lewis Carroll, and see what Lewis Carroll would do with the modern world, because if you think about things like relativity, quantum mechanics, and chaos theory and stuff like that, he'd love it." In the novel Noon has the southern-county Alice confront the northern oddity of Manchester, lost in the strange words of the Mancunian dialect. This encounter enables Noon to play with words as Alice mishears them, and to make the most of a myriad of puns, from Alice's encounters with the "Civil Serpents" to her research in the "librarinth." Even the title of the book, which was the first thing that came to Noon, is a pun on the title of Martin Gardner's critical edition of Carroll's Alice novels, *The Annotated Alice: Alice's Adventures in Wonderland & Through the Looking Glass* (1960).

Some critics also noted the postmodern quality of Noon's novel. Rather than a parody of the two Alice books, it is a pastiche, using Carroll's ideas and voice as points of extension, not critique. Noon also highlights the metafictional aspect of Carroll's novels. As Carroll turned young Alice Liddell into a character for his novels, Noon incorporates himself—or rather, his fictional counterpart, Zenith O'Clock—into his own novel. O'Clock tells Alice of his admiration for Carroll's novels, his love of language ("That's my desire, you see, Alice: I make play with old words, twice nightly—why, sometimes even thrice nightly!—just so they can breed new words"), and he mentions his own books, *Shurt* and *Solumn,* puns on Noon's first two titles, which have been ravaged by the Crickets. Even Alice's pursuit of her parrot, which led her into the grandfather clock, allows Noon another self-referential parody, since young Alice finds herself chasing feathers, as do the characters in Vurt. Animal/human hybrids fill the novel, and Alice's identity is cast in doubt as her doll Celia, an anagram of Alice, becomes an android-like version of herself. By the end of the novel the reader is left with three Alices: the real Alice, Alice Liddell, Carroll's inspiration; the fictional Alice, Carroll's character; and the automated Alice, Alice's robotic twin; or, as Noon puts it, the real, the unreal, and the "nureal." As Noon defines it, *nureality* is "a place where things can live halfway between reality and unreality."

As usual, critics were split over *Automated Alice,* primarily in terms of the language. While the majority of reviewers responded positively to Noon's puns, some felt the language games to be heavy handed. In an interview for the on-line journal *Cold Print* (1988), Noon was also asked whether his book fit the current trend of writing sequels to classic literary works, such as Emma Tennant's sequels to Jane Austen's novels. In his interview for *Albedo,* Noon was asked to reflect on the connection of his work to the shift in cyberpunk science fiction to Victorian settings seen, for example, in the "steampunk" of Gibson and Bruce Sterling's *The Differ-*

ence Engine (1991). In both cases, Noon observed that his goal was not a nostalgic turn to the past but an attempt to see aspects of the future in the present day. He also distanced himself further from science fiction when he told Kuismanen and van de Kruisweg in their interview for *Albedo* (1997) that he saw his writing in the tradition of Carroll and C. S. Lewis, "it is coming from a stream of the English fantasy; whimsy." He noted that imagination is foremost in his writing, which runs against the mainstream of contemporary British literature:

> You have to remember that I'm writing in England, which is not the most imaginative country in the world. Ninety-nine percent of the books that British people write are very tightly controlled middle class books about manners and marriage problems written in a very tightly controlled prose style. Which is great, we're very good at that. But when people like me come along who want to experiment with language it's quite difficult for us to get established. What I'm determined to promote is the idea that the imagination is actually a very good thing, a sexy thing.

Noon's next novel continued to explore the imagination as it extended his experimentation with language.

If *Alice* marked a break in the *Vurt* series, then Noon's next novel, *Nymphomation* (1997), marked a return. Noon's fourth novel, which was nominated for the Arthur C. Clarke Award, is a prequel to *Vurt* rather than a sequel to *Pollen.* After writing *Alice,* he went back to the abandoned draft of the book he had begun writing after *Pollen.* In that draft there was a section about a domino game that becomes a national fixation. Noon expanded this idea to create an elaborate satire of Britain's obsession with the National Lottery in the 1990s. In the novel the people of near-future Manchester watch the *AnnoDomino* television show to see if the dots that appear on Lady Cookie Luck's dress match the configuration on the domino they have bought for the week. Noon has the main characters of the novel, a group of mathematics students, seek an orderly pattern behind the seemingly chance-nature of the dominoes, using probability and chaos theories. They discover the sinister plot of The Company, which hosts the game, and how it uses "nymphomation," self-replicating information that can be used to control dreams and desire.

Nymphomation attempts to explain the origins of the Vurt as it brings together the many strands of Noon's first three novels. Even the apparent intermission of *Automated Alice* gets thrown in the mix. In "Where the Stories Come From" he states, "I'd come up with the mad idea of carrying on *Automated Alice*'s story into the future, and the two ideas came together. It became a book about the origin of *Vurt* feathers, and

Dust jacket for the U.S. edition of Noon's 1996 book, in which Lewis Carroll's best-known character is hurled into a surreal near-future Manchester and encounters her robotic twin (Richland County Public Library)

Alice's role in that creation." In *Nymphomation* there is a character named Celia Hobart, who is a young Alice-like figure, and her first name is the same as Alice's automated twin. She is also the young version of Miss Hobart, the mysterious leader of *Vurt,* and accidentally creates the Vurt feathers at the end of the prequel. Even the last line of *Nymphomation,* "The young boy puts the feather into his mouth," repeats the first line of *Vurt,* helping to unify the cycle.

After the book was finished, Noon stated in "Where the Stories Come From" that the four books "connect in weird ways, a web of connections." In interviews of the time, Noon predicted another book that would complete the series, but, in a 2000 interview with Antony Johnston for *Spike Magazine,* he has indicated that he is finished. He also noted that *Nymphomation* was a difficult book for him to write, that it was "definitely a watershed." Johnston contended that the novel feels "very self-analytical in places," almost a deconstruction, rather than an extension of *Vurt.* Noon agreed that it is a "self-conscious book," but one that was also important in his development as a writer: "I think if anybody looked back at the progression of what I've done, *Nymphomation* is definitely where things started to change."

Since *Nymphomation,* Noon has stated repeatedly that he wants to move away from overt science fiction.

Despite the otherworldliness of *Nymphomation,* there are already indications of Noon's shift from science fiction to more realistic work that also makes use of experimental language. The characters are more realistic in that there are no human/animal hybrids like those found in *Vurt* and *Pollen.* Whereas the first two novels use fantastic characters to present abstract ideas about identity, *Nymphomation* shows more concrete conflicts in identity through scenes with the Indian character Jazir Malik and the white-supremacist League of Zero. The novel is also more directly political in its satire of government and consumer culture, especially advertising. The police force and university are sponsored by the fast-food company Whoomphy MegaBurgers. The air is filled with "blurbflies," bio-mechanical creatures that spread advertising messages wherever they go. Even the formal layout of the novel includes an advertising look as blurbfly advertisements and the phrase "Play to Win" pop up on nearly every page.

Even as the characters and politics in *Nymphomation* move in a relatively more realistic direction, the language becomes more heightened and stylized. The language of the novel is fast and filled with many invented words. This linguistic inventiveness can be seen in a parody of Carroll's "Jabberwocky" (1871):

"Twas nine-ish, and the slimy hordes did clack and gamble in the wave. All dotty were the game-parades, and the telebox did crave." Noon's language also continued to divide his critics. Chris Mitchell's positive review in *Spike Magazine* (October 1997) noted that "it's Noon's overdrive prose style that carries the reader through *Nymphomation*–the author seems to be unable to get his sentences out fast enough, continually playing with and subverting his own writing, exploiting every pun, allusion and innuendo that comes to mind." Amy Mandeville, in the *New Statesman* (12 December 1997), gave a generally positive review, but concluded that Noon's use of language is too "cool" for its own good, and most likely would make the novel seem outdated quickly. Victoria Moore, also in the *New Statesman* (23 October 1998), even commented, in an article on the launch party for Noon's next project, *Pixel Juice: Stories from the Avant Pulp* (1998), that "I like listening to his voice, warm and tough as whisky. But I hate reading his words off the page; they seem as bizarre, harsh and unforgiving as dance music when you're trying to relax in a hot bath. . . ."

Nymphomation was difficult for Noon to write. When he finished, his editor at Transworld, Bill Scott Kerr, suggested that he take it easy on himself for his next project by assembling a collection of his short stories. This project eventually became *Pixel Juice*. While Noon agreed to the idea, he found himself immensely displeased as he began rereading his earlier stories. In "Juicing the Pixels," an essay posted on the www.jeff-noon.com website in which Noon discusses the process of writing the collection, he says, "I found myself shaking my head in despair. Can I really have written such rubbish?" He wondered whether he could successfully write short stories since he had become accustomed to the space of a novel, which allowed him "to go mad, to overindulge." Rather than resurrect stories he did not care much for, he decided to write a series of new stories as a way of exploring the form. At first a chance to relax, the collection became instead a major new project.

Some of the ideas that arose were new, while others were inspired by scraps and abandoned concepts from his files. "I was determined to create something that would show off all my various writing skills, a book that revelled in style, in language, in meaning." As the stories emerged, Noon also decided that he wanted some kind of pattern or arrangement for the stories. In the end Noon constructed a work of fifty short stories organized into four sections, titled "Illusion's Perfume," "Infection's Courtship," "Poison's Flightpath," and "Reflection's Embrace." The stories in each section generally move from pieces that are relatively normal to ones that are increasingly strange. The final product is

a collection that provides an introduction to the range of themes and styles that persistently preoccupy Noon. There are Borgesian fantasies, cyberpunk adventures, stories of gritty realism, tales of youth culture, a few returns to the dream universe of *Vurt,* and examples of Noon's dub fiction "re-mixes."

In "Juicing the Pixels," Noon lists two stories, "Solace" and "The Cabinet of Night Unlocked," as favorites. "Solace" concerns a boy, Nesbit, whose life is overcome by an addiction to a brand of soda, which allows the user to choose the flavor by twisting the cap. The boy creates new flavors by turning the cap just so. Noon describes this story as a "'typical' Jeff Noon story, in that it takes a mundane reality, follows the consequences of it all the way through the darkness, and ends up (in the last sentence) reaching for the stars." The story ends with an old friend, the nameless narrator, encountering Nesbit as an older man. The narrator samples one of Nesbit's obsessive mixtures and says, "Tasted like heaven, I tell you. Like heaven was washing over my tongue." Even as the story is permeated by a sense of tragedy, of a life destroyed by consumer culture, it provides an ironic ending that is reminiscent of Ballard's work.

Noon lists "The Cabinet of Night Unlocked" as a personal favorite. "If I had to choose just one example of my writing to preserve, this would be a serious contender." The story is about a medieval document that may kill the person who reads the entire text out loud. A reflection on suicide and the relationship between language and death, the story shares with "Solace" Noon's characteristic dark mood tempered in the end by an appeal to the transcendent. It is this quality that also makes Noon's work optimistic and hopeful. As Noon writes in "Juicing the Pixels": "I view my work as being essentially moral. I think that's why I'll never be 'controversial,' no matter how far down I go into the darkness, somehow or other I try to allow the narrative to pull me back out. A glimmer of hope."

The stories in *Pixel Juice* help clarify a quality present in all of Noon's works, the sense that although his characters struggle in strange, desperate environments, they manage to find release through the very strangeness of the world that was at first so alienating. *Pixel Juice* also features Noon's first full experiments in remix or dub fiction. "Dub Karaoke" is the first of four remixes and consists of a kind of poetry: "drumsoft mechanisms / endazzlements of rhythm / shimmering system." In "Juicing the Pixels," Noon describes the process of writing this piece: "What happens here, I take the 'Homo Karaoke' story, I strip it down on screen to its essential images. Break these into words, phrases, juggle them around, looking for a new hit. Start to build it up again. The phrases started to naturally fall into three-line stanzas, and it came to me that I was actually trying to write haiku, the Japanese poetry form. Then it's just a matter of getting them to work as a page, as a text, as a shimmer of meaning."

In the four remixes, language becomes fragmented and distorted, similar to the music of Dub Reggae. The concept of dub began with Jamaican producers, such as Lee "Scratch" Perry and King Tubby, who used the recording studio as an instrument, playing with the final mix of a recording. As Noon says in "Cobralingus: Origins of a Dub Fiction," a note published on the official Codex Books website for *Cobralingus: Metamorphiction* (2001), "they punched holes in the sound; they let instruments drop away, only to return at some later moment; they added sound effects to the mix. Very often the track revealed its skeleton, the bass and drums; at other times a ghost seemed to be haunting the mix. Music had become a liquid experience." Beyond writing about popular and electronic music, as he does in such stories as "Homo Karaoke" and "DJNA," Noon adopts a mode of writing from these musical sources. He has even stated in "Juicing the Pixels" that, though he cannot sing well, he thinks of his writing as an attempt to sing. Noon says, "Keep that in mind as you read my stuff, it's the real key." The experiments in dub and the attempt to create writing that sings comes to fruition in Noon's fifth novel, *Needle in the Groove* (2000), as does his desire to move toward something "more real, a bit more character-based," as he puts it in "Where the Stories Come From."

Noon surprised many of his readers when, in June 1999, he moved to Brighton. The writer who had written almost exclusively about Manchester, and who had become completely associated with that city, left. Noon had stated years before that he did not want to be seen solely as a Mancunian author, as when he remarked in his 1996 interview with Griffin that "I'd hate people to think of me as a Mancunian writer." Noon's move to Brighton expressed a desire for freedom from constraints, similar to his rejection of the label of science-fiction writer. While he found it hard to write after he first arrived, he then felt that he had fast become part of an artistic community in Brighton, which he never felt in Manchester since it was more of a musical than literary city. *Needle in the Groove* is Noon's farewell to Manchester, a novel about the postwar history of underground and popular music in that city. Even the street names are renamed for its pop stars, from Joy Division Terrace and Magazine Boulevard to Hollies Road and Happy Mondays Arcade. In the spirit of farewell Noon also stated in his 2000 interview with Johnston that *Needle*

in the Groove could be considered the fourth and final *Vurt* novel, "Because all the books in the *Vurt* sequence have been about the same thing. Which has got nothing to do with feathers, nothing to do with anything 'science fictional' at all. It's to do with the search for a new family. The escape from a broken family, the setting up of a new, alternative family, and the search to repair a broken family." In these ways, *Needle in the Groove,* as does *Nymphomation,* has the feel of a transitional text in Noon's body of work; it looks backward through the history of a city and its music as it looks forward in language and style.

The novel follows Elliot Hill, a bass player, who has had little success in the music business, until he is asked to audition for a band called Glam Damage. Singer Donna, DJ Jody, and drummer 2spot are creating a new kind of techno-dance music that makes use of a new experimental technology, a liquid-containing sphere that records music. When shaken, the sphere remixes the recorded material. Remixing serves as a metaphor in the book for revision and the way public and private histories change with each new telling and each new listening. The novel resembles *Vurt* when the band uses the liquid music as a drug. They drink, smoke, and eventually inject it, and enter a collective hallucination. Halfway through the novel, 2spot disappears and commits suicide. The band falls apart, but Elliot and the other band members use the drug to go back into the past to find 2spot. The novel fuses the history of 2spot's family with the history of popular music in Britain. His grandfather Georgie played in a skiffle group and then a beat band, which evolved into psychedelic and progressive rock groups. 2spot's father, Deezil, played in a punk group.

Aside from making punk and dub music the content of his novel, Noon uses music to craft the style and shape of the text. The entire work is written without periods, with phrases divided by diagonals, or solidi, the slash marks usually used to cite poetry or lyrics: "the nightclub / a stonecold zombie with a look of shock on its face, the kind that happens when nocturnals get caught in the daylight / check that feeling / something about turned-off neon always does it for me, turns on the sadness, gets me thinking about where all the shine goes to / like it should've been raining, like it should've always been raining." As a few reviewers noted, the style could have easily produced an awkward reading experience, but it actually generates a text that is fast-paced, smooth, and extremely musical in rhythm and sound. The book also features more examples of the kind of dub remixes used in *Pixel Juice;* in this case several of the prose chapters of *Needle in the Groove* reappear in a revised poetic form. Noon has stated that he is increasingly concerned with finding better ways to match style and content. In his *Spike Magazine* interview with Johnston, he said, "I have this idea that every story has its own particular language. A lot of writers don't consider this at all; they've got their style and they do it. But for me, easily the longest part of the process is discovering the language. Once I've done that, the book just goes." Noon extended the stylistic experimentation of the novel *Needle in the Groove* by working with electronic musician David Toop to record a CD that uses Noon's voice as a sample for the music.

Noon's next work, *Cobralingus,* was released in 2001 by the small Brighton publisher Codex Books. Extending the dub and remix idea begun in *Pixel Juice* and *Needle in the Groove,* Noon uses his own writing and "samples" from other texts, such as works by William Shakespeare, Emily Dickinson, and Zane Grey, Manchester street names, and a shipping forecast, as sources for generating new pieces. In the preface to *Cobralingus,* "Cobralingus: Instructions," Noon says that the process "imagines text to be a signal, which can be passed through various filter gates, each of which has a specific effect upon the language. Each gate allows the writer to access different creative responses within his or her imagination." There is also a key that describes the general process behind such filter gates as "decay," "explode," "purify," and "search & replace." The result is a set of ten experimental texts with such titles as "Exploding Horse Generator Unit" and "Boa Conscriptor Breeding System." Each piece consists of several variations of how the source materials have been remixed. Many of the texts resemble concrete poetry since words and letters take on graphic form, which is reinforced by Daniel Allington's illustrations. Michael Bracewell notes in his introductory essay that though the systematic approach of the book may seem mechanical, it offers "a set of systems and devices which trigger the warmth and imaginative fancy of classic romanticism." This collection also illustrates how Noon uses modernist-style experiments to reflect his concerns with the "liquid culture" of postmodernism, its fluid sense of language, reality, and identity.

Noon, who began his artistic life as a musician and painter, has come full circle in *Cobralingus,* which uses the techniques of electronic dance music to create a work that integrates text, sound, and image. Since *Cobralingus,* Noon has worked on two projects that further display his flexibility as a writer. *Mappalujo* is an on-line, collaborative project with Steve Beard, author of *Digital Leatherette* (2000), that

jeff noon/nymphomation

'An imaginative and linguistic tour de force' *Independent*

Cover for the 2000 paperback edition of Noon's 1997 novel, about a sinister company that controls people's dreams (Richland County Public Library)

extends the textual experimentation of *Cobralingus.* In contrast, *Falling Out of Cars* (2002) is a road novel, published by the Doubleday division of Transworld Publishers, Ltd., that relies on more conventional narrative forms. As a writer, Noon has undergone many changes over the course of his career. He has moved from psychedelic mythology to avant-garde explorations of language. Using the term "Avant Pulp" to describe his work, he has tried to produce experimental imaginative fiction by writing within popular genres, such as mystery and science fiction, and by adopting the techniques of popular music. Drawing inspiration from youth culture, Noon also has a youthful audience, who communicate their enthusiasm for his work through e-mail discussion groups and on Internet fan sites. Reviewers have praised and criticized him for his unconventional imagination and experimental view of language. Noon parodies his work and its reception in "Pixel Dub Juice (sublimerix remix)," which closes the last remix in *Pixel Juice:*

In style it's manic-frenetic,
With language mistreated genetic;
Brings K. Dick alive,
To join Famous Five
In acrobatic alphabetics.
Oh, there's weirdo perversions galore!
Guns, hookers and drugs by the score;
Critics should pan it,
They really should ban it,
Or at least put it front of the store.

Jeff Noon is a writer who experiments with style and content. He sees himself writing against the grain of the sort of novels that win the Booker Prize. In a manifesto written for *The Guardian* (10 January 2001), "Film-makers use jump cuts, freeze frames, slow motion. Musicians remix, scratch, sample. Can't we writers have some fun as well?" he criticizes the mainstream of contemporary British novels for a conservatism that prevents the novel from advancing in form. Rather than settle for a style or genre with which he or his readers may feel comfortable, Noon has made clear that he wishes to move forward and to use each book as a way to "revel in the wild excitement of language."

Interviews:

Nile Southern and Mark Amerika, "As Per Vurt," *Alt-X,* 1995 <www.altx.com/interviews/jeff.noon.html>;

Caroline Griffin, "Jeff Noon," *Pure Fiction,* 1996 <www.purefiction.com/pages/authors/noon/noon.htm>;

Bethan Roberts, "Fairytales from the Future," *Spike Magazine,* 1996 <www.spikemagazine.com/1196noon.htm>;

David V. Barrett, "The Lucidity Switch: Jeff Noon Interviewed," *Interzone,* 115 (1997): 46–49;

Eya Kuismanen and Ruud van de Kruisweg, "An Interview with Jeff Noon," *Albedo,* 14 (1997): 8–12;

Chris Wood, "Chris Wood interviews Jeff Noon," *Pure Fiction,* 1998 <www.purefiction.com/newrev/intervie/noon.htm>;

"The Mancunian Candidate: Jeff Noon Discusses *Automated Alice,*" *Cold Print,* 3 (1998) <www.coldprint.freeserve.co.uk/jeff.html>;

Polly Marshall, "Dub Til It Bleeds," *Interzone,* 142 (April 1999); republished *Spike Magazine* <www.spikemagazine.com/0800jeffnooninterzone.htm>;

Sean Coughlan, "Voice of a Conurbation," *Times* (London), 6 May 2000, Metro section, pp. 16–17;

Antony Johnston, "Liquid Culture," *Spike Magazine,* 2000 <www.spikemagazine.com/0800jeffnoon. htm>.

References:

Andrew M. Butler, *Cyberpunk* (Harpender, U.K.: Pocket Essentials, 2000), pp. 65–68;

Cobralingus Web Site, 2001 <www.codexbooks.co.uk/cobraindex.html>;

Val Gough, "A Crossbreed Loneliness? Jeff Noon's Feminist Cyberpunk," in *Future Females, The Next Generation: New Voices and Velocities in Feminist Science Fiction Criticism,* edited by Marleen S. Barr (Lanham, Md.: Rowman & Littlefield, 2000), pp. 109–127;

Jeff Noon Web Page, 17 February 2002 <www.jeffnoon.com>.

Lawrence Norfolk

(1 October 1963 –   )

Barry Lewis
University of Sunderland

BOOKS: *Lemprière's Dictionary* (London: Sinclair-Stevenson, 1991; New York: Harmony, 1992); translated into German by Hanswilhelm Haefs as *Lemprière's Wörterbuch: Roman* (Munich: Knaus, 1992);
The Pope's Rhinoceros (London: Sinclair-Stevenson, 1996; New York: Harmony, 1996);
In the Shape of a Boar (London: Weidenfeld & Nicolson, 2000; New York: Grove, 2001).

OTHER: *New Writing 8,* edited by Norfolk and Tibor Fischer (London: Vintage/British Council, 1999);
"Being Translated; or, The Virgin Mary's Hair," in *New Writing 9,* edited by John Fowles and A. L. Kennedy (London: Vintage, 2000), pp. 149–156;
The Oxford and Cambridge May Anthologies 2000: Short Stories, selected and introduced by Norfolk (Cambridge: Varsity/Cherwell, 2000);
Virginia Woolf, *Jacob's Room,* introductions by Norfolk and Elisabeth Bronfen (London: Vintage, 2000).

SELECTED PERIODICAL PUBLICATIONS–
UNCOLLECTED: "A Bosnian Alphabet," *Granta,* 43 (Spring 1993): 213–222;
"The Honesty of Pagemonsters," *TLS: The Times Literary Supplement* (2 September 1994): 6.

Lawrence Norfolk (photograph © Ulf Anderson–GAMMA; courtesy of the author)

"Lawrence Norfolk was born in London in 1963. This is his first novel." These lines comprise the sum total of the information Norfolk divulged about himself on the inside flap of the dust jacket for *Lemprière's Dictionary* (1991). He repeated this reticent formula on the dust jackets of his second and third novels. As does Thomas Pynchon, the American novelist with whom he has been most often compared, Norfolk chooses to keep his private life private. He has granted few interviews in Britain and the United States, though his extensive popularity on the Continent (especially in Germany) has resulted in several appearances in the media.

Norfolk was born 1 October 1963. His early life was not without drama. His parents, Michael Norfolk and Shirley Kathleen Blake Norfolk, moved to Baghdad in Iraq in 1965, where his father was a civil engineer. The outbreak of the 1967 Six Day War in the Middle East and the ensuing hostilities between Israel and the Arab states meant that the Norfolks had to be quickly evacuated, and the family returned to England. Lawrence attended the King Edward VI private school in Bath until 1981 and began reading books by such authors as Evelyn Waugh and Aleksandr Solzhenitsyn. He left home at nineteen in 1983 to study English at King's College, London. Graduating in 1986, he took up several temporary posts as a barman, a construction laborer, and a teacher, while also beginning study for a Ph.D. that he never completed. His life moved in a new direction when—encouraged by a girlfriend who was convinced of his potential as a writer—he attended the London Book Fair and handed a one-page synopsis to the first agent he saw, Carol Blake of Blake Friedman. Prompted to submit more, he spent the next three weeks writing what later became the first sixty pages of his novel *Lemprière's Dictionary*. Using this opening chapter, Blake quickly sold the publication rights, convincing Sinclair-Stevenson that Norfolk would soon deliver the finished typescript.

Although *Lemprière's Dictionary* took four years to write—during which time the anxious publishers were "doing their nut," as Norfolk put it in a 15 July 2001 interview with Michelle Griffin of *The Age* (Melbourne)—upon publication in 1991 the book was instantly hailed by reviewers as an astonishing debut. It received the Somerset Maugham Award in 1992 and the following year prompted the inclusion of Norfolk as one of the twenty writers in the "Best Young British Novelists" list published by the prestigious *Granta* magazine. Nearly a quarter-of-a-million words long, the novel was widely admired for its plot pyrotechnics, thematic scope, and sheer linguistic daring. Michael Dirda in *The Washington Post Book World* (20 September 1992) said it was an "extravagantly spectacular first novel." Moreover, *Lemprière's Dictionary* established Norfolk as one of the leading British practitioners of what Linda Hutcheon calls "historiographic metafiction" in her *Poetics of Postmodernism: History, Theory, Fiction* (1988), a form of writing that takes actual events from the past as the basis for self-reflective experiment and postmodernist meditation. Other novelists in this category include Julian Barnes, Salman Rushdie, and Graham Swift in the United Kingdom, and John Barth, Don DeLillo, and Pynchon in the United States. Norfolk's novel transforms the life of a rather ordinary late-eighteenth- and early-nineteenth-century cleric and scholar and involves him in a worldwide conspiracy.

The historical John Lemprière was born in 1765 into a family that held prominent positions in Jersey under Elizabeth I, James I, and Oliver Cromwell. Lemprière attended Oxford University before becoming headmaster of Abingdon School in 1792. Financial irregularities resulted in his resigning that post in 1809 to become headmaster of Exeter Grammar School. He died in 1824 and was largely forgotten. Lemprière's *Classical Dictionary of Proper Names Mentioned in Ancient Authors Writ Large* (1788), commonly called *Lemprière's Dictionary,* however, was a significant influence upon writers of the Romantic school, especially John Keats, and is still a standard reference work on Greek and Roman mythology. The dictionary appeared at the very cusp of the transition between the Age of Reason and the Age of Romanticism. One of the definitive texts of the neoclassical period was Samuel Johnson's *Dictionary of the English Language* (1755), whose aim was nothing less than to fix pronunciations and definitions according to the rational ideal of a circumscribed and controlled knowledge. *Lemprière's Dictionary,* on the other hand, deals with the nonexistent figures of mythology, a body of symbolic possibilities that is by its very nature uncircumscribable.

Lemprière, as depicted by Norfolk, is himself transformed into a mythical figure who is a product of his changing times. His head is steeped in classical lore, and it rarely rises from his beloved books about the heroes and gods of the ancient world. Yet, Lemprière is also a young man beset by vague fantasies and longings, with a latent urge to travel abroad and savor the irrational flavors of life firsthand. One of the symptoms of Lemprière's unstable classical/Romantic temperament is his tendency to hallucinate when under stress. The first major hallucination occurs after he successfully chooses a selection of classical texts for the library of Viscount Nicolas Casterleigh. As a reward Lemprière is presented with a fine volume of Ovid's *Metamorphoses* (circa 8 A.D.). The book is illustrated throughout, but the picture accompanying the legend of Diana and Actaeon is in a different style than the others. He dwells for some time upon its singularity. Later, to his horror, Lemprière witnesses this scene come to life. The viscount's daughter, Juliette, bathes naked in a pool, as did Diana, while on the far bank Lemprières father, Charles, suffers the fate of Actaeon and is mauled to death by Casterleigh's dogs. The reader is left uncertain as to what has happened—are Lemprière's fantasies causing events to occur in the real world? Such breakdowns between the factual and the fictive are a common feature in works of historiographic metafiction.

Lemprière visits two "doctors of the mind" in London, where he travels to settle his father's will. Ernst Kalkbrenner and Elmore Clementi, otherwise known as Ernst and Elly, diagnose that John is afflicted with "projective-objective palilexic echopraxia"; that is, he has a vivd imagination and tends to recreate what he reads in the real world. They recommend that he write something about the ancients as an outlet for his meandering mind. They run through an alphabet of possibilities—from "almanac" to "year-book"—before they suggest that Lemprière compile a dictionary of classical references.

Lemprière throws himself into the task, beginning, naturally, with the letter *A.* As he approaches Christmastime and the letter *D,* the worlds of his imagination and the reality outside merge once more. Lemprière realizes that the entry on Danae—who gave birth to Perseus after Zeus visited her in the form of a shower of gold—is central to his task in some obscure way. What Lemprière does not foresee, however, is that he will again become the witness of a sinister ritual murder. A prostitute called Rosalie is suffocated by a cascade of the precious molten metal on the grounds of the estate of Edmund de Vere, twelfth Earl of Braith.

The murders of his father and Rosalie are part of a mystery that Lemprière investigates, only to find that he himself has become the subject of investigation by several parties. The detective Sir John Fielding—reminiscent of Umberto Eco's medieval sleuth, Brother William of Baskerville, in his *Name of the Rose* (1981)—enters the proceedings to solve the murder of the woman. He is the brother of novelist Henry Fielding, the author of *Joseph Andrews* (1742) and *Tom Jones* (1749), who helped establish the very conventions of novelistic realism that Norfolk so ably contravenes. Sir John, a blind Bow Street magistrate, believes that every crime has a rational solution. Aided only by his guide-boy, and a capacity for deduction that prefigures the greater penetration of Sherlock Holmes, Sir John begins to suspect Lemprière after the discovery of the corpse of solicitor George Peppard. The net draws in more tightly after the body of a young woman is found at the top of the King's Arms stairs near the Thames. The corpse is wrapped in the hide of a goat, and the echoes between this latest ritual murder and the slaying of Iphigenia in Greek myth again implicate Lemprière, who is oblivious to the fact that the signing and dating of his dictionary entries—linked so closely to these grisly crimes—constitute incriminating evidence about his involvement.

Sir John is not the only person on the trail of Lemprière. He is also stalked by Nazim-ud-Dowlah, an Indian noble known as the Nawab, with a mission to track down nine anonymous men responsible for secret financial embezzlements in the East. His only clue to their whereabouts is a single name: "Lemprière." Once Nazim—a shadowy figure cloaked all in black—reaches London, he launches a vigil over a ship called the *Vendragon* (formerly the *Falmouth*). It is loaded with classical statues from the Coade Stone Manufactory. Only later is it revealed that the casts contain gold intended to finance the French Revolution. Nazim struggles to make sense of what he encounters, and this struggle connects him with most of the other characters in the book, who are also engaged in hermeneutic activities of one kind or another. Before his death, Charles Lem-

Dust jacket for the 1992 U.S. edition of Norfolk's 1991 novel, about a classical scholar investigating a mysterious eighteenth-century British secret society (Richland County Public Library)

prière had pored over maps, charts, and documents, trying to find a particular ship, a clue that would be the "key to the pattern" of his investigation. His son, John, continues the inquiries and ponders a written agreement between his ancestor François Lemprière and Thomas de Vere, fourth Earl of Braith, "as if it were a fragment of something much larger," which indeed it is. The deeper Lemprière goes into this matter, the more convinced he becomes that he is on the threshold of something portentous, a feeling that the reader of the novel shares with its protagonist.

Lemprière stumbles across a tangled conspiracy whose roots lie in the luckless expedition of the Honorable Company of Merchants to the East Indies in 1600. Nine English entrepreneurs backed this voyage, convinced that it would make their fortune; however, the nine Englishmen became bankrupt by the time their ship returned with a cargo full of pepper, as there was a glut in the market for pepper. They were then helped by nine Frenchmen from La Rochelle, Huguenots who were not allowed by the Catholic court to further their own entrepreneurial ambitions. The nine Frenchmen relieved the debt of the original investors under a secret agreement that nine-tenths of the profits of the second and subsequent voyages would go to them.

All went well until the siege of La Rochelle in 1627. This small port on the west coast of France, where the nine Frenchmen stored their treasure, attracted the wrath of Cardinal Richelieu and Louis XIV, as it had become an enclave of Protestant independence. The siege lasted until the following year and killed more than two-thirds of the citizens. Eventually, the eight remaining Frenchmen (the ninth conspirator, Lemprière's ancestor, is in England, seeking help to raise the siege) decide that it is time to escape via a subterranean lake, even if it means leaving their riches behind. Before leaving, they convene a meeting for the people of La Rochelle in the citadel, and then set fire to it. As the escapees watch the human conflagration from a safe distance, they see a small child thrown into the air who dips toward the sea, then soars up again. This sole survivor of the inferno is Septimus Praeceps, the seventh son of a seventh son, otherwise known as the mythical Sprite of Rochelle.

The rest of Norfolk's narrative covers ground that is familiar to readers of Pynchon, a writer who specializes in paranoid "alternative histories." (There is even a sly allusion to Pynchon in Lemprière's Dictionary when Mister O'Tristero, a character who appears for one line only, is introduced to Lemprière as a rival scribe.) The French conspirators form the Cabbala, a version of the sinister underground organization named the Tristero in Pynchon's The Crying of Lot 49 (1966). Like the Tristero, the Cabbala secretly controls important world events. After losing their fortunes at La Rochelle, the Frenchmen regrouped in secret caverns beneath London and infiltrated East India House. From this hub they sponsored despots and dictators, so that the profits of the East India Company could be siphoned off for themselves. The Cabbala also engaged in a war lasting several generations with the Lemprière family, some of whom perished in the Rochelle fires. Despite the tremendous power of the Cabbala, Lemprière—aided by Septimus, the Sprite of Rochelle who has lived for several generations in order to exact revenge—manages to outwit his antagonists.

Lemprière's Dictionary ends with a series of spectacular set pieces and surprises. The version that was published in the United States in 1992 was approximately one-fifth shorter than the British original and streamlined some of the plot. Subsequently, several of the revelations about double identities were missing in the U.S. edition. This abridged version was nowhere near

as controversial, however, as the translation that appeared in Germany that same year. Within the first five months Lemprière's Wörterbuch had sold approximately 150,000 copies. By this time, however, it was also at the center of a fierce debate. The German translation by Hanswilhelm Haefs, sent to reviewers along with a copy of the original, was the subject of an open letter sent by eleven literary translators (known as the Straelen group) to the press, publishers, and booksellers' associations. The Straelen group denounced the translation and called for it to be withdrawn, on the grounds of Haefs's incompetence in both the source and target languages, and inadequate editing. By June 1993 the group had compiled a thirty-page list of serious errors. The response to the charges by Norfolk's German publishers was curt. They accused the eleven translators of a personal vendetta and argued that a book as idiosyncratic as Lemprière's Dictionary demanded a creative, source-centered translation.

Norfolk's second novel, The Pope's Rhinoceros (1996), was composed during his three years of residence in Chicago from 1993. His wife, Vineeta Rayan, whom he married 30 April 1994, was a medical researcher there; they have a son, Lucas, born 30 November 2000. Like his first novel, this book is essentially an historiographic metafiction. In other words, The Pope's Rhinoceros is a self-reflexive work that applies to historical narrative all the techniques and generic devices associated with postmodernist writing. Norfolk's research is again meticulous. At the center of the novel is an outrage, an equivalent to the burning of the citizens of La Rochelle that anchored his previous book. This time it is the sacking of Prato, a small town in northern Italy, that generates the moral unease. The town was invaded in 1512 by Spanish soldiers in an orgy of looting and rape during the successful campaign to restore the Medici family to power. The Medici triumph in Florence was consolidated the following year when Giovanni de' Medici ascended to the papacy as Pope Leo X.

Norfolk cleverly braids these historical events with a fictive extravaganza centering on two mercenaries named Salvestro and Bernardo, both of whom were witnesses (and unwilling accomplices) to the rapes and murders at Prato. Salvestro, Bernardo, and a fellow mercenary called Groot are dragooned into guarding the family of Tedaldi, the mayor of Prato, during the sacking of the city. Tedaldi and his family are murdered, and the blame is cast upon the three guards. Salvestro, Bernardo, and Groot narrowly escape death themselves, though Groot is later caught, tortured, and blackmailed into betraying Salvestro and Bernardo when they later turn up in Rome.

The rhinoceros at the heart of the novel is familiar from Albrecht Dürer's 1515 woodcut of the beast. Less well-known, however, are the circumstances that led to the production of this image. Dürer worked from a sketch of an animal that King Manuel I of Portugal sent as a gift to Pope Leo X in Rome. From out of this historical incident, Norfolk develops another huge, sprawling narrative.

Salvestro and Bernardo become involved in a dispute between two ambassadors who wish to gain favor with the Pope. Dom João de Faria is a representative of Dom Manolon of Portugal, and Don Jerónimo da Vich is the spokesman for Fernando, king of Spain. Both countries are vying for a Papal Bull that will grant them territorial advantage from their voyages of exploration. The Pope decides to grant this favor to the country that can obtain for him a rhinoceros to fight the elephant he already possesses, in order to test the theory of Plinius that the two beasts are natural enemies. Faria and Vich conspire together to produce the illusion of a rivalry between them for the benefit of the Pope. But what starts as a mock competition becomes a real one. Two ships—the *Santa Lucia* and the *Ajuda*—battle with each other to be the first to bring a rhinoceros to Rome.

Against all odds, Salvestro and Bernardo do catch the rhinoceros. But capturing the rhinoceros is one thing—transporting it safely back to Rome is another thing altogether, and the beast perishes en route. Nevertheless, the battle between the two animals goes ahead. In a farcical climax, Salvestro stuffs the rhino with bread in an ad hoc attempt at taxidermy. When the beast enters the lake where the conflict is to take place, it explodes after the dough rises and bursts.

A great deal of *The Pope's Rhinoceros* hinges around the two central characters, Salvestro and Bernardo, who are physical and temperamental opposites, reminiscent in many ways of George and Lennie from John Steinbeck's *Of Mice and Men* (1937). Salvestro is thin and cunning; Bernardo is dim-witted and strong. They are dependent upon each other, both practically and emotionally, and often have to help each other out when they are in trouble. For instance, Bernardo saves Salvestro from a mob of villagers on Usedom, who almost drown him because they believe he is the son of a witch. Conversely, on several occasions Salvestro is able to protect the simpleton Bernardo from exploitation by the many hustlers and con artists they meet on their travels.

Many of the reviewers of *The Pope's Rhinoceros* again were dazzled by Norfolk's narrative dexterity and command of period detail but disappointed by what appeared to be the two-dimensionality of its central characters. Phil Baker of *The Sunday Times* (London) even went so far as to say, in a 28 April 1996 review,

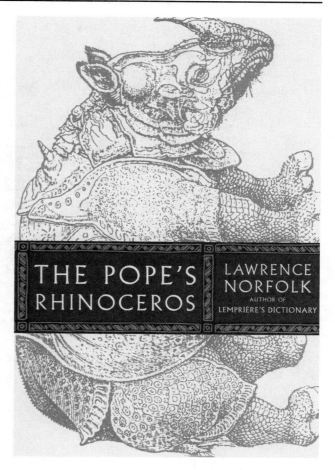

Dust jacket for the U.S. edition of Norfolk's 1996 novel, about two sixteenth-century mercenaries who become involved in an expedition to capture a rhinoceros for Pope Leo X (Richland County Public Library)

that Salvestro and Bernardo were no more convincing than cartoon characters such as Asterix the Gaul and Hagar the Horrible. While this criticism is valid, it ignores how this kind of flat characterization is appropriate to the text. They are a comic device, and that is enough for the purposes of the plot.

In the Shape of a Boar (2000), named after a poem by Paul Celan, is a new departure in Norfolk's fiction, but one that develops several of his preoccupations. Based upon recognizable historical facts concerning the life of Celan, a poet whose work nagged at the twin issues of authenticity and unrepresentability, its intricate structure unfolds a delicate probing into the past. It was short-listed for the James Tait Black Memorial Fiction Prize in 2000. Reviews were mixed. Ruth Scurr, in a 20 September 2000 review in *The Times* (London), thought it was "intelligent, innovative, erudite, elegant, witty, lyrical and serious," while Hugo Barnacle, in a 5 November 2000 review in *The Sunday Times* (London)

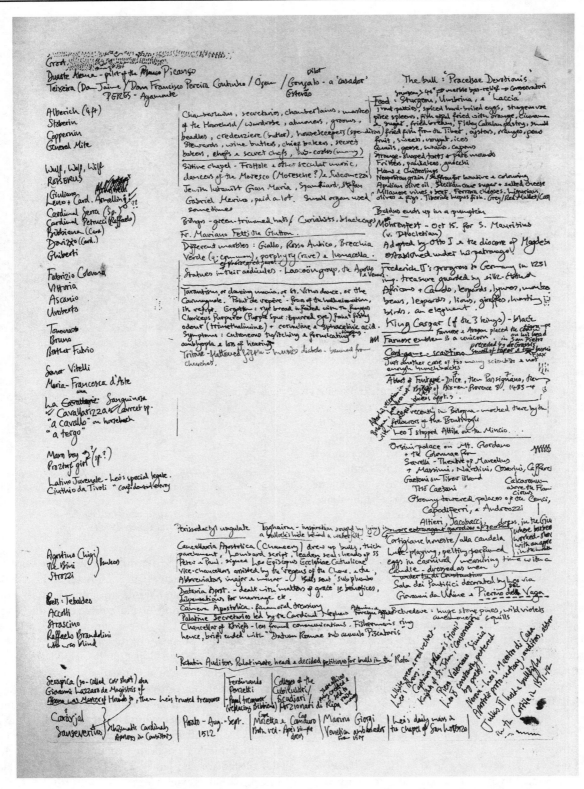

Pages from Norfolk's notebook for In the Shape of a Boar *(2000); the page at right includes a street plan of the Romanian town of Czernowitz, circa 1930, birthplace of the poet Paul Celan, after whom Norfolk modeled his protagonist (Collection of Lawrence Norfolk).*

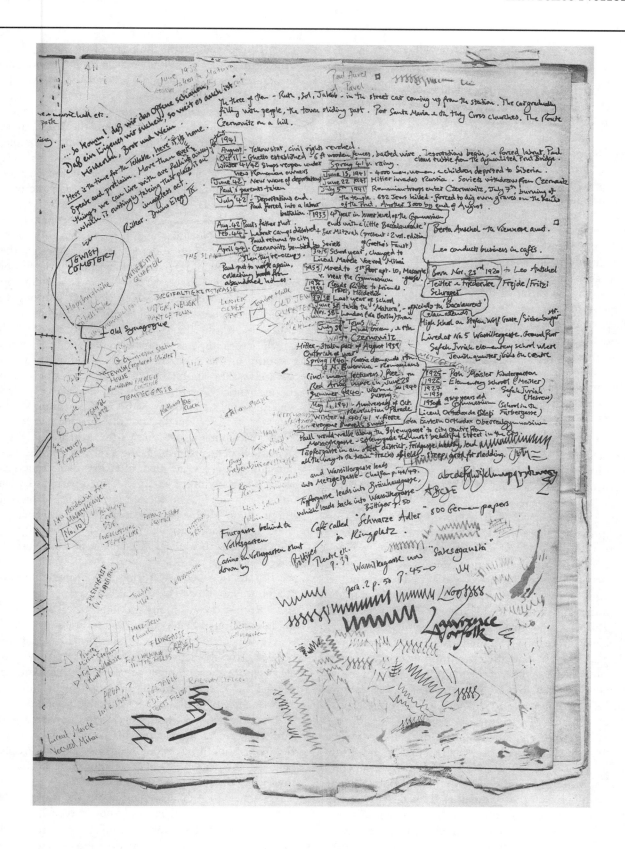

titled "Making a Pig's Ear of the Classics," merely found it "solemn" and "somewhat overwritten."

The book opens with a retelling of the Greek legend of the hunt for the boar of Kalydon, a beast sent by the goddess Artemis to ravage the land as revenge for the failure of King Oeneus of Aetolia to honor her with sacrifices. The king's son, Meleager, gathers a group of Greek heroes to track down the boar and kill it. The only female member of the band is Atalanta, and she and Meleager share a mutual attraction. This relationship arouses the jealousy of Meilanion, another member of the party, who strikes off on his own in pursuit of the boar. Meanwhile, the number of heroes dwindles as a result of an ambush and a flood. Eventually, only Meleager and Atalanta enter the cave in which the boar dwells, watched from a distance by Meilanion. What happens next is not recorded, though nearly every other detail in the story has been fastidiously documented by more than 250 footnotes. Norfolk revealed in a 20 September 2000 interview with Jerome Boyd Maunsell for *The Times* (London) that all of these scholarly annotations are accurate. They took more than two years to research, and they consolidate the concreteness and immediacy of the first part of the novel.

The narrative then lurches forward to the twentieth century and oscillates between several distinct historical moments. Part 2 is titled "Paris," and it centers around a Romanian Jew, Solomon Memel, who recalls his experiences during World War II and the decades following the war from the vantage point of the "present," Paris in the 1970s. Memel is a fictional re-creation of Celan. Like Celan, he is from Czernowitz, a town in the Bukovina region of Romania that was occupied twice during World War II, first by the Russians and then the Germans. His idyllic love triangle in the late 1930s with his friends, Jakob Feuerstein and Ruth Lackner, is shattered by the advent of war. The Jews were first rounded-up into a ghetto, then released, only to find their community decimated by "actions" in the middle of the night that result in transportation of their loved ones to concentration camps. Memel's parents are so transported, as were Celan's. Lackner helps Memel escape from this nightmare, while Feuerstein is left behind. In real life Celan escaped the Nazis with the help of his friend Ruth Lackner, an actress. Painfully walking across the Carpathian Mountains to Greece, Memel becomes a pawn in a feud between partisan bands. Thyella, the female leader of a group of resistance fighters, betrays her comrades to the Nazi colonel Heinrich Eberhardt to secure the safety of her lover, Xanthos. She is subsequently tracked down and executed by Geraxos, Xanthos's grandfather, for her disloyalty .

These events form the basis of the poem Memel writes after the war that makes him famous and becomes a set-text in schools around the world, "Die Kielerjagd" (The Boar Hunt). The poem uses the Kalydonian myth as a metaphor for the tragedies that he witnessed during the war. Although the reader never sees a section of the poem firsthand, it is clearly implied that it is in some way an analogue of the opening part of the novel. This isomorphism is strengthened when the "Memel Affair" erupts in the 1950s after the publication of a scholarly edition of the poem by Memel's old friend, Feuerstein. This version is peppered with footnotes, as is Norfolk's text in part 1, but these annotations have a much different status. Although they start out as textual references, they quickly mushroom into increasingly larger paragraphs as Feuerstein comments on the veracity of Memel's text. Among the details he disputes are the likelihood of dolphins in the Gulf of Corinth; the types of weapons used by the Greek heroes; the unseasonable apples; and the erroneous flora of the mountain regions. Although trivial in themselves, the abundance of errors casts doubt upon the authenticity of Memel's poem. Articles appear in which Memel's encounter with Greek partisans during the war is questioned, and the prominent scholar Walter Reichmann also doubts its authenticity. Feuerstein, however, is far from being a reliable commentator himself. Ruth reveals that after the war Feuerstein wrote her many crazy letters, inflamed perhaps by jealousy, declaring that he wanted to track down the truth in relation to Memel and his poem. In short, Feuerstein is possibly mad, and his insanity is seemingly confirmed by his suicide in 1955. This aspect of Norfolk's novel, with its games of pursuit and penmanship, recalls another book featuring an insane annotator, Vladimir Nabokov's *Pale Fire* (1962).

Ruth—now a famous motion-picture director living in the United States—has come to France to make a movie version of Memel's poem. Despite a lingering bond, the two of them are never quite able to revive the electricity of their younger selves. Ruth, after catching Memel in a compromising situation with her lead actress, challenges him to speak the truth. She believes that he invented the whole story about the Greek partisans because he thinks that his own townspeople in Bukovina should have fought against the catastrophes befalling them as did Thyella, whom she believes is mythical. Memel remains silent. It is only when she leaves that he ruminates aloud about the impossibility of bearing witness to what could not be seen.

There are biographical similarities between the historical Celan and his fictional avatar, Memel; however, the most important similarity lies in the nature of their poetry. Memel's poem "Die Kielerjagd"

Dust jacket for the 2001 U.S. edition of Norfolk's 2000 novel, which features retellings of the Greek myth
about the hunt for the boar Kalydon (Richland County Public Library)

uses motifs from the Greek legend of the hunting of the boar in Kalydon to investigate evil and the powerlessness of language to describe it. As described in the novel, it is reminiscent of Celan's poem "Todesfuge" (Fugue of Death, 1948), which also addresses in an oblique manner the implications of the Holocaust, using the German language and a complex web of allusions to German literature to indict the horrors that the Germans perpetrated. It too became a set-text in schools and was subject to revisionist criticism for allegedly deriving aesthetic beauty from the horrors of Auschwitz and thus trivializing the Holocaust.

During the period in which Norfolk was writing his third novel, the question of authenticity in relation to the Holocaust was brought into sharp focus with the publication of Binjamin Wilkomirski's *Bruchstücke, aus einer Kindheit 1939–1948* (1995; translated as *Fragments: Memories of a Wartime Childhood*, 1996). This book presented itself as an autobiographical account of a Jewish author's experiences within a concentration camp during World War II. Swiss author Daniel Ganzfried later alleged that these claims were fabricated

and that the author was not a Latvian Jew, as he claimed. The original German publisher, Suhrkamp Verlag, finally withdrew all copies of the book from bookstores in 1999 in response to an independent report that documented that Wilkomirski was in fact Bruno Dösseker, a Swiss Christian who had never left Switzerland during World War II. The Wilkomirski scandal mirrored the charges of falsity raised against Memel in relation to the poem that makes him famous, a situation that also resonates with the accusations of plagiarism made against Celan in 1960, the so-called Goll Affair in which Claire Goll falsely alleged that Celan had plagiarized the work of her husband, Yvan Goll. Literature faces a thorny challenge when dealing with events as momentous as those of the Final Solution. Theodor W. Adorno's famous statement that it would be barbaric to write poetry after Auschwitz pinpoints the problems of representation in Memel's poem. How can such extreme barbarity be embodied within literature? Simply to verbalize something in fictional form is to aestheticize it, to render even the most horrific actuality palatable to the imagination. Memel's solution is to choose the boar as a negative symbol of that which cannot be expressed directly. As one of the characters states in the novel, "Evil inhabits the boar. He is the principal of violence, of license." In the Greek legend the heroes Atalanta, Meleager and Meilanion hunt the boar, but its eventual demise is not described since it takes place within the darkness of a cave. Norfolk writes in his footnotes: "There the record halts. The trails of 'Atalanta,' 'Meilanion' and 'Meleager' run out." Sol and his friends Ruth and Jakob–each of whom reacted to the German occupation in different ways–hunt the boar too, a boar that represents the truth of their wartime experiences. Memel's desire to find a meaning in his tragic past leads also to a cave. This one is located in Agrapha–an imaginary place in the Greek mountains, with a name that means "unwritten"–where he flees after the Jews are persecuted in his homeland. Here Memel purportedly observed the end of yet another three-way relationship, involving the Greek partisans Xanthos, Thyella, and Geraxos. These characters are bound together by bonds of love and hate. Geraxos killed Thyella at the cave, believing that she betrayed her comrades in order to set free Xanthos, her lover, who was captured by the Germans.

The three triangular relationships of Norfolk's *In the Shape of a Boar* (Geraxos-Thyella-Xanthos, Meleager-Atalanta-Meilanion, and Sol-Ruth-Jakob) suggest that there are strong parallels between the present and the past; however, Lawrence Norfolk's novels all render the present and the past equally elusive. In *Lemprière's Dictionary, The Pope's Rhinoceros,* and *In the Shape of a Boar* Norfolk plays with notions of discovering and inventing history. The periods described in those books are lavishly re-created thanks to his relentless research. For his first novel he cross-referenced eighteenth-century shipping reports and tide tables to faithfully record details of the weather; for his second novel he carefully researched the city plans and building practices of sixteenth-century Rome. Yet, at the same time, the "facts" become the platform to launch some of the wildest flights of fancy in contemporary British fiction. Myth and truth are allowed to interfuse with each other at every point, so that what the reader is left with is a sense (frequently encountered in historiographical metafiction) of the impenetrability of the past. Norfolk's novels, like the acts of the heroes we create, "take place in darkness and silence . . . in the cave."

Interviews:

Jerome Boyd Maunsell, "Lost in the Labyrinth of Untold Tales," *Times* (London), 20 September 2000, p. 8;

Michelle Griffin, "An Eye for Detail," *Age* (Melbourne), 15 July 2001.

References:

Amy J. Elias, "The Pynchon Intertext of *Lemprière's Dictionary*," *Pynchon Notes,* 41, no. 4 (1997): 28–40;

Julie C. Hayes, "Fictions of Enlightenment: Sontag, Süskind, Norfolk, Kurzweil," *Bucknell Review,* 41, no. 2 (1998): 21–36;

David Hurton, "Literary Translation between Equivalence and Manipulation: Lawrence Norfolk's *Lemprière's Dictionary* in German," *Neophilologus,* 78, no. 2 (1994): 175–194;

Linda Hutcheon, *A Poetics of Postmodernism: History, Theory, Fiction* (London & New York: Routledge, 1988);

Barry Lewis, *Lawrence Norfolk: Myth, Truth and Fantasy* (London: Peter Lang, 2003);

Denise Eileen McCoskey, "Murder by Letters: Interpretation, Identity and the Instability of Text in Norfolk's *Lemprière's Dictionary*," *Classical and Modern Literature,* 20, no. 2 (2000): 39–59.

Joseph O'Connor

(20 September 1963 –   )

Tim Middleton
Bath Spa University College

BOOKS: *Cowboys & Indians* (London: Sinclair-Stevenson, 1991);

True Believers (London: Sinclair-Stevenson, 1991);

Desperadoes (London: Flamingo, 1993);

Even the Olives Are Bleeding: The Life and Times of Charles Donnelly (Dublin: New Island Books, 1993);

The Secret World of the Irish Male (Dublin: New Island Books, 1994; London: Minerva, 1995);

Red Roses and Petrol (London: Methuen, 1995);

The Irish Male at Home and Abroad (Dublin: New Island Books, 1996; London: Minerva, 1996);

Sweet Liberty: Travels in Irish America (London: Picador, 1996; Boulder, Colo.: Roberts Rinehart, 1996);

Finbar's Hotel, by O'Connor, Dermot Bolger, Roddy Doyle, Anne Enright, Hugo Hamilton, Jennifer Johnston, and Colm Tóibín, edited by Bolger (London: Picador, 1997);

The Salesman (London: Secker & Warburg, 1998; New York: Picador USA, 1999);

The Comedian (Dublin: New Island Books, 2000);

Inishowen (London: Secker & Warburg, 2000);

The Last of the Irish Males (Dublin: New Island Books, 2001; London: Review, 2001);

Yeats is Dead! A Novel by Fifteen Irish Writers, by O'Connor and others, edited by O'Connor (London: Cape, 2001); republished as *Yeats is Dead! A Mystery by Fifteen Irish Writers* (New York: Knopf, 2001).

PLAY PRODUCTIONS: *Red Roses and Petrol,* Dublin, Project Arts Centre, 9 May 1995; London, Tricycle Theatre, 1995;

The Weeping of Angels, Dublin, Gate Theatre, 1997.

PRODUCED SCRIPTS: *A Stone of the Heart,* motion picture, adapted by O'Connor from his short story of the same title, independent production, 1991;

Ailsa, motion picture, adapted by O'Connor from his short story of the same title, Temple Films, 1994;

Joseph O'Connor (photograph by Martin Morrel; from the dust jacket for the U.S. edition of The Salesman, *1999)*

The Long Way Home, motion picture, adapted by O'Connor from his short story of the same title, Treasure Films, 1995.

Joseph O'Connor's output is varied, including novels, a novella, a short-story collection, two plays, a biography, three works of prose nonfiction, a travelogue, and four screenplays. As a novelist, O'Connor's main themes are exile and family relationships. His work has been particularly successful in presenting the beliefs and values of a new generation of Irish men.

O'Connor's work has been written in a culture undergoing tremendous change and in which the certainties of the past are subject to revision. As critic Richard Kearney has suggested in his *Transitions: Narratives in Modern Irish Culture* (1988), "A central problem facing contemporary Irish culture is how to mediate between the images of past and future; how to avoid the petrification of tradition and the alienation of modernity." O'Connor's work may readily be located as part of what, in his *Ireland's Literature: Selected Essays* (1988), Terence Brown calls the "vital energy of contemporary Irish art in its engagement . . . with crises of identity, violence and historical consciousness." O'Connor argues in his *The Secret World of the Irish Male* (1994) that slavishly adhering to the perceived stereotypes of traditional Irishness is wholly misguided "when modern Ireland is crying out to be celebrated, imagined and changed." For O'Connor it is no longer possible to speak of Irishness as a single category; rather, one should note the existence of competing accounts of Irishness, a pluralistic sense of national identity contingent upon specific intersections of place and time. O'Connor's work has centered upon the urban Ireland of Dublin and its suburbs: this milieu is a location marked by violence, oppression, and reckless hedonism while simultaneously being a place shaped by compassion, conviviality, and community feeling.

Joseph Victor O'Connor was born 20 September 1963 in the south Dublin suburb of Glenageary. By the time his mother, Joanna Marie (O'Grady) O'Connor, died in an automobile accident in 1985, his parents had divorced, and his father, John Oliver Vincent O'Connor had remarried. His sisters are the controversial rock singer Sinead O'Connor and the painter Eimear. He also has two brothers, John and Eoin. O'Connor was educated at University College, Dublin, from 1981 to 1986, attaining two first-class honors degrees, a B.A. in English and modern American literature and an M.A. in Anglo-Irish literature. In the summer of 1985 he worked as a freelance journalist in Nicaragua before returning to Dublin to finish work on his M.A. He then spent October 1985 until summer 1986 at Oxford University before working in London for the British Nicaraguan Solidarity Campaign. He gave up this job in 1988 to concentrate on writing, and his first publications, the stories "Last of the Mohicans" and "Aisla," were published in the Dublin *Sunday Tribune* in January and November of 1989. He won the *Sunday Tribune* First Fiction and New Irish Writer of the Year Awards in 1989. In 1991 he earned an M.A. in screenwriting from the Northern School of Film and Television, University of Leeds.

O'Connor's first novel, *Cowboys & Indians* (1991), tells the story of self-interested recent graduate Eddie Virago. Taking the stock plot device of emigration, O'Connor updates the experience for the 1990s in a bittersweet comic tale of Virago's hopeless attempts to secure fame. Virago's stable world has become dis-

jointed following his graduation. His parents have separated, his girlfriend has gone to work in Nicaragua, and when the reader first meets Eddie he is hungover on the ferry to England, where he hopes to find success. Misfits, including Marion Mangan, whom he meets on the ferry, people Eddie's world. Marion is traveling to England to secure an abortion; she is from Ballybracken, a "black little turfsmelling secretive town" in Donegal, and O'Connor uses his central characters' different backgrounds to explore modern Irish values from rural and urban perspectives. Yet, this novel does not rely upon stock Irish characters; indeed, it goes out of its way to critique such conventions. An instance of this critique occurs when Eddie's best friend and aspiring author Dean Bean dismisses the "Great Irish Novel" as "A bit of motherlove, a touch of suppressed lust, a soupcon of masochistic Catholic guilt, a bit of token Britbashing, whole shitloads of limpid eyes and flared nostrils and sweaty Celtic thighs, all wrapped up in a sauce of snotgreen Joycean wank." Narrated in the third person but from Eddie's point of view, the novel was justly acclaimed for its evocation of feckless 1990s masculinity:

> They talked about their friends. Fergus wanted to be a film director. Now he was unemployed. Casey wanted to be a novelist. He was illegal in New York, working as a hospital clerk. Jimmy Sterne, the great future criminal lawyer and defender of the poor, was now working in a television repair shop in Auckland. Paul O'Brien, Ireland's first anarchist Taoiseach, was managing a disco bar in Carrickmacross. Tim Stoker, the man who put the Boomtown Rats on at Belfield when he was Ents Officer, now ran his uncle's pornographic video store. . . . The girls were all doing fine. But the guys, Jesus, the guys. A collection of primadonnas and hasbeens and neverweres and casualties and out and out chancers.

In summary the novel sounds an unlikely comedy, but O'Connor handles his material with an ironic wit. *Cowboys & Indians* is a slight, enjoyable novel that resists the temptation to take itself too seriously. The book offers a sardonic view of youthful aspiration and can be read as an indictment of the folly of youthful idealism. There are some effective scenes of parent and child relationships and a wry deflation of the conventions of Irish writing.

The book was generally well received by the critics. Robert Nye's review in *The Guardian* (21 March 1991) suggested that this first novel was "much better than most" and "works because the author is passionately involved in what he dislikes." *Cowboys & Indians* was shortlisted for the Whitbread Prize and awarded a writing prize by the London listings magazine *Time Out*.

O'Connor's next book was *True Believers* (1991), a collection of thirteen short stories in which he continues to explore the lives of the young émigré Irish. Many of these stories predate his first novel, and characters and ideas from *Cowboys & Indians* are found in "Last of the Mohicans" and "Mothers Were All the Same." O'Connor eschews the modernist moment of insight so central to many twentieth-century Irish short stories in favor of a postmodernist recounting of the superficialities of the everyday that pointedly avoids showing characters attaining moments of vision or even just a deeper understanding of their predicaments. In this approach the influence of one of his heroes, American author Raymond Carver, is clear. Through an often-bittersweet comedy, O'Connor intimates the alienation and self-doubt at the heart of the new Ireland.

"Last of the Mohicans" offers readers a different view of Eddie Virago from that provided in *Cowboys & Indians*. In this story the unnamed narrator shares aspects of the Virago character from the novel: a girlfriend who is going to work for charity in a faraway place (in this case Ethiopia) and a dead-end job selling rubbish bags. The narrator meets Eddie in London, and his seeing the college idol, "the kind of guy I tried to hang around with . . . Suave, cynical, dressed like a Sunday supplement," reduced to frying burgers provides the basis for this wry tale of failed ambition.

"Mothers Were All the Same" is another tale of young emigrants that, as does *Cowboys & Indians,* begins with a chance meeting in transit. The narrator, Eddie, meets Catriona at Luton Airport, and they decide to stay at a low-rent hotel in London where they enjoy a night of lovemaking. Catriona is in England to secure an abortion, but Eddie is crassly oblivious to this fact. The story ends with Catriona returning alone to Ireland after her abortion and Eddie arriving, late, at his aunt's home to be met with scolding. Although Eddie is now aware of Catriona's abortion, he is unable to put his feelings into words. The story closes with him lying in bed wrapping a blanket around himself: "Really tight. Over my head. So tight that it felt like a second skin. And the whole world was shut out now, on the other side of the darkness." The male inability to articulate emotions is a theme that recurs in this collection and is developed further in later fiction.

Several stories in the collection also focus on failed communication. "Ailsa" is the first-person narrative of an unemployed, alcoholic, abusive, predatory man who spies on his neighbor Caitlin Rourke and beats up his girlfriend, Sara. Ailsa is the name of Caitlin's baby, whose birth comes near the end of the narrative. A story of failed communication between men and women, this narrative closes with the narrator lying in the bath listening to his breathing and heartbeat: "I lay there perfectly still until the grey water went cold around me." O'Connor adapted the short story for a motion picture directed by Paddy Breathnach; released in 1994, the movie won the

Euskal Media Prize for best first film at the San Sebastian International Film Festival that year. "Phantom" is a flat, pointless story about people who have drifted apart but cannot quite see it; again, none of the characters is able to clearly express what he or she feels toward the others. In "Glass Houses" Dublin taxi driver Fred Murray hits a young woman with his cab. The girl refuses to go to the hospital but agrees to be taken to her mother's house, and during the journey she confides that she is pregnant. When they arrive, the girl appears to have fallen asleep. Fred thinks that she is dead, but she is just playing a sick joke on him. The story ends with another contemplative moment in which Frank wonders if "it was possible to turn such an unspeakable thing into words."

The title story, "True Believers," is also about failed communication, narrated retrospectively from a child's perspective. O'Connor exploits the limited point of view of his child narrator by allowing the reader to see that the parents are drifting apart, while the children are only partially aware of this fact: one sign is that the mother no longer accompanies them to church. Returning from church one day, the family meets an old woman called Agnes. Gradually, they come to know more about Agnes, a passionately religious and seemingly crazy woman who douses her home in holy water to keep the devil away. The mother walks out on the marriage while the rest of the family are out with Agnes at the seaside, and the resulting domestic complications and the father's despair lead to his losing his job and staying at home to care for the children. One Sunday Agnes is not at church, so they all go to see if she is all right and discover that she has died of pneumonia. The growing unhappiness of his father and the death of the God-fearing Agnes prompt the narrator into feeling that "my childhood ended" and that "God died in my life." The story ends with father and son sitting together listening to the sound of the rain.

Other stories in the collection offer perspectives on the emigrant Irish. "The Wizard of Oz" tells the story of Ed, a N.I.P.P.L.E–"New Irish Professional Person in London, England"–who believes in the reality of the life he is trying to live but is relentlessly brought down to earth by the narrator, Dave, who is in England seeking work after returning from traveling in Australia. In "The Greater of These is Love" Father Martin Flanagan, a much different sort of emigrant, is a parish priest in north London, where his small congregation is composed mostly of old women. When one morning a girl comes into his church during Mass, Father Flanagan is prompted to recall a girlfriend from his childhood. He is interrupted by his housekeeper to go and help a young man who has been arrested, and his success here breaks his mood; the story ends with him at peace with himself and his role.

Another tale of reconciliation is presented in "The Long Way Home," which begins with Ray Priest leaving his wife in the middle of the night after several years of discord. Ray picks up a hitchhiker, and shortly afterward the car runs over something; stopping to investigate, the two get caught up in preventing cattle escaping from a field. The farmer thanks them and offers to put them up for the night. The young man accepts, but Ray decides to return home and arrives back at dawn to make something of a reconciliation with Marion: "He knew in those moments that love is not always about freedom. He could see that love is often just a homecoming, and little more. And that the journey home of the heart is sometimes the longest of all." O'Connor adapted the short story into a motion picture; again directed by Breathnach, the movie was released in 1995.

There are also stories dealing with loss, such as "Freedom of the Press," which begins with the death in a train crash of Eileen Guthrie and deals with her husband's attempts to come to terms with her death. Also in this category is "Sink," in which a husband returns home to find that his wife has left him.

Finally, there are stories of betrayal, such as "The Bedouin Feast," in which the recently separated narrator is taken by his friends Joseph and Marie on a truly dreadful package holiday to Tunisia where "the stench of sewage drifted in from the bay." During a Bedouin feast laid on for the tourists Joseph argues with an elderly Englishman, a fight breaks out, and Joseph ends up in jail. Later that night, the narrator and Marie have sex, during which the narrator admits that "secretly I wished that this was over, and already part of the past." In "The Hills Are Alive," Danny Sullivan, a member of the Irish Republican Army (IRA), meets an English soldier, Henry Woods, in the public lavatory where he has gone in search of gay sex. The two men continue to meet, unaware that they are on opposing sides in the conflict or that Danny is being watched by the secret services. Danny discovers that Henry is English but cannot bring himself to kill him, and the two meet repeatedly until they fall in love. They plan to leave Ireland but are killed; each, ironically, by his own side, in that Henry is gunned down by a British patrol while Danny is blown up by an IRA car bomb.

True Believers sold well and received generally favorable reviews. Norman Shrapnel, writing in *The Guardian* (31 October 1991), found the collection moving and declared that O'Connor "admirably reveals the power of the short story to speak for our time." An unsigned review in *Publishers Weekly* (8 February 1993) called O'Connor's style "terse and graphic, attuned to the voices of his young characters," noting that this style sometimes "proves a powerful literary tool" but "more often it shows off a tiresome alienation that works well when a story's plot is strong enough to justify it" but "sags" in the character-driven stories.

O'Connor's second novel, *Desperadoes* (1993), draws upon his time in Nicaragua. It is a more ambitious work than his first novel, as O'Connor tries to deal with another culture and with central characters from another generation. Set in 1985 at the height of the Sandinistas' struggle with the Contras, the novel tells the story of Frank and Eleanor Little, an estranged couple who travel to Nicaragua to collect the body of their son, who has been reported killed in a Contra raid. Interspersed with the account of their search for their son are the life stories of the central characters, which allow O'Connor to write about Irish history as well as Nicaraguan politics. However, the central concern of the novel is people, and the reader is provided with a detailed account of the Little family and Johnny's difficult relationship with each of his parents.

In Nicaragua the Littles meet their son's best friend, Smokes Morrison, a larger-than-life American who was in a band with Johnny, and Morrison's long-suffering girlfriend, Cherry Balducci. Smokes helps the Littles steer their way through the Sandinista bureaucracy. Frank Little becomes increasingly bitter, at times castigating his son's generation for their easy attitude toward life and work. He also lashes out at his estranged wife, blaming Johnny's behavior on her past alcoholism. The novel, however, reveals that Johnny was something of a spoiled and self-centered child. Forced together by bitter circumstance, the Littles discover that despite their many differences they still have much in common, though there is no suggestion of a reconciliation. The novel draws on autobiographical material in its depictions of Nicaragua and the Littles, who may be seen as an exaggerated version of the O'Connors in that both families live in the Dublin suburb of Gleanageary and experience bitter family rows that end in a separation.

Shortly after arriving in Managua, the Littles are presented with a body, but it is not that of their son. After some investigations the authorities discover that there is a man in jail in the northern town of Corinto who might be Johnny, but the Littles cannot travel there since the Contras are active in that region. Unwilling to wait for official clearance, the Littles travel north with the rest of Smokes's band—Guapo and the blind Lorenzo, both native Nicaraguans—into the war zone, where they hope to find Johnny. This journey allows O'Connor to describe the people and places of rural Nicaragua. The country people they meet are unfailingly kind and, despite crushing poverty, always generous. Nicaragua is often presented as similar to Ireland, both by the Littles and by the Nicaraguans. As one woman they meet puts it: "Ireland . . . She's saying that the ordinary people in Ireland have suffered a lot too. All the bloodshed. And they always have to leave their country, like the people here."

On arrival in Corinto the Littles meet Johnny's girlfriend, Pilar, who is four months pregnant. They find Johnny has lost his identity papers and is in prison, having been arrested for involvement in drug smuggling. If the Littles turn to the authorities for help, Johnny will face a lengthy jail sentence; and their only other option is to pay a bribe of $4,000 to secure his release, but they do not have the cash. Contra forces attack the city, and in the ensuing upheaval the Littles are arrested, and Johnny escapes from the damaged jail. Frank and Eleanor are taken back to Managua, where he is held in jail while she is placed under house arrest in the Imperial Hotel. Johnny is soon recaptured by the authorities, who are prepared to be lenient since Pilar is the daughter of a famous revolutionary, but Johnny refuses to provide the names of his contacts in the drug-smuggling ring. Johnny is sentenced to one year in prison while his parents are expelled from the country. The novel focuses upon the parent-child relationship but treats this relationship from the perspective of the parents. While there are several successfully drawn younger characters, the central figures are the Littles, whose disintegrated relationship O'Connor carefully charts.

The novel received mixed reviews. Daniel Cairns in *The Guardian* (6 March 1994) complained that "Sentimentality insinuates itself too often for the characters to break free from cliché. . . . There is too much salvation and nowhere near enough just desserts." In *The Guardian* (5 July 1995) Fiachra Gibbons summarized the novel as "a typical O'Connor send up of political pretensions—mostly his own—but it is also about death, guilt," and, Gibbons suggested, a strong authorial vein of catharsis, in what he called its replaying of his "childhood wish fulfilment" of "bringing warring parents together." In *New Statesman & Society* (18 March 1994) Douglas Kennedy called the book a "compulsive and astonishingly confident novel" that "operates on several intriguing levels," summing it up as "a ferociously ambitious novel that aims high and, by and large, succeeds wonderfully."

In 1993 O'Connor was awarded the Irish Arts Council Macauly Fellowship. He returned to Ireland, and his master's thesis was published as *Even the Olives Are Bleeding: The Life and Times of Charles Donnelly* (1993). Between 1993 and 1998 O'Connor published mostly nonfiction, including travel writing and humorous pieces in periodicals. His first play, *Red Roses and Petrol,* premiered 9 May 1995 in Dublin and was published later that year. During this period O'Connor collaborated with Breathnach on movie projects and also began to write a weekly column for the *Irish Sunday Tribune.* The two collections of journalism, *The Secret World of the Irish Male* and *The Irish Male at Home and Abroad* (1996), were

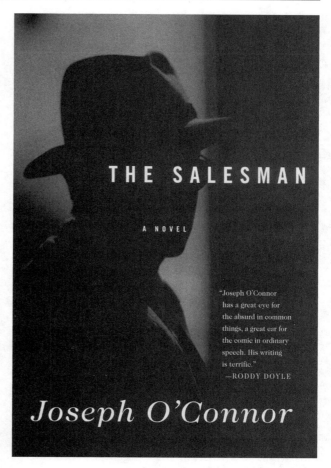

Dust jacket for the U.S. edition of O'Connor's 1998 novel, about a father who attempts to murder the escaped criminal who assaulted his daughter and ends up as the man's hostage (Richland County Public Library)

popular in Ireland, where they topped the best-seller lists, but British reviews were mixed. In *The Guardian* (7 July 1995) Nicholas Lezard dismissed the humor content of *The Secret World of the Irish Male,* suggesting that O'Connor's "comic writing tries too hard," but he praised his "astute comments on James Joyce, the Irish, and silly British attitudes." Reviewing the collection in *The New Statesman & Society* (14 July 1995), Patricia Craig called the book "as relentlessly jokey as an album of seaside postcards" but concluded that *The Secret World of the Irish Male* "is written with energy and aplomb, and in a spirit as right-on as it's head on." As the titles suggest, these works offer comic meditations on Irish masculinity in the vein of *Cowboys & Indians*—that is, wry reflections on the Irish twenty-something generation. Within these collections, however, there are some strong pieces on the changing nature of Irish culture.

Of particular interest in *The Secret World of the Irish Male* is the sequence of articles on Irish fiction that forms

"The Write Stuff: Irish Writers and Writing," as these pieces offer an informative account of new trends in Irish writing, identifying a "new concentration on the dignity of individual lives" as what is "so powerful—and so profoundly political—in the work of the new Irish writers" of the late twentieth century. For O'Connor, Irish fiction has emerged from the shade of its modernist fathers. He claims that the "version of Irish history known as the Irish literary tradition" has "more to do with tourism than art" and suggests that Irish writing is outstripping English fiction, which "is in a critical, perhaps terminal, state of decline." O'Connor highlights Roddy Doyle as his exemplar of all that is right about the modern Irish novel: he is a great storyteller, and his works are "deeply iconoclastic" and "passionately moral."

The Irish Male at Home and Abroad is a collection of mostly lightweight, humorous journalism. The final piece, "Banana Republic, recollections of a suburban Irish childhood," however, is an unflinching and at times poignant account of what O'Connor calls "my difficult childhood." The material may shed further light on the Eleanor/Johnny relationship in *Desperadoes*. O'Connor describes his mother as possessing "a capacity for doing great harm to people she loved," and, like Johnny, O'Connor recalls spending "a good deal of the very hot summer of 1977 just wandering around the streets of Dublin" avoiding his mother. O'Connor also reveals a youthful facility for prevarication—"I had the habit of telling people bare faced lies"—which echoes that of both Eddie Virago and Smokes Morrison.

O'Connor's other major work from this period is the travel book *Sweet Liberty: Travels in Irish America* (1996). Loosely based on a journey that encompasses all the places named Dublin in the United States, this book is often uncertain in tone—veering from historical recounting to O'Connor's more usual lighthearted style. The book was given a pasting in a May 1996 issue of *The Observer* (London), with reviewer Will Hobson harshly suggesting that it was so bad that its "real intention is to drive a final nail into the travel writing genre's coffin." Yet, positive reviews in *The New York Times Book Review, The Sunday Telegraph* (London), *The Mail on Sunday* (London), and the *Irish-American Magazine* praised O'Connor's humor and powers of observation.

O'Connor was invited by editor Dermot Bolger to contribute a chapter to the serial novel *Finbar's Hotel* (1997). The novel is set in a once grand, now decrepit, Dublin hotel scheduled for demolition, and the chapters comprise a series of interlocking narratives about individuals in the hotel. In addition to O'Connor and Bolger (novelist and founder of New Island Books), the other contributors were fellow Irish writers Doyle, Anne Enright, Hugo Hamilton, Jennifer Johnston, and Colm Tóibín. Since each chapter is unsigned, the novel

attracted much speculation as to which author had written which chapter. Reviews were generally favorable, with Katherine Weber noting in *The New York Times Book Review* (2 May 1999) that "American readers will probably be far less intent than their Irish counterparts on guessing the identity of the author of each unsigned chapter. Instead, readers here . . . will be drawn in by the novel itself," remarking that the book "brings together a good deal of distinctive writing with energy and charm—and surprising harmony," and concluding that "this unusual novel is far more than a curiosity, although no one—its own authors included—would presume to call it an important work of literature."

O'Connor's second novel, *The Salesman* (1998), was written after a lengthy break from long fiction. As with *Desperadoes,* the parent-child relationship is central to the novel. Once again, O'Connor portrays an alcoholic parent—in this case it is the father—and a broken marriage. There are also links with earlier works; for example, the narrator's best friend is a more glamorous individual—Seánie Ronan—recalling the relationship between Eddie and Dean Bean in *Cowboys & Indians.* Here the rivalry is tempered by the fact that Ronan becomes a priest, but, later in life, Sweeney discovers that his best friend is actually the father of his wife's first child, Lizzie. Readers in search of autobiographical resonances need not look long: the difficult family breakup, the mother winning custody, and the teenage daughter seeking a home with her father are all things that occurred in O'Connor's childhood and are detailed in "Banana Republic, recollections of a suburban Irish childhood" in *The Irish Male at Home and Abroad.*

The first-person narrative of the novel is divided into four parts. Parts 1, 3, and 4 are presented as a letter written by Billy Sweeney, the salesman of the title, to his daughter, Maeve, who lies in a coma after being beaten and raped during a petrol station robbery. Part 2 comprises Sweeney's diary from 12 to 25 July 1994. In part Sweeney writes the letter to assuage a sense of guilt, hoping that his words "might help you to understand something small of where you came from, the bright mad love we felt for you, the evanescent love we had for each other. I confess I do hope for that little, or that much." Sweeney uses the letter as a means of setting out his side of the story of his failed marriage, and thus the reader is given a powerful account of an alcoholic's descent into addiction and a poignant tale of family breakup. The reader is also given another of O'Connor's histories of modern Ireland as Sweeney recounts the story of his life.

The novel begins at the trial of Maeve's attackers, where, during a recess, one of the gang, Donal Quinn, escapes. Some weeks later Sweeney spots a heavily disguised Quinn in the seaside town of Bray, and, having watched his movements for some time, he decides to revenge himself on Quinn by arranging for him to be murdered. The murder attempt fails, and Sweeney ends up holding Quinn hostage. In a reversal of fortune, Quinn escapes, but, reluctant to leave because he is sought by the IRA, he then holds Sweeney hostage in his own home. The novel ends with Quinn shot by the IRA for drug dealing and Sweeney reunited with his family.

There are potential flaws in the narrative. While the diary section is wholly convincing, it strains the reader's credulity to accept that Sweeney could actually recall and then write in such detail the events of his life, particularly because he was a chronic alcoholic for a significant part of it. At times the first-person narrative drifts toward an unlikely omniscience, and O'Connor does not take advantage of the limitations of a single point of view to characterize his narrator—as, for example, Patrick McCabe is able to do in *The Butcher Boy* (1992). What is effective, however, is the well-judged reliance upon the assumption that Sweeney is writing for his daughter, which results in certain facts being taken for granted by the narrative. Thus, the reader is casually introduced to the fact that Grace dies in a car crash and that Sweeney is an alcoholic well before the characters have been fully established or these events occur in Sweeney's retelling of his life story to Maeve. This delivery is not only part of the realism of the novel but also a means of engaging readers and encouraging them to continue reading to find out more.

The botched-revenge aspect of the narrative introduces a thriller dimension to what otherwise would be a poignant family saga. There is a marked shift in tone in the scenes dealing with Quinn and then Sweeney's incarceration that at times sits uneasily with the more realistic sequences concerning Sweeney's life. What sustains the novel is the narrative voice of Billy Sweeney and the way in which this voice offers a personal view of a changing Ireland. As he did earlier in *Desperadoes* with Frank Little, O'Connor again shows great skill in creating the idiom and mind-set of a middle-aged Irish man.

Reviews of *The Salesman* were positive. Nicholas Royle, writing in the *Literary Review* (January 1998), commented that the "transition from a light-hearted mood to doom-laden tragedy is handled with a confidence and skill unusual in a thirty-four-year-old. Likewise the depth of suffering. O'Connor's narrator is a good twenty years his senior, yet we never feel that the author is striving for authority of experience. He's a natural, a reader of other men's and women's minds and hearts." In *The New York Times Book Review* (11 July 1999) James Saynor called the novel "brutal yet contrite" and praised the author's use of dialogue, remarking that "O'Connor's writing can be long-winded, but it is also freewheeling and supple, switching between the comic, the candid and the profane."

The Comedian (2000) is a novella that O'Connor contributed to the Open Door series, an initiative by New Island Books and the City of Dublin Vocational Education Committee. The idea behind the series is to provide fiction with adult themes for adults who have difficulty with reading and are too embarrassed to read children's books. The story is a reworking of "True Believers" from O'Connor's 1991 short-story collection—though the narrator's family is much poorer and presented in more detail than it is in the earlier story. The father is more fully drawn and—as one might expect with O'Connor—emerges as the hero in this tale of family disintegration. As befits a story aimed at less adept readers, the narrative spells out what the earlier story left for the reader to deduce. In its new form the story is reminiscent of Doyle's *Paddy Clarke, Ha, Ha, Ha* (1993) inasmuch as it tells the tale of a family breakup through the eyes of a child.

Inishowen (2000) is a substantial and ambitious novel that tells the interlinked stories of an alcoholic police inspector, Martin Aitken; a New York plastic surgeon, Milton Amery; and his terminally ill wife, Ellen. O'Connor's wealthy New Yorkers are competently drawn, but this shift to a new fictional terrain does not mark any great departure. O'Connor keeps to familiar emotional ground, as the Amerys are another dysfunctional middle-class family. Ellen abruptly leaves the family home days before Christmas to return to Ireland, the country of her birth, and seek the mother who gave her up for adoption as a baby. The novel shares the Dublin milieu of *The Salesman,* and the detective who worked on Quinn's case appears again, now as Detective Superintendent Duigan.

O'Connor uses an omniscient narrator to tell the stories of three people between 23 December 1994 and 1 January 1995. The book is divided into eleven sections of unequal length and forty chapters. In many copies of the original U.K. edition there was a printing error that mistitled the eleventh section "Saturday 31 January 1994," whereas the section should be titled "Saturday 31 December 1994." O'Connor's use of third-person narrative in *Inishowen* is more sophisticated than in *Desperadoes.* He makes effective use of free indirect discourse to allow characters to present themselves by means of their prejudices, especially in his presentation of Milton Amery, whose banal jealous fantasies regarding his wife help underscore his shallowness. O'Connor also returns to the detailed and convincing portrayal of a middle-aged woman in the depiction of Ellen, reminiscent of Eleanor Little in *Desperadoes* in her caring but independent ways. As with the earlier novel, O'Connor uses a journey as a device to bring together two people who, in helping the other, find that they still have a capacity for human warmth despite all their past troubles.

Both Aitken and Ellen have a link with Inishowen, a remote country town in County Donegal. Aitken's former wife came from the town, and their son, Robbie, who was killed in a car accident at the age of nine, is buried there, while Ellen's birth mother lives in the town. Inishowen and Valerie's republican father are reminiscent of Marion Mangan's father and her hometown of Ballybracken in *Cowboys & Indians*. Together, in a snowbound Ireland, Aitken and Ellen make the awkward journey to their past, to go to Inishowen, where his child is buried and her birth mother lives. In order to avoid Aitken's questions, Ellen pretends to be a nun, but toward the end of the journey north Aitken discovers the truth about Ellen from a newspaper report. Intermixed with this journey is the pursuit of Aitken by a disgruntled criminal sworn to avenge a public humiliation and the increasingly unlikely attempts of the Amery family to track down the missing Ellen.

O'Connor presents a knowing deflation of the tourist myths of Ireland: for Amery the mythic West of Ireland is "bleakness and Becketty nothingness" and "the main talent the Irish had now, and the main one they had always had, was for beating the living bejesus out of each other." O'Connor also depicts the power of an unhappy marriage psychologically to warp and deform all involved, while still managing to work in well-drawn humorous scenes, such as the Amery family's disastrous Christmas dinner.

In 2001 Jonathan Cape Ltd. published *Yeats is Dead! A Novel by Fifteen Irish Writers,* a collaborative novel to which O'Connor contributed and that he edited. O'Connor spent some four years on the project, which he began after Amnesty International asked him if he were interested in compiling an anthology of Irish short fiction. Demurring, O'Connor instead asked fellow Irish writers to participate in writing a group novel, which in this case is more accurately described as a collection of seven unsigned, interlinked short stories. In addition to the novelists Doyle and Hamilton, who had also contributed to that earlier novel, O'Connor succeeded in enlisting the Irish American novelist Frank McCourt, playwright and screenwriter Conor McPherson, journalist Gene Kerrigan, playwright and actress Gina Moxley, best-selling novelist Marian Keyes, literary biographer Anthony Cronin, writer and stand-up comedian Owen O'Neill, sportswriter Tom Humphries, actress Pauline McLynn (best known for her role as Mrs. Doyle in the Channel 4 television comedy *Father Ted*), playwrights Charlie O'Neill and Donal O'Kelly, and the director and screenwriter Gerard Stembridge.

Doyle wrote the first chapter and McCourt the final chapter for the novel, a murder mystery set in Dublin that centers around the search for the manuscript of unpublished work by James Joyce. Reviewing the novel in *Book* (July–August 2001), Kevin Greenberg remarked that "all the chapters are turbulent, and most of the writers take ample license in introducing new characters and fortifying old ones with remarkable, slapstick indiscretion," saying that a "generous amount of credit must be given to editor Joseph O'Connor, who manages to keep things cohesive throughout." O'Connor told Andre Mayer in a telephone interview for the Toronto weekly newspaper *eye* (21 June 2001) that editing the book was "absolutely hell on earth," particularly in establishing continuity, since the contributors "tried to make it as difficult as possible for the person coming after them. . . . The body count is pretty high because people were fond of murdering all of the characters created by a previous author." He told Mayer, "we don't make very high literary claims" for the novel; however, as Emma Brockes noted in a group interview with O'Connor and seven of his co-authors for *The Guardian* (12 June 2001), the book "is worth reading for the fun-factor of watching the last three authors scramble to pull 15 storylines together; for the blatant squeamishness of the first six authors, who would rather slay the entire cast list than take up second-hand characters; and for the sense of enjoyment that infuses the thing from start to finish." The authors donated all of their royalties to Amnesty International: the book earned more than £500,000 in advance sales. It debuted at number two on the Irish best-seller list and was number one on the list for two months.

Joseph O'Connor continues to live in Dublin with his wife and child. He is a popular writer who can weave a complex and compelling story about vivid characters caught up in real human problems. O'Connor declares in *The Secret World of the Irish Male* that "People want to read stories which inform their lives, which bring us news from the world of the writer to the world which the rest of us inhabit," and he has developed from a writer mostly concerned with people of his own generation to an author whose works deal with a wide variety of Irish life.

Interviews:

Emma Brockes, "Character Assassins," *Guardian,* 12 June 2001;

Andre Mayer, "Irish mob mentality," *eye* (Toronto), 21 June 2001.

References:

Terence Brown, *Ireland's Literature: Selected Essays* (Mullingar, Ireland: Lilliput Press / Totowa, N.J.: Barnes & Noble, 1988);

Liam Harte, "A Kind of Scab: Irish Identity in the writings of Dermot Bolger and Joseph O'Connor," *Irish Studies Review,* 20 (Autumn 1997): 17–22;

Richard Kearney, *Transitions: Narratives in Modern Irish Culture* (Dublin: Wolfhound Press, 1988).

Kate O'Riordan

(26 March 1960 –)

Kersti Tarien
St Hugh's College, Oxford University

BOOKS: *Involved* (London: Flamingo, 1995);
The Boy in the Moon (London: Flamingo, 1997);
Ladies' Night at Finbar's Hotel, by O'Riordan, Maeve Binchy, Clare Boylan, Emma Donoghue, Anne Haverty, Éilis Ní Dhuibhne, and Deirdre Purcell, edited by Dermot Bolger (London: Picador, 1999; Dublin: New Island, 1999; San Diego: Harcourt Brace, 2000)–includes "Room 102–Da Da Da–Daa" by O'Riordan;
The Angel in the House (London: Flamingo, 2000).

PLAY PRODUCTIONS: *The Jaws of Darkness,* London, Orange Tree Theatre, 1995;
She'll Be Wearing Silk Pyjamas, London, Orange Tree Theatre, 1997.

PRODUCED SCRIPTS: "The Homecoming," television, *Capital Lives,* Carlton Television, 1995;
Involved, television, adapted by O'Riordan from her novel of that title, HTV, 1996;
In the Beginning, television, RTÉ, 1999;
The Boy in the Moon, television, Salt Productions / BBC Northern Ireland, 2000.

Kate O'Riordan (photograph by Jerry Bauer; from the cover for the paperback edition of The Boy in the Moon, *1998)*

Kate O'Riordan, an Irish-born writer who lives and works in England, has written novels, short stories, and dramatic pieces. Her writings, centered on an in-depth exploration of human relationships, focus on the importance of boundaries between past and present and the unearthing of repressed traumas and buried secrets. Often based around an apparent conflict between different cultural stereotypes–Northern Ireland and the Republic of Ireland or Ireland and Britain–O'Riordan's work frequently includes a disturbing vein of barely suppressed violence hidden beneath the veneer of day-to-day life. Her concern with the hidden, and often darker, side of human life sets O'Riordan's work alongside that of other young Irish women writers such as Mary Morrissy, Anne Haverty, and Mary O'Donnell, who, as did O'Riordan, emerged during the 1990s. All of these authors use neo-Gothic portray-als of family relationships and transgenerational conflicts in order to reflect upon the problematic nature of personal identity. The uncanny family secrets that distort familiar domestic spaces in this literature and its practitioners' attempts to articulate repressed scandals suggest that these psychological battlegrounds are much different territory from the romantic ground explored, for example, in Maeve Binchy's fiction.

O'Riordan's interest in psychological and physical violence finds a parallel in the work of Northern Irish writers such as Eoin McNamee, Glenn Patterson, and Robert McLiam Wilson.

Kate McCarthy was born in London on 26 March 1960 to an Irish couple, Frank and Phyl McCarthy, the first of four children. A year later, the McCarthys returned to Bantry, a small town in the west of Ireland, where Frank McCarthy took over the family business, a butcher's shop. Having failed to realize his ambition to become a poet, he was determined to help his children to an appreciation of what he considered to be good literature. His influence on the young Kate was considerable, especially as a guide to reading matter. The range of her reading was huge: from Margaret Mitchell's *Gone with the Wind* (1936)—her first non-children's book—to Virginia Woolf and the great Russian novels of Ivan Turgenev, Leo Tolstoy, and Fyodor Dostoevsky, which became and remain her favorites.

McCarthy began to compose stories as soon as she learned to write, and her earliest literary ambition was to compose the "ultimate collection of fairy stories," often in the same macabre vein as her later fiction. As she recalled in an interview given to Arminta Wallace of *The Irish Times* (19 August 1997): "I started by writing fairy stories. I still have a copy of one, which must have been the first, or maybe the second, story that I ever wrote, and at the end I've got: 'By the way, the mother was dead.'"

Following her early education at a local convent primary school and secondary school, McCarthy was sent to boarding school in Roscarberry. Never a particularly conscientious pupil, she nevertheless won several essay awards, an indication, perhaps, that her English teachers recognized a gift not yet fully realized. Graduating from Mount St. Michael School in 1978, she decided not to continue her studies at university, and instead she applied for a position in a local travel agency. She spent a year selling pilgrimages—religious package tours—in agencies in Bantry, Clonakilty, and Skibbereen, then moved to Los Angeles for a year, where she worked for a travel agent who catered to the Irish American market. Her encounters with different cultures left their mark on her later fiction. She returned to Ireland, and in 1984 she married her childhood sweetheart, Donal O'Riordan. Originally intending to settle in Canada, the young couple failed to obtain work permits and instead chose London as their new home.

After settling in London, O'Riordan began to write more seriously, and during the late 1980s her short stories regularly appeared in literary magazines such as *Acumen* and *Staple* and newspapers such as *The Mail on Sunday* (London) and *The Sunday Tribune* (Dublin). She experimented with a range of genres and stylistic techniques, from stream of consciousness to spoofs on Bible stories. At the same time she joined several writing groups, which became useful sources of practical information as well as opportunities to encounter other writers and their works. In 1991 O'Riordan won the Sunday Tribune/Hennessy Best Emerging Writer Award. As well as writing short stories, during this period she wrote several plays, and she performed several rehearsed readings in small fringe theaters. This interest in dramatic literature forms a constant parallel to her activity as a novelist and has attracted equally favorable criticism; she was invited to attend the prestigious Carlton Screenwriters Course in 1995, the same year in which her play *The Jaws of Darkness* was produced by the Orange Tree Theatre in London.

The impulse that led O'Riordan to write her first novel was linked to the birth of her first son when, as she recalled in an unpublished 27 June 2001 interview with Kersti Tarien, a "kind of panic set in." Encouraged by the success of her short stories and first plays, she sent a few chapters and a plot summary to Maggie Phillips of the literary agency Ed Victor Ltd., who later became her agent and whose support O'Riordan acknowledges as crucial in the completion of her novel. *Involved* (1995) was written while O'Riordan was at home caring for her newborn baby, during the short intervals while the baby slept.

The idea for *Involved* derived from O'Riordan's experiences as an Irish woman in the United States, where she encountered a view of Ireland based primarily on the Troubles, as the sectarian violence endemic in Northern Ireland since 1968 is known. Her encounter with this common misconception, that all Irish people have been personally affected by this sectarian violence, led O'Riordan to reflect on the real differences between Northern Ireland and the Irish Republic; in fact, having grown up in the Irish Republic, O'Riordan has never been to "the North," as Northern Ireland is known. In the United States, people believed her childhood to have been a time of permanent conflict, in which bombs and ambushes were a part of everyday life, whereas in reality, she told Tarien, "the people from the North seemed wild, strange, and mad to us."

In *Involved* O'Riordan set out to explore the differences within Ireland through the juxtaposition of two much different Irish characters. As Aisling Foster in *TLS: The Times Literary Supplement* (17 February 1995) succinctly summarized her aims in the novel: "Kate O'Riordan ignores the well-trodden areas of tribes and sovereignty. Instead, she explores a very different characteristic: that ancient mentality gap which separates Ulster from the rest of the island and keeps Ireland like a bear with a sore head. In a new version of familiar troubles thriller mixed with a love story, O'Riordan pours out her exasperation at Northern insularity and poses some interesting questions about just how united Ireland or its inhabitants can be."

Involved is the story of a young Irish couple. Kitty Fitzgerald, a young publisher from a middle-class Cork family, and Danny O'Neill, a junior solicitor from a Belfast ghetto, meet and fall in love in Dublin. Against the background of two different worlds–the relaxed and affluent South, the violent and hermetic North–O'Riordan investigates two different family settings, both disturbing. The O'Neills, a close-knit family, are intimately involved in IRA paramilitary activities, and the opening scenes of the novel depict Danny's elder brother, Eamon, killing a puppy, described in chilling detail. Kitty's family, only superficially "normal," proves to be no less disturbed than is Danny's: her mother is an alcoholic with an unexplained hatred of her daughter, and her father is terminally ill. Under the combined forces of social and family pressure, Danny and Kitty's relationship falls apart. Confronted with the shocking evidence of the depth of Danny's family's involvement in paramilitary activities, and convinced of Danny's neglect of her, Kitty finally decides to inform the police about Eamon O'Neill's involvement with the IRA. The novel closes with a suggestion of further violence as the reader learns that Eamon has discovered the location of Kitty's new home in Canada.

The realist style of *Involved* makes the personal tale of Kitty and Danny's failed romance emblematic of the divide between the North and the South. The political division is reflected through the personal divide that needs to be transcended in order to achieve an unfractured future. Framed by the scenes reflected through Eamon's ice-cold point of view, Kitty's story, filtered through her often bewildered mind, achieves poignancy and human warmth, offering a contrast with the outbreak of violence. O'Riordan's novel leaves little hope for reconciliation between the conflicting communities. As Gerry Smythe said in his review of *Involved* for the *Irish Studies Review* (Spring 1997): "The 'national romance' in O'Riordan's novel has evolved to the stage where the damaging rift is no longer imagined in terms of the conflicting communities *within* Northern Ireland, but rather the breach that has emerged between North and South, and indeed the cultural divide *between* both parts of Ireland and Great Britain." As do Bernard MacLaverty's *Cal* (1983), Brian Moore's *Lies of Silence* (1990), and McNamee's *Resurrection Man* (1994), O'Riordan's first novel uses political subject matter to explore how Irish politics can be defined in ways other than just matters of public policy, including public and individual expressions of ideology, sexual displacement, and domestic desire.

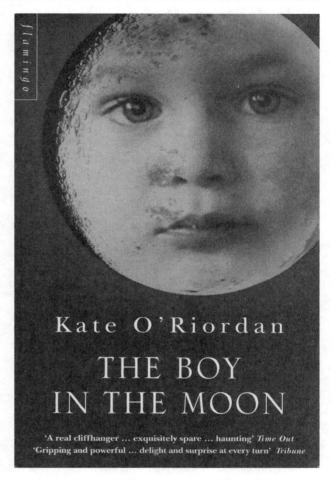

Cover for the paperback edition of O'Riordan's 1997 novel, about a couple driven apart by the accidental death of their young son (Bruccoli Clark Layman Archives)

Although her novel exemplifies the same addictive excitement of violence that characterizes the "bloody poetry" of McNamee's *Resurrection Man,* which rendered political Belfast as a mythical hinterland, O'Riordan's evocation of Northern Ireland in her debut novel is, according to the reviewers, less successful. Writing for *The Irish Times* (1 April 1995), Eamonn Sweeney noted that "ironically, it is the Troubles background of her book that proves the one weakness in an otherwise exemplary debut novel." In his *TLS* review Foster said, "O'Riordan appears as baffled as any outsider by Ulster intransigence. She shows her disgust at the refusal of citizens like Danny to rail against the terror and is so infuriated by the self-importance which their war has brought, sometimes allowing the twists of story to knot and get lost." Despite these shortcomings, the novel Sweeney called an "unusually assured debut" was nominated for the Dillon's First Novel Prize. The author started to be talked about as an "acutely interesting writer whose future work should bear watching."

Following the publication of her first novel O'Riordan began writing full-time. After *Involved* was published, she completed two plays—*A Drawing Down of Blinds* (reading in Soho Theatre and Orange Tree Theatre in 1996) and *She'll Be Wearing Silk Pyjamas* (produced by Orange Tree Theatre in 1997). In the 1990s O'Riordan also worked for television, including writing an episode for the popular hospital drama *Casualty,* for which she got only a "storyline credit." The experiment does not, however, appear to have been particularly successful; O'Riordan's comments in her 1997 interview for *The Irish Times* on her difficulties in writing for this television program reveal an important element in her writing technique: "It was a total disaster. I just couldn't get it right. I'd been trained all along to do everything possible not to make characters say what they're feeling; to find ways to show it through the action or in a roundabout way—a facial expression, or a glance—but in Casualty there is always a moment where they just spill their guts."

In 1997 O'Riordan's second novel, *The Boy in the Moon,* was published. Once again, the novel was inspired by personal experience, in this case an incident in which her small son's life appeared to be endangered. As she said in her interview with Wallace:

It's purely fiction but it all came from a moment when my husband put my son on a bridge—small stone bridge outside Lismore Castle in Co. Waterford—and I turned and saw him. And I just completely froze, because it is about a forty-foot drop, and a kid moves so fast . . . I don't know whether men are less vigilant or whether it's to do with wanting their children—sons, particularly—not to be afraid. Although obviously it's wrong to generalise. Anyway, I couldn't get it out of my head all of that Christmas—I had started another novel, but that image kept eating away at me.

The novel centers on the portrayal of adult and childhood grief, the need to recover repressed emotions and discover the hidden pattern of one's personal past in order to come to terms with the present. *The Boy in the Moon* depicts the rigid Englishwoman Julia and her seemingly relaxed Irish husband, Brian, and their different ways of learning to accept the accidental death of their young son, Sam. In her 1997 interview O'Riordan acknowledged having deliberately chosen protagonists who represent the stereotypical characteristic traits of the Irish and the English: "I did want the central characters in this book to represent stereotyped ideas of Ireland and England—the husband is apparently very easy-going, a chatty kind of guy, whereas the wife is much more reserved and uptight." While the family is

on its way to a holiday in Ireland, Sam accidentally slips from his father's grip while standing on a bridge and falls to his death. Stunned by grief, Julia and Brian part company, with Julia eventually seeking refuge on the farm run by Jeremiah, Brian's patriarchal father, who leads a frugal and monotonous life, governed by household chores and unremitting Bible reading. While living on the farm, Julia comes upon Brian's mother's journal, which reveals that Sam's death has an eerie parallel in Brian's childhood, when Brian's twin brother, Noel, fell over a cliff. Brian, meanwhile, racked by guilt at the death of his son, is also haunted by memories of the death of his brother, for which he believes himself also to be responsible. Julia's detective work uncovers the real culprit for Noel's death, the tyrannical Jeremiah, thus bringing about an emotional release: "For now, all they could do was cling and weep: for Sam, for Noel, for themselves, for the possibility of love enduring without forgiveness—and for the blind, trusting love of constantly betrayed children everywhere."

In *The Boy in the Moon,* O'Riordan portrays human relationships as a complex web, where the present is intricately interwoven with the past. Shifting between English and Irish registers, Brian's and Julia's narrating voices, their childhood and present, O'Riordan's skillful deployment of multiple points of view accentuates the theme of memory. The characters' gradual awakening to a fuller understanding of their lives necessarily means accepting the unsettling as a part of one's personal past. The intricate temporal structure of the novel was carefully planned and executed. O'Riordan explained to Wallace: "I was trying to do it in layers, so there are three stories running in tandem—and then once I opened it up and brought in the 1960s it became great fun for me, because that was my time too. And I'd totally forgotten the era of mini-skirts and Muriel Spark. It was a real turning point for Ireland—I mean, I know mini-skirts were probably shocking in England too, but they had more resonance in Ireland."

Despite O'Riordan's care with the setting, Ruth Scurr, reviewing the novel for *TLS* (5 September 1997), found the Irish setting contingent, claiming that: "This is a timeless, placeless story with deprivation its only real context." Impressed by the convincing depiction of the "avatars of trauma," Scurr compared O'Riordan to Thomas Hardy, saying that "As with Hardy, one is awed by the novelist's unflinching grasp on suffering."

The overall positive reception with which *The Boy in the Moon* met can be summarized with Louise East's words in her review in *The Irish Times* (19 September 1997). Citing the "satisfyingly knotty plot," "the gradual awakenings and epiphanies of O'Riordan's well-turned characters," and "the depiction of tragedies which never descends into the mawkish or

Emma Donoghue, Éilis Ní Dhuibhne, O'Riordan, Anne Haverty, Maeve Binchy, Clare Boylan,
and Deirdre Purcell (photograph by Colm Henry; from the paperback cover for the
U.S. edition of Ladies' Night at Finbar's Hotel, 2000)

glib," East chose *The Boy in the Moon* for the Book of the Week, declaring "I am already looking forward to her next novel."

O'Riordan's growing fame and reputation in the Irish literary world was further confirmed when Dermot Bolger invited her and six other well-known Irish women authors–Binchy, Clare Boylan, Emma Donoghue, Haverty, Éilis Ní Dhuibhne, and Deirdre Purcell –each to submit a chapter about one night in the lives of the (mostly) female guests of a hotel. For the group novel *A Night at Finbar's Hotel,* published in 1997, Bolger had asked several Irish writers, including Roddy Doyle, Anne Enright, Hugo Hamilton, and Joseph O'Connor, each to contribute unsigned chapters portraying the clientele of a shabby Dublin hotel slated for demolition. In the sequel, *Ladies' Night at Finbar's Hotel* (1999), the anonymous chapters depict the reopening of the formerly seedy establishment, now resplendently redecorated. As Carolyn See noted in the *International Herald Tribune* (27 March 2000), the refurbished Finbar's Hotel is "too trendy for words," which could also be said about the jacket photo that has the seven writers "jammed companionably into a foaming jacuzzi." Bolger increased the mischievous playfulness of this fictional enterprise by leaving the readers to guess which author wrote which chapter. O'Riordan's contribution, "Room 102–Da Da Da–Daa," relates the story of a clothing designer, surprised by her manic-depressive father's unexpected appearance in the hotel. Bolger adapted the novel into a radio play for the British Broadcasting Corporation (BBC), which aired on BBC Radio 4 on 10 May 2000.

The powerful grip that family can have over personal fate is again among the central thematic interests in O'Riordan's third novel, *The Angel in the House* (2000). Compared to *Involved* and *The Boy in the Moon,* this novel is notably lighter in tone. Angela, a novice nun working in a center for the homeless, is an Irish girl who is unquestioningly following the career path chosen for her by her domineering aunts. Robert, a charming art restorer with an unrequited passion for the creative arts, leads a lonely life in Isleworth, where his daily existence is a balancing act between the demands of his American mother and the supposedly perfect family of his best friend, Peter. During his weekly lecture at the Victoria and Albert Museum, Robert meets Angela and falls in love. Multiple twists and turns complicate the protagonists' path toward true love. Robert is unaware of Angela's vocation, and Angela mistakenly assumes Robert to have a rather complicated role to fulfill in Peter's family, believing him to be the biological father of Peter's two daughters. The meddling of Robert's mother, Bonnie, and Peter keep the two apart until the romantic and rather predictable happy ending. O'Riordan evokes a range of colorful characters, among whom are the foul-mouthed, all-too-often inebriated Mother Superior; Angela's aunts, whose domineering voices accompany both her waking hours and her dreams; and Bonnie, Robert's embarrassing hippie (and American) mother.

Although governed by the generic rules of romantic comedy, the protagonists' pursuit of personal happiness indicates that this goal cannot be accomplished without first coming to terms with one's past. While explaining the intricacies of the restoration process to Angela, Robert exults in the creative possibilities of his occupation: "I've found the reality, the truth of the thing itself, detected every flaw, every crack, every pathetic fissure—and made it whole again." While reassessing their lives, O'Riordan's characters wonder whether their true self-images lie in the present or past. Thus, Angela asks Robert, "Are you saying the reality is when you've it all stripped back to the bare essentials, what's really left, or is the reality the new restored work just because it looks exactly as it did once before?"

Reviewers were disappointed to find the disturbing darkness of O'Riordan's previous novels to have been replaced with a brighter and more hopeful tone in *The Angel in the House.* In an undated online review posted on www.ireland.com, Eve Patten summarized what some critics saw as the weaknesses of the novel: "The humour is fatigued, the narrative grinding, and I would go so far as to suggest that some of the caricatures might be described as misogynistic were they not protected by the conventions of the 'non-serious' genre." In a 20 May 2000 review in *The Times* (London), however, Gill Hornby was notably less critical, remarking upon the darker subplots that enrich the narrative and the plethora of colorful characters evoked in the novel. According to her verdict, while *The Angel in the House* may seem a little overcrowded at times, "none of these people can be accused of being boring."

In *The Angel in the House* Angela and Robert's highly human quest for personal happiness evokes O'Riordan's central thematic interests: human relationships and the necessary journey into one's past in order to accept and understand the present. Although the conventions of romantic comedy make the end of such a quest perhaps rather predictable, this journey nevertheless entails passing through disturbingly unfamiliar territories. Herein lies O'Riordan's real strength—making the eerie, frightening, and unspeakable an organic part of everyday experience. Familiarizing, however, does not entail domesticating. Thus, O'Riordan's fiction retains the disturbingly chilling twists and turns of the fairy tales she composed as a child. One has to agree with the reviewers—Kate O'Riordan is an author whose future work bears watching.

Interviews:

Arminta Wallace, "Home is where hurt is: Interview with Kate O'Riordan," *Irish Times,* 19 August 1997, p. 6;

Stephen Saunders, "Writing which has time to meander: Interview with Kate O'Riordan," *Canberra Times,* 13 June 1999, p. 18.

Deirdre Purcell

(22 April 1945 –)

Ellen Crowell
University of Texas at Austin

BOOKS: *Ethiopia: The Dark Hunger,* by Purcell and
Pat Langan (Dublin: Magill, 1984);
On Lough Derg, with photographs by Liam Blake and
commentary by Bishop Joseph Duffy (Dublin:
Veritas, 1988);
The Time of My Life: An Autobiography, by Purcell and
Gay Byrne (Dublin: Gill & Macmillan, 1989);
A Place of Stones (Dublin: Town House / London:
Macmillan, 1991; New York: Signet, 1993);
That Childhood Country (Dublin: Town House / Lon-
don: Macmillan, 1992; New York: Signet,
1994);
Falling for a Dancer (Dublin: Town House / London:
Macmillan, 1993); republished as *Ashes of Roses*
(New York: Signet, 1994);
Francey (Dublin: Town House / London: Macmillan,
1994); republished as *Roses After Rain* (New
York: Signet, 1996);
Sky (Dublin: Town House / London: Macmillan,
1995; New York: Signet, 1997);
Love Like Hate Adore (Dublin: Town House / London:
Macmillan, 1997);
Ladies' Night at Finbar's Hotel, by Purcell, Clare Boy-
lan, Kate O'Riordan, Maeve Binchy, Emma
Donoghue, Anne Haverty, and Éilis Ní
Dhuibhne, edited by Dermot Bolger (London:
Picador / Dublin: New Island, 1999; San Diego:
Harcourt Brace, 2000);
Jesus and Billy Are Off to Barcelona, Open Door Series,
no. 3 (Dublin: New Island, 1999);
Entertaining Ambrose (Dublin: Town House, 2000;
Dublin: Town House / London: Macmillan,
2001);
Marble Gardens (London: Headline, 2002; Dublin:
New Island, 2002);
Has Anyone Here Seen Larry? Open Door Series (Dub-
lin: New Island, 2002).

PRODUCED SCRIPT: *Falling for a Dancer,* television, adapted by Purcell from her novel of that
title, BBC Northern Ireland / RTÉ, 1998.

Deirdre Purcell (from the dust jacket for
Love Like Hate Adore, *1997)*

OTHER: *Write Here! Write Now! Footprints from the Second
Millennium: A Record of the Lives, Thought and Hopes
of a Selection of Young People in Ireland as the Second
Millennium Turns to the Third,* edited by Purcell and
others (Dublin: National Millennium Committee,
1999);
James Gleason, *Contemplating Ireland,* introduction by
Purcell (Washington, D.C.: Atlantic Ireland,
2000; Dublin: New Island, 2001).

Since publishing her first novel, *A Place of Stones*
(1991), Deirdre Purcell has marshaled diverse narrative
styles to produce texts centered squarely within contemporary Irish cultural debates. Known most widely
first as an acclaimed journalist and then as a successful

writer of best-selling romance fiction, Purcell has gained further recognition as a literary novelist and screenwriter. Her novels are distributed in Ireland, England, and the United States and have been translated into eleven different languages.

Persistent comparisons between Purcell and Maeve Binchy, perhaps the most popular writer of Irish popular fiction, have prompted Purcell to define and differentiate her own writing. In a 22 February 1995 interview with a reporter for the New Zealand newspaper *The Dominion* (Wellington), Purcell observed that comparisons between Binchy and herself constituted "a kind of journalistic shorthand." She argued that these comparisons stem from superficial similarities: both writers are women, both are writing about Ireland, and both write about the same era. "But outside that," Purcell maintained, "we're not very similar." She insisted that her novels, unlike Binchy's "lovely, warm fireside books," are more "dramatic." And though her first five novels are most easily categorized within the genre of popular romance and therefore often dismissed as "airport fare," Purcell's particular brand of drama consistently pits private life against public discourse in Ireland, thereby connecting her heroines' personal struggles with social issues affecting contemporary Irish women.

Purcell was born 22 April 1945 in Dublin, Ireland. She was educated at Scoil Mhuire, Marlborough Street, Dublin, and Gortnor Abbey, Crossmolina, County Mayo. She was employed by Aer Lingus in the early 1960s, when increased air travel from the United States created a rapid expansion in Irish tourism. Purcell was at this time interested in acting and theater, and as a result of her roles in several amateur productions on Dublin stages, in 1965 she was offered a position in the Abbey Theatre Company under the direction of Ernest Blythe. Purcell stayed with the Abbey Theatre for three years. In 1968 Purcell left Dublin for Loyola University in Chicago, Illinois, where she had been offered a theater fellowship. At Loyola she met her first husband, actor Rob Weckler. They married in 1969 and remained in Chicago, where their son Adrian was born in 1973, moving to Dublin when Adrian was seven weeks old. She and her husband separated when their second son, Simon (born in Ireland in 1975), was eighteen months old, soon after Purcell began working for Radio Telefis Éireann (RTÉ), the Irish national broadcasting service, as a radio newsreader. Her skills on the radio news quickly established her prominence in the Irish press, and in 1977 Purcell was offered a job as a newsreader on RTÉ television. This offer was an historic one; Purcell was the first woman newsreader for RTÉ television. Her television feature stories gained the attention of print news sources, and she began writing for *The Irish Press* (Dublin) in 1983 while still working for RTÉ television. Then, Vincent Browne, at that time editor of *The Sunday Tribune* (Dublin), enticed her to leave *The Irish Press* (Dublin) for his newspaper.

Prior experience in every aspect of Irish media made Purcell an impressive and respected voice for *The Sunday Tribune* (Dublin). She was careful not to allow her stories to follow the media trend toward invasive journalism. In Medb Ruane's 7 May 1998 interview with Purcell for *The Irish Times* (Dublin), the author described her journalistic style as ruled by a sense of fairness and privacy: "Who's perfect: are you perfect, am I perfect? No. Are we perfect mothers, wives, lovers, girlfriends? No. But . . . we should be entitled to some privacy." During her time at *The Sunday Tribune* (Dublin) Purcell received the two most prestigious awards in Irish journalism: the Benson & Hedges Award and the A. T. Cross Award. Three books grew out of her work for this newspaper: *Ethiopia: The Dark Hunger* (1984), which addresses famine in that African country, *On Lough Derg* (1988), which documents the yearly Irish Catholic pilgrimage to Lough Derg, a remote mountain lake island in Donegal, and *The Time of My Life: An Autobiography* (1989), the life story of the popular Irish television personality, Gabriel "Gay" Byrne, which Purcell largely wrote. These three publications show the breadth of Purcell's reporting skills as well as her preference for human-interest stories. Ruane remarked that Purcell's interviews for *The Sunday Tribune* (Dublin) "kept their eye on the target: people relaxed into her easy company, opening their hearts rather than spilling their guts." Purcell called the relationship between writer and subject "almost sacred" and depicted her own role as more of facilitator than interpreter. "I kind of believe that if I were interviewing myself," Purcell mused, "I would suspect I don't have an ego that gets between me and the subject, or the reader and the subject. My skill is to show people the person."

On Lough Derg is an example of this kind of subject-driven, human-interest writing. In this book Purcell acts as a documentarian, recording the movements, conversations, and professions of faith made by penitents en route to Lough Derg. There, on an island in the middle of the mountain lake, an annual summer pilgrimage of penance commences. This island is known as Saint Patrick's Purgatory, because Patrick visited the island in A.D. 445 to spend solitary time in fasting and prayer. Historically, Lough Derg held two meanings for pilgrims. Throughout medieval Europe, the island acquired fame as a place to test the Catholic faithful: penitents would descend into a cave on the island to replicate the horrors of purgatory. Irish penitents viewed Lough Derg as a retreat for intensive prayer, penance, and professions of devotion. Every year, between 13 June and 15 August, the island attracts approximately thirty thousand people for a three-day pilgrimage. Contemporary pilgrims recite 280 prayers at each of the nine stations, say night prayer and benediction, renew their baptismal vows, and receive confession. They eat only one meal a day, consisting of dry bread or oatcakes, and they may only drink black tea or coffee. Purcell and photographer Liam Blake accompanied pilgrims to St. Patrick's Purgatory, and she recorded the voices of these modern penitents. She often writes in dialect to preserve the sound of pilgrims' voices, and some of the comments she records are unexpected and enlightening:

Actually I'd no notion of coming here—no thought of coming here at all. It was Gracie here who said she was away to Lough Derg and she said would I like to go . . .
                                        —pilgrim

You rarely know why you are here at Lough Derg. But God knows.
                                        —priest at the Holy Hour

Gracie: "Well you're cairtainly no havin' a holiday!"
                                        —pilgrim

In *On Lough Derg,* Purcell practices the kind of noninvasive reporting style she prefers: she allows individuals to tell their own stories with minimal commentary. By recording the voices at the Lough Derg retreat, Purcell also provides a glimpse into the way an ancient Irish Catholic ritual is preserved and practiced in contemporary Ireland. Readers who know Purcell only through her novels will notice some continuity between this kind of reporting on Irish culture and her novelistic sensitivity to the many ways contemporary and past Irish cultures are in dramatic dialogue.

On the basis of her successful writing style, developed first on radio, then on television, and finally in feature writing, Purcell was approached by Treasa Coady, the publisher of Town House/Country House, a small Irish press that publishes Irish fiction for a mainstream readership, usually in conjunction with London-based publishers. Coady "asked me to write a blockbuster, and that's what I tried to do," Purcell recalled in her 1998 interview with Ruane. "I could have written on subjects that would have pleased the consensus, but I didn't."

The central thematic taboo at the center of *A Place of Stones,* Purcell's first novel, is incest. The protagonist is a small-town Irish girl named Molly O'Brien who becomes the internationally famous movie star Margo Bryan. Margo/Molly is attracted to a young, sophisticated American named Christian whom she meets abroad but remains in love with a young Irishman from her hometown, her brother Conor. This novel utilizes traditional elements of the Gothic romance: the potentially scandalous love between Molly and Conor is, true to Gothic narrative convention, ultimately sanctioned after a case of mistaken identity is righted. The novel is set in contemporary Chicago and contemporary Ireland, and Purcell uses references to Irish tourism, Irish and American pop culture, and Irish/American relations to bring these Gothic conventions into a pop-culture arena.

A Place of Stones was a best-seller in Ireland and England, and Purcell followed this first novel with two other Irish romances that take place in 1950s Ireland. In a 26 September 1998 article for *The Irish Times* (Dublin) titled "Gone With the Wind of Change," Binchy describes this decade as "a different country." "Life for women since 1922 should have been joyful and optimistic," Binchy argues, "but too often it was blighted by the fear of raising a head too high over a parapet: a woman who called too much attention to herself was a woman who would not win." In her novels depicting this era, however, Purcell takes this fear of social attack and makes it erotic; the very landscape of Irish repressiveness that Binchy decries in her essay becomes the perfect popular-romance setting for breaking sexual taboos. Most contemporary popular romance novels include sexual encounters, and when these encounters appear in Purcell's 1950s novels, readers are forced to imagine illicit sex in Binchy's "different country." In this way Purcell's historical romances both make use of this era as setting and critique the ways in which its attitudes toward sexuality, reproduction, and social propriety handicapped both men and women.

That Childhood Country (1992) opens in the fictional Irish town of Drumboola in 1953, where John and Derek Flynn, twins from a poor family, are planning to immigrate to Canada to avoid a life of poverty. Derek, who has been having an illicit relationship with Rose O'Beirne Moffat, Protestant member of the declining Anglo-Irish gentry, mourns over leaving her behind. Their last night together ends in Rose's pregnancy and begins this maze of forbidden love that extends into the next generation. In this novel Purcell uses a relationship between a lower-class Catholic man and a woman from the Anglo-Irish upper class to create Gothic tension, and this theme is one she later picks up in *Love Like Hate Adore* (1997).

Falling for a Dancer (1993; U.S. edition published as *Ashes of Roses,* 1994) again takes place in the 1950s and is set first in Cork, where heroine Elizabeth Sullivan lives with her strict, upper-middle-class Catholic family. On a day trip to Dublin with a friend, she meets and is seduced by a traveling actor, George Gallagher, who that night is playing Captain Molyneaux in Dion Boucicault's *The Shaughran* (1874). After discovering their daughter is pregnant, Elizabeth's parents and the local priest offer her two options: either enter the Cork city Magdalen Home for unmarried mothers or marry a middle-aged widower farmer from western County Cork and raise his children.

*Dust jacket for Purcell's 1991 novel, about a small-town Irishwoman who
becomes a famous actress (Bruccoli Clark Layman Archives)*

After visiting the Magdalen Home, Elizabeth chooses the option that will allow her the most freedom and moves to the Beara Peninsula in western County Cork. There, her much older husband and his children must adjust to a wife and mother who still wants to be a young woman and have her sexual freedom.

In her next two romances, Purcell returns again to the terrain of contemporary Ireland and Irish popular culture, while also setting some action in England and the United States. *Francey* (1994; U.S. edition published as *Roses After Rain*, 1996) is the story of Francey Sullivan, an isolated young Dubliner who has never met his biological father. When he meets Hazel Slye, a famous pop singer who was involved with his father years before, he falls in love with her and gets much-needed information about his father's whereabouts. When he arrives in England, however, he is just in time for his father's funeral. There he meets his half brothers and falls in love with another of his father's mistresses, Fleur. *Francey* is another novel in which Purcell plays with themes of incest and adultery.

In *Sky* (1995) the protagonist is Sky McPherson, an Irish American woman who is a newspaper reporter in a small Montana town. Divorced after an unhappy marriage, bored with her dead-end job, and restless in a relationship that seems to be going nowhere, Sky stumbles onto a mystery involving intrigue and international crime. Assigned to write the obituary of Midge Treacy, wife of one of the most prominent citizens of the community, she discovers that something sinister lies behind the woman's death. Purcell maintains a high level of suspense in a narrative set in Ireland, England, and Montana with such plot elements as Sky's mother, an aging hippie, apparently concealing something about her past in Ireland; the arrival of a mysterious stranger from Ireland; and hints of a conspiracy involving the upcoming visit to Ireland of Charles, Prince of Wales.

Purcell's first five novels—*A Place of Stones, That Childhood Country, Falling for a Dancer, Francey,* and *Sky*—were commercial successes that attracted a wide and devoted readership. But despite their commercial success, these novels were not widely reviewed at the time of their publication. However, her next novel, *Love Like Hate Adore,* attracted a great deal of critical attention when it was published in 1997 and it marked a shift in Purcell's writing career. In it Purcell abandons the third-person narrative style she had employed in her early novels and instead takes up the voice of Angela Devine, an inner-city Dubliner in her mid thirties who is forced to confront the media, her friends' prejudices, and her own fears about men when her younger brother, James, is accused of rape. This novel is rooted in Angela's sometimes stream-of-consciousness observations about her inner life and her Dublin surroundings. "The first thirty pages are hard going," Purcell commented in her 1998 interview with Ruane, "but then Angela's discursive ramblings start to take shape. I absolutely loved the first-person narrative–I found it exhilarating." The novel opens: "Every second of this summer hammered a spike into my memory. It is bizarre that so much could have happened. It is just August and the first intimations of disaster came on a Saturday in early May. Three months, as slow as a century. I thought I'd tell all to you before the finer details blow it away like dandelion clocks."

The novel, then, is essentially the story of these three months, told through a candid and sometimes repetitive first-person voice. What Purcell has constructed here is an extended confession of sorts; a woman trying to make sense of a crime, her reaction to the crime, and the public frenzy the crime provokes, by narrating her experience. Purcell seems to identify and gently poke fun at the confessional mode of storytelling when she has Angela herself consider current Irish trends toward confessional art and reportage: "But what I think is really gas is that they all make money out of giving out. Their childhoods and their upbringings and their abuse and their deprivation. The whole shebang." Angela herself, though, is a woman slow to admit that the problems in her own childhood, including extreme poverty, neglect, and a mother with severe drug problems, affect her present life. She lives and works in Dublin, supports her younger brother James whom she raised almost from infancy, and tells herself that she and her brother are getting along well. But when she learns that her brother has been accused of rape, Angela must reassess her beliefs, priorities, and relationships.

"I wouldn't say that I am or am not a feminist," mused Purcell in her interview with Ruane. "I think I lived feminism without knowing it. But I think some feminism has been very harsh, and some of what went into *Love Like Hate Adore* came out of that distinction. Women had to push very hard and continue to have to push hard, but I'd love to take a breath and look round and gather up the lost, and I feel like some of the young men are part of the lost." Angela is a character who from the first seems strong and outspoken. She works both at the counter of a delicatessen in Ballsbridge, an affluent Dublin neighborhood on the south side of the city, and as a "kissogram" (kissing telegram) girl in her spare time. At the time of the accusation she has been going to adult education classes, studying Irish and English literature. Her politics seem liberal, but above all she believes in the supremacy of family; namely, her own. But when her brother is accused of date rape, Angela is forced to look at this crime from the male perspective, much to the shock of most of her friends who instinctively side with the woman who was allegedly raped. Purcell researched many aspects of this novel, including the largely increased interest in adult education in Dublin and the sexual-assault prevention networks and centers in the city. *Love Like Hate Adore* introduces readers to the Dublin Rape Crisis Services, the inner workings of a sexual-assault case within the Irish legal system, and the way the Irish media can use an assault case as material for radio reportage, talk-show debate, call-in commentary, and roundtable television discussions. In these ways Purcell asks her readers to consider feminist issues from many perspectives and to assess the ways in which black and white stances on controversial social issues are rarely adequate in telling individuals' stories. The media is a constant presence in this novel, and certainly Purcell drew on her own experience in the Irish press to flesh out these voices that echo for the public the private interactions between Angela, James, and their lawyers. Newspapers and broadcasters characterize her brother as a monster and characterize the woman who accused him of rape as a martyr for all rape victims everywhere. The threat of media exposure, attacks from the public, and surveillance follow Angela through the novel.

Critical response to *Love Like Hate Adore* was mixed, but all who reviewed this novel noted Purcell's dramatic narrative shift. In a 21 May 1998 review in *The Irish Times* (Dublin) Arminta Wallace remarked that though the novel occasionally runs into difficulties such as a "rambling" and "maddeningly circuitous" narrative style and weak character development, she allowed that "for pop fiction to tackle such subjects as date rape, media harassment, poverty and dysfunctional families in contemporary Ireland is courageous, to say the least." Another reviewer for *The Irish Times* (Dublin), Lucile Redmond, observed in her 20 September 1998 notice that the novel is "immense" in its scope but complained that the flashbacks to Angela's childhood "can become tedious" and have "little sense of risk or urgency to drive them, tempting the reader to skip pages to get back to the story of James and his accuser." However, despite such lukewarm reviews, *Love Like Hate Adore* was short-listed for the 1998 Orange Prize for Fiction, an award for women writers that at that time was the most remunerative literary award for a single novel in the United Kingdom. Purcell was pleased with her novel but legitimately stunned to be short-listed for the Orange Prize. Although she did not win the 1998 prize, her nomination established her on the Dublin literary scene. Because one of the goals of the Orange Prize is to celebrate "accessible" novels, it is not surprising that judges singled out Purcell's writing for recognition.

One of Purcell's early novels, *Falling for a Dancer,* was optioned by Parallel Films for a television miniseries, broadcast in 1998 by the BBC in Northern Ireland and RTÉ in the Republic of Ireland. Purcell adapted the screenplay from her novel, and the miniseries was directed by Richard Standeven, who also directed the television mysteries *Cracker* (1996–1998). Although Purcell's script stays close to the novel and close to the formula for the best-selling Irish romance, the miniseries also dramatizes the ways in which Elizabeth's struggles mirror those that contemporary women are still saddled with in Ireland and elsewhere; namely, reproductive and childbearing options, domestic violence, and rape. When the producer of the television adaptation, Peter Norris, remarked in an 18 October 1997 interview with *The Irish Times* (Dublin), "What I love about this series is that there's not a mention of history or the troubles," he was missing Purcell's point entirely. In *Falling for a Dancer* Purcell illuminates those facets of Irish history that most affected Irish women, such as the Magdalen Laundries and arranged marriages.

The miniseries was shot on location in West Cork on the Beara Peninsula—a part of Ireland that is remote enough to look like Ireland in the 1950s without too many camera tricks, and stunning enough to offer audiences majestic and evocative shots of the Irish landscape. Towns on the Beara Peninsula, such as Eyeries, Allihies, and Castletownbere, cooperated with the television crew by repainting storefronts, antiquing hotel interiors for dance scenes, and hiding electrical generators in haystacks. But some locations, such as Claonach, were so remote and unpopulated that they had no electrical sources to hide from cameras.

Audiences in Ireland, Northern Ireland, and Great Britain raved about this version of Purcell's novel. Sara Caden reported in *Film West,* the Irish cinema quarterly, that "*Falling for a Dancer* is enormously popular. RTÉ had every reason to make an advance fuss, what they created was a hit. And the people who count are not those who have column inches to fill, but those who sat down every Sunday for four weeks, submerged themselves in a good story and found plenty of material for critical analysis among friends the next day." Despite this commercial success, some critics were concerned that the depiction of Irish life and history in the production was not directed at an Irish audience but instead pandered to American and English audiences by offering stereotypes as narrative shorthand. Rosita Boland titled her 5 September 1998 review for *The Irish Times* (Dublin) "Falling for Something Else Entirely," and asked, "Just who is the target audience that RTÉ has in mind for . . . *Falling for a Dancer?*" Her answer: "RTÉ's autumn series does not seem intended solely, or even primarily, for an RTÉ audience at all. It

has been made with both eyes fixed on a much wider and more lucrative global Irish-roots audience, using all the cliché'd cultural short cuts en route, which conveniently pass as period drama. Hence the presence of dancehalls, horses and carts, remote seaside locations, multiple pregnancies, priests, nuns, misty hillsides, and, of course, lots of sheep."

But in response to this kind of critical reaction to *Falling for a Dancer,* Caden argued that "people watched because they were mad to know what happened next. This qualifies as quality drama." She continued, "Deirdre Purcell's characters were something of a change from the norm, however. There was little of the standard bowing and scraping to the church, an individuality, a cheekiness in the people that rang true. These were not your usual Irish crowd resigned to their lot, dead in their souls." Caden linked critical responses to the miniseries to the critical response Purcell's fiction had generally received when she argued that although Purcell's novel "was a classic tale of love and treachery" and could even be called "the standard tale of love and treachery," she asserted that "the charm and mastery lie in the telling of any tale." "That Purcell's novel is now number two in the Irish Paperback Bestsellers second time around," Camden observes, "is a credit to her skill, but she also made a fine job of adapting her work to a screenplay."

Purcell joined six other well-known Irish women authors—Binchy, Clare Boylan, Kate O'Riordan, Emma Donoghue, Anne Haverty, and Éilis Ní Dhuibhne—in contributing to a collaborative novel, *Ladies' Night at Finbar's Hotel* (1999). Edited by Dermot Bolger, the group novel was a sequel to *A Night at Finbar's Hotel* (1997), which Bolger had also edited. This earlier work had featured anonymous contributions by several (mostly male) Irish writers, such as Roddy Doyle, Anne Enright, Hugo Hamilton, and Joseph O'Connor, forming a loose-knit narrative about the guests and staff of a formerly grand, now decrepit, Dublin hotel about to be demolished. *Ladies' Night at Finbar's Hotel* is also set in the hotel, now modishly refurbished and reopened, and the unsigned chapters recount the often humourous escapades of a new set of characters. Bolger adapted the novel for the British Broadcasting Corporation (BBC) into a radio play, which was broadcast on BBC Radio 4 on 10 May 2000.

New Island Books, publisher of the Open Door book series for adult literacy students, recognized Purcell's clear voice and wide appeal by asking her to produce a novella for the series, which included contributions by such authors as John Banville, Doyle, Sheila O'Flanagan, and Patricia Scanlan. Purcell wrote a short novella aimed at a diverse audience, including but not limited to teenagers, English as a Second Language students, and elderly literacy students. *Jesus and Billy Are Off to Barcelona* (1999) is on the surface a simple story; in it two young men from Barcelona fly to Dublin to participate in a student exchange. They are each bound for a family in Dublin: one lower-class and one upper-class. Jesus, an exceptionally attractive, intelligent, and cosmopolitan young man, has been hand-selected to stay with the upper-class Dublin family. But after a mix-up at the overcrowded Dublin airport, he goes home with the poorer family by mistake. Billy, the Irish boy who, as part of the exchange, is scheduled to fly back to Barcelona with Jesus, is proud to have such a refined-looking young man live with his family; he suffers from a typical adolescent anxiety over his family's lack of tact and decorum. But when Jesus and Billy become too close, Billy's family's homophobia forces Jesus back home to Barcelona, without Billy.

The story is narrated in straightforward, colloquial language and is printed in bold, large type. The editors for the Open Door Series take great care in making these novellas accessible to a wide readership, and Purcell's style fits this genre well. But true to her previous thematic approaches, Purcell chose subject matter—class identity and homophobia in contemporary Dublin—that is unexpected and challenging for a public literacy book series. This deceptively simple narrative in the end questions the subtle ways in which an adolescent can be made to feel ashamed of his sexuality because of homophobia expressed within the family. By making homophobia the focus of *Jesus and Billy Are Off to Barcelona,* Purcell again pushes the limits of genre to tap into currents in contemporary Irish culture.

Purcell served on the National Millennium Committee in the late 1990s; chaired by Séamus Brennan, the committee was responsible for recommending projects to celebrate or document the millennium in Ireland. Purcell devised and implemented the Millennium Book Writership, a project that had students in schools around the country write about how they saw Ireland at the millennium. A selection of these works, which included essays, poems, and pictures, was compiled into twenty-three manuscript volumes and deposited at the National Library of Ireland in 1999. The index was published that same year as *Write Here! Write Now! Footprints from the Second Millennium: A Record of the Lives, Thought and Hopes of a Selection of Young People in Ireland as the Second Millennium Turns to the Third.* She told Linda Flood in a 24 June 2001 interview for *The Sunday Business Post* (Dublin) that she felt this project was her most satisfying accomplishment: "The instant I thought of the idea I saw the finished product and I set to it and I did it and on time and on target I presented these beautiful books to Mary McAleese to be held in the National Library for the next 1,000 years. It was shepherding something from conception through to completion through that visualisation that gave me such tremendous satisfaction."

Dust jacket for Purcell's novel about a woman whose beloved younger brother is accused of rape (Bruccoli Clark Layman Archives)

Purcell's subsequent full-length novel, *Entertaining Ambrose* (2000), is again told through the voice of a first-person narrator. May Lanigan, an upper-middle-class Dublin housewife, tells the story of her husband's arrest on charges of participating in organized crime, and her son's brutal murder. Lanigan, like the narrator of *Love Like Hate Adore,* Angela Devine, is involved in community adult education. She had been attending a local writer's group before this chain of events turned her life upside down, and Purcell uses the conceit of a woman speaking into a tape recorder and telling her life story as justification for the existence of her loosely episodic narrative. Again, Purcell asks some pointed questions about the role of the press in individuals' tragedies. When Lanigan's son is targeted as an informer and killed by a gang of men involved with organized crime, his body left as a warning to other would-be informants, Purcell carefully documents how the family members of supposed criminals are not allowed privacy to grieve. Instead, the Lanigan household is besieged by reporters, police, lawyers, and news crews. No mourners come to the funeral, and the death of Lanigan's son is exploited for use in public discussions on the topic of gang violence. As in *Love Like Hate Adore,* Purcell is here concerned with the largely untold story of the families of the accused, and how they deal with private grief and public stigma.

But unlike other narrative explorations of this split between public and private life, in this novel Purcell introduces an element of the supernatural into contemporary Dublin: the Ambrose of the title. May Lanigan is visited daily by a guardian angel named Ambrose, who arrives early to help her through the chain of griefs she will face before the end of the story. This unexpected incursion of angelic support left many critics reeling. Helen Falconer of *The Guardian* (21 April 2001) commented: "Having already read Purcell's 1998 novel *Love, Like, Hate, Adore,* [*sic*] about an uneducated cleaning lady who stands by her brother when he's accused of rape, I thought when I began *Entertaining Ambrose* that Purcell was making another refreshingly brave contribution to the neglected genre of social realism. That was until the angel walked in."

Falconer admitted that the angel startled her out of her original sense of Purcell as a social realist but that she finally realized that in *Entertaining Ambrose,* Purcell was trying to create a modern, female Job character, replacing the devil of the biblical story with "a more complex catalog of human evils, of which self-delusion tops the list." Purcell's "version of the path to heaven," Falconer continued, "is a ruthlessly modern one of independence and individuality, a process not of martyrdom but of letting go." Sara Hudson of *The Times* (London) was not fazed by the presence of the angel and remarked in her 3 March 2000 review that, as did Purcell's *Love Like Hate Adore,* "this new book shows a similarly deft handling of themes central to women's fiction." Other critics similarly appreciated Purcell's daring in creating a character like Ambrose to preside over a novel that is essentially an example of social realism, but critiqued the book on the grounds that its "gritty social realism" was not gritty enough. On the RTÉ television program *Imprint* (12 November 2000), Mary Coll noted that the novel was a change of tone for Purcell; rather than being light romantic fiction, the novel attempted a serious examination of the Dublin crime world and its consequences for families. But Coll suggested that Purcell had trouble balancing the two elements of the narrative, "the angel and the criminal." The "gentleness of Deirdre Purcell's writing style," Coll argued, made it difficult for readers to imagine the crime world she is trying to evoke.

Although responses to Purcell's more "literary" novels have ranged from lukewarm reviews to high praise, and they have garnered nominations for literary prizes, one thing was clear from an economic standpoint: these novels do not sell the same number of copies as her popular romance novels did. But Purcell seems comfortable with the trade-off she is making in exchanging wide distribution and best-seller status for the freedom of a more literary writing style. This stylistic shift in Purcell's writing is perhaps indicated by her move from Town House and Macmillan, general publishers of best-selling Irish popular fiction in Ireland and Great Britain, respectively, to New Island Books and Headline, publishers of literary fiction and nonfiction in Ireland and Great Britain. In an 11 March 2001 interview with John Burns of *The Sunday Times* (London) Purcell's agent, Clare Alexander, described the reason for this shift: "Deirdre started out as a romance writer. That changed, and she got literary recognition. Macmillan was baffled with that. Her sales were in decline in Britain as her literary recognition was on the rise. Headline/New Island is very comfortable with the more issue-driven novels she is now doing." In a 7 April 2002 interview with Patricia Deevy for *The Sunday Independent* (Dublin), however, Purcell dismissed speculation that the change in publishers came about because *Love Like Hate Adore* and *Entertaining Ambrose* "were so unlike their conventional commercial predecessors that Macmillan was not happy." Deevy reported that "Purcell says it was nothing of the sort. Just a better deal negotiated by a new agent with a new publisher." Purcell remarked, "The books I'm writing now are the books I want to write now. I'm not writing them to be commercial. I'm not writing them to be literary. They just are the books that are in my mind now." She went on to express her disdain for the division of fiction into commercial and literary categories. "I absolutely hate it. People who do these categorisations, I wonder what gives them the right, really. And why is it only women?"

On 14 September 2001 Purcell married for a second time, to her longtime partner, Kevin Healy, director of public affairs for RTÉ. The marriage came shortly before the death of Purcell's mother, Maureen Purcell, in October 2001. According to Deevy, Purcell continued working on her next novel during her mother's illness, but it was "written in the early hours of the morning, between about 4.30am and 10am, because by day she was on call to her mother."

Published in April 2002, *Marble Gardens* centers around the relationship between two women, Sophie and Riba, lifelong friends. When Riba's teenage daughter, Zelda, becomes seriously ill, Riba becomes exasperated by the seeming incapability of conventional medicine to help and instead turns to alternative medicine, traveling with her daughter to the Caribbean to seek the treatment of the New Age guru Daniel Street. The childless Sophie loves Zelda as if she were her own daughter and finds herself grappling with the competing pulls of her loyalty to her best friend, Riba—who regards any criticism of Street, an obvious (to Sophie) charlatan, as criticism of herself—and her fear that Zelda's life is in danger. An added complication is the mutual attraction that arises between Sophie and Riba's husband, Brian, who is also concerned about Zelda. Deevy observed that the novel is about the nature of friendship, the effects that terminal illness can have on a family, and "the crumbling nature of untended marriages." She remarked that "*Marble Gardens*'s skewering of new-age excess is one of its strengths." Purcell said, "I struggled with my own view about this. I figured: 'Am I intolerant? Am I a know-all, that I know better than anybody else?' And I really don't think so because none of these gurus, certainly the American ones, none of them are poor. And it's usually vulnerable people that are targeted by these quacks and gurus." Soon after publication the novel hit the number one spot on *The Irish Times* (Dublin) fiction best-seller list.

In 2002 Purcell also published another novella in the Open Door series, *Has Anyone Here Seen Larry?* The title character, Larissa (or Larry), is an eighty-seven-year-old widow who lives with her two daughters, Martha and Mary, and the story centers around the jealousy that the controlling Martha, who has shouldered the burden of caring for their infirm mother, feels toward the carefree Mary, her mother's favorite.

Historically, the "popular romance" has been a genre dominated by women writers. Although popular romance attracts a consistent, avid, and lucrative readership, literary critics widely dismiss these novels as unworthy of critical attention. Aine McCarthy, in an 11 June 1996 feature article in *The Irish Times* (Dublin) surveying contemporary women's writing in Ireland, calls this dismissal "an occupational hazard for the writer of mass-market women's fiction." She argues that this genre is more often subjected to snobbery than forms of popular fiction associated with male writers; critics do not similarly stigmatize novels that fall under the categories of crime, espionage, or science fiction. McCarthy interviewed Purcell, who responded to this critical dismissal:

> I think it's a subcutaneous form of anti-feminism. Genres like spy fiction or science fiction are mostly read by men, and written by men and this form of escapism is seen as more serious because of a subconscious assumption that whatever men read must be more serious than what women read. But this is totally skewed. It is women's fiction which deals with the fundamentals—love, sex, birth, death, family—and men's popular fiction that deals with the peripherals like espionage or politics.

While not all popular-romance fiction lends itself to scholarly analysis, many writers of popular romances use this genre as a platform from which to imagine women's lives and to critique cultural ideologies that affect these women. Scholars sometimes dismiss these romances for their very popularity; their thematic concerns are seen as market driven and therefore not engaged in legitimate imaginative dialogues with the world. But though mass-market fiction targeted toward female readers is generally realistic, straightforward, and written in simple, nonexperimental prose, some of these novels are concerned with social and psychological themes that fall far outside the standard seduction plot.

Starting with her first best-seller, Deirdre Purcell has gone further than most popular-romance writers in her attempt to weave contemporary and sometimes controversial Irish social concerns through her novels. Her themes have included incest, adultery, rape, gang crime, abortion, and homophobia. Readers who expect a purely escapist plot may criticize Purcell's inclusion of such volatile issues in her works; but it is this kind of thematic range and daring that makes Purcell one of the most interesting contemporary Irish writers. Purcell has not yet attracted much critical attention. As Una Bradley observed in a short interview with Purcell for *The Belfast Telegraph* (27 April 2002), "Despite her great success . . . there is a sense in which she struggles with an image problem. In the media, she is often regarded as the writer of 'beach' fiction, the kind of pulp that one enjoys, but doesn't take seriously." In response, Purcell pointed out that "Journalists who pigeon-hole me often haven't read my books. . . . I know a lot of writers but I don't know any who deliberately 'dumb down.' We are all simply producing the best we can."

Interviews:

"Irish Novelist Purcell on Fleeting New Zealand Visit," *The Dominion* (Wellington), 22 February 1995, 16;

Shirley Kelly, "A Change of Direction," *Books Ireland* (September 1997): 201–203;

Medb Ruane, "The Gentle Rebel," *Irish Times* (Dublin), 7 May 1998, p. 15;

Linda Flood, "Unlocking Your Talent," *Sunday Business Post* (Dublin), 24 June 2001;

Patricia Deevy, "The Dramas of Deirdre," *Sunday Independent* (Dublin), 7 April 2002, p. 4;

Una Bradley, "The Luck of Deirdre Purcell," *Belfast Telegraph,* 27 April 2002.

References:

Maeve Binchy, "Gone With the Wind of Change," *Irish Times* (Dublin), 26 September 1998, p. 7;

John Burns, "Purcell Picks Up Binchy's Mantle," *Sunday Times* (London), 11 March 2001, p. 8;

Aine McCarthy, "All Human Life Is There," *Irish Times* (Dublin), 11 June 1996.

Ian Rankin
(Jack Harvey)
(28 April 1960 –)

Mariadele Boccardi
Emmanuel College, University of Cambridge

BOOKS: *The Flood* (Edinburgh: Polygon, 1986);
Knots & Crosses (London: Bodley Head, 1987; Garden City, N.Y.: Doubleday, 1987);
Watchman (London: Bodley Head, 1988; New York: Doubleday, 1991);
Westwind (London: Barrie & Jenkins, 1990);
Hide & Seek (London: Barrie & Jenkins, 1991; New York: Otto Penzler, 1994);
Wolfman (London: Century, 1992); republished as *Tooth & Nail* (New York: St. Martin's Press, 1996; London: Orion, 1998);
Strip Jack (London: Orion, 1992; New York: St. Martin's Press, 1994);
A Good Hanging and Other Stories (London: Century, 1992); republished as *A Good Hanging: Short Stories* (New York: St. Martin's Press, 2002);
The Black Book (London: Orion, 1993; New York: Otto Penzler, 1994);
Witch Hunt, as Jack Harvey (London: Headline, 1993);
Mortal Causes (London: Orion, 1994; New York: Simon & Schuster, 1994);
Bleeding Hearts, as Harvey (London: Headline, 1994);
Let It Bleed (London: Orion, 1995; New York: Simon & Schuster, 1996);
Blood Hunt, as Harvey (London: Headline, 1995);
Black & Blue (London: Orion, 1997; New York: St. Martin's Press, 1997);
Herbert in Motion and Other Stories (London: Revolver, 1997);
The Hanging Garden (London: Orion, 1998; New York: St. Martin's Press, 1998);
Death Is Not The End: An Inspector Rebus Novella (London: Orion, 1998; New York: St. Martin's Press, 2000);
Dead Souls (London: Orion, 1999; New York: St. Martin's Press, 1999);
Set in Darkness (London: Orion, 2000; New York: St. Martin's Press, 2000);

Ian Rankin (photograph by Susan Greenhill; from the cover for the U.S. paperback edition of The Hanging Garden, *1999)*

The Falls (London: Orion, 2001; New York: St. Martin's Press, 2001);
Resurrection Men (London: Orion, 2002; Boston: Little, Brown, 2003);
Beggar's Banquet (London: Orion, 2002).
Collections: *Rebus: The Early Years,* introduction by Rankin (London: Orion, 1999)—comprises *Knots & Crosses, Hide & Seek,* and *Tooth & Nail;*

The Jack Harvey Novels (London: Orion, 2000)—comprises *Witch Hunt, Bleeding Hearts,* and *Blood Hunt;*
Rebus: The St. Leonard's Years (London: Orion, 2001)—comprises *Strip Jack, The Black Book,* and *Mortal Causes.*

OTHER: *Ian Rankin Presents Criminal Minded: A Collection of Short Fiction from Canongate Crime,* edited by Rankin (Edinburgh: Canongate Crime, 2000);
Robert Greenfield, *A Journey Through America with the Rolling Stones,* introduction by Rankin (London: Helter Skelter, 2001).

SELECTED PERIODICAL PUBLICATIONS–
UNCOLLECTED: "Surface and Structure: Reading Muriel Spark's *The Driver's Seat,*" *Journal of Narrative Technique,* 15 (1985): 146–155;
"A Scottish Journey," *Observer* (London), 11 April 1999, Features section, p. 3.
"The Perfect Villain," *Observer* (London), 25 February 2001, Features section, p. 8.
"Ian Rankin: Welcome to the Spook Capital of the World," *Independent* (London), 22 April 2001, p. 26.

Ian Rankin is one of the most successful crime writers in Great Britain and, increasingly, in the United States. The series of novels featuring Inspector John Rebus has garnered praise from reviewers commensurate to a commercial success so widespread that, at one point, eight volumes from the series appeared in the top-ten list of best-sellers in Scotland, a feat that earned the author a citation from the *Guinness Book of Records.* The popularity of Rankin's books has led to their adaptation for broadcast on British television. Each new addition to the series over the years has been greeted by further critical and popular acclaim, while the series as a whole has been hailed for the complexity and ingenuity of the plots, the depth of characterization, and the insightfulness of its depiction of contemporary Scotland. The same characteristics that make the novels outstanding examples of the crime genre also signal Rankin's desire to transcend its limitations, a desire accompanied by his willingness to experiment with other forms as well as within the form.

Although his most accomplished and successful works belong to the crime genre, to define Rankin purely as a crime novelist and dismiss his books as genre fiction because they display the distinctive traits of an identifiable genre is both misleading and reductive. Misleading in that Rankin has written other types of fiction; reductive in that his novels primarily belong to a Scottish literary tradition and only secondarily to a crime one. Even in the Rebus books, which form the largest and better-known part of Rankin's literary production, the investigation of a crime forms only one layer of the narrative. The crime is used as a pretext for an inquiry into contemporary Scotland, embracing both its rich historical and cultural heritage and the social and political reality of sectarian violence, poverty, and corruption, and it is conducted from a city, Edinburgh, which becomes in the novels the epitome and exacerbation of these contrasting aspects.

Edinburgh is the author's adoptive city: in an 18 March 2001 interview with Robert McCrum for *The Observer* (London) Rankin explained that he arrived there "as an outsider" to go to university from Cardenden, Fife, thirty miles north of Edinburgh. Ian James Rankin was born there on 28 April 1960, the younger son of James Hill Rankin, a dockyard worker, and Isobel Rankin, a dinner lady (a person who serves food in a school or factory cafeteria). A small mining town, Cardenden was a tightly knit community that, by the time of Rankin's birth, was already starting to feel the consequences of the first mining-pit closures. These closures gave rise to unemployment and a general sense of hopelessness that earned the town the nickname Car-dead-end by the local youth. For the young people living there, the only alternatives to gangs were a cinema and a library, and Rankin made ample use of the latter. His family's house did not have many books, but his father enjoyed reading novels of espionage by Ian Fleming and John Le Carré; this taste influenced his son's career: one of the reasons Rankin cites on the website created by his U.S. publisher, St. Martin's Press (www.ianrankin.com), for his choice of the crime genre is his desire to write something his father would want to read. As a boy Rankin was encouraged to take regular trips to the local library, where he read voraciously, taking full advantage of the absence of age restrictions on the lending of books: among his borrowings were Mario Puzo's *The Godfather* (1969) and Anthony Burgess's *A Clockwork Orange* (1962). Echoes of both resurface in his novels, in the depiction of often-graphic violence and in the psychological dimensions of his villains.

Rankin's precocious interest in writing, which he told Nick Hasted in an interview for *The Guardian* (21 April 2001) started when he was only four years old with the creation of his own comic books, was set against this background of limited opportunities. At secondary school in Cowdenbeath, Rankin met a young working-class teacher, Ron Gillespie, who considered his pupil's writing to be already of publishable quality. The decision on Rankin's part to embark on a literary career owes something to this early appreciation. Rankin's first move in the chosen direction was to go to the University of Edinburgh in late 1978 to study for a degree in English literature, specializing in American literature.

Dust jacket for the U.S. edition of Rankin's 1987 novel,
in which he introduced Inspector John Rebus
(Richland County Public Library)

This period was a politically significant time in Scottish history, with consequences reverberating onto the cultural and literary landscapes. A year after Rankin's arrival in the Scottish capital, the British government asked the people of Scotland to cast their votes in a referendum on the option of devolved government through an elected Scottish parliament. The prospect of self-determination generated a wide-ranging debate on the characteristics of Scottish identity and the possibility of a national culture separate from both English and British ones, which continued with renewed vigor even after the voters narrowly rejected devolution, in an attempt to explain the reasons for the defeat. As a student during these years, Rankin found himself in a privileged position to survey the tradition of the Scottish novel, both in its nineteenth-century peak in the persons of Sir Walter Scott, Robert Louis Stevenson, and James Hogg and more recently in Muriel Spark and representatives of the so-called Scottish Renaissance: James Kelman, William McIlvanney, Iain Banks, and Alasdair Gray. All are

influences on Rankin's writing; on the *Tangled Web UK* website (www.twbooks.co.uk), as well as in his interview with McCrum, Rankin has explicitly acknowledged Scott for his attempt to explain the dynamics of Scottish history in adventurous novels, and he identifies Stevenson and Hogg as the major exponents of the Gothic genre. Kelman and McIlvanney use a form of gritty yet humorous realism to describe contemporary Scotland, a form not dissimilar from Rankin's own, with McIlvanney in particular using detective plots in his books featuring Jack Laidlaw, while Spark constitutes a specifically literary influence for her formal innovations and her experiments with genres.

When Rankin began his career as a novelist, the vibrancy of the cultural scene and his own familiarity with the literature of Scotland favored the choice of a Scottish setting for his works. After obtaining a first-class degree, Rankin worked toward completing a Ph.D., writing his thesis on Spark between 1983 and 1986, but he never completed it. He used the time and financial support for the research to write his own books. The first novel he sent to publishers, "Summer Rites," written in 1983, remains as yet unpublished. He describes it in "Exile on Princes Street: Inspector Rebus & I," a 1998 piece posted on the *Tangled Web UK* website, as "a surrealistic comedy set in a Highland hotel," but under the deceptively light tone it already introduced the setting and serious themes that recur in his later production, since its plot centered on a kidnapping by the Scottish Liberation Army. Between 1983 and 1984 Rankin wrote *The Flood* (1986), published by Polygon, a small independent publishing house that was owned by Edinburgh University Students' Association, a student cooperative. The novel is a semi-autobiographical coming-of-age tale: its protagonist is a young man from a village in Fife whose main ambition is to leave his native town and move to Edinburgh. The novel is especially interesting for the wryly sympathetic portrait of a community faced with all the problems resulting from economic decline. A reader can glean information on the author's teenage years in Cardenden from this early work. In 1985 Rankin wrote *Knots & Crosses,* in which the character of Detective Sergeant John Rebus, later Inspector John Rebus, makes his first appearance.

Published in 1987, *Knots & Crosses* occupies an important place in Rankin's career, not only because it marks the beginning of the series for which he has acquired fame but also because it both reveals his interests at the time of writing and includes elements pointing to the future development of the series. The plot centers on the murders of young girls by a man who sends Rebus strings tied in knots and minuscule crosses as clues; the murderer is eventually revealed to be Gordon Reeve, a friend from Rebus's army and Special Air Service (SAS) days, aiming to take revenge for a perceived betrayal by his friend through killing Rebus's daughter, Samantha, whose name the initials of the previous victims spell. The close relationship that existed in the past between policeman and criminal makes a final, deadly confrontation between the two inevitable.

The name of the protagonist–"a smart-arse undergraduate joke," says Rankin whenever he is asked where it came from–the nature of the clues, and the genre of the novel were influenced by Rankin's knowledge of Scottish literature and by his familiarity with literary theory, in particular with semiology, a theory of the interpretation of signs that was popular among academics in the 1980s. Rankin demonstrated his adeptness at using semiology as an interpretative tool in an academic article on Spark's *The Driver's Seat* (1970), which was published in the same year as *Knots & Crosses* in *The Journal of Narrative Technique*. The word *rebus*, in fact, indicates a puzzle whose solution rests with the interpretation of visual signs in phonetic combination with letters; the choice of victims by their names makes of them pieces in a living puzzle, with the word *Samantha* as its solution. True to his name, interpreting clues is precisely what Rebus is invited, and initially fails, to do by the murderer: the knots and crosses the latter sends are, in the language of semiology, *signifiers,* meaningful not in themselves but insofar as they in turn refer to the games of noughts and crosses (or tic-tac-toe) that in the past the policeman used to play with the murderer. The reference to the games signifies the murderer's identity, and the solution to the mystery is reached when the passages from the surface of the sign's appearance to its reference and finally to what is being represented are completed. A similar narrative strategy had been used a few years before by Umberto Eco, an important figure in the field of semiology, in *Il nome della rosa* (1980; translated as *The Name of the Rose*, 1983). Eco's book is a literary detective novel set in the Middle Ages, whose plot revolves on the decipherment of verbal and nonverbal clues and that succeeds in molding the familiar detective genre to convey an impressive amount of historical information on the social and political reality of the time based on real events, and to discuss several philosophical questions.

Eco's novel is an influential precedent to Rankin's own. He remarked to Boyd Tonkin in a 5 January 2002 interview for *The Independent* (London), "It was jam-packed full of stuff that I thought Umberto Eco would like if he read it." At the same time, however, after the book was published he did not wholeheartedly accept that *Knots & Crosses* belonged to the crime genre, insisting that it was meant as a rewriting of Stevenson's *The Strange Case of Dr. Jekyll and Mr. Hyde* (1886) in a modern setting: as such, it owed more to the Scottish Gothic tradition of the nineteenth century than to what he perceived as an English genre–namely, the crime story on the model of Agatha Christie, which flourished in the

years between World War I and World War II and that Rankin thought had remained unchanged since then.

In 1986 the grant Rankin was receiving for the Ph.D. ran out. Rankin decided to abandon the project, marry his long-term girlfriend, Miranda Harvey, and move to London. Miranda Rankin worked for Conservative member of Parliament Francis Maude, while Ian Rankin initially decided to devote himself to writing full-time. The experiment, however, did not succeed, and after a year Rankin resumed outside employment, first as secretary to the National Folktale Center, then as a journalist and editor of a monthly music magazine, *Hi-Fi Review*. During this period, from 1987 to 1990, Rankin experimented with other forms and genres before returning to the crime novel. He wrote two novels: the first, *Watchman,* a spy novel in the style of Graham Greene and Le Carré, appeared in 1988, the same year in which Rankin was elected a Hawthornden Fellow, which offered him a residency at the International Writers' Retreat at Hawthornden Castle; the second novel, *Westwind,* published two years later, is a thriller about arms dealing and the space race.

In 1990 Rankin and his wife left England for the French region of the Dordogne. There he took up the character of Rebus again and, with this second novel in which Rebus featured as protagonist, the series truly began. *Hide & Seek* (1991) introduces some of the characters who figure in the later novels, such as Brian Holmes, Rebus's first assistant, and "Farmer" Watson and Frank Lauderdale, his superiors. The jokingly literary references to Scottish literature continue in the names of Holmes and Watson, which add an allusion to the characters Sherlock Holmes and Dr. John Watson from the works of Sir Arthur Conan Doyle, another eminent Scottish writer of detective stories. The borrowed names, however, do not deduct from their fullness of characterization: Rankin's skills in this area are evident from the first appearance of these personages, and they are briefly yet deftly sketched as believable individuals. The novel centers on the investigation into the death of a drug addict in a dilapidated housing project, which leads Rebus to expose the less savory aspects of outwardly respectable Edinburgh. The death, in fact, is connected to the secret activities of the exclusive Hyde club, where successful professionals and businessmen gather to indulge their illegal desires. The plot moves between the two sides of Edinburgh: the wealthy, genteel capital inhabited by powerful men and the seedy, deprived environment of the high-rise estates that surround it, which, as Rankin writes in "A Scottish Journey," a 1999 article published in *The Observer* (London), have "effectively isolated Edinburgh's less flush populace." Both are represented in equal measure in the novel and are finally brought together in the solution of the crime.

Introduced by an epigraph taken from *The Strange Case of Dr. Jekyll and Mr. Hyde,* and with the name of the club providing a further literary echo and a clue to the themes of duplicity, appearances, and deception in the novel, *Hide & Seek* presents itself as another homage to the Scottish Gothic tradition: as is Stevenson's story, this book is a moral tale about talented individuals overreaching themselves in the belief that they can fashion their own rules of behavior. In it Rankin returns to the motif of the double already exploited in the first Rebus book, but while in *Knots & Crosses* he explored the formal aspects of doubleness, in *Hide & Seek* he concentrates on its moral implications. In the earlier work the criminal functions as the policeman's double; however, in the second Rebus novel doubles and duplicity exist in individual characters: the distance between the businessmen's public personae and private vices reproduces the split between Jekyll and Hyde. This split is, in turn, magnified in the depiction of Edinburgh as a city of opposites or, as John Lanchester calls it in an essay on Rankin's novels published in the *London Review of Books* (27 April 2000), a city "of appearances and division and of almost structural hypocrisy." This feature of the city remains a constant for the whole series. With this book, in fact, Rankin offers the first of several portraits of Edinburgh, focusing on one aspect at a time but attempting to encompass the complexity of the whole.

The Scottish setting is temporarily abandoned in the next novel, *Wolfman* (1992), published in the United States as *Tooth & Nail* (1996), which title was retained for all subsequent editions in the United Kingdom. In this novel Rebus travels to London to help capture a serial killer who bites off parts of his victim's bodies. Within the series, this book stands out as an oddity insofar as it does not confront the human and social dimensions of crime but exploits its most sensationalistic aspects.

For Rankin, 1992 was a significant and productive year. His first child, Jack, was born; he received the Chandler-Fulbright Prize, which gave him $20,000 and a round-trip ticket to the United States. He, his wife, and infant son spent six months traveling in the United States. That same year the next Rebus novel, *Strip Jack,* was published, as was *A Good Hanging and Other Stories,* a collection of short stories also featuring the character.

In *Strip Jack,* Rebus is trying to untangle the political web woven around Gregor Jack, an independent member of Parliament caught in a brothel during a police raid and whose wife is murdered shortly afterward. The plot allows the author the opportunity to examine a contemporary issue, in this case the role of the press in exposing the private lives of public figures, and to provide the story with a moral dimension exploring the dangers of being driven by personal ambition in a career of public service. *A Good Hanging and Other Stories* groups

together twelve mysteries solved by Rebus. In a condensed form they reiterate the themes and settings of the novels in the series.

Witch Hunt (1993), the first in a trilogy of thrillers with professional assassins for protagonists, was written under the name Jack Harvey (a combination of the first name of his eldest son and his wife's last name). For the next three years Rankin published under both this pseudonym and his real name, alternating between the crime novels and the thrillers. *The Black Book,* the fifth novel in the Rebus series, also appeared in 1993. A savage attack on his colleague Holmes and the discovery that he was collecting information about a crime committed several years before lead Rebus to confront the reality of organized crime in Edinburgh and allows the author to turn his attention to another facet of life in the city. The novel marks the appearance in the series of two new characters who progressively acquire major roles in the books that follow: Siobhan Clarke is a young policewoman who soon becomes Rebus's regular assistant, and Morris Gerald "Big Ger" Cafferty is the master criminal who controls the Edinburgh underworld and slowly becomes the protagonist's alter ego. In "The Perfect Villain," a 25 February 2001 article for *The Observer* (London), Rankin defines the characteristics of the perfect fictional villain: he must be three-dimensional, unpredictable, evil to the core, and yet fascinating. And Cafferty is a well-rounded character, interesting in his own right and not just as the inspector's adversary; his actions are always dictated by self-interest, but it is not clear where the self-interest rests, so that he becomes utterly unpredictable; the author gives him opinions and a certain outlook on life that have much in common with Rebus's own, so that he becomes, as Lanchester suggests, a "delicately drawn Hyde figure" to the detective's Jekyll. The nuanced relationship between the two, characterized by the rivalry of being on opposite sides but equally by the grudging mutual respect of those who know one another to be fundamentally alike, could thus be developed over the course of several novels.

In *Mortal Causes* (1994) Cafferty's son is tortured and murdered in a sectarian revenge attack during the time of the Edinburgh International Festival. The resulting investigation sees the two enemies on the same side: with Cafferty in prison and therefore unable to carry out his own inquiry he has to trust the police, in the person of Rebus, to find the culprits. The nature of the killing means that the novel explores the existence in Scotland of religious fanaticism and paramilitary organizations, more commonly mentioned in relation to Northern Ireland; its timing allows Rankin to portray the city at its yearly privileged best and contrast this pageantry with the unchanged hopelessness of its deprived areas. Although criminal and thwarted by the police, the plan by a gang of youths from the housing estates to explode a bomb on the closing day of the festival is presented as in some way understandable.

Rankin published *Bleeding Hearts* (1994) and *Blood Hunt* (1995) using his Harvey pseudonym. The latter novel is an interesting case of a character from one novel being brought back to life in another: the protagonist, in fact, is Gordon Reeve, the murderer in *Knots & Crosses,* here in a different role. With *Let It Bleed* (1995) Rankin introduces the stylistic conceit of naming a novel after a vintage rock title, in this case the title song of the Rolling Stones's 1969 album. In Rankin's novel Rebus returns to the world of politics, this time for an investigation into corruption at the highest levels of the Civil Service. The following year the author and his family, now including two sons, returned to Edinburgh for good, though they still maintain their home in France. Rankin's younger son, Kit, was born in 1994 with Angelman Syndrome, a rare genetic disorder that causes speech impairment, learning difficulties, and problems with balance. Rankin has since become a campaigner for the rights of disabled persons.

Black & Blue, the ninth novel in the series (with a title taken from that of the Rolling Stones's 1976 album), was published in 1997, the same year as a second collection of short stories, *Herbert in Motion and Other Stories,* appeared in a limited edition of two hundred signed copies. *Black & Blue* won the Crime Writers' Association Gold Dagger Award for best novel of the year and constituted a dramatic leap in quality and a comparable change in fortune for the creator of Inspector Rebus. In a 1 April 2001 article in *The Independent* (London) Andrew Taylor calls it "the breakthrough novel that brought him commercial as well as critical success." As Lanchester points out, "the first Rebus books were well above average crime novels; from *Black & Blue* onwards there is an extra sense of range and ambition about Rankin's work." Hasted, in *The Guardian* interview, called the novel "the turning point, as Rankin borrowed James Ellroy's staccato style and ambition." The complexity of the narrative marks the difference from previous works in the series, with the plot joining three story lines that Rankin skillfully juggles. The first concerns the hunt for a serial killer of women whose actions aim to repeat the criminal exploits of Bible John, a killer of near mythical status active in Scotland in the 1960s and never caught. In the course of this investigation Rebus uncovers a trail of corruption flowing from the Aberdeen-based oil industry that taints the police force of that city. The second story line centers on Bible John himself, as Rankin daringly brings him back in the present as a businessman who is also hunting his younger imitator, and even devises an accidental meeting between him and Rebus at an oil conference. While this side of the story owes a debt to Andrew O'Hagan's book *The Missing* (1995) for the factual information about Bible John, the latter's second life as an oilman is the most striking invention of the novel and

wholly Rankin's own. The third strand in the plot involves an investigation from Rebus's past that is reopened in the suspicion that it resulted in a miscarriage of justice: this episode is the first time in the series that the reader is allowed a glimpse of the character's early days as a policeman.

With *Black & Blue* Rankin widens his subject beyond present-day Edinburgh. On the one hand, he includes significant aspects of contemporary Scotland outside the city, most notably the consequences, economic and otherwise, of the discovery of oil in the North Sea; on the other, through the fictional policemen's memories of Bible John he explores a specific period in recent Scottish history. The interaction of past and present, real and fictional events, private and public concerns, is maintained in subsequent novels; so is, formally, the structure of multiple plots.

The Hanging Garden (1998) depicts Rebus facing the consequences of international organized crime in Scotland: he becomes involved in the plight of a Bosnian immigrant forced into prostitution by a drug-running Chechen boss who is trying to replace Big Ger Cafferty's organization with his own crime syndicate. When Rebus's daughter, Samantha, is the victim of a hit-and-run accident that leaves her in a coma, Rebus forges a pact with Cafferty by which he will pursue the latter's rivals in exchange for information on the person responsible for Samantha's accident. The plot thus presents side by side the realistic depiction of a gang war and the moral questions of whether to compromise one's integrity for personal revenge; equally, it provides the reader with a further exploration of Rebus's past, as his daughter's state becomes the opportunity for reminiscences. The title is taken from that of a song by The Cure, which appeared in the 1982 album *Pornography.*

Moral questions and real events combine in a separate strand of the plot that concerns a suspected war criminal from World War II living in Edinburgh, a situation inspired by a real-life case. In 1996 an elderly man living in London was accused of war crimes committed during the Nazi occupation of Belarus; he was subsequently tried and convicted. Rankin's novel moves the setting of the events from England to Scotland to examine not only the difficulty of establishing the truth at such distance in time from the events but also the contrasting needs of justice for the victims and compassion for an elderly man, and finally the possibility of redemption for even the worst crimes.

This latter problem recurs with relation to pedophilia in *Dead Souls* (1999). The title of Rankin's novel is taken from that of a 1981 song by Joy Division, which in turn was taken from the title of Nikolai Gogol's epic prose poem *Pokhozhdeniia Chichikova, ili Mertvye dushi* (The Adventures of Chichikov, or Dead Souls, 1842). Some elements of Rankin's 1999 novel are present in a previous novella, *Death Is Not The End* (1998). When Rebus spots a convicted pedophile taking pictures of children at a zoo and then traces him to a housing estate where many children live, he does not hesitate to let the residents know about the man's past. The move has disastrous consequences, as the residents organize vigilante squads and then set fire to the pedophile's apartment. Upon further inquiry, however, the detective discovers that the man had himself been abused as a child and that his case is connected to the apparently inexplicable suicide of a police officer. While this story line delves into the possible causes of pedophilia, from genetic predisposition to abuse suffered in the past, and poses the questions of whether pedophiles are to be held responsible for their actions and what place in society they should be given, an initially separate inquiry reveals new aspects of Rebus's early life in Fife. An old flame asks Rebus to help her trace her son, who has disappeared in Edinburgh; in the course of the investigation Rebus finds himself remembering the past, in what are tones close to those of *The Flood,* and imagining what might have happened had he stayed in his hometown, only to conclude that returning to the past is impossible as well as undesirable. The strand of the plot of *Dead Souls* involving the missing boy and glimpses of Rebus's past in Carenden is transferred from the novella *Death is Not The End,* with one important change: in the earlier work it is an old male friend of the policeman who asks for his help rather than an old flame. With the change, the recollections of Rebus's youth acquire a more nostalgic tinge, but at the same time his renunciation of the past is more strongly affirmed. Compared with the vague nostalgia of this side of the plot and the topical urgency of the other, the third story, about a serial killer released from prison in the United States and seeking revenge in Scotland, is less engrossing. Reviewers praised the bravery of the choice of a difficult topic, but also suggested, as did Sean O'Brien in *TLS: The Times Literary Supplement* (5 February 1999), that "the author has outgrown his chosen form" and seems to be seeking a novel of social realism that sits uneasily with the requirements of the crime genre.

Despite these reservations, however, the series continued to enjoy popular acclaim: a single volume collecting the first three Rebus books was published in 1999 under the title *Rebus: The Early Years,* while the following year, Independent Television (ITV) disclosed plans to film *Black & Blue.* The omnibus volume includes an informative authorial introduction discussing the crime genre in relation to the literary novel. In it Rankin explains that with his choice of genre he had aimed to distance himself from high literature to reach beyond a small circle of devotees and have a wider audience for what he considered a necessary enterprise, namely, to give an updated portrayal of Scotland at the turn of the twentieth century and into the twenty-first. The changed political scene in Scot-

land provided him with the ideal opportunity to fulfill this ambition.

If in the two previous novels the issues explored–the fate of war criminals, forced prostitution, and the attitude of society toward pedophiles–had a resonance beyond the Scottish borders, *Set in Darkness* (2000) owes its conception to contemporary political events in Britain that directly affected Scotland. In 1997, after eighteen years of Conservative government, the Labour Party won the general election. One of the key Labour pledges was to grant Scotland, Wales, and Northern Ireland devolved government. A referendum was held on the issue; this time, unlike in 1979, the majority in favor of devolution was overwhelming, elections for the Scottish parliament were duly held, and the institution officially opened in July 1999. The parliament was hosted in a temporary building, while a new site was being developed around the historic Queensberry House.

Rankin adopts this real background for his novel, setting it in the period between the referendum and the elections. Its plot ambitiously surveys three hundred years of national history by means of three separate crimes, one real, the others fictional, all taking place at significant moments. In 1707 Queensberry House was the site of the signing of the Act of Union between Scotland and England, which effectively ended Scottish independence; while the signers were at a Thanksgiving service, in the kitchens an act of cannibalism was being committed, as a deranged man roasted a servant on a spit in a fireplace. During a guided tour of the site, Rebus, in charge of security for the new parliament, discovers a mummified corpse when the same fireplace is uncovered, this one apparently walled into the fireplace around the time of the first devolution referendum; he takes charge of the inquiry to discover the identity of the body but is soon confronted with another corpse, that of a Labour candidate from one of the most important families in the country. The investigations into the two deaths soon appear to be connected, as the political and economic interests roused by the prospect of the parliament have remained the same for twenty years, as have the criminals controlling them. Once again, in fact, Rebus finds himself face to face with Cafferty, now out of prison, and even receives his help in finding the culprit, Barry Hutton, a member of a criminal gang with a legitimate business front, only to discover that Cafferty's goal is to take the man's place.

As on the occasion of the previous referendum, the possibility of partial self-government, this time realized, was accompanied by a reflection on the state of Scotland, in which Rankin took part with appearances on news programs and contributions to the newspapers. In "A Scottish Journey" he writes that "as the Parliament approaches Scotland itself stands naked. For so long, we have defined ourselves by what we are not: we are not English. Now, we begin the far harder task of defining just exactly what we are." *Set in Darkness* may be seen as Rankin's attempt at doing just that, and the panorama he sketches is gloomy. The title of the novel, taken from the poem "The Old Astronomer to His Pupil" by the nineteenth-century American writer Sarah Williams, suggests that it proposes a vision of unrelenting darkness: the whole history of Scotland since the loss of independence is seen as a sequence of crimes and prevarication; its future, signaled by the newly established devolved institutions, begins in the same vein. The title of the novel also suggests hope, however, as the line in Williams's poem from which it is taken reads in full, "Though my soul may set in darkness, it will rise in perfect light." Rankin has suggested, in a 2000 interview for the on-line periodical *January Magazine,* that "the new Parliament could be leading Scotland into the light after 300 years of being linked to England. And Rebus, you know, has his moments of darkness, but always he seems to finally reach a point of light."

The very scope of the book—which aims to provide the interpretation of an entire nation in its past, present, and future states—has withheld from *Set in Darkness* the critical acclaim lavished on the other novels in the series. The novel was well received in *The Observer* (12 March 2000), with reviewer Peter Guttridge observing that writers have often "chafed against the limitations a long-running mystery series imposes on them" but remarking that if Rankin "is feeling constrained, there's no sign of it here." Less favorable was the review by Heather O'Donoghue in *TLS* (25 February 2000), while Jane Jakeman, in a 14 March 2000 review in *The Independent* (London), in a not wholly negative appraisal, nevertheless saw this book as "a development that overstretches Rebus and cramps the talents of his creator" and wondered if the subject that preoccupies Rankin, "to chart the development of modern Scotland," is compatible with his chosen form: the author "is sharply aware of the possibilities for corruption that the new order brings, but the truth is that bureaucracy not only stuffs the text with acronyms, it also makes for uninteresting crime." Jakeman suggested that Rankin's role as "chronicler" of contemporary Scotland might be better performed through a different genre.

Rankin seems to have partly heeded her critique: though his next novel again falls with the genre of crime fiction, in it Rankin abandons contemporary political concerns to return to the mythical quality of the Scottish past and its most notorious protagonists. The plot of *The Falls* (2001) makes use of the real-life Arthur's Seat coffins: in 1836 five boys playing in the largest park in Edinburgh entered a cave, where they found seventeen miniature coffins containing wooden dolls. Ever since their discovery the coffins, now housed in the Museum of Scotland, gave rise to speculations as to their provenance and meaning: the current consensus is that they were built, with a shoe-maker's tools, to give some form of burial to the victims of William Burke and William Hare, two early-nineteenth-century murderers who killed people to sell their bodies to the anatomy professors of the medical school.

New coffins appear in *The Falls* on the sites where women have died or disappeared, the latest at the house of Flip, a wealthy student at Edinburgh University. As in *Set in Darkness,* the present is superimposed on two layers of the past, the nineteenth-century one of the original coffins and an intermediate one from the 1970s, when three women died in drownings that were ruled as accidental or suicide, though Rebus begins to suspect that they may have been the victims of one killer. While Rebus investigates the coffins, his assistant, Clarke, follows a parallel line of inquiry: the missing student was in fact involved in an Internet role-playing game run by a mysterious "quizmaster." By the end of the novel a connection has been discovered between the two inquiries, and both are brought to successful conclusions. However, though the historical strand of the plot is the less relevant to the discovery of the student's murderer, it is the more engrossing: as Guttridge remarked in an 18 March 2001 review in *The Observer* (London), "Rebus, decidedly lo-tech, is a denizen of a physically tangible, wholly believable real world. The virtual reality conjured up by the game pales by comparison."

Rankin's endeavor to give a portrait of his country by means of one of Rebus's investigations continues with *Resurrection Men,* published in 2002. His interest in exploring the connections between past events and present situations also continues in this novel. Past and present are initially separated in the plot and, with a narrative device similar to that used in *The Falls,* they are investigated by Rebus and Clarke, respectively. The division of the cases occurs at the start of the novel, when, after insulting his superior, Rebus is sent to the Scottish Police College for retraining; here, with other policemen also in disgrace with their superiors (they are the "Resurrection Men" of the title, all given one last chance to redeem themselves), he is set to work on the old case, in which he was himself involved. This side of the plot affords occasional insights into the policeman's past and offers an interesting variation in methods and scope with respect to the investigations described in previous books. Given the distance from the object of the investigation and the restrictions of action at the Police College, Rebus becomes engaged in an intellectual, vaguely academic puzzle-solving exercise. Clarke, on the other hand, is assigned to the case of a murdered art dealer among whose clients was Rebus's old adversary, Big Ger Cafferty. This investigation proceeds along more-predictable lines, until a connection is revealed between the two crimes, past and present, and the novel reaches a surprising but satisfactory conclusion.

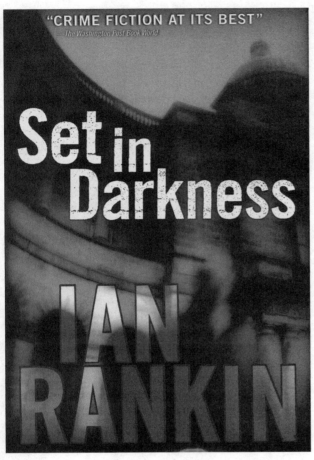

"CRIME FICTION AT ITS BEST"
The Washington Post Book World

Set in Darkness

IAN RANKIN

*Dust jacket for the U.S. edition of Rankin's 2000 novel,
about Rebus's investigations into murders linked to the
building that will house the Scottish Parliament
(Richland County Public Library)*

Partly owing to the renewed interest in Scottish affairs that followed the opening of the parliament, Rankin's role as chronicler and interpreter of contemporary Scotland has earned him several invitations to participate in television programs and write contributions for the national newspapers. ITV dedicated the entire space of the prestigious, highbrow *South Bank Show* to Rankin's (and Rebus's) Edinburgh. The hour-long program, which aired 1 July 2001, featured Rankin touring Edinburgh with the program host, Melvyn Bragg. It thus pointed to the two most appealing, and consistently praised, elements in the novels: their protagonist and setting.

Rebus's name was the self-referential gesture of a student of literary theory to signal the nature of the plot of *Knots & Crosses,* rather than a starting point for characterization, and Rankin had not intended to use it in more than one novel. Nevertheless, the author had unwittingly created a potentially perfect protagonist for a series. In the first novel he was a forty-year-old divorced man with a teenage daughter; he had been in the army, where he had

served in Northern Ireland but had resigned following a nervous breakdown—one of whose consequences, excessive drinking, remained with him—and entered the police, where he showed an antagonism toward authority that made him a loner. Both the outline of his past and the present condition of his life provided ample scope for further representation. Rebus does not change significantly in the course of the series, though he does age in real time, and a few details are modified to suit an increasingly more minute definition of the character: his SAS background is progressively abandoned (in the beginning of *Knots & Crosses* it is implied that he served with this elite commando unit, but it eventually turns out that he only underwent basic training); his former wife becomes less important but his daughter more so; he acquires a taste in rock music at the same time as rock songs punctuate mood and events in the novels; his drinking problem worsens, then improves, then worsens again; likewise his relationships with women. The series format allows for near-infinite opportunities for greater definition, especially insofar as his past is concerned, and by the time of the later novels Rebus has become interesting in himself, not only as a vehicle for the description of an investigation. Yet, through all the changes, Rebus's pessimistic attitude toward the world has remained the same, and he finds confirmation in the fact that frequently, at the end of a case, he has discovered the truth but has been unable to arrest the culprit. His actions in the novels, whether they denote unbreakable integrity of the incorruptible or a surprising willingness to come to terms with criminals, are guided by a Calvinist belief in the inevitability of events despite human attempts at intervention: integrity and compromise are only there to provide the illusion of having some power over reality.

For Lanchester this unchangeable core reflects the character's own stubbornness, which in turn reproduces a typically Scottish attitude, so that this highly believable character is also a metaphor for his country. Taylor, on the other hand, writes that "at first John Rebus falls into a familiar mould for a detective in crime fiction: he is a hard-drinking misfit, frequently at odds with his superiors, his private life littered with the debris of broken relationships. But the depth of characterization makes him anything but formulaic." The depth and realism of the depiction rest on the constant reminder, novel after novel, that the past makes the present what it is: the character of Rebus is, therefore, defined as much by what successive novels reveal of his past as by the events in which he is involved in the present. This technique is also a clue to the author's own view not only of individuals but also of events: a favorite plot device of Rankin's, in fact, is to have a case explained by delving into the past of the people involved.

Inevitably, the success of Rebus has led to questions regarding the degree of similarity between creator and creation. Some biographical similarities (both men are originally from Cardenden) and shared tastes, in rock music, Edinburgh pubs, and whiskey, do not prevent Rankin from distancing himself from his character: the latter is, of course, fictional and "much darker." Rebus was born a man in his forties, with a real job, a failed marriage and a child, from the mind of a young, unmarried student aged twenty-five. At the same time, however, Rankin admitted to Hasted that "I'm probably closer to him now than when I started the series. There was a period of me getting to know him, and him getting to know me. He does a lot of the things I'd like to do but daren't. I keep myself in control, most of the time, and let him run."

The inextricable connection between the past and the present is true of Edinburgh as well as of Rebus or the crimes in the novels and explains Rankin's fascination with the city that, in a 22 April 2001 article published in *The Independent* (London), "Ian Rankin: Welcome to the Spook Capital of the World," he calls "a city steeped in history, and that history is bloody indeed." The history of Edinburgh is rich in mysteries, ghosts, and criminals, with many examples of double lives in the manner of Jekyll and Hyde. The history of Edinburgh has also established in the architecture of the city the present condition of divisiveness so frequently represented by Rankin, whose own perception, as reported in a 25 March 2001 review of *The Falls* by Peter Kemp in *The Sunday Times* (London), is of "a city with a schizophrenically split personality." In the eighteenth century the wealthy families of the city moved from the crowded and chaotic Old Town to a purpose-built New Town, elegant and spacious; in so doing, they added physical distance to the existing class division between themselves and the poorer part of the population. In the 1960s and 1970s a similar move was effected, this time of the lower classes, with the construction of the housing estates at the periphery of the New Town.

The situation described in the Rebus novels is the consequence of such historical events. Rankin's forays into the past of Edinburgh, as well as those of his characters, have the purpose of making the present intelligible. Edinburgh is one of the recurring characters in the series, whose professed aim is to provide a comprehensive depiction of all the aspects of contemporary Scotland. As with a character, the city is given a psychological dimension characterized by desires pulling it in opposite directions; it interacts with other characters, particularly with Rebus, influencing their behavior by its presence.

In their 2001 interview Hasted asserted that "with each book, Rebus's ghosts, and Rankin's interest in the skeletons mouldering under Edinburgh's haughty surface, have grown, till the series no longer seems about solving crimes, but investigating one man's soul and one city."

Although Rankin's concerns may exceed the limited scope of the genre, a crime plot is ideally suited to this aim, in that it can explore any social environment and draw connections between them. In the Queen's Jubilee Birthday Honours List in June 2002, Rankin was made an Officer of the Order of the British Empire (OBE). With characteristic self-deprecation, he commented to a BBC interviewer at the time that his son Jack thought the title sounded "nerdy," remarking "I am trying to convince him that the way to pronounce my name now is Ian Rankinobe, to rhyme with Obi wan Kinobe. That is the only way to get round it." On a more serious note, he said of the award that "It is good for Scottish fiction, Scottish writers, and for crime fiction in general, that we are getting recognised as writing proper, good literature, that is worth being honoured."

Ian Rankin has fashioned his personal brand of crime writing, characterized by stylistic flair, complex plotting, and realistic representation, which the American novelist James Ellroy, an author with whom he has much in common, has called "tartan noir." With it, he is successfully pursuing his goal of becoming the official chronicler of Scotland.

Interviews:

J. Kinston Pierce, "Ian Rankin: The Accidental Crime Writer," *January Magazine* (2000) <http://januarymagazine.com/profiles/ianrankin.html>;

Robert McCrum, "Gothic Scot," *Observer* (London), 18 March 2001, p. 17;

Nick Hasted, "The Detective of Darkness," *Guardian*, 21 April 2001, p. 11;

Mel Gussow, "'Lone Cop' of Edinburgh Has Alter Ego At the Pub," *New York Times*, 3 January 2002;

Boyd Tonkin, "Ian Rankin: Rewards of an Inspector's Remorse," *Independent* (London), 5 January 2002.

References:

Ian Rankin Official Site <http://www.ianrankin.net> [8 August 2002];

Ian Rankin Website <http://www.ianrankin.com> [8 August 2002];

John Lanchester, "Secrets and Lies: The Impossible World of DI John Rebus," *London Review of Books* (27 April 2000), pp. 18–20;

Gill Plain, *Ian Rankin's* Black and Blue: *A Reader's Guide* (New York: Continuum, 2002);

Tangled Web UK: Ian Rankin Pages (19 July 2002) <http://www.twbooks.co.uk/authors/irankin.html>;

Andrew Taylor, "Ian Rankin: The King of Tartan Noir," *Independent* (London), 1 April 2001, p. 18;

Gavin Wallace and Randall Stevenson, eds., *The Scottish Novel Since the Seventies: New Visions, Old Dreams* (Edinburgh: Edinburgh University Press, 1993).

James Ryan

(5 May 1952 –)

Moira E. Casey
University of Connecticut

BOOKS: *Home from England* (London: Phoenix House, 1995);

Dismantling Mr. Doyle (London: Phoenix House, 1997)—extract translated into Italian by Maria Giosa as "P.S. I Love You," in *Linea D'Ombra,* 131 (March 1998): 38–43;

Seeds of Doubt (London: Weidenfeld & Nicolson, 2001).

James Ryan was an unknown when his first novel, *Home from England,* appeared on the Irish literary scene in 1995, but he was a well-connected unknown; since his late mother-in-law was the renowned Irish short-story writer Mary Lavin, and his wife, Caroline Walsh, is the literary editor of the *Irish Times,* he was not exactly a stranger to the world of professional Irish writing. Ryan has earned a great deal of notice, by both reviewers and his fellow writers, since his literary debut. His first three novels all received favorable reviews, and reviewers and literary critics alike have associated Ryan with a long and illustrious list of Irish literary notables. His thematic interests in issues such as the dysfunctional Irish family unit, the domestic sphere, emigration from and return to Ireland, and the clash between traditional, conservative Irish ways of life and a more modern, cosmopolitan sensibility have resulted in Ryan's being linked with the similar interests of established Irish writers such as John McGahern, Seamus Deane, and William Trevor, as well as with such newer writers as Colm Tóibín.

James Kevin Ryan was born 5 May 1952 in Rathdowney, County Laois, where he also attended primary school. His father, Paul Ryan, was a lawyer, and his mother, Kathleen (née Kirwan) Ryan, a homemaker. He went to secondary school in Rockwell College, Cashel, in County Tipperary. At Rockwell College, Ryan demonstrated a writer's mind for careful observation and creativity. Michael Ryan, a close, lifelong friend of Ryan's, who shared a room with him at Rockwell, was quoted in a 20 September 1997 article in *The Irish Times* as saying that Ryan would stay awake at night, making humorous analyses of the

James Ryan (courtesy of the author)

events of the previous day: "His observations were always sharp and funny."

Ryan's education continued at Trinity College in Dublin, where he earned a bachelor of arts degree in 1975. There he read widely in a variety of literature, particularly enjoying French, English, and Russian novels of the nineteenth century. Ryan also read Marcel Proust as well as American writers J. D. Salinger and Susan Minot. In 1976 Ryan received an education degree, also from Trinity, and he joined the teaching staff at Newpark Comprehensive School in Blackrock, Dublin. After Ryan took a study leave in 1981, his thesis, which he described to Moira E. Casey in an unpublished 22 June 2001 interview as dealing with the "recollections and viewpoints of a selection of contemporary Irish painters and sculptors," earned him a master's degree in education, again from Trinity.

Since, as Ryan told Eileen Battersby, *Home from England* took him about seven years to write, he would have begun writing it around 1988. He was able to write the novel while teaching full-time and raising two children with his wife, Caroline Walsh. His son, Mathew, was born 8 May 1983, and his daughter, Alice, was born 21 November 1986. Getting his first novel published was apparently a simple matter for Ryan. When the novel was ready for publication, he mailed it to Maggie McKernan, an editor at Phoenix House. In the early 1990s McKernan had worked with two Irish writers, Colum McCann and Michael Collins, both of whom Ryan admired, and Ryan felt that she might be a good choice for his own work. In a 25 May 1995 article in *The Irish Times* Eileen Battersby quoted Ryan as saying that he also wanted a British publisher as a "kind of personal test" to see if his writing would have an appeal outside of Ireland. After receiving and reading the manuscript for *Home from England,* McKernan at first assumed that such a high-quality novel had been written by a more established and experienced writer, and she suspected that the name "James Ryan" might be a pseudonym. Once Ryan's actual identity as a new novelist had been established, McKernan indicated that she was interested in working with him, and a contract for the novel was quickly signed.

Home from England traces one rural Irish family's move from Ireland to England in 1963 and their resulting sense of conflicted national identity. The family returns to Ireland twice—once in 1966 for a fiftieth anniversary celebration of the Easter Uprising and then again in the early 1980s for the father's funeral. Both returns serve to highlight the ever-growing distance of the family from their native land as well as the changes occurring both in Ireland and on the world stage, with the counterculture movements of the 1960s. The narrative is focused through the first-person perspective of the family son, whose relationship to his father (as well as to both of his nations, Ireland and England) evolves throughout the novel as he matures.

Ryan's focus on the issue of emigration in *Home from England* came as a result of his teaching experiences. He found that the history textbooks he was using in his secondary-school history courses did not fully explore the experience of emigration, which he feels to be "one of the most prevalent experiences" for Irish families during the 1950s and early 1960s. Although he admitted to Shirley Kelley in an interview for *Books Ireland* (March 2001) that "the experience of emigration and dislocation" was "not part of my personal experience, growing up in Portlaoise I was surrounded by it." Ryan also found that while the history books tended to neglect the subject, it seemed to him that Irish fiction had not devoted much attention to emigration either. He told Kelley that the experience of emigration not only lacked treatment by the history books, but "it wasn't greatly reflected in Irish fiction either." Consequently, Kelley reported, Ryan wrote his first novel "with almost a pioneering spirit."

Upon the publication of *Home from England,* a celebration was held at the Dublin Writers' Museum for the new novelist and his debut work. It was an auspicious beginning, with fellow writers Tim Pat Coogan and Ferdia MacAnna in attendance, as well as former Irish *taoiseach* (prime minister) Garret Fitzgerald. The subsequent critical response to *Home from England* was overwhelmingly positive; in *The Irish Times* (24 May 1995), reviewer Kevin Casey called it a "first novel of unusual accomplishment" and lauded Ryan's "gift for characterisation." In a 28 May 1995 review in *The Independent on Sunday* (London), Roy Foster, the eminent Irish historian, also praised *Home from England,* commending its pacing and Ryan's psychological insight. Echoing McKernan's sentiments upon first receiving the manuscript, Aisling Foster, in *TLS: The Times Literary Supplement* (26 May 1995), declared that "it is hard to believe that this is Ryan's first novel."

In May of 1995, the same month in which the novel was published, Ryan read an excerpt at the Laois Literary Festival. In 1996 excerpts from the novel appeared in *Home: An Anthology of Modern Irish Writing,* edited by Siobhan Parkinson, and *The Letter Box: An Anthology of Writing from County Laois,* edited by Mary O'Donnell. The warm reception of the novel by the literary press earned Ryan a two-book deal with Phoenix House. At a signing session for *Home from England* in Kenny's Bookshop & Art Gallery in Galway, Ryan met the Irish-born movie actor and producer Gabriel Byrne. Byrne felt the novel had strong prospects as a motion picture, and Ryan was commissioned by Byrne's production company, Plurabelle Films, to write the screenplay. The screenplay was accepted by Plurabelle Films in 1997, but it has since "disappeared into the Hollywood void," as Ryan told Casey in their 2001 interview. Also in 1997, Irish literature scholar Gerry Smyth discussed the treatment in *Home from England* of the effect of emi-

JAMES RYAN

Home
from England

*Cover for the paperback edition of Ryan's 1995 novel, about a family that emigrates
from rural Ireland to England (Bruccoli Clark Layman Archives)*

gration on modern Irish identity in his analytic work *The Novel and the Nation: Studies in New Irish Fiction.*

The success of *Home from England* helped Ryan to earn an Irish Arts Council Bursary award. He then took up an option to job share in the comprehensive school in which he teaches, an option that allows him more time to devote to writing. The combination of the bursary award and the job share allowed him to produce his second novel, *Dismantling Mr. Doyle* (1997), relatively quickly, only two years following the publication of *Home from England.*

As he did in *Home from England,* Ryan addresses the theme of contradictory cultural identities in *Dismantling Mr. Doyle,* but in a much different manner than in his first novel. The protagonist, Eve Doyle, does not permanently emigrate from Ireland, but the time she spends outside of the country dramatically changes her perspective on her homeland in general and her family in particular. In *Dismantling Mr. Doyle,*

Ryan examines how a young Irishwoman's return to Ireland following her feminist education in the United States changes her family members' long-standing patterns of relating to one another. Eve Doyle returns during the Christmas holidays to learn that her father has an illegitimate daughter about whom no one in the family has known. When she goes back to school, she enlists the help and advice of two of her feminist school friends who are experienced with popular psychological trends. The end result is a climactic and slightly ridiculous confrontation in the Doyle family home, during which Eve's American friends try to orchestrate a mediated group-therapy session. The session is designed to force all the parties—including Eve's subservient and self-effacing mother—to face squarely Mr. Doyle's past actions and their own denial. The effect is humorous, although not entirely unsuccessful, as the Doyle family does resolve some of its conflicts and

Eve manages to break free mentally and emotionally from her family's psychological grasp.

Dismantling Mr. Doyle was launched in September of 1997 with a book-signing party at Eason's bookstore in Dublin, where journalist and novelist Nuala O'Faolain gave a speech in which she suggested that she was invited to speak because her works address feminist issues and the focus in the book is on the clash between traditional Irish family values and American feminism. Other writers at the launching were Thomas Keneally, the author of *Schindler's List* (1982), and popular Irish novelist Maeve Binchy. In November of 1997 Ryan participated in the Umbria Libri festival, and an extract from *Dismantling Mr. Doyle,* translated into Italian by Maria Giosa, was subsequently published in the March 1998 issue of *Linea d'Ombra,* the festival publication.

The reviews for *Dismantling Mr. Doyle* were decidedly more mixed than those for *Home from England* had been, but none seemed to be outright negative. Most of the critics seemed to have recognized both the skills that Ryan successfully employed as well as the ambitious goal of trying to trace the Doyle family's psychological intricacies. Nevertheless, several critics found that Ryan had in some way failed in this novel. For example, Alison Dye, in *The Irish Times* (20 September 1997), stated that she felt the novel was less about the dismantling of the Doyle patriarch than about the story of the Doyle daughter Eve. Dye also found weaknesses in Ryan's character development, stating that she "felt hurried on from one character to another before his or her experiences had been sufficiently probed." She did admit that the "huge internal shifts" that the Doyle family experience, and the "emotions that attend them," are challenging territory for any writer. Whatever the reason, from a variety of critics' perspectives, the knack for characterization and realistic psychological portraits that Ryan had demonstrated in *Home from England,* and for which critics had lauded him, seem weaker in *Dismantling Mr. Doyle.*

Between 1998 and 2000 Ryan was working on his third novel, *Seeds of Doubt* (2001), a lengthy and ambitious triptych, which subtly addresses the experience of the emigrant but perhaps looks more squarely at the difficulties faced by the individual just within the individual's native country. The novel was published early in 2001, and an extract was published 3 March 2001 in the *Irish Times* fiction page, *Write Now,* edited by Katie Donovan.

Seeds of Doubt is a complicated and challenging novel, divided into three sections, each devoted to revealing a segment of the larger plot. The first section primarily tells the story of Nora Macken, the second

oldest of five sisters who grow up on the family farm, Templeard, in County Tipperary. The story begins in 1978, with the sisters coming together to discuss the oldest sister's plan to sell the family home. Through a series of flashbacks, Ryan explores the childhood lives of the sisters in the 1930s and 1940s, eventually revealing Nora's rape by a young priest and her subsequent pregnancy and childbirth. The child is swiftly removed by the nuns who attend Nora during the birth. Nora's infamy among the townspeople ruins her chances of marriage, and the shame she brings to the family places her in disfavor with her father.

The second part of the triptych shows Ryan's ambition as a writer; here he abandons the first-person narrator in order to give the reader a style that is more emotionally detached from the subject. He said to Casey that he also wanted to "wrench the story from the context in which it was set"—the context established in the opening section of the novel. This fable-like section tells the story of Nora's child, Angelo, who mysteriously ends up in a small village in Italy, where he is raised by three servant women. He is already about seven years old when he arrives in the village, and nothing is known about his infancy. Over time he falls in love with Maria Stella, the youngest of the women who are raising him, and when she agrees to marry a young lawyer, Angelo—now about eighteen—murders the prospective groom and commits suicide.

If the second section of the novel is unsettling in its leap into another culture, different characters, a different style of storytelling, and a gruesome finale, the third section helps to resolve the reader's unease. The final section of the novel is narrated by Nora's nephew Patrick, who helps Nora to confront her past. This section links together the first and second sections and explains some of the missing elements of Angelo's history.

Seeds of Doubt received overwhelmingly positive criticism. Reviewers recognized Ryan's objectives; as with the focus on emigration in his first novel, he wanted to tell a story that he felt was a familiar one—a mid-twentieth-century Irishwoman's life nearly ruined both by an unwanted child and by the sexual hypocrisy of the Catholic Church—but that was infrequently told in the literature. Ryan told Kelley in their *Books Ireland* interview that he was partly motivated by "how silence operates and how it shapes people's lives. With the collusion of so many parties—in this case Nora's mother and father, her sisters, the nuns at her boarding school, the priest and his superiors—it becomes a subversive force. Nora . . . is the carrier of so much unspoken history, a history that, I think, is most likely to emerge in fiction."

From Seeds of Doubt, Chpt. 3

Unwitting complicity, but complicity none the less.

Lurking with uncertainty among the fragments of our cruelty to Aunt Cassie is the spectre of Daddo and Ammie's complicity. They preached kindness but there was often a hollow ring to it, prompting us to look behind the scenes in search of a more credible sentiment. What we absorbed in the course of that search was their ~~secret~~ resentment at having Cassie under their roof, witness to their every move. And because our search was unsupervised we grasped that resentment in its rawest form, as children will, collectively becoming its mouthpiece.

unvoiced

Indent par → *Now Flossie would never say something like that about herself…*

Aunt Cassie ended her days staring into the fire, her eyes as bright as moonstones, her ~~bony~~ hands clamped to the frayed arms of her basket chair, waiting for death. A whole decade, virtually silent. Very occasionally, maybe once or twice in a year, she laughed loudly, a terrorised hee-haw of a laugh, casting about the kitchen as if in her dark meanderings she had stumbled across something as funny as it was sad. A great irony maybe, which out of some kind of washed up, residual loyalty to the living she vowed to take with her to the grave.

Knobbly

In her own view of herself Cassie was first and foremost a Macken of Templeard, a share cropper of sorts in whatever it produced while she remained within its confines. That was her birthright. Although far from beautiful, she frequently boasted of my mother, Ammie's great beauty. This she seemed to do in good faith, never hankering after beauty herself because she had a sister-in-law in whose beauty she had a recognised stake.

This she did?

, the bedrock on which her whole life was built.

'Bea Coady', she used to say, always calling Ammie by her full maiden name, 'turned more heads in this parish than the rest of them put together.' And here she might stop whatever she was doing, savouring we supposed, the pride she felt in Ammie's beauty, secure that she herself had been adequately compensated for her own lack of it.

Page from the revised typescript for Ryan's 2001 novel (Collection of James Ryan)

Ryan, perhaps more successfully so than with *Dismantling Mr. Doyle,* is able with *Seeds of Doubt* to write that history and narrate the workings of silence and denial on the Irish psyche. In *The Irish Times* (10 March 2001), Liam Harte wrote that "*Seeds of Doubt* is a novel which deftly illuminates the devastating human consequences of denial and deception in society which forces its citizens to live up to a false, idealised image of itself." Additionally, some critics found a degree of maturation of Ryan's style in his third novel. John Kenny, in *TLS* (6 April 2001), noted that "*Seeds of Doubt* has the emotionally implosive effect and economy of style of Ryan's earlier work, but there is an added expansiveness, both in terms of language and thematic resonance." Just as other reviewers did with *Home from England,* Kenny went on to compare *Seeds of Doubt* to the work of McGahern.

In Ryan's first three novels the emigration and return of one or all of the protagonists radically alters both the characters' perspectives on Ireland and on the family unit. In *The Irish Times* (24 May 1995), Kevin Casey wrote that *Home from England* "attempts to contemplate the damage done to his [the protagonist's] family not only by emigration but by the stubborn unwillingness to recognise that there is almost no way of going back and never to a place that has remained unchanged." In *Dismantling Mr. Doyle* daughter Eve's feminist education in America nearly serves to dismantle not only her father, Mr. Doyle, but their entire family as well. And in *Seeds of Doubt,* Nora Macken's rape as a young girl by a priest and her subsequent pregnancy force her eventually to leave Ireland for England, as well as to leave the narrow trajectory of her life that her father and family have carefully planned out and that she has internalized. In his *Irish Times* review Harte stated that *Seeds of Doubt* "deserves to take its place alongside [Tóibín's] *The Heather Blazing* [1992] and [Deane's] *Reading in the Dark* [1996] as a text which indicts the oppressive power of the national meta-narrative to suppress realities which cannot be accommodated within the officially authorised version of Irishness." In his first three novels Ryan centers the plot on various types of conflict between such national metanarratives and unaccommodatable realities; these conflicts frequently arise directly from the experiences of the character or characters who leave Ireland, only to return greatly changed.

In 2001 Ryan presented a paper at a symposium held at University College, Cork. The conference theme was "The Lost Decade," and the papers presented focused on emigration from Ireland during the 1950s. The paper that Ryan presented, "Inadmissable Departures," will be included in a publication of the conference proceedings scheduled to be published by Cork University Press in the fall of 2002. The paper deals with the Irish tradition of literature that addresses the emigrant experience, and Ryan told Moira Casey that he is becoming "increasingly aware of how extensive that tradition is." However, he has identified a lack of first-person narratives about the emigrant experience between the formation of the Irish Free State in 1922 and the early 1960s, a lack that he explores in that paper. In 2001 Ryan also participated in both the Dublin Literary Festival and a Franco-Irish literary festival, "Etonnants Voyageurs" (Astonishing Travelers). As James Ryan continues to write, he will no doubt continue to expound in fiction on the themes of emigration and the particular psychological conflicts of Irish men and women.

Interview:

Shirley Kelley, "The Silence of Unspoken History," *Books Ireland* (March 2001): 51.

References:

Eileen Battersby, "Making their fiction debuts," *Irish Times,* 25 May 1995, p. 14;

Gerry Smyth, *The Novel and the Nation: Studies in New Irish Fiction* (London: Pluto, 1997), pp. 148–150;

"Who's on the Books?" *Irish Times,* 20 September 1997, p. 61.

Madeleine St John

(1942 –   )

Shannon Forbes
Marquette University

BOOKS: *The Women in Black* (London: Deutsch, 1993);
A Pure Clear Light (London: Fourth Estate, 1996; New
York: Carroll & Graf, 2000);
The Essence of the Thing (London: Fourth Estate, 1997;
New York: Carroll & Graf, 1998);
A Stairway to Paradise (London: Fourth Estate, 1999;
New York: Carroll & Graf, 1999).

Madeleine St John (pronounced "Sin-jin") is an
extremely private figure who came to sudden and
unwelcome public attention with the surprise nomination of her third novel, *The Essence of the Thing* (1997),
for the prestigious Booker Prize. St John has given few
interviews and has revealed few details of her personal
life. One interviewer, Emma Cook, noted in *The Independent* (London) on 21 September 1997 that "people
assume that St John must be a recluse because she has
such a low profile." Because St John guards her privacy,
little information concerning her cultural or literary
influences, thoughts about her books and style of composition, or personal history is publically available.

St John was born in 1942 into a wealthy
Anglo-Australian family in Sydney, Australia. St John
"guardedly" described her childhood to Libby Brooks
in an interview for *The Guardian* (18 September 1997)
as "not one long laugh." Her mother died when she
was twelve, which, St John said in her interview with
Cook, "obviously changed everything." She studied
first at the Queenwood School for Girls, a boarding
school in Mosman, New South Wales, and later at
Sydney University, graduating in 1963; her contemporaries included Germaine Greer and Clive James. St
John left Australia in 1965 at the age of twenty-three.
When asked by Brooks if she was eager to leave, St
John responded, "Who wouldn't be? Really, there's
nothing unusual in leaving Australia. Suddenly one
day there was no one left under the age of 35." St John
first moved to the United States, where her new husband began graduate studies, while she worked at the
university bookstore. Two years later the marriage
was over. St John at that point moved to England and

*Madeleine St John (photograph by Steve Gorton;
from the dust jacket for the U.S. edition of* The
Essence of the Thing, *1998)*

subsequently spent what Louise Robson described in
an interview distributed on the Australian Associated
Press wire service on 15 October 1997 as "thirty Bohemian and reclusive years in London." St John told
Robson that she no longer thought of herself as Australian: "If someone came to me with a gun I'd have to
say British."

As she told Brooks, St John supported herself by
working at several "stupid little part-time jobs," including one job at a left-wing bookshop. St John described
the shop to Cook as "full of earnest, dedicated social-
ists. I didn't believe a word they said—I knew that life

wasn't that simple." She explained to Brooks that "It never struck me that I wanted to write. There just came a point in my life when I realized there was nothing else I could do to try to earn a few quid. It wasn't a burning need, which is an awful thing to confess. I thought I'd have a crack at this writing thing." She remarked in her interview with Cook that she had previously considered writing, but "the thing that stopped me for so many years was the realization that I couldn't be that good. Then it percolated through that I could be as good at least as some of the people who were getting away with it."

The result of St John's newfound confidence was her first book, *The Women in Black* (1993). Set in the 1950s, this novel is about the loneliness and boredom of three department-store employees. These women wear the black dresses that serve as uniforms in the Ladies' Frocks Department at Goode's, a store in Sydney, Australia. Each of the three women experiences extreme unhappiness as a result of problems stemming from relations with the opposite sex. Patty—"thin, straw-coloured and unloved"—suffers in a failed marriage. Fay, who has become bored with the wild single life, longs to find one decent man. Lisa is an intelligent teenager—though she has "the body and the mien of a child of around fifteen, and an immature one at that"—whose father believes women should not attend college. The novel maintains an optimistic tone, in that each woman, during the hectic Christmas shopping season, in some way confronts her problem and obtains some semblance of comfort and satisfaction.

The novel received positive notices. In a 20 April 1993 review in *The Independent* (London) Shena Mackay described *The Women in Black* as "graceful and charming . . . If there are tears in the eyes, they will be tears of pleasure at the resolution and consummate workmanship of a small masterpiece." The reviewer for *Publishers Weekly* (20 September 1993) wrote that "St John writes in a mannerly, witty style and in spite of her characters' stereotypical girlishness . . . an essentially lighthearted tone sustains this tale." The novel was even rumored to have been long-listed for the Booker Prize in 1993 and was optioned in 1997 for a motion-picture adaptation by Australian director Bruce Beresford, known for such movies as *Breaker Morant* (1980) and *Driving Miss Daisy* (1989). In an interview published in *Reel West* (January–February 2000), Beresford mentioned that he had written a screenplay and hoped to begin work on the movie in 2001. Kate Bochner adapted the novel for the radio program *The Book Reading,* in a production read by Tammy McCarthy and broadcast by the Australian Broadcasting Corporation on 13 November 2000.

St John's second novel, *A Pure Clear Light* (1996), explores the way Gillian Selkirk's life is lacking despite her house in West London, vacations in France, three bright children, and successful career as an accountant. Her married lover, Simon Beaufort, is a television director who fell in love with Gillian after his wife, Flora, a lapsed Catholic, left with their three children for a holiday in France. Simon, an agnostic, is determined not to leave Flora, though he finds Gillian irresistible. When Flora's friend discovers the secret affair, Flora becomes determined that her marriage must endure in spite of her fears that her world is now transitory.

A Pure Clear Light received positive reviews. The novel was described by Victoria Walker in a 4 October 1997 review in *The Times* (London) as "A triumph of the minimalist, it appraises love, both sacred and profane, desire, pain and the disappointments of this earth with a laser eye." Similarly, an unsigned review in *Publishers Weekly* (22 May 2000) compared *A Pure Clear Light* to Graham Greene's *The Power and the Glory* (1940) and André Gide's *La Porte étroite* (1909; translated as *Strait is the Gate,* 1924) in its exploration of "the tension between worldly and religious love." This reviewer asserted that St John's "prose is swift and beautifully spare; the dialogue is sharp and witty; yet the tone of the narrative is chilly, like white winter light, more of a hedge against emotional suicide than a life-affirming renewal of love."

These two novels, though well received, did little to further St John's career as a novelist, and she spent many hours in her flat in Notting Hill contemplating more practical ways to earn a living, even as she composed her third book, *The Essence of the Thing.* St John was, she told Cook, "seriously worried about what I could possibly do next. I mean, my sales were so pathetic that with the best will in the world no one would want to take me on. I thought I could be a check-out girl, but I'm probably too old. However, I did really talk myself into being a tea-lady."

Published in 1997, *The Essence of the Thing* tells the story of how Nicola, who has been living for six years with Jonathan, a London lawyer in his thirties, hears from Jonathan one day "out of the blue" that they must split up because he feels the relationship "just isn't working." Nicola, stunned, moves out of the apartment as Jonathan requests, and desperately tries to understand why the relationship failed. The novel focuses on the way Nicola experiences, at various stages in this grieving process, confusion, denial, and finally acceptance and optimism as she moves forward to explore other possibilities for romance and fulfillment.

The Essence of the Thing was extremely well received by the critics. An unsigned review in the 20 July 1998

*Dust jacket for the U.S. edition of St John's 1997 novel,
which critic Gardner McFall called "a brisk,
sophisticated and artful narrative"
(Richland County Public Library)*

issue of *Publishers Weekly* noted that "the difficulties of committing to a relationship make wonderful fodder for St John's insightful, often hilarious third novel." The reviewer commented that "using spare prose, sparkling dialogue and painfully true observations on family life, St John creates a winning combination of humor and pathos." Similarly, in *The New York Times Book Review* (24 January 1999) Gardner McFall remarked that St John "shapes what might have been a bathetic story into a brisk, sophisticated and artful narrative buoyed by an ironic use of the religious imagery of hell, salvation and resurrection." Ron Charles in *The Christian Science Monitor* (20 August 1998) identified the strengths of St John's prose style: "In the perfectly captured dialogue between these friends, St John explores a sad gulf between those secure in relationships and those who consider themselves adrift."

Yet, the attention St John received for this novel caused her to long for the obscurity she had previously experienced. *The Essence of the Thing* was nominated for the Booker Prize, and, according to Cook, "overnight

everything changed," and St John became "a subject of media curiosity and attention." Brooks described St John's life before the nomination as "a tale untold," but the announcement of the nomination "raised eyebrows among the literary cognoscenti" and resulted in hordes of journalists wanting to probe the "obscure history" of this "wild-card choice." St John was overwhelmed by this attention, telling Brooks that "'I am gob-smacked, truly. I think we'd all like to get attention, but when we've got it we're in a very equivocal position, despising ourselves for wanting it." She told Brooks that "All this changes one's perception. I don't know what it will be like to return to real life." She stated that "God knows who this creature is who is going to emerge out of all this. The only thing I'm sure of is that it won't be me, and it won't be the person who wrote the book." St John remarked in her interview with Brooks that "I've looked from a distance at what is done to writers in the public eye. Nothing could be more deleterious to writing fiction."

According to Robson, St John was, therefore, happy to have lost the Booker Prize, stating that "You get a lot of attention and publicity that you're simply not used to so the publicity you would get for a win would be too much." St John went on to say that "I have just been catapulted to a slight degree of stardom after total obscurity. Enough is enough," while also, however, adding that she would soon be commencing work on another novel. St John told Robson that she had begun a new book but, as a result of the commotion of attention showered upon her after having been nominated for the Booker Prize, doubted she could continue.

St John's antipathy to the publicity connected with the Booker Prize is not surprising considering the way many critics reacted when her nomination was announced. In the 21 September 1997 issue of *The Sunday Telegraph* (London) for instance, David Robson dismissed St John completely: "As for *The Essence of the Thing*, it is hard to remember a more insubstantial novel making the Booker shortlist. It reads like a runner-up in a short story competition in *Cosmopolitan*. Madeleine St John has a good ear for dialogue but, once she has reminded you for the umpteenth time that men are bastards, you wonder why she bothers. It is common knowledge, isn't it?" St John was not dismayed about criticism that seemed to focus on the superficial, however. She commented to Cook that "I mean to write about something beyond those details. They are just there to lead you to another place. That's just the surface. I know some people can't see that. They see some dreary little account of a couple breaking up, but what the hell."

St John did manage to overcome the writer's block that the Booker Prize nomination apparently induced. *A Stairway to Paradise* (1999) is a novel describing the predicaments of three intertwined lovers. Andrew Flynn leaves a failed marriage and a young daughter in the United States and returns to London. His friend Alex is a journalist who suffers in a loveless marriage. Both men fall in love with a woman named Barbara who is charming but indecisive. None of the three main characters in this novel wallow in self-pity; rather, they all simply move through life with low expectations.

This novel also received mainly positive reviews. Beth Gibbs wrote in a review for *The Library Journal* (July 1999), for example, that "St John, who has been compared to Iris Murdoch and Mary Wesley, captures the mixture of emotions that result from lust, longing, and deceit." An unsigned review in *Publishers Weekly* (5 July 1999) commented that St John "casts a droll eye over sentimental entanglements in this sophisticated novel."

Nicholas Clee, who in 1997 was one of the most outspoken critics of St John's Booker nomination, reviewed the novel for *The New Statesman* (19 April 1999). He noted that the book "has 49 chapters in 185 pages, a good many of which contain a lot of white space. A cursory glance suggests flimsy plotting, functional prose and shallow characters." Clee went on to say, however, that "this is a novel with much more substance, craft and imaginative sympathy than its surface reveals." In *Commonweal* (11 February 2000), Elizabeth Kirkland Cahill also pointed out the craft involved in the novel, but noted that "while the plot is carefully structured and the novel's forty-nine chapters nicely organized into four parts, the writing is so good that it almost doesn't matter what happens." Cahill called St John's prose "spare but rich, like a desert flower in bloom. Not a word is wasted. She is a frequent elider, accurately replicating the spoken shorthand that passes for conversation in Britain."

Sylvia Brownrigg in *The Guardian* (24 April 1999) remarked that "It's a familiar scenario, yet in St John's adroit handling the story becomes quietly affecting." She praised St John's achievement in depicting "the poignant comedy in the ways people mask their unhappiness with their materialism: when frustrated Alex looks around his north London house, he reflects that, 'it made up for a lot, an awful lot, that skirting,'" though Brownrigg tempered her praise somewhat when she called the novel a "pleasing if light confection." Mary Allen's 10 April 1999 review in *The Spectator* (London) is typical of the simultaneously positive and negative reviews St John receives: "The main problem is that none of the characters appears to learn anything from their misfortunes, and it is Madeleine St John's considerable technical skills that keep the attention, not any sense of development on the part of the central trio. . . . *A Stairway to Paradise* never really gets moving, leaving the characters engaged in a circumlocutory amble

Dust jacket for the U.S. edition of St John's 1999 novel, in which two friends fall in love with the same woman (Richland County Public Library)

around what one of them refers to as 'a salubrious suburb of hell.'"

While Madeleine St John's novels have received virtually no scholarly attention, most reviews of the novels are generally positive. Critics appreciate her accurately rendered dialogue and thought processes, and the way in which St John depicts the emotions of characters who have failed in some way—or have been failed—as well as those who are hopeful about the future. Certainly there are many readers who, unlike some reviewers, recognize the depth behind St John's focus on everyday minutiae.

Interviews:

Libby Brooks, "Women: Stranger Than Fiction," *Guardian,* 18 September 1997, p. T5;

Emma Cook, "Tea lady, check-out girl? No, I'll stick to writing," *Independent* (London), 21 September 1997, News section, p. 8;

Louise Robson, "Publicity Shy Aussie Author Happy to Miss out on Booker," *AAP Newsfeed* (15 October 1997).

Ahdaf Soueif

(1950 –)

Geoffrey P. Nash
University of Sunderland

BOOKS: *Aisha* (London: Cape, 1983);
In the Eye of the Sun (London: Bloomsbury, 1992; New York: Pantheon, 1993);
Sandpiper (London: Bloomsbury, 1996);
The Map of Love (London: Bloomsbury, 1999; New York: Anchor/Doubleday, 2000);
Mukhtarat min a'mal Ahdaf Suwayf (Cairo: al-Hay'ah al-Misriyah al-'Ammah lil-Kitab, 1999).

TRANSLATION: Mourid Barghouti, *I Saw Ramallah,* foreword by Edward W. Said (Cairo & New York: American University in Cairo Press, 2000).

SELECTED PERIODICAL PUBLICATION– UNCOLLECTED: "Nile Blues," *Guardian,* 6 November 2001.

Ahdaf Soueif (photograph by Robert Lyons; courtesy of the author)

In addition to writing novels and short stories published in both English and Arabic, the Anglo-Egyptian writer Ahdaf Soueif is a translator of Arabic writing into English, and she has engaged in the promotion and mediation of Arab culture in association with several cultural organizations. She is a regular contributor to literary magazines and newspapers as well as appearing on radio and television in England, the United States, and the Arab world. Soueif describes her time as being divided between London and Cairo, thus accenting the cultural dualities that have been formative in the creation of her fiction. Although Soueif is a British citizen and thus a British novelist, Egypt figures large in her work, and she draws upon both Arabic and English literary traditions.

In comparison to the introduction of the English language into India and sub-Saharan Africa, its appearance in Arabic-speaking countries was desultory, to say the least. "By the middle of the nineteenth century," writes the historian Albert Hourani in his *A History of the Arab Peoples* (1991), "French had replaced Italian as the *lingua franca* of trade and the cities; knowledge of English scarcely existed in the Maghrib and was less widespread than French further east." While France,

which seized a foothold in Algeria in the 1830s, was quick to promote its imperial sway over the Arab world, it was not until British armies defeated the popular revolution of Ahmad 'Urābī Pasha in 1882 and occupied Egypt that Britain came to exercise firsthand control over a large Arabic-speaking land. By the end of World War I, however, the British controlled a de facto empire in the Middle East, stretching from the Red Sea to the Persian Gulf and incorporating Mesopotamia (modern Iraq) to the north.

Whereas the French were keen to spread their language and culture throughout their spheres of interest in the Levant, it was not the British but rather the Americans who actively introduced English-medium education into the Middle East. Founded by American missionaries in Beirut in 1866, the Syrian Protestant College was renamed the American University of Beirut in 1920 and between the two world wars was responsible for educating a generation of Arab and other Middle-East future political and cultural leaders. In Egypt, however, as Soueif points out in her novel *The Map of Love* (1999), tertiary education was blocked by the British agent and consul general Evelyn Baring, Lord Cromer, until his retirement in 1907. The following year King Fu'ād I founded Egyptian University, which was later called Fu'ād I University and is now Cairo University. But if the British did little in Egypt—in contrast to all they did in India—to foster the spread of their language and literature (allowing French to retain its pre-occupation ascendancy among the educated classes), their writers often adopted an Egyptian background for their novels. Lawrence Durrell's tetralogy, *The Alexandria Quartet* (1957–1960), concerned as it is with the European and Levantine colony in the second largest Egyptian city, does little more than that. Cairo University was, however, the setting for several novels of the 1950s—including D. J. Enright's *Academic Year* (1955) and P. H. Newby's *Picnic at Sakkara* (1955)—that attempt to comprehend the interface of the different minorities, nationalities, classes, and sects in Egypt, before the British epoch eventually ended with the Officers' Revolution of 1952, the coup that overthrew the monarchy and resulted in the expulsion of most foreigners.

Given the strategic placement of Egypt at the junction of the continents of Europe, Africa, and Asia, it is unsurprising that Egyptian writers should so often have been the purveyors of Western ideas and culture to the Arab/Islamic lands to the east. *Zaynab* (1913), which is generally called the first novel in Arabic, was written by an Egyptian, Muhammad Husayn Haykal, and an early practitioner of the modern Arabic short story, Mustāfā Lutfī al-Manfalūtī, was also an Egyptian. The Arabic literary tradition may be resplendent and ancient but is one with which contemporary Arab writers have not found it easy to live. The major problem to be faced is the gulf that separates classical and received standard Arabic from the many different vernaculars operative throughout the modern Arab world. The Egyptian vernacular, for example, has gained a wide audience beyond its borders through motion pictures, and yet the most celebrated Egyptian novelist of the twentieth and early-twenty-first centuries, the winner of the 1988 Nobel Prize in literature, Naguib Mahfouz, has avoided its direct incorporation into his novels, even in dialogue. Although classical Arabic literature possesses its own narrative forms, the novel itself is a Western importation, albeit one that Arab writers have sometimes seen fit to modify according to these traditional forms. Arabic literature has been translated only sparingly, with Mahfouz being one of the few Arab writers in Arabic known in the West, even though the modern Arabic novel and short story now have a rich corpus from which to draw.

Soueif was born in Cairo in 1950 to academic parents. Her mother, Fatma Moussa, became the first woman lecturer in the English department of Fu'ād I University in 1952; she eventually became head of the department of English at Cairo University in 1972, retiring in 1987. Her father, Mustafa Soueif, was a philosophy graduate who later became a professor of psychology at Cairo University. Ahdaf Soueif lived in London between the ages of four and eight, while her mother was earning a Ph.D. in English literature at London University and her father was pursuing postdoctoral work toward a diploma in clinical psychology. The family returned to Egypt, where Soueif completed her education, graduating from Cairo University with a B.A. in English literature in 1971. She continued her studies in English and American literature at the American University in Cairo, obtaining her M.A. degree in 1973. She then took up doctoral work in literary stylistics at the University of Lancaster, the cold, northern England university campus that forms the setting for part of Souief's novel *In the Eye of the Sun* (1992). The next six years were spent lecturing at Cairo University, as well as being editor-in-chief of the Collier Macmillan Ltd. Arabic educational texts project in Cairo and London.

Soueif's first published book, *Aisha* (1983), is experimental in several key respects. According to the Arabic-literature specialist Hilary Fitzpatrick, it is neither a novel nor a collection of independent stories. In a 1992 essay, "Arabic Fiction in English: A Case of Dual Nationality," Fitzpatrick describes the piece as being connected with the handful of writings published by earlier Arab writers in English. The main character, Aisha, is a middle-class Egyptian who is partly educated in a London state school, where her superior English sets her apart from the local students. The duality of her English and Egyptian experiences is expressed in Aisha's mastery of standard English, on the one hand, and her immersion in traditional Egyptian cultural practice through her nurse, Zeina, on the other. The nurse's stories reveal a world of raw emotion, realism, and religious fatalism, that pulls Aisha away from the rationally ordered life of her parents. In the end, having experienced a ceremony of exorcism at which psychologically scarred women desperately seek healing, Aisha dies in childbirth. Fitzpatrick points out that the cultural schizophrenia of the book is not untypical of Arabic literature, as is the frame of eight interconnected narratives. Soueif's use of stream of consciousness and

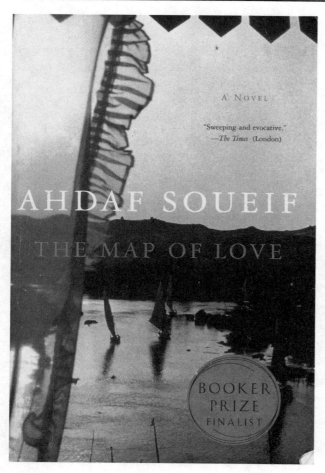

*Paperback cover for the 2000 U.S. edition of Soueif's 1999 novel,
about a pair of early-twentieth-century Anglo-Egyptian lovers
and their late-twentieth-century American descendant
(Richland County Public Library)*

flashback is, in contrast, a modernist device, albeit one that had been adopted into the Arabic novel by the Egyptian writer Mahfouz some twenty years earlier in *Al-Liss w'al-Kilab'* (1962; translated as *The Thief and the Dogs,* 1984).

Between 1987 and 1989 Soueif continued her academic career at King Saud University in Riyadh, Saudi Arabia, where she taught linguistics. She married the British literary critic Ian Hamilton in 1981. They had two sons, Omar Robert, born in 1984, and Ismail Richard, born in 1989. Hamilton died on 27 December 2001.

In the Eye of the Sun represents a much more ambitious fictional project than Soueif's earlier volume. Reviewers have discerned in it a Victorian richness, going so far as to link the novel with George Eliot's *Middlemarch* (1871–1872) or with Mahfouz's *Al-Thulathiyya* (1956–1957; translated as *The Cairo Trilogy,* 1990–1992). As in *Aisha,* Soueif has clearly drawn on autobiographical material.

At the center of the novel is a failed relationship that might be said to build on "Returning," the first story in *Aisha*. In the novel, however, a political dimension has been added to the greatly amplified Egyptian domestic setting. The novel sets out to trace the formation of its central protagonist, Asya Ulama–literally translated, "Asia of the learned clerics" or "Asia of the scientists"– against the background of Egyptian and Arab affairs between May 1967 and April 1980. These thirteen years, which encompass the Arab-Israeli wars of June 1967 and October 1973, the decline of Nasserite Arab socialism, and the emergence of a Palestinian national resistance, are a defining period in modern Egyptian and Arab history. They begin with the last years of Gamal Abdel Nasser–who died three years after the catastrophic Arab defeat of 1967–and extend through almost the entire presidency of Anwar Sadat, whose time as Egyptian leader was marked by huge social upheaval. According to Edward W. Said, in his review of the novel in *TLS: The Times Literary Supplement* (19 June 1992), "nowhere is the intersection between the public and the private more interesting than when Asya considers the difference between her mother Lateefa (also a lecturer in English literature) and herself as each abandons Arabic for English."

If Asya adopts English literature as a vocation in the first part of the novel, the second part develops the unraveling of her marriage to Saif against her erotic but destructive affair with the British student, Gerald Stone. What Said terms the "Anglo-Arab encounter" was rarely so prominent a feature of earlier Arabic fiction, even though it appeared as a crucial external dimension in the Sudanese author Tayeb Salih's influential *Mawsim al-hijrah ilá al-Shamāl* (1967; translated as *Season of Migration to the North,* 1969). For Said, the section of *In the Eye of the Sun* set in England marks the emergence of a form of writing by Arabs that is "about being in England, having to do intimately with English people and so on." This setting, he implied, makes the use of English as the medium of transmission appropriate, in contrast to what he terms "the oddness of the enterprise" in *Aisha,* which is predominantly set in an Arab Muslim context.

Asya has been described as a liberal and an elitist Arab Egyptian woman. Although she is a Muslim, her privileged background enables her to indulge in sexual experimentation, covertly in her own land, but more freely abroad, where she travels as a student, and in Beirut, Damascus, and London, in the company of her fiancé, Saif. Asya's premarital intimacy with Saif stops short of complete sexual congress, however, and once the pair have accomplished the traditional marriage rituals, they find themselves unable to consummate their union, though Saif is not impotent nor is Asya frigid.

From Asya's point of view, her relationship with Saif, who is unable to accept her on her own terms, seems to represent the limitations of her cultural inheritance, and the need she feels to go beyond this inheritance finds expression in her search for emotional and sexual fulfillment with European men. Excluding her early experiences, Asya's first attraction is to Saif's friend Mario, a South African of Italian extraction whom she meets when she goes to England to study. The affair is frustrated on both sides by each character's sense of honor and loyalty. But Asya later plunges into a liaison with the Englishman Gerald Stone. Technically, Gerald is not responsible for Asya's loss of virginity; she had actually miscarried Saif's baby, though conception had taken place without penetration. However, he is the first man to satisfy her sexually. Their physical relationship quickly intensifies into an obsession on his part. If Saif signifies the virtues and limitations of home, Gerald can be seen as a predator who, without being conscious of his Orientalist tastes and sadistic urges, nevertheless subdues and enslaves his "eastern butterfly" as the Western imperialists had conquered the East. In one scene, while walking beside the River Thames in London, Asya meditates on the fact that she and her mother both adopted English: "A middle-aged spinster came out to Cairo in the 1930s to teach English. A small, untidy twelve-year-old girl fell in love with her and lived and breathed English Literature from that day on. That girl was my mother, and here, now, am I."

While aware of the postcolonial overtones to this relationship, Soueif does not allow her characters to degenerate into crude stereotypes. Neither does the obvious feminist dimension to the novel develop out of step with the cultural boundaries of Asya's Arab Islamic society. When she eventually succeeds in breaking free of Gerald, she returns to Egypt, still in love with Saif but unable ever again to live with him. At the end of the novel Asya comes across a recently discovered statue of a dancer from the age of Ramses II. The female figure, which is "in complete possession of herself," signifies a primordial Egyptian feminine identity against which Asya is able to locate a facet of her own nature.

Sandpiper (1996) is a collection of seven short stories, three of which date from the 1980s. Unlike her earlier collection, *Aisha,* in Soueif's second collection there is no apparent interconnectedness between the stories, and each of them seems to be a distinct narrative. "Mandy" appears to be a sketch of the Asya-Saif relationship that sits at the center of *In the Eye of the Sun.* Indeed, its closeness to a specific series of incidents in the novel makes its inclusion in the subsequently published volume of short stories somewhat puzzling. Several of the Alexandrian Greek characters in "Chez Milou" also made their appearance in similar

circumstances in the novel. In the opening and closing stories, "Melody" and "I Think of You," both of which have expatriate contexts, Soueif appears to be drawing on her experience of living on the Arabian Peninsula. Overall, the stories establish the typical themes of Soueif's fiction: fraught, sometimes cross-cultural personal relationships between men and women, in situations characterized by cultural as well as gender confusion, both of which contribute to the dislocation of the main female protagonists. In "Melody" a Turkish mother, whose child is run over by a speeding Arab motorist and whose husband shows videos of the child's dead body to outsiders, is observed by an uncomprehending Western woman, who nevertheless shares her cultural displacement, living as she does in the same expatriate compound. A cross-cultural marriage between a European woman and an Egyptian in the title story, "Sandpiper," begins as a love match but then dissolves against the background of his family's holiday home west of Alexandria: "My foreignness, which had been so charming, began to irritate him. My inability to remember names, to follow the minutiae of politics, my struggles with his language . . . He was back home, and needed someone he could be at home with, at home. It took perhaps a year. His heart was broken in two. Mine was simply broken." Even within the Arabic-speaking world, cultural and religious differences intrude. In "I Think of You," an Egyptian academic, married to an estranged Englishman, awaits the delivery of her second baby in a hospital on the Arabian Peninsula. Her fellow patients are not even sure if she speaks Arabic, while their processes of covering and uncovering in the presence of doctors and male visitors are culturally alien to her. As in *Aisha,* the stories seem to be testing out ways of escape from cultural confusion.

In her next novel, published in 1999, Soueif explores an even closer connection between an Egyptian historical dimension and the Anglo-Arab encounter. In *The Map of Love* she joins these two preoccupations as intimately as her subject, a love match between a widowed Victorian British lady and an Egyptian aristocrat, can allow. But whereas her first novel has the freshness and immediacy of lived contemporary history, the later work bears the imprint of historical reading grafted onto the genre of romance. A reference in *In the Eye of the Sun* to Ruth Prawer Jhbvala's *Heat and Dust* (1975) suggests that, half-consciously at least, Soueif may have already had the Indian novel at the back of her mind, to surface in her depiction of two generations of Anglo-Egyptian lovers in *The Map of Love.*

Within the novel, the discovery in 1997 of a trunk containing old letters, notebooks, journals, and

هنا، عند قدمي، يمتد النيل في كتلة سيالة مضيئة، تعكس مياهه أضواء المراكب

الصغيرة، والمطاعم العائمة، والجسور المنثورة عبر النهر، وفي الوسط تقوم الجزيرة الزمالك ،

الأوبرا تضوي في الظلام وإلى جانبها برج القاهرة القائم كزهرة

اللوتس الرشيقة. هنلللنظر لتضلهير في روعته وعليه يقبع الغيام الذي يطلق عليه

أهل القاهرة «السحابة السوداء». لا يجزم أحد من أين جاءت. يقولون أن الفلاحين

يحرقون الأرز في الشرقية. يقولون أنها قمامة القاهرة تحترق ــ وبدون ضابط في

موضعين. يقولون أن السبب في أحد مكونات البترول الخالي من الرصاص، تقبع فوق

كل شيء، ويتعايش معها أهل القاهرة لأنهم ــ إلى الآن ــ لازالوا قادرين على التنفس.

«لا أدري عمن أشعر بالتباعد أكثر: الأمريكان أم الطالبان؟ تشبك نادرة كعبها في

حرف المقعد وتضم ركبتها إلى صدرها: «لغتهم تتميز بإعجاب بالنفس من نوع دنئ».

نادرة وزوجها الأمريكي يعملان بالتصوير، له الآن ثلاثة أشهر في سان دييجو وكان

التخطيط أن تلحق به في ١٥ سبتمبر حتى يعودا معا في يناير. والآن لا تطاوعها

نفسها على المغادرة. تسألني إن كنت أشاهد سي إن إن وتستطرد «هل من واجب

الصحفيين التعاون مع الحكومة؟ أم هل للإعلام برنامجاً مختلفاً؟ إنهم يحاولون

إخافتنا حتى يبقى كل منا في حفرة الصغير لا يكلم الآخر. تقص لي أنها يوم ١٢

سبتمبر تلقت سبع مكالمات دولية من وكالات تعمل لحساب أمريكية يطلبون

منها أن تخرج إلى الشوارع لتلتقط صوراً الناس يحتفلون. قالت لهم لا أحد يحتفل في

الشوارع. قالوا «في القهاوي إذن. ألا تدركين كم سيتغير عالمك؟ صوري الناس تضحك

مبتهجة في القهاوي.» أخبرتهم أن الشعب كله في حالة صدمة، ملتصق بالتلفزيون،

وحين ظللوا على إصرارهم اقترحت عليهم أن يرسلوها إلى بلدة جنين في الضفة العربية

لتصور الاحتلال الإسرائيلي.

أمسيتي الأولى في القاهرة. المدينة كالمعتاد تنطق بالطاقة. مهرجان القاهرة

للسينما يهدي جائزته الخاصة إلى تاهمينا، المخرجة الإيرانية التي يسبب لها مشهد

في فيلمها الأخير، النصف المختفي، مشاكل في إيران حيث تصور فتاتين

محجبتين توزعان المنشورات الشيوعية. مسرح الهناجر يعرض «فيدرا» مصرية،

ويصل مولد السيدة زينب إلى ذروته حيث يؤم الآلاف مسجدها الكريم. تتزاحم

الملصقات على جدران مباني وسط البلد مشيرة إلى اقتراب موعد انتخابات النقابات

*Pages from the typescripts for the Arabic and English versions of "Nile Blues," an article that appeared
in* al-Quds *(London) and* The Guardian *in November 2001 (Collection of Ahdaf Soueif)*

Right there, at my feet, the Nile spreads out in a shimmering, flowing mass. The water reflects the lights of small boats, of floating restaurants, of the bridges flung across the river. From the centre rises Gezira island, on it the lit up dome of the Opera House and the tall slim lotus of the Cairo tower. The scene is spectacularly beautiful and over it all hangs the thick pall Cairenes call the Black Cloud. No-one seems certain where it comes from. They say it's the farmers burning husks of rice in Sharqiyya province. They say it's Cairo rubbish burning in several places - two of them out of control. They say it's a component in the new unleaded petrol. It hangs over everything but Cairenes live with it, because - so far - they can still breathe.

"I don't know who I feel more alienated from, the Americans or the Taliban," Nadra hitches her heel to the seat of her chair, hugs her knee to her chest: "Their language is so sleazily self-laudatory." Nadra and her American husband are photographers. He has been in San Diego for three months. She was supposed to join him on 15th September and they would come back together in January. But now she can't bring herself to go. "Do you watch CNN?" she asks. "Should journalists collude with government? Or do the media have an agenda of their own? They're trying to frighten us all so we each stay in our little hole and don't talk to each other." She tells me that on September 12 she received international calls from seven agencies, all working for clients in the American media. "Go out," they said "and photograph the people rejoicing in the streets." But nobody's rejoicing in the streets she said. "In the coffee-shops then. Photograph the people laughing and celebrating in the coffee-shops." "People are glued to their TVs," she told them,"Everybody's in shock." Still they pressed her. Eventually she said if they wanted her photographs they could send her to Jenin (on the West Bank) and she'd photograph Israeli tanks entering the city.

That was my first night in Cairo. The city is as usual humming with energy. The Cairo film festival awards its Special Jury Prize to Iranian woman director Tahmina who is in trouble in Iran for including a shot of two chador-clad women handing out communist leaflets in her film The Hidden Half. The Hanager theatre workshop is showing an Egyptian Phaedre. The feast of the Lady Zeinab, grand-daughter of the Prophet and one of the most popular members of his household is reaching its climax with thousands of people from all over the country converging on al-Sayyida, the district which contains her mosque and bears her name. The walls of downtown Cairo are chaotic with posters for the Trade Union elections due to take place in a few days. The demonstrations that have so far been contained within the campuses of Cairo's five universities ebb and flow with news of Afghani civilian casualties and new Israeli incursions into Palestinian towns.

Over the next two weeks I sense a mood that is not explosive but tense, expectant. There is also puzzlement, a deep exhaustion and a cold, amused cynicism. Nobody even bothers to discuss the 'Clash of Civilisations' theory except to marvel that the West wastes any time on it at all. Can't they see how much of their culture we've adopted? people ask. Practically every major work of Western literature or thought is translated into Arabic. The Cairo Opera House is home to the Cairo Symphony Orchestra and the Egyptian Ballet as well as the Arab Music Ensemble. English is taught in every school and the British Council in Cairo is the largest of their operations worldwide because of its English Language courses. Yes there are aspects of western society that we don't like, they say, but they are the aspects that the west itself regards as problematic: widespread drug abuse, violent crime, the disintegration of the family, teenage pregnancies, lack of sense of community, rampant consumerism .. What's wrong with not wanting those for ourselves?

The Islam versus the West theory is dismissed by both Muslim and Christian clerics. In an interview with al-Jazeera, Sheikh Qaradawi echoes what Nadra has been saying: "It is unfair to lump people together in one basket," he says, "The American people are the prisoners of their media. They're ordinary people, concerned with their daily lives, with earning a living. We must try to reach them through debate, not through hostility." Sayed

personal relics from the turn of the twentieth century intertwines the histories of different generations of Anglo-Americans and Egyptians, connected by the marriage of Lady Anna Winterbourne and Sharif Pasha al-Baroudi. The story begins when Isabel Parkman, an American divorcée and descendent of Anna and Sharif, meets and falls in love with Omar al-Ghamrawi, a New York-based Egyptian who also has blood links with the Anna-Sharif marriage. Isabel travels to Egypt to deliver the trunk to Omar's sister, Amal, who acts as the editor of the Anna-Sharif story, piecing together the primary sources while supplying research and sympathetic guesswork to fill in the gaps. The two Western female protagonists, Anna and Isabel, are initiated into Egyptian and Arab perspectives, propelled by their intimacy with their Egyptian lovers while being immersed in the political events of their respective epochs.

The Map of Love takes its place alongside a whole corpus of postcolonial literature in which the terms of empire have been renegotiated and the history of the colonized subject asserted alongside that of the imperial power. In his *Culture and Imperialism* (1993) Said terms the commonality of this experience, fractured as it is according to whichever perspective is adopted, the colonizer's or the colonized's, "Overlapping Territories, Intertwined Histories." Said argues for "contrapuntal" readings of literature, in which a canonical text would be set beside a postcolonial text, so that the latter might supply perspectives omitted or occluded in the former. Soueif's concern in *The Map of Love,* however, seems not only to be about rewriting a colonial encounter from the point of view of the colonized, but also to posit an alternative, a meeting of equals, as embodied in the coming together of the mixed, aristocratic couple. Soueif engineers Anna's meeting with Sharif by having her travel to the desert disguised as a man, only to be kidnapped en route by patriots who take her to the pasha's house.

Anna and Sharif's relationship develops on Egyptian soil and is seen to validate Egyptian national aspirations. Hovering in the background is the Cardinal Richelieu-like figure of Lord Cromer—ostensibly the British agent and consul general, but effectually the sole ruler of Egypt—who actually appears onstage in the scene in which Anna and Sharif go to the British Agency to get their marriage registered. Anna is connected through her father-in-law, Sir Charles Winterbourne, to a tiny group of British anti-imperialists centered on another historical figure, Wilfrid Scawen Blunt, the Tory advocate for oppressed nationalities. She is, therefore, predisposed to accept Egyptians on their own terms. The time frame of the Anna-Sharif story is

from 1897, when Anna comes to Egypt freshly widowed, until 1911, when she returns to England after the assassination of her second husband. Encompassing the last decade of Lord Cromer's rule, this period marked both a culmination of the British domination set in motion by the events of 1882 and the inception of a fully self-aware Egyptian nationalist movement that reached its watershed after World War I under the leadership of Sa'd Zaghlūl.

Soueif has made her fictional character Sharif the nephew of an historical figure, 'Urabi's prime minister Mahmoud Sami Pasha, of whom Blunt writes in his *Secret History of the English Occupation of Egypt: Being a Personal Narrative of Events* (1907): "His part, as I see it, throughout the troubles that were coming was a perfectly loyal one, both to the Constitutional and the National cause, and he paid dearer for his constancy, for he was a rich man and so had more to lose, than any other concerned in the rebellion." Sharif is shown throughout to be as worthy a patriot as his uncle, though an increasingly isolated one, as the British entrench themselves in his country and the Egyptians are polarized between the pro-British Constitutionalists, on one hand, and the extreme forces that ultimately accomplish his death, on the other. Although Sharif is married to an Englishwoman, Soueif is at pains to establish him as entirely independent of the British.

Some readers have felt the character of Anna to be somewhat two-dimensional, and it is true that little development is seen in her marriage with Sharif beyond the occasional early argument. Her relationship with her sister-in-law, Layla, is closely paralleled by that between Isabel and Amal. Both Western women are eager to speak Arabic and learn about Arab culture. Isabel is invited by Amal to the family estate in the south and is caught up in the Islamist insurgency and the government's draconian response. The state of the contemporary Arab world, discussed by the more-articulate and highborn characters within both time frames, is seen to be affected by a continuing intrusive Western presence and the emerging threat of Zionism, seen at its beginning in the Anna/Sharif section of the novel. Soueif ensures that both Anna and Isabel come to sympathize with the Egyptian/Arab cause, but the death of Sharif, doubled by the hinted-at assassination of Omar at the end, indicates both the author's pessimistic appraisal of the "Arab predicament" and an almost Forsterian recognition that the time for a wider brotherhood between Anglo-Americans and Arabs has not yet come.

In an interview with Mohammed Shaheen published in *Banipal: Magazine of Modern Arab Literature* (2001), the Sudanese writer Salih said of Arabs who write in English, "It is a compromise ultimately. They have inevitably to lean towards the language they are writing in, a language which has its own rationale, its own logic. And their drawing of characters, even the mode of expressing ideas, how much they are daring in their writing, is limited by this medium." Interesting though her translation of the idioms used in her novels by lower-class or older Egyptian characters is, Soueif has increasingly conformed to the demands of her English medium. While she began by experimenting with Arabic forms of storytelling in *Aisha,* with *The Map of Love* she has clearly reached the stage where her mode of writing is dictated by a well-established genre of English writing—the historical romance. Here she has adopted the diary form, also used in *In the Eye of the Sun,* as well as flashback and an editor-narrator. By adopting the medium of English, Soueif gained a much wider readership than any contemporary Egyptian writer would dare hope for. *The Map of Love* was even short-listed for the Booker Prize for fiction in England.

In addition, through a female character such as Asya, whose relative freedom and choice of sexual experimentation goes far beyond the experience of most Islamic Arab women, Soueif would seem to be linked to a discourse of feminism that scarcely exists in any collective form in the Arab world, where, as Leila Ahmed and Deniz Kandiyoti have both argued, the issue of women's rights is still confused by the Islamic world's relations with the West. It is true that her compatriot Nawal al-Saadawi has gone much further in challenging traditional religious axioms as patriarchal and inimical to the development of Arab women. Soueif's writings, however, do not criticize the Islamic religion, other than in *In the Eye of the Sun,* when the practice of veiling adopted by lower-middle-class university students was critiqued.

Hanan Mahmud Ibrahim, in her 1999 dissertation on feminism in the novels of Soueif, the Lebanese writer Hanan al-Shaykh, and the British writers Michelle Roberts and Sara Maitland, concludes that in the works of Soueif and al-Shaykh, "Islam and Islamic men and women are relegated to a peripheral narrative space." It is likely that future scholarly work on Ahdaf Soueif's writings will want to interrogate the uses she makes of English for the presentation of Arab issues and themes to her readers.

Interviews:
Libby Brooks, "Lifting the Veil," *Guardian,* 2 August 1999, p. T4;
Yasmin Alibhai-Brown, "I long for Egypt. I feel that I am in this place but not of it," *Independent* (London), 28 September 1999, p. S8.

References:
Leila Ahmed, *Women and Gender in Islam: Historical Roots of a Modern Debate* (New Haven: Yale University Press, 1992);
Fouad Ajami, *The Arab Predicament: Arab Political Thought and Practice Since 1967,* revised edition (Cambridge & New York: Cambridge University Press, 1992);
Wilfrid Scawen Blunt, *Secret History of the English Occupation of Egypt: Being a Personal Narrative of Events* (London: Unwin, 1907);
Hilary Fitzpatrick, "Arabic Fiction in English: A Case of Dual Nationality," *New Comparison,* 13 (Spring 1992): 46–55;
Albert Hourani, *A History of the Arab Peoples* (London: Faber & Faber, 1991);
Hanan Mahmud Ibrahim, "Tales of Two Houses: A Comparative Study between Some Arab and British Feminist Novels," Ph.D. thesis, University of Kent at Canterbury, 1999;
Deniz Kandiyoti, "Contemporary Feminist Scholarship and Middle East Studies," in *Gendering the Middle East: Emerging Perspectives,* edited by Kandiyoti (London: Tauris, 1996), pp. 1–27;
Joseph Massad, "The Politics of Desire in the Writings of Ahdaf Soueif," *Journal of Palestine Studies,* 28 (Summer 1999): 74–85;
Geoffrey Nash, *The Arab Writer in English, Arab Themes in a Metropolitan Language, 1908–1958* (Brighton: Sussex Academic Press, 1998);
Edward W. Said, "The Anglo-Arab Encounter: *In the Eye of the Sun,*" *TLS: The Times Literary Supplement* (19 June 1992): 91–92;
Said, *Culture and Imperialism* (New York: Knopf, 1993);
Mohammed Shaheen, "Interview with Tayeb Salih," *Banipal: Magazine of Modern Arab Literature,* 10/11 (Spring/Summer 2001): 82–84.

Rupert Thomson

(5 November 1955 –   )

Ben Saunders
University of Oregon

BOOKS: *Dreams of Leaving* (London: Bloomsbury, 1987; New York: Atheneum, 1988);

The Five Gates of Hell (London: Bloomsbury, 1991; New York & Toronto: Knopf, 1991);

Air & Fire (London: Bloomsbury, 1993; New York: Knopf, 1994);

The Insult (London: Bloomsbury, 1996; New York: Knopf, 1996);

Soft (London: Bloomsbury, 1998); republished as *Soft!* (New York: Knopf, 1998);

The Book of Revelation (London: Bloomsbury, 1999; New York: Knopf, 2000).

OTHER: "Look, The Monkey's Laughing," in *Soho Square: Stories, Essays, Poems, Pictures,* volume 1, edited by Isabel Fonseca (London: Bloomsbury, 1988), pp. 257–267;

"No Girl," in *20 under 35,* edited by Peter Strauss (London: Sceptre, 1988); pp. 279–290.

Rupert Thomson is generally acknowledged to be one of the finest literary stylists now working in the United Kingdom. Since the publication of his first novel he has been consistently lauded by reviewers for the brilliance of his prose, which is most often characterized as "lyrical" or "poetic" and is scattered with striking, unusual, and sometimes risky images, such as the description of twilight in London in his first book, *Dreams of Leaving* (1987):

> Moses shaded his eyes. There was a big bucket in the sky at the end of the King's Road. This bucket was overflowing with molten gold light. The light was called sunset, and this is how it worked. The bucket slowly emptied of light. As the bucket emptied, the light slowly darkened—gold to orange, orange to red, red to purple—until, after hours of pouring, only the sediment remained: black light or, in other words, night.

In his most successful writings, however, Thomson is able to combine this ambitious "high" literary idiom with the compulsive narrative power of the most gripping genre fictions, creating masterpieces of suspense as well as triumphs of memorable descriptive detail.

Thomson has also earned something of a reputation as an author who resists easy categorization. For example, an unsigned review of his novel *Soft!* (1998) in *Publishers Weekly* (6 July 1998) described him as "a hugely talented but hard-to-classify British writer whose books so far have had little in common beyond their soaring imagination and startling vividness of style." The point may be further illustrated by the fact that Thomson has been compared to such varied authors as Charles Dickens, Joseph Conrad, Graham Greene, Mervyn Peake, Gabriel García Márquez, Oliver Sacks, Edgar Allan Poe, Elmore Leonard, Martin Amis, and Don DeLillo. Moreover, Thomson's novels partake variously and sometimes simultaneously in the traditions of the picaresque, the Gothic, the historical epic, the roman noir, science fiction, detective fiction, and magic realism—without ever quite conforming to the received conventions of any of these diverse novelistic idioms. Thomson acknowledges that his writings often seem to violate reader expectations, but he also says that these violations are not necessarily intentional and that he does not write with any kind of "ideal reader" in mind. Similarly, when questioned about his attitude toward genre by Ben Saunders in an unpublished 19 April 2001 interview, he remarked disarmingly: "I don't really think about it." Yet, it is nevertheless possible to discern the presence of recurring ideas and themes across his body of work. These themes include: the persistence of memory and the relation of the present to the past; the blurring of the boundaries between subjectivity and objectivity; the relation of dreams to "reality"; and the transformations wrought by the experience of profound disappointment and loss. In Thomson's own words he is fascinated by "lives that have been derailed—with journeys that begin in the experience of trauma," and at some level all of his novels so far can be described as accounts of such journeys.

Rupert William Farquhar-Thomson was born on 5 November 1955 in Eastbourne, England. His father, Rodney George Farquhar-Thomson, served in the

Rupert Thomson (from the dust jacket for the U.S. edition of The Five Gates of Hell, *1991)*

Royal Navy and was discharged after contracting severe pneumonia; he was subsequently hospitalized for an extended period and underwent radical surgery, during which portions of his damaged lungs were removed. While recovering from these operations, he met and fell in love with Wendy Winifred Chute Gausden, Rupert's mother, who was working as a nurse, and the couple married shortly thereafter. Although necessarily restricted in his physical activities after leaving hospital, Rodney Farquhar-Thomson had a strong and lifelong interest in all the creative arts. Sustained by a small disability pension, he was able to devote much of his time to poetry and painting, while occasionally supplementing his income as a part-time teacher of art and English. Thomson's own passion for literature and the arts arose in part from his father's early influence. Overall, the first years of Thomson's childhood seem to have been happy, but tragedy struck the family in 1964 when his mother died suddenly. Rupert Thomson, just eight years old, was so deeply affected by this loss that today he has almost no memories of his life before this period.

Thomson's father eventually married again–to the family au pair, a woman just a few years older than his son Rupert–and shortly thereafter Thomson was sent to Christ's Hospital School, a charity boarding school in Horsham, Sussex. From there Thomson won a scholarship to Cambridge University, matriculating at Sidney Sussex College when he was seventeen years old. Already an avid reader with ambitions as a poet, Thomson nevertheless decided to take his degree in medieval history rather than the perhaps more obvious choice of English literature: "I deliberately didn't study English because I knew that I was always going to do it," he told Saunders in April 2001. "But I liked the gaps [in Medieval History]. They provided opportunities to be creative. . . . I enjoyed the room for speculation in going back to people like Bede." Thomson's literary work during this period was mostly confined to the writing of poetry for student magazines.

Eager to see the world, he traveled to New York City within a week of graduating from Cambridge and spent some time afterward exploring both the United

States and Mexico. Thomson then moved back to Europe, spending almost a year in Athens, where he taught English and wrote a first novel, based in part upon his experiences in the United States. He eventually abandoned this work, however, describing it in the April 2001 interview as "too personal and too impenetrable." Returning to London in 1976, Thomson "noticed that most of his friends from university were wearing suits," as the author's note in *Dreams of Leaving* says, and decided to get "a proper job," entering the advertising industry as a copywriter, in part because it was "a profession that would at least involve some kind of writing," as he remarked to Saunders in April 2001. For almost five years he worked for various agencies around London, but in 1982 he was inspired to abandon the professional life and returned to the creatively peripatetic existence of his postuniversity years.

Thomson now sees travel as an important part of his creative process; when interviewed by James Delingpole for the 9 November 1999 *Daily Telegraph* (London), he stated that these journeys "stimulate your ability to absorb things. . . . It reawakens you. Whereas if you live somewhere for a long time, you start to take things for granted." During this period Thomson took on almost any kind of work that would also allow him the freedom to write. "I'd do anything," he recalled in his April 2001 interview with Saunders, "the more ordinary or bizarre, the better." Thus, between 1982 and 1987 Thomson spent time in the Italian countryside, as well as the cities of Berlin, New York, Tokyo, and Sydney, working variously as a caretaker, a farmhand, a bookseller, and a barman. All the while Thomson was writing what became his first novel, *Dreams of Leaving*, published in June 1987. By turns fascinating and frustrating, *Dreams of Leaving* follows the wayward progress of Moses Highness, a character whose earliest personal history is, for him at least, a mysterious blank.

Moses' story actually begins in the sinister and surreal village of New Egypt—a tiny, isolated, and self-contained police state located somewhere in the south of England. An open-air jail from which no one escapes, New Egypt strongly resembles "The Village" of the 1960s British television show *The Prisoner* (although Thomson told Saunders he has not seen the show and was not directly influenced by it); it has its own culture, history, and folklore, and its boundaries are constantly patrolled by members of the local constabulary—a series of economical studies in darkly comic characterization, with names such as Hazard, Marlpit, Damage, and Dolphin. These village policemen are themselves under the command of Chief Inspector Peach, a villain whose brutal authoritarian tendencies are rooted in his own overwhelming need for order and control. Moses' parents, unhappy inhabitants of New Egypt who lack the will to attempt escape, place their appropriately named child in a basket of bullrushes and send him downriver; Moses is thus the first person to get away from New Egypt, although this necessarily remains unknown to anyone, including Moses himself, for some time.

The novel continues with Moses in his twenties, living in London, and leading a hedonistic, directionless life of drinking and parties, occasionally scanning directories without success for someone else with his own last name. However, a small suitcase, left in his basket by his parents and presented to him on his twenty-fifth birthday by his foster family, contains a dress and a photograph album that provide him with his first concrete clues as to his origins, and these eventually lead him back to New Egypt. Moses' slow process of recollection and discovery provides Thomson with an opportunity to explore in several haunting passages his interest in the deceptive quality of memory. For example, staring at the photos of his parents, Moses comments:

> "I'm trying so hard to remember that sometimes, just sometimes, I fool myself into thinking that I do remember. It's hazy but I can't tell the difference . . . And what about this dress?" He reached out and touched the hem. "When I first opened the suitcase I thought I remembered it. It was like a flash. A gut-reaction. Very sudden. I remembered my mother, my real mother, bending over me, wearing that dress. But the more I thought about it, the more I realized that all I could really see in my memory was the dress. Just the dress bending over me. Nobody inside it."

As Moses comes closer to the truth of his origins, Chief Inspector Peach discovers the truth of Moses' disappearance from the village as a baby and decides that Moses must be killed in order to preserve his perfect record of "no escapees." A cat-and-mouse game begins, with Moses as the ignorant mouse. Peach ultimately falls victim to his own obsessiveness, and the novel ends on a note of ambivalent optimism.

Moses' recovery of his past, however, does not provide him with the sense of direction he has hitherto lacked. Instead, the lesson he learns is more subtle. Once able to attribute his lack of direction to the lacunae of his personal history, Moses finally discovers that knowledge of the past is no more a guarantee of guidance in the present than if his origins had indeed remained shrouded in mystery. In short, the only difference between not knowing and knowing turns out to be that the former condition provided an excuse for his sense of being adrift, and at the end of the novel he no longer has that excuse. Or, as Madame Zola—famous clairvoyant and an apparent allusion to Madame Sosostris from T. S. Eliot's *The Waste Land* (1922)—puts it: "The past is always clear. It's only the future that is unclear." Armed with this "knowledge," Moses appears ready to embrace that murky future and looks forward to a "Happy New Year."

Critical reactions to *Dreams of Leaving* were mixed. Nicholas Lezard raved in *The Guardian* (9 October 1988) that "this excellent first novel . . . deserves to become a mini-cult classic," but Andrew Hislop, writing for *TLS: The Times Literary Supplement* (17 July 1987), found the novel equal parts "brilliant" and "muddled." Thomson was consistently praised, however, for the "lyrical" figurative style of the work. Apart from the general quality of the prose, the greatest strength of *Dreams of Leaving* is its large cast of unusual secondary characters, which include Madame Zola and Moses' poignantly tragic parents. Also among the secondary characters are other denizens of New Egypt, including a greengrocer who attempts to escape by disguising himself as a section of plowed field and Moses' London friends, such as Eddie, a man so beautiful Moses imagines he must be a statue come to life, and Ridley, a nightclub bouncer who whistles like a bird. In the final analysis the novel resembles its central protagonist in both his best and worst qualities: oversized and occasionally given to rudderless, dreamy drifting, it is also possessed of a distinctive vision of the world that is strangely charming and compelling.

Thomson's second novel, *The Five Gates of Hell* (1991), is significantly shorter and far more tightly structured than *Dreams of Leaving*. In a series of alternating chapters, *The Five Gates of Hell* tells the story of the intertwined lives of two much different men: Nathan Christian—middle-class, physically beautiful, emotionally sensitive, sexually ambiguous—and Jed Morgan—working-class, strikingly ugly, accustomed to human cruelty, and heterosexual, with a menstruation fetish. Both boys grow up in different parts of the seaside town of Moon Beach, and the novel begins with two separate naturalistic portraits of key traumatic moments in each of their childhoods—the sudden death of Nathan's mother and the destruction of Jed's prized collection of radios at the hands of his own mother. This latter episode is particularly representative of Thomson at his most compelling and assured best, as in the passage wherein Jed's youthful passion is evoked through similes that manage to be distinctive without ostentatiously detracting from the emotional content:

By the time he was ten he had more than a hundred radios, radios of every size, make and year. Some didn't work at all; these he dismantled. Others produced only static, but that was all right too; he could still switch them on and watch the lights come up behind the

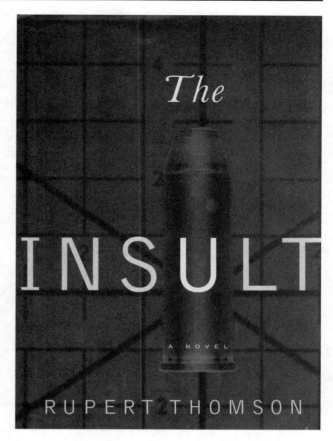

Dust jacket for the U.S. edition of Thomson's 1996 novel, a psychological thriller about a blind man who discovers he can see in the dark (Richland County Public Library)

names like some kind of miniature simulated dawn. A few of the old radios still worked, and he was addicted to the way the voices grew in volume as the set warmed up, and how the voices always sound so warm, so cosy, like people wrapped up against cold weather; though it was the present he was listening to, somehow it always sounded like the past. Other boys his age had model aeroplanes or toy soldiers or guns. He looked down on them. A model aeroplane had no previous life, a toy soldier had no soul, a gun couldn't talk to you. But a radio.

The fact that this warmly nostalgic evocation of childhood lies at the center of a chapter full of casual cruelty, concluding with an episode of viciously comic revenge, also reveals something of Thomson's typically deft handling of widely different emotional registers.

The two opening chapters of *The Five Gates of Hell* can be read as freestanding short stories in the realist tradition—each displays an acute sensitivity to the mental processes of childhood, and each has its own distinct and self-contained narrative arc—but as the novel continues, odd background details make it clear that the setting is actually not quite that of this world, but perhaps that of a parallel or near-future universe in which death and burial have become enormous moneymaking industries (some descriptions of holidays and festivals in this seaside town evoke accounts of the Mexican celebration of the Day of the Dead). Moon Beach is for all intents and purposes owned and run by the Paradise Corporation, a kind of corporate undertakers service, and the city skyline is dominated by the weirdly spooky image of high-rise graveyards, while the surrounding sea is scattered with "memory buoys" marking the locations of "ocean cemeteries." The sinister director of the Paradise Corporation, Neville Creed, is a charismatic sadist. The title of the novel comes from a piece of sadomasochist bondage gear—"an assembly of metal rings and leather straps"—that Creed owns. Both Jed and Nathan eventually come under Creed's spell; Jed commits a murder for Creed and spends the remainder of the novel trying to expiate himself of the crime, while Nathan, ignorant of both Creed's true identity and Jed's connection to him, becomes Creed's lover for a short time. The carefully plotted climax of the novel brings Nathan's and Jed's narratives together, with disturbing and violent consequences.

Reviews of *The Five Gates of Hell* were extremely positive, with many readers complimenting Thomson for his skillful integration of emotionally poignant elements, such as the portrayal of relationships within the Christian family, with episodes of nightmarish sexual violence. But, perhaps surprisingly, this "seductive *roman noir*," as Bruce Allen called it in *The New York Times Book Review* (16 October 1991), with its otherworldly setting and nightmarish villains, is also Thomson's most obviously autobiographical work; the sections describing Nathan's early life, including the account of the loss of his mother, the portrait of his invalid father, and even the detail of his father's remarriage to a young au pair, clearly parallel episodes in Thomson's own personal history. Thomson described this novel to Saunders as beginning "as an experiment in autobiography." After his father died in February 1984, Thomson and his two brothers (one with his wife and baby daughter) returned to the family home, where they had been born and raised, living there together for what he called "an extraordinary summer," remarking, "We had the unruliness, the untrammelled violence, of children, and yet we had no parents to control us. Everyone was dead." He told Saunders that he originally planned on writing a novel about that summer,

> But within a few weeks of starting work on the book, two things happened. Firstly, I began to feel that it was too soon to be addressing such potentially explosive material. I simply did not have sufficient distance, sufficient hindsight. On a more practical level, if I had written about the experience with any degree of accuracy or truth, then it would only have served to heighten family

tensions that were already running pretty high. Secondly, and more importantly, perhaps . . . Jed Morgan appeared from nowhere and hijacked the whole project. . . . Jed took his rightful place at the heart of the book and Nathan became a witness to events, a kind of Nick Carraway to Jed's Gatsby. I say 'importantly' because once Jed had arrived I could only keep the autobiographical material if it served the narrative.

Of the events that initially inspired *The Five Gates of Hell*, Thomson remarked to Saunders that

> I still have a book to write about what happened that year, but I want it to be non-fiction. It's become a secret book, one that will be written slowly and published posthumously. Three brothers return to the house where they were born following the sudden death of their father. It's material I find irresistible . . . a story that seems to have the architecture and power of a myth.

Thomson's next novel, *Air & Fire* (1993), differs significantly from either of his previous works, owing more to the genres of romance and historical epic. Set in "Lower California" at the end of the nineteenth century, the plot concerns an attempt by a band of French colonialists—including a student of Gustave Eiffel named Theophile Valance—to construct a modern Christian church in a remote desert mining town chiefly populated by "pagan" Indians. Valance's wife, the beautiful Suzanne, inspires the passionate but ultimately unrequited love of two other nonnative denizens of this colonial outpost, a Mexican army officer given to slightly ludicrous, melodramatic posturing and a down-at-the-heels American prospector named Wilson Pharaoh, who carries the burden of his father's failed dreams of striking it rich. Suzanne herself is reminiscent of one of Thomas Hardy's notorious heroines: a hyper-feminine object of desire, she chafes at the restrictions of her bourgeois life but is at the same time enormously naive and somewhat irresponsible.

The details of setting are more fully realized in this novel than in either of Thomson's previous works, and the imaginative representation of tensions among and toward the various ethnic and national groups that inhabit this colonial world—French, Mexican, Indian, and American—are persuasively and at times archly observed. Once again, the novel is remarkable for its memorable cast of secondary characters—such as the French doctor who owns a vast collection of decorative waistcoats and Jesus, the Mexican baker, who spends almost the entire novel attempting to produce a palatable baguette. In *Air & Fire* Thomson also refines the dream symbolism already evident in both of his previous novels, using dream imagery to draw parts of his narrative together. For example, before Wilson has ever seen Suzanne, he dreams "that all his veins were filled with gold; he only had to cut his wrists and he would be rich." Pages later, the fact that his desire for Suzanne has taken the place of his desire for gold is figured in language that subtly echoes the symbolism of this earlier dream: "The sight of that woman had run into him like something molten, had run into every part of him, and would set."

As David Murray noted in his favorable review in *The New York Times Book Review* (13 March 1994), the plot of *Air & Fire* matters less than does the overall "haunting atmosphere" of the book. Among the most poetically descriptive of Thomson's works, it is also perhaps the least narratively compelling. Nonetheless, critics were once again unanimous on the question of Thomson's style. The reviewer for *The New Yorker* (28 March 1994), for example, remarked, "More than anything else it is the prose . . . that, with the concentration of a magnifying glass, kindles this novel's fire." In a further sign of Thomson's growing reputation, *Air & Fire* was also shortlisted for the Writer's Guild Fiction Prize in 1993.

Critical acclaim translated into significant commercial success for Thomson with the publication of his fourth novel, *The Insult* (1996), which sold a remarkable 50,000 copies in the United Kingdom, largely on the basis of word-of-mouth recommendation, as Delingpole noted in his 1999 interview with Thomson. A highly original psychological thriller, which draws from, or perhaps ironizes, the techniques of magic realism, the book is divided into three unequal sections and turns on a seductive, simple premise. On the first page, the protagonist, Martin Blom, is gunned down in an apparently motiveless and random assault. Upon waking, Martin is told that his brain injury–the "insult" of the title–has rendered him totally and permanently blind, although he is otherwise quite unharmed. Then, late one evening, while learning how to walk again with his blind man's cane in the gardens of the hospital, Martin experiences what he considers a genuine miracle: as the sun goes down, and the light fades, his sight returns. When his doctor dismisses the notion of returning vision as a common delusion among the newly blind, Martin decides to keep his gift a secret. Released from the hospital, Martin swiftly loses himself in a hallucinatory nocturnal underworld in which his fantasies and "reality" become blurred and indistinct. The reader is encouraged to accept Martin's strange new vision of the world and also invited to question that vision, until he or she is almost as disoriented as the protagonist. As Suzi Feay noted in her 1 February 1996 review in *The Independent* (London), Martin is "a spectacularly chilling example of the unreliable narrator." Just how unreliable is made clear from the much different reactions that readers had to Martin's personality. Some, such as Richard Davenport-Hines in *TLS* (8

March 1996), admired his courage and imagination, while others, as did Feay, saw something "elegantly cold and misogynistic about the narrative's treatment of women who are neither slim, young nor beautiful." Feay interpreted these and related passages as Thomson's sly critique of Martin's "ludicrous pickiness." The ironic possibilities of the novel are indeed manifold; once a question mark has been placed over Martin's version of events, many of the relations between various characters might appear in retrospect as structured by mutual misunderstanding.

In the course of "Nightlife," the title of this first section of the book, Martin becomes involved with a girl named Nina, who is apparently attracted to him because of his blindness. When she suddenly disappears under sinister circumstances, Martin becomes a suspect and vows to find her. Martin eventually makes his way to Nina's family home, where he learns her history from her grandmother Edith Hekmann. The narrative voice of the novel switches from Martin to that of Edith at this point, for a section of some one hundred pages titled "Carving Babies." The revelations of this section are as disturbing as the title might lead one to expect. Finally, in the short and ultimately moving final section, "Silver Skin," a metaphor for Martin's personal transformation over the course of the events of the novel, Martin again takes up the story and resolves the questions regarding his perceptions that have lingered throughout. Davenport-Hines accurately described this conclusion as "a series of brutal and bleak surprises which will leave readers feeling incriminated by their own stupidity and weak need of comfortable solutions."

Although the transformation in narrative voice at the center of the novel was considered distracting by a small number of readers, including the reviewer for *Publishers Weekly* (3 June 1996), Thomson said in 2001 that he ranked "Carving Babies" among his own personal favorite pieces of sustained writing; and in general, *The Insult* was accorded a rapturous critical reception, acclaimed by authors Jay McInerney and Michael Ondaatje, as well as by the reviewers, and eventually short-listed for the prestigious Guardian Fiction Prize in 1996.

Thomson's use of dream imagery is again exploited to great effect in this fourth novel. When asked in May 2001 about the significant place of dreams in his work, Thomson's comments reveal some interesting facts about his individual creative process:

Whenever I start a new book I have nightmares. Night after night. For a long time I didn't understand why. Recently I came up with a theory. To write fiction of any power and authenticity you have to draw on the deepest, most secret parts of yourself. That's where fiction comes from, but it's also where dreams are made.

Dust jacket for the U.S. edition of Thomson's 1998 novel, about a soft-drink company plot to promote a new product with subliminal advertising (Richland County Public Library)

Small wonder, then, if there's a certain amount of cross-fertilisation between the two. I often think of Louise Bourgeois in this context. She once said, I trust my unconscious. The unconscious is my friend. . . . You might say that I want my fiction to have that relationship to reality. I want to be able to look at reality from a standpoint that feels unpredictable, surreal, and yet, at the same time, entirely cogent. I seem to be attracted to ideas that allow me to do this, *The Insult* being an obvious example.

Thomson's fifth novel, *Soft,* which, like *The Insult,* can also be described as a "literary thriller," describes a campaign to promote a new soft drink that goes terribly, violently wrong. The book returns to the third-person narrative "parallel lives" structure Thomson previously exploited so effectively in *The Five Gates of Hell,* and it is plotted with similar precision—as the writer of the 16 March 1998 review in *The Independent* (London) remarked, "Thomson's characters are as deeply implicated in each other's lives as in a novel by Dickens." This time, however,

there are three principal points of view: first, that of Barker Dodds, a strong-arm criminal who would prefer to leave the world of crime behind; second, that of Glade Spencer, a pretty young waitress; and third, that of Jimmy Lyle, an ambitious marketing director for a soft-drink company. To supplement her income, Glade volunteers for what she believes is a paid scientific study of sleeping patterns but is actually a program of experimental subliminal advertising, designed to turn consumers into "ambassadors" for a new orange soda named *Soft!* In the aftermath of her exposure to these subliminal messages, Glade starts to behave strangely, and the soft drink company, fearing exposure, decides that she must be eliminated. Thomson's lightness of touch and deft characterizations keep the plot credible. For example, Thomson resists the obvious temptation to make Jimmy—the architect of the subliminal ad campaign—into a caricature greedy corporate capitalist villain. Jimmy is in fact a quite likeable young man, motivated by nothing more unpleasant than "healthy" career ambitions. In terms of its setting, local detail, and characters, *Soft* is also Thomson's most distinctly "English" book since *Dreams of Leaving,* a fact that explains the comparison some readers have made between the novel and the work of Martin Amis; for example, Christopher Hart in a 14 March 1998 review for *The Independent* (London) compared Thomson's novel to Amis's *Money: A Suicide Note* (1984). *Soft* was generally well received by reviewers. Hart wrote that "Thomson has the storyteller's knack of keeping you glued to the page," and he called the novel "impressive" though "not entirely successful," arguing that "only towards the very end do the characters begin to exert any real emotional pull on the reader." In *The San Francisco Chronicle* (3 January 1999) Michael Sragow praised Thomson for building suspense "from personality and emotion" and not from twists in the plot, but remarked that in the last part of the book "the narrative winds down and succumbs to hopelessness." Reviewing the novel for *The New York Times* (10 November 1998), Michiko Kakutani remarked, "Mr. Thomson likes to mix up sociological observation, irreverent humor and dreamlike surreal riffs with some surprisingly lyrical meditations on the passing pageant of contemporary life. This time, he's fused these elements into a tight, hypnotic story, and given us his most powerful novel yet."

Thomson has said that the idea for his sixth novel, *The Book of Revelation* (1999), came to him with such compelling force that he actually began writing it before he had even finished *Soft.* A press release from his British publisher quoted him as remarking, "There was no sense of having that 'area of interest' in my head, no process of germination. The book was just suddenly there. It was for that reason, perhaps, that it felt, quite literally, unprecedented." The novel differs from Thomson's previous works in other ways, too; although it is written in both the third and first person, it is focused upon the internal life of a single male character whose name is never revealed, and while Thomson had written frankly about sexual matters in his previous works, *The Book of Revelation* is the first of his novels to make issues of gender, sexuality, and power its principal themes. The first half of the novel delineates the kidnapping, sexual humiliation, and torture of a physically beautiful male ballet dancer at the hands of three women, while the remainder of the text explores the psychic aftermath and consequences of this experience for the victim.

Thomson's prose style in this novel is less obviously marked by the kinds of figurative elaboration that characterize his other books, and this spare, meditative quality has the eerie effect of making the sense of alienation that arises from the experience of sexual abuse all the more palpable. The reversal of obvious traditional gender roles in terms of oppressor and oppressed also provides obvious material for critical speculation on the complex relationship between gender and power. Thomson himself feels that the novel represents almost a distillation of his previous work; the narrative dualism that structures *The Five Gates of Hell* and *The Insult* is still present but unified within a single character; and while the more deliberately cool and limpid prose style of the novel may be less self-consciously "literary," the haunting "poetic" effect of his earlier work is retained. Reviews of the novel were once again unanimously positive. Writing in the 18 September 1999 issue of *The Independent* (London), Nicholas Royle remarked, "The writing is full of surprises, as if on Thomson's desk there's a card-index full of original similes and descriptions to make you look at the world afresh." Moreover, *The Book of Revelation* has garnered more attention in the United States than any of Thomson's previous books. Anthony Bourdain, reviewing the novel in *The New York Times* (12 March 2000), said of the plot that "It's an unlikely scenario—probably even an offensive one to some—but it's a premise made terrifyingly real by a hugely talented writer." In fact, there seems to be some interest in adapting *The Book of Revelation* as a motion picture.

Rupert Thomson remains modest about these achievements, however, and the suggestion that his readership seems to be growing in size. He remarked that while expanding his readership would undoubtedly be "great," his main concern is to be able to support himself, and now his wife, Katherine Norbury, and their child, doing the work that he loves to do. "I need to write," he told Saunders in their April 2001 interview. "It's like a compulsion, almost a physical thing." When asked how he saw the role of the writer, Thomson cited Flannery O'Connor—an author whose work, like Thomson's, is often invested in uncovering the fabulous in the ordinary, the transcendent in the grotesque, and whom he described as a major influence—"a personal literary heroine." He recollected that O'Connor remarked that the novelist is ultimately concerned with "the concrete details of life that make actual the mystery of our position on earth." Thomson hopes to continue to actualize the mystery in many more books. "I've always had a sense of time being short. And there are so many novels I want to write."

Interview:

James Delingpole, "Telling Tales of the Unexpected," *Daily Telegraph* (London), 9 November 1999, p. 15.

Reference:

Burton Raffel, "Novelists to Watch: Thomson, Timm, and Forbes," *Literary Review: An International Journal of Contemporary Writing,* 43, no. 4 (2000): 585–601.

Jonathan Treitel
(1959 –   )

Peter Brigg
University of Guelph

BOOKS: *The Red Cabbage Café* (London: Bloomsbury, 1990; New York: Pantheon, 1990);
Emma Smart (London: Bloomsbury, 1992).

OTHER: "I Want the State to Construct Me," "The Foundry," "Dog in Jerusalem," "A Marble in Jerusalem," "Mobilization," "Reach," "Hide and Seek," "Bricklaying for You," "An Interpretation of Dreams," "Chamber of Horrors," and "Extract from 'Mrs Potter Remembers Some Nice Moral Tales,'" in *Poetry Introduction 7* (London: Faber & Faber, 1990), pp. 81–92;
"Waltz Time," in *Best Short Stories 1992,* edited by Giles Gordon and David Hughes (London: Heinemann, 1992); republished as *Best English Short Stories IV* (New York: Norton, 1993);
"Stalin, Stalin, and Stalin," in *Best Short Stories 1993,* edited by Gordon and Hughes (London: Heinemann, 1993); republished as *Best English Short Stories V* (New York: Norton, 1994), pp. 292–299;
"Graffiti," in *New Writing 4,* edited by A. S. Byatt and Alan Hollinghurst (London: British Council/Vintage, 1995), pp. 128–134;
"A Great Exhibition," in *New Writing 8,* edited by Tibor Fischer and Lawrence Norfolk (London: British Council/Vintage, 1999), pp. 307–318;
"A Romance Meat," in *New Writing 9,* edited by John Fowles and A. L. Kennedy (London: British Council/Vintage, 2000), pp. 204–211.

SELECTED PERIODICAL PUBLICATIONS– UNCOLLECTED: "The Parable of the Two Cultures," *Critical Quarterly,* 31, no. 3 (1989): 22–25;
"The Polar Bear Murders," *Critical Quarterly,* 34, no. 1 (1992): 88–92;
"Ice Worship in America," *Critical Quarterly,* 37, no. 2 (1995): 63–68;
"Bless Minsky," *Tikkun,* 13, no. 4 (1998): 51–55, 66–67.

Jonathan Treitel is more than a writer of promise for the twenty-first century, having already written

Jonathan Treitel (photograph by Nigel Parry; from the dust jacket for Emma Smart, *1992)*

sophisticated novels and compiled a body of shorter work including stories, radio scripts, and poetry. He is not so much searching for a style as trying out stylistic positions, but in what he has produced there is a consistent concern with language and with the sense of the uncertain ground of reality in modern times. He appears to be finding ways in which his gift for humor and wit can be employed to focus on comedy in the old sense, not the laughable but the panorama of life in which all humans engage.

Jonathan Alexander Treitel was born in London in 1959. He completed his formal education in California, where he earned a Ph.D degree at Stanford University on the philosophy of science. He has lived in San Francisco, Paris, Jerusalem, London, and Tokyo and traveled in more than seventy countries. He now resides in the New York City area. He has been active in writer's workshops, and he has held residencies at the MacDowell Colony, Yaddo, the Blue Mountain Center, Ledig House International Writers' Colony, Villa Montalvo, Helene Wurlitzer Foundation, Ragdale Foundation, Millay Colony for the Arts, and Djerassi Resident Artists Program in the United States, at Chateau de Lavigny in Lausanne, Switzerland, and at the Rockefeller Foundation Bellagio Study and Conference Center in Bellagio, Italy. He was awarded The Arts Council of England Literature Award in 1995.

Treitel's stylistic approach is in early evidence in "The Parable of the Two Cultures," a short story published in *Critical Quarterly* (1989). The title alludes to C. P. Snow's *The Two Cultures and The Scientific Revolution* (1959), in which Snow argues that modern intellectual culture has been divided into the world of art (specifically, literature) and the world of science, and that literary thinkers and scientists cannot communicate with or understand one another. The unnamed first-person narrator of Treitel's story is an accountant whose wife has left him. He manages a group of chemists and decides to learn Greek because he did not go to university and wants to impress the chemists. He gets a senior student of Greek, Penelope, to tutor him, and Greek ideas and words slip into the story. At the same time he finds himself trying to learn the Second Law of Thermodynamics and is talking chemistry with Penelope. When his company transfers him, the chemists give him a pseudo-Greek going-away party with retsina and plastic vine leaves, and Penelope cries and says she loves him. The story closes while the protagonist contemplates Plato's suggestion that human beings were originally creatures with two heads and eight limbs; now divided into male and female, the sciences and the arts. The protagonist asserts that he is in the middle and will never be loved.

The deft touches of humor are what make this story work. There is a consistent parallel between the narrator's failed marriage and the fact that the scientists love the arts but cannot stay with them. The ingenuity and wit of the story is used to good purpose to reflect on the more serious split between kinds of thinking and experience.

The Red Cabbage Café (1990) is a first novel that balances a cartoon-like quality of events against frighteningly real moments in the Soviet Union between 1919 and 1939, with a shocking coda in Berlin a year later. The novel revolves around reality and masks, featuring wax figures, the dying Lenin, bizarre artists trying to discover how art and revolution can mix, and a communist-style romantic triangle in which a woman is shared by two men. One of the lovers is the first-person narrator, Humphrey Veil, a German-Jewish engineer educated in Britain who leaves his job on the New York subway system to help the Russian Revolution by assisting in the design of the Moscow subway. Despite his devotion to communism he is eventually falsely denounced as a German spy near the beginning of Joseph Stalin's purges, and after spending fifteen years in the Siberian gulags Humphrey is traded to Nazi Germany for a Russian spy. In Germany, Humphrey is lionized as a suffering hero of the Fatherland and featured in a propaganda movie, but he must be replaced by Heinz Deutsch, the Aryan actor who portrayed him in the movie. Humphrey is murdered by Deutsch at the end of the book, fulfilling in a strange way the epigraph of the book, a quotation from Karl Marx: "History repeats itself, the first time as tragedy and the second time as farce." Readers are left to ponder Treitel's thoughts about the quotation, for the Russian portions of the novel have approached the farcical, and the abrupt and suddenly agonizing German scene of the ending is closer to tragedy.

Characteristic of the text are the sequences involving Lenin. Humphrey is first taken to see Lenin because Sophia, the wax artist who is his lover, is making a wax Lenin to appear in place of the real Soviet leader, now crippled by strokes. Humphrey is to fix a wax-cylinder recording machine so Lenin can record revolutionary exhortations to be broadcast when the wax figure is displayed in shadows on the Kremlin battlements. However, Lenin is unable to speak, though Humphrey records a patriotic declaration himself while testing the machine, and he later hears the recording of his own voice, slowed down and deepened in pitch to resemble Lenin's, broadcast over loudspeakers as he attends a political rally in Red Square.

Humphrey is later driven in a car into the room where the speechless, dying Lenin wants Humphrey—since his speaking voice apparently sounds like

Dust jacket for the U.S. edition of Treitel's 1990 novel, about an idealistic British-born German Jewish engineer who goes to the Soviet Union after the Russian Revolution (Richland County Public Library)

Lenin's—to make a recording of his last will and testament, in which Lenin criticizes Stalin's lust for power. Then Gritz, the nearly mad poet with whom Humphrey has been sharing Sophia, bursts from the trunk of the car, blames Lenin for his poems being censored, and fakes shooting himself, only to be shot by Lenin's guards. Lenin expires, and Stalin enters through a secret door and takes the wax-cylinder recording of the will. Humphrey later discovers that a taxidermist friend of Sophia's is trying to stuff and preserve Lenin so he may be exhibited in his tomb in Red Square, but even Sophia's skill with wax is inadequate to restore the face. So they disguise the corpse of Gritz, whom the taxidermist had promised to preserve in exchange for a tin of tobacco, to look like Lenin, and it is placed in Lenin's tomb. Humphrey is finally arrested when he breaks through the line of people waiting to enter the tomb and shouts insults at his dead friend Gritz.

This mind-twisting sequence of events is funny, but it is always haunted by impending violence. Near the close of the narrative Humphrey "turns" to the reader and cautions him that the events depicted in the novel do not agree with history: "Either I am a composer of fiction—for whatever reasons of ambition, craziness, artistic urge and self-delusion—or Stalin is. Reader: which seems to you the more likely?" The playfulness of this postmodern self-consciousness is counterbalanced by the reader's absorption in the character, in the narrative, in the history portrayed, and in the slightly garish rendition of the historical context.

Michael Harris made the case for the novel in his review for the *Los Angeles Times* (20 January 1991), declaring that the book was effective because of Treitel's "unusually delicate sense of tone. He tells outrageous lies but remains true to the underlying reality." Harris remarked that "oppression and betrayal creep up on the merry threesome, as they crept up on millions of others . . . but Treitel keeps our eyes on the fancy footwork of his skaters, not on the rapidly thinning ice beneath them." In her 15 July 1990 review for *The Observer* (London) Victoria Cunningham commented: "History, in Treitel's book, is all faking, dodgy substitution, lies. Historiography is wacky and iconoclastic, keen to live up to Marx's dictum about history returning first as tragedy then as farce. The result is pleasant, low-budget, Magic Realism. You mustn't, as the knowing Conclusion advises, believe a word of it." Beatrice Wilson in a 28 July 1990 review in *The Spectator* (London) remarked that the "greatest weakness" of the book was that "Treitel is not yet a skilled enough writer to make his characters seem consistently believable. Some of the time, especially in the first part, they come across merely as transparent creations, as garishly colourful and yet as lifeless as the waxworks in Sophia's exhibition"; she went on to declare, however, that "this is not as important a problem as it might sound. . . . The author is at his best when giving creatively warped accounts of historical figures and events," and called *The Red Cabbage Café* a "remarkable book," explaining that the novel works because of its "surrealist black humour, with the power to make death seem funny and falsehoods true."

In 1990 Treitel had ten of his poems, along with a fragment of a longer poem, published in the anthology *Poetry Introduction 7*. These poems showcase Treitel's consistently thoughtful use of language. His verbal cleverness and wit are never trivial; he is always seeking to work with words to make them reveal reality, to clarify perceptions. The longest of these poems, "The Foundry," is built on the fact that the word *ghetto* is derived from the Italian *ghèto,* the Venetian dialect word for *foundry,* referring to the island in Venice where the Jews were forced to live in the Middle Ages. The poem features sensuous descriptions of the place and of Jewish life in medieval Venice, but it ends with a telling vision of the state of contemporary Jews:

> and the Jews
> do not live within the old constraints.
> Roads lead in and out. You can no longer tell
> where the Ghetto ends and where the world begins.

The poems reflect the slightly surreal quality of Treitel's stories and novels. "Hide and Seek" centers around the strange moment in World War I when "Drury Lane backdrop painters" were brought to the front lines to camouflage military trucks, a moment when theater and war touched. "Chamber of Horrors" recounts an episode during World War II when the artisans at Madame Tussaud's Wax Museum ran out of blue glass eyes while making the wax figures of Prime Minister Winston Churchill and Princess Elizabeth. The solution to this crisis was to use "a sharpened teaspoon" to remove the eyes from the wax effigies of minor aristocrats killed during the Reign of Terror, formerly exhibited in the Chamber of Horrors of the title. Treitel's poetry is intellectually sinuous, demonstrating the same quality of reality seen as

though refracted through a cracked mirror that pervades his prose writing.

"Waltz Time," published in *The New Yorker* (11 February 1991) and collected in *Best Short Stories 1992,* is a two-page gem of a story with the tightest of twists. At a grand ball in Vienna a colonel's wife is longing for a perfect lover when that lover, Rudolf, walks across the dance floor and sweeps her away from a Prussian officer. But, as she waltzes in Rudolf's arms, he speaks of an anarchist bomb in his head and becomes progressively more violent a dancer, until the floor clears around them and she realizes she is dancing with a madman "across the polished floor of a ballroom on the first floor of a palace in the middle of a city at the heart of an empire in the spring of that year." Cued by the reference to an anarchist's bomb and by the military husbands discussing the Balkans, the reader realizes that the disruption of this ball foreshadows the chaos and carnage of World War I. Treitel's touch here is light and exact.

"The Polar Bear Murders," a short story published in *Critical Quarterly* (1992), is a stylistic experiment of a much different sort. In an Eighty-ninth Street bar the narrator listens to Toucerman tell bits of several tales. The central story is of two Puerto Rican boys who sneak into the Bronx Zoo at night. One boy is suddenly and brutally mauled to death by one of the two polar bears he is teasing. A policeman, pointedly named Robert Reagan, then appears on the scene and apparently shoots the bears. The "apparently" is important, because the polar bear narrative never finishes, as Toucerman switches instead to discussing his impending divorce and then recounts some anecdotes about people suffering in strange ways. The story ends with the narrator observing that life is not fair and "sometimes you just want to scream all day and night." As in "Waltz Time," Treitel encodes several suggestions into his fragmented narrative, including dissatisfaction with the presidency of Ronald Reagan and the power of urban legends. And the prose can flare into vivid horror, as in the line "one of the bears patted Matty on the face, tearing off his nose and an eye."

In the short story "Stalin, Stalin, and Stalin," published in *The New Yorker* (21 September 1992) and collected the following year in *Best Short Stories 1993,* Treitel comically describes a series of annual reunions of the impersonators that Stalin used to give speeches and make public appearances on his behalf, sometimes simultaneously with one another, as he sought to maintain the cult of personality and seeming omnipresence that gave him power. At the first meeting, which takes place soon after Stalin's death, there are many of the Stalin impersonators, but over the next few years there are fewer and fewer of them

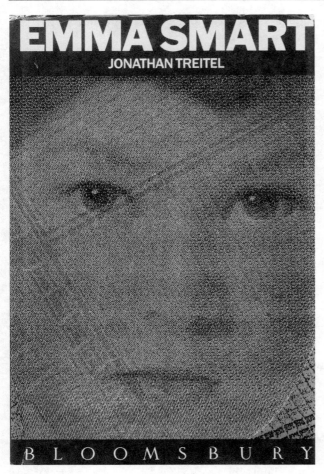

Dust jacket for Treitel's 1992 novel, in which a biographer tries to murder his Nobel Prize–winning subject (Bruccoli Clark Layman Archives)

life. On a research year in New York City Emma is taken by Frank, an American scholar she met at Cambridge, to a café frequented by Eastern European exiles. At the café a Nobel Prize–winning writer named L. Z. Allgrobsch suffers a stroke and sinks into a coma when Emma remarks that everyone else in the café must admire him. Frank sets out to write a biography of the comatose writer, and as the novel unfolds, Allgrobsch's life and involvements provide much of the story line. Emma discovers that much of Allgrobsch's known biography is false. Finally, Frank tries to kill Allgrobsch in the hospital by making him laugh, so that Frank can publish his biography without permission. Ironically, it is Emma, who caused the stroke in the first place, who now causes Allgrobsch's death by explaining Frank's ruse to him. At the conclusion of the novel Emma gets an appointment at the University of California in Berkeley and leaves the chaos of New York behind.

Treitel has many satirical targets in this text. Emma is a pompous English girl, a victim of a country upbringing who is unable to understand much beyond mathematics, which she sees as a strange game of great importance that only a few can play. The text incorporates many stories purportedly written by Allgrobsch, and they are takes on the works of Eastern European writers typified by the Polish-born Isaac Bashevis Singer, winner of the 1978 Nobel Prize in literature, who wrote little parables set in a tiny peasant village. Frank is a practitioner of the worst sort of pseudointellectual contemporary literary theory, who thinks nothing of murdering a Nobel Prize winner in order to get tenure.

Balancing the satire is the sheer pleasure of a high-speed comic romp. Emma is a prototypical British newcomer to New York who gets all of the surprises that greet such visitors. The narrative moves at breakneck speed, interrupted only by the Allgrobsch tales, and Treitel has an excellent eye for a comic situation. Critics were not uniformly approving, however; for example, Patrick Gale contended in his 4 April 1992 review of *Emma Smart* in *The Daily Telegraph* (London), "Treitel plays stimulating games with ideas of mathematical, biographical and fictional truth, but encloses them in a relentlessly 'comic' matter of the most put-downable kind."

Since the publication of *Emma Smart,* Treitel has continued to hone the fine balance of the comic absurd and the dark absurd in his writing. Collected in *New Writing 4* (1995), "Graffiti" is set in a future Rome where every unprotected surface is covered with indelible "Superpaint" graffiti. In the story a leader takes a group of juvenile delinquents to expunge graffiti with a new "supersolvent," but ironi-

as Stalin's memory falls out of official favor. Throughout the story the doubles reveal aspects of the real Stalin. First, they disclose little human details—such as that he had a boil on his back—but later they reflect on his coldness, his violence, and on his betrayals of others. The doubles then admit that they too performed acts of violence in what they took to be the spirit of Stalin, and they wonder if these acts were excessive. Treitel thus uses these doubles to reflect on the man whom they impersonated, in a sense to perform a "self-examination" of Stalin, a man who was probably incapable of self-examination.

Treitel's second novel, *Emma Smart* (1992), is a cleverly plotted comic novel that introduces a stronger element of satire into his work. The title character is a twenty-one-year-old British mathematician from a British landowning family who uses the pompous formulation "One feels" or "One wanted" throughout, creating the effect that she is outside herself watching events unfold and is emotionally uninvolved in her

cally they instead remove Michelangelo's painting from the ceiling of the Sistine Chapel.

Published in the summer 1995 issue of *Critical Quarterly,* "Ice Worship in America" is a cleverly pitched American regional tale that has both satiric and mythic dimensions. In it Treitel describes the town of New Eden, New York, where the power fails and a culture dependent upon generated cold—for drinks, freezers, air conditioning—suddenly finds its food rotting. The story vividly delves into the history of cutting ice from the river in winter in former times. When the power does come back on, the citizens of New Eden no longer trust their manufactured ice, for they know it could fail them again. The story indulges in long catalogues of what Americans keep in freezers and in rich caricatures of figures in the town. But Treitel once again has a gentle, slightly pulled punch here, for this story is about a loss of faith in New Eden, a near-biblical loss of innocence and trust. It gently skewers consumerism and gadget-minded modern America.

In "Bless Minsky," published in *Tikkun* (1998), an aged Jewish tailor from New York who has retired to Miami is commissioned to make a gigantic box kite for a strange, powerful man who then refuses to accept it. At the end of the story the narrative becomes surreal, as Minsky is, apparently, slowly wafted aloft while carrying the kite away from his unsuccessful transaction. This magic realist touch closes a story rich with details of the Jewish New York-Miami culture, juxtaposing realism, caricature, and myth.

"A Great Exhibition,"collected in *New Writing 8* (1999), depicts two Victorian sisters who purchase two of the first hoop-skirted crinolines, put them on, and feel as though they are floating above the earth. After some giggling and jokes they dare to venture out in them and float through London on invisible feet. One of them rips her crinoline and hides inside her sister's so they flow together down the street. The story ends on a pseudo-Victorian note, moralizing about one of the sisters later being "ruined," and, in fact, the style of the whole story is a parodic echo of such Victorian pornography as the anonymous nineteenth-century book *My Secret Life.* Treitel demonstrates an astute ear for Victorian speech and manners throughout.

Jonathan Treitel has experimented successfully with a considerable variety of styles. He has deftly depicted various cultural, historical, and social settings, whether Soviet Russia, contemporary New York, Victorian London, or pre–World War I Vienna. His stories and novels are both clever and highly original. The biographical note to *New Writing 8* (1999) reports that he was working on another novel, about Albert Einstein in America. Readers of his earlier works will anticipate that in this new project he will turn his stylistic gifts and his skill in creating events just past the edges of realism into something wonderful and strange.

Robert McLiam Wilson

(24 February 1964 –   )

Gregory Dobbins
University of California, Davis

BOOKS: *Ripley Bogle* (London: Deutsch, 1989; New York: Arcade, 1998);

The Dispossessed, by Wilson and Donovan Wylie (London: Picador, 1992);

Manfred's Pain (London: Picador, 1992);

Eureka Street (London: Secker & Warburg, 1996); republished as *Eureka Street: A Novel of Ireland Like No Other* (New York: Arcade, 1997); translated into French by Brice Matthieussent as *Eureka Street* (Paris: Editions Christian Bourgois, 1997).

PRODUCED SCRIPT: "Baseball in Irish History," television, by Wilson, Carlo Gebler, and Glenn Patterson, *War Cries,* Channel Four, July 1996.

OTHER: "Guns," in *Signals: An Anthology of Poetry and Prose,* edited by Adrian Rice (Newry, County Down, N. Ireland: Abbey Press, 1997), pp. 59–63.

SELECTED PERIODICAL PUBLICATIONS–UNCOLLECTED: "The Way Forward for Ireland," *Fortnight* (February 1992): 2;

"Rhythm Method: Maurice Leitch's *Gilchrist,*" *Fortnight* (September 1994): 45–46;

"Sticks and Stones: The Irish Identity," *Grand Street,* 62 (1997): 135–139;

"Belfast Surrenders to Drama," *Guardian,* 12 September 1999, p. 2.

As works written by a Northern Irish writer, there is an implicit pressure to regard the novels of Belfast-born Robert McLiam Wilson in terms of their connection to the Troubles that have characterized Northern Ireland since the late 1960s, especially since most of his books are either in part or directly concerned with sectarian tension and violence in Belfast. Similarly, there is an implicit pressure to place Wilson himself in relation to one of the contending identities within the context of Northern Irish society. Wilson addresses this issue himself in the essay "Sticks and Stones: The Irish Iden-

tity"(1997): "Like most of the citizens of Belfast, my identity is the subject of some dispute. Some say I'm British, some say I'm Irish, some even say that there's no way I'm five eleven and that I'm five foot ten at best. In many ways I'm not permitted to contribute to this debate. If the controversy is ever satisfactorily concluded, I will be whatever the majority of people tell me I am."

Wilson's apparent disregard for the customary dualistic sets of identities that characterize Northern Irish political life–such as Irish/British, republican/loyalist, or Catholic/Protestant–should not be construed as flippancy or a reluctance to participate in political debate. While Wilson is reluctant to identity himself in such reduced terms, he acknowledges that perhaps such reductions are unavoidable in Northern Ireland, where ethnic or national understandings of identity have been so frequently connected to violence: "I'm five foot eleven. I weigh around 170 pounds. I have brown hair, green eyes, and so on. Irish or British is very far down on my list–somewhere below my favorite color. Nonetheless, I must concede that nationality is tenacious." Wilson's response is to satirize ruthlessly the legitimacy of any position or ideology that justifies itself through violence–and Wilson is evenhanded in his approach, as his equally satirical representations of both Irishness and Britishness, of both Irish republicanism and Unionism indicate. Wilson's novels cannot be called political in any strict sense of the word. But if his work is considered in more strictly ethical terms, then Wilson can be understood as one of the most engaged Irish/British/Northern Irish writers to publish since the 1980s.

Wilson's account of his background has not always been consistent in interviews. As Candida Crewe wrote in a 7 September 1996 interview in *The Times* (London), "Wilson is a mesmerizing storyteller. And not just in print–in conversation with friends he is an inveterate peddler of tales, which may or may not exaggerate the truth. He is also an impossibly romantic figure."

Robert McLiam Wilson (photograph by David Barker; from the dust jacket
for the U.S. edition of Ripley Bogle, *1998)*

Robert Wilson was born 24 February 1964 in Belfast, Northern Ireland. His father was Robert Wilson, who worked in a bread factory when not unemployed, and his mother was Patricia Wilson, a health worker. At various times Wilson has suggested that he does not know his biological father and that most of his six siblings had different fathers. This strain within his family has affected his writing. As he told Topaz Amoore in an 11 September 1999 interview for *The Daily Express* (London), "there are no typical families in my books. No fathers, just a lot of fractured relationships." Raised as a Catholic, he spent the first twelve years of his life in a working-class neighborhood called Turf Lodge in predominantly Catholic West Belfast. During the 1970s Turf Lodge was strongly nationalist, supporting the republican Sinn Féin political party as well as being a hotbed for the Irish Republican Army (IRA). Wilson was soon introduced to the political tension that has come to characterize Northern Irish life, though his family refrained from connections to organized republicanism. Wilson himself took solace in literature, claiming to have begun reading deeply within the tradition of the nineteenth-century novel before the age

of ten. As he told Crewe, "I was already nicking books from the library. You couldn't steal the kid's books because there was always someone watching, but it was free rein in the adult section. They thought, what's some snotty seven year old going to do with Stendahl? So I stole [William Makepeace] Thackeray, George Eliot, Jane Austen."

When Wilson was twelve, his family moved to a largely rural, Protestant area north of Belfast in County Antrim. Wilson suggested to Crewe that the absence of local members of the IRA as male role models (as well as his already apparent satirical bent) took away any possible interest in active republicanism and helped him to develop ecumenical sympathies. "Boys are most vulnerable to that bullshit between 14 and 20 and are easily led. There's that necrophiliac tradition of Irish republicanism in which death is so honoured and definitive of the movement. Young men wanting to make their mark have corrosive fantasies about heroism and self-immolation. . . . It wasn't likely to have happened to me anyway because the vain, egotistic, or confident are much less likely to be seduced. And a sense of humour helps. I'm not earnest enough." Wilson's secondary education was at the prestigious St. Malachy's College in Belfast, a school that had also produced the writers Brian Moore, Michael McLaverty, and Bernard MacLaverty. Wilson's adolescence proved difficult. At age sixteen he began dating a Protestant girl, and his mother reportedly threw him out of the family home as a result–allegedly, Wilson has not spoken to his mother since the incident. He continued to attend school but began two years of alternating between homelessness and low-rent housing while supporting himself by menial labor. Although he did poorly on his A levels–a poor performance that Wilson attributed to the number of night jobs he was then working–the administration of St. Malachy's arranged for Wilson to take the entrance exams to Cambridge University. To just about everyone's surprise Wilson was accepted to St. Catherine's College, Cambridge.

At Cambridge, Wilson's academic career took a subordinate place not only to his literary ambitions but also to the romanticization of his own background. Around this time Wilson added "McLiam" to his name: *Mc* is an abbreviation of the Irish word for *son,* and *Liam* is the Irish version of *William;* hence *McLiam* means "son of William" or "Will's son." The addition gave his name a more Celtic air than the decidedly Protestant-sounding "Robert Wilson." In a 1992 interview with Crewe for *The Guardian,* Wilson revealed that "I played on the whole prole paddy bit. By the end I had a life story that lasted 27 minutes–exactly the time between the entrée and the main dish. But I didn't complete my degree. It was time to be a novelist." Wilson dropped out of Cambridge and took several low-paying jobs–refuse collector, bartender, security guard, and kilt salesman, among others–in order to support his attempts at writing a novel. Wilson already had been working on a massive novel since his teenage years. As Wilson told Richard Mills in an interview for *Irish Studies Review* (1999), "I wrote five versions of the novel before I drafted it. And the first version was a five-hundred page, third person narrative: past-tense, with no homelessness. It was useless, but there was something that could work." After several revisions and the crucially important addition of a homeless first-person narrator, Wilson's novel was eventually published in 1989 as *Ripley Bogle.* Wilson moved back to Belfast not long after the publication of *Ripley Bogle* and his marriage to his wife, Mary Ann, a Belfast teacher.

Regarded by critics such as Gerry Smyth, in his *The Novel and the Nation: Studies in the New Irish Fiction* (1997), "as one of the most precocious debuts of any Irish writer," *Ripley Bogle* received outstanding reviews. Set in a London summer sometime in the late 1980s, the novel concerns a four-day period in the life of the title character, a homeless twenty-one-year-old Cam-

bridge dropout from Belfast. Written from Ripley Bogle's perspective, the narrative alternates between often harrowing firsthand accounts of homeless life and the various events in Ripley's youth in Belfast that helped bring him to his current condition. Although he frequently self-consciously alludes to his influences–Charles Dickens is often mentioned, and an entire chapter set in a Kilburn pub is written as a prolonged satire of the "Nighttown" section of James Joyce's *Ulysses* (1922)–Wilson's combination of style and subject matter is distinctively his own. Since Ripley has a fairly erudite education, the vocabulary and style employed by Wilson in the narration of Ripley's account of his condition are nuanced and pronounced. Despite the horror of many facets of his life and experience, Ripley's narration is characterized by a frequently cynical wit that serves to make the bleaker facets of his existence even more horrible. By portraying the effects of homelessness and violence on the human body in a graphic manner, Wilson's description of the effects of poverty, the elements, and public opinion upon a human life is vivid and extreme. A long description of the sort of hunger experienced by the homeless is emblematic of Wilson's lurid and occasionally hallucinatory style:

> It suddenly comes to me that I'm hungry. Well perhaps, "hungry" is not quite the right word. Bowelwitheringly fucking ravenous might be a well more just and measured phrase to describe what I am currently experiencing. . . . Hunger is hitting me hard. Hunger is tickling me hard with a crowbar and Hunger is enjoying it. . . .And just as you think you've had it, just as you think you're all finally fucked-up, the calm comes again. . . . But what's this? Why strap me vitals, it's Agony again! He is truly pissed off now and desires to do you harm. He starts off with a spot of resolute bowelboiling before going to work on your stomach wall with a brillo pad. In a moment of inspiration, he ties your pancreas to your bladder with a cheesewire. Phantasmagoria is now the name of the game and suddenly Kafka seems like P.G. Wodehouse. The Devil comes to call as a fetchingly giant spider with suppurating boils and diarrhea sweat. His monstrous, quivering maw pouts invitingly at you as he squats in his own shimmering, steaming obscenity. Aroused now, he snogs with you for a while before lunching on your lungs and liver.

Elsewhere Wilson presents vomiting, respiratory disorders, and the prolonged effects of shock after Ripley is stabbed by another homeless man, in similar extensive detail.

If the narration of *Ripley Bogle* that takes place in the present tense is primarily a prolonged exposition on the experience of homelessness, most of the plot to the novel is to be found in Ripley's account of his past. Ripley's background and experiences have much in common with the details of Wilson's life. Like Wilson, Ripley was born in the Turf Lodge area of West Belfast, begins reading precociously at an early age—Ripley claims to have mastered the complete works of Dickens and Thackeray by the age of five—is expelled from his family's house as an adolescent for having a Protestant girlfriend, and endures a brief period of homelessness and poverty before beginning, and not completing, a degree at Cambridge. The similarities seem to have ended there, however, as these events are exaggerated and recast in a bitter and satirical manner that enables Wilson to make several points about both the Northern Ireland of his youth and Britain during the Margaret Thatcher era. As Smyth suggests in his 1997 monograph on Irish fiction, "Bogle's cultural inheritance mirrors his own experiences and the general perspective of the text as a whole, caught between specifically English and Irish ways of seeing, and moving towards a cynical, albeit impotent, repudiation of both." A general subtext to the sections set in Belfast concerns Ripley's rejection of the various political explanations of violence in Northern Ireland. Wilson is careful to focus largely on victims of the Troubles who are only peripherally involved with the conflict itself. Rather than focusing on any of the combatants themselves, Ripley graphically describes events from his memory—such as the story of Muire Ginchy, a young neighbor of Ripley's, whose genitals are torn apart after he falls on a stretch of barbed wire upon being frightened by a British soldier on Internment Night (the 9 August 1971 British military crackdown on the IRA in Belfast); the connected stories of Ripley's father, Bobby, and Mary Sharkey: she is brutally tarred and feathered by the IRA for dating a member of the British army, and Bobby Bogle is eventually shot and killed by the IRA for attempting to defend her; or two unnamed schoolmates assassinated by Protestant terrorists for being able to recite the Ave Maria. Wilson's focus on such victims demonstrates the manner in which he prefers to divert discussions of the Troubles away from the ideological arguments used to justify political violence toward an emphasis on the horror suffered by innocent bystanders who are guilty only of living in Northern Ireland. But Wilson's sympathies extend to victims in general, whether in the depiction of the neurosis suffered by Ripley's adolescent girlfriend, Deirdre, after a botched abortion performed by Ripley with a paintbrush or in the description of the death of Maurice, one of Ripley's few friends.

Maurice is a youthful member of the IRA—his arguments that justify violence against "legitimate targets" prompt Ripley to deliver several antirepublican rants—but he eventually becomes targeted for assassination by a rival republican faction. Ripley helps to hide Maurice but quickly reveals the hiding place when threatened by the assassination squad. Maurice is shot several times, and Ripley is cast adrift in a small boat with the dying Maurice. The graphic description of Maurice's death centers upon the fragility of human life in the aftermath of political violence:

> When I removed my hands, he shuddered violently, a great wretching spasm of agony. I smelt the unmistakable odour of liquid shite, squeezed from his ripped guts. This was both repulsive and touching. It was bitter to see my friend's youth ebb so easily away. It was disheartening to see the blood spew and belch in great gouts of life. It seemed a surprisingly anarchic business in the end, dying. An arbitrary mechanical breakdown. I felt a great surge of pity and compassion.

Ripley withholds the fact of his complicity in Maurice's death from his narration until the end of the novel. Ultimately, three of the central stories drawn from Ripley's past—Maurice's death, Ripley's relationship with Deirdre and his complicity in her abortion, and a romantic relationship with the upper-class Laura while at Cambridge—are revealed to be stories that either manipulate actual events in order to make Ripley appear as a hero or are complete fabrications. These events, and Ripley's lies about them, contribute to Ripley's abject condition throughout the novel, and Ripley's inability to admit these lies provides the basis for one of the central targets of Wilson's satirical critique, male narcissism. As Wilson told Jonathan Coe in an interview in *The Guardian* (1989) not long after the publication of *Ripley Bogle,* "It's about egoism." Wilson returns to the theme of male narcissism and its negative consequences, whether rendered tragically or comically, in his subsequent novels.

On the whole *Ripley Bogle* received a largely positive critical appraisal upon its publication. "This ebullient, grotesque debut is at times irritatingly affected in its unashamed eclecticism," Peter Reading wrote in *TLS: The Times Literary Supplement* (21–27 July 1989), "But the prevalent quality is haunting and horrific, an updated Thomsonian portrayal of nocturnal dreadfulness in the metropolis." Some critics found the characterization of Ripley and the disjointed qualities to his narration to be the strongest part of the book. "The novel's qualities are those of immodest youth: it is ambitious, energetic, self-absorbed, bursting with hormonal vehemence and self-consciousness," Zachary Taylor stated in *The London Review of Books* (22 June 1989). "Structure and sequence (and plot) are not its strong points. The good bits are bits, hit you straight on, and mostly have to do with the narrator-protagonist, his wishes, delusions, comical pretensions, and embarrassments." While many critics praised the ribald and graphic style of the novel, some critics felt it to be over-written. "Its one problem is that of verbal diarrhea," suggested Richard Pine in the *Irish Literary Supplement* (Fall 1993). "Wilson's garrulous and spicily jaunty manner often allowed him to paint scenes of misery and inhumanity even more purplish than the situation required."

Regardless of such criticisms, *Ripley Bogle* quickly acquired an impressive reputation and received several literary awards. It won the Rooney Prize (1989), the Hughes Prize (1989), the Irish Book Award (1990), and the prestigious Betty Trask Prize (1990). The last award David Montrose regarded in *TLS* (19 June 1992) as surprising, "because the Trask is reserved for debuts of a traditional or romantic nature, and *Ripley Bogle* came across as a collaboration between James Joyce and Charles Bukowski." The hitherto unknown Wilson soon rose in status. Along with such writers as Glenn Patterson, Colin Bateman, and Francis Molloy, he began to be recognized as part of an emerging generation of what critic Eve Patten terms "prodigal novelists" that represent a new voice in Northern Irish writing. According to Patten, these writers could be characterized by their common satirical awareness of the limitations of earlier Northern Irish writing; as she puts it in her 1995 essay: "Their self-conscious relationship to an exhausted literary inheritance and to the pitfalls of the provincial cliché has been an enabling feature of their writing while the tactics they have developed, from dialect to pastiche and satire to historicity, have helped to expose the images of Northern Irish society which disrupt pietistic or complacent narratives."

Initially, Wilson played up the biographical similarities between Ripley and himself. In 1989, for example, he went so far as to take interviewer Coe on a walk through central London in which he described a homeless period in London and alluded to various homeless people they encountered as former "colleagues." In his interview with Mills for *Irish Studies Review* a decade later, Wilson suggested that this description was perhaps an exaggeration. When asked about the degree to which *Ripley Bogle* was autobiographical, Wilson responded, "A considerable portion, although things were hugely altered for fictional purposes, like the London homelessness. In actual fact, I was homeless in Belfast." Regardless of whether the experiences Wilson described in *Ripley Bogle* were his own or not, the theme of homelessness was perhaps formally crucial for the representation of Ripley's impoverishment and abjection.

In his next book, *The Dispossessed* (1992), Wilson suggests that "perhaps homelessness is the single aspect of poverty that fiction tackles best. The revealed truth of fiction is sometimes a stronger truth than a fact too outrageous fully to comprehend. . . . Maybe the necessary empathy of the novel is one of the few routes to understanding such a predicament." The general subject of *The Dispossessed* is the widespread poverty of Britain at the beginning of the 1990s. Although Ripley Bogle had sardonically referred to the efforts of Dickens and George Orwell to document the experience of extreme poverty, Wilson attempted to follow their example in *The Dispossessed,* a documentary collaboration with the Northern Irish photographer Donovan Wylie. Its approach can be summarized as a prolonged attempt to call into question a growing consensus regarding poverty that Wilson identifies in the final sentences of the book: "the idea that the poor will always be with us." He argues that acceptance of this view makes poverty "ever more tolerable" and that "The notion of its permanence is making poverty's marshy foundations adamantine." *The Dispossessed* bears some resemblance to James Agee and Walker Evans's Depression-era book *Let Us Now Praise Famous Men* (1941). In *The Dispossessed* the authors chronicle the lives of the indigent in the cities of London, Glasgow, and Belfast through Wylie's photographs and Wilson's accounts of the experiences of the people he encounters. Wilson's style and tone reflect the seriousness of his subject matter. His writing is much more restrained and less sarcastically ebullient than in *Ripley Bogle,* and from the beginning Wilson openly doubts his abilities to represent the depth of experience that he would witness:

> I don't know precisely what I was thinking about when I decided to write this book. I'm not sure why I chose to write about London, Glasgow, and Belfast. I can barely remember what I hoped for, dreaded or expected. I recall that when Donovan and I arrived in London, I was hugely pessimistic . . . I felt fraudulent already. I was the last man qualified to write about the "dispossessed." I felt like a mountebank, I was a novelist. A paid liar. What was I doing here?

As Wilson comes into contact with an increasing number of impoverished people, for whom he develops an honest affection during his time spent among the poor of London, Wilson finds it increasingly difficult to write. He frequently worries about the degree to which a journalistic sense of distance is even possible given the testimonies of the poor that he meets: "Things got out of hand. The merest notion of writerly objectivity or structure collapsed. Penless, undisciplined, I got involved."

Poverty in itself represents one moment of the failure of contemporary British society. But perhaps a greater failure, Wilson suggests, is that the same society is unable to tell itself the truth. In such conditions the narrative representation of failure to some degree must present itself as a formal failure as well:

> I have said that this book is a failure or, at best, a book about failure. The more I've written, the greater this conviction has grown. . . . I never really discovered how to write this book. A year and more ago, it seemed a fairly simple undertaking. I already felt so much about poverty—I set out with chapterfuls of opinions and theories. None of them survived actual contact with the newest mutations of British poverty. I had spent much of my own life in poverty but the deprivation that I encountered in the past year was very different. . . . If anything, this book is simply a complaint. We'd like to complain, please. We have no answers and our understanding of the issues is perhaps rudimentary but we'd still like to complain.

Despite Wilson's sense of failure, such sentiment did not carry over to the critical reception of the book. *The Dispossessed* was not as popular as *Ripley Bogle* but received generally favorable reviews.

While *The Dispossessed* might have seemed to be a nonfiction extension of some of the central thematic concerns of *Ripley Bogle,* Wilson's next novel was a complete departure from his debut. *Manfred's Pain* (1992), published two months after *The Dispossessed,* centers on the last days of an elderly man named Manfred, as he dies of a variety of ailments in contemporary London. If there are biographical details in common between Wilson and Ripley Bogle, the character of Manfred could not be more different: Manfred is elderly rather than young, Jewish rather than Catholic, and reticent rather than extroverted. In addition, there are absolutely no connections between Northern Irish political or social conditions and the novel; in writing *Manfred's Pain* Wilson seems to have gone out of his way to distance it from his own Northern Irish background. The novel is stylistically different than *Ripley Bogle* as well. Whereas *Ripley Bogle* is characterized by a self-conscious, wordy, and frequently tragicomic first-person narration, the third-person narration of *Manfred's Pain* is understated almost to the point of minimalism and is more or less bereft of humor. As Natasha Fairweather wrote in an 18 June 1992 review in *The Times* (London), "Gone are the endless neologisms and Joycean amalgamated words. Gone is the uneasy marriage of high literacy and the dog-dirty vernacular. Linguistic self-indulgence has given way to an understated use of English prose which is masterly."

Despite these differences, there are certain similarities between the two novels. As in *Ripley Bogle, Manfred's Pain* is concerned with a marginal figure isolated from the rest of society, and the plot of the novel pro-

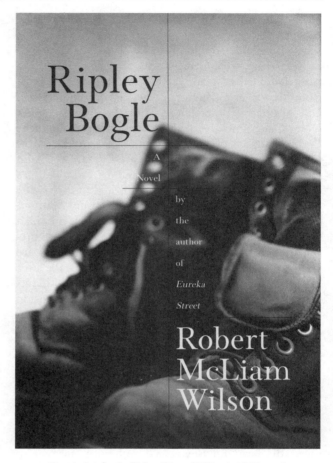

Dust jacket for the U.S. edition of Wilson's 1989 novel, about a Belfast-born Cambridge dropout living on the streets of London (Richland County Public Library)

ceeds by alternating between descriptions of the physical pain and stoic anticipation of death that characterizes Manfred's life in the present and a recounting of the events in his past that led to his current condition. Furthermore, Manfred comes to embody another example of the destructively self-obsessed male. One of Wilson's central targets in the novel is the casual and frequent brutality inflicted upon women, a theme that he had raised in the much different context of *The Dispossessed.* In *Manfred's Pain* the primary cause of Manfred's considerable abjection is his brutally violent abuse of his wife thirty years earlier. This abuse is predicated upon a desire for mastery of his wife that arises out of another form of male self-obsession: a desire for the complete possession of every facet of his wife's identity.

As a character, Manfred bears some resemblance to the characters of Samuel Beckett. He spends his days preparing for death in willful solitude, contemplating the various types of pain he feels; since he believes that he deserves this pain as a punishment for the pain he inflicted upon his wife in his younger days, he refuses to seek medical attention. His connection with the outside world is confined to occasional visits from his son and daughter-in-law (whom he despises) and neighborly interactions with the friendly black nurse Garth and the slightly comical drunken racist Webb, "a part of the great mindless underclass of England, the most witless and depressing proletariat in Europe." Manfred's life is structured around two types of incommunicative contact with his former wife, Emma: weekly telephone calls in which only Manfred speaks and monthly meetings in Hyde Park in which Manfred is not permitted to look at Emma. The representation of Manfred's past experiences, as they are related in alternating chapters, attempts to take in a broad swath of twentieth-century British Jewish history. His childhood takes place within the tension between his mother's desire for cultural assimilation and his father's resistance to assimilation. As a young man Manfred enlists in the British army and sees action through much of World War II, enabling Wilson to present a resolutely unheroic and disillusioning description of modern warfare.

After the war Manfred takes a job as a rent collector for a real estate firm run by a former army associate that provides housing for displaced Jewish refugees. He meets the beautiful Emma, a Czech-born survivor of the Nazi concentration camp Birkenau. The couple fall in love and briefly have a happy life together. Manfred desires to have access to every aspect of Emma's being, however, and her refusal to speak about her past before the war makes Manfred increasingly jealous. Indeed, Emma does not really speak about anything in the book, despite her centrality to the novel, and with the notable exception in which she finally does provide an account of her experience of the Holocaust, Emma is given little dialogue throughout the book. In order to express his jealousy, Manfred begins to beat Emma routinely, and Wilson's almost casual representation of the brutality of spousal violence serves to make this facet of the book all the more shocking.

Manfred's jealousy ultimately connects to his general sense of guilt for witnessing the suffering of the Holocaust without experiencing its horrors:

> In truth, he had always been jealous of Emma's nameless wartime past. He was jealous of other things. He was jealous of the bus in which she had ridden to school. He was jealous of the skirts and shoes she had worn, of the sounds she had heard, sights she had seen and thoughts she had thought. In the face of her unimpeachable sexual fidelity, he could only be jealous of everything . . . But most of all, he was jealous of the war, of the camps. He had beaten her first because of a suspicion of some childhood violation or rape at Birkenau. He was jealous of Birkenau.

As a form of self-punishment, Manfred eventually leaves Emma in order to let himself gradually decay into his present moribund condition. Wilson carries forth the narration until the exact moment of Manfred's death, graphically detailing the experience of the breakdown of the human body in a manner that evokes some of the passages of *Ripley Bogle*. Wilson adds some darkly comic touches to the death scene that play upon Manfred's muted narcissistic qualities. Having collapsed outside his apartment in the final moments of his life, Manfred is joined by the completely drunken Webb:

> To Manfred's horror, Webb seemed to be settling himself down for a long exchange . . . All Manfred's plans for an elegant, private death were destroyed. He had not imagined dying to Webb's gross accompaniment. The injustice was monstrous. He had done nothing to merit this. Impotently, Manfred raged. Lying satisfied beside him, Webb oozed woozy comradeship.

The critical response to *Manfred's Pain* was much more mixed than it had been to *Ripley Bogle*. On the one hand, there were several enthusiastic responses to the novel that regarded *Manfred's Pain* as a worthy successor to *Ripley Bogle*. "This novelist is for real," suggested Robbie Dinwoodie in *The Glasgow Herald* (11 June 1992). "Now and henceforth Robert McLiam Wilson is unignorable." Penny Perrick, in a 14 June 1992 review for *The Times* (London), emphasized the stylistic differences from *Ripley Bogle:* "The stiff choppy style is well matched to the strange and horrible story of Wilson's second novel, which is about the treacherous and unavailing demands that love makes on the love object. . . . This is a writer that makes you wonder what he will do next; you anticipate his next book with excitement, curiosity and quite a bit of trepidation." Generally positive reviews such as this were enough to provide *Manfred's Pain* with a high enough reputation for it to be shortlisted for the Whitbread Award.

On the other hand, those reviews of the novel that were less enthusiastic were far more critical than anything that had been levied at *Ripley Bogle*. Writing for *The Guardian* (4 June 1992), Claire Messud went so far as to suggest that "as there is a fine line between boldness and foolhardiness, so there is one between the best writing and some of the worst. In his immature ambition, Wilson has perhaps lost sight of that line. *Manfred's Pain,* as a result, does neither its subject nor its author justice." Wilson has developed mixed feelings about the novel since it was published and has come to concur to some extent with such negative assessments.

As he revealed to Tom Adair in an interview for *Scotland on Sunday* (1996), "I'm proud of the marital violence. It was well written. . . . The gap between intent and execution will always be here. But I didn't do enough work on it. Those inadequacies, they somehow, you know, make me feel I should be arrested." In his 1999 interview with Mills, Wilson spoke about the novel in far harsher terms: "I didn't write that novel when I should have. I was distracted by the publication of my first novel, I was collecting prizes . . . I don't really talk about that novel." Despite Wilson's own misgivings about perceived flaws of the novel, critical consensus about *Manfred's Pain* suggests that the novel nevertheless demonstrates Wilson's literary ability. As Guy Mannes-Abbott stated in a review in *The New Statesman & Society* (26 June 1992), "the novel is certainly flawed from overreaching; but that does not, finally, obscure a very singular talent."

From 1991 to 1994 Wilson served as writer-in-residence at the University of Ulster, Coleraine, a position that allowed him to devote a considerable amount of attention to his next novel. Wilson worked on other projects during this time as well, most notably within the field of television. The decision by the IRA to announce a complete cessation of military activity in August 1994 and the subsequent cease-fire announced by Unionist paramilitary groups had a strong influence on Wilson's two most notable projects of this period: the novel *Eureka Street* (1996) and the television documentary "Baseball in Irish History" (1996).

"Baseball in Irish History," which Wilson made with fellow Irish novelists Carlo Gebler and Patterson for the Channel Four program *War Cries,* focuses on the persistence of IRA "punishment beatings" after the cease-fire. Punishment beatings result from the belief of the IRA that it is the legitimate police force of Catholic Northern Ireland; they occur when paramilitaries brutally attack fellow Catholics for supposed "social crimes." As he told Crewe in their interview in *The Times* (London) not long after the documentary aired, Wilson has serious grievances with this practice: "I won't call them punishment beatings because that suggests that a punishment is warranted. They are for such crimes as drugs, burglary, joy-riding; having a brother or sister who does drugs, burglary, or joyriding; chatting up the wrong woman in the bar, not paying a snooker debt to a prominent paramilitary, wearing the wrong type of shoes, and so on. There are some flaws in this, I feel, as a system of jurisprudence." Despite the serious nature of the program, Wilson took a satirical approach to his subject matter by pretending to focus on the history of baseball in Northern Ireland. That history is extremely slight—Northern Ireland had only one amateur baseball team at the time the documentary was

made—but more baseball bats are sold in sporting-goods shops in Northern Ireland than in all other regions of Great Britain combined. The fact that baseball bats are common weapons in punishment beatings enabled Wilson to focus on the persistence of IRA brutality after its supposed cessation of violent activity.

The program, which aired only weeks after the end of the first IRA cease-fire, foreshadowed the content of the novel that appeared a few months later. *Eureka Street* is perhaps the first novel to have the cease-fire and the subsequent inception of the Northern Irish peace process as its historical context. In the spirit of this moment, the novel focuses on the friendship between two men in their early thirties—one Catholic, one Protestant—and their life in contemporary Belfast. The city of Belfast might also be regarded as the central character of the novel, as *Eureka Street* represents a prolonged reconciliation between Wilson and his native city. As he told Mills, "I'm in love with it and you get to do a bit of fancy writing. This journalist . . . wrote in her feature that I had the attitude to Belfast of the boy who was in love with the ugliest girl in the class. I thought that was perfect." Midway through the novel Wilson interrupts his narrative in order to include a self-contained chapter that serves as a sort of meditative prose poem on the beauty and ugliness of Belfast. At one point Wilson makes the connection between the city and the novel explicit:

> The city's surface is thick with its living citizens. Its earth is richly sown with its many dead. The city is a repository of narratives, of stories. Present tense, past tense or future. The city is a novel. . . . The men and women there are narratives, endlessly complex and intriguing. The most humdrum of them constitutes a narrative that would defeat Tolstoy at his best and most voluminous.

Wilson suggests that there is something utopian to the city when it is configured in such terms: "For as you look around the perimeter of your illuminated vision, you can see the buildings and streets in which a dark hundred thousand, a million, ten million stories as vivid and complex as your own reside. It doesn't get more divine than that." This idealistic version of Belfast, however, does not necessarily represent the reality of Belfast. In order to love Belfast, one must also acknowledge its history of political violence. Even if people are as crucial to a city as characters are to a novel, this symbiotic relationship does not necessarily protect either from harm; as Wilson suggests at the end of the chapter, "They are epic, these citizens, they are murderable." This observation provides a clue to the primary theme of the novel. As the novel ends, one of the characters looks out over the city of Belfast and meditates upon his love for his native city in language that directly recalls Wilson's earlier comparison of the city to the novel: "Tender is a small word for what I feel for this town. I think of my city's conglomerate of bodies. . . . Sometimes, this frail cityful of organs makes me seethe and boil with tenderness. They seem so unmurderable and, because I think of them, they belong to me." At least two crucial things have happened to this character: he has just fallen in love, with a former enemy, and a more general form of love symbolized by the cease-fire and the peace process has come to characterize his city.

Eureka Street presents a prolonged inquiry into the possibilities of love amid the culture of death that routine political violence produces. By the end of the novel Wilson suggests that love is the crucial foundation necessary for the termination of sectarian strife in Northern Ireland. The novel begins with the sentence "All stories are love stories" and proceeds to catalogue over the next four hundred pages as many types and variations of love as possible: romantic love, both heterosexual and homosexual sexual love, familial love, maternal love, paternal or step-paternal love, comradely love, and basic humanitarian love in general. In each case love is represented as a sort of triumph in which boundaries are broken down and the hatred that motivates sectarian violence is confronted. *Eureka Street* is thus a considerably more positive work than Wilson's earlier novels.

The evocative tone demonstrated in Wilson's poetic chapter on Belfast is somewhat characteristic of the novel as a whole, and there is far less concern with the representation of pain, decay, and the breakdown of the human body in *Eureka Street* than there had been in his earlier novels. Even in moments in which he represents violence or destruction, Wilson's descriptive skills are directed toward narrative goals involving love and sympathy. In the chapter that succeeds his meditation upon Belfast, Wilson briefly introduces several new characters in order to develop his suggestion that the citizens of Belfast are narratives-in-motion. Midway though the chapter, however, these new characters are killed by the explosion of a bomb planted by the IRA. The description of the effect of the explosion on the bodies of these characters is rendered in horribly graphic detail and is as disturbing as descriptions of human decay in *Ripley Bogle* or *Manfred's Pain*. Unlike those novels, in which Wilson focused upon the suffering of characters whom he had already taken great pains to represent as unsympathetic, the passage is possibly even more shocking in that the explosion kills likable characters capable of love; the story of Rosemary Daye, the most developed of these ephemeral characters, centers on her thoughts about the beginning of a new love affair.

Eureka Street nevertheless retains the satirical tone that is evident throughout Wilson's novels. The bulk of this satire is directed against violent republicanism. "I rail against the republican myth because it's believed," Wilson told Crewe in their 1996 interview. "The world thinks loyalist paramilitaries are right-wing arseholes. I wish that it would wake up to the fact that the republicans are too. It's that classic thing of people being sympathetic towards who they see as the underdog, a sort of misplaced political correctness by the left-wing." Wilson parodies several specific figures associated with organized republicanism. Gerry Adams, leader of the Sinn Féin political party, is represented as Jimmy Eve, leader of the Just Us party—a loose translation of the Irish phrase *sinn féin amháin* that emphasizes what Wilson feels to be Sinn Féin's intolerance of other political positions. Despite this thinly veiled critique, Adams chose *Eureka Street* as one of his favorite books of 1996. Wilson's satire is somewhat evenhanded in that many other political positions, organizations, or people are also satirized, including nonviolent Irish nationalism, Unionism, loyalist paramilitaries, Amnesty International, and, perhaps, Seamus Heaney, the best-known Northern Irish writer. While the fictional poet Shague Ghinthoss bears more than a passing resemblance to Heaney, Wilson insisted to Mills that "if people draw parallels with him it's their concern, not mine."

The intent of Wilson's parodies is revealed most strongly in a satirical subplot involving graffiti bearing the initials "OTG." The initials first appear near the end of the opening chapter of the novel, when Jake Jackson, one of the two central characters of the book, notices a new graffito on the wall outside his house: "The local kids would write things there for the purposes of bravado or initiation. . . . It was an epic and somehow touching battle, very Belfast. The kids wrote the usual stuff of both sides: IRA, INLA, UVF, UFF, UDA, IPLO, FTP (Fuck the Pope), FTQ (Fuck the Queen), and one FTNP (Fuck the Next Pope). But tonight's graffito was a new one on me. . . . someone had chosen to write in white three-foot-high letters: OTG." This acronym is unusual because, as another character reflects to himself upon first encountering the initials, "the letter O didn't feature much in Irish or Ulster graffiti." As the initials become more widespread throughout the city during the course of the novel, the government, the police, republican and loyalist paramilitaries, and almost all of the characters wonder what the initials could possibly stand for and about the ideological makeup of this apparent organization. Ultimately, the graffiti is revealed to be the work of a single figure who makes a brief cameo near the end of the novel; the

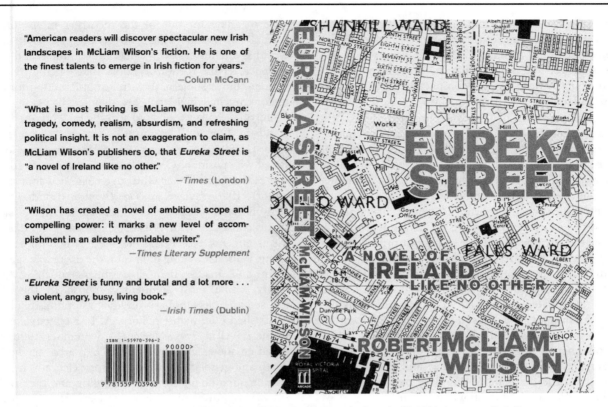

"American readers will discover spectacular new Irish landscapes in McLiam Wilson's fiction. He is one of the finest talents to emerge in Irish fiction for years."
—Colum McCann

"What is most striking is McLiam Wilson's range: tragedy, comedy, realism, absurdism, and refreshing political insight. It is not an exaggeration to claim, as McLiam Wilson's publishers do, that *Eureka Street* is "a novel of Ireland like no other."
—*Times* (London)

"Wilson has created a novel of ambitious scope and compelling power: it marks a new level of accomplishment in an already formidable writer."
—*Times Literary Supplement*

"*Eureka Street* is funny and brutal and a lot more . . . a violent, angry, busy, living book."
—*Irish Times* (Dublin)

ISBN 1-55970-396-2

Dust jacket for the 1997 U.S. edition of Wilson's 1996 novel, about the friendship between a Catholic and a Protestant in Belfast (Richland County Public Library)

initials are meaningful precisely for their meaninglessness. As Jake reflects:

> You want to know what OTG means? Almost everything. That was the point. All of the other letters written on our walls were dark minority stuff. The world's grand, lazy majority will never be arsed writing anything anywhere and, anyway, they wouldn't know what to write. They would change their permissive, clement, heterogeneous minds half-way through. That's why OTG was written for them. It could mean anything they wanted. It *did* mean anything they wanted. Order the Gammon. Octogenarians Tote Guns. Openly Titular Gesture. One True God.

This realization encapsulates the politics of *Eureka Street*. In a sense Wilson's relation to his novel, which was originally to be titled "OTG," is similar to the anonymous painter's relation to his acronymic graffito: *Eureka Street* seeks to be an open-ended expression on behalf of non-aligned Northern Irish society in general. As Wilson told Amoore in their 1999 interview, "Violence is a part of the material of the city and its citizens have to work around it. An awful lot of people in Northern Ireland simply don't care whether it is Irish, British, or independent. Yet no one speaks for them and no one reflects their views or even demonstrates the fact that they exist."

Jake Jackson and Chuckie Lurgan, the primary characters of the book, around whose friendship the novel is structured, present two examples of such ordinary Belfast citizens. Jake's story is written in the first person and bears some biographical similarities to Wilson, a Catholic from West Belfast opposed to republicanism, but these connections are not developed as extensively as Wilson's apparent similarities to Ripley Bogle, who makes a brief cameo appearance in the novel. The plot involving Jake primarily focuses on his unsuccessful attempts to find love and commitment, and his general ineptitude in his relationships with women provides another site for Wilson's recurring theme regarding the emotional and psychological limitations of male narcissism. Because of Jake's strong humanitarian impulses, expressed in such subplots as his attempt to care for the abused street-child Roche, he makes a much more sympathetic character than Wilson's earlier male narcissists. Chuckie, a Protestant whose story is written in the third person, presents a departure from characters such as Jake or Ripley. In a 1994 review of the novel *Gilchrist* by the Northern Irish Protestant writer Maurice Leitch, a strong influence, Wilson reflected upon the devalued status of Protestant perspectives in considerations of Irish culture: "There is a definite and ill-managed difference in how the non-Irish view Catholics and Protestants. Bizarrely, this distinction is beginning to show itself most clearly in the realms of cultural comment. The Protestant vision, the Protestant version, isn't popular. It's got no rhythm. It's white South African. It's too complicated. The Catholic vision is familiar, *more* Irish somehow."

The character of Chuckie Lurgan presents Wilson's attempt to rectify this situation. Chuckie embodies several stereotypes regarding Ulster Protestant identity but is ultimately one of the most sympathetic and successful characters of the novel. The plot involving Chuckie focuses on the manner in which he becomes spectacularly wealthy through his amazing ability to attract large amounts of investment capital, despite the fact that he neither works nor produces anything of great value. In one typical scheme he pays local children a small amount of money to collect and varnish several twigs; he then sells the twigs in the United States at inflated prices as "Leprechaun Walking-Sticks." This plot gives Wilson the opportunity to make several satirical observations about the various developmental schemes in Northern Ireland designed to attract investment from the United States and elsewhere, as well as to raise the issue of the place of Northern Ireland in a globalized international economy.

The initial critical reaction to *Eureka Street* was much more positive, though occasionally qualified, than it had been for Wilson's previous novel, *Manfred's Pain*. One of the more frequent reactions centered upon its similarities to large Victorian novels or to the love stories of William Shakespeare's comedies. As Richard Kirkland suggests in his 2000 essay on the fiction of Wilson and fellow Belfast novelist Patterson, "*Eureka Street* owes its greatest structural debt to the novels of Dickens, and the fantastical, carnivalesque, sentimental vision of Wilson's Belfast enables a breadth of vision which at many points appears to be aspiring to the condition of epic." These influences led some critics to qualify their praise of the novel with mild criticisms directed toward the feasibility of those influences; as Eileen Battersby noted in a 10 August 1996 interview in *The Irish Times* (Dublin): "There are some shortcomings: it is too long, and, as with most Shakespearian comedies, some of the plot outlines are detectable long before the closing pages. Still as a comic novel of Belfast now, this is stylish, funny, black, and memorable." Wilson is aware of some of the limitations of his debt to the Victorian novel; as he wrote in an article concerning attempts to adapt *Eureka Street* for television, "Novels are messy and shapeless things at the best of times, and mine particularly so." Other critics objected to the characters of the novel, regarding them as caricatures or as sexist. Along these lines, Trevor Lewis, in an 18 August 1996 review in *The Sunday Times* (London), found a pos-

sible meaning for one of the recurring motifs of the novel: "For the novel has an overriding laddishness: its world is circumscribed by masculine humor and male violence. This is not a book that openly dislikes women, but it subjects them to an unflattering form of metonymy in which they are denoted by teeth, hips, 'callipygian' curves, or cold ideologies. Perhaps OTG stands for One for The Guys."

Despite this criticism, the general response to the novel was positive. On the issue of the perceived sexism of the novel, Peter Guttridge suggested in a 1 September 1996 review in *The Observer* (London) that Wilson invokes sexism in order to satirize it, a position that is consistent with Wilson's earlier works: "It is boy meets girl, not vice versa, but there is nothing laddish about Wilson's writing of lads on the make. He satirizes them and makes their boorishness touching. And funny." The most frequent response to the book focused upon its emphasis on love, its optimism, and its unabashedly humanist politics. A. L. Kennedy's praise of the novel in *The Scotsman* (14 September 1996) is a paradigmatic example: "In the face of arbitrary violent death and genocidal conflict, Wilson celebrates humanity, the quixotic humor of the last gasp and the private, subversive power of sexuality and sex. He offers us no solutions, but shows us our best and our worst with a redemptive tenderness and common sense."

Although *Eureka Street* did not attain the prizes and honors allotted to *Ripley Bogle*, this sort of praise helped the book to be short-listed for both the *Irish Times* Irish Literature Prize and the *Irish Times* International Fiction Prize in 1997. In 1999 *Eureka Street* was adapted into a successful television miniseries for the British Broadcasting Corporation that aired on BBC2. The book has since been warmly received in translation in Germany, Italy, and, most especially, France. Wilson and his translator Brice Matthieussent won the 1999 UNESCO Françoise Gallimand Prize for the French translation of *Eureka Street*. The book has also acquired a respectable cult following in the United States.

As Vivian Valvano Lynch suggested in a review in *The Irish Literary Supplement* (Fall 1997), *Eureka Street* runs the risk of becoming dated by the historical specificity of its satire: "Without specifying dates, the author utilizes such precise information from the political, social, and cultural news circa 1994 that it may be difficult to identify the butts of his satire as time goes on." Nevertheless, Valvano Lynch recognized that the humanitarian pragmatism of *Eureka Street* might contribute to the importance of the novel in critical discussions of Northern Irish culture: "there is not, and there never will be, any mistaking his central thrust: sectarian violence is ruining Belfast; reactions ranging from the hypocritical to the inept are complicating the situation and compounding atrocities. McLiam Wilson alternates between naming names and cagey fictionalizing." The novel has continued to attract scholarly attention and is frequently included on the course syllabi of classes on Irish literature in the United States.

In an insightful review of *Eureka Street* in the Northern Irish cultural and political journal *Fortnight* (October 1996) the eminent Belfast-based critic Edna Longley praised the novel for its humanism and positive iconoclasm. "This is a brave, brilliant essay into the dark. Despite the laid back characters who seem close to the narrative voice of his fiction, Wilson is a writer who believes in moral agency, in action for good or evil . . . he is one of the few writers who really disturb clichés of the North, who shake up stale perceptions." This observation might be seen as applicable to the bulk of Robert McLiam Wilson's writing. There is an occasionally graphic or brutal quality to his language and to the turns of his plots, and Wilson's frequent commitment to satire and comedy occasionally seems shocking when juxtaposed against the more horrible or tragic aspects of his work. Nevertheless, it is impossible to deny the humanitarian impulse behind his representation of the effect of violence and social marginalization upon a young person's psyche in *Ripley Bogle*, the effects of spiraling poverty upon society's most vulnerable people in *The Dispossessed*, the lingering effects of historical violence and the immediate effects of spousal violence in *Manfred's Pain*, or the effects that love might have in the face of political violence in *Eureka Street*.

Interviews:

Jonathan Coe, "Out on the Mean Streets," *Guardian*, 13 June 1989; Weekend Arts section, p. 1.

Candida Crewe, "Belfast Slabbers Pave a Literary Way," *Guardian*, 18 February 1992, p. 32;

Tom Adair, "Unsuitable Boy," *Scotland on Sunday*, 18 August 1996, p. 10;

Crewe, "Biting the Bullet," *Times* (London), 7 September 1996, p. 18;

Paul Vallely, "Belfast Boy," *Independent* (London), 25 October 1997, p. 22;

Richard Mills, "'All Stories Are Love Stories,'" *Irish Studies Review*, 7, no. 1 (1999): 73–77;

Topaz Amoore, "'If You Repeat What I'm About to Say, You'll Get Me Shot,'" *Daily Express* (London), 11 September 1999.

References:

Ellen-Raïssa Jackson, "Gender, Violence and Hybridity: Reading the Postcolonial in Three Irish Novels," *Irish Studies Review*, 7, no. 2 (1999): 221–231;

Richard Kirkland, "Bourgeois Redemptions: The Fictions of Glenn Patterson and Robert McLiam Wilson," in *Contemporary Irish Fiction: Themes, Tropes, Theories*, edited by Liam Harte and Michael Parker (New York: St. Martin's Press, 2000), pp. 213–231;

Eve Patten, "Fiction in Conflict: Northern Ireland's Prodigal Novelists," in *Peripheral Visions: Images of Nationhood in Contemporary British Fiction*, edited by Ian A. Bell (Cardiff: University of Wales Press, 1995), pp. 128–148;

Laura Pelaschiar, "Transforming Belfast: The Evolving Role of the City in Northern Irish Fiction," *Irish University Review*, 30, no. 1 (2000): 117–131;

Gerry Smyth, *The Novel and the Nation: Studies in the New Irish Fiction* (London: Pluto, 1997), pp. 132–134.

Books for Further Reading

Acheson, James, ed. *The British and Irish Novel Since 1960*. New York: St. Martin's Press, 1991.

Bell, Ian A., ed. *Peripheral Visions: Images of Nationhood in Contemporary British Fiction*. Cardiff: University of Wales Press, 1995.

Bloom, Clive, and Gary Day, eds. *Literature and Culture in Modern Britain,* volume 3, *1956–1999*. Harlow, U.K.: Longman, 2000.

Booker, M. Keith. *The Modern British Novel of the Left: A Research Guide*. Westport, Conn.: Greenwood Press, 1998.

Bradbury, Malcolm. *Dangerous Pilgrimages: Transatlantic Mythologies and the Novel*. London: Secker & Warburg, 1995; New York: Viking, 1996.

Bradbury. *The Modern British Novel*. London: Secker & Warburg, 1993.

Bradbury. *No, Not Bloomsbury*. London: Deutsch, 1987; New York: Columbia University Press, 1988.

Bradbury, ed. *Class Work: The Best of Contemporary Short Fiction*. London: Sceptre, 1995.

Brînzeu, Pia. *Corridors of Mirrors: The Spirit of Europe in Contemporary British and Romanian Fiction*. Lanham, Md.: University Press of America, 2000.

British Council. *The Novel in Britain and Ireland Since 1970: A Select Bibliography,* third edition. London: British Council, 1994.

Byatt, A. S., and Alan Hollinghurst, eds. *New Writing 4*. London: Vintage, 1995.

Byatt, and Peter Porter, eds. *New Writing 6*. London: Vintage, 1997.

Cahalan, James M. *Double Visions: Women and Men in Modern and Contemporary Irish Fiction*. Syracuse, N.Y.: Syracuse University Press, 1999.

Callil, Carmen, and Craig Raine, eds. *New Writing 7*. London: Vintage, 1998.

D'Haen, Theo, and Hans Bertens, eds. *British Postmodern Fiction*. Postmodern Studies, no. 6. Amsterdam & Atlanta: Rodopi, 1993.

Dhar, T. N. *History-fiction Interface in Indian English Novel: Mulk Raj Anand, Nayantara Sahgal, Salman Rushdie, Shashi Tharoor, O.V. Vijayan*. New Delhi: Prestige, 1999; London: Sangam, 1999.

Eckstein, Barbara J. *The Language of Fiction in a World of Pain: Reading Politics as Paradox*. Philadelphia: University of Pennsylvania Press, 1990.

Edwards, Brian. *Theories of Play and Postmodern Fiction*. New York & London: Garland, 1998.

Elias, Amy J. *Sublime Desire: History and Post-1960s Fiction*. Baltimore: Johns Hopkins University Press, 2001.

Fokkema, Aleid. *Postmodern Characters: A Study of Characterization in British and American Postmodern Fiction*. Amsterdam & Atlanta: Rodopi, 1991.

Fowles, John, and A. L. Kennedy, eds. *New Writing 9*. London: Vintage/British Council, 2001.

Gerard, David. *Fallen among Scribes: Conversations with Novelists, Poets, Critics*. Wilmslow, U.K.: Elvet Press, 1998.

Gorra, Michael. *After Empire: Scott, Naipaul, Rushdie*. Chicago: University of Chicago Press, 1997.

Harte, Liam, and Michael Parker, eds. *Contemporary Irish Fiction: Themes, Tropes, Theories*. New York: St. Martin's Press, 2000; Basingstoke, U.K.: Macmillan, 2000.

Harvey, David. *The Condition of Postmodernity: An Enquiry into the Origins of Cultural Change*. Cambridge, Mass. & Oxford: Blackwell, 1989.

Hassam, Andrew. *Writing and Reality: A Study of Modern British Diary Fiction*. Contributions to the Study of World Literature Series, no. 47. Westport, Conn.: Greenwood Press, 1993.

Hawthorn, Jeremy, ed. *The British Working-Class Novel in the Twentieth Century*. London & Baltimore: Arnold, 1984.

Head, Dominic. *The Cambridge Introduction to Modern British Fiction, 1950–2000*. Cambridge & New York: Cambridge University Press, 2002.

Higdon, David Leon. *Shadows of the Past in Contemporary British Fiction*. Athens: University of Georgia Press, 1985.

Holmes, Frederick M. *The Historical Imagination: Postmodernism and the Treatment of the Past in Contemporary British Fiction*. Victoria, B.C.: University of Victoria Press, 1997.

Hosmer, Robert E., Jr., ed. *Contemporary British Women Writers: Narrative Strategies*. New York: St. Martin's Press, 1993.

Kirkland, Richard. *Literature and Culture in Northern Ireland since 1965: Moments of Danger*. London & New York: Longman, 1996.

Korte, Barbara, and Klaus Peter Müller, eds. *Unity in Diversity Revisited? British Literature and Culture in the 1990s*. Tübingen, Germany: Narr, 1998.

Koza, Kimberly Ann. "Women as Images of History: Contemporary Anglophone Fiction by Minority and Post-colonial Women Writers." Ph.D. thesis. University of Indiana, Bloomington, 1988.

Langford, Larry L. *Fiction and the Social Contract: Genocide, Pornography, and the Deconstruction of History*. New York: Peter Lang, 1998.

Lee, Alison. *Realism and Power: Postmodern British Fiction*. London & New York: Routledge, 1990.

Lee, Robert A., ed. *Other Britain, Other British: Contemporary Multicultural Fiction*. London & East Haven, Conn.: Pluto, 1995.

Lively, Penelope, and George Szirtes, eds. *New Writing 10*. London: Picador, 2001.

Lord, Geoffrey William. *Postmodernism and Notions of National Difference: A Comparison of Postmodern Fiction in Britain and America*. Postmodern Studies, no. 18. Amsterdam & Atlanta: Rodopi, 1996.

Marshall, Alan, and Neil Sammells, eds. *Irish Encounters: Poetry, Politics and Prose*. Bath, U.K.: Sulis, 1998.

McCaffery, Larry, ed. *Postmodern Fiction: A Bio-Bibliographical Guide*. New York & London: Greenwood Press, 1986.

McCaffery, ed. *Storming the Reality Studio: A Casebook of Cyberpunk and Postmodern Science Fiction*. Durham, N.C.: Duke University Press, 1991.

Mengham, Rod, ed. *An Introduction to Contemporary Fiction: International Writing in English since 1970*. Cambridge: Polity / Malden, Mass.: Blackwell, 1999.

Middeke, Martin, and Werner Huber, eds. *Biofictions: The Rewriting of Romantic Lives in Contemporary Fiction and Drama*. Columbia, S.C.: Camden House, 1999.

Moses, Michael Valdez. *The Novel and the Globalization of Culture*. New York & Oxford: Oxford University Press, 1995.

Motion, Andrew, and Candice Rodd, eds. *New Writing 3*. London: Minerva/British Council, 1994.

Nash, Cristopher. *World Postmodern Fiction: A Guide*. New York & London: Longman, 1993.

Norfolk, Lawrence, and Tibor Fischer, eds. *New Writing 8*. London: Vintage/British Council, 1999.

Parker, Peter. *The Reader's Companion to the Twentieth Century Novel*. London: Fourth Estate/Oxford: Helicon, 1994.

Philips, Deborah, and Ian Haywood. *Brave New Causes: Women in British Postwar Fictions*. London & Washington, D.C.: Leicester University Press, 1998.

Porter, and Christopher Hope, eds. *New Writing 5*. London: Vintage, 1996.

Rogers, Jane, ed. *Good Fiction Guide*. New York & Oxford: Oxford University Press, 2001.

Scanlan, Margaret S. *Traces of Another Time: History and Politics in Postwar British Fiction*. Princeton: Princeton University Press, 1990.

Shaffer, Brian W. *The Blinding Torch: Modern British Fiction and the Discourse of Civilization*. Amherst: University of Massachusetts Press, 1993.

Sizemore, Christine Wick. *Negotiating Identities in Women's Lives: English Postcolonial and Contemporary British Novels*. Westport, Conn.: Greenwood Press, 2002.

Skinner, John. *The Stepmother Tongue: An Introduction to New Anglophone Fiction*. New York: St. Martin's Press, 1998.

Smyth, Gerry. *The Novel and the Nation: Studies in the New Irish Fiction*. London: Pluto, 1997.

Todd, Richard. *Consuming Fictions: The Booker Prize and Fiction in Britain Today*. London: Bloomsbury, 1996.

Todd, and Luisa Flora, eds. *Theme Parks, Rainforests and Sprouting Wastelands: European Essays on Theory and Performance in Contemporary British Fiction*. Amsterdam & Atlanta: Rodopi, 2000.

Wallace, Gavin, and Randall Stevenson, eds. *The Scottish Novel since the Seventies: New Visions, Old Dreams*. Edinburgh: Edinburgh University Press, 1993.

Werlock, Abby H. P., ed. *British Women Writing Fiction*. Tuscaloosa: University of Alabama Press, 2000.

Wheeler, Kathleen. *A Guide to Twentieth-Century Women Novelists*. Oxford & Cambridge, Mass.: Blackwell, 1997.

Contributors

R. Victoria Arana . . . . Howard University

Steven Belletto . . . . University of Wisconsin–Madison

Stacia L. Bensyl . . . . Missouri Western State College

Mariadele Boccardi . . . . Emmanuel College, University of Cambridge

Mary L. Bogumil . . . . Southern Illinois University, Carbondale

Peter Brigg . . . . University of Guelph

Moira E. Casey . . . . University of Connecticut

Roger Clark . . . . York St John College

Ellen Crowell . . . . University of Texas at Austin

Rocío G. Davis . . . . University of Navarre

Gregory Dobbins . . . . University of California, Davis

Mary Robertson Ellen . . . . University of East Anglia

Desmond Fitzgibbon . . . . National University of Ireland, Maynooth

Shannon Forbes . . . . Marquette University

Annette Gilson . . . . Oakland University

Ann Hancock . . . . University of the West of England, Bristol

Roxanne Harde . . . . Queen's University

Dominic Head . . . . Brunel University

Dirk Van Hulle . . . . University of Antwerp

Benjamin G. Lanier-Nabors . . . . Louisiana State University

Joseph Lennon . . . . Manhattan College

Barry Lewis . . . . University of Sunderland

Tim Middleton . . . . Bath Spa University College

Michael R. Molino . . . . Southern Illinois University, Carbondale

Caitriona Moloney . . . . Bradley University

Robert A. Morace . . . . Daemen College

Geoffrey P. Nash . . . . University of Sunderland

Anne-Marie Obilade . . . . Southern Illinois University, Carbondale

David Ian Paddy . . . . Whittier College

Annette Rubery . . . . University of Warwick

Ben Saunders . . . . University of Oregon

Philip Lockwood Simpson . . . . Brevard Community College, Palm Bay Campus

Claire Squires . . . . Oxford Brookes University

Kersti Tarien . . . . St Hugh's College, Oxford University

Ann Owens Weekes . . . . University of Arizona

Eva Roa White . . . . Southern Illinois University, Carbondale

Aiping Zhang . . . . California State University, Chico

Cumulative Index

Dictionary of Literary Biography, Volumes 1-267
Dictionary of Literary Biography Yearbook, 1980-2001
Dictionary of Literary Biography Documentary Series, Volumes 1-19
Concise Dictionary of American Literary Biography, Volumes 1-7
Concise Dictionary of British Literary Biography, Volumes 1-8
Concise Dictionary of World Literary Biography, Volumes 1-4

Cumulative Index

DLB before number: *Dictionary of Literary Biography*, Volumes 1-267
Y before number: *Dictionary of Literary Biography Yearbook*, 1980-2001
DS before number: *Dictionary of Literary Biography Documentary Series*, Volumes 1-19
CDALB before number: *Concise Dictionary of American Literary Biography*, Volumes 1-7
CDBLB before number: *Concise Dictionary of British Literary Biography*, Volumes 1-8
CDWLB before number: *Concise Dictionary of World Literary Biography*, Volumes 1-4

A

Aakjær, Jeppe 1866-1930 . . . . DLB-214

Abbey, Edward 1927-1989. . . . . DLB-256

Abbey, Edwin Austin 1852-1911 . . . . DLB-188

Abbey, Maj. J. R. 1894-1969 . . . . DLB-201

Abbey Press DLB-49

The Abbey Theatre and Irish Drama,
    1900-1945 . . . . DLB-10

Abbot, Willis J. 1863-1934. . . . . DLB-29

Abbott, Jacob 1803-1879 . . . . DLB-1, 42, 243

Abbott, Lee K. 1947- DLB-130

Abbott, Lyman 1835-1922 . . . . DLB-79

Abbott, Robert S. 1868-1940 . . . . DLB-29, 91

Abe Kōbō 1924-1993 . . . . DLB-182

Abelard, Peter circa 1079-1142? DLB-115, 208

Abelard-Schuman. DLB-46

Abell, Arunah S. 1806-1888. . . . . DLB-43

Abell, Kjeld 1901-1961. . . . . DLB-214

Abercrombie, Lascelles 1881-1938. . . . . . . DLB-19

Aberdeen University Press Limited DLB-106

Abish, Walter 1931- DLB-130, 227

Ablesimov, Aleksandr Onisimovich
    1742-1783. . . . . DLB-150

Abraham à Sancta Clara 1644-1709 . . . . . DLB-168

Abrahams, Peter
    1919- DLB-117, 225; CDWLB-3

Abrams, M. H. 1912- DLB-67

Abramson, Jesse 1904-1979 . . . . DLB-241

Abrogans circa 790-800 . . . . DLB-148

Abschatz, Hans Aßmann von
    1646-1699 . . . . DLB-168

Abse, Dannie 1923- DLB-27, 245

Abutsu-ni 1221-1283 . . . . DLB-203

Academy Chicago Publishers DLB-46

Accius circa 170 B.C.-circa 80 B.C. DLB-211

Accrocca, Elio Filippo 1923- DLB-128

Ace Books DLB-46

Achebe, Chinua 1930- DLB-117; CDWLB-3

Achtenberg, Herbert 1938- DLB-124

Ackerman, Diane 1948- DLB-120

Ackroyd, Peter 1949- DLB-155, 231

Acorn, Milton 1923-1986. . . . . DLB-53

Acosta, Oscar Zeta 1935?- DLB-82

Acosta Torres, José 1925- DLB-209

Actors Theatre of Louisville DLB-7

Adair, Gilbert 1944- DLB-194

Adair, James 1709?-1783?. DLB-30

Adam, Graeme Mercer 1839-1912 . . . . DLB-99

Adam, Robert Borthwick, II 1863-1940 . . DLB-187

Adame, Leonard 1947- DLB-82

Adameşteanu, Gabriel 1942- DLB-232

Adamic, Louis 1898-1951 . . . . DLB-9

Adams, Abigail 1744-1818 . . . . DLB-200

Adams, Alice 1926-1999 . . . . DLB-234; Y-86

Adams, Bertha Leith (Mrs. Leith Adams,
    Mrs. R. S. de Courcy Laffan)
    1837?-1912 . . . . DLB-240

Adams, Brooks 1848-1927. . . . . DLB-47

Adams, Charles Francis, Jr. 1835-1915 . . . . DLB-47

Adams, Douglas 1952- DLB-261; Y-83

Adams, Franklin P. 1881-1960. . . . . DLB-29

Adams, Hannah 1755-1832 . . . . DLB-200

Adams, Henry 1838-1918 . . . . DLB-12, 47, 189

Adams, Herbert Baxter 1850-1901 . . . . DLB-47

Adams, J. S. and C. [publishing house] DLB-49

Adams, James Truslow
    1878-1949 . . . . DLB-17; DS-17

Adams, John 1735-1826 . . . . DLB-31, 183

Adams, John 1735-1826 and
    Adams, Abigail 1744-1818. . . . . DLB-183

Adams, John Quincy 1767-1848 . . . . DLB-37

Adams, Léonie 1899-1988 . . . . DLB-48

Adams, Levi 1802-1832 . . . . DLB-99

Adams, Richard 1920- DLB-261

Adams, Samuel 1722-1803 . . . . DLB-31, 43

Adams, Sarah Fuller Flower
    1805-1848 . . . . DLB-199

Adams, Thomas 1582 or 1583-1652 . . . . . DLB-151

Adams, William Taylor 1822-1897 . . . . DLB-42

Adamson, Sir John 1867-1950 . . . . DLB-98

Adamson, Harold 1906-1980. . . . . DLB-265

Adcock, Arthur St. John 1864-1930. . . . . . DLB-135

Adcock, Betty 1938- DLB-105

"Certain Gifts". DLB-105

Adcock, Fleur 1934- DLB-40

Addison, Joseph 1672-1719 . . . DLB-101; CDBLB-2

Ade, George 1866-1944. . . . . DLB-11, 25

Adeler, Max (see Clark, Charles Heber)

Adlard, Mark 1932- DLB-261

Adler, Richard 1921- and
    Ross, Jerry 1926-1955. . . . . DLB-265

Adonias Filho 1915-1990 . . . . DLB-145

Adorno, Theodor W. 1903-1969. . . . . DLB-242

Advance Publishing Company DLB-49

Ady, Endre 1877-1919 . . . . . . DLB-215; CDWLB-4

AE 1867-1935 . . . . DLB-19; CDBLB-5

Ælfric circa 955-circa 1010. . . . . DLB-146

Aeschines
    circa 390 B.C.-circa 320 B.C. DLB-176

Aeschylus 525-524 B.C.-456-455 B.C.
    . . . . DLB-176; CDWLB-1

Afro-American Literary Critics:
    An Introduction DLB-33

After Dinner Opera Company. Y-92

Agassiz, Elizabeth Cary 1822-1907 . . . . . . DLB-189

Agassiz, Louis 1807-1873 . . . . DLB-1, 235

Agee, James
    1909-1955 . . . . DLB-2, 26, 152; CDALB-1

The Agee Legacy: A Conference at the University
    of Tennessee at Knoxville. Y-89

Aguilera Malta, Demetrio 1909-1981 . . . . DLB-145

Ahlin, Lars 1915-1997 . . . . DLB-257

Ai 1947- DLB-120

Aichinger, Ilse 1921- DLB-85

Aickman, Robert 1914-1981 . . . . DLB-261

Aidoo, Ama Ata 1942- DLB-117; CDWLB-3

Aiken, Conrad
    1889-1973 . . . . DLB-9, 45, 102; CDALB-5

Aiken, Joan 1924- DLB-161

Aikin, Lucy 1781-1864 . . . . DLB-144, 163

Ainsworth, William Harrison 1805-1882 . . DLB-21

Aistis, Jonas 1904-1973 . . . . . DLB-220; CDWLB-4

Aitken, George A. 1860-1917. . . . . DLB-149

Aitken, Robert [publishing house] DLB-49

Akenside, Mark 1721-1770. . . . . DLB-109

Akins, Zoë 1886-1958 . . . . DLB-26

Aksahov, Sergei Timofeevich
          1791-1859 . . . . DLB-198

Akutagawa, Ryūsuke 1892-1927 . . . . . . DLB-180

Alabaster, William 1568-1640 . . . . DLB-132

Alain de Lille circa 1116-1202/1203 . . . . . DLB-208

Alain-Fournier 1886-1914 . . . . DLB-65

Alanus de Insulis (see Alain de Lille)

Alarcón, Francisco X. 1954- DLB-122

Alarcón, Justo S. 1930- DLB-209

Alba, Nanina 1915-1968 . . . . DLB-41

Albee, Edward 1928- . . . DLB-7, 266; CDALB-1

Albert the Great circa 1200-1280 . . . . . . DLB-115

Albert, Octavia 1853-ca. 1889 . . . . DLB-221

Alberti, Rafael 1902-1999 . . . . DLB-108

Albertinus, Aegidius circa 1560-1620 . . . . DLB-164

Alcaeus born circa 620 B.C. DLB-176

Alcott, Bronson 1799-1888 . . . . DLB-1, 223

Alcott, Louisa May 1832-1888
      . . . DLB-1, 42, 79, 223, 239; DS-14; CDALB-3

Alcott, William Andrus 1798-1859 . . . . DLB-1, 243

Alcuin circa 732-804 . . . . DLB-148

Alden, Beardsley and Company DLB-49

Alden, Henry Mills 1836-1919 . . . . DLB-79

Alden, Isabella 1841-1930 . . . . DLB-42

Alden, John B. [publishing house] DLB-49

Aldington, Richard
      1892-1962 . . . . .DLB-20, 36, 100, 149

Aldis, Dorothy 1896-1966 . . . . DLB-22

Aldis, H. G. 1863-1919 . . . . DLB-184

Aldiss, Brian W. 1925- DLB-14, 261

Aldrich, Thomas Bailey
      1836-1907 . . . . .DLB-42, 71, 74, 79

Alegría, Ciro 1909-1967 . . . . DLB-113

Alegría, Claribel 1924- DLB-145

Aleixandre, Vicente 1898-1984 . . . . DLB-108

Aleksandravičius, Jonas (see Aistis, Jonas)

Aleksandrov, Aleksandr Andreevich
      (see Durova, Nadezhda Andreevna)

Aleramo, Sibilla 1876-1960 . . . . DLB-114, 264

Alexander, Cecil Frances 1818-1895 . . . . . DLB-199

Alexander, Charles 1868-1923 . . . . DLB-91

Alexander, Charles Wesley
      [publishing house] DLB-49

Alexander, James 1691-1756 . . . . DLB-24

Alexander, Lloyd 1924- DLB-52

Alexander, Sir William, Earl of Stirling
      1577?-1640 . . . . DLB-121

Alexie, Sherman 1966- DLB-175, 206

Alexis, Willibald 1798-1871 . . . . DLB-133

Alfred, King 849-899 . . . . DLB-146

Alger, Horatio, Jr. 1832-1899 . . . . DLB-42

Algonquin Books of Chapel Hill DLB-46

Algren, Nelson
      1909-1981 . . . . .DLB-9; Y-81, Y-82; CDALB-1

Nelson Algren: An International
      Symposium Y-00

"All the Faults of Youth and Inexperience":
      A Reader's Report on
      Thomas Wolfe's *O Lost* Y-01

Allan, Andrew 1907-1974 . . . . DLB-88

Allan, Ted 1916-1995 . . . . DLB-68

Allbeury, Ted 1917- DLB-87

Alldritt, Keith 1935- DLB-14

Allen, Ethan 1738-1789 . . . . DLB-31

Allen, Frederick Lewis 1890-1954 . . . . . . DLB-137

Allen, Gay Wilson 1903-1995 . . . . .DLB-103; Y-95

Allen, George 1808-1876 . . . . DLB-59

Allen, George [publishing house] DLB-106

Allen, George, and Unwin Limited DLB-112

Allen, Grant 1848-1899 . . . . .DLB-70, 92, 178

Allen, Henry W. 1912- Y-85

Allen, Hervey 1889-1949 . . . . DLB-9, 45

Allen, James 1739-1808 . . . . DLB-31

Allen, James Lane 1849-1925 . . . . DLB-71

Allen, Jay Presson 1922- DLB-26

Allen, John, and Company DLB-49

Allen, Paula Gunn 1939- DLB-175

Allen, Samuel W. 1917- DLB-41

Allen, Woody 1935- DLB-44

Allende, Isabel 1942- DLB-145; CDWLB-3

Alline, Henry 1748-1784 . . . . DLB-99

Allingham, Margery 1904-1966 . . . . DLB-77

Allingham, William 1824-1889 . . . . DLB-35

Allison, W. L. [publishing house] DLB-49

The *Alliterative Morte Arthure and the Stanzaic
      Morte Arthur* circa 1350-1400 . . . . DLB-146

Allott, Kenneth 1912-1973 . . . . DLB-20

Allston, Washington 1779-1843 . . . . . . DLB-1, 235

Almon, John [publishing house] DLB-154

Alonzo, Dámaso 1898-1990 . . . . DLB-108

Alsop, George 1636-post 1673 . . . . DLB-24

Alsop, Richard 1761-1815 . . . . DLB-37

Altemus, Henry, and Company DLB-49

Altenberg, Peter 1885-1919 . . . . DLB-81

Althusser, Louis 1918-1990 . . . . DLB-242

Altolaguirre, Manuel 1905-1959 . . . . DLB-108

Aluko, T. M. 1918- DLB-117

Alurista 1947- DLB-82

Alvarez, A. 1929- DLB-14, 40

Alvaro, Corrado 1895-1956 . . . . DLB-264

Alver, Betti 1906-1989 . . . . . DLB-220; CDWLB-4

Amadi, Elechi 1934- DLB-117

Amado, Jorge 1912- DLB-113

Ambler, Eric 1909-1998 . . . . DLB-77

American Conservatory Theatre DLB-7

American Fiction and the 1930s DLB-9

American Humor: A Historical Survey
      East and Northeast
      South and Southwest
      Midwest
      West DLB-11

The American Library in Paris Y-93

American News Company DLB-49

The American Poets' Corner: The First
      Three Years (1983-1986) Y-86

American Publishing Company DLB-49

American Stationers' Company DLB-49

American Sunday-School Union DLB-49

American Temperance Union DLB-49

American Tract Society DLB-49

The American Trust for the
      British Library Y-96

The American Writers Congress
      (9-12 October 1981) Y-81

The American Writers Congress: A Report
      on Continuing Business Y-81

Ames, Fisher 1758-1808 . . . . DLB-37

Ames, Mary Clemmer 1831-1884 . . . . DLB-23

Amiel, Henri-Frédéric 1821-1881 . . . . . . .DLB-217

Amini, Johari M. 1935- DLB-41

Amis, Kingsley 1922-1995
      . . . . . . DLB-15, 27, 100, 139, Y-96; CDBLB-7

Amis, Martin 1949- DLB-194

Ammianus Marcellinus
      circa A.D. 330-A.D. 395 . . . . DLB-211

Ammons, A. R. 1926- DLB-5, 165

Amory, Thomas 1691?-1788 . . . . DLB-39

Anania, Michael 1939- DLB-193

Anaya, Rudolfo A. 1937- DLB-82, 206

Ancrene Riwle circa 1200-1225 . . . . DLB-146

Andersch, Alfred 1914-1980 . . . . DLB-69

Andersen, Benny 1929- DLB-214

Anderson, Alexander 1775-1870 . . . . DLB-188

Anderson, David 1929- DLB-241

Anderson, Frederick Irving 1877-1947 . . . DLB-202

Anderson, Margaret 1886-1973 . . . . DLB-4, 91

Anderson, Maxwell 1888-1959 . . . . . . .DLB-7, 228

Anderson, Patrick 1915-1979 . . . . DLB-68

Anderson, Paul Y. 1893-1938 . . . . DLB-29

Anderson, Poul 1926- DLB-8

Anderson, Robert 1750-1830 . . . . DLB-142

Anderson, Robert 1917- DLB-7

Anderson, Sherwood
      1876-1941 . . . . . DLB-4, 9, 86; DS-1; CDALB-4

Andreae, Johann Valentin 1586-1654 . . . . DLB-164

Andreas Capellanus
      flourished circa 1185 . . . . DLB-208

Andreas-Salomé, Lou 1861-1937 . . . . DLB-66

Andres, Stefan 1906-1970 . . . . DLB-69

Andreu, Blanca 1959- DLB-134

Andrewes, Lancelot 1555-1626 . . . . .DLB-151, 172

Andrews, Charles M. 1863-1943 . . . . .DLB-17

Andrews, Miles Peter ?-1814 . . . . DLB-89

Andrews, Stephen Pearl 1812-1886 . . . . . DLB-250

Andrian, Leopold von 1875-1951 . . . . DLB-81

Andrić, Ivo 1892-1975 . . . . . .DLB-147; CDWLB-4

Andrieux, Louis (see Aragon, Louis)

Andrus, Silas, and Son DLB-49

Andrzejewski, Jerzy 1909-1983 . . . . DLB-215

Angell, James Burrill 1829-1916. . . . . .DLB-64

Angell, Roger 1920- DLB-171, 185

Angelou, Maya 1928- DLB-38; CDALB-7

Anger, Jane flourished 1589. . . . . .DLB-136

Angers, Félicité (see Conan, Laure)

Anglo-Norman Literature in the Development
    of Middle English Literature DLB-146

The Anglo-Saxon Chronicle circa 890-1154 . . .DLB-146

The "Angry Young Men" DLB-15

Angus and Robertson (UK) Limited DLB-112

Anhalt, Edward 1914-2000 . . . . .DLB-26

Anners, Henry F. [publishing house] DLB-49

Annolied between 1077 and 1081. . . . . . . .DLB-148

Annual Awards for *Dictionary of Literary
    Biography* Editors
    and Contributors. Y-98, Y-99, Y-00, Y-01

Anscombe, G. E. M. 1919-2001. . . . . . . .DLB-262

Anselm of Canterbury 1033-1109 . . . . . .DLB-115

Anstey, F. 1856-1934 . . . . DLB-141, 178

Anthony, Michael 1932- DLB-125

Anthony, Piers 1934- DLB-8

Anthony, Susanna 1726-1791. . . . . .DLB-200

Antin, David 1932- DLB-169

Antin, Mary 1881-1949 . . . . DLB-221; Y-84

Anton Ulrich, Duke of Brunswick-Lüneburg
    1633-1714 .DLB-168

Antschel, Paul (see Celan, Paul)

Anyidoho, Kofi 1947- DLB-157

Anzaldúa, Gloria 1942- DLB-122

Anzengruber, Ludwig 1839-1889 . . . . . . .DLB-129

Apess, William 1798-1839 . . . . DLB-175, 243

Apodaca, Rudy S. 1939- DLB-82

Apollinaire, Guillaume 1880-1918 . . . . . .DLB-258

Apollonius Rhodius third century B.C. DLB-176

Apple, Max 1941- DLB-130

Appleton, D., and Company DLB-49

Appleton-Century-Crofts. DLB-46

Applewhite, James 1935- DLB-105

Applewood Books DLB-46

April, Jean-Pierre 1948- DLB-251

Apuleius circa A.D. 125-post A.D. 164
    . . . . .DLB-211; CDWLB-1

Aquin, Hubert 1929-1977 . . . . .DLB-53

Aquinas, Thomas 1224 or 1225-1274 . . . .DLB-115

Aragon, Louis 1897-1982. . . . . .DLB-72, 258

Aralica, Ivan 1930- DLB-181

Aratus of Soli
    circa 315 B.C.-circa 239 B.C. DLB-176

Arbasino, Alberto 1930- DLB-196

Arbor House Publishing Company DLB-46

Arbuthnot, John 1667-1735 . . . . .DLB-101

Arcadia House. .DLB-46

Arce, Julio G. (see Ulica, Jorge)

Archer, William 1856-1924 . . . . .DLB-10

Archilochhus
    mid seventh century B.C.E. DLB-176

The Archpoet circa 1130?-? DLB-148

Archpriest Avvakum (Petrovich)
    1620?-1682 . . . . .DLB-150

Arden, John 1930- DLB-13, 245

Arden of Faversham DLB-62

Ardis Publishers. Y-89

Ardizzone, Edward 1900-1979 . . . . .DLB-160

Arellano, Juan Estevan 1947- DLB-122

The Arena Publishing Company. DLB-49

Arena Stage DLB-7

Arenas, Reinaldo 1943-1990 . . . . .DLB-145

Arendt, Hannah 1906-1975 . . . . .DLB-242

Arensberg, Ann 1937- Y-82

Arghezi, Tudor 1880-1967. . .DLB-220; CDWLB-4

Arguedas, José María 1911-1969 . . . . . . .DLB-113

Argueta, Manilio 1936- DLB-145

Arias, Ron 1941- DLB-82

Arishima, Takeo 1878-1923. . . . . .DLB-180

Aristophanes circa 446 B.C.-circa 386 B.C.
    . . . . DLB-176; CDWLB-1

Aristotle 384 B.C.-322 B.C.
    . . . . DLB-176; CDWLB-1

Ariyoshi Sawako 1931-1984 . . . . .DLB-182

Arland, Marcel 1899-1986. . . . . .DLB-72

Arlen, Michael 1895-1956 . . . . . . DLB-36, 77, 162

Armah, Ayi Kwei 1939- . . . DLB-117; CDWLB-3

Armantrout, Rae 1947- DLB-193

Der arme Hartmann ?-after 1150. . . . . . . .DLB-148

Armed Services Editions DLB-46

Armitage, G. E. (Robert Edric) 1956- . .DLB-267

Armstrong, Martin Donisthorpe
    1882-1974 . . . . .DLB-197

Armstrong, Richard 1903- DLB-160

Armstrong, Terence Ian Fytton (see Gawsworth, John)

Arndt, Ernst Moritz 1769-1860 . . . . .DLB-90

Arnim, Achim von 1781-1831 . . . . .DLB-90

Arnim, Bettina von 1785-1859. . . . . .DLB-90

Arnim, Elizabeth von (Countess Mary
    Annette Beauchamp Russell)
    1866-1941 . . . . .DLB-197

Arno Press. DLB-46

Arnold, Edward [publishing house] DLB-112

Arnold, Edwin 1832-1904 . . . . .DLB-35

Arnold, Edwin L. 1857-1935 . . . . .DLB-178

Arnold, Matthew
    1822-1888 . . . . .DLB-32, 57; CDBLB-4

Preface to *Poems* (1853) DLB-32

Arnold, Thomas 1795-1842. . . . . .DLB-55

Arnott, Peter 1962- DLB-233

Arnow, Harriette Simpson 1908-1986 . . . . .DLB-6

Arp, Bill (see Smith, Charles Henry)

Arpino, Giovanni 1927-1987 . . . . .DLB-177

Arreola, Juan José 1918- DLB-113

Arrian circa 89-circa 155 . . . . .DLB-176

Arrowsmith, J. W. [publishing house] DLB-106

The Art and Mystery of Publishing:
    Interviews Y-97

Artaud, Antonin 1896-1948. . . . . .DLB-258

Arthur, Timothy Shay
    1809-1885 . . . . DLB-3, 42, 79, 250; DS-13

The Arthurian Tradition and
    Its European Context DLB-138

Artmann, H. C. 1921-2000 . . . . .DLB-85

Arvin, Newton 1900-1963 . . . . .DLB-103

Asch, Nathan 1902-1964. . . . . .DLB-4, 28

Ascham, Roger 1515 or 1516-1568 . . . . .DLB-236

Ash, John 1948- DLB-40

Ashbery, John 1927- DLB-5, 165; Y-81

Ashbridge, Elizabeth 1713-1755 . . . . .DLB-200

Ashburnham, Bertram Lord
    1797-1878 . . . . .DLB-184

Ashendene Press DLB-112

Asher, Sandy 1942- Y-83

Ashton, Winifred (see Dane, Clemence)

Asimov, Isaac 1920-1992. . . . . DLB-8; Y-92

Askew, Anne circa 1521-1546 . . . . .DLB-136

Aspazija 1865-1943 . . . . .DLB-220; CDWLB-4

Asselin, Olivar 1874-1937 . . . . .DLB-92

The Association of American Publishers Y-99

The Association for Documentary Editing . . . Y-00

Astell, Mary 1666-1731 . . . . .DLB-252

Astley, William (see Warung, Price)

Asturias, Miguel Angel
    1899-1974 . . . . DLB-113; CDWLB-3

At Home with Albert Erskine Y-00

Atheneum Publishers. DLB-46

Atherton, Gertrude 1857-1948. . . . . DLB-9, 78, 186

Athlone Press. .DLB-112

Atkins, Josiah circa 1755-1781 . . . . .DLB-31

Atkins, Russell 1926- DLB-41

Atkinson, Kate 1951- DLB-267

Atkinson, Louisa 1834-1872 . . . . .DLB-230

The Atlantic Monthly Press. DLB-46

Attaway, William 1911-1986 . . . . .DLB-76

Atwood, Margaret 1939- DLB-53, 251

Aubert, Alvin 1930- DLB-41

Aubert de Gaspé, Phillipe-Ignace-François
    1814-1841 .DLB-99

Aubert de Gaspé, Phillipe-Joseph
    1786-1871 .DLB-99

Aubin, Napoléon 1812-1890 . . . . .DLB-99

Aubin, Penelope
    1685-circa 1731 . . . . .DLB-39

Preface to *The Life of Charlotta
    du Pont* (1723) DLB-39

Aubrey-Fletcher, Henry Lancelot (see Wade, Henry)

Auchincloss, Louis 1917- DLB-2, 244; Y-80

Auden, W. H. 1907-1973 . . .DLB-10, 20; CDBLB-6

Audio Art in America: A Personal Memoir. . . Y-85

Audubon, John James 1785-1851. . . . . . .DLB-248

Audubon, John Woodhouse
    1812-1862 . . . . .DLB-183

Auerbach, Berthold 1812-1882 . . . . .DLB-133

Auernheimer, Raoul 1876-1948 . . . . DLB-81

Augier, Emile 1820-1889 . . . . DLB-192

Augustine 354-430 . . . . DLB-115

Responses to Ken Auletta Y-97

Aulus Cellius
  circa A.D. 125-circa A.D. 180? DLB-211

Austen, Jane
  1775-1817 . . . . DLB-116; CDBLB-3

Auster, Paul 1947- DLB-227

Austin, Alfred 1835-1913 . . . . DLB-35

Austin, J. L. 1911-1960 . . . . DLB-262

Austin, Jane Goodwin 1831-1894 . . . . . . DLB-202

Austin, John 1790-1859 . . . . DLB-262

Austin, Mary 1868-1934 . . . . . DLB-9, 78, 206, 221

Austin, William 1778-1841 . . . . DLB-74

Australie (Emily Manning)
  1845-1890 . . . . DLB-230

Author-Printers, 1476–1599 . . . . DLB-167

Author Websites Y-97

Authors and Newspapers Association DLB-46

Authors' Publishing Company DLB-49

Avallone, Michael 1924-1999 . . . . Y-99

Avalon Books DLB-46

Avancini, Nicolaus 1611-1686 . . . . DLB-164

Avendaño, Fausto 1941- DLB-82

Averroëó 1126-1198 . . . . DLB-115

Avery, Gillian 1926- DLB-161

Avicenna 980-1037 . . . . DLB-115

Avison, Margaret 1918- DLB-53

Avon Books DLB-46

Avyžius, Jonas 1922-1999 . . . . DLB-220

Awdry, Wilbert Vere 1911-1997 . . . . DLB-160

Awoonor, Kofi 1935- DLB-117

Ayckbourn, Alan 1939- DLB-13, 245

Ayer, A. J. 1910-1989 . . . . DLB-262

Aymé, Marcel 1902-1967 . . . . DLB-72

Aytoun, Sir Robert 1570-1638 . . . . DLB-121

Aytoun, William Edmondstoune
  1813-1865 . . . . DLB-32, 159

B

B. V. (see Thomson, James)

Babbitt, Irving 1865-1933 . . . . DLB-63

Babbitt, Natalie 1932- DLB-52

Babcock, John [publishing house] DLB-49

Babits, Mihály 1883-1941 . . . DLB-215; CDWLB-4

Babrius circa 150-200 . . . . DLB-176

Baca, Jimmy Santiago 1952- DLB-122

Bacchelli, Riccardo 1891-1985 . . . . DLB-264

Bache, Benjamin Franklin 1769-1798 . . . . . DLB-43

Bacheller, Irving 1859-1950 . . . . DLB-202

Bachmann, Ingeborg 1926-1973 . . . . DLB-85

Bačinskaitė-Bučienė, Salomėja (see Nėris, Salomėja)

Bacon, Delia 1811-1859 . . . . DLB-1, 243

Bacon, Francis
  1561-1626 . . . . DLB-151, 236, 252; CDBLB-1

Bacon, Sir Nicholas circa 1510-1579 . . . . . DLB-132

Bacon, Roger circa 1214/1220-1292 . . . . . DLB-115

Bacon, Thomas circa 1700-1768 . . . . DLB-31

Bacovia, George
  1881-1957 . . . . DLB-220; CDWLB-4

Badger, Richard G., and Company DLB-49

Bagaduce Music Lending Library Y-00

Bage, Robert 1728-1801 . . . . DLB-39

Bagehot, Walter 1826-1877 . . . . DLB-55

Bagley, Desmond 1923-1983 . . . . DLB-87

Bagley, Sarah G. 1806-1848 . . . . DLB-239

Bagnold, Enid 1889-1981 . . . DLB-13, 160, 191, 245

Bagryana, Elisaveta
  1893-1991 . . . . DLB-147; CDWLB-4

Bahr, Hermann 1863-1934 . . . . DLB-81, 118

Bailey, Abigail Abbot 1746-1815 . . . . DLB-200

Bailey, Alfred Goldsworthy 1905- DLB-68

Bailey, Francis [publishing house] DLB-49

Bailey, H. C. 1878-1961 . . . . DLB-77

Bailey, Jacob 1731-1808 . . . . DLB-99

Bailey, Paul 1937- DLB-14

Bailey, Philip James 1816-1902 . . . . DLB-32

Baillargeon, Pierre 1916-1967 . . . . DLB-88

Baillie, Hugh 1890-1966 . . . . DLB-29

Baillie, Joanna 1762-1851 . . . . DLB-93

Bailyn, Bernard 1922- DLB-17

Bainbridge, Beryl 1933- DLB-14, 231

Baird, Irene 1901-1981 . . . . DLB-68

Baker, Augustine 1575-1641 . . . . DLB-151

Baker, Carlos 1909-1987 . . . . DLB-103

Baker, David 1954- DLB-120

Baker, George Pierce 1866-1935 . . . . DLB-266

Baker, Herschel C. 1914-1990 . . . . DLB-111

Baker, Houston A., Jr. 1943- DLB-67

Baker, Nicholson 1957- DLB-227

Baker, Samuel White 1821-1893 . . . . DLB-166

Baker, Thomas 1656-1740 . . . . DLB-213

Baker, Walter H., Company
  ("Baker's Plays") DLB-49

The Baker and Taylor Company DLB-49

Bakhtin, Mikhail Mikhailovich
  1895-1975 . . . . DLB-242

Balaban, John 1943- DLB-120

Bald, Wambly 1902- DLB-4

Balde, Jacob 1604-1668 . . . . DLB-164

Balderston, John 1889-1954 . . . . DLB-26

Baldwin, James 1924-1987
  . . . . DLB-2, 7, 33, 249; Y-87; CDALB-1

Baldwin, Joseph Glover
  1815-1864 . . . . DLB-3, 11, 248

Baldwin, Louisa (Mrs. Alfred Baldwin)
  1845-1925 . . . . DLB-240

Baldwin, Richard and Anne
  [publishing house] DLB-170

Baldwin, William circa 1515-1563 . . . . . . DLB-132

Bale, John 1495-1563 . . . . DLB-132

Balestrini, Nanni 1935- DLB-128, 196

Balfour, Sir Andrew 1630-1694 . . . . DLB-213

Balfour, Arthur James 1848-1930 . . . . . . DLB-190

Balfour, Sir James 1600-1657 . . . . DLB-213

Ballantine Books DLB-46

Ballantyne, R. M. 1825-1894 . . . . DLB-163

Ballard, J. G. 1930- DLB-14, 207, 261

Ballard, Martha Moore 1735-1812 . . . . . . DLB-200

Ballerini, Luigi 1940- DLB-128

Ballou, Maturin Murray
  1820-1895 . . . . DLB-79, 189

Ballou, Robert O. [publishing house] DLB-46

Balzac, Honoré de 1799-1855 . . . . DLB-119

Bambara, Toni Cade
  1939- DLB-38, 218; CDALB-7

Bamford, Samuel 1788-1872 . . . . DLB-190

Bancroft, A. L., and Company DLB-49

Bancroft, George 1800-1891 . . . DLB-1, 30, 59, 243

Bancroft, Hubert Howe 1832-1918 . . . DLB-47, 140

Bandelier, Adolph F. 1840-1914 . . . . DLB-186

Bangs, John Kendrick 1862-1922 . . . . . . DLB-11, 79

Banim, John 1798-1842 . . . . DLB-116, 158, 159

Banim, Michael 1796-1874 . . . . DLB-158, 159

Banks, Iain 1954- DLB-194, 261

Banks, John circa 1653-1706 . . . . DLB-80

Banks, Russell 1940- DLB-130

Bannerman, Helen 1862-1946 . . . . DLB-141

Bantam Books DLB-46

Banti, Anna 1895-1985 . . . . DLB-177

Banville, John 1945- DLB-14

Banville, Théodore de 1823-1891 . . . . . . DLB-217

Baraka, Amiri
  1934- DLB-5, 7, 16, 38; DS-8; CDALB-1

Barańczak, Stanisław 1946- DLB-232

Baratynsky, Evgenii Abramovich
  1800-1844 . . . . DLB-205

Barbauld, Anna Laetitia
  1743-1825 . . . . DLB-107, 109, 142, 158

Barbeau, Marius 1883-1969 . . . . DLB-92

Barber, John Warner 1798-1885 . . . . DLB-30

Bàrberi Squarotti, Giorgio 1929- DLB-128

Barbey d'Aurevilly, Jules-Amédée
  1808-1889 . . . . DLB-119

Barbier, Auguste 1805-1882 . . . . DLB-217

Barbilian, Dan (see Barbu, Ion)

Barbour, John circa 1316-1395 . . . . DLB-146

Barbour, Ralph Henry 1870-1944 . . . . . . DLB-22

Barbu, Ion 1895-1961 . . . . . . DLB-220; CDWLB-4

Barbusse, Henri 1873-1935 . . . . DLB-65

Barclay, Alexander circa 1475-1552 . . . . . DLB-132

Barclay, E. E., and Company DLB-49

Bardeen, C. W. [publishing house] DLB-49

Barham, Richard Harris 1788-1845 . . . . . DLB-159

Barich, Bill 1943- DLB-185

Baring, Maurice 1874-1945 . . . . DLB-34

Baring-Gould, Sabine
  1834-1924 . . . . DLB-156, 190

Barker, A. L. 1918- DLB-14, 139

Barker, Arthur, Limited..............DLB-112

Barker, Clive 1952- DLB-261

Barker, George 1913-1991...............DLB-20

Barker, Harley Granville 1877-1946......DLB-10

Barker, Howard 1946- DLB-13, 233

Barker, James Nelson 1784-1858 ....DLB-37

Barker, Jane 1652-1727 ....DLB-39, 131

Barker, Lady Mary Anne 1831-1911.....DLB-166

Barker, William circa 1520-after 1576 ....DLB-132

Barkov, Ivan Semenovich 1732-1768 .....DLB-150

Barks, Coleman 1937- DLB-5

Barlach, Ernst 1870-1938..........DLB-56, 118

Barlow, Joel 1754-1812...............DLB-37

The Prospect of Peace (1778)...............DLB-37

Barnard, John 1681-1770 ....DLB-24

Barnard, Marjorie 1879-1987 and Eldershaw, Flora
(M. Barnard Eldershaw) 1897-1956...DLB-260

Barne, Kitty (Mary Catherine Barne)
1883-1957 ....DLB-160

Barnes, A. S., and Company DLB-49

Barnes, Barnabe 1571-1609 ....DLB-132

Barnes, Djuna 1892-1982..........DLB-4, 9, 45

Barnes, Jim 1933- DLB-175

Barnes, Julian 1946- DLB-194; Y-93

Julian Barnes Checklist Y-01

Barnes, Margaret Ayer 1886-1967.........DLB-9

Barnes, Peter 1931- DLB-13, 233

Barnes, William 1801-1886 ....DLB-32

Barnes and Noble Books DLB-46

Barnet, Miguel 1940- DLB-145

Barney, Natalie 1876-1972 ....DLB-4

Barnfield, Richard 1574-1627..........DLB-172

Baron, Richard W.,
Publishing Company...............DLB-46

Barr, Amelia Edith Huddleston
1831-1919 ....DLB-202, 221

Barr, Robert 1850-1912.............DLB-70, 92

Barral, Carlos 1928-1989.............DLB-134

Barrax, Gerald William 1933- DLB-41, 120

Barrès, Maurice 1862-1923 ....DLB-123

Barrett, Eaton Stannard 1786-1820 ......DLB-116

Barrie, J. M.
1860-1937 ......DLB-10, 141, 156; CDBLB-5

Barrie and Jenkins DLB-112

Barrio, Raymond 1921- DLB-82

Barrios, Gregg 1945- DLB-122

Barry, Philip 1896-1949......... DLB-7, 228

Barry, Robertine (see Françoise)

Barry, Sebastian 1955- DLB-245

Barse and Hopkins................DLB-46

Barstow, Stan 1928- DLB-14, 139

Barth, John 1930- DLB-2, 227

Barthelme, Donald
1931-1989 .... DLB-2, 234; Y-80, Y-89

Barthelme, Frederick 1943- DLB-244; Y-85

Bartholomew, Frank 1898-1985 ....DLB-127

Bartlett, John 1820-1905 ....DLB-1, 235

Bartol, Cyrus Augustus 1813-1900 ....DLB-1, 235

Barton, Bernard 1784-1849 ....DLB-96

Barton, John ca. 1610-1675 ....DLB-236

Barton, Thomas Pennant 1803-1869.....DLB-140

Bartram, John 1699-1777 ....DLB-31

Bartram, William 1739-1823 ....DLB-37

Basic Books DLB-46

Basille, Theodore (see Becon, Thomas)

Bass, Rick 1958- DLB-212

Bass, T. J. 1932- Y-81

Bassani, Giorgio 1916- DLB-128, 177

Basse, William circa 1583-1653.........DLB-121

Bassett, John Spencer 1867-1928 ....DLB-17

Bassler, Thomas Joseph (see Bass, T. J.)

Bate, Walter Jackson 1918-1999 .....DLB-67, 103

Bateman, Christopher
[publishing house]...............DLB-170

Bateman, Stephen circa 1510-1584 ......DLB-136

Bates, H. E. 1905-1974...........DLB-162, 191

Bates, Katharine Lee 1859-1929 ....DLB-71

Batiushkov, Konstantin Nikolaevich
1787-1855......................DLB-205

Batsford, B. T. [publishing house]......DLB-106

Battiscombe, Georgina 1905- DLB-155

The Battle of Maldon circa 1000 ....DLB-146

Baudelaire, Charles 1821-1867 ....DLB-217

Bauer, Bruno 1809-1882 ....DLB-133

Bauer, Wolfgang 1941- DLB-124

Baum, L. Frank 1856-1919 ....DLB-22

Baum, Vicki 1888-1960...............DLB-85

Baumbach, Jonathan 1933- Y-80

Bausch, Richard 1945- DLB-130

Bausch, Robert 1945- DLB-218

Bawden, Nina 1925- DLB-14, 161, 207

Bax, Clifford 1886-1962 ....DLB-10, 100

Baxter, Charles 1947- DLB-130

Bayer, Eleanor (see Perry, Eleanor)

Bayer, Konrad 1932-1964 ....DLB-85

Bayley, Barrington J. 1937- DLB-261

Baynes, Pauline 1922- DLB-160

Baynton, Barbara 1857-1929 ....DLB-230

Bazin, Hervé 1911-1996..............DLB-83

Beach, Sylvia 1887-1962...........DLB-4; DS-15

Beacon Press DLB-49

Beadle and Adams DLB-49

Beagle, Peter S. 1939- Y-80

Beal, M. F. 1937- Y-81

Beale, Howard K. 1899-1959...........DLB-17

Beard, Charles A. 1874-1948 ....DLB-17

A Beat Chronology: The First Twenty-five
Years, 1944-1969.................DLB-16

Periodicals of the Beat Generation........DLB-16

The Beats in New York City DLB-237

The Beats in the West DLB-237

Beattie, Ann 1947- DLB-218; Y-82

Beattie, James 1735-1803 ....DLB-109

Beatty, Chester 1875-1968..........DLB-201

Beauchemin, Nérée 1850-1931 ....DLB-92

Beauchemin, Yves 1941- DLB-60

Beaugrand, Honoré 1848-1906 ....DLB-99

Beaulieu, Victor-Lévy 1945- DLB-53

Beaumont, Francis circa 1584-1616
and Fletcher, John 1579-1625
.....................DLB-58; CDBLB-1

Beaumont, Sir John 1583?-1627.........DLB-121

Beaumont, Joseph 1616-1699 ....DLB-126

Beauvoir, Simone de 1908-1986 .... DLB-72; Y-86

Becher, Ulrich 1910- DLB-69

Becker, Carl 1873-1945 ....DLB-17

Becker, Jurek 1937-1997...............DLB-75

Becker, Jurgen 1932- DLB-75

Beckett, Samuel 1906-1989
.........DLB-13, 15, 233; Y-90; CDBLB-7

Beckford, William 1760-1844 ....DLB-39

Beckham, Barry 1944- DLB-33

Becon, Thomas circa 1512-1567 ....DLB-136

Becque, Henry 1837-1899 ....DLB-192

Beddoes, Thomas 1760-1808...........DLB-158

Beddoes, Thomas Lovell 1803-1849......DLB-96

Bede circa 673-735....................DLB-146

Bedford-Jones, H. 1887-1949 ....DLB-251

Beecher, Catharine Esther 1800-1878 ..DLB-1, 243

Beecher, Henry Ward 1813-1887 ..DLB-3, 43, 250

Beer, George L. 1872-1920 ....DLB-47

Beer, Johann 1655-1700 ....DLB-168

Beer, Patricia 1919-1999 ....DLB-40

Beerbohm, Max 1872-1956 ....DLB-34, 100

Beer-Hofmann, Richard 1866-1945.......DLB-81

Beers, Henry A. 1847-1926 ....DLB-71

Beeton, S. O. [publishing house] DLB-106

Bégon, Elisabeth 1696-1755 ....DLB-99

Behan, Brendan
1923-1964 ....DLB-13, 233; CDBLB-7

Behn, Aphra 1640?-1689........DLB-39, 80, 131

Behn, Harry 1898-1973 ....DLB-61

Behrman, S. N. 1893-1973 .... DLB-7, 44

Belaney, Archibald Stansfeld (see Grey Owl)

Belasco, David 1853-1931 ....DLB-7

Belford, Clarke and Company DLB-49

Belinksy, Vissarion Grigor'evich
1811-1848 ....DLB-198

Belitt, Ben 1911- DLB-5

Belknap, Jeremy 1744-1798 ....DLB-30, 37

Bell, Adrian 1901-1980 ....DLB-191

Bell, Clive 1881-1964...............DS-10

Bell, Daniel 1919- DLB-246

Bell, George, and Sons. DLB-106

Bell, Gertrude Margaret Lowthian
1868-1926 ....DLB-174

Bell, James Madison 1826-1902 .... DLB-50

Bell, Madison Smartt 1957- DLB-218

Bell, Marvin 1937- DLB-5

Bell, Millicent 1919- DLB-111

Bell, Quentin 1910-1996............. DLB-155

Bell, Robert [publishing house]......... DLB-49

Bell, Vanessa 1879-1961 ....DS-10

Bellamy, Edward 1850-1898............ DLB-12

Bellamy, John [publishing house] DLB-170

Bellamy, Joseph 1719-1790 .... DLB-31

La Belle Assemblée 1806-1837 .... DLB-110

Bellezza, Dario 1944-1996 .... DLB-128

Belloc, Hilaire 1870-1953 .... DLB-19, 100, 141, 174

Belloc, Madame (see Parkes, Bessie Rayner)

Bellonci, Maria 1902-1986 .... DLB-196

Bellow, Saul
1915- DLB-2, 28; Y-82; DS-3; CDALB-1

Belmont Productions DLB-46

Bels, Alberts 1938- DLB-232

Belševica, Vizma 1931- ... DLB-232; CDWLB-4

Bemelmans, Ludwig 1898-1962 .... DLB-22

Bemis, Samuel Flagg 1891-1973 .... DLB-17

Bemrose, William [publishing house] DLB-106

Ben no Naishi 1228?-1271?............. DLB-203

Benchley, Robert 1889-1945............ DLB-11

Bencúr, Matej (see Kukučin, Martin)

Benedetti, Mario 1920- DLB-113

Benedict, Pinckney 1964- DLB-244

Benedict, Ruth 1887-1948............. DLB-246

Benedictus, David 1938- DLB-14

Benedikt, Michael 1935- DLB-5

Benediktov, Vladimir Grigor'evich
1807-1873 .... DLB-205

Benét, Stephen Vincent
1898-1943 .... DLB-4, 48, 102, 249

Benét, William Rose 1886-1950 .... DLB-45

Benford, Gregory 1941- Y-82

Benjamin, Park 1809-1864 .... DLB-3, 59, 73, 250

Benjamin, S. G. W. 1837-1914 .... DLB-189

Benjamin, Walter 1892-1940 .... DLB-242

Benlowes, Edward 1602-1676.......... DLB-126

Benn Brothers Limited DLB-106

Benn, Gottfried 1886-1956 .... DLB-56

Bennett, Arnold
1867-1931.... DLB-10, 34, 98, 135; CDBLB-5

Bennett, Charles 1899-1995 .... DLB-44

Bennett, Emerson 1822-1905 .... DLB-202

Bennett, Gwendolyn 1902- DLB-51

Bennett, Hal 1930- DLB-33

Bennett, James Gordon 1795-1872 .... DLB-43

Bennett, James Gordon, Jr. 1841-1918 .... DLB-23

Bennett, John 1865-1956 .... DLB-42

Bennett, Louise 1919- DLB-117; CDWLB-3

Benni, Stefano 1947- DLB-196

Benoit, Jacques 1941- DLB-60

Benson, A. C. 1862-1925 .... DLB-98

Benson, E. F. 1867-1940 .... DLB-135, 153

Benson, Jackson J. 1930- DLB-111

Benson, Robert Hugh 1871-1914 .... DLB-153

Benson, Stella 1892-1933 .... DLB-36, 162

Bent, James Theodore 1852-1897.......DLB-174

Bent, Mabel Virginia Anna ?-?.........DLB-174

Bentham, Jeremy 1748-1832.... DLB-107, 158, 252

Bentley, E. C. 1875-1956 .... DLB-70

Bentley, Phyllis 1894-1977 .... DLB-191

Bentley, Richard 1662-1742 .... DLB-252

Bentley, Richard [publishing house] DLB-106

Benton, Robert 1932-   and Newman,
David 1937- DLB-44

Benziger Brothers DLB-49

Beowulf circa 900-1000 or 790-825
.... DLB-146; CDBLB-1

Berent, Wacław 1873-1940........... DLB-215

Beresford, Anne 1929- DLB-40

Beresford, John Davys
1873-1947............... DLB-162, 178, 197

"Experiment in the Novel" (1929) DLB-36

Beresford-Howe, Constance 1922- DLB-88

Berford, R. G., Company.............. DLB-49

Berg, Stephen 1934- DLB-5

Bergengruen, Werner 1892-1964 .... DLB-56

Berger, John 1926- DLB-14, 207

Berger, Meyer 1898-1959............. DLB-29

Berger, Thomas 1924- DLB-2; Y-80

Bergman, Hjalmar 1883-1931......... DLB-259

Bergman, Ingmar 1918- DLB-257

Berkeley, Anthony 1893-1971 .... DLB-77

Berkeley, George 1685-1753.... DLB-31, 101, 252

The Berkley Publishing Corporation DLB-46

Berlin, Irving 1888-1989 .... DLB-265

Berlin, Lucia 1936- DLB-130

Berman, Marshall 1940- DLB-246

Bernal, Vicente J. 1888-1915 .... DLB-82

Bernanos, Georges 1888-1948 .... DLB-72

Bernard, Harry 1898-1979 .... DLB-92

Bernard, John 1756-1828 .... DLB-37

Bernard of Chartres circa 1060-1124? ... DLB-115

Bernard of Clairvaux 1090-1153 .... DLB-208

The Bernard Malamud Archive at the
Harry Ransom Humanities
Research Center.................... Y-00

Bernard Silvestris
flourished circa 1130-1160........ DLB-208

Bernari, Carlo 1909-1992............. DLB-177

Bernhard, Thomas
1931-1989 ....DLB-85, 124; CDWLB-2

Bernstein, Charles 1950- DLB-169

Berriault, Gina 1926-1999 .... DLB-130

Berrigan, Daniel 1921- DLB-5

Berrigan, Ted 1934-1983 .... DLB-5, 169

Berry, Wendell 1934- DLB-5, 6, 234

Berryman, John 1914-1972.... DLB-48; CDALB-1

Bersianik, Louky 1930- DLB-60

Berthelet, Thomas [publishing house] DLB-170

Berto, Giuseppe 1914-1978.............DLB-177

Bertolucci, Attilio 1911- DLB-128

Berton, Pierre 1920- DLB-68

Bertrand, Louis "Aloysius"
1807-1841.....................DLB-217

Besant, Sir Walter 1836-1901...... DLB-135, 190

Bessette, Gerard 1920- DLB-53

Bessie, Alvah 1904-1985............. DLB-26

Bester, Alfred 1913-1987 .... DLB-8

Besterman, Theodore 1904-1976 .... DLB-201

The Bestseller Lists: An Assessment........ Y-84

Bestuzhev, Aleksandr Aleksandrovich
(Marlinsky) 1797-1837 .... DLB-198

Bestuzhev, Nikolai Aleksandrovich
1791-1855..................... DLB-198

Betham-Edwards, Matilda Barbara (see Edwards,
Matilda Barbara Betham-)

Betjeman, John
1906-1984 .... DLB-20; Y-84; CDBLB-7

Betocchi, Carlo 1899-1986........... DLB-128

Bettarini, Mariella 1942- DLB-128

Betts, Doris 1932- DLB-218; Y-82

Beùkoviù, Matija 1939- DLB-181

Beveridge, Albert J. 1862-1927..........DLB-17

Beverley, Robert circa 1673-1722.... DLB-24, 30

Bevilacqua, Alberto 1934- DLB-196

Bevington, Louisa Sarah 1845-1895..... DLB-199

Beyle, Marie-Henri (see Stendhal)

Białoszewski, Miron 1922-1983 .... DLB-232

Bianco, Margery Williams 1881-1944 ... DLB-160

Bibaud, Adèle 1854-1941 .... DLB-92

Bibaud, Michel 1782-1857 .... DLB-99

Bibliographical and Textual Scholarship
Since World War II.................. Y-89

Bichsel, Peter 1935- DLB-75

Bickerstaff, Isaac John 1733-circa 1808.... DLB-89

Biddle, Drexel [publishing house]........ DLB-49

Bidermann, Jacob
1577 or 1578-1639 .... DLB-164

Bidwell, Walter Hilliard 1798-1881 ...... DLB-79

Bienek, Horst 1930- DLB-75

Bierbaum, Otto Julius 1865-1910 .... DLB-66

Bierce, Ambrose 1842-1914?
.......DLB-11, 12, 23, 71, 74, 186; CDALB-3

Bigelow, William F. 1879-1966.......... DLB-91

Biggle, Lloyd, Jr. 1923- DLB-8

Bigiaretti, Libero 1905-1993...........DLB-177

Bigland, Eileen 1898-1970 .... DLB-195

Biglow, Hosea (see Lowell, James Russell)

Bigongiari, Piero 1914- DLB-128

Bilenchi, Romano 1909-1989 .... DLB-264

Billinger, Richard 1890-1965 .... DLB-124

Billings, Hammatt 1818-1874 .... DLB-188

Billings, John Shaw 1898-1975 ....DLB-137

Billings, Josh (see Shaw, Henry Wheeler)

Binding, Rudolf G. 1867-1938 . . . . .DLB-66

Bingay, Malcolm 1884-1953 . . . . .DLB-241

Bingham, Caleb 1757-1817 . . . . .DLB-42

Bingham, George Barry 1906-1988 . . . . . .DLB-127

Bingham, Sallie 1937- DLB-234

Bingley, William [publishing house] DLB-154

Binyon, Laurence 1869-1943 . . . . .DLB-19

Biographia Brittanica DLB-142

Biographical Documents I Y-84

Biographical Documents II Y-85

Bioren, John [publishing house] DLB-49

Bioy Casares, Adolfo 1914- DLB-113

Bird, Isabella Lucy 1831-1904 . . . . .DLB-166

Bird, Robert Montgomery 1806-1854 . . . .DLB-202

Bird, William 1888-1963 . . . . .DLB-4; DS-15

Birken, Sigmund von 1626-1681 . . . . . . .DLB-164

Birney, Earle 1904-1995 . . . . .DLB-88

Birrell, Augustine 1850-1933 . . . . .DLB-98

Bisher, Furman 1918- DLB-171

Bishop, Elizabeth
1911-1979 . . . . .DLB-5, 169; CDALB-6

Bishop, John Peale 1892-1944 . . . . . .DLB-4, 9, 45

Bismarck, Otto von 1815-1898 . . . . .DLB-129

Bisset, Robert 1759-1805 . . . . .DLB-142

Bissett, Bill 1939- DLB-53

Bitzius, Albert (see Gotthelf, Jeremias)

Bjørnvig, Thorkild 1918- DLB-214

Black, David (D. M.) 1941- DLB-40

Black, Walter J. [publishing house] DLB-46

Black, Winifred 1863-1936 . . . . .DLB-25

The Black Aesthetic: Background DS-8

Black Theaters and Theater Organizations in
America, 1961-1982:
A Research List DLB-38

Black Theatre: A Forum [excerpts] DLB-38

Blackamore, Arthur 1679-? DLB-24, 39

Blackburn, Alexander L. 1929- Y-85

Blackburn, John 1923- DLB-261

Blackburn, Paul 1926-1971 . . . . .DLB-16; Y-81

Blackburn, Thomas 1916-1977 . . . . .DLB-27

Blackmore, R. D. 1825-1900 . . . . .DLB-18

Blackmore, Sir Richard 1654-1729 . . . . . .DLB-131

Blackmur, R. P. 1904-1965 . . . . .DLB-63

Blackwell, Basil, Publisher DLB-106

Blackwood, Algernon Henry
1869-1951 . . . . DLB-153, 156, 178

Blackwood, Caroline 1931-1996 . . . . .DLB-14, 207

Blackwood, William, and Sons, Ltd. DLB-154

Blackwood's Edinburgh Magazine
1817-1980 . . . . .DLB-110

Blades, William 1824-1890 . . . . .DLB-184

Blaga, Lucian 1895-1961 . . . . .DLB-220

Blagden, Isabella 1817?-1873 . . . . .DLB-199

Blair, Eric Arthur (see Orwell, George)

Blair, Francis Preston 1791-1876 . . . . .DLB-43

Blair, James circa 1655-1743 . . . . .DLB-24

Blair, John Durburrow 1759-1823 . . . . . . .DLB-37

Blais, Marie-Claire 1939- DLB-53

Blaise, Clark 1940- DLB-53

Blake, George 1893-1961 . . . . .DLB-191

Blake, Lillie Devereux 1833-1913 . . .DLB-202, 221

Blake, Nicholas 1904-1972 . . . . .DLB-77
(see Day Lewis, C.)

Blake, William
1757-1827 . . . . . .DLB-93, 154, 163; CDBLB-3

The Blakiston Company DLB-49

Blanchard, Stephen 1950- DLB-267

Blanchot, Maurice 1907- DLB-72

Blanckenburg, Christian Friedrich von
1744-1796 . . . . .DLB-94

Blandiana, Ana 1942- DLB-232; CDWLB-4

Blaser, Robin 1925- DLB-165

Blaumanis, Rudolfs 1863-1908 . . . . .DLB-220

Bleasdale, Alan 1946- DLB-245

Bledsoe, Albert Taylor 1809-1877 . . DLB-3, 79, 248

Bleecker, Ann Eliza 1752-1783 . . . . .DLB-200

Blelock and Company DLB-49

Blennerhassett, Margaret Agnew
1773-1842 . . . . .DLB-99

Bles, Geoffrey [publishing house] DLB-112

Blessington, Marguerite, Countess of
1789-1849 . . . . .DLB-166

Blew, Mary Clearman 1939- DLB-256

The Blickling Homilies circa 971 . . . . .DLB-146

Blind, Mathilde 1841-1896 . . . . .DLB-199

Blish, James 1921-1975. . . . . .DLB-8

Bliss, E., and E. White
[publishing house] DLB-49

Bliven, Bruce 1889-1977 . . . . .DLB-137

Blixen, Karen 1885-1962 . . . . .DLB-214

Bloch, Robert 1917-1994 . . . . .DLB-44

Block, Lawrence 1938- DLB-226

Block, Rudolph (see Lessing, Bruno)

Blondal, Patricia 1926-1959 . . . . .DLB-88

Bloom, Harold 1930- DLB-67

Bloomer, Amelia 1818-1894 . . . . .DLB-79

Bloomfield, Robert 1766-1823 . . . . .DLB-93

Bloomsbury Group DS-10

Blotner, Joseph 1923- DLB-111

Blount, Thomas 1618?-1679 . . . . .DLB-236

Bloy, Léon 1846-1917 . . . . .DLB-123

Blume, Judy 1938- DLB-52

Blunck, Hans Friedrich 1888-1961 . . . . . . .DLB-66

Blunden, Edmund 1896-1974 . . . DLB-20, 100, 155

Blundeville, Thomas 1522?-1606 . . . . . . .DLB-236

Blunt, Lady Anne Isabella Noel
1837-1917 . . . . .DLB-174

Blunt, Wilfrid Scawen 1840-1922 . . . . DLB-19, 174

Bly, Nellie (see Cochrane, Elizabeth)

Bly, Robert 1926- DLB-5

Blyton, Enid 1897-1968 . . . . .DLB-160

Boaden, James 1762-1839 . . . . .DLB-89

Boas, Frederick S. 1862-1957 . . . . .DLB-149

The Bobbs-Merrill Archive at the
Lilly Library, Indiana University Y-90

Boborykin, Petr Dmitrievich 1836-1921 . .DLB-238

The Bobbs-Merrill Company DLB-46

Bobrov, Semen Sergeevich
1763?-1810 . . . . .DLB-150

Bobrowski, Johannes 1917-1965 . . . . .DLB-75

The Elmer Holmes Bobst Awards in Arts
and Letters Y-87

Bodenheim, Maxwell 1892-1954 . . . . . . .DLB-9, 45

Bodenstedt, Friedrich von 1819-1892 . . . .DLB-129

Bodini, Vittorio 1914-1970. . . . . .DLB-128

Bodkin, M. McDonnell 1850-1933 . . . . . .DLB-70

Bodley, Sir Thomas 1545-1613 . . . . .DLB-213

Bodley Head DLB-112

Bodmer, Johann Jakob 1698-1783 . . . . . . .DLB-97

Bodmershof, Imma von 1895-1982 . . . . . .DLB-85

Bodsworth, Fred 1918- DLB-68

Boehm, Sydney 1908- DLB-44

Boer, Charles 1939- DLB-5

Boethius circa 480-circa 524 . . . . .DLB-115

Boethius of Dacia circa 1240-? DLB-115

Bogan, Louise 1897-1970 . . . . .DLB-45, 169

Bogarde, Dirk 1921- DLB-14

Bogdanovich, Ippolit Fedorovich
circa 1743-1803 . . . . .DLB-150

Bogue, David [publishing house] DLB-106

Böhme, Jakob 1575-1624 . . . . .DLB-164

Bohn, H. G. [publishing house] DLB-106

Bohse, August 1661-1742 . . . . .DLB-168

Boie, Heinrich Christian 1744-1806. . . . . . .DLB-94

Bok, Edward W. 1863-1930 . . . . . .DLB-91; DS-16

Boland, Eavan 1944- DLB-40

Boldrewood, Rolf (Thomas Alexander Browne)
1826?-1915 . . . . .DLB-230

Bolingbroke, Henry St. John, Viscount
1678-1751 . . . . .DLB-101

Böll, Heinrich
1917-1985 . . . . .DLB-69; Y-85; CDWLB-2

Bolling, Robert 1738-1775 . . . . .DLB-31

Bolotov, Andrei Timofeevich
1738-1833 . . . . .DLB-150

Bolt, Carol 1941- DLB-60

Bolt, Robert 1924-1995 . . . . .DLB-13, 233

Bolton, Herbert E. 1870-1953 . . . . .DLB-17

Bonaventura DLB-90

Bonaventure circa 1217-1274 . . . . .DLB-115

Bonaviri, Giuseppe 1924- DLB-177

Bond, Edward 1934- DLB-13

Bond, Michael 1926- DLB-161

Boni, Albert and Charles
[publishing house] DLB-46

Boni and Liveright. DLB-46

Bonnefoy, Yves 1923- DLB-258

Bonner, Marita 1899-1971 . . . . .DLB-228

Bonner, Paul Hyde 1893-1968 . . . . .DS-17

Bonner, Sherwood (see McDowell, Katharine
    Sherwood Bonner)

Robert Bonner's Sons DLB-49

Bonnin, Gertrude Simmons (see Zitkala-Ša)

Bonsanti, Alessandro 1904-1984 . . . . .DLB-177

Bontempelli, Massimo 1878-1960 . . . . . . DLB-264

Bontemps, Arna 1902-1973 . . . . DLB-48, 51

The Book Arts Press at the University
    of Virginia Y-96

The Book League of America DLB-46

Book Publishing Accounting: Some Basic
    Concepts Y-98

Book Reviewing in America: I Y-87

Book Reviewing in America: II Y-88

Book Reviewing in America: III. Y-89

Book Reviewing in America: IV Y-90

Book Reviewing in America: V Y-91

Book Reviewing in America: VI. Y-92

Book Reviewing in America: VII Y-93

Book Reviewing in America: VIII Y-94

Book Reviewing in America and the
    Literary Scene .Y-95

Book Reviewing and the
    Literary Scene Y-96, Y-97

Book Supply Company Y-93

The Book Trade History Group Y-93

The Book Trade and the Internet Y-00

The Booker Prize Y-96

Address by Anthony Thwaite,
    Chairman of the Booker Prize Judges
    Comments from Former Booker
    Prize Winners .Y-86

The Books of George V. Higgins:
    A Checklist of Editions and Printings Y-00

Boorde, Andrew circa 1490-1549 . . . . DLB-136

Boorstin, Daniel J. 1914- DLB-17

Booth, Franklin 1874-1948 . . . . DLB-188

Booth, Mary L. 1831-1889 . . . . DLB-79

Booth, Philip 1925- Y-82

Booth, Wayne C. 1921- DLB-67

Booth, William 1829-1912 . . . . DLB-190

Borchardt, Rudolf 1877-1945 . . . . DLB-66

Borchert, Wolfgang 1921-1947 . . . . . . DLB-69, 124

Borel, Pétrus 1809-1859 . . . . DLB-119

Borges, Jorge Luis
    1899-1986 . . . . . . .DLB-113; Y-86; CDWLB-3

Borgese, Giuseppe Antonio 1882-1952 . . . DLB-264

Börne, Ludwig 1786-1837 . . . . DLB-90

Bornstein, Miriam 1950- DLB-209

Borowski, Tadeusz
    1922-1951 . . . . DLB-215; CDWLB-4

Borrow, George 1803-1881 . . . . . DLB-21, 55, 166

Bosanquet, Bernard 1848-1923 . . . . DLB-262

Bosch, Juan 1909- DLB-145

Bosco, Henri 1888-1976 . . . . DLB-72

Bosco, Monique 1927- DLB-53

Bosman, Herman Charles 1905-1951 . . . . DLB-225

Bostic, Joe 1908-1988 . . . . DLB-241

Boston, Lucy M. 1892-1990 . . . . DLB-161

Boswell, James
    1740-1795 . . . . DLB-104, 142; CDBLB-2

Boswell, Robert 1953- DLB-234

Bote, Hermann
    circa 1460-circa 1520 . . . . .DLB-179

Botev, Khristo 1847-1876 . . . . DLB-147

Botta, Anne C. Lynch 1815-1891 . . . . . DLB-3, 250

Botto, Ján (see Krasko, Ivan)

Bottome, Phyllis 1882-1963 . . . . DLB-197

Bottomley, Gordon 1874-1948 . . . . DLB-10

Bottoms, David 1949- DLB-120; Y-83

Bottrall, Ronald 1906- DLB-20

Bouchardy, Joseph 1810-1870 . . . . DLB-192

Boucher, Anthony 1911-1968 . . . . DLB-8

Boucher, Jonathan 1738-1804 . . . . DLB-31

Boucher de Boucherville, George
    1814-1894 . . . . DLB-99

Boudreau, Daniel (see Coste, Donat)

Bourassa, Napoléon 1827-1916 . . . . DLB-99

Bourget, Paul 1852-1935 . . . . DLB-123

Bourinot, John George 1837-1902 . . . . DLB-99

Bourjaily, Vance 1922- DLB-2, 143

Bourne, Edward Gaylord
    1860-1908 . . . . DLB-47

Bourne, Randolph 1886-1918 . . . . DLB-63

Bousoño, Carlos 1923- DLB-108

Bousquet, Joë 1897-1950 . . . . DLB-72

Bova, Ben 1932- Y-81

Bovard, Oliver K. 1872-1945 . . . . DLB-25

Bove, Emmanuel 1898-1945 . . . . DLB-72

Bowen, Elizabeth
    1899-1973 . . . . DLB-15, 162; CDBLB-7

Bowen, Francis 1811-1890 . . . . DLB-1, 59, 235

Bowen, John 1924- DLB-13

Bowen, Marjorie 1886-1952 . . . . DLB-153

Bowen-Merrill Company DLB-49

Bowering, George 1935- DLB-53

Bowers, Bathsheba 1671-1718 . . . . DLB-200

Bowers, Claude G. 1878-1958 . . . . DLB-17

Bowers, Edgar 1924-2000 . . . . DLB-5

Bowers, Fredson Thayer
    1905-1991 . . . . .DLB-140; Y-80, 91

Bowles, Paul 1910-1999 . . . . . DLB-5, 6, 218; Y-99

Bowles, Samuel, III 1826-1878 . . . . DLB-43

Bowles, William Lisles 1762-1850 . . . . DLB-93

Bowman, Louise Morey 1882-1944 . . . . . . DLB-68

Boyd, James 1888-1944 . . . . DLB-9; DS-16

Boyd, John 1919- DLB-8

Boyd, Martin 1893-1972 . . . . DLB-260

Boyd, Thomas 1898-1935 . . . . DLB-9; DS-16

Boyd, William 1952- DLB-231

Boye, Karin 1900-1941 . . . . DLB-259

Boyesen, Hjalmar Hjorth
    1848-1895 . . . . .DLB-12, 71; DS-13

Boylan, Clare 1948- DLB-267

Boyle, Kay 1902-1992 . . . . .DLB-4, 9, 48, 86; Y-93

Boyle, Roger, Earl of Orrery 1621-1679 . . . DLB-80

Boyle, T. Coraghessan 1948- DLB-218; Y-86

Božić, Mirko 1919- DLB-181

Brackenbury, Alison 1953- DLB-40

Brackenridge, Hugh Henry
    1748-1816. . . . . .DLB-11, 37

Brackett, Charles 1892-1969 . . . . DLB-26

Brackett, Leigh 1915-1978 . . . . DLB-8, 26

Bradburn, John [publishing house] DLB-49

Bradbury, Malcolm 1932-2000 . . . . . .DLB-14, 207

Bradbury, Ray 1920- DLB-2, 8; CDALB-6

Bradbury and Evans DLB-106

Braddon, Mary Elizabeth
    1835-1915 . . . . .DLB-18, 70, 156

Bradford, Andrew 1686-1742 . . . . DLB-43, 73

Bradford, Gamaliel 1863-1932 . . . . .DLB-17

Bradford, John 1749-1830 . . . . DLB-43

Bradford, Roark 1896-1948 . . . . DLB-86

Bradford, William 1590-1657 . . . . DLB-24, 30

Bradford, William, III 1719-1791 . . . . . DLB-43, 73

Bradlaugh, Charles 1833-1891 . . . . DLB-57

Bradley, David 1950- DLB-33

Bradley, F. H. 1846-1924 . . . . DLB-262

Bradley, Ira, and Company DLB-49

Bradley, J. W., and Company DLB-49

Bradley, Katherine Harris (see Field, Michael)

Bradley, Marion Zimmer 1930-1999 . . . . . . DLB-8

Bradley, William Aspenwall 1878-1939 . . . . DLB-4

Bradshaw, Henry 1831-1886 . . . . DLB-184

Bradstreet, Anne
    1612 or 1613-1672 . . . . . . .DLB-24; CDABL-2

Bradūnas, Kazys 1917- DLB-220

Bradwardine, Thomas circa
    1295-1349 . . . . DLB-115

Brady, Frank 1924-1986 . . . . DLB-111

Brady, Frederic A. [publishing house] DLB-49

Bragg, Melvyn 1939- DLB-14

Brainard, Charles H. [publishing house] . . DLB-49

Braine, John 1922-1986 . DLB-15; Y-86; CDBLB-7

Braithwait, Richard 1588-1673 . . . . DLB-151

Braithwaite, William Stanley
    1878-1962. . . . . DLB-50, 54

Braker, Ulrich 1735-1798 . . . . DLB-94

Bramah, Ernest 1868-1942 . . . . DLB-70

Branagan, Thomas 1774-1843 . . . . DLB-37

Brancati, Vitaliano 1907-1954 . . . . DLB-264

Branch, William Blackwell 1927- DLB-76

Brand, Max (see Faust, Frederick Schiller)

Branden Press DLB-46

Branner, H.C. 1903-1966 . . . . DLB-214

Brant, Sebastian 1457-1521 . . . . .DLB-179

Brassey, Lady Annie (Allnutt)
    1839-1887 . . . . DLB-166

Brathwaite, Edward Kamau
 1930- DLB-125; CDWLB-3

Brault, Jacques 1933- DLB-53

Braun, Matt 1932- DLB-212

Braun, Volker 1939- DLB-75

Brautigan, Richard
 1935-1984 .... DLB-2, 5, 206; Y-80, Y-84

Braxton, Joanne M. 1950- DLB-41

Bray, Anne Eliza 1790-1883...........DLB-116

Bray, Thomas 1656-1730.............DLB-24

Brazdžionis, Bernardas 1907- DLB-220

Braziller, George [publishing house] DLB-46

The Bread Loaf Writers' Conference 1983 ... Y-84

Breasted, James Henry 1865-1935.......DLB-47

Brecht, Bertolt
 1898-1956 .... DLB-56, 124; CDWLB-2

Bredel, Willi 1901-1964...............DLB-56

Bregendahl, Marie 1867-1940 ....DLB-214

Breitinger, Johann Jakob 1701-1776 ......DLB-97

Bremser, Bonnie 1939- DLB-16

Bremser, Ray 1934- DLB-16

Brennan, Christopher 1870-1932.......DLB-230

Brentano, Bernard von 1901-1964.......DLB-56

Brentano, Clemens 1778-1842 ....DLB-90

Brentano's DLB-49

Brenton, Howard 1942- DLB-13

Breslin, Jimmy 1929-1996 ....DLB-185

Breton, André 1896-1966 ....DLB-65, 258

Breton, Nicholas circa 1555-circa 1626 ...DLB-136

The Breton Lays
 1300-early fifteenth century........DLB-146

Brewer, Luther A. 1858-1933 ....DLB-187

Brewer, Warren and Putnam...........DLB-46

Brewster, Elizabeth 1922- DLB-60

Breytenbach, Breyten 1939- DLB-225

Bridge, Ann (Lady Mary Dolling Sanders
 O'Malley) 1889-1974..............DLB-191

Bridge, Horatio 1806-1893 ....DLB-183

Bridgers, Sue Ellen 1942- DLB-52

Bridges, Robert
 1844-1930 ....DLB-19, 98; CDBLB-5

The Bridgewater Library..............DLB-213

Bridie, James 1888-1951 ....DLB-10

Brieux, Eugene 1858-1932............DLB-192

Brigadere, Anna 1861-1933 ....DLB-220

Briggs, Charles Frederick
 1804-1877 ....DLB-3, 250

Brighouse, Harold 1882-1958 ....DLB-10

Bright, Mary Chavelita Dunne (see Egerton, George)

Brimmer, B. J., Company DLB-46

Brines, Francisco 1932- DLB-134

Brink, André 1935- DLB-225

Brinley, George, Jr. 1817-1875 ....DLB-140

Brinnin, John Malcolm 1916-1998.......DLB-48

Brisbane, Albert 1809-1890 ....DLB-3, 250

Brisbane, Arthur 1864-1936...........DLB-25

British Academy DLB-112

The British Critic 1793-1843 ....DLB-110

The British Library and the Regular
 Readers' Group....................Y-91

British Literary Prizes Y-98

*The British Review and London Critical
 Journal 1811-1825* DLB-110

British Travel Writing, 1940-1997......DLB-204

Brito, Aristeo 1942- DLB-122

Brittain, Vera 1893-1970 ....DLB-191

Brizeux, Auguste 1803-1858 ....DLB-217

Broadway Publishing Company DLB-46

Broch, Hermann
 1886-1951 ....DLB-85, 124; CDWLB-2

Brochu, André 1942- DLB-53

Brock, Edwin 1927- DLB-40

Brockes, Barthold Heinrich 1680-1747 ...DLB-168

Brod, Max 1884-1968 ....DLB-81

Brodber, Erna 1940- DLB-157

Brodhead, John R. 1814-1873 ....DLB-30

Brodkey, Harold 1930-1996 ....DLB-130

Brodsky, Joseph 1940-1996.............. Y-87

Brodsky, Michael 1948- DLB-244

Broeg, Bob 1918- DLB-171

Brøgger, Suzanne 1944- DLB-214

Brome, Richard circa 1590-1652 ....DLB-58

Brome, Vincent 1910- DLB-155

Bromfield, Louis 1896-1956 ....DLB-4, 9, 86

Bromige, David 1933- DLB-193

Broner, E. M. 1930- DLB-28

Bronk, William 1918-1999 ....DLB-165

Bronnen, Arnolt 1895-1959...........DLB-124

Brontë, Anne 1820-1849 ....DLB-21, 199

Brontë, Charlotte
 1816-1855 ......DLB-21, 159, 199; CDBLB-4

Brontë, Emily
 1818-1848 ...... DLB-21, 32, 199; CDBLB-4

Brook, Stephen 1947- DLB-204

Brook Farm 1841-1847 ....DLB-223

Brooke, Frances 1724-1789 ....DLB-39, 99

Brooke, Henry 1703?-1783.............DLB-39

Brooke, L. Leslie 1862-1940 ....DLB-141

Brooke, Margaret, Ranee of Sarawak
 1849-1936 ....DLB-174

Brooke, Rupert
 1887-1915 ....DLB-19, 216; CDBLB-6

Brooker, Bertram 1888-1955...........DLB-88

Brooke-Rose, Christine 1923- DLB-14, 231

Brookner, Anita 1928- DLB-194; Y-87

Brooks, Charles Timothy 1813-1883...DLB-1, 243

Brooks, Cleanth 1906-1994 ....DLB-63; Y-94

Brooks, Gwendolyn
 1917-2000 ....DLB-5, 76, 165; CDALB-1

Brooks, Jeremy 1926- DLB-14

Brooks, Mel 1926- DLB-26

Brooks, Noah 1830-1903........DLB-42; DS-13

Brooks, Richard 1912-1992 ....DLB-44

Brooks, Van Wyck
 1886-1963 ....DLB-45, 63, 103

Brophy, Brigid 1929-1995 ....DLB-14

Brophy, John 1899-1965 ....DLB-191

Brossard, Chandler 1922-1993 ....DLB-16

Brossard, Nicole 1943- DLB-53

Broster, Dorothy Kathleen 1877-1950 ....DLB-160

Brother Antoninus (see Everson, William)

Brotherton, Lord 1856-1930 ....DLB-184

Brougham and Vaux, Henry Peter Brougham,
 Baron 1778-1868.............DLB-110, 158

Brougham, John 1810-1880.............DLB-11

Broughton, James 1913-1999............DLB-5

Broughton, Rhoda 1840-1920 ....DLB-18

Broun, Heywood 1888-1939 ....DLB-29, 171

Brown, Alice 1856-1948 ....DLB-78

Brown, Bob 1886-1959 ....DLB-4, 45

Brown, Cecil 1943- DLB-33

Brown, Charles Brockden
 1771-1810 .... DLB-37, 59, 73; CDALB-2

Brown, Christy 1932-1981 ....DLB-14

Brown, Dee 1908- Y-80

Brown, Frank London 1927-1962 ....DLB-76

Brown, Fredric 1906-1972 ....DLB-8

Brown, George Mackay
 1921-1996 .... DLB-14, 27, 139

Brown, Harry 1917-1986 ....DLB-26

Brown, Larry 1951- DLB-234

Brown, Lew (see DeSylva, Buddy)

Brown, Marcia 1918- DLB-61

Brown, Margaret Wise 1910-1952.......DLB-22

Brown, Morna Doris (see Ferrars, Elizabeth)

Brown, Oliver Madox 1855-1874 ....DLB-21

Brown, Sterling 1901-1989 ....DLB-48, 51, 63

Brown, T. E. 1830-1897 ....DLB-35

Brown, Thomas Alexander (see Boldrewood, Rolf)

Brown, Warren 1894-1978 ....DLB-241

Brown, William Hill 1765-1793 ....DLB-37

Brown, William Wells
 1815-1884 ....DLB-3, 50, 183, 248

Browne, Charles Farrar 1834-1867 ....DLB-11

Browne, Frances 1816-1879...........DLB-199

Browne, Francis Fisher 1843-1913.......DLB-79

Browne, Howard 1908-1999 ....DLB-226

Browne, J. Ross 1821-1875 ....DLB-202

Browne, Michael Dennis 1940- DLB-40

Browne, Sir Thomas 1605-1682 ....DLB-151

Browne, William, of Tavistock
 1590-1645 ....DLB-121

Browne, Wynyard 1911-1964.......DLB-13, 233

Browne and Nolan..................DLB-106

Brownell, W. C. 1851-1928............DLB-71

Browning, Elizabeth Barrett
 1806-1861 ....DLB-32, 199; CDBLB-4

Browning, Robert
 1812-1889 ....DLB-32, 163; CDBLB-4

Introductory Essay: *Letters of Percy Bysshe Shelley* (1852). DLB-32

Brownjohn, Allan 1931- DLB-40

Brownson, Orestes Augustus 1803-1876. . . . . DLB-1, 59, 73, 243

Bruccoli, Matthew J. 1931- DLB-103

Bruce, Charles 1906-1971. . . . . DLB-68

John Edward Bruce: Three Documents . . . DLB-50

Bruce, Leo 1903-1979. . . . . DLB-77

Bruce, Mary Grant 1878-1958 . . . . DLB-230

Bruce, Philip Alexander 1856-1933 . . . . . . DLB-47

Bruce Humphries [publishing house] DLB-46

Bruce-Novoa, Juan 1944- DLB-82

Bruckman, Clyde 1894-1955 . . . . DLB-26

Bruckner, Ferdinand 1891-1958. . . . . . . DLB-118

Brundage, John Herbert (see Herbert, John)

Brunner, John 1934-1995 . . . . DLB-261

Brutus, Dennis 1924- DLB-117, 225; CDWLB-3

Bryan, C. D. B. 1936- DLB-185

Bryant, Arthur 1899-1985 . . . . DLB-149

Bryant, William Cullen 1794-1878 . . . . DLB-3, 43, 59, 189, 250; CDALB-2

Bryce Echenique, Alfredo 1939- DLB-145; CDWLB-3

Bryce, James 1838-1922 . . . . DLB-166, 190

Bryden, Bill 1942- DLB-233

Brydges, Sir Samuel Egerton 1762-1837 . . DLB-107

Bryskett, Lodowick 1546?-1612. . . . . . . DLB-167

Buchan, John 1875-1940. . . . . .DLB-34, 70, 156

Buchanan, George 1506-1582. . . . . DLB-132

Buchanan, Robert 1841-1901. . . . . . . DLB-18, 35

"The Fleshly School of Poetry and Other Phenomena of the Day" (1872), by Robert Buchanan. DLB-35

"The Fleshly School of Poetry: Mr. D. G. Rossetti" (1871), by Thomas Maitland (Robert Buchanan). DLB-35

Buchman, Sidney 1902-1975. . . . . DLB-26

Buchner, Augustus 1591-1661 . . . . DLB-164

Büchner, Georg 1813-1837 . . DLB-133; CDWLB-2

Bucholtz, Andreas Heinrich 1607-1671 . . . DLB-168

Buck, Pearl S. 1892-1973 . . DLB-9, 102; CDALB-7

Bucke, Charles 1781-1846 . . . . DLB-110

Bucke, Richard Maurice 1837-1902 . . . . . . DLB-99

Buckingham, Joseph Tinker 1779-1861 and Buckingham, Edwin 1810-1833 . . . . . . DLB-73

Buckler, Ernest 1908-1984 . . . . DLB-68

Buckley, William F., Jr. 1925- DLB-137; Y-80

Buckminster, Joseph Stevens 1784-1812 . . . . DLB-37

Buckner, Robert 1906- DLB-26

Budd, Thomas ?-1698 . . . . DLB-24

Budrys, A. J. 1931- DLB-8

Buechner, Frederick 1926- Y-80

Buell, John 1927- DLB-53

Bufalino, Gesualdo 1920-1996 . . . . DLB-196

Buffum, Job [publishing house]. DLB-49

Bugnet, Georges 1879-1981 . . . . DLB-92

Buies, Arthur 1840-1901 . . . . DLB-99

Building the New British Library at St Pancras. Y-94

Bukowski, Charles 1920-1994 . . . DLB-5, 130, 169

Bulatović, Miodrag 1930-1991 . . . . DLB-181; CDWLB-4

Bulgarin, Faddei Venediktovich 1789-1859. . . . . DLB-198

Bulger, Bozeman 1877-1932 . . . . .DLB-171

Bullein, William between 1520 and 1530-1576. . . . . . . DLB-167

Bullins, Ed 1935- DLB-7, 38, 249

Bulwer, John 1606-1656 . . . . DLB-236

Bulwer-Lytton, Edward (also Edward Bulwer) 1803-1873. . . . . DLB-21

"On Art in Fiction "(1838) DLB-21

Bumpus, Jerry 1937- Y-81

Bunce and Brother DLB-49

Bunner, H. C. 1855-1896. . . . . .DLB-78, 79

Bunting, Basil 1900-1985 . . . . DLB-20

Buntline, Ned (Edward Zane Carroll Judson) 1821-1886 . . . . DLB-186

Bunyan, John 1628-1688 . . . . . DLB-39; CDBLB-2

Burch, Robert 1925- DLB-52

Burciaga, José Antonio 1940- DLB-82

Burdekin, Katharine 1896-1963 . . . . DLB-255

Bürger, Gottfried August 1747-1794 . . . . . . DLB-94

Burgess, Anthony 1917-1993 . . . . . DLB-14, 194, 261; CDBLB-8

The Anthony Burgess Archive at the Harry Ransom Humanities Research Center. Y-98

Anthony Burgess's 99 Novels: An Opinion Poll. Y-84

Burgess, Gelett 1866-1951 . . . . DLB-11

Burgess, John W. 1844-1931 . . . . DLB-47

Burgess, Thornton W. 1874-1965 . . . . . . DLB-22

Burgess, Stringer and Company DLB-49

Burick, Si 1909-1986. . . . . .DLB-171

Burk, John Daly circa 1772-1808 . . . . DLB-37

Burk, Ronnie 1955- DLB-209

Burke, Edmund 1729?-1797 . . . . . . DLB-104, 252

Burke, James Lee 1936- DLB-226

Burke, Johnny 1908-1964. . . . . DLB-265

Burke, Kenneth 1897-1993 . . . . DLB-45, 63

Burke, Thomas 1886-1945. . . . . DLB-197

Burley, Dan 1907-1962. . . . . DLB-241

Burlingame, Edward Livermore 1848-1922 . . . . DLB-79

Burman, Carina 1960- DLB-257

Burnet, Gilbert 1643-1715. . . . . DLB-101

Burnett, Frances Hodgson 1849-1924 . . . . .DLB-42, 141; DS-13, 14

Burnett, W. R. 1899-1982 . . . . DLB-9, 226

Burnett, Whit 1899-1973 and Martha Foley 1897-1977 . . . . DLB-137

Burney, Fanny 1752-1840. . . . . DLB-39

Dedication, *The Wanderer* (1814). DLB-39

Preface to *Evelina* (1778) DLB-39

Burns, Alan 1929- DLB-14, 194

Burns, John Horne 1916-1953 . . . . .Y-85

Burns, Robert 1759-1796 . . . . DLB-109; CDBLB-3

Burns and Oates. DLB-106

Burnshaw, Stanley 1906- DLB-48

Burr, C. Chauncey 1815?-1883 . . . . DLB-79

Burr, Esther Edwards 1732-1758 . . . . DLB-200

Burroughs, Edgar Rice 1875-1950 . . . . . . DLB-8

Burroughs, John 1837-1921 . . . . DLB-64

Burroughs, Margaret T. G. 1917- DLB-41

Burroughs, William S., Jr. 1947-1981 . . . . . DLB-16

Burroughs, William Seward 1914-1997 . . . . DLB-2, 8, 16, 152, 237; Y-81, Y-97

Burroway, Janet 1936- DLB-6

Burt, Maxwell Struthers 1882-1954 . . . . DLB-86; DS-16

Burt, A. L., and Company DLB-49

Burton, Hester 1913- DLB-161

Burton, Isabel Arundell 1831-1896. . . . . . DLB-166

Burton, Miles (see Rhode, John)

Burton, Richard Francis 1821-1890 . . . . .DLB-55, 166, 184

Burton, Robert 1577-1640. . . . . DLB-151

Burton, Virginia Lee 1909-1968. . . . . DLB-22

Burton, William Evans 1804-1860 . . . . DLB-73

Burwell, Adam Hood 1790-1849 . . . . DLB-99

Bury, Lady Charlotte 1775-1861 . . . . DLB-116

Busch, Frederick 1941- DLB-6, 218

Busch, Niven 1903-1991. . . . . DLB-44

Bushnell, Horace 1802-1876. . . . . .DS-13

Bussieres, Arthur de 1877-1913. . . . . DLB-92

Butler, Charles ca. 1560-1647. . . . . DLB-236

Butler, Guy 1918- DLB-225

Butler, E. H., and Company. DLB-49

Butler, Joseph 1692-1752 . . . . DLB-252

Butler, Josephine Elizabeth 1828-1906 . . . . DLB-190

Butler, Juan 1942-1981 . . . . DLB-53

Butler, Judith 1956- DLB-246

Butler, Octavia E. 1947- DLB-33

Butler, Pierce 1884-1953. . . . . .DLB-187

Butler, Robert Olen 1945- DLB-173

Butler, Samuel 1613-1680. . . . . .DLB-101, 126

Butler, Samuel 1835-1902. . . . . DLB-18, 57, 174

Butler, William Francis 1838-1910 . . . . DLB-166

Butor, Michel 1926- DLB-83

Butter, Nathaniel [publishing house] DLB-170

Butterworth, Hezekiah 1839-1905 . . . . . . DLB-42

Buttitta, Ignazio 1899- DLB-114

Butts, Mary 1890-1937. . . . . DLB-240

Buzzati, Dino 1906-1972. . . . . .DLB-177

Byars, Betsy 1928- DLB-52

Byatt, A. S. 1936- DLB-14, 194

Byles, Mather 1707-1788. . . . . .DLB-24

Bynneman, Henry
[publishing house] DLB-170

Bynner, Witter 1881-1968. . . . . .DLB-54

Byrd, William circa 1543-1623 . . . . .DLB-172

Byrd, William, II 1674-1744. . . . . . . .DLB-24, 140

Byrne, John Keyes (see Leonard, Hugh)

Byron, George Gordon, Lord
1788-1824 . . . . .DLB-96, 110; CDBLB-3

Byron, Robert 1905-1941 . . . . .DLB-195

C

Caballero Bonald, José Manuel
1926- DLB-108

Cabañero, Eladio 1930- DLB-134

Cabell, James Branch 1879-1958 . . . . . . .DLB-9, 78

Cabeza de Baca, Manuel 1853-1915 . . . . .DLB-122

Cabeza de Baca Gilbert, Fabiola
1898- DLB-122

Cable, George Washington
1844-1925 . . . . DLB-12, 74; DS-13

Cable, Mildred 1878-1952 . . . . .DLB-195

Cabrera, Lydia 1900-1991 . . . . .DLB-145

Cabrera Infante, Guillermo
1929- DLB-113; CDWLB-3

Cadell [publishing house]. DLB-154

Cady, Edwin H. 1917- DLB-103

Caedmon flourished 658-680. . . . . .DLB-146

Caedmon School circa 660-899 . . . . .DLB-146

Caesar, Irving 1895-1996. . . . . .DLB-265

Cafés, Brasseries, and Bistros. DS-15

Cage, John 1912-1992 . . . . .DLB-193

Cahan, Abraham 1860-1951 . . . . . .DLB-9, 25, 28

Cahn, Sammy 1913-1993. . . . . .DLB-265

Cain, George 1943- DLB-33

Cain, James M. 1892-1977 . . . . .DLB-226

Caird, Edward 1835-1908 . . . . .DLB-262

Caird, Mona 1854-1932. . . . . .DLB-197

Čaks, Aleksandrs
1901-1950 . . . . .DLB-220; CDWLB-4

Caldecott, Randolph 1846-1886 . . . . . . .DLB-163

Calder, John (Publishers), Limited. DLB-112

Calderón de la Barca, Fanny
1804-1882 . . . . .DLB-183

Caldwell, Ben 1937- DLB-38

Caldwell, Erskine 1903-1987 . . . . .DLB-9, 86

Caldwell, H. M., Company DLB-49

Caldwell, Taylor 1900-1985 . . . . DS-17

Calhoun, John C. 1782-1850 . . . . . . .DLB-3, 248

Călinescu, George 1899-1965 . . . . .DLB-220

Calisher, Hortense 1911- DLB-2, 218

A Call to Letters and an Invitation
to the Electric Chair,
by Siegfried Mandel DLB-75

Callaghan, Mary Rose 1944- DLB-207

Callaghan, Morley 1903-1990 . . . . .DLB-68

Callahan, S. Alice 1868-1894 . . . . . . .DLB-175, 221

Callaloo Y-87

Callimachus circa 305 B.C.-240 B.C. DLB-176

Calmer, Edgar 1907- DLB-4

Calverley, C. S. 1831-1884 . . . . .DLB-35

Calvert, George Henry
1803-1889 . . . . .DLB-1, 64, 248

Calvino, Italo 1923-1985 . . . . .DLB-196

Cambridge, Ada 1844-1926. . . . . .DLB-230

Cambridge Press DLB-49

Cambridge Songs (Carmina Cantabrigensia)
circa 1050 .DLB-148

Cambridge University Press DLB-170

Camden, William 1551-1623. . . . . .DLB-172

Camden House: An Interview with
James Hardin Y-92

Cameron, Eleanor 1912- DLB-52

Cameron, George Frederick
1854-1885 . . . . .DLB-99

Cameron, Lucy Lyttelton 1781-1858. . . . .DLB-163

Cameron, Peter 1959- DLB-234

Cameron, William Bleasdell 1862-1951 . . .DLB-99

Camm, John 1718-1778 . . . . .DLB-31

Camon, Ferdinando 1935- DLB-196

Camp, Walter 1859-1925 . . . . .DLB-241

Campana, Dino 1885-1932 . . . . .DLB-114

Campbell, Bebe Moore 1950- DLB-227

Campbell, David 1915-1979. . . . . .DLB-260

Campbell, Gabrielle Margaret Vere
(see Shearing, Joseph, and Bowen, Marjorie)

Campbell, James Dykes 1838-1895 . . . . . .DLB-144

Campbell, James Edwin 1867-1896 . . . . . .DLB-50

Campbell, John 1653-1728. . . . . .DLB-43

Campbell, John W., Jr. 1910-1971 . . . . . . .DLB-8

Campbell, Ramsey 1946- DLB-261

Campbell, Roy 1901-1957 . . . . .DLB-20, 225

Campbell, Thomas 1777-1844 . . . . . .DLB-93, 144

Campbell, William Wilfred 1858-1918 . . . .DLB-92

Campion, Edmund 1539-1581 . . . . .DLB-167

Campion, Thomas
1567-1620 . . . . .DLB-58, 172; CDBLB-1

Campton, David 1924- DLB-245

Camus, Albert 1913-1960 . . . . .DLB-72

The Canadian Publishers' Records
Database Y-96

Canby, Henry Seidel 1878-1961 . . . . .DLB-91

Candelaria, Cordelia 1943- DLB-82

Candelaria, Nash 1928- DLB-82

Canetti, Elias
1905-1994 . . . . .DLB-85, 124; CDWLB-2

Canham, Erwin Dain 1904-1982. . . . . . . .DLB-127

Canitz, Friedrich Rudolph Ludwig von
1654-1699 . . . . .DLB-168

Cankar, Ivan 1876-1918. . . . . DLB-147; CDWLB-4

Cannan, Gilbert 1884-1955 . . . . .DLB-10, 197

Cannan, Joanna 1896-1961 . . . . .DLB-191

Cannell, Kathleen 1891-1974. . . . . .DLB-4

Cannell, Skipwith 1887-1957 . . . . .DLB-45

Canning, George 1770-1827. . . . . .DLB-158

Cannon, Jimmy 1910-1973 . . . . .DLB-171

Cano, Daniel 1947- DLB-209

Cantú, Norma Elia 1947- DLB-209

Cantwell, Robert 1908-1978 . . . . .DLB-9

Cape, Jonathan, and Harrison Smith
[publishing house]. DLB-46

Cape, Jonathan, Limited DLB-112

Čapek, Karel 1890-1938 . . . .DLB-215; CDWLB-4

Capen, Joseph 1658-1725. . . . . .DLB-24

Capes, Bernard 1854-1918 . . . . .DLB-156

Capote, Truman 1924-1984
. . . . . DLB-2, 185, 227; Y-80, Y-84; CDALB-1

Capps, Benjamin 1922- DLB-256

Caproni, Giorgio 1912-1990 . . . . .DLB-128

Caragiale, Mateiu Ioan 1885-1936. . . . . . .DLB-220

Cardarelli, Vincenzo 1887-1959. . . . . . . .DLB-114

Cárdenas, Reyes 1948- DLB-122

Cardinal, Marie 1929- DLB-83

Carew, Jan 1920- DLB-157

Carew, Thomas 1594 or 1595-1640. . . . .DLB-126

Carey, Henry circa 1687-1689-1743. . . . . .DLB-84

Carey, M., and Company DLB-49

Carey, Mathew 1760-1839. . . . . . . .DLB-37, 73

Carey and Hart DLB-49

Carlell, Lodowick 1602-1675. . . . . .DLB-58

Carleton, William 1794-1869. . . . . .DLB-159

Carleton, G. W. [publishing house]. DLB-49

Carlile, Richard 1790-1843 . . . . .DLB-110, 158

Carlson, Ron 1947- DLB-244

Carlyle, Jane Welsh 1801-1866 . . . . .DLB-55

Carlyle, Thomas
1795-1881 . . . . .DLB-55, 144; CDBLB-3

"The Hero as Man of Letters: Johnson,
Rousseau, Burns" (1841) [excerpt] DLB-57

The Hero as Poet. Dante;
Shakspeare (1841). DLB-32

Carman, Bliss 1861-1929. . . . . .DLB-92

Carmina Burana circa 1230 . . . . .DLB-138

Carnero, Guillermo 1947- DLB-108

Carossa, Hans 1878-1956 . . . . .DLB-66

Carpenter, Humphrey
1946- DLB-155; Y-84, Y-99

The Practice of Biography III: An Interview
with Humphrey Carpenter Y-84

Carpenter, Stephen Cullen ?-1820?. DLB-73

Carpentier, Alejo
1904-1980 . . . . .DLB-113; CDWLB-3

Carr, Marina 1964- DLB-245

Carrier, Roch 1937- DLB-53

Carrillo, Adolfo 1855-1926 . . . . .DLB-122

Carroll, Gladys Hasty 1904- DLB-9

Carroll, John 1735-1815 . . . . .DLB-37

Carroll, John 1809-1884 . . . . .DLB-99

Carroll, Lewis
1832-1898 . . . . . .DLB-18, 163, 178; CDBLB-4

The Lewis Carroll Centenary Y-98

Carroll, Paul 1927- DLB-16

Carroll, Paul Vincent 1900-1968 .... DLB-10

Carroll and Graf Publishers DLB-46

Carruth, Hayden 1921- DLB-5, 165

Carryl, Charles E. 1841-1920.......... DLB-42

Carson, Anne 1950- DLB-193

Carswell, Catherine 1879-1946........ DLB-36

Cărtărescu, Mirea 1956- DLB-232

Carter, Angela 1940-1992......DLB-14, 207, 261

Carter, Elizabeth 1717-1806 .... DLB-109

Carter, Henry (see Leslie, Frank)

Carter, Hodding, Jr. 1907-1972........ DLB-127

Carter, John 1905-1975............. DLB-201

Carter, Landon 1710-1778............ DLB-31

Carter, Lin 1930- Y-81

Carter, Martin 1927-1997 ....DLB-117; CDWLB-3

Carter, Robert, and Brothers DLB-49

Carter and Hendee.................. DLB-49

Cartwright, Jim 1958- DLB-245

Cartwright, John 1740-1824 .... DLB-158

Cartwright, William circa 1611-1643 .... DLB-126

Caruthers, William Alexander
    1802-1846 .... DLB-3, 248

Carver, Jonathan 1710-1780 .... DLB-31

Carver, Raymond
    1938-1988 ....DLB-130; Y-83, Y-88

First Strauss "Livings" Awarded to Cynthia
    Ozick and Raymond Carver
    An Interview with Raymond Carver Y-83

Cary, Alice 1820-1871............... DLB-202

Cary, Joyce 1888-1957 ... DLB-15, 100; CDBLB-6

Cary, Patrick 1623?-1657 .... DLB-131

Casey, Gavin 1907-1964............. DLB-260

Casey, Juanita 1925- DLB-14

Casey, Michael 1947- DLB-5

Cassady, Carolyn 1923- DLB-16

Cassady, Neal 1926-1968 .... DLB-16, 237

Cassell and Company................ DLB-106

Cassell Publishing Company DLB-49

Cassill, R. V. 1919- DLB-6, 218

Cassity, Turner 1929- DLB-105

Cassius Dio circa 155/164-post 229 ...... DLB-176

Cassola, Carlo 1917-1987.............DLB-177

The Castle of Perserverance circa 1400-1425 . DLB-146

Castellano, Olivia 1944- DLB-122

Castellanos, Rosario
    1925-1974........... DLB-113; CDWLB-3

Castillo, Ana 1953- DLB-122, 227

Castillo, Rafael C. 1950- DLB-209

Castlemon, Harry (see Fosdick, Charles Austin)

Čašule, Kole 1921- DLB-181

Caswall, Edward 1814-1878 .... DLB-32

Catacalos, Rosemary 1944- DLB-122

Cather, Willa 1873-1947
    .... DLB-9, 54, 78, 256; DS-1; CDALB-3

Catherine II (Ekaterina Alekseevna), "The Great,"
    Empress of Russia 1729-1796 ...... DLB-150

Catherwood, Mary Hartwell 1847-1902... DLB-78

Catledge, Turner 1901-1983 .... DLB-127

Catlin, George 1796-1872 .... DLB-186, 189

Cato the Elder 234 B.C.-149 B.C. DLB-211

Cattafi, Bartolo 1922-1979 .... DLB-128

Catton, Bruce 1899-1978 .... DLB-17

Catullus circa 84 B.C.-54 B.C.
    .... DLB-211; CDWLB-1

Causley, Charles 1917- DLB-27

Caute, David 1936- DLB-14, 231

Cavendish, Duchess of Newcastle,
    Margaret Lucas 1623-1673 .... DLB-131, 252

Cawein, Madison 1865-1914 .... DLB-54

Caxton, William [publishing house]......DLB-170

The Caxton Printers, Limited DLB-46

Caylor, O. P. 1849-1897............. DLB-241

Cayrol, Jean 1911- DLB-83

Cecil, Lord David 1902-1986.......... DLB-155

Cela, Camilo José 1916- Y-89

Celan, Paul 1920-1970 ...... DLB-69; CDWLB-2

Celati, Gianni 1937- DLB-196

Celaya, Gabriel 1911-1991........... DLB-108

A Celebration of Literary Biography Y-98

Céline, Louis-Ferdinand 1894-1961 ...... DLB-72

The Celtic Background to Medieval English
    Literature..................... DLB-146

Celtis, Conrad 1459-1508..............DLB-179

Cendrars, Blaise 1887-1961........... DLB-258

Center for Bibliographical Studies and
    Research at the University of
    California, Riverside Y-91

The Center for the Book in the Library
    of Congress Y-93

Center for the Book Research Y-84

Centlivre, Susanna 1669?-1723.......... DLB-84

The Centre for Writing, Publishing and
    Printing History at the University
    of Reading Y-00

The Century Company DLB-49

Cernuda, Luis 1902-1963............. DLB-134

Cervantes, Lorna Dee 1954- DLB-82

de Céspedes, Alba 1911-1997 .... DLB-264

Ch., T. (see Marchenko, Anastasiia Iakovlevna)

Chaadaev, Petr Iakovlevich
    1794-1856..................... DLB-198

Chacel, Rosa 1898- DLB-134

Chacón, Eusebio 1869-1948........... DLB-82

Chacón, Felipe Maximiliano 1873-? DLB-82

Chadwick, Henry 1824-1908 .... DLB-241

Chadwyck-Healey's Full-Text Literary Databases:
    Editing Commercial Databases of
    Primary Literary Texts Y-95

Challans, Eileen Mary (see Renault, Mary)

Chalmers, George 1742-1825 .... DLB-30

Chaloner, Sir Thomas 1520-1565 ...... DLB-167

Chamberlain, Samuel S. 1851-1916 ...... DLB-25

Chamberland, Paul 1939- DLB-60

Chamberlin, William Henry 1897-1969 ... DLB-29

Chambers, Charles Haddon 1860-1921 ... DLB-10

Chambers, María Cristina (see Mena, María Cristina)

Chambers, Robert W. 1865-1933 ...... DLB-202

Chambers, W. and R.
    [publishing house] DLB-106

Chamisso, Albert von 1781-1838 ...... DLB-90

Champfleury 1821-1889.............. DLB-119

Chandler, Harry 1864-1944........... DLB-29

Chandler, Norman 1899-1973 ....DLB-127

Chandler, Otis 1927- DLB-127

Chandler, Raymond
    1888-1959 ... DLB-226, 253; DS-6; CDALB-5

Raymond Chandler Centenary Tributes
    from Michael Avallone, James Ellroy,
    Joe Gores, and William F. Nolan........ Y-88

Channing, Edward 1856-1931 ....DLB-17

Channing, Edward Tyrrell
    1790-1856................. DLB-1, 59, 235

Channing, William Ellery
    1780-1842 .... DLB-1, 59, 235

Channing, William Ellery, II
    1817-1901.................... DLB-1, 223

Channing, William Henry
    1810-1884 .... DLB-1, 59, 243

Chaplin, Charlie 1889-1977 .... DLB-44

Chapman, George
    1559 or 1560-1634............ DLB-62, 121

Chapman, John DLB-106

Chapman, Olive Murray 1892-1977..... DLB-195

Chapman, R. W. 1881-1960 .... DLB-201

Chapman, William 1850-1917 .... DLB-99

Chapman and Hall.................. DLB-106

Chappell, Fred 1936- DLB-6, 105

"A Detail in a Poem" DLB-105

Chappell, William 1582-1649......... DLB-236

Char, René 1907-1988 .... DLB-258

Charbonneau, Jean 1875-1960 .... DLB-92

Charbonneau, Robert 1911-1967........ DLB-68

Charles, Gerda 1914- DLB-14

Charles, William [publishing house]...... DLB-49

Charles d'Orléans 1394-1465 .... DLB-208

Charley (see Mann, Charles)

Charteris, Leslie 1907-1993............ DLB-77

Chartier, Alain circa 1385-1430 .... DLB-208

Charyn, Jerome 1937- Y-83

Chase, Borden 1900-1971............. DLB-26

Chase, Edna Woolman 1877-1957 ...... DLB-91

Chase, Mary Coyle 1907-1981 .... DLB-228

Chase-Riboud, Barbara 1936- DLB-33

Chateaubriand, François-René de
    1768-1848 .... DLB-119

Chatterton, Thomas 1752-1770 .... DLB-109

Essay on Chatterton (1842), by
    Robert Browning................. DLB-32

Chatto and Windus DLB-106

Chatwin, Bruce 1940-1989........ DLB-194, 204

Chaucer, Geoffrey
1340?-1400 . . . . DLB-146; CDBLB-1

Chaudhuri, Amit 1962- DLB-267

Chauncy, Charles 1705-1787 . . . . .DLB-24

Chauveau, Pierre-Joseph-Olivier
1820-1890 . . . . .DLB-99

Chávez, Denise 1948- DLB-122

Chávez, Fray Angélico 1910- DLB-82

Chayefsky, Paddy 1923-1981 . . . . DLB-7, 44; Y-81

Cheesman, Evelyn 1881-1969 . . . . .DLB-195

Cheever, Ezekiel 1615-1708 . . . . .DLB-24

Cheever, George Barrell 1807-1890 . . . . . .DLB-59

Cheever, John 1912-1982
. . . . . DLB-2, 102, 227; Y-80, Y-82; CDALB-1

Cheever, Susan 1943- Y-82

Cheke, Sir John 1514-1557 . . . . .DLB-132

Chelsea House .DLB-46

Chênedollé, Charles de 1769-1833. . . . . . .DLB-217

Cheney, Ednah Dow 1824-1904 . . . . .DLB-1, 223

Cheney, Harriet Vaughn 1796-1889 . . . . . .DLB-99

Chénier, Marie-Joseph 1764-1811 . . . . . . .DLB-192

Chernyshevsky, Nikolai Gavrilovich
1828-1889 . . . . .DLB-238

Cherry, Kelly 1940 . . . . Y-83

Cherryh, C. J. 1942- Y-80

Chesebro', Caroline 1825-1873 . . . . .DLB-202

Chesney, Sir George Tomkyns
1830-1895 . . . . .DLB-190

Chesnut, Mary Boykin 1823-1886. . . . . .DLB-239

Chesnutt, Charles Waddell
1858-1932 . . . . DLB-12, 50, 78

Chesson, Mrs. Nora (see Hopper, Nora)

Chester, Alfred 1928-1971 . . . . .DLB-130

Chester, George Randolph 1869-1924 . . . .DLB-78

The Chester Plays circa 1505-1532;
revisions until 1575 . . . . .DLB-146

Chesterfield, Philip Dormer Stanhope,
Fourth Earl of 1694-1773 . . . . .DLB-104

Chesterton, G. K. 1874-1936
. . DLB-10, 19, 34, 70, 98, 149, 178; CDBLB-6

Chettle, Henry circa 1560-circa 1607 . . . . .DLB-136

Cheuse, Alan 1940- DLB-244

Chew, Ada Nield 1870-1945 . . . . .DLB-135

Cheyney, Edward P. 1861-1947 . . . . .DLB-47

Chiara, Piero 1913-1986 . . . . .DLB-177

Chicano History DLB-82

Chicano Language DLB-82

Child, Francis James 1825-1896 . . . .DLB-1, 64, 235

Child, Lydia Maria 1802-1880 . . . .DLB-1, 74, 243

Child, Philip 1898-1978 . . . . .DLB-68

Childers, Erskine 1870-1922 . . . . .DLB-70

Children's Book Awards and Prizes DLB-61

Children's Illustrators, 1800-1880 . . . . . . .DLB-163

Childress, Alice 1916-1994 . . . . . DLB-7, 38, 249

Childs, George W. 1829-1894 . . . . .DLB-23

Chilton Book Company DLB-46

Chin, Frank 1940- DLB-206

Chinweizu 1943- DLB-157

Chitham, Edward 1932- DLB-155

Chittenden, Hiram Martin 1858-1917 . . . . .DLB-47

Chivers, Thomas Holley 1809-1858 . . .DLB-3, 248

Cholmondeley, Mary 1859-1925 . . . . . . .DLB-197

Chomsky, Noam 1928- DLB-246

Chopin, Kate 1850-1904 . . .DLB-12, 78; CDALB-3

Chopin, Rene 1885-1953 . . . . .DLB-92

Choquette, Adrienne 1915-1973 . . . . .DLB-68

Choquette, Robert 1905- DLB-68

Choyce, Lesley 1951- DLB-251

Chrétien de Troyes
circa 1140-circa 1190 . . . . .DLB-208

Christensen, Inger 1935- DLB-214

The Christian Publishing Company DLB-49

Christie, Agatha
1890-1976 . . . . DLB-13, 77, 245; CDBLB-6

Christine de Pizan
circa 1365-circa 1431 . . . . .DLB-208

Christopher, John 1922- DLB-255

Christus und die Samariterin circa 950 . . . . .DLB-148

Christy, Howard Chandler 1873-1952 . . .DLB-188

Chulkov, Mikhail Dmitrievich
1743?-1792 . . . . .DLB-150

Church, Benjamin 1734-1778 . . . . .DLB-31

Church, Francis Pharcellus 1839-1906 . . . .DLB-79

Church, Peggy Pond 1903-1986 . . . . .DLB-212

Church, Richard 1893-1972 . . . . .DLB-191

Church, William Conant 1836-1917 . . . . . .DLB-79

Churchill, Caryl 1938- DLB-13

Churchill, Charles 1731-1764 . . . . .DLB-109

Churchill, Winston 1871-1947 . . . . .DLB-202

Churchill, Sir Winston
1874-1965 . . . . . .DLB-100; DS-16; CDBLB-5

Churchyard, Thomas 1520?-1604 . . . . . . .DLB-132

Churton, E., and Company DLB-106

Chute, Marchette 1909-1994 . . . . .DLB-103

Ciardi, John 1916-1986 . . . . .DLB-5; Y-86

Cibber, Colley 1671-1757 . . . . .DLB-84

Cicero
106 B.C.-43 B.C. DLB-211, CDWLB-1

Cima, Annalisa 1941- DLB-128

Čingo, Živko 1935-1987 . . . . .DLB-181

Cioran, E. M. 1911-1995 . . . . .DLB-220

Čipkus, Alfonsas (see Nyka-Niliūnas, Alfonsas)

Cirese, Eugenio 1884-1955 . . . . .DLB-114

Cīrulis, Jānis (see Bels, Alberts)

Cisneros, Sandra 1954- DLB-122, 152

City Lights Books DLB-46

Cixous, Hélène 1937- DLB-83, 242

The Claims of Business and Literature:
An Undergraduate Essay by
Maxwell Perkins Y-01

Clampitt, Amy 1920-1994 . . . . .DLB-105

Clancy, Tom 1947- DLB-227

Clapper, Raymond 1892-1944 . . . . .DLB-29

Clare, John 1793-1864 . . . . .DLB-55, 96

Clarendon, Edward Hyde, Earl of
1609-1674 .DLB-101

Clark, Alfred Alexander Gordon (see Hare, Cyril)

Clark, Ann Nolan 1896- DLB-52

Clark, C. E. Frazer, Jr. 1925- DLB-187; Y-01

Clark, C. M., Publishing Company DLB-46

Clark, Catherine Anthony 1892-1977 . . . . .DLB-68

Clark, Charles Heber 1841-1915 . . . . .DLB-11

Clark, Davis Wasgatt 1812-1871 . . . . .DLB-79

Clark, Eleanor 1913- DLB-6

Clark, J. P. 1935- DLB-117; CDWLB-3

Clark, Lewis Gaylord
1808-1873 . . . . .DLB-3, 64, 73, 250

Clark, Walter Van Tilburg
1909-1971 . . . . .DLB-9, 206

Clark, William (see Lewis, Meriwether)

Clark, William Andrews, Jr. 1877-1934 . . .DLB-187

Clarke, Sir Arthur C. 1917- DLB-261

Clarke, Austin 1896-1974 . . . . .DLB-10, 20

Clarke, Austin C. 1934- DLB-53, 125

Clarke, Gillian 1937- DLB-40

Clarke, James Freeman
1810-1888 . . . . .DLB-1, 59, 235

Clarke, Lindsay 1939- DLB-231

Clarke, Marcus 1846-1881 . . . . .DLB-230

Clarke, Pauline 1921- DLB-161

Clarke, Rebecca Sophia 1833-1906 . . . . . . .DLB-42

Clarke, Robert, and Company DLB-49

Clarke, Samuel 1675-1729 . . . . .DLB-252

Clarkson, Thomas 1760-1846 . . . . .DLB-158

Claudel, Paul 1868-1955 . . . . .DLB-192, 258

Claudius, Matthias 1740-1815 . . . . .DLB-97

Clausen, Andy 1943- DLB-16

Clawson, John L. 1865-1933 . . . . .DLB-187

Claxton, Remsen and Haffelfinger DLB-49

Clay, Cassius Marcellus 1810-1903 . . . . . . .DLB-43

Cleage, Pearl 1948- DLB-228

Cleary, Beverly 1916- DLB-52

Cleary, Kate McPhelim 1863-1905 . . . . . .DLB-221

Cleaver, Vera 1919- and
Cleaver, Bill 1920-1981 . . . . .DLB-52

Cleland, John 1710-1789 . . . . .DLB-39

Clemens, Samuel Langhorne (Mark Twain)
1835-1910 . . . . .DLB-11, 12, 23, 64, 74,
186, 189; CDALB-3

Mark Twain on Perpetual Copyright Y-92

Clement, Hal 1922- DLB-8

Clemo, Jack 1916- DLB-27

Clephane, Elizabeth Cecilia
1830-1869 .DLB-199

Cleveland, John 1613-1658 . . . . .DLB-126

Cliff, Michelle 1946- DLB-157; CDWLB-3

Clifford, Lady Anne 1590-1676 . . . . .DLB-151

Clifford, James L. 1901-1978 . . . . .DLB-103

Clifford, Lucy 1853?-1929 . . . . .DLB-135, 141, 197

Clift, Charmian 1923-1969 . . . . .DLB-260

Clifton, Lucille 1936- DLB-5, 41

Clines, Francis X. 1938- DLB-185

Clive, Caroline (V) 1801-1873 . . . . DLB-199

Clode, Edward J. [publishing house] DLB-46

Clough, Arthur Hugh 1819-1861 . . . . DLB-32

Cloutier, Cécile 1930- DLB-60

Clouts, Sidney 1926-1982 . . . . DLB-225

Clutton-Brock, Arthur 1868-1924 . . . . . . DLB-98

Coates, Robert M. 1897-1973 . . . . . DLB-4, 9, 102

Coatsworth, Elizabeth 1893- DLB-22

Cobb, Charles E., Jr. 1943- DLB-41

Cobb, Frank I. 1869-1923 . . . . DLB-25

Cobb, Irvin S. 1876-1944 . . . . DLB-11, 25, 86

Cobbe, Frances Power 1822-1904 . . . . . . DLB-190

Cobbett, William 1763-1835 . . . . .DLB-43, 107

Cobbledick, Gordon 1898-1969 . . . . .DLB-171

Cochran, Thomas C. 1902- DLB-17

Cochrane, Elizabeth 1867-1922 . . . . . DLB-25, 189

Cockerell, Sir Sydney 1867-1962 . . . . . . DLB-201

Cockerill, John A. 1845-1896 . . . . DLB-23

Cocteau, Jean 1889-1963 . . . . DLB-65, 258

Coderre, Emile (see Jean Narrache)

Coe, Jonathan 1961- DLB-231

Coetzee, J. M. 1940- DLB-225

Coffee, Lenore J. 1900?-1984 . . . . DLB-44

Coffin, Robert P. Tristram 1892-1955 . . . . DLB-45

Coghill, Mrs. Harry (see Walker, Anna Louisa)

Cogswell, Fred 1917- DLB-60

Cogswell, Mason Fitch 1761-1830 . . . . . . DLB-37

Cohan, George M. 1878-1942 . . . . DLB-249

Cohen, Arthur A. 1928-1986 . . . . DLB-28

Cohen, Leonard 1934- DLB-53

Cohen, Matt 1942- DLB-53

Colbeck, Norman 1903-1987 . . . . DLB-201

Colden, Cadwallader 1688-1776 . . . . . . DLB-24, 30

Colden, Jane 1724-1766 . . . . DLB-200

Cole, Barry 1936- DLB-14

Cole, George Watson 1850-1939 . . . . . . DLB-140

Colegate, Isabel 1931- DLB-14, 231

Coleman, Emily Holmes 1899-1974 . . . . . . DLB-4

Coleman, Wanda 1946- DLB-130

Coleridge, Hartley 1796-1849 . . . . DLB-96

Coleridge, Mary 1861-1907 . . . . DLB-19, 98

Coleridge, Samuel Taylor
1772-1834 . . . . DLB-93, 107; CDBLB-3

Coleridge, Sara 1802-1852 . . . . DLB-199

Colet, John 1467-1519 . . . . DLB-132

Colette 1873-1954 . . . . DLB-65

Colette, Sidonie Gabrielle (see Colette)

Colinas, Antonio 1946- DLB-134

Coll, Joseph Clement 1881-1921 . . . . . . DLB-188

Collier, John 1901-1980 . . . . .DLB-77, 255

Collier, John Payne 1789-1883 . . . . DLB-184

Collier, Mary 1690-1762 . . . . DLB-95

Collier, P. F. [publishing house] DLB-49

Collier, Robert J. 1876-1918 . . . . DLB-91

Collin and Small DLB-49

Collingwood, R. G. 1889-1943 . . . . DLB-262

Collingwood, W. G. 1854-1932 . . . . DLB-149

Collins, An floruit circa 1653 . . . . DLB-131

Collins, Anthony 1676-1729 . . . . DLB-252

Collins, Isaac [publishing house] DLB-49

Collins, Merle 1950- DLB-157

Collins, Michael 1964- DLB-267

Collins, Mortimer 1827-1876 . . . . DLB-21, 35

Collins, Tom (see Furphy, Joseph)

Collins, Wilkie
1824-1889 . . . . . . DLB-18, 70, 159; CDBLB-4

Collins, William 1721-1759 . . . . DLB-109

Collins, William, Sons and Company . . . DLB-154

Collis, Maurice 1889-1973 . . . . DLB-195

Collyer, Mary 1716?-1763? DLB-39

Colman, Benjamin 1673-1747 . . . . DLB-24

Colman, George, the Elder 1732-1794 . . . . DLB-89

Colman, George, the Younger
1762-1836 . . . . DLB-89

Colman, S. [publishing house] DLB-49

Colombo, John Robert 1936- DLB-53

Colquhoun, Patrick 1745-1820 . . . . DLB-158

Colter, Cyrus 1910- DLB-33

Colum, Padraic 1881-1972 . . . . DLB-19

Columella fl. first century A.D. DLB-211

Colvin, Sir Sidney 1845-1927 . . . . DLB-149

Colwin, Laurie 1944-1992 . . . . . . .DLB-218; Y-80

Comden, Betty 1919- and
Green, Adolph 1918- DLB-44, 265

Come to Papa Y-99

Comi, Girolamo 1890-1968 . . . . DLB-114

The Comic Tradition Continued
[in the British Novel] DLB-15

Comisso, Giovanni 1895-1969 . . . . DLB-264

Commager, Henry Steele 1902-1998 . . . . . DLB-17

The Commercialization of the Image of
Revolt, by Kenneth Rexroth DLB-16

Community and Commentators: Black
Theatre and Its Critics DLB-38

Commynes, Philippe de
circa 1447-1511 . . . . DLB-208

Compton, D. G. 1930- DLB-261

Compton-Burnett, Ivy 1884?-1969 . . . . . . DLB-36

Conan, Laure 1845-1924 . . . . DLB-99

Concord History and Life DLB-223

Concord Literary History of a Town DLB-223

Conde, Carmen 1901- DLB-108

Conference on Modern Biography Y-85

Congreve, William
1670-1729 . . . . DLB-39, 84; CDBLB-2

Preface to Incognita (1692) DLB-39

Conkey, W. B., Company DLB-49

Conn, Stewart 1936- DLB-233

Connell, Evan S., Jr. 1924- DLB-2; Y-81

Connelly, Marc 1890-1980 . . . . .DLB-7; Y-80

Connolly, Cyril 1903-1974 . . . . DLB-98

Connolly, James B. 1868-1957 . . . . DLB-78

Connor, Ralph 1860-1937 . . . . DLB-92

Connor, Tony 1930- DLB-40

Conquest, Robert 1917- DLB-27

Conrad, John, and Company DLB-49

Conrad, Joseph
1857-1924 . . . . DLB-10, 34, 98, 156; CDBLB-5

Conroy, Jack 1899-1990 . . . . Y-81

Conroy, Pat 1945- DLB-6

Considine, Bob 1906-1975 . . . . DLB-241

The Consolidation of Opinion: Critical
Responses to the Modernists DLB-36

Consolo, Vincenzo 1933- DLB-196

Constable, Archibald, and Company DLB-154

Constable, Henry 1562-1613 . . . . DLB-136

Constable and Company Limited DLB-112

Constant, Benjamin 1767-1830 . . . . DLB-119

Constant de Rebecque, Henri-Benjamin de
(see Constant, Benjamin)

Constantine, David 1944- DLB-40

Constantin-Weyer, Maurice 1881-1964 . . . DLB-92

Contempo Caravan: Kites in a Windstorm . . . Y-85

A Contemporary Flourescence of Chicano
Literature Y-84

Continental European Rhetoricians,
1400-1600 . . . . DLB-236

The Continental Publishing Company DLB-49

Conversations with Editors Y-95

Conversations with Publishers I: An Interview
with Patrick O'Connor Y-84

Conversations with Publishers II: An Interview
with Charles Scribner III Y-94

Conversations with Publishers III: An Interview
with Donald Lamm Y-95

Conversations with Publishers IV: An Interview
with James Laughlin Y-96

Conversations with Rare Book Dealers I: An
Interview with Glenn Horowitz Y-90

Conversations with Rare Book Dealers II: An
Interview with Ralph Sipper Y-94

Conversations with Rare Book Dealers
(Publishers) III: An Interview with
Otto Penzler Y-96

The Conversion of an Unpolitical Man,
by W. H. Bruford DLB-66

Conway, Anne 1631-1679 . . . . DLB-252

Conway, Moncure Daniel
1832-1907 . . . . DLB-1, 223

Cook, David C., Publishing Company . . . DLB-49

Cook, Ebenezer circa 1667-circa 1732 . . . . DLB-24

Cook, Edward Tyas 1857-1919 . . . . DLB-149

Cook, Eliza 1818-1889 . . . . DLB-199

Cook, George Cram 1873-1924 . . . . DLB-266

Cook, Michael 1933-1994 . . . . DLB-53

Cooke, George Willis 1848-1923 . . . . DLB-71

Cooke, Increase, and Company DLB-49

Cooke, John Esten 1830-1886 . . . . DLB-3, 248

Cooke, Philip Pendleton
  1816-1850 . . . . .DLB-3, 59, 248

Cooke, Rose Terry 1827-1892 . . . . . . .DLB-12, 74

Cook-Lynn, Elizabeth 1930- DLB-175

Coolbrith, Ina 1841-1928. . . . . .DLB-54, 186

Cooley, Peter 1940- DLB-105

"Into the Mirror" DLB-105

Coolidge, Clark 1939- DLB-193

Coolidge, George [publishing house] DLB-49

Coolidge, Susan (see Woolsey, Sarah Chauncy)

Cooper, Anna Julia 1858-1964. . . . . . . .DLB-221

Cooper, Edith Emma (see Field, Michael)

Cooper, Giles 1918-1966 . . . . .DLB-13

Cooper, J. California 19??- DLB-212

Cooper, James Fenimore
  1789-1851 . . . . . . .DLB-3, 183, 250; CDALB-2

Cooper, Kent 1880-1965 . . . . .DLB-29

Cooper, Susan 1935- DLB-161, 261

Cooper, Susan Fenimore 1813-1894 . . . . .DLB-239

Cooper, William [publishing house] DLB-170

Coote, J. [publishing house] DLB-154

Coover, Robert 1932- DLB-2, 227; Y-81

Copeland and Day. DLB-49

Ćopić, Branko 1915-1984 . . . . .DLB-181

Copland, Robert 1470?-1548 . . . . .DLB-136

Coppard, A. E. 1878-1957 . . . . .DLB-162

Coppée, François 1842-1908 . . . . .DLB-217

Coppel, Alfred 1921- Y-83

Coppola, Francis Ford 1939- DLB-44

Copway, George (Kah-ge-ga-gah-bowh)
  1818-1869 . . . . DLB-175, 183

Corazzini, Sergio 1886-1907 . . . . .DLB-114

Corbett, Richard 1582-1635 . . . . .DLB-121

Corbière, Tristan 1845-1875 . . . . .DLB-217

Corcoran, Barbara 1911- DLB-52

Cordelli, Franco 1943- DLB-196

Corelli, Marie 1855-1924. . . . . .DLB-34, 156

Corle, Edwin 1906-1956 . . . . Y-85

Corman, Cid 1924- DLB-5, 193

Cormier, Robert 1925-2000. . . .DLB-52; CDALB-6

Corn, Alfred 1943- DLB-120; Y-80

Cornford, Frances 1886-1960 . . . . .DLB-240

Cornish, Sam 1935- DLB-41

Cornish, William circa 1465-circa 1524. . .DLB-132

Cornwall, Barry (see Procter, Bryan Waller)

Cornwallis, Sir William, the Younger
  circa 1579-1614 . . . . .DLB-151

Cornwell, David John Moore (see le Carré, John)

Corpi, Lucha 1945- DLB-82

Corrington, John William
  1932-1988 . . . . .DLB-6, 244

Corriveau, Monique 1927-1976 . . . . .DLB-251

Corrothers, James D. 1869-1917 . . . . .DLB-50

Corso, Gregory 1930- DLB-5, 16, 237

Cortázar, Julio 1914-1984 . . .DLB-113; CDWLB-3

Cortéz, Carlos 1923- DLB-209

Cortez, Jayne 1936- DLB-41

Corvinus, Gottlieb Siegmund
  1677-1746. . . . . .DLB-168

Corvo, Baron (see Rolfe, Frederick William)

Cory, Annie Sophie (see Cross, Victoria)

Cory, William Johnson 1823-1892 . . . . . . .DLB-35

Coryate, Thomas 1577?-1617 . . . . . . DLB-151, 172

Ćosić, Dobrica 1921- DLB-181; CDWLB-4

Cosin, John 1595-1672. . . . . .DLB-151, 213

Cosmopolitan Book Corporation DLB-46

The Cost of *The Cantos:* William Bird
  to Ezra Pound Y-01

Costain, Thomas B. 1885-1965 . . . . .DLB-9

Coste, Donat 1912-1957 . . . . .DLB-88

Costello, Louisa Stuart 1799-1870 . . . . . . .DLB-166

Cota-Cárdenas, Margarita 1941- DLB-122

Côté, Denis 1954- DLB-251

Cotten, Bruce 1873-1954 . . . . .DLB-187

Cotter, Joseph Seamon, Sr. 1861-1949. . . .DLB-50

Cotter, Joseph Seamon, Jr. 1895-1919 . . . .DLB-50

Cottle, Joseph [publishing house]. DLB-154

Cotton, Charles 1630-1687 . . . . .DLB-131

Cotton, John 1584-1652. . . . . .DLB-24

Cotton, Sir Robert Bruce 1571-1631 . . . . .DLB-213

Coulter, John 1888-1980 . . . . .DLB-68

Cournos, John 1881-1966 . . . . .DLB-54

Courteline, Georges 1858-1929 . . . . .DLB-192

Cousins, Margaret 1905-1996 . . . . .DLB-137

Cousins, Norman 1915-1990. . . . . .DLB-137

Couvreur, Jessie (see Tasma)

Coventry, Francis 1725-1754 . . . . .DLB-39

Dedication, *The History of Pompey
  the Little* (1751) DLB-39

Coverdale, Miles 1487 or 1488-1569. . . . .DLB-167

Coverly, N. [publishing house] DLB-49

Covici-Friede DLB-46

Cowan, Peter 1914- DLB-260

Coward, Noel
  1899-1973 . . . . .DLB-10, 245; CDBLB-6

Coward, McCann and Geoghegan DLB-46

Cowles, Gardner 1861-1946 . . . . .DLB-29

Cowles, Gardner "Mike", Jr.
  1903-1985 . . . . DLB-127, 137

Cowley, Abraham 1618-1667 . . . . . .DLB-131, 151

Cowley, Hannah 1743-1809 . . . . .DLB-89

Cowley, Malcolm
  1898-1989 . . . . DLB-4, 48; Y-81, Y-89

Cowper, Richard 1926-2002 . . . . .DLB-261

Cowper, William 1731-1800 . . . . . . .DLB-104, 109

Cox, A. B. (see Berkeley, Anthony)

Cox, James McMahon 1903-1974 . . . . . . .DLB-127

Cox, James Middleton 1870-1957 . . . . . . .DLB-127

Cox, Leonard ca. 1495-ca. 1550 . . . . .DLB-236

Cox, Palmer 1840-1924. . . . . .DLB-42

Coxe, Louis 1918-1993 . . . . .DLB-5

Coxe, Tench 1755-1824. . . . . .DLB-37

Cozzens, Frederick S. 1818-1869 . . . . . . .DLB-202

Cozzens, James Gould
  1903-1978 . . . . .DLB-9; Y-84; DS-2; CDALB-1

James Gould Cozzens—A View from Afar. Y-97

James Gould Cozzens Case Re-opened Y-97

James Gould Cozzens: How to Read Him Y-97

Cozzens's *Michael Scarlett* Y-97

James Gould Cozzens Symposium and
  Exhibition at the University of
  South Carolina, Columbia Y-00

Crabbe, George 1754-1832 . . . . .DLB-93

Crace, Jim 1946- DLB-231

Crackanthorpe, Hubert 1870-1896 . . . . . .DLB-135

Craddock, Charles Egbert (see Murfree, Mary N.)

Cradock, Thomas 1718-1770 . . . . .DLB-31

Craig, Daniel H. 1811-1895. . . . . .DLB-43

Craik, Dinah Maria 1826-1887 . . . . . .DLB-35, 136

Cramer, Richard Ben 1950- DLB-185

Cranch, Christopher Pearse
  1813-1892 . . . . .DLB-1, 42, 243

Crane, Hart 1899-1932 . . . . .DLB-4, 48; CDALB-4

Crane, R. S. 1886-1967 . . . . .DLB-63

Crane, Stephen
  1871-1900 . . . . .DLB-12, 54, 78; CDALB-3

Crane, Walter 1845-1915 . . . . .DLB-163

Cranmer, Thomas 1489-1556 . . . . . .DLB-132, 213

Crapsey, Adelaide 1878-1914. . . . . .DLB-54

Crashaw, Richard 1612 or 1613-1649 . . . .DLB-126

Craven, Avery 1885-1980 . . . . .DLB-17

Crawford, Charles 1752-circa 1815 . . . . . . .DLB-31

Crawford, F. Marion 1854-1909 . . . . .DLB-71

Crawford, Isabel Valancy 1850-1887 . . . . .DLB-92

Crawley, Alan 1887-1975 . . . . .DLB-68

Crayon, Geoffrey (see Irving, Washington)

Crayon, Porte (see Strother, David Hunter)

Creamer, Robert W. 1922- DLB-171

Creasey, John 1908-1973 . . . . .DLB-77

Creative Age Press. DLB-46

Creech, William [publishing house]. DLB-154

Creede, Thomas [publishing house] DLB-170

Creel, George 1876-1953 . . . . .DLB-25

Creeley, Robert 1926- . . . DLB-5, 16, 169; DS-17

Creelman, James 1859-1915 . . . . .DLB-23

Cregan, David 1931- DLB-13

Creighton, Donald Grant 1902-1979 . . . . .DLB-88

Cremazie, Octave 1827-1879 . . . . .DLB-99

Crémer, Victoriano 1909?- DLB-108

Crescas, Hasdai circa 1340-1412? DLB-115

Crespo, Angel 1926- DLB-134

Cresset Press DLB-112

Cresswell, Helen 1934- DLB-161

Crèvecoeur, Michel Guillaume Jean de
  1735-1813 . . . . .DLB-37

Crewe, Candida 1964- DLB-207

Crews, Harry 1935- DLB-6, 143, 185

Crichton, Michael 1942- Y-81

A Crisis of Culture: The Changing Role
of Religion in the New Republic DLB-37

Crispin, Edmund 1921-1978 . . . . DLB-87

Cristofer, Michael 1946- DLB-7

Crnjanski, Miloš
1893-1977 . . . . DLB-147; CDWLB-4

Crocker, Hannah Mather 1752-1829 . . . . DLB-200

Crockett, David (Davy)
1786-1836 . . . . DLB-3, 11, 183, 248

Croft-Cooke, Rupert (see Bruce, Leo)

Crofts, Freeman Wills 1879-1957 . . . . DLB-77

Croker, John Wilson 1780-1857 . . . . DLB-110

Croly, George 1780-1860 . . . . DLB-159

Croly, Herbert 1869-1930 . . . . DLB-91

Croly, Jane Cunningham 1829-1901 . . . . . DLB-23

Crompton, Richmal 1890-1969 . . . . DLB-160

Cronin, A. J. 1896-1981 . . . . DLB-191

Cros, Charles 1842-1888 . . . . DLB-217

Crosby, Caresse 1892-1970 . . . . DLB-48

Crosby, Caresse 1892-1970
and Crosby, Harry
1898-1929 . . . . DLB-4; DS-15

Crosby, Harry 1898-1929 . . . . DLB-48

Crosland, Camilla Toulmin
(Mrs. Newton Crosland)
1812-1895 . . . . DLB-240

Cross, Gillian 1945- DLB-161

Cross, Victoria 1868-1952 . . . . DLB-135, 197

Crossley-Holland, Kevin 1941- . . . DLB-40, 161

Crothers, Rachel 1870-1958 . . . . DLB-7, 266

Crowell, Thomas Y., Company DLB-49

Crowley, John 1942- Y-82

Crowley, Mart 1935- DLB-7, 266

Crown Publishers DLB-46

Crowne, John 1641-1712 . . . . DLB-80

Crowninshield, Edward Augustus
1817-1859 . . . . DLB-140

Crowninshield, Frank 1872-1947 . . . . DLB-91

Croy, Homer 1883-1965 . . . . DLB-4

Crumley, James 1939- DLB-226; Y-84

Cruse, Mary Anne 1825?-1910 . . . . DLB-239

Cruz, Migdalia 1958- DLB-249

Cruz, Victor Hernández 1949- DLB-41

Csokor, Franz Theodor 1885-1969 . . . . . . DLB-81

Csoóri, Sándor 1930- DLB-232; CDWLB-4

Cuala Press DLB-112

Cudworth, Ralph 1617-1688 . . . . DLB-252

Cullen, Countee
1903-1946 . . . . DLB-4, 48, 51; CDALB-4

Culler, Jonathan D. 1944- DLB-67, 246

Cullinan, Elizabeth 1933- DLB-234

The Cult of Biography
Excerpts from the Second Folio Debate:
"Biographies are generally a disease of
English Literature" — Germaine Greer,
Victoria Glendinning, Auberon Waugh,
and Richard Holmes Y-86

Culverwel, Nathaniel 1619?-1651? DLB-252

Cumberland, Richard 1732-1811 . . . . DLB-89

Cummings, Constance Gordon
1837-1924 . . . . .DLB-174

Cummings, E. E.
1894-1962 . . . . DLB-4, 48; CDALB-5

Cummings, Ray 1887-1957 . . . . DLB-8

Cummings and Hilliard DLB-49

Cummins, Maria Susanna
1827-1866 . . . . DLB-42

Cumpián, Carlos 1953- DLB-209

Cunard, Nancy 1896-1965 . . . . DLB-240

Cundall, Joseph [publishing house] DLB-106

Cuney, Waring 1906-1976 . . . . DLB-51

Cuney-Hare, Maude 1874-1936 . . . . DLB-52

Cunningham, Allan 1784-1842 . . . . . DLB-116, 144

Cunningham, J. V. 1911- DLB-5

Cunningham, Peter 1947- DLB-267

Cunningham, Peter F.
[publishing house] DLB-49

Cunquiero, Alvaro 1911-1981 . . . . DLB-134

Cuomo, George 1929- Y-80

Cupples, Upham and Company DLB-49

Cupples and Leon DLB-46

Cuppy, Will 1884-1949 . . . . DLB-11

Curiel, Barbara Brinson 1956- DLB-209

Curll, Edmund [publishing house] DLB-154

Currie, James 1756-1805 . . . . DLB-142

Currie, Mary Montgomerie Lamb Singleton,
Lady Currie
(see Fane, Violet)

Cursor Mundi circa 1300 . . . . DLB-146

Curti, Merle E. 1897- DLB-17

Curtis, Anthony 1926- DLB-155

Curtis, Cyrus H. K. 1850-1933 . . . . DLB-91

Curtis, George William
1824-1892 . . . . DLB-1, 43, 223

Curzon, Robert 1810-1873 . . . . DLB-166

Curzon, Sarah Anne 1833-1898 . . . . DLB-99

Cusack, Dymphna 1902-1981 . . . . DLB-260

Cushing, Harvey 1869-1939 . . . . DLB-187

Custance, Olive (Lady Alfred Douglas)
1874-1944 . . . . DLB-240

Cynewulf circa 770-840 . . . . DLB-146

Czepko, Daniel 1605-1660 . . . . DLB-164

Czerniawski, Adam 1934- DLB-232

D

Dabit, Eugène 1898-1936 . . . . DLB-65

Daborne, Robert circa 1580-1628 . . . . DLB-58

Dąbrowska, Maria
1889-1965 . . . . DLB-215; CDWLB-4

Dacey, Philip 1939- DLB-105

"Eyes Across Centuries: Contemporary
Poetry and 'That Vision Thing,'" . . . DLB-105

Dach, Simon 1605-1659 . . . . DLB-164

Dagerman, Stig 1923-1954 . . . . DLB-259

Daggett, Rollin M. 1831-1901 . . . . DLB-79

D'Aguiar, Fred 1960- DLB-157

Dahl, Roald 1916-1990 . . . . DLB-139, 255

Dahlberg, Edward 1900-1977 . . . . DLB-48

Dahn, Felix 1834-1912 . . . . DLB-129

Dal', Vladimir Ivanovich (Kazak Vladimir
Lugansky) 1801-1872 . . . . DLB-198

Dale, Peter 1938- DLB-40

Daley, Arthur 1904-1974 . . . . .DLB-171

Dall, Caroline Healey 1822-1912 . . . . . DLB-1, 235

Dallas, E. S. 1828-1879 . . . . DLB-55

From *The Gay Science* (1866) DLB-21

The Dallas Theater Center DLB-7

D'Alton, Louis 1900-1951 . . . . DLB-10

Daly, Carroll John 1889-1958 . . . . DLB-226

Daly, T. A. 1871-1948 . . . . DLB-11

Damon, S. Foster 1893-1971 . . . . DLB-45

Damrell, William S. [publishing house] . . . DLB-49

Dana, Charles A. 1819-1897 . . . . . . DLB-3, 23, 250

Dana, Richard Henry, Jr.
1815-1882 . . . . DLB-1, 183, 235

Dandridge, Ray Garfield DLB-51

Dane, Clemence 1887-1965 . . . . .DLB-10, 197

Danforth, John 1660-1730 . . . . DLB-24

Danforth, Samuel, I 1626-1674 . . . . DLB-24

Danforth, Samuel, II 1666-1727 . . . . DLB-24

Dangerous Years: London Theater,
1939-1945 . . . . DLB-10

Daniel, John M. 1825-1865 . . . . DLB-43

Daniel, Samuel 1562 or 1563-1619 . . . . . . DLB-62

Daniel Press DLB-106

Daniells, Roy 1902-1979 . . . . DLB-68

Daniels, Jim 1956- DLB-120

Daniels, Jonathan 1902-1981 . . . . .DLB-127

Daniels, Josephus 1862-1948 . . . . DLB-29

Daniels, Sarah 1957- DLB-245

Danilevsky, Grigorii Petrovich
1829-1890 . . . . DLB-238

Dannay, Frederic 1905-1982 and
Manfred B. Lee 1905-1971 . . . . .DLB-137

Danner, Margaret Esse 1915- DLB-41

Danter, John [publishing house] DLB-170

Dantin, Louis 1865-1945 . . . . DLB-92

Danzig, Allison 1898-1987 . . . . .DLB-171

D'Arcy, Ella circa 1857-1937 . . . . DLB-135

Dark, Eleanor 1901-1985 . . . . DLB-260

Darke, Nick 1948- DLB-233

Darley, Felix Octavious Carr 1822-1888 . DLB-188

Darley, George 1795-1846 . . . . DLB-96

Darmesteter, Madame James
(see Robinson, A. Mary F.)

Darwin, Charles 1809-1882 . . . . .DLB-57, 166

Darwin, Erasmus 1731-1802 . . . . DLB-93

Daryush, Elizabeth 1887-1977 . . . . DLB-20

Dashkova, Ekaterina Romanovna
(née Vorontsova) 1743-1810 . . . . DLB-150

Dashwood, Edmée Elizabeth Monica de la Pasture
(see Delafield, E. M.)

Daudet, Alphonse 1840-1897 . . . . DLB-123

d'Aulaire, Edgar Parin 1898- and
   d'Aulaire, Ingri 1904- DLB-22

Davenant, Sir William 1606-1668 . . . .DLB-58, 126

Davenport, Guy 1927- DLB-130

Davenport, Marcia 1903-1996 . . . . DS-17

Davenport, Robert ?-? DLB-58

Daves, Delmer 1904-1977 . . . . .DLB-26

Davey, Frank 1940- DLB-53

Davidson, Avram 1923-1993 . . . . .DLB-8

Davidson, Donald 1893-1968 . . . . .DLB-45

Davidson, John 1857-1909 . . . . .DLB-19

Davidson, Lionel 1922- DLB-14

Davidson, Robyn 1950- DLB-204

Davidson, Sara 1943- DLB-185

Davie, Donald 1922- DLB-27

Davie, Elspeth 1919- DLB-139

Davies, Sir John 1569-1626 . . . . .DLB-172

Davies, John, of Hereford 1565?-1618 . . . .DLB-121

Davies, Peter, Limited DLB-112

Davies, Rhys 1901-1978 . . . . .DLB-139, 191

Davies, Robertson 1913-1995 . . . . .DLB-68

Davies, Samuel 1723-1761 . . . . .DLB-31

Davies, Thomas 1712?-1785 . . . . . . .DLB-142, 154

Davies, W. H. 1871-1940 . . . . DLB-19, 174

Daviot, Gordon 1896?-1952 . . . . .DLB-10
   (see also Tey, Josephine)

Davis, Arthur Hoey (see Rudd, Steele)

Davis, Charles A. 1795-1867 . . . . .DLB-11

Davis, Clyde Brion 1894-1962 . . . . .DLB-9

Davis, Dick 1945- DLB-40

Davis, Frank Marshall 1905-? DLB-51

Davis, H. L. 1894-1960 . . . . .DLB-9, 206

Davis, John 1774-1854 . . . . .DLB-37

Davis, Lydia 1947- DLB-130

Davis, Margaret Thomson 1926- DLB-14

Davis, Ossie 1917- DLB-7, 38, 249

Davis, Owen 1874-1956 . . . . .DLB-249

Davis, Paxton 1925-1994 . . . . Y-89

Davis, Rebecca Harding 1831-1910 . . .DLB-74, 239

Davis, Richard Harding 1864-1916
   . . . . DLB-12, 23, 78, 79, 189; DS-13

Davis, Samuel Cole 1764-1809 . . . . .DLB-37

Davis, Samuel Post 1850-1918 . . . . .DLB-202

Davison, Frank Dalby 1893-1970 . . . . . . .DLB-260

Davison, Peter 1928- DLB-5

Davydov, Denis Vasil'evich
   1784-1839 . . . . .DLB-205

Davys, Mary 1674-1732 . . . . .DLB-39

   Preface to The Works of
   Mrs. Davys (1725) DLB-39

DAW Books DLB-46

Dawson, Ernest 1882-1947 . . . . .DLB-140

Dawson, Fielding 1930- DLB-130

Dawson, Sarah Morgan 1842-1909 . . . . .DLB-239

Dawson, William 1704-1752 . . . . .DLB-31

Day, Angel flourished 1583-1599 . . . DLB-167, 236

Day, Benjamin Henry 1810-1889 . . . . .DLB-43

Day, Clarence 1874-1935 . . . . .DLB-11

Day, Dorothy 1897-1980 . . . . .DLB-29

Day, Frank Parker 1881-1950 . . . . .DLB-92

Day, John circa 1574-circa 1640 . . . . .DLB-62

Day, John [publishing house] DLB-170

Day, The John, Company DLB-46

Day Lewis, C. 1904-1972 . . . . .DLB-15, 20
   (see also Blake, Nicholas)

Day, Mahlon [publishing house] DLB-49

Day, Thomas 1748-1789 . . . . .DLB-39

Dazai Osamu 1909-1948 . . . . .DLB-182

Deacon, William Arthur 1890-1977 . . . . . .DLB-68

Deal, Borden 1922-1985 . . . . .DLB-6

de Angeli, Marguerite 1889-1987 . . . . . . .DLB-22

De Angelis, Milo 1951- DLB-128

De Bow, J. D. B.
   1820-1867 . . . . .DLB-3, 79, 248

de Bruyn, Günter 1926- DLB-75

de Camp, L. Sprague 1907-2000 . . . . .DLB-8

De Carlo, Andrea 1952- DLB-196

De Casas, Celso A. 1944- DLB-209

Dechert, Robert 1895-1975 . . . . .DLB-187

Dedications, Inscriptions, and Annotations . . . Y-01

Dee, John 1527-1608 or 1609 . . . . . .DLB-136, 213

Deeping, George Warwick 1877-1950 . . . .DLB 153

Defoe, Daniel
   1660-1731 . . . . . . .DLB-39, 95, 101; CDBLB-2

   Preface to Colonel Jack (1722) DLB-39

   Preface to The Farther Adventures of
   Robinson Crusoe (1719) DLB-39

   Preface to Moll Flanders (1722) DLB-39

   Preface to Robinson Crusoe (1719) DLB-39

   Preface to Roxana (1724) DLB-39

de Fontaine, Felix Gregory 1834-1896 . . . .DLB-43

De Forest, John William 1826-1906 . . .DLB-12, 189

DeFrees, Madeline 1919- DLB-105

"The Poet's Kaleidoscope: The Element
   of Surprise in the Making of
   the Poem" .DLB-105

DeGolyer, Everette Lee 1886-1956 . . . . . .DLB-187

de Graff, Robert 1895-1981 . . . . Y-81

de Graft, Joe 1924-1978 . . . . .DLB-117

De Heinrico circa 980? DLB-148

Deighton, Len 1929- DLB-87; CDBLB-8

DeJong, Meindert 1906-1991 . . . . .DLB-52

Dekker, Thomas
   circa 1572-1632 . . . . . .DLB-62, 172; CDBLB-1

Delacorte, George T., Jr. 1894-1991 . . . . .DLB-91

Delafield, E. M. 1890-1943 . . . . .DLB-34

Delahaye, Guy 1888-1969 . . . . .DLB-92

de la Mare, Walter 1873-1956
   . . . . .DLB-19, 153, 162, 255; CDBLB-6

Deland, Margaret 1857-1945 . . . . .DLB-78

Delaney, Shelagh 1939- DLB-13; CDBLB-8

Delano, Amasa 1763-1823 . . . . .DLB-183

Delany, Martin Robinson 1812-1885 . . . . .DLB-50

Delany, Samuel R. 1942- DLB-8, 33

de la Roche, Mazo 1879-1961 . . . . .DLB-68

Delavigne, Jean François Casimir
   1793-1843 . . . . .DLB-192

Delbanco, Nicholas 1942- DLB-6, 234

Delblanc, Sven 1931-1992 . . . . .DLB-257

Del Castillo, Ramón 1949- DLB-209

Deledda, Grazia 1871-1936 . . . . .DLB-264

De León, Nephtal 1945- DLB-82

Delfini, Antonio 1907-1963 . . . . .DLB-264

Delgado, Abelardo Barrientos 1931- . . .DLB-82

Del Giudice, Daniele 1949- DLB-196

De Libero, Libero 1906-1981 . . . . .DLB-114

DeLillo, Don 1936- DLB-6, 173

de Lint, Charles 1951- DLB-251

de Lisser H. G. 1878-1944 . . . . .DLB-117

Dell, Floyd 1887-1969 . . . . .DLB-9

Dell Publishing Company DLB-46

delle Grazie, Marie Eugene 1864-1931 . . . .DLB-81

Deloney, Thomas died 1600 . . . . .DLB-167

Deloria, Ella C. 1889-1971 . . . . .DLB-175

Deloria, Vine, Jr. 1933- DLB-175

del Rey, Lester 1915-1993 . . . . .DLB-8

Del Vecchio, John M. 1947- DS-9

Del'vig, Anton Antonovich 1798-1831 . . . .DLB-205

de Man, Paul 1919-1983 . . . . .DLB-67

DeMarinis, Rick 1934- DLB-218

Demby, William 1922- DLB-33

De Mille, James 1833-1880 . . . . .DLB-251

de Mille, William 1878-1955 . . . . .DLB-266

Deming, Philander 1829-1915 . . . . .DLB-74

Deml, Jakub 1878-1961 . . . . .DLB-215

Demorest, William Jennings 1822-1895 . . .DLB-79

De Morgan, William 1839-1917 . . . . .DLB-153

Demosthenes 384 B.C.-322 B.C. DLB-176

Denham, Henry [publishing house] DLB-170

Denham, Sir John 1615-1669 . . . . . . .DLB-58, 126

Denison, Merrill 1893-1975 . . . . .DLB-92

Denison, T. S., and Company DLB-49

Dennery, Adolphe Philippe 1811-1899 . . .DLB-192

Dennie, Joseph 1768-1812 . . . . . DLB-37, 43, 59, 73

Dennis, C. J. 1876-1938 . . . . .DLB-260

Dennis, John 1658-1734 . . . . .DLB-101

Dennis, Nigel 1912-1989 . . . . DLB-13, 15, 233

Denslow, W. W. 1856-1915 . . . . .DLB-188

Dent, J. M., and Sons DLB-112

Dent, Tom 1932-1998 . . . . .DLB-38

Denton, Daniel circa 1626-1703 . . . . .DLB-24

DePaola, Tomie 1934- DLB-61

Department of Library, Archives, and Institutional
   Research, American Bible Society Y-97

De Quille, Dan 1829-1898 . . . . .DLB-186

De Quincey, Thomas
   1785-1859 . . . . .DLB-110, 144; CDBLB-3

"Rhetoric" (1828; revised, 1859)
[excerpt] DLB-57

Derby, George Horatio 1823-1861 . . . . DLB-11

Derby, J. C., and Company DLB-49

Derby and Miller DLB-49

De Ricci, Seymour 1881-1942 . . . . DLB-201

Derleth, August 1909-1971 . . . . DLB-9; DS-17

Derrida, Jacques 1930- DLB-242

The Derrydale Press DLB-46

Derzhavin, Gavriil Romanovich
1743-1816 . . . . DLB-150

Desaulniers, Gonsalve 1863-1934 . . . . DLB-92

Desbordes-Valmore, Marceline
1786-1859 . . . . DLB-217

Deschamps, Emile 1791-1871 . . . . DLB-217

Deschamps, Eustache 1340?-1404 . . . . . . DLB-208

Desbiens, Jean-Paul 1927- DLB-53

des Forêts, Louis-Rene 1918- DLB-83

Desiato, Luca 1941- DLB-196

Desnica, Vladan 1905-1967 . . . . DLB-181

Desnos, Robert 1900-1945 . . . . DLB-258

DesRochers, Alfred 1901-1978 . . . . DLB-68

Desrosiers, Léo-Paul 1896-1967 . . . . DLB-68

Dessì, Giuseppe 1909-1977 . . . . DLB-177

Destouches, Louis-Ferdinand
(see Céline, Louis-Ferdinand)

DeSylva, Buddy 1895-1950 and
Brown, Lew 1893-1958 . . . . DLB-265

De Tabley, Lord 1835-1895 . . . . DLB-35

Deutsch, André, Limited DLB-112

Deutsch, Babette 1895-1982 . . . . DLB-45

Deutsch, Niklaus Manuel (see Manuel, Niklaus)

Devanny, Jean 1894-1962 . . . . DLB-260

Deveaux, Alexis 1948- DLB-38

The Development of the Author's Copyright
in Britain DLB-154

The Development of Lighting in the Staging
of Drama, 1900-1945 . . . . DLB-10

"The Development of Meiji Japan" DLB-180

De Vere, Aubrey 1814-1902 . . . . DLB-35

Devereux, second Earl of Essex, Robert
1565-1601 . . . . DLB-136

The Devin-Adair Company DLB-46

De Vinne, Theodore Low 1828-1914 . . . . DLB-187

Devlin, Anne 1951- DLB-245

De Voto, Bernard 1897-1955 . . . . DLB-9, 256

De Vries, Peter 1910-1993 . . . . DLB-6; Y-82

Dewdney, Christopher 1951- DLB-60

Dewdney, Selwyn 1909-1979 . . . . DLB-68

Dewey, John 1859-1952 . . . . DLB-246

Dewey, Orville 1794-1882 . . . . DLB-243

Dewey, Thomas B. 1915-1981 . . . . DLB-226

DeWitt, Robert M., Publisher DLB-49

DeWolfe, Fiske and Company DLB-49

Dexter, Colin 1930- DLB-87

de Young, M. H. 1849-1925 . . . . DLB-25

Dhlomo, H. I. E. 1903-1956 . . . . DLB-157, 225

Dhuoda circa 803-after 843 . . . . DLB-148

The Dial 1840-1844 . . . . DLB-223

The Dial Press DLB-46

Diamond, I. A. L. 1920-1988 . . . . DLB-26

Dibble, L. Grace 1902-1998 . . . . DLB-204

Dibdin, Thomas Frognall 1776-1847 . . . . . DLB-184

Di Cicco, Pier Giorgio 1949- DLB-60

Dick, Philip K. 1928-1982 . . . . DLB-8

Dick and Fitzgerald DLB-49

Dickens, Charles 1812-1870
. . . . DLB-21, 55, 70, 159, 166; CDBLB-4

Dickey, James 1923-1997
. . . . DLB-5, 193; Y-82, Y-93, Y-96;
DS-7, DS-19; CDALB-6

James Dickey Tributes Y-97

The Life of James Dickey: A Lecture to
the Friends of the Emory Libraries,
by Henry Hart Y-98

Dickey, William 1928-1994 . . . . DLB-5

Dickinson, Emily
1830-1886 . . . . DLB-1, 243; CDWLB-3

Dickinson, John 1732-1808 . . . . DLB-31

Dickinson, Jonathan 1688-1747 . . . . DLB-24

Dickinson, Patric 1914- DLB-27

Dickinson, Peter 1927- DLB-87, 161

Dicks, John [publishing house] DLB-106

Dickson, Gordon R. 1923- DLB-8

Dictionary of Literary Biography Yearbook Awards
. . . . . Y-92, Y-93, Y-97, Y-98, Y-99, Y-00, Y-01

The Dictionary of National Biography DLB-144

Didion, Joan 1934-
. . . . . DLB-2, 173, 185; Y-81, Y-86; CDALB-6

Di Donato, Pietro 1911- DLB-9

Die Fürstliche Bibliothek Corvey Y-96

Diego, Gerardo 1896-1987 . . . . DLB-134

Dietz, Howard 1896-1983 . . . . DLB-265

Digges, Thomas circa 1546-1595 . . . . DLB-136

The Digital Millennium Copyright Act:
Expanding Copyright Protection in
Cyberspace and Beyond Y-98

Diktonius, Elmer 1896-1961 . . . . DLB-259

Dillard, Annie 1945- Y-80

Dillard, R. H. W. 1937- DLB-5, 244

Dillingham, Charles T., Company DLB-49

The Dillingham, G. W., Company DLB-49

Dilly, Edward and Charles
[publishing house] DLB-154

Dilthey, Wilhelm 1833-1911 . . . . DLB-129

Dimitrova, Blaga 1922- . . . DLB-181; CDWLB-4

Dimov, Dimitr 1909-1966 . . . . DLB-181

Dimsdale, Thomas J. 1831?-1866 . . . . DLB-186

Dinescu, Mircea 1950- DLB-232

Dinesen, Isak (see Blixen, Karen)

Dingelstedt, Franz von 1814-1881 . . . . . . DLB-133

Dintenfass, Mark 1941- Y-84

Diogenes, Jr. (see Brougham, John)

Diogenes Laertius circa 200 . . . . DLB-176

DiPrima, Diane 1934- DLB-5, 16

Disch, Thomas M. 1940- DLB-8

Disney, Walt 1901-1966 . . . . DLB-22

Disraeli, Benjamin 1804-1881 . . . . DLB-21, 55

D'Israeli, Isaac 1766-1848 . . . . DLB-107

Ditlevsen, Tove 1917-1976 . . . . DLB-214

Ditzen, Rudolf (see Fallada, Hans)

Dix, Dorothea Lynde 1802-1887 . . . . . DLB-1, 235

Dix, Dorothy (see Gilmer, Elizabeth Meriwether)

Dix, Edwards and Company DLB-49

Dix, Gertrude circa 1874-? DLB-197

Dixie, Florence Douglas 1857-1905 . . . . . DLB-174

Dixon, Ella Hepworth
1855 or 1857-1932 . . . . DLB-197

Dixon, Paige (see Corcoran, Barbara)

Dixon, Richard Watson 1833-1900 . . . . . . DLB-19

Dixon, Stephen 1936- DLB-130

Dmitriev, Ivan Ivanovich 1760-1837 . . . . . DLB-150

Do They Or Don't They?
Writers Reading Book Reviews Y-01

Dobell, Bertram 1842-1914 . . . . DLB-184

Dobell, Sydney 1824-1874 . . . . DLB-32

Dobie, J. Frank 1888-1964 . . . . DLB-212

Döblin, Alfred 1878-1957 . . . . DLB-66; CDWLB-2

Dobson, Austin 1840-1921 . . . . DLB-35, 144

Dobson, Rosemary 1920- DLB-260

Doctorow, E. L.
1931- DLB-2, 28, 173; Y-80; CDALB-6

Documents on Sixteenth-Century
Literature DLB-167, 172

Dodd, Anne [publishing house] DLB-154

Dodd, Mead and Company DLB-49

Dodd, Susan M. 1946- DLB-244

Dodd, William E. 1869-1940 . . . . DLB-17

Doderer, Heimito von 1896-1968 . . . . DLB-85

Dodge, B. W., and Company DLB-46

Dodge, Mary Abigail 1833-1896 . . . . DLB-221

Dodge, Mary Mapes
1831?-1905 . . . . DLB-42, 79; DS-13

Dodge Publishing Company DLB-49

Dodgson, Charles Lutwidge (see Carroll, Lewis)

Dodsley, R. [publishing house] DLB-154

Dodsley, Robert 1703-1764 . . . . DLB-95

Dodson, Owen 1914-1983 . . . . DLB-76

Dodwell, Christina 1951- DLB-204

Doesticks, Q. K. Philander, P. B.
(see Thomson, Mortimer)

Doheny, Carrie Estelle 1875-1958 . . . . . . DLB-140

Doherty, John 1798?-1854 . . . . DLB-190

Doig, Ivan 1939- DLB-206

Doinaş, Ştefan Augustin 1922- DLB-232

Domínguez, Sylvia Maida 1935- DLB-122

Donahoe, Patrick [publishing house] DLB-49

Donald, David H. 1920- DLB-17

The Practice of Biography VI: An
Interview with David Herbert Donald Y-87

Donaldson, Scott 1928- DLB-111

Doni, Rodolfo 1919- DLB-177

Donleavy, J. P. 1926- DLB-6, 173

Donnadieu, Marguerite (see Duras, Marguerite)

Donne, John
    1572-1631 . . . . .DLB-121, 151; CDBLB-1

Donnelley, R. R., and Sons Company. DLB-49

Donnelly, Ignatius 1831-1901 . . . . .DLB-12

Donoghue, Emma 1969- DLB-267

Donohue and Henneberry. DLB-49

Donoso, José 1924-1996 . . . . DLB-113; CDWLB-3

Doolady, M. [publishing house]. DLB-49

Dooley, Ebon (see Ebon)

Doolittle, Hilda 1886-1961. . . . . .DLB-4, 45

Doplicher, Fabio 1938- DLB-128

Dor, Milo 1923- DLB-85

Doran, George H., Company DLB-46

Dorgelès, Roland 1886-1973 . . . . .DLB-65

Dorn, Edward 1929-1999 . . . . .DLB-5

Dorr, Rheta Childe 1866-1948 . . . . .DLB-25

Dorris, Michael 1945-1997. . . . . .DLB-175

Dorset and Middlesex, Charles Sackville,
    Lord Buckhurst, Earl of 1643-1706. . . .DLB-131

Dorsey, Candas Jane 1952- DLB-251

Dorst, Tankred 1925- DLB-75, 124

Dos Passos, John 1896-1970
    . . . . .DLB-4, 9; DS-1, DS-15; CDALB-5

John Dos Passos: Artist Y-99

John Dos Passos: A Centennial
    Commemoration. Y-96

Dostoevsky, Fyodor 1821-1881 . . . . .DLB-238

Doubleday and Company DLB-49

Dougall, Lily 1858-1923 . . . . .DLB-92

Doughty, Charles M.
    1843-1926 . . . . DLB-19, 57, 174

Douglas, Lady Alfred (see Custance, Olive)

Douglas, Gavin 1476-1522. . . . . .DLB-132

Douglas, Keith 1920-1944 . . . . .DLB-27

Douglas, Norman 1868-1952. . . . . . .DLB-34, 195

Douglass, Frederick 1818-1895
    . . . . .DLB-1, 43, 50, 79, 243; CDALB-2

Frederick Douglass Creative Arts Center . . Y-01

Douglass, William circa 1691-1752 . . . . . . .DLB-24

Dourado, Autran 1926- DLB-145

Dove, Arthur G. 1880-1946. . . . . .DLB-188

Dove, Rita 1952- DLB-120; CDALB-7

Dover Publications. DLB-46

Doves Press DLB-112

Dowden, Edward 1843-1913 . . . . . . .DLB-35, 149

Dowell, Coleman 1925-1985 . . . . .DLB-130

Dowland, John 1563-1626 . . . . .DLB-172

Downes, Gwladys 1915- DLB-88

Downing, J., Major (see Davis, Charles A.)

Downing, Major Jack (see Smith, Seba)

Dowriche, Anne
    before 1560-after 1613. . . . . .DLB-172

Dowson, Ernest 1867-1900 . . . . .DLB-19, 135

Doxey, William [publishing house] DLB-49

Doyle, Sir Arthur Conan
    1859-1930 . . . DLB-18, 70, 156, 178; CDBLB-5

Doyle, Kirby 1932- DLB-16

Doyle, Roddy 1958- DLB-194

Drabble, Margaret
    1939- DLB-14, 155, 231; CDBLB-8

Drach, Albert 1902- DLB-85

Dragojević, Danijel 1934- DLB-181

Drake, Samuel Gardner 1798-1875 . . . . . .DLB-187

The Dramatic Publishing Company DLB-49

Dramatists Play Service DLB-46

Drant, Thomas early 1540s?-1578 . . . . . . .DLB-167

Draper, John W. 1811-1882 . . . . .DLB-30

Draper, Lyman C. 1815-1891 . . . . .DLB-30

Drayton, Michael 1563-1631 . . . . .DLB-121

Dreiser, Theodore 1871-1945
    . . . . . . DLB-9, 12, 102, 137; DS-1; CDALB-3

Dresser, Davis 1904-1977 . . . . .DLB-226

Drewitz, Ingeborg 1923-1986 . . . . .DLB-75

Drieu La Rochelle, Pierre 1893-1945. . . . . .DLB-72

Drinker, Elizabeth 1735-1807. . . . . .DLB-200

Drinkwater, John
    1882-1937 . . . . DLB-10, 19, 149

Droste-Hülshoff, Annette von
    1797-1848. . . . . DLB-133; CDWLB-2

The Drue Heinz Literature Prize
    Excerpt from "Excerpts from a Report
    of the Commission," in David
    Bosworth's *The Death of Descartes*
    An Interview with David Bosworth Y-82

Drummond, William, of Hawthornden
    1585-1649 . . . . .DLB-121, 213

Drummond, William Henry
    1854-1907 . . . . .DLB-92

Druzhinin, Aleksandr Vasil'evich
    1824-1864 . . . . .DLB-238

Dryden, Charles 1860?-1931. . . . . DLB-171

Dryden, John
    1631-1700 . . . . . .DLB-80, 101, 131; CDBLB-2

Držić, Marin
    circa 1508-1567 . . . . DLB-147; CDWLB-4

Duane, William 1760-1835 . . . . .DLB-43

Dubé, Marcel 1930- DLB-53

Dubé, Rodolphe (see Hertel, François)

Dubie, Norman 1945- DLB-120

Dubin, Al 1891-1945 . . . . .DLB-265

Dubois, Silvia
    1788 or 1789?-1889 . . . . .DLB-239

Du Bois, W. E. B.
    1868-1963 . . . . DLB-47, 50, 91, 246; CDALB-3

Du Bois, William Pène 1916-1993. . . . . . . .DLB-61

Dubrovina, Ekaterina Oskarovna
    1846-1913 . . . . .DLB-238

Dubus, Andre 1936-1999. . . . . .DLB-130

Ducange, Victor 1783-1833 . . . . .DLB-192

Du Chaillu, Paul Belloni 1831?-1903. . . . .DLB-189

Ducharme, Réjean 1941- DLB-60

Dučić, Jovan
    1871-1943 . . . . DLB-147; CDWLB-4

Duck, Stephen 1705?-1756. . . . . .DLB-95

Duckworth, Gerald, and Company
    Limited DLB-112

Duclaux, Madame Mary (see Robinson, A. Mary F.)

Dudek, Louis 1918- DLB-88

Duell, Sloan and Pearce. DLB-46

Duerer, Albrecht 1471-1528. . . . . .DLB-179

Duff Gordon, Lucie 1821-1869 . . . . .DLB-166

Dufferin, Helen Lady, Countess of Gifford
    1807-1867 . . . . .DLB-199

Duffield and Green DLB-46

Duffy, Maureen 1933- DLB-14

Dufief, Nicholas Gouin 1776-1834. . . . . . .DLB-187

Dugan, Alan 1923- DLB-5

Dugard, William [publishing house] DLB-170

Dugas, Marcel 1883-1947 . . . . .DLB-92

Dugdale, William [publishing house]. DLB-106

Duhamel, Georges 1884-1966 . . . . .DLB-65

Dujardin, Edouard 1861-1949. . . . . .DLB-123

Dukes, Ashley 1885-1959 . . . . .DLB-10

Dumas, Alexandre *père* 1802-1870 . . . . .DLB-119, 192

Dumas, Alexandre *fils*
    1824-1895 . . . . .DLB-192

Dumas, Henry 1934-1968 . . . . .DLB-41

du Maurier, Daphne 1907-1989 . . . . .DLB-191

Du Maurier, George
    1834-1896 . . . . DLB-153, 178

Dummett, Michael 1925- DLB-262

Dunbar, Paul Laurence
    1872-1906 . . . . .DLB-50, 54, 78; CDALB-3

Dunbar, William
    circa 1460-circa 1522. . . . . .DLB-132, 146

Duncan, Dave 1933- DLB-251

Duncan, David James 1952- DLB-256

Duncan, Norman 1871-1916 . . . . .DLB-92

Duncan, Quince 1940- DLB-145

Duncan, Robert 1919-1988 . . . . . . .DLB-5, 16, 193

Duncan, Ronald 1914-1982. . . . . .DLB-13

Duncan, Sara Jeannette 1861-1922 . . . . . . .DLB-92

Dunigan, Edward, and Brother DLB-49

Dunlap, John 1747-1812. . . . . .DLB-43

Dunlap, William 1766-1839. . . . . . .DLB-30, 37, 59

Dunmore, Helen 1952- DLB-267

Dunn, Douglas 1942- DLB-40

Dunn, Harvey Thomas 1884-1952 . . . . . .DLB-188

Dunn, Stephen 1939- DLB-105

"The Good, The Not So Good" DLB-105

Dunne, Finley Peter 1867-1936 . . . . . . .DLB-11, 23

Dunne, John Gregory 1932- Y-80

Dunne, Philip 1908-1992. . . . . .DLB-26

Dunning, Ralph Cheever 1878-1930 . . . . . . .DLB-4

Dunning, William A. 1857-1922 . . . . .DLB-17

Dunsany, Lord (Edward John Moreton
    Drax Plunkett, Baron Dunsany)
    1878-1957 . . . . DLB-10, 77, 153, 156, 255

Duns Scotus, John
    circa 1266-1308. . . . . .DLB-115

Dunton, John [publishing house] DLB-170

Dunton, W. Herbert 1878-1936 . . . . DLB-188

Dupin, Amantine-Aurore-Lucile (see Sand, George)

Dupuy, Eliza Ann 1814-1880 . . . . DLB-248

Durack, Mary 1913-1994 . . . . DLB-260

Durand, Lucile (see Bersianik, Louky)

Duranti, Francesca 1935- DLB-196

Duranty, Walter 1884-1957 . . . . DLB-29

Duras, Marguerite 1914-1996 . . . . DLB-83

Durfey, Thomas 1653-1723 . . . . DLB-80

Durova, Nadezhda Andreevna
(Aleksandr Andreevich Aleksandrov)
1783-1866 . . . . DLB-198

Durrell, Lawrence 1912-1990
. . . . .DLB-15, 27, 204; Y-90; CDBLB-7

Durrell, William [publishing house] DLB-49

Dürrenmatt, Friedrich
1921-1990 . . . . DLB-69, 124; CDWLB-2

Duston, Hannah 1657-1737 . . . . DLB-200

Dutt, Toru 1856-1877 . . . . DLB-240

Dutton, E. P., and Company DLB-49

Duvoisin, Roger 1904-1980 . . . . DLB-61

Duyckinck, Evert Augustus
1816-1878 . . . . DLB-3, 64, 250

Duyckinck, George L.
1823-1863 . . . . DLB-3, 250

Duyckinck and Company DLB-49

Dwight, John Sullivan 1813-1893 . . . . . DLB-1, 235

Dwight, Timothy 1752-1817 . . . . DLB-37

Dybek, Stuart 1942- DLB-130

Dyer, Charles 1928- DLB-13

Dyer, Sir Edward 1543-1607 . . . . DLB-136

Dyer, George 1755-1841 . . . . DLB-93

Dyer, John 1699-1757 . . . . DLB-95

Dyk, Viktor 1877-1931 . . . . DLB-215

Dylan, Bob 1941- DLB-16

E

Eager, Edward 1911-1964 . . . . DLB-22

Eagleton, Terry 1943- DLB-242

Eames, Wilberforce 1855-1937 . . . . DLB-140

Earle, Alice Morse 1853-1911 . . . . DLB-221

Earle, James H., and Company DLB-49

Earle, John 1600 or 1601-1665 . . . . DLB-151

Early American Book Illustration,
by Sinclair Hamilton DLB-49

Eastlake, William 1917-1997 . . . . DLB-6, 206

Eastman, Carol ?- DLB-44

Eastman, Charles A. (Ohiyesa)
1858-1939 .DLB-175

Eastman, Max 1883-1969 . . . . DLB-91

Eaton, Daniel Isaac 1753-1814 . . . . DLB-158

Eaton, Edith Maude 1865-1914 . . . . DLB-221

Eaton, Winnifred 1875-1954 . . . . DLB-221

Eberhart, Richard 1904- DLB-48; CDALB-1

Ebner, Jeannie 1918- DLB-85

Ebner-Eschenbach, Marie von
1830-1916 . . . . DLB-81

Ebon 1942- DLB-41

E-Books Turn the Corner Y-98

Ecbasis Captivi circa 1045 . . . . DLB-148

Ecco Press DLB-46

Eckhart, Meister circa 1260-circa 1328. . . DLB-115

The Eclectic Review 1805-1868 . . . . DLB-110

Eco, Umberto 1932- DLB-196, 242

Eddison, E. R. 1882-1945 . . . . DLB-255

Edel, Leon 1907-1997 . . . . DLB-103

Edelfeldt, Inger 1956- DLB-257

Edes, Benjamin 1732-1803 . . . . DLB-43

Edgar, David 1948- DLB-13, 233

Edgeworth, Maria
1768-1849 . . . . .DLB-116, 159, 163

The Edinburgh Review 1802-1929 . . . . DLB-110

Edinburgh University Press DLB-112

The Editor Publishing Company DLB-49

Editorial Institute at Boston University Y-00

Editorial Statements DLB-137

Edmonds, Randolph 1900- DLB-51

Edmonds, Walter D. 1903-1998 . . . . DLB-9

Edric, Robert (see Armitage, G. E.)

Edschmid, Kasimir 1890-1966 . . . . DLB-56

Edson, Margaret 1961- DLB-266

Edson, Russell 1935- DLB-244

Edwards, Amelia Anne Blandford
1831-1892 .DLB-174

Edwards, Dic 1953- DLB-245

Edwards, Edward 1812-1886 . . . . DLB-184

Edwards, James [publishing house] DLB-154

Edwards, Jonathan 1703-1758 . . . . DLB-24

Edwards, Jonathan, Jr. 1745-1801 . . . . DLB-37

Edwards, Junius 1929- DLB-33

Edwards, Matilda Barbara Betham
1836-1919 .DLB-174

Edwards, Richard 1524-1566 . . . . DLB-62

Edwards, Sarah Pierpont 1710-1758 . . . . . DLB-200

Effinger, George Alec 1947- DLB-8

Egerton, George 1859-1945 . . . . DLB-135

Eggleston, Edward 1837-1902 . . . . DLB-12

Eggleston, Wilfred 1901-1986 . . . . DLB-92

Eglītis, Anšlavs 1906-1993 . . . . DLB-220

Ehrenreich, Barbara 1941- DLB-246

Ehrenstein, Albert 1886-1950 . . . . DLB-81

Ehrhart, W. D. 1948- DS-9

Ehrlich, Gretel 1946- DLB-212

Eich, Günter 1907-1972 . . . . DLB-69, 124

Eichendorff, Joseph Freiherr von
1788-1857 . . . . DLB-90

Eifukumon'in 1271-1342 . . . . DLB-203

1873 Publishers' Catalogues DLB-49

Eighteenth-Century Aesthetic
Theories DLB-31

Eighteenth-Century Philosophical
Background DLB-31

Eigner, Larry 1926-1996 . . . . DLB-5, 193

Eikon Basilike 1649 . . . . DLB-151

Eilhart von Oberge
circa 1140-circa 1195 . . . . DLB-148

Einhard circa 770-840 . . . . DLB-148

Eiseley, Loren 1907-1977 . . . . .DS-17

Eisenberg, Deborah 1945- DLB-244

Eisenreich, Herbert 1925-1986 . . . . DLB-85

Eisner, Kurt 1867-1919 . . . . DLB-66

Ekelöf, Gunnar 1907-1968 . . . . DLB-259

Eklund, Gordon 1945- Y-83

Ekman, Kerstin 1933- DLB-257

Ekwensi, Cyprian
1921- DLB-117; CDWLB-3

Elaw, Zilpha circa 1790-?- DLB-239

Eld, George [publishing house] DLB-170

Elder, Lonne, III 1931- DLB-7, 38, 44

Elder, Paul, and Company DLB-49

The Electronic Text Center and the Electronic
Archive of Early American Fiction at the
University of Virginia Library Y-98

Eliade, Mircea 1907-1986 . . . DLB-220; CDWLB-4

Elie, Robert 1915-1973 . . . . DLB-88

Elin Pelin 1877-1949 . . . . . . .DLB-147; CDWLB-4

Eliot, George
1819-1880 . . . . DLB-21, 35, 55; CDBLB-4

Eliot, John 1604-1690 . . . . DLB-24

Eliot, T. S. 1888-1965
. . . . .DLB-7, 10, 45, 63, 245; CDALB-5

T. S. Eliot Centennial Y-88

Eliot's Court Press DLB-170

Elizabeth I 1533-1603 . . . . DLB-136

Elizabeth of Nassau-Saarbrücken
after 1393-1456 . . . . .DLB-179

Elizondo, Salvador 1932- DLB-145

Elizondo, Sergio 1930- DLB-82

Elkin, Stanley 1930-1995 . . . .DLB-2, 28, 218; Y-80

Elles, Dora Amy (see Wentworth, Patricia)

Ellet, Elizabeth F. 1818?-1877 . . . . DLB-30

Elliot, Ebenezer 1781-1849 . . . . DLB-96, 190

Elliot, Frances Minto (Dickinson)
1820-1898 . . . . DLB-166

Elliott, Charlotte 1789-1871 . . . . DLB-199

Elliott, George 1923- DLB-68

Elliott, George P. 1918-1980 . . . . DLB-244

Elliott, Janice 1931- DLB-14

Elliott, Sarah Barnwell 1848-1928 . . . . . . DLB-221

Elliott, Thomes and Talbot DLB-49

Elliott, William, III 1788-1863 . . . . DLB-3, 248

Ellis, Alice Thomas (Anna Margaret Haycraft)
1932- DLB-194

Ellis, Edward S. 1840-1916 . . . . DLB-42

Ellis, Frederick Staridge
[publishing house] DLB-106

The George H. Ellis Company DLB-49

Ellis, Havelock 1859-1939 . . . . DLB-190

Ellison, Harlan 1934- DLB-8

Ellison, Ralph
1914-1994 ... DLB-2, 76, 227; Y-94; CDALB-1

Ellmann, Richard 1918-1987 ...... DLB-103; Y-87

Ellroy, James 1948- DLB-226; Y-91

Eluard, Paul 1895-1952 ....DLB-258

Elyot, Thomas 1490?-1546 ....DLB-136

Emanuel, James Andrew 1921- DLB-41

Emecheta, Buchi 1944- .. DLB-117; CDWLB-3

Emendations for *Look Homeward, Angel*....... Y-00

The Emergence of Black Women Writers.... DS-8

Emerson, Ralph Waldo 1803-1882
........DLB-1, 59, 73, 183, 223; CDALB-2

Ralph Waldo Emerson in 1982........... Y-82

Emerson, William 1769-1811...........DLB-37

Emerson, William 1923-1997 ....Y-97

Emin, Fedor Aleksandrovich
circa 1735-1770 ....DLB-150

Emmanuel, Pierre 1916-1984...........DLB-258

Empedocles fifth century B.C...........DLB-176

Empson, William 1906-1984 ....DLB-20

Enchi Fumiko 1905-1986...............DLB-182

"Encounter with the West" DLB-180

The End of English Stage Censorship,
1945-1968 ....DLB-13

Ende, Michael 1929-1995 ....DLB-75

Endō Shūsaku 1923-1996 ....DLB-182

Engel, Marian 1933-1985...............DLB-53

Engels, Friedrich 1820-1895...........DLB-129

Engle, Paul 1908- DLB-48

English, Thomas Dunn 1819-1902 .....DLB-202

English Composition and Rhetoric (1866),
by Alexander Bain [excerpt] DLB-57

The English Language: 410 to 1500 .....DLB-146

Ennius 239 B.C.-169 B.C................DLB-211

Enquist, Per Olov 1934- DLB-257

Enright, Anne 1962- DLB-267

Enright, D. J. 1920- DLB-27

Enright, Elizabeth 1909-1968...........DLB-22

Epic and Beast Epic DLB-208

Epictetus circa 55-circa 125-130........DLB-176

Epicurus 342/341 B.C.-271/270 B.C. DLB-176

Epps, Bernard 1936- DLB-53

Epstein, Julius 1909- and
Epstein, Philip 1909-1952 ....DLB-26

Equiano, Olaudah
circa 1745-1797 ....DLB-37, 50; DWLB-3

Olaudah Equiano and Unfinished Journeys:
The Slave-Narrative Tradition and
Twentieth-Century Continuities, by
Paul Edwards and Pauline T.
Wangman DLB-117

The E-Researcher: Possibilities and Pitfalls ... Y-00

Eragny Press DLB-112

Erasmus, Desiderius 1467-1536........DLB-136

Erba, Luciano 1922- DLB-128

Erdrich, Louise
1954- DLB-152, 175, 206; CDALB-7

Erichsen-Brown, Gwethalyn Graham
(see Graham, Gwethalyn)

Eriugena, John Scottus circa 810-877 .....DLB-115

Ernst, Paul 1866-1933 ....DLB-66, 118

Ershov, Petr Pavlovich 1815-1869......DLB-205

Erskine, Albert 1911-1993 ....Y-93

Erskine, John 1879-1951 ....DLB-9, 102

Erskine, Mrs. Steuart ?-1948 ....DLB-195

Ertel', Aleksandr Ivanovich
1855-1908 ....DLB-238

Ervine, St. John Greer 1883-1971 ....DLB-10

Eschenburg, Johann Joachim 1743-1820 ...DLB-97

Escoto, Julio 1944- DLB-145

Esdaile, Arundell 1880-1956 ....DLB-201

Eshleman, Clayton 1935- DLB-5

Espriu, Salvador 1913-1985...........DLB-134

Ess Ess Publishing Company...........DLB-49

Essex House Press DLB-112

Esson, Louis 1878-1993 ....DLB-260

Essop, Ahmed 1931- DLB-225

Esterházy, Péter 1950- DLB-232; CDWLB-4

Estes, Eleanor 1906-1988 ....DLB-22

Estes and Lauriat....................DLB-49

Estleman, Loren D. 1952- DLB-226

Eszterhas, Joe 1944- DLB-185

Etherege, George 1636-circa 1692.......DLB-80

Ethridge, Mark, Sr. 1896-1981 ....DLB-127

Ets, Marie Hall 1893- DLB-22

Etter, David 1928- DLB-105

Ettner, Johann Christoph 1654-1724 .....DLB-168

Eugene Gant's Projected Works Y-01

Eupolemius flourished circa 1095 ....DLB-148

Euripides circa 484 B.C.-407/406 B.C.
.... DLB-176; CDWLB-1

Evans, Augusta Jane 1835-1909........DLB-239

Evans, Caradoc 1878-1945............DLB-162

Evans, Charles 1850-1935 ....DLB-187

Evans, Donald 1884-1921 ....DLB-54

Evans, George Henry 1805-1856.......DLB-43

Evans, Hubert 1892-1986 ....DLB-92

Evans, M., and Company DLB-46

Evans, Mari 1923- DLB-41

Evans, Mary Ann (see Eliot, George)

Evans, Nathaniel 1742-1767 ....DLB-31

Evans, Sebastian 1830-1909...........DLB-35

Evans, Ray 1915- and
Livingston, Jay 1915-2001.........DLB-265

Evaristi, Marcella 1953- DLB-233

Everett, Alexander Hill 1790-1847.......DLB-59

Everett, Edward 1794-1865 ....DLB-1, 59, 235

Everson, R. G. 1903- DLB-88

Everson, William 1912-1994 ......DLB-5, 16, 212

Ewart, Gavin 1916-1995 ....DLB-40

Ewing, Juliana Horatia 1841-1885....DLB-21, 163

The Examiner 1808-1881 ....DLB-110

Exley, Frederick 1929-1992 ...... DLB-143; Y-81

von Eyb, Albrecht 1420-1475...........DLB-179

Eyre and Spottiswoode DLB-106

Ezera, Regīna 1930- DLB-232

Ezzo ?-after 1065 ....DLB-148

F

Faber, Frederick William 1814-1863 ......DLB-32

Faber and Faber Limited DLB-112

Faccio, Rena (see Aleramo, Sibilla)

Fagundo, Ana María 1938- DLB-134

Fair, Ronald L. 1932- DLB-33

Fairfax, Beatrice (see Manning, Marie)

Fairlie, Gerard 1899-1983 ....DLB-77

Fallada, Hans 1893-1947 ....DLB-56

Fancher, Betsy 1928- Y-83

Fane, Violet 1843-1905 ....DLB-35

Fanfrolico Press DLB-112

Fanning, Katherine 1927 ....DLB-127

Fanshawe, Sir Richard 1608-1666 ....DLB-126

Fantasy Press Publishers DLB-46

Fante, John 1909-1983 ....DLB-130; Y-83

Al-Farabi circa 870-950................DLB-115

Farabough, Laura 1949- DLB-228

Farah, Nuruddin 1945- ...DLB-125; CDWLB-3

Farber, Norma 1909-1984 ....DLB-61

Fargue, Léon-Paul 1876-1947 ....DLB-258

Farigoule, Louis (see Romains, Jules)

Farjeon, Eleanor 1881-1965...........DLB-160

Farley, Harriet 1812-1907 ....DLB-239

Farley, Walter 1920-1989 ....DLB-22

Farmborough, Florence 1887-1978.......DLB-204

Farmer, Penelope 1939- DLB-161

Farmer, Philip José 1918- DLB-8

Farnaby, Thomas 1575?-1647 ....DLB-236

Farningham, Marianne (see Hearn, Mary Anne)

Farquhar, George circa 1677-1707 ....DLB-84

Farquharson, Martha (see Finley, Martha)

Farrar, Frederic William 1831-1903......DLB-163

Farrar and Rinehart..................DLB-46

Farrar, Straus and Giroux DLB-46

Farrell, J. G. 1935-1979 ....DLB-14

Farrell, James T. 1904-1979 ....DLB-4, 9, 86; DS-2

Fast, Howard 1914- DLB-9

Faulkner, George [publishing house] DLB-154

Faulkner, William 1897-1962
...DLB-9, 11, 44, 102; DS-2; Y-86; CDALB-5

William Faulkner Centenary...............Y-97

"Faulkner 100—Celebrating the Work,"
University of South Carolina, Columbia ..Y-97

Impressions of William Faulkner.........Y-97

Faulkner and Yoknapatawpha Conference,
Oxford, Mississippi..................Y-97

Faulks, Sebastian 1953- DLB-207

Fauset, Jessie Redmon 1882-1961 ....DLB-51

Faust, Frederick Schiller (Max Brand) 1892-1944 .... DLB-256

Faust, Irvin 1924- DLB-2, 28, 218; Y-80

Fawcett, Edgar 1847-1904 .... DLB-202

Fawcett, Millicent Garrett 1847-1929 .... DLB-190

Fawcett Books DLB-46

Fay, Theodore Sedgwick 1807-1898 ..... DLB-202

Fearing, Kenneth 1902-1961 .... DLB-9

Federal Writers' Project DLB-46

Federman, Raymond 1928- Y-80

Fedorov, Innokentii Vasil'evich (see Omulevsky, Innokentii Vasil'evich)

Feiffer, Jules 1929- DLB-7, 44

Feinberg, Charles E. 1899-1988 ....DLB-187; Y-88

Feind, Barthold 1678-1721 .... DLB-168

Feinstein, Elaine 1930- DLB-14, 40

Feiss, Paul Louis 1875-1952 .... DLB-187

Feldman, Irving 1928- DLB-169

Felipe, Léon 1884-1968 .... DLB-108

Fell, Frederick, Publishers DLB-46

Felltham, Owen 1602?-1668 .... DLB-126, 151

Felman, Soshana 1942- DLB-246

Fels, Ludwig 1946- DLB-75

Felton, Cornelius Conway 1807-1862 .. DLB-1, 235

Fenn, Harry 1837-1911 .... DLB-188

Fennario, David 1947- DLB-60

Fenner, Dudley 1558?-1587? DLB-236

Fenno, Jenny 1765?-1803 .... DLB-200

Fenno, John 1751-1798 .... DLB-43

Fenno, R. F., and Company DLB-49

Fenoglio, Beppe 1922-1963 ....DLB-177

Fenton, Geoffrey 1539?-1608 .... DLB-136

Fenton, James 1949- DLB-40

Ferber, Edna 1885-1968 ..... DLB-9, 28, 86, 266

Ferdinand, Vallery, III (see Salaam, Kalamu ya)

Ferguson, Sir Samuel 1810-1886 .... DLB-32

Ferguson, William Scott 1875-1954 ...... DLB-47

Fergusson, Robert 1750-1774 .... DLB-109

Ferland, Albert 1872-1943 .... DLB-92

Ferlinghetti, Lawrence 1919- DLB-5, 16; CDALB-1

Fermor, Patrick Leigh 1915- DLB-204

Fern, Fanny (see Parton, Sara Payson Willis)

Ferrars, Elizabeth 1907- DLB-87

Ferré, Rosario 1942- DLB-145

Ferret, E., and Company DLB-49

Ferrier, Susan 1782-1854 .... DLB-116

Ferril, Thomas Hornsby 1896-1988 ..... DLB-206

Ferrini, Vincent 1913- DLB-48

Ferron, Jacques 1921-1985 .... DLB-60

Ferron, Madeleine 1922- DLB-53

Ferrucci, Franco 1936- DLB-196

Fetridge and Company DLB-49

Feuchtersleben, Ernst Freiherr von 1806-1849 .... DLB-133

Feuchtwanger, Lion 1884-1958 .... DLB-66

Feuerbach, Ludwig 1804-1872 .... DLB-133

Feuillet, Octave 1821-1890 .... DLB-192

Feydeau, Georges 1862-1921 .... DLB-192

Fichte, Johann Gottlieb 1762-1814 ...... DLB-90

Ficke, Arthur Davison 1883-1945 .... DLB-54

Fiction Best-Sellers, 1910-1945 .... DLB-9

Fiction into Film, 1928-1975: A List of Movies Based on the Works of Authors in British Novelists, 1930-1959 .... DLB-15

Fiedler, Leslie A. 1917- DLB-28, 67

Field, Barron 1789-1846 .... DLB-230

Field, Edward 1924- DLB-105

Field, Joseph M. 1810-1856 .... DLB-248

Field, Michael (Katherine Harris Bradley [1846-1914] and Edith Emma Cooper [1862-1913]) DLB-240

"The Poetry File" DLB-105

Field, Eugene 1850-1895 .... DLB-23, 42, 140; DS-13

Field, John 1545?-1588 .... DLB-167

Field, Marshall, III 1893-1956 .... DLB-127

Field, Marshall, IV 1916-1965 .... DLB-127

Field, Marshall, V 1941- DLB-127

Field, Nathan 1587-1619 or 1620 .... DLB-58

Field, Rachel 1894-1942 .... DLB-9, 22

A Field Guide to Recent Schools of American Poetry Y-86

Fielding, Helen 1958- DLB-231

Fielding, Henry 1707-1754 .... DLB-39, 84, 101; CDBLB-2

"Defense of *Amelia*" (1752) DLB-39

From *The History of the Adventures of Joseph Andrews* (1742) DLB-39

Preface to *Joseph Andrews* (1742) DLB-39

Preface to Sarah Fielding's *The Adventures of David Simple* (1744) DLB-39

Preface to Sarah Fielding's *Familiar Letters* (1747) [excerpt] DLB-39

Fielding, Sarah 1710-1768 .... DLB-39

Preface to *The Cry* (1754) DLB-39

Fields, Annie Adams 1834-1915 .... DLB-221

Fields, Dorothy 1905-1974 .... DLB-265

Fields, James T. 1817-1881 ..... DLB-1, 235

Fields, Julia 1938- DLB-41

Fields, Osgood and Company DLB-49

Fields, W. C. 1880-1946 .... DLB-44

Fierstein, Harvey 1954- DLB-266

Fifty Penguin Years Y-85

Figes, Eva 1932- DLB-14

Figuera, Angela 1902-1984 .... DLB-108

Filmer, Sir Robert 1586-1653 .... DLB-151

Filson, John circa 1753-1788 .... DLB-37

Finch, Anne, Countess of Winchilsea 1661-1720 .... DLB-95

Finch, Robert 1900- DLB-88

Findley, Timothy 1930- DLB-53

Finlay, Ian Hamilton 1925- DLB-40

Finley, Martha 1828-1909 .... DLB-42

Finn, Elizabeth Anne (McCaul) 1825-1921 .... DLB-166

Finnegan, Seamus 1949- DLB-245

Finney, Jack 1911-1995 .... DLB-8

Finney, Walter Braden (see Finney, Jack)

Firbank, Ronald 1886-1926 .... DLB-36

Firmin, Giles 1615-1697 .... DLB-24

First Edition Library/Collectors' Reprints, Inc. Y-91

Fischart, Johann 1546 or 1547-1590 or 1591 .....DLB-179

Fischer, Karoline Auguste Fernandine 1764-1842 .... DLB-94

Fischer, Tibor 1959- DLB-231

Fish, Stanley 1938- DLB-67

Fishacre, Richard 1205-1248 .... DLB-115

Fisher, Clay (see Allen, Henry W.)

Fisher, Dorothy Canfield 1879-1958 ... DLB-9, 102

Fisher, Leonard Everett 1924- DLB-61

Fisher, Roy 1930- DLB-40

Fisher, Rudolph 1897-1934 .... DLB-51, 102

Fisher, Steve 1913-1980 .... DLB-226

Fisher, Sydney George 1856-1927 ...... DLB-47

Fisher, Vardis 1895-1968 .... DLB-9, 206

Fiske, John 1608-1677 .... DLB-24

Fiske, John 1842-1901 ....DLB-47, 64

Fitch, Thomas circa 1700-1774 .... DLB-31

Fitch, William Clyde 1865-1909 .... DLB-7

FitzGerald, Edward 1809-1883 .... DLB-32

Fitzgerald, F. Scott 1896-1940 .... DLB-4, 9, 86, 219; Y-81, Y-92; DS-1, 15, 16; CDALB-4

F. Scott Fitzgerald Centenary Celebrations Y-96

F. Scott Fitzgerald: A Descriptive Bibliography, Supplement (2001) Y-01

F. Scott Fitzgerald Inducted into the American Poets' Corner at St. John the Divine; Ezra Pound Banned Y-99

"F. Scott Fitzgerald: St. Paul's Native Son and Distinguished American Writer": University of Minnesota Conference, 29-31 October 1982 .... Y-82

First International F. Scott Fitzgerald Conference Y-92

Fitzgerald, Penelope 1916- DLB-14, 194

Fitzgerald, Robert 1910-1985 .... Y-80

FitzGerald, Robert D. 1902-1987 .... DLB-260

Fitzgerald, Thomas 1819-1891 .... DLB-23

Fitzgerald, Zelda Sayre 1900-1948 .... Y-84

Fitzhugh, Louise 1928-1974 .... DLB-52

Fitzhugh, William circa 1651-1701 .... DLB-24

Flagg, James Montgomery 1877-1960 .... DLB-188

Flanagan, Thomas 1923- Y-80

Flanner, Hildegarde 1899-1987 .... DLB-48

Flanner, Janet 1892-1978 .... DLB-4

Flannery, Peter 1951- DLB-233

Flaubert, Gustave 1821-1880 . . . . .DLB-119

Flavin, Martin 1883-1967. . . . . .DLB-9

Fleck, Konrad
(flourished circa 1220) DLB-138

Flecker, James Elroy 1884-1915. . . . . . .DLB-10, 19

Fleeson, Doris 1901-1970. . . . . .DLB-29

Fleißer, Marieluise 1901-1974 . . . . . . .DLB-56, 124

Fleischer, Nat 1887-1972. . . . . .DLB-241

Fleming, Abraham 1552?-1607 . . . . .DLB-236

Fleming, Ian 1908-1964 . . . DLB-87, 201; CDBLB-7

Fleming, Paul 1609-1640 . . . . .DLB-164

Fleming, Peter 1907-1971 . . . . .DLB-195

Fletcher, Giles, the Elder 1546-1611 . . . . .DLB-136

Fletcher, Giles, the Younger
1585 or 1586-1623 . . . . .DLB-121

Fletcher, J. S. 1863-1935. . . . . .DLB-70

Fletcher, John (see Beaumont, Francis)

Fletcher, John Gould 1886-1950 . . . . . . .DLB-4, 45

Fletcher, Phineas 1582-1650 . . . . .DLB-121

Flieg, Helmut (see Heym, Stefan)

Flint, F. S. 1885-1960 . . . . .DLB-19

Flint, Timothy 1780-1840 . . . . DLB-73, 186

Flores-Williams, Jason 1969- DLB-209

Florio, John 1553?-1625. . . . . .DLB-172

Fo, Dario 1926- Y-97

Foden, Giles 1967- DLB-267

Foix, J. V. 1893-1987 . . . . .DLB-134

Foley, Martha (see Burnett, Whit, and Martha Foley)

Folger, Henry Clay 1857-1930. . . . . .DLB-140

Folio Society. DLB-112

Follain, Jean 1903-1971 . . . . .DLB-258

Follen, Charles 1796-1840 . . . . .DLB-235

Follen, Eliza Lee (Cabot) 1787-1860 . . . .DLB-1, 235

Follett, Ken 1949- DLB-87; Y-81

Follett Publishing Company. DLB-46

Folsom, John West [publishing house]. DLB-49

Folz, Hans
between 1435 and 1440-1513 . . . . . . .DLB-179

Fontane, Theodor
1819-1898 . . . . .DLB-129; CDWLB-2

Fontes, Montserrat 1940- DLB-209

Fonvisin, Denis Ivanovich
1744 or 1745-1792 . . . . .DLB-150

Foote, Horton 1916- DLB-26, 266

Foote, Mary Hallock
1847-1938 . . . . .DLB-186, 188, 202, 221

Foote, Samuel 1721-1777 . . . . .DLB-89

Foote, Shelby 1916- DLB-2, 17

Forbes, Calvin 1945- DLB-41

Forbes, Ester 1891-1967. . . . . .DLB-22

Forbes, Rosita 1893?-1967 . . . . .DLB-195

Forbes and Company. DLB-49

Force, Peter 1790-1868. . . . . .DLB-30

Forché, Carolyn 1950- DLB-5, 193

Ford, Charles Henri 1913- DLB-4, 48

Ford, Corey 1902-1969 . . . . .DLB-11

Ford, Ford Madox
1873-1939 . . . . . . .DLB-34, 98, 162; CDBLB-6

Ford, J. B., and Company DLB-49

Ford, Jesse Hill 1928-1996 . . . . .DLB-6

Ford, John 1586-?. DLB-58; CDBLB-1

Ford, R. A. D. 1915- DLB-88

Ford, Richard 1944- DLB-227

Ford, Worthington C. 1858-1941 . . . . . . .DLB-47

Fords, Howard, and Hulbert DLB-49

Foreman, Carl 1914-1984 . . . . .DLB-26

Forester, C. S. 1899-1966. . . . . .DLB-191

Forester, Frank (see Herbert, Henry William)

Forman, Harry Buxton 1842-1917. . . . . . .DLB-184

Fornés, María Irene 1930- DLB-7

Forrest, Leon 1937-1997. . . . . .DLB-33

Forster, E. M.
1879-1970 . . . . .DLB-34, 98, 162, 178, 195;
DS-10; CDBLB-6

Forster, Georg 1754-1794 . . . . .DLB-94

Forster, John 1812-1876 . . . . .DLB-144

Forster, Margaret 1938- DLB-155

Forsyth, Frederick 1938- DLB-87

Forten, Charlotte L. 1837-1914 . . . . . .DLB-50, 239

Charlotte Forten: Pages from
her Diary. DLB-50

Fortini, Franco 1917- DLB-128

Fortune, Mary ca. 1833-ca. 1910 . . . . . . .DLB-230

Fortune, T. Thomas 1856-1928. . . . . .DLB-23

Fosdick, Charles Austin 1842-1915 . . . . . .DLB-42

Foster, Genevieve 1893-1979 . . . . .DLB-61

Foster, Hannah Webster 1758-1840. . . DLB-37, 200

Foster, John 1648-1681 . . . . .DLB-24

Foster, Michael 1904-1956. . . . . .DLB-9

Foster, Myles Birket 1825-1899 . . . . .DLB-184

Foucault, Michel 1926-1984. . . . . .DLB-242

Foulis, Robert and Andrew / R. and A.
[publishing house] DLB-154

Fouqué, Caroline de la Motte
1774-1831 . . . . .DLB-90

Fouqué, Friedrich de la Motte
1777-1843. . . . . .DLB-90

Four Seas Company. DLB-46

Four Winds Press DLB-46

Fournier, Henri Alban (see Alain-Fournier)

Fowler, Christopher 1953- DLB-267

Fowler and Wells Company DLB-49

Fowles, John
1926- DLB-14, 139, 207; CDBLB-8

Fox, John 1939- DLB-245

Fox, John, Jr. 1862 or 1863-1919 . . . .DLB-9; DS-13

Fox, Paula 1923- DLB-52

Fox, Richard K. [publishing house] DLB-49

Fox, Richard Kyle 1846-1922 . . . . .DLB-79

Fox, William Price 1926- DLB-2; Y-81

Foxe, John 1517-1587 . . . . .DLB-132

Fraenkel, Michael 1896-1957 . . . . .DLB-4

France, Anatole 1844-1924 . . . . .DLB-123

France, Richard 1938- DLB-7

Francis, C. S. [publishing house] DLB-49

Francis, Convers 1795-1863. . . . . .DLB-1, 235

Francis, Dick 1920- DLB-87

Francis, Sir Frank 1901-1988 . . . . .DLB-201

Francis, Jeffrey, Lord 1773-1850 . . . . .DLB-107

François 1863-1910 . . . . .DLB-92

François, Louise von 1817-1893. . . . . . . .DLB-129

Franck, Sebastian 1499-1542 . . . . .DLB-179

Francke, Kuno 1855-1930 . . . . .DLB-71

Frank, Bruno 1887-1945 . . . . .DLB-118

Frank, Leonhard 1882-1961 . . . . .DLB-56, 118

Frank, Melvin (see Panama, Norman)

Frank, Waldo 1889-1967. . . . . .DLB-9, 63

Franken, Rose 1895?-1988 . . . . . .DLB-228, Y-84

Franklin, Benjamin
1706-1790 . . . .DLB-24, 43, 73, 183; CDALB-2

Franklin, James 1697-1735 . . . . .DLB-43

Franklin, Miles 1879-1954 . . . . .DLB-230

Franklin Library .DLB-46

Frantz, Ralph Jules 1902-1979 . . . . .DLB-4

Franzos, Karl Emil 1848-1904 . . . . .DLB-129

Fraser, G. S. 1915-1980 . . . . .DLB-27

Fraser, Kathleen 1935- DLB-169

Frattini, Alberto 1922- DLB-128

Frau Ava ?-1127 . . . . .DLB-148

Fraunce, Abraham 1558?-1592 or 1593. . .DLB-236

Frayn, Michael 1933- DLB-13, 14, 194, 245

Frederic, Harold
1856-1898 . . . . .DLB-12, 23; DS-13

Freed, Arthur 1894-1973 . . . . .DLB-265

Freeling, Nicolas 1927- DLB-87

Freeman, Douglas Southall
1886-1953 . . . . .DLB-17; DS-17

Freeman, Judith 1946- DLB-256

Freeman, Legh Richmond 1842-1915 . . . . .DLB-23

Freeman, Mary E. Wilkins
1852-1930 . . . . .DLB-12, 78, 221

Freeman, R. Austin 1862-1943 . . . . .DLB-70

Freidank circa 1170-circa 1233. . . . . .DLB-138

Freiligrath, Ferdinand 1810-1876 . . . . . . .DLB-133

Frémont, John Charles 1813-1890. . . . . . .DLB-186

Frémont, John Charles 1813-1890 and
Frémont, Jessie Benton 1834-1902 . . .DLB-183

French, Alice 1850-1934 . . . . .DLB-74; DS-13

French Arthurian Literature DLB-208

French, David 1939- DLB-53

French, Evangeline 1869-1960. . . . . .DLB-195

French, Francesca 1871-1960 . . . . .DLB-195

French, James [publishing house]. DLB-49

French, Samuel [publishing house] DLB-49

Samuel French, Limited. DLB-106

Freneau, Philip 1752-1832 . . . . DLB-37, 43

Freni, Melo 1934- DLB-128

Freshfield, Douglas W. 1845-1934 . . . . . .DLB-174

Freytag, Gustav 1816-1895 . . . . .DLB-129

Fridegård, Jan 1897-1968 . . . . DLB-259

Fried, Erich 1921-1988 . . . . DLB-85

Friedan, Betty 1921- DLB-246

Friedman, Bruce Jay 1930- DLB-2, 28, 244

Friedrich von Hausen circa 1171-1190 . . . DLB-138

Friel, Brian 1929- DLB-13

Friend, Krebs 1895?-1967? DLB-4

Fries, Fritz Rudolf 1935- DLB-75

Fringe and Alternative Theater in
    Great Britain DLB-13

Frisch, Max
    1911-1991 . . . . DLB-69, 124; CDWLB-2

Frischlin, Nicodemus 1547-1590 . . . . .DLB-179

Frischmuth, Barbara 1941- DLB-85

Fritz, Jean 1915- DLB-52

Froissart, Jean circa 1337-circa 1404 . . . . DLB-208

From John Hall Wheelock's Oral Memoir Y-01

Fromentin, Eugene 1820-1876 . . . . DLB-123

Frontinus circa A.D. 35-A.D. 103/104 . . . DLB-211

Frost, A. B. 1851-1928 . . . . DLB-188; DS-13

Frost, Robert
    1874-1963 . . . . DLB-54; DS-7; CDALB-4

Frostenson, Katarina 1953- DLB-257

Frothingham, Octavius Brooks
    1822-1895 . . . . DLB-1, 243

Froude, James Anthony
    1818-1894 . . . . .DLB-18, 57, 144

Fruitlands 1843-1844 . . . . DLB-223

Fry, Christopher 1907- DLB-13

Fry, Roger 1866-1934 . . . . .DS-10

Fry, Stephen 1957- DLB-207

Frye, Northrop 1912-1991 . . . . . . .DLB-67, 68, 246

Fuchs, Daniel 1909-1993 . . . . .DLB-9, 26, 28; Y-93

Fuentes, Carlos 1928- DLB-113; CDWLB-3

Fuertes, Gloria 1918- DLB-108

Fugard, Athol 1932- DLB-225

The Fugitives and the Agrarians:
    The First Exhibition Y-85

Fujiwara no Shunzei 1114-1204 . . . . DLB-203

Fujiwara no Tameaki 1230s?-1290s? DLB-203

Fujiwara no Tameie 1198-1275 . . . . DLB-203

Fujiwara no Teika 1162-1241 . . . . DLB-203

Fulbecke, William 1560-1603? DLB-172

Fuller, Charles H., Jr. 1939- DLB-38, 266

Fuller, Henry Blake 1857-1929 . . . . DLB-12

Fuller, John 1937- DLB-40

Fuller, Margaret (see Fuller, Sarah)

Fuller, Roy 1912-1991 . . . . DLB-15, 20

Fuller, Samuel 1912- DLB-26

Fuller, Sarah 1810-1850
    . . . . DLB-1, 59, 73, 183, 223, 239; CDALB-2

Fuller, Thomas 1608-1661 . . . . DLB-151

Fullerton, Hugh 1873-1945 . . . . .DLB-171

Fullwood, William flourished 1568 . . . . . DLB-236

Fulton, Alice 1952- DLB-193

Fulton, Len 1934- .Y-86

Fulton, Robin 1937- DLB-40

Furbank, P. N. 1920- DLB-155

Furman, Laura 1945- Y-86

Furness, Horace Howard
    1833-1912 . . . . DLB-64

Furness, William Henry
    1802-1896 . . . . DLB-1, 235

Furnivall, Frederick James
    1825-1910 . . . . DLB-184

Furphy, Joseph
    (Tom Collins) 1843-1912 . . . . DLB-230

Furthman, Jules 1888-1966 . . . . DLB-26

Furui Yoshikichi 1937- DLB-182

Fushimi, Emperor 1265-1317 . . . . DLB-203

Futabatei, Shimei
    (Hasegawa Tatsunosuke)
    1864-1909 . . . . DLB-180

The Future of the Novel (1899), by
    Henry James DLB-18

Fyleman, Rose 1877-1957 . . . . DLB-160

G

Gadallah, Leslie 1939- DLB-251

Gadda, Carlo Emilio 1893-1973 . . . . .DLB-177

Gaddis, William 1922-1998 . . . . .DLB-2, Y-99

Gág, Wanda 1893-1946 . . . . DLB-22

Gagarin, Ivan Sergeevich 1814-1882 . . . . DLB-198

Gagnon, Madeleine 1938- DLB-60

Gaiman, Neil 1960- DLB-261

Gaine, Hugh 1726-1807 . . . . DLB-43

Gaine, Hugh [publishing house] DLB-49

Gaines, Ernest J.
    1933- DLB-2, 33, 152; Y-80; CDALB-6

Gaiser, Gerd 1908-1976 . . . . DLB-69

Gaitskill, Mary 1954- DLB-244

Galarza, Ernesto 1905-1984 . . . . DLB-122

Galaxy Science Fiction Novels DLB-46

Gale, Zona 1874-1938 . . . . .DLB-9, 228, 78

Galen of Pergamon 129-after 210 . . . . . . .DLB-176

Gales, Winifred Marshall 1761-1839 . . . . DLB-200

Gall, Louise von 1815-1855 . . . . DLB-133

Gallagher, Tess 1943- DLB-120, 212, 244

Gallagher, Wes 1911- DLB-127

Gallagher, William Davis 1808-1894 . . . . . DLB-73

Gallant, Mavis 1922- DLB-53

Gallegos, María Magdalena 1935- DLB-209

Gallico, Paul 1897-1976 . . . . .DLB-9, 171

Gallop, Jane 1952- DLB-246

Galloway, Grace Growden 1727-1782 . . . . DLB-200

Gallup, Donald 1913- DLB-187

Galsworthy, John 1867-1933
    . . . . . DLB-10, 34, 98, 162; DS-16; CDBLB-5

Galt, John 1779-1839 . . . . DLB-99, 116

Galton, Sir Francis 1822-1911 . . . . DLB-166

Galvin, Brendan 1938- DLB-5

Gambit DLB-46

Gamboa, Reymundo 1948- DLB-122

Gammer Gurton's Needle DLB-62

Gan, Elena Andreevna (Zeneida R-va)
    1814-1842 . . . . DLB-198

Gannett, Frank E. 1876-1957 . . . . DLB-29

Gao Xingjian 1940- Y-00

Gaos, Vicente 1919-1980 . . . . DLB-134

García, Andrew 1854?-1943 . . . . DLB-209

García, Lionel G. 1935- DLB-82

García, Richard 1941- DLB-209

García-Camarillo, Cecilio 1943- DLB-209

García Lorca, Federico 1898-1936 . . . . . . DLB-108

García Márquez, Gabriel
    1928- DLB-113; Y-82; CDWLB-3

Gardam, Jane 1928- DLB-14, 161, 231

Gardell, Jonas 1963- DLB-257

Garden, Alexander circa 1685-1756 . . . . . DLB-31

Gardiner, John Rolfe 1936- DLB-244

Gardiner, Margaret Power Farmer
    (see Blessington, Marguerite, Countess of)

Gardner, John
    1933-1982 . . . . DLB-2; Y-82; CDALB-7

Garfield, Leon 1921-1996 . . . . DLB-161

Garis, Howard R. 1873-1962 . . . . DLB-22

Garland, Hamlin 1860-1940 . . .DLB-12, 71, 78, 186

Garneau, Francis-Xavier 1809-1866 . . . . . DLB-99

Garneau, Hector de Saint-Denys
    1912-1943 . . . . DLB-88

Garneau, Michel 1939- DLB-53

Garner, Alan 1934- DLB-161, 261

Garner, Hugh 1913-1979 . . . . DLB-68

Garnett, David 1892-1981 . . . . DLB-34

Garnett, Eve 1900-1991 . . . . DLB-160

Garnett, Richard 1835-1906 . . . . DLB-184

Garrard, Lewis H. 1829-1887 . . . . DLB-186

Garraty, John A. 1920- DLB-17

Garrett, George
    1929- DLB-2, 5, 130, 152; Y-83

Fellowship of Southern Writers Y-98

Garrett, John Work 1872-1942 . . . . .DLB-187

Garrick, David 1717-1779 . . . . DLB-84, 213

Garrison, William Lloyd
    1805-1879 . . . . DLB-1, 43, 235; CDALB-2

Garro, Elena 1920-1998 . . . . DLB-145

Garth, Samuel 1661-1719 . . . . DLB-95

Garve, Andrew 1908- DLB-87

Gary, Romain 1914-1980 . . . . DLB-83

Gascoigne, George 1539?-1577 . . . . DLB-136

Gascoyne, David 1916- DLB-20

Gaskell, Elizabeth Cleghorn
    1810-1865 . . . . . DLB-21, 144, 159; CDBLB-4

Gaskell, Jane 1941- DLB-261

Gaspey, Thomas 1788-1871 . . . . DLB-116

Gass, William H. 1924- DLB-2, 227

Gates, Doris 1901- DLB-22

Gates, Henry Louis, Jr. 1950- DLB-67

Gates, Lewis E. 1860-1924 . . . . DLB-71

Gatto, Alfonso 1909-1976 . . . . DLB-114

Gault, William Campbell 1910-1995 . . . . .DLB-226

Gaunt, Mary 1861-1942 . . . . DLB-174, 230

Gautier, Théophile 1811-1872 . . . . .DLB-119

Gauvreau, Claude 1925-1971 . . . . .DLB-88

The *Gawain*-Poet
flourished circa 1350-1400 . . . . .DLB-146

Gawsworth, John (Terence Ian Fytton Armstrong)
1912-1970 . . . . .DLB-255

Gay, Ebenezer 1696-1787 . . . . .DLB-24

Gay, John 1685-1732 . . . . .DLB-84, 95

Gayarré, Charles E. A. 1805-1895 . . . . . . .DLB-30

Gaylord, Charles [publishing house] DLB-49

Gaylord, Edward King 1873-1974 . . . . . . .DLB-127

Gaylord, Edward Lewis 1919- DLB-127

Geda, Sigitas 1943- DLB-232

Geddes, Gary 1940- DLB-60

Geddes, Virgil 1897- DLB-4

Gedeon (Georgii Andreevich Krinovsky)
circa 1730-1763 . . . . .DLB-150

Gee, Maggie 1948- DLB-207

Gee, Shirley 1932- DLB-245

Geßner, Salomon 1730-1788 . . . . .DLB-97

Geibel, Emanuel 1815-1884 . . . . .DLB-129

Geiogamah, Hanay 1945- DLB-175

Geis, Bernard, Associates DLB-46

Geisel, Theodor Seuss 1904-1991 . . .DLB-61; Y-91

Gelb, Arthur 1924- DLB-103

Gelb, Barbara 1926- DLB-103

Gelber, Jack 1932- DLB-7, 228

Gelinas, Gratien 1909- DLB-88

Gellert, Christian Füerchtegott
1715-1769 . . . . .DLB-97

Gellhorn, Martha 1908-1998 . . . . .Y-82, Y-98

Gems, Pam 1925- DLB-13

Genet, Jean 1910-1986 . . . . .DLB-72; Y-86

Genette, Gérard 1930- DLB-242

Genevoix, Maurice 1890-1980 . . . . .DLB-65

Genovese, Eugene D. 1930- DLB-17

Gent, Peter 1942- Y-82

Geoffrey of Monmouth
circa 1100-1155 . . . . .DLB-146

George, Henry 1839-1897 . . . . .DLB-23

George, Jean Craighead 1919- DLB-52

George, W. L. 1882-1926 . . . . .DLB-197

George III, King of Great Britain and Ireland
1738-1820 . . . . .DLB-213

George V. Higgins to Julian Symons Y-99

Georgslied 896? .DLB-148

Gerber, Merrill Joan 1938- DLB-218

Gerhardie, William 1895-1977 . . . . .DLB-36

Gerhardt, Paul 1607-1676 . . . . .DLB-164

Gérin, Winifred 1901-1981 . . . . .DLB-155

Gérin-Lajoie, Antoine 1824-1882 . . . . . . .DLB-99

German Drama 800-1280 . . . . .DLB-138

German Drama from Naturalism
to Fascism: 1889-1933 . . . . .DLB-118

German Literature and Culture from Charlemagne
to the Early Courtly Period
. . . . .DLB-148; CDWLB-2

German Radio Play, The DLB-124

German Transformation from the Baroque
to the Enlightenment, The DLB-97

The Germanic Epic and Old English
Heroic Poetry: *Widsith, Waldere,*
and *The Fight at Finnsburg* DLB-146

Germanophilism, by Hans Kohn DLB-66

Gernsback, Hugo 1884-1967 . . . . DLB-8, 137

Gerould, Katharine Fullerton
1879-1944 . . . . .DLB-78

Gerrish, Samuel [publishing house] DLB-49

Gerrold, David 1944- DLB-8

Gershwin, Ira 1896-1983 . . . . .DLB-265

The Ira Gershwin Centenary Y-96

Gerson, Jean 1363-1429 . . . . .DLB-208

Gersonides 1288-1344 . . . . .DLB-115

Gerstäcker, Friedrich 1816-1872 . . . . . . .DLB-129

Gerstenberg, Heinrich Wilhelm von
1737-1823 . . . . .DLB-97

Gervinus, Georg Gottfried
1805-1871 . . . . .DLB-133

Geston, Mark S. 1946- DLB-8

Al-Ghazali 1058-1111 . . . . .DLB-115

Gibbings, Robert 1889-1958 . . . . .DLB-195

Gibbon, Edward 1737-1794 . . . . .DLB-104

Gibbon, John Murray 1875-1952 . . . . . . .DLB-92

Gibbon, Lewis Grassic (see Mitchell, James Leslie)

Gibbons, Floyd 1887-1939 . . . . .DLB-25

Gibbons, Reginald 1947- DLB-120

Gibbons, William ?-? DLB-73

Gibson, Charles Dana
1867-1944 . . . . .DLB-188; DS-13

Gibson, Graeme 1934- DLB-53

Gibson, Margaret 1944- DLB-120

Gibson, Margaret Dunlop 1843-1920 . . . .DLB-174

Gibson, Wilfrid 1878-1962 . . . . .DLB-19

Gibson, William 1914- DLB-7

Gibson, William 1948- DLB-251

Gide, André 1869-1951 . . . . .DLB-65

Giguère, Diane 1937- DLB-53

Giguère, Roland 1929- DLB-60

Gil de Biedma, Jaime 1929-1990 . . . . . . .DLB-108

Gil-Albert, Juan 1906- DLB-134

Gilbert, Anthony 1899-1973 . . . . .DLB-77

Gilbert, Sir Humphrey 1537-1583 . . . . . . .DLB-136

Gilbert, Michael 1912- DLB-87

Gilbert, Sandra M. 1936- DLB-120, 246

Gilchrist, Alexander 1828-1861 . . . . .DLB-144

Gilchrist, Ellen 1935- DLB-130

Gilder, Jeannette L. 1849-1916 . . . . .DLB-79

Gilder, Richard Watson 1844-1909 . . . .DLB-64, 79

Gildersleeve, Basil 1831-1924 . . . . .DLB-71

Giles of Rome circa 1243-1316 . . . . .DLB-115

Giles, Henry 1809-1882 . . . . .DLB-64

Gilfillan, George 1813-1878 . . . . .DLB-144

Gill, Eric 1882-1940 . . . . .DLB-98

Gill, Sarah Prince 1728-1771 . . . . .DLB-200

Gill, William F., Company DLB-49

Gillespie, A. Lincoln, Jr. 1895-1950 . . . . . . .DLB-4

Gillespie, Haven 1883-1975 . . . . .DLB-265

Gilliam, Florence ?-? DLB-4

Gilliatt, Penelope 1932-1993 . . . . .DLB-14

Gillott, Jacky 1939-1980 . . . . .DLB-14

Gilman, Caroline H. 1794-1888 . . . . . DLB-3, 73

Gilman, Charlotte Perkins 1860-1935 . . . .DLB-221

Gilman, W. and J. [publishing house] DLB-49

Gilmer, Elizabeth Meriwether 1861-1951 . .DLB-29

Gilmer, Francis Walker 1790-1826 . . . . . . .DLB-37

Gilmore, Mary 1865-1962 . . . . .DLB-260

Gilroy, Frank D. 1925- DLB-7

Gimferrer, Pere (Pedro) 1945- DLB-134

Gingrich, Arnold 1903-1976 . . . . .DLB-137

Ginsberg, Allen
1926-1997 . . . .DLB-5, 16, 169, 237; CDALB-1

Ginzburg, Natalia 1916-1991 . . . . .DLB-177

Ginzkey, Franz Karl 1871-1963 . . . . .DLB-81

Gioia, Dana 1950- DLB-120

Giono, Jean 1895-1970 . . . . .DLB-72

Giotti, Virgilio 1885-1957 . . . . .DLB-114

Giovanni, Nikki 1943- DLB-5, 41; CDALB-7

Gipson, Lawrence Henry 1880-1971 . . . . . .DLB-17

Girard, Rodolphe 1879-1956 . . . . .DLB-92

Giraudoux, Jean 1882-1944 . . . . .DLB-65

Gissing, George 1857-1903 . . . . .DLB-18, 135, 184

The Place of Realism in Fiction (1895) DLB-18

Giudici, Giovanni 1924- DLB-128

Giuliani, Alfredo 1924- DLB-128

Glackens, William J. 1870-1938 . . . . .DLB-188

Gladstone, William Ewart
1809-1898 . . . . .DLB-57, 184

Glaeser, Ernst 1902-1963 . . . . .DLB-69

Glancy, Diane 1941- DLB-175

Glanvill, Joseph 1636-1680 . . . . .DLB-252

Glanville, Brian 1931- DLB-15, 139

Glapthorne, Henry 1610-1643? DLB-58

Glasgow, Ellen 1873-1945 . . . . .DLB-9, 12

Glasier, Katharine Bruce 1867-1950 . . . . .DLB-190

Glaspell, Susan 1876-1948 . . . . . .DLB-7, 9, 78, 228

Glass, Montague 1877-1934 . . . . .DLB-11

Glassco, John 1909-1981 . . . . .DLB-68

Glauser, Friedrich 1896-1938 . . . . .DLB-56

F. Gleason's Publishing Hall DLB-49

Gleim, Johann Wilhelm Ludwig
1719-1803 . . . . .DLB-97

Glendinning, Victoria 1937- DLB-155

The Cult of Biography
Excerpts from the Second Folio Debate:
"Biographies are generally a disease of
English Literature" Y-86

Glidden, Frederick Dilley (Luke Short)
1908-1975 . . . . DLB-256

Glinka, Fedor Nikolaevich 1786-1880. . . . DLB-205

Glover, Keith 1966- DLB-249

Glover, Richard 1712-1785 . . . . DLB-95

Glück, Louise 1943- DLB-5

Glyn, Elinor 1864-1943 . . . . DLB-153

Gnedich, Nikolai Ivanovich 1784-1833 . . . DLB-205

Gobineau, Joseph-Arthur de
1816-1882 . . . . DLB-123

Godber, John 1956- DLB-233

Godbout, Jacques 1933- DLB-53

Goddard, Morrill 1865-1937 . . . . DLB-25

Goddard, William 1740-1817 . . . . DLB-43

Godden, Rumer 1907-1998 . . . . DLB-161

Godey, Louis A. 1804-1878 . . . . DLB-73

Godey and McMichael DLB-49

Godfrey, Dave 1938- DLB-60

Godfrey, Thomas 1736-1763 . . . . DLB-31

Godine, David R., Publisher DLB-46

Godkin, E. L. 1831-1902 . . . . DLB-79

Godolphin, Sidney 1610-1643 . . . . DLB-126

Godwin, Gail 1937- DLB-6, 234

Godwin, M. J., and Company DLB-154

Godwin, Mary Jane Clairmont
1766-1841 . . . . DLB-163

Godwin, Parke 1816-1904 . . . . DLB-3, 64, 250

Godwin, William 1756-1836 . . . . .DLB-39, 104,
. . . . .142, 158, 163, 262; CDBLB-3

Preface to *St. Leon* (1799) DLB-39

Goering, Reinhard 1887-1936 . . . . DLB-118

Goes, Albrecht 1908- DLB-69

Goethe, Johann Wolfgang von
1749-1832 . . . . DLB-94; CDWLB-2

Goetz, Curt 1888-1960 . . . . DLB-124

Goffe, Thomas circa 1592-1629 . . . . DLB-58

Goffstein, M. B. 1940- DLB-61

Gogarty, Oliver St. John 1878-1957 . . . DLB-15, 19

Gogol, Nikolai Vasil'evich 1809-1852 . . . DLB-198

Goines, Donald 1937-1974 . . . . DLB-33

Gold, Herbert 1924- DLB-2; Y-81

Gold, Michael 1893-1967 . . . . DLB-9, 28

Goldbarth, Albert 1948- DLB-120

Goldberg, Dick 1947- DLB-7

Golden Cockerel Press DLB-112

Golding, Arthur 1536-1606 . . . . DLB-136

Golding, Louis 1895-1958 . . . . DLB-195

Golding, William 1911-1993
. . . . DLB-15, 100, 255; Y-83; CDBLB-7

Goldman, Emma 1869-1940 . . . . DLB-221

Goldman, William 1931- DLB-44

Goldring, Douglas 1887-1960 . . . . DLB-197

Goldsmith, Oliver 1730?-1774
. . . . . . DLB-39, 89, 104, 109, 142; CDBLB-2

Goldsmith, Oliver 1794-1861 . . . . DLB-99

Goldsmith Publishing Company DLB-46

Goldstein, Richard 1944- DLB-185

Gollancz, Sir Israel 1864-1930 . . . . DLB-201

Gollancz, Victor, Limited DLB-112

Gombrowicz, Witold
1904-1969 . . . . DLB-215; CDWLB-4

Gómez-Quiñones, Juan 1942- DLB-122

Gomme, Laurence James
[publishing house] DLB-46

Goncharov, Ivan Aleksandrovich
1812-1891 . . . . DLB-238

Goncourt, Edmond de 1822-1896 . . . . . . DLB-123

Goncourt, Jules de 1830-1870 . . . . DLB-123

Gonzales, Rodolfo "Corky" 1928- DLB-122

González, Angel 1925- DLB-108

Gonzalez, Genaro 1949- DLB-122

Gonzalez, Ray 1952- DLB-122

Gonzales-Berry, Erlinda 1942- DLB-209

"Chicano Language" DLB-82

González de Mireles, Jovita
1899-1983 . . . . DLB-122

González-T., César A. 1931- DLB-82

Goodbye, Gutenberg? A Lecture at the
New York Public Library,
18 April 1995, by Donald Lamm Y-95

Goodis, David 1917-1967 . . . . DLB-226

Goodison, Lorna 1947- DLB-157

Goodman, Allegra 1967- DLB-244

Goodman, Paul 1911-1972 . . . . DLB-130, 246

The Goodman Theatre DLB-7

Goodrich, Frances 1891-1984 and
Hackett, Albert 1900-1995 . . . . DLB-26

Goodrich, Samuel Griswold
1793-1860 . . . . .DLB-1, 42, 73, 243

Goodrich, S. G. [publishing house] DLB-49

Goodspeed, C. E., and Company DLB-49

Goodwin, Stephen 1943- Y-82

Googe, Barnabe 1540-1594 . . . . DLB-132

Gookin, Daniel 1612-1687 . . . . DLB-24

Goran, Lester 1928- DLB-244

Gordimer, Nadine 1923- DLB-225; Y-91

Gordon, Adam Lindsay 1833-1870 . . . . . DLB-230

Gordon, Caroline
1895-1981 . . . . . . .DLB-4, 9, 102; DS-17; Y-81

Gordon, Charles F. (see OyamO)

Gordon, Giles 1940- DLB-14, 139, 207

Gordon, Helen Cameron, Lady Russell
1867-1949 . . . . DLB-195

Gordon, Lyndall 1941- DLB-155

Gordon, Mack 1904-1959 . . . . DLB-265

Gordon, Mary 1949- DLB-6; Y-81

Gordone, Charles 1925-1995 . . . . DLB-7

Gore, Catherine 1800-1861 . . . . DLB-116

Gore-Booth, Eva 1870-1926 . . . . DLB-240

Gores, Joe 1931- DLB-226

Gorey, Edward 1925-2000 . . . . DLB-61

Gorgias of Leontini
circa 485 B.C.-376 B.C. DLB-176

Görres, Joseph 1776-1848 . . . . DLB-90

Gosse, Edmund 1849-1928 . . . . .DLB-57, 144, 184

Gosson, Stephen 1554-1624 . . . . .DLB-172

The Schoole of Abuse (1579) DLB-172

Gotanda, Philip Kan 1951- DLB-266

Gotlieb, Phyllis 1926- DLB-88, 251

Go-Toba 1180-1239 . . . . DLB-203

Gottfried von Straßburg
died before 1230 . . . . . . .DLB-138; CDWLB-2

Gotthelf, Jeremias 1797-1854 . . . . DLB-133

Gottschalk circa 804/808-869 . . . . DLB-148

Gottsched, Johann Christoph
1700-1766 . . . . DLB-97

Götz, Johann Nikolaus 1721-1781 . . . . DLB-97

Goudge, Elizabeth 1900-1984 . . . . DLB-191

Gough, John B. 1817-1886 . . . . DLB-243

Gould, Wallace 1882-1940 . . . . DLB-54

Govoni, Corrado 1884-1965 . . . . DLB-114

Gower, John circa 1330-1408 . . . . DLB-146

Goyen, William 1915-1983 . . . . .DLB-2, 218; Y-83

Goytisolo, José Augustín 1928- DLB-134

Gozzano, Guido 1883-1916 . . . . DLB-114

Grabbe, Christian Dietrich 1801-1836 . . . DLB-133

Gracq, Julien 1910- DLB-83

Grady, Henry W. 1850-1889 . . . . DLB-23

Graf, Oskar Maria 1894-1967 . . . . DLB-56

Graf Rudolf
between circa 1170 and circa 1185 . . . DLB-148

Graff, Gerald 1937- DLB-246

Grafton, Richard [publishing house] DLB-170

Grafton, Sue 1940- DLB-226

Graham, Frank 1893-1965 . . . . DLB-241

Graham, George Rex 1813-1894 . . . . DLB-73

Graham, Gwethalyn 1913-1965 . . . . DLB-88

Graham, Jorie 1951- DLB-120

Graham, Katharine 1917- DLB-127

Graham, Lorenz 1902-1989 . . . . DLB-76

Graham, Philip 1915-1963 . . . . .DLB-127

Graham, R. B. Cunninghame
1852-1936 . . . . .DLB-98, 135, 174

Graham, Shirley 1896-1977 . . . . DLB-76

Graham, Stephen 1884-1975 . . . . DLB-195

Graham, W. S. 1918- DLB-20

Graham, William H. [publishing house] . . . DLB-49

Graham, Winston 1910- DLB-77

Grahame, Kenneth
1859-1932 . . . . .DLB-34, 141, 178

Grainger, Martin Allerdale 1874-1941 . . . . DLB-92

Gramatky, Hardie 1907-1979 . . . . DLB-22

Grand, Sarah 1854-1943 . . . . .DLB-135, 197

Grandbois, Alain 1900-1975 . . . . DLB-92

Grandson, Oton de circa 1345-1397 . . . . DLB-208

Grange, John circa 1556-? DLB-136

Granich, Irwin (see Gold, Michael)

Granovsky, Timofei Nikolaevich
1813-1855 . . . . DLB-198

Grant, Anne MacVicar 1755-1838 . . . . . . DLB-200

Grant, Duncan 1885-1978 . . . . DS-10

Grant, George 1918-1988 . . . . .DLB-88

Grant, George Monro 1835-1902 . . . . . . .DLB-99

Grant, Harry J. 1881-1963. . . . . .DLB-29

Grant, James Edward 1905-1966 . . . . .DLB-26

Grass, Günter 1927- . . . DLB-75, 124; CDWLB-2

Grasty, Charles H. 1863-1924 . . . . .DLB-25

Grau, Shirley Ann 1929- DLB-2, 218

Graves, John 1920- Y-83

Graves, Richard 1715-1804 . . . . .DLB-39

Graves, Robert 1895-1985
  . . .DLB-20, 100, 191; DS-18; Y-85; CDBLB-6

Gray, Alasdair 1934- DLB-194, 261

Gray, Asa 1810-1888 . . . . .DLB-1, 235

Gray, David 1838-1861 . . . . .DLB-32

Gray, Simon 1936- DLB-13

Gray, Thomas 1716-1771 . . . .DLB-109; CDBLB-2

Grayson, Richard 1951- DLB-234

Grayson, William J. 1788-1863 . . . .DLB-3, 64, 248

The Great Bibliographers Series Y-93

The Great Modern Library Scam Y-98

The Great War and the Theater, 1914-1918
  [Great Britain] DLB-10

The Great War Exhibition and Symposium at
  the University of South Carolina Y-97

Grech, Nikolai Ivanovich 1787-1867 . . . . .DLB-198

Greeley, Horace 1811-1872 . . .DLB-3, 43, 189, 250

Green, Adolph (see Comden, Betty)

Green, Anna Katharine
  1846-1935 . . . . .DLB-202, 221

Green, Duff 1791-1875 . . . . .DLB-43

Green, Elizabeth Shippen 1871-1954 . . . . .DLB-188

Green, Gerald 1922- DLB-28

Green, Henry 1905-1973 . . . . .DLB-15

Green, Jonas 1712-1767 . . . . .DLB-31

Green, Joseph 1706-1780 . . . . .DLB-31

Green, Julien 1900-1998 . . . . .DLB-4, 72

Green, Paul 1894-1981 . . . . . . DLB-7, 9, 249; Y-81

Green, T. and S. [publishing house] DLB-49

Green, T. H. 1836-1882 . . . . .DLB-262

Green, Terence M. 1947- DLB-251

Green, Thomas Hill 1836-1882 . . . . .DLB-190, 262

Green, Timothy [publishing house] DLB-49

Greenaway, Kate 1846-1901 . . . . .DLB-141

Greenberg: Publisher DLB-46

Green Tiger Press DLB-46

Greene, Asa 1789-1838 . . . . .DLB-11

Greene, Belle da Costa 1883-1950 . . . . . .DLB-187

Greene, Benjamin H.
  [publishing house] DLB-49

Greene, Graham 1904-1991
  . . . . .DLB-13, 15, 77, 100, 162, 201, 204;
  Y-85, Y-91; CDBLB-7

Greene, Robert 1558-1592 . . . . .DLB-62, 167

Greene, Robert Bernard (Bob), Jr.
  1947- DLB-185

Greenfield, George 1917-2000 . . . . Y-00

Greenhow, Robert 1800-1854 . . . . .DLB-30

Greenlee, William B. 1872-1953 . . . . .DLB-187

Greenough, Horatio 1805-1852 . . . . . . .DLB-1, 235

Greenwell, Dora 1821-1882 . . . . .DLB-35, 199

Greenwillow Books DLB-46

Greenwood, Grace (see Lippincott, Sara Jane Clarke)

Greenwood, Walter 1903-1974 . . . . . .DLB-10, 191

Greer, Ben 1948- DLB-6

Greflinger, Georg 1620?-1677 . . . . .DLB-164

Greg, W. R. 1809-1881 . . . . .DLB-55

Greg, W. W. 1875-1959 . . . . .DLB-201

Gregg, Josiah 1806-1850 . . . . .DLB-183, 186

Gregg Press DLB-46

Gregory, Isabella Augusta Persse, Lady
  1852-1932 . . . . .DLB-10

Gregory, Horace 1898-1982 . . . . .DLB-48

Gregory of Rimini circa 1300-1358 . . . . . .DLB-115

Gregynog Press .DLB-112

Greiffenberg, Catharina Regina von
  1633-1694 . . . . .DLB-168

Greig, Noël 1944- DLB-245

Grenfell, Wilfred Thomason
  1865-1940 . . . . .DLB-92

Gress, Elsa 1919-1988 . . . . .DLB-214

Greve, Felix Paul (see Grove, Frederick Philip)

Greville, Fulke, First Lord Brooke
  1554-1628 .DLB-62, 172

Grey, Sir George, K.C.B. 1812-1898 . . . . .DLB-184

Grey, Lady Jane 1537-1554 . . . . .DLB-132

Grey Owl 1888-1938 . . . . .DLB-92; DS-17

Grey, Zane 1872-1939 . . . . .DLB-9, 212

Grey Walls Press DLB-112

Griboedov, Aleksandr Sergeevich
  1795?-1829 . . . . .DLB-205

Grier, Eldon 1917- DLB-88

Grieve, C. M. (see MacDiarmid, Hugh)

Griffin, Bartholomew flourished 1596 . . . .DLB-172

Griffin, Gerald 1803-1840 . . . . .DLB-159

The Griffin Poetry Prize Y-00

Griffith, Elizabeth 1727?-1793 . . . . .DLB-39, 89

  Preface to *The Delicate Distress* (1769) DLB-39

Griffith, George 1857-1906 . . . . .DLB-178

Griffiths, Ralph [publishing house] DLB-154

Griffiths, Trevor 1935- DLB-13, 245

Griggs, S. C., and Company DLB-49

Griggs, Sutton Elbert 1872-1930 . . . . .DLB-50

Grignon, Claude-Henri 1894-1976 . . . . . . .DLB-68

Grigorovich, Dmitrii Vasil'evich
  1822-1899 . . . . .DLB-238

Grigson, Geoffrey 1905- DLB-27

Grillparzer, Franz
  1791-1872 . . . . .DLB-133; CDWLB-2

Grimald, Nicholas
  circa 1519-circa 1562 . . . . .DLB-136

Grimké, Angelina Weld 1880-1958 . . . .DLB-50, 54

Grimké, Sarah Moore 1792-1873 . . . . . . .DLB-239

Grimm, Hans 1875-1959 . . . . .DLB-66

Grimm, Jacob 1785-1863 . . . . .DLB-90

Grimm, Wilhelm
  1786-1859 . . . . .DLB-90; CDWLB-2

Grimmelshausen, Johann Jacob Christoffel von
  1621 or 1622-1676 . . . . .DLB-168; CDWLB-2

Grimshaw, Beatrice Ethel 1871-1953 . . . . .DLB-174

Grindal, Edmund 1519 or 1520-1583 . . . .DLB-132

Gripe, Maria (Kristina) 1923- DLB-257

Griswold, Rufus Wilmot
  1815-1857 . . . . .DLB-3, 59, 250

Grosart, Alexander Balloch 1827-1899 . . .DLB-184

Gross, Milt 1895-1953 . . . . .DLB-11

Grosset and Dunlap DLB-49

Grossman, Allen 1932- DLB-193

Grossman Publishers DLB-46

Grosseteste, Robert circa 1160-1253 . . . . .DLB-115

Grosvenor, Gilbert H. 1875-1966 . . . . .DLB-91

Groth, Klaus 1819-1899 . . . . .DLB-129

Groulx, Lionel 1878-1967 . . . . .DLB-68

Grove, Frederick Philip 1879-1949 . . . . . . .DLB-92

Grove Press DLB-46

Grubb, Davis 1919-1980 . . . . .DLB-6

Gruelle, Johnny 1880-1938 . . . . .DLB-22

von Grumbach, Argula
  1492-after 1563? DLB-179

Grymeston, Elizabeth
  before 1563-before 1604 . . . . .DLB-136

Gryphius, Andreas
  1616-1664 . . . . .DLB-164; CDWLB-2

Gryphius, Christian 1649-1706 . . . . .DLB-168

Guare, John 1938- DLB-7, 249

Guerra, Tonino 1920- DLB-128

Guest, Barbara 1920- DLB-5, 193

Guèvremont, Germaine 1893-1968 . . . . . .DLB-68

Guglielminetti, Amalia 1881-1941 . . . . . . .DLB-264

Guidacci, Margherita 1921-1992 . . . . .DLB-128

Guide to the Archives of Publishers, Journals,
  and Literary Agents in North American
  Libraries Y-93

Guillén, Jorge 1893-1984 . . . . .DLB-108

Guilloux, Louis 1899-1980 . . . . .DLB-72

Guilpin, Everard
  circa 1572-after 1608? DLB-136

Guiney, Louise Imogen 1861-1920 . . . . . . .DLB-54

Guiterman, Arthur 1871-1943 . . . . .DLB-11

Günderrode, Caroline von
  1780-1806 . . . . .DLB-90

Gundulić, Ivan
  1589-1638 . . . . .DLB-147; CDWLB-4

Gunesekera, Romesh 1954- DLB-267

Gunn, Bill 1934-1989 . . . . .DLB-38

Gunn, James E. 1923- DLB-8

Gunn, Neil M. 1891-1973 . . . . .DLB-15

Gunn, Thom 1929- DLB-27; CDBLB-8

Gunnars, Kristjana 1948- DLB-60

Günther, Johann Christian
  1695-1723 . . . . .DLB-168

Gurik, Robert 1932- DLB-60

Gurney, A. R. 1930- DLB-266

Gustafson, Ralph 1909-1995 . . . . DLB-88

Gustafsson, Lars 1936- DLB-257

Gütersloh, Albert Paris 1887-1973. . . . . . . DLB-81

Guthrie, A. B., Jr. 1901-1991 . . . . DLB-6, 212

Guthrie, Ramon 1896-1973 . . . . DLB-4

The Guthrie Theater DLB-7

Guthrie, Thomas Anstey (see Anstey, FC)

Gutzkow, Karl 1811-1878 . . . . DLB-133

Guy, Ray 1939- DLB-60

Guy, Rosa 1925- DLB-33

Guyot, Arnold 1807-1884 . . . . .DS-13

Gwynne, Erskine 1898-1948. . . . . DLB-4

Gyles, John 1680-1755 . . . . DLB-99

Gyllensten, Lars 1921- DLB-257

Gysin, Brion 1916- DLB-16

H

H.D. (see Doolittle, Hilda)

Habermas, Jürgen 1929- DLB-242

Habington, William 1605-1654 . . . . DLB-126

Hacker, Marilyn 1942- DLB-120

Hackett, Albert (see Goodrich, Frances)

Hacks, Peter 1928- DLB-124

Hadas, Rachel 1948- DLB-120

Hadden, Briton 1898-1929 . . . . DLB-91

Hagedorn, Friedrich von 1708-1754 . . . . . DLB-168

Hagelstange, Rudolf 1912-1984 . . . . DLB-69

Haggard, H. Rider
　1856-1925 . . . . DLB-70, 156, 174, 178

Haggard, William 1907-1993 . . . . .Y-93

Hagy, Alyson 1960- DLB-244

Hahn-Hahn, Ida Gräfin von
　1805-1880 . . . . DLB-133

Haig-Brown, Roderick 1908-1976. . . . . DLB-88

Haight, Gordon S. 1901-1985. . . . . DLB-103

Hailey, Arthur 1920- DLB-88; Y-82

Haines, John 1924- DLB-5, 212

Hake, Edward flourished 1566-1604 . . . . DLB-136

Hake, Thomas Gordon 1809-1895. . . . . . . DLB-32

Hakluyt, Richard 1552?-1616. . . . . DLB-136

Halas, František 1901-1949 . . . . DLB-215

Halbe, Max 1865-1944. . . . . DLB-118

Halberstam, David 1934- DLB-241

Haldane, J. B. S. 1892-1964 . . . . DLB-160

Haldeman, Joe 1943- DLB-8

Haldeman-Julius Company. DLB-46

Haldone, Charlotte 1894-1969 . . . . DLB-191

Hale, E. J., and Son. DLB-49

Hale, Edward Everett
　1822-1909 . . . . .DLB-1, 42, 74, 235

Hale, Janet Campbell 1946- DLB-175

Hale, Kathleen 1898- DLB-160

Hale, Leo Thomas (see Ebon)

Hale, Lucretia Peabody 1820-1900 . . . . . . DLB-42

Hale, Nancy
　1908-1988 . . . . DLB-86; DS-17; Y-80, Y-88

Hale, Sarah Josepha (Buell)
　1788-1879 . . . . .DLB-1, 42, 73, 243

Hale, Susan 1833-1910 . . . . DLB-221

Hales, John 1584-1656 . . . . DLB-151

Halévy, Ludovic 1834-1908 . . . . DLB-192

Haley, Alex 1921-1992 . . . . . . DLB-38; CDALB-7

Haliburton, Thomas Chandler
　1796-1865. . . . . DLB-11, 99

Hall, Anna Maria 1800-1881 . . . . DLB-159

Hall, Donald 1928- DLB-5

Hall, Edward 1497-1547 . . . . DLB-132

Hall, Halsey 1898-1977. . . . . DLB-241

Hall, James 1793-1868 . . . . .DLB-73, 74

Hall, Joseph 1574-1656 . . . . DLB-121, 151

Hall, Radclyffe 1880-1943 . . . . DLB-191

Hall, Samuel [publishing house] DLB-49

Hall, Sarah Ewing 1761-1830 . . . . DLB-200

Hall, Stuart 1932- DLB-242

Hallam, Arthur Henry 1811-1833 . . . . DLB-32

On Some of the Characteristics of Modern
　Poetry and On the Lyrical Poems of
　Alfred Tennyson (1831). DLB-32

Halleck, Fitz-Greene 1790-1867 . . . . . . DLB-3, 250

Haller, Albrecht von 1708-1777. . . . . DLB-168

Halliday, Brett (see Dresser, Davis)

Halliwell-Phillipps, James Orchard
　1820-1889 . . . . DLB-184

Hallmann, Johann Christian
　1640-1704 or 1716? DLB-168

Hallmark Editions DLB-46

Halper, Albert 1904-1984. . . . . DLB-9

Halperin, John William 1941- DLB-111

Halstead, Murat 1829-1908 . . . . DLB-23

Hamann, Johann Georg 1730-1788. . . . . . . DLB-97

Hamburger, Michael 1924- DLB-27

Hamilton, Alexander 1712-1756 . . . . DLB-31

Hamilton, Alexander 1755?-1804 . . . . DLB-37

Hamilton, Cicely 1872-1952. . . . . .DLB-10, 197

Hamilton, Edmond 1904-1977 . . . . DLB-8

Hamilton, Elizabeth 1758-1816 . . . . . DLB-116, 158

Hamilton, Gail (see Corcoran, Barbara)

Hamilton, Gail (see Dodge, Mary Abigail)

Hamilton, Hamish, Limited DLB-112

Hamilton, Hugo 1953- DLB-267

Hamilton, Ian 1938- DLB-40, 155

Hamilton, Janet 1795-1873 . . . . DLB-199

Hamilton, Mary Agnes 1884-1962 . . . . . DLB-197

Hamilton, Patrick 1904-1962 . . . . . . DLB-10, 191

Hamilton, Virginia 1936- DLB-33, 52

Hamilton-Paterson, James 1941- DLB-267

Hamilton, Sir William 1788-1856 . . . . . . DLB-262

Hammerstein, Oscar, II 1895-1960 . . . . DLB-265

Hammett, Dashiell
　1894-1961 . . . . DLB-226; DS-6; CDALB-5

The Glass Key and Other Dashiell Hammett
　Mysteries Y-96

Dashiell Hammett: An Appeal in TAC. Y-91

Hammon, Jupiter 1711-died between
　1790 and 1806 . . . . DLB-31, 50

Hammond, John ?-1663 . . . . DLB-24

Hamner, Earl 1923- DLB-6

Hampson, John 1901-1955. . . . . DLB-191

Hampton, Christopher 1946- DLB-13

Handel-Mazzetti, Enrica von 1871-1955. . . DLB-81

Handke, Peter 1942- DLB-85, 124

Handlin, Oscar 1915- DLB-17

Hankin, St. John 1869-1909 . . . . DLB-10

Hanley, Clifford 1922- DLB-14

Hanley, James 1901-1985 . . . . DLB-191

Hannah, Barry 1942- DLB-6, 234

Hannay, James 1827-1873 . . . . DLB-21

Hano, Arnold 1922- DLB-241

Hansberry, Lorraine
　1930-1965 . . . . .DLB-7, 38; CDALB-1

Hansen, Martin A. 1909-1955 . . . . DLB-214

Hansen, Thorkild 1927-1989 . . . . DLB-214

Hanson, Elizabeth 1684-1737 . . . . DLB-200

Hapgood, Norman 1868-1937 . . . . DLB-91

Happel, Eberhard Werner 1647-1690. . . . DLB-168

The Harbinger 1845-1849 . . . . DLB-223

Harburg, E. Y. "Yip" 1896-1981 . . . . . . DLB-265

Harcourt Brace Jovanovich DLB-46

Hardenberg, Friedrich von (see Novalis)

Harding, Walter 1917- DLB-111

Hardwick, Elizabeth 1916- DLB-6

Hardy, Frank 1917-1994. . . . . DLB-260

Hardy, Thomas
　1840-1928 . . . . . . DLB-18, 19, 135; CDBLB-5

"Candour in English Fiction" (1890) DLB-18

Hare, Cyril 1900-1958 . . . . DLB-77

Hare, David 1947- DLB-13

Hare, R. M. 1919-2002. . . . . DLB-262

Hargrove, Marion 1919- DLB-11

Häring, Georg Wilhelm Heinrich
　(see Alexis, Willibald)

Harington, Donald 1935- DLB-152

Harington, Sir John 1560-1612. . . . . DLB-136

Harjo, Joy 1951- DLB-120, 175

Harkness, Margaret (John Law)
　1854-1923 . . . . .DLB-197

Harley, Edward, second Earl of Oxford
　1689-1741 . . . . DLB-213

Harley, Robert, first Earl of Oxford
　1661-1724. . . . . DLB-213

Harlow, Robert 1923- DLB-60

Harman, Thomas flourished 1566-1573. . DLB-136

Harness, Charles L. 1915- DLB-8

Harnett, Cynthia 1893-1981. . . . . DLB-161

Harnick, Sheldon 1924- DLB-265

Harper, Edith Alice Mary (see Wickham, Anna)

Harper, Fletcher 1806-1877 . . . . .DLB-79

Harper, Frances Ellen Watkins
   1825-1911 . . . . .DLB-50, 221

Harper, Michael S. 1938- DLB-41

Harper and Brothers DLB-49

Harpur, Charles 1813-1868 . . . . .DLB-230

Harraden, Beatrice 1864-1943 . . . . .DLB-153

Harrap, George G., and Company
   Limited DLB-112

Harriot, Thomas 1560-1621 . . . . .DLB-136

Harris, Alexander 1805-1874 . . . . .DLB-230

Harris, Benjamin ?-circa 1720 . . . . . . .DLB-42, 43

Harris, Christie 1907- DLB-88

Harris, Frank 1856-1931 . . . . .DLB-156, 197

Harris, George Washington
   1814-1869 . . . . .DLB-3, 11, 248

Harris, Joel Chandler
   1848-1908 . . . . DLB-11, 23, 42, 78, 91

Harris, Mark 1922- DLB-2; Y-80

Harris, Wilson 1921- DLB-117; CDWLB-3

Harrison, Mrs. Burton
   (see Harrison, Constance Cary)

Harrison, Charles Yale 1898-1954. . . . . . .DLB-68

Harrison, Constance Cary 1843-1920 . . . .DLB-221

Harrison, Frederic 1831-1923 . . . . . . .DLB-57, 190

"On Style in English Prose" (1898) DLB-57

Harrison, Harry 1925- DLB-8

Harrison, James P., Company DLB-49

Harrison, Jim 1937- Y-82

Harrison, M. John 1945- DLB-261

Harrison, Mary St. Leger Kingsley
   (see Malet, Lucas)

Harrison, Paul Carter 1936- DLB-38

Harrison, Susan Frances 1859-1935. . . . . .DLB-99

Harrison, Tony 1937- DLB-40, 245

Harrison, William 1535-1593 . . . . .DLB-136

Harrison, William 1933- DLB-234

Harrisse, Henry 1829-1910 . . . . .DLB-47

The Harry Ransom Humanities
   Research Center at the University
   of Texas at Austin Y-00

Harryman, Carla 1952- DLB-193

Harsdörffer, Georg Philipp 1607-1658. . . .DLB-164

Harsent, David 1942- DLB-40

Hart, Albert Bushnell 1854-1943 . . . . .DLB-17

Hart, Anne 1768-1834 . . . . .DLB-200

Hart, Elizabeth 1771-1833 . . . . .DLB-200

Hart, Julia Catherine 1796-1867. . . . . .DLB-99

Hart, Lorenz 1895-1943. . . . . .DLB-265

The Lorenz Hart Centenary Y-95

Hart, Moss 1904-1961 . . . . .DLB-7, 266

Hart, Oliver 1723-1795 . . . . .DLB-31

Hart-Davis, Rupert, Limited DLB-112

Harte, Bret 1836-1902
   . . . . DLB-12, 64, 74, 79, 186; CDALB-3

Harte, Edward Holmead 1922- DLB-127

Harte, Houston Harriman 1927- DLB-127

Hartlaub, Felix 1913-1945 . . . . .DLB-56

Hartlebon, Otto Erich 1864-1905 . . . . . . .DLB-118

Hartley, David 1705-1757 . . . . .DLB-252

Hartley, L. P. 1895-1972 . . . . .DLB-15, 139

Hartley, Marsden 1877-1943 . . . . .DLB-54

Hartling, Peter 1933- DLB-75

Hartman, Geoffrey H. 1929- DLB-67

Hartmann, Sadakichi 1867-1944 . . . . .DLB-54

Hartmann von Aue
   circa 1160-circa 1205. . . . DLB-138; CDWLB-2

Harvey, Gabriel 1550?-1631 . . . DLB-167, 213, 236

Harvey, Jack (see Rankin, Ian)

Harvey, Jean-Charles 1891-1967 . . . . .DLB-88

Harvill Press Limited. DLB-112

Harwood, Lee 1939- DLB-40

Harwood, Ronald 1934- DLB-13

Hašek, Jaroslav 1883-1923. . .DLB-215; CDWLB-4

Haskins, Charles Homer 1870-1937 . . . . . .DLB-47

Haslam, Gerald 1937- DLB-212

Hass, Robert 1941- DLB-105, 206

Hasselstrom, Linda M. 1943- DLB-256

Hastings, Michael 1938- DLB-233

Hatar, Győző 1914- DLB-215

The Hatch-Billops Collection. DLB-76

Hathaway, William 1944- DLB-120

Hauff, Wilhelm 1802-1827 . . . . .DLB-90

A Haughty and Proud Generation (1922),
   by Ford Madox Hueffer DLB-36

Haugwitz, August Adolph von
   1647-1706. . . . . .DLB-168

Hauptmann, Carl 1858-1921. . . . . . .DLB-66, 118

Hauptmann, Gerhart
   1862-1946 . . . . . . .DLB-66, 118; CDWLB-2

Hauser, Marianne 1910- Y-83

Havel, Václav 1936- DLB-232; CDWLB-4

Haven, Alice B. Neal 1827-1863 . . . . .DLB-260

Havergal, Frances Ridley 1836-1879 . . . . .DLB-199

Hawes, Stephen 1475?-before 1529 . . . . . .DLB-132

Hawker, Robert Stephen 1803-1875 . . . . . .DLB-32

Hawkes, John
   1925-1998 . . . . .DLB-2, 7, 227; Y-80, Y-98

John Hawkes: A Tribute Y-98

Hawkesworth, John 1720-1773. . . . . .DLB-142

Hawkins, Sir Anthony Hope (see Hope, Anthony)

Hawkins, Sir John 1719-1789 . . . . . .DLB-104, 142

Hawkins, Walter Everette 1883-? DLB-50

Hawthorne, Nathaniel
   1804-1864 . . . .DLB-1, 74, 183, 223; CDALB-2

Hawthorne, Nathaniel 1804-1864 and
   Hawthorne, Sophia Peabody
   1809-1871 .DLB-183

Hawthorne, Sophia Peabody
   1809-1871 . . . . .DLB-183, 239

Hay, John 1835-1905. . . . . DLB-12, 47, 189

Hayashi, Fumiko 1903-1951 . . . . .DLB-180

Haycox, Ernest 1899-1950 . . . . .DLB-206

Haycraft, Anna Margaret (see Ellis, Alice Thomas)

Hayden, Robert
   1913-1980 . . . . .DLB-5, 76; CDALB-1

Haydon, Benjamin Robert
   1786-1846 . . . . .DLB-110

Hayes, John Michael 1919- DLB-26

Hayley, William 1745-1820 . . . . .DLB-93, 142

Haym, Rudolf 1821-1901 . . . . .DLB-129

Hayman, Robert 1575-1629. . . . . .DLB-99

Hayman, Ronald 1932- DLB-155

Hayne, Paul Hamilton
   1830-1886 . . . . .DLB-3, 64, 79, 248

Hays, Mary 1760-1843 . . . . .DLB-142, 158

Hayward, John 1905-1965. . . . . .DLB-201

Haywood, Eliza 1693?-1756 . . . . .DLB-39

From the Dedication, *Lasselia* (1723) DLB-39

From *The Tea-Table* *DLB-39*

From the Preface to *The Disguis'd
   Prince* (1723). DLB-39

Hazard, Willis P. [publishing house] DLB-49

Hazlitt, William 1778-1830 . . . . .DLB-110, 158

Hazzard, Shirley 1931- Y-82

Head, Bessie
   1937-1986 . . . . DLB-117, 225; CDWLB-3

Headley, Joel T. 1813-1897 . . .DLB-30, 183; DS-13

Heaney, Seamus
   1939- DLB-40; Y-95; CDBLB-8

Heard, Nathan C. 1936- DLB-33

Hearn, Lafcadio 1850-1904 . . . . . . DLB-12, 78, 189

Hearn, Mary Anne (Marianne Farningham,
   Eva Hope) 1834-1909 . . . . .DLB-240

Hearne, John 1926- DLB-117

Hearne, Samuel 1745-1792. . . . . .DLB-99

Hearne, Thomas 1678?-1735 . . . . .DLB-213

Hearst, William Randolph 1863-1951 . . . . .DLB-25

Hearst, William Randolph, Jr.
   1908-1993 . . . . .DLB-127

Heartman, Charles Frederick
   1883-1953 . . . . .DLB-187

Heath, Catherine 1924- DLB-14

Heath, James Ewell 1792-1862. . . . . .DLB-248

Heath, Roy A. K. 1926- DLB-117

Heath-Stubbs, John 1918- DLB-27

Heavysege, Charles 1816-1876 . . . . .DLB-99

Hebbel, Friedrich
   1813-1863 . . . . .DLB-129; CDWLB-2

Hebel, Johann Peter 1760-1826 . . . . .DLB-90

Heber, Richard 1774-1833 . . . . .DLB-184

Hébert, Anne 1916-2000 . . . . .DLB-68

Hébert, Jacques 1923- DLB-53

Hecht, Anthony 1923- DLB-5, 169

Hecht, Ben 1894-1964 . . . DLB-7, 9, 25, 26, 28, 86

Hecker, Isaac Thomas 1819-1888 . . . . .DLB-1, 243

Hedge, Frederic Henry
   1805-1890 . . . . .DLB-1, 59, 243

Hefner, Hugh M. 1926- DLB-137

Hegel, Georg Wilhelm Friedrich
   1770-1831 . . . . .DLB-90

Heide, Robert 1939- DLB-249

Heidish, Marcy 1947- Y-82

Heißenbüttel, Helmut 1921-1996 . . . . DLB-75

Heike monogatari DLB-203

Hein, Christoph 1944- . . . DLB-124; CDWLB-2

Hein, Piet 1905-1996 . . . . DLB-214

Heine, Heinrich 1797-1856 . . . DLB-90; CDWLB-2

Heinemann, Larry 1944- DS-9

Heinemann, William, Limited DLB-112

Heinesen, William 1900-1991 . . . . DLB-214

Heinlein, Robert A. 1907-1988 . . . . DLB-8

Heinrich Julius of Brunswick
1564-1613 . . . . DLB-164

Heinrich von dem Türlîn
flourished circa 1230 . . . . DLB-138

Heinrich von Melk
flourished after 1160 . . . . DLB-148

Heinrich von Veldeke
circa 1145-circa 1190 . . . . DLB-138

Heinrich, Willi 1920- DLB-75

Heinse, Wilhelm 1746-1803 . . . . DLB-94

Heinz, W. C. 1915- DLB-171

Heiskell, John 1872-1972 . . . . DLB-127

Hejinian, Lyn 1941- DLB-165

Heliand circa 850 . . . . DLB-148

Heller, Joseph
1923-1999 . . . . DLB-2, 28, 227; Y-80, Y-99

Heller, Michael 1937- DLB-165

Hellman, Lillian 1906-1984 . . . . . DLB-7, 228; Y-84

Hellwig, Johann 1609-1674 . . . . DLB-164

Helprin, Mark 1947- Y-85; CDALB-7

Helwig, David 1938- DLB-60

Hemans, Felicia 1793-1835 . . . . DLB-96

Hemenway, Abby Maria 1828-1890 . . . . . DLB-243

Hemingway, Ernest 1899-1961
. . . . . DLB-4, 9, 102, 210; Y-81, Y-87, Y-99;
DS-1, DS-15, DS-16; CDALB-4

The Hemingway Centenary Celebration at the
JFK Library Y-99

Ernest Hemingway: A Centennial
Celebration. Y-99

The Ernest Hemingway Collection at the
John F. Kennedy Library Y-99

Ernest Hemingway Declines to Introduce
War and Peace Y-01

Ernest Hemingway's Reaction to James Gould
Cozzens Y-98

Ernest Hemingway's Toronto Journalism
Revisited: With Three Previously
Unrecorded Stories Y-92

Falsifying Hemingway Y-96

Hemingway: Twenty-Five Years Later Y-85

Not Immediately Discernible . . . but Eventually
Quite Clear: The *First Light* and *Final Years*
of Hemingway's Centenary Y-99

Hemingway Salesmen's Dummies Y-00

Second International Hemingway Colloquium:
Cuba Y-98

Hémon, Louis 1880-1913 . . . . DLB-92

Hempel, Amy 1951- DLB-218

Hemphill, Paul 1936- Y-87

Hénault, Gilles 1920- DLB-88

Henchman, Daniel 1689-1761 . . . . DLB-24

Henderson, Alice Corbin 1881-1949 . . . . DLB-54

Henderson, Archibald 1877-1963 . . . . . . DLB-103

Henderson, David 1942- DLB-41

Henderson, George Wylie 1904- DLB-51

Henderson, Zenna 1917-1983 . . . . DLB-8

Henighan, Tom 1934- DLB-251

Henisch, Peter 1943- DLB-85

Henley, Beth 1952- Y-86

Henley, William Ernest 1849-1903 . . . . . . DLB-19

Henning, Rachel 1826-1914 . . . . DLB-230

Henningsen, Agnes 1868-1962 . . . . DLB-214

Henniker, Florence 1855-1923 . . . . DLB-135

Henry, Alexander 1739-1824 . . . . DLB-99

Henry, Buck 1930- DLB-26

Henry VIII of England 1491-1547 . . . . . . DLB-132

Henry of Ghent
circa 1217-1229 - 1293 . . . . DLB-115

Henry, Marguerite 1902-1997 . . . . DLB-22

Henry, O. (see Porter, William Sydney)

Henry, Robert Selph 1889-1970 . . . . DLB-17

Henry, Will (see Allen, Henry W.)

Henryson, Robert
1420s or 1430s-circa 1505 . . . . DLB-146

Henschke, Alfred (see Klabund)

Hensher, Philip 1965- DLB-267

Hensley, Sophie Almon 1866-1946 . . . . . . DLB-99

Henson, Lance 1944- DLB-175

Henty, G. A. 1832?-1902 . . . . DLB-18, 141

Hentz, Caroline Lee 1800-1856 . . . . . . DLB-3, 248

Heraclitus
flourished circa 500 B.C. DLB-176

Herbert, Agnes circa 1880-1960 . . . . DLB-174

Herbert, Alan Patrick 1890-1971 . . . . DLB-10, 191

Herbert, Edward, Lord, of Cherbury
1582-1648 . . . . DLB-121, 151, 252

Herbert, Frank 1920-1986 . . . . . DLB-8; CDALB-7

Herbert, George 1593-1633 . . DLB-126; CDBLB-1

Herbert, Henry William 1807-1858 . . . . DLB-3, 73

Herbert, John 1926- DLB-53

Herbert, Mary Sidney, Countess of Pembroke
(see Sidney, Mary)

Herbert, Xavier 1901-1984 . . . . DLB-260

Herbert, Zbigniew
1924-1998 . . . . DLB-232; CDWLB-4

Herbst, Josephine 1892-1969 . . . . DLB-9

Herburger, Gunter 1932- DLB-75, 124

Hercules, Frank E. M. 1917-1996 . . . . DLB-33

Herder, Johann Gottfried 1744-1803 . . . . . DLB-97

Herder, B., Book Company DLB-49

Heredia, José-María de 1842-1905 . . . . . . DLB-217

Herford, Charles Harold 1853-1931 . . . DLB-149

Hergesheimer, Joseph 1880-1954 . . . . DLB-9, 102

Heritage Press DLB-46

Hermann the Lame 1013-1054 . . . . DLB-148

Hermes, Johann Timotheus
1738-1821 . . . . DLB-97

Hermlin, Stephan 1915-1997 . . . . DLB-69

Hernández, Alfonso C. 1938- DLB-122

Hernández, Inés 1947- DLB-122

Hernández, Miguel 1910-1942 . . . . DLB-134

Hernton, Calvin C. 1932- DLB-38

Herodotus circa 484 B.C.-circa 420 B.C.
. . . . DLB-176; CDWLB-1

Heron, Robert 1764-1807 . . . . DLB-142

Herr, Michael 1940- DLB-185

Herrera, Juan Felipe 1948- DLB-122

Herrick, E. R., and Company DLB-49

Herrick, Robert 1591-1674 . . . . DLB-126

Herrick, Robert 1868-1938 . . . . DLB-9, 12, 78

Herrick, William 1915- Y-83

Herrmann, John 1900-1959 . . . . DLB-4

Hersey, John 1914-1993 . . . DLB-6, 185; CDALB-7

Hertel, François 1905-1985 . . . . DLB-68

Hervé-Bazin, Jean Pierre Marie (see Bazin, Hervé)

Hervey, John, Lord 1696-1743 . . . . DLB-101

Herwig, Georg 1817-1875 . . . . DLB-133

Herzog, Emile Salomon Wilhelm
(see Maurois, André)

Hesiod eighth century B.C. DLB-176

Hesse, Hermann
1877-1962 . . . . DLB-66; CDWLB-2

Hessus, Helius Eobanus 1488-1540 . . . . . DLB-179

Hewat, Alexander circa 1743-circa 1824 . . . DLB-30

Hewitt, John 1907- DLB-27

Hewlett, Maurice 1861-1923 . . . . DLB-34, 156

Heyen, William 1940- DLB-5

Heyer, Georgette 1902-1974 . . . . DLB-77, 191

Heym, Stefan 1913- DLB-69

Heyse, Paul 1830-1914 . . . . DLB-129

Heytesbury, William
circa 1310-1372 or 1373 . . . . DLB-115

Heyward, Dorothy 1890-1961 . . . . DLB-7, 249

Heyward, DuBose 1885-1940 . . . DLB-7, 9, 45, 249

Heywood, John 1497?-1580? DLB-136

Heywood, Thomas
1573 or 1574-1641 . . . . DLB-62

Hibbs, Ben 1901-1975 . . . . DLB-137

Hichens, Robert S. 1864-1950 . . . . DLB-153

Hickey, Emily 1845-1924 . . . . DLB-199

Hickman, William Albert 1877-1957 . . . . DLB-92

Hicks, Granville 1901-1982 . . . . DLB-246

Hidalgo, José Luis 1919-1947 . . . . DLB-108

Hiebert, Paul 1892-1987 . . . . DLB-68

Hieng, Andrej 1925- DLB-181

Hierro, José 1922- DLB-108

Higgins, Aidan 1927- DLB-14

Higgins, Colin 1941-1988 . . . . DLB-26

Higgins, George V.
1939-1999 . . . . DLB-2; Y-81, Y-98, Y-99

George V. Higgins to Julian Symons Y-99

Higginson, Thomas Wentworth
   1823-1911 . . . . .DLB-1, 64, 243

Highwater, Jamake 1942?- DLB-52; Y-85

Hijuelos, Oscar 1951- DLB-145

Hildegard von Bingen 1098-1179. . . . . . .DLB-148

Das Hildesbrandslied
   circa 820 . . . . .DLB-148; CDWLB-2

Hildesheimer, Wolfgang
   1916-1991 . . . . .DLB-69, 124

Hildreth, Richard 1807-1865 . . .DLB-1, 30, 59, 235

Hill, Aaron 1685-1750 . . . . .DLB-84

Hill, Geoffrey 1932- DLB-40; CDBLB-8

Hill, George M., Company DLB-49

Hill, "Sir" John 1714?-1775. . . . . .DLB-39

Hill, Lawrence, and Company,
   Publishers .DLB-46

Hill, Leslie 1880-1960 . . . . .DLB-51

Hill, Susan 1942- DLB-14, 139

Hill, Walter 1942- DLB-44

Hill and Wang. .DLB-46

Hillberry, Conrad 1928- DLB-120

Hillerman, Tony 1925- DLB-206

Hilliard, Gray and Company. DLB-49

Hills, Lee 1906- DLB-127

Hillyer, Robert 1895-1961 . . . . .DLB-54

Hilton, James 1900-1954 . . . . .DLB-34, 77

Hilton, Walter died 1396. . . . . .DLB-146

Hilton and Company. DLB-49

Himes, Chester 1909-1984. . . .DLB-2, 76, 143, 226

Hindmarsh, Joseph [publishing house]. . . .DLB-170

Hine, Daryl 1936- DLB-60

Hingley, Ronald 1920- DLB-155

Hinojosa-Smith, Rolando 1929- DLB-82

Hinton, S. E. 1948- CDALB-7

Hippel, Theodor Gottlieb von
   1741-1796. . . . . .DLB-97

Hippocrates of Cos flourished circa 425 B.C.
   . . . . .DLB-176; CDWLB-1

Hirabayashi, Taiko 1905-1972. . . . . .DLB-180

Hirsch, E. D., Jr. 1928- DLB-67

Hirsch, Edward 1950- DLB-120

Hoagland, Edward 1932- DLB-6

Hoagland, Everett H., III 1942- DLB-41

Hoban, Russell 1925- DLB-52; Y-90

Hobbes, Thomas 1588-1679 . . . . . . .DLB-151, 252

Hobby, Oveta 1905- DLB-127

Hobby, William 1878-1964 . . . . .DLB-127

Hobsbaum, Philip 1932- DLB-40

Hobson, Laura Z. 1900- DLB-28

Hobson, Sarah 1947- DLB-204

Hoby, Thomas 1530-1566. . . . . .DLB-132

Hoccleve, Thomas
   circa 1368-circa 1437. . . . . .DLB-146

Hochhuth, Rolf 1931- DLB-124

Hochman, Sandra 1936- DLB-5

Hocken, Thomas Morland
   1836-1910 . . . . .DLB-184

Hodder and Stoughton, Limited DLB-106

Hodgins, Jack 1938- DLB-60

Hodgman, Helen 1945- DLB-14

Hodgskin, Thomas 1787-1869 . . . . .DLB-158

Hodgson, Ralph 1871-1962 . . . . .DLB-19

Hodgson, William Hope
   1877-1918 . . . . DLB-70, 153, 156, 178

Hoe, Robert, III 1839-1909. . . . . .DLB-187

Hoeg, Peter 1957- DLB-214

Højholt, Per 1928- DLB-214

Hoffenstein, Samuel 1890-1947 . . . . .DLB-11

Hoffman, Charles Fenno 1806-1884 . . .DLB-3, 250

Hoffman, Daniel 1923- DLB-5

Hoffmann, E. T. A.
   1776-1822 . . . . .DLB-90; CDWLB-2

Hoffman, Frank B. 1888-1958. . . . . .DLB-188

Hoffman, William 1925- DLB-234

Hoffmanswaldau, Christian Hoffman von
   1616-1679 .DLB-168

Hofmann, Michael 1957- DLB-40

Hofmannsthal, Hugo von
   1874-1929 . . . . DLB-81, 118; CDWLB-2

Hofstadter, Richard 1916-1970 . . . . . . DLB-17, 246

Hogan, Desmond 1950- DLB-14

Hogan, Linda 1947- DLB-175

Hogan and Thompson DLB-49

Hogarth Press .DLB-112

Hogg, James 1770-1835 . . . . .DLB-93, 116, 159

Hohberg, Wolfgang Helmhard Freiherr von
   1612-1688 . . . . .DLB-168

von Hohenheim, Philippus Aureolus
   Theophrastus Bombastus (see Paracelsus)

Hohl, Ludwig 1904-1980. . . . . .DLB-56

Holbrook, David 1923- DLB-14, 40

Holcroft, Thomas 1745-1809 . . . . .DLB-39, 89, 158

Preface to *Alwyn* (1780) DLB-39

Holden, Jonathan 1941- DLB-105

"Contemporary Verse Story-telling" DLB-105

Holden, Molly 1927-1981 . . . . .DLB-40

Hölderlin, Friedrich 1770-1843 DLB-90; CDWLB-2

Holdstock, Robert 1948- DLB-261

Holiday House. .DLB-46

Holinshed, Raphael died 1580. . . . . .DLB-167

Holland, J. G. 1819-1881. . . . . DS-13

Holland, Norman N. 1927- DLB-67

Hollander, John 1929- DLB-5

Holley, Marietta 1836-1926. . . . . .DLB-11

Hollinghurst, Alan 1954- DLB-207

Hollingsworth, Margaret 1940- DLB-60

Hollo, Anselm 1934- DLB-40

Holloway, Emory 1885-1977. . . . . .DLB-103

Holloway, John 1920- DLB-27

Holloway House Publishing Company DLB-46

Holme, Constance 1880-1955 . . . . .DLB-34

Holmes, Abraham S. 1821?-1908 . . . . . . .DLB-99

Holmes, John Clellon 1926-1988. . . . .DLB-16, 237

"Four Essays on the Beat Generation". DLB-16

Holmes, Mary Jane 1825-1907 . . . . .DLB-202, 221

Holmes, Oliver Wendell
   1809-1894 . . . . . . .DLB-1, 189, 235; CDALB-2

Holmes, Richard 1945- DLB-155

The Cult of Biography
   Excerpts from the Second Folio Debate:
   "Biographies are generally a disease of
   English Literature" Y-86

Holmes, Thomas James 1874-1959 . . . . . .DLB-187

Holroyd, Michael 1935- DLB-155; Y-99

Holst, Hermann E. von 1841-1904 . . . . . . .DLB-47

Holt, Henry, and Company DLB-49

Holt, John 1721-1784 . . . . .DLB-43

Holt, Rinehart and Winston DLB-46

Holtby, Winifred 1898-1935 . . . . .DLB-191

Holthusen, Hans Egon 1913- DLB-69

Hölty, Ludwig Christoph Heinrich
   1748-1776. . . . . .DLB-94

Holub, Miroslav
   1923-1998 . . . . .DLB-232; CDWLB-4

Holz, Arno 1863-1929. . . . . .DLB-118

Home, Henry, Lord Kames
   (see Kames, Henry Home, Lord)

Home, John 1722-1808 . . . . .DLB-84

Home, William Douglas 1912- DLB-13

Home Publishing Company DLB-49

Homer circa eighth-seventh centuries B.C.
   . . . . DLB-176; CDWLB-1

Homer, Winslow 1836-1910 . . . . .DLB-188

Homes, Geoffrey (see Mainwaring, Daniel)

Honan, Park 1928- DLB-111

Hone, William 1780-1842 . . . . .DLB-110, 158

Hongo, Garrett Kaoru 1951- DLB-120

Honig, Edwin 1919- DLB-5

Hood, Hugh 1928- DLB-53

Hood, Mary 1946- DLB-234

Hood, Thomas 1799-1845. . . . . .DLB-96

Hook, Theodore 1788-1841. . . . . .DLB-116

Hooker, Jeremy 1941- DLB-40

Hooker, Richard 1554-1600 . . . . .DLB-132

Hooker, Thomas 1586-1647 . . . . .DLB-24

hooks, bell 1952- DLB-246

Hooper, Johnson Jones
   1815-1862 . . . . .DLB-3, 11, 248

Hope, Anthony 1863-1933 . . . . .DLB-153, 156

Hope, Christopher 1944- DLB-225

Hope, Eva (see Hearn, Mary Anne)

Hope, Laurence (Adela Florence
   Cory Nicolson) 1865-1904 . . . . .DLB-240

Hopkins, Ellice 1836-1904. . . . . .DLB-190

Hopkins, Gerard Manley
   1844-1889 . . . . .DLB-35, 57; CDBLB-5

Hopkins, John (see Sternhold, Thomas)

Hopkins, John H., and Son DLB-46

Hopkins, Lemuel 1750-1801 . . . . .DLB-37

Hopkins, Pauline Elizabeth 1859-1930 . . . .DLB-50

Hopkins, Samuel 1721-1803 . . . . .DLB-31

Hopkinson, Francis 1737-1791 . . . . DLB-31

Hopkinson, Nalo 1960- DLB-251

Hopper, Nora (Mrs. Nora Chesson)
1871-1906 . . . . DLB-240

Hoppin, Augustus 1828-1896 . . . . DLB-188

Hora, Josef 1891-1945 . . . . . DLB-215; CDWLB-4

Horace 65 B.C.-8 B.C. DLB-211; CDWLB-1

Horgan, Paul 1903-1995 . . . . . .DLB-102, 212; Y-85

Horizon Press DLB-46

Hornby, C. H. St. John 1867-1946 . . . . . . DLB-201

Hornby, Nick 1957- DLB-207

Horne, Frank 1899-1974 . . . . DLB-51

Horne, Richard Henry (Hengist)
1802 or 1803-1884 . . . . DLB-32

Horney, Karen 1885-1952 . . . . DLB-246

Hornung, E. W. 1866-1921 . . . . DLB-70

Horovitz, Israel 1939- DLB-7

Horton, George Moses 1797?-1883? DLB-50

Horváth, Ödön von 1901-1938 . . . . . DLB-85, 124

Horwood, Harold 1923- DLB-60

Hosford, E. and E. [publishing house] DLB-49

Hoskens, Jane Fenn 1693-1770? DLB-200

Hoskyns, John 1566-1638 . . . . DLB-121

Hosokawa Yūsai 1535-1610 . . . . DLB-203

Hostovský, Egon 1908-1973 . . . . DLB-215

Hotchkiss and Company DLB-49

Hough, Emerson 1857-1923 . . . . DLB-9, 212

Houghton, Stanley 1881-1913 . . . . DLB-10

Houghton Mifflin Company. DLB-49

Household, Geoffrey 1900-1988 . . . . DLB-87

Housman, A. E. 1859-1936 . . . DLB-19; CDBLB-5

Housman, Laurence 1865-1959 . . . . DLB-10

Houston, Pam 1962- DLB-244

Houwald, Ernst von 1778-1845 . . . . DLB-90

Hovey, Richard 1864-1900 . . . . DLB-54

Howard, Donald R. 1927-1987 . . . . DLB-111

Howard, Maureen 1930- Y-83

Howard, Richard 1929- DLB-5

Howard, Roy W. 1883-1964 . . . . DLB-29

Howard, Sidney 1891-1939 . . . .DLB-7, 26, 249

Howard, Thomas, second Earl of Arundel
1585-1646 . . . . DLB-213

Howe, E. W. 1853-1937 . . . . DLB-12, 25

Howe, Henry 1816-1893 . . . . DLB-30

Howe, Irving 1920-1993 . . . . DLB-67

Howe, Joseph 1804-1873 . . . . DLB-99

Howe, Julia Ward 1819-1910 . . . . DLB-1, 189, 235

Howe, Percival Presland 1886-1944 . . . . . DLB-149

Howe, Susan 1937- DLB-120

Howell, Clark, Sr. 1863-1936 . . . . DLB-25

Howell, Evan P. 1839-1905 . . . . DLB-23

Howell, James 1594?-1666 . . . . DLB-151

Howell, Soskin and Company DLB-46

Howell, Warren Richardson
1912-1984. . . . . DLB-140

Howells, William Dean 1837-1920
. . . . .DLB-12, 64, 74, 79, 189; CDALB-3

Introduction to Paul Laurence Dunbar,
Lyrics of Lowly Life (1896) DLB-50

Howitt, Mary 1799-1888 . . . . .DLB-110, 199

Howitt, William 1792-1879 and
Howitt, Mary 1799-1888 . . . . DLB-110

Hoyem, Andrew 1935- DLB-5

Hoyers, Anna Ovena 1584-1655 . . . . DLB-164

Hoyle, Fred 1915-2001 . . . . DLB-261

Hoyos, Angela de 1940- DLB-82

Hoyt, Henry [publishing house] DLB-49

Hoyt, Palmer 1897-1979 . . . . DLB-127

Hrabal, Bohumil 1914-1997 . . . . DLB-232

Hrabanus Maurus 776?-856 . . . . DLB-148

Hronský, Josef Cíger 1896-1960. . . . . DLB-215

Hrotsvit of Gandersheim
circa 935-circa 1000 . . . . DLB-148

Hubbard, Elbert 1856-1915 . . . . DLB-91

Hubbard, Kin 1868-1930 . . . . DLB-11

Hubbard, William circa 1621-1704 . . . . . . DLB-24

Huber, Therese 1764-1829 . . . . DLB-90

Huch, Friedrich 1873-1913 . . . . DLB-66

Huch, Ricarda 1864-1947 . . . . DLB-66

Huck at 100: How Old Is
Huckleberry Finn? Y-85

Huddle, David 1942- DLB-130

Hudgins, Andrew 1951- DLB-120

Hudson, Henry Norman 1814-1886 . . . . . DLB-64

Hudson, Stephen 1868?-1944 . . . . DLB-197

Hudson, W. H. 1841-1922 . . . . . .DLB-98, 153, 174

Hudson and Goodwin DLB-49

Huebsch, B. W. [publishing house] DLB-46

Oral History: B. W. Huebsch. Y-99

Hueffer, Oliver Madox 1876-1931 . . . . . . DLB-197

Hugh of St. Victor circa 1096-1141 . . . . DLB-208

Hughes, David 1930- DLB-14

Hughes, Dusty 1947- DLB-233

Hughes, Hatcher 1881-1945. . . . . DLB-249

Hughes, John 1677-1720 . . . . DLB-84

Hughes, Langston 1902-1967
. . . . .DLB-4, 7, 48, 51, 86, 228; CDALB-5

Hughes, Richard 1900-1976 . . . . DLB-15, 161

Hughes, Ted 1930-1998. . . . . DLB-40, 161

Hughes, Thomas 1822-1896 . . . . DLB-18, 163

Hugo, Richard 1923-1982 . . . . DLB-5, 206

Hugo, Victor 1802-1885. . . . . . .DLB-119, 192, 217

Hugo Awards and Nebula Awards DLB-8

Hull, Richard 1896-1973. . . . . DLB-77

Hulme, T. E. 1883-1917 . . . . DLB-19

Hulton, Anne ?-1779? DLB-200

Humboldt, Alexander von 1769-1859 . . . . DLB-90

Humboldt, Wilhelm von 1767-1835 . . . . . DLB-90

Hume, David 1711-1776 . . . . DLB-104, 252

Hume, Fergus 1859-1932 . . . . DLB-70

Hume, Sophia 1702-1774 . . . . DLB-200

Hume-Rothery, Mary Catherine
1824-1885 . . . . DLB-240

Humishuma (see Mourning Dove)

Hummer, T. R. 1950- DLB-120

Humorous Book Illustration. DLB-11

Humphrey, Duke of Gloucester
1391-1447 . . . . DLB-213

Humphrey, William
1924-1997 . . . . DLB-6, 212, 234

Humphreys, David 1752-1818 . . . . DLB-37

Humphreys, Emyr 1919- DLB-15

Huncke, Herbert 1915-1996. . . . . DLB-16

Huneker, James Gibbons
1857-1921. . . . . DLB-71

Hunold, Christian Friedrich 1681-1721 . . DLB-168

Hunt, Irene 1907- DLB-52

Hunt, Leigh 1784-1859. . . . . . . .DLB-96, 110, 144

Hunt, Violet 1862-1942 . . . . .DLB-162, 197

Hunt, William Gibbes 1791-1833 . . . . DLB-73

Hunter, Evan 1926- Y-82

Hunter, Jim 1939- DLB-14

Hunter, Kristin 1931- DLB-33

Hunter, Mollie 1922- DLB-161

Hunter, N. C. 1908-1971 . . . . DLB-10

Hunter-Duvar, John 1821-1899 . . . . DLB-99

Huntington, Henry E. 1850-1927 . . . . DLB-140

Huntington, Susan Mansfield
1791-1823. . . . . DLB-200

Hurd and Houghton DLB-49

Hurst, Fannie 1889-1968 . . . . DLB-86

Hurst and Blackett DLB-106

Hurst and Company DLB-49

Hurston, Zora Neale
1901?-1960. . . . . DLB-51, 86; CDALB-7

Husson, Jules-François-Félix (see Champfleury)

Huston, John 1906-1987. . . . . DLB-26

Hutcheson, Francis 1694-1746 . . . . . . DLB-31, 252

Hutchinson, Ron 1947- DLB-245

Hutchinson, R. C. 1907-1975 . . . . DLB-191

Hutchinson, Thomas 1711-1780
. . . . DLB-30, 31

Hutchinson and Company
(Publishers) Limited. DLB-112

Hutton, Richard Holt 1826-1897 . . . . DLB-57

von Hutton, Ulrich 1488-1523. . . . . .DLB-179

Huxley, Aldous 1894-1963
. . . . . . DLB-36, 100, 162, 195, 255; CDBLB-6

Huxley, Elspeth Josceline
1907-1997. . . . . .DLB-77, 204

Huxley, T. H. 1825-1895. . . . . DLB-57

Huyghue, Douglas Smith
1816-1891 . . . . DLB-99

Huysmans, Joris-Karl 1848-1907 . . . . DLB-123

Hwang, David Henry
1957- DLB-212, 228

Hyde, Donald 1909-1966 and
Hyde, Mary 1912- DLB-187

Hyman, Trina Schart 1939- DLB-61

I

Iavorsky, Stefan 1658-1722 . . . . .DLB-150

Iazykov, Nikolai Mikhailovich
1803-1846 . . . . .DLB-205

Ibáñez, Armando P. 1949- DLB-209

Ibn Bajja circa 1077-1138 . . . . .DLB-115

Ibn Gabirol, Solomon
circa 1021-circa 1058. . . . . .DLB-115

Ibuse, Masuji 1898-1993 . . . . .DLB-180

Ichijō Kanera
(see Ichijō Kaneyoshi)

Ichijō Kaneyoshi (Ichijō Kanera)
1402-1481 .DLB-203

The Iconography of Science-Fiction Art DLB-8

Iffland, August Wilhelm 1759-1814 . . . . . . .DLB-94

Ignatieff, Michael 1947- DLB-267

Ignatow, David 1914-1997. . . . . .DLB-5

Ike, Chukwuemeka 1931- DLB-157

Ikkyū Sōjun 1394-1481 . . . . .DLB-203

Iles, Francis (see Berkeley, Anthony)

Illich, Ivan 1926- DLB-242

The Illustration of Early German Literar
Manuscripts, circa 1150-circa 1300 . . .DLB-148

Illyés, Gyula 1902-1983 . . . . . DLB-215; CDWLB-4

Imbs, Bravig 1904-1946. . . . . .DLB-4

Imbuga, Francis D. 1947- DLB-157

Immermann, Karl 1796-1840. . . . . .DLB-133

Inchbald, Elizabeth 1753-1821 . . . . . . .DLB-39, 89

Ingamells, Rex 1913-1955 . . . . .DLB-260

Inge, William 1913-1973 . . . DLB-7, 249; CDALB-1

Ingelow, Jean 1820-1897 . . . . .DLB-35, 163

Ingersoll, Ralph 1900-1985 . . . . .DLB-127

The Ingersoll Prizes Y-84

Ingoldsby, Thomas (see Barham, Richard Harris)

Ingraham, Joseph Holt 1809-1860 . . . . .DLB-3, 248

Inman, John 1805-1850 . . . . .DLB-73

Innerhofer, Franz 1944- DLB-85

Innis, Harold Adams 1894-1952 . . . . .DLB-88

Innis, Mary Quayle 1899-1972 . . . . .DLB-88

Inō Sōgi 1421-1502 . . . . .DLB-203

Inoue Yasushi 1907-1991 . . . . .DLB-181

International Publishers Company DLB-46

Interviews:

Adoff, Arnold and Virginia Hamilton Y-01

Anastas, Benjamin Y-98

Baker, Nicholson Y-00

Bank, Melissa Y-98

Bernstein, Harriet Y-82

Betts, Doris Y-82

Bosworth, David Y-82

Bottoms, David Y-83

Bowers, Fredson Y-80

Burnshaw, Stanley. Y-97

Carpenter, Humphrey Y-84, Y-99

Carr, Virginia Spencer. Y-00

Carver, Raymond Y-83

Cherry, Kelly. Y-83

Coppel, Alfred Y-83

Cowley, Malcolm Y-81

Davis, Paxton Y-89

De Vries, Peter Y-82

Dickey, James Y-82

Donald, David Herbert Y-87

Ellroy, James. Y-91

Fancher, Betsy Y-83

Faust, Irvin. Y-00

Fulton, Len Y-86

Furst, Alan Y-01

Garrett, George Y-83

Greenfield, George. Y-91

Griffin, Bryan Y-81

Groom, Winston Y-01

Guilds, John Caldwell Y-92

Hardin, James Y-92

Harrison, Jim Y-82

Hazzard, Shirley. Y-82

Herrick, William Y-01

Higgins, George V. Y-98

Hoban, Russell. Y-90

Holroyd, Michael. Y-99

Horowitz, Glen Y-90

Iggulden, John Y-01

Jakes, John Y-83

Jenkinson, Edward B. Y-82

Jenks, Tom Y-86

Kaplan, Justin. Y-86

King, Florence Y-85

Klopfer, Donald S. Y-97

Krug, Judith. Y-82

Lamm, Donald. Y-95

Laughlin, James Y-96

Lindsay, Jack Y-84

Mailer, Norman Y-97

Manchester, William Y-85

McCormack, Thomas Y-98

McNamara, Katherine Y-97

McTaggart, J. M. E. 1866-1925 . . . . .DLB-262

Mellen, Joan. Y-94

Menaher, Daniel Y-97

Mooneyham, Lamarr. Y-82

Murray, Les Y-01

Nosworth, David Y-82

O'Connor, Patrick Y-84, Y-99

Ozick, Cynthia. Y-83

Penner, Jonathan Y-83

Pennington, Lee Y-82

Penzler, Otto Y-96

Plimpton, George Y-99

Potok, Chaim. Y-84

Powell, Padgett Y-01

Prescott, Peter S. Y-86

Rabe, David. Y-91

Rallyson, Carl Y-97

Rechy, John Y-82

Reid, B. L. Y-83

Reynolds, Michael. Y-95, Y-99

Schlafly, Phyllis Y-82

Schroeder, Patricia. Y-99

Schulberg, Budd Y-81, Y-01

Scribner, Charles, III. Y-94

Sipper, Ralph. Y-94

Staley, Thomas F. Y-00

Styron, William Y-80

Toth, Susan Allen Y-86

Tyler, Anne Y-82

Vaughan, Samuel. Y-97

Von Ogtrop, Kristin Y-92

Wallenstein, Barry Y-92

Weintraub, Stanley Y-82

Williams, J. Chamberlain. Y-84

Editors, Conversations with Y-95

Interviews on E-Publishing Y-00

Into the Past: William Jovanovich's
Reflections in Publishing. Y-01

Irving, John 1942- DLB-6; Y-82

Irving, Washington 1783-1859
. . . . .DLB-3, 11, 30, 59, 73, 74,
183, 186, 250; CDALB-2

Irwin, Grace 1907- DLB-68

Irwin, Will 1873-1948 . . . . .DLB-25

Isaksson, Ulla 1916-2000. . . . . .DLB-257

Iser, Wolfgang 1926- DLB-242

Isherwood, Christopher
1904-1986 . . . . DLB-15, 195; Y-86

The Christopher Isherwood Archive,
The Huntington Library. Y-99

Ishiguro, Kazuo
1954- DLB-194

Ishikawa Jun 1899-1987. . . . . .DLB-182

The Island Trees Case: A Symposium on
School Library Censorship
An Interview with Judith Krug
An Interview with Phyllis Schlafly
An Interview with Edward B. Jenkinson
An Interview with Lamarr Mooneyham
An Interview with Harriet Bernstein. Y-82

Islas, Arturo
1938-1991 .DLB-122

Issit, Debbie 1966- DLB-233

Ivanišević, Drago
|1907-1981 .DLB-181

Ivaska, Astrīde 1926- DLB-232

Ivers, M. J., and Company DLB-49

Iwaniuk, Wacław 1915- DLB-215

Iwano, Hōmei 1873-1920. . . . . .DLB-180

Iwaszkiewicz, Jarosław 1894-1980 . . . . . . .DLB-215

Iyayi, Festus 1947- DLB-157

Izumi, Kyōka 1873-1939 . . . . .DLB-180

J

Jackmon, Marvin E. (see Marvin X)

Jacks, L. P. 1860-1955 . . . . DLB-135

Jackson, Angela 1951- DLB-41

Jackson, Charles 1903-1968 . . . . DLB-234

Jackson, Helen Hunt
1830-1885 . . . . DLB-42, 47, 186, 189

Jackson, Holbrook 1874-1948 . . . . DLB-98

Jackson, Laura Riding 1901-1991 . . . . DLB-48

Jackson, Shirley
1916-1965 . . . . DLB-6, 234; CDALB-1

Jacob, Max 1876-1944 . . . . DLB-258

Jacob, Naomi 1884?-1964 . . . . DLB-191

Jacob, Piers Anthony Dillingham
(see Anthony, Piers)

Jacob, Violet 1863-1946 . . . . DLB-240

Jacobi, Friedrich Heinrich 1743-1819 . . . . . DLB-94

Jacobi, Johann Georg 1740-1841 . . . . DLB-97

Jacobs, George W., and Company DLB-49

Jacobs, Harriet 1813-1897 . . . . DLB-239

Jacobs, Joseph 1854-1916 . . . . DLB-141

Jacobs, W. W. 1863-1943 . . . . DLB-135

Jacobsen, Jørgen-Frantz 1900-1938 . . . . . . DLB-214

Jacobsen, Josephine 1908- DLB-244

Jacobson, Dan 1929- DLB-14, 207, 225

Jacobson, Howard 1942- DLB-207

Jacques de Vitry circa 1160/1170-1240 . . . DLB-208

Jæger, Frank 1926-1977 . . . . DLB-214

Jaggard, William [publishing house] DLB-170

Jahier, Piero 1884-1966 . . . . DLB-114, 264

Jahnn, Hans Henny 1894-1959 . . . . . DLB-56, 124

Jakes, John 1932- Y-83

Jakobson, Roman 1896-1982 . . . . DLB-242

James, Alice 1848-1892 . . . . DLB-221

James, C. L. R. 1901-1989 . . . . DLB-125

James, George P. R. 1801-1860 . . . . DLB-116

James, Henry 1843-1916
. . . . . . DLB-12, 71, 74, 189; DS-13; CDALB-3

James, John circa 1633-1729 . . . . DLB-24

James, M. R. 1862-1936 . . . . DLB-156, 201

James, Naomi 1949- DLB-204

James, P. D. 1920- . . . DLB-87; DS-17; CDBLB-8

James VI of Scotland, I of England
1566-1625 . . . . DLB-151, 172

*Ane Schort Treatise Conteining Some Revlis
and Cautelis to Be Obseruit and Eschewit
in Scottis Poesi* (1584) DLB-172

James, Thomas 1572?-1629 . . . . DLB-213

James, U. P. [publishing house] DLB-49

James, Will 1892-1942 . . . . DS-16

Jameson, Anna 1794-1860 . . . . DLB-99, 166

Jameson, Fredric 1934- DLB-67

Jameson, J. Franklin 1859-1937 . . . . DLB-17

Jameson, Storm 1891-1986 . . . . DLB-36

Jančar, Drago 1948- DLB-181

Janés, Clara 1940- DLB-134

Janevski, Slavko 1920- . . . DLB-181; CDWLB-4

Jansson, Tove 1914-2001 . . . . DLB-257

Janvier, Thomas 1849-1913 . . . . DLB-202

Jaramillo, Cleofas M. 1878-1956 . . . . DLB-122

Jarman, Mark 1952- DLB-120

Jarrell, Randall 1914-1965 . DLB-48, 52; CDALB-1

Jarrold and Sons DLB-106

Jarry, Alfred 1873-1907 . . . . DLB-192, 258

Jarves, James Jackson 1818-1888 . . . . DLB-189

Jasmin, Claude 1930- DLB-60

Jaunsudrabiņš, Jānis 1877-1962 . . . . DLB-220

Jay, John 1745-1829 . . . . DLB-31

Jean de Garlande (see John of Garland)

Jefferies, Richard 1848-1887 . . . . DLB-98, 141

Jeffers, Lance 1919-1985 . . . . DLB-41

Jeffers, Robinson
1887-1962 . . . . DLB-45, 212; CDALB-4

Jefferson, Thomas
1743-1826 . . . . DLB-31, 183; CDALB-2

Jégé 1866-1940 . . . . DLB-215

Jelinek, Elfriede 1946- DLB-85

Jellicoe, Ann 1927- DLB-13, 233

Jemison, Mary circa 1742-1833 . . . . DLB-239

Jenkins, Dan 1929- DLB-241

Jenkins, Elizabeth 1905- DLB-155

Jenkins, Robin 1912- DLB-14

Jenkins, William Fitzgerald (see Leinster, Murray)

Jenkins, Herbert, Limited DLB-112

Jennings, Elizabeth 1926- DLB-27

Jens, Walter 1923- DLB-69

Jensen, Johannes V. 1873-1950 . . . . DLB-214

Jensen, Merrill 1905-1980 . . . . DLB-17

Jensen, Thit 1876-1957 . . . . DLB-214

Jephson, Robert 1736-1803 . . . . DLB-89

Jerome, Jerome K. 1859-1927 . . . . DLB-10, 34, 135

Jerome, Judson 1927-1991 . . . . DLB-105

Jerrold, Douglas 1803-1857 . . . . DLB-158, 159

Jersild, Per Christian 1935- DLB-257

Jesse, F. Tennyson 1888-1958 . . . . DLB-77

Jewel, John 1522-1571 . . . . DLB-236

Jewett, John P., and Company DLB-49

Jewett, Sarah Orne 1849-1909 . . . . DLB-12, 74, 221

The Jewish Publication Society DLB-49

Jewitt, John Rodgers 1783-1821 . . . . DLB-99

Jewsbury, Geraldine 1812-1880 . . . . DLB-21

Jewsbury, Maria Jane 1800-1833 . . . . DLB-199

Jhabvala, Ruth Prawer 1927- DLB-139, 194

Jiménez, Juan Ramón 1881-1958 . . . . DLB-134

Jimmy, Red, and Others: Harold Rosenthal
Remembers the Stars of the Press Box Y-01

Jin, Ha 1956- DLB-244

Joans, Ted 1928- DLB-16, 41

Jōha 1525-1602 . . . . DLB-203

Johannis de Garlandia (see John of Garland)

John, Errol 1924-1988 . . . . DLB-233

John, Eugenie (see Marlitt, E.)

John of Dumbleton
circa 1310-circa 1349 . . . . DLB-115

John of Garland (Jean de Garlande, Johannis de
Garlandia) circa 1195-circa 1272 . . . . DLB-208

Johns, Captain W. E. 1893-1968 . . . . DLB-160

Johnson, Mrs. A. E. ca. 1858-1922 . . . . . . DLB-221

Johnson, Amelia (see Johnson, Mrs. A. E.)

Johnson, B. S. 1933-1973 . . . . DLB-14, 40

Johnson, Benjamin [publishing house] DLB-49

Johnson, Benjamin, Jacob, and
Robert [publishing house] DLB-49

Johnson, Charles 1679-1748 . . . . DLB-84

Johnson, Charles R. 1948- DLB-33

Johnson, Charles S. 1893-1956 . . . . . . DLB-51, 91

Johnson, Denis 1949- DLB-120

Johnson, Diane 1934- Y-80

Johnson, Dorothy M. 1905–1984 . . . . DLB-206

Johnson, E. Pauline (Tekahionwake)
1861-1913 . . . . DLB-175

Johnson, Edgar 1901-1995 . . . . DLB-103

Johnson, Edward 1598-1672 . . . . DLB-24

Johnson, Eyvind 1900-1976 . . . . DLB-259

Johnson, Fenton 1888-1958 . . . . DLB-45, 50

Johnson, Georgia Douglas
1877?-1966 . . . . DLB-51, 249

Johnson, Gerald W. 1890-1980 . . . . DLB-29

Johnson, Greg 1953- DLB-234

Johnson, Helene 1907-1995 . . . . DLB-51

Johnson, Jacob, and Company DLB-49

Johnson, James Weldon
1871-1938 . . . . DLB-51; CDALB-4

Johnson, John H. 1918- DLB-137

Johnson, Joseph [publishing house] DLB-154

Johnson, Linton Kwesi 1952- DLB-157

Johnson, Lionel 1867-1902 . . . . DLB-19

Johnson, Nunnally 1897-1977 . . . . DLB-26

Johnson, Owen 1878-1952 . . . . Y-87

Johnson, Pamela Hansford 1912- DLB-15

Johnson, Pauline 1861-1913 . . . . DLB-92

Johnson, Ronald 1935-1998 . . . . DLB-169

Johnson, Samuel 1696-1772 . . . DLB-24; CDBLB-2

Johnson, Samuel
1709-1784 . . . . DLB-39, 95, 104, 142, 213

Johnson, Samuel 1822-1882 . . . . DLB-1, 243

Johnson, Susanna 1730-1810 . . . . DLB-200

Johnson, Terry 1955- DLB-233

Johnson, Uwe 1934-1984 . . . . . DLB-75; CDWLB-2

Johnston, Annie Fellows 1863-1931 . . . . . . DLB-42

Johnston, Basil H. 1929- DLB-60

Johnston, David Claypole 1798?-1865 . . . DLB-188

Johnston, Denis 1901-1984 . . . . DLB-10

Johnston, Ellen 1835-1873 . . . . DLB-199

Johnston, George 1912-1970 . . . . DLB-260

Johnston, George 1913- DLB-88

Johnston, Sir Harry 1858-1927 . . . . DLB-174

Johnston, Jennifer 1930- DLB-14

Johnston, Mary 1870-1936. . . . . .DLB-9

Johnston, Richard Malcolm 1822-1898 . . . . DLB-74

Johnstone, Charles 1719?-1800?. DLB-39

Johst, Hanns 1890-1978 . . . . DLB-124

Jolas, Eugene 1894-1952 . . . . .DLB-4, 45

Jones, Alice C. 1853-1933 . . . . .DLB-92

Jones, Charles C., Jr. 1831-1893 . . . . DLB-30

Jones, D. G. 1929- DLB-53

Jones, David 1895-1974 . . .DLB-20, 100; CDBLB-7

Jones, Diana Wynne 1934- DLB-161

Jones, Ebenezer 1820-1860 . . . . .DLB-32

Jones, Ernest 1819-1868. . . . . .DLB-32

Jones, Gayl 1949- DLB-33

Jones, George 1800-1870 . . . . .DLB-183

Jones, Glyn 1905- DLB-15

Jones, Gwyn 1907- DLB-15, 139

Jones, Henry Arthur 1851-1929. . . . . .DLB-10

Jones, Hugh circa 1692-1760 . . . . .DLB-24

Jones, James 1921-1977 . . . . . . .DLB-2, 143; DS-17

James Jones Papers in the Handy Writers'
   Colony Collection at the University of
   Illinois at Springfield Y-98

The James Jones Society Y-92

Jones, Jenkin Lloyd 1911- DLB-127

Jones, John Beauchamp 1810-1866 . . . . . .DLB-202

Jones, LeRoi (see Baraka, Amiri)

Jones, Lewis 1897-1939 . . . . .DLB-15

Jones, Madison 1925- DLB-152

Jones, Major Joseph
   (see Thompson, William Tappan)

Jones, Marie 1955- DLB-233

Jones, Preston 1936-1979 . . . . .DLB-7

Jones, Rodney 1950- DLB-120

Jones, Thom 1945- DLB-244

Jones, Sir William 1746-1794 . . . . .DLB-109

Jones, William Alfred
   1817-1900 . . . . .DLB-59

Jones's Publishing House. DLB-49

Jong, Erica 1942- DLB-2, 5, 28, 152

Jonke, Gert F. 1946- DLB-85

Jonson, Ben
   1572?-1637. . . . . .DLB-62, 121; CDBLB-1

Jordan, June 1936- DLB-38

Joseph and George. Y-99

Joseph, Jenny 1932- DLB-40

Joseph, Michael, Limited DLB-112

Josephson, Matthew 1899-1978 . . . . .DLB-4

Josephus, Flavius 37-100. . . . . .DLB-176

Josiah Allen's Wife (see Holley, Marietta)

Josipovici, Gabriel 1940- DLB-14

Josselyn, John ?-1675 . . . . .DLB-24

Joudry, Patricia 1921- DLB-88

Jouve, Pierre-Jean 1887-1976 . . . . .DLB-258

Jovanovich, William
   1920-2001 . . . . Y-01

Into the Past: William Jovanovich's
   Reflections on Publishing Y-01

Jovine, Francesco 1902-1950 . . . . .DLB-264

Jovine, Giuseppe 1922- DLB-128

Joyaux, Philippe (see Sollers, Philippe)

Joyce, Adrien (see Eastman, Carol)

Joyce, James 1882-1941
   . . . . DLB-10, 19, 36, 162, 247; CDBLB-6

James Joyce Centenary: Dublin, 1982 . . . . Y-82

James Joyce Conference. Y-85

A Joyce (Con)Text: Danis Rose and the
   Remaking of *Ulysses* Y-97

The New *Ulysses* Y-84

Jozsef, Attila
   1905-1937 . . . . .DLB-215; CDWLB-4

Judd, Orange, Publishing Company DLB-49

Judd, Sylvester 1813-1853 . . . . .DLB-1, 243

Judith circa 930 . . . . .DLB-146

Julian Barnes Checklist Y-01

Julian of Norwich
   1342-circa 1420. . . . . .DLB-1146

Julius Caesar
   100 B.C.-44 B.C. DLB-211; CDWLB-1

June, Jennie
   (see Croly, Jane Cunningham)

Jung, Franz 1888-1963. . . . . .DLB-118

Jünger, Ernst 1895- DLB-56; CDWLB-2

Der jüngere Titurel circa 1275 . . . . .DLB-138

Jung-Stilling, Johann Heinrich
   1740-1817 . . . . .DLB-94

Justice, Donald 1925- Y-83

Juvenal circa A.D. 60-circa A.D. 130
   . . . . .DLB-211; CDWLB-1

The Juvenile Library
   (see Godwin, M. J., and Company)

K

Kacew, Romain (see Gary, Romain)

Kafka, Franz 1883-1924. . . . . .DLB-81; CDWLB-2

Kahn, Gus 1886-1941 . . . . .DLB-265

Kahn, Roger 1927- DLB-171

Kaikō Takeshi 1939-1989 . . . . .DLB-182

Kaiser, Georg 1878-1945 . . . . DLB-124; CDWLB-2

Kaiserchronik circca 1147 . . . . .DLB-148

Kaleb, Vjekoslav 1905- DLB-181

Kalechofsky, Roberta 1931- DLB-28

Kaler, James Otis 1848-1912 . . . . .DLB-12

Kalmar, Bert 1884-1947 . . . . .DLB-265

Kames, Henry Home, Lord
   1696-1782 . . . . .DLB-31, 104

Kamo no Chōmei (Kamo no Nagaakira)
   1153 or 1155-1216 . . . . .DLB-203

Kamo no Nagaakira (see Kamo no Chōmei)

Kampmann, Christian 1939-1988 . . . . . . .DLB-214

Kandel, Lenore 1932- DLB-16

Kanin, Garson 1912-1999 . . . . .DLB-7

Kant, Hermann 1926- DLB-75

Kant, Immanuel 1724-1804 . . . . .DLB-94

Kantemir, Antiokh Dmitrievich
   1708-1744 . . . . .DLB-150

Kantor, MacKinlay 1904-1977. . . . . . . .DLB-9, 102

Kanze Kōjirō Nobumitsu 1435-1516 . . . . .DLB-203

Kanze Motokiyo (see Zeimi)

Kaplan, Fred 1937- DLB-111

Kaplan, Johanna 1942- DLB-28

Kaplan, Justin 1925- DLB-111; Y-86

The Practice of Biography V:
   An Interview with Justin Kaplan. Y-86

Kaplinski, Jaan 1941- DLB-232

Kapnist, Vasilii Vasilevich 1758?-1823 . . .DLB-150

Karadžić, Vuk Stefanović
   1787-1864. . . . . DLB-147; CDWLB-4

Karamzin, Nikolai Mikhailovich
   1766-1826 . . . . .DLB-150

Karinthy, Frigyes 1887-1938 . . . . .DLB-215

Karsch, Anna Louisa 1722-1791. . . . . .DLB-97

Kasack, Hermann 1896-1966 . . . . .DLB-69

Kasai, Zenzō 1887-1927 . . . . .DLB-180

Kaschnitz, Marie Luise 1901-1974 . . . . . . .DLB-69

Kassák, Lajos 1887-1967 . . . . .DLB-215

Kaštelan, Jure 1919-1990 . . . . .DLB-147

Kästner, Erich 1899-1974. . . . . .DLB-56

Katenin, Pavel Aleksandrovich
   1792-1853 . . . . .DLB-205

Kattan, Naim 1928- DLB-53

Katz, Steve 1935- Y-83

Kauffman, Janet 1945- DLB-218; Y-86

Kauffmann, Samuel 1898-1971 . . . . .DLB-127

Kaufman, Bob 1925- DLB-16, 41

Kaufman, George S. 1889-1961. . . . . .DLB-7

Kavan, Anna 1901-1968 . . . . .DLB-255

Kavanagh, P. J. 1931- DLB-40

Kavanagh, Patrick 1904-1967 . . . . . . .DLB-15, 20

Kawabata, Yasunari 1899-1972 . . . . .DLB-180

Kay, Guy Gavriel 1954- DLB-251

Kaye-Smith, Sheila 1887-1956 . . . . .DLB-36

Kazin, Alfred 1915-1998 . . . . .DLB-67

Keane, John B. 1928- DLB-13

Keary, Annie 1825-1879 . . . . .DLB-163

Keary, Eliza 1827-1918 . . . . .DLB-240

Keating, H. R. F. 1926- DLB-87

Keatley, Charlotte 1960- DLB-245

Keats, Ezra Jack 1916-1983 . . . . .DLB-61

Keats, John 1795-1821 . . . .DLB-96, 110; CDBLB-3

Keble, John 1792-1866. . . . . .DLB-32, 55

Keckley, Elizabeth 1818?-1907 . . . . .DLB-239

Keeble, John 1944- Y-83

Keeffe, Barrie 1945- DLB-13, 245

Keeley, James 1867-1934 . . . . .DLB-25

W. B. Keen, Cooke and Company DLB-49

Keillor, Garrison 1942- Y-87

Keith, Marian 1874?-1961 . . . . .DLB-92

Keller, Gary D. 1943- DLB-82

Keller, Gottfried
1819-1890. . . . . DLB-129; CDWLB-2

Kelley, Edith Summers 1884-1956 . . . . DLB-9

Kelley, Emma Dunham ?-?. DLB-221

Kelley, William Melvin 1937- DLB-33

Kellogg, Ansel Nash 1832-1886 . . . . DLB-23

Kellogg, Steven 1941- DLB-61

Kelly, George E. 1887-1974. . . . . .DLB-7, 249

Kelly, Hugh 1739-1777 . . . . DLB-89

Kelly, Piet and Company DLB-49

Kelly, Robert 1935- DLB-5, 130, 165

Kelman, James 1946- DLB-194

Kelmscott Press. DLB-112

Kelton, Elmer 1926- DLB-256

Kemble, E. W. 1861-1933 . . . . DLB-188

Kemble, Fanny 1809-1893 . . . . DLB-32

Kemelman, Harry 1908- DLB-28

Kempe, Margery circa 1373-1438. . . . . . . DLB-146

Kempner, Friederike 1836-1904 . . . . DLB-129

Kempowski, Walter 1929- DLB-75

Kendall, Claude [publishing company]. . . . DLB-46

Kendall, Henry 1839-1882 . . . . DLB-230

Kendall, May 1861-1943 . . . . DLB-240

Kendell, George 1809-1867 . . . . DLB-43

Kenedy, P. J., and Sons. DLB-49

Kenkō circa 1283-circa 1352. . . . . DLB-203

Kennan, George 1845-1924 . . . . DLB-189

Kennedy, Adrienne 1931- DLB-38

Kennedy, John Pendleton 1795-1870 . . DLB-3, 248

Kennedy, Leo 1907- DLB-88

Kennedy, Margaret 1896-1967 . . . . DLB-36

Kennedy, Patrick 1801-1873. . . . . DLB-159

Kennedy, Richard S. 1920- DLB-111

Kennedy, William 1928- DLB-143; Y-85

Kennedy, X. J. 1929- DLB-5

Kennelly, Brendan 1936- DLB-40

Kenner, Hugh 1923- DLB-67

Kennerley, Mitchell [publishing house] . . . DLB-46

Kenny, Maurice 1929- DLB-175

Kent, Frank R. 1877-1958 . . . . DLB-29

Kenyon, Jane 1947-1995 . . . . DLB-120

Keough, Hugh Edmund 1864-1912 . . . . .DLB-171

Keppler and Schwartzmann DLB-49

Ker, John, third Duke of Roxburghe
1740-1804. DLB-213

Ker, N. R. 1908-1982 . . . . DLB-201

Kerlan, Irvin 1912-1963 . . . . DLB-187

Kermode, Frank 1919- DLB-242

Kern, Jerome 1885-1945. . . . . DLB-187

Kernaghan, Eileen 1939- DLB-251

Kerner, Justinus 1776-1862 . . . . DLB-90

Kerouac, Jack
1922-1969 . . DLB-2, 16, 237; DS-3; CDALB-1

The Jack Kerouac Revival Y-95

"Re-meeting of Old Friends":
The Jack Kerouac Conference. Y-82

Auction of Jack Kerouac's *On the Road* Scroll . . Y-01

Kerouac, Jan 1952-1996 . . . . DLB-16

Kerr, Charles H., and Company DLB-49

Kerr, Orpheus C. (see Newell, Robert Henry)

Kersh, Gerald 1911-1968 . . . . DLB-255

Kesey, Ken
1935-2001 . . . . DLB-2, 16, 206; CDALB-6

Kessel, Joseph 1898-1979 . . . . DLB-72

Kessel, Martin 1901- DLB-56

Kesten, Hermann 1900- DLB-56

Keun, Irmgard 1905-1982 . . . . DLB-69

Key, Ellen 1849-1926 . . . . DLB-259

Key and Biddle. DLB-49

Keynes, Sir Geoffrey 1887-1982 . . . . DLB-201

Keynes, John Maynard 1883-1946. . . . . . . .DS-10

Keyserling, Eduard von 1855-1918 . . . . . . DLB-66

Khan, Ismith 1925- DLB-125

Khaytov, Nikolay 1919- DLB-181

Khemnitser, Ivan Ivanovich
1745-1784 . . . . DLB-150

Kheraskov, Mikhail Matveevich
1733-1807. DLB-150

Khomiakov, Aleksei Stepanovich
1804-1860 . . . . DLB-205

Khristov, Boris 1945- DLB-181

Khvoshchinskaia, Nadezhda Dmitrievna
1824-1889 . . . . DLB-238

Khvostov, Dmitrii Ivanovich
1757-1835 . . . . DLB-150

Kidd, Adam 1802?-1831. . . . . DLB-99

Kidd, William [publishing house]. DLB-106

Kidder, Tracy 1945- DLB-185

Kiely, Benedict 1919- DLB-15

Kieran, John 1892-1981 . . . . .DLB-171

Kiggins and Kellogg DLB-49

Kiley, Jed 1889-1962. . . . . DLB-4

Kilgore, Bernard 1908-1967 . . . . DLB-127

Kilian, Crawford 1941- DLB-251

Killens, John Oliver 1916- DLB-33

Killigrew, Anne 1660-1685. . . . . DLB-131

Killigrew, Thomas 1612-1683 . . . . DLB-58

Kilmer, Joyce 1886-1918. . . . . DLB-45

Kilroy, Thomas 1934- DLB-233

Kilwardby, Robert circa 1215-1279 . . . . . DLB-115

Kilworth, Garry 1941- DLB-261

Kimball, Richard Burleigh 1816-1892 . . . DLB-202

Kincaid, Jamaica 1949-
. . . . . . .DLB-157, 227; CDALB-7; CDWLB-3

King, Charles 1844-1933 . . . . DLB-186

King, Clarence 1842-1901 . . . . DLB-12

King, Florence 1936 . . . . .Y-85

King, Francis 1923- DLB-15, 139

King, Grace 1852-1932. . . . . .DLB-12, 78

King, Harriet Hamilton 1840-1920. . . . . . DLB-199

King, Henry 1592-1669 . . . . DLB-126

King, Solomon [publishing house] DLB-49

King, Stephen 1947- DLB-143; Y-80

King, Susan Petigru 1824-1875. . . . . DLB-239

King, Thomas 1943- DLB-175

King, Woodie, Jr. 1937- DLB-38

Kinglake, Alexander William
1809-1891 . . . . DLB-55, 166

Kingsbury, Donald 1929- DLB-251

Kingsley, Charles
1819-1875. . . . . . .DLB-21, 32, 163, 178, 190

Kingsley, Henry 1830-1876 . . . . DLB-21, 230

Kingsley, Mary Henrietta 1862-1900 . . . . .DLB-174

Kingsley, Sidney 1906- DLB-7

Kingsmill, Hugh 1889-1949 . . . . DLB-149

Kingsolver, Barbara
1955- DLB-206; CDALB-7

Kingston, Maxine Hong
1940- DLB-173, 212; Y-80; CDALB-7

Kingston, William Henry Giles
1814-1880 . . . . DLB-163

Kinnan, Mary Lewis 1763-1848 . . . . DLB-200

Kinnell, Galway 1927- DLB-5; Y-87

Kinsella, Thomas 1928- DLB-27

Kipling, Rudyard 1865-1936
. . . . DLB-19, 34, 141, 156; CDBLB-5

Kipphardt, Heinar 1922-1982. . . . . DLB-124

Kirby, William 1817-1906. . . . . DLB-99

Kircher, Athanasius 1602-1680 . . . . DLB-164

Kireevsky, Ivan Vasil'evich 1806-1856 . . DLB-198

Kireevsky, Petr Vasil'evich 1808-1856. . . DLB-205

Kirk, Hans 1898-1962 . . . . DLB-214

Kirk, John Foster 1824-1904. . . . . DLB-79

Kirkconnell, Watson 1895-1977 . . . . DLB-68

Kirkland, Caroline M.
1801-1864 . . . . .DLB-3, 73, 74, 250; DS-13

Kirkland, Joseph 1830-1893 . . . . DLB-12

Kirkman, Francis [publishing house] DLB-170

Kirkpatrick, Clayton 1915- DLB-127

Kirkup, James 1918- DLB-27

Kirouac, Conrad (see Marie-Victorin, Frère)

Kirsch, Sarah 1935- DLB-75

Kirst, Hans Hellmut 1914-1989 . . . . DLB-69

Kiš, Danilo 1935-1989 . . . . . .DLB-181; CDWLB-4

Kita Morio 1927- DLB-182

Kitcat, Mabel Greenhow 1859-1922. . . . . DLB-135

Kitchin, C. H. B. 1895-1967. . . . . DLB-77

Kittredge, William 1932- DLB-212, 244

Kiukhel'beker, Vil'gel'm Karlovich
1797-1846 . . . . DLB-205

Kizer, Carolyn 1925- DLB-5, 169

Klabund 1890-1928 . . . . DLB-66

Klaj, Johann 1616-1656 . . . . DLB-164

Klappert, Peter 1942- DLB-5

Klass, Philip (see Tenn, William)

Klein, A. M. 1909-1972 . . . . DLB-68

Kleist, Ewald von 1715-1759 . . . . DLB-97

Kleist, Heinrich von
1777-1811..............DLB-90; CDWLB-2

Klinger, Friedrich Maximilian
1752-1831 ....DLB-94

Klíma, Ivan 1931- DLB-232; CDWLB-4

Kliushnikov, Viktor Petrovich
1841-1892 ....DLB-238

Oral History Interview with Donald S.
Klopfer Y-97

Klopstock, Friedrich Gottlieb
1724-1803 ....DLB-97

Klopstock, Meta 1728-1758 ....DLB-97

Kluge, Alexander 1932- DLB-75

Knapp, Joseph Palmer 1864-1951 ....DLB-91

Knapp, Samuel Lorenzo 1783-1838 ......DLB-59

Knapton, J. J. and P.
[publishing house] DLB-154

Kniazhnin, Iakov Borisovich
1740-1791......................DLB-150

Knickerbocker, Diedrich (see Irving, Washington)

Knigge, Adolph Franz Friedrich Ludwig,
Freiherr von 1752-1796 ....DLB-94

Knight, Charles, and Company.........DLB-106

Knight, Damon 1922- DLB-8

Knight, Etheridge 1931-1992...........DLB-41

Knight, John S. 1894-1981..............DLB-29

Knight, Sarah Kemble 1666-1727.....DLB-24, 200

Knight-Bruce, G. W. H. 1852-1896......DLB-174

Knister, Raymond 1899-1932 ....DLB-68

Knoblock, Edward 1874-1945 ....DLB-10

Knopf, Alfred A. 1892-1984..............Y-84

Knopf, Alfred A. [publishing house] DLB-46

Knopf to Hammett: The Editoral
Correspondence Y-00

Knorr von Rosenroth, Christian
1636-1689 ....DLB-168

"Knots into Webs: Some Autobiographical
Sources," by Dabney Stuart DLB-105

Knowles, John 1926- DLB-6; CDALB-6

Knox, Frank 1874-1944 ....DLB-29

Knox, John circa 1514-1572...........DLB-132

Knox, John Armoy 1850-1906..........DLB-23

Knox, Lucy 1845-1884 ....DLB-240

Knox, Ronald Arbuthnott 1888-1957 .....DLB-77

Knox, Thomas Wallace 1835-1896......DLB-189

Kobayashi Takiji 1903-1933 ....DLB-180

Kober, Arthur 1900-1975..............DLB-11

Kobiakova, Aleksandra Petrovna
1823-1892 ....DLB-238

Kocbek, Edvard 1904-1981 ... DLB-147; CDWB-4

Koch, Howard 1902- DLB-26

Koch, Kenneth 1925- DLB-5

Kōda, Rohan 1867-1947...............DLB-180

Koehler, Ted 1894-1973 ....DLB-265

Koenigsberg, Moses 1879-1945 ....DLB-25

Koeppen, Wolfgang 1906-1996..........DLB-69

Koertge, Ronald 1940- DLB-105

Koestler, Arthur 1905-1983 ...... Y-83; CDBLB-7

Kohn, John S. Van E. 1906-1976 and
Papantonio, Michael 1907-1978......DLB-187

Kokoschka, Oskar 1886-1980 ....DLB-124

Kolb, Annette 1870-1967 ....DLB-66

Kolbenheyer, Erwin Guido
1878-1962 ....DLB-66, 124

Kolleritsch, Alfred 1931- DLB-85

Kolodny, Annette 1941- DLB-67

Kol'tsov, Aleksei Vasil'evich
1809-1842 ....DLB-205

Komarov, Matvei circa 1730-1812......DLB-150

Komroff, Manuel 1890-1974 ....DLB-4

Komunyakaa, Yusef 1947- DLB-120

Kondoleon, Harry 1955-1994 ....DLB-266

Koneski, Blaže 1921-1993 ...DLB-181; CDWLB-4

Konigsburg, E. L. 1930- DLB-52

Konparu Zenchiku 1405-1468?.........DLB-203

Konrád, György 1933- DLB-232; CDWLB-4

Konrad von Würzburg
circa 1230-1287 ....DLB-138

Konstantinov, Aleko 1863-1897........DLB-147

Konwicki, Tadeusz 1926- DLB-232

Kooser, Ted 1939- DLB-105

Kopit, Arthur 1937- DLB-7

Kops, Bernard 1926?- DLB-13

Kornbluth, C. M. 1923-1958............DLB-8

Körner, Theodor 1791-1813 ....DLB-90

Kornfeld, Paul 1889-1942 ....DLB-118

Kosinski, Jerzy 1933-1991 ....DLB-2; Y-82

Kosmač, Ciril 1910-1980..............DLB-181

Kosovel, Srečko 1904-1926 ....DLB-147

Kostrov, Ermil Ivanovich 1755-1796 .....DLB-150

Kotzebue, August von 1761-1819 ....DLB-94

Kotzwinkle, William 1938- DLB-173

Kovačić, Ante 1854-1889..............DLB-147

Kovič, Kajetan 1931- DLB-181

Kozlov, Ivan Ivanovich 1779-1840........DLB-205

Kraf, Elaine 1946- Y-81

Kramer, Jane 1938- DLB-185

Kramer, Larry 1935- DLB-249

Kramer, Mark 1944- DLB-185

Kranjčević, Silvije Strahimir
1865-1908 ....DLB-147

Krasko, Ivan 1876-1958...............DLB-215

Krasna, Norman 1909-1984 ....DLB-26

Kraus, Hans Peter 1907-1988..........DLB-187

Kraus, Karl 1874-1936...............DLB-118

Krause, Herbert 1905-1976 ....DLB-256

Krauss, Ruth 1911-1993 ....DLB-52

Kreisel, Henry 1922- DLB-88

Krestovsky V. (see Khvoshchinskaia,
Nadezhda Dmitrievna)

Krestovsky, Vsevolod Vladimirovich
1839-1895 ....DLB-238

Kreuder, Ernst 1903-1972 ....DLB-69

Krėvė-Mickevičius, Vincas 1882-1954....DLB-220

Kreymborg, Alfred 1883-1966.........DLB-4, 54

Krieger, Murray 1923- DLB-67

Krim, Seymour 1922-1989 ....DLB-16

Kristensen, Tom 1893-1974...........DLB-214

Kristeva, Julia 1941- DLB-242

Krleža, Miroslav 1893-1981.. DLB-147; CDWLB-4

Krock, Arthur 1886-1974..............DLB-29

Kroetsch, Robert 1927-...............DLB-53

Kross, Jaan 1920- DLB-232

Krúdy, Gyula 1878-1933 ....DLB-215

Krutch, Joseph Wood
1893-1970..................DLB-63, 206

Krylov, Ivan Andreevich
1769-1844 ....DLB-150

Kubin, Alfred 1877-1959 ....DLB-81

Kubrick, Stanley 1928-1999.............DLB-26

Kudrun circa 1230-1240 ....DLB-138

Kuffstein, Hans Ludwig von
1582-1656 ....DLB-164

Kuhlmann, Quirinus 1651-1689 ....DLB-168

Kuhnau, Johann 1660-1722 ....DLB-168

Kukol'nik, Nestor Vasil'evich
1809-1868 ....DLB-205

Kukučín, Martin
1860-1928 ....DLB-215; CDWLB-4

Kumin, Maxine 1925- DLB-5

Kuncewicz, Maria 1895-1989 ....DLB-215

Kundera, Milan 1929- DLB-232; CDWLB-4

Kunene, Mazisi 1930- DLB-117

Kunikida, Doppo 1869-1908............DLB-180

Kunitz, Stanley 1905- DLB-48

Kunjufu, Johari M. (see Amini, Johari M.)

Kunnert, Gunter 1929-...............DLB-75

Kunze, Reiner 1933- DLB-75

Kupferberg, Tuli 1923- DLB-16

Kurahashi Yumiko 1935- DLB-182

Kureishi, Hanif 1954- DLB-194, 245

Kürnberger, Ferdinand 1821-1879......DLB-129

Kurz, Isolde 1853-1944 ....DLB-66

Kusenberg, Kurt 1904-1983.............DLB-69

Kushchevsky, Ivan Afanas'evich
1847-1876.......................DLB-238

Kushner, Tony 1956- DLB-228

Kuttner, Henry 1915-1958 ....DLB-8

Kyd, Thomas 1558-1594 ....DLB-62

Kyffin, Maurice circa 1560?-1598 ....DLB-136

Kyger, Joanne 1934- DLB-16

Kyne, Peter B. 1880-1957 ....DLB-78

Kyōgoku Tamekane 1254-1332 ....DLB-203

Kyrklund, Willy 1921- DLB-257

L

L. E. L. (see Landon, Letitia Elizabeth)

Laberge, Albert 1871-1960.............DLB-68

Laberge, Marie 1950- DLB-60

Labiche, Eugène 1815-1888............DLB-192

Labrunie, Gerard (see Nerval, Gerard de)

La Capria, Raffaele 1922- DLB-196

Lacombe, Patrice
(see Trullier-Lacombe, Joseph Patrice)

Lacretelle, Jacques de 1888-1985 .... DLB-65

Lacy, Ed 1911-1968 .... DLB-226

Lacy, Sam 1903- DLB-171

Ladd, Joseph Brown 1764-1786 .... DLB-37

La Farge, Oliver 1901-1963 .... DLB-9

Laffan, Mrs. R. S. de Courcy (see Adams,
Bertha Leith)

Lafferty, R. A. 1914- DLB-8

La Flesche, Francis 1857-1932..........DLB-175

Laforge, Jules 1860-1887............. DLB-217

Lagerkvist, Pär 1891-1974 .... DLB-259

Lagerlöf, Selma 1858-1940 .... DLB-259

Lagorio, Gina 1922- DLB-196

La Guma, Alex
1925-1985 ....DLB-117, 225; CDWLB-3

Lahaise, Guillaume (see Delahaye, Guy)

Lahontan, Louis-Armand de Lom d'Arce,
Baron de 1666-1715? DLB-99

Laing, Kojo 1946- DLB-157

Laird, Carobeth 1895- Y-82

Laird and Lee DLB-49

Lalić, Ivan V. 1931-1996 .... DLB-181

Lalić, Mihailo 1914-1992 .... DLB-181

Lalonde, Michèle 1937- DLB-60

Lamantia, Philip 1927- DLB-16

Lamartine, Alphonse de 1790-1869 ..... DLB-217

Lamb, Lady Caroline 1785-1828 .... DLB-116

Lamb, Charles
1775-1834.......DLB-93, 107, 163; CDBLB-3

Lamb, Mary 1764-1874............... DLB-163

Lambert, Betty 1933-1983 .... DLB-60

Lamming, George 1927- .. DLB-125; CDWLB-3

L'Amour, Louis 1908-1988 ...... DLB-206; Y-80

Lampman, Archibald 1861-1899 .... DLB-92

Lamson, Wolffe and Company DLB-49

Lancer Books DLB-46

Lanchester, John 1962- DLB-267

Landesman, Jay 1919-   and
Landesman, Fran 1927- DLB-16

Landolfi, Tommaso 1908-1979..........DLB-177

Landon, Letitia Elizabeth 1802-1838 ..... DLB-96

Landor, Walter Savage 1775-1864 ....DLB-93, 107

Landry, Napoléon-P. 1884-1956........ DLB-92

Lane, Charles 1800-1870 .... DLB-1, 223

Lane, F. C. 1885-1984 .... DLB-241

Lane, John, Company............... DLB-49

Lane, Laurence W. 1890-1967 .... DLB-91

Lane, M. Travis 1934- DLB-60

Lane, Patrick 1939- DLB-53

Lane, Pinkie Gordon 1923- DLB-41

Laney, Al 1896-1988 ....DLB-4, 171

Lang, Andrew 1844-1912..... DLB-98, 141, 184

Langevin, André 1927- DLB-60

Langford, David 1953- DLB-261

Langgässer, Elisabeth 1899-1950 ... DLB-69

Langhorne, John 1735-1779 .... DLB-109

Langland, William
circa 1330-circa 1400 .... DLB-146

Langton, Anna 1804-1893 .... DLB-99

Lanham, Edwin 1904-1979............. DLB-4

Lanier, Sidney 1842-1881....... DLB-64; DS-13

Lanyer, Aemilia 1569-1645 .... DLB-121

Lapointe, Gatien 1931-1983 .... DLB-88

Lapointe, Paul-Marie 1929- DLB-88

Larcom, Lucy 1824-1893 .... DLB-221, 243

Lardner, John 1912-1960 ....DLB-171

Lardner, Ring 1885-1933
......DLB-11, 25, 86, 171; DS-16; CDALB-4

Lardner 100: Ring Lardner
Centennial Symposium Y-85

Lardner, Ring, Jr. 1915-2000 ......DLB-26, Y-00

Larkin, Philip 1922-1985 ..... DLB-27; CDBLB-8

La Roche, Sophie von 1730-1807 .... DLB-94

La Rocque, Gilbert 1943-1984 .... DLB-60

Laroque de Roquebrune, Robert
(see Roquebrune, Robert de)

Larrick, Nancy 1910- DLB-61

Larsen, Nella 1893-1964............... DLB-51

Larson, Clinton F. 1919-1994......... DLB-256

La Sale, Antoine de
circa 1386-1460/1467............. DLB-208

Lasch, Christopher 1932-1994 .... DLB-246

Lasker-Schüler, Else 1869-1945 ..... DLB-66, 124

Lasnier, Rina 1915- DLB-88

Lassalle, Ferdinand 1825-1864 .... DLB-129

Latham, Robert 1912-1995............ DLB-201

Lathrop, Dorothy P. 1891-1980 .... DLB-22

Lathrop, George Parsons 1851-1898 ..... DLB-71

Lathrop, John, Jr. 1772-1820........... DLB-37

Latimer, Hugh 1492?-1555........... DLB-136

Latimore, Jewel Christine McLawler
(see Amini, Johari M.)

La Tour du Pin, Patrice de 1911-1975 ... DLB-258

Latymer, William 1498-1583 .... DLB-132

Laube, Heinrich 1806-1884 .... DLB-133

Laud, William 1573-1645 .... DLB-213

Laughlin, James 1914-1997........DLB-48; Y-96

James Laughlin Tributes................. Y-97

Conversations with Publishers IV:
An Interview with James Laughlin....... Y-96

Laumer, Keith 1925- DLB-8

Lauremberg, Johann 1590-1658 .... DLB-164

Laurence, Margaret 1926-1987......... DLB-53

Laurentius von Schnüffis 1633-1702..... DLB-168

Laurents, Arthur 1918- DLB-26

Laurie, Annie (see Black, Winifred)

Laut, Agnes Christiana 1871-1936 .... DLB-92

Lauterbach, Ann 1942- DLB-193

Lautreamont, Isidore Lucien Ducasse, Comte de
1846-1870.......................DLB-217

Lavater, Johann Kaspar 1741-1801....... DLB-97

Lavin, Mary 1912-1996 .... DLB-15

Law, John (see Harkness, Margaret)

Lawes, Henry 1596-1662 .... DLB-126

Lawless, Anthony (see MacDonald, Philip)

Lawless, Emily (The Hon. Emily Lawless) 1845-1913
DLB-240

Lawrence, D. H. 1885-1930
......DLB-10, 19, 36, 98, 162, 195; CDBLB-6

Lawrence, David 1888-1973........... DLB-29

Lawrence, Jerome 1915-   and
Lee, Robert E. 1918-1994 .... DLB-228

Lawrence, Seymour 1926-1994 ....Y-94

Lawrence, T. E. 1888-1935 .... DLB-195

Lawson, George 1598-1678 .... DLB-213

Lawson, Henry 1867-1922 .... DLB-230

Lawson, John ?-1711................. DLB-24

Lawson, John Howard 1894-1977 .... DLB-228

Lawson, Louisa Albury 1848-1920....... DLB-230

Lawson, Robert 1892-1957............ DLB-22

Lawson, Victor F. 1850-1925 .... DLB-25

Layard, Sir Austen Henry
1817-1894......................DLB-166

Layton, Irving 1912- DLB-88

LaZamon flourished circa 1200 .... DLB-146

Lazarević, Laza K. 1851-1890 ....DLB-147

Lazarus, George 1904-1997 .... DLB-201

Lazhechnikov, Ivan Ivanovich
1792-1869....................... DLB-198

Lea, Henry Charles 1825-1909 .... DLB-47

Lea, Sydney 1942- DLB-120

Lea, Tom 1907- DLB-6

Leacock, John 1729-1802 .... DLB-31

Leacock, Stephen 1869-1944 .... DLB-92

Lead, Jane Ward 1623-1704 .... DLB-131

Leadenhall Press................... DLB-106

Leakey, Caroline Woolmer 1827-1881... DLB-230

Leapor, Mary 1722-1746............. DLB-109

Lear, Edward 1812-1888 ....DLB-32, 163, 166

Leary, Timothy 1920-1996 .... DLB-16

Leary, W. A., and Company DLB-49

Léautaud, Paul 1872-1956 .... DLB-65

Leavis, F. R. 1895-1978.............. DLB-242

Leavitt, David 1961- DLB-130

Leavitt and Allen DLB-49

Le Blond, Mrs. Aubrey 1861-1934......DLB-174

le Carré, John 1931- DLB-87; CDBLB-8

Lécavelé, Roland (see Dorgeles, Roland)

Lechlitner, Ruth 1901- DLB-48

Leclerc, Félix 1914- DLB-60

Le Clézio, J. M. G. 1940- DLB-83

Lectures on Rhetoric and Belles Lettres (1783),
by Hugh Blair [excerpts] DLB-31

Leder, Rudolf (see Hermlin, Stephan)

Lederer, Charles 1910-1976 . . . . .DLB-26

Ledwidge, Francis 1887-1917 . . . . .DLB-20

Lee, Dennis 1939- DLB-53

Lee, Don L. (see Madhubuti, Haki R.)

Lee, George W. 1894-1976 . . . . .DLB-51

Lee, Harper 1926- DLB-6; CDALB-1

Lee, Harriet (1757-1851) and
    Lee, Sophia (1750-1824) DLB-39

Lee, Laurie 1914-1997 . . . . .DLB-27

Lee, Leslie 1935- DLB-266

Lee, Li-Young 1957- DLB-165

Lee, Manfred B. (see Dannay, Frederic, and
    Manfred B. Lee)

Lee, Nathaniel circa 1645-1692 . . . . .DLB-80

Lee, Sir Sidney 1859-1926 . . . . .DLB-149, 184

Lee, Sir Sidney, "Principles of Biography," in
    Elizabethan and Other Essays DLB-149

Lee, Tanith 1947- DLB-261

Lee, Vernon
    1856-1935 . . . . .DLB-57, 153, 156, 174, 178

Lee and Shepard DLB-49

Le Fanu, Joseph Sheridan
    1814-1873 . . . . DLB-21, 70, 159, 178

Leffland, Ella 1931- Y-84

le Fort, Gertrud von 1876-1971 . . . . .DLB-66

Le Gallienne, Richard 1866-1947 . . . . .DLB-4

Legaré, Hugh Swinton
    1797-1843 . . . . .DLB-3, 59, 73, 248

Legaré, James Mathewes 1823-1859 . . .DLB-3, 248

The Legends of the Saints and a Medieval
    Christian Worldview DLB-148

Léger, Antoine-J. 1880-1950 . . . . .DLB-88

Leggett, William 1801-1839 . . . . .DLB-250

Le Guin, Ursula K.
    1929- DLB-8, 52, 256; CDALB-6

Lehman, Ernest 1920- DLB-44

Lehmann, John 1907- DLB-27, 100

Lehmann, John, Limited DLB-112

Lehmann, Rosamond 1901-1990 . . . . .DLB-15

Lehmann, Wilhelm 1882-1968 . . . . .DLB-56

Leiber, Fritz 1910-1992 . . . . .DLB-8

Leibniz, Gottfried Wilhelm 1646-1716 . . . .DLB-168

Leicester University Press DLB-112

Leigh, Carolyn 1926-1983 . . . . .DLB-265

Leigh, W. R. 1866-1955 . . . . .DLB-188

Leinster, Murray 1896-1975 . . . . .DLB-8

Leiser, Bill 1898-1965 . . . . .DLB-241

Leisewitz, Johann Anton 1752-1806 . . . . . .DLB-94

Leitch, Maurice 1933- DLB-14

Leithauser, Brad 1943- DLB-120

Leland, Charles G. 1824-1903 . . . . .DLB-11

Leland, John 1503?-1552 . . . . .DLB-136

Lemay, Pamphile 1837-1918 . . . . .DLB-99

Lemelin, Roger 1919-1992 . . . . .DLB-88

Lemercier, Louis-Jean-Népomucène
    1771-1840 . . . . .DLB-192

Le Moine, James MacPherson
    1825-1912 . . . . .DLB-99

Lemon, Mark 1809-1870 . . . . .DLB-163

Le Moyne, Jean 1913-1996 . . . . .DLB-88

Lemperly, Paul 1858-1939 . . . . .DLB-187

L'Engle, Madeleine 1918- DLB-52

Lennart, Isobel 1915-1971 . . . . .DLB-44

Lennox, Charlotte
    1729 or 1730-1804 . . . . .DLB-39

Lenox, James 1800-1880 . . . . .DLB-140

Lenski, Lois 1893-1974 . . . . .DLB-22

Lentricchia, Frank 1940- DLB-246

Lenz, Hermann 1913-1998 . . . . .DLB-69

Lenz, J. M. R. 1751-1792 . . . . .DLB-94

Lenz, Siegfried 1926- DLB-75

Leonard, Elmore 1925- DLB-173, 226

Leonard, Hugh 1926- DLB-13

Leonard, William Ellery 1876-1944 . . . . . .DLB-54

Leonowens, Anna 1834-1914 . . . . . . .DLB-99, 166

LePan, Douglas 1914- DLB-88

Lepik, Kalju 1920-1999 . . . . .DLB-232

Leprohon, Rosanna Eleanor 1829-1879 . . . .DLB-99

Le Queux, William 1864-1927 . . . . .DLB-70

Lermontov, Mikhail Iur'evich
    1814-1841 . . . . .DLB-205

Lerner, Alan Jay 1918-1986 . . . . .DLB-265

Lerner, Max 1902-1992 . . . . .DLB-29

Lernet-Holenia, Alexander 1897-1976 . . . . .DLB-85

Le Rossignol, James 1866-1969 . . . . .DLB-92

Lescarbot, Marc circa 1570-1642 . . . . .DLB-99

LeSeur, William Dawson 1840-1917 . . . . . .DLB-92

LeSieg, Theo. (see Geisel, Theodor Seuss)

Leskov, Nikolai Semenovich 1831-1895 . .DLB-238

Leslie, Doris before 1902-1982 . . . . .DLB-191

Leslie, Eliza 1787-1858 . . . . .DLB-202

Leslie, Frank 1821-1880 . . . . DLB-43, 79

Leslie, Frank, Publishing House DLB-49

Leśmian, Bolesław 1878-1937 . . . . .DLB-215

Lesperance, John 1835?-1891 . . . . .DLB-99

Lessing, Bruno 1870-1940 . . . . .DLB-28

Lessing, Doris
    1919- DLB-15, 139; Y-85; CDBLB-8

Lessing, Gotthold Ephraim
    1729-1781 . . . . DLB-97; CDWLB-2

Lettau, Reinhard 1929- DLB-75

Letter from Japan Y-94, Y-98

Letter from London Y-96

Letter to [Samuel] Richardson on *Clarissa*
    (1748), by Henry Fielding DLB-39

A Letter to the Editor of *The Irish Times* Y-97

Lever, Charles 1806-1872 . . . . .DLB-21

Lever, Ralph ca. 1527-1585 . . . . .DLB-236

Leverson, Ada 1862-1933 . . . . .DLB-153

Levertov, Denise
    1923-1997 . . . . .DLB-5, 165; CDALB-7

Levi, Peter 1931- DLB-40

Levi, Primo 1919-1987 . . . . .DLB-177

Lévi-Strauss, Claude 1908- DLB-242

Levien, Sonya 1888-1960 . . . . .DLB-44

Levin, Meyer 1905-1981 . . . . DLB-9, 28; Y-81

Levine, Norman 1923- DLB-88

Levine, Philip 1928- DLB-5

Levis, Larry 1946- DLB-120

Levy, Amy 1861-1889 . . . . .DLB-156, 240

Levy, Benn Wolfe 1900-1973 . . . . . . DLB-13; Y-81

Lewald, Fanny 1811-1889 . . . . .DLB-129

Lewes, George Henry 1817-1878 . . . . .DLB-55, 144

"Criticism In Relation To
    Novels" (1863) DLB-21

The Principles of Success in Literature
    (1865) [excerpt] DLB-57

Lewis, Agnes Smith 1843-1926 . . . . .DLB-174

Lewis, Alfred H. 1857-1914 . . . . .DLB-25, 186

Lewis, Alun 1915-1944 . . . . .DLB-20, 162

Lewis, C. Day (see Day Lewis, C.)

Lewis, C. S. 1898-1963
    . . . . .DLB-15, 100, 160, 255; CDBLB-7

Lewis, Charles B. 1842-1924 . . . . .DLB-11

Lewis, Henry Clay 1825-1850 . . . . . . .DLB-3, 248

Lewis, Janet 1899-1999 . . . . .Y-87

Lewis, Matthew Gregory
    1775-1818 . . . . DLB-39, 158, 178

Lewis, Meriwether 1774-1809 and
    Clark, William 1770-1838 . . . . . .DLB-183, 186

Lewis, Norman 1908- DLB-204

Lewis, R. W. B. 1917- DLB-111

Lewis, Richard circa 1700-1734 . . . . .DLB-24

Lewis, Sinclair
    1885-1951 . . . . . .DLB-9, 102; DS-1; CDALB-4

Sinclair Lewis Centennial Conference Y-85

Lewis, Wilmarth Sheldon 1895-1979 . . . . .DLB-140

Lewis, Wyndham 1882-1957 . . . . .DLB-15

Lewisohn, Ludwig 1882-1955 . . . DLB-4, 9, 28, 102

Leyendecker, J. C. 1874-1951 . . . . .DLB-188

Lezama Lima, José 1910-1976 . . . . .DLB-113

L'Heureux, John 1934- DLB-244

Libbey, Laura Jean 1862-1924 . . . . .DLB-221

The Library of America DLB-46

Library History Group Y-01

The Licensing Act of 1737 . . . . .DLB-84

Lichfield, Leonard I [publishing house] . . .DLB-170

Lichtenberg, Georg Christoph 1742-1799 . .DLB-94

The Liddle Collection Y-97

Lidman, Sara 1923- DLB-257

Lieb, Fred 1888-1980 . . . . .DLB-171

Liebling, A. J. 1904-1963 . . . . DLB-4, 171

Lieutenant Murray (see Ballou, Maturin Murray)

Lighthall, William Douw 1857-1954 . . . . . .DLB-92

Lilar, Françoise (see Mallet-Joris, Françoise)

Lili'uokalani, Queen 1838-1917 . . . . .DLB-221

Lillo, George 1691-1739 . . . . .DLB-84

Lilly, J. K., Jr. 1893-1966 . . . . .DLB-140

Lilly, Wait and Company. DLB-49

Lily, William circa 1468-1522 . . . . DLB-132

Limited Editions Club DLB-46

Limón, Graciela 1938- DLB-209

Lincoln and Edmands. DLB-49

Lindesay, Ethel Forence
(see Richardson, Henry Handel)

Lindgren, Astrid 1907-2002 . . . . DLB-257

Lindgren, Torgny 1938- DLB-257

Lindsay, Alexander William, Twenty-fifth Earl
of Crawford 1812-1880 . . . . DLB-184

Lindsay, Sir David circa 1485-1555 . . . . . DLB-132

Lindsay, David 1878-1945 . . . . DLB-255

Lindsay, Jack 1900- Y-84

Lindsay, Lady (Caroline Blanche Elizabeth Fitzroy
Lindsay) 1844-1912 . . . . DLB-199

Lindsay, Norman 1879-1969 . . . . DLB-260

Lindsay, Vachel 1879-1931. . . . DLB-54; CDALB-3

Linebarger, Paul Myron Anthony
(see Smith, Cordwainer)

Link, Arthur S. 1920-1998 . . . . DLB-17

Linn, Ed 1922-2000 . . . . DLB-241

Linn, John Blair 1777-1804 . . . . DLB-37

Lins, Osman 1924-1978 . . . . DLB-145

Linton, Eliza Lynn 1822-1898 . . . . DLB-18

Linton, William James 1812-1897. . . . . . . DLB-32

Lintot, Barnaby Bernard
[publishing house] DLB-170

Lion Books DLB-46

Lionni, Leo 1910-1999 . . . . DLB-61

Lippard, George 1822-1854 . . . . DLB-202

Lippincott, J. B., Company. DLB-49

Lippincott, Sara Jane Clarke 1823-1904 . . . DLB-43

Lippmann, Walter 1889-1974. . . . . DLB-29

Lipton, Lawrence 1898-1975 . . . . DLB-16

Liscow, Christian Ludwig 1701-1760 . . . . . DLB-97

Lish, Gordon 1934- DLB-130

Lisle, Charles-Marie-René Leconte de
1818-1894. . . . . DLB-217

Lispector, Clarice
1925-1977. . . . . DLB-113; CDWLB-3

LitCheck Website. Y-01

A Literary Archaeologist Digs On: A Brief
Interview with Michael Reynolds by
Michael Rogers Y-99

*The Literary Chronicle and Weekly Review
1819-1828* DLB-110

Literary Documents: William Faulkner
and the People-to-People Program Y-86

Literary Documents II: *Library Journal*
Statements and Questionnaires from
First Novelists. Y-87

Literary Effects of World War II
[British novel]. DLB-15

Literary Prizes. Y-00

Literary Prizes [British]. DLB-15

Literary Research Archives: The Humanities
Research Center, University of Texas Y-82

Literary Research Archives II: Berg Collection
of English and American Literature of
the New York Public Library. Y-83

Literary Research Archives III:
The Lilly Library. Y-84

Literary Research Archives IV:
The John Carter Brown Library Y-85

Literary Research Archives V:
Kent State Special Collections Y-86

Literary Research Archives VI: The Modern
Literary Manuscripts Collection in the
Special Collections of the Washington
University Libraries. Y-87

Literary Research Archives VII:
The University of Virginia Libraries Y-91

Literary Research Archives VIII:
The Henry E. Huntington Library Y-92

Literary Research Archives IX:
Special Collections at Boston University . . Y-99

The Literary Scene and Situation and . . . Who
(Besides Oprah) Really Runs American
Literature?. Y-99

Literary Societies Y-98, Y-99, Y-00, Y-01

"Literary Style" (1857), by William
Forsyth [excerpt] DLB-57

Literatura Chicanesca: The View From
Without DLB-82

Literature at Nurse, or Circulating Morals (1885),
by George Moore. DLB-18

The Literature of Boxing in England
through Arthur Conan Doyle Y-01

The Literature of the
Modern Breakthrough. DLB-259

Litt, Toby 1968- DLB-267

Littell, Eliakim 1797-1870 . . . . DLB-79

Littell, Robert S. 1831-1896 . . . . DLB-79

Little, Brown and Company. DLB-49

Little Magazines and Newspapers DS-15

The Little Review 1914-1929. . . . . .DS-15

Littlewood, Joan 1914- DLB-13

Lively, Penelope 1933- DLB-14, 161, 207

Liverpool University Press. DLB-112

The Lives of the Poets DLB-142

Livesay, Dorothy 1909- DLB-68

Livesay, Florence Randal 1874-1953 . . . . . DLB-92

"Living in Ruin," by Gerald Stern DLB-105

Livings, Henry 1929-1998 . . . . DLB-13

Livingston, Anne Howe 1763-1841 . . .DLB-37, 200

Livingston, Jay (see Evans, Ray)

Livingston, Myra Cohn 1926-1996 . . . . . . DLB-61

Livingston, William 1723-1790. . . . . DLB-31

Livingstone, David 1813-1873 . . . . DLB-166

Livingstone, Douglas 1932-1996 . . . . DLB-225

Livy 59 B.C.-A.D. 17 . . . . . . DLB-211; CDWLB-1

Liyong, Taban lo (see Taban lo Liyong)

Lizárraga, Sylvia S. 1925- DLB-82

Llewellyn, Richard 1906-1983 . . . . DLB-15

Lloyd, Edward [publishing house] DLB-106

Lobel, Arnold 1933- DLB-61

Lochridge, Betsy Hopkins (see Fancher, Betsy)

Locke, David Ross 1833-1888 . . . . DLB-11, 23

Locke, John 1632-1704. . . . .DLB-31, 101, 213, 252

Locke, Richard Adams 1800-1871 . . . . DLB-43

Locker-Lampson, Frederick
1821-1895 . . . . DLB-35, 184

Lockhart, John Gibson
1794-1854. . . . . DLB-110, 116 144

Lockridge, Ross, Jr. 1914-1948. . . . .DLB-143; Y-80

Locrine and Selimus DLB-62

Lodge, David 1935- DLB-14, 194

Lodge, George Cabot 1873-1909 . . . . DLB-54

Lodge, Henry Cabot 1850-1924. . . . . DLB-47

Lodge, Thomas 1558-1625. . . . . .DLB-172

From *Defence of Poetry* (1579) DLB-172

Loeb, Harold 1891-1974. . . . . DLB-4

Loeb, William 1905-1981. . . . . .DLB-127

Loesser, Frank 1919-1986. . . . . DLB-265

Lofting, Hugh 1886-1947. . . . . DLB-160

Logan, Deborah Norris 1761-1839. . . . . . DLB-200

Logan, James 1674-1751 . . . . DLB-24, 140

Logan, John 1923- DLB-5

Logan, Martha Daniell 1704?-1779. . . . . . DLB-200

Logan, William 1950- DLB-120

Logau, Friedrich von 1605-1655 . . . . DLB-164

Logue, Christopher 1926- DLB-27

Lohenstein, Daniel Casper von
1635-1683 . . . . DLB-168

Lo-Johansson, Ivar 1901-1990 . . . . DLB-259

Lomonosov, Mikhail Vasil'evich
1711-1765. . . . . DLB-150

London, Jack
1876-1916. . . . . .DLB-8, 12, 78, 212; CDALB-3

The London Magazine 1820-1829. . . . . DLB-110

Long, David 1948- DLB-244

Long, H., and Brother DLB-49

Long, Haniel 1888-1956. . . . . DLB-45

Long, Ray 1878-1935 . . . . .DLB-137

Longfellow, Henry Wadsworth
1807-1882. . . . . DLB-1, 59, 235; CDALB-2

Longfellow, Samuel 1819-1892. . . . . DLB-1

Longford, Elizabeth 1906- DLB-155

Longinus circa first century DLB-176

Longley, Michael 1939- DLB-40

Longman, T. [publishing house]. DLB-154

Longmans, Green and Company. DLB-49

Longmore, George 1793?-1867. . . . . DLB-99

Longstreet, Augustus Baldwin
1790-1870. . . . . .DLB-3, 11, 74, 248

Longworth, D. [publishing house] DLB-49

Lonsdale, Frederick 1881-1954. . . . . DLB-10

A Look at the Contemporary Black Theatre
Movement DLB-38

Loos, Anita 1893-1981. . . . .DLB-11, 26, 228; Y-81

Lopate, Phillip 1943- Y-80

Lopez, Barry 1945- DLB-256

López, Diana
(see Isabella, Ríos)

López, Josefina 1969- DLB-209

Loranger, Jean-Aubert 1896-1942 . . . . .DLB-92

Lorca, Federico García 1898-1936 . . . . . .DLB-108

Lord, John Keast 1818-1872. . . . . .DLB-99

The Lord Chamberlain's Office and Stage
    Censorship in England DLB-10

Lorde, Audre 1934-1992 . . . . .DLB-41

Lorimer, George Horace 1867-1939 . . . . . .DLB-91

Loring, A. K. [publishing house] DLB-49

Loring and Mussey DLB-46

Lorris, Guillaume de (see *Roman de la Rose*)

Lossing, Benson J. 1813-1891 . . . . .DLB-30

Lothar, Ernst 1890-1974 . . . . .DLB-81

Lothrop, D., and Company DLB-49

Lothrop, Harriet M. 1844-1924 . . . . .DLB-42

Loti, Pierre 1850-1923 . . . . .DLB-123

Lotichius Secundus, Petrus 1528-1560. . . . DLB-179

Lott, Emeline ?-? DLB-166

Louisiana State University Press Y-97

The Lounger, no. 20 (1785), by Henry
    Mackenzie DLB-39

Lounsbury, Thomas R. 1838-1915 . . . . . . .DLB-71

Louÿs, Pierre 1870-1925 . . . . .DLB-123

Lovelace, Earl 1935- DLB-125; CDWLB-3

Lovelace, Richard 1618-1657 . . . . .DLB-131

Lovell, Coryell and Company DLB-49

Lovell, John W., Company DLB-49

Lover, Samuel 1797-1868 . . . . .DLB-159, 190

Lovesey, Peter 1936- DLB-87

Lovinescu, Eugen
    1881-1943 . . . . .DLB-220; CDWLB-4

Lovingood, Sut
    (see Harris, George Washington)

Low, Samuel 1765-? DLB-37

Lowell, Amy 1874-1925 . . . . .DLB-54, 140

Lowell, James Russell 1819-1891
    . . . . . .DLB-1, 11, 64, 79, 189, 235; CDALB-2

Lowell, Robert 1917-1977. . .DLB-5, 169; CDALB-7

Lowenfels, Walter 1897-1976 . . . . .DLB-4

Lowndes, Marie Belloc 1868-1947 . . . . . . .DLB-70

Lowndes, William Thomas 1798-1843 . . .DLB-184

Lownes, Humphrey [publishing house] . . .DLB-170

Lowry, Lois 1937- DLB-52

Lowry, Malcolm 1909-1957 . . .DLB-15; CDBLB-7

Lowther, Pat 1935-1975 . . . . .DLB-53

Loy, Mina 1882-1966 . . . . .DLB-4, 54

Lozeau, Albert 1878-1924 . . . . .DLB-92

Lubbock, Percy 1879-1965 . . . . .DLB-149

Lucan A.D. 39-A.D. 65 . . . . .DLB-211

Lucas, E. V. 1868-1938 . . . . . . .DLB-98, 149, 153

Lucas, Fielding, Jr. [publishing house] DLB-49

Luce, Clare Booth 1903-1987 . . . . .DLB-228

Luce, Henry R. 1898-1967 . . . . .DLB-91

Luce, John W., and Company DLB-46

Lucian circa 120-180 . . . . .DLB-176

Lucie-Smith, Edward 1933- DLB-40

Lucilius circa 180 B.C.-102/101 B.C. DLB-211

Lucini, Gian Pietro 1867-1914 . . . . .DLB-114

Lucretius circa 94 B.C.-circa 49 B.C.
    . . . . .DLB-211; CDWLB-1

Luder, Peter circa 1415-1472 . . . . .DLB-179

Ludlam, Charles 1943-1987 . . . . .DLB-266

Ludlum, Robert 1927- Y-82

Ludus de Antichristo circa 1160 . . . . .DLB-148

Ludvigson, Susan 1942- DLB-120

Ludwig, Jack 1922- DLB-60

Ludwig, Otto 1813-1865 . . . . .DLB-129

Ludwigslied 881 or 882 . . . . .DLB-148

Luera, Yolanda 1953- DLB-122

Luft, Lya 1938- DLB-145

Lugansky, Kazak Vladimir
    (see Dal', Vladimir Ivanovich)

Lugn, Kristina 1948- DLB-257

Lukács, Georg (see Lukács, György)

Lukács, György
    1885-1971 . . . . .DLB-215, 242; CDWLB-4

Luke, Peter 1919- DLB-13

Lummis, Charles F. 1859-1928 . . . . .DLB-186

Lundkvist, Artur 1906-1991 . . . . .DLB-259

Lupton, F. M., Company DLB-49

Lupus of Ferrières
    circa 805-circa 862 . . . . .DLB-148

Lurie, Alison 1926- DLB-2

Lussu, Emilio 1890-1975 . . . . .DLB-264

Lustig, Arnošt 1926- DLB-232

Luther, Martin 1483-1546 . . . DLB-179; CDWLB-2

Luzi, Mario 1914- DLB-128

L'vov, Nikolai Aleksandrovich 1751-1803 . .DLB-150

Lyall, Gavin 1932- DLB-87

Lydgate, John circa 1370-1450 . . . . .DLB-146

Lyly, John circa 1554-1606 . . . . .DLB-62, 167

Lynch, Patricia 1898-1972 . . . . .DLB-160

Lynch, Richard flourished 1596-1601 . . . .DLB-172

Lynd, Robert 1879-1949 . . . . .DLB-98

Lyon, Matthew 1749-1822 . . . . .DLB-43

Lyotard, Jean-François 1924-1998 . . . . . . .DLB-242

Lysias circa 459 B.C.-circa 380 B.C. DLB-176

Lytle, Andrew 1902-1995 . . . . .DLB-6; Y-95

Lytton, Edward
    (see Bulwer-Lytton, Edward)

Lytton, Edward Robert Bulwer
    1831-1891 . . . . .DLB-32

M

Maass, Joachim 1901-1972 . . . . .DLB-69

Mabie, Hamilton Wright 1845-1916 . . . . . .DLB-71

Mac A'Ghobhainn, Iain (see Smith, Iain Crichton)

MacArthur, Charles 1895-1956 . . . . .DLB-7, 25, 44

Macaulay, Catherine 1731-1791 . . . . .DLB-104

Macaulay, David 1945- DLB-61

Macaulay, Rose 1881-1958 . . . . .DLB-36

Macaulay, Thomas Babington
    1800-1859 . . . . .DLB-32, 55; CDBLB-4

Macaulay Company DLB-46

MacBeth, George 1932- DLB-40

Macbeth, Madge 1880-1965 . . . . .DLB-92

MacCaig, Norman 1910-1996 . . . . .DLB-27

MacDiarmid, Hugh
    1892-1978 . . . . .DLB-20; CDBLB-7

MacDonald, Cynthia 1928- DLB-105

MacDonald, George 1824-1905 . . . .DLB-18, 163, 178

MacDonald, John D. 1916-1986 . . . . .DLB-8; Y-86

MacDonald, Philip 1899?-1980 . . . . .DLB-77

Macdonald, Ross (see Millar, Kenneth)

Macdonald, Sharman 1951- DLB-245

MacDonald, Wilson 1880-1967 . . . . .DLB-92

Macdonald and Company (Publishers) . . .DLB-112

MacEwen, Gwendolyn 1941-1987 . . . .DLB-53, 251

Macfadden, Bernarr 1868-1955 . . . . . .DLB-25, 91

MacGregor, John 1825-1892 . . . . .DLB-166

MacGregor, Mary Esther (see Keith, Marian)

Machado, Antonio 1875-1939 . . . . .DLB-108

Machado, Manuel 1874-1947 . . . . .DLB-108

Machar, Agnes Maule 1837-1927 . . . . .DLB-92

Machaut, Guillaume de
    circa 1300-1377 . . . . .DLB-208

Machen, Arthur Llewelyn Jones
    1863-1947 . . . . .DLB-36, 156, 178

MacInnes, Colin 1914-1976 . . . . .DLB-14

MacInnes, Helen 1907-1985 . . . . .DLB-87

Mac Intyre, Tom 1931- DLB-245

Mačiulis, Jonas (see Maironis, Jonas)

Mack, Maynard 1909- DLB-111

Mackall, Leonard L. 1879-1937 . . . . .DLB-140

MacKaye, Percy 1875-1956 . . . . .DLB-54

Macken, Walter 1915-1967 . . . . .DLB-13

Mackenzie, Alexander 1763-1820 . . . . .DLB-99

Mackenzie, Alexander Slidell
    1803-1848 . . . . .DLB-183

Mackenzie, Compton 1883-1972 . . . . .DLB-34, 100

Mackenzie, Henry 1745-1831 . . . . .DLB-39

Mackenzie, Kenneth (Seaforth)
    1913-1955 . . . . .DLB-260

Mackenzie, William 1758-1828 . . . . .DLB-187

Mackey, Nathaniel 1947- DLB-169

Mackey, Shena 1944- DLB-231

Mackey, William Wellington
    1937- DLB-38

Mackintosh, Elizabeth (see Tey, Josephine)

Mackintosh, Sir James 1765-1832 . . . . . . .DLB-158

Maclaren, Ian (see Watson, John)

Macklin, Charles 1699-1797 . . . . .DLB-89

MacLaverty, Bernard 1942- DLB-267

MacLean, Katherine Anne 1925- DLB-8

Maclean, Norman 1902-1990 . . . . .DLB-206

MacLeish, Archibald 1892-1982
    . . . . DLB-4, 7, 45, 228; Y-82; CDALB-7

MacLennan, Hugh 1907-1990 . . . . .DLB-68

MacLeod, Alistair 1936- DLB-60

Macleod, Fiona (see Sharp, William)

Macleod, Norman 1906-1985 .... DLB-4

Mac Low, Jackson 1922- DLB-193

Macmillan and Company DLB-106

The Macmillan Company DLB-49

Macmillan's English Men of Letters,
First Series (1878-1892) DLB-144

MacNamara, Brinsley 1890-1963 .... DLB-10

MacNeice, Louis 1907-1963 .... DLB-10, 20

MacPhail, Andrew 1864-1938 .... DLB-92

Macpherson, James 1736-1796 .... DLB-109

Macpherson, Jay 1931- DLB-53

Macpherson, Jeanie 1884-1946 .... DLB-44

Macrae Smith Company DLB-46

MacRaye, Lucy Betty (see Webling, Lucy)

Macrone, John [publishing house] DLB-106

MacShane, Frank 1927-1999 .... DLB-111

Macy-Masius DLB-46

Madden, David 1933- DLB-6

Madden, Sir Frederic 1801-1873 .... DLB-184

Maddow, Ben 1909-1992 .... DLB-44

Maddux, Rachel 1912-1983 ...... DLB-234; Y-93

Madgett, Naomi Long 1923- DLB-76

Madhubuti, Haki R. 1942- DLB-5, 41; DS-8

Madison, James 1751-1836 .... DLB-37

Madsen, Svend Åge 1939- DLB-214

Maeterlinck, Maurice 1862-1949 ...... DLB-192

Mafūz, Najīb 1911- Y-88

Magee, David 1905-1977 .... DLB-187

Maginn, William 1794-1842 .... DLB-110, 159

Magoffin, Susan Shelby 1827-1855 ...... DLB-239

Mahan, Alfred Thayer 1840-1914 .... DLB-47

Maheux-Forcier, Louise 1929- DLB-60

Mahin, John Lee 1902-1984 .... DLB-44

Mahon, Derek 1941- DLB-40

Maikov, Vasilii Ivanovich 1728-1778 .... DLB-150

Mailer, Norman 1923-
........DLB-2, 16, 28, 185; Y-80, Y-83, Y-97;
DS-3; CDALB-6

Maillart, Ella 1903-1997 .... DLB-195

Maillet, Adrienne 1885-1963 .... DLB-68

Maillet, Antonine 1929- DLB-60

Maillu, David G. 1939- DLB-157

Maimonides, Moses 1138-1204 ...... DLB-115

Main Selections of the Book-of-the-Month
Club, 1926-1945 .... DLB-9

Main Trends in Twentieth-Century Book
Clubs DLB-46

Mainwaring, Daniel 1902-1977 .... DLB-44

Mair, Charles 1838-1927 .... DLB-99

Maironis, Jonas
1862-1932 .... DLB-220; CDWLB-4

Mais, Roger 1905-1955 ..... DLB-125; CDWLB-3

Major, Andre 1942- DLB-60

Major, Charles 1856-1913 .... DLB-202

Major, Clarence 1936- DLB-33

Major, Kevin 1949- DLB-60

Major Books DLB-46

Makemie, Francis circa 1658-1708 ...... DLB-24

The Making of Americans Contract Y-98

The Making of a People, by
J. M. Ritchie DLB-66

Maksimović, Desanka
1898-1993 .... DLB-147; CDWLB-4

Malamud, Bernard 1914-1986
......DLB-2, 28, 152; Y-80, Y-86; CDALB-1

Mălăncioiu, Ileana 1940- DLB-232

Malaparte, Curzio 1898-1957 .... DLB-264

Malerba, Luigi 1927- DLB-196

Malet, Lucas 1852-1931 .... DLB-153

Mallarmé, Stéphane 1842-1898 .... DLB-217

Malleson, Lucy Beatrice (see Gilbert, Anthony)

Mallet-Joris, Françoise 1930- DLB-83

Mallock, W. H. 1849-1923 ....DLB-18, 57

"Every Man His Own Poet; or,
The Inspired Singer's Recipe
Book" (1877) DLB-35

Malone, Dumas 1892-1986 .... DLB-17

Malone, Edmond 1741-1812 .... DLB-142

Malory, Sir Thomas
circa 1400-1410 - 1471 ... DLB-146; CDBLB-1

Malpede, Karen 1945- DLB-249

Malraux, André 1901-1976 .... DLB-72

Malthus, Thomas Robert
1766-1834 ....DLB-107, 158

Maltz, Albert 1908-1985 .... DLB-102

Malzberg, Barry N. 1939- DLB-8

Mamet, David 1947- DLB-7

Mamin, Dmitrii Narkisovich 1852-1912.. DLB-238

Manaka, Matsemela 1956- DLB-157

Manchester University Press DLB-112

Mandel, Eli 1922-1992 .... DLB-53

Mandeville, Bernard 1670-1733 .... DLB-101

Mandeville, Sir John
mid fourteenth century DLB-146

Mandiargues, André Pieyre de 1909- ... DLB-83

Manea, Norman 1936- DLB-232

Manfred, Frederick 1912-1994 .... DLB-6, 212, 227

Manfredi, Gianfranco 1948- DLB-196

Mangan, Sherry 1904-1961 .... DLB-4

Manganelli, Giorgio 1922-1990 ...... DLB-196

Manilius fl. first century A.D. DLB-211

Mankiewicz, Herman 1897-1953 .... DLB-26

Mankiewicz, Joseph L. 1909-1993 ...... DLB-44

Mankowitz, Wolf 1924-1998 .... DLB-15

Manley, Delarivière 1672?-1724 ...... DLB-39, 80

Preface to *The Secret History, of Queen Zarah,
and the Zarazians* (1705) DLB-39

Mann, Abby 1927- DLB-44

Mann, Charles 1929-1998 .... Y-98

Mann, Emily 1952- DLB-266

Mann, Heinrich 1871-1950 .... DLB-66, 118

Mann, Horace 1796-1859 .... DLB-1, 235

Mann, Klaus 1906-1949 .... DLB-56

Mann, Mary Peabody 1806-1887 .... DLB-239

Mann, Thomas 1875-1955 ... DLB-66; CDWLB-2

Mann, William D'Alton 1839-1920 ..... DLB-137

Mannin, Ethel 1900-1984 .... DLB-191, 195

Manning, Emily (see Australie)

Manning, Frederic 1882-1935 .... DLB-260

Manning, Laurence 1899-1972 .... DLB-251

Manning, Marie 1873?-1945 .... DLB-29

Manning and Loring DLB-49

Mannyng, Robert
flourished 1303-1338 .... DLB-146

Mano, D. Keith 1942- DLB-6

Manor Books DLB-46

Mansfield, Katherine 1888-1923 .... DLB-162

Manuel, Niklaus circa 1484-1530 ......DLB-179

Manzini, Gianna 1896-1974 ....DLB-177

Mapanje, Jack 1944- DLB-157

Maraini, Dacia 1936- DLB-196

Marcel Proust at 129 and the Proust Society
of America Y-00

Marcel Proust's *Remembrance of Things Past*:
The Rediscovered Galley Proofs Y-00

March, William 1893-1954 .... DLB-9, 86

Marchand, Leslie A. 1900-1999 .... DLB-103

Marchant, Bessie 1862-1941 .... DLB-160

Marchant, Tony 1959- DLB-245

Marchenko, Anastasiia Iakovlevna
1830-1880 .... DLB-238

Marchessault, Jovette 1938- DLB-60

Marcinkevičius, Justinas 1930- DLB-232

Marcus, Frank 1928- DLB-13

Marcuse, Herbert 1898-1979 .... DLB-242

Marden, Orison Swett 1850-1924 ......DLB-137

Marechera, Dambudzo 1952-1987 ......DLB-157

Marek, Richard, Books DLB-46

Mares, E. A. 1938- DLB-122

Margulies, Donald 1954- DLB-228

Mariani, Paul 1940- DLB-111

Marie de France flourished 1160-1178 ... DLB-208

Marie-Victorin, Frère 1885-1944 .... DLB-92

Marin, Biagio 1891-1985 .... DLB-128

Marincovič, Ranko
1913- DLB-147; CDWLB-4

Marinetti, Filippo Tommaso
1876-1944 .... DLB-114, 264

Marion, Frances 1886-1973 .... DLB-44

Marius, Richard C. 1933-1999 .... Y-85

Markevich, Boleslav Mikhailovich
1822-1884 .... DLB-238

Markfield, Wallace 1926- DLB-2, 28

Markham, Edwin 1852-1940 ...... DLB-54, 186

Markle, Fletcher 1921-1991 ....DLB-68; Y-91

Marlatt, Daphne 1942- DLB-60

Marlitt, E. 1825-1887 .... DLB-129

Marlowe, Christopher
  1564-1593 . . . . DLB-62; CDBLB-1

Marlyn, John 1912- DLB-88

Marmion, Shakerley 1603-1639. . . . . .DLB-58

Der Marner before 1230-circa 1287. . . . . .DLB-138

Marnham, Patrick 1943- DLB-204

The *Marprelate Tracts* 1588-1589 . . . . . . .DLB-132

Marquand, John P. 1893-1960. . . . . . .DLB-9, 102

Marqués, René 1919-1979 . . . . .DLB-113

Marquis, Don 1878-1937 . . . . .DLB-11, 25

Marriott, Anne 1913- DLB-68

Marryat, Frederick 1792-1848 . . . . . . .DLB-21, 163

Marsh, Capen, Lyon and Webb DLB-49

Marsh, George Perkins
  1801-1882 . . . . .DLB-1, 64, 243

Marsh, James 1794-1842 . . . . .DLB-1, 59

Marsh, Narcissus 1638-1713 . . . . .DLB-213

Marsh, Ngaio 1899-1982 . . . . .DLB-77

Marshall, Alan 1902-1984 . . . . .DLB-260

Marshall, Edison 1894-1967 . . . . .DLB-102

Marshall, Edward 1932- DLB-16

Marshall, Emma 1828-1899 . . . . .DLB-163

Marshall, James 1942-1992 . . . . .DLB-61

Marshall, Joyce 1913- DLB-88

Marshall, Paule 1929- DLB-33, 157, 227

Marshall, Tom 1938-1993 . . . . .DLB-60

Marsilius of Padua
  circa 1275-circa 1342 . . . . .DLB-115

Mars-Jones, Adam 1954- DLB-207

Marson, Una 1905-1965 . . . . .DLB-157

Marston, John 1576-1634. . . . . DLB-58, 172

Marston, Philip Bourke 1850-1887 . . . . . . .DLB-35

Martens, Kurt 1870-1945 . . . . .DLB-66

Martial circa A.D. 40-circa A.D. 103
  .DLB-211; CDWLB-1

Martien, William S. [publishing house] DLB-49

Martin, Abe (see Hubbard, Kin)

Martin, Catherine ca. 1847-1937 . . . . . . .DLB-230

Martin, Charles 1942- DLB-120

Martin, Claire 1914- DLB-60

Martin, David 1915-1997 . . . . .DLB-260

Martin, Jay 1935- DLB-111

Martin, Johann (see Laurentius von Schnüffis)

Martin, Thomas 1696-1771 . . . . .DLB-213

Martin, Violet Florence (see Ross, Martin)

Martin du Gard, Roger 1881-1958 . . . . . . .DLB-65

Martineau, Harriet
  1802-1876 . . . . DLB-21, 55, 159, 163, 166, 190

Martínez, Demetria 1960- DLB-209

Martínez, Eliud 1935- DLB-122

Martínez, Max 1943- DLB-82

Martínez, Rubén 1962- DLB-209

Martinson, Harry 1904-1978 . . . . .DLB-259

Martinson, Moa 1890-1964 . . . . .DLB-259

Martone, Michael 1955- DLB-218

Martyn, Edward 1859-1923 . . . . .DLB-10

Marvell, Andrew
  1621-1678 . . . . .DLB-131; CDBLB-2

Marvin X 1944- DLB-38

Marx, Karl 1818-1883 . . . . .DLB-129

Marzials, Theo 1850-1920 . . . . .DLB-35

Masefield, John
  1878-1967 . . .DLB-10, 19, 153, 160; CDBLB-5

Masham, Damaris Cudworth Lady
  1659-1708 . . . . .DLB-252

Masino, Paola 1908-1989. . . . . .DLB-264

Mason, A. E. W. 1865-1948 . . . . .DLB-70

Mason, Bobbie Ann
  1940- DLB-173; Y-87; CDALB-7

Mason, William 1725-1797. . . . . .DLB-142

Mason Brothers DLB-49

Massey, Gerald 1828-1907. . . . . .DLB-32

Massey, Linton R. 1900-1974 . . . . .DLB-187

Massinger, Philip 1583-1640 . . . . .DLB-58

Masson, David 1822-1907 . . . . .DLB-144

Masters, Edgar Lee
  1868-1950 . . . . .DLB-54; CDALB-3

Masters, Hilary 1928- DLB-244

Mastronardi, Lucio 1930-1979. . . . . .DLB-177

Matevski, Mateja 1929- . . . DLB-181; CDWLB-4

Mather, Cotton
  1663-1728 . . . . . . .DLB-24, 30, 140; CDALB-2

Mather, Increase 1639-1723 . . . . .DLB-24

Mather, Richard 1596-1669. . . . . .DLB-24

Matheson, Annie 1853-1924 . . . . .DLB-240

Matheson, Richard 1926- DLB-8, 44

Matheus, John F. 1887- DLB-51

Mathews, Cornelius 1817?-1889 . . .DLB-3, 64, 250

Mathews, Elkin [publishing house] DLB-112

Mathews, John Joseph 1894-1979 . . . . . . .DLB-175

Mathias, Roland 1915- DLB-27

Mathis, June 1892-1927 . . . . .DLB-44

Mathis, Sharon Bell 1937- DLB-33

Matković, Marijan 1915-1985 . . . . .DLB-181

Matoš, Antun Gustav 1873-1914. . . . . . . .DLB-147

Matsumoto Seichō 1909-1992 . . . . .DLB-182

The Matter of England 1240-1400 . . . . . .DLB-146

The Matter of Rome early twelfth to late
  fifteenth century DLB-146

Matthew of Vendôme
  circa 1130-circa 1200 . . . . .DLB-208

Matthews, Brander
  1852-1929 . . . . .DLB-71, 78; DS-13

Matthews, Jack 1925- DLB-6

Matthews, Victoria Earle 1861-1907 . . . . .DLB-221

Matthews, William 1942-1997. . . . . .DLB-5

Matthiessen, F. O. 1902-1950 . . . . .DLB-63

Matthiessen, Peter 1927- DLB-6, 173

Maturin, Charles Robert 1780-1824 . . . . . DLB-178

Maugham, W. Somerset 1874-1965
  . . . . DLB-10, 36, 77, 100, 162, 195; CDBLB-6

Maupassant, Guy de 1850-1893 . . . . .DLB-123

Mauriac, Claude 1914-1996. . . . . .DLB-83

Mauriac, François 1885-1970 . . . . .DLB-65

Maurice, Frederick Denison
  1805-1872 .DLB-55

Maurois, André 1885-1967 . . . . .DLB-65

Maury, James 1718-1769 . . . . .DLB-31

Mavor, Elizabeth 1927- DLB-14

Mavor, Osborne Henry (see Bridie, James)

Maxwell, Gavin 1914-1969 . . . . .DLB-204

Maxwell, H. [publishing house] DLB-49

Maxwell, John [publishing house] DLB-106

Maxwell, William 1908- DLB-218; Y-80

May, Elaine 1932- DLB-44

May, Karl 1842-1912. . . . . .DLB-129

May, Thomas 1595 or 1596-1650 . . . . .DLB-58

Mayer, Bernadette 1945- DLB-165

Mayer, Mercer 1943- DLB-61

Mayer, O. B. 1818-1891 . . . . .DLB-3, 248

Mayes, Herbert R. 1900-1987 . . . . .DLB-137

Mayes, Wendell 1919-1992 . . . . .DLB-26

Mayfield, Julian 1928-1984 . . . . DLB-33; Y-84

Mayhew, Henry 1812-1887 . . . . . . DLB-18, 55, 190

Mayhew, Jonathan 1720-1766 . . . . .DLB-31

Mayne, Ethel Colburn 1865-1941 . . . . . . .DLB-197

Mayne, Jasper 1604-1672. . . . . .DLB-126

Mayne, Seymour 1944- DLB-60

Mayor, Flora Macdonald 1872-1932 . . . . . .DLB-36

Mayröcker, Friederike 1924- DLB-85

Mazrui, Ali A. 1933- DLB-125

Mažuranić, Ivan 1814-1890 . . . . .DLB-147

Mazursky, Paul 1930- DLB-44

McAlmon, Robert 1896-1956 . . .DLB-4, 45; DS-15

Robert McAlmon's "A Night at Bricktop's" . Y-01

McArthur, Peter 1866-1924. . . . . .DLB-92

McAuley, James 1917-1976 . . . . .DLB-260

McBride, Robert M., and Company DLB-46

McCabe, Patrick 1955- DLB-194

McCaffrey, Anne 1926- DLB-8

McCann, Colum, 1965- DLB-267

McCarthy, Cormac 1933- DLB-6, 143, 256

McCarthy, Mary 1912-1989 . . . . .DLB-2; Y-81

McCay, Winsor 1871-1934 . . . . .DLB-22

McClane, Albert Jules 1922-1991 . . . . . . DLB-171

McClatchy, C. K. 1858-1936 . . . . .DLB-25

McClellan, George Marion 1860-1934 . . . .DLB-50

McCloskey, Robert 1914- DLB-22

McClung, Nellie Letitia 1873-1951 . . . . . .DLB-92

McClure, Joanna 1930- DLB-16

McClure, Michael 1932- DLB-16

McClure, Phillips and Company. DLB-46

McClure, S. S. 1857-1949 . . . . .DLB-91

McClurg, A. C., and Company DLB-49

McCluskey, John A., Jr. 1944- DLB-33

McCollum, Michael A. 1946 . . . . .Y-87

McConnell, William C. 1917- DLB-88

McCord, David 1897-1997 . . . . DLB-61

McCord, Louisa S. 1810-1879 . . . . DLB-248

McCorkle, Jill 1958- DLB-234; Y-87

McCorkle, Samuel Eusebius
1746-1811 . . . . DLB-37

McCormick, Anne O'Hare 1880-1954 . . . . DLB-29

Kenneth Dale McCormick Tributes Y-97

McCormick, Robert R. 1880-1955 . . . . . . DLB-29

McCourt, Edward 1907-1972 . . . . DLB-88

McCoy, Horace 1897-1955 . . . . DLB-9

McCrae, Hugh 1876-1958 . . . . DLB-260

McCrae, John 1872-1918 . . . . DLB-92

McCullagh, Joseph B. 1842-1896 . . . . DLB-23

McCullers, Carson
1917-1967 . . . . . .DLB-2, 7, 173, 228; CDALB-1

McCulloch, Thomas 1776-1843 . . . . DLB-99

McDonald, Forrest 1927- DLB-17

McDonald, Walter 1934- DLB-105, DS-9

"Getting Started: Accepting the Regions
You Own—or Which Own You," . . . DLB-105

McDougall, Colin 1917-1984 . . . . DLB-68

McDowell, Katharine Sherwood Bonner
1849-1883 . . . . DLB-202, 239

McDowell, Obolensky DLB-46

McEwan, Ian 1948- DLB-14, 194

McFadden, David 1940- DLB-60

McFall, Frances Elizabeth Clarke
(see Grand, Sarah)

McFarlane, Leslie 1902-1977 . . . . DLB-88

McFarland, Ronald 1942- DLB-256

McFee, William 1881-1966 . . . . DLB-153

McGahern, John 1934- DLB-14, 231

McGee, Thomas D'Arcy 1825-1868 . . . . . . DLB-99

McGeehan, W. O. 1879-1933 . . . . . . .DLB-25, 171

McGill, Ralph 1898-1969 . . . . DLB-29

McGinley, Phyllis 1905-1978 . . . . DLB-11, 48

McGinniss, Joe 1942- DLB-185

McGirt, James E. 1874-1930 . . . . DLB-50

McGlashan and Gill DLB-106

McGough, Roger 1937- DLB-40

McGrath, John 1935- DLB-233

McGrath, Patrick 1950- DLB-231

McGraw-Hill. DLB-46

McGuane, Thomas 1939- DLB-2, 212; Y-80

McGuckian, Medbh 1950- DLB-40

McGuffey, William Holmes 1800-1873 . . . DLB-42

McGuinness, Frank 1953- DLB-245

McHenry, James 1785-1845 . . . . DLB-202

McIlvanney, William 1936- DLB-14, 207

McIlwraith, Jean Newton 1859-1938 . . . . . DLB-92

McIntosh, Maria Jane 1803-1878 . . . DLB-239, 248

McIntyre, James 1827-1906 . . . . DLB-99

McIntyre, O. O. 1884-1938 . . . . DLB-25

McKay, Claude 1889-1948 . . . . .DLB-4, 45, 51, 117

The David McKay Company DLB-49

McKean, William V. 1820-1903 . . . . DLB-23

McKenna, Stephen 1888-1967 . . . . DLB-197

The McKenzie Trust Y-96

McKerrow, R. B. 1872-1940. . . . . DLB-201

McKinley, Robin 1952- DLB-52

McKnight, Reginald 1956- DLB-234

McLachlan, Alexander 1818-1896 . . . . . . DLB-99

McLaren, Floris Clark 1904-1978 . . . . . . DLB-68

McLaverty, Michael 1907- DLB-15

McLean, Duncan 1964- DLB-267

McLean, John R. 1848-1916. . . . . DLB-23

McLean, William L. 1852-1931 . . . . DLB-25

McLennan, William 1856-1904 . . . . DLB-92

McLoughlin Brothers DLB-49

McLuhan, Marshall 1911-1980 . . . . DLB-88

McMaster, John Bach 1852-1932 . . . . DLB-47

McMurtry, Larry 1936-
. . . . . .DLB-2, 143, 256; Y-80, Y-87; CDALB-6

McNally, Terrence 1939- DLB-7, 249

McNeil, Florence 1937- DLB-60

McNeile, Herman Cyril 1888-1937 . . . . . . DLB-77

McNickle, D'Arcy 1904-1977 . . . . . .DLB-175, 212

McPhee, John 1931- DLB-185

McPherson, James Alan 1943- DLB-38, 244

McPherson, Sandra 1943- Y-86

McTaggart, J. M. E. 1866-1925 . . . . DLB-262

McWhirter, George 1939- DLB-60

McWilliam, Candia 1955- DLB-267

McWilliams, Carey 1905-1980. . . . . DLB-137

Mda, Zakes 1948- DLB-225

Mead, L. T. 1844-1914. . . . . DLB-141

Mead, Matthew 1924- DLB-40

Mead, Taylor ?- DLB-16

Meany, Tom 1903-1964 . . . . .DLB-171

Mechthild von Magdeburg
circa 1207-circa 1282 . . . . DLB-138

Medieval French Drama. DLB-208

Medieval Travel Diaries. DLB-203

Medill, Joseph 1823-1899 . . . . DLB-43

Medoff, Mark 1940- DLB-7

Meek, Alexander Beaufort
1814-1865 . . . . DLB-3, 248

Meeke, Mary ?-1816? DLB-116

Meinke, Peter 1932- DLB-5

Mejia Vallejo, Manuel 1923- DLB-113

Melanchthon, Philipp 1497-1560 . . . . . .DLB-179

Melançon, Robert 1947- DLB-60

Mell, Max 1882-1971 . . . . DLB-81, 124

Mellow, James R. 1926-1997 . . . . DLB-111

Mel'nikov, Pavel Ivanovich 1818-1883 . . DLB-238

Meltzer, David 1937- DLB-16

Meltzer, Milton 1915- DLB-61

Melville, Elizabeth, Lady Culross
circa 1585-1640 . . . . .DLB-172

Melville, Herman
1819-1891 . . . . . . DLB-3, 74, 250; CDALB-2

Memoirs of Life and Literature (1920),
by W. H. Mallock [excerpt] DLB-57

Mena, María Cristina 1893-1965 . . . DLB-209, 221

Menander 342-341 B.C.-circa 292-291 B.C.
. . . . .DLB-176; CDWLB-1

Menantes (see Hunold, Christian Friedrich)

Mencke, Johann Burckhard
1674-1732. . . . . DLB-168

Mencken, H. L. 1880-1956
. . . . .DLB-11, 29, 63, 137, 222; CDALB-4

H. L. Mencken's "Berlin, February, 1917" Y-00

Mencken and Nietzsche: An Unpublished
Excerpt from H. L. Mencken's My Life
as Author and Editor Y-93

Mendelssohn, Moses 1729-1786 . . . . DLB-97

Mendes, Catulle 1841-1909 . . . . .DLB-217

Méndez M., Miguel 1930- DLB-82

Mens Rea (or Something). Y-97

The Mercantile Library of New York Y-96

Mercer, Cecil William (see Yates, Dornford)

Mercer, David 1928-1980. . . . . DLB-13

Mercer, John 1704-1768 . . . . DLB-31

Mercer, Johnny 1909?-1976 . . . . DLB-265

Meredith, George
1828-1909 . . . .DLB-18, 35, 57, 159; CDBLB-4

Meredith, Louisa Anne 1812-1895 . . DLB-166, 230

Meredith, Owen
(see Lytton, Edward Robert Bulwer)

Meredith, William 1919- DLB-5

Mergerle, Johann Ulrich
(see Abraham ä Sancta Clara)

Mérimée, Prosper 1803-1870 . . . . . . .DLB-119, 192

Merivale, John Herman 1779-1844. . . . . . DLB-96

Meriwether, Louise 1923- DLB-33

Merlin Press DLB-112

Merriam, Eve 1916-1992 . . . . DLB-61

The Merriam Company DLB-49

Merril, Judith 1923-1997 . . . . DLB-251

Merrill, James 1926-1995 . . . . . .DLB-5, 165; Y-85

Merrill and Baker. DLB-49

The Mershon Company. DLB-49

Merton, Thomas 1915-1968. . . . . . .DLB-48; Y-81

Merwin, W. S. 1927- DLB-5, 169

Messner, Julian [publishing house] DLB-46

Mészöly, Miklós 1921- DLB-232

Metcalf, J. [publishing house] DLB-49

Metcalf, John 1938- DLB-60

The Methodist Book Concern DLB-49

Methuen and Company DLB-112

Meun, Jean de (see Roman de la Rose)

Mew, Charlotte 1869-1928 . . . . DLB-19, 135

Mewshaw, Michael 1943- Y-80

Meyer, Conrad Ferdinand 1825-1898 . . . DLB-129

Meyer, E. Y. 1946- DLB-75

Meyer, Eugene 1875-1959 . . . . DLB-29

Meyer, Michael 1921-2000 . . . . DLB-155

Meyers, Jeffrey 1939- DLB-111

Meynell, Alice 1847-1922 . . . . .DLB-19, 98

Meynell, Viola 1885-1956 . . . . .DLB-153

Meyrink, Gustav 1868-1932 . . . . .DLB-81

Mézières, Philipe de circa 1327-1405 . . . . .DLB-208

Michael, Ib 1945- DLB-214

Michael, Livi 1960- DLB-267

Michaëlis, Karen 1872-1950 . . . . .DLB-214

Michaels, Leonard 1933- DLB-130

Michaux, Henri 1899-1984 . . . . .DLB-258

Micheaux, Oscar 1884-1951 . . . . .DLB-50

Michel of Northgate, Dan
    circa 1265-circa 1340 . . . . .DLB-146

Micheline, Jack 1929-1998 . . . . .DLB-16

Michener, James A. 1907?-1997 . . . . .DLB-6

Micklejohn, George
    circa 1717-1818 . . . . .DLB-31

Middle English Literature:
    An Introduction. DLB-146

The Middle English Lyric DLB-146

Middle Hill Press DLB-106

Middleton, Christopher 1926- DLB-40

Middleton, Richard 1882-1911 . . . . .DLB-156

Middleton, Stanley 1919- DLB-14

Middleton, Thomas 1580-1627 . . . . .DLB-58

Miegel, Agnes 1879-1964 . . . . .DLB-56

Mieželaitis, Eduardas 1919-1997 . . . . . . .DLB-220

Mihailović, Dragoslav 1930- DLB-181

Mihalić, Slavko 1928- DLB-181

Mikhailov, A. (see Sheller, Aleksandr
    Konstantinovich)

Mikhailov, Mikhail Larionovich
    1829-1865 .DLB-238

Miles, Josephine 1911-1985 . . . . .DLB-48

Miles, Susan (Ursula Wyllie Roberts)
    1888-1975 .DLB-240

Miliković, Branko 1934-1961 . . . . .DLB-181

Milius, John 1944- DLB-44

Mill, James 1773-1836 . . . . .DLB-107, 158, 262

Mill, John Stuart
    1806-1873 . . . . . .DLB-55, 190, 262; CDBLB-4

Millar, Andrew [publishing house] DLB-154

Millar, Kenneth
    1915-1983 . . . . .DLB-2, 226; Y-83; DS-6

Millay, Edna St. Vincent
    1892-1950 . . . . .DLB-45, 249; CDALB-4

Millen, Sarah Gertrude 1888-1968 . . . . . .DLB-225

Miller, Andrew 1960- DLB-267

Miller, Arthur
    1915- DLB-7, 266; CDALB-1

Miller, Caroline 1903-1992 . . . . .DLB-9

Miller, Eugene Ethelbert 1950- DLB-41

Miller, Heather Ross 1939- DLB-120

Miller, Henry
    1891-1980 . . . . . . .DLB-4, 9; Y-80; CDALB-5

Miller, Hugh 1802-1856 . . . . .DLB-190

Miller, J. Hillis 1928- DLB-67

Miller, James [publishing house] DLB-49

Miller, Jason 1939- DLB-7

Miller, Joaquin 1839-1913 . . . . .DLB-186

Miller, May 1899- DLB-41

Miller, Paul 1906-1991 . . . . .DLB-127

Miller, Perry 1905-1963 . . . . DLB-17, 63

Miller, Sue 1943- DLB-143

Miller, Vassar 1924-1998 . . . . .DLB-105

Miller, Walter M., Jr. 1923- DLB-8

Miller, Webb 1892-1940 . . . . .DLB-29

Millett, Kate 1934- DLB-246

Millhauser, Steven 1943- DLB-2

Millican, Arthenia J. Bates 1920- DLB-38

Milligan, Alice 1866-1953 . . . . .DLB-240

Mills and Boon DLB-112

Mills, Magnus 1954- DLB-267

Milman, Henry Hart 1796-1868 . . . . .DLB-96

Milne, A. A. 1882-1956 . . . . . DLB-10, 77, 100, 160

Milner, Ron 1938- DLB-38

Milner, William [publishing house] DLB-106

Milnes, Richard Monckton (Lord Houghton)
    1809-1885 . . . . .DLB-32, 184

Milton, John
    1608-1674 . . . . .DLB-131, 151; CDBLB-2

Miłosz, Czesław 1911- DLB-215; CDWLB-4

Minakami Tsutomu 1919- DLB-182

Minamoto no Sanetomo 1192-1219 . . . . .DLB-203

The Minerva Press DLB-154

Minnesang circa 1150-1280 . . . . .DLB-138

Minns, Susan 1839-1938 . . . . .DLB-140

Minor Illustrators, 1880-1914 . . . . .DLB-141

Minor Poets of the Earlier Seventeenth
    Century DLB-121

Minton, Balch and Company DLB-46

Mirbeau, Octave 1848-1917 . . . . . . .DLB-123, 192

Mirk, John died after 1414? DLB-146

Miron, Gaston 1928- DLB-60

A Mirror for Magistrates DLB-167

Mishima Yukio 1925-1970 . . . . .DLB-182

Mitchel, Jonathan 1624-1668 . . . . .DLB-24

Mitchell, Adrian 1932- DLB-40

Mitchell, Donald Grant
    1822-1908 . . . . .DLB-1, 243; DS-13

Mitchell, Gladys 1901-1983 . . . . .DLB-77

Mitchell, James Leslie 1901-1935 . . . . .DLB-15

Mitchell, John (see Slater, Patrick)

Mitchell, John Ames 1845-1918 . . . . .DLB-79

Mitchell, Joseph 1908-1996 . . . . . . .DLB-185; Y-96

Mitchell, Julian 1935- DLB-14

Mitchell, Ken 1940- DLB-60

Mitchell, Langdon 1862-1935 . . . . .DLB-7

Mitchell, Loften 1919- DLB-38

Mitchell, Margaret 1900-1949 . . .DLB-9; CDALB-7

Mitchell, S. Weir 1829-1914 . . . . .DLB-202

Mitchell, W. J. T. 1942- DLB-246

Mitchell, W. O. 1914- DLB-88

Mitchison, Naomi Margaret (Haldane)
    1897-1999 . . . . .DLB-160, 191, 255

Mitford, Mary Russell 1787-1855 . . . .DLB-110, 116

Mitford, Nancy 1904-1973 . . . . .DLB-191

Mittelholzer, Edgar
    1909-1965 . . . . DLB-117; CDWLB-3

Mitterer, Erika 1906- DLB-85

Mitterer, Felix 1948- DLB-124

Mitternacht, Johann Sebastian
    1613-1679 .DLB-168

Miyamoto, Yuriko 1899-1951 . . . . .DLB-180

Mizener, Arthur 1907-1988 . . . . .DLB-103

Mo, Timothy 1950- DLB-194

Moberg, Vilhelm 1898-1973 . . . . .DLB-259

Modern Age Books DLB-46

"Modern English Prose" (1876),
    by George Saintsbury DLB-57

The Modern Language Association of America
    Celebrates Its Centennial Y-84

The Modern Library DLB-46

"Modern Novelists – Great and Small" (1855),
    by Margaret Oliphant DLB-21

"Modern Style" (1857), by Cockburn
    Thomson [excerpt] DLB-57

The Modernists (1932),
    by Joseph Warren Beach DLB-36

Modiano, Patrick 1945- DLB-83

Moffat, Yard and Company DLB-46

Moffet, Thomas 1553-1604 . . . . .DLB-136

Mohr, Nicholasa 1938- DLB-145

Moix, Ana María 1947- DLB-134

Molesworth, Louisa 1839-1921 . . . . .DLB-135

Möllhausen, Balduin 1825-1905 . . . . .DLB-129

Molnár, Ferenc
    1878-1952 . . . . .DLB-215; CDWLB-4

Molnár, Miklós (see Mészöly, Miklós)

Momaday, N. Scott
    1934- DLB-143, 175, 256; CDALB-7

Monkhouse, Allan 1858-1936 . . . . .DLB-10

Monro, Harold 1879-1932 . . . . .DLB-19

Monroe, Harriet 1860-1936 . . . . .DLB-54, 91

Monsarrat, Nicholas 1910-1979 . . . . .DLB-15

Montagu, Lady Mary Wortley
    1689-1762 . . . . .DLB-95, 101

Montague, C. E. 1867-1928 . . . . .DLB-197

Montague, John 1929- DLB-40

Montale, Eugenio 1896-1981 . . . . .DLB-114

Montalvo, José 1946-1994 . . . . .DLB-209

Monterroso, Augusto 1921- DLB-145

Montesquiou, Robert de 1855-1921 . . . . .DLB-217

Montgomerie, Alexander
    circa 1550?-1598 . . . . .DLB-167

Montgomery, James 1771-1854 . . . . . .DLB-93, 158

Montgomery, John 1919- DLB-16

Montgomery, Lucy Maud
    1874-1942 . . . . .DLB-92; DS-14

Montgomery, Marion 1925- DLB-6

Montgomery, Robert Bruce (see Crispin, Edmund)

Montherlant, Henry de 1896-1972 . . . . . . .DLB-72

The Monthly Review 1749-1844 . . . . .DLB-110

Montigny, Louvigny de 1876-1955. . . . . . DLB-92

Montoya, José 1932- DLB-122

Moodie, John Wedderburn Dunbar
1797-1869 . . . . DLB-99

Moodie, Susanna 1803-1885. . . . . DLB-99

Moody, Joshua circa 1633-1697 . . . . DLB-24

Moody, William Vaughn 1869-1910 . . . .DLB-7, 54

Moorcock, Michael 1939- DLB-14, 231, 261

Moore, Alan 1953- DLB-261

Moore, Brian 1921-1999. . . . . DLB-251

Moore, Catherine L. 1911- DLB-8

Moore, Clement Clarke 1779-1863. . . . . . DLB-42

Moore, Dora Mavor 1888-1979 . . . . DLB-92

Moore, G. E. 1873-1958 . . . . DLB-262

Moore, George 1852-1933 . . . . DLB-10, 18, 57, 135

Moore, Lorrie 1957- DLB-234

Moore, Marianne
1887-1972 . . . . DLB-45; DS-7; CDALB-5

Moore, Mavor 1919- DLB-88

Moore, Richard 1927- DLB-105

Moore, T. Sturge 1870-1944. . . . . DLB-19

Moore, Thomas 1779-1852. . . . . . . DLB-96, 144

Moore, Ward 1903-1978 . . . . DLB-8

Moore, Wilstach, Keys and Company DLB-49

Moorehead, Alan 1901-1983 . . . . DLB-204

Moorhouse, Geoffrey 1931- DLB-204

The Moorland-Spingarn Research
Center DLB-76

Moorman, Mary C. 1905-1994 . . . . DLB-155

Mora, Pat 1942- DLB-209

Moraga, Cherríe 1952- DLB-82, 249

Morales, Alejandro 1944- DLB-82

Morales, Mario Roberto 1947- DLB-145

Morales, Rafael 1919- DLB-108

Morality Plays: *Mankind* circa 1450-1500 and
Everyman circa 1500 . . . . DLB-146

Morante, Elsa 1912-1985 . . . . .DLB-177

Morata, Olympia Fulvia 1526-1555 . . . . . .DLB-179

Moravia, Alberto 1907-1990 . . . . .DLB-177

Mordaunt, Elinor 1872-1942 . . . . .DLB-174

Mordovtsev, Daniil Lukich 1830-1905. . . DLB-238

More, Hannah
1745-1833. . . . . DLB-107, 109, 116, 158

More, Henry 1614-1687 . . . . DLB-126, 252

More, Sir Thomas
1477 or 1478-1535 . . . . DLB-136

Moreno, Dorinda 1939- DLB-122

Morency, Pierre 1942- DLB-60

Moretti, Marino 1885-1979. . . . . . . DLB-114, 264

Morgan, Berry 1919- DLB-6

Morgan, Charles 1894-1958. . . . . . . DLB-34, 100

Morgan, Edmund S. 1916- DLB-17

Morgan, Edwin 1920- DLB-27

Morgan, John Pierpont 1837-1913 . . . . . . DLB-140

Morgan, John Pierpont, Jr. 1867-1943 . . . DLB-140

Morgan, Robert 1944- DLB-120

Morgan, Sydney Owenson, Lady
1776?-1859 . . . . DLB-116, 158

Morgner, Irmtraud 1933- DLB-75

Morhof, Daniel Georg 1639-1691 . . . . . . DLB-164

Mori, Ōgai 1862-1922 . . . . DLB-180

Móricz, Zsigmond 1879-1942 . . . . DLB-215

Morier, James Justinian
1782 or 1783?-1849 . . . . DLB-116

Mörike, Eduard 1804-1875. . . . . DLB-133

Morin, Paul 1889-1963. . . . . DLB-92

Morison, Richard 1514?-1556 . . . . DLB-136

Morison, Samuel Eliot 1887-1976 . . . . . . DLB-17

Morison, Stanley 1889-1967. . . . . DLB-201

Moritz, Karl Philipp 1756-1793 . . . . DLB-94

Moriz von Craûn circa 1220-1230 . . . . DLB-138

Morley, Christopher 1890-1957 . . . . DLB-9

Morley, John 1838-1923. . . . . . . DLB-57, 144, 190

Morris, George Pope 1802-1864 . . . . DLB-73

Morris, James Humphrey (see Morris, Jan)

Morris, Jan 1926- DLB-204

Morris, Lewis 1833-1907 . . . . DLB-35

Morris, Margaret 1737-1816 . . . . DLB-200

Morris, Richard B. 1904-1989 . . . . DLB-17

Morris, William 1834-1896
. . . . . DLB-18, 35, 57, 156, 178, 184; CDBLB-4

Morris, Willie 1934-1999 . . . . Y-80

Morris, Wright
1910-1998 . . . . .DLB-2, 206, 218; Y-81

Morrison, Arthur 1863-1945 . . . .DLB-70, 135, 197

Morrison, Charles Clayton 1874-1966 . . . . DLB-91

Morrison, John 1904-1988 . . . . DLB-260

Morrison, Toni 1931-
. . . . . . .DLB-6, 33, 143; Y-81, Y-93; CDALB-6

Morrissy, Mary 1957- DLB-267

Morrow, William, and Company. DLB-46

Morse, James Herbert 1841-1923. . . . . . . DLB-71

Morse, Jedidiah 1761-1826 . . . . DLB-37

Morse, John T., Jr. 1840-1937 . . . . DLB-47

Morselli, Guido 1912-1973 . . . . .DLB-177

Mortimer, Favell Lee 1802-1878 . . . . DLB-163

Mortimer, John
1923- DLB-13, 245; CDBLB-8

Morton, Carlos 1942- DLB-122

Morton, H. V. 1892-1979 . . . . DLB-195

Morton, John P., and Company DLB-49

Morton, Nathaniel 1613-1685 . . . . DLB-24

Morton, Sarah Wentworth 1759-1846 . . . . DLB-37

Morton, Thomas circa 1579-circa 1647 . . . DLB-24

Moscherosch, Johann Michael
1601-1669 . . . . DLB-164

Moseley, Humphrey
[publishing house] DLB-170

Möser, Justus 1720-1794 . . . . DLB-97

Mosley, Nicholas 1923- DLB-14, 207

Moss, Arthur 1889-1969. . . . . DLB-4

Moss, Howard 1922-1987 . . . . DLB-5

Moss, Thylias 1954- DLB-120

The Most Powerful Book Review
in America
[*New York Times Book Review*] Y-82

Motion, Andrew 1952- DLB-40

Motley, John Lothrop
1814-1877. . . . . DLB-1, 30, 59, 235

Motley, Willard 1909-1965 . . . . .DLB-76, 143

Mott, Lucretia 1793-1880 . . . . DLB-239

Motte, Benjamin, Jr. [publishing house] . . DLB-154

Motteux, Peter Anthony 1663-1718 . . . . . . DLB-80

Mottram, R. H. 1883-1971 . . . . DLB-36

Mount, Ferdinand 1939- DLB-231

Mouré, Erin 1955- DLB-60

Mourning Dove (Humishuma) between
1882 and 1888?-1936. . . . . .DLB-175, 221

Movies from Books, 1920-1974 . . . . DLB-9

Mowat, Farley 1921- DLB-68

Mowbray, A. R., and Company,
Limited. DLB-106

Mowrer, Edgar Ansel 1892-1977 . . . . DLB-29

Mowrer, Paul Scott 1887-1971 . . . . DLB-29

Moxon, Edward [publishing house] DLB-106

Moxon, Joseph [publishing house] DLB-170

Mphahlele, Es'kia (Ezekiel)
1919- DLB-125; CDWLB-3

Mrożek, Sławomir 1930- . . DLB-232; CDWLB-4

Mtshali, Oswald Mbuyiseni 1940- DLB-125

Mucedorus DLB-62

Mudford, William 1782-1848 . . . . DLB-159

Mueller, Lisel 1924- DLB-105

Muhajir, El (see Marvin X)

Muhajir, Nazzam Al Fitnah (see Marvin X)

Mühlbach, Luise 1814-1873 . . . . DLB-133

Muir, Edwin 1887-1959 . . . . . . .DLB-20, 100, 191

Muir, Helen 1937- DLB-14

Muir, John 1838-1914 . . . . DLB-186

Muir, Percy 1894-1979 . . . . DLB-201

Mujū Ichien 1226-1312. . . . . DLB-203

Mukherjee, Bharati 1940- DLB-60, 218

Mulcaster, Richard
1531 or 1532-1611. . . . . DLB-167

Muldoon, Paul 1951- DLB-40

Müller, Friedrich (see Müller, Maler)

Müller, Heiner 1929-1995 . . . . DLB-124

Müller, Maler 1749-1825 . . . . DLB-94

Muller, Marcia 1944- DLB-226

Müller, Wilhelm 1794-1827 . . . . DLB-90

Mumford, Lewis 1895-1990 . . . . DLB-63

Munby, A. N. L. 1913-1974 . . . . DLB-201

Munby, Arthur Joseph 1828-1910 . . . . DLB-35

Munday, Anthony 1560-1633 . . . . . .DLB-62, 172

Mundt, Clara (see Mühlbach, Luise)

Mundt, Theodore 1808-1861 . . . . DLB-133

Munford, Robert circa 1737-1783 . . . . DLB-31

Mungoshi, Charles 1947- DLB-157

Munk, Kaj 1898-1944. . . . . DLB-214

Munonye, John 1929- DLB-117

Munro, Alice 1931- DLB-53

Munro, George [publishing house] DLB-49

Munro, H. H.
1870-1916 . . . . .DLB-34, 162; CDBLB-5

Munro, Neil 1864-1930 . . . . .DLB-156

Munro, Norman L.
[publishing house] DLB-49

Munroe, James, and Company DLB-49

Munroe, Kirk 1850-1930 . . . . .DLB-42

Munroe and Francis DLB-49

Munsell, Joel [publishing house] DLB-49

Munsey, Frank A. 1854-1925 . . . . . . .DLB-25, 91

Munsey, Frank A., and Company DLB-49

Murakami Haruki 1949- DLB-182

Murav'ev, Mikhail Nikitich
1757-1807 .DLB-150

Murdoch, Iris 1919-1999
. . . . .DLB-14, 194, 233; CDBLB-8

Murdoch, Rupert 1931- DLB-127

Murfree, Mary N. 1850-1922 . . . . .DLB-12, 74

Murger, Henry 1822-1861 . . . . .DLB-119

Murger, Louis-Henri (see Murger, Henry)

Murner, Thomas 1475-1537 . . . . .DLB-179

Muro, Amado 1915-1971 . . . . .DLB-82

Murphy, Arthur 1727-1805 . . . . .DLB-89, 142

Murphy, Beatrice M. 1908- DLB-76

Murphy, Dervla 1931- DLB-204

Murphy, Emily 1868-1933 . . . . .DLB-99

Murphy, Jack 1923-1980 . . . . .DLB-241

Murphy, John, and Company DLB-49

Murphy, John H., III 1916- DLB-127

Murphy, Richard 1927-1993 . . . . .DLB-40

Murray, Albert L. 1916- DLB-38

Murray, Gilbert 1866-1957 . . . . .DLB-10

Murray, Jim 1919-1998 . . . . .DLB-241

Murray, John [publishing house] DLB-154

Murry, John Middleton 1889-1957 . . . . .DLB-149

"The Break-Up of the Novel" (1922) DLB-36

Murray, Judith Sargent
1751-1820 . . . . DLB-37, 200

Murray, Pauli 1910-1985 . . . . .DLB-41

Musäus, Johann Karl August 1735-1787 . . . .DLB-97

Muschg, Adolf 1934- DLB-75

The Music of *Minnesang* DLB-138

Musil, Robert
1880-1942 . . . . .DLB-81, 124; CDWLB-2

Muspilli circa 790-circa 850 . . . . .DLB-148

Musset, Alfred de 1810-1857 . . . . . . .DLB-192, 217

Mussey, Benjamin B., and Company DLB-49

Mutafchieva, Vera 1929- DLB-181

Mwangi, Meja 1948- DLB-125

My Summer Reading Orgy: Reading for Fun
and Games: One Reader's Report
on the Summer of 2001 . . . . Y-01

Myers, Frederic W. H. 1843-1901 . . . . . .DLB-190

Myers, Gustavus 1872-1942 . . . . .DLB-47

Myers, L. H. 1881-1944 . . . . .DLB-15

Myers, Walter Dean 1937- DLB-33

Myerson, Julie 1960- DLB-267

Mykolaitis-Putinas, Vincas 1893-1967 . . . .DLB-220

Myles, Eileen 1949- DLB-193

Myrdal, Jan 1927- DLB-257

N

Na Prous Boneta circa 1296-1328 . . . . . . .DLB-208

Nabl, Franz 1883-1974 . . . . .DLB-81

Nabokov, Vladimir 1899-1977
. . . . DLB-2, 244; Y-80, Y-91; DS-3; CDALB-1

The Vladimir Nabokov Archive
in the Berg Collection Y-91

Nabokov Festival at Cornell Y-83

Nádaši, Ladislav (see Jégé)

Naden, Constance 1858-1889 . . . . .DLB-199

Nadezhdin, Nikolai Ivanovich
1804-1856 . . . . .DLB-198

Naevius circa 265 B.C.-201 B.C. DLB-211

Nafis and Cornish DLB-49

Nagai, Kafū 1879-1959 . . . . .DLB-180

Naipaul, Shiva 1945-1985 . . . . DLB-157; Y-85

Naipaul, V. S. 1932-
. . . . .DLB-125, 204, 207; Y-85, Y-01;
CDBLB-8; CDWLB-3

Nakagami Kenji 1946-1992 . . . . .DLB-182

Nakano-in Masatada no Musume (see Nijō, Lady)

Nałkowska, Zofia 1884-1954 . . . . .DLB-215

Nancrede, Joseph [publishing house] DLB-49

Naranjo, Carmen 1930- DLB-145

Narezhny, Vasilii Trofimovich
1780-1825 . . . . .DLB-198

Narrache, Jean 1893-1970 . . . . .DLB-92

Nasby, Petroleum Vesuvius (see Locke, David Ross)

Nash, Eveleigh [publishing house] DLB-112

Nash, Ogden 1902-1971 . . . . .DLB-11

Nashe, Thomas 1567-1601? DLB-167

Nason, Jerry 1910-1986 . . . . .DLB-241

Nast, Conde 1873-1942 . . . . .DLB-91

Nast, Thomas 1840-1902 . . . . .DLB-188

Nastasijević, Momčilo 1894-1938 . . . . . . .DLB-147

Nathan, George Jean 1882-1958 . . . . . . .DLB-137

Nathan, Robert 1894-1985 . . . . .DLB-9

National Book Critics Circle Awards Y-00; Y-01

The National Jewish Book Awards Y-85

The National Theatre and the Royal
Shakespeare Company: The
National Companies DLB-13

Natsume, Sōseki 1867-1916 . . . . .DLB-180

Naughton, Bill 1910- DLB-13

Navarro, Joe 1953- DLB-209

Naylor, Gloria 1950- DLB-173

Nazor, Vladimir 1876-1949 . . . . .DLB-147

Ndebele, Njabulo 1948- DLB-157

Neagoe, Peter 1881-1960 . . . . .DLB-4

Neal, John 1793-1876 . . . . .DLB-1, 59, 243

Neal, Joseph C. 1807-1847 . . . . .DLB-11

Neal, Larry 1937-1981 . . . . .DLB-38

The Neale Publishing Company DLB-49

Nebel, Frederick 1903-1967 . . . . .DLB-226

Neely, F. Tennyson [publishing house] DLB-49

Negoiţescu, Ion 1921-1993 . . . . .DLB-220

Negri, Ada 1870-1945 . . . . .DLB-114

"The Negro as a Writer," by
G. M. McClellan DLB-50

"Negro Poets and Their Poetry," by
Wallace Thurman DLB-50

Neidhart von Reuental
circa 1185-circa 1240 . . . . .DLB-138

Neihardt, John G. 1881-1973 . . . . . .DLB-9, 54, 256

Neilson, John Shaw 1872-1942 . . . . .DLB-230

Neledinsky-Meletsky, Iurii Aleksandrovich
1752-1828 . . . . .DLB-150

Nelligan, Emile 1879-1941 . . . . .DLB-92

Nelson, Alice Moore Dunbar 1875-1935 . . .DLB-50

Nelson, Antonya 1961- DLB-244

Nelson, Kent 1943- DLB-234

Nelson, Thomas, and Sons [U.K.] DLB-106

Nelson, Thomas, and Sons [U.S.] DLB-49

Nelson, William 1908-1978 . . . . .DLB-103

Nelson, William Rockhill 1841-1915 . . . . .DLB-23

Nemerov, Howard 1920-1991 . . . . . DLB-5, 6; Y-83

Németh, László 1901-1975 . . . . .DLB-215

Nepos circa 100 B.C.-post 27 B.C. DLB-211

Nėris, Salomėja
1904-1945 . . . . DLB-220; CDWLB-4

Nerval, Gerard de 1808-1855 . . . . .DLB-217

Nesbit, E. 1858-1924 . . . . DLB-141, 153, 178

Ness, Evaline 1911-1986 . . . . .DLB-61

Nestroy, Johann 1801-1862 . . . . .DLB-133

Nettleship, R. L. 1846-1892 . . . . .DLB-262

Neugeboren, Jay 1938- DLB-28

Neukirch, Benjamin 1655-1729 . . . . .DLB-168

Neumann, Alfred 1895-1952 . . . . .DLB-56

Neumann, Ferenc (see Molnár, Ferenc)

Neumark, Georg 1621-1681 . . . . .DLB-164

Neumeister, Erdmann 1671-1756 . . . . . . .DLB-168

Nevins, Allan 1890-1971 . . . . DLB-17; DS-17

Nevinson, Henry Woodd 1856-1941 . . . .DLB-135

The New American Library DLB-46

New Approaches to Biography: Challenges
from Critical Theory, USC Conference
on Literary Studies, 1990 . . . . Y-90

New Directions Publishing Corporation . . .DLB-46

A New Edition of *Huck Finn* Y-85

New Forces at Work in the American Theatre:
1915-1925 . . . . .DLB-7

New Literary Periodicals:
A Report for 1987 . . . . .Y-87

New Literary Periodicals:
A Report for 1988 . . . . .Y-88

New Literary Periodicals:
A Report for 1989 . . . . .Y-89

New Literary Periodicals:
A Report for 1990 . . . . Y-90

New Literary Periodicals:
A Report for 1991 . . . . Y-91

New Literary Periodicals:
A Report for 1992 . . . . Y-92

New Literary Periodicals:
A Report for 1993 . . . . Y-93

The New Monthly Magazine
1814-1884. DLB-110

The New Variorum Shakespeare Y-85

A New Voice: The Center for the Book's First
Five Years. Y-83

The New Wave [Science Fiction] DLB-8

New York City Bookshops in the 1930s and 1940s:
The Recollections of Walter Goldwater. . . Y-93

Newbery, John [publishing house] DLB-154

Newbolt, Henry 1862-1938 . . . . DLB-19

Newbound, Bernard Slade (see Slade, Bernard)

Newby, Eric 1919- DLB-204

Newby, P. H. 1918- DLB-15

Newby, Thomas Cautley
[publishing house] DLB-106

Newcomb, Charles King 1820-1894 . . . DLB-1, 223

Newell, Peter 1862-1924. . . . . DLB-42

Newell, Robert Henry 1836-1901. . . . . . . DLB-11

Newhouse, Samuel I. 1895-1979. . . . . . . DLB-127

Newman, Cecil Earl 1903-1976 . . . . DLB-127

Newman, David (see Benton, Robert)

Newman, Frances 1883-1928 . . . . Y-80

Newman, Francis William 1805-1897. . . . DLB-190

Newman, John Henry
1801-1890 . . . . DLB-18, 32, 55

Newman, Mark [publishing house]. DLB-49

Newmarch, Rosa Harriet 1857-1940. . . . . DLB-240

Newnes, George, Limited DLB-112

Newsome, Effie Lee 1885-1979. . . . . DLB-76

Newspaper Syndication of American
Humor DLB-11

Newton, A. Edward 1864-1940 . . . . DLB-140

Newton, Sir Isaac 1642-1727. . . . . DLB-252

Nexø, Martin Andersen 1869-1954 . . . . . DLB-214

Nezval, Vítěslav
1900-1958. . . . . DLB-215; CDWLB-4

Ngugi wa Thiong'o
1938- DLB-125; CDWLB-3

Niatum, Duane 1938- DLB-175

The *Nibelungenlied* and the *Klage*
circa 1200. . . . . DLB-138

Nichol, B. P. 1944-1988 . . . . DLB-53

Nicholas of Cusa 1401-1464. . . . . DLB-115

Nichols, Ann 1891?-1966 . . . . DLB-249

Nichols, Beverly 1898-1983 . . . . DLB-191

Nichols, Dudley 1895-1960 . . . . DLB-26

Nichols, Grace 1950- DLB-157

Nichols, John 1940- Y-82

Nichols, Mary Sargeant (Neal) Gove
1810-1884. . . . . DLB-1, 243

Nichols, Peter 1927- DLB-13, 245

Nichols, Roy F. 1896-1973 . . . . DLB-17

Nichols, Ruth 1948- DLB-60

Nicholson, Edward Williams Byron
1849-1912 . . . . DLB-184

Nicholson, Norman 1914- DLB-27

Nicholson, William 1872-1949 . . . . DLB-141

Ní Chuilleanáin, Eiléan 1942- DLB-40

Nicol, Eric 1919- DLB-68

Nicolai, Friedrich 1733-1811. . . . . DLB-97

Nicolas de Clamanges circa 1363-1437. . . DLB-208

Nicolay, John G. 1832-1901 and
Hay, John 1838-1905. . . . . DLB-47

Nicolson, Adela Florence Cory (see Hope, Laurence)

Nicolson, Harold 1886-1968. . . . . . .DLB-100, 149

Nicolson, Harold, "The Practice of Biography," in
*The English Sense of Humour and
Other Essays* DLB-149

Nicolson, Nigel 1917- DLB-155

Niebuhr, Reinhold 1892-1971. . . . . .DLB-17; DS-17

Niedecker, Lorine 1903-1970 . . . . DLB-48

Nieman, Lucius W. 1857-1935 . . . . DLB-25

Nietzsche, Friedrich
1844-1900 . . . . DLB-129; CDWLB-2

Nievo, Stanislao 1928- DLB-196

Niggli, Josefina 1910- Y-80

Nightingale, Florence 1820-1910 . . . . DLB-166

Nijō, Lady (Nakano-in Masatada no Musume)
1258-after 1306 . . . . DLB-203

Nijō Yoshimoto 1320-1388. . . . . DLB-203

Nikolev, Nikolai Petrovich
1758-1815. . . . . DLB-150

Niles, Hezekiah 1777-1839 . . . . DLB-43

Nims, John Frederick 1913-1999 . . . . DLB-5

Nin, Anaïs 1903-1977 . . . . DLB-2, 4, 152

1985: The Year of the Mystery:
A Symposium. Y-85

The 1997 Booker Prize. Y-97

The 1998 Booker Prize. Y-98

Niño, Raúl 1961- DLB-209

Nissenson, Hugh 1933- DLB-28

Niven, Frederick John 1878-1944 . . . . DLB-92

Niven, Larry 1938- DLB-8

Nixon, Howard M. 1909-1983 . . . . DLB-201

Nizan, Paul 1905-1940 . . . . DLB-72

Njegoš, Petar II Petrović
1813-1851 . . . . .DLB-147; CDWLB-4

Nkosi, Lewis 1936- DLB-157

"The No Self, the Little Self, and the Poets,"
by Richard Moore DLB-105

Noah, Mordecai M. 1785-1851. . . . . DLB-250

Noailles, Anna de 1876-1933 . . . . DLB-258

Nobel Peace Prize

The 1986 Nobel Peace Prize: Elie Wiesel. Y-86

The Nobel Prize and Literary Politics Y-86

Nobel Prize in Literature

The 1982 Nobel Prize in Literature:
Gabriel García Márquez. Y-82

The 1983 Nobel Prize in Literature:
William Golding Y-83

The 1984 Nobel Prize in Literature:
Jaroslav Seifert Y-84

The 1985 Nobel Prize in Literature:
Claude Simon Y-85

The 1986 Nobel Prize in Literature:
Wole Soyinka Y-86

The 1987 Nobel Prize in Literature:
Joseph Brodsky Y-87

The 1988 Nobel Prize in Literature:
Najīb Mahfūz. Y-88

The 1989 Nobel Prize in Literature:
Camilo José Cela Y-89

The 1990 Nobel Prize in Literature:
Octavio Paz Y-90

The 1991 Nobel Prize in Literature:
Nadine Gordimer. Y-91

The 1992 Nobel Prize in Literature:
Derek Walcott. Y-92

The 1993 Nobel Prize in Literature:
Toni Morrison. Y-93

The 1994 Nobel Prize in Literature:
Kenzaburō Ōe Y-94

The 1995 Nobel Prize in Literature:
Seamus Heaney Y-95

The 1996 Nobel Prize in Literature:
Wisława Szymborsha. Y-96

The 1997 Nobel Prize in Literature:
Dario Fo. Y-97

The 1998 Nobel Prize in Literature:
José Saramago Y-98

The 1999 Nobel Prize in Literature:
Günter Grass Y-99

The 2000 Nobel Prize in Literature:
Gao Xingjian Y-00

The 2001 Nobel Prize in Literature:
V. S. Naipaul Y-01

Nodier, Charles 1780-1844. . . . . DLB-119

Noël, Marie 1883-1967. . . . . DLB-258

Noel, Roden 1834-1894 . . . . DLB-35

Nogami, Yaeko 1885-1985. . . . . DLB-180

Nogo, Rajko Petrov 1945- DLB-181

Nolan, William F. 1928- DLB-8

Noland, C. F. M. 1810?-1858. . . . . DLB-11

Noma Hiroshi 1915-1991. . . . . DLB-182

Nonesuch Press DLB-112

Noon, Jeff 1957- DLB-267

Noonan, Robert Phillipe (see Tressell, Robert)

Noonday Press DLB-46

Noone, John 1936- DLB-14

Nora, Eugenio de 1923- DLB-134

Nordan, Lewis 1939- DLB-234

Nordbrandt, Henrik 1945- DLB-214

Nordhoff, Charles 1887-1947 . . . . DLB-9

Norén, Lars 1944- DLB-257

Norfolk, Lawrence 1963- DLB-267

Norman, Charles 1904-1996 . . . . DLB-111

Norman, Marsha 1947- DLB-266; Y-84

Norris, Charles G. 1881-1945 . . . . DLB-9

Norris, Frank
1870-1902 . . . . DLB-12, 71, 186; CDALB-3

Norris, John 1657-1712 . . . . DLB-252

Norris, Leslie 1921- DLB-27, 256

Norse, Harold 1916- DLB-16

Norte, Marisela 1955- DLB-209

North, Marianne 1830-1890 . . . . DLB-174

North Point Press DLB-46

Nortje, Arthur 1942-1970 . . . . DLB-125

Norton, Alice Mary (see Norton, Andre)

Norton, Andre 1912- DLB-8, 52

Norton, Andrews 1786-1853 . . . . DLB-1, 235

Norton, Caroline 1808-1877 . . . . DLB-21, 159, 199

Norton, Charles Eliot 1827-1908 . . . DLB-1, 64, 235

Norton, John 1606-1663 . . . . DLB-24

Norton, Mary 1903-1992 . . . . DLB-160

Norton, Thomas (see Sackville, Thomas)

Norton, W. W., and Company DLB-46

Norwood, Robert 1874-1932 . . . . DLB-92

Nosaka Akiyuki 1930- DLB-182

Nossack, Hans Erich 1901-1977 . . . . DLB-69

Not Immediately Discernible . . . but Eventually
Quite Clear: The *First Light* and *Final Years*
of Hemingway's Centenary Y-99

A Note on Technique (1926), by
Elizabeth A. Drew [excerpts] DLB-36

Notes from the Underground
of *Sister Carrie* Y-01

Notker Balbulus circa 840-912 . . . . DLB-148

Notker III of Saint Gall
circa 950-1022 . . . . DLB-148

Notker von Zweifalten ?-1095 . . . . DLB-148

Nourse, Alan E. 1928- DLB-8

Novak, Slobodan 1924- DLB-181

Novak, Vjenceslav 1859-1905 . . . . DLB-147

Novakovich, Josip 1956- DLB-244

Novalis 1772-1801 . . . . DLB-90; CDWLB-2

Novaro, Mario 1868-1944 . . . . DLB-114

Novás Calvo, Lino
1903-1983 . . . . DLB-145

"The Novel in [Robert Browning's]
'The Ring and the Book'" (1912),
by Henry James DLB-32

The Novel of Impressionism,
by Jethro Bithell DLB-66

Novel-Reading: *The Works of
Charles Dickens, The Works of
W. Makepeace Thackeray*
(1879), by Anthony Trollope DLB-21

Novels for Grown-Ups Y-97

The Novels of Dorothy Richardson (1918),
by May Sinclair DLB-36

Novels with a Purpose (1864), by
Justin M'Carthy DLB-21

Noventa, Giacomo 1898-1960 . . . . DLB-114

Novikov, Nikolai
Ivanovich 1744-1818 . . . . DLB-150

Novomeský, Laco 1904-1976 . . . . DLB-215

Nowlan, Alden 1933-1983 . . . . DLB-53

Noyes, Alfred 1880-1958 . . . . DLB-20

Noyes, Crosby S. 1825-1908 . . . . DLB-23

Noyes, Nicholas 1647-1717 . . . . DLB-24

Noyes, Theodore W. 1858-1946 . . . . DLB-29

N-Town Plays circa 1468 to early
sixteenth century DLB-146

Nugent, Frank 1908-1965 . . . . DLB-44

Nugent, Richard Bruce 1906- DLB-151

Nušić, Branislav 1864-1938 . . DLB-147; CDWLB-4

Nutt, David [publishing house] DLB-106

Nwapa, Flora
1931-1993 . . . . DLB-125; CDWLB-3

Nye, Bill 1850-1896 . . . . DLB-186

Nye, Edgar Wilson (Bill)
1850-1896 . . . . DLB-11, 23

Nye, Naomi Shihab 1952- DLB-120

Nye, Robert 1939- DLB-14

Nyka-Niliūnas, Alfonsas
1919- DLB-220

O

Oakes Smith, Elizabeth
1806-1893 . . . . DLB-1, 239, 243

Oakes, Urian circa 1631-1681 . . . . DLB-24

Oakley, Violet 1874-1961 . . . . DLB-188

Oates, Joyce Carol 1938- . . . DLB-2, 5, 130; Y-81

Ōba Minako 1930- DLB-182

Ober, Frederick Albion 1849-1913 . . . . . . DLB-189

Ober, William 1920-1993 . . . . Y-93

Oberholtzer, Ellis Paxson 1868-1936 . . . . . DLB-47

Obradović, Dositej 1740?-1811 . . . . DLB-147

O'Brien, Charlotte Grace 1845-1909 . . . . . DLB-240

O'Brien, Edna 1932- . . . DLB-14, 231; CDBLB-8

O'Brien, Fitz-James 1828-1862 . . . . DLB-74

O'Brien, Flann (see O'Nolan, Brian)

O'Brien, Kate 1897-1974 . . . . DLB-15

O'Brien, Tim
1946- DLB-152; Y-80; DS-9; CDALB-7

O'Casey, Sean 1880-1964 . . . . . DLB-10; CDBLB-6

Occom, Samson 1723-1792 . . . . DLB-175

Ochs, Adolph S. 1858-1935 . . . . DLB-25

Ochs-Oakes, George Washington
1861-1931 . . . . DLB-137

O'Connor, Flannery 1925-1964
. . . . DLB-2, 152; Y-80; DS-12; CDALB-1

O'Connor, Frank 1903-1966 . . . . DLB-162

O'Connor, Joseph 1963- DLB-267

Octopus Publishing Group DLB-112

Oda Sakunosuke 1913-1947 . . . . DLB-182

Odell, Jonathan 1737-1818 . . . . DLB-31, 99

O'Dell, Scott 1903-1989 . . . . DLB-52

Odets, Clifford 1906-1963 . . . . DLB-7, 26

Odhams Press Limited DLB-112

Odoevsky, Aleksandr Ivanovich
1802-1839 . . . . DLB-205

Odoevsky, Vladimir Fedorovich
1804 or 1803-1869 . . . . DLB-198

O'Donnell, Peter 1920- DLB-87

O'Donovan, Michael (see O'Connor, Frank)

O'Dowd, Bernard 1866-1953 . . . . DLB-230

Ōe Kenzaburō 1935- DLB-182; Y-94

O'Faolain, Julia 1932- DLB-14, 231

O'Faolain, Sean 1900- DLB-15, 162

Off Broadway and Off-Off Broadway DLB-7

Off-Loop Theatres DLB-7

Offord, Carl Ruthven 1910- DLB-76

O'Flaherty, Liam 1896-1984 . . . DLB-36, 162; Y-84

Ogilvie, J. S., and Company DLB-49

Ogilvy, Eliza 1822-1912 . . . . DLB-199

Ogot, Grace 1930- DLB-125

O'Grady, Desmond 1935- DLB-40

Ogunyemi, Wale 1939- DLB-157

O'Hagan, Howard 1902-1982 . . . . DLB-68

O'Hara, Frank 1926-1966 . . . . DLB-5, 16, 193

O'Hara, John
1905-1970 . . . . DLB-9, 86; DS-2; CDALB-5

John O'Hara's Pottsville Journalism Y-88

O'Hegarty, P. S. 1879-1955 . . . . DLB-201

Okara, Gabriel 1921- DLB-125; CDWLB-3

O'Keeffe, John 1747-1833 . . . . DLB-89

Okes, Nicholas [publishing house] DLB-170

Okigbo, Christopher
1930-1967 . . . . DLB-125; CDWLB-3

Okot p'Bitek 1931-1982 . . . . . DLB-125; CDWLB-3

Okpewho, Isidore 1941- DLB-157

Okri, Ben 1959- DLB-157, 231

Olaudah Equiano and Unfinished Journeys:
The Slave-Narrative Tradition and
Twentieth-Century Continuities, by
Paul Edwards and Pauline T.
Wangman DLB-117

Old English Literature:
An Introduction DLB-146

Old English Riddles
eighth to tenth centuries DLB-146

Old Franklin Publishing House DLB-49

Old German Genesis and *Old German Exodus*
circa 1050-circa 1130 . . . . DLB-148

Old High German Charms and
Blessings DLB-148; CDWLB-2

The *Old High German Isidor*
circa 790-800 . . . . DLB-148

The Old Manse DLB-223

Older, Fremont 1856-1935 . . . . DLB-25

Oldham, John 1653-1683 . . . . DLB-131

Oldman, C. B. 1894-1969 . . . . DLB-201

Olds, Sharon 1942- DLB-120

Olearius, Adam 1599-1671 . . . . DLB-164

O'Leary, Ellen 1831-1889 . . . . DLB-240

Oliphant, Laurence 1829?-1888 . . . . . . DLB-18, 166

Oliphant, Margaret 1828-1897 . . . DLB-18, 159, 190

Oliver, Chad 1928- DLB-8

Oliver, Mary 1935- DLB-5, 193

Ollier, Claude 1922- DLB-83

Olsen, Tillie 1912 or 1913-
.... DLB-28, 206; Y-80; CDALB-7

Olson, Charles 1910-1970 .... DLB-5, 16, 193

Olson, Elder 1909- DLB-48, 63

Omotoso, Kole 1943- DLB-125

Omulevsky, Innokentii Vasil'evich
1836 [or 1837]-1883 .... DLB-238

On Learning to Write.................... Y-88

Ondaatje, Michael 1943- DLB-60

O'Neill, Eugene 1888-1953..... DLB-7; CDALB-5

Eugene O'Neill Memorial Theater
Center DLB-7

Eugene O'Neill's Letters: A Review Y-88

Onetti, Juan Carlos
1909-1994 .... DLB-113; CDWLB-3

Onions, George Oliver 1872-1961 ...... DLB-153

Onofri, Arturo 1885-1928 .... DLB-114

O'Nolan, Brian 1911-1966 .... DLB-231

Opie, Amelia 1769-1853 .... DLB-116, 159

Opitz, Martin 1597-1639............. DLB-164

Oppen, George 1908-1984 .... DLB-5, 165

Oppenheim, E. Phillips 1866-1946 ...... DLB-70

Oppenheim, James 1882-1932 .... DLB-28

Oppenheimer, Joel 1930-1988 ...... DLB-5, 193

Optic, Oliver (see Adams, William Taylor)

Oral History: B. W. Huebsch............. Y-99

Oral History Interview with Donald S.
Klopfer......................... Y-97

Orczy, Emma, Baroness 1865-1947 ...... DLB-70

Oregon Shakespeare Festival Y-00

Origo, Iris 1902-1988 .... DLB-155

Orlovitz, Gil 1918-1973 .... DLB-2, 5

Orlovsky, Peter 1933- DLB-16

Ormond, John 1923- DLB-27

Ornitz, Samuel 1890-1957 .... DLB-28, 44

O'Riordan, Kate 1960- DLB-267

O'Rourke, P. J. 1947- DLB-185

Orten, Jiří 1919-1941 .... DLB-215

Ortese, Anna Maria 1914- DLB-177

Ortiz, Simon J. 1941- DLB-120, 175, 256

Ortnit and *Wolfdietrich* circa 1225-1250.... DLB-138

Orton, Joe 1933-1967 .... DLB-13; CDBLB-8

Orwell, George (Eric Arthur Blair)
1903-1950 .. DLB-15, 98, 195, 255; CDBLB-7

The Orwell Year...................... Y-84

(Re-)Publishing Orwell.................. Y-86

Ory, Carlos Edmundo de 1923- DLB-134

Osbey, Brenda Marie 1957- DLB-120

Osbon, B. S. 1827-1912............... DLB-43

Osborn, Sarah 1714-1796 .... DLB-200

Osborne, John 1929-1994..... DLB-13; CDBLB-7

Osgood, Frances Sargent 1811-1850..... DLB-250

Osgood, Herbert L. 1855-1918.......... DLB-47

Osgood, James R., and Company DLB-49

Osgood, McIlvaine and Company DLB-112

O'Shaughnessy, Arthur 1844-1881...... DLB-35

O'Shea, Patrick [publishing house] DLB-49

Osipov, Nikolai Petrovich
1751-1799 .... DLB-150

Oskison, John Milton 1879-1947 ....DLB-175

Osler, Sir William 1849-1919 ...... DLB-184

Osofisan, Femi 1946- DLB-125; CDWLB-3

Ostenso, Martha 1900-1963 .... DLB-92

Ostrauskas, Kostas 1926- DLB-232

Ostriker, Alicia 1937- DLB-120

Osundare, Niyi
1947- DLB-157; CDWLB-3

Oswald, Eleazer 1755-1795 .... DLB-43

Oswald von Wolkenstein
1376 or 1377-1445 ....DLB-179

Otero, Blas de 1916-1979 .... DLB-134

Otero, Miguel Antonio 1859-1944 ...... DLB-82

Otero, Nina 1881-1965............. DLB-209

Otero Silva, Miguel 1908-1985........ DLB-145

Otfried von Weißenburg
circa 800-circa 875? DLB-148

Otis, Broaders and Company.......... DLB-49

Otis, James (see Kaler, James Otis)

Otis, James, Jr. 1725-1783 .... DLB-31

Ottaway, James 1911- DLB-127

Ottendorfer, Oswald 1826-1900........ DLB-23

Ottieri, Ottiero 1924- DLB-177

Otto-Peters, Louise 1819-1895 .... DLB-129

Otway, Thomas 1652-1685 .... DLB-80

Ouellette, Fernand 1930- DLB-60

Ouida 1839-1908 .... DLB-18, 156

Outing Publishing Company DLB-46

Outlaw Days, by Joyce Johnson........ DLB-16

Overbury, Sir Thomas
circa 1581-1613 .... DLB-151

The Overlook Press DLB-46

Overview of U.S. Book Publishing,
1910-1945 .... DLB-9

Ovid 43 B.C.-A.D. 17...... DLB-211; CDWLB-1

Owen, Guy 1925- DLB-5

Owen, John 1564-1622............. DLB-121

Owen, John [publishing house]......... DLB-49

Owen, Peter, Limited DLB-112

Owen, Robert 1771-1858 ....DLB-107, 158

Owen, Wilfred
1893-1918 .... DLB-20; DS-18; CDBLB-6

The Owl and the Nightingale
circa 1189-1199 .... DLB-146

Owsley, Frank L. 1890-1956 .... DLB-17

Oxford, Seventeenth Earl of, Edward
de Vere 1550-1604.................DLB-172

OyamO (Charles F. Gordon
1943- DLB-266

Ozerov, Vladislav Aleksandrovich
1769-1816..................... DLB-150

Ozick, Cynthia 1928- DLB-28, 152; Y-83

First Strauss "Livings" Awarded to Cynthia
Ozick and Raymond Carver
An Interview with Cynthia Ozick Y-83

P

Pace, Richard 1482?-1536 .... DLB-167

Pacey, Desmond 1917-1975 .... DLB-88

Pack, Robert 1929- DLB-5

Packaging Papa: *The Garden of Eden* Y-86

Padell Publishing Company DLB-46

Padgett, Ron 1942- DLB-5

Padilla, Ernesto Chávez 1944- DLB-122

Page, L. C., and Company............ DLB-49

Page, Louise 1955- DLB-233

Page, P. K. 1916- DLB-68

Page, Thomas Nelson
1853-1922 ....DLB-12, 78; DS-13

Page, Walter Hines 1855-1918........DLB-71, 91

Paget, Francis Edward 1806-1882 ..... DLB-163

Paget, Violet (see Lee, Vernon)

Pagliarani, Elio 1927- DLB-128

Pain, Barry 1864-1928 ....DLB-135, 197

Pain, Philip ?-circa 1666 .... DLB-24

Paine, Robert Treat, Jr. 1773-1811 ..... DLB-37

Paine, Thomas
1737-1809 .... DLB-31, 43, 73, 158; CDALB-2

Painter, George D. 1914- DLB-155

Painter, William 1540?-1594 .... DLB-136

Palazzeschi, Aldo 1885-1974....... DLB-114, 264

Paley, Grace 1922- DLB-28, 218

Paley, William 1743-1805............. DLB-251

Palfrey, John Gorham 1796-1881 .. DLB-1, 30, 235

Palgrave, Francis Turner 1824-1897...... DLB-35

Palmer, Joe H. 1904-1952...............DLB-171

Palmer, Michael 1943- DLB-169

Palmer, Nettie 1885-1964 .... DLB-260

Palmer, Vance 1885-1959............. DLB-260

Paltock, Robert 1697-1767 .... DLB-39

Paludan, Jacob 1896-1975............. DLB-214

Pan Books Limited.................. DLB-112

Panama, Norman 1914- and
Frank, Melvin 1913-1988.......... DLB-26

Panaev, Ivan Ivanovich 1812-1862...... DLB-198

Panaeva, Avdot'ia Iakovlevna
1820-1893 .... DLB-238

Pancake, Breece D'J 1952-1979........ DLB-130

Panduro, Leif 1923-1977 .... DLB-214

Panero, Leopoldo 1909-1962 .... DLB-108

Pangborn, Edgar 1909-1976........... DLB-8

"Panic Among the Philistines": A Postscript,
An Interview with Bryan Griffin Y-81

Panizzi, Sir Anthony 1797-1879 .... DLB-184

Panneton, Philippe (see Ringuet)

Panshin, Alexei 1940- DLB-8

Pansy (see Alden, Isabella)

Pantheon Books DLB-46

Papadat-Bengescu, Hortensia
1876-1955..................... DLB-220

Papantonio, Michael (see Kohn, John S. Van E.)

Paperback Library .DLB-46

Paperback Science Fiction DLB-8

Papini, Giovanni 1881-1956 . . . . .DLB-264

Paquet, Alfons 1881-1944 . . . . .DLB-66

Paracelsus 1493-1541 . . . . .DLB-179

Paradis, Suzanne 1936- DLB-53

Páral, Vladimír, 1932- DLB-232

Pardoe, Julia 1804-1862 . . . . .DLB-166

Paredes, Américo 1915-1999 . . . . .DLB-209

Pareja Diezcanseco, Alfredo 1908-1993 . . .DLB-145

Parents' Magazine Press DLB-46

Parfit, Derek 1942- DLB-262

Parise, Goffredo 1929-1986 . . . . .DLB-177

Parisian Theater, Fall 1984: Toward
     A New Baroque Y-85

Parish, Mitchell 1900-1993 . . . . .DLB-265

Parizeau, Alice 1930- DLB-60

Park, Ruth 1923- DLB-260

Parke, John 1754-1789 . . . . .DLB-31

Parker, Dan 1893-1967 . . . . .DLB-241

Parker, Dorothy 1893-1967 . . . . . . .DLB-11, 45, 86

Parker, Gilbert 1860-1932 . . . . .DLB-99

Parker, J. H. [publishing house] DLB-106

Parker, James 1714-1770 . . . . .DLB-43

Parker, John [publishing house] DLB-106

Parker, Matthew 1504-1575 . . . . .DLB-213

Parker, Stewart 1941-1988 . . . . .DLB-245

Parker, Theodore 1810-1860 . . . . .DLB-1, 235

Parker, William Riley 1906-1968 . . . . . . .DLB-103

Parkes, Bessie Rayner (Madame Belloc)
     1829-1925 . . . . .DLB-240

Parkman, Francis
     1823-1893 . . . . .DLB-1, 30, 183, 186, 235

Parks, Gordon 1912- DLB-33

Parks, Tim 1954- DLB-231

Parks, William 1698-1750 . . . . .DLB-43

Parks, William [publishing house] DLB-49

Parley, Peter (see Goodrich, Samuel Griswold)

Parmenides
     late sixth-fifth century B.C. DLB-176

Parnell, Thomas 1679-1718 . . . . .DLB-95

Parnicki, Teodor 1908-1988 . . . . .DLB-215

Parr, Catherine 1513?-1548 . . . . .DLB-136

Parrington, Vernon L. 1871-1929 . . . . .DLB-17, 63

Parrish, Maxfield 1870-1966 . . . . .DLB-188

Parronchi, Alessandro 1914- DLB-128

Parton, James 1822-1891 . . . . .DLB-30

Parton, Sara Payson Willis
     1811-1872 . . . . .DLB-43, 74, 239

Partridge, S. W., and Company DLB-106

Parun, Vesna 1922- DLB-181; CDWLB-4

Pasinetti, Pier Maria 1913- DLB-177

Pasolini, Pier Paolo 1922- DLB-128, 177

Pastan, Linda 1932- DLB-5

Paston, George (Emily Morse Symonds)
     1860-1936 . . . . .DLB-149, 197

The Paston Letters 1422-1509 . . . . .DLB-146

Pastorius, Francis Daniel
     1651-circa 1720 . . . . .DLB-24

Patchen, Kenneth 1911-1972 . . . . .DLB-16, 48

Pater, Walter
     1839-1894 . . . . DLB-57, 156; CDBLB-4

Aesthetic Poetry (1873) DLB-35

Paterson, A. B. "Banjo" 1864-1941 . . . . . .DLB-230

Paterson, Katherine 1932- DLB-52

Patmore, Coventry 1823-1896 . . . . . . .DLB-35, 98

Paton, Alan 1903-1988 . . . . DS-17

Paton, Joseph Noel 1821-1901 . . . . .DLB-35

Paton Walsh, Jill 1937- DLB-161

Patrick, Edwin Hill ("Ted") 1901-1964 . . .DLB-137

Patrick, John 1906-1995 . . . . .DLB-7

Pattee, Fred Lewis 1863-1950 . . . . .DLB-71

Pattern and Paradigm: History as
     Design, by Judith Ryan DLB-75

Patterson, Alicia 1906-1963 . . . . .DLB-127

Patterson, Eleanor Medill 1881-1948 . . . . .DLB-29

Patterson, Eugene 1923- DLB-127

Patterson, Joseph Medill 1879-1946 . . . . . .DLB-29

Pattillo, Henry 1726-1801 . . . . .DLB-37

Paul, Elliot 1891-1958 . . . . .DLB-4

Paul, Jean (see Richter, Johann Paul Friedrich)

Paul, Kegan, Trench, Trubner and
     Company Limited DLB-106

Paul, Peter, Book Company DLB-49

Paul, Stanley, and Company Limited DLB-112

Paulding, James Kirke
     1778-1860 . . . . DLB-3, 59, 74, 250

Paulin, Tom 1949- DLB-40

Pauper, Peter, Press DLB-46

Pavese, Cesare 1908-1950 . . . . DLB-128, 177

Pavić, Milorad 1929- DLB-181; CDWLB-4

Pavlov, Konstantin 1933- DLB-181

Pavlov, Nikolai Filippovich 1803-1864 . . . .DLB-198

Pavlova, Karolina Karlovna 1807-1893 . . . .DLB-205

Pavlović, Miodrag
     1928- DLB-181; CDWLB-4

Paxton, John 1911-1985 . . . . .DLB-44

Payn, James 1830-1898 . . . . .DLB-18

Payne, John 1842-1916 . . . . .DLB-35

Payne, John Howard 1791-1852 . . . . .DLB-37

Payson and Clarke DLB-46

Paz, Octavio 1914-1998 . . . . .Y-90, Y-98

Pazzi, Roberto 1946- DLB-196

Pea, Enrico 1881-1958 . . . . .DLB-264

Peabody, Elizabeth Palmer 1804-1894 . .DLB-1, 223

Peabody, Elizabeth Palmer
     [publishing house] DLB-49

Peabody, Josephine Preston 1874-1922 . . .DLB-249

Peabody, Oliver William Bourn
     1799-1848 . . . . .DLB-59

Peace, Roger 1899-1968 . . . . .DLB-127

Peacham, Henry 1578-1644? DLB-151

Peacham, Henry, the Elder
     1547-1634 . . . . DLB-172, 236

Peachtree Publishers, Limited DLB-46

Peacock, Molly 1947- DLB-120

Peacock, Thomas Love 1785-1866 . . .DLB-96, 116

Pead, Deuel ?-1727 . . . . .DLB-24

Peake, Mervyn 1911-1968 . . . . . .DLB-15, 160, 255

Peale, Rembrandt 1778-1860 . . . . .DLB-183

Pear Tree Press DLB-112

Pearce, Philippa 1920- DLB-161

Pearson, H. B. [publishing house] DLB-49

Pearson, Hesketh 1887-1964 . . . . .DLB-149

Pechersky, Andrei (see Mel'nikov, Pavel Ivanovich)

Peck, George W. 1840-1916 . . . . .DLB-23, 42

Peck, H. C., and Theo. Bliss
     [publishing house] DLB-49

Peck, Harry Thurston 1856-1914 . . . . .DLB-71, 91

Peden, William 1913-1999 . . . . .DLB-234

Peele, George 1556-1596 . . . . .DLB-62, 167

Pegler, Westbrook 1894-1969 . . . . .DLB-171

Péguy, Charles Pierre 1873-1914 . . . . . . .DLB-258

Pekić, Borislav 1930-1992 . . .DLB-181; CDWLB-4

Pellegrini and Cudahy DLB-46

Pelletier, Aimé (see Vac, Bertrand)

Pelletier, Francine 1959- DLB-251

Pemberton, Sir Max 1863-1950 . . . . .DLB-70

de la Peña, Terri 1947- DLB-209

Penfield, Edward 1866-1925 . . . . .DLB-188

Penguin Books [U.K.] DLB-112

Penguin Books [U.S.] DLB-46

Penn Publishing Company DLB-49

Penn, William 1644-1718 . . . . .DLB-24

Penna, Sandro 1906-1977 . . . . .DLB-114

Pennell, Joseph 1857-1926 . . . . .DLB-188

Penner, Jonathan 1940- Y-83

Pennington, Lee 1939- Y-82

Penton, Brian 1904-1951 . . . . .DLB-260

Pepys, Samuel
     1633-1703 . . . . .DLB-101, 213; CDBLB-2

Percy, Thomas 1729-1811 . . . . .DLB-104

Percy, Walker 1916-1990 . . . . . DLB-2; Y-80, Y-90

Percy, William 1575-1648 . . . . .DLB-172

Perec, Georges 1936-1982 . . . . .DLB-83

Perelman, Bob 1947- DLB-193

Perelman, S. J. 1904-1979 . . . . .DLB-11, 44

Perez, Raymundo "Tigre" 1946- DLB-122

Peri Rossi, Cristina 1941- DLB-145

Perkins, Eugene 1932- DLB-41

Perkoff, Stuart Z. 1930-1974 . . . . .DLB-16

Perley, Moses Henry 1804-1862 . . . . .DLB-99

Permabooks DLB-46

Perovsky, Aleksei Alekseevich
     (Antonii Pogorel'sky) 1787-1836 . . . . .DLB-198

Perri, Henry 1561-1617 . . . . .DLB-236

Perrin, Alice 1867-1934 . . . . .DLB-156

Perry, Bliss 1860-1954 . . . . DLB-71

Perry, Eleanor 1915-1981 . . . . DLB-44

Perry, Henry (see Perri, Henry)

Perry, Matthew 1794-1858 . . . . DLB-183

Perry, Sampson 1747-1823 . . . . DLB-158

Perse, Saint-John 1887-1975 . . . . DLB-258

Persius A.D. 34-A.D. 62 . . . . DLB-211

Perutz, Leo 1882-1957 . . . . DLB-81

Pesetsky, Bette 1932- DLB-130

Pestalozzi, Johann Heinrich 1746-1827 . . . . DLB-94

Peter, Laurence J. 1919-1990 . . . . DLB-53

Peter of Spain circa 1205-1277 . . . . DLB-115

Peterkin, Julia 1880-1961 . . . . DLB-9

Peters, Lenrie 1932- DLB-117

Peters, Robert 1924- DLB-105

"Foreword to *Ludwig of Bavaria*" DLB-105

Petersham, Maud 1889-1971 and
    Petersham, Miska 1888-1960 . . . . DLB-22

Peterson, Charles Jacobs 1819-1887 . . . . . . DLB-79

Peterson, Len 1917- DLB-88

Peterson, Levi S. 1933- DLB-206

Peterson, Louis 1922-1998 . . . . DLB-76

Peterson, T. B., and Brothers DLB-49

Petitclair, Pierre 1813-1860 . . . . DLB-99

Petrescu, Camil 1894-1957 . . . . DLB-220

Petronius circa A.D. 20-A.D. 66
    . . . . DLB-211; CDWLB-1

Petrov, Aleksandar 1938- DLB-181

Petrov, Gavriil 1730-1801 . . . . DLB-150

Petrov, Valeri 1920- DLB-181

Petrov, Vasilii Petrovich 1736-1799 . . . . . DLB-150

Petrović, Rastko
    1898-1949 . . . . DLB-147; CDWLB-4

Petruslied circa 854? DLB-148

Petry, Ann 1908-1997 . . . . DLB-76

Pettie, George circa 1548-1589 . . . . DLB-136

Peyton, K. M. 1929- DLB-161

Pfaffe Konrad flourished circa 1172 . . . . . DLB-148

Pfaffe Lamprecht flourished circa 1150 . . DLB-148

Pfeiffer, Emily 1827-1890 . . . . DLB-199

Pforzheimer, Carl H. 1879-1957 . . . . DLB-140

Phaedrus circa 18 B.C.-circa A.D. 50 . . . . DLB-211

Phaer, Thomas 1510?-1560 . . . . DLB-167

Phaidon Press Limited DLB-112

Pharr, Robert Deane 1916-1992 . . . . DLB-33

Phelps, Elizabeth Stuart 1815-1852 . . . . . DLB-202

Phelps, Elizabeth Stuart 1844-1911 . . . DLB-74, 221

Philander von der Linde
    (see Mencke, Johann Burckhard)

Philby, H. St. John B. 1885-1960 . . . . . . DLB-195

Philip, Marlene Nourbese 1947- DLB-157

Philippe, Charles-Louis 1874-1909 . . . . . . DLB-65

Philips, John 1676-1708 . . . . DLB-95

Philips, Katherine 1632-1664 . . . . DLB-131

Phillipps, Sir Thomas 1792-1872 . . . . DLB-184

Phillips, Caryl 1958- DLB-157

Phillips, David Graham 1867-1911 . . . . . DLB-9, 12

Phillips, Jayne Anne 1952- Y-80

Phillips, Robert 1938- DLB-105

"Finding, Losing, Reclaiming: A Note
    on My Poems" DLB-105

Phillips, Sampson and Company DLB-49

Phillips, Stephen 1864-1915 . . . . DLB-10

Phillips, Ulrich B. 1877-1934 . . . . DLB-17

Phillips, Wendell 1811-1884 . . . . DLB-235

Phillips, Willard 1784-1873 . . . . DLB-59

Phillips, William 1907- DLB-137

Phillpotts, Adelaide Eden (Adelaide Ross)
    1896-1993 . . . . DLB-191

Phillpotts, Eden 1862-1960 . . . DLB-10, 70, 135, 153

Philo circa 20-15 B.C.-circa A.D. 50 . . . . . DLB-176

Philosophical Library DLB-46

Phinney, Elihu [publishing house] DLB-49

Phoenix, John (see Derby, George Horatio)

PHYLON (Fourth Quarter, 1950),
    The Negro in Literature:
    The Current Scene DLB-76

Physiologus circa 1070-circa 1150 . . . . . DLB-148

Piccolo, Lucio 1903-1969 . . . . DLB-114

Pickard, Tom 1946- DLB-40

Pickering, William [publishing house] . . . DLB-106

Pickthall, Marjorie 1883-1922 . . . . DLB-92

Pictorial Printing Company DLB-49

Pielmeier, John 1949- DLB-266

Piercy, Marge 1936- DLB-120, 227

Pierro, Albino 1916- DLB-128

Pignotti, Lamberto 1926- DLB-128

Pike, Albert 1809-1891 . . . . DLB-74

Pike, Zebulon Montgomery
    1779-1813 . . . . DLB-183

Pillat, Ion 1891-1945 . . . . DLB-220

Pilon, Jean-Guy 1930- DLB-60

Pinckney, Eliza Lucas 1722-1793 . . . . DLB-200

Pinckney, Josephine 1895-1957 . . . . DLB-6

Pindar circa 518 B.C.-circa 438 B.C.
    . . . . DLB-176; CDWLB-1

Pindar, Peter (see Wolcot, John)

Pineda, Cecile 1942- DLB-209

Pinero, Arthur Wing 1855-1934 . . . . DLB-10

Piñero, Miguel 1946-1988 . . . . DLB-266

Pinget, Robert 1919-1997 . . . . DLB-83

Pinkney, Edward Coote 1802-1828 . . . . . DLB-248

Pinnacle Books DLB-46

Piñon, Nélida 1935- DLB-145

Pinsky, Robert 1940- Y-82

Robert Pinsky Reappointed Poet Laureate Y-98

Pinter, Harold 1930- DLB-13; CDBLB-8

Piontek, Heinz 1925- DLB-75

Piozzi, Hester Lynch [Thrale]
    1741-1821 . . . . DLB-104, 142

Piper, H. Beam 1904-1964 . . . . DLB-8

Piper, Watty DLB-22

Pirandello, Luigi 1868-1936 . . . . DLB-264

Pirckheimer, Caritas 1467-1532 . . . . DLB-179

Pirckheimer, Willibald 1470-1530 . . . . . . DLB-179

Pisar, Samuel 1929- Y-83

Pisemsky, Aleksai Feofilaktovich
    1821-1881 . . . . DLB-238

Pitkin, Timothy 1766-1847 . . . . DLB-30

The Pitt Poetry Series: Poetry Publishing
    Today Y-85

Pitter, Ruth 1897- DLB-20

Pix, Mary 1666-1709 . . . . DLB-80

Pixérécourt, René Charles Guilbert de
    1773-1844 . . . . DLB-192

Plaatje, Sol T. 1876-1932 . . . . DLB-125, 225

Plante, David 1940- Y-83

Platen, August von 1796-1835 . . . . DLB-90

Plath, Sylvia
    1932-1963 . . . . DLB-5, 6, 152; CDALB-1

Plato circa 428 B.C.-348-347 B.C.
    . . . . DLB-176; CDWLB-1

Plato, Ann 1824?-? DLB-239

Platon 1737-1812 . . . . DLB-150

Platt, Charles 1945- DLB-261

Platt and Munk Company DLB-46

Plautus circa 254 B.C.-184 B.C.
    . . . . DLB-211; CDWLB-1

Playboy Press DLB-46

Playford, John [publishing house] DLB-170

Plays, Playwrights, and Playgoers DLB-84

Playwrights on the Theater DLB-80

Der Pleier flourished circa 1250 . . . . DLB-138

Pleijel, Agneta 1940- DLB-257

Plenzdorf, Ulrich 1934- DLB-75

Plessen, Elizabeth 1944- DLB-75

Pletnev, Petr Aleksandrovich
    1792-1865 . . . . DLB-205

Pliekšāne, Elza Rozenberga (see Aspazija)

Pliekšāns, Jānis (see Rainis, Jānis)

Plievier, Theodor 1892-1955 . . . . DLB-69

Plimpton, George 1927- DLB-185, 241; Y-99

Pliny the Elder A.D. 23/24-A.D. 79 . . . . . DLB-211

Pliny the Younger
    circa A.D. 61-A.D. 112 . . . . DLB-211

Plomer, William
    1903-1973 . . . . DLB-20, 162, 191, 225

Plotinus 204-270 . . . . DLB-176; CDWLB-1

Plowright, Teresa 1952- DLB-251

Plume, Thomas 1630-1704 . . . . DLB-213

Plumly, Stanley 1939- DLB-5, 193

Plumpp, Sterling D. 1940- DLB-41

Plunkett, James 1920- DLB-14

Plutarch
    circa 46-circa 120 . . . . . . DLB-176; CDWLB-1

Plymell, Charles 1935- DLB-16

Pocket Books DLB-46

Poe, Edgar Allan 1809-1849
    . . . . DLB-3, 59, 73, 74, 248; CDALB-2

Poe, James 1921-1980 . . . . .DLB-44

The Poet Laureate of the United States
Statements from Former Consultants
in Poetry Y-86

Pogodin, Mikhail Petrovich
1800-1875 . . . . .DLB-198

Pogorel'sky, Antonii
(see Perovsky, Aleksei Alekseevich)

Pohl, Frederik 1919- DLB-8

Poirier, Louis (see Gracq, Julien)

Poláček, Karel 1892-1945 . . .DLB-215; CDWLB-4

Polanyi, Michael 1891-1976 . . . . .DLB-100

Pole, Reginald 1500-1558 . . . . .DLB-132

Polevoi, Nikolai Alekseevich
1796-1846 .DLB-198

Polezhaev, Aleksandr Ivanovich
1804-1838 .DLB-205

Poliakoff, Stephen 1952- DLB-13

Polidori, John William 1795-1821 . . . . . .DLB-116

Polite, Carlene Hatcher 1932- DLB-33

Pollard, Alfred W. 1859-1944 . . . . .DLB-201

Pollard, Edward A. 1832-1872 . . . . .DLB-30

Pollard, Graham 1903-1976 . . . . .DLB-201

Pollard, Percival 1869-1911 . . . . .DLB-71

Pollard and Moss .DLB-49

Pollock, Sharon 1936- DLB-60

Polonsky, Abraham 1910-1999 . . . . .DLB-26

Polotsky, Simeon 1629-1680 . . . . .DLB-150

Polybius circa 200 B.C.-118 B.C. DLB-176

Pomialovsky, Nikolai Gerasimovich
1835-1863 .DLB-238

Pomilio, Mario 1921-1990 . . . . .DLB-177

Ponce, Mary Helen 1938- DLB-122

Ponce-Montoya, Juanita 1949- DLB-122

Ponet, John 1516?-1556 . . . . .DLB-132

Ponge, Francis 1899-1988 . . . . .DLB-258

Poniatowski, Elena
1933- DLB-113; CDWLB-3

Ponsard, François 1814-1867 . . . . .DLB-192

Ponsonby, William [publishing house] . . .DLB-170

Pontiggia, Giuseppe 1934- DLB-196

Pony Stories DLB-160

Poole, Ernest 1880-1950 . . . . .DLB-9

Poole, Sophia 1804-1891 . . . . .DLB-166

Poore, Benjamin Perley 1820-1887 . . . . . .DLB-23

Popa, Vasko 1922-1991 . . . . .DLB-181; CDWLB-4

Pope, Abbie Hanscom 1858-1894 . . . . . .DLB-140

Pope, Alexander
1688-1744 . . . . . .DLB-95, 101, 213; CDBLB-2

Popov, Mikhail Ivanovich
1742-circa 1790 . . . . .DLB-150

Popović, Aleksandar 1929-1996 . . . . .DLB-181

Popper, Sir Karl R. 1902-1994 . . . . .DLB-262

Popular Library .DLB-46

Porete, Marguerite ?-1310 . . . . .DLB-208

Porlock, Martin (see MacDonald, Philip)

Porpoise Press .DLB-112

Porta, Antonio 1935-1989 . . . . .DLB-128

Porter, Anna Maria 1780-1832 . . . . .DLB-116, 159

Porter, Cole 1891-1964 . . . . .DLB-265

Porter, David 1780-1843 . . . . .DLB-183

Porter, Eleanor H. 1868-1920 . . . . .DLB-9

Porter, Gene Stratton (see Stratton-Porter, Gene)

Porter, Hal 1911-1984 . . . . .DLB-260

Porter, Henry ?-? DLB-62

Porter, Jane 1776-1850 . . . . .DLB-116, 159

Porter, Katherine Anne 1890-1980
. . . . .DLB-4, 9, 102; Y-80; DS-12; CDALB-7

Porter, Peter 1929- DLB-40

Porter, William Sydney
1862-1910 . . . . . . .DLB-12, 78, 79; CDALB-3

Porter, William T. 1809-1858 . . . . .DLB-3, 43, 250

Porter and Coates DLB-49

Portillo Trambley, Estela 1927-1998 . . . . .DLB-209

Portis, Charles 1933- DLB-6

Posey, Alexander 1873-1908 . . . . .DLB-175

Postans, Marianne circa 1810-1865 . . . . . .DLB-166

Postl, Carl (see Sealsfield, Carl)

Poston, Ted 1906-1974 . . . . .DLB-51

Potekhin, Aleksei Antipovich 1829-1908 . .DLB-238

Potok, Chaim 1929- DLB-28, 152

A Conversation with Chaim Potok Y-84

Potter, Beatrix 1866-1943 . . . . .DLB-141

Potter, David M. 1910-1971 . . . . .DLB-17

Potter, Dennis 1935-1994 . . . . .DLB-233

The Harry Potter Phenomenon Y-99

Potter, John E., and Company DLB-49

Pottle, Frederick A. 1897-1987 . . . . .DLB-103; Y-87

Poulin, Jacques 1937- DLB-60

Pound, Ezra 1885-1972
. . . . .DLB-4, 45, 63; DS-15; CDALB-4

Poverman, C. E. 1944- DLB-234

Povich, Shirley 1905-1998 . . . . .DLB-171

Powell, Anthony 1905-2000 . . .DLB-15; CDBLB-7

The Anthony Powell Society: Powell and
the First Biennial Conference Y-01

Dawn Powell, Where Have You Been All
Our Lives? Y-97

Powell, John Wesley 1834-1902 . . . . .DLB-186

Powell, Padgett 1952- DLB-234

Powers, J. F. 1917-1999 . . . . .DLB-130

Powers, Jimmy 1903-1995 . . . . .DLB-241

Pownall, David 1938- DLB-14

Powys, John Cowper 1872-1963 . . . . .DLB-15, 255

Powys, Llewelyn 1884-1939 . . . . .DLB-98

Powys, T. F. 1875-1953 . . . . .DLB-36, 162

Poynter, Nelson 1903-1978 . . . . .DLB-127

The Practice of Biography: An Interview
with Stanley Weintraub Y-82

The Practice of Biography II: An Interview
with B. L. Reid Y-83

The Practice of Biography III: An Interview
with Humphrey Carpenter Y-84

The Practice of Biography IV: An Interview with
William Manchester Y-85

The Practice of Biography VI: An Interview with
David Herbert Donald Y-87

The Practice of Biography VII: An Interview with
John Caldwell Guilds Y-92

The Practice of Biography VIII: An Interview
with Joan Mellen Y-94

The Practice of Biography IX: An Interview
with Michael Reynolds Y-95

Prados, Emilio 1899-1962 . . . . .DLB-134

Praed, Mrs. Caroline (see Praed, Rosa)

Praed, Rosa (Mrs. Caroline Praed)
1851-1935 .DLB-230

Praed, Winthrop Mackworth 1802-1839 . . .DLB-96

Praeger Publishers DLB-46

Praetorius, Johannes 1630-1680 . . . . .DLB-168

Pratolini, Vasco 1913-1991 . . . . .DLB-177

Pratt, E. J. 1882-1964 . . . . .DLB-92

Pratt, Samuel Jackson 1749-1814 . . . . .DLB-39

Preciado Martin, Patricia 1939- DLB-209

Preface to The History of Romances (1715), by
Pierre Daniel Huet [excerpts] DLB-39

Préfontaine, Yves 1937- DLB-53

Prelutsky, Jack 1940- DLB-61

Premisses, by Michael Hamburger DLB-66

Prentice, George D. 1802-1870 . . . . .DLB-43

Prentice-Hall DLB-46

Prescott, Orville 1906-1996 . . . . Y-96

Prescott, William Hickling
1796-1859 . . . . .DLB-1, 30, 59, 235

The Present State of the English Novel (1892),
by George Saintsbury DLB-18

Prešeren, Franče
1800-1849 . . . . .DLB-147; CDWLB-4

Preston, Margaret Junkin
1820-1897 . . . . .DLB-239, 248

Preston, May Wilson 1873-1949 . . . . .DLB-188

Preston, Thomas 1537-1598 . . . . .DLB-62

Prévert, Jacques 1900-1977 . . . . .DLB-258

Prichard, Katharine Susannah
1883-1969 .DLB-260

Price, Reynolds 1933- DLB-2, 218

Price, Richard 1723-1791 . . . . .DLB-158

Price, Richard 1949- Y-81

Prideaux, John 1578-1650 . . . . .DLB-236

Priest, Christopher 1943- DLB-14, 207, 261

Priestley, J. B. 1894-1984
. . .DLB-10, 34, 77, 100, 139; Y-84; CDBLB-6

Priestley, Joseph 1733-1804 . . . . .DLB-252

Primary Bibliography: A Retrospective Y-95

Prime, Benjamin Young 1733-1791 . . . . . . .DLB-31

Primrose, Diana floruit circa 1630 . . . . . . .DLB-126

Prince, F. T. 1912- DLB-20

Prince, Nancy Gardner 1799-? DLB-239

Prince, Thomas 1687-1758 . . . . .DLB-24, 140

Pringle, Thomas 1789-1834 . . . . .DLB-225

Printz, Wolfgang Casper 1641-1717 . . . . . .DLB-168

Prior, Matthew 1664-1721 .... DLB-95

Prisco, Michele 1920- DLB-177

Pritchard, William H. 1932- DLB-111

Pritchett, V. S. 1900-1997.......... DLB-15, 139

Probyn, May 1856 or 1857-1909 .... DLB-199

Procter, Adelaide Anne 1825-1864... DLB-32, 199

Procter, Bryan Waller 1787-1874 .... DLB-96, 144

Proctor, Robert 1868-1903 .... DLB-184

Producing Dear Bunny, Dear Volodya: The Friendship and the Feud Y-97

The Profession of Authorship:
   Scribblers for Bread Y-89

Prokopovich, Feofan 1681?-1736 .... DLB-150

Prokosch, Frederic 1906-1989 .... DLB-48

The Proletarian Novel DLB-9

Pronzini, Bill 1943- DLB-226

Propertius circa 50 B.C.-post 16 B.C.
   .... DLB-211; CDWLB-1

Propper, Dan 1937- DLB-16

Prose, Francine 1947- DLB-234

Protagoras circa 490 B.C.-420 B.C. DLB-176

Proud, Robert 1728-1813 .... DLB-30

Proust, Marcel 1871-1922............ DLB-65

Prynne, J. H. 1936- DLB-40

Przybyszewski, Stanislaw 1868-1927 ..... DLB-66

Pseudo-Dionysius the Areopagite floruit
   circa 500..................... DLB-115

Public Domain and the Violation of Texts.... Y-97

The Public Lending Right in America Statement by Sen. Charles McC. Mathias, Jr. PLR and the Meaning of Literary Property Statements on PLR by American Writers............. Y-83

The Public Lending Right in the United Kingdom Public Lending Right: The First Year in the United Kingdom Y-83

The Publication of English
   Renaissance Plays DLB-62

Publications and Social Movements
   [Transcendentalism]................ DLB-1

Publishers and Agents: The Columbia
   Connection....................... Y-87

Publishing Fiction at LSU Press Y-87

The Publishing Industry in 1998:
   Sturm-und-drang.com Y-98

The Publishing Industry in 1999 .... Y-99

Pückler-Muskau, Hermann von
   1785-1871 ....DLB-133

Pufendorf, Samuel von 1632-1694 ...... DLB-168

Pugh, Edwin William 1874-1930 .... DLB-135

Pugin, A. Welby 1812-1852........... DLB-55

Puig, Manuel 1932-1990.... DLB-113; CDWLB-3

Pulitzer, Joseph 1847-1911 .... DLB-23

Pulitzer, Joseph, Jr. 1885-1955 ...... DLB-29

Pulitzer Prizes for the Novel,
   1917-1945...................... DLB-9

Pulliam, Eugene 1889-1975........ DLB-127

Purcell, Deirdre 1945- DLB-267

Purchas, Samuel 1577?-1626......... DLB-151

Purdy, Al 1918-2000................ DLB-88

Purdy, James 1923- DLB-2, 218

Purdy, Ken W. 1913-1972 .... DLB-137

Pusey, Edward Bouverie 1800-1882..... DLB-55

Pushkin, Aleksandr Sergeevich
   1799-1837..................... DLB-205

Pushkin, Vasilii L'vovich
   1766-1830..................... DLB-205

Putnam, George Palmer
   1814-1872..............DLB-3, 79, 250, 254

G. P. Putnam [publishing house] DLB-254

G. P. Putnam's Sons [U.K.] DLB-106

G. P. Putnam's Sons [U.S.] DLB-49

A Publisher's Archives: G. P. Putnam Y-92

Putnam, Samuel 1892-1950 .... DLB-4

Puzo, Mario 1920-1999 .... DLB-6

Pyle, Ernie 1900-1945................ DLB-29

Pyle, Howard
   1853-1911 .... DLB-42, 188; DS-13

Pym, Barbara 1913-1980 ......DLB-14, 207; Y-87

Pynchon, Thomas 1937- DLB-2, 173

Pyramid Books.................... DLB-46

Pyrnelle, Louise-Clarke 1850-1907...... DLB-42

Pythagoras circa 570 B.C.-? DLB-176

Q

Quad, M. (see Lewis, Charles B.)

Quaritch, Bernard 1819-1899......... DLB-184

Quarles, Francis 1592-1644 .... DLB-126

The Quarterly Review 1809-1967 ...... DLB-110

Quasimodo, Salvatore 1901-1968....... DLB-114

Queen, Ellery (see Dannay, Frederic, and Manfred B. Lee)

Queen, Frank 1822-1882 .... DLB-241

The Queen City Publishing House DLB-49

Queneau, Raymond 1903-1976 ..... DLB-72, 258

Quennell, Sir Peter 1905-1993 ..... DLB-155, 195

Quesnel, Joseph 1746-1809 .... DLB-99

The Question of American Copyright
   in the Nineteenth Century
      Preface, by George Haven Putnam
      The Evolution of Copyright, by
         Brander Matthews
      Summary of Copyright Legislation in
         the United States, by R. R. Bowker
      Analysis of the Provisions of the
         Copyright Law of 1891, by
         George Haven Putnam
      The Contest for International Copyright,
         by George Haven Putnam
      Cheap Books and Good Books,
         by Brander Matthews........ DLB-49

Quiller-Couch, Sir Arthur Thomas
   1863-1944 ....DLB-135, 153, 190

Quin, Ann 1936-1973............ DLB-14, 231

Quincy, Samuel, of Georgia ?-? DLB-31

Quincy, Samuel, of Massachusetts
   1734-1789 .... DLB-31

Quinn, Anthony 1915- DLB-122

The Quinn Draft of James Joyce's
   Circe Manuscript Y-00

Quinn, John 1870-1924............. DLB-187

Quiñónez, Naomi 1951- DLB-209

Quintana, Leroy V. 1944- DLB-82

Quintana, Miguel de 1671-1748
   A Forerunner of Chicano Literature . DLB-122

Quintillian
   circa A.D. 40-circa A.D. 96 .... DLB-211

Quintus Curtius Rufus fl. A.D. 35 ...... DLB-211

Quist, Harlin, Books.............. DLB-46

Quoirez, Françoise (see Sagan, Françoise)

R

R-va, Zeneida (see Gan, Elena Andreevna)

Raabe, Wilhelm 1831-1910 .... DLB-129

Raban, Jonathan 1942- DLB-204

Rabe, David 1940- DLB-7, 228

Raboni, Giovanni 1932- DLB-128

Rachilde 1860-1953 .... DLB-123, 192

Racin, Kočo 1908-1943 ....DLB-147

Rackham, Arthur 1867-1939 .... DLB-141

Radauskas, Henrikas
   1910-1970........... DLB-220; CDWLB-4

Radcliffe, Ann 1764-1823 ....DLB-39, 178

Raddall, Thomas 1903-1994 .... DLB-68

Radford, Dollie 1858-1920........... DLB-240

Radichkov, Yordan 1929- DLB-181

Radiguet, Raymond 1903-1923 .... DLB-65

Radishchev, Aleksandr Nikolaevich
   1749-1802.................... DLB-150

Radnóti, Miklós
   1909-1944 ....DLB-215; CDWLB-4

Radványi, Netty Reiling (see Seghers, Anna)

Rahv, Philip 1908-1973 ....DLB-137

Raich, Semen Egorovich 1792-1855..... DLB-205

Raičković, Stevan 1928- DLB-181

Raimund, Ferdinand Jakob 1790-1836 .... DLB-90

Raine, Craig 1944- DLB-40

Raine, Kathleen 1908- DLB-20

Rainis, Jānis 1865-1929 .... DLB-220; CDWLB-4

Rainolde, Richard
   circa 1530-1606 .... DLB-136, 236

Rakić, Milan 1876-1938 .....DLB-147; CDWLB-4

Rakosi, Carl 1903- DLB-193

Ralegh, Sir Walter
   1554?-1618........... DLB-172; CDBLB-1

Ralin, Radoy 1923- DLB-181

Ralph, Julian 1853-1903 .... DLB-23

Ramat, Silvio 1939- DLB-128

Rambler, no. 4 (1750), by Samuel Johnson
   [excerpt]................... DLB-39

Ramée, Marie Louise de la (see Ouida)

Ramírez, Sergío 1942- DLB-145

Ramke, Bin 1947- DLB-120

Ramler, Karl Wilhelm 1725-1798........ DLB-97

Ramon Ribeyro, Julio 1929- DLB-145

Ramos, Manuel 1948- DLB-209

Ramous, Mario 1924- DLB-128

Rampersad, Arnold 1941- DLB-111

Ramsay, Allan 1684 or 1685-1758 . . . . .DLB-95

Ramsay, David 1749-1815 . . . . .DLB-30

Ramsay, Martha Laurens 1759-1811 . . . . .DLB-200

Ramsey, Frank P. 1903-1930 . . . . .DLB-262

Ranck, Katherine Quintana 1942- DLB-122

Rand, Avery and Company DLB-49

Rand, Ayn 1905-1982 . . . . . . .DLB-227; CDALB-7

Rand McNally and Company DLB-49

Randall, David Anton 1905-1975 . . . . . . .DLB-140

Randall, Dudley 1914- DLB-41

Randall, Henry S. 1811-1876 . . . . .DLB-30

Randall, James G. 1881-1953 . . . . .DLB-17

The Randall Jarrell Symposium:
   A Small Collection of Randall Jarrells
   Excerpts From Papers Delivered at the
   Randall Jarrel Symposium Y-86

Randolph, A. Philip 1889-1979 . . . . .DLB-91

Randolph, Anson D. F.
   [publishing house] DLB-49

Randolph, Thomas 1605-1635 . . . . . .DLB-58, 126

Random House DLB-46

Rankin, Ian (Jack Harvey) 1960- DLB-267

Ranlet, Henry [publishing house] DLB-49

Ransom, Harry 1908-1976 . . . . .DLB-187

Ransom, John Crowe
   1888-1974 . . . . .DLB-45, 63; CDALB-7

Ransome, Arthur 1884-1967 . . . . .DLB-160

Raphael, Frederic 1931- DLB-14

Raphaelson, Samson 1896-1983 . . . . .DLB-44

Rashi circa 1040-1105 . . . . .DLB-208

Raskin, Ellen 1928-1984 . . . . .DLB-52

Rastell, John 1475?-1536 . . . . DLB-136, 170

Rattigan, Terence
   1911-1977 . . . . DLB-13; CDBLB-7

Rawlings, Marjorie Kinnan 1896-1953
   . . . . .DLB-9, 22, 102; DS-17; CDALB-7

Rawlinson, Richard 1690-1755 . . . . .DLB-213

Rawlinson, Thomas 1681-1725 . . . . .DLB-213

Raworth, Tom 1938- DLB-40

Ray, David 1932- DLB-5

Ray, Gordon Norton 1915-1986 . . . . DLB-103, 140

Ray, Henrietta Cordelia 1849-1916 . . . . . .DLB-50

Raymond, Ernest 1888-1974 . . . . .DLB-191

Raymond, Henry J. 1820-1869 . . . . . . .DLB-43, 79

Razaf, Andy 1895-1973 . . . . .DLB-265

Michael M. Rea and the Rea Award for the
   Short Story Y-97

Reach, Angus 1821-1856 . . . . .DLB-70

Read, Herbert 1893-1968 . . . . .DLB-20, 149

Read, Martha Meredith DLB-200

Read, Opie 1852-1939 . . . . .DLB-23

Read, Piers Paul 1941- DLB-14

Reade, Charles 1814-1884 . . . . .DLB-21

Reader's Digest Condensed Books DLB-46

Readers Ulysses Symposium Y-97

Reading, Peter 1946- DLB-40

Reading Series in New York City Y-96

The Reality of One Woman's Dream:
   The de Grummond Children's
   Literature Collection Y-99

Reaney, James 1926- DLB-68

Rebhun, Paul 1500?-1546 . . . . .DLB-179

Rèbora, Clemente 1885-1957 . . . . .DLB-114

Rebreanu, Liviu 1885-1944 . . . . .DLB-220

Rechy, John 1934- DLB-122; Y-82

The Recovery of Literature:
   Criticism in the 1990s: A Symposium Y-91

Redding, J. Saunders 1906-1988 . . . . . .DLB-63, 76

Redfield, J. S. [publishing house] DLB-49

Redgrove, Peter 1932- DLB-40

Redmon, Anne 1943- Y-86

Redmond, Eugene B. 1937- DLB-41

Redpath, James [publishing house] DLB-49

Reed, Henry 1808-1854 . . . . .DLB-59

Reed, Henry 1914- DLB-27

Reed, Ishmael
   1938- DLB-2, 5, 33, 169, 227; DS-8

Reed, Rex 1938- DLB-185

Reed, Sampson 1800-1880 . . . . .DLB-1, 235

Reed, Talbot Baines 1852-1893 . . . . .DLB-141

Reedy, William Marion 1862-1920 . . . . . . .DLB-91

Reese, Lizette Woodworth 1856-1935 . . . . .DLB-54

Reese, Thomas 1742-1796 . . . . .DLB-37

Reeve, Clara 1729-1807 . . . . .DLB-39

Preface to *The Old English Baron* (1778) DLB-39

The Progress of Romance (1785) [excerpt] DLB-39

Reeves, James 1909-1978 . . . . .DLB-161

Reeves, John 1926- DLB-88

Reeves-Stevens, Garfield 1953- DLB-251

"Reflections: After a Tornado,"
   by Judson Jerome DLB-105

Regnery, Henry, Company DLB-46

Rehberg, Hans 1901-1963 . . . . .DLB-124

Rehfisch, Hans José 1891-1960 . . . . .DLB-124

Reich, Ebbe Kløvedal 1940- DLB-214

Reid, Alastair 1926- DLB-27

Reid, B. L. 1918-1990 . . . . DLB-111; Y-83

The Practice of Biography II:
   An Interview with B. L. Reid Y-83

Reid, Christopher 1949- DLB-40

Reid, Forrest 1875-1947 . . . . .DLB-153

Reid, Helen Rogers 1882-1970 . . . . .DLB-29

Reid, James ?-? DLB-31

Reid, Mayne 1818-1883 . . . . .DLB-21, 163

Reid, Thomas 1710-1796 . . . . .DLB-31, 252

Reid, V. S. (Vic) 1913-1987 . . . . .DLB-125

Reid, Whitelaw 1837-1912 . . . . .DLB-23

Reilly and Lee Publishing Company DLB-46

Reimann, Brigitte 1933-1973 . . . . .DLB-75

Reinmar der Alte
   circa 1165-circa 1205 . . . . .DLB-138

Reinmar von Zweter
   circa 1200-circa 1250 . . . . .DLB-138

Reisch, Walter 1903-1983 . . . . .DLB-44

Reizei Family DLB-203

Remarks at the Opening of "The Biographical
   Part of Literature" Exhibition, by
   William R. Cagle Y-98

Remarque, Erich Maria
   1898-1970 . . . . .DLB-56; CDWLB-2

Remington, Frederic
   1861-1909 . . . . DLB-12, 186, 188

Reminiscences, by Charles Scribner, Jr. DS-17

Renaud, Jacques 1943- DLB-60

Renault, Mary 1905-1983 . . . . Y-83

Rendell, Ruth 1930- DLB-87

Rensselaer, Maria van Cortlandt van
   1645-1689 . . . . .DLB-200

Repplier, Agnes 1855-1950 . . . . .DLB-221

Representative Men and Women: A Historical
   Perspective on the British Novel,
   1930-1960 . . . . .DLB-15

Research in the American Antiquarian Book
   Trade Y-97

Reshetnikov, Fedor Mikhailovich
   1841-1871 . . . . .DLB-238

Rettenbacher, Simon 1634-1706 . . . . .DLB-168

Reuchlin, Johannes 1455-1522 . . . . .DLB-179

Reuter, Christian 1665-after 1712 . . . . . . .DLB-168

Revell, Fleming H., Company DLB-49

Reverdy, Pierre 1889-1960 . . . . .DLB-258

Reuter, Fritz 1810-1874 . . . . .DLB-129

Reuter, Gabriele 1859-1941 . . . . .DLB-66

Reventlow, Franziska Gräfin zu
   1871-1918 . . . . .DLB-66

Review of Nicholson Baker's *Double Fold:
   Libraries and the Assault on Paper* Y-00

Review of Reviews Office DLB-112

Review of [Samuel Richardson's] *Clarissa* (1748),
   by Henry Fielding DLB-39

The Revolt (1937), by Mary Colum
   [excerpts] DLB-36

Rexroth, Kenneth 1905-1982
   . . . . . DLB-16, 48, 165, 212; Y-82; CDALB-1

Rey, H. A. 1898-1977 . . . . .DLB-22

Reynal and Hitchcock DLB-46

Reynolds, G. W. M. 1814-1879 . . . . .DLB-21

Reynolds, John Hamilton 1794-1852 . . . . . .DLB-96

Reynolds, Sir Joshua 1723-1792 . . . . .DLB-104

Reynolds, Mack 1917- DLB-8

A Literary Archaeologist Digs On: A Brief
   Interview with Michael Reynolds by
   Michael Rogers Y-99

Reznikoff, Charles 1894-1976 . . . . .DLB-28, 45

Rhett, Robert Barnwell 1800-1876 . . . . . . .DLB-43

Rhode, John 1884-1964 . . . . .DLB-77

Rhodes, Eugene Manlove 1869-1934 . . . .DLB-256

Rhodes, James Ford 1848-1927 . . . . .DLB-47

Rhodes, Richard 1937- DLB-185

Rhys, Jean 1890-1979
   . . . . DLB-36, 117, 162; CDBLB-7; CDWLB-3

Ricardo, David 1772-1823 . . . . DLB-107, 158

Ricardou, Jean 1932- DLB-83

Rice, Elmer 1892-1967 . . . . .DLB-4, 7

Rice, Grantland 1880-1954 . . . . .DLB-29, 171

Rich, Adrienne 1929- DLB-5, 67; CDALB-7

Richard de Fournival
1201-1259 or 1260 . . . . DLB-208

Richard, Mark 1955- DLB-234

Richards, David Adams 1950- DLB-53

Richards, George circa 1760-1814 . . . . DLB-37

Richards, Grant [publishing house] DLB-112

Richards, I. A. 1893-1979 . . . . DLB-27

Richards, Laura E. 1850-1943 . . . . DLB-42

Richards, William Carey 1818-1892 . . . . . DLB-73

Richardson, Charles F. 1851-1913 . . . . DLB-71

Richardson, Dorothy M. 1873-1957 . . . . . DLB-36

Richardson, Henry Handel
(Ethel Florence Lindesay
Robertson) 1870-1946 . . . . .DLB-197, 230

Richardson, Jack 1935- DLB-7

Richardson, John 1796-1852 . . . . DLB-99

Richardson, Samuel
1689-1761 . . . . DLB-39, 154; CDBLB-2

Introductory Letters from the Second
Edition of *Pamela* (1741) DLB-39

Postscript to [the Third Edition of]
Clarissa (1751) DLB-39

Preface to the First Edition of
Pamela (1740) DLB-39

Preface to the Third Edition of
Clarissa (1751) [excerpt] DLB-39

Preface to Volume 1 of *Clarissa* (1747) DLB-39

Preface to Volume 3 of *Clarissa* (1748) DLB-39

Richardson, Willis 1889-1977 . . . . DLB-51

Riche, Barnabe 1542-1617 . . . . DLB-136

Richepin, Jean 1849-1926 . . . . DLB-192

Richler, Mordecai 1931- DLB-53

Richter, Conrad 1890-1968 . . . . DLB-9, 212

Richter, Hans Werner 1908- DLB-69

Richter, Johann Paul Friedrich
1763-1825 . . . . DLB-94; CDWLB-2

Rickerby, Joseph [publishing house] DLB-106

Rickword, Edgell 1898-1982 . . . . DLB-20

Riddell, Charlotte 1832-1906 . . . . DLB-156

Riddell, John (see Ford, Corey)

Ridge, John Rollin 1827-1867 . . . . .DLB-175

Ridge, Lola 1873-1941 . . . . DLB-54

Ridge, William Pett 1859-1930 . . . . DLB-135

Riding, Laura (see Jackson, Laura Riding)

Ridler, Anne 1912- DLB-27

Ridruejo, Dionisio 1912-1975 . . . . DLB-108

Riel, Louis 1844-1885 . . . . DLB-99

Riemer, Johannes 1648-1714 . . . . DLB-168

Rifbjerg, Klaus 1931- DLB-214

Riffaterre, Michael 1924- DLB-67

Riggs, Lynn 1899-1954 . . . . .DLB-175

Riis, Jacob 1849-1914 . . . . DLB-23

Riker, John C. [publishing house] DLB-49

Riley, James 1777-1840 . . . . DLB-183

Riley, John 1938-1978 . . . . DLB-40

Rilke, Rainer Maria
1875-1926 . . . . DLB-81; CDWLB-2

Rimanelli, Giose 1926- DLB-177

Rimbaud, Jean-Nicolas-Arthur
1854-1891 . . . . DLB-217

Rinehart and Company DLB-46

Ringuet 1895-1960 . . . . DLB-68

Ringwood, Gwen Pharis 1910-1984 . . . . . . DLB-88

Rinser, Luise 1911- DLB-69

Ríos, Alberto 1952- DLB-122

Ríos, Isabella 1948- DLB-82

Ripley, Arthur 1895-1961 . . . . DLB-44

Ripley, George 1802-1880 . . . . .DLB-1, 64, 73, 235

The Rising Glory of America:
Three Poems DLB-37

The Rising Glory of America:
Written in 1771 (1786),
by Hugh Henry Brackenridge and
Philip Freneau DLB-37

Riskin, Robert 1897-1955 . . . . DLB-26

Risse, Heinz 1898- DLB-69

Rist, Johann 1607-1667 . . . . DLB-164

Ristikivi, Karl 1912-1977 . . . . DLB-220

Ritchie, Anna Mowatt 1819-1870 . . . . . DLB-3, 250

Ritchie, Anne Thackeray 1837-1919 . . . . . DLB-18

Ritchie, Thomas 1778-1854 . . . . DLB-43

Rites of Passage [on William Saroyan] Y-83

The Ritz Paris Hemingway Award Y-85

Rivard, Adjutor 1868-1945 . . . . DLB-92

Rive, Richard 1931-1989 . . . . DLB-125, 225

Rivera, José 1955- DLB-249

Rivera, Marina 1942- DLB-122

Rivera, Tomás 1935-1984 . . . . DLB-82

Rivers, Conrad Kent 1933-1968 . . . . DLB-41

Riverside Press DLB-49

Rivington, Charles [publishing house] . . . DLB-154

Rivington, James circa 1724-1802 . . . . DLB-43

Rivkin, Allen 1903-1990 . . . . DLB-26

Roa Bastos, Augusto 1917- DLB-113

Robbe-Grillet, Alain 1922- DLB-83

Robbins, Tom 1936- Y-80

Roberts, Charles G. D. 1860-1943 . . . . DLB-92

Roberts, Dorothy 1906-1993 . . . . DLB-88

Roberts, Elizabeth Madox
1881-1941 . . . . DLB-9, 54, 102

Roberts, James [publishing house] DLB-154

Roberts, Keith 1935-2000 . . . . DLB-261

Roberts, Kenneth 1885-1957 . . . . DLB-9

Roberts, Michèle 1949- DLB-231

Roberts, Ursula Wyllie (see Miles, Susan)

Roberts, William 1767-1849 . . . . DLB-142

Roberts Brothers DLB-49

Robertson, A. M., and Company DLB-49

Robertson, Ethel Florence Lindesay
(see Richardson, Henry Handel)

Robertson, William 1721-1793 . . . . DLB-104

Robin, Leo 1895-1984 . . . . DLB-265

Robins, Elizabeth 1862-1952 . . . . .DLB-197

Robinson, A. Mary F. (Madame James
Darmesteter, Madame Mary
Duclaux) 1857-1944 . . . . DLB-240

Robinson, Casey 1903-1979 . . . . DLB-44

Robinson, Edwin Arlington
1869-1935 . . . . DLB-54; CDALB-3

Robinson, Henry Crabb 1775-1867 . . . . . .DLB-107

Robinson, James Harvey 1863-1936 . . . . . DLB-47

Robinson, Lennox 1886-1958 . . . . DLB-10

Robinson, Mabel Louise 1874-1962 . . . . . . DLB-22

Robinson, Marilynne 1943- DLB-206

Robinson, Mary 1758-1800 . . . . DLB-158

Robinson, Richard circa 1545-1607 . . . . . DLB-167

Robinson, Therese 1797-1870 . . . . DLB-59, 133

Robison, Mary 1949- DLB-130

Roblès, Emmanuel 1914-1995 . . . . DLB-83

Roccatagliata Ceccardi, Ceccardo
1871-1919 . . . . DLB-114

Roche, Billy 1949- DLB-233

Rochester, John Wilmot, Earl of
1647-1680 . . . . DLB-131

Rochon, Esther 1948- DLB-251

Rock, Howard 1911-1976 . . . . .DLB-127

Rockwell, Norman Perceval 1894-1978 . . DLB-188

Rodgers, Carolyn M. 1945- DLB-41

Rodgers, W. R. 1909-1969 . . . . DLB-20

Rodney, Lester 1911- DLB-241

Rodríguez, Claudio 1934-1999 . . . . DLB-134

Rodríguez, Joe D. 1943- DLB-209

Rodríguez, Luis J. 1954- DLB-209

Rodriguez, Richard 1944- DLB-82, 256

Rodríguez Julia, Edgardo 1946- DLB-145

Roe, E. P. 1838-1888 . . . . DLB-202

Roethke, Theodore
1908-1963 . . . . DLB-5, 206; CDALB-1

Rogers, Jane 1952- DLB-194

Rogers, Pattiann 1940- DLB-105

Rogers, Samuel 1763-1855 . . . . DLB-93

Rogers, Will 1879-1935 . . . . DLB-11

Rohmer, Sax 1883-1959 . . . . DLB-70

Roiphe, Anne 1935- Y-80

Rojas, Arnold R. 1896-1988 . . . . DLB-82

Rolfe, Frederick William
1860-1913 . . . . DLB-34, 156

Rolland, Romain 1866-1944 . . . . DLB-65

Rolle, Richard circa 1290-1300 - 1340 . . . DLB-146

Rölvaag, O. E. 1876-1931 . . . . DLB-9, 212

Romains, Jules 1885-1972 . . . . DLB-65

Roman, A., and Company DLB-49

Roman de la Rose: Guillaume de Lorris
1200 to 1205-circa 1230, Jean de Meun
1235-1240-circa 1305 . . . . DLB-208

Romano, Lalla 1906- DLB-177

Romano, Octavio 1923- DLB-122

Rome, Harold 1908-1993 . . . . DLB-265

Romero, Leo 1950- DLB-122

Romero, Lin 1947- DLB-122

Romero, Orlando 1945- DLB-82

Rook, Clarence 1863-1915 ....DLB-135

Roosevelt, Theodore 1858-1919 .....DLB-47, 186

Root, Waverley 1903-1982 ....DLB-4

Root, William Pitt 1941- DLB-120

Roquebrune, Robert de 1889-1978 ......DLB-68

Rorty, Richard 1931- DLB-246

Rosa, João Guimarães 1908-1967......DLB-113

Rosales, Luis 1910-1992 ....DLB-134

Roscoe, William 1753-1831 ....DLB-163

Danis Rose and the Rendering of *Ulysses* Y-97

Rose, Reginald 1920- DLB-26

Rose, Wendy 1948- DLB-175

Rosegger, Peter 1843-1918 ....DLB-129

Rosei, Peter 1946- DLB-85

Rosen, Norma 1925- DLB-28

Rosenbach, A. S. W. 1876-1952.......DLB-140

Rosenbaum, Ron 1946- DLB-185

Rosenberg, Isaac 1890-1918.........DLB-20, 216

Rosenfeld, Isaac 1918-1956 ....DLB-28

Rosenthal, Harold 1914-1999 ....DLB-241

Jimmy, Red, and Others: Harold Rosenthal
   Remembers the Stars of the Press Box... Y-01

Rosenthal, M. L. 1917-1996..........DLB-5

Rosenwald, Lessing J. 1891-1979.......DLB-187

Ross, Alexander 1591-1654..........DLB-151

Ross, Harold 1892-1951 ....DLB-137

Ross, Jerry (see Adler, Richard)

Ross, Leonard Q. (see Rosten, Leo)

Ross, Lillian 1927- DLB-185

Ross, Martin 1862-1915..............DLB-135

Ross, Sinclair 1908-1996 ....DLB-88

Ross, W. W. E. 1894-1966 ....DLB-88

Rosselli, Amelia 1930-1996 ....DLB-128

Rossen, Robert 1908-1966............DLB-26

Rossetti, Christina 1830-1894 ...DLB-35, 163, 240

Rossetti, Dante Gabriel
   1828-1882 ....DLB-35; CDBLB-4

Rossner, Judith 1935- DLB-6

Rostand, Edmond 1868-1918 ....DLB-192

Rosten, Leo 1908-1997 ....DLB-11

Rostenberg, Leona 1908- DLB-140

Rostopchina, Evdokiia Petrovna
   1811-1858 ....DLB-205

Rostovsky, Dimitrii 1651-1709 ....DLB-150

Rota, Bertram 1903-1966.............DLB-201

   Bertram Rota and His Bookshop........ Y-91

Roth, Gerhard 1942- DLB-85, 124

Roth, Henry 1906?-1995..............DLB-28

Roth, Joseph 1894-1939..............DLB-85

Roth, Philip 1933-
   ....DLB-2, 28, 173; Y-82; CDALB-6

Rothenberg, Jerome 1931- DLB-5, 193

Rothschild Family DLB-184

Rotimi, Ola 1938- DLB-125

Routhier, Adolphe-Basile 1839-1920 .....DLB-99

Routier, Simone 1901-1987 ....DLB-88

Routledge, George, and Sons..........DLB-106

Roversi, Roberto 1923- DLB-128

Rowe, Elizabeth Singer 1674-1737 ....DLB-39, 95

Rowe, Nicholas 1674-1718.............DLB-84

Rowlands, Samuel circa 1570-1630 ......DLB-121

Rowlandson, Mary
   circa 1637-circa 1711 ....DLB-24, 200

Rowley, William circa 1585-1626 ....DLB-58

Rowse, A. L. 1903-1997..............DLB-155

Rowson, Susanna Haswell
   circa 1762-1824 ....DLB-37, 200

Roy, Camille 1870-1943..............DLB-92

Roy, Gabrielle 1909-1983 ....DLB-68

Roy, Jules 1907- DLB-83

The G. Ross Roy Scottish Poetry Collection
   at the University of South Carolina Y-89

The Royal Court Theatre and the English
   Stage Company....................DLB-13

The Royal Court Theatre and the New
   Drama..........................DLB-10

The Royal Shakespeare Company
   at the Swan Y-88

Royall, Anne Newport 1769-1854 ....DLB-43, 248

The Roycroft Printing Shop DLB-49

Royde-Smith, Naomi 1875-1964 ....DLB-191

Royster, Vermont 1914- DLB-127

Royston, Richard [publishing house].....DLB-170

Różewicz, Tadeusz 1921- DLB-232

Ruark, Gibbons 1941- DLB-120

Ruban, Vasilii Grigorevich 1742-1795 ....DLB-150

Rubens, Bernice 1928- DLB-14, 207

Rudd and Carleton DLB-49

Rudd, Steele (Arthur Hoey Davis) DLB-230

Rudkin, David 1936- DLB-13

Rudnick, Paul 1957- DLB-266

Rudolf von Ems circa 1200-circa 1254 ...DLB-138

Ruffin, Josephine St. Pierre
   1842-1924 ....DLB-79

Ruganda, John 1941- DLB-157

Ruggles, Henry Joseph 1813-1906.......DLB-64

Ruiz de Burton, María Amparo
   1832-1895 ....DLB-209, 221

Rukeyser, Muriel 1913-1980 ....DLB-48

Rule, Jane 1931- DLB-60

Rulfo, Juan 1918-1986......DLB-113; CDWLB-3

Rumaker, Michael 1932- DLB-16

Rumens, Carol 1944- DLB-40

Rummo, Paul-Eerik 1942- DLB-232

Runyon, Damon 1880-1946 .....DLB-11, 86, 171

Ruodlieb circa 1050-1075..............DLB-148

Rush, Benjamin 1746-1813 ....DLB-37

Rush, Rebecca 1779-?.................DLB-200

Rushdie, Salman 1947- DLB-194

Rusk, Ralph L. 1888-1962.............DLB-103

Ruskin, John
   1819-1900 ......DLB-55, 163, 190; CDBLB-4

Russ, Joanna 1937- DLB-8

Russell, B. B., and Company...........DLB-49

Russell, Benjamin 1761-1845 ....DLB-43

Russell, Bertrand 1872-1970........DLB-100, 262

Russell, Charles Edward 1860-1941 ......DLB-25

Russell, Charles M. 1864-1926 ....DLB-188

Russell, Eric Frank 1905-1978 ....DLB-255

Russell, Fred 1906- DLB-241

Russell, George William (see AE)

Russell, Countess Mary Annette Beauchamp
   (see Arnim, Elizabeth von)

Russell, R. H., and Son DLB-49

Russell, Willy 1947- DLB-233

Rutebeuf flourished 1249-1277 ....DLB-208

Rutherford, Mark 1831-1913..........DLB-18

Ruxton, George Frederick
   1821-1848 ....DLB-186

Ryan, James 1952- DLB-267

Ryan, Michael 1946- Y-82

Ryan, Oscar 1904- DLB-68

Ryder, Jack 1871-1936...............DLB-241

Ryga, George 1932- DLB-60

Rylands, Enriqueta Augustina Tennant
   1843-1908 ....DLB-184

Rylands, John 1801-1888.............DLB-184

Ryle, Gilbert 1900-1976...............DLB-262

Ryleev, Kondratii Fedorovich
   1795-1826 ....DLB-205

Rymer, Thomas 1643?-1713 ....DLB-101

Ryskind, Morrie 1895-1985...........DLB-26

Rzhevsky, Aleksei Andreevich
   1737-1804 ....DLB-150

S

The Saalfield Publishing Company DLB-46

Saba, Umberto 1883-1957 ....DLB-114

Sábato, Ernesto 1911- DLB-145; CDWLB-3

Saberhagen, Fred 1930- DLB-8

Sabin, Joseph 1821-1881 ....DLB-187

Sacer, Gottfried Wilhelm 1635-1699.....DLB-168

Sachs, Hans 1494-1576 .....DLB-179; CDWLB-2

Sack, John 1930- DLB-185

Sackler, Howard 1929-1982 ....DLB-7

Sackville, Lady Margaret 1881-1963 .....DLB-240

Sackville, Thomas 1536-1608 ....DLB-132

Sackville, Thomas 1536-1608
   and Norton, Thomas 1532-1584......DLB-62

Sackville-West, Edward 1901-1965 ......DLB-191

Sackville-West, V. 1892-1962 ......DLB-34, 195

Sadlier, D. and J., and Company........DLB-49

Sadlier, Mary Anne 1820-1903 ....DLB-99

Sadoff, Ira 1945- DLB-120

Sadoveanu, Mihail 1880-1961 ....DLB-220

Sáenz, Benjamin Alire 1954- DLB-209

Saenz, Jaime 1921-1986 . . . . DLB-145

Saffin, John circa 1626-1710 . . . . DLB-24

Sagan, Françoise 1935- DLB-83

Sage, Robert 1899-1962 . . . . DLB-4

Sagel, Jim 1947- DLB-82

Sagendorph, Robb Hansell 1900-1970 . . . DLB-137

Sahagún, Carlos 1938- DLB-108

Sahkomaapii, Piitai (see Highwater, Jamake)

Sahl, Hans 1902- DLB-69

Said, Edward W. 1935- DLB-67

Saigyō 1118-1190 . . . . DLB-203

Saiko, George 1892-1962 . . . . DLB-85

St. Dominic's Press DLB-112

Saint-Exupéry, Antoine de 1900-1944 . . . . DLB-72

St. John, J. Allen 1872-1957 . . . . DLB-188

St John, Madeleine 1942- DLB-267

St. Johns, Adela Rogers 1894-1988 . . . . . . DLB-29

The St. John's College Robert Graves Trust . . Y-96

St. Martin's Press DLB-46

St. Omer, Garth 1931- DLB-117

Saint Pierre, Michel de 1916-1987 . . . . DLB-83

Sainte-Beuve, Charles-Augustin
1804-1869 . . . . DLB-217

Saints' Lives DLB-208

Saintsbury, George 1845-1933 . . . . . . DLB-57, 149

Saiokuken Sōchō 1448-1532 . . . . DLB-203

Saki (see Munro, H. H.)

Salaam, Kalamu ya 1947- DLB-38

Šalamun, Tomaž 1941-   . . . DLB-181; CDWLB-4

Salas, Floyd 1931- DLB-82

Sálaz-Marquez, Rubén 1935- DLB-122

Salemson, Harold J. 1910-1988 . . . . DLB-4

Salinas, Luis Omar 1937- DLB-82

Salinas, Pedro 1891-1951 . . . . DLB-134

Salinger, J. D.
1919- DLB-2, 102, 173; CDALB-1

Salkey, Andrew 1928- DLB-125

Sallust circa 86 B.C.-35 B.C.
. . . . DLB-211; CDWLB-1

Salt, Waldo 1914- DLB-44

Salter, James 1925- DLB-130

Salter, Mary Jo 1954- DLB-120

Saltus, Edgar 1855-1921 . . . . DLB-202

Saltykov, Mikhail Evgrafovich
1826-1889 . . . . DLB-238

Salustri, Carlo Alberto (see Trilussa)

Salverson, Laura Goodman 1890-1970 . . . . DLB-92

Samain, Albert 1858-1900 . . . . DLB-217

Sampson, Richard Henry (see Hull, Richard)

Samuels, Ernest 1903-1996 . . . . DLB-111

Sanborn, Franklin Benjamin
1831-1917 . . . . DLB-1, 223

Sánchez, Luis Rafael 1936- DLB-145

Sánchez, Philomeno "Phil" 1917- DLB-122

Sánchez, Ricardo 1941-1995 . . . . DLB-82

Sánchez, Saúl 1943- DLB-209

Sanchez, Sonia 1934- DLB-41; DS-8

Sand, George 1804-1876 . . . . DLB-119, 192

Sandburg, Carl
1878-1967 . . . . DLB-17, 54; CDALB-3

Sanders, Edward 1939- DLB-16, 244

Sandoz, Mari 1896-1966 . . . . DLB-9, 212

Sandwell, B. K. 1876-1954 . . . . DLB-92

Sandy, Stephen 1934- DLB-165

Sandys, George 1578-1644 . . . . DLB-24, 121

Sangster, Charles 1822-1893 . . . . DLB-99

Sanguineti, Edoardo 1930- DLB-128

Sanjōnishi Sanetaka 1455-1537 . . . . DLB-203

Sansay, Leonora ?-after 1823 . . . . DLB-200

Sansom, William 1912-1976 . . . . DLB-139

Santayana, George
1863-1952 . . . . DLB-54, 71, 246; DS-13

Santiago, Danny 1911-1988 . . . . DLB-122

Santmyer, Helen Hooven 1895-1986 . . . . Y-84

Sanvitale, Francesca 1928- DLB-196

Sapidus, Joannes 1490-1561 . . . . DLB-179

Sapir, Edward 1884-1939 . . . . DLB-92

Sapper (see McNeile, Herman Cyril)

Sappho circa 620 B.C.-circa 550 B.C.
. . . . DLB-176; CDWLB-1

Saramago, José 1922- Y-98

Sarban (John F. Wall) 1910-1989 . . . . . . DLB-255

Sardou, Victorien 1831-1908 . . . . DLB-192

Sarduy, Severo 1937- DLB-113

Sargent, Pamela 1948- DLB-8

Saro-Wiwa, Ken 1941- DLB-157

Saroyan, William
1908-1981 . . . . . DLB-7, 9, 86; Y-81; CDALB-7

Sarraute, Nathalie 1900-1999 . . . . DLB-83

Sarrazin, Albertine 1937-1967 . . . . DLB-83

Sarris, Greg 1952- DLB-175

Sarton, May 1912-1995 . . . . DLB-48; Y-81

Sartre, Jean-Paul 1905-1980 . . . . DLB-72

Sassoon, Siegfried
1886-1967 . . . . DLB-20, 191; DS-18

Siegfried Loraine Sassoon:
A Centenary Essay
Tributes from Vivien F. Clarke and
Michael Thorpe Y-86

Sata, Ineko 1904- DLB-180

Saturday Review Press DLB-46

Saunders, James 1925- DLB-13

Saunders, John Monk 1897-1940 . . . . DLB-26

Saunders, Margaret Marshall
1861-1947 . . . . DLB-92

Saunders and Otley DLB-106

Saussure, Ferdinand de 1857-1913 . . . . . . DLB-242

Savage, James 1784-1873 . . . . DLB-30

Savage, Marmion W. 1803?-1872 . . . . DLB-21

Savage, Richard 1697?-1743 . . . . DLB-95

Savard, Félix-Antoine 1896-1982 . . . . DLB-68

Savery, Henry 1791-1842 . . . . DLB-230

Saville, (Leonard) Malcolm 1901-1982 . . . DLB-160

Savinio, Alberto 1891-1952 . . . . DLB-264

Sawyer, Robert J. 1960- DLB-251

Sawyer, Ruth 1880-1970 . . . . DLB-22

Sayers, Dorothy L.
1893-1957 . . . . DLB-10, 36, 77, 100; CDBLB-6

Sayle, Charles Edward 1864-1924 . . . . . . DLB-184

Sayles, John Thomas 1950- DLB-44

Sbarbaro, Camillo 1888-1967 . . . . DLB-114

Scalapino, Leslie 1947- DLB-193

Scannell, Vernon 1922- DLB-27

Scarry, Richard 1919-1994 . . . . DLB-61

Schaefer, Jack 1907-1991 . . . . DLB-212

Schaeffer, Albrecht 1885-1950 . . . . DLB-66

Schaeffer, Susan Fromberg 1941- DLB-28

Schaff, Philip 1819-1893 . . . . DS-13

Schaper, Edzard 1908-1984 . . . . DLB-69

Scharf, J. Thomas 1843-1898 . . . . DLB-47

Schede, Paul Melissus 1539-1602 . . . . DLB-179

Scheffel, Joseph Viktor von 1826-1886 . . . DLB-129

Scheffler, Johann 1624-1677 . . . . DLB-164

Schelling, Friedrich Wilhelm Joseph von
1775-1854 . . . . DLB-90

Scherer, Wilhelm 1841-1886 . . . . DLB-129

Scherfig, Hans 1905-1979 . . . . DLB-214

Schickele, René 1883-1940 . . . . DLB-66

Schiff, Dorothy 1903-1989 . . . . DLB-127

Schiller, Friedrich
1759-1805 . . . . DLB-94; CDWLB-2

Schirmer, David 1623-1687 . . . . DLB-164

Schlaf, Johannes 1862-1941 . . . . DLB-118

Schlegel, August Wilhelm 1767-1845 . . . . DLB-94

Schlegel, Dorothea 1763-1839 . . . . DLB-90

Schlegel, Friedrich 1772-1829 . . . . DLB-90

Schleiermacher, Friedrich 1768-1834 . . . . DLB-90

Schlesinger, Arthur M., Jr. 1917- DLB-17

Schlumberger, Jean 1877-1968 . . . . DLB-65

Schmid, Eduard Hermann Wilhelm
(see Edschmid, Kasimir)

Schmidt, Arno 1914-1979 . . . . DLB-69

Schmidt, Johann Kaspar (see Stirner, Max)

Schmidt, Michael 1947- DLB-40

Schmidtbonn, Wilhelm August
1876-1952 . . . . DLB-118

Schmitz, Aron Hector (see Svevo, Italo)

Schmitz, James H. 1911- DLB-8

Schnabel, Johann Gottfried
1692-1760 . . . . DLB-168

Schnackenberg, Gjertrud 1953- DLB-120

Schnitzler, Arthur
1862-1931 . . . . DLB-81, 118; CDWLB-2

Schnurre, Wolfdietrich 1920-1989 . . . . DLB-69

Schocken Books DLB-46

Scholartis Press DLB-112

Scholderer, Victor 1880-1971 . . . . DLB-201

The Schomburg Center for Research
in Black Culture DLB-76

Schönbeck, Virgilio (see Giotti, Virgilio)

Schönherr, Karl 1867-1943.............DLB-118

Schoolcraft, Jane Johnston 1800-1841 ....DLB-175

School Stories, 1914-1960 ....DLB-160

Schopenhauer, Arthur 1788-1860 ....DLB-90

Schopenhauer, Johanna 1766-1838 ....DLB-90

Schorer, Mark 1908-1977.............DLB-103

Schottelius, Justus Georg 1612-1676 .....DLB-164

Schouler, James 1839-1920 ....DLB-47

Schoultz, Solveig von 1907-1996 ....DLB-259

Schrader, Paul 1946- DLB-44

Schreiner, Olive
1855-1920 .... DLB-18, 156, 190, 225

Schroeder, Andreas 1946- DLB-53

Schubart, Christian Friedrich Daniel
1739-1791 ....DLB-97

Schubert, Gotthilf Heinrich 1780-1860 ....DLB-90

Schücking, Levin 1814-1883 ....DLB-133

Schulberg, Budd 1914- DLB-6, 26, 28; Y-81

Schulte, F. J., and Company.............DLB-49

Schulz, Bruno 1892-1942....DLB-215; CDWLB-4

Schulze, Hans (see Praetorius, Johannes)

Schupp, Johann Balthasar 1610-1661.....DLB-164

Schurz, Carl 1829-1906 ....DLB-23

Schuyler, George S. 1895-1977 ....DLB-29, 51

Schuyler, James 1923-1991 ....DLB-5, 169

Schwartz, Delmore 1913-1966 ....DLB-28, 48

Schwartz, Jonathan 1938- Y-82

Schwartz, Lynne Sharon 1939- DLB-218

Schwarz, Sibylle 1621-1638 ....DLB-164

Schwerner, Armand 1927-1999 ....DLB-165

Schwob, Marcel 1867-1905 ....DLB-123

Sciascia, Leonardo 1921-1989 ....DLB-177

Science Fantasy DLB-8

Science-Fiction Fandom and Conventions ...DLB-8

Science-Fiction Fanzines: The Time
Binders DLB-8

Science-Fiction Films DLB-8

Science Fiction Writers of America and the
Nebula Awards DLB-8

Scot, Reginald circa 1538-1599 ....DLB-136

Scotellaro, Rocco 1923-1953 ....DLB-128

Scott, Alicia Anne (Lady John Scott)
1810-1900 ....DLB-240

Scott, Catharine Amy Dawson
1865-1934 ....DLB-240

Scott, Dennis 1939-1991 ....DLB-125

Scott, Dixon 1881-1915 ....DLB-98

Scott, Duncan Campbell 1862-1947.......DLB-92

Scott, Evelyn 1893-1963 ....DLB-9, 48

Scott, F. R. 1899-1985 ....DLB-88

Scott, Frederick George 1861-1944 ....DLB-92

Scott, Geoffrey 1884-1929 ....DLB-149

Scott, Harvey W. 1838-1910 ....DLB-23

Scott, Lady Jane (see Scott, Alicia Anne)

Scott, Paul 1920-1978.............DLB-14, 207

Scott, Sarah 1723-1795 ....DLB-39

Scott, Tom 1918- DLB-27

Scott, Sir Walter 1771-1832
...... DLB-93, 107, 116, 144, 159; CDBLB-3

Scott, Walter, Publishing
Company Limited...............DLB-112

Scott, William Bell 1811-1890 ....DLB-32

Scott, William R. [publishing house] DLB-46

Scott-Heron, Gil 1949- DLB-41

Scribe, Eugene 1791-1861 ....DLB-192

Scribner, Arthur Hawley 1859-1932 .... DS-13, 16

Scribner, Charles 1854-1930 .... DS-13, 16

Scribner, Charles, Jr. 1921-1995 ....Y-95

Reminiscences DS-17

Charles Scribner's Sons DLB-49; DS-13, 16, 17

Scripps, E. W. 1854-1926 ....DLB-25

Scudder, Horace Elisha 1838-1902 ....DLB-42, 71

Scudder, Vida Dutton 1861-1954 ......DLB-71

Scupham, Peter 1933- DLB-40

Seabrook, William 1886-1945 ....DLB-4

Seabury, Samuel 1729-1796 ....DLB-31

Seacole, Mary Jane Grant 1805-1881....DLB-166

The Seafarer circa 970 ....DLB-146

Sealsfield, Charles (Carl Postl)
1793-1864 ....DLB-133, 186

Sears, Edward I. 1819?-1876 ....DLB-79

Sears Publishing Company DLB-46

Seaton, George 1911-1979 ....DLB-44

Seaton, William Winston 1785-1866 ......DLB-43

Secker, Martin [publishing house] DLB-112

Secker, Martin, and Warburg Limited....DLB-112

The Second Annual New York Festival
of Mystery......................Y-00

Second-Generation Minor Poets of the
Seventeenth Century DLB-126

Sedgwick, Arthur George 1844-1915......DLB-64

Sedgwick, Catharine Maria
1789-1867 .... DLB-1, 74, 183, 239, 243

Sedgwick, Ellery 1872-1930............DLB-91

Sedgwick, Eve Kosofsky 1950- DLB-246

Sedley, Sir Charles 1639-1701 ....DLB-131

Seeberg, Peter 1925-1999.............DLB-214

Seeger, Alan 1888-1916 ....DLB-45

Seers, Eugene (see Dantin, Louis)

Segal, Erich 1937- Y-86

Šegedin, Petar 1909- DLB-181

Seghers, Anna 1900-1983 ....DLB-69; CDWLB-2

Seid, Ruth (see Sinclair, Jo)

Seidel, Frederick Lewis 1936- Y-84

Seidel, Ina 1885-1974.................DLB-56

Seifert, Jaroslav
1901-1986 .... DLB-215; Y-84; CDWLB-4

Seigenthaler, John 1927- DLB-127

Seizin Press DLB-112

Séjour, Victor 1817-1874 ....DLB-50

Séjour Marcou et Ferrand, Juan Victor
(see Séjour, Victor)

Sekowski, Jósef-Julian, Baron Brambeus
(see Senkovsky, Osip Ivanovich)

Selby, Bettina 1934- DLB-204

Selby, Hubert, Jr. 1928- DLB-2, 227

Selden, George 1929-1989.............DLB-52

Selden, John 1584-1654 ....DLB-213

Selected English-Language Little Magazines
and Newspapers [France, 1920-1939] ...DLB-4

Selected Humorous Magazines
(1820-1950)....................DLB-11

Selected Science-Fiction Magazines and
Anthologies......................DLB-8

Selenić, Slobodan 1933-1995 ....DLB-181

Self, Edwin F. 1920- DLB-137

Self, Will 1961- DLB-207

Seligman, Edwin R. A. 1861-1939.......DLB-47

Selimović, Meša
1910-1982 ....DLB-181; CDWLB-4

Sellings, Arthur 1911-1968 ....DLB-261

Selous, Frederick Courteney
1851-1917 ....DLB-174

Seltzer, Chester E. (see Muro, Amado)

Seltzer, Thomas [publishing house] DLB-46

Selvon, Sam 1923-1994 .....DLB-125; CDWLB-3

Semmes, Raphael 1809-1877 ....DLB-189

Senancour, Etienne de 1770-1846 ....DLB-119

Sendak, Maurice 1928- DLB-61

Seneca the Elder
circa 54 B.C.-circa A.D. 40 ....DLB-211

Seneca the Younger
circa 1 B.C.-A.D. 65 ....DLB-211; CDWLB-1

Senécal, Eva 1905- DLB-92

Sengstacke, John 1912- DLB-127

Senior, Olive 1941- DLB-157

Senkovsky, Osip Ivanovich
(Józef-Julian Sekowski, Baron Brambeus)
1800-1858.....................DLB-198

Šenoa, August 1838-1881 ... DLB-147; CDWLB-4

"Sensation Novels" (1863), by
H. L. Manse DLB-21

Sepamla, Sipho 1932- DLB-157, 225

Serao, Matilde 1856-1927 ....DLB-264

Seredy, Kate 1899-1975 ....DLB-22

Sereni, Vittorio 1913-1983.............DLB-128

Seres, William [publishing house] DLB-170

Serling, Rod 1924-1975 ....DLB-26

Sernine, Daniel 1955- DLB-251

Serote, Mongane Wally 1944- DLB-125, 225

Serraillier, Ian 1912-1994.............DLB-161

Serrano, Nina 1934- DLB-122

Service, Robert 1874-1958.............DLB-92

Sessler, Charles 1854-1935 ....DLB-187

Seth, Vikram 1952- DLB-120

Seton, Elizabeth Ann 1774-1821........DLB-200

Seton, Ernest Thompson
1860-1942 ....DLB-92; DS-13

Setouchi Harumi 1922- DLB-182

Settle, Mary Lee 1918- DLB-6

Seume, Johann Gottfried 1763-1810 . . . . . DLB-94

Seuse, Heinrich 1295?-1366 . . . . .DLB-179

Seuss, Dr. (see Geisel, Theodor Seuss)

The Seventy-fifth Anniversary of the Armistice:
    The Wilfred Owen Centenary and
    the Great War Exhibit
    at the University of Virginia Y-93

Severin, Timothy 1940- DLB-204

Sewall, Joseph 1688-1769 . . . . DLB-24

Sewall, Richard B. 1908- DLB-111

Sewell, Anna 1820-1878 . . . . DLB-163

Sewell, Samuel 1652-1730 . . . . DLB-24

Sex, Class, Politics, and Religion [in the
    British Novel, 1930-1959] DLB-15

Sexton, Anne 1928-1974 . . . DLB-5, 169; CDALB-1

Seymour-Smith, Martin 1928-1998 . . . . . . DLB-155

Sgorlon, Carlo 1930- DLB-196

Shaara, Michael 1929-1988 . . . . Y-83

Shabel'skaia, Aleksandra Stanislavovna
    1845-1921 . . . . DLB-238

Shadwell, Thomas 1641?-1692 . . . . DLB-80

Shaffer, Anthony 1926- DLB-13

Shaffer, Peter 1926- DLB-13, 233; CDBLB-8

Shaftesbury, Anthony Ashley Cooper,
    Third Earl of 1671-1713 . . . . DLB-101

Shairp, Mordaunt 1887-1939 . . . . DLB-10

Shakespeare, Nicholas 1957- DLB-231

Shakespeare, William
    1564-1616 . . . . . . DLB-62, 172, 263; CDBLB-1

$6,166,000 for a *Book!* Observations on
    *The Shakespeare First Folio: The History
    of the Book* Y-01

The Shakespeare Globe Trust Y-93

Shakespeare Head Press DLB-112

Shakhovskoi, Aleksandr Aleksandrovich
    1777-1846 . . . . DLB-150

Shange, Ntozake 1948- DLB-38, 249

Shapiro, Karl 1913-2000 . . . . DLB-48

Sharon Publications DLB-46

Sharp, Margery 1905-1991 . . . . DLB-161

Sharp, William 1855-1905 . . . . DLB-156

Sharpe, Tom 1928- DLB-14, 231

Shaw, Albert 1857-1947 . . . . DLB-91

Shaw, George Bernard
    1856-1950 . . . . . . .DLB-10, 57, 190, CDBLB-6

Shaw, Henry Wheeler 1818-1885 . . . . DLB-11

Shaw, Joseph T. 1874-1952 . . . . DLB-137

Shaw, Irwin
    1913-1984 . . . . . . DLB-6, 102; Y-84; CDALB-1

Shaw, Mary 1854-1929 . . . . DLB-228

Shaw, Robert 1927-1978 . . . . DLB-13, 14

Shaw, Robert B. 1947- DLB-120

Shawn, Wallace 1943- DLB-266

Shawn, William 1907-1992 . . . . DLB-137

Shay, Frank [publishing house] DLB-46

Shchedrin, N. (see Saltykov, Mikhail Evgrafovich)

Shea, John Gilmary 1824-1892 . . . . DLB-30

Sheaffer, Louis 1912-1993 . . . . DLB-103

Shearing, Joseph 1886-1952 . . . . DLB-70

Shebbeare, John 1709-1788 . . . . DLB-39

Sheckley, Robert 1928- DLB-8

Shedd, William G. T. 1820-1894 . . . . DLB-64

Sheed, Wilfred 1930- DLB-6

Sheed and Ward [U.S.] DLB-46

Sheed and Ward Limited [U.K.] DLB-112

Sheldon, Alice B. (see Tiptree, James, Jr.)

Sheldon, Edward 1886-1946 . . . . DLB-7

Sheldon and Company DLB-49

Sheller, Aleksandr Konstantinovich
    1838-1900 . . . . DLB-238

Shelley, Mary Wollstonecraft 1797-1851
    . . . . .DLB-110, 116, 159, 178; CDBLB-3

Shelley, Percy Bysshe
    1792-1822 . . . . . . DLB-96, 110, 158; CDBLB-3

Shelnutt, Eve 1941- DLB-130

Shenstone, William 1714-1763 . . . . DLB-95

Shepard, Clark and Brown DLB-49

Shepard, Ernest Howard 1879-1976 . . . . . DLB-160

Shepard, Sam 1943- DLB-7, 212

Shepard, Thomas I, 1604 or 1605-1649 . . . DLB-24

Shepard, Thomas, II, 1635-1677 . . . . DLB-24

Shepherd, Luke
    flourished 1547-1554 . . . . DLB-136

Sherburne, Edward 1616-1702 . . . . DLB-131

Sheridan, Frances 1724-1766 . . . . DLB-39, 84

Sheridan, Richard Brinsley
    1751-1816 . . . . DLB-89; CDBLB-2

Sherman, Francis 1871-1926 . . . . DLB-92

Sherman, Martin 1938- DLB-228

Sherriff, R. C. 1896-1975 . . . . . . .DLB-10, 191, 233

Sherrod, Blackie 1919- DLB-241

Sherry, Norman 1935- DLB-155

Sherry, Richard 1506-1551 or 1555 . . . . . DLB-236

Sherwood, Mary Martha 1775-1851 . . . . . DLB-163

Sherwood, Robert E. 1896-1955 . . . .DLB-7, 26, 249

Shevyrev, Stepan Petrovich
    1806-1864 . . . . DLB-205

Shiel, M. P. 1865-1947 . . . . DLB-153

Shiels, George 1886-1949 . . . . DLB-10

Shiga, Naoya 1883-1971 . . . . DLB-180

Shiina Rinzō 1911-1973 . . . . DLB-182

Shikishi Naishinnō 1153?-1201 . . . . DLB-203

Shillaber, Benjamin Penhallow
    1814-1890 . . . . DLB-1, 11, 235

Shimao Toshio 1917-1986 . . . . DLB-182

Shimazaki, Tōson 1872-1943 . . . . DLB-180

Shine, Ted 1931- DLB-38

Shinkei 1406-1475 . . . . DLB-203

Ship, Reuben 1915-1975 . . . . DLB-88

Shirer, William L. 1904-1993 . . . . DLB-4

Shirinsky-Shikhmatov, Sergii Aleksandrovich
    1783-1837 . . . . DLB-150

Shirley, James 1596-1666 . . . . DLB-58

Shishkov, Aleksandr Semenovich
    1753-1841 . . . . DLB-150

Shockley, Ann Allen 1927- DLB-33

Shōno Junzō 1921- DLB-182

Shore, Arabella 1820?-1901 and
    Shore, Louisa 1824-1895 . . . . DLB-199

Short, Luke (see Glidden, Frederick Dilley)

Short, Peter [publishing house] DLB-170

Shorter, Dora Sigerson 1866-1918 . . . . . . DLB-240

Shorthouse, Joseph Henry 1834-1903 . . . . DLB-18

Shōtetsu 1381-1459 . . . . DLB-203

Showalter, Elaine 1941- DLB-67

Shulevitz, Uri 1935- DLB-61

Shulman, Max 1919-1988 . . . . DLB-11

Shute, Henry A. 1856-1943 . . . . DLB-9

Shute, Nevil 1899-1960 . . . . DLB-255

Shuttle, Penelope 1947- DLB-14, 40

Sibbes, Richard 1577-1635 . . . . DLB-151

Sibiriak, D. (see Mamin, Dmitrii Narkisovich)

Siddal, Elizabeth Eleanor 1829-1862 . . . . DLB-199

Sidgwick, Ethel 1877-1970 . . . . .DLB-197

Sidgwick, Henry 1838-1900 . . . . DLB-262

Sidgwick and Jackson Limited DLB-112

Sidney, Margaret (see Lothrop, Harriet M.)

Sidney, Mary 1561-1621 . . . . DLB-167

Sidney, Sir Philip
    1554-1586 . . . . DLB-167; CDBLB-1

An Apologie for Poetrie (the Olney
    edition, 1595, of *Defence of Poesie*) DLB-167

Sidney's Press DLB-49

Sierra, Rubén 1946- DLB-122

Sierra Club Books DLB-49

Siger of Brabant circa 1240-circa 1284 . . . DLB-115

Sigourney, Lydia Huntley
    1791-1865 . . . . . . .DLB-1, 42, 73, 183, 239, 243

Silkin, Jon 1930- DLB-27

Silko, Leslie Marmon 1948- . . DLB-143, 175,256

Silliman, Benjamin 1779-1864 . . . . DLB-183

Silliman, Ron 1946- DLB-169

Silliphant, Stirling 1918- DLB-26

Sillitoe, Alan 1928- DLB-14, 139; CDBLB-8

Silman, Roberta 1934- DLB-28

Silone, Ignazio (Secondino Tranquilli)
    1900-1978 . . . . DLB-264

Silva, Beverly 1930- DLB-122

Silverberg, Robert 1935- DLB-8

Silverman, Kaja 1947- DLB-246

Silverman, Kenneth 1936- DLB-111

Simak, Clifford D. 1904-1988 . . . . DLB-8

Simcoe, Elizabeth 1762-1850 . . . . DLB-99

Simcox, Edith Jemima 1844-1901 . . . . DLB-190

Simcox, George Augustus 1841-1905 . . . . . DLB-35

Sime, Jessie Georgina 1868-1958 . . . . DLB-92

Simenon, Georges 1903-1989 . . . . . . .DLB-72; Y-89

Simic, Charles 1938- DLB-105

"Images and 'Images,'" DLB-105

Simionescu, Mircea Horia 1928- DLB-232

Simmel, Johannes Mario 1924- DLB-69

Simmes, Valentine [publishing house] DLB-170

Simmons, Ernest J. 1903-1972 . . . . DLB-103

Simmons, Herbert Alfred 1930- DLB-33

Simmons, James 1933- DLB-40

Simms, William Gilmore
1806-1870 . . . . DLB-3, 30, 59, 73, 248

Simms and M'Intyre DLB-106

Simon, Claude 1913- DLB-83; Y-85

Simon, Neil 1927- DLB-7, 266

Simon and Schuster DLB-46

Simons, Katherine Drayton Mayrant
1890-1969 . . . . Y-83

Simović, Ljubomir 1935- DLB-181

Simpkin and Marshall
[publishing house] DLB-154

Simpson, Helen 1897-1940 . . . . DLB-77

Simpson, Louis 1923- DLB-5

Simpson, N. F. 1919- DLB-13

Sims, George 1923- DLB-87; Y-99

Sims, George Robert 1847-1922 . . . DLB-35, 70, 135

Sinán, Rogelio 1904- DLB-145

Sinclair, Andrew 1935- DLB-14

Sinclair, Bertrand William 1881-1972 . . . . . DLB-92

Sinclair, Catherine 1800-1864 . . . . DLB-163

Sinclair, Jo 1913-1995 . . . . DLB-28

Sinclair, Lister 1921- DLB-88

Sinclair, May 1863-1946 . . . . DLB-36, 135

Sinclair, Upton 1878-1968 . . . . . DLB-9; CDALB-5

Sinclair, Upton [publishing house] DLB-46

Singer, Isaac Bashevis
1904-1991 . . . . DLB-6, 28, 52; Y-91; CDALB-1

Singer, Mark 1950- DLB-185

Singmaster, Elsie 1879-1958 . . . . DLB-9

Sinisgalli, Leonardo 1908-1981 . . . . DLB-114

Siodmak, Curt 1902-2000 . . . . DLB-44

Sîrbu, Ion D. 1919-1989 . . . . DLB-232

Siringo, Charles A. 1855-1928 . . . . DLB-186

Sissman, L. E. 1928-1976 . . . . DLB-5

Sisson, C. H. 1914- DLB-27

Sitwell, Edith 1887-1964 . . . . . . DLB-20; CDBLB-7

Sitwell, Osbert 1892-1969 . . . . DLB-100, 195

Skácel, Jan 1922-1989 . . . . DLB-232

Skalbe, Kārlis 1879-1945 . . . . DLB-220

Skármeta, Antonio
1940- DLB-145; CDWLB-3

Skavronsky, A. (see Danilevsky, Grigorii Petrovich)

Skeat, Walter W. 1835-1912 . . . . DLB-184

Skeffington, William
[publishing house] DLB-106

Skelton, John 1463-1529 . . . . DLB-136

Skelton, Robin 1925- DLB-27, 53

Škéma, Antanas 1910-1961 . . . . DLB-220

Skinner, Constance Lindsay
1877-1939 . . . . DLB-92

Skinner, John Stuart 1788-1851 . . . . DLB-73

Skipsey, Joseph 1832-1903 . . . . DLB-35

Skou-Hansen, Tage 1925- DLB-214

Škvorecký, Josef 1924- DLB-232; CDWLB-4

Slade, Bernard 1930- DLB-53

Slamnig, Ivan 1930- DLB-181

Slančeková, Božena (see Timrava)

Slataper, Scipio 1888-1915 . . . . DLB-264

Slater, Patrick 1880-1951 . . . . DLB-68

Slaveykov, Pencho 1866-1912 . . . . DLB-147

Slaviček, Milivoj 1929- DLB-181

Slavitt, David 1935- DLB-5, 6

Sleigh, Burrows Willcocks Arthur
1821-1869 . . . . DLB-99

A Slender Thread of Hope:
The Kennedy Center Black
Theatre Project DLB-38

Slesinger, Tess 1905-1945 . . . . DLB-102

Slessor, Kenneth 1901-1971 . . . . DLB-260

Slick, Sam (see Haliburton, Thomas Chandler)

Sloan, John 1871-1951 . . . . DLB-188

Sloane, William, Associates DLB-46

Small, Maynard and Company DLB-49

Small Presses in Great Britain and Ireland,
1960-1985 . . . . DLB-40

Small Presses I: Jargon Society Y-84

Small Presses II: The Spirit That Moves
Us Press Y-85

Small Presses III: Pushcart Press Y-87

Smart, Christopher 1722-1771 . . . . DLB-109

Smart, David A. 1892-1957 . . . . DLB-137

Smart, Elizabeth 1913-1986 . . . . DLB-88

Smart, J. J. C. 1920- DLB-262

Smedley, Menella Bute 1820?-1877 . . . . . DLB-199

Smellie, William [publishing house] DLB-154

Smiles, Samuel 1812-1904 . . . . DLB-55

Smiley, Jane 1949- DLB-227, 234

Smith, A. J. M. 1902-1980 . . . . DLB-88

Smith, Adam 1723-1790 . . . . DLB-104, 252

Smith, Adam (George Jerome Waldo Goodman)
1930- DLB-185

Smith, Alexander 1829-1867 . . . . DLB-32, 55

"On the Writing of Essays" (1862) DLB-57

Smith, Amanda 1837-1915 . . . . DLB-221

Smith, Betty 1896-1972 . . . . Y-82

Smith, Carol Sturm 1938- Y-81

Smith, Charles Henry 1826-1903 . . . . DLB-11

Smith, Charlotte 1749-1806 . . . . DLB-39, 109

Smith, Chet 1899-1973 . . . . DLB-171

Smith, Cordwainer 1913-1966 . . . . DLB-8

Smith, Dave 1942- DLB-5

Smith, Dodie 1896- DLB-10

Smith, Doris Buchanan 1934- DLB-52

Smith, E. E. 1890-1965 . . . . DLB-8

Smith, Elder and Company DLB-154

Smith, Elihu Hubbard 1771-1798 . . . . DLB-37

Smith, Elizabeth Oakes (Prince)
(see Oakes Smith, Elizabeth)

Smith, Eunice 1757-1823 . . . . DLB-200

Smith, F. Hopkinson 1838-1915 . . . . DS-13

Smith, George D. 1870-1920 . . . . DLB-140

Smith, George O. 1911-1981 . . . . DLB-8

Smith, Goldwin 1823-1910 . . . . DLB-99

Smith, H. Allen 1907-1976 . . . . DLB-11, 29

Smith, Harrison, and Robert Haas
[publishing house] DLB-46

Smith, Harry B. 1860-1936 . . . . DLB-187

Smith, Hazel Brannon 1914- DLB-127

Smith, Henry circa 1560-circa 1591 . . . . . DLB-136

Smith, Horatio (Horace) 1779-1849 . . . . . DLB-116

Smith, Horatio (Horace) 1779-1849 and
James Smith 1775-1839 . . . . DLB-96

Smith, Iain Crichton 1928- DLB-40, 139

Smith, J. Allen 1860-1924 . . . . DLB-47

Smith, J. Stilman, and Company DLB-49

Smith, Jessie Willcox 1863-1935 . . . . DLB-188

Smith, John 1580-1631 . . . . DLB-24, 30

Smith, John 1618-1652 . . . . DLB-252

Smith, Josiah 1704-1781 . . . . DLB-24

Smith, Ken 1938- DLB-40

Smith, Lee 1944- DLB-143; Y-83

Smith, Logan Pearsall 1865-1946 . . . . DLB-98

Smith, Margaret Bayard 1778-1844 . . . . . DLB-248

Smith, Mark 1935- Y-82

Smith, Michael 1698-circa 1771 . . . . DLB-31

Smith, Pauline 1882-1959 . . . . DLB-225

Smith, Red 1905-1982 . . . . DLB-29, 171

Smith, Roswell 1829-1892 . . . . DLB-79

Smith, Samuel Harrison 1772-1845 . . . . . DLB-43

Smith, Samuel Stanhope 1751-1819 . . . . . DLB-37

Smith, Sarah (see Stretton, Hesba)

Smith, Sarah Pogson 1774-1870 . . . . DLB-200

Smith, Seba 1792-1868 . . . . DLB-1, 11, 243

Smith, Stevie 1902-1971 . . . . DLB-20

Smith, Sydney 1771-1845 . . . . DLB-107

Smith, Sydney Goodsir 1915-1975 . . . . . . DLB-27

Smith, Sir Thomas 1513-1577 . . . . DLB-132

Smith, W. B., and Company DLB-49

Smith, W. H., and Son DLB-106

Smith, Wendell 1914-1972 . . . . DLB-171

Smith, William flourished 1595-1597 . . . . DLB-136

Smith, William 1727-1803 . . . . DLB-31

A General Idea of the College of Mirania
(1753) [excerpts] DLB-31

Smith, William 1728-1793 . . . . DLB-30

Smith, William Gardner 1927-1974 . . . . . DLB-76

Smith, William Henry 1808-1872 . . . . DLB-159

Smith, William Jay 1918- DLB-5

Smithers, Leonard [publishing house] DLB-112

Smollett, Tobias
1721-1771 . . . . DLB-39, 104; CDBLB-2

Dedication, *Ferdinand Count
Fathom* (1753) DLB-39

Preface to *Ferdinand Count Fathom* (1753) DLB-39

Preface to *Roderick Random* (1748) DLB-39

Smythe, Francis Sydney 1900-1949 . . . . . DLB-195

Snelling, William Joseph 1804-1848 . . . . . DLB-202

Snellings, Rolland (see Touré, Askia Muhammad)

Snodgrass, W. D. 1926- DLB-5

Snow, C. P.
1905-1980 . . . . DLB-15, 77; DS-17; CDBLB-7

Snyder, Gary 1930- DLB-5, 16, 165, 212, 237

Sobiloff, Hy 1912-1970 . . . . DLB-48

The Society for Textual Scholarship and
TEXT Y-87

The Society for the History of Authorship,
Reading and Publishing Y-92

Söderberg, Hjalmar 1869-1941 . . . . DLB-259

Södergran, Edith 1892-1923 . . . . DLB-259

Soffici, Ardengo 1879-1964 . . . . DLB-114, 264

Sofola, 'Zulu 1938- DLB-157

Solano, Solita 1888-1975 . . . . DLB-4

Soldati, Mario 1906-1999 . . . . DLB-177

Šoljan, Antun 1932-1993 . . . . DLB-181

Sollers, Philippe 1936- DLB-83

Sollogub, Vladimir Aleksandrovich
1813-1882. . . . . DLB-198

Sollors, Werner 1943- DBL-246

Solmi, Sergio 1899-1981 . . . . DLB-114

Solomon, Carl 1928- DLB-16

Solway, David 1941- DLB-53

Solzhenitsyn and America. Y-85

Somerville, Edith Œnone 1858-1949 . . . . DLB-135

Somov, Orest Mikhailovich
1793-1833 . . . . DLB-198

Sønderby, Knud 1909-1966 . . . . DLB-214

Song, Cathy 1955- DLB-169

Sonnevi, Göran 1939- DLB-257

Sono Ayako 1931- DLB-182

Sontag, Susan 1933- DLB-2, 67

Sophocles 497/496 B.C.-406/405 B.C.
. . . . DLB-176; CDWLB-1

Šopov, Aco 1923-1982 . . . . DLB-181

Sørensen, Villy 1929- DLB-214

Sorensen, Virginia 1912-1991 . . . . DLB-206

Sorge, Reinhard Johannes 1892-1916 . . . . DLB-118

Sorrentino, Gilbert 1929- DLB-5, 173; Y-80

Sotheby, James 1682-1742 . . . . DLB-213

Sotheby, John 1740-1807 . . . . DLB-213

Sotheby, Samuel 1771-1842 . . . . DLB-213

Sotheby, Samuel Leigh 1805-1861 . . . . . . DLB-213

Sotheby, William 1757-1833 . . . . . DLB-93, 213

Soto, Gary 1952- DLB-82

Sources for the Study of Tudor and Stuart
Drama DLB-62

Soueif, Ahdaf 1950- DLB-267

Souster, Raymond 1921- DLB-88

The *South English Legendary circa thirteenth-fifteenth*
centuries DLB-146

Southerland, Ellease 1943- DLB-33

Southern, Terry 1924-1995 . . . . DLB-2

Southern Illinois University Press Y-95

Southern Writers Between the Wars DLB-9

Southerne, Thomas 1659-1746 . . . . DLB-80

Southey, Caroline Anne Bowles
1786-1854. . . . . DLB-116

Southey, Robert 1774-1843 . . . . . DLB-93, 107, 142

Southwell, Robert 1561?-1595 . . . . DLB-167

Southworth, E. D. E. N. 1819-1899 . . . . . DLB-239

Sowande, Bode 1948- DLB-157

Sowle, Tace [publishing house]. DLB-170

Soyfer, Jura 1912-1939 . . . . DLB-124

Soyinka, Wole
1934- DLB-125; Y-86, Y-87; CDWLB-3

Spacks, Barry 1931- DLB-105

Spalding, Frances 1950- DLB-155

Spark, Muriel 1918- . . . DLB-15, 139; CDBLB-7

Sparke, Michael [publishing house] DLB-170

Sparks, Jared 1789-1866 . . . . DLB-1, 30, 235

Sparshott, Francis 1926- DLB-60

Späth, Gerold 1939- DLB-75

Spatola, Adriano 1941-1988 . . . . DLB-128

Spaziani, Maria Luisa 1924- DLB-128

Special Collections at the University of Colorado
at Boulder Y-98

The Spectator 1828- DLB-110

Spedding, James 1808-1881 . . . . DLB-144

Spee von Langenfeld, Friedrich
1591-1635 . . . . DLB-164

Speght, Rachel 1597-after 1630 . . . . DLB-126

Speke, John Hanning 1827-1864 . . . . DLB-166

Spellman, A. B. 1935- DLB-41

Spence, Catherine Helen 1825-1910 . . . . . DLB-230

Spence, Thomas 1750-1814 . . . . DLB-158

Spencer, Anne 1882-1975 . . . . DLB-51, 54

Spencer, Charles, third Earl of Sunderland
1674-1722 . . . . DLB-213

Spencer, Elizabeth 1921- DLB-6, 218

Spencer, George John, Second Earl Spencer
1758-1834 . . . . DLB-184

Spencer, Herbert 1820-1903 . . . . .DLB-57, 262

"The Philosophy of Style" (1852) DLB-57

Spencer, Scott 1945- Y-86

Spender, J. A. 1862-1942 . . . . DLB-98

Spender, Stephen 1909-1995 . . DLB-20; CDBLB-7

Spener, Philipp Jakob 1635-1705 . . . . DLB-164

Spenser, Edmund
circa 1552-1599 . . . . DLB-167; CDBLB-1

Envoy from The Shepheardes Calender DLB-167

"The Generall Argument of the
Whole Booke," from
The Shepheardes Calender. DLB-167

"A Letter of the Authors Expounding
His Whole Intention in the Course
of this Worke: Which for that It Giueth
Great Light to the Reader, for the Better
Vnderstanding Is Hereunto Annexed,"
from The Faerie Qveene (1590) DLB-167

"To His Booke," from
The Shepheardes Calender (1579) DLB-167

"To the Most Excellent and Learned Both
Orator and Poete, Mayster Gabriell Haruey,
His Verie Special and Singular Good Frend
E. K. Commendeth the Good Lyking of
This His Labour, and the Patronage of
the New Poete," from
The Shepheardes Calender. DLB-167

Sperr, Martin 1944- DLB-124

Spewack, Samuel 1899-1971 and
Bella 1899-1990 . . . . DLB-266

Spicer, Jack 1925-1965 . . . . .DLB-5, 16, 193

Spielberg, Peter 1929- Y-81

Spielhagen, Friedrich 1829-1911 . . . . DLB-129

"Spielmannsepen" (circa 1152-circa 1500) . . DLB-148

Spier, Peter 1927- DLB-61

Spillane, Mickey 1918- DLB-226

Spink, J. G. Taylor 1888-1962 . . . . DLB-241

Spinrad, Norman 1940- DLB-8

Spires, Elizabeth 1952- DLB-120

Spitteler, Carl 1845-1924 . . . . DLB-129

Spivak, Lawrence E. 1900- DLB-137

Spofford, Harriet Prescott
1835-1921 . . . . .DLB-74, 221

Sprigge, T. L. S. 1932- DLB-262

Spring, Howard 1889-1965 . . . . DLB-191

Squibob (see Derby, George Horatio)

Squier, E. G. 1821-1888 . . . . DLB-189

Stableford, Brian 1948- DLB-261

Stacpoole, H. de Vere 1863-1951 . . . . DLB-153

Staël, Germaine de 1766-1817 . . . . . .DLB-119, 192

Staël-Holstein, Anne-Louise Germaine de
(see Staël, Germaine de)

Stafford, Jean 1915-1979 . . . . .DLB-2, 173

Stafford, William 1914-1993. . . . . DLB-5, 206

Stage Censorship: "The Rejected Statement"
(1911), by Bernard Shaw [excerpts] . . . DLB-10

Stallings, Laurence 1894-1968 . . . . .DLB-7, 44

Stallworthy, Jon 1935- DLB-40

Stampp, Kenneth M. 1912- DLB-17

Stănescu, Nichita 1933-1983 . . . . DLB-232

Stanev, Emiliyan 1907-1979 . . . . DLB-181

Stanford, Ann 1916- DLB-5

Stangerup, Henrik 1937-1998 . . . . DLB-214

Stanitsky, N. (see Panaeva, Avdot'ia Iakovlevna)

Stankevich, Nikolai Vladimirovich
1813-1840 . . . . DLB-198

Stanković, Borisav ("Bora")
1876-1927 . . . . .DLB-147; CDWLB-4

Stanley, Henry M. 1841-1904 . . . DLB-189; DS-13

Stanley, Thomas 1625-1678 . . . . DLB-131

Stannard, Martin 1947- DLB-155

Stansby, William [publishing house]. DLB-170

Stanton, Elizabeth Cady 1815-1902 . . . . . DLB-79

Stanton, Frank L. 1857-1927 . . . . DLB-25

Stanton, Maura 1946- DLB-120

Stapledon, Olaf 1886-1950 . . . . DLB-15, 255

Star Spangled Banner Office. DLB-49

Stark, Freya 1893-1993 . . . . DLB-195

Starkey, Thomas circa 1499-1538 . . . . . . .DLB-132

Starkie, Walter 1894-1976 . . . . .DLB-195

Starkweather, David 1935- DLB-7

Starrett, Vincent 1886-1974 . . . . .DLB-187

The State of Publishing Y-97

Statements on the Art of Poetry DLB-54

Stationers' Company of London, The DLB-170

Statius circa A.D. 45-A.D. 96 . . . . .DLB-211

Stead, Christina 1902-1983 . . . . .DLB-260

Stead, Robert J. C. 1880-1959 . . . . .DLB-92

Steadman, Mark 1930- DLB-6

The Stealthy School of Criticism (1871), by
    Dante Gabriel Rossetti DLB-35

Stearns, Harold E. 1891-1943 . . . . .DLB-4

Stebnitsky, M. (see Leskov, Nikolai Semenovich)

Stedman, Edmund Clarence 1833-1908 . . .DLB-64

Steegmuller, Francis 1906-1994 . . . . .DLB-111

Steel, Flora Annie 1847-1929 . . . . . . .DLB-153, 156

Steele, Max 1922- Y-80

Steele, Richard
    1672-1729 . . . . .DLB-84, 101; CDBLB-2

Steele, Timothy 1948- DLB-120

Steele, Wilbur Daniel 1886-1970 . . . . .DLB-86

Steere, Richard circa 1643-1721 . . . . .DLB-24

Stefanovski, Goran 1952- DLB-181

Stegner, Wallace 1909-1993 . . . .DLB-9, 206; Y-93

Stehr, Hermann 1864-1940 . . . . .DLB-66

Steig, William 1907- DLB-61

Stein, Gertrude 1874-1946
    . . . . . .DLB-4, 54, 86, 228; DS-15; CDALB-4

Stein, Leo 1872-1947 . . . . .DLB-4

Stein and Day Publishers DLB-46

Steinbeck, John
    1902-1968 . . . .DLB-7, 9, 212; DS-2; CDALB-5

John Steinbeck Research Center Y-85

Steinem, Gloria 1934- DLB-246

Steiner, George 1929- DLB-67

Steinhoewel, Heinrich 1411/1412-1479 . . .DLB-179

Steloff, Ida Frances 1887-1989 . . . . .DLB-187

Stendhal 1783-1842 . . . . .DLB-119

Stephen Crane: A Revaluation Virginia
    Tech Conference, 1989 . . . . Y-89

Stephen, Leslie 1832-1904 . . . . . .DLB-57, 144, 190

Stephen Vincent Benét Centenary Y-97

Stephens, A. G. 1865-1933 . . . . .DLB-230

Stephens, Alexander H. 1812-1883 . . . . . .DLB-47

Stephens, Alice Barber 1858-1932 . . . . . . .DLB-188

Stephens, Ann 1810-1886 . . . . . . .DLB-3, 73, 250

Stephens, Charles Asbury 1844?-1931 . . . . .DLB-42

Stephens, James 1882?-1950 . . . .DLB-19, 153, 162

Stephens, John Lloyd 1805-1852 . . . .DLB-183, 250

Stephens, Michael 1946- DLB-234

Stephenson, P. R. 1901-1965 . . . . .DLB-260

Sterling, George 1869-1926 . . . . .DLB-54

Sterling, James 1701-1763 . . . . .DLB-24

Sterling, John 1806-1844 . . . . .DLB-116

Stern, Gerald 1925- DLB-105

Stern, Gladys B. 1890-1973 . . . . .DLB-197

Stern, Madeleine B. 1912- DLB-111, 140

Stern, Richard 1928- DLB-218; Y-87

Stern, Stewart 1922- DLB-26

Sterne, Laurence
    1713-1768 . . . . DLB-39; CDBLB-2

Sternheim, Carl 1878-1942 . . . . .DLB-56, 118

Sternhold, Thomas ?-1549 and
    John Hopkins ?-1570 . . . . .DLB-132

Steuart, David 1747-1824 . . . . .DLB-213

Stevens, Henry 1819-1886 . . . . .DLB-140

Stevens, Wallace 1879-1955 . . . .DLB-54; CDALB-5

Stevenson, Anne 1933- DLB-40

Stevenson, D. E. 1892-1973 . . . . .DLB-191

Stevenson, Lionel 1902-1973 . . . . .DLB-155

Stevenson, Robert Louis
    1850-1894 . . . . . . .DLB-18, 57, 141, 156, 174;
                                          DS-13; CDBLB-5

"On Style in Literature:
    Its Technical Elements" (1885) DLB-57

Stewart, Donald Ogden
    1894-1980 . . . . .DLB-4, 11, 26

Stewart, Douglas 1913-1985 . . . . .DLB-260

Stewart, Dugald 1753-1828 . . . . .DLB-31

Stewart, George, Jr. 1848-1906 . . . . .DLB-99

Stewart, George R. 1895-1980 . . . . .DLB-8

Stewart, Harold 1916-1995 . . . . .DLB-260

Stewart, Maria W. 1803?-1879 . . . . .DLB-239

Stewart, Randall 1896-1964 . . . . .DLB-103

Stewart, Sean 1965- DLB-251

Stewart and Kidd Company DLB-46

Stickney, Trumbull 1874-1904 . . . . .DLB-54

Stieler, Caspar 1632-1707 . . . . .DLB-164

Stifter, Adalbert
    1805-1868 . . . . .DLB-133; CDWLB-2

Stiles, Ezra 1727-1795 . . . . .DLB-31

Still, James 1906- DLB-9; Y01

Stirling, S. M. 1954- DLB-251

Stirner, Max 1806-1856 . . . . .DLB-129

Stith, William 1707-1755 . . . . .DLB-31

Stock, Elliot [publishing house] DLB-106

Stockton, Frank R.
    1834-1902 . . . . .DLB-42, 74; DS-13

Stockton, J. Roy 1892-1972 . . . . .DLB-241

Stoddard, Ashbel [publishing house] DLB-49

Stoddard, Charles Warren
    1843-1909 . . . . .DLB-186

Stoddard, Elizabeth 1823-1902 . . . . .DLB-202

Stoddard, Richard Henry
    1825-1903 . . . . .DLB-3, 64, 250; DS-13

Stoddard, Solomon 1643-1729 . . . . .DLB-24

Stoker, Bram
    1847-1912 . . . . . . .DLB-36, 70, 178; CDBLB-5

Stokes, Frederick A., Company DLB-49

Stokes, Thomas L. 1898-1958 . . . . .DLB-29

Stokesbury, Leon 1945- DLB-120

Stolberg, Christian Graf zu 1748-1821 . . . . .DLB-94

Stolberg, Friedrich Leopold Graf zu
    1750-1819 . . . . .DLB-94

Stone, Herbert S., and Company DLB-49

Stone, Lucy 1818-1893 . . . . .DLB-79, 239

Stone, Melville 1848-1929 . . . . .DLB-25

Stone, Robert 1937- DLB-152

Stone, Ruth 1915- DLB-105

Stone, Samuel 1602-1663 . . . . .DLB-24

Stone, William Leete 1792-1844 . . . . .DLB-202

Stone and Kimball DLB-49

Stoppard, Tom
    1937- DLB-13, 233; Y-85; CDBLB-8

Playwrights and Professors DLB-13

Storey, Anthony 1928- DLB-14

Storey, David 1933- DLB-13, 14, 207, 245

Storm, Theodor 1817-1888 . .DLB-129; CDWLB-2

Story, Thomas circa 1670-1742 . . . . .DLB-31

Story, William Wetmore 1819-1895 . . .DLB-1, 235

Storytelling: A Contemporary Renaissance . . . Y-84

Stoughton, William 1631-1701 . . . . .DLB-24

Stow, John 1525-1605 . . . . .DLB-132

Stow, Randolph 1935- DLB-260

Stowe, Harriet Beecher 1811-1896
    . . DLB-1, 12, 42, 74, 189, 239, 243; CDALB-3

Stowe, Leland 1899- DLB-29

Stoyanov, Dimitr Ivanov (see Elin Pelin)

Strabo 64 or 63 B.C.-circa A.D. 25 . . . . . .DLB-176

Strachey, Lytton 1880-1932 . . . . . .DLB-149; DS-10

Strachey, Lytton, Preface to Eminent
    Victorians DLB-149

Strahan, William [publishing house] DLB-154

Strahan and Company DLB-106

Strand, Mark 1934- DLB-5

The Strasbourg Oaths 842 . . . . .DLB-148

Stratemeyer, Edward 1862-1930 . . . . .DLB-42

Strati, Saverio 1924- DLB-177

Stratton and Barnard DLB-49

Stratton-Porter, Gene
    1863-1924 . . . . .DLB-221; DS-14

Straub, Peter 1943- Y-84

Strauß, Botho 1944- DLB-124

Strauß, David Friedrich 1808-1874 . . . . . .DLB-133

The Strawberry Hill Press DLB-154

Strawson, P. F. 1919- DLB-262

Streatfeild, Noel 1895-1986 . . . . .DLB-160

Street, Cecil John Charles (see Rhode, John)

Street, G. S. 1867-1936 . . . . .DLB-135

Street and Smith DLB-49

Streeter, Edward 1891-1976 . . . . .DLB-11

Streeter, Thomas Winthrop 1883-1965 . . .DLB-140

Stretton, Hesba 1832-1911 . . . . .DLB-163, 190

Stribling, T. S. 1881-1965 . . . . .DLB-9

Der Stricker circa 1190-circa 1250 . . . . . .DLB-138

Strickland, Samuel 1804-1867 . . . . .DLB-99

Strindberg, August 1849-1912 . . . . .DLB-259

Stringer, Arthur 1874-1950 . . . . .DLB-92

Stringer and Townsend DLB-49

Strittmatter, Erwin 1912- DLB-69

Strniša, Gregor 1930-1987 . . . . DLB-181

Strode, William 1630-1645 . . . . DLB-126

Strong, L. A. G. 1896-1958 . . . . DLB-191

Strother, David Hunter (Porte Crayon)
    1816-1888 . . . . DLB-3, 248

Strouse, Jean 1945- DLB-111

Stuart, Dabney 1937- DLB-105

Stuart, Jesse 1906-1984 . . . . . DLB-9, 48, 102; Y-84

Stuart, Lyle [publishing house] DLB-46

Stuart, Ruth McEnery 1849?-1917 . . . . . . DLB-202

Stubbs, Harry Clement (see Clement, Hal)

Stubenberg, Johann Wilhelm von
    1619-1663 . . . . DLB-164

Studebaker, William V. 1947- DLB-256

Studio DLB-112

The Study of Poetry (1880), by
    Matthew Arnold DLB-35

Stump, Al 1916-1995 . . . . DLB-241

Sturgeon, Theodore 1918-1985 . . . . . DLB-8; Y-85

Sturges, Preston 1898-1959 . . . . DLB-26

"Style" (1840; revised, 1859), by
    Thomas de Quincey [excerpt] DLB-57

"Style" (1888), by Walter Pater DLB-57

Style (1897), by Walter Raleigh
    [excerpt] DLB-57

"Style" (1877), by T. H. Wright
    [excerpt] DLB-57

"Le Style c'est l'homme" (1892), by
    W. H. Mallock DLB-57

Styron, William
    1925- DLB-2, 143; Y-80; CDALB-6

Suárez, Mario 1925- DLB-82

Such, Peter 1939- DLB-60

Suckling, Sir John 1609-1641? DLB-58, 126

Suckow, Ruth 1892-1960 . . . . DLB-9, 102

Sudermann, Hermann 1857-1928 . . . . . . DLB-118

Sue, Eugène 1804-1857 . . . . DLB-119

Sue, Marie-Joseph (see Sue, Eugène)

Suetonius circa A.D. 69-post A.D. 122 . . . DLB-211

Suggs, Simon (see Hooper, Johnson Jones)

Sui Sin Far (see Eaton, Edith Maude)

Suits, Gustav 1883-1956 . . . . DLB-220; CDWLB-4

Sukenick, Ronald 1932- DLB-173; Y-81

Suknaski, Andrew 1942- DLB-53

Sullivan, Alan 1868-1947 . . . . DLB-92

Sullivan, C. Gardner 1886-1965 . . . . DLB-26

Sullivan, Frank 1892-1976 . . . . DLB-11

Sulte, Benjamin 1841-1923 . . . . DLB-99

Sulzberger, Arthur Hays 1891-1968 . . . . . DLB-127

Sulzberger, Arthur Ochs 1926- DLB-127

Sulzer, Johann Georg 1720-1779 . . . . DLB-97

Sumarokov, Aleksandr Petrovich
    1717-1777 . . . . DLB-150

Summers, Hollis 1916- DLB-6

A Summing Up at Century's End Y-99

Sumner, Charles 1811-1874 . . . . DLB-235

Sumner, Henry A. [publishing house] DLB-49

Sundman, Per Olof 1922-1992 . . . . DLB-257

Supervielle, Jules 1884-1960 . . . . DLB-258

Surtees, Robert Smith 1803-1864 . . . . DLB-21

Survey of Literary Biographies Y-00

A Survey of Poetry Anthologies,
    1879-1960 . . . . DLB-54

Surveys: Japanese Literature,
    1987-1995 . . . . DLB-182

Sutherland, Efua Theodora
    1924-1996 . . . . DLB-117

Sutherland, John 1919-1956 . . . . DLB-68

Sutro, Alfred 1863-1933 . . . . DLB-10

Svendsen, Hanne Marie 1933- DLB-214

Svevo, Italo (Aron Hector Schmitz)
    1861-1928 . . . . DLB-264

Swados, Harvey 1920-1972 . . . . DLB-2

Swain, Charles 1801-1874 . . . . DLB-32

Swallow Press DLB-46

Swan Sonnenschein Limited DLB-106

Swanberg, W. A. 1907- DLB-103

Swenson, May 1919-1989 . . . . DLB-5

Swerling, Jo 1897- DLB-44

Swift, Graham 1949- DLB-194

Swift, Jonathan
    1667-1745 . . . . DLB-39, 95, 101; CDBLB-2

Swinburne, A. C.
    1837-1909 . . . . DLB-35, 57; CDBLB-4

Swineshead, Richard
    floruit circa 1350 . . . . DLB-115

Swinnerton, Frank 1884-1982 . . . . DLB-34

Swisshelm, Jane Grey 1815-1884 . . . . DLB-43

Swope, Herbert Bayard 1882-1958 . . . . . . DLB-25

Swords, T. and J., and Company DLB-49

Swords, Thomas 1763-1843 and
    Swords, James ?-1844 . . . . DLB-73

Sykes, Ella C. ?-1939 . . . . DLB-174

Sylvester, Josuah
    1562 or 1563-1618 . . . . DLB-121

Symonds, Emily Morse (see Paston, George)

Symonds, John Addington
    1840-1893 . . . . DLB-57, 144

"Personal Style" (1890) DLB-57

Symons, A. J. A. 1900-1941 . . . . DLB-149

Symons, Arthur 1865-1945 . . . . . . DLB-19, 57, 149

Symons, Julian
    1912-1994 . . . . DLB-87, 155; Y-92

Julian Symons at Eighty Y-92

Symons, Scott 1933- DLB-53

A Symposium on The Columbia History of
    the Novel Y-92

Synge, John Millington
    1871-1909 . . . . DLB-10, 19; CDBLB-5

Synge Summer School: J. M. Synge and the
    Irish Theater, Rathdrum, County Wiclow,
    Ireland Y-93

Syrett, Netta 1865-1943 . . . . DLB-135, 197

Szabó, Lőrinc 1900-1957 . . . . DLB-215

Szabó, Magda 1917- DLB-215

Szymborska, Wisława
    1923- DLB-232, Y-96; CDWLB-4

T

Taban lo Liyong 1939?- DLB-125

Tabori, George 1914- DLB-245

Tabucchi, Antonio 1943- DLB-196

Taché, Joseph-Charles 1820-1894 . . . . DLB-99

Tachihara Masaaki 1926-1980 . . . . DLB-182

Tacitus circa A.D. 55-circa A.D. 117
    . . . . DLB-211; CDWLB-1

Tadijanović, Dragutin 1905- DLB-181

Tafdrup, Pia 1952- DLB-214

Tafolla, Carmen 1951- DLB-82

Taggard, Genevieve 1894-1948 . . . . DLB-45

Taggart, John 1942- DLB-193

Tagger, Theodor (see Bruckner, Ferdinand)

Taiheiki late fourteenth century DLB-203

Tait, J. Selwin, and Sons DLB-49

Tait's Edinburgh Magazine 1832-1861 . . . . . DLB-110

The Takarazaka Revue Company Y-91

Talander (see Bohse, August)

Talese, Gay 1932- DLB-185

Talev, Dimitr 1898-1966 . . . . DLB-181

Taliaferro, H. E. 1811-1875 . . . . DLB-202

Tallent, Elizabeth 1954- DLB-130

TallMountain, Mary 1918-1994 . . . . . . DLB-193

Talvj 1797-1870 . . . . DLB-59, 133

Tamási, Áron 1897-1966 . . . . DLB-215

Tammsaare, A. H.
    1878-1940 . . . . DLB-220; CDWLB-4

Tan, Amy 1952- DLB-173; CDALB-7

Tandori, Dezső 1938- DLB-232

Tanner, Thomas 1673/1674-1735 . . . . DLB-213

Tanizaki Jun'ichirō 1886-1965 . . . . DLB-180

Tapahonso, Luci 1953- DLB-175

The Mark Taper Forum DLB-7

Taradash, Daniel 1913- DLB-44

Tarbell, Ida M. 1857-1944 . . . . DLB-47

Tardivel, Jules-Paul 1851-1905 . . . . DLB-99

Targan, Barry 1932- DLB-130

Tarkington, Booth 1869-1946 . . . . DLB-9, 102

Tashlin, Frank 1913-1972 . . . . DLB-44

Tasma (Jessie Couvreur) 1848-1897 . . . . DLB-230

Tate, Allen 1899-1979 . . . . . . DLB-4, 45, 63; DS-17

Tate, James 1943- DLB-5, 169

Tate, Nahum circa 1652-1715 . . . . DLB-80

Tatian circa 830 . . . . DLB-148

Taufer, Veno 1933- DLB-181

Tauler, Johannes circa 1300-1361 . . . . DLB-179

Tavčar, Ivan 1851-1923 . . . . DLB-147

Taverner, Richard ca. 1505-1575 . . . . . . DLB-236

Taylor, Ann 1782-1866 . . . . DLB-163

Taylor, Bayard 1825-1878 . . . . . . DLB-3, 189, 250

Taylor, Bert Leston 1866-1921 . . . . .DLB-25

Taylor, Charles H. 1846-1921. . . . . .DLB-25

Taylor, Edward circa 1642-1729 . . . . .DLB-24

Taylor, Elizabeth 1912-1975 . . . . .DLB-139

Taylor, Henry 1942- DLB-5

Taylor, Sir Henry 1800-1886. . . . . .DLB-32

Taylor, Jane 1783-1824 . . . . .DLB-163

Taylor, Jeremy circa 1613-1667 . . . . .DLB-151

Taylor, John 1577 or 1578 - 1653 . . . . . . .DLB-121

Taylor, Mildred D. ?- DLB-52

Taylor, Peter 1917-1994. . . . . DLB-218; Y-81, Y-94

Taylor, Susie King 1848-1912 . . . . .DLB-221

Taylor, William Howland 1901-1966 . . . .DLB-241

Taylor, William, and Company DLB-49

Taylor-Made Shakespeare? Or Is "Shall I Die?" the
Long-Lost Text of Bottom's Dream? Y-85

Teasdale, Sara 1884-1933 . . . . .DLB-45

Telles, Lygia Fagundes 1924- DLB-113

Temple, Sir William 1628-1699 . . . . .DLB-101

Temple, William F. 1914-1989 . . . . .DLB-255

Temrizov, A. (see Marchenko, Anastasia Iakovlevna)

Tench, Watkin ca. 1758-1833 . . . . .DLB-230

Tenn, William 1919- DLB-8

Tennant, Emma 1937- DLB-14

Tenney, Tabitha Gilman
1762-1837 . . . . DLB-37, 200

Tennyson, Alfred
1809-1892 . . . . DLB-32; CDBLB-4

Tennyson, Frederick 1807-1898 . . . . .DLB-32

Tenorio, Arthur 1924- DLB-209

Tepliakov, Viktor Grigor'evich
1804-1842 . . . . .DLB-205

Terence circa 184 B.C.-159 B.C. or after
. . . . DLB-211; CDWLB-1

Terhune, Albert Payson 1872-1942 . . . . . . .DLB-9

Terhune, Mary Virginia
1830-1922 . . . . DS-13, DS-16

Terry, Megan 1932- DLB-7, 249

Terson, Peter 1932- DLB-13

Tesich, Steve 1943-1996 . . . . Y-83

Tessa, Delio 1886-1939 . . . . .DLB-114

Testori, Giovanni 1923-1993 . . . . DLB-128, 177

Tey, Josephine 1896?-1952 . . . . .DLB-77

Thacher, James 1754-1844 . . . . .DLB-37

Thackeray, William Makepeace
1811-1863 . . .DLB-21, 55, 159, 163; CDBLB-4

Thames and Hudson Limited DLB-112

Thanet, Octave (see French, Alice)

Thatcher, John Boyd 1847-1909 . . . . . . .DLB-187

Thaxter, Celia Laighton 1835-1894 . . . . . .DLB-239

Thayer, Caroline Matilda Warren
1785-1844 . . . . .DLB-200

Thayer, Douglas 1929- DLB-256

The Theatre Guild DLB-7

The Theater in Shakespeare's Time DLB-62

Thegan and the Astronomer
flourished circa 850 . . . . .DLB-148

Thelwall, John 1764-1834 . . . . .DLB-93, 158

Theocritus circa 300 B.C.-260 B.C. DLB-176

Theodorescu, Ion N. (see Arghezi, Tudor)

Theodulf circa 760-circa 821 . . . . .DLB-148

Theophrastus circa 371 B.C.-287 B.C. DLB-176

Theriault, Yves 1915-1983. . . . . .DLB-88

Thério, Adrien 1925- DLB-53

Theroux, Paul 1941- DLB-2, 218; CDALB-7

Thesiger, Wilfred 1910- DLB-204

They All Came to Paris DS-16

Thibaudeau, Colleen 1925- DLB-88

Thielen, Benedict 1903-1965 . . . . .DLB-102

Thiong'o Ngugi wa (see Ngugi wa Thiong'o)

Third-Generation Minor Poets of the
Seventeenth Century DLB-131

This Quarter 1925-1927, 1929-1932 . . . . DS-15

Thoma, Ludwig 1867-1921 . . . . .DLB-66

Thoma, Richard 1902- DLB-4

Thomas, Audrey 1935- DLB-60

Thomas, D. M. 1935- . .DLB-40, 207; CDBLB-8

D. M. Thomas: The Plagiarism
Controversy Y-82

Thomas, Dylan
1914-1953 . . . . . . .DLB-13, 20, 139; CDBLB-7

The Dylan Thomas Celebration Y-99

Thomas, Edward
1878-1917 . . . . .DLB-19, 98, 156, 216

Thomas, Frederick William 1806-1866 . . .DLB-202

Thomas, Gwyn 1913-1981 . . . . .DLB-15, 245

Thomas, Isaiah 1750-1831 . . . . DLB-43, 73, 187

Thomas, Isaiah [publishing house] DLB-49

Thomas, Johann 1624-1679 . . . . .DLB-168

Thomas, John 1900-1932 . . . . .DLB-4

Thomas, Joyce Carol 1938- DLB-33

Thomas, Lorenzo 1944- DLB-41

Thomas, R. S. 1915-2000 . . . . .DLB-27; CDBLB-8

Thomasîn von Zerclære
circa 1186-circa 1259 . . . . .DLB-138

Thomasius, Christian 1655-1728 . . . . . . .DLB-168

Thompson, Daniel Pierce 1795-1868 . . . . .DLB-202

Thompson, David 1770-1857 . . . . .DLB-99

Thompson, Dorothy 1893-1961 . . . . .DLB-29

Thompson, E. P. 1924-1993 . . . . .DLB-242

Thompson, Flora 1876-1947 . . . . .DLB-240

Thompson, Francis
1859-1907 . . . . .DLB-19; CDBLB-5

Thompson, George Selden (see Selden, George)

Thompson, Henry Yates 1838-1928 . . . . .DLB-184

Thompson, Hunter S. 1939- DLB-185

Thompson, Jim 1906-1977 . . . . .DLB-226

Thompson, John 1938-1976 . . . . .DLB-60

Thompson, John R. 1823-1873 . . . . DLB-3, 73, 248

Thompson, Lawrance 1906-1973 . . . . . . .DLB-103

Thompson, Maurice 1844-1901 . . . . . . DLB-71, 74

Thompson, Ruth Plumly 1891-1976 . . . . . .DLB-22

Thompson, Thomas Phillips 1843-1933 . . .DLB-99

Thompson, William 1775-1833 . . . . .DLB-158

Thompson, William Tappan
1812-1882 . . . . .DLB-3, 11, 248

Thomson, Edward William 1849-1924 . . . .DLB-92

Thomson, James 1700-1748 . . . . .DLB-95

Thomson, James 1834-1882 . . . . .DLB-35

Thomson, Joseph 1858-1895 . . . . DLB-174

Thomson, Rupert 1955- DLB-267

Thomson, Mortimer 1831-1875 . . . . .DLB-11

Thon, Melanie Rae 1957- DLB-244

Thoreau, Henry David
1817-1862 . . . . . . .DLB-1, 183, 223; CDALB-2

The Thoreauvian Pilgrimage: The Structure of an
American Cult DLB-223

Thorpe, Adam 1956- DLB-231

Thorpe, Thomas Bangs
1815-1878 . . . . .DLB-3, 11, 248

Thorup, Kirsten 1942- DLB-214

Thoughts on Poetry and Its Varieties (1833),
by John Stuart Mill DLB-32

Thrale, Hester Lynch
(see Piozzi, Hester Lynch [Thrale])

Thubron, Colin 1939- DLB-204, 231

Thucydides
circa 455 B.C.-circa 395 B.C. DLB-176

Thulstrup, Thure de 1848-1930 . . . . .DLB-188

Thümmel, Moritz August von
1738-1817 . . . . .DLB-97

Thurber, James
1894-1961 . . . . .DLB-4, 11, 22, 102; CDALB-5

Thurman, Wallace 1902-1934 . . . . .DLB-51

Thwaite, Anthony 1930- DLB-40

The Booker Prize
Address by Anthony Thwaite,
Chairman of the Booker Prize Judges
Comments from Former Booker
Prize Winners Y-86

Thwaites, Reuben Gold 1853-1913 . . . . . . .DLB-47

Tibullus circa 54 B.C.-circa 19 B.C. DLB-211

Ticknor, George 1791-1871 . . . DLB-1, 59, 140, 235

Ticknor and Fields DLB-49

Ticknor and Fields (revived) DLB-46

Tieck, Ludwig 1773-1853 . . . . DLB-90; CDWLB-2

Tietjens, Eunice 1884-1944 . . . . .DLB-54

Tikkanen, Märta 1935- DLB-257

Tilghman, Christopher circa 1948 . . . . . . .DLB-244

Tilney, Edmund circa 1536-1610 . . . . . . .DLB-136

Tilt, Charles [publishing house] DLB-106

Tilton, J. E., and Company DLB-49

Time and Western Man (1927), by Wyndham
Lewis [excerpts] DLB-36

Time-Life Books DLB-46

Times Books DLB-46

Timothy, Peter circa 1725-1782 . . . . .DLB-43

Timrava 1867-1951 . . . . .DLB-215

Timrod, Henry 1828-1867 . . . . .DLB-3, 248

Tindal, Henrietta 1818?-1879 . . . . .DLB-199

Tinker, Chauncey Brewster 1876-1963 . . .DLB-140

Tinsley Brothers DLB-106

Tiptree, James, Jr. 1915-1987 . . . . DLB-8

Tišma, Aleksandar 1924- DLB-181

Titus, Edward William
1870-1952 . . . . DLB-4; DS-15

Tiutchev, Fedor Ivanovich 1803-1873 . . . DLB-205

Tlali, Miriam 1933- DLB-157, 225

Todd, Barbara Euphan 1890-1976 . . . . . . DLB-160

Todorov, Tzvetan 1939- DLB-242

Tofte, Robert
1561 or 1562-1619 or 1620 . . . . DLB-172

Toklas, Alice B. 1877-1967 . . . . DLB-4

Tokuda, Shūsei 1872-1943 . . . . DLB-180

Toland, John 1670-1722 . . . . DLB-252

Tolkien, J. R. R.
1892-1973 . . . . . . DLB-15, 160, 255; CDBLB-6

Toller, Ernst 1893-1939 . . . . DLB-124

Tollet, Elizabeth 1694-1754 . . . . DLB-95

Tolson, Melvin B. 1898-1966 . . . . DLB-48, 76

Tolstoy, Aleksei Konstantinovich
1817-1875 . . . . DLB-238

Tolstoy, Leo 1828-1910 . . . . DLB-238

Tom Jones (1749), by Henry Fielding
[excerpt] DLB-39

Tomalin, Claire 1933- DLB-155

Tomasi di Lampedusa, Giuseppe
1896-1957 . . . . DLB-177

Tomlinson, Charles 1927- DLB-40

Tomlinson, H. M. 1873-1958 . . . . DLB-36, 100, 195

Tompkins, Abel [publishing house] DLB-49

Tompson, Benjamin 1642-1714 . . . . DLB-24

Tomson, Graham R.
(see Watson, Rosamund Marriott)

Ton'a 1289-1372 . . . . DLB-203

Tondelli, Pier Vittorio 1955-1991 . . . . DLB-196

Tonks, Rosemary 1932- DLB-14, 207

Tonna, Charlotte Elizabeth 1790-1846 . . . DLB-163

Tonson, Jacob the Elder
[publishing house] DLB-170

Toole, John Kennedy 1937-1969 . . . . Y-81

Toomer, Jean 1894-1967 . . DLB-45, 51; CDALB-4

Tor Books DLB-46

Torberg, Friedrich 1908-1979 . . . . DLB-85

Torrence, Ridgely 1874-1950 . . . . . . DLB-54, 249

Torres-Metzger, Joseph V. 1933- DLB-122

Toth, Susan Allen 1940- Y-86

Tottell, Richard [publishing house] DLB-170

"The Printer to the Reader," (1557)
by Richard Tottell DLB-167

Tough-Guy Literature DLB-9

Touré, Askia Muhammad 1938- DLB-41

Tourgée, Albion W. 1838-1905 . . . . DLB-79

Tournemir, Elizaveta Sailhas de (see Tur, Evgeniia)

Tourneur, Cyril circa 1580-1626 . . . . DLB-58

Tournier, Michel 1924- DLB-83

Tousey, Frank [publishing house] DLB-49

Tower Publications DLB-46

Towne, Benjamin circa 1740-1793 . . . . DLB-43

Towne, Robert 1936- DLB-44

The Townely Plays fifteenth and sixteenth
centuries DLB-146

Townshend, Aurelian
by 1583-circa 1651 . . . . DLB-121

Toy, Barbara 1908- DLB-204

Tozzi, Federigo 1883-1920 . . . . DLB-264

Tracy, Honor 1913- DLB-15

Traherne, Thomas 1637?-1674 . . . . DLB-131

Traill, Catharine Parr 1802-1899 . . . . DLB-99

Train, Arthur 1875-1945 . . . . DLB-86; DS-16

Tranquilli, Secondino (see Silone, Ignazio)

The Transatlantic Publishing Company . . . DLB-49

The Transatlantic Review 1924-1925 . . . . DS-15

The Transcendental Club 1836-1840 . . . . DLB-223

Transcendentalism DLB-223

Transcendentalists, American DS-5

A Transit of Poets and Others: American
Biography in 1982 . . . . Y-82

transition 1927-1938 . . . . DS-15

Translators of the Twelfth Century: Literary Issues
Raised and Impact Created DLB-115

Tranströmer, Tomas 1931- DLB-257

Travel Writing, 1837-1875 . . . . DLB-166

Travel Writing, 1876-1909 . . . . DLB-174

Travel Writing, 1910-1939 . . . . DLB-195

Traven, B. 1882? or 1890?-1969? DLB-9, 56

Travers, Ben 1886-1980 . . . . DLB-10, 233

Travers, P. L. (Pamela Lyndon)
1899-1996 . . . . DLB-160

Trediakovsky, Vasilii Kirillovich
1703-1769 . . . . DLB-150

Treece, Henry 1911-1966 . . . . DLB-160

Treitel, Jonathan 1959- DLB-267

Trejo, Ernesto 1950- DLB-122

Trelawny, Edward John
1792-1881 . . . . DLB-110, 116, 144

Tremain, Rose 1943- DLB-14

Tremblay, Michel 1942- DLB-60

Trends in Twentieth-Century
Mass Market Publishing DLB-46

Trent, William P. 1862-1939 . . . . DLB-47

Trescot, William Henry 1822-1898 . . . . . . DLB-30

Tressell, Robert (Robert Phillipe Noonan)
1870-1911 . . . . DLB-197

Trevelyan, Sir George Otto
1838-1928 . . . . DLB-144

Trevisa, John circa 1342-circa 1402 . . . . . DLB-146

Trevor, William 1928- DLB-14, 139

Trierer Floyris circa 1170-1180 . . . . DLB-138

Trillin, Calvin 1935- DLB-185

Trilling, Lionel 1905-1975 . . . . DLB-28, 63

Trilussa 1871-1950 . . . . DLB-114

Trimmer, Sarah 1741-1810 . . . . DLB-158

Triolet, Elsa 1896-1970 . . . . DLB-72

Tripp, John 1927- DLB-40

Trocchi, Alexander 1925- DLB-15

Troisi, Dante 1920-1989 . . . . DLB-196

Trollope, Anthony
1815-1882 . . . . DLB-21, 57, 159; CDBLB-4

Trollope, Frances 1779-1863 . . . . DLB-21, 166

Trollope, Joanna 1943- DLB-207

Troop, Elizabeth 1931- DLB-14

Trotter, Catharine 1679-1749 . . . . . . DLB-84, 252

Trotti, Lamar 1898-1952 . . . . DLB-44

Trottier, Pierre 1925- DLB-60

Trotzig, Birgitta 1929- DLB-257

Troubadours, *Trobaíritz,* and Trouvères . . DLB-208

Troupe, Quincy Thomas, Jr. 1943- DLB-41

Trow, John F., and Company DLB-49

Trowbridge, John Townsend 1827-1916 . DLB-202

Trudel, Jean-Louis 1967- DLB-251

Truillier-Lacombe, Joseph-Patrice
1807-1863 . . . . DLB-99

Trumbo, Dalton 1905-1976 . . . . DLB-26

Trumbull, Benjamin 1735-1820 . . . . DLB-30

Trumbull, John 1750-1831 . . . . DLB-31

Trumbull, John 1756-1843 . . . . DLB-183

Truth, Sojourner 1797?-1883 . . . . DLB-239

Tscherning, Andreas 1611-1659 . . . . DLB-164

Tsubouchi, Shōyō 1859-1935 . . . . DLB-180

Tucholsky, Kurt 1890-1935 . . . . DLB-56

Tucker, Charlotte Maria
1821-1893 . . . . DLB-163, 190

Tucker, George 1775-1861 . . . . DLB-3, 30, 248

Tucker, James 1808?-1866? DLB-230

Tucker, Nathaniel Beverley
1784-1851 . . . . DLB-3, 248

Tucker, St. George 1752-1827 . . . . DLB-37

Tuckerman, Frederick Goddard
1821-1873 . . . . DLB-243

Tuckerman, Henry Theodore 1813-1871 . . DLB-64

Tumas, Juozas (see Vaizgantas)

Tunis, John R. 1889-1975 . . . . DLB-22, 171

Tunstall, Cuthbert 1474-1559 . . . . DLB-132

Tunström, Göran 1937-2000 . . . . DLB-257

Tuohy, Frank 1925- DLB-14, 139

Tupper, Martin F. 1810-1889 . . . . DLB-32

Tur, Evgeniia 1815-1892 . . . . DLB-238

Turbyfill, Mark 1896- DLB-45

Turco, Lewis 1934- Y-84

Turgenev, Aleksandr Ivanovich
1784-1845 . . . . DLB-198

Turgenev, Ivan Sergeevich 1818-1883 . . . DLB-238

Turnball, Alexander H. 1868-1918 . . . . . DLB-184

Turnbull, Andrew 1921-1970 . . . . DLB-103

Turnbull, Gael 1928- DLB-40

Turner, Arlin 1909-1980 . . . . DLB-103

Turner, Charles (Tennyson)
1808-1879 . . . . DLB-32

Turner, Ethel 1872-1958 . . . . DLB-230

Turner, Frederick 1943- DLB-40

Turner, Frederick Jackson
1861-1932 . . . . DLB-17, 186

Turner, Joseph Addison 1826-1868......DLB-79

Turpin, Waters Edward 1910-1968......DLB-51

Turrini, Peter 1944- DLB-124

Tutuola, Amos 1920-1997...DLB-125; CDWLB-3

Twain, Mark (see Clemens, Samuel Langhorne)

Tweedie, Ethel Brilliana circa 1860-1940. . DLB-174

The 'Twenties and Berlin, by Alex Natan . . DLB-66

Two Hundred Years of Rare Books and
    Literary Collections at the
    University of South Carolina Y-00

Twombly, Wells 1935-1977...........DLB-241

Twysden, Sir Roger 1597-1672 ....DLB-213

Tyler, Anne
    1941- DLB-6, 143; Y-82; CDALB-7

Tyler, Mary Palmer 1775-1866 ....DLB-200

Tyler, Moses Coit 1835-1900 .... DLB-47, 64

Tyler, Royall 1757-1826...............DLB-37

Tylor, Edward Burnett 1832-1917......DLB-57

Tynan, Katharine 1861-1931......DLB-153, 240

Tyndale, William circa 1494-1536......DLB-132

U

Uchida, Yoshika 1921-1992...........CDALB-7

Udall, Nicholas 1504-1556.............DLB-62

Ugrêsić, Dubravka 1949- DLB-181

Uhland, Ludwig 1787-1862 ....DLB-90

Uhse, Bodo 1904-1963 ....DLB-69

Ujević, Augustin ("Tin") 1891-1955 .....DLB-147

Ulenhart, Niclas flourished circa 1600....DLB-164

Ulibarrí, Sabine R. 1919- DLB-82

Ulica, Jorge 1870-1926...............DLB-82

Ulivi, Ferruccio 1912- DLB-196

Ulizio, B. George 1889-1969 ....DLB-140

Ulrich von Liechtenstein
    circa 1200-circa 1275 ....DLB-138

Ulrich von Zatzikhoven
    before 1194-after 1214.............DLB-138

Ulysses, Reader's Edition Y-97

Unaipon, David 1872-1967 ....DLB-230

Unamuno, Miguel de 1864-1936.......DLB-108

Under, Marie 1883-1980
    ....DLB-220; CDWLB-4

Under the Microscope (1872), by
    A. C. Swinburne DLB-35

Underhill, Evelyn
    1875-1941 ....DLB-240

Ungaretti, Giuseppe 1888-1970 ....DLB-114

Unger, Friederike Helene 1741-1813 .....DLB-94

United States Book Company DLB-49

Universal Publishing and Distributing
    Corporation......................DLB-46

The University of Iowa
    Writers' Workshop
    Golden Jubilee Y-86

University of Missouri Press Y-01

The University of South Carolina Press Y-94

University of Wales Press DLB-112

University Press of Florida Y-00

University Press of Kansas Y-98

University Press of Mississippi Y-99

"The Unknown Public" (1858), by
    Wilkie Collins [excerpt]............DLB-57

Uno, Chiyo 1897-1996................DLB-180

Unruh, Fritz von 1885-1970........DLB-56, 118

Unspeakable Practices II:
    The Festival of Vanguard
    Narrative at Brown University Y-93

Unsworth, Barry 1930- DLB-194

Unt, Mati 1944- DLB-232

The Unterberg Poetry Center of the
    92nd Street Y Y-98

Unwin, T. Fisher [publishing house] DLB-106

Upchurch, Boyd B. (see Boyd, John)

Updike, John 1932-
    ....DLB-2, 5, 143, 218, 227; Y-80, Y-82;
                        DS-3; CDALB-6

John Updike on the Internet Y-97

Upīts, Andrejs 1877-1970 ....DLB-220

Upton, Bertha 1849-1912 ....DLB-141

Upton, Charles 1948- DLB-16

Upton, Florence K. 1873-1922.........DLB-141

Upward, Allen 1863-1926 ....DLB-36

Urban, Milo 1904-1982 ....DLB-215

Urista, Alberto Baltazar (see Alurista)

Urquhart, Fred 1912- DLB-139

Urrea, Luis Alberto 1955- DLB-209

Urzidil, Johannes 1896-1976 ....DLB-85

The Uses of Facsimile Y-90

Usk, Thomas died 1388 ....DLB-146

Uslar Pietri, Arturo 1906- DLB-113

Ussher, James 1581-1656.............DLB-213

Ustinov, Peter 1921- DLB-13

Uttley, Alison 1884-1976 ....DLB-160

Uz, Johann Peter 1720-1796...........DLB-97

V

Vac, Bertrand 1914- DLB-88

Vācietis, Ojārs 1933-1983 ....DLB-232

Vaičiulaitis, Antanas 1906-1992 ....DLB-220

Vaculík, Ludvík 1926- DLB-232

Vaičiūnaite, Judita 1937- DLB-232

Vail, Laurence 1891-1968 ....DLB-4

Vailland, Roger 1907-1965.............DLB-83

Vaižgantas 1869-1933 ....DLB-220

Vajda, Ernest 1887-1954 ....DLB-44

Valdés, Gina 1943- DLB-122

Valdez, Luis Miguel 1940- DLB-122

Valduga, Patrizia 1953- DLB-128

Valente, José Angel 1929-2000 ....DLB-108

Valenzuela, Luisa 1938- ...DLB-113; CDWLB-3

Valeri, Diego 1887-1976..............DLB-128

Valerius Flaccus fl. circa A.D. 92......DLB-211

Valerius Maximus fl. circa A.D. 31......DLB-211

Valéry, Paul 1871-1945 ....DLB-258

Valesio, Paolo 1939- DLB-196

Valgardson, W. D. 1939- DLB-60

Valle, Víctor Manuel 1950- DLB-122

Valle-Inclán, Ramón del 1866-1936......DLB-134

Vallejo, Armando 1949-..............DLB-122

Vallès, Jules 1832-1885 ....DLB-123

Vallette, Marguerite Eymery (see Rachilde)

Valverde, José María 1926-1996 ....DLB-108

Van Allsburg, Chris 1949- DLB-61

Van Anda, Carr 1864-1945............DLB-25

van der Post, Laurens 1906-1996 ....DLB-204

Van Dine, S. S. (see Wright, Williard Huntington)

Van Doren, Mark 1894-1972...........DLB-45

van Druten, John 1901-1957 ....DLB-10

Van Duyn, Mona 1921- DLB-5

Van Dyke, Henry 1852-1933 .....DLB-71; DS-13

Van Dyke, Henry 1928- DLB-33

Van Dyke, John C. 1856-1932 ....DLB-186

van Gulik, Robert Hans 1910-1967........DS-17

van Itallie, Jean-Claude 1936- DLB-7

Van Loan, Charles E. 1876-1919........DLB-171

Van Rensselaer, Mariana Griswold
    1851-1934 ....DLB-47

Van Rensselaer, Mrs. Schuyler
    (see Van Rensselaer, Mariana Griswold)

Van Vechten, Carl 1880-1964.........DLB-4, 9

van Vogt, A. E. 1912-2000 ....DLB-8, 251

Vanbrugh, Sir John 1664-1726 ....DLB-80

Vance, Jack 1916?- DLB-8

Vančura, Vladislav
    1891-1942...........DLB-215; CDWLB-4

Vane, Sutton 1888-1963 ....DLB-10

Vanguard Press DLB-46

Vann, Robert L. 1879-1940...........DLB-29

Vargas Llosa, Mario
    1936- DLB-145; CDWLB-3

Varley, John 1947- Y-81

Varnhagen von Ense, Karl August
    1785-1858 ....DLB-90

Varnhagen von Ense, Rahel
    1771-1833 ....DLB-90

Varro 116 B.C.-27 B.C...............DLB-211

Vasiliu, George (see Bacovia, George)

Vásquez, Richard 1928- DLB-209

Vásquez Montalbán, Manuel 1939- ...DLB-134

Vassa, Gustavus (see Equiano, Olaudah)

Vassalli, Sebastiano 1941- DLB-128, 196

Vaughan, Henry 1621-1695 ....DLB-131

Vaughan, Thomas 1621-1666..........DLB-131

Vaughn, Robert 1592?-1667 ....DLB-213

Vaux, Thomas, Lord 1509-1556 ....DLB-132

Vazov, Ivan 1850-1921 .....DLB-147; CDWLB-4

Véa, Alfredo, Jr. 1950-..............DLB-209

Veblen, Thorstein 1857-1929..........DLB-246

Vega, Janine Pommy 1942- DLB-16

Veiller, Anthony 1903-1965 ....DLB-44

Velásquez-Trevino, Gloria 1949- DLB-122

Veley, Margaret 1843-1887 . . . . DLB-199

Velleius Paterculus
circa 20 B.C.-circa A.D. 30. . . . . DLB-211

Veloz Maggiolo, Marcio 1936- DLB-145

Vel'tman Aleksandr Fomich
1800-1870 . . . . DLB-198

Venegas, Daniel ?-? DLB-82

Venevitinov, Dmitrii Vladimirovich
1805-1827 . . . . DLB-205

Vergil, Polydore circa 1470-1555 . . . . DLB-132

Veríssimo, Erico 1905-1975 . . . . DLB-145

Verlaine, Paul 1844-1896 . . . . DLB-217

Verne, Jules 1828-1905 . . . . DLB-123

Verplanck, Gulian C. 1786-1870 . . . . DLB-59

Very, Jones 1813-1880 . . . . DLB-1, 243

Vian, Boris 1920-1959 . . . . DLB-72

Viazemsky, Petr Andreevich
1792-1878 . . . . DLB-205

Vicars, Thomas 1591-1638 . . . . DLB-236

Vickers, Roy 1888?-1965 . . . . DLB-77

Vickery, Sukey 1779-1821 . . . . DLB-200

Victoria 1819-1901 . . . . DLB-55

Victoria Press DLB-106

Vidal, Gore 1925- DLB-6, 152; CDALB-7

Vidal, Mary Theresa 1815-1873 . . . . DLB-230

Vidmer, Richards 1898-1978 . . . . DLB-241

Viebig, Clara 1860-1952 . . . . DLB-66

Viereck, George Sylvester
1884-1962 . . . . DLB-54

Viereck, Peter 1916- DLB-5

Viets, Roger 1738-1811 . . . . DLB-99

Viewpoint: Politics and Performance, by
David Edgar DLB-13

Vigil-Piñon, Evangelina 1949- DLB-122

Vigneault, Gilles 1928- DLB-60

Vigny, Alfred de
1797-1863 . . . . .DLB-119, 192, 217

Vigolo, Giorgio 1894-1983 . . . . DLB-114

The Viking Press DLB-46

Vilde, Eduard 1865-1933 . . . . DLB-220

Vilinskaia, Mariia Aleksandrovna
(see Vovchok, Marko)

Villanueva, Alma Luz 1944- DLB-122

Villanueva, Tino 1941- DLB-82

Villard, Henry 1835-1900 . . . . DLB-23

Villard, Oswald Garrison
1872-1949 . . . . DLB-25, 91

Villarreal, Edit 1944- DLB-209

Villarreal, José Antonio 1924- DLB-82

Villaseñor, Victor 1940- DLB-209

Villegas de Magnón, Leonor
1876-1955 . . . . DLB-122

Villehardouin, Geoffroi de
circa 1150-1215 . . . . DLB-208

Villemaire, Yolande 1949- DLB-60

Villena, Luis Antonio de 1951- DLB-134

Villiers, George, Second Duke
of Buckingham 1628-1687 . . . . DLB-80

Villiers de l'Isle-Adam, Jean-Marie Mathias
Philippe-Auguste, Comte de
1838-1889 . . . . DLB-123, 192

Villon, François 1431-circa 1463?. DLB-208

Vine Press DLB-112

Viorst, Judith ?- DLB-52

Vipont, Elfrida (Elfrida Vipont Foulds,
Charles Vipont) 1902-1992 . . . . DLB-160

Viramontes, Helena María 1954- DLB-122

Virgil 70 B.C.-19 B.C. DLB-211; CDWLB-1

Virtual Books and Enemies of Books Y-00

Vischer, Friedrich Theodor 1807-1887 . . . DLB-133

Vitruvius circa 85 B.C.-circa 15 B.C. DLB-211

Vitry, Philippe de 1291-1361 . . . . DLB-208

Vittorini, Elio 1908-1966 . . . . DLB-264

Vivanco, Luis Felipe 1907-1975 . . . . DLB-108

Vivian, E. Charles 1882-1947 . . . . DLB-255

Viviani, Cesare 1947- DLB-128

Vivien, Renée 1877-1909 . . . . DLB-217

Vizenor, Gerald 1934- DLB-175, 227

Vizetelly and Company DLB-106

Voaden, Herman 1903- DLB-88

Voß, Johann Heinrich 1751-1826 . . . . DLB-90

Voigt, Ellen Bryant 1943- DLB-120

Vojnović, Ivo 1857-1929 . . . . .DLB-147; CDWLB-4

Volkoff, Vladimir 1932- DLB-83

Volland, P. F., Company DLB-46

Vollbehr, Otto H. F.
1872?-1945 or 1946 . . . . DLB-187

Vologdin (see Zasodimsky, Pavel Vladimirovich)

Volponi, Paolo 1924- DLB-177

Vonarburg, Élisabeth 1947- DLB-251

von der Grün, Max 1926- DLB-75

Vonnegut, Kurt 1922-
. . . . . . DLB-2, 8, 152; Y-80; DS-3; CDALB-6

Voranc, Prežihov 1893-1950 . . . . DLB-147

Vovchok, Marko 1833-1907. . . . . DLB-238

Voynich, E. L. 1864-1960 . . . . DLB-197

Vroman, Mary Elizabeth
circa 1924-1967 . . . . DLB-33

W

Wace, Robert ("Maistre")
circa 1100-circa 1175 . . . . DLB-146

Wackenroder, Wilhelm Heinrich
1773-1798 . . . . DLB-90

Wackernagel, Wilhelm 1806-1869 . . . . . . DLB-133

Waddell, Helen 1889-1965 . . . . DLB-240

Waddington, Miriam 1917- DLB-68

Wade, Henry 1887-1969 . . . . DLB-77

Wagenknecht, Edward 1900- DLB-103

Wägner, Elin 1882-1949 . . . . DLB-259

Wagner, Heinrich Leopold 1747-1779 . . . . DLB-94

Wagner, Henry R. 1862-1957 . . . . DLB-140

Wagner, Richard 1813-1883 . . . . DLB-129

Wagoner, David 1926- DLB-5, 256

Wah, Fred 1939- DLB-60

Waiblinger, Wilhelm 1804-1830 . . . . DLB-90

Wain, John
1925-1994 . . .DLB-15, 27, 139, 155; CDBLB-8

Wainwright, Jeffrey 1944- DLB-40

Waite, Peirce and Company DLB-49

Wakeman, Stephen H. 1859-1924 . . . . . . .DLB-187

Wakoski, Diane 1937- DLB-5

Walahfrid Strabo circa 808-849 . . . . DLB-148

Walck, Henry Z. DLB-46

Walcott, Derek
1930- DLB-117; Y-81, Y-92; CDWLB-3

Waldegrave, Robert [publishing house] . . .DLB-170

Waldman, Anne 1945- DLB-16

Waldrop, Rosmarie 1935- DLB-169

Walker, Alice 1900-1982 . . . . DLB-201

Walker, Alice
1944- DLB-6, 33, 143; CDALB-6

Walker, Annie Louisa (Mrs. Harry Coghill)
circa 1836-1907 . . . . DLB-240

Walker, George F. 1947- DLB-60

Walker, John Brisben 1847-1931 . . . . DLB-79

Walker, Joseph A. 1935- DLB-38

Walker, Margaret 1915- DLB-76, 152

Walker, Ted 1934- DLB-40

Walker and Company DLB-49

Walker, Evans and Cogswell Company. . . DLB-49

Wall, John F. (see Sarban)

Wallace, Alfred Russel 1823-1913 . . . . . . DLB-190

Wallace, Dewitt 1889-1981 and
Lila Acheson Wallace 1889-1984. . . . .DLB-137

Wallace, Edgar 1875-1932 . . . . DLB-70

Wallace, Lew 1827-1905. . . . . DLB-202

Wallace, Lila Acheson
(see Wallace, Dewitt, and Lila Acheson Wallace)

Wallace, Naomi 1960- DLB-249

Wallant, Edward Lewis
1926-1962 . . . . DLB-2, 28, 143

Waller, Edmund 1606-1687 . . . . DLB-126

Walpole, Horace 1717-1797. . . . .DLB-39, 104, 213

Preface to the First Edition of
The Castle of Otranto (1764). DLB-39

Preface to the Second Edition of
The Castle of Otranto (1765). DLB-39

Walpole, Hugh 1884-1941 . . . . DLB-34

Walrond, Eric 1898-1966. . . . . DLB-51

Walser, Martin 1927- DLB-75, 124

Walser, Robert 1878-1956 . . . . DLB-66

Walsh, Ernest 1895-1926 . . . . DLB-4, 45

Walsh, Robert 1784-1859. . . . . DLB-59

Walters, Henry 1848-1931 . . . . DLB-140

Waltharius circa 825 . . . . DLB-148

Walther von der Vogelweide
circa 1170-circa 1230 . . . . DLB-138

Walton, Izaak
1593-1683 . . . . DLB-151, 213; CDBLB-1

Wambaugh, Joseph 1937- DLB-6; Y-83

Wand, Alfred Rudolph 1828-1891 . . . . . .DLB-188

Waniek, Marilyn Nelson 1946- DLB-120

Wanley, Humphrey 1672-1726 . . . . .DLB-213

Warburton, William 1698-1779 . . . . .DLB-104

Ward, Aileen 1919- DLB-111

Ward, Artemus (see Browne, Charles Farrar)

Ward, Arthur Henry Sarsfield (see Rohmer, Sax)

Ward, Douglas Turner 1930- DLB-7, 38

Ward, Mrs. Humphry 1851-1920 . . . . . . .DLB-18

Ward, James 1843-1925 . . . . .DLB-262

Ward, Lynd 1905-1985 . . . . .DLB-22

Ward, Lock and Company DLB-106

Ward, Nathaniel circa 1578-1652 . . . . . . .DLB-24

Ward, Theodore 1902-1983 . . . . .DLB-76

Wardle, Ralph 1909-1988 . . . . .DLB-103

Ware, Henry, Jr. 1794-1843 . . . . .DLB-235

Ware, William 1797-1852 . . . . .DLB-1, 235

Warfield, Catherine Ann 1816-1877 . . . . . .DLB-248

Waring, Anna Letitia 1823-1910 . . . . .DLB-240

Warne, Frederick, and Company [U.K.] . . .DLB-106

Warne, Frederick, and Company [U.S.] DLB-49

Warner, Anne 1869-1913 . . . . .DLB-202

Warner, Charles Dudley 1829-1900 . . . . . .DLB-64

Warner, Marina 1946- DLB-194

Warner, Rex 1905- DLB-15

Warner, Susan 1819-1885 . . . . DLB-3, 42, 239, 250

Warner, Sylvia Townsend
1893-1978 . . . . .DLB-34, 139

Warner, William 1558-1609 . . . . .DLB-172

Warner Books .DLB-46

Warr, Bertram 1917-1943 . . . . .DLB-88

Warren, John Byrne Leicester (see De Tabley, Lord)

Warren, Lella 1899-1982 . . . . Y-83

Warren, Mercy Otis 1728-1814 . . . . . .DLB-31, 200

Warren, Robert Penn 1905-1989
. . . . . . DLB-2, 48, 152; Y-80, Y-89; CDALB-6

Warren, Samuel 1807-1877 . . . . .DLB-190

Die Wartburgkrieg circa 1230-circa 1280 . . .DLB-138

Warton, Joseph 1722-1800 . . . . .DLB-104, 109

Warton, Thomas 1728-1790 . . . . . . .DLB-104, 109

Warung, Price (William Astley)
1855-1911 .DLB-230

Washington, George 1732-1799 . . . . .DLB-31

Washington, Ned 1901-1976 . . . . .DLB-265

Wassermann, Jakob 1873-1934 . . . . .DLB-66

Wasserstein, Wendy 1950- DLB-228

Wasson, David Atwood 1823-1887 . . . .DLB-1, 223

Watanna, Onoto (see Eaton, Winnifred)

Waterhouse, Keith 1929- DLB-13, 15

Waterman, Andrew 1940- DLB-40

Waters, Frank 1902-1995 . . . . . . .DLB-212; Y-86

Waters, Michael 1949- DLB-120

Watkins, Tobias 1780-1855 . . . . .DLB-73

Watkins, Vernon 1906-1967 . . . . .DLB-20

Watmough, David 1926- DLB-53

Watson, Ian 1943- DLB-261

Watson, James Wreford (see Wreford, James)

Watson, John 1850-1907 . . . . .DLB-156

Watson, Rosamund Marriott
(Graham R. Tomson) 1860-1911 . . . .DLB-240

Watson, Sheila 1909- DLB-60

Watson, Thomas 1545?-1592 . . . . .DLB-132

Watson, Wilfred 1911- DLB-60

Watt, W. J., and Company DLB-46

Watten, Barrett 1948- DLB-193

Watterson, Henry 1840-1921 . . . . .DLB-25

Watts, Alan 1915-1973 . . . . .DLB-16

Watts, Franklin [publishing house] DLB-46

Watts, Isaac 1674-1748 . . . . .DLB-95

Waugh, Alec 1898-1981 . . . . .DLB-191

Waugh, Auberon 1939-2000 . . . DLB-14, 194; Y-00

The Cult of Biography
Excerpts from the Second Folio Debate:
"Biographies are generally a disease of
English Literature" Y-86

Waugh, Evelyn
1903-1966 . . . . . .DLB-15, 162, 195; CDBLB-6

Way and Williams DLB-49

Wayman, Tom 1945- DLB-53

We See the Editor at Work Y-97

Weatherly, Tom 1942- DLB-41

Weaver, Gordon 1937- DLB-130

Weaver, Robert 1921- DLB-88

Webb, Beatrice 1858-1943 and
Webb, Sidney 1859-1947 . . . . .DLB-190

Webb, Francis 1925-1973 . . . . .DLB-260

Webb, Frank J. ?-? DLB-50

Webb, James Watson 1802-1884 . . . . .DLB-43

Webb, Mary 1881-1927 . . . . .DLB-34

Webb, Phyllis 1927- DLB-53

Webb, Walter Prescott 1888-1963 . . . . . . .DLB-17

Webbe, William ?-1591 . . . . .DLB-132

Webber, Charles Wilkins 1819-1856? DLB-202

Webling, Lucy (Lucy Betty MacRaye)
1877-1952 .DLB-240

Webling, Peggy (Arthur Weston)
1871-1949 .DLB-240

Webster, Augusta 1837-1894 . . . . .DLB-35, 240

Webster, Charles L., and Company DLB-49

Webster, John
1579 or 1580-1634? DLB-58; CDBLB-1

John Webster: The Melbourne
Manuscript Y-86

Webster, Noah
1758-1843 . . . . DLB-1, 37, 42, 43, 73, 243

Webster, Paul Francis 1907-1984 . . . . .DLB-265

Weckherlin, Georg Rodolf 1584-1653 . . . .DLB-164

Wedekind, Frank
1864-1918 . . . . .DLB-118; CDBLB-2

Weeks, Edward Augustus, Jr.
1898-1989 .DLB-137

Weeks, Stephen B. 1865-1918 . . . . .DLB-187

Weems, Mason Locke 1759-1825 . . DLB-30, 37, 42

Weerth, Georg 1822-1856 . . . . .DLB-129

Weidenfeld and Nicolson DLB-112

Weidman, Jerome 1913-1998 . . . . .DLB-28

Weiß, Ernst 1882-1940 . . . . .DLB-81

Weigl, Bruce 1949- DLB-120

Weinbaum, Stanley Grauman 1902-1935 . . .DLB-8

Weiner, Andrew 1949- DLB-251

Weintraub, Stanley 1929- DLB-111; Y82

The Practice of Biography: An Interview
with Stanley Weintraub Y-82

Weise, Christian 1642-1708 . . . . .DLB-168

Weisenborn, Gunther 1902-1969 . . . .DLB-69, 124

Weiss, John 1818-1879 . . . . .DLB-1, 243

Weiss, Peter 1916-1982 . . . . .DLB-69, 124

Weiss, Theodore 1916- DLB-5

Weisse, Christian Felix 1726-1804 . . . . . . .DLB-97

Weitling, Wilhelm 1808-1871 . . . . .DLB-129

Welch, James 1940- DLB-175, 256

Welch, Lew 1926-1971? DLB-16

Weldon, Fay 1931- DLB-14, 194; CDBLB-8

Wellek, René 1903-1995 . . . . .DLB-63

Wells, Carolyn 1862-1942 . . . . .DLB-11

Wells, Charles Jeremiah circa 1800-1879 . . .DLB-32

Wells, Gabriel 1862-1946 . . . . .DLB-140

Wells, H. G.
1866-1946 . . . DLB-34, 70, 156, 178; CDBLB-6

Wells, Helena 1758?-1824 . . . . .DLB-200

Wells, Robert 1947- DLB-40

Wells-Barnett, Ida B. 1862-1931 . . . . .DLB-23, 221

Welty, Eudora 1909- DLB-2, 102, 143;
. . . . Y-87, Y-01; DS-12; CDALB-1

Eudora Welty: Eye of the Storyteller Y-87

Eudora Welty Newsletter Y-99

Eudora Welty's Funeral Y-01

Eudora Welty's Ninetieth Birthday Y-99

Wendell, Barrett 1855-1921 . . . . .DLB-71

Wentworth, Patricia 1878-1961 . . . . .DLB-77

Wentworth, William Charles
1790-1872 .DLB-230

Werder, Diederich von dem 1584-1657 . .DLB-164

Werfel, Franz 1890-1945 . . . . .DLB-81, 124

Werner, Zacharias 1768-1823 . . . . .DLB-94

The Werner Company DLB-49

Wersba, Barbara 1932- DLB-52

Wescott, Glenway 1901- DLB-4, 9, 102

Wesker, Arnold 1932- DLB-13; CDBLB-8

Wesley, Charles 1707-1788 . . . . .DLB-95

Wesley, John 1703-1791 . . . . .DLB-104

Wesley, Mary 1912- DLB-231

Wesley, Richard 1945- DLB-38

Wessels, A., and Company DLB-46

Wessobrunner Gebet circa 787-815 . . . . . . .DLB-148

West, Anthony 1914-1988 . . . . .DLB-15

West, Cheryl L. 1957- DLB-266

West, Cornel 1953- DLB-246

West, Dorothy 1907-1998. . . . . DLB-76

West, Jessamyn 1902-1984. . . . . DLB-6; Y-84

West, Mae 1892-1980. . . . . DLB-44

West, Michelle Sagara 1963- DLB-251

West, Nathanael
1903-1940 . . . . . DLB-4, 9, 28; CDALB-5

West, Paul 1930- DLB-14

West, Rebecca 1892-1983. . . . . DLB-36; Y-83

West, Richard 1941- DLB-185

West and Johnson DLB-49

Westcott, Edward Noyes 1846-1898 . . . . DLB-202

The Western Messenger 1835-1841 . . . . DLB-223

Western Publishing Company DLB-46

Western Writers of America Y-99

The Westminster Review 1824-1914 . . . . . . DLB-110

Weston, Arthur (see Webling, Peggy)

Weston, Elizabeth Jane circa 1582-1612. . .DLB-172

Wetherald, Agnes Ethelwyn 1857-1940 . . . DLB-99

Wetherell, Elizabeth (see Warner, Susan)

Wetherell, W. D. 1948- DLB-234

Wetzel, Friedrich Gottlob 1779-1819 . . . . DLB-90

Weyman, Stanley J. 1855-1928. . . . DLB-141, 156

Wezel, Johann Karl 1747-1819 . . . . DLB-94

Whalen, Philip 1923- DLB-16

Whalley, George 1915-1983. . . . . DLB-88

Wharton, Edith 1862-1937
. . .DLB-4, 9, 12, 78, 189; DS-13; CDALB-3

Wharton, William 1920s?- Y-80

"What You Lose on the Swings You Make Up
on the Merry-Go-Round" Y-99

Whately, Mary Louisa 1824-1889 . . . . . . DLB-166

Whately, Richard 1787-1863. . . . . DLB-190

From *Elements of Rhetoric* (1828;
revised, 1846). DLB-57

What's Really Wrong With Bestseller Lists . . . Y-84

Wheatley, Dennis 1897-1977. . . . . . . .DLB-77, 255

Wheatley, Phillis
circa 1754-1784. . . . . . . DLB-31, 50; CDALB-2

Wheeler, Anna Doyle 1785-1848? DLB-158

Wheeler, Charles Stearns 1816-1843 . . DLB-1, 223

Wheeler, Monroe 1900-1988 . . . . DLB-4

Wheelock, John Hall 1886-1978. . . . . DLB-45

From John Hall Wheelock's Oral Memoir Y-01

Wheelwright, J. B. 1897-1940 . . . . DLB-45

Wheelwright, John circa 1592-1679 . . . . . DLB-24

Whetstone, George 1550-1587 . . . . DLB-136

Whetstone, Colonel Pete (see Noland, C. F. M.)

Whewell, William 1794-1866 . . . . DLB-262

Whichcote, Benjamin 1609?-1683 . . . . . DLB-252

Whicher, Stephen E. 1915-1961. . . . . . . DLB-111

Whipple, Edwin Percy 1819-1886 . . . . . DLB-1, 64

Whitaker, Alexander 1585-1617 . . . . DLB-24

Whitaker, Daniel K. 1801-1881 . . . . DLB-73

Whitcher, Frances Miriam
1812-1852. . . . . DLB-11, 202

White, Andrew 1579-1656 . . . . DLB-24

White, Andrew Dickson 1832-1918 . . . . . . DLB-47

White, E. B. 1899-1985 . . . DLB-11, 22; CDALB-7

White, Edgar B. 1947- DLB-38

White, Edmund 1940- DLB-227

White, Ethel Lina 1887-1944 . . . . DLB-77

White, Hayden V. 1928- DLB-246

White, Henry Kirke 1785-1806 . . . . DLB-96

White, Horace 1834-1916 . . . . DLB-23

White, James 1928-1999. . . . . DLB-261

White, Patrick 1912-1990. . . . . DLB-260

White, Phyllis Dorothy James (see James, P. D.)

White, Richard Grant 1821-1885. . . . . . . DLB-64

White, T. H. 1906-1964. . . . . DLB-160, 255

White, Walter 1893-1955. . . . . DLB-51

White, William, and Company DLB-49

White, William Allen 1868-1944 . . . . . DLB-9, 25

White, William Anthony Parker
(see Boucher, Anthony)

White, William Hale (see Rutherford, Mark)

Whitechurch, Victor L. 1868-1933. . . . . . DLB-70

Whitehead, Alfred North 1861-1947 . . . . DLB-100

Whitehead, James 1936- Y-81

Whitehead, William 1715-1785. . . . . DLB-84, 109

Whitfield, James Monroe 1822-1871 . . . . . DLB-50

Whitfield, Raoul 1898-1945 . . . . DLB-226

Whitgift, John circa 1533-1604. . . . . . . DLB-132

Whiting, John 1917-1963 . . . . DLB-13

Whiting, Samuel 1597-1679 . . . . DLB-24

Whitlock, Brand 1869-1934 . . . . DLB-12

Whitman, Albert, and Company DLB-46

Whitman, Albery Allson 1851-1901. . . . . . DLB-50

Whitman, Alden 1913-1990 . . . . Y-91

Whitman, Sarah Helen (Power)
1803-1878. . . . . DLB-1, 243

Whitman, Walt
1819-1892 . . . DLB-3, 64, 224, 250; CDALB-2

Whitman Publishing Company DLB-46

Whitney, Geoffrey 1548 or 1552?-1601. . DLB-136

Whitney, Isabella flourished 1566-1573 . . DLB-136

Whitney, John Hay 1904-1982. . . . . DLB-127

Whittemore, Reed 1919-1995. . . . . DLB-5

Whittier, John Greenleaf
1807-1892 . . . . DLB-1, 243; CDALB-2

Whittlesey House. DLB-46

Who Runs American Literature?. Y-94

Whose *Ulysses*? The Function of Editing. Y-97

Wickham, Anna (Edith Alice Mary Harper)
1884-1947. . . . . DLB-240

Wicomb, Zoë 1948- DLB-225

Wideman, John Edgar 1941- DLB-33, 143

Widener, Harry Elkins 1885-1912 . . . . . . DLB-140

Wiebe, Rudy 1934- DLB-60

Wiechert, Ernst 1887-1950 . . . . DLB-56

Wied, Martina 1882-1957. . . . . DLB-85

Wiehe, Evelyn May Clowes (see Mordaunt, Elinor)

Wieland, Christoph Martin 1733-1813. . . . DLB-97

Wienbarg, Ludolf 1802-1872 . . . . DLB-133

Wieners, John 1934- DLB-16

Wier, Ester 1910- DLB-52

Wiesel, Elie
1928- DLB-83; Y-86, 87; CDALB-7

Wiggin, Kate Douglas 1856-1923. . . . . . . DLB-42

Wigglesworth, Michael 1631-1705 . . . . . . DLB-24

Wilberforce, William 1759-1833. . . . . . . DLB-158

Wilbrandt, Adolf 1837-1911. . . . . DLB-129

Wilbur, Richard
1921- DLB-5, 169; CDALB-7

Wild, Peter 1940- DLB-5

Wilde, Lady Jane Francesca Elgee
1821?-1896. . . . . DLB-199

Wilde, Oscar 1854-1900
. . . . .DLB-10, 19, 34, 57, 141, 156, 190;
CDBLB-5

"The Critic as Artist" (1891) DLB-57

Oscar Wilde Conference at Hofstra
University Y-00

From "The Decay of Lying" (1889) DLB-18

"The English Renaissance of
Art" (1908). DLB-35

"L'Envoi" (1882) DLB-35

Wilde, Richard Henry 1789-1847. . . . . . DLB-3, 59

Wilde, W. A., Company DLB-49

Wilder, Billy 1906- DLB-26

Wilder, Laura Ingalls 1867-1957. . . . DLB-22, 256

Wilder, Thornton
1897-1975. . . . . . . .DLB-4, 7, 9, 228; CDALB-7

Thornton Wilder Centenary at Yale Y-97

Wildgans, Anton 1881-1932. . . . . DLB-118

Wiley, Bell Irvin 1906-1980 . . . . .DLB-17

Wiley, John, and Sons DLB-49

Wilhelm, Kate 1928- DLB-8

Wilkes, Charles 1798-1877 . . . . DLB-183

Wilkes, George 1817-1885 . . . . DLB-79

Wilkins, John 1614-1672 . . . . DLB-236

Wilkinson, Anne 1910-1961. . . . . DLB-88

Wilkinson, Eliza Yonge
1757-circa 1813. . . . . DLB-200

Wilkinson, Sylvia 1940- Y-86

Wilkinson, William Cleaver 1833-1920. . . DLB-71

Willard, Barbara 1909-1994. . . . . DLB-161

Willard, Emma 1787-1870. . . . . DLB-239

Willard, Frances E. 1839-1898. . . . . DLB-221

Willard, L. [publishing house] DLB-49

Willard, Nancy 1936- DLB-5, 52

Willard, Samuel 1640-1707. . . . . DLB-24

Willeford, Charles 1919-1988 . . . . DLB-226

William of Auvergne 1190-1249 . . . . . . DLB-115

William of Conches
circa 1090-circa 1154 . . . . DLB-115

William of Ockham circa 1285-1347 . . . . DLB-115

William of Sherwood
1200/1205-1266/1271. . . . . DLB-115

The William Chavrat American Fiction Collection
at the Ohio State University Libraries Y-92

Williams, A., and Company DLB-49

Williams, Ben Ames 1889-1953. . . . . . . .DLB-102

Williams, C. K. 1936- DLB-5

Williams, Chancellor 1905- DLB-76

Williams, Charles 1886-1945. . .DLB-100, 153, 255

Williams, Denis 1923-1998 . . . . .DLB-117

Williams, Emlyn 1905-1987. . . . . .DLB-10, 77

Williams, Garth 1912-1996 . . . . .DLB-22

Williams, George Washington
1849-1891 . . . . .DLB-47

Williams, Heathcote 1941- DLB-13

Williams, Helen Maria 1761-1827 . . . . . .DLB-158

Williams, Hugo 1942- DLB-40

Williams, Isaac 1802-1865 . . . . .DLB-32

Williams, Joan 1928- DLB-6

Williams, Joe 1889-1972 . . . . .DLB-241

Williams, John A. 1925- DLB-2, 33

Williams, John E. 1922-1994 . . . . .DLB-6

Williams, Jonathan 1929- DLB-5

Williams, Miller 1930- DLB-105

Williams, Nigel 1948- DLB-231

Williams, Raymond 1921- DLB-14, 231, 242

Williams, Roger circa 1603-1683 . . . . .DLB-24

Williams, Rowland 1817-1870 . . . . .DLB-184

Williams, Samm-Art 1946- DLB-38

Williams, Sherley Anne 1944-1999 . . . . . . .DLB-41

Williams, T. Harry 1909-1979 . . . . .DLB-17

Williams, Tennessee
1911-1983 . . . . .DLB-7; Y-83; DS-4; CDALB-1

Williams, Terry Tempest 1955- DLB-206

Williams, Ursula Moray 1911- DLB-160

Williams, Valentine 1883-1946 . . . . .DLB-77

Williams, William Appleman 1921- DLB-17

Williams, William Carlos
1883-1963 . . . . . .DLB-4, 16, 54, 86; CDALB-4

Williams, Wirt 1921- DLB-6

Williams Brothers DLB-49

Williamson, Henry 1895-1977 . . . . .DLB-191

Williamson, Jack 1908- DLB-8

Willingham, Calder Baynard, Jr.
1922-1995 .DLB-2, 44

Williram of Ebersberg circa 1020-1085 . . .DLB-148

Willis, Nathaniel Parker 1806-1867
. . . . .DLB-3, 59, 73, 74, 183, 250; DS-13

Willkomm, Ernst 1810-1886 . . . . .DLB-133

Willumsen, Dorrit 1940- DLB-214

Wills, Garry 1934- DLB-246

Willson, Meredith 1902-1984 . . . . .DLB-265

Wilmer, Clive 1945- DLB-40

Wilson, A. N. 1950- DLB-14, 155, 194

Wilson, Angus 1913-1991 . . . . . .DLB-15, 139, 155

Wilson, Arthur 1595-1652 . . . . .DLB-58

Wilson, August 1945- DLB-228

Wilson, Augusta Jane Evans 1835-1909 . . .DLB-42

Wilson, Colin 1931- DLB-14, 194

Wilson, Edmund 1895-1972 . . . . .DLB-63

Wilson, Effingham [publishing house] DLB-154

Wilson, Ethel 1888-1980 . . . . .DLB-68

Wilson, F. P. 1889-1963. . . . . .DLB-201

Wilson, Harriet E.
1827/1828?-1863? DLB-50, 239, 243

Wilson, Harry Leon 1867-1939 . . . . .DLB-9

Wilson, John 1588-1667 . . . . .DLB-24

Wilson, John 1785-1854 . . . . .DLB-110

Wilson, John Dover 1881-1969 . . . . .DLB-201

Wilson, Lanford 1937- DLB-7

Wilson, Margaret 1882-1973 . . . . .DLB-9

Wilson, Michael 1914-1978 . . . . .DLB-44

Wilson, Mona 1872-1954. . . . . .DLB-149

Wilson, Robert Charles 1953- DLB-251

Wilson, Robert McLiam 1964- DLB-267

Wilson, Robley 1930- DLB-218

Wilson, Romer 1891-1930 . . . . .DLB-191

Wilson, Thomas 1524-1581 . . . . . .DLB-132, 236

Wilson, Woodrow 1856-1924 . . . . .DLB-47

Wimsatt, William K., Jr. 1907-1975 . . . . . .DLB-63

Winchell, Walter 1897-1972. . . . . .DLB-29

Winchester, J. [publishing house]. DLB-49

Winckelmann, Johann Joachim
1717-1768 . . . . .DLB-97

Winckler, Paul 1630-1686 . . . . .DLB-164

Wind, Herbert Warren 1916- DLB-171

Windet, John [publishing house] DLB-170

Windham, Donald 1920- DLB-6

Wing, Donald Goddard 1904-1972 . . . . . .DLB-187

Wing, John M. 1844-1917 . . . . .DLB-187

Wingate, Allan [publishing house] DLB-112

Winnemucca, Sarah 1844-1921 . . . . .DLB-175

Winnifrith, Tom 1938- DLB-155

Winning an Edgar Y-98

Winsloe, Christa 1888-1944 . . . . .DLB-124

Winslow, Anna Green 1759-1780 . . . . . . .DLB-200

Winsor, Justin 1831-1897 . . . . .DLB-47

John C. Winston Company. DLB-49

Winters, Yvor 1900-1968 . . . . .DLB-48

Winterson, Jeanette 1959- DLB-207, 261

Winthrop, John 1588-1649 . . . . .DLB-24, 30

Winthrop, John, Jr. 1606-1676. . . . . .DLB-24

Winthrop, Margaret Tyndal 1591-1647 . .DLB-200

Winthrop, Theodore 1828-1861 . . . . .DLB-202

Wirt, William 1772-1834 . . . . .DLB-37

Wise, John 1652-1725 . . . . .DLB-24

Wise, Thomas James 1859-1937 . . . . .DLB-184

Wiseman, Adele 1928-1992 . . . . .DLB-88

Wishart and Company DLB-112

Wisner, George 1812-1849 . . . . .DLB-43

Wister, Owen 1860-1938. . . . . DLB-9, 78, 186

Wister, Sarah 1761-1804 . . . . .DLB-200

Wither, George 1588-1667 . . . . .DLB-121

Witherspoon, John 1723-1794 . . . . .DLB-31

Withrow, William Henry 1839-1908 . . . . .DLB-99

Witkacy (see Witkiewicz, Stanisław Ignacy)

Witkiewicz, Stanisław Ignacy
1885-1939 . . . . .DLB-215; CDWLB-4

Wittgenstein, Ludwig 1889-1951 . . . . . . .DLB-262

Wittig, Monique 1935- DLB-83

Wodehouse, P. G.
1881-1975 . . . . .DLB-34, 162; CDBLB-6

Wohmann, Gabriele 1932- DLB-75

Woiwode, Larry 1941- DLB-6

Wolcot, John 1738-1819 . . . . .DLB-109

Wolcott, Roger 1679-1767 . . . . .DLB-24

Wolf, Christa 1929- DLB-75; CDWLB-2

Wolf, Friedrich 1888-1953. . . . . .DLB-124

Wolfe, Gene 1931- DLB-8

Wolfe, John [publishing house] DLB-170

Wolfe, Reyner (Reginald)
[publishing house] DLB-170

Wolfe, Thomas
1900-1938 . . . . .DLB-9, 102, 229; Y-85;
DS-2, DS-16; CDALB-5

"All the Faults of Youth and Inexperience":
A Reader's Report on
Thomas Wolfe's *O Lost* Y-01

Eugene Gant's Projected Works Y-01

The Thomas Wolfe Collection at the University
of North Carolina at Chapel Hill Y-97

Thomas Wolfe Centennial
Celebration in Asheville Y-00

Fire at Thomas Wolfe Memorial. Y-98

The Thomas Wolfe Society. Y-97

Wolfe, Tom 1931- DLB-152, 185

Wolfenstein, Martha 1869-1906 . . . . .DLB-221

Wolff, Helen 1906-1994 . . . . Y-94

Wolff, Tobias 1945- DLB-130

Wolfram von Eschenbach
circa 1170-after 1220 . . . .DLB-138; CDWLB-2

Wolfram von Eschenbach's *Parzival*:
Prologue and Book 3 . . . . .DLB-138

Wolker, Jiří 1900-1924 . . . . .DLB-215

Wollstonecraft, Mary 1759-1797
. . . . .DLB-39, 104, 158, 252; CDBLB-3

Wondratschek, Wolf 1943- DLB-75

Wong, Elizabeth 1958- DLB-266

Wood, Anthony à 1632-1695 . . . . .DLB-213

Wood, Benjamin 1820-1900 . . . . .DLB-23

Wood, Charles 1932- DLB-13

Wood, Mrs. Henry 1814-1887 . . . . .DLB-18

Wood, Joanna E. 1867-1927 . . . . .DLB-92

Wood, Sally Sayward Barrell Keating
1759-1855 . . . . .DLB-200

Wood, Samuel [publishing house] DLB-49

Wood, William ?-? DLB-24

The Charles Wood Affair:
A Playwright Revived Y-83

Woodberry, George Edward
1855-1930 . . . . .DLB-71, 103

Woodbridge, Benjamin 1622-1684 . . . . . . .DLB-24

Woodcock, George 1912-1995 . . . . .DLB-88

Woodhull, Victoria C. 1838-1927 . . . . . . .DLB-79

Woodmason, Charles circa 1720-? DLB-31

Woodress, Jr., James Leslie 1916- DLB-111

Woods, Margaret L. 1855-1945 . . . . DLB-240

Woodson, Carter G. 1875-1950 . . . . . . DLB-17

Woodward, C. Vann 1908-1999 . . . . DLB-17

Woodward, Stanley 1895-1965 . . . . .DLB-171

Woodworth, Samuel 1785-1842 . . . . DLB-260

Wooler, Thomas 1785 or 1786-1853 . . . . DLB-158

Woolf, David (see Maddow, Ben)

Woolf, Douglas 1922-1992 . . . . DLB-244

Woolf, Leonard 1880-1969 . . . . . DLB-100; DS-10

Woolf, Virginia 1882-1941
. . . . DLB-36, 100, 162; DS-10; CDBLB-6

Woolf, Virginia, "The New Biography," *New York
Herald Tribune,* 30 October 1927. . . . . DLB-149

Woollcott, Alexander 1887-1943 . . . . DLB-29

Woolman, John 1720-1772 . . . . DLB-31

Woolner, Thomas 1825-1892. . . . . DLB-35

Woolrich, Cornell 1903-1968 . . . . DLB-226

Woolsey, Sarah Chauncy 1835-1905 . . . . . DLB-42

Woolson, Constance Fenimore
1840-1894 . . . . .DLB-12, 74, 189, 221

Worcester, Joseph Emerson
1784-1865. . . . . DLB-1, 235

Worde, Wynkyn de [publishing house] . . .DLB-170

Wordsworth, Christopher 1807-1885 . . . . DLB-166

Wordsworth, Dorothy 1771-1855 . . . . . . DLB-107

Wordsworth, Elizabeth 1840-1932 . . . . . . DLB-98

Wordsworth, William
1770-1850 . . . . DLB-93, 107; CDBLB-3

Workman, Fanny Bullock 1859-1925 . . . . DLB-189

The Works of the Rev. John Witherspoon
(1800-1801) [excerpts] DLB-31

A World Chronology of Important Science
Fiction Works (1818-1979). DLB-8

World Literatue Today: A Journal for the
New Millennium Y-01

World Publishing Company. DLB-46

World War II Writers Symposium
at the University of South Carolina,
12–14 April 1995 . . . . .Y-95

Worthington, R., and Company DLB-49

Wotton, Sir Henry 1568-1639 . . . . DLB-121

Wouk, Herman 1915- Y-82; CDALB-7

Wreford, James 1915- DLB-88

Wren, Sir Christopher 1632-1723. . . . . . DLB-213

Wren, Percival Christopher
1885-1941 . . . . DLB-153

Wrenn, John Henry 1841-1911 . . . . DLB-140

Wright, C. D. 1949- DLB-120

Wright, Charles 1935- DLB-165; Y-82

Wright, Charles Stevenson 1932- DLB-33

Wright, Frances 1795-1852. . . . . DLB-73

Wright, Harold Bell 1872-1944 . . . . DLB-9

Wright, James
1927-1980. . . . . DLB-5, 169; CDALB-7

Wright, Jay 1935- DLB-41

Wright, Judith 1915-2000 . . . . DLB-260

Wright, Louis B. 1899-1984 . . . . DLB-17

Wright, Richard
1908-1960 . . . . DLB-76, 102; DS-2; CDALB-5

Wright, Richard B. 1937- DLB-53

Wright, S. Fowler 1874-1965 . . . . DLB-255

Wright, Sarah Elizabeth 1928- DLB-33

Wright, Willard Huntington ("S. S. Van Dine")
1888-1939 . . . . .DS-16

Wrigley, Robert 1951- DLB-256

A Writer Talking: A Collage Y-00

Writers and Politics: 1871-1918,
by Ronald Gray DLB-66

Writers and their Copyright Holders:
the WATCH Project Y-94

Writers' Forum. Y-85

Writing for the Theatre,
by Harold Pinter DLB-13

Wroth, Lawrence C. 1884-1970 . . . . DLB-187

Wroth, Lady Mary 1587-1653 . . . . DLB-121

Wurlitzer, Rudolph 1937- DLB-173

Wyatt, Sir Thomas circa 1503-1542. . . . . DLB-132

Wycherley, William
1641-1715. . . . . DLB-80; CDBLB-2

Wyclif, John
circa 1335-31 December 1384 . . . . . . DLB-146

Wyeth, N. C. 1882-1945 . . . . DLB-188; DS-16

Wylie, Elinor 1885-1928 . . . . DLB-9, 45

Wylie, Philip 1902-1971 . . . . DLB-9

Wyllie, John Cook 1908-1968 . . . . DLB-140

Wyman, Lillie Buffum Chace
1847-1929. DLB-202

Wymark, Olwen 1934- DLB-233

Wyndham, John 1903-1969 . . . . DLB-255

Wynne-Tyson, Esmé 1898-1972. . . . . . . DLB-191

X

Xenophon circa 430 B.C.-circa 356 B.C. . . .DLB-176

Y

Yasuoka Shōtarō 1920- DLB-182

Yates, Dornford 1885-1960 . . . . .DLB-77, 153

Yates, J. Michael 1938- DLB-60

Yates, Richard
1926-1992 . . . . DLB-2, 234; Y-81, Y-92

Yau, John 1950- DLB-234

Yavorov, Peyo 1878-1914. . . . . DLB-147

The Year in Book Publishing Y-86

The Year in Book Reviewing and the Literary
Situation. Y-98

The Year in British Drama Y-99, Y-00, Y-01

The Year in British Fiction Y-99, Y-00, Y-01

The Year in Children's
Books Y-92–Y-96, Y-98, Y-99, Y-00, Y-01

The Year in Children's Literature Y-97

The Year in Drama Y-82-Y-85, Y-87–Y-96

The Year in Fiction. . . Y-84–Y-86, Y-89, Y-94–Y-99

The Year in Fiction: A Biased View Y-83

The Year in Literary
Biography. Y-83–Y-98, Y-00, Y-01

The Year in Literary Theory Y-92–Y-93

The Year in London Theatre Y-92

The Year in the Novel Y-87, Y-88, Y-90–Y-93

The Year in Poetry . .Y-83–Y-92, Y-94, Y-95, Y-96,
. . . . .Y-97, Y-98, Y-99, Y-00, Y-01

The Year in Science Fiction
and Fantasy Y-00, Y-01

The Year in Short Stories Y-87

The Year in the Short Story Y-88, Y-90–Y-93

The Year in Texas Literature. Y-98

The Year in U.S. Drama Y-00

The Year in U.S. Fiction. Y-00, Y-01

The Year's Work in American Poetry Y-82

The Year's Work in Fiction: A Survey. Y-82

Yearsley, Ann 1753-1806 . . . . DLB-109

Yeats, William Butler
1865-1939 . . . DLB-10, 19, 98, 156; CDBLB-5

Yellen, Jack 1892-1991 . . . . DLB-265

Yep, Laurence 1948- DLB-52

Yerby, Frank 1916-1991 . . . . DLB-76

Yezierska, Anzia
1880-1970 . . . . DLB-28, 221

Yolen, Jane 1939- DLB-52

Yonge, Charlotte Mary
1823-1901 . . . . DLB-18, 163

The York Cycle circa 1376-circa 1569 . . . DLB-146

A Yorkshire Tragedy DLB-58

Yoseloff, Thomas [publishing house] DLB-46

Young, A. S. "Doc" 1919-1996. . . . . DLB-241

Young, Al 1939- DLB-33

Young, Arthur 1741-1820. . . . . DLB-158

Young, Dick 1917 or 1918 - 1987. . . . . . .DLB-171

Young, Edward 1683-1765 . . . . DLB-95

Young, Frank A. "Fay" 1884-1957 . . . . . . DLB-241

Young, Francis Brett 1884-1954 . . . . DLB-191

Young, Gavin 1928- DLB-204

Young, Stark 1881-1963 . . . . . .DLB-9, 102; DS-16

Young, Waldeman 1880-1938 . . . . DLB-26

Young, William
publishing house] DLB-49

Young Bear, Ray A. 1950- DLB-175

Yourcenar, Marguerite
1903-1987 . . . . .DLB-72; Y-88

"You've Never Had It So Good," Gusted by
"Winds of Change": British Fiction in the
1950s, 1960s, and After DLB-14

Yovkov, Yordan 1880-1937 . .DLB-147; CDWLB-4

Z

Zachariä, Friedrich Wilhelm 1726-1777 . . . DLB-97

Zagajewski, Adam 1945- DLB-232

Zagoskin, Mikhail Nikolaevich
1789-1852. DLB-198

Zajc, Dane 1929- DLB-181

Zālīte, Māra 1952- DLB-232

Zamora, Bernice 1938- DLB-82

Zand, Herbert 1923-1970 . . . . DLB-85

Zangwill, Israel 1864-1926 . . . . . .DLB-10, 135, 197

Zanzotto, Andrea 1921- DLB-128

Zapata Olivella, Manuel 1920- DLB-113

Zasodimsky, Pavel Vladimirovich
1843-1912 . . . . DLB-238

Zebra Books DLB-46

Zebrowski, George 1945- DLB-8

Zech, Paul 1881-1946. . . . . DLB-56

Zeidner, Lisa 1955- DLB-120

Zeidonis, Imants 1933- DLB-232

Zeimi (Kanze Motokiyo) 1363-1443 .....DLB-203

Zelazny, Roger 1937-1995 ....DLB-8

Zenger, John Peter 1697-1746..........DLB-24, 43

Zepheria..........................DLB-172

Zesen, Philipp von 1619-1689 ....DLB-164

Zhukovsky, Vasilii Andreevich
    1783-1852 ....DLB-205

Zieber, G. B., and Company DLB-49

Ziedonis, Imants 1933- CDWLB-4

Zieroth, Dale 1946- DLB-60

Zigler und Kliphausen, Heinrich
    Anshelm von 1663-1697 ....DLB-168

Zimmer, Paul 1934- DLB-5

Zinberg, Len (see Lacy, Ed)

Zindel, Paul 1936- DLB-7, 52; CDALB-7

Zingref, Julius Wilhelm 1591-1635 .....DLB-164

Zinnes, Harriet 1919- DLB-193

Zinzendorf, Nikolaus Ludwig von
    1700-1760.......................DLB-168

Zitkala-Ša 1876-1938 ....DLB-175

Zīverts, Mārtiņš 1903-1990 ....DLB-220

Zlatovratsky, Nikolai Nikolaevich
    1845-1911 ....DLB-238

Zola, Emile 1840-1902...............DLB-123

Zolla, Elémire 1926- DLB-196

Zolotow, Charlotte 1915- DLB-52

Zschokke, Heinrich 1771-1848..........DLB-94

Zubly, John Joachim 1724-1781 ....DLB-31

Zu-Bolton, Ahmos, II 1936- DLB-41

Zuckmayer, Carl 1896-1977 ....DLB-56, 124

Zukofsky, Louis 1904-1978 ....DLB-5, 165

Zupan, Vitomil 1914-1987............DLB-181

Župančič, Oton 1878-1949... DLB-147; CDWLB-4

zur Mühlen, Hermynia 1883-1951 ....DLB-56

Zweig, Arnold 1887-1968..............DLB-66

Zweig, Stefan 1881-1942 ....DLB-81, 118

ISBN 0-7876-6016-7

90000

9 780787 660161